PSYCHOLOGY

PSYCHOLOGY

KELLY G. SHAVER
COLLEGE OF WILLIAM & MARY

ROGER M. TARPY
BUCKNELL UNIVERSITY

MACMILLAN PUBLISHING COMPANY
NEW YORK

MAXWELL MACMILLAN CANADA
TORONTO

Editor: **Christine Cardone**
Development Editors: **David Chodoff** and **Carolyn Smith**
Production Supervisor: **Katherine Mara Evancie**
Production Manager: **Sandra Moore**
Art Director: **Pat Smythe**
Text and Cover Designer: **Sheree L. Goodman**
Cover Photograph: **Constantin Brancusi.** *A Muse,* **1917.**
The Museum of Fine Arts, Houston. Museum purchase with
funds provided by Mrs. Herman Brown and Mrs. William
Stamps Farish (62.1).
Photo Researchers: **Dallas Chang/Chris Migdol**
Illustrations by **York Graphic Services** and **Carlyn Iverson**

This book was set in Times Roman by York Graphic Services, Inc., and was printed and bound by Von Hoffman
Press, Inc. The cover was printed by The Lehigh Press, Inc.

Macmillan Publishing Company
866 Third Avenue, New York, New York 10022

Macmillan Publishing Company is part of
the Maxwell Communication Group of Companies.

Maxwell Macmillan Canada, Inc.
1200 Eglinton Avenue East
Suite 200
Don Mills, Ontario M3C 3N1

LIBRARY OF CONGRESS CATALOGING-IN-PUBLICATION DATA

Shaver, Kelly G.
    Psychology / Kelly G. Shaver, Roger M. Tarpy.
        p.   cm.
    Includes bibliographical references and indexes.
    ISBN 0-02-409622-9
    1. Psychology.   I. Tarpy, Roger M.   II. Title.
BF121.S465   1993
150—dc20   92-16181
                      CIP

Copyright acknowledgments begin on p. C-1, following the References, which constitutes an extension of the copyright page.

Printing: 1   2   3   4   5   6   7   Year: 3   4   5   6   7   8   9

To our wives
Carole and Jean

And to our children
Vicky, Betsy, Elizabeth, and David

ABOUT THE AUTHORS

KELLY G. SHAVER is professor of psychology at the College of William & Mary. He holds B.S. and M.S. degrees in psychology from the University of Washington, and a Ph.D. in psychology from Duke University. From 1977 to 1979, Dr. Shaver was program director for social and developmental psychology in the Division of Behavioral and Neural Sciences at the National Science Foundation. He has served on research review committees for the National Science Foundation, the National Institute of Mental Health, and on a small business innovation research review committee at the National Institutes of Health. Dr. Shaver has served on the editorial boards of the *Journal of Personality and Social Psychology* and the *Journal of Personality,* and currently serves on the program committee of the Eastern Psychological Association and the editorial boards of the *Journal of Applied Social Psychology* and *Entrepreneurship Theory and Practice.* He is the author of three books on social psychology, co-author of two others, and is author or co-author of more than 80 papers and research articles on attribution processes, psycholegal issues, and entrepreneurship. His book, *An Introduction to Attribution Processes,* has been translated into Japanese, his most recent book is *The Attribution of Blame: Causality, Responsibility, and Blameworthiness.* In 1989, he was an honored nominee in the Council for Advancement and Support of Education's Professor of the Year program.

ROGER M. TARPY is professor of psychology at Bucknell University and served as chairperson of that department from 1975 to 1979. He received a B.A. degree from Amherst College, an M.A. from the College of William & Mary, and an M.A. and Ph.D. from Princeton University. Dr. Tarpy has taught at Williams College and has been a visiting professor at the Universities of Oxford and Exeter. An expert in basic learning processes, he has received a number of grants and awards, and regularly reviews for the National Science Foundation as well as for several journals in psychology. He has published more than 50 papers and articles and is author or co-author of five books whose topics include learning, motivation, and most recently, behavioral economics. His book *Basic Principles of Learning* has been translated into Spanish and German; his most recent book is *The Individual in the Economy: A Survey of Economic Psychology* (1987), co-authored with S. E. G. Lea and P. Webley. In 1982, Professor Tarpy received the Lindback Award for Distinguished Teaching.

BRIEF CONTENTS

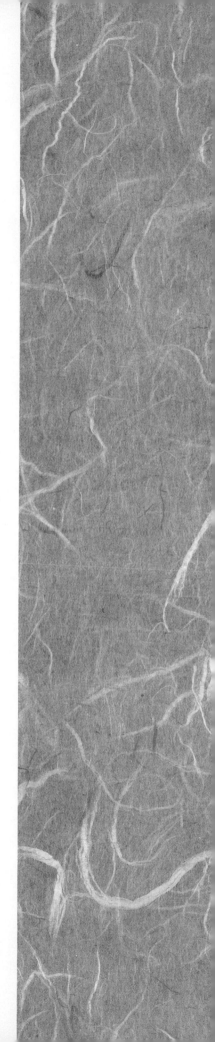

CONTENTS

xi

PART THREE
FREE WILL VERSUS BEHAVIORAL DETERMINISM
193

PART FOUR

THE ORIGINS OF KNOWLEDGE

289

PART FIVE
THE ROLE OF NATURE AND
NURTURE IN DEVELOPMENT
403

PREFACE

Most students who take a psychology course take only one. That course at a minimum should introduce them to the field and maintain their intrinsic interest in it. We feel that in doing so it should also increase their understanding of human nature and, by tying psychology to its intellectual roots and to other areas of intellectual exploration, enhance their overall education. We wrote this book with both these narrow and broader goals in mind. We wanted to show how psychology is beginning to answer questions about human behavior that have concerned philosophers and scientists for centuries:

- Are mind and body one entity, or are they separate and distinct?
- Do actions result from the free exercise of will, or are they determined?
- How do people obtain knowledge about the world around them?
- Which is more important in shaping behavior: heredity or environment?
- How do people participate in groups without losing their individual identity?
- What aspects of behavior remain stable over time, and why or how do other aspects change?

We use these six timeless questions as a framework for organizing our presentation of the research and theory of modern psychology.

A TEXTBOOK THAT TEACHES

In writing this book we have taken seriously our role as *teachers*. With that role comes the responsibility to organize, select, and simplify. There are many ways this can be done. We have elected to minimize distractions to let the enduring ideas of psychology speak for themselves. We cover all important topics directly in the text, not in digressive "boxes." The research literature in psychology is vast and growing geometrically, but we try to show how crucial research fits into the broader concerns of the discipline without overwhelming students with a detailed mass of findings. We have attempted to write a text that respects the various points of view within psychology while presenting the field as a whole, a text that describes current research and theory while remaining true to psychology's place in the history of ideas.

ORGANIZATION

This book organizes all the material found in an introductory psychology course around the six enduring questions listed at the beginning of this Preface. The number of chapters has been dictated by our desire to present topics clearly, coherently, and from a variety of perspectives. We have separate chapters, for example, on hunger and thirst, sexual and aggressive behaviors, and social motives, allowing us to examine the interaction of biological and social factors on each. Other books combine these topics in various ways, with the result that the context of the larger chapters in which they appear often constrains the way they can be presented. Likewise, in our book we treat two major areas of interest in social psychology—social cognition and interpersonal behavior—separately. Many books combine these two topics. A close look at the Contents will reveal many similar examples. Our chapters vary in length but not in depth. They can be combined flexibly to meet the needs of any course schedule.

The book is divided into seven parts, each consisting of two or more chapters. **Part One, "A Historical Overview of Psychology,"** consists of two chapters—"Foundations for Understanding Behavior" (Chapter 1) and "Psychology as a Science" (Chapter 2)—that describe the intellectual roots of the discipline. Each of the following six parts addresses one of the questions listed at the beginning of the Preface.

Part Two, "The Study of Mind and Body," addresses the question: How do mind and body interact? It consists of five chapters—"Sensation" (Chapter 3), "Perception" (Chapter 4), "Neuropsychology" (Chapter 5), "Emotion" (Chapter 6), and "States of Consciousness" (Chapter 7)—that examine how physical events relate to mental events. These chapters show how events in the world are represented (sensation) and given meaning (perception), how the brain functions (neuropsychology), how emotional states are triggered and experienced (emotion), and how mind and body come together in consciousness (states of consciousness).

Part Three, "Free Will Versus Behavioral Determinism," addresses the question: Are people capable of free choice, or is their behavior determined? It consists of four chapters—"Ethology and Behavior Genetics" (Chapter 8), "Basic Needs" (Chapter 9), "Biosocial Motives" (Chapter 10), and "Social Motives" (Chapter 11)—that describe the biological and social influences on behavior. Chapter 8 examines the implications of evolutionary theory and genetics for behavior (ethology and behavior genetics). This biological perspective continues in a discussion of the behaviors related to hunger and thirst (basic needs). Next we turn to sexual behavior and aggression, behaviors that humans share with other animals but that are also strongly influenced by social factors (biosocial motives). The last chapter in Part Three examines motives that are more specifically characteristic of humans, such as affiliation and achievement (social motives).

Part Four, "The Origins of Knowledge," addresses the question: How is knowledge organized and structured? It consists of four chapters—"Learning" (Chapter 12), "Information Processing and Memory" (Chapter 13), "Cognitive Structure and Organization" (Chapter 14), and "Thinking and Problem Solving" (Chapter 15)—that examine how knowledge is acquired and used. These chapters describe the basic building blocks of knowledge (learning), the way information is stored (information processing and memory), how it is organized into units and systems (cognitive structure and organization), and how it is manipulated to solve problems (thinking and problem solving).

Part Five, "The Role of Nature and Nurture in Development," addresses the question: How much of human behavior can be accounted for by heredity and how much by environment? It consists of three chapters—"Cognitive Development" (Chapter 16), "Language and Communication" (Chapter 17), and "Social Development" (Chapter 18)—that show how the rudimentary skills of the infant become the sophisticated capabilities of the adult. These chapters describe the hereditary and environmental influences on growth in cognitive abilities (cognitive development), nativist and empiricist approaches to the acquisition and use of language (language and communication), and the environmental factors that affect the development of social skills (social development).

Part Six, "Individual and Group Processes," addresses the question: What is the role of the individual in the larger group? It consists of two chapters—"Social Cognition, Attitudes, and the Self" (Chapter 19) and "Interpersonal Behavior" (Chapter 20)—that describe individual social behavior and interpersonal relations. These chapters show how social reality is perceived, organized, and reflected in the self (social cognition, attitudes, and the self) and how people interact with and influence one another (interpersonal behavior).

Part Seven, "Stability and Change in Behavior," addresses the question: How can people change without losing their individual identities? It consists of five chapters—"Personality Structure and Function" (Chapter 21), "Individual Differences" (Chapter 22), "Stress and Coping" (Chapter 23), "Psychological Disorders" (Chapter 24), and "Treatment of Disorders" (Chapter 25)—that deal with the issue of stability versus change in behavior. Chapter 21 describes what is presumed to be the stable core of the individual (personality structure and function), then Chapter 22 examines variations among people (individual differences). Chapter 23 discusses ways people adjust to life's demands (stress and coping). Chapter 24 describes the profound changes inherent in serious psychological disorder (psychological disorders), and the last chapter discusses ways in which normal functioning can be restored (treatment of psychopathology).

The appendix, **"An Introduction to Research Methods and Statistics in Psychology,"** acquaints students with some of the fundamental concepts of scientific methodology and statistical reasoning that are so central to modern psychology.

FEATURES OF THE BOOK

Our book presents the content of a first course in psychology in the context of *timeless questions about human nature.* The six themes do more than organize that content, however; each acts as a strong thread that weaves through chapters to provide a coherent view of the discipline.

Other features complement this organizational approach. Each part opens with an *introduction to the theme* and the way it relates to the following chapters. The opening paragraphs of each chapter relate the content of that chapter to the theme and to broader issues in psychology. Each chapter begins with an *outline* and ends with a concise *Summary* of key points. Within each chapter, *Interim Summaries* at the conclusion of each major section immediately reinforce what has just been covered. *End-of-chapter Focus Questions* are designed to provoke thought about the issues raised in the chapter. *Key terms* are indicated throughout the chapters in boldface type and are included in the *Glossary* at the end of the book.

The *illustrations* in the text reflect our commitment to teaching. Photographs have been chosen to reinforce points made in the text, not merely to make the book more appealing. Figures and tables support discussions in the text of particular research studies. All the figures and tables as well as the many superb anatomical drawings have been produced especially for this book. As a result, the text and illustrations work together without distractions to convey the excitement and intellectual wealth of psychology.

SUPPLEMENTARY MATERIALS

A complete package of carefully developed supplementary materials is available to assist students, instructors, and teaching assistants.

The *Instructor's Manual* provides learning objectives, lecture aids, suggested classroom demonstrations, and a list of relevant audiovisual material for each chapter.

The *Test Bank* includes multiple-choice and essay questions that test students' grasp both of concepts and of facts and definitions. It is available in book form and on disk for IBM, Apple II, and Macintosh computers. The computerized testing system allows instructors to generate tests in a variety of configurations and to add their own questions.

The *Study Guide,* by Roberta Kestenbaum of the University of Michigan, includes a variety of material—key terms, summary and review exercises, self-tests, and questions for study and review—designed to help students get the most from the text-book.

Computer simulations of experiments and demonstrations are available on request, as are *transparencies, slides, and videos.*

ACKNOWLEDGMENTS

From its inception, this book has been a true collaboration. In this spirit, we determined the order of authorship by flipping a coin. From our discussion of possible organizing themes, through the trading back and forth of multiple drafts of chapters, to the final selection of photographs, we have considered ourselves a team. On rare instances, accepting that psychology accommodates divergent viewpoints, we have agreed to disagree. For the most part, however, we have tried to produce a coherent description of the field that speaks with a single voice. We could not have accomplished this goal without the help of many others. It is a pleasure to acknowledge their contributions here.

We are especially grateful to our colleagues and family members who have given generously of their time to discuss the book's approach and to provide constructive criticism on portions of the manuscript. These include Nancy Caine (ethology), Owen Floody (neuropsychology and needs), and Andrea Halpern (cognitive) of Bucknell University; Linda Duke (cognitive) of the University of Alabama, Birmingham; Mary Louise Kean (language and communication) of the University of California, Irvine; and Jean Roberts (chapters too numerous to mention) of the Pennsylvania College of Technology. We obtained a college student's eye view of portions of the manuscript from David Tarpy and Vicky Shaver. Vicky also provided original drawings for some of the illustrations. We received expert secretarial assistance from Kay Ocker and Ruth Craven; David Hindelang helped in checking references.

Each draft of the text was also reviewed by teachers of the introductory course and experts in specific areas. We are grateful for their many thoughtful, thorough comments.

William A. Barnard, *University of Northern Colorado*
John K. Bare, *Carleton College*
Bernard C. Beins, *Ithaca College*
Michael Best, *Southern Methodist University*
Charles F. Bond, *Texas Christian University*
Stanley Coren, *University of British Columbia*
Richard B. Day, *McMaster University*
Grace Galliano, *Kennesaw State College*
John Governale, *Portland State University*
David A. F. Haaga, *The American University*
Martin Kaplan, *Northern Illinois University*
Mary-Louise Kean, *University of California-Irvine*
Frank C. Keil, *Cornell University*
D. Brett King, *University of Colorado-Boulder*
Jon A. Krosnick, *Ohio State University*
Joanne Lindoerfer, *Lamar University*
Alexandra Logue, *SUNY–Stonybrook*
Richard Mayer, *University of California–Santa Barbara*
Dan P. McAdams, *Northwestern University*
Thomas E. McGill, *Williams College*

John McKinney, *Michigan State University*
Steve Meier, *University of Idaho*
William Moorcroft, *Luther College*
David Pittenger, *Marietta College*
Janet D. Proctor, *Purdue University*
Milton Rosenbaum, *University of Iowa*
Steven R. Sabat, *Georgetown University*
John Santelli, *Fairleigh Dickinson University*
Matthew J. Sharps, *California State University–Fresno*
Joseph P. Sidowski, *University of South Florida*
Aaron Smith, *University of Michigan (Emeritus)*
Robert F. Smith, *George Mason University*
C. R. Snyder, *University of Kansas*
Sheldon Solomon, *Skidmore College*
Kenneth Springer, *Southern Methodist University*
Donald Vardiman, *William Paterson College*
Wayne Viney, *Colorado State University*
Robert L. Weiss, *University of Oregon*

We would like to thank Janet Proctor (Purdue University) in particular for her invaluable comments on the book's art program. Her suggestions helped substantially to improve the pedagogical impact of the illustrations.

The talent, commitment, and hard work of many people associated with Macmillan Publishing Company made this book possible. Christine Cardone, the psychology editor, recognized the value of using enduring questions about human nature to organize this book. Her unwavering support for this approach and her persistent efforts to move the entire project forward have helped turn a vision into a reality. D. Anthony English, editor-in-chief for social science and the humanities, provided invaluable commitment and support at crucial times during the book's development. We would also like to thank Scott Rubin, marketing manager, for his many helpful insights and his ongoing support.

We are grateful to Katherine Evancie for her work as production supervisor. Producing a book of this complexity is a daunting task that requires diplomacy, attention to detail, and enduring good humor. Katherine exhibits all three in abundance. Chris Migdol, head of Macmillan's photo research department, and Dallas Chang, our photo researcher, unerringly translated our sometimes vague requests into outstanding photographs that complement the text. Sandy Moore, the manufacturing manager, kept the whole team on schedule.

Carolyn Smith provided invaluable editorial guidance. The book reads far better than it would have without her efforts.

Our final thanks go to David Chodoff, whose title, Development Editor, does not do justice to his contributions. His wide-ranging intellectual curiosity has been an asset to the entire project, his suggestions for organizational changes have improved the flow of ideas within chapters, and his deft editing has added clarity and impact. We consider him a valued colleague.

K.G.S.
R.M.T.

PSYCHOLOGY

PART ONE

A HISTORICAL OVERVIEW
OF PSYCHOLOGY

For as long as there have been written records, philosophers and scientists have wondered about human nature. Are the mind and body one entity, or are they separate and distinct? Do actions result from the free exercise of will, or are they determined? How do people obtain knowledge about the world around them? Which is more important in behavior, heredity or environment? How do people participate in groups without losing their individual identity? What aspects of behavior remain stable over time, and why or how do people change? These six timeless questions are part of the foundation for understanding behavior, and so they constitute the framework for our presentation of the research and theory of modern psychology. Each question provides the organizing principle for a different part of the book.

Although psychology can trace its roots to philosophy and science from antiquity through the early nineteenth century, the beginning of psychology as an independent discipline is usually considered 1879, the year in which the first psychological laboratory was established. Today, psychology is a vibrant intellectual endeavor whose methods have advanced considerably and whose theories have become ever more precise in the past hundred years. And yet the same basic questions are still at the heart of the discipline.

CHAPTER 1   FOUNDATIONS FOR UNDERSTANDING BEHAVIOR

CHAPTER 2   PSYCHOLOGY AS A SCIENCE

CHAPTER 1

FOUNDATIONS FOR UNDERSTANDING BEHAVIOR

 How can we define "psychology"? This question can be answered three ways, beginning with the derivation of the word itself. *Psychology* is a compound of two Greek words: *psyche,* meaning "breath," "life," or "soul," and *logos,* meaning "thought" or "reason." As this derivation suggests, psychology involves reasoning about, or studying, the human spirit or soul. Because spirit and soul are generally viewed as being beyond the reach of scientific inquiry, psychology is usually understood to refer to the study of thought and behavior.

Second, psychology can be distinguished from related disciplines, including sociology, anthropology, and biology, by its focus of inquiry (Figure 1-1). Like sociology and anthropology, psychology is concerned with human behavior. Where sociology and anthropology concentrate on the behavior and interactions of groups and larger social systems, however, psychology focuses on the behavior of individual human beings. Describing the similarities among cultures is a task for anthropology, but showing how a culture becomes represented in the mind of an individual is a task for psychology. Like biology, psychology is concerned with the physical basis of life. Where biology encompasses the study of the life processes in both plants and animals, however, psychology focuses exclusively on the biological factors implicated in human and animal behavior. Principles of genetic transmission fall into the province of biology, but the degree to which a specific human faculty like intelligence might be inherited is a psychological question. As these examples suggest, psychology can be distinguished from related disciplines by virtue of its concentration on individual behavior.

Finally, the domain of psychology can be illustrated by the activities of psychologists in their academic and professional settings. In research, psychologists study how the senses and the central nervous system interact to provide information to the organism. Psychologists investigate processes of learning, memory, and decision making to determine how information is organized, and how education can be accomplished more effectively. Psychologists examine individual differences in intellectual ability, physical skills, and personality characteristics to identify the dimensions common to us all without losing sight of the fact that each person is unique. Psychologists study the antecedents and consequences of aggression, attrac-

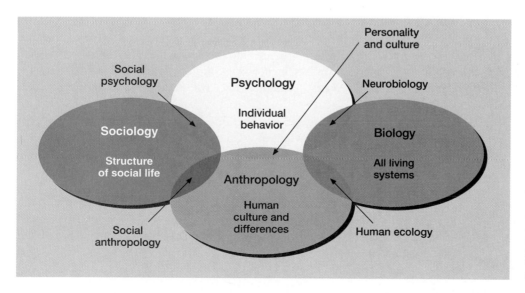

FIGURE 1-1 Psychology and related disciplines. As the study of individual human behavior, psychology is closely related to three other social and life sciences: sociology, anthropology, and biology. Entire fields have developed at the intersections between the four parent disciplines. Five examples of these are shown in the figure. Social psychology examines individual behavior in the context of social relationships; neurobiology is the study of biological processes at the level of the cell that are involved in neural transmission; human ecology is the study of the interactions between human societies and the larger ecological systems of which they are a part; social anthropology is the cross-cultural study of human social systems; and the field of personality and culture involves the study of the effect of cultural differences on the individual personality.

3

tion, and social attitudes. Psychologists chart the development of the person through life, and investigate the causes and treatment of emotional disorders. In professional roles, psychologists provide therapy for people with psychological disorders, serve as school counselors, and work in a variety of health-care settings. In business, psychologists are involved in advertising, marketing, training, and personnel services. In all of these settings, psychologists apply their interest in individual human behavior to the solution of practical problems.

PSYCHOLOGY IN THE HISTORY OF IDEAS

Each of these three answers to the question, "What is psychology?" tells us something about the field, but none of them provides a complete picture. When you have finished this text, we hope you will have a better understanding of the rich and varied field that is modern psychology. But to understand the discipline fully, you also need to know its place in the history of ideas.

The underlying views of human nature that shape contemporary psychological theory and research derive directly from those of the past; no radical changes have yet occurred that would make those prior views irrelevant. In this regard psychology differs from other disciplines. For example, Copernicus's realization that the sun, not the earth, was the center of the solar system marked the beginning of modern astronomy, and made prior theory obsolete. More recently, the description of deoxyribonucleic acid (DNA) revolutionized biology and genetics. Such critical discoveries redefine the way science is done within a discipline, making a return to previous ideas impossible (Kuhn, 1962). Astronomy cannot be taught competently by anyone who still believes the earth to be the center of the universe; genetics cannot be taught competently without reference to DNA.

In contrast to fields whose direction has been dramatically altered by a single insight, psychology has developed gradually. Although psychologists have made many important advances in the study of human nature, no *single* new idea has made all prior study of the subject irrelevant. Rather, psychology continues to evolve ever more sophisticated means for addressing timeless questions about human behavior. Six such questions have played an important role in the development of psychology, and we use each of these as the central theme for one of the next six Parts of this textbook, as follows:

1. What is the relationship of the mind to the body? This question provides the theme for Part II, "The Study of Mind and Body" (Chapter 3, "Sensation"; Chapter 4, "Perception"; Chapter 5, "Neuropsychology"; Chapter 6, "Emotion"; and Chapter 7, "States of Consciousness").

2. Do people act with free will, or is their behavior determined by forces outside their control? This question provides the theme for Part III, "Free Will Versus Behavioral Determinism" (Chapter 8, "Ethology and Behavior Genetics"; Chapter 9, "Basic Needs"; Chapter 10, "Biosocial Motives"; Chapter 11, "Social Motives").

3. What is the origin of knowledge? This question provides the theme for Part IV, "The Origins of Knowledge" (Chapter 12, "Learning"; Chapter 13, "Information Processing and Memory"; Chapter 14, "Cognitive Structure and Organization"; Chapter 15, "Thinking and Problem Solving").

4. How much of human behavior can be accounted for by heredity, and how much by environment? This question provides the theme for Part V, "The Role of Nature and Nurture in Development" (Chapter 16, "Cognitive Development"; Chapter 17, "Language and Communication"; Chapter 18, "Social Development").

5. What is the role of the individual in the larger group? This question provides the theme for Part VI, "Individual and Group Processes" (Chapter 19, "Social Cognition, Attitudes, and the Self"; Chapter 20, "Interpersonal Behavior").

6. To what extent, or in what sense, is behavior stable over time? This question provides the theme for Part VII, "Stability and Change in Behavior" (Chapter 21, "Personality Structure and Function"; Chapter 22, "Individual Differences"; Chapter 23, "Stress and Coping"; Chapter 24, "Psychological Disorders"; Chapter 25, "Treatment of Psychopathology").

Traditionally these questions have produced sharply contrasting answers—that mind and body are completely separate entities or that the mind and the brain are the same thing, for example; or that the way we are is entirely determined by heredity or entirely determined by environment. To make the issues raised as clear as possible, we shall begin our discussion of each question by outlining these contrasting answers. As we shall see in the chapters to come, however, the "truth" is typically found somewhere between the extremes.

MIND VERSUS BODY

How do physical events, such as lights and sounds, give rise to subjective mental experiences? Conversely, how are mental states, such as a decision to climb stairs or swing a baseball bat, translated into physical events like movements of the legs or arms? And is the mind something entirely separate from the body, or are they the same thing? Questions like these lie at the core of what is often referred to as the mind–body problem.

DUALISM: MIND AND BODY AS SEPARATE ENTITIES

The relationship between mind and body has been a subject of speculation since Aristotle's time, but historians agree that the first clear statement of the mind–body problem was made by the seventeenth-century philosopher René Descartes. Born in France and educated in a Jesuit college, Descartes (1596–1650) developed a strong desire to establish a unified science based on the principles of mathematics. His studies of the nature of human existence and the foundations of knowledge convinced him that there are two separate realities. One reality is the physical world, which obeys the natural laws of physics and chemistry. This is the reality of animal life and tangible objects such as the human body. The other reality is the world of conscious experience, which lacks tangible form. This is the reality of the mind. Not subject to the laws of physics and chemistry, the mind is free. As proof of the claim that mind and body are separate, Descartes pointed out that cutting off a person's foot would diminish the body but not the mind. This view that mind and body are separate is known as **dualism.**

René Descartes (1596–1650), the French philosopher and mathematician, argued that the body and the mind were separate entities.

According to Descartes, the mind has two primary functions: understanding and will. Understanding results from the reasoning processes through which the mind contemplates ideas. Some ideas are derived from the senses, whereas others are innate and not based on sensory experience. As an example of an innate idea, Descartes noted that humans can have an idea of God despite the fact that they have never in their experience encountered God (Descartes, 1952/1641).

Will is the means by which the mind governs the movements and activities of the body. According to Descartes, the specific physical site at which the mind interacts with the body is the pineal gland, a small lobe of tissue near the base of the brain. When the mind wills an action to occur, the pineal gland changes orientation, exerting pressure on a fluid in the nerves and thereby activating muscle tissue. This hydraulic model of mind–body interaction is shown in Figure 1-2.

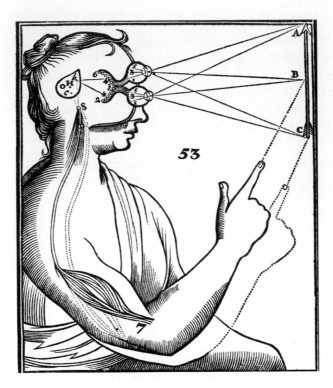

FIGURE 1-2 The role of the pineal gland in Descartes's physiology. According to Descartes, the pineal gland is the specific site at which the mind interacts with the body. As illustrated here, an image is transmitted from the eyes to the pineal gland. If the mind wills an action to occur in response, it changes the orientation of the pineal gland, exerting pressure on a fluid in the nerves and activating the muscles.

Today we think of Descartes's explanation for mind–body interaction as quaint or naive, but the theory of dualism continues to have a strong appeal. The idea that the mind and body are separate is consistent with our subjective experiences. We can appreciate the sweet smell of jasmine without being aware of the odor molecules contacting the interior of our nostrils. We can think through the answer to a problem while remaining oblivious to the electrochemical brain activity involved in such thought. Thus, dualism seems to be an accurate reflection of the relationship between mental and physical events.

MONISM: MIND AND BODY AS A SINGLE ENTITY

Almost as soon as it was proposed, the theory of dualism was subjected to strong challenges. The major opposing position is **monism,** the claim that there is only one reality: physical reality. There are several versions of monism (Churchland, 1988). One that has been important in the development of psychology is **materialist identity theory,** in which the mind is equated with the brain.

The first coherent statement of the identity theory is credited to the political philosopher Thomas Hobbes (Churchland, 1988; Robinson, 1979). Hobbes (1588–1679) was a contemporary of Descartes who rebelled against dualism because of its religious and supernatural implications (Watson, 1968). Hobbes believed that all mental activity (sensations, perceptions, thoughts, and emotions) can be explained entirely in terms of physical activities in the brain. Mental states, therefore, are physical states, and nothing more.

The arguments in support of identity theory fit quite well with what science has taught us about the brain. We cannot deny that we have a physical basis. Moreover, we know that mental phenomena depend on, or are controlled by, the neurochemical activity of the brain. Epileptic seizures can be reduced by surgically altering the way brain structures communicate with one another; the bizarre thoughts that accompany some severe psychological disorders can be managed with medications that affect brain function. The success of such treatments indicates that the physical brain affects both thought and behavior. The fact that surgery or drugs can alter mental states does not, however, prove that *every* mental state has a corresponding physical state in the brain.

The English philosopher Thomas Hobbes (1588–1679) laid the foundation for the materialist identity theory by arguing that mental states could be traced to the physical activity of the brain.

An alternative theory that has developed in the twentieth century, **functional materialism,** focuses on the functions performed by the mind (Churchland, 1988). This approach attempts to explain mental functioning by drawing an analogy to information processing by computers. Computers, although they contain no living tissue, can perform functions commonly thought of as "mental." Computers, for example, can perform complex calculations, make decisions after assessing the risks involved in alternative courses of action, or arrive at a medical diagnosis after interviewing a patient. According to functional materialism, such artificial reasoning processes can be considered the *functional equivalent* of human reasoning processes.

The computer analogy has two implications. First, mental processes presume the existence of some physical structure, so dualism, in which the mind is independent of the body, cannot be correct. Second, the physical structure in which those processes occur need not be a human brain, so the materialist identity theory cannot be correct. The functional materialist theory has gained widespread acceptance among psychologists who study the processes by which people gain and use knowledge. Despite the force of the functional materialist claims, the question of whether computers can really *think* is far from settled.

SCIENTIFIC STUDY OF THE MIND–BODY RELATIONSHIP

Psychophysics

Dualism, identity theory, and functional materialism are philosophical theories about how mind and body interact. Though each can advance some compelling arguments in its favor, none attempts to measure *directly* the relationship between physical events and mental experience. Such direct measurement became the province of **psychophysics,** the scientific study of the relationship between physical states (such as sound) and psychological events (such as the experience of loudness).

The psychophysical method was first used by Ernst Weber (1795–1878), a German physiologist who taught at Leipzig University and was interested in the physiology of the senses. Weber created a method for determining the **sensory threshold,** that is, the point at which a physical stimulus becomes strong enough to trigger a psychological sensation. In the case of the auditory threshold, for example, a subject wearing headphones listens to a series of tones that begin so softly they cannot be heard and then gradually increase in intensity. At some point the subject begins to hear the tones, and this psychological experience can be defined in terms of the physical intensity of the sound. In other words, psychophysics provided a method for connecting a specific mental event (hearing a tone) to a particular physical event (the intensity, measured in units called decibels, of a sound).

Building on Weber's work, Gustav Fechner (1801–1887) developed a psychophysical theory that specified quantitative relationships between changes in mental sensations and changes in external stimuli. This theory will be described in more detail in Chapter 3. What is important here is that psychophysics moved the mind-body debate beyond its origins in philosophy to the scientific methods of psychology.

Specific Nerve Energies

The nineteenth century saw dramatic advances in scientific knowledge. From the standpoint of the mind–body question, the most notable advances were the discoveries of biologists, especially in the area of sensory processes and the nervous system. In 1833 the physiologist Johannes Müller (1801–1858) proposed the theory of **specific nerve energies.** This theory assigned to the nerves a predominant role in determining sensory experience. Specifically, the nature of a sensation depends more on which kind of nerve is stimulated than on the characteristics of external objects. Vastly different stimuli might act on the same kind of nerve and therefore give rise to the same sensation. For example, the eye is normally sensitive to visual stimuli. If,

Johannes Müller (1801–1858), the German physiologist whose theory of specific nerve energies claimed that the nature of a sensation depended more on the nerve stimulated than on the characteristics of external objects.

however, one presses gently on the side of the eyeball with the eyelid closed, a visual experience is produced even though the stimulus is not light but pressure. Thus, the sensation depends on the type of nerve stimulated, not on the source of the stimulus.

The theory of specific nerve energies was a significant step toward clarifying the relationship between external reality and sensation. It suggested that one can gain important insights into the origins of mental experience by studying the nerves. It also implied that knowledge about the mind could be derived from the study of the body.

INTERIM SUMMARY

Perhaps the oldest of the central questions of psychology is the question of how the mind and the body are related. Dualists consider the mind to be fundamentally different from, and separate from, the body. Monists, in contrast, believe that mind and body are not separate entities. One monist view, the materialist identity theory, holds that mental experience (mind) and physical substance (brain) are one and the same. An alternative monist view, functional materialism, argues that the identity theory is inadequate because computers (which have no living tissue) can perform operations that are the functional equivalent of human reasoning processes. The first scientific approach to the study of the relationship between mind and body was psychophysics, in which mental experiences were defined in terms of the physical stimulation required to produce those experiences. The theory of specific nerve energies suggested that sensation depends on the type of nerve stimulated rather than the source of the stimulus.

FREE WILL VERSUS DETERMINISM

Scientific study of any domain assumes that the events under consideration are caused, and that regularities in these causes can be detected. Yet few human beliefs are as cherished as the idea that people possess freedom of choice. Common sense tells us that the "behavior" of physical objects is *determined*—a rock dropped from a bridge will fall into the water; it will not hover in the air or move upward. The same laws of gravity also apply to human beings as physical objects. A person jumping off a diving board will fall into the water just as surely as would the dropped rock. Common sense also tells us, however, that human behavior involves freely made choices whose outcomes cannot be known in advance. If a person decides to drop a rock, the rock cannot on its own choose not to fall. In contrast, a person can consider diving, and then decide not to do so. Thus, human beings seem at once both to be governed by physical laws and yet able to choose between alternative courses of action. How can both of these commonsense views be true? This seeming paradox is at the core of the issue of free will versus **determinism.**

HARD DETERMINISM

There are two extreme positions on the issue of free will versus determinism, each related to a different view of the mind–body problem. The first is derived from the materialist identity theory and holds that if all mental events are physical (that is, neurological) events, then mental events follow the same laws as physical systems. Every action therefore is determined; there is no such thing as free will. This view is called **hard determinism.**

The psychological theories of B. F. Skinner and Sigmund Freud are both examples

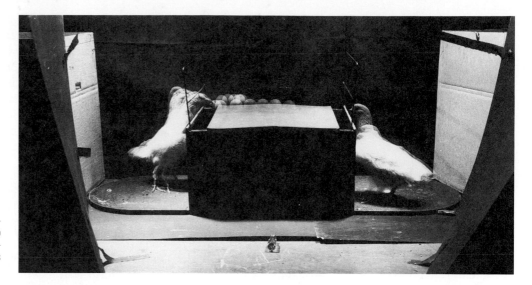

An illustration of the power of reinforcement: The pigeons have been trained to play Ping-Pong for a reward. Demonstrations like this one support B. F. Skinner's deterministic view of behavior.

of hard determinism. Skinner (1971) maintained that the behavior of any animal, humans included, is fully determined by the animal's past history and the stimuli in its immediate environment. Behaviors that are rewarded will recur, behaviors that are not rewarded will tend not to recur. For example, if a rat pushes on a bar in a box and food appears, we can predict that it will push on the bar again. The animal's history of interaction with its environment—the fact that it was rewarded for a particular behavior—*determines* its later behavior—to push on the bar again. According to Skinner, human behavior is determined in the same way. Although society emphasizes such concepts as freedom, initiative, and responsibility, behavior is actually determined by the rewards and punishments experienced by the individual in the past. The concept of free will is a myth that has no place in a truly scientific study of behavior: "The free inner man . . . is only a prescientific substitute for the kinds of causes which are discovered in the course of a scientific analysis" (Skinner, 1953, p. 447).

Sigmund Freud also had a deterministic view of human behavior, believing actions to be the consequence of unconscious desires. These unconscious motivations are presumed to arise from the individual's biological heritage, including aggressive and sexual instincts. Like Skinner, Freud noted how deeply people believe in "psychic freedom and choice," but he argued that this belief "is quite unscientific, and that it must give ground before the claims of a determinism which governs even mental life" (1952/1917, p. 486).

The problem with each of these views, and with hard determinism more generally, is that we do not "feel" that our actions are wholly constrained; we believe we are capable of making choices. As one observer has pointed out, "Those learned professors of philosophy or psychology who deny the existence of free will do so only in their professional moments and in their studies and lecture rooms. For when it comes to doing anything practical, even of the most trivial kind, they invariably behave as if they and others were free" (Stace, 1952, p. 248).

INDETERMINISM

The other extreme position on the question of free will versus determinism was expressed by Descartes and is closely related to dualism. Physical reality—the body—conforms to the same physical laws that affect the inanimate world. But the psychological reality—the mind—is not subject to physical laws. Thus the human mind is undetermined; its free will is infinite. This position, called **indeterminism,** identifies a realm of mental activities, including choices, to which the rules of determinism do not apply.

9

The problem with this position is that if the mind governs behavior, and the mind is undetermined, then behavior should also be undetermined. But from a common-sense point of view, human behavior hardly seems random. To a large extent, it seems to be caused by something. People follow plans to achieve goals; they show remarkable consistency in their actions; and they respond to and are affected even by biological conditions such as hunger and thirst. It appears, therefore, that behavior is organized or determined in some way, rather than stemming entirely from free will.

SOFT DETERMINISM

According to hard determinism, or indeterminism, determinism and free will are incompatible. Either human behavior is determined (in which case there is no room for free will), or there is utterly unconstrained will (in which case there is no room for determinism). Many writers have attempted to resolve this dilemma by taking a position termed **soft determinism** (Churchland, 1988). This approach sees human behavior as both determined and subject to free will. Thomas Hobbes, for example, distinguished between voluntary and involuntary actions. Voluntary actions are caused by internal events such as intentions, desires, and motives; involuntary actions are caused by external agents. Voluntary behaviors are not entirely undetermined, but they are under the control of the individual.

David Hume (1711–1776) took a somewhat different approach. He believed that the issue of free will versus determinism is really a matter of semantics. Our actions are both determined and free because they spring from our motives rather than being caused by external agents. Hume also believed that free actions are not necessarily predictable: People act "out of character" on occasion; the motive for such behavior is not clear, but the behavior is nonetheless motivated.

Another way of stating the idea of soft determinism is to say that people are a source or cause of their own actions. This view is exemplified in the writings of the Scottish philosopher Thomas Reid (1710–1796). Reid (1863) based his view on examples like the following: Imagine that you are faced with a significant moral decision. You grapple with the alternatives, trying to decide which course of action to take. Do you ever doubt that you *could* decide either way? And regardless of the choice you make, do you ever doubt that it is *your* choice? Of course, it would be possible to claim that other people forced you to do what you did, but that would be a rationalization. According to Reid, hard determinism is incompatible with the concepts of morality, deliberation, and the pursuit of goals.

Soft determinism has a central place in modern psychology. Any contemporary theory in which cognition plays a major role presumes that people are able to make choices. For example, in attempting to explain how humans store information, retrieve it, and use it to direct their behavior, psychologists describe a process termed *executive control* (Greeno & Bjork, 1973) or *plans* (Miller, Galanter, & Pribram, 1960). Neither control nor planning makes any sense unless there is "a means of controlling the actions to be performed" (Norman, 1981, p. 247). Control implies choice, and choice requires freedom of will.

INTERIM SUMMARY

Philosophers have long debated whether human actions are wholly determined or are subject to free will. There are two extreme positions on this question. Hard determinism denies the existence of free will, whereas indeterminism holds that mental activities are entirely free from physical laws. Soft determinism attempts to resolve the problem by allowing human motives or choices to serve as the causes of behavior.

ORIGINS OF KNOWLEDGE

What do we know, and how do we come to know it? To put it another way, What are the contents of mind, and how do they get there? In one form or another, this question has occupied philosophers for thousands of years. Answers have generally reflected a position between two extremes: on the one hand, that we are born with no knowledge and acquire it all from experience; on the other, that knowledge is innate—we are born with it. If knowledge is held to be innate, then another question arises—how did it get there? Because one answer to this question is that "God put it there," the origins-of-knowledge theme has been inextricably linked to religious thought.

THE ANCIENT GREEK PHILOSOPHERS

Plato

The foundations of **epistemology,** the philosophical study of the nature and origins of knowledge, were established in ancient Greece in the works of Plato and Aristotle. Plato (427–347 B.C.) developed a theory of knowledge that was presented in one of his famous dialogues, the *Republic.*

In making the case for innate knowledge, Plato argued that humans may be compared to a group of prisoners chained to a low wall of a cave. Light is provided by a fire above and behind them. As animals pass, and as people carry objects by, the firelight casts shadows on the cave wall opposite the prisoners. These shadows provide only fleeting impressions of reality. But should a prisoner be released and allowed to view the objects directly, then to see them outside the cave, and finally to look at the heavens and the sun directly, the prisoner will come to know, through reason and intuition, the relationship of the real world to the world of the shadows. Plato's point is that there are two psychological worlds, a world of phenomena and a world of Forms (eternal ideas inherent in every person). The sensory world is changing and unreal, like the flickering shadows on the wall of the cave. The world of Forms is unchanging and eternal, like the sun, and is known through reason, not through sensory experience.

As another demonstration that knowledge is inherent in every person, regardless of experience, Plato noted (in the *Meno*) that through careful questioning, Socrates was able to lead a slave boy who had received no schooling to solve a geometric equation. Because Socrates had not revealed the solution, Plato argued that the boy must have been born with knowledge of it. In summary, for Plato knowledge was the possession of truth, an understanding that relied on reasoning, but not at all on sensory experience.

Like the prisoners in Plato's cave, what you see in this Balinese shadow puppet show is not the object itself, but rather only the shadow it casts on the screen. Plato believed that we cannot contact the world directly, so we must understand it through the application of reason.

Aristotle

Although Plato's student Aristotle (384–322 B.C.) initially defended his teacher's views, he soon developed a quite different theory of knowledge. In his *Metaphysics* he writes, "All men by nature desire to know. An indication of this is the delight we take in our senses ..." (1952, p. 499). Throughout this work he emphasized the role of the senses in the acquisition of knowledge. In another treatise, *On the Soul,* he describes the mind as a writing tablet on which nothing is written before the individual begins thinking and having sensory experiences. This image of an empty writing tablet—a **tabula rasa**—was later popularized by John Locke in his *Essay on Human Understanding:* "Let us then suppose the mind to be, as we say, white paper, void of all characters, without any ideas: How comes it to be furnished? ... I answer in one word, from *experience*" (1952/1690, p. 121).

For Aristotle and those who followed his lead, all knowledge was derived from the senses, that is, through experience. Aristotle's interest in broad experience was also reflected in his approach to science. He collected biological specimens and wrote extensively on the classification of plants and animals. Such activity was an important legacy for modern psychology, because it presupposed that knowledge would be based on observations gathered from the external world (Robinson, 1979).

THE MIDDLE AGES: RELIGION AND KNOWLEDGE

Augustine

Through the next thousand years, the writings of Plato and Aristotle were nearly lost. There was very little examination of the origins of human knowledge, and what there was tended to emphasize religious doctrine rather than independent inquiry. Science declined with the decline of the Roman Empire, reaching a low ebb in the second century A.D. (Watson, 1968). And as Christianity changed from being an obscure sect to a major religion, it began to defend itself from non-Christian thought, including philosophical inquiry into human nature. In 313 the Emperor Constantine issued the

Artist's conception of Aristotle (right) and his teacher Plato (left) engaged in a philosophical discussion.

Edict of Milan, which secured the toleration of Christianity. Official recognition of Christianity had one crucial consequence for philosophical inquiry: "Heresy was born. Unlike the 'easy-going' religions of old ... Christianity demanded uncompromising adherence to the one God who through the voices of the Hebrew prophets and through Christ had made manifest the Truth" (Watson, 1968, p. 89). This dogmatic view, coupled with the prevailing preoccupation with sin, had three implications for psychological thought. First, the mind–body problem became of critical importance. How could reason be used to bring the passions of the body under control? Second, human beings—whose reasoning ability made them morally accountable—were clearly distinguished from animals assumed not to possess reason. And third, emphasis on an afterlife made people suspicious of natural phenomena because they were of this world (Watson, 1968).

From the perspective of psychology, the most important figure during the first few centuries A.D. was Aurelius Augustine (354–430). After training in Carthage, Augustine became a teacher of rhetoric, first in Carthage, then in Rome, and then in Milan. Early in his intellectual life Augustine embraced what is known as **Neoplatonism,** a philosophical position that rests on Plato's distinction between the sensory world and the world of Forms. When Augustine moved to Milan, his thinking was dramatically influenced by his friendship with Ambrose, the Bishop of Milan. Within two or three years, Augustine had undergone a religious conversion, been baptized by Ambrose, and resigned his teaching position to organize a monastery in Africa.

Like Plato, Augustine distinguished between a sensory world, known through the sense organs, and an "intelligible" world, known through the mind (or, in the Christian parlance of the time, the soul). It was a small step from Plato's world of Forms to a world of spiritual truth provided by a deity. Thus, whereas for Plato ultimate truth was found through reason, for Augustine ultimate truth was derived from faith.

Preservation of the Ancient Wisdom

During the fifth century the Roman Empire began to collapse. A society that had been cemented together by a uniform system of Roman law fell into chaos. Local customs replaced central authority, the social fabric was torn by internal strife and invasions by barbarians, cities and towns virtually disappeared. During this period from about 500 A.D. to 900 A.D., often described as the Dark Ages, there was little scholarship of any kind, religious or philosophical, in what had been the Roman Empire.

The philosophy of the ancient Greeks might have been lost forever if it had not been preserved in translations made by followers of a very different religion—Islam. In 570 A.D. Mahomet was born in Mecca, Arabia. When he was an adult he received a revelation from God, began preaching the principles based on this revelation, and in 622 had to flee from Mecca to Medina, where he died 10 years later. He called his religion Islam and his followers Muslims; his teachings are contained in a holy book called the Koran.

Mahomet's followers took up the task of spreading his teachings and were tremendously successful. At its height a hundred years after Mahomet's death, the Muslim Empire encompassed an area larger than had the Roman Empire. With so many lands under domination, translation was an important tool in the diffusion of Muslim culture, and many of the works translated were from the ancient Greek and Roman writings. From the eighth century to the twelfth, it was Muslim culture, not Western culture, that preserved the theory of knowledge inherent in the philosophy and science of the ancients.

In the twelfth century, during a period often called the High Middle Ages, the works of the Greek philosophers were rediscovered in the West. Works of Aristotle and Plato were again translated into Latin, many from Arabic, and some from the original Greek. In this epoch universities were founded in Bologna, Paris, and Oxford, and scholars once again examined the wisdom of the ancients, thus reestablishing a Western link to the past. Religion still influenced views of the origins of

During the early Middle Ages in Europe, the wisdom of the ancient Greeks was preserved in translations made by Islamic scholars.

knowledge, but the universities had begun to lay the foundation for scientific inquiry.

THE RENAISSANCE AND THE REEMERGENCE OF SCIENCE

Religion retained much of its authority during the Renaissance (ca. 1450–1600), but during the seventeenth century it was confronted by a number of challenges arising out of scientific inquiry. The most dramatic of those challenges was Copernicus's "heretical" notion that the earth and the other planets revolve around the sun. This idea met with an immediate and heated reaction, partly because it violated what everyone "knows." We do not see the earth revolving, nor do we feel ourselves spinning. What we see are the stars and planets traveling through the skies. It is obvious, therefore, that the universe revolves around the earth. More serious, however, was the fact that Copernicus's heliocentric system flew in the face of theology. If the earth rotated around the sun, humanity lost its privileged position in the universe; thus the idea that human beings had been created by God was called into question. The church was so adamantly opposed to the heliocentric theory that the astronomer Galileo was forced to recant his belief in Copernicus's theory to avoid the punishment given to heretics—being burned at the stake.

Francis Bacon (1561–1626) is the English baron whose four "tables" of comparisons helped to establish the foundation of the modern experimental method in science.

Another influential figure in the reemergence of science was Francis Bacon (1561–1626). Bacon's main contribution to the history of science was his use of the experiment as a method of gaining knowledge. Where the followers of Aristotle had emphasized the study of objects themselves, Bacon argued for the importance of making comparisons between objects in order to discover abstract dimensions on which the objects might be similar or different.

For example, in his *Novum Organum* Bacon described the use of four "tables" to study a phenomenon such as heat. The first, called the table of existence and presence, would list all the instances of the phenomenon under study. (Thus, instances of heat include the sun's rays, flames of all kinds, and a spark created by friction.) The second table, called the table of deviation or absence, would list all the corresponding instances in which the phenomenon is absent. (In the case of heat, only the sun's rays have a corresponding negative, the rays of the moon.) The third table, the table of comparative instances, would show variations in the phenomenon under study. (Spices are not warm to the touch but are hot to the palate; certain animals are cold

14

externally but warm internally; the motion of a bellows increases the heat of a fire.) Finally, all the information from the first three tables would be combined into a fourth, the exclusive table. (For example, heat cannot be merely terrestrial, or the sun's rays would not be warm; it cannot be an enduring aspect of objects, or objects warmed by friction would be warm all the time; it cannot be confined to flames, or animals and spices would be cold.) In sum, Bacon believed that knowledge could be gained by making comparisons among phenomena experienced by the senses.

EMPIRICISM

Bacon's approach set the stage for **empiricism,** the doctrine that all knowledge (with the possible exceptions of logic and mathematics) is derived from experience. During the seventeenth and eighteenth centuries empiricism became a key characteristic of scientific inquiry. Although the strong version of empiricism described here has been challenged, its emphasis on the collection of data through experimentation remains a guiding principle of psychology and other scientific disciplines.

The great British philosopher John Locke (1632–1704) is generally regarded as the founder of empiricism. Locke asserted that all knowledge is derived from sensations. He also mounted a strong attack against the Platonic notion of innate ideas, which was being defended by Descartes. For Locke, ideas and all other elements of mental life come from experience. Hence his insistence, as we noted earlier, that at birth the mind is like a blank page, a tabula rasa, to be written on by experience.

If knowledge is derived from the senses, there must be some means of transforming sensory experience into new ideas. Another British philosopher, David Hume (1711–1776), attempted to discover the processes by which this occurs. Hume claimed that the contents of the mind take two forms. The first consists of *impressions,* the forceful and vivid perceptions that occur when we hear, see, feel, love, hate, desire, or will. The second consists of *ideas,* the thoughts and memories derived from impressions; ideas are faint copies of impressions. To explain how the contents of the mind are created or combined, Hume proposed three "principles of association."

According to the law of resemblance or similarity, an impression may trigger a particular idea because the two are similar. For example, a picture of a house (impression) may elicit a thought of the actual house (idea).

According to the law of contiguity, one idea may trigger the memory of another if the sensations on which the ideas were based were close to each other in space or time. This is the principle behind the pairing of glossary terms with their definitions, of dates with the historical events that they signify, or of words from a foreign language with the words they represent in the native language.

According to the law of cause and effect, if two events are contiguous in space or time, with one always preceding the other, the person experiencing the events will come to believe (perhaps mistakenly) that the first event is the cause of the second. This is the origin of the "lucky charm." An article of jewelry or clothing always worn before a successful academic performance, for example, may come to be seen as the cause of the success.

Engraving of David Hume (1711–1776), one of the philosophers known as the British empiricists. Empiricists argued that all knowledge was derived from the senses, and Hume proposed three "principles of association" by which this might occur.

CRITIQUES OF EMPIRICISM

Empiricism as embodied in the views of Bacon, Locke, and Hume is the opposite of Plato's belief that knowledge can be gained through reasoning alone. But some eighteenth-century philosophers came to the defense of Plato's view and opposed the empiricist claim that all knowledge originates from experience. Foremost among empiricism's critics was the German philosopher Immanuel Kant (1724–1804).

Kant believed that some knowledge is obtained through experience. He called this *empirical knowledge* and distinguished it from fundamental principles that must underlie experience. These principles exist *a priori,* a Latin term for "from what is before." These a priori principles are independent of experience, universal, and necessary. To illustrate the difference between the kinds of things we learn from experience and the kinds of things we know from a priori principles, Kant compared the way we might view a house to the way we would be forced to view a passing ship. If you were standing outside a house, you could begin to look at it at the level of the foundation and then direct your gaze upward to the roof. Or you could look at the house in the reverse order. Because the house is stationary, with all its parts visible at the same time, you can look at its parts in any order you wish. But if you were standing on the edge of a canal and a ship passed in front of you, you would see the bow of the ship first, the beam next, and the stern last. The order in which you can see the parts is dictated by the direction in which the ship passes you, and you cannot reverse that order.

Kant's point is that you do not need to have seen a ship sail down a canal in order to know the difference between perceiving something that is stationary and perceiving something that is moving in a single direction. The ability to recognize the difference between the two situations is derived from an a priori understanding of what Kant called the "principle of necessity": The passing of the ship *of necessity* means that its parts can be perceived in only one order. Thus, where the empiricists rejected all claims for the existence of innate knowledge, Kant proposed a version of the Platonic view, asserting that at least the idea of causality (and others, such as space and time) is known a priori rather than as a result of experience.

Thomas Reid (1863, Vol. 1), another influential critic of empiricism, argued that the understanding of cause and effect is not, as the empiricists argued, an inference we draw from the constant conjunction of events, but rather is a conviction based on the inner experience of the exercise of will. This argument embodies two elements that are significant for psychology. First, causality involves more than a constant conjunction of events. For example, day always follows night, but no one believes that day *causes* night. Second, the kind of causality involved in human behavior is fundamentally different from the causality observed in physical systems. Events merely happen in physical systems. If a car with its engine off is given a push at the top of a hill, it will roll down the hill, partway up the other side, back down to the bottom, up the original slope, back down again, and so forth, coming to rest at the bottom as if it had been a pendulum released at the top of its arc. In contrast, people *create* events in response to their own intentions: If the car is being driven by a person, where it comes to rest will depend on where the driver was planning to go. Thus, intention is the fundamental element of personal (as opposed to physical) causality.

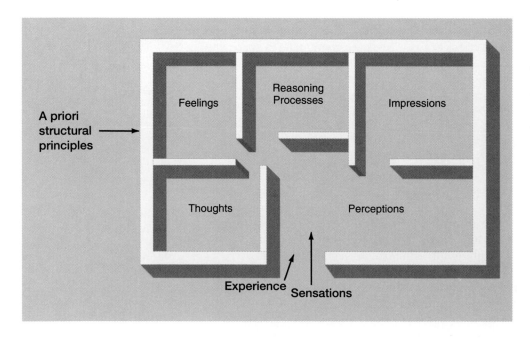

A priori structural principles

Feelings

Reasoning Processes

Impressions

Thoughts

Perceptions

Experience   Sensations

FIGURE 1-3 The mind as a room. Modern psychology views knowledge as resulting from a combination of experience and innate structures. In this view, the mind is like a room: It has certain preexisting structures like floors, walls, ceilings, and doors, but the way the empty structure is furnished depends on what the individual occupant brings to it.

Modern psychology takes a middle position on the question of whether knowledge is innate or derived from experience. Its predominant techniques are based on empiricism, and many of its areas of interest, such as learning and social development, are founded on the assumption that experience plays a crucial role in human behavior. Other areas of interest, such as the inheritance of intelligence, or the study of language, are based on the assumption that some elements of knowledge are present at birth. In sum, psychology assumes that much of the "furniture" of the mind is brought in from outside through experience, but it enters a room that already has a floor, walls, and a ceiling (see Figure 1-3).

INTERIM SUMMARY

Where does knowledge come from? The ancient Greek philosophers had opposing views on this question, with Plato arguing that knowledge can be gained only through reason and intuition, and Aristotle emphasizing the importance of the senses in the acquisition of knowledge. With the rise of Christianity, the notion of truth derived from faith became dominant and scientific inquiry was discouraged. During the seventeenth century a burgeoning interest in science produced major challenges to religious authority. Francis Bacon's emphasis on the importance of studying the relationships among objects laid the groundwork for the rise of empiricism, the doctrine that all knowledge is derived from experience. John Locke and David Hume carried forward the empiricist tradition, but Immanuel Kant and Thomas Reid argued that some knowledge may be innate.

NATURE VERSUS NURTURE

The fragile line between "civilized" behavior and savagery has been crossed many times throughout history. The frequency of war, murder, and torture stands as eloquent testimony to the human potential for violence. Why is this dark side of human nature so apparent in some individuals and so effectively restrained in others? Are some people born killers, or has their behavior been molded by a bad environment? If there can be born killers, can there also be born healers? More broadly, what accounts for the differences among individuals: heredity (nature) or environment (nurture)? This nature–nurture controversy has been at the center of psychological debate for centuries.

DARWIN'S THEORY OF EVOLUTION

From the time of the ancient Greeks through the Middle Ages, no one questioned the notion that humans are inherently superior to all other animals. This belief was the target of the theory of evolution proposed by Charles Darwin in 1859. If the Copernican revolution removed humanity from the center of the universe, the Darwinian revolution eroded humanity's special place on the earth. For the ancient Greeks, the human capacity for contemplation and reason set people apart from animals. In the dogma of Christianity and other religions, humans were the only creatures capable of entertaining the idea of a supreme deity; they were the only ones for whom moral responsibility, sin, and redemption were possible. In terms of the theory of evolution, however, humans became merely a highly evolved animal species.

Darwin was interested in the question of how traits such as eye color or body shape are passed from one generation to the next. Others knew that traits could be inherited, if only on the practical level of breeding plants or livestock, but Darwin

Charles Darwin (1809–1882), the British naturalist, proposed a theory of natural selection that had three basic propositions: More animals are born than live to sexual maturity, there are variations among individuals within a species, and the environment poses a challenge. Individuals best prepared to cope with this challenge will be the most likely to survive to pass on their traits.

was the first to envision a detailed and systematic theory to explain heredity. In 1835 he set sail from England as the ship's naturalist aboard HMS *Beagle*. His primary duties were to record the flora and fauna in the newly explored lands of South America, but the observations he made during the five-year voyage became the basis for his theory of evolution.

Darwin's observations of the animal inhabitants of the Galapagos Islands provided crucial evidence for his theory. Because the islands were isolated from the South American continent, animals stranded there were unable to escape; they had to adapt to conditions on the islands or perish. But the islands contained a number of distinct habitats, each of which posed vastly different challenges. On the coast the terrain was harsh and dry; inland, at a higher elevation, there were tropical rain forests. The variety of habitats, each with its own animal inhabitants, suggested to Darwin that any creature must adapt to very specific conditions in order to survive.

On the basis of his observations in the Galapagos, Darwin outlined the three fundamental principles of what he called *natural selection:*

1. Many more animals are born than live to sexual maturity.
2. There are variations among individuals within a given species. Some are born somewhat larger than normal, others are smaller; some are slightly faster, others are slower; some have keener eyesight than others.
3. The environment poses a challenge. There is only so much food to be found and only so much time in which to hunt or forage. There are predators and there are competitors for mates. Coping with these challenges is a matter of life and death.

Together these conditions give rise to natural selection. On the average, animals whose unique collection of inherited traits give them even a slight advantage in the struggle for survival within their environmental niche are more likely to survive and reproduce and to pass that advantage on to their offspring. Animals whose inherited traits do not help them meet the challenges posed by their environment will not pass on those traits. Not every unfit individual will die before reaching sexual maturity, nor will every fit individual survive long enough to reproduce. But the chances are higher that those most capable of meeting the challenges of their environment will survive to reproduce and pass their traits on to the next generation. Nature thus "selects" the most advantageous mutations.

Painting of the HMS *Beagle*. Charles Darwin was the ship's naturalist on its voyage to the Galapagos Islands; Darwin used his observations in the islands as evidence for his theory of evolution.

THE CONCEPT OF INSTINCTS

It did not take long for Darwin's ideas to find their way into psychology. They first appeared in the works of the influential American psychologist and philosopher William James (1842–1910). James had been invited by Henry Holt, the publisher, to write a psychology textbook that took evolutionary theory into account. The result was James's two-volume textbook, *The Principles of Psychology,* published in 1890. It described the "science of mental life," including topics ranging from neural processes to the exercise of will, as a natural science in which evolution played a significant role. A shorter version of the text for classroom use, *Psychology: Briefer Course* was published in 1892. This book was soon translated into French and German and continued to be reprinted until 1945. Read by thousands of students, both works helped establish psychology as an independent discipline based on natural science.

James and other contemporary writers (for example, McDougall, 1908) were interested in discovering exactly how the evolutionary principles stated by Darwin are represented in specific animal and human behaviors. They suggested that part of the answer may lie in instincts. James defined an instinct as a "faculty of acting in such a way as to produce certain ends, without foresight of the ends, and without previous education in the performance" (1984/1892, p. 339). This definition suggests that instincts—insofar as they influence behavior "without previous education," that is, without experience—are innate. Two aspects of the definition deserve comment.

First, instinctive behavior is engaged in for purposes that are outside the conscious awareness of the organism. In the case of animals this point was viewed as self-evident on the presumption that animals do not possess the ability to reflect on their behavior. Even in the case of humans, however, behaviors aimed at securing warmth, sex, or food were believed to be nonconscious in nature. James argued that if one asks a man *why* he is eating what admittedly tastes good, "instead of revering you as a philosopher he will probably laugh at you for a fool" (1984/1892, p. 341).

Second, only the first instance of an instinctive behavior must occur without prior education. Once an instinctive behavior has been performed, instinct may be modified by experience. In other words, the organism may initially respond to the demands of its environment by engaging in an instinctive behavior, but on subsequent occasions that behavior may be modified on the basis of what has been learned on previous occasions. Moreover, James believed that as animals evolved into more complex creatures they developed many more instincts, some of which might compete with one another. Thus, whereas a lower animal's instinctive behavior would

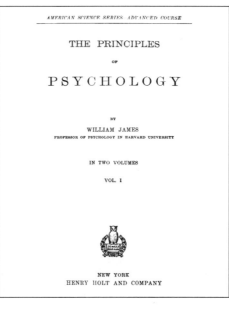

AMERICAN SCIENCE SERIES: ADVANCED COURSE

THE PRINCIPLES

OF

PSYCHOLOGY

BY

WILLIAM JAMES
PROFESSOR OF PSYCHOLOGY IN HARVARD UNIVERSITY

IN TWO VOLUMES

VOL. I

NEW YORK
HENRY HOLT AND COMPANY

Left: Portrait of William James (1842–1910), the American scholar who wrote the first text in psychology. *Right:* Opening page of William James's text in psychology. This two-volume book described the "science of mental life" in terms based in part on Darwin's theory of natural selection.

Instincts in action: The ocelot instinctively hunts a small field mouse, but a human's instinctive reaction to the mouse might be tempered by experience.

be triggered immediately by a particular stimulus, a human's instinctive behavior might involve some hesitation, caused either by the existence of a competing instinct or by a learned association. For example, when a cat sees a mouse it pounces on it immediately, but a human might wonder how to kill the mouse without touching it.

In sum, James's view represents a combination of the nature and nurture perspectives, because it takes into account both inherited instincts and learned responses to the demands of the environment.

BEHAVIORISM

Another description of psychology as a natural science—*behaviorism*—rejects "nature" entirely, claiming that all behavior is learned. Behaviorism is described more fully in Chapter 2; here we focus on its relevance to the nature–nurture debate.

In the early 1900s the chief proponent of behaviorism was John B. Watson (1878–1958). Like James, Watson was impressed by Darwin's insights, especially the importance of considering human beings a highly evolved animal species, rather than unique organisms different in kind from all other animals. Watson initially endorsed the concept of instinct, although he considered it ambiguous (Watson, 1914). But by 1924 he had thoroughly rejected the idea that any behavior might have a hereditary basis, whether that basis was instinct or something else. Instead, he claimed that human behavior is shaped entirely by the environment. This view is vividly expressed in an often-quoted passage from his book *Behaviorism:*

> Give me a dozen healthy infants, well-formed, and my own specified world to bring them up in and I'll guarantee to take any one at random and train him to become any type of specialist I might select—doctor, lawyer, artist, merchant-chief and, yes, even beggar-man and thief, regardless of his talents, penchants, tendencies, abilities, vocations, and race of his ancestors. (1924, p. 104)

Clearly, this position is at the "nurture" extreme of the nature–nurture debate. Only the infant's health is left to heredity.

Today most psychologists agree that a thorough understanding of human behavior requires an analysis of both inherited and learned factors. The individual's genetic heritage sets limits on his or her behavior. Within those limits, behavior is shaped by the person's environment. No one has ever seriously defended the position that all human traits are inherited, and the other extreme, represented by Watson's claim, is no longer viewed as credible. When nature–nurture arguments occur in various subfields of psychology, they have to do with the relative contributions of genetic heritage and environmental influences.

INTERIM SUMMARY

Psychologists have long debated the question of whether the differences among individuals are attributable to heredity (nature) or environment (nurture). The argument for inherited traits is based on Darwin's principles of natural selection, in which inherited traits that give an organism an advantage in the struggle for survival are passed on to subsequent generations. In attempting to explain how those principles are represented in specific behaviors, William James emphasized the role of instincts. John B. Watson, in contrast, claimed that the environment alone shapes human behavior, a view that is termed *behaviorism.* Modern psychologists believe that both inherited and learned factors play a role in human behavior.

INDIVIDUAL AND GROUP

As noted earlier, Darwin's theory of evolution eroded humankind's claim to a special place among the animals on earth. There are, however, a few areas in which humans seem to be unique—to be different in kind, not just degree, from other animals. One of these qualitative differences can be seen in the organization of human societies, specifically the relationship between the individual and the group.

Although a good deal of animal behavior also takes place in a social context—witness the social stratification in a beehive, or the cooperative hunting of a pack of wild dogs—there remain two essential points of contrast. First, human societies possess structures for the regulation of conduct, sets of group-created expectations about how individuals should behave. These expectations may take the form of legends designed to transmit culture or morality, abstract moral principles (such as the "golden rule"), formally codified laws, or the unspoken desires of a person's romantic partner. Second, because of the human's capacity for abstract thinking, people create for themselves personal identities that depend in part on other people. The "self" is a particularly human construction, and it incorporates both one's place in relation to others (family, ethnic background, cultural heritage) and what many of those others think of one.

The importance of social structure in the lives of humans can be seen in two related areas: the role of other people in the development of the self (to what extent is the self molded and maintained by interactions with others?) and the formal and informal exchanges that occur between individuals (what do people seek in their exchanges with others, and how can it be determined whether those exchanges are fair?).

DEVELOPMENT OF THE SELF

What exactly is the self, and to what extent is it determined by other individuals in the person's environment? For the ancient Greeks, the self was equivalent to the soul, which included such things as reason, desire, and passion. Whether the soul could be influenced by external agents depended on the soul's relationship to the body. Some philosophers, such as Plato, believed that the soul is immortal, existing prior to the existence of the body and continuing to exist after the body has perished. At least the second half of this belief is found in Christianity and other religious doctrines that include the idea of an afterlife. Other philosophers, such as Descartes, believed that the soul is inextricably bound to the body.

Only a soul linked to the body can be influenced to any great degree by people with whom that body comes in contact. Consequently, it is not surprising that Descartes's work, which helped to crystallize the mind–body debate, also marked an important turning point from prior discussion of "the soul" to discussion of "the self." In the second of his *Meditations,* Descartes disagreed with the Platonic view that the soul includes reason, passion, and desire. Instead, he equated the soul with the mind, which he went on to treat as interchangeable with the self—"I think, therefore I am." Thus, for Descartes the human capacity for reflective thought was both the essential feature of the soul and the defining characteristic of the self.

In the same book that brought evolutionary theory to bear on psychological thought, William James (1890) attempted to combine Descartes's ideas with the Platonic notion of a soul that also includes passion and desire. He divided the self into two basic components, the *I* and the *Me.* The *I* represents the "pure ego," the self as knower, as organized stream of consciousness. In this respect James's *I* is similar to the mind–self–soul concept proposed by Descartes, but there is a critical difference: For Descartes and other philosophers, the soul included not only the conscious reflections occurring at the present moment but also those that had occurred in the past. But James (1890) dismissed the past—and future—of the soul by arguing that *psychology* needed only to deal with the present consciousness. For James, whether or not there was going to be a conscious future for the self after the mortal death of the body was not a psychological question. Moreover, James claimed that whatever past reflections there might be are stored in the other part of the self, the *Me.* Thus the *I* is self-as-process, whereas the *Me* is the "empirical self," or the self-as-content.

James thus offered a solution to the problems created by the notion of an immortal soul. A soul that exists after the death of the body cannot be studied by the methods of scientific inquiry, but a present state of consciousness can be studied, for example, by the psychophysical methods outlined earlier. Moreover, if we assume like Plato that desires and passions are included in the soul, or like Descartes that all thinking, past and present, is included in the mind–self–soul, these additional elements are beyond the reach of science. Alternatively, if we assume with James that past thinking, present emotions, and present desires are all included in the *Me,* which is available for empirical study, the research problem is solved.

Social and cultural influence on the self begins with the birth of the human being. Like the young of many species, the human child depends on its parents for food and protection until it is able to care for itself. But the human child also depends on its parents (or caregivers) for knowledge about human society. Indeed, the educator and social commentator Jean-Jacques Rousseau (1712–1778), in a description of the social ties among individuals, noted that "the most ancient of all societies, and the only one that is natural, is the family" (1952/1762, p. 387).

When a child first experiences the distinction between self and other, the other is typically a parent. When the child first learns that actions have consequences (which are not always pleasant), that some individuals have a position in the group that is different from the child's, or that there are informal rules for sharing and exchanges, the lessons are provided within the context of the family. In psychological terms, the child's cognitive, social, and moral development begins in the first social group it encounters—the family.

Jean-Jacques Rousseau (1712–1778), the French philosopher, argued that in a state of nature, humans would pursue their own interests with a minimum of conflict.

RULES OF SOCIAL EXCHANGE

Throughout the history of Western thought it has been generally agreed that the external social environment influences the development of the self. Even believers in an immortal soul have viewed the soul as capable of perfecting itself. The fact that such perfection is possible indicates that the person must have at least some com-

The family is the first human society to which an individual (the child) must adapt. The child's encounters are the beginning of cognitive, social, and moral development.

merce with the external environment, if only to discover in what ways to change. What is at issue is the *value* (positive or negative) of the external influence. Specifically, does participation in group activities with other people benefit or harm the individual? This question has frequently been answered in terms of the exercise of power and the effort to establish principles for fair social exchange between individuals, or between an individual and the larger society.

The State of Nature

Are individuals better off or worse off because they live in organized societies? One way to answer this question is to think about what humans might be like without social organization. Here Rousseau's description of the primitive human is instructive. Although preceding Darwin's theory of evolution by almost a hundred years, Rousseau's work had a decidedly evolutionary flavor. Stripping mankind of all acquired faculties, "we behold in him an animal weaker than some, and less agile than others, but, taking him all round, the most advantageously organized of any" (1952/1762, p. 334). Humans in a state of nature (that is, not living in societies) would begin life equal in physical and mental capacity. They would develop a "robust and almost unalterable constitution" (1952/1762, p. 335) as a result of their daily struggle to survive. Sexual contacts would carry no commitment. Strong and well-formed children would survive until they could leave their mothers and forage on their own, but weaker ones would perish. Whatever language there was would be highly individualized and would be instigated by the children to make their needs known.

One might think that people existing under such conditions would have no obligations to one another and hence would be neither virtuous nor vicious. But Rousseau argued that natural human compassion, not the social group, "supplies the place of laws, morals, and virtues" (1952/1762, p. 345). He recognized that society serves to regulate sexual relations and the dominance of one person or another. But he believed that for man in a state of nature, physical needs, not love or admiration, would be the reason for sexual intercourse, "so every woman equally answers his purpose." Similarly, Rousseau asserted that without mutual dependence there could be no domination or servitude; there would be no way to force obedience from an equal. Thus, for Rousseau participation in society is harmful to humans: Society began with the first man who enclosed a piece of land and said *This is mine,* and found people simple enough to believe him" (1952/1762, p. 348). War and murder are creations of organized society. People left to their own devices would satisfy their simple needs with as little harm to others as possible.

The Need for Social Control

The opposite point of view, to which Rousseau was replying, was expressed by Thomas Hobbes. Hobbes began with the same first assumption as Rousseau, namely that human beings are created equal in terms of physical and mental endowments. But he believed that out of this equality of ability would arise "equality of hope in the attaining of our ends. And therefore if any two men desire the same thing, which nevertheless they cannot both enjoy, they become enemies . . . [endeavoring] to destroy or subdue one another" (1952/1651, p. 84). Even in a state of nature, people would use violence to gain domination over others or to prevent such domination, or to gain respect that they would not otherwise receive. Consequently, Hobbes believed that "during the time men live without a common power to keep them all in awe, they are in that condition which is called *war,* and such a war is of every man against every man" (1952/1651, p. 85).

To avoid annihilation, according to Hobbes, humans must form a "commonwealth." In such a commonwealth, each individual relinquishes some of his or her liberty in exchange for protection against violence at the hands of others. The commonwealth was empowered to regulate conduct by passing laws, imposing punishments on those who broke the laws, and providing rewards to those who performed valued functions. Without such controls, Hobbes believed, life would be "solitary, poor, brutish, nasty, and short" (1952/1651, p. 85).

Today the state of nature, if it ever existed, cannot be recaptured. Social groups are mere threads in the fabric of a global human society. Social exchange is regulated by informal customs that have been honored for centuries, local and national legal systems, and by international treaties. Because of these controls on behavior, individual actions must be considered in the context of the social groups to which the person belongs.

INTERIM SUMMARY

Philosophers have viewed the self as identical with the soul and/or the mind, but modern psychologists generally agree with William James that the self has two parts: the conscious reflection occurring at any given moment, and past thoughts, present emotions, and present desires. Although it has generally been agreed that the external social environment influences the development of the self, the value of that influence has been debated. Whereas Rousseau believed that without social organization the human would be admirably independent, Hobbes held that society was necessary to prevent humans from becoming enmeshed in a condition of constant warfare. Today social organization is so pervasive that individual behavior must be considered in the context of the groups to which the person belongs.

STABILITY VERSUS CHANGE

Life represents a balance between stability and change. Comparing the original "state of nature" to today's complex industrialized societies suggests that the living conditions of human beings have changed dramatically. Yet a child's first experience with society is still likely to be in a family. At the societal level, then, some things have remained the same despite tremendous change. The same is true for an individual person: some aspects change, others remain the same. Although changing from infant to child to adult, a human being remains in an important way the same person. Despite the fact that one's moods and behavior can change dramatically from moment to moment, the core of the self remains relatively constant. On the other hand, coping with a major personal tragedy can lead to profound changes in one's personality or psychological health. Our sixth and final theme, stability versus change, addresses these issues.

In psychology, questions of stability and change are most likely to arise in connection with the study of personality and abnormal behavior. We tend to value stability when referring to personality; for example, we expect our friends to behave in predictable ways and we become concerned when we notice that they have changed. On the other hand, psychotherapy rests on the assumption that individuals can change in order to meet the demands of the social world. To understand these psychological applications, we need first to examine more general perspectives on stability and change.

PERSPECTIVES ON CHANGE

Plato's view of change was consistent with his assertion that the soul is immortal. Change is like the body; it can be perceived by the senses. Stability in such matters as truth or virtue may be understood only through the power of reason. Aristotle agreed with Plato that change is inherently more difficult to understand than constancy, but he believed that change could be understood through reason. He believed that there were enduring principles that govern change. Entities may change in size (a tree grows from a sapling), in quality (a leaf turns red in the fall), in place (the leaf falls and is blown elsewhere by the wind), or through birth or death. In each case the thing that is changing may be understood by examining the "contraries"—the initial state of the object and the final state into which it was changing. The object had an original "actuality" and a "potential" that was not fully realized until the change was complete.

The transformation of a caterpillar into a butterfly illustrates the balance between stability and change: Although the outward state of the butterfly is entirely different from that of the caterpillar, it is still the same individual.

Seventeenth-century philosophers, including Locke and especially Descartes, roundly criticized the view that change is the partial realization of an as-yet-unfulfilled potential. We cannot view a leaf as real (and alive) on the tree and real (but dead) on the ground, yet somehow not real during the time that it is changing color before falling. This is an important criticism of Aristotle's position, because all human behavior takes place during the transition from conception to death. It would be absurd to consider behavior unreal because it occurs during this long transitional time.

William James also related change to the passage of time. James argued that "awareness of *change* is ... the condition on which our perception of time's flow depends" (1984/1892, p. 247). But these changes that are available to perception will depend on *what* is measured, and on *how* the measurement procedure is conducted. Keeping these two factors in mind, we now turn to psychological approaches to stability and change.

PSYCHOLOGICAL APPROACHES TO STABILITY AND CHANGE

Modern psychologists believe that objects, animals, and people exist in a state that is best described as relative permanence. From the level of single cells to the level of social structures, stability and change exist as complementaries. Cells die and are replaced, but the replacements carry the same genetic code as the originals. A baby becomes a child, and that child becomes an adult, but the person remains the same human individual despite the often dramatic changes that accompany such development. Nations change entire political and economic systems, and yet somehow retain a common national identity.

How can change be distinguished from stability? To keep the analysis manageable, let us begin by looking at change in an inanimate object such as a tree. The atoms in a tree are constantly moving. The tree itself is constantly growing. Through the seasons its leaves sprout, grow, and die. But we do not expect to wake up to find that the tree has moved from where it was yesterday. Is the tree changing or is it stable? The answer depends on what is chosen for study. If we compare the size of the tree as it is today to its size a year ago, we say it has changed. But if we consider a different aspect, such as its location, we say the tree is stable.

Some human characteristics are as stable as the location of a tree, whereas other human characteristics are more transient than the most changeable aspect of a tree. A person's genetic structure is established at conception and does not change through the person's life. When that genetic background completely determines a characteristic (such as eye color), the characteristic will also remain fixed throughout life. On the other hand, when genetic endowment merely sets a range of possibilities (as is the case with human intelligence), there is an opportunity for environmental influence within the genetically established limits. If genetically based capacities are relatively fixed, motivationally based behaviors can change from moment to moment. Successful performance on ability-linked tasks requires more than genetic inheritance, it also requires a drive to succeed that can vary dramatically from one task to another. And a person's emotional reaction to progress (or lack of progress) on the task can change in the blink of an eye. All of this indicates that some behaviors are inherently more variable than others.

MEASUREMENT OF STABILITY AND CHANGE

Some behaviors have long time frames and others short ones, the same is true of the methods used by psychological science. The longest time frames found in psychological research are typically those of life-span developmental psychology, in which individuals are compared across periods of years at different stages in their cognitive and social growth. In contrast, some of the shortest time spans occur in studies of the

----

ERRATA SHEET

Page 27, the complete INTERIM SUMMARY *should read:*

A sixth major theme of psychology is stability versus change: To what extent do entities (people, trees, social groups) remain the same and yet change over time? Stability and change can generally be understood as complementary aspects of the same entity. In psychology, questions of stability and change are most likely to arise in relation to the study of personality and abnormal behavior. The time span chosen and the aspects of a phenomenon selected for observation affect the observer's judgment regarding stability or change. The view of stability and change as complementary also has methodological implications: Time enters into the description of any psychological phenomenon; conclusions are presumed to apply as long as conditions remain the same. And the coexistence of stability and change within an individual may require the use of special statistical measures to separate them.

Page 104, second paragraph under The Moon Illusion *should read:*

Many explanations of the moon illusion have been offered. Several investigators have claimed that Emmert's law accounts for this illusion (Rock, 1975). As shown in part *a* of Figure 4-23, the perceived size of an object on the horizon can be strongly affected by depth cues. The retinal image of the moon is actually the same size in both parts of the figure, but the perceived distance is not. (In part *a* the moon looks farther away because of linear perspective.) Therefore, because the inferred distance is greater but the actual retinal image is the same, the moon is perceived to be larger when it is on the horizon.

effects of drugs on the neurochemistry of the brain, in which observations may last only a few thousandths of a second.

One of the fundamental measurement problems for psychological science is to choose research procedures whose duration is appropriate for the phenomenon under study. This challenge is the same whether the behavior is a neural response that lasts a fraction of a second or the gradual increase in social skill that occurs across years of a child's development. On one hand, the procedure selected must first be short enough to discover change when it occurs. Measurements taken every few minutes will likely be frequent enough to detect changes in expressed emotional behavior, but will not be frequent enough to record many of the neural processes involved in emotion. On the other hand, the procedure must extend over a period long enough to ensure that the process of change has been completed. In this case, measures taken every few minutes can detect momentary variations in mood, but not the overall improvement in emotional tone that might accompany months of psychotherapy.

The coexistence of stability and change in behavior requires psychological science to do more than select a duration-appropriate procedure. It also dictates particular kinds of experimental designs and statistical methods. For example, experimental methods that contain a sequence of events (say, a sequence of sounds) may reverse the sequence so that the effects of time can be measured or eliminated. As another example, a phenomenon may be measured many times, or in many different ways. These separate instances will then be combined statistically to reveal an overall pattern in what might otherwise appear to be nothing more than random fluctuation.

In sum, psychology faces the difficult task of deriving general principles from behavior that is both stable and continually changing. An individual's characteristics and actions will change over time. And some aspects of the individual will be relatively more permanent than others. One methodological solution to this problem is to employ statistical measures that take random variation into account.

INTERIM SUMMARY

A sixth major theme of psychology is stability versus change: To what extent do entities (people, trees, social groups) remain the same and yet change over time? Stability and change can generally be understood as complementary aspects of the same entity. In psychology, questions of stability and change are most likely to arise in relation to the study of personality and abnormal behavior. The time span chosen and the aspects of a phenomenon selected for observation affect the observer's judgment regarding stability or change. The view of stability and change as complementary also has methodological implications: Time enters into the description of any psychological phenomenon; conclusions are presumed to apply as long as conditions remain the same. And the coexistence of stability and change within an individual

SUMMARY

1. Psychology can be defined in terms of its derivation as a discipline involved in the study of human thought and behavior; it can be distinguished from other related disciplines like sociology, anthropology, and biology by virtue of its concentration on individual behavior; and the breadth of its interests can be seen in the wide range of activities that psychologists perform in their academic and professional settings.

2. In contrast to fields that have been revolutionized by a single discovery, psychology has developed gradually. The field can be seen as grounded on six timeless questions: What is the relationship of the mind to the body? Do people act with free will, or is their behavior determined by forces outside their control? What is the origin of knowledge? How much of human behavior can be accounted for by heredity, and how much by environment? What is the role of the individual in the larger group? To what extent is behavior stable over time? Each of these questions serves as the organizing theme for a group of related chapters in the text.

3. Two philosophical positions lie at the heart of the mind–body problem. These are *dualism,* which holds that mind and body constitute separate realities, and *materialism,* a monistic view that mind and body are the same. The first truly psychological method was *psychophysics,* which described psychological phenomena (for example, sensations) in terms of the physical stimulation (for example, light or sound) that produced the sensation.

4. There are three major positions on the question of free will versus determinism. The first, *hard determinism,* traces all causes of behavior to factors outside the person, thus eliminating the possibility of free will. The second, *indeterminism,* asserts that within the mental realm, the deterministic rules for physical systems do not apply. The third alternative, *soft determinism,* agrees with the deterministic principle that all events have causes but gives personal choices the status of a cause.

5. Are the contents of mind innate, or learned? Plato's world of Forms, Descartes's notion of innate ideas, and Kant's postulation that some cognitive relations and categories are known a priori all argue for some cognitive "furniture" known without experience. Alternatively, Aristotle and Locke argue that initially the human mind is a blank writing tablet, or *tabula rasa,* on which char-

acters are written by experience alone. The scientific doctrine of *empiricism* holds that experience is no less important as a source of scientific truth than as a source of human knowledge. Empiricism and the *principles of association* have been influential specifically in the study of learning, and generally in psychology as a discipline.

6. What accounts for individual differences among people—heredity or environment? On the heredity side, Darwin's *theory of evolution* holds that in the "struggle to survive" those best able to adapt to changing circumstances will live to sexual maturity and pass on their inherited traits. Evolutionary principles, and the "natural science" view of psychology they embody, were first broadly introduced by William James in his influential psychology textbook. The extreme of the environmentalist position is represented in the claim by Watson, the founder of *behaviorism,* that any individual differences among adults can be created by a lifetime of experiences. Although modern psychological theory no longer endorses this extreme view, behaviorism has been an influential guide to research methods.

7. Rousseau argued that in the absence of society people existed as independent beings, living in peace. In contrast, Hobbes argued that humankind's natural state involves war and aggression, both of which can only be regulated by the power of the state. In modern society humans participate in, and are influenced by, a wide range of social groups, from the family to the state. Other people affect the development of *self,* and the exchange between person and group involves rules for determining whether these interchanges have been fair.

8. There is a dynamic relationship between stability and change, with individuals existing in what is best regarded as relative permanence. Alterations of the person through time, and comparisons of different aspects of the same person, are best examined through statistical procedures.

FOCUS QUESTIONS

1. How is the functional materialist theory of mind/body different from the materialist identity theory, and how are both of these different from the dualist theory?

2. What is psychophysics? Why did it play an important role in the beginnings of the field of psychology?

3. Distinguish between hard determinism and soft determinism. Which of these provides the better explanation for human behavior? Defend your answer.

4. What does it mean to say that the mind is a *tabula rasa*? Would Plato have agreed with this description?

5. Compare the religious view of knowledge espoused by Augustine to the scientific view put forward by Copernicus and Bacon.

6. What are the *principles of association*?

7. Hume and Kant differ in their accounts of how people get the contents of their minds. What is the most critical element in this difference?

8. Describe Darwin's theory of evolution, and say what its implications are for the study of psychology as a natural science.

9. What does Rousseau consider to be the most natural of ancient societies? How does Rousseau's vision of the state of nature contrast with Hobbes's view of the function of society?

10. How is it possible that a person can change attitudes and opinions from one day to the next, and yet remain the same person?

CHAPTER 2

PSYCHOLOGY AS A SCIENCE

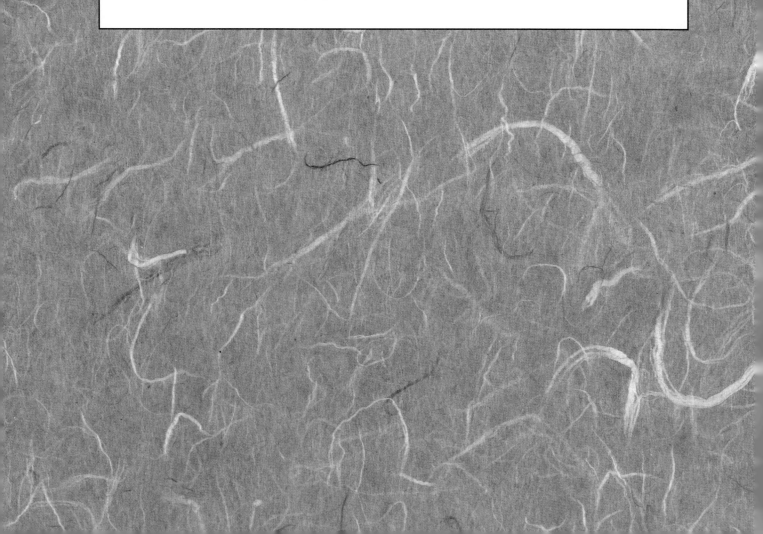

Although the origins of psychology may be found in philosophical and scientific thought since the time of the ancient Greeks, the beginning of psychology as a separate discipline is traced to 1879, when Wilhelm Wundt is said to have founded the first psychological laboratory, at the University of Leipzig. Wundt (1832–1920) had received an M.D. from the University of Heidelberg in 1856, specializing in physiology. In 1858 he became an assistant to Hermann von Helmholtz, a physiologist who became renowned for his theory of color vision. In 1867 Wundt offered a course entitled "Physiological Psychology," and in 1873–74 he published his *Principles of Physiological Psychology,* which described experimental psychology as a separate laboratory science with its own focus and methodology. In 1875 he received a professorship at the University of Leipzig and in 1879 opened his own laboratory. This date "has somehow become 'official' as the beginning of a university-based [psychological] laboratory devoted to research" (Hilgard, 1987, p. 39).

The history of psychology in the United States is intertwined with the beginnings of graduate education in America. One of Wundt's first two students was G. Stanley Hall, who had come to Leipzig for advanced training after receiving his Ph.D. from Harvard University. William James had been Hall's doctoral advisor; Hall's was only the eighteenth Ph.D. granted by Harvard in any subject. Hall founded the first psychological laboratory in the United States in 1883 at Johns Hopkins University, and later went on to become the first president of Clark University, at the time one of the two universities in the United States exclusively devoted to graduate education. Between 1883 and 1900, 41 psychological laboratories were established in the United States; nearly half of them were founded by students of Wundt or Hall. As a result, Wundt had a considerable influence on the early development of American psychology (Hilgard, 1987).

If Wundt was the dean of experimental psychologists, William James was the emerging discipline's philosopher. As noted in Chapter 1, James's *Principles of Psychology* (1890) set forth a wide array of topics to be addressed by psychology. Some, such as sensation and habit, could be investigated by experimental means; others, such as consciousness and the self, remained tantalizingly out of reach.

Wilhelm Wundt (1832–1920) is the German physiologist credited with establishing the first experimental laboratory in psychology in 1879 at the University of Leipzig.

The biological laboratory in 1883 at Johns Hopkins University in which G. Stanley Hall performed some of the first psychology experiments conducted in America.

The rise of psychology as a discipline in the United States coincided with the development of graduate education. In this image from 1893, scholars at Clark University, which was devoted exclusively to graduate education, use a kinesimeter, developed by G. S. Hall.

SCHOOLS OF PSYCHOLOGICAL THOUGHT

From the beginning, the discipline of psychology grappled with the question of how to examine the contents of mind, especially conscious experience, in a scientifically rigorous fashion. Two approaches emerged, developing into the first two schools of psychological thought in the United States: structuralism and functionalism. **Structuralism** was concerned with the building blocks of mental life, whereas **functionalism** emphasized the adaptive value of mental processes. Where a structuralist would ask "What is the essence of the color 'red'?" a functionalist would ask "What good does it do humans to be able to distinguish red from other colors?"

We saw in Chapter 1 that much eighteenth-century philosophy dealt with the origins of knowledge. Hume and other British empiricists argued that all the contents of the mind are constructed from sensory experience. Other philosophers, such as Kant, asserted that some elements of the mind are present at birth and serve to organize sensory experience. Supporters of the latter view are known as idealists because of their belief in the existence of innate "ideas" such as causality, time, and three-dimensional space.

Wundt accepted this position and devoted his research to a search for the ideas that serve to organize the contents of the mind. He believed that these could be identified through **introspection,** the controlled examination of inner perception. He used laboratory instruments to produce precise changes in sensory stimuli and asked subjects to respond to yes-or-no questions about their sensory experiences. For example, a subject might be shown a series of lights that differed slightly in wavelength. For each new display the subject would be asked, "Is this red?"

STRUCTURALISM

Wundt asserted that the elements of sensory experience are combined through a process that he termed *creative synthesis.* This process not only creates new mental contents but also directs cognition or thought (Hilgard, 1987). An example is deciding to solve arithmetic problems. Solving such problems requires thought, and deciding to solve problems instead of doing something else also involves nothing but thought. Thus one thought process is produced by another in an act of creative synthesis. It is important to note that creative synthesis is a voluntary act, in contrast to the passive associations among mental events described by Locke and other empiricists. New mental contents are created not merely by association (for example, through contiguity or similarity) but by an active, voluntary process.

One of Wundt's foremost students was E. B. Titchener (1867–1927), an Englishman who received a Ph.D. from Leipzig in 1892 and spent his academic career at Cornell University. In contrast to Wundt, who concentrated on how sensations might be combined to create the contents of the mind, Titchener emphasized analysis of the sensations themselves. Because of this emphasis on the building blocks of the "structure" of consciousness, the school of psychology associated with Titchener came to be known as structuralism.

Structuralists noted that chemistry had succeeded in discovering the irreducible elements of the physical world. They believed that the mental world could similarly be divided into a set of irreducible elements. But whereas chemistry had discovered 91 naturally occurring elements by 1880, structuralism could identify only three kinds of mental elements: sensations, affections, and images. According to structuralists, *sensations* arise from sensory stimulation and are categorized by modality (for example, vision, hearing, touch), and by their properties (for example, intensity and duration). *Affections,* such as tension or pleasure, accompany sensations and are the elements underlying emotional experiences. *Images* are mental elements, such as memories of past experiences, that are not directly triggered by external stimuli present at the time they are recalled. As such, they provide a context for evaluating sensations.

FUNCTIONALISM

Whereas structuralists focused on the contents of the mind, other psychologists focused on the goals that may be achieved through behavior. Although European psychology had begun to consider "acts" as well as structure, the action-oriented cultural temperament of the United States was especially congenial to this new focus. A number of American psychologists became interested in how the mind might aid the individual in the struggle for survival. For example, an ability to distinguish animals that pose an immediate threat to humans from those that merely look unpleasant would have helped primitive human beings protect themselves from attack. This emphasis on the adaptive character of the mind came to be known as functionalism.

Functionalism was not recognized as a coherent psychological school until Titchener contrasted "functional psychology" with structuralism. Structuralism as Titchener defined it excluded habits and human physiology from the domain of psychology. He maintained that the only truly psychological phenomena are those that have to do with the contents of conscious experience. Titchener's views generated an intense controversy that became a contest for dominance of the discipline of psychology as well as a scientific dispute.

The contest centered on the interpretation of a particular kind of experiment that was frequently used to measure the speed of mental operations. In this kind of experiment, a subject would be seated in a chair facing a table containing a light and a device like a telegraph key. The subject's finger would be resting on the telegraph key, and the subject's task was to lift his or her finger as quickly as possible when the light came on. This procedure provided what was known as **reaction time,** the amount of time it takes to make a muscular response (such as lifting a finger) after receiving a sensory input (such as a light flash).

Reaction time was thought to consist of the time required for a sensory message to reach the brain and for the brain to react to the stimulus and activate the appropriate muscles. Structuralists typically did not take measurements until the subjects had been highly trained in repeated presentations of the light. When measurements were finally recorded among these subjects, those who described themselves as concentrating on the muscular preparation needed to lift a finger as quickly as possible produced consistently shorter reaction times than did those who said they were concentrating on the display where the stimulus was presented.

In 1895, however, James M. Baldwin, a psychologist identified with the functionalist school, conducted the same research with *untrained* subjects (Baldwin & Shaw, 1895). Some of these subjects displayed the typical pattern, but others had faster reaction times when they concentrated on the stimulus display. From the structuralist perspective, these differences were attributable to the procedural error of using

Timing of responses in an early psychometric technique. The same general principles are used in modern reaction-time studies to investigate the operation of cognitive processes.

untrained subjects. From the functionalist point of view, however, they represented different patterns of adaptation. More important, in 1896 James R. Angell, another psychologist associated with the functionalist school, showed that these patterns could be altered through training; subjects who reacted more quickly when they concentrated on the stimulus display could be trained to react more quickly when they concentrated on muscular preparation (Angell & Moore, 1896). To functionalists this suggested that behavior could be changed, or adapted, to fit new circumstances.

Titchener disputed this interpretation, arguing that only expert and practiced observers were capable of producing data that met scientific standards. In other words, for structuralists only "professional" subjects would do. In 1906 Angell defined, and defended, functionalism in his presidential address to the American Psychological Association (Hilgard, 1987; Watson, 1968). Angell objected to Titchener's rejection of physical processes, and drew three points of contrast between functionalism and structuralism. First, he argued that functionalism was a science of mental operations rather than mental contents. Second, he noted that the purpose of the mind was to enable the person to deal effectively with the demands of the environment. And third, he argued that the mind was *psychophysical,* thus linking the contents of the mind to the activities of the body. Angell later became president of the Carnegie Corporation and of Yale University. His illustrious students included John B. Watson, who as noted in Chapter 1 is the founder of behaviorism, L. L. Thurstone, who was responsible for many of the quantitative methods used in psychological research, and three other presidents of the American Psychological Association. Not surprisingly, Angell's defense of functionalism played a significant role in the development of psychology in the United States.

Functionalism can be seen as a transitional step between structuralism's concentration on mental elements and modern psychology's emphasis on the study of behavior in all its varied forms. Unlike structuralism, functional psychology was open to new ideas, problems, and methods of investigation. One result was increased interest in animal psychology. (The study of animal behavior was inconsistent with structuralism's focus on human consciousness.) Functionalism held that because all species must adapt to environmental constraints, adaptive behaviors can be studied in other species besides humans. Functionalists also broadened the scope of psychology to include the study of children, abnormal behavior, and applied fields such as education. Table 2-1 summarizes the differences between structuralism and functionalism.

TABLE 2-1   Comparing structuralism and functionalism. Structuralism takes its inspiration from chemistry, functionalism draws more on biology. Thus for structuralists, study of conscious experience was an end in itself, whereas for functionalists, the end was to discover the adaptive value of all forms of both human and animal behavior.

Kind of Comparison	Structuralism	Functionalism
Analogy to:	Chemistry	Biology
Building blocks:	Elements Sensations Affections Images	Processes Adaptive purpose
Objects of study:	Conscious experience	Development Learning Animal models

INTERIM SUMMARY

Wilhelm Wundt founded the first psychological laboratory in 1879. Through introspection, the controlled examination of inner perception, he hoped to identify the elements of consciousness and discover how they are combined. One of his students, E. B. Titchener, emphasized analysis of sensations as the building blocks of consciousness; this approach came to be known as structuralism. Other American psychologists became more interested in the usefulness or function of the mind, giving rise to an approach known as functionalism. This approach was more open to new ideas, broadened the scope of psychology, and served as the transition between the study of mind for its own sake and the study of behavior in all its forms.

THE BEHAVIORIST REVOLUTION

There were two major centers of functionalism in the United States. One was at the University of Chicago, where Angell and John Dewey taught, and the other at Columbia University, whose faculty included James McKeen Cattell (a student of Wundt) and two of Cattell's students, E. L. Thorndike and Robert S. Woodworth. These two universities had a substantial impact on the development of American psychology.

STIMULUS–RESPONSE PSYCHOLOGY

At Columbia, Thorndike investigated how adaptive behaviors like securing food are learned. Believing in the value of animal models, Thorndike studied the behavior of cats, using "puzzle boxes" like the one shown in Figure 2-1. The cat was enclosed in the box and had to press a pedal to open the door and obtain food placed outside the box. The cat learned to do this in a few trials. What began as random movement became a coherent response that was "stamped in" by the cat's success in gaining access to the food.

FIGURE 2-1 The puzzle box Thorndike used to study how cats might learn a functionally adaptive response, such as securing food.

The process observed by Thorndike was a form of associative learning. The stimulus situation—being enclosed in the box—was associated with the adaptive response of pressing a pedal. (Thorndike labeled these S for stimulus and R for response.) Responses followed by "satisfaction" (obtaining the food) would be stamped in, whereas responses followed by "discomfort" would be stamped out. The stimulus–response (S–R) association was established by the consequences produced by the response. Thorndike referred to this as the **law of effect.**

BEHAVIORISM

Photograph of John B. Watson (1878–1958), the founder of the scientific approach to psychology known as behaviorism.

At about the same time, an energetic young psychologist at the University of Chicago was developing ideas that would revolutionize psychology in the United States. John B. Watson had come to Chicago to study with Angell during the time that Angell was defending functionalism against Titchener's attacks. After receiving his Ph.D. in 1903, Watson remained at the University of Chicago as an instructor until 1908; he then moved to Johns Hopkins University.

In 1913 Watson published a famous paper in which he presented an articulate argument against introspection as used by the structuralists. He suggested that psychology should discard all mentalistic concepts, even those assumed by the functionalists. In his view, conscious experience was a subjective notion that could not be observed objectively and therefore could not be studied scientifically: "The time seems to have come when psychology must discard all reference to consciousness; when it need no longer delude itself into thinking that it is making mental states the object of observation" (Watson 1913, p. 163). Although he did not deny the *existence* of the kind of reflective consciousness described by Descartes, Watson asserted that psychology should not *study* consciousness.

Watson believed, instead, that psychology should concentrate on *behavior,* in an attempt to become "a purely objective experimental branch of natural science" (1913, p. 158). Wundt certainly thought that his own research was experimental, but Watson would have excluded this kind of investigation because it dealt with the contents of mind. For Watson, acceptable research methods included observation and experimentation with both animals and humans, so long as the phenomena chosen for study were externally available. The theoretical goal of psychological research, Watson believed, was "the prediction and control of behavior" (1913, p. 158). This could be achieved by studying **conditioned reflexes,** or stimulus–response connections established through learning. Although this view drew upon the famous experiments of the Russian physiologist Ivan Pavlov, in which dogs learned to salivate at the sound of a bell, Watson expanded the domain of conditioned reflexes to encompass all aspects of behavior, including emotions, language, thought, motor skills, and personality. His approach became known as **behaviorism.**

Watson's insistence on objective research methods and his reliance on the conditioned reflex led him to emphasize the role of learning in all animal and human behavior. In his view, the contents of the mind were constructed through learning. But Watson still faced the problem of how to describe the manipulation of those contents—what we call "thinking." The existence of thought could not be denied, but thinking could not be studied using objective methods. Watson attempted to solve the problem by arguing that thinking is implicit, subvocal speech. According to his theory, humans learn to talk at an early age through conditioning; as they mature, speech becomes internalized and silent. Thinking is really silent speech.

Although many of Watson's views have now been rejected, behaviorism's impact on psychology as a science cannot be exaggerated. Within a few years after the publication of Watson's 1913 paper, psychology had abandoned much of its past and embraced this radically new viewpoint, at least as far as methods were concerned. There was less enthusiasm for Watson's theoretical ideas, such as the idea that thinking is simply silent speech or that emotions are no more than racing hearts or sweaty palms. Even critics of behaviorism, however, avoid the use of introspection and take observable behaviors as the point of departure for theorizing about mental events.

S–O–R PSYCHOLOGY

Most psychologists today differ from Watson in believing that mental phenomena are important and are legitimate objects of study. They would agree that only overt behavior can be observed directly, but would assert that it is possible to use overt behavior to make inferences about mental phenomena that are not directly observable. In contrast to Watson's S–R model, this alternative has been labeled the **S–O–R** model (Stimulus–Organism–Response). Features of the organism (O) deemed to be important would include such things as thought processes, personality variables, or emotional reactions.

The S–O–R model (see Figure 2-2) can be traced to Robert Woodworth, a functionalist psychologist who was Thorndike's colleague and friend. Woodworth had earlier written a textbook (1921) encouraging students to describe behavior as

FIGURE 2-2 Comparing the S–R and the S–O–R models of behavior. The original S–R model (a) considered only observable stimuli and observable responses, ruling out inferences about anything that might be found between S and R. In contrast, the S–O–R model (b) presumes that stimuli affect processes within the organism that in turn influence the observed responses.

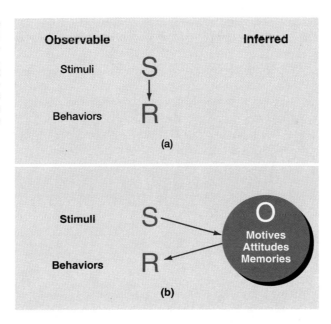

involving S–R connections. But Woodworth had always been interested in motivation, and he recognized that S–R connections do not adequately explain motivational processes. For example, the banquet table that looks so enticing when you are hungry loses its attraction after you have eaten as much as you can hold. The banquet table has not changed as a stimulus, so what is affecting your response must be some process or state that is internal to you. Woodworth therefore modified the S–R formula to include the potential for motivation within the individual.

The resulting S–O–R model is a prevalent form of explanation in nearly all of psychology. Psychologists specify and label the stimulus conditions (S) presented in their research, make objective measurements of the resulting behavior (R), and infer psychological properties or states (O), such as personality or motivation, that help explain the relationship between S and R. In this sense nearly all modern psychologists are behaviorists; their inferences are always based on some form of behavior.

Where psychologists differ is in which internal properties they choose to emphasize. These differences have given rise to four major psychological perspectives: the biopsychological approach, theoretical behaviorism, the cognitive approach, and the psychodynamic perspective. Although each major perspective has at least one scientific journal devoted to its viewpoint, because of the diversity in the discipline no perspective constitutes a well-defined school. The American Psychological Association, which at the turn of the century had some 500–700 members, now has well over 50,000 members. In the late 1980s another major national organization, the American Psychological Society, was formed; it now has over 15,000 members. In 1900 there were fewer than 50 laboratories in experimental psychology; now some 350 universities grant in excess of 1,000 doctorates in psychology every year, in clinical as well as academic areas. Psychologists today are much more likely to identify themselves by their topical specialty than by perspective. Within a topical specialty such as neuropsychology, cognitive psychology, or social psychology, however, the overall perspective still affects choice of problem and method, and often implies a particular position on one or more of the six organizing themes discussed in Chapter 1. For example, we have already noted that Watsonian behaviorism takes an extreme nurture position on the question of whether behavior is more heavily influenced by nature or nurture. For all of these reasons, it is useful to describe the broad outline of each perspective, which we will do in the rest of this chapter.[1]

INTERIM SUMMARY

Stimulus–response psychology originated with Thorndike's experiments on the learning of adaptive behaviors. This approach was carried further by Watson, who claimed that consciousness could not be studied scientifically and that psychologists should limit their studies to observable behavior, a view that became known as behaviorism. Focusing on the conditioned reflex, Watson emphasized the role of learning in all animal and human behavior. Modern psychology has expanded the stimulus–response model to include an intervening level; current theories are defined as S–O–R models, with O referring to features of the organism. Modern psychological perspectives differ in terms of what properties or states are thought to intervene between the stimulus and the response.

[1]Some psychologists believe that there is a fifth perspective, the humanistic approach. Because historians of the discipline (for example, Robinson, 1979) argue that on a theoretical level this perspective is not equivalent to the other four, it will be described in Chapter 22 rather than here.

THE BIOLOGICAL PERSPECTIVE

The biological perspective in psychology begins with the fact that human beings are animals and asserts that all human behavior, including mental activities, has a biological basis. The roots of this perspective may be found in the ideas of Descartes, Hobbes, and Darwin as discussed in Chapter 1. We now know that the brain, not the pineal gland as Descartes believed, is the organ that directs human behavior. The brain is a complex electrochemical device consisting of tens of billions of interacting nerve cells. Much of what goes on in the brain occurs in response to stimuli received through the senses. The operation of the brain and the nervous and sensory systems therefore is of great interest to psychologists who approach the discipline from a biological perspective. But the biological approach is applied to other topics besides the brain and the senses, including inherited characteristics, physical needs, emotions, learning, development from infancy to adulthood, and responses to stress.

Because of the ethical and methodological difficulties involved in conducting biologically oriented research with human beings, this perspective makes extensive use of animal models. The theory of evolution provides a justification for comparisons across species, but such comparisons need to take into consideration the limits of the biological systems involved. For example, studies of the large nerve in the horseshoe crab provide important insights into the functioning of a single nerve cell but do not indicate how hundreds of thousands of cells might interact in a complex thought process.

REDUCTIONISM

The biological perspective raises the issue of **reductionism.** In its most sweeping form, the principle of reductionism asserts that theories about any system should be expressed in terms of the most elementary units involved. For example, if all behavior necessarily involves neural communication within the brain, then all behavior—including complex acts such as learning, motivation, or the formation of friendships—should be explained in terms of neural communication within the brain. Because this extreme form of reductionism would severely limit the explanatory power of theories, it is rarely applied. There is, however, a moderate version of reductionism involved in a variety of psychological debates. An example is the debate about whether human beings are capable of intentional action. Materialists would argue that there can be no action, voluntary or involuntary, without neurochemical activity; therefore, action can be described entirely in terms of such activity, and calling a behavior intentional adds nothing to the explanation. In contrast, the commonsense philosophy of Reid (1863) asserts that intention is a critical element for the understanding of human action; therefore, an explanation solely in terms of neurochemical activity misses the point.

INTERIM SUMMARY

The biological perspective in psychology emphasizes the fact that human action has a biological basis. Psychologists who use this approach are especially interested in discovering how the brain and the senses work, but they also explore such topics as inherited characteristics, learning, and responses to stress. Biologically oriented psychologists often use animal models to explain human behavior. The biological approach is associated with reductionism, in which a theory is expressed in the most elementary units involved. In this case, the issue is whether or not mental phenomena can be understood entirely in terms of the neurochemical activity of the brain.

THE PERSPECTIVE OF BEHAVIORISM

Although behaviorism originated with Watson, it has become identified with the work of B. F. Skinner. Whereas Watson focused on physiological reflexes produced by external stimulation, Skinner concentrated on behavior that is not elicited by external stimuli. For example, if you are sitting with one leg crossed over the other, a light tap just below the kneecap will cause a reflex contraction that moves the leg. The specific external stimulus is necessary for the reflex to occur. But you could also move your leg yourself. If you did so, and someone paid you five dollars for doing so, you probably would do it again. This behavior does not require a reflex. Skinner assumed that when an animal's or human's behavior is rewarded, or **reinforced,** the likelihood of the behavior's being repeated increases. He used the term **operant conditioning** to describe this process, which applies to complex learning as well as to simple behaviors. The principles of conditioning are discussed in more detail in Chapter 12; the important point here is that operant conditioning provides a much broader base for the behavioral perspective than the notion of the conditioned reflex. Indeed, principles of operant conditioning have been applied to such diverse areas as education, clinical treatment, and the organization of society.

As a *methodological* orientation, behaviorism insists that stimulus variables and responses be measured objectively. This can be done whether or not one assumes that there are O-variables in between the S and the R. In contrast, as a *theoretical* position Skinner's behaviorist approach avoids explanations involving internal processes. Recall that the British empiricists, especially Locke, regarded all the contents of the mind as originating from experience. Skinner agrees that experience plays a crucial role in behavior, but goes a step further and argues that the contents of the mind are not part of the explanation. If the contents of the mind originate entirely from the organism's experience in the world, talking about the contents of the mind adds nothing to our understanding of behavior.

In contrast to Watson and Skinner, other behavioral theorists are willing to infer internal states that mediate between stimuli and responses. In the area of learning—the central concern of behavioral theorists—these internal variables have been specified in a theory proposed by Hull (1943) and modified by Spence (1956). For exam-

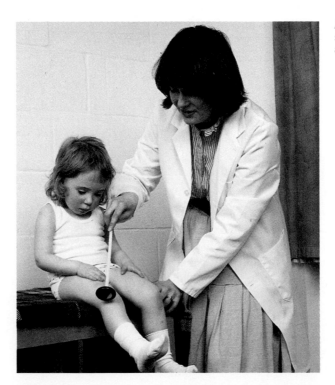

A pediatrician tests for the presence of a simple reflex behavior by gently tapping a patellar tendon.

B. F. Skinner as a young man (1933), shortly after his selection by Harvard University as a fellow in a special academic program

ple, suppose that through repeated reinforcement (that is, rewards) an animal has learned to press a bar in order to receive food. Will the animal press the bar constantly even when it is not hungry, gradually filling its cage with uneaten food? Obviously not. To account for such situations, Hull proposed that the number of reinforcements for bar pressing creates an O variable, "habit strength," and that the number of hours the animal has been deprived of food determines the value of a different O variable, "drive." When drive is high enough, it combines with habit strength to create yet another O variable, "excitatory potential," which leads to the observed behavior.

Hull's model and other S–O–R theories could be criticized as being mentalistic because they infer internal states that cannot be directly observed or measured. But provided the stimuli and responses are measured accurately, the investigation of psychological states is no more dependent on inference than other sciences. Astronomers infer the gravitational force of heavenly bodies from the way observable light bends around them. Physicists infer the nature of the forces holding atoms together by observing what happens when atoms are split apart. Archaeologists infer the social structure of entire communities from the limited evidence available from excavations.

In psychology, a valid inference for any O variable requires that the stimulus and the response be defined in terms as objective and detailed as possible. Consequently, all psychologists rely on **operational definitions,** which define O variables in terms of the experimental procedures used to produce stimuli and measure responses. In the case of Hull's theory, "hours of food deprivation" is the operational definition of drive. Such definitions permit other researchers, regardless of their perspective, to repeat, or **replicate,** the procedures. Successful replications increase our confidence in the reported findings, although no experiment can *prove* the truth of a theory.

Although Watson succeeded in getting psychologists to abandon the study of mental content through introspection, they have continued to study internal psychological states, albeit in a more objective way. The various O variables in psychological theories are simply concepts about which scientists can agree, given the objectively specified conditions under which the observations were made.

Inference from observation: Psychologists infer the operation of psychological processes from observed behavior just as archaeologists infer the social structure of a prior civilization from its artifacts.

41

INTERIM SUMMARY

Theoretical behaviorism is associated with B. F. Skinner, who focused on behavior that is voluntarily emitted by the organism. Skinner held that when behavior is reinforced, the likelihood that it will be repeated increases; he referred to this process as operant conditioning. Although both Watson and Skinner were critical of "mentalism," more recent behavioral theories infer internal states in the organism that mediate between stimulus and response. Such inferences are considered valid provided the stimulus and response are defined in terms as detailed and objective as possible; these operational definitions allow other researchers to replicate an experiment.

THE COGNITIVE PERSPECTIVE

In contrast to extreme behaviorism, which denies the existence of the mind, the cognitive perspective in psychology views the mind as its principal subject matter. This is not the same as studying the brain as a biological entity, although theories about cognition take account of recent discoveries in neuropsychology. Nor does it involve studying all the various states within the organism that might mediate between a stimulus and a response, although cognition is obviously involved in much human motivation. Instead, the cognitive perspective is concerned with the mental contents and processes that enable organisms to make rational choices among alternative behaviors.

Consider an example. At some point in your college career you will be asked to select a major, if you have not already done so. The request to "return this form, indicating your major, to the Registrar by 5:00 P.M. Friday" can be regarded as the stimulus (S), and your compliance with the request can be thought of as the response (R). But this description of the process of selecting a major leaves out a great deal of important information. How do you decide what to write on the form? Do you begin comparing all the possible majors when you receive the form, or do you search your memory for information about various majors? To whom do you talk before making a decision, and how do you weigh the advice you receive?

If you are like many people, your choice of a major will involve a search for information, storage and retrieval of that information, informal computation of the risks of various choices (will choosing to major in a subject you enjoy decrease your chances of finding a good job?), and evaluation of the positive aspects of each alternative. The cognitive approach is interested in the ways you categorize the possible majors, in how and what you remember of what other people have told you, and in

Selection of a college major may begin with a conversation with a faculty advisor. But making the selection requires a series of cognitive processes that lead to the final decision.

how you balance the risks and benefits in order to make your final decision. Categorization, memory, problem solving, and decision making are all topics of interest to the cognitive approach.

COGNITION AND COMPUTERS

The development of the cognitive perspective, the most recent of the major viewpoints in psychology, coincided with the advent of computers. In many disciplines the computer serves as no more than an adding machine. To be sure, it is a very powerful adding machine, capable of performing a tremendous number of calculations in a very short time. But the structure and operation of the computer do not, for example, serve as a model for the organization of the galaxy, for the composition of DNA, or for the structure of matter. By contrast, many of the principles involved in the operation of computers have helped to change the way cognitive psychology views the process of human thought. For example, computer programs (software) provide instructions by which physical elements of the machine (computer hardware) solve problems. This relationship between software and hardware provides an analogy for cognitive psychologists who seek to identify the logical rules that might guide the operation of the physical brain. Indeed, one of the influential cognitive psychology textbooks describes "human information processing" as a discipline with a close relationship to computer science (Lindsay & Norman, 1977).

Two publications in the late 1940s helped lay the foundation for cognitive psychology. The first, by Wiener (1948), described **cybernetics,** the study of control processes in animals and machines. One of the central ideas of cybernetics is the notion of feedback, which can be illustrated with the example of a thermostat. When the temperature in a house falls below a specific preset level, the thermostat turns on the furnace and monitors the resulting change in temperature until the preset level is regained. In psychology, feedback occurs when an organism performs a behavior and receives a reinforcement (which provides information about the results of the behavior), and either maintains or alters its actions accordingly.

The second publication was a book by Shannon and Weaver (1949) that outlines a mathematical theory of communication. It introduced the term *bit* (short for "binary digit") as a measure of the information value of communications. The receiver of a communication is seen as being in a state of uncertainty; a bit is the amount of information that reduces the receiver's uncertainty by half. For example, if you are trying to locate another person in the continental United States and are told that the person lives "west of the Mississippi River," your uncertainty has been reduced by roughly 50% and you have received one bit of information.

These industrial robots are a modern application of the principle of feedback that underlies many of the cognitive theories of psychology.

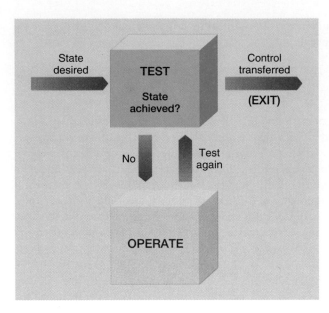

FIGURE 2-3 The Test-Operate-Test-Exit (TOTE) model of control through feedback. This model is useful for describing both reflex and intentional behaviors.

THE TOTE MODEL

The idea of feedback and the view of the person as an information processor seeking to reduce uncertainty were first combined into a model of human behavior in 1960 by Miller, Galanter, and Pribram. Their model, called the TOTE (Test-Operate-Test-Exit) model, replaced Watson's conditioned reflex with a feedback loop. The use of a conceptual unit instead of a physical unit made it possible to describe both physiological reflexes and intentional behavior as involving the control of behavior through feedback (see Figure 2-3).

The TOTE model begins with some desired state (ranging from, say, removal of a piece of grit from the surface of the eye to the publication of a novel). There is an initial test to determine whether the desired state has been achieved. If it has not, there is an operation (an eye blink or another month of writing) designed to bring about the desired state. Then there is another test. If the desired state has been achieved, control is transferred to another system or activity. In the case of a reflex action like blinking, the necessary operations may be carried out in fractions of a second without conscious thought. In the case of an intentional behavior like publishing a novel, there may be many comparisons between the desired state and the actual state, extending over a long period, before the desired state is achieved.

Regardless of the particular topic studied, the cognitive approach views people as primarily *rational* decision makers. To be sure, human rationality is imperfect and subject to various kinds of error, but the emphasis of cognitive psychology is on the rules or principles of rational thought.

INTERIM SUMMARY

The cognitive perspective concentrates on mental structures and processes, such as memory, thinking, and the rules people use to solve problems, make decisions, and direct their behavior. It often makes use of analogies with information processing by computers. The idea of feedback and the conception of the receiver of communication as an information processor seeking to reduce uncertainty are central to cognitive psychology. They are combined in the TOTE model, in which the organism conducts tests to determine whether a desired state has been achieved and directs its behavior accordingly. The cognitive approach views people as primarily rational decision makers.

THE PSYCHODYNAMIC PERSPECTIVE

Like the cognitive perspective, the psychodynamic perspective assumes that a thorough understanding of human behavior requires "mentalism," or the consideration of mental events. But whereas the cognitive perspective describes people as rational information processors and decision makers, the psychodynamic perspective focuses on failures of rationality. People are seen not as rational decision makers who occasionally make errors but, rather, as individuals whose rationality is scarcely able to keep unconscious motives under control.

The intellectual force behind the psychodynamic perspective is Sigmund Freud (1856–1939), whose collected works comprise 24 volumes (edited and translated by Strachey, 1953–1974). When Freud was four years old, his family moved to Vienna, Austria, where he lived and worked throughout his life. Freud entered the University of Vienna to study medicine, receiving a medical degree in 1881 (Watson, 1968). Freud's thinking was influenced not only by Aristotle, Darwin, and the German poet Goethe, but also by Fechner's "iceberg" metaphor for the mind (specifically, that the mind is mostly below the surface and moved by hidden currents; see Figure 2-4), and by his study in France of hypnosis with the renowned neurologist, Jean-Martin Charcot (Watson, 1968).

THE UNCONSCIOUS

The psychodynamic perspective parts company with the cognitive approach in its view of the relative importance of unconscious motivation. Freud's influential first book, *The Interpretation of Dreams* (1913/1900), was based on the assumption that the secrets of the unconscious are revealed during dreams, when the conscious mind has loosened its control over the expression of "unacceptable" motives. Even in a waking state, a person may express unconscious impulses in "slips of the tongue" (Freud, 1960/1901). An example would be a political candidate who, meaning to say "I have every confidence in my running mate's capabilities," stumbles over the word "confidence."

Freud's views were based on observations of patients in his practice of psychotherapy. In that practice, as well as in his descriptions of normal behavior, Freud

Sigmund Freud (1856–1939) looking at a manuscript in the office of his Vienna home.

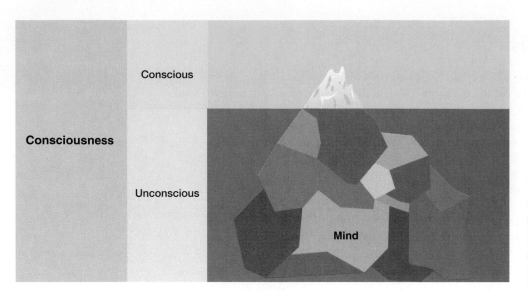

FIGURE 2-4 The mind as an iceberg. According to the psychodynamic perspective, the human mind is like an iceberg: Most of it is below the surface (not available to consciousness) and it is moved by unseen currents (unconscious processes).

attempted to discover the influence of unconscious processes. His studies with Charcot in France acquainted him with the use of hypnosis in the treatment of hysteria, an emotional disorder characterized by sleepwalking, multiple personality, and a variety of physical symptoms such as paralysis. At first Freud used hypnosis in treating patients with hysteria. Soon, however, he began combining hypnosis with a therapy developed by Josef Breuer in which patients were encouraged to talk about unpleasant events in order to release pent-up emotions. Eventually Freud renounced the clinical use of hypnosis in favor of **psychoanalysis,** a therapeutic technique based on **free association,** in which the patient is required to say, without censorship, everything that comes to mind. Where hypnosis required that the patient be put into a deep trance, psychoanalysis achieved comparable results with the patient wide awake. Psychoanalysis remains an important technique for the treatment of psychopathology.

CHILDHOOD SEXUALITY

In the course of their treatment for hysteria, several of Freud's patients revealed what at first seemed to be instances of seduction during childhood by an older relative. Most of the patients were women, and the older relative was usually the father. As far as the patients were concerned, the trauma associated with these incidents had precipitated the symptoms. But when patients who had no difficulty discussing other sensitive topics were unable to describe these seductions in any detail, Freud concluded that for the most part they had never taken place; they were fantasies.

This conclusion led Freud to search for evidence of sexuality in children before puberty. On the basis of this evidence he developed the theory of **psychosexual stages,** which is described in detail in Chapter 18. Children of both sexes were presumed to pass through these stages, and psychological problems were thought to result from difficulty in making the transitions between stages. For example, Freud believed that during one of these stages every child would experience sexual desire for the parent of the opposite sex and would thereby be placed in competition with the parent of the same sex. Drawing upon characters in ancient Greek legend, Freud termed this condition the **Oedipus complex** among males (after the king of Thebes, who unwittingly killed his father and married his mother); and the **Electra complex** among females (after the character in a Greek tragedy who persuaded her brother to kill their mother). In both males and females this conflict with the parents could be resolved only when the child internalized moral prescriptions and identified with the parent of the same sex.

Although Freud's ideas pervade popular culture, psychologists regard them with a degree of caution bordering on skepticism. Critics of Freud have concentrated on the fact that his ideas have fared badly in a variety of scientific tests. Even some of Freud's original followers, who remained committed to a psychodynamic approach, criticized important aspects of his theories. For example, Carl Gustav Jung (1875–1961) rejected Freud's emphasis on childhood sexuality. Alfred Adler (1870–1937) agreed with Freud that childhood conflicts influence the adult personality, but he believed that the central issue is the child's feeling of powerlessness or inferiority, not childhood sexuality. Still others such as Karen Horney (1885–1952), Erich Fromm (1900–1979), and Harry Stack Sullivan (1892–1949) rejected the idea of an Oedipus complex and emphasized the social (rather than sexual) nature of psychological development.

USE OF INDIVIDUAL CASES

An important feature of the psychodynamic approach is its use of individual cases in developing theories. Freud's experiences in treating a woman suffering from hysteria led him to recognize the value of allowing a patient to talk without interruption. The case of a little boy who was terrified of horses played a crucial role in the development of his theory of psychosexual stages. Yet despite their origins in clinical case histories, Freud's theories were intended to describe the development and behavior of all individuals, regardless of whether they were psychologically normal or emotionally disturbed.

In this respect the psychodynamic approach differs radically from the biological, behavioral, and cognitive perspectives. Theories about the biological functioning of an organism are generally based on multiple observations of normal individuals; the same is true of cognitive theories. In the Skinnerian version of behaviorism there are numerous studies based on the behavior of a single subject, but they include many separate procedures performed in predetermined sequence, thus generating multiple observations. It is clearly appropriate to base explanations of emotional disorders on material gleaned from clinical experience. But the use of such material as the foundation for theories about normal functioning is controversial, both because of the small numbers of individuals involved, and because of the fact that those individuals were suffering from psychological disorders.

INTERIM SUMMARY

The psychodynamic approach assumes that a thorough understanding of human behavior requires the consideration of mental events, especially unconscious motives. This approach is associated with Sigmund Freud. Freud's observations of patients in his clinical practice convinced him of the existence of unconscious sexual motives in young children. He developed a theory of psychosexual development that included the idea of the Oedipus/Electra complex, in which the child experiences sexual desire for the parent of the opposite sex and is in competition with the parent of the same sex. Other psychodynamic theorists have challenged these ideas while retaining Freud's emphasis on unconscious motives and the influence of childhood experiences on adult personality. A controversial feature of the psychodynamic approach is its use of individual cases to develop theories about normal as well as emotionally disturbed people.

THE PSYCHOLOGICAL VIEWPOINT

In its short history as an independent discipline, psychology has drawn strength from its philosophical and scientific roots, and has branched off into uncharted territory. It now views the organism as part biological creature, part response producer, and part thinker; limited by biological faculties; driven by conscious and unconscious motives. This very diversity of opinion is one reason the discipline is vibrant. We trust that you will get a sense of this excitement in the pages to come.

SUMMARY

1. The first psychological laboratory was established by Wilhelm Wundt in 1879 at Leipzig University. In the United States, the first laboratory was established at Johns Hopkins University in 1883 by G. Stanley Hall.

2. The rise of psychology as a separate discipline coincided with the beginning of graduate education in the United States. William James's influential book, *Principles of Psychology,* set forth the wide array of topics available to the new discipline.

3. The first two "schools" of psychology in the United States were *structuralism,* which concentrated on identifying the irreducible mental elements needed to construct consciousness, and *functionalism,* which emphasized the role that consciousness could play in better enabling people to adapt to changes in their environments.

4. In experiments with cats, E. L. Thorndike discovered that responses followed by "satisfaction" would be "stamped in," whereas responses followed by "discomfort" would be "stamped out." This relationship between stimulus and response *(S–R)* is known as the *law of effect.*

5. In 1913 John B. Watson published a paper attacking the method of *introspection* that had been used by the structuralists. Arguing that psychology should set aside its interest in consciousness, Watson asserted that *behaviorism*—the study of objectively observable behavior—should be the method of choice for psychology.

6. Although modern psychology has generally adopted the methodological prescriptions of behaviorism, current theories are based on an *S–O–R* model, in which features of the internal organism (O) are inferred from the observed relationships between stimuli (S) and responses (R).

7. The *biopsychological* approach in psychology takes seriously the idea that human beings, and animals, are biological organisms. The brain and sensory systems, inherited characteristics, and the physical needs of both animals and humans are of particular interest to biopsychologists.

8. The *behavioral* perspective, following Watson's lead, emphasizes *operant conditioning* and other processes that are external to the person. Behavior is seen to be guided, or changed, by the reward, or *reinforcement,* it produces. The behavioral perspective is thus very interested in processes of learning.

9. The *cognitive* perspective concentrates on the internal and mental structures and processes that Watsonian behaviorism would have declared off limits. Cognitive psychologists draw on analogies to computer information-processing and feedback systems to develop models of such cognitive processes as memory, problem solving, and decision making.

10. Where the cognitive approach concentrates on rational decision making, the *psychodynamic* perspective emphasizes the unconscious processes that can affect behavior. This approach was initiated by Sigmund Freud, who used a technique of *free association* in his clinical practice to reveal the unconscious roots of his patients' problems. Freud's theories have been criticized because they were developed from case studies of a small

number of disturbed individuals, and many of his conclusions have fared badly in scientific tests. The general therapeutic technique of *psychoanalysis,* however, remains a force in contemporary treatment of psychopathology.

FOCUS QUESTIONS

1. What is the fundamental disagreement between structuralism and functionalism?

2. Describe the law of effect.

3. What are the similarities and differences between Watsonian behaviorism and S–O–R psychology?

4. Describe the biological perspective in psychology. What is its position on the issue of reductionism?

5. Describe the principles of operant conditioning.

6. What is the cognitive perspective in psychology? Why is the notion of feedback important to this perspective?

7. Describe the psychodynamic perspective in psychology. Why does the unconscious play such a substantial role in this view of psychological functioning?

THE STUDY OF
MIND AND BODY

One of the earliest, and perhaps still the most fundamental problem for psychology is to show how the mind and the body interact. How do physical events, such as lights and sounds, give rise to mental experience? Conversely, how do mental states, such as a person's conscious choice to swing a tennis racket, get translated into physical events like bodily movements? Although the **mind/body distinction** is the organizing theme for the next five chapters, each has a somewhat different perspective. Chapter 3 describes the study of human senses—sight, hearing, smell, touch, and taste—showing how physical stimuli become represented in the mind. Chapter 4, on perception, considers how objects are understood in their totality, and how external events are given meaning. Chapter 5, on neuropsychology, then discusses details of how the brain—the physical representation of mind—processes information. Returning from the physical to the psychological, Chapter 6 describes emotion, as it is experienced in the mind and as it is reflected in activity of the body. Finally, the section concludes with Chapter 7 on consciousness, a problem at the heart of the dichotomy between mind and body.

CHAPTER 3   SENSATION

CHAPTER 4   PERCEPTION

CHAPTER 5   NEUROPSYCHOLOGY

CHAPTER 6   EMOTION

CHAPTER 7   STATES OF CONSCIOUSNESS

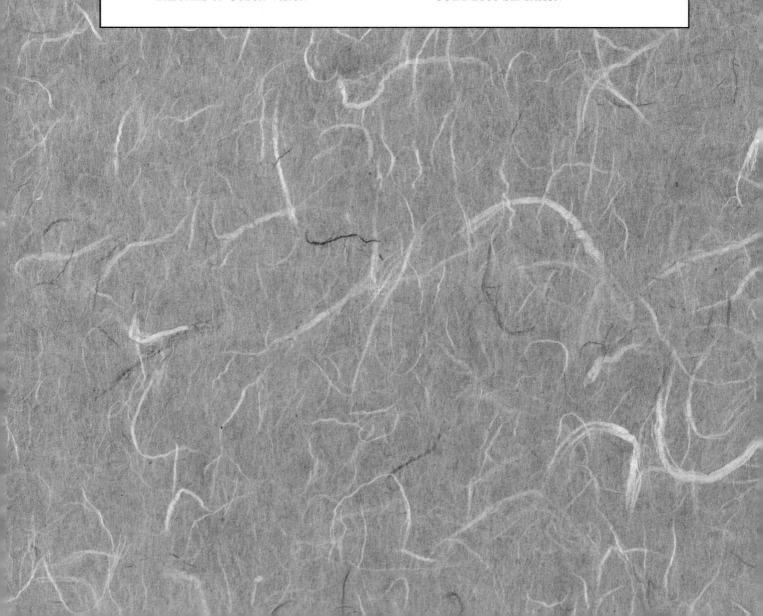

CHAPTER 3

SENSATION

 As you read these words, you are being bombarded by thousands of stimuli. Light strikes the page and is reflected to your eyes; noises swirl around your head; the temperature of the air, the pressure of the chair against your legs, the taste of the snack you are munching—all combine to form an intricate mosaic of stimulation. In psychology this phenomenon is termed **sensation.**

Although we may be aware of various sensations, we rarely stop to think about how or why those sensations occur. Why, for example, do we see shadows, contours, and colors? Why does a noise seem loud or soft or musical? Why does boiling water feel hot and painful? Why does the aroma of pizza differ from that of a flower? These are the kinds of questions investigated by sensory psychologists.

As we saw in Chapter 1, sensation was among the first phenomena to be investigated by psychologists. They hoped that their studies would shed light on the mind body question. Today sensory psychologists continue to study how physical energy is translated into sensory feeling—that is, the processes by which physical events impinging on the body give rise to psychological events in the mind.

PSYCHOPHYSICS

In sensory psychology, the study of the quantitative relationship between physical stimuli and the psychological sensations to which the stimuli give rise is called **psychophysics.** Few issues have received more attention in psychophysics than the study of the threshold, the point along a physical continuum that corresponds to a particular sensory reaction such as detection of a stimulus. Let us illustrate the traditional approach to this issue with the following example. Assume that the intensity of an auditory tone is gradually increased from zero to some higher level. At a certain point the intensity will be great enough to cause the listener to say "Yes, I hear it." This is the **absolute threshold** of sensation, the point at which the stimulus is first detected, the onset of a psychological sensation. Thus, a sensation can be specified in terms of the physical energy required to produce it. Once a stimulus has been detected, if the intensity is increased once again there will be a second point at which the listener will say, "It is louder than it was." This is the **difference threshold,** the stimulus increment that produces a **just noticeable difference (jnd)** from a previous value. Again, the psychological experience (the jnd) is expressed in units based on the physical stimulation.

PSYCHOPHYSICAL LAWS

Psychologists typically wish to go beyond the mere measurement of sensory thresholds; their goal is to formulate laws that describe the *general* way that sensation changes as a function of changes in the physical stimulation.

Weber's Law

One of the earliest and most important laws was proposed by Ernst Weber in 1846. Weber made the following observation: It is much easier to detect a difference between two pieces of metal weighing 25 and 26 ounces than it is to detect a difference between two other pieces of metal weighing 100 and 101 ounces. From this, Weber speculated that the increase in intensity needed to reach the difference threshold would be a constant *proportion* of the initial intensity, not simply a constant absolute amount. If, for example, the difference threshold was reached by increasing the weight of a 25-ounce piece of metal by 1/25 of its weight (to 26 ounces), then the same *proportional* increase would be needed to reach the difference threshold when starting with a 100-ounce weight, namely an increase of 1/25 or 2.5 ounces.

Weber's law is, generally speaking, quite accurate, although the proportional change in intensity needed to reach the difference threshold is usually larger when the initial stimulus is either very weak or very strong. Moreover, the Weber fractions differ for the various sense modalities. For example, the proportional increase required to detect a change in pitch from a 2,000-hertz tone is 1/333; an increase of 1/53 is required to detect that a weight is heavier than a 300-gram original; and an increase of 1/11 decibels is needed to detect a difference in loudness from a 100 decibel noise.

Fechner's Law

Starting with Weber's law, Gustav Fechner derived a more general formulation between mind and body. He argued that each increment in sensation, each jnd, was equivalent regardless of how much physical energy was needed to produce the jnd. Stated in terms of Weber's law, each proportional increment in physical intensity would create one extra unit of sensation. Let us consider an example. Assume that the absolute threshold for a stimulus falls at 10 units of intensity, and that a Weber fraction of 1/2 is required to produce a jnd. This means that the first difference threshold would be reached when a stimulus of 15 units of intensity is presented. Using 15 as a new starting point, an additional jnd would occur for a stimulus of 22.5 units of intensity; a third for 33.75 units; and so forth. The general relationship between the growth of sensation and the increase in stimulus intensity can be seen when these successive jnds are plotted as a function of stimulus intensity (see Figure 3-1). Fechner's law is a mathematical equation that summarizes the relationship depicted in this figure. It expresses the general relationship between stimulus intensity (body) and sensation (mind).

Stevens's Law

Fechner's law assumed that each jnd was psychologically equivalent. For example, a stimulus that was four jnds above the absolute threshold would be judged to be

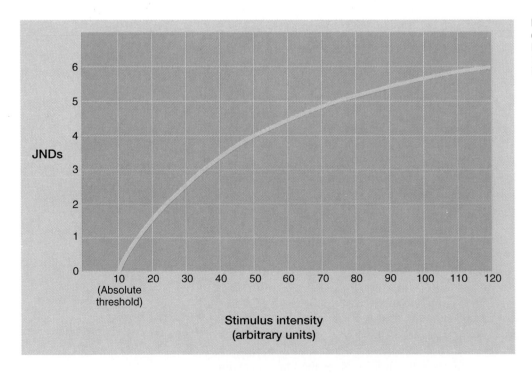

FIGURE 3-1 Successive just noticeable differences (jnds) as a function of stimulus intensity. The absolute threshold is 10 units of intensity and the Weber ratio is 1/2.

twice as intense as a stimulus that was only two jnds above. Yet such a result is not found. A stimulus falling at the four-jnd point is typically sensed as being *more* than twice as intense as one falling at the two-jnd point. In other words, each proportional increase in physical intensity does not create an equivalent unit of strength of sensation.

A more modern formulation relating sensation to stimulus intensity, which avoids this assumption of Fechner's law, is found in the work of S. S. Stevens. Stevens claimed that sensation should be measured directly, not indirectly as Fechner had done (Stevens, 1957). When direct measurements are taken, a different relationship between mind and body is found. Although the mathematical details of Stevens's law are beyond the scope of this book, we briefly describe some of his methodology.

Stevens pioneered the use of four direct sensory-scaling techniques: *ratio production, ratio estimation, magnitude estimation,* and *magnitude production.* With the ratio-production technique, the subject is given one stimulus and asked to make adjustments to a second stimulus so that the intensity of the second stands in a particular relation to the intensity of the first. For example, the subject may be asked to adjust the second stimulus so that it is 1/2 as intense as the first, or 1/3, or even twice as intense (Stevens, 1936). Ratio estimation is very similar. Rather than manipulating a second stimulus directly, however, the subject is given two stimuli and simply asked to estimate the ratio between them. For example, two tones may be sounded and the subject must decide whether the first tone is, say, twice (or 1/2, or 1/3) as loud as the second. For the magnitude-estimation technique, a subject assigns a numerical estimate to the stimulus intensity (Stevens, 1958). In one experiment, subjects were given different concentrations of a taste solution (sugar, salt, quinine) and were asked to give a number that corresponded to the intensity of the flavor. Although this task seems impossibly ambiguous, nevertheless subjects have no difficulty in providing an answer. Finally, in magnitude production, the subject is given a numerical value and then asked to produce a stimulus that equals that value (Stevens & Guirao, 1962). For example, the experimenter might ask the subject to produce a sound whose intensity corresponds to the number 50.

It is important to note that these techniques ask the subjects to report their sensations *directly.* The magnitude of the sensation is not calculated simply by counting the number of jnds between the absolute threshold and the stimulus value. Furthermore, the intensity of sensations arising from different sense modalities can be compared. For example, subjects may be asked to adjust the intensity of a tone so that it matches the intensity of a light, or to squeeze a handgrip so that the intensity of the force exerted by the hand matches the intensity of an electric shock (Stevens, 1966).

SIGNAL-DETECTION THEORY

The underlying assumption in Fechner's and Stevens's approach to psychophysics is that reaching the difference threshold is achieved simply by adding intensity to a stimulus. There are problems with this assumption, because a person's attitude may also affect detection. For example, imagine that you are in charge of monitoring a radar scope. Your job is to alert officials if an incoming missile is within 200 miles of New York City. You do not want to sound the alert every time you see a faint blip, because a false alarm (claiming a missile is on its way when in fact it is not) would trigger an unjustified retaliation. You therefore must be cautious in interpreting your observations in order to guarantee that the blip you identify as a missile is, indeed, a missile and not a flock of birds or a weather balloon. Your ability to detect the visual stimulus will be influenced not only by the physical strength of the signal but also by your cautious attitude.

Now imagine a different situation. You are a biologist scanning a microscope slide for evidence of cancer cells. Assume that the cancer cells are imbedded among other healthy cells, so they are difficult to detect, at least with complete certainty. Your inclination in this situation would be the reverse of the previous example. *Any* vague

United States Air Force radar tracking center. Detection of various signals is affected by the signal's strength and the observer's bias.

image of a cancerous cell, no matter how uncertain you are, would cause you to sound the alert, because failing to do so would jeopardize the health of a person who might genuinely need treatment.

The examples cited above suggest that detection of a stimulus is influenced by much more than the physical strength of the stimulus. It is also influenced by a subject's expectation or bias. The radar operator wants to be very sure that the target is a missile and so has a bias against responding too readily, whereas the biologist is eager to detect any sign of cancer whatsoever and so is biased in favor of detecting a signal.

Subjects have different expectations or biases because they face very different consequences for making an error. Let us discuss this point further by considering the matrix of outcomes shown in Figure 3-2. As the figure shows, any instance of signal detection involves four possible outcomes, or decisions. If a signal is present, and the subject says "Yes," then a correct decision has been made, a hit. Similarly, if the signal is absent, and the subject says "No," then a correct decision has also been made, a correct negative. If, however, the stimulus is present and the subject fails to detect it, then the subject has missed. Alternatively, if no signal is present but the subject claims that it is, then the subject has raised a false alarm. The respective consequences of making these two types of errors, misses or false alarms, influence the subject's response pattern by causing the subject to have either a more cautious or more risky response bias.

ROC and Sensitivity

The effects of the subject's expectations or bias is illustrated by a **receiver-operating characteristic curve (ROC curve).** Such a curve is shown in Figure 3-3. As we just discussed, when a subject is asked to identify the presence of a stimulus, a "Yes" response is either a hit or a false alarm. An ROC curve plots the proportion of hits (on the y axis) against the proprotion of false alarms (on the x axis) for a group of subjects asked to detect a particular stimulus. The strength of the stimulus determines the overall position of the curve. The stronger the signal, the more likely a hit and the less likely a miss, and the closer the curve comes to the upper-left-hand corner (where the probability of a hit is 1.0 and the probability of a false alarm is 0). Conversely, the weaker the signal, the more likely a false alarm and the closer the curve approximates chance performance (the diagonal line that runs from lower left to upper right).

Subject bias in signal-detection studies creates bowed curves like those shown in Figure 3-3. The performance of a subject with a conservative bias (a subject inclined

FIGURE 3-2 Matrix showing the outcomes for a subject's answer ("Yes, the stimulus is present" versus "No, the stimulus is not present") as a function of whether or not the stimulus is actually present.

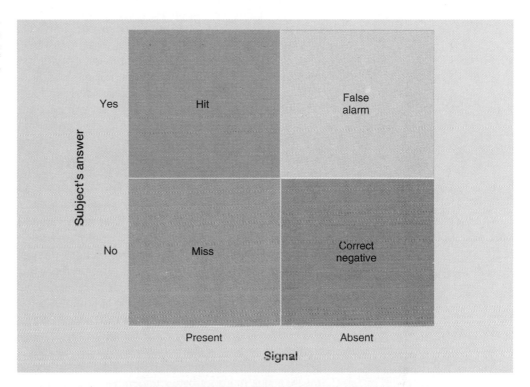

FIGURE 3-3 Typical receiver-operating characteristic (ROC) curves. Each curve represents performance for a stimulus of a particular intensity.

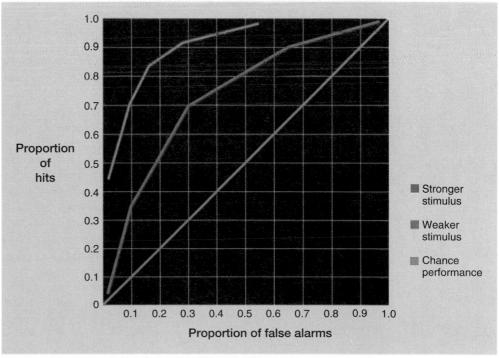

to minimize false alarms) falls in the lower left of a given curve, with a high ratio of hits to false alarms. The performance of a subject with a riskier bias (one inclined to maximize hits) will fall in the upper right, with a lower ratio of hits to false alarms.

The factor that influences where one's performance actually falls on the ROC curve is the payoff or consequence of being wrong. If there is a heavy penalty for a false alarm, such as an unjustified nuclear retaliation, then the subject is conservatively biased and performance is shifted toward the lower left of the ROC curve. If the penalty is greater for misses, for example failing to detect a cancer cell, then the subject is biased in the opposite direction and performance is shifted toward the right of the ROC curve.

Consider an experiment that demonstrated subject bias (Stunkard & Koch, 1964). Obese and normal-weight people swallowed stomach balloons that could then be inflated and used to record the pressure of stomach contractions. The subject's task was to report when he or she felt the sensation of hunger. Presumably such a psychological sensation would stem from the intensity of the physical stimulus, the stomach contractions. The authors found that normal-weight men and women tended to report hunger when the stomach contractions were, in fact, present but not when the contractions were absent. In contrast, obese women tended to say "No" even when contractions were present (they missed fairly frequently), whereas obese men tended to say "Yes" even when contractions were absent (they had many more false alarms). This bias in responding meant that the performance of the obese men shifted toward the upper-right-hand corner of the ROC curve. The opposite bias in the obese women meant that their performance shifted toward the lower-left-hand corner of the ROC curve. If this experiment had been conducted using traditional psychophysical techniques, then the obese men would have been judged to be most sensitive to stomach contractions (they said "Yes" most often), and the obese women would have been judged to be the least sensitive to contractions (they said "Yes" least often). But such a conclusion would be incorrect because performance was based as much on subject bias as it was on stimulus intensity. The signal detection method was able to separate the effects of subject bias from those of stimulus intensity.

In addition to the issues raised in the study of psychophysics, such as specifying the limits of our senses by measuring thresholds, sensory psychologists are interested in describing how sensations are produced—the physiological mechanisms by which physical energy is translated into psychological sensations. The examination of these mechanisms helps us better understand the relationship between body and mind. In the rest of this chapter we explore several such mechanisms, beginning with vision.

INTERIM SUMMARY

The study of the quantitative relationship between physical stimuli and the psychological sensations to which the stimuli give rise is called psychophysics. According to Weber's law, the increase in physical intensity needed to produce a just noticeable difference in sensation is a constant proportion of the original stimulus. According to Fechner's law, each increment in sensation (each just noticeable difference) is psychologically equivalent regardless of the amount of energy needed to produce it. In contrast to Weber and Fechner, S. S. Stevens demonstrated that it is possible to obtain direct estimates of sensation from subjects. According to signal detection theory, stimulus intensity is not the only determinant of psychological sensation; expectations (or bias) also play a role. When the consequences of missing a signal are costly, a subject will be more inclined to sense a signal that has not occurred (raise a false alarm). When the consequences of incorrectly detecting a signal are costly, a subject will be more inclined to miss a signal that has in fact occurred.

VISION

Vision is in many respects our most important sense (Coren, Porac, & Ward, 1984). Not all species are dominated by vision to the extent that humans are. In humans, mobility and defenses are severely compromised when the sense of vision is impaired.

VISUAL STIMULI

The stimulus that creates a visual sensation is light. A light source emits a stream of photons that may be described as a wave of energy (Graham, 1965). As shown in Figure 3-4, light waves have three important characteristics: **amplitude,** the height of the wave measured from peak to trough; **wavelength,** the distance between peaks; and **frequency,** the number of peaks per unit of time. Wavelength and frequency are closely related: the longer the wavelength, the fewer waves per unit of time and the lower the frequency. These characteristics of light affect the kind of sensation it cre-

FIGURE 3-4 A schematic diagram of a simple wave showing amplitude (peak to trough distance) and wavelength (peak to peak distance). Frequency is the number of waves per unit of time.

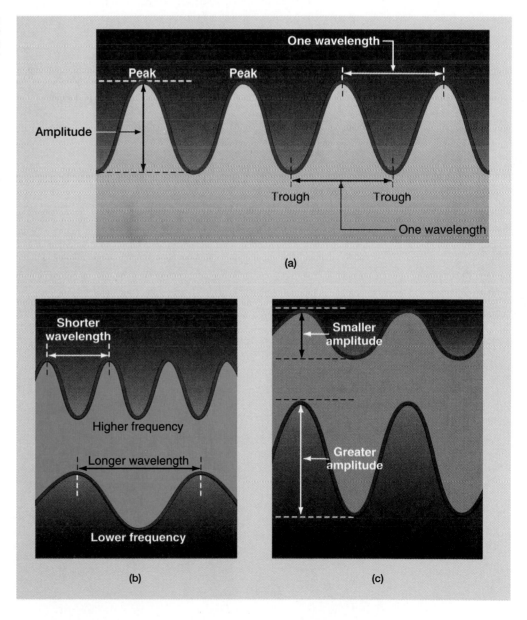

ates. The intensity, or **brightness,** of a visual stimulus is determined by the amplitude of the light waves (or the number of photons striking the eye). The color, or **hue,** of the stimulus is determined by the wavelength.

Light waves are a form of electromagnetic radiation. As shown in Figure 3-5, the wavelength of electromagnetic radiation can vary greatly. Cosmic rays have wavelengths of about 10-trillionths of an inch, whereas long radio waves can be many miles long. The radiation that is visible to the human eye covers only a small fraction of the continuum; visible wavelengths range from about 380 to about 760 nanometers (nm) (a nanometer is one-billionth of a meter). Radiation within this range of wavelengths constitutes the **visible spectrum,** ranging from violet (at the low end) to red (at the high end). White light is a mixture of all the visible wavelengths.

ANATOMY OF THE EYE

Although the eye is much more complex than a camera, many of its structures perform functions similar to those performed by the parts of a camera (see Figure 3-6). The opening of the eye, or diaphragm, is called the **pupil.** Light travels through it to the inner, light-sensitive surface of the eye. Behind the pupil is the **lens,** which, like the lens of a camera, focuses the light onto the inner surface. It does this by changing its thickness as a result of being stretched by the **ciliary muscle.**

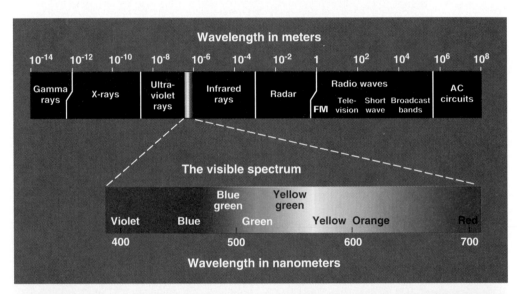

FIGURE 3-5 The electromagnetic spectrum. The visible spectrum represents only one small range within the entire spectrum. Gamma rays and X-rays and radar and radio waves overlap slightly.

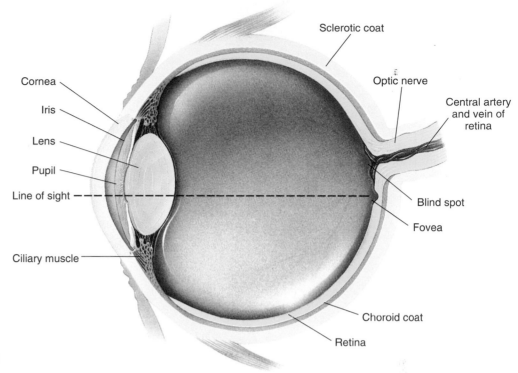

FIGURE 3-6 A cross-section of the human eye.

The eye is covered by three layers of tissue. The outermost, the **sclerotic coat,** is a protective layer. A transparent portion of this layer, the **cornea,** admits light to the inner portions of the eye. The second layer, the **choroid coat,** contains blood vessels and pigmentation. At the front of the eye, the choroid coat forms the **iris.** The interior layer, the area of the eye most important for our discussion, is the **retina.** This surface contains the receptors that are sensitive to light.

Rods and Cones

Figure 3-7 is a cross-sectional diagram of the retina, which consists of several structures. The most important of these are the **rods** and **cones,** specialized cells that are sensitive to light energy (Cornsweet, 1970). The rods are smaller than the cones, but they outnumber the cones by nearly 20 to 1 (about 125 million rods compared to 6 or 7 million cones).

There are a number of differences between rods and cones. First, many adjacent rods converge onto a single **bipolar cell,** which, in turn, converge onto **ganglion cells.** Cones, in contrast, are more likely to be individually connected to a ganglion cell through a single bipolar cell. Second, rods are distributed throughout most of the retina, especially toward the periphery, whereas cones tend to be clustered toward the center. In fact, the central part of the retina, called the **fovea,** contains only cones. Finally, rods and cones differ in their chemical makeup. Although both kinds of receptors contain visual pigments (light-sensitive chemicals), rods contain larger quantities of the pigment **rhodopsin.** The rhodopsin in the rods is depleted when they are exposed to light; it returns to its preexposure level only after 15 minutes or more of total darkness. The process of depletion and restoration determines sensitivity to light—the less rhodopsin available, the lower the sensitivity. Thus, a person who has just been exposed to bright light is less sensitive to changes in illumination than one who has remained in the dark for some period of time (who has been **dark-adapted**). This explains why a person who enters a darkened theater has trouble "seeing"; the rhodopsin in the rods must first be replenished.

Rods and cones differ not only anatomically but also in function. For example, rods, with more rhodopsin than cones, are extremely sensitive, responding even to

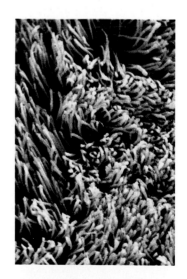

View of the rods in a human retina taken by a scanning electron microscope.

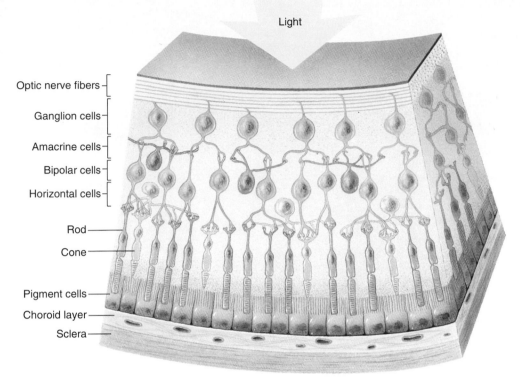

Light

Optic nerve fibers

Ganglion cells

Amacrine cells

Bipolar cells

Horizontal cells

Rod

Cone

Pigment cells

Choroid layer

Sclera

FIGURE 3-7 A cross-sectional schematic view of the human retina. Note that the visual receptors, the rods and the cones, are actually pointed away from the direction of the oncoming light. Note also the various levels in the retina. Rods and cones connect to bipolar cells, which in turn connect to ganglion cells and the optic-nerve fibers. The amacrine cells form interconnections between ganglion and bipolar cells; the horizontal cells form interconnections between the rods and cones and bipolar cells. The optic-nerve fibers carry visual signals to the brain.

the faintest light; cones are less sensitive. If the eye is dark-adapted and the fovea (which contains only cones) is stimulated by a faint light, the subject reports less light than if a peripheral portion of the retina (containing relatively few cones) is stimulated (Hecht, Shlaer, & Pirenne, 1942). As can be seen in Figure 3-8, at the fovea, sensitivity to light is very low. Sensitivity is absent entirely at the blind spot, the point on the retina where the visual nerves converge and exit from the eye; there are no light receptors at that point. Points lying farther from the fovea, however, contain more rods and are more sensitive. This is why it is easier to see a faint star if one looks slightly to the side of the star (stimulating the rods in the periphery of the retina) rather than straight at the star (stimulating only the cones in the fovea).

Another way to demonstrate the difference in sensitivity of the rods and cones is to stimulate each type of receptor with varying intensities of light, recording whether each intensity was sufficient to activate the receptor. This method determines the threshold intensity for each type of receptor—that is, the minimum amount of light needed for activation. Such a threshold intensity graph is shown in Figure 3-9. The two curves indicate that the cones are much less sensitive than the rods even after a long dark-adaptation period (Hecht & Shlaer, 1938). The threshold for the cones is well above the threshold for the rods.

There is another important difference between rods and cones: Rods produce colorless sensations, whereas cones produce the sensation of color. Evidence for this difference is found in the **Purkinje effect,** in which the brightness of one color changes more dramatically with a decrease in illumination than the brightness of another color. For example, red and green patches of color may look equally bright under normal light, but when they are viewed under dim light the green patch suddenly looks brighter. As we saw earlier, the rods are more sensitive to dim light than the cones, but the rods are less sensitive than the cones to light at the red end of the spectrum. Therefore, when the patches are viewed under dim light the rods contribute more than the cones to the resulting sensation, but because the rods are less sensitive to red light, the green patch looks brighter.

In sum, rods are smaller and more sensitive than cones, contain larger amounts of rhodopsin, and are involved in vision at low levels of illumination. Cones are larger but less numerous (although the fovea contains only cones) and much less sensitive than rods; they are involved in color vision.

VISUAL PHENOMENA

In this section we consider five visual phenomena that have been studied by sensory psychologists: sensitivity, spatial acuity, temporal acuity, brightness contrast, and color mixture.

Sensitivity

In one experiment on sensitivity to visual stimuli, subjects were placed in a dark room for about 30 minutes so that their eyes would become dark-adapted (Bouman, 1955; Hecht, Shlaer, & Pirenne, 1942). Then a small patch of light was flashed for one millisecond and the subjects were asked whether or not they had seen it. The researchers found that the smallest possible unit of light energy (a single quantum) falling on the retina for a millisecond was sufficient to activate a rod receptor (Cornsweet, 1970). This finding indicates that the human eye has evolved to be maximally sensitive to light. (To appreciate this high degree of sensitivity, consider the fact that a typical flashlight radiates an amount of light energy, in quanta, represented by the number 2 followed by 30 zeros. Only one quantum is needed to activate a rod receptor.)

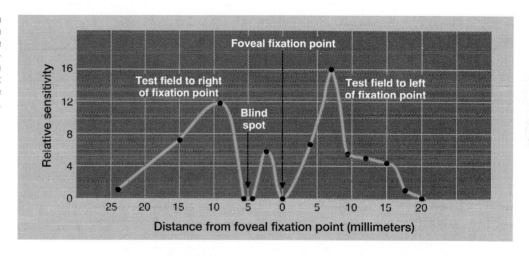

FIGURE 3-8 Relative sensitivity to a blue light as a function of the position on the retina stimulated by the light. The horizontal axis indicates distance (in millimeters) on either side of the fixation point (the fovea). The insensitive spot that appears at about 5 millimeters is the blind spot. (Adapted from Hecht, Shlaer, & Pirenne, 1942.)

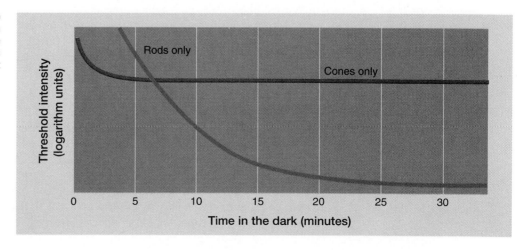

FIGURE 3-9 Light intensity required to trigger the visual receptors as a function of the length of dark-adaptation. Note that there are two curves, one for rods and one for cones. (Adapted from Hecht & Shlaer, 1938.)

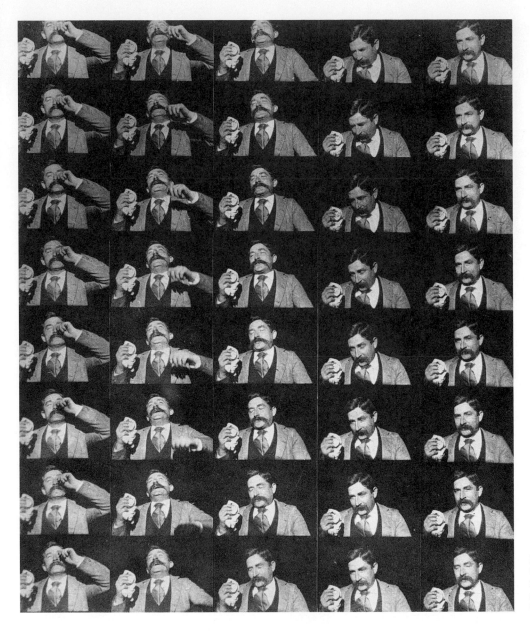

Kinescopic record of a sneeze illustrating the flicker fusion phenomenon. If these discrete images were displayed in quick succession, they would appear as a continuous moving action.

Spatial Acuity

The term **spatial acuity** refers to the extent to which we can distinguish between different objects or forms in space. Acuity improves as the intensity of a stimulus increases; that is, we see brighter objects more accurately (Hecht, 1931). This is why two closely spaced bright stars appear as distinct points of light whereas two dimmer stars, equally near to each other, appear as a single point of light. The relationship between intensity and spatial acuity also explains why we find it much easier to read very small print in a bright light than in a dim light.

Temporal Acuity

When two lights are flashed on the retina one after the other, they are normally experienced as discrete visual sensations. This is an example of **temporal acuity,** the extent to which we can distinguish between visual stimuli separated in time. If the time between the two flashes is short enough, however, the lights are seen as a single flash. In fact, if a stream of flashes is presented at a high frequency, the subject sees a single continuous light. This is referred to as the **flicker fusion phenomenon,** which accounts for the fact that we experience a sense of motion when we watch a movie

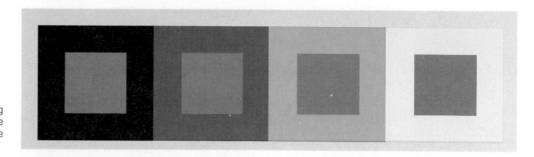

FIGURE 3-10 Patches demonstrating the effect of brightness contrast. The actual brightness of the gray area in the center is the same in all four patches.

even though our eyes are actually being stimulated by a series of discrete, motionless images.

The frequency of flashes that produces the fusion phenomenon is known as the **critical fusion frequency (CFF).** But temporal acuity is also affected by the intensity of the flashes (Graham, 1965); in fact, frequency and intensity interact to create the CFF. At high intensities, temporal gaps between flashes are more noticeable and the frequency of flashes must be increased to maintain the fusion effect. At lower intensities the CFF is reached with a lower frequency of flashes.

Brightness Contrast

Most of the light that strikes the eye is uneven in intensity; it forms complex mosaics of lightness and darkness rather than uniform fields of illumination. When less intense portions of a stimulus border on more intense portions, they appear even dimmer than they would if they were viewed in isolation (Heinemann, 1955). This effect is termed **brightness contrast** and is illustrated in Figure 3-10. The small patches in the centers of the squares appear to be different shades of gray, but in reality they are the same shade. The illumination of each central patch is influenced by the brightness of the surrounding field; when the surrounding field is dark, the gray patch appears lighter than when the surrounding field is light. Thus, the brightness of a stimulus is a function not only of the wave amplitude of that stimulus but also of the brightness of the surrounding stimuli.

Color Mixture

One of the most striking characteristics of almost every visual experience is the sensation of color. Human beings are able to discriminate among a vast number of hues. Most colored stimuli, of course, are not pure hues but mixtures. Color mixtures can be represented on the color circle shown in Figure 3-11. At the perimeter of the circle are the various wavelengths of light, which correspond to hues. The purity, or **saturation,** of the color is represented by the radius; saturation increases toward the edges of the circle, where pure hues are found, and decreases toward the center, where mixtures of hues are found. Colors that are at exactly opposite points on the color circle are called **complementary colors;** they combine to produce gray.

It has long been known that new colors can be produced by combining various other colors. Such combinations can be achieved in two ways. In **color mixture by addition,** two colored light beams overlap or fuse. In contrast, **color mixture by subtraction** occurs when colored paints, which reflect some wavelengths and absorb others, are mixed. In either case the color that results is determined not by what is mixed, light beams or paint, but by the wavelength of the light that eventually reaches the eye.

The additive procedure, in which colored lights are mixed, produces a new color that can be placed somewhere between the positions of the two original colors on the color circle. For example, mixing a 609-nanometer orange light and a 510-nanometer green light will produce a yellow-green sensation. The exact hue depends on the intensities of the two component lights. If the orange light is more intense, the result-

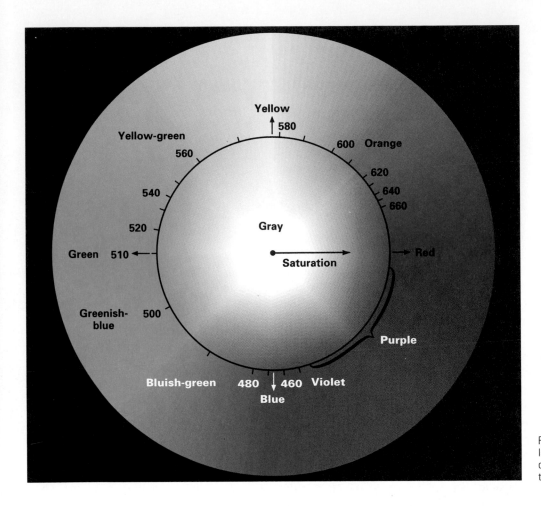

FIGURE 3-11 The color circle. Wavelength varies around the circumference of the circle; saturation increases from the center out.

ing light will be yellowish; if the green light is more intense, the resulting color will be closer to green. (See Figure 3-12.)

The subtractive process is similar except that the resulting color is that of the light reflected from the surface. (See Figure 3-13.) A red fire engine looks red because it absorbs all wavelengths *except* red; the red wavelength is reflected. Similarly, a green leaf looks green because it absorbs all light except light with a wavelength of about 510 nanometers—that is, green light—which is reflected from the leaf's surface. When we mix paints, therefore, the resulting color is a combination of the wavelengths that are not absorbed by the paint mixture but instead are reflected back to the eye. If, for example, one mixes blue and yellow paint in equal amounts and then shines white light onto the mixture, the blue paint will absorb all wavelengths except those in the green-blue-violet range and the yellow paint will absorb all but the green-yellow wavelengths. The only light reflected back will be a shade of green.

THEORIES OF COLOR VISION

We noted earlier that color vision depends on the cone receptors in the retina. But how do the cones work? Do people have a separate kind of cone for each wavelength of light? This seems unlikely, because we experience such a vast number of different colors that it would require the presence of thousands of different kinds of cones in each tiny region of the retina. But if there are fewer types of cones than there are distinguishable colors, how many types are there?

Trichromatic Theory

The oldest theory of color vision, the **trichromatic theory,** dates from the work of Thomas Young in 1807 and Hermann von Helmholtz in 1866 and therefore is often called the Young–Helmholtz theory. Young and Helmholtz argued that the eye con-

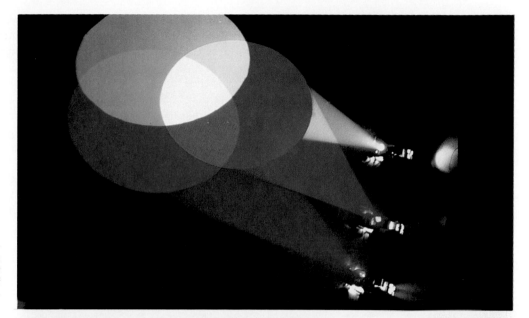

FIGURE 3-12 An example of color mixture by addition. Here, the overlapping circles of colored light show how new colors can be created by the mixture of the three primary colors: red (or red-orange), green, and violet (or blue-violet).

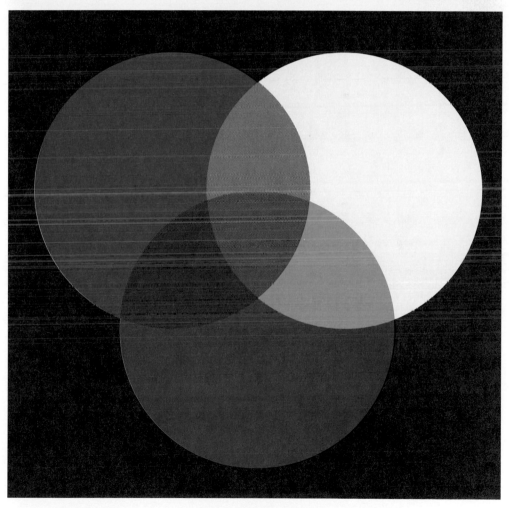

FIGURE 3-13 An example of color mixture by subtraction. Here, the reflected light from various mixtures of colored paints combine to create new hues. For example, green is produced because the yellow pigments absorb wavelengths to about 500 nanometers, whereas the blue pigment absorbs wavelengths from 550 nanometers, and higher. This means that when the two are combined, the only wavelengths remaining that can reflect off white paper lie between about 500 and 550 nanometers, which is in the green portion of the spectrum.

tains three types of cone receptors, each of which is sensitive to one of three **primary colors:** red (or red-orange), green, and blue (or blue-violet). When colored light strikes the retina, each type of cone receptor is activated to a certain degree; the resulting experience of color then is determined by the combined action of all three types of receptors.

The principal evidence for the trichromatic theory was derived from experiments

67

on color mixture. Because virtually all the hues that we can identify can be obtained by mixing red, green, and blue in various proportions, it seemed reasonable to assume that there are three kinds of cones corresponding to these colors. In this view, the colors that we see are created because each type of cone contributes differentially to the visual experience, with the amount contributed by each type depending on the amount of each primary color present in the stimulus. For example, when a yellow light falls on the retina, the red and green receptors react most; in effect, a yellow sensation occurs when these two types of receptors are activated equally strongly. (See Figure 3-14.) Similarly, when a blue light strikes the retina, the blue and green receptors are activated but the red receptors are not.

Although such evidence supports the trichromatic theory, a more convincing test would consist of isolating single cones in the retina, stimulating them with light of a specific wavelength, and observing how they respond. If the trichromatic theory is correct, one would expect to find cones that respond only to red, only to blue, and only to green wavelengths.

It is obviously impossible to do this with the normal intact eye, but analogous tests

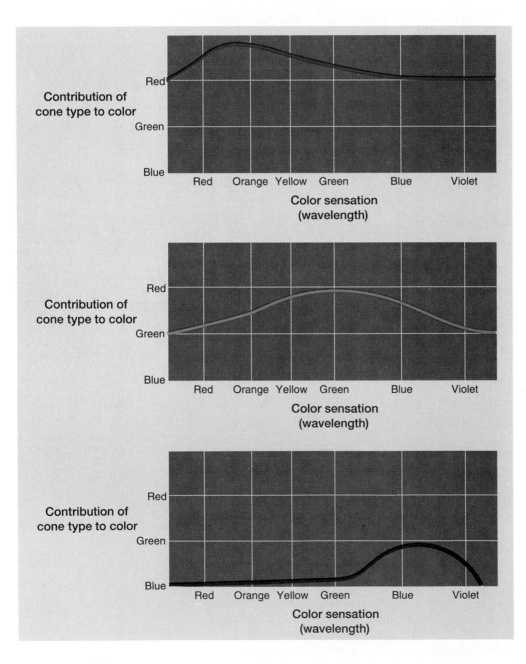

FIGURE 3-14 Relative contributions of the three kinds of cone receptors—red, green, and blue—to various color sensations, based upon color mixture experiments. (Adapted from Geldard, 1972.)

have been conducted using retinas from victims of fatal automobile accidents (Brown & Wald, 1964; Marks, Dobelle, & MacNichol, 1964). Before any nerve degeneration could occur, the retinas were placed under a specialized microscope and slender beams of colored light were directed at individual cones. Beneath the microscope was a spectrophotometer, an instrument that measures the wavelength of light; it was used to determine which wavelengths were being absorbed by the cone. Three kinds of cones were identified in this way. As predicted by the trichromatic theory, they absorbed wavelengths of 450, 530, and 570 nanometers, corresponding to the blue, green, and red portions of the spectrum.

Although it is simple and appealing, there are some problems with the Young–Helmholtz theory. For one thing, colors seem to change when their brightness changes; yellowish colors, for example, seem to change toward a purer yellow when intensity is increased, and violet and blue-green become bluer. This phenomenon, called the **Bezhold–Brücke effect,** poses a problem for the Young–Helmholtz theory because changes in brightness alone should not alter the relative contributions of the three primary receptors and therefore should not affect hue (Cornsweet, 1962).

Opponent-Process Theory

Another theory of color vision, the **opponent-process theory** (see Figure 3-15), suggests that color vision occurs not because combinations of three types of color receptors are activated but because three separate systems, each reacting to a *pair* of colors, are activated (Hering, 1964/1877). One of those systems, the black/white sys-

FIGURE 3-15 How the red/green and blue/yellow opponent-process systems combine to produce a color sensation. The separate panels in this figure are described in the text.

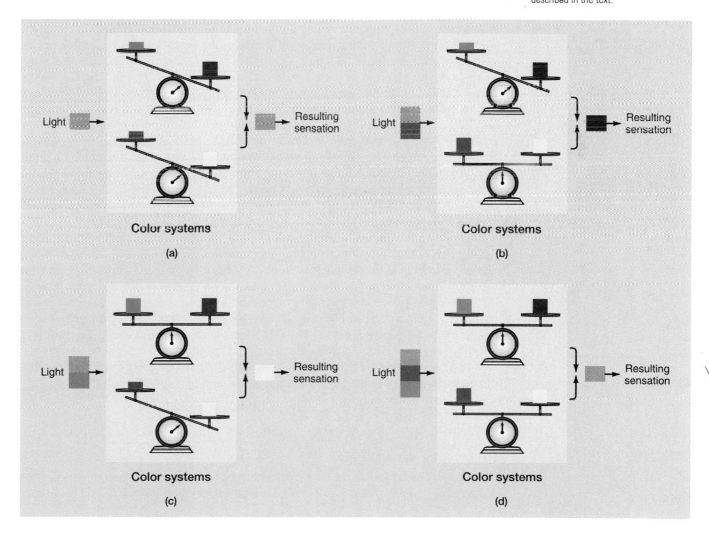

tem, detects the luminance or brightness of light and contributes little to the sensation of color. The other two systems, however, produce color experience by responding to red/green and yellow/blue wavelengths. When activated by light, each system produces both a primary and an opponent process. These processes operate like a simple balance: When light activates one process, the balance is tipped in its favor and the opponent process is inhibited.

The opponent-process theory is illustrated in Figure 3-15. When the eye is exposed to pure red light, the red process in the red/green system is activated and the opponent (green) process is inhibited. If green light is added to the red light, the red becomes desaturated and eventually looks gray. The blue/yellow system works in a similar fashion. When pure blue light strikes the eye, the blue process is activated and the yellow process is inhibited. If yellow light is added, the blue becomes desaturated; when the two processes are in balance, the resulting sensation is gray.

According to this theory, the various hues among which we differentiate are produced by the combination of processes in these systems. An orange sensation, for instance, is produced by a combination of the yellow and red processes—the yellow stemming from the blue/yellow system and the red from the red/green system (see Figure 3-15a). We know this because when we add blue light to the original orange stimulus, so that the blue/yellow system comes into balance, producing a neutral gray, the resulting sensation is pure red (see Figure 3-15b). If, on the other hand, we add green light so that the red/green system comes into balance, the resulting sensation is yellow (see Figure 3-15c). Finally, if blue and green are added, so that both systems are balanced, the resulting sensation is one of gray (see Figure 3-15d).

This approach was used in a study that confirmed the opponent-process theory (Hurvich & Jameson, 1957). By adding pure colors to existing light stimuli, the researchers were able to balance one system or the other (or both), thereby showing that certain colors belong to the same system. The results are presented in Figure 3-16. The zero level, or baseline, corresponds to the balance point for a given color system—that is, the point at which the subject reports seeing a neutral gray. Points away from the baseline indicate where each color system is not in balance. Points above the line indicate a stronger sensation of red or yellow; points below the baseline indicate stronger green or blue sensations. The farther a point is from the baseline in either direction, the stronger the experience of that color and the greater the amount of the opponent color that must be added to produce the sensation of gray. For instance, more pure red must be added to green light with a wavelength of about 540 nanometers than to green light with a wavelength of about 560 nanometers to produce gray; similarly, less yellow is needed to balance a blue light with a wavelength of about 440 nanometers than to balance a blue light with a wavelength of about 475 nanometers.

The two color systems act together, of course, to produce the various hues. Their joint action is shown in Figure 3-16c. Note that the pure colors are produced when one color system is out of balance while the other is balanced. Thus, light with a wavelength of about 475 nanometers causes the red/green system to be in balance but causes the blue/yellow system to favor blue; the resulting sensation is blue. Similarly, light with a wavelength of about 490 nanometers causes the blue/yellow system to be in balance but causes the red/green system to favor green; the resulting sensation is green. At any given point along the spectrum, we can predict which hue will be experienced by combining the action of the two color systems. The fact that red and green cancel each other and that yellow and blue cancel each other strongly supports the notion that there are two color systems rather than the three suggested by the trichromatic theory.

Reconciling the Theories

How can the evidence for the trichromatic theory be so strong when the evidence for the opponent-process theory is equally strong? Which theory is correct? The answer

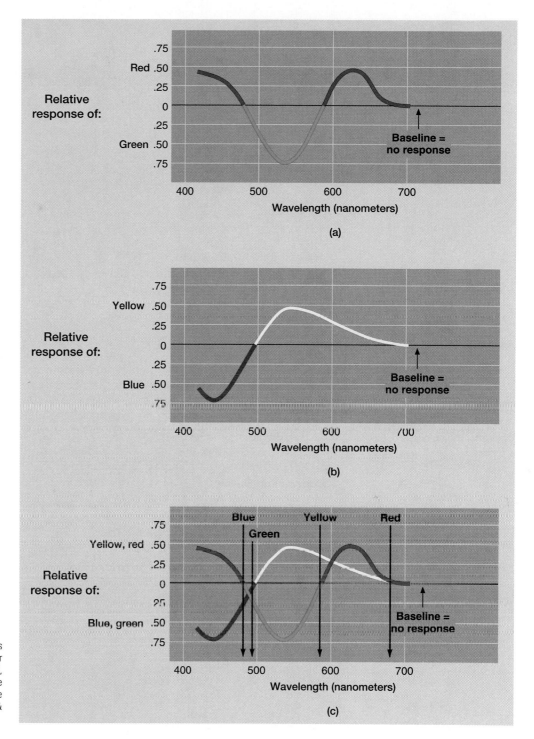

FIGURE 3-16 Relative visual responses as a function of wavelength of light for red and green (a), blue and yellow (b), and the two systems combined (c). The zero line is the balance point for the color systems. (Adapted from Hurvich & Jameson, 1957.)

is that both theories are correct to a degree; in fact, they complement each other. Part of the visual system operates according to the trichromatic theory, whereas other parts operate in accordance with the opponent-process theory.

Figure 3-17 illustrates how the two theories can be reconciled. The trichromatic theory provides an accurate description of how the retinal cones react to light. At that level of visual processing there are indeed three kinds of cone receptors corresponding to the three primary colors. The opponent-process theory, however, more accurately describes the functioning of the ganglion cells in the retina and the

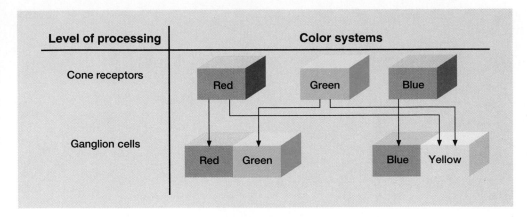

FIGURE 3-17 A schematic diagram illustrating how the trichromatic and opponent-process theories combine to produce color vision. At one level of visual processing—the cones—the system operates according to the trichromatic theory. At a higher level, however—the ganglion cells—it operates according to the opponent-process theory. (Adapted from Hurvich & Jameson, 1957.)

lateral geniculate nucleus (LGN) of the brain. (The LGN is the area of the brain that receives visual information from the retina and relays it to other parts of the brain.) The ganglion cells and the LGN receive the red-green-blue information from the cones and recode the information as indicated in the opponent-process theory.

This recoding process has been demonstrated in a number of experiments (DeValois & DeValois, 1975). In one series of studies, extremely thin wire electrodes were placed in single nerve cells within the LGN of a monkey. Light of a specific wavelength was then flashed at the monkey's eye, and the rate of nerve impulses from the LGN was observed. (A change in the rate of nerve impulses indicates visual activity.) The results confirmed that an opponent process was occurring in the LGN.

Figure 3-18 shows how the red/green and blue/yellow cells in the LGN responded to light of various wavelengths. When the stimulus wavelength was below about 600 nanometers (blue-green-yellow), the red/green LGN cells were inhibited. When the wavelength was above 600 nanometers (orange-red), those cells were activated. In other words, red light activated the cells and green light reduced their rate of firing. A comparable effect was observed in the blue/yellow cells: When the stimulus wavelength was below about 500 nanometers (blue end of the spectrum), neural activity

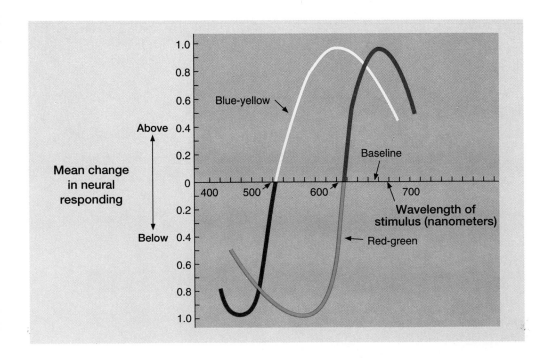

FIGURE 3-18 Mean change in neural activity (number of nerve firings per second) in the lateral geniculate nucleus as a function of the wavelength of light stimulating the cone receptor. (Adapted from DaValois & DaValois, 1975.)

was inhibited; when it was above that level (yellow), neural activity was increased. The same kind of recoding has been found to occur in the retinal ganglion cells (Cornsweet, 1970; Ganz, 1975).

INTERIM SUMMARY

Light waves are characterized by amplitude, wavelength, and frequency. The brightness of a visual stimulus is roughly proportional to the amplitude of the light waves; the color or hue is determined by the wavelength. The most important structures in the eye are the rods and cones, which are embedded in the retina. Rods contain larger quantities of rhodopsin, a visual pigment that is depleted by exposure to light. Rods are more sensitive to light, but cones produce the sensation of color. The trichromatic theory of color vision states that the eye contains three kinds of cone receptors, each of which is sensitive to one of three primary colors: red, green, and blue. The opponent-process theory suggests that color vision results from the activation of three separate color systems, each reacting to a pair of colors (black/white, red/green, and yellow/blue); various hues are produced by the combination of processes in these systems. It appears that both theories are accurate but that they apply to different levels of the visual processing system. The trichromatic theory describes the cone receptors found in the retina, whereas the opponent-process theory describes the coding of visual information by the retinal ganglion cells and the lateral geniculate nucleus of the brain.

AUDITION

Most people would agree that audition (hearing) is our second most important sense. Sensory psychologists have devoted considerable study to audition, focusing on many of the same problems that are of interest in the study of vision (Gulick, 1989).

AUDITORY STIMULI

Sound is generated by vibrating objects that create waves of air pressure. As an object vibrates, it bumps against the air, causing a radiating pressure wave. The pressure wave bounces against the eardrum, causing it to vibrate and produce nerve impulses.

Like light waves, sound waves are characterized by amplitude (wave height), wavelength (distance from one wave peak to the next), and frequency (number of waves per unit time). The frequency of a sound wave, measured in **hertz (Hz),** or waves per second, gives rise to the sensation of pitch, that is, the sense that the sound is high or low. The amplitude of the wave is measured in **decibels (db)** and is experienced as intensity or loudness.

ANATOMY OF THE EAR

The ear is divided into three parts—external, middle, and inner. (See Figure 3-19.) The external ear collects sound waves and funnels them toward the middle ear, where they bounce against the **tympanic membrane** (eardrum), causing it to vibrate. Located behind the eardrum, in the middle ear, are three tiny bones: the

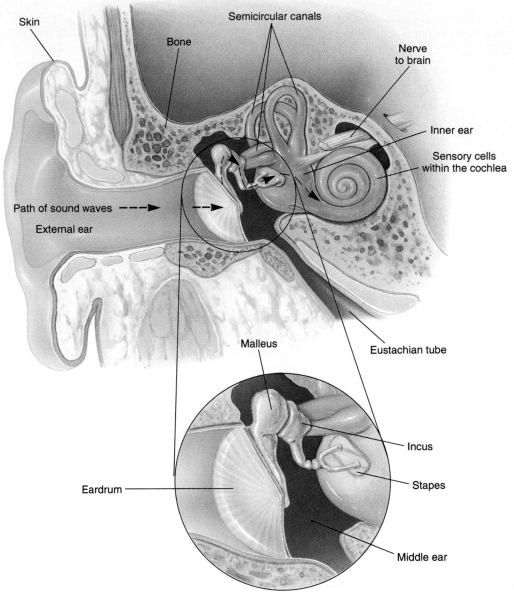

Skin

Bone

Semicircular canals

Nerve
to brain

Inner ear

Sensory cells
within the cochlea

Path of sound waves ⇢

External ear

Malleus

Eustachian tube

Eardrum

Incus

Stapes

Middle ear

FIGURE 3-19 A schematic drawing of
the human ear.

malleus, incus, and **stapes.** The malleus is attached to the eardrum and vibrates along with it. The other two bones are attached to each other by ligaments and form a kind of lever that beats against the **oval window** of the inner ear. Thus, as the eardrum vibrates, so do the three bones, and so, in turn, does the oval window.

The inner ear has three main sections: the **cochlea,** the **vestibule,** and the **semicircular canals.** The cochlea contains the specialized structures that convert vibrations into nerve impulses.

The Cochlea

The cochlea is aptly named; the term is derived from the Latin word for "snail," and the organ looks like a coiled-up shell. If it were unrolled, the cochlea would be 1/8 inch wide and 1/3 inch long and would appear as shown in Figure 3-20 (Geldard, 1972). Note that the cochlea is not uniform in width; it is wide at the basal end, where the inner ear is connected to the middle ear, and narrower at the apical end (or apex). The **cochlear partition** divides the cochlea lengthwise into two main sections: the **scala vestibuli** and the **scala tympani;** both are filled with a thick substance called **perilymph fluid.** The partition itself has two sections: a bony portion and the **basilar membrane,** whose surface contains specialized hair cells connected

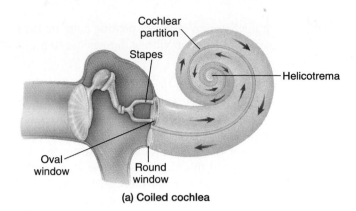

(a) Coiled cochlea

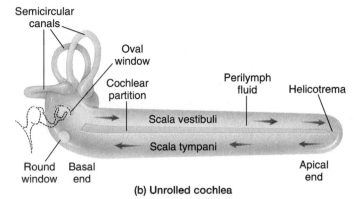

FIGURE 3-20 A schematic diagram of the cochlea. This organ is coiled much like a snail's shell (*a*). The bottom diagram (*b*) shows what it would look like if it were "unrolled." Note that the cochlear partition does not extend fully to the apical end

(b) Unrolled cochlea

to auditory nerve fibers below the surface. There are about 23,500 hair cells, ranging in length from 0.05 millimeter at the basal end of the membrane to about 0.1 millimeter at the apical end. Taken together, these structures—the cochlear partition, basilar membrane, and hair cells—are called the **organ of Corti.**

The cochlea is stimulated by vibrations of the oval window. Slow vibrations displace the perilymph fluid in the scala vestibuli, creating a wave that moves toward the apical end of the cochlea, travels through the opening in the partition, and returns toward the **round window,** which bulges outward to accommodate the pressure. More rapid vibrations affect the system in a different way. The fluid does not have time to travel from the oval window to the apex and back to the round window. Instead, a sharp vibration of the oval window causes the cochlear partition to act like a buggy whip: It bends downward, first near the basal end and then, after about 3 milliseconds, at the apical end. This causes the hair cells on the membrane to move, and their movement, in turn, creates nerve impulses in the auditory tract.

THEORIES OF AUDITION

The sequence of events by which waves of air pressure are converted into nerve impulses does not tell us why we hear different pitches. A number of theories have attempted to explain this phenomenon.

Place-Resonance Theory

One of the earliest theories—the **place-resonance theory**—was proposed by Hermann von Helmholtz (who also contributed to the development of the trichromatic theory of color vision). Helmholtz knew that the hair cells on the basilar membrane vary in length and tension. On the basis of this knowledge, he argued that the hair cells act as resonators: Whenever the membrane vibrates at a certain frequency, the hair cells vibrate as well. But because of the differences in the length and tension of hairs at different locations on the membrane, not all of the hairs vibrate in response to every sound. Only the hairs of the "appropriate" length and tension vibrate in response to a sound of a given frequency. The sensation of pitch therefore depends on the location of the resonating hairs on the basilar membrane; that is, the hairs at a particular location vibrate in response to pressure waves at a particular frequency.

Frequency Theory

A second theory of audition, the **frequency theory,** holds that the basilar membrane vibrates as a whole, acting more or less like a microphone. Pitch is a function of the frequency of vibration—the higher the frequency, the higher the pitch; loudness is a function of the amplitude—the greater the wave amplitude the louder the sound.

Although this theory is simple and appealing, it has a serious flaw: Nerve fibers cannot fire at rates of more than about 1,000 times per second, yet we are able to hear sounds with frequencies well above that rate. An additional principle, known as the **volley principle,** has been suggested in an attempt to resolve this problem (Wever, 1949). According to the volley principle, individual nerve fibers fire in unison up to a certain rate—say, 1,000 times per second. When the sound waves are at higher frequencies, however, the individual nerves do not respond to every peak of the wave. Instead, they respond to every second or third or tenth peak. (See Figure 3-21.) This creates a staggered pattern in which nerves fire intermittently rather than in unison, producing "volleys" of impulses at a rate well in excess of 1,000 per seond.

The volley principle suggests how individual nerves can function together to produce a rate of firing many times the individual frequency. When the vibrations caused by the incoming stimuli are too rapid for the nerves to convert them into indi-

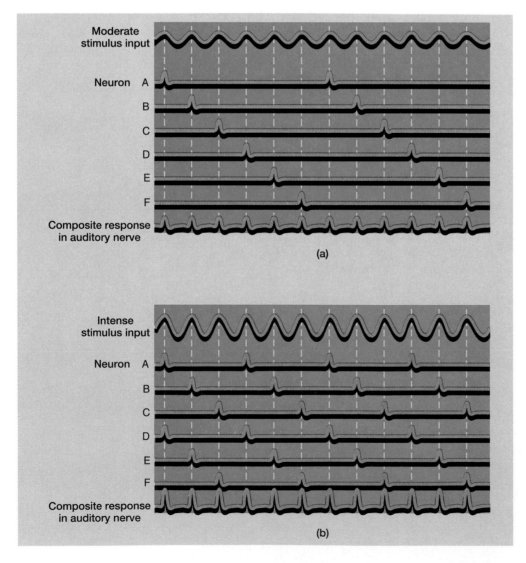

FIGURE 3-21 Diagram showing how the volley principle works to produce high-frequency sounds. Note that the frequency produced in the auditory nerve depends on the staggered firing of individual neurons, whereas the overall intensity depends on the total number of neurons firing at one time.

vidual impulses, the nerves begin to fire in a staggered way, thereby increasing the overall rate of impulses (Rose, Brugge, Anderson, & Hind, 1967).

Békésy's Theory

Békésy (1960) in effect combined the two theories just described. He first established that the basilar membrane varies in stiffness; it is quite stiff near the basal end and more elastic toward the apical end. In response to very low-frequency stimuli (about 400 hertz or below), all parts of the membrane seem to vibrate together and pitch is determined by the overall frequency of vibration. This response supports the frequency theory of hearing. In response to higher frequencies, however, the vibrating basilar membrane sets up a traveling wave (see Figure 3-22a) similar to the

FIGURE 3-22 Diagram showing how the traveling wave (*a*) reaches its peak at different points along the basilar membrane depending upon the frequency of the sound (*b*).

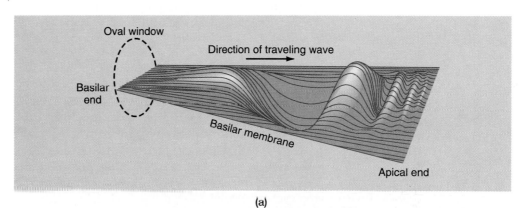

(a)

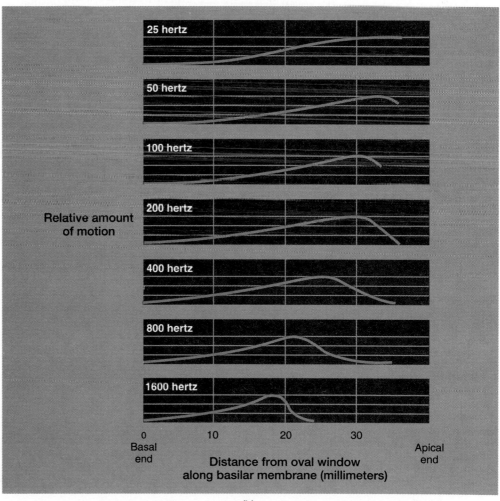

(b)

77

effect one obtains by yanking up and down on a slack rope. The wave begins at the basal end of the membrane, increases in amplitude as it travels along the membrane, and subsides as it nears the apex.

The important point here is that the *position* on the basilar membrane at which the wave reaches its maximum amplitude depends on the frequency of the wave. For low frequencies, the highest amplitude occurs near the apical end. For high frequencies, the point of greatest amplitude occurs nearer to the basal end. For midrange sounds (about 1,600 hertz), the highest amplitude occurs at about the middle of the membrane. (See Figure 3-22b.)

Research indicates that both the place and the frequency theories are correct, especially for frequencies from about 500 to 4,000 hertz. The place along the membrane at which the traveling wave reaches its maximum strength does indeed vary with the frequency of the sound. But the overall rate of nerve firing is also related to the frequency of the sound.

INTERIM SUMMARY

Like light waves, sound waves are characterized by amplitude, wavelength, and frequency. Amplitude creates the sensation of loudness, whereas frequency creates the sensation of pitch. The most important portion of the ear is the cochlea, which contains the specialized structures that convert sound waves into nerve impulses. One of the earliest theories of audition was Helmholtz's place-resonance theory, according to which hairs at different locations on the basilar membrane vibrate in response to sounds of different frequencies. Another theory, the frequency theory, holds that the basilar membrane vibrates as a whole. These two theories were combined by Békésy, who showed that the basilar membrane vibrates as a unit in response to low-frequency stimuli but that at higher frequencies the membrane sets up a traveling wave; the position at which the wave reaches its maximum amplitude depends on the frequency of the sound.

SECONDARY SENSES

Although vision and audition have been studied more extensively than the other senses, considerable research has been done on the secondary senses. These include olfaction (smell), gustation (taste), and cutaneous sensation (the skin senses).

OLFACTION

Although some animals, such as dogs, have many more olfactory receptors than humans (Marshall & Moulton, 1981), the human sense of **olfaction** is highly developed. In fact, it has been claimed that human olfactory receptors can be triggered by a single odorous molecule—that is, by the smallest possible physical stimulus (DeVries & Stuiver, 1961).

The starting point for understanding olfaction is the physical and chemical nature of odor molecules (Brown, 1975). It is very difficult to specify the properties of those molecules, because there is no single physical continuum (analogous to the wavelength of light, for instance) on which odorous molecules can be placed. It appears, however, that the odor of a substance is related both to its volatility (how easily it becomes gaseous) and to its solubility (how easily it dissolves). But it is not clear whether an odorous substance must be volatile. Water, for example, is volatile but not odorous, whereas musk is not very volatile but very odorous.

Olfactory Receptors

Odorous molecules enter the nose and repeatedly stick to and are released from the surface of the mucous membrane, triggering the olfactory receptors (Figure 3-23). The receptors are located on the surface of the **olfactory epithelium,** the sensitive tissue at the top of each nostril. At the ends of the nerve fibers are projections,

FIGURE 3-23 A schematic diagram of the olfactory receptors.

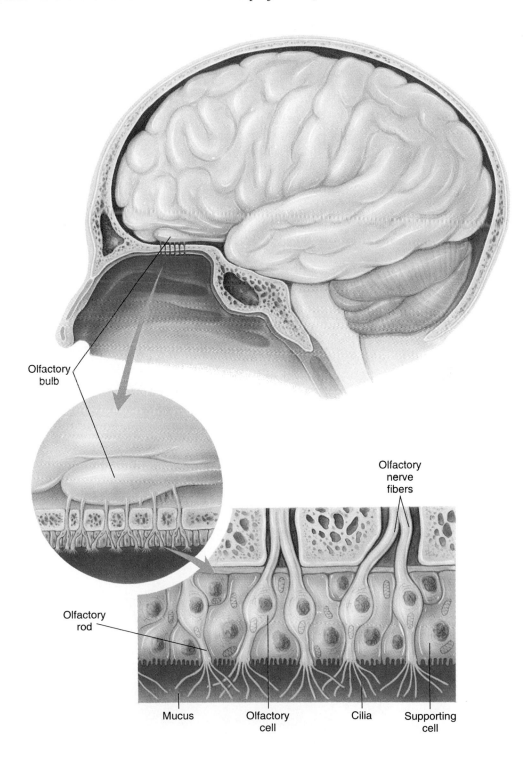

Olfactory bulb

Olfactory nerve fibers

Olfactory rod

Mucus   Olfactory cell   Cilia   Supporting cell

called **olfactory rods,** that extend through the supporting **sustentacular cells** to the surface of the epithelium. Each rod is extremely small, perhaps one-millionth of a meter in diameter, and each has 10 to 12 small hairs, called **cilia,** projecting from its tip about 1 to 2 micrometers into the mucous membrane. Somehow—it is not known exactly how—the odor molecules are trapped in the mucous membrane and cause the cilia to produce a nerve impulse.

Odor Quality

One might think that it should be possible to classify odors according to primary categories (for example, menthol, burnt, turpentine) much as hues can be classified according to primary colors. Odors, however, are far more difficult to classify than colors. Estimates have placed the number of primary odors at anywhere from four to about 40 (Amoore, 1969). Because so many odors do not fit neatly into any one category, there is no single classification system.

Theories of Olfaction

Given the difficulty of classifying odors, it is not surprising that no single theory of olfaction accounts for all the known facts (Moncrieff, 1967). The most widely accepted theory of smell is the **stereochemical theory** (Amoore, 1970). As illustrated in Figure 3-24, this is a "lock-and-key" theory: It holds that there is a physical match between the shape of the odorous molecule and that of the receptor. Researchers have tested this theory by correlating the shapes of various odorous molecules with their odors. The results indicate that there may be seven classes of odors—camphorous, musky, floral, minty, ethereal, pungent, and putrid—although the evidence is still far from being clear-cut (Davies & Taylor, 1965).

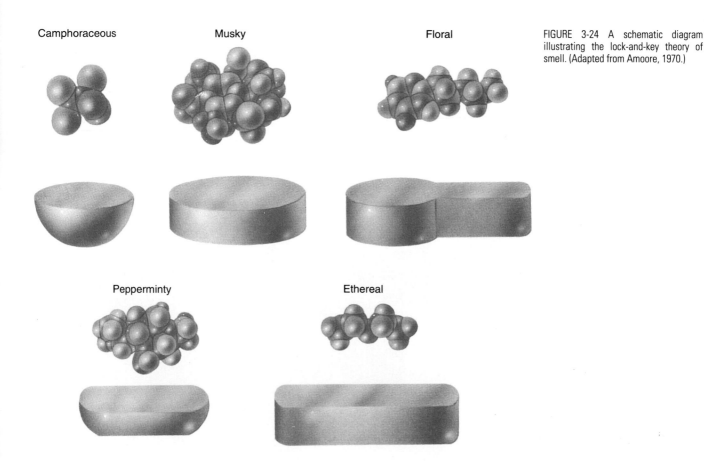

Camphoraceous   Musky   Floral

Pepperminty   Ethereal

FIGURE 3-24 A schematic diagram illustrating the lock-and-key theory of smell. (Adapted from Amoore, 1970.)

GUSTATION

Taste, or **gustation,** has been called the poor relation of the family of senses because it contributes relatively little to human sensory experience (Geldard, 1972). Even though taste seems to be the primary means of appreciating foods, the smell of the food actually dominates this sensation. In fact, if the nasal cavities are blocked and food is pureed so that it cannot be identified on the basis of texture and temperature, humans have a difficult time identifying food by taste alone.

Taste Stimuli

Like odorous stimuli, taste stimuli cannot be categorized on a single dimension. Scientists agree, however, that there are four basic or primary tastes: salt, bitter, sweet, and sour. The problem with this classification scheme is that no one knows for sure how molecules of substances with these characteristics affect the receptors. Moreover, the taste of a substance sometimes depends on its concentration. For example, potassium chloride tastes sweet at very low concentrations, bitter at somewhat higher concentrations, and salty at the highest concentration levels (Dzendolet & Meiselman, 1967).

Taste Receptors

The basic receptor for taste sensations is the **taste bud** (see Figure 3-25). Taste buds are located not only on the tongue but also on the palate, pharynx, tonsils, lips, and cheeks, as well as on the underside of the tongue. The densest concentrations of taste buds are in the **papillae,** the lobes of tissue on the surface of the tongue. Each papillus contains 200 or more buds.

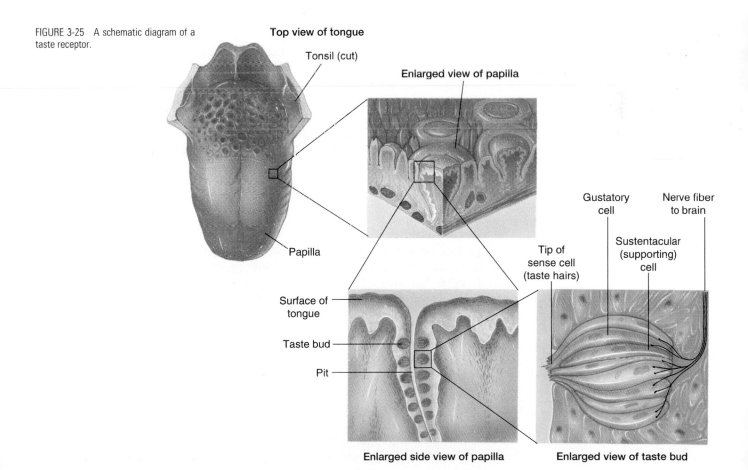

FIGURE 3-25   A schematic diagram of a taste receptor.

Top view of tongue

Tonsil (cut)

Enlarged view of papilla

Papilla

Gustatory cell

Nerve fiber to brain

Sustentacular (supporting) cell

Tip of sense cell (taste hairs)

Surface of tongue

Taste bud

Pit

Enlarged side view of papilla

Enlarged view of taste bud

Each taste bud contains between 2 and 24 spindle-shaped nerve fibers called **gustatory cells** in addition to sustentacular (supporting) cells. The tips of the gustatory cells protrude slightly beyond the surrounding tissue into the cavities on the papillae; this allows them to come into contact with the molecules of the substance being ingested.

Scientists generally believe that sensitivity to taste varies as a function of the location of the taste buds on the tongue. The tip of the tongue, for instance, is said to be especially sensitive to sweet solutions, the back of the tongue to bitter ones, and the edges to acidic ones; salt receptors are located uniformly throughout the surface of the tongue. Particular taste sensations are not, however, localized in one place. In fact, sensitivity to bitter and sour tastes is even greater on the palate than on the tongue (Brown, 1975).

Papillae may differ in terms of the taste to which they are most sensitive. Some research has shown that individual papillae respond to all four basic tastes (McCutcheon & Saunders, 1972), but other studies, in which individual papillae were isolated under a microscope, have found that certain papillae respond to only one taste (Békésy, 1966). Clearly, the issue is not fully resolved (Brown, 1975).

Taste Interactions

Many factors affect the experience of taste; these include not only the type of molecule and the location of the receptor but also the combination of tastes in question (Moskowitz, 1970; Stevens, 1969). A sweet solution, for example, reduces bitterness and sourness. People who put sugar in their coffee or lemonade can attest to this fact. Caffeine, on the other hand, enhances sourness. Another factor is temperature: When sweet and salty solutions are warmed, the sweet flavor is enhanced but the salty taste is diminished (Békésy, 1964).

Theories of Gustation

Scientists agree that a dissolved substance somehow acts on a particular receptor, but beyond that little is known for sure. Indeed, any theory of taste must overcome some significant problems (Pfaffmann, 1962). One problem is that receptors may respond to more than one taste, thereby ruling out the theory that the sensation depends on which receptor is stimulated. Another problem is that distilled water, which contains no chemicals, can elicit tastes. It is difficult to see how any chemical-receptor relationship could account for this finding. In short, the development of an adequate theory of taste must await further research.

CUTANEOUS SENSATION

The surface of the skin covers about two square meters, making the **cutaneous sense** the largest of the sensory systems. Scientists have traditionally agreed that the skin mediates three types of sensation: temperature, pressure, and pain (Janal, Clark, & Carroll, 1991; Verrillo, 1975). Only recently, however, has it become possible to understand how the skin receptors transform physical energy into sensation.

Skin Receptors

As shown in Figure 3-26, the skin consists of three layers: the **epidermis,** which lies nearest the surface; the **dermis,** beneath the epidermis; and the **subcutaneous tissue,** the lowest layer. Within these layers are several types of nerve fibers. Originally it was believed that the **Krause end bulbs** create the sensation of cold, the **Ruffini endings** that of heat, the **Meissner's corpuscles** and hair follicles that of touch, and the **free nerve endings** that of pain (Verillo, 1975). In other words, scientists once believed that the sensation created by a particular stimulus was attributable to the

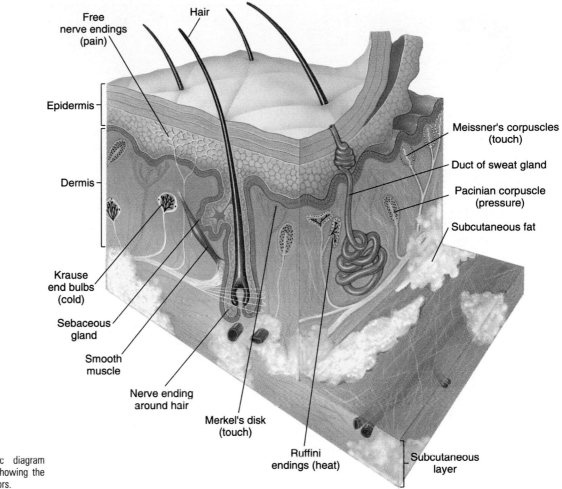

FIGURE 3-26 A schematic diagram (cross-section) of the skin, showing the various kinds of sense receptors.

type of nerve stimulated rather than to characteristics of the stimulus. This view was first raised in Müller's doctrine of specific nerve energies (discussed in Chapter 2) but has now generally been discredited. There are instances in which a receptor responds to a particular type of stimulus (for example, free nerve endings do appear to produce the sensation of pain), but it is now known that most of the structures in the skin respond to more than one kind of stimulus (Kenshalo & Nafe, 1962; Melzack & Wall, 1962).

Touch

In studying the sense of touch, researchers measure spatial discrimination thresholds at various points on the skin (Weinstein, 1968). The skin is touched with two bristles and the minimum distance between them that can be felt as two distinct pressure points (as opposed to a single point) is measured. As shown in Figure 3-27, the middle finger is extremely sensitive; a distance of only 2.5 millimeters between bristles will be felt as two pressure points. The calf is considerably less sensitive; a distance of 47 millimeters is required before the subject will feel two pressure points instead of one (Sherrick, 1968; see also Katz, 1989; Schiff & Foulke, 1983).

Temperature

An important function of the cutaneous system is the detection of temperature. The baseline temperature of the human body typically ranges from about 28°C at the earlobe to about 37°C on the forearm. The change in temperature required to produce a

83

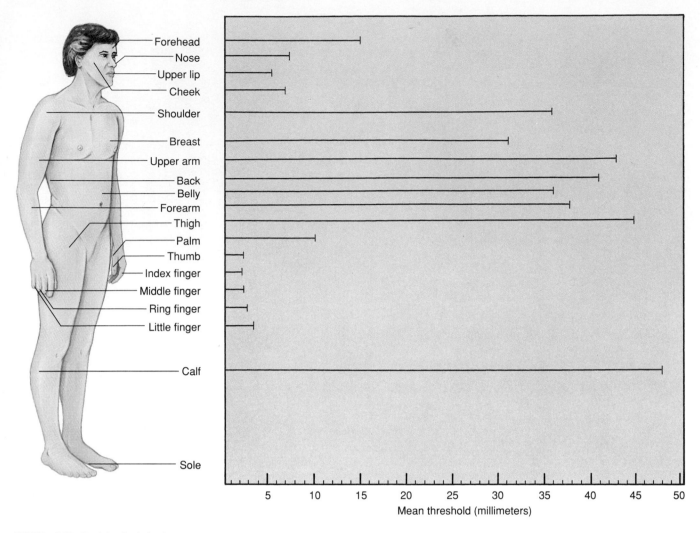

FIGURE 3-27 Spatial discrimination thresholds, expressed in millimeters, for various parts of the body. The numbers reflect the distance between two points required to produce the sensation of two discrete points of stimulation. (Adapted from Weinstein, 1968.)

noticeable difference can vary from as little as 0.01°C to about 8°C, depending on the baseline temperature, the size of the area stimulated, and other variables. In general, the greater the surface area stimulated, the greater its sensitivity to temperature changes (Kenshalo, Decker, & Hamilton, 1967).

Historically, the sensation of heat was thought to depend on the activation of the Ruffini nerve endings, whereas the sensation of cold was believed to occur in response to stimulation of the Krause end bulbs. The evidence for this theory is not, however, very compelling. It depends primarily on the fact that the areas of the skin especially sensitive to heat and cold are those areas that have a relatively large concentration of Ruffini and Krause nerve endings (Geldard, 1972).

A more contemporary theory of temperature sensation is the **neurovascular theory** (Kenshalo & Nafe, 1962). According to this theory, the sensation of a change in temperature is produced by the mechanical stimulation of free nerve endings in the walls of the vascular system. As the blood vessels cool and warm, they contract and expand. This mechanical stimulation creates nerve impulses that we experience as changes in temperature. The emphasis here is on the spatial and temporal patterns of nerve impulses to the brain rather than on the kind of nerve ending that is stimulated. Presumably there are areas in the brain that respond to such patterns, producing the sensation of heat or cold depending on the kind of pattern received. The problem with this theory, however, is that the time it takes for a person to feel warm differs from the time it takes to feel cold. If these sensations were created by the stimulation of the same free nerve endings, the time required to feel the sensation should be the same for both (Gagge & Stevens, 1968).

The secondary senses include olfaction (smell), gustation (taste), and the cutaneous (of the skin) senses. The odor of a substance is related to both its volatility and its solubility. According to the stereochemical theory, there is a physical match between the shape of an odorous molecule and the shape of the receptor, but it is still not clear why we can distinguish among many kinds of odors. Tastes are easier to classify than smells—the basic tastes being salt, bitter, sweet, and sour—but the taste of a substance sometimes depends on its concentration. Scientists agree that a dissolved substance acts on receptors in the taste buds to create the sensation of taste, but there is no adequate theory to account for how the quality of a taste is determined. The cutaneous sensations include temperature, pressure, and pain. It appears that particular receptors in the skin are involved in the creation of these sensations, but it is not yet known whether they are unique in that respect or whether other structures are involved as well.

SUMMARY

1. *Sensation* is the study of sensory abilities, the processes by which physical energy is translated into psychological experience.

2. *Psychophysics* is primarily concerned with the quantitative relationship between stimulus intensity and the psychological sensations to which the stimuli give rise. The most central problem in psychophysics is the specification of threshold. The *absolute threshold* is the minimum stimulus intensity that produces a noticeable sensation; the *difference threshold,* or *just noticeable difference (jnd),* is the minimal increment of intensity that causes the subject to sense a difference between two stimuli.

3. According to Weber's law, a difference threshold for a particular type of stimulus is always a constant proportion of the stimulus intensity. Fechner's law expresses the general relationship between the intensity of a stimulus and the intensity of the resulting sensation. It assumes that each jnd for a stimulus represents the same increment in the intensity of sensation.

4. Breaking with the traditional psychophysics of Weber and Fechner, Stevens proposed that the strength of a sensation should be measured directly, for example by having a person assign to the stimulus a number corresponding to its intensity, or by having the subject alter the stimulus intensity so that it was twice, or half, as intense.

5. *Signal-detection theory* emphasizes that stimulus intensity is not the only factor that influences sensory thresholds; subjects' expectations also bias their sensitivity to stimulation. Subject bias is created by the consequences of making an error in judgment, either claiming that a stimulus is present when it is not (false alarm) or that a stimulus is not present when it is (miss). A *receiver-operating characteristic curve* depicts a subject's performance and the extent to which detection is influenced by bias.

6. Visible light waves are one form of electromagnetic radiation. Their *amplitude* gives rise to the intensity, or *brightness,* of a visual stimulus, and their *wavelength* to its *hue.*

7. The most important part of the eye is the *retina,* which contains the visual receptors, *rods* and *cones.* Rods are smaller but more numerous than cones. They are also more sensitive to light than cones. Rods produce colorless sensations whereas cones produce the sensation of color.

8. The *Purkinje effect* confirms that rods and cones perform different functions. The effect occurs when, viewed in normal light, red and green patches look equally bright (because cones contribute more to the sensation under brightly lit

conditions), but when viewed in dim light, the green looks brighter (because rods contribute more when the light is dim and are less sensitive to red).

9. *Spatial* and *temporal acuity* are affected by the intensity of the visual stimulus. Moreover, when visual stimuli are presented in close temporal proximity, they tend to fuse into a single sensation. This *flicker fusion phenomenon* depends on the *critical fusion frequency* as well as the intensity of the stimulus.

10. *Brightness contrast* occurs when adjacent portions of a stimulus differ in brightness—the less intense part looks even dimmer than it would if it were viewed alone.

11. Virtually all of the colors we discriminate can be produced by mixing the three *primary colors*—red, green, and blue—in various proportions. Color mixtures can be obtained by combining colored lights *(additive process)* or from the reflection of light from a mixture of pigments *(subtractive process)*.

12. According to the *trichromatic theory* of color vision, color sensations are produced from the activation of three primary color receptors. According to the *opponent-process theory*, three pairs of color receptors exist, each leading to opposing kinds of color experience— black/white, red/green, and yellow/blue. There is good evidence for both of these theories. In fact, the retinal cones appear to be organized according to the trichromatic theory, whereas the *ganglion cells* of the retina and the *lateral geniculate nucleus* of the brain are organized according to the opponent-process theory.

13. Sound is generated when vibrating objects create waves of air pressure. The sensation of sound results when pressure waves in the air beat against the *tympanic membrane* in the ear, stimulating the *cilia* on the *basilar membrane* in the *cochlea* and thus establishing auditory nerve impulses.

14. According to the *place-resonance theory,* hair cells on the basilar membrane vary in length and tension and thus vibrate at different frequencies. When the basilar membrane vibrates at the frequency of a particular hair, the hair resonates, giving rise to the sensation of pitch. According to the *frequency theory,* the sensation of pitch is a function of the frequency of vibration of the basilar membrane as a whole. According to proponents of the frequency theory, the *volley principle* accounts for the sensation of pitches that result from frequencies greater than the rate at which nerve fibers can fire. *Békésy's theory* combines the place-resonance and the frequency theories. Békésy found that the place along the membrane at which a traveling wave reaches its maximum strength varies with the frequency of the sound, but that the overall rate of nerve firing is also related to the frequency of the sound.

15. Although a good deal is known about the secondary senses, *olfaction, gustation,* and the *cutaneous senses,* psychologists are less certain about how these senses work than they are about the workings of vision and audition. For example, it has been difficult to identify primary odors and to state how tasted substances affect the *taste buds.* For the cutaneous senses, there are several receptor types, but the specificity between receptor and stimulus does not appear to be as great as was once thought.

FOCUS QUESTIONS

1. How does the study of sensory abilities reflect modern psychology's interest in the mind–body problem?

2. What evidence exists for arguing that the rods and cones play distinctly different roles in visual sensation?

3. Describe some of the factors that affect visual acuity.

4. Describe the evidence for and against the two major theories of color vision, and discuss how this theoretical issue has been resolved.

5. Discuss the frequency and place theories of hearing and how the volley principle contributes to these theories.

6. Discuss why psychologists have virtually no complete or authoritative theory of gustation and olfaction.

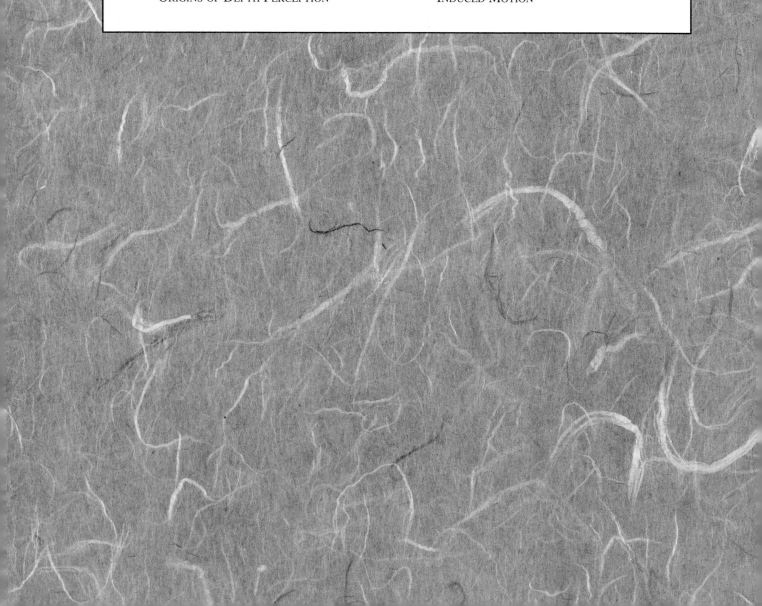

CHAPTER 4

PERCEPTION

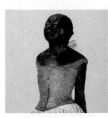 We saw in Chapter 3 that stimuli in the environment impinge on the sense organs and give rise to psychological sensations. The sense organs function as transformers of energy; light waves, for example, are transformed into neural impulses that, in turn, create psychological sensations. **Perception** goes beyond the transformation of physical energy into psychological experience. It involves the interpretation of sensory inputs: assessing the meaning of events and understanding objects in their totality. Thus, the study of perception is the study of the phenomenological world—the world as it *appears* to the observer, as it is individually experienced by each person.

Suppose that we arrange for light to be reflected from an object and move across a person's line of vision. We could think of the object as simply a source of stimulation. The light reflected from it strikes the person's retina and is transformed into neural energy. Furthermore, we could manipulate the stimulus—by changing its speed, for example—and study the effect on the person's ability to detect the stimulus. Now suppose that the object is an oncoming truck. Light waves from the object still stimulate the retina and are transformed into neural energy, but now the object has *meaning:* It is familiar yet menacing; it may be out of control and dangerous. In other words, the eye *senses* the light stimulus—its color, velocity, and other characteristics—but the person as interpreter of the stimulus *perceives* it as a meaningful object. A fundamental challenge for the study of perception is to show how meaning is added to sensation.

In our everyday experience we are usually unaware of this phenomenological aspect of perception. You can, however, demonstrate it for yourself (Gordon, 1989). Choose a brightly colored object in your room—perhaps a lampshade or a book cover—and study it for a moment. Notice its color; get a feel for how the color appears to you (for example, is it vivid?). Notice how much the color is part of the object—that is, how difficult it is to divorce the color from the object. Now take a piece of notebook paper, punch a small (1/4-inch) hole in the center, hold the page about 12 inches from your eye, and look at the object through the hole. The phenomenological *experience* of viewing the object is noticeably different. The color no longer appears to belong to the object but seems to float in space just behind the paper. In a sense, the patch of color that you view through the hole in the paper is an element of the object and provides raw material for your perception of that object. But viewing this element in isolation is entirely different from viewing the colored object in its totality.

PERCEPTION OF FORM

Before we can understand why a particular pattern of visual stimulation is perceived as a meaningful object, we need to ask a more fundamental question: How do we know that a pattern of stimulation is an object at all? What causes a retinal image to be perceived as a discrete, nameable figure or form?

PERCEIVING OBJECTS

Imagine slicing a Ping-Pong ball in half and placing one half over each eye. You would see an undifferentiated field of light—a vast, formless expanse of luminance. Like people caught in a heavy snowstorm, subjects who experience this effect report a total "blankout" (comparable to snow blindness) in which they feel virtually blind (Avant, 1965).

Contours

This experience of feeling blind suggests that visual perception depends on the presence of contours. A contour is an abrupt change in luminance, an edge between light and dark areas. Contours do not have to be explicitly present in a visual stimulus; they can be subjective or implied. In Figure 4-1, for example, we see an object shaped like a rectangle even though parts of the figure lack an abrupt transition from light to dark (Coren, 1972). We infer the "missing" parts of the contour because the background appears to contain whole, coherent objects that are hidden by a rectangle in the foreground (Shank & Walker, 1989).

Figure and Ground

Once contours are perceived, objects or figures can be distinguished from the background. **Figure** and **ground** (also called background) differ in a number of ways. First, a figure is an integrated unit of perception, a cohesive group of contours. It has a shape, coherence, and unity. The ground, on the other hand, does not have shape; it

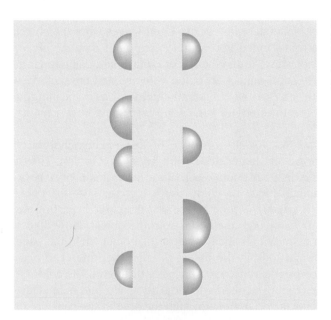

FIGURE 4-1 A subjective contour. We perceive an object in the shape of a flat strip even though, in the places where it is not defined by the round objects, the "edges" of the strip are indistinguishable from the background.

This striking image by the artist M. C. Escher exploits an ambiguous figure-ground relationship.

is formless. Second, a figure is perceived to lie in front of the ground, which seems to extend in all directions behind it. Third and most important, the figure has meaning. Even though we may not be able to give it a name, it nevertheless appears to be *nameable*. The ground, in contrast, is uniform and meaningless.

The separation of the information striking our retina into figure and ground is so fundamental to perception that we take it entirely for granted. But the importance of this distinction is dramatically illustrated by reversible figure–ground images like the one shown in Figure 4-2. What makes this figure reversible is the fact that the information provided by the image does not distinguish between figure and ground. If one focuses on the white portion and perceives it as the figure, one sees the outline of a vase. If, however, one thinks of the black portion as the figure and the white portion as ground, one sees two faces looking at each other. In either case the figure is unified and meaningful whereas the ground is an undifferentiated expanse lying behind the figure and extending indefinitely in all directions.

ORGANIZATION AND OBJECT PERCEPTION

The preceding discussion suggests that we automatically differentiate between figure and ground, but it does not specify how we know that a collection of contours is actually a figure. The first major steps in this direction were taken by the **Gestalt** psychologists in the early decades of the twentieth century (Koffka, 1935; Köhler, 1947; Wertheimer, 1976). The Gestalt psychologists rebelled against the prevailing idea that perceptions can be understood in terms of their elements. In fact, the German word *Gestalt* is roughly translated as "unified whole" or "configuration." These psychologists believed that one's holistic perception, the Gestalt, is greater than the sum of the individual elements making up the image. In other words, they wanted to study the phenomenological world—the world as we actually perceive it—not the elements that combine to create perceptions. In addition, they wished to specify the laws that govern perception and identify the processes in the brain that organize perceptual information. They developed the following five laws.

Law of Proximity

According to the **law of proximity,** several elements are seen as a coherent object by virtue of being spatially close to one another. For example, the pattern shown in part *a* of Figure 4-3 is perceived as three distinct columns of dots. We organize the dots in this way because the vertical distance between the dots is less than the horizontal distance; spatial proximity determines their perceptual organization. The pattern in part *b* of the figure is seen simply as a field of nine scattered dots; the equal spacing between the dots in both directions prevents us from grouping them together in any particular way.

Law of Similarity

According to the **law of similarity,** an image is organized by similarities among its elements. In the example shown in Figure 4-4, the circles are similar to each other, so we tend to see them as representing a coherent and discrete object. They are not part of the background but rather constitute a figure in and of themselves.

FIGURE 4-2 A reversible figure-ground. We perceive either a vase or the silhouette of two faces.

FIGURE 4-3 The law of proximity. In part (*a*) we perceive three columns of dots because the vertical distance between the dots is less than the horizontal distance. In (*b*) we perceived a field of nine scattered dots because the dots are spaced equally in all directions.

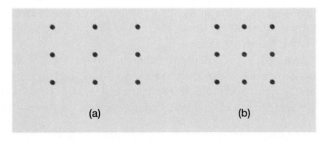

(a)   (b)

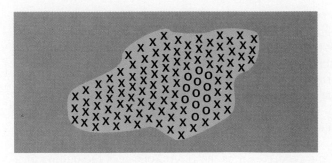

FIGURE 4-4 The law of similarity. Because the circles are similar to each other, we perceive them as a coherent and discrete object.

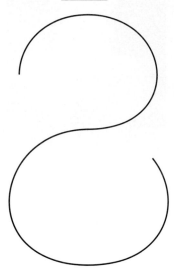

FIGURE 4-5 The law of good continuation. We perceive a figure 8 because of our tendency to continue the line implied by the curves.

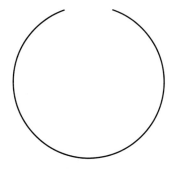

FIGURE 4-6 The law of closure. We perceive an enclosed circle because we tend to complete the contour of the circle.

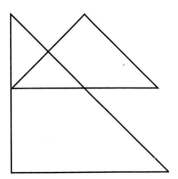

FIGURE 4-7 The law of Prägnanz. We tend to perceive two overlapping triangles instead of two small triangles and two irregular quadrilaterals because we tend to interpret a stimulus in the simplest terms.

Law of Good Continuation

The **law of good continuation** states that the perceiver will continue contours whenever the elements of the pattern establish an implied direction. Thus, the image shown in Figure 4-5 is seen as a figure 8 because we continue the curved line implied by the pattern.

Law of Closure

The **law of closure** states that humans tend to enclose a space by completing a contour and ignoring gaps in the figure. For example, one perceives the figure shown in Figure 4-6 as a circle even though it has a distinct gap in its contour.

Law of Prägnanz

According to the **law of Prägnanz,** a stimulus will be organized into as good a figure as possible. Although not well defined originally, the term "good" in this sense implies symmetrical, simple, and regular. For instance, one could think of the image shown in Figure 4-7 as a single figure composed of two small triangles and two quadrilaterals. People invariably see it, however, as two large, overlapping triangles. The law of Prägnanz impels us to see the stimulus in the simplest terms rather than in a complex or irregular way.

Visual Information and Object Perception

One of the criticisms of the law of Prägnanz was that the Gestalt psychologists did not clearly define "goodness." Modern research has addressed this problem, focusing on the complexity of the visual stimulus. One approach suggests that goodness can be expressed in terms of symmetry (Attneave, 1954, 1955; Yodogawa, 1982). If we are presented with an image of only half of a symmetrical figure, we can interpret the whole image because we automatically know the shape of the other half. In fact, the more symmetrical a figure, the less one needs to know about its shape in order to recognize it. According to this position, then, the greater the symmetry of a figure, the less its complexity and the greater its goodness.

Another approach relates the goodness of an image not to symmetry in and of itself but rather to the number of different orientations the figure can assume. The fewer the possible orientations of the figure, the greater its goodness (Garner, 1962, 1974). This idea is illustrated in Figure 4-8. Three patterns are shown on the left. They differ in terms of the number of possible orientations they can assume (these are shown to the right of the figure). No matter how the topmost pattern is rotated or inverted, the same image is seen; the figure has only one unique orientation. The pattern at the bottom, however, has eight possible orientations and thus is said to be visually more complex.

Several studies demonstrated the importance of the number of possible orientations by asking subjects to rate the goodness of figures on a scale from 1 to 7 (Garner & Clement, 1963; Handel & Garner, 1966). Figures with fewer possible orientations were judged to have greater goodness than figures with more possible orientations.

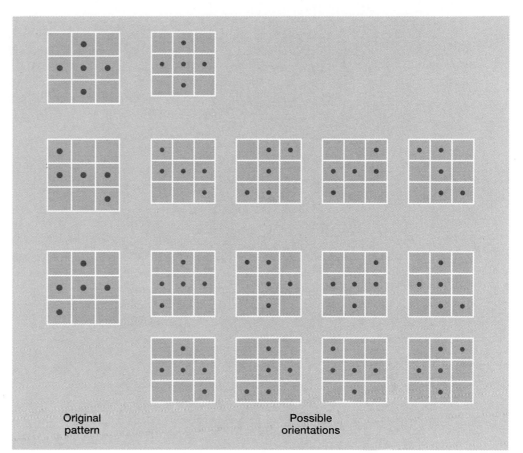

FIGURE 4-8 According to one interpretation of the term, the fewer the number of different orientations a figure can assume, the greater its "goodness." The three original patterns on the left differ in the number of orientations they can assume when rotated or inverted (flipped over). The top pattern has only one orientation; the middle pattern has four; and the bottom pattern has eight. (Adapted from Handel & Garner, 1966.)

Original pattern

Possible orientations

Origins of Object Perception

An important question in the study of perception is whether perceptions are learned or innate. Many studies have addressed this question. For example, experiments have been conducted using subjects who had been blind from birth but had undergone cataract surgery and were then able to see. Many of these subjects had great difficulty recognizing objects. Specifically, subjects were unable to identify simple geometric figures such as squares and circles, although they could see the forms and could identify them if they were allowed to touch them (Senden, 1960; Valvo, 1971). In other words, although the subjects had trouble naming the objects, they did see contours and organize their visual world into figure and ground.

Another approach to the question of whether perceptions are innate or learned is to study visual experience in infants before they have had an opportunity to learn about particular stimuli. Evidence from such studies suggests that humans have the ability to recognize coherent forms soon after birth (Salapatek, 1975). For example, one-month-old babies tend to fixate on the outline of a human face. By the time they are two months old, they begin to fixate on the facial features within the outline (Maurer & Salapatek, 1976). Clearly, the ability to differentiate between figure and ground—and thus to perceive objects—is present very early in life.

INTERIM SUMMARY

Visual perception depends on the presence of contours, or abrupt changes in luminance. Contours may be implied as well as explicitly present. Once contours are perceived, a figure can be distinguished from the ground or background. The Gestalt psychologists specified five laws that govern the organization of perceptual information: the law of proximity, the law of similarity, the law of good continuation, the law of closure, and the law of Prägnanz (which states that a stimulus will be organized into as good a figure as possible). Attempts to define the "goodness" of a figure have focused on the figure's symmetry and the number of unique orientations it may assume. Experimental evidence indicates that the ability to perceive contours and organize the visual world into figure and ground is present very early in life.

PERCEPTION OF DEPTH

One of the most interesting—and puzzling—topics in the study of perception is the perception of depth (Hochberg, 1971; Rock, 1975). Humans perceive objects in three dimensions, yet there is nothing three-dimensional about the pattern of stimulation striking the retina. Clearly, there must be characteristics of the visual system or of the images themselves that provide cues for the perception of depth. Researchers have identified several such characteristics. Some of these are aspects of the visual system or the position from which an object is viewed; others are pictorial cues, that is, aspects of the object or scene being viewed.

PHYSIOLOGICAL CUES

Two physiological reactions that provide cues for depth are accommodation and convergence. **Accommodation** refers to the changes that occur in the shape of the lens when images at varying distances from the observer are viewed. In order to keep an image focused on the retina, the lens must change its thickness as its distance from the object varies. This is accomplished by the contraction of the ciliary muscle. The action of the muscle and the resulting stretching of the lens create a signal in the brain that provides a feeling of depth associated with the image. The sense of depth arising from accommodation, however, can occur only when an object is less than about 3 meters from the lens. When objects are farther away the lens is maximally relaxed, so variations in distance do not cause changes in the shape of the lens.

A second physiological cue stems from **convergence,** rotation of the eyes inward to focus on a nearby object. The change in the position of the eyes is achieved through the contraction of various muscles attached to the eyeballs. Again, feedback from these muscles to the brain provides a cue for depth. It is easy to demonstrate the effect of convergence. Hold your finger at arm's length. Now move your hand toward your face while continuing to focus on your finger. You should be able to feel your eyes turn inward as your finger gets closer to your face.

Like accommodation, convergence is of limited value as a cue for depth because it works only for objects that are relatively close to the viewer (Hochberg, 1971). The eyes do not change their position when observing distant objects.

PARALLAX CUES

Compared to eye muscle movements, the depth cues stemming from **parallax,** the difference in the appearance of an object that results when one views it from different positions, are more important. There are two kinds of parallax cues: binocular disparity and motion parallax.

Binocular Disparity

Because of the separation between the eye sockets, each eye has a slightly different view of an object. This **binocular disparity** provides a cue for depth. In other words, when the brain receives two disparate views of an object it is able to position that

FIGURE 4-9   A stereoscope.

object. In phenomenological terms, we experience the object as being located at a particular point in space.

You can easily demonstrate the effect of binocular disparity. Hold one index finger at arm's length and the other about 6 inches in front of your eyes, lining up both fingers with your nose. Now open and close each eye alternately. Note that both fingers appear to jump back and forth relative to a fixed point on the opposite wall. Note also that the closer finger jumps more than the farther one. This effect occurs because the distance of an object determines the extent of the disparity between the views obtained by the two eyes—the closer the object, the greater the disparity.

Evidence that binocular disparity provides a cue for depth can be obtained using a **stereoscope.** This device, which was popular toward the end of the nineteenth century, presents the eyes with views of the same scene photographed from slightly different positions. (See Figure 4-9.) The views are more or less the same as those that would be obtained in actually viewing the scene. In the stereoscope, each eye sees only one of the two pictures but the scene is perceived as three-dimensional.

Motion Parallax

As we move about, an image occupies different positions on the retina. This **motion parallax** also gives rise to the perception of depth. Imagine that you are riding in a car and looking out the window. If you focus on the horizon, all the objects in view will seem to be passing in the opposite direction to the one in which you are moving. Nearby objects seem to pass more rapidly than distant objects. (See Figure 4-10.) If

FIGURE 4-10   Motion parallax. As the arrows indicate, when we look out the window of a moving vehicle our perception of the direction in which objects appear to be moving relative to each other depends upon the point in the scene upon which we fix our attention.

(a)

(b)

you focus on an intermediate point, nearby objects will still seem to move rapidly in the opposite direction to the one in which you are moving, but distant objects will seem to move (more slowly) in the same direction as you are moving. This *differential* rate of movement provides a powerful cue for depth. We perceive objects as being located at various distances from us because as we move about they pass before us at different speeds—the closer they are, the faster they pass through our field of vision (see Rivest, Ono, & Saida, 1989).

PICTORIAL CUES

Many cues for depth are properties of the scene being viewed.

Relative Size

One such cue is the relative size of the image on the retina. As illustrated in Figure 4-11, objects of the same size cast a smaller image on the retina when they are far away than when they are nearby. Investigators have demonstrated the importance of retinal image size in creating a sense of depth. In one experiment, playing cards were shown to observers who were then asked to judge how far away they were (Ittelson, 1951). The observers were required to look at the cards through a small opening in a partition, using only one eye; thus other cues for depth, such as binocular disparity and motion parallax, were absent. The cards were always the same distance from the

FIGURE 4-11 Relative size. The farther an object is from the eye, the smaller the image it casts on the retina, providing an important cue for depth perception.

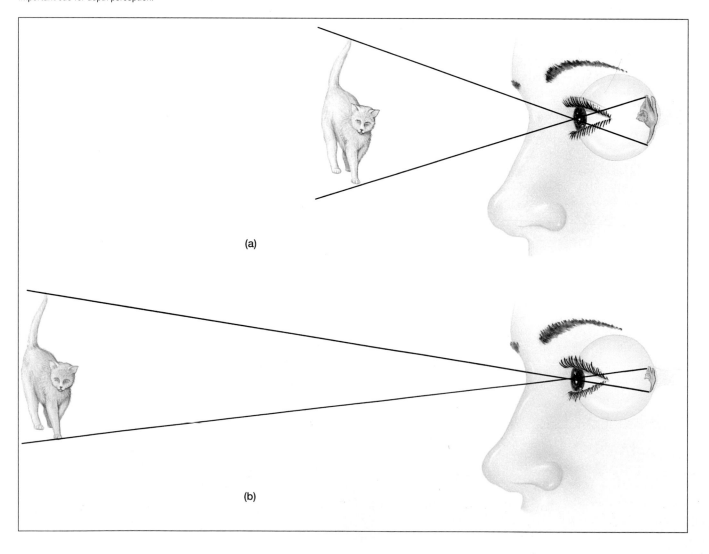

(a)

(b)

viewer, but they differed in size; therefore, the corresponding retinal images also differed in size. As predicted, cards that were twice the normal size were perceived as being only half as far away, whereas cards that were half the normal size were perceived to be twice as far away.

Interposition

A sense of relative depth, but not absolute distance, is created when one object partially blocks the view of another; this is referred to as **interposition.** In part *a* of Figure 4-12, the triangle is perceived as closer than the square because it partially blocks one's view of the square. Closer objects can block one's view of farther objects, but not vice versa. As shown in part *b* of Figure 4-12, the two objects do not have to be recognizable forms for interposition to produce a sense of depth; they simply have to be seen as coherent figures with a shared boundary.

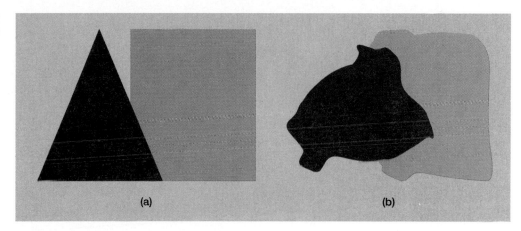

FIGURE 4-12 Interposition. A figure that appears partially to block another will also appear to be in front of it.

(a)   (b)

Shadowing

Depth may also be perceived as a result of **shadowing.** As shown in Figure 4-13, shadows can consist of gradations in brightness on the object itself or can be cast by the object onto other surfaces. We learn from our experience that shadows are part of uneven surfaces. For example, a bump normally has a shadow at the bottom because light usually arrives from above. Indentations, on the other hand, typically have a shadow at the top. (See Figure 4-14.)

Linear Perspective

One of the most important cues for depth is **linear perspective,** the apparent convergence of parallel lines toward a point in the distance. Again, we perceive depth because experience has taught us that converging lines of this sort are associated with distant points. As shown in Figure 4-15, linear perspective can produce a startling sense of depth and is frequently employed by artists to create this effect.

Aerial Perspective

A sense of depth is obtained when distant objects appear hazy; this effect is termed **aerial perspective.** Air contains particles that scatter and absorb light. As this occurs, the light becomes more desaturated (that is, less vividly colored) and contours become less distinct. (See Figure 4-16.) Because there are more light-scattering particles between the viewer and very distant objects, those objects appear hazy in contrast to nearby objects.

FIGURE 4-13 Both gradations of shadow on an object and the shadow the object casts onto other surfaces contribute to the perception of depth.

FIGURE 4-14 Bumps and dents have characteristic shadow patterns. As this high-speed photograph of a drop of water shows, dents tend to have shadows at the top and bumps at the bottom.

FIGURE 4-15 Linear perspective. The apparent convergence of parallel lines toward a point in the distance provides a strong cue for depth perception.

FIGURE 4-16 Aerial perspective. As this photograph shows, the hazy quality of distant points relative to nearby points contributes to depth perception.

Texture Gradient

An important factor in depth perception is the **texture gradient**—a change in the density of the elements that make up an image (Gibson, 1950). Consider the images in Figure 4-17. Part *a* shows two relatively uniform patterns, one denser than the other. Because the elements of the patterns are uniformly distributed, there is no sense of depth. As shown in part *b*, however, when there is a *change* in density—that is, a gradient of texture—a sense of depth is obtained. In this example the denser portion of the image appears more distant than the less dense portion. Part of the explanation for this effect is that the space between elements of more distant objects corresponds to a smaller retinal image than the space between elements of nearby objects.

A number of experiments have confirmed the effect of a texture gradient on depth perception. In one study, subjects looked at a pattern of dots through an opening in a screen (Gruber & Clark, 1956). The dots were more or less evenly spaced, like those in part *a* of Figure 4-17, but the entire target was rotated slightly toward one side, placing that side farther from the subject's eyes than the other side of the target. From a perceptual standpoint, therefore, the pattern of dots *looked* more like the one in part *b* of Figure 4-17. To demonstrate that the target was perceived as slanted simply because the dots produced a texture gradient, the experimenters asked the subjects to manipulate a rod located below the opening in the screen so that the plane of the rod was parallel to what they perceived to be the plane of the target. (See Figure 4-18 on page 100.) In doing so, the subjects consistently matched the plane of the rod to the actual plane of the target, indicating that they perceived the dot pattern as slanted. The only reason they perceived such a slant in the stimulus was that the texture or density of the dots varied.

Interaction of Cues

As the preceding discussion has shown, there are many kinds of cues for depth; those cues arise from the physical characteristics of the visual system as well as from the pictorial characteristics of the images themselves. Normally, of course, a scene

FIGURE 4-17   Texture gradient. The dot patterns in part (*a*) provide no indication of depth. In (*b*) the change in the density of dots creates the perception that the denser portion is more distant. The photograph (*c*) shows the same effect.

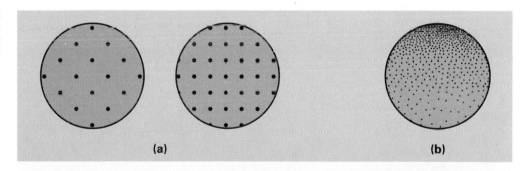

(a) (b)

(c)

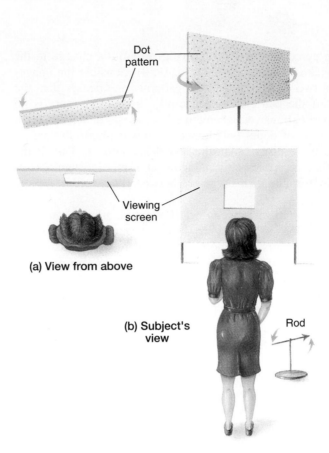

Dot pattern

Viewing screen

(a) View from above

(b) Subject's view

Rod

FIGURE 4-18 The apparatus used to study the effect of texture gradients on the perception of depth. (Adapted from Gruber & Clark, 1956.)

contains more than one cue for depth. Interposition may be combined with relative size, shadowing with changes in density of texture, linear perspective with binocular disparity. Figure 4-19 provides an example of both linear perspective and aerial perspective. It is important to realize that all the available cues contribute to the perception of depth (Jameson & Hurvich, 1959; van der Meer, 1979).

ORIGINS OF DEPTH PERCEPTION

As with the perception of form, researchers have long wondered whether people learn to perceive depth or whether they are born with this ability. This is not an easy question to answer, because humans cannot be isolated from birth (thus depriving them of opportunities to learn about depth cues), and later tested on their ability to perceive depth. Such studies have been done using animals, but the results must be interpreted cautiously because animals reared in isolation may be abnormal.

Evidence for Innate Factors

In one experiment, chicks were raised in an environment in which the light always came from below (Hershberger, 1970); shadows therefore were reversed from their normal pattern. The chicks were taught to discriminate between bumps and dents that had been hammered into an aluminum panel. For some of the chicks, pecking at the bump, but not the dent, produced food; for the others, the reverse was true. Care was taken to produce an even level of lighting so that there would be no special shadows associated with either bumps or dents. The chicks were then tested with photographs of bumps or dents, in which shadows appeared either at the top or at the bottom. The chicks responded to the photographs according to how they look in a normal environment; that is, pictures with shadows at the top were responded to as dents and pictures with shadows at the bottom were responded to as bumps. One might have predicted the opposite outcome—that the subjects would respond to the

FIGURE 4-19 Most of the time, depth perception results from the interaction of many cues for depth. This painting, for example, takes advantage of the effects of both linear and aerial perspective to create the illusion of depth.

pictures according to the way bumps and dents appeared when they were being reared—that is, when light came from beneath. These results suggest that depth perception is innate.

Another approach to the study of innate factors in depth perception utilizes the **visual cliff** apparatus shown in Figure 4-20 (Gibson, 1969; Gibson & Walk, 1960). The apparatus consists of two checkerboard patterns beneath a glass surface. One pattern is close to the surface, whereas the other is much lower, creating a "shallow" side and a "deep" side. Subjects are placed on the glass over the shallow side and encouraged to venture onto the deep side. The results indicate that many species, including rats, chickens, sheep, goats, kittens, monkeys, and humans, tend to avoid the deep side (Walk & Gibson, 1961).

Other research has shown that avoidance of the deep side occurs very early in life, when there has been little opportunity to learn about the world. For example, two-month-old infants were placed on the shallow side of the visual cliff and then were moved to the deep side (Campos, Langer, & Krowitz, 1970). The infants' heart rate changed dramatically following the move, indicating that they perceived a difference between the two sides.

FIGURE 4-20 The visual cliff apparatus.

Other kinds of studies also suggest that depth perception is innate. In one experiment, infants were fitted with special goggles; one eye was covered with a red filter and the other with a green filter (Fox, Aslin, Shea, & Dumais, 1980). The infants were then shown a display on a television screen that to the naked eye appeared to be a random pattern of red and green dots. But when the goggles were worn, each eye was stimulated by a different pattern of dots. The red filter absorbed or masked the light emanating from the red dots, thus allowing the eye covered by that filter to be stimulated only by the green dots. The green filter masked the green dots, leaving only the red dots visible to the eye covered with that filter. When viewed in this way, the dots in the display were not random but instead formed a square pattern. Recall our earlier discussion of the effect of binocular disparity: Stereoscopic depth perception occurs when each eye receives a slightly different view of the pattern. In this study, the image of the square was created by just such an effect. Viewed together, the red and green dots seemed to be randomly distributed, but when each eye received a different image, a three-dimensional square pattern was evident.

The researchers then moved the square back and forth across the field of vision while observing the subjects' gaze. The infants' eyes followed the square pattern. The researchers concluded that if the infants could see the square pattern, they must have been experiencing depth perception, because the pattern was apparent only under stereoscopic viewing conditions. Thus, the study seems to confirm that depth perception is innate or at least is present very soon after birth (Petrig, Julesz, Kropfl, Baumgartner, & Anliker, 1981).

Evidence for Learned Factors

Studies like those just described provide strong evidence in support of the idea that depth perception is innate, but experience or learning can also play a significant role. Animal subjects deprived of light early in life do not avoid the deep side of the visual cliff. They begin to show the normal avoidance reaction only after they have experienced depth (Mitchell, 1981; Tees & Midgley, 1978; Walk & Gibson, 1961). Another demonstration of the role of experience in depth perception used figures made of wire (Wallach, O'Connell, & Neisser, 1953). (See Figure 4-21.) Initially the subjects reported that the figures looked two-dimensional. The figures were then placed behind a translucent screen and rotated so that the shadow cast on the screen changed shape, giving the impression of depth. Then subjects were again shown the stationary figures in front of the screen. They now saw the figures as three-dimensional. The experience of seeing the objects in three dimensions while they were rotated caused them to perceive depth later, when the objects were stationary. This is known as the **kinetic depth effect.** Interestingly, other wire patterns not used in the

FIGURE 4-21 Random wire figures like those used to demonstrate the kinetic depth effect. When subjects initially viewed these figures in front of a screen, they saw them as two dimensional. After the figures were placed behind a translucent screen and rotated so that they cast a changing shadow on the screen, subjects perceived them as three dimensional. (Adapted from Wallach, O'Connell, & Neisser, 1953.)

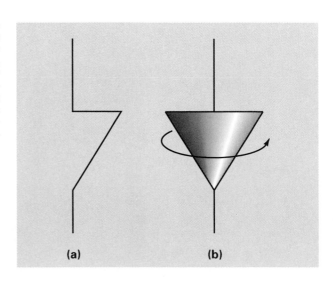

(a)   (b)

rotation phase of the experiment continued to be seen as two-dimensional; the creation of perceived depth occurred only for figures that had been rotated.

INTERIM SUMMARY

The cues that create a perception of depth are contained in the physiological reactions of the eyes, the differences in the appearance of an object when viewed from different positions (parallax), and the characteristics of objects themselves. The physiological cues are accommodation (the change in the shape of the lens when viewing objects at different distances) and convergence (rotation of the eyes inward to focus on a nearby object). An important parallax cue is binocular disparity: The eyes have slightly disparate views of an object, enabling the brain to position the object. Motion parallax—the differential rate of movement of the viewer relative to near and far objects—also provides a powerful cue for depth. Cues for depth are also contained in several pictorial characteristics of images: relative size, interposition or partial blocking, shadowing, linear perspective, aerial perspective, and texture gradient (changes in the density of elements in the image). There is considerable evidence that the ability to perceive depth is innate or present shortly after birth, but experience can also play a significant role in depth perception.

CONSTANCY

Constancy refers to the fact that one's perception of an object remains constant even though the conditions under which it is viewed may change. Of the several kinds of constancy, the most important for the purposes of this section is size constancy.

SIZE CONSTANCY

One might expect that the perceived size of an object would depend directly on the size of the retinal image: The larger the retinal image, the greater the perceived size. We saw in Figure 4-11 that object size and retinal image size vary systematically. When two objects are the same size and differ only in their distance from the eye, the farther object creates a smaller retinal image than the closer object. Objects that are farther away do look smaller than nearby objects, but this is true only to a limited extent. The phenomenon termed **size constancy** causes objects at a greater distance from the viewer, which produce smaller retinal images, to *appear* to be more or less the same size as closer objects. This phenomenon is illustrated in Figure 4-22. In part *a*, the more distant figure appears larger than the retinal image size would indicate; in fact, the two people seem to be more or less the same size. To appreciate this fact, look at part *b*. The figure in the bottom left corner is physically the same size as the distant figure in part *a*, yet it appears to be much smaller. In short, constancy occurs when something looks larger than would be indicated by retinal image size alone. The phenomenological experience of the stimulus is dramatically different from what would be expected on the basis of sensory input alone.

Emmert's Law

It is clear from Figure 4-22 that size constancy depends on the perceived distance of an object. The relationship between perceived size, retinal image, and distance is known as Emmert's law. In formal terms, that law is as follows:

Perceived size $=$ retinal image size $\times$ perceived distance.

(a)   (b)

FIGURE 4-22 Size constancy. The retinal image of the more distant figure in
part (a) is much smaller than the retinal
image of the closer figure, but we
nonetheless perceive them as of approximately the same size. Placing the distant
figure next to the closer figure, as in (b),
without changing its size shows the
strength of this effect.

If the size of the retinal image decreases (as would be true of more distant objects), but
at the same time perceived distance increases (because of, say, linear perspective), the perceived size tends to remain constant. If, on the other hand, retinal image size stays the
same but distance increases, as in part a of Figure 4-22, the perceived size tends to increase.

The Moon Illusion

One of the best-known illusions involving size constancy is the **moon illusion**
(Kaufman & Rock, 1962; Rock & Kaufman, 1962): The moon looks very much
larger when it is on the horizon than when it is viewed at the zenith, the highest point
in the sky. Clearly, the size of the retinal image does not change as the moon travels
through the sky, yet in phenomenological terms the moon is perceived as being much
larger on the horizon than at the zenith.

Many explanations of the moon illusion have been offered. Several investigators have a
of Figure 4-23, the perceived size of an object on the horizon can be strongly affected
by depth cues. The retinal image of the moon is actually the same size in both parts of the
figure, but the perceived distance is not. (In part a the moon looks farther away
because of linear perspective.) Therefore, because the inferred distance is greater but
the actual retinal image is the same, the moon is perceived to be larger when it is on the
horizon.

Other theorists disagree with this explanation. They point out that the moon looks
closer, not farther away, when it is on the horizon. According to Emmert's law, an
object that *looks* closer than another object of the same actual size should appear
smaller, not larger.

The issue is not fully settled at this point, but a number of promising ideas have
been offered (Reed, 1984). One suggests that the human visual system causes objects
that are perceived to be near to loom larger than objects perceived to be more distant
(Hershenson, 1982). Regardless of which explanation is finally accepted, it is clear
that the moon illusion depends, in part, on the interaction between perceptions of
size and distance.

104

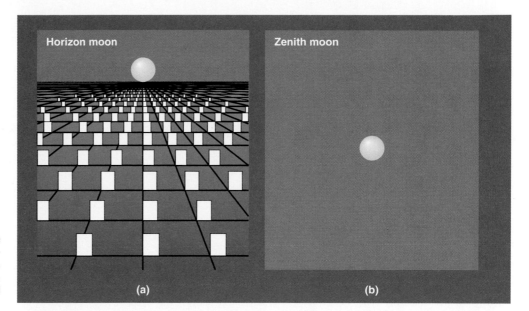

FIGURE 4-23 The moon illusion. The picture of the moon in part (a) looks bigger than the picture of the moon in (b), although they are actually the same size. The photograph shows the moon rising over Dallas, Texas.

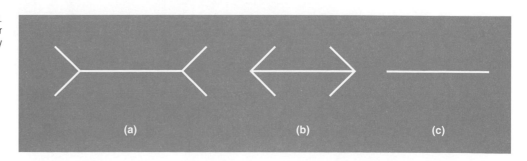

Spatial Illusions

Another well-known and widely studied illusion, the **Müller–Lyer illusion,** named after the psychologists who first studied it, has also been related to depth cues (see also Parks & Hui, 1989). This illusion is illustrated in Figure 4-24. Although the horizontal lines appear to be of different lengths, in fact they are not. Obviously, the fact that the arrows point inward in one case and outward in the other is an important factor in creating the illusion.

One explanation of the Müller–Lyer illusion is based on the phenomena of linear perspective and size constancy (Madden & Burt, 1981). It argues that the illusion contains depth cues (linear perspective) that affect the perceived distance of the hori-

FIGURE 4-24 The Müller-Lyer illusion. The horizontal line in part (a) looks longer than the horizontal line in (b), but they are both actually the same length as (c).

105

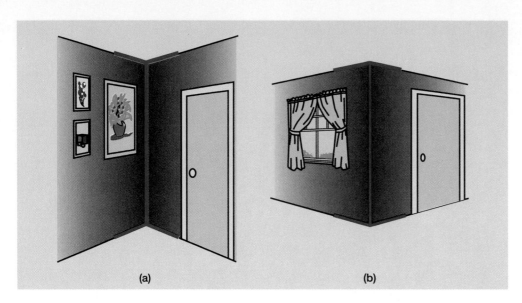

FIGURE 4-25 How Emmert's Law may account for the Müller-Lyer illusion.

(a)   (b)

zontal lines. According to Emmert's law, if two objects appear to differ in distance from the observer, yet their retinal images are the same size, the one that appears to be farther away will appear larger. Figure 4-25 illustrates this idea. When the "arrows" point outward, as in part *a,* we know that they are extending toward us; we therefore judge the vertical edge (the corner of the room) to be farther away. When the "arrows" point inward, as in part *b,* we know that they are receding from us, so we judge the vertical edge to be closer. In sum, in the absence of differences in retinal image size, differences in perceived distance create differences in the perception of size.

There are some problems with this explanation. Other versions of the Müller–Lyer illusion produce the same illusion of differences in size yet do not contain depth cues. (See Figure 4-26.) In fact, the Müller–Lyer illusion can actually be reversed when the horizontal lines are shorter than the distances between the arrows. (See Figure 4-27.) In Figure 4-27 part *b,* the line with the inward-pointing arrows, looks longer than part *a,* the line with the outward-pointing arrows (Fellows, 1967).

Another explanation of the Müller–Lyer illusion is the confusion theory. According to this theory, subjects are confused in judging the length of the horizontal line because they respond to the whole figure—the horizontal line plus the arrows—rather than to the horizontal line by itself. As a result, their judgments are biased in the direction of the overall pattern. For example, the overall image in part *a* of Figure 4-24 (horizontal line plus outward-pointing arrows) is actually longer than the images in parts *b* and *c* of the figure. The viewer unconsciously infers that this difference in overall size is attributable in part to a difference in the size of the horizontal

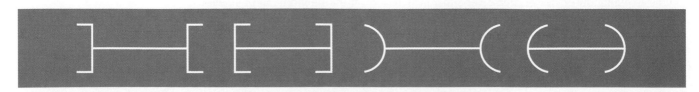

FIGURE 4-26 Versions of the Müller-Lyer illusion (above) that have no depth cues that could be explained by Emmert's law.

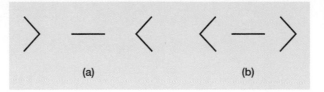

(a)   (b)

FIGURE 4-27 A configuration that produces the opposite effect of the standard Müller-Lyer illusion (left). The horizontal line in (*a*) appears shorter than the horizontal line in (*b*).

line. Similarly, the confusion theory argues that the horizontal line in part *b* of Figure 4-24 looks shorter than the line in part *c* because the viewer is influenced by the distance between the tips of the arrows, not just by the end points of the horizontal line (Coren & Girgus, 1972; Holding, 1970).

In an experiment that supported this explanation, the angle of the arrows and the distance between the tips of the arrows were systematically varied (Erlebacher & Sekuler, 1969). As shown in Figure 4-28, a smaller angle generally creates a greater illusion: The horizontal line in part *b* appears shorter than the one in part *c*, and both appear shorter than the one in part *a;* yet all are the same length. But note that the distance between the tips of the arrows also changes as the angle is varied. When these distances are made equal, the illusion disappears: The horizontal lines in parts *d* and *e* of Figure 4-28 appear to be about the same length. The magnitude of the illusion therefore depends on the distance between the tips of the arrows rather than on the angle of the arrows. In fact, if the distance between the inward-pointing tips is varied while the angle remains constant, a smaller distance creates a stronger illusion. This is shown in parts *f* and *g* of Figure 4-28.

SHAPE CONSTANCY

Besides size constancy, there are several other kinds of constancy, including shape, color, and brightness constancies. **Shape constancy** is based on the same principle as size constancy—that is, it is explained by Emmert's law. It occurs when we perceive an object as maintaining the same shape when we view it from another angle, despite the fact that the shape of the retinal image has changed. Consider the object shown in

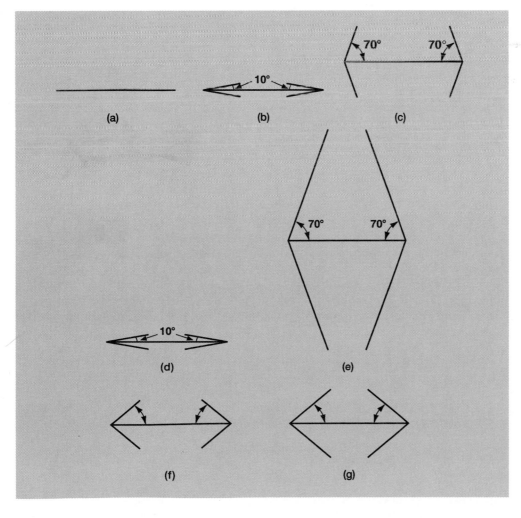

FIGURE 4-28 These figures show how the strength of the Müller-Lyer illusion is affected by the angle of the arrows and the length of the distance between the outer tips of the arrows.

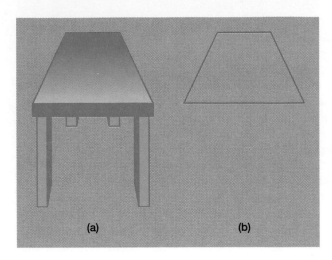

FIGURE 4-29 Shape constancy. We perceive a table top as having a constant rectangular shape, no matter the position from which we view it. The retinal image of the table top in part (*a*) is not rectangular, however, but, trapezoidal, as in (*b*).

Figure 4-29. The top of the table is perceived as being rectangular even though, as shown in part *b* of the figure, the shape of the retinal image is trapezoidal. The perception of a rectangular shape remains constant, despite the difference in the shape of the retinal image, because the parts of the image that are perceived as farther away, such as the farther edge of the table, are perceived as larger owing to size constancy. And as Emmert's law would predict, if the farther edge is perceived as being larger, its size is maintained, and so too is its shape.

ORIGINS OF CONSTANCY

Is the perception of constancy learned or innate? One experiment tested the perception of size constancy in rats (Heller, 1968). The rats were reared in darkness for 34 days. They were then taught to discriminate between two circles of different sizes. The rats were allowed to view the circles from a particular vantage point in an alleyway and to receive a food reward at the end of the alleyway for choosing the larger circle. Once the rats had mastered this task, the larger circle was moved farther away so that the retinal image it created was approximately the same as that created by the smaller circle. Again the animals were allowed to choose between the two circles to obtain a food reward. Now, however, the rats chose randomly rather than always selecting the larger circle. The results therefore suggested that the rats did not perceive size constancy; they had reacted to the larger circle on the basis of its retinal-image size. On the other hand, after the rats were kept in a lighted room for a week they appeared to perceive size constancy.

The study just described suggests that size constancy depends on experience, but a similar study using humans produced different results (Bower, 1964, 1965). Six- to eight-week-old infants were rewarded by the experimenter's saying "peek-a-boo" when they turned their heads to look at a small cube placed 1 meter away. They were then tested using a larger cube placed 3 meters away. The infants did not respond to the larger stimulus, even though its retinal image was the same as that of the original cube. When the smaller cube was placed 3 meters away, however, the infants responded. Thus, it appears that size constancy in humans either is innate or develops within the first two months of life.

INTERIM SUMMARY

Constancy refers to the tendency to perceive an object as the same even when the conditions under which it is viewed have changed. In size constancy, objects at different distances from the viewer appear to be the same size despite the difference in size of their retinal images. According to Emmert's law, perceived size results from the interaction between retinal-image size and perceived distance, such that if retinal-image size decreases as perceived distance increases, perceived size remains constant. This law has been used to explain various optical illusions, such as the moon illusion and the Müller–Lyer illusion, but other explanations have also been suggested for these phenomena. Other kinds of perceptual constancy include shape, color, and brightness constancy; Emmert's law can be applied to explain shape constancy. Research on whether perceptual constancy is learned or innate has produced contradictory results: Experiments with animals indicate that constancy is learned, whereas experiments with human infants suggest that it is innate or develops shortly after birth.

MOTION PERCEPTION

One would expect the perception of motion to depend simply on whether an image moves across the retina, but motion perception is more complicated than that.

Figure 4-30 illustrates three situations that are relevant to the perception of movement. Part *a* shows that an object may move across the visual field, thereby causing its image to move across a stationary retina. Under these conditions the viewer would perceive that the object itself had changed position, and thus would perceive motion. Part *b* of the figure indicates that an object may move and that the eyes may follow it, so that the retinal image is maintained at more or less the same position. If the detection of movement depended merely on a change in the position of an image on the retina, we would not perceive movement when we follow an object with our eyes, and yet we do. For example, if we watch a car move down the street, following it with our eyes, we perceive movement even though the position of the car's image on the retina does not change. Part *c* of the figure illustrates the situation in which an object remains stationary while the head and/or eyes move, thereby causing the image on the retina to move. Although the image on the retina is changing its position, we do not perceive the object as moving. In all three conditions, the perception

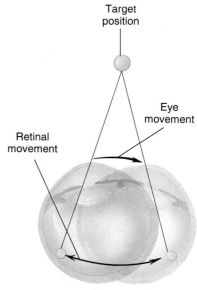

FIGURE 4-30 Three situations relevant to the perception of motion. In part (*a*), the eye is stationary, but the object moves. In (*b*), the eye follows the moving object. In (*c*), the eye moves but the object remains stationary.

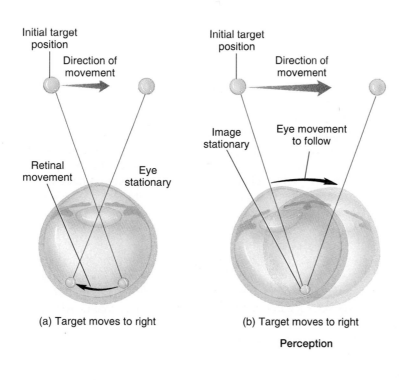

(a) Target moves to right

(b) Target moves to right

(c) Target is seen as stationary

Perception

of motion depends on whether the object is seen to change its location relative to the observer, not simply on whether the retinal image changes position.

But if the retinal image remains stationary, as in part *b* of Figure 4-30, how does the viewer know that the object has changed its location? One answer is that the brain responds to neural feedback from the muscles of the eyes and head. In the absence of movement of the retinal image, the muscle movements are interpreted as evidence of movement in the visual field. Researchers have found cells in the cat's brain whose rate of firing depends on eye movement—the greater the eye movement, the higher the rate of firing of these specialized cells (Donaldson & Long, 1980). Movement of the eyes and head thus may be sufficient to produce the perception of movement of an object in the visual field.

MOTION DETECTORS

When the eyes and head do not move, the movement of an image across the retina provides the stimulus for the perception of motion. Detection of this movement (by cats and monkeys and, by inference, human beings) occurs by means of specialized **motion detectors** in the brain (Hubel & Wiesel, 1962, 1968). The presence of these detectors was established by experiments in which electrodes were placed in specific neurons (nerve cells) in a cat's brain and stimuli were moved across the cat's visual field. The results showed that certain neurons were activated only when vertical lines were moved across the visual field; those neurons did not fire when the lines were slanted at 45 degrees. Other neurons were activated only when horizontal lines were moved across the visual field. This response is even more specific in other animals; for example, certain cells in the monkey brain are activated only when the monkey is shown the shape of a hand (Gross, Rocha-Miranda, & Bender, 1972).

Analogous results have been obtained in experiments with humans, although those experiments could not use implanted electrodes. In one study, the electrical patterns of the brain were recorded by electrodes placed on the surface of the skull (Campbell & Maffei, 1974). The subjects were repeatedly exposed to a particular stimulus, such as a vertical line. This procedure, called **habituation,** causes the electrical brain activity triggered by the stimulus to subside. Once the brain activity had decreased, the orientation of the stimulus was changed; for example, the subjects were shown lines slanted at 45 degrees. The subjects' brain activity became intense again, indicating that the new orientation had been detected. It thus appears that humans also have motion detectors in the brain (Sekuler, 1975).

APPARENT MOTION

Motion detectors undoubtedly provide information about the movement of an image across the retina, but a physiological reaction of this sort cannot explain many other aspects of motion perception, such as the fact that we perceive movement even when we move our eyes and head to follow a moving object (Rock, 1975). Nor do they explain the **apparent motion (Phi) phenomenon.** Imagine the following situation: A subject is placed in a dimly lit room and shown two small points of light placed several inches apart. The lights flash briefly in an alternating pattern. Depending on the distance between the lights and the rate of flashing, what the subject perceives is not an alternating pattern of flashes but movement by a single light from left to right and back again. In other words, the viewer sees movement even though from an objective point of view the retina is merely being alternately stimulated by two different lights (see Mack, Klein, Hill, & Palumbo, 1989).

The tendency to experience the apparent motion phenomenon appears to be innate. It has been documented not only in newborn human infants but also in fish and even in newly hatched insects (Rock, Tauber, & Heller, 1965; Tauber & Koffler, 1966). Moreover, research has shown that the Phi phenomenon occurs for entire patterns of stimulation, not just for single points of light. For example, if the two pat-

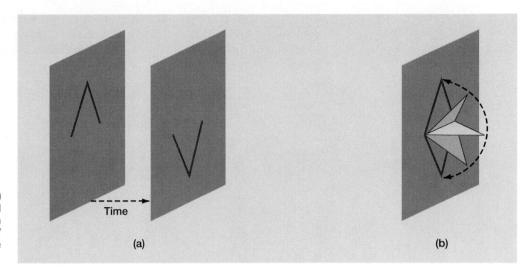

FIGURE 4-31 The apparent motion (Phi) phenomenon. When the two V-shaped patterns of light in part (*a*) are turned on and off in an alternating pattern, the V pattern appears to rotate toward the viewer, as in (*b*).

Time

(a)

(b)

terns shown in Figure 4-31 are illuminated alternately, the viewer not only perceives movement but sees the patterns moving in three dimensions, that is, rotating 180 degrees through the plane perpendicular to the patterns.

The Phi phenomenon has been shown to occur for patterns that differ not only in location but also in color, brightness, and form. For example, if one of two alternating points of light is green and the other yellow, the point appears to move from one position to the other *and* to change color, from green to yellow and back, as it does so (Bundesen, Larsen, & Farrell, 1983; Kolers & von Grunau, 1976).

INDUCED MOTION

A final aspect of motion perception deserving of mention is the phenomenon of **induced movement.** Imagine that a single point of light is surrounded by a rectangular frame in an otherwise darkened room, and that the frame moves in one direction. The subject does not perceive the frame as moving but instead sees the point of light moving in the direction opposite to that in which the frame is moving. An everyday example of this phenomenon is the effect one sees when the moon is partially hidden by clouds. The clouds provide a frame for the moon and, when moving slowly in one direction, cause the moon to appear to move in the opposite direction.

Induced motion can also occur when the viewer's body is an object in the visual field. When there is a frame around the body that moves, the viewer may have the sensation of moving. This effect occurs when, for example, one looks out the window of a car while stopped at a traffic light and observes the car in the next lane moving slowly forward. The illusion is that one's own car is rolling backward; in fact, people who experience this induced motion often needlessly apply their brakes.

The experience of induced motion provides further evidence that the perception of motion is relative. Motion depends not merely on the occurrence of movement in space but on the perceiver's point of view.

INTERIM SUMMARY

If the image of an object on the retina remains stationary, movement of the eyes and head produces the perception of movement of an object in the visual field. When the eyes and head do not move, movement of the image across the retina provides the stimulus for the perception of motion. Detection of this movement occurs by means of specialized motion detectors in the brain. The experience of apparent motion (the

Phi phenomenon) occurs when two patterns are illuminated alternately; experimental evidence suggests that the ability to perceive apparent motion is inborn. The phenomenon of induced motion provides further evidence that the perception of motion depends not merely on the fact of movement in space but on the perceiver's point of view.

SUMMARY

1. Perception is the study of the sensory world as we experience it. This approach was emphasized by the *Gestalt* psychologists who argued that perception is a phenomenological experience.

2. Visual perception depends on the presence of contours. Once contours are perceived, the *figure* (an integrated, meaningful unit of perception) can be distinguished from the *ground* (the uniform and meaningless background).

3. Gestalt theorists hypothesized that perception is organized according to a number of laws—*the law of proximity, the law of similarity, the law of good continuation, the law of closure,* and *the law of Prägnanz.* According to the law of Prägnanz, humans will organize a stimulus into as good a figure as possible. "Good" in this sense has been interpreted to mean symmetrical and with the fewest possible orientations.

4. Studies showing that human infants can distinguish between stimuli that contain facelike features from those that have random features suggest that the ability to differentiate figure and ground is innate.

5. Depth perception is created in a number of ways. Some cues for depth (*accommodation, convergence,* and *parallax*) result from the way our visual system is constructed. Others (*linear* and *aerial perspective, shadowing, interposition,* and *texture gradients*) result from properties of the scene viewed.

6. Experimental evidence suggests that the ability to perceive depth is innate, but that experience also plays a role.

7. *Constancy* refers to the fact that one's perception of an object remains constant even though conditions under which it is viewed may change. Size constancy refers to our ability to perceive an object as of a constant size no matter what its distance. According to one explanation of size constancy—*Emmert's Law*—when the perceived distance of an object changes, but the retinal image does not, then the perceived size increases. Two well-known illusions, the *moon illusion* and the *Müller–Lyer illusion,* involve size constancy. Various explanations have been offered for these illusions, including Emmert's law, but none has proved conclusive. Shape constancy, which refers to our ability to perceive an object as of a constant shape no matter what the angle from which we view it, can be explained by Emmert's law.

8. The perception of constancy appears to be attributable to both innate and learned factors.

9. Motion perception occurs when an object is perceived to move relative to the viewer. A variety of cues contribute to motion perception. These include a change in the position of the retinal image of an object and feedback from the head and neck muscles.

10. Animals, including humans, have neurons in the brain that detect moving contours.

11. The *Phi phenomenon* occurs when alternating lights appear to be a single light moving back and forth. *Induced movement* results when the motion of the frame surrounding a motionless object produces the illusion that the object itself is moving in the opposite direction. Both of these effects clearly illustrate the phenomenological nature of perception.

======

FOCUS QUESTION

1. Define the study of perception and contrast the concerns of perception with those of sensation.

2. Describe what is needed for perceiving forms and comparing the features of a figure with those of the background.

3. Why does the perception of depth pose an interesting and challenging problem in the study of perception?

4. Discuss the various conditions, both physiological properties of the visual system and properties of the scene being viewed, that give rise to the perception of depth.

5. How does perceived distance relate to the size constancy phenomenon?

6. Discuss the critical conditions that give rise to the perception of motion.

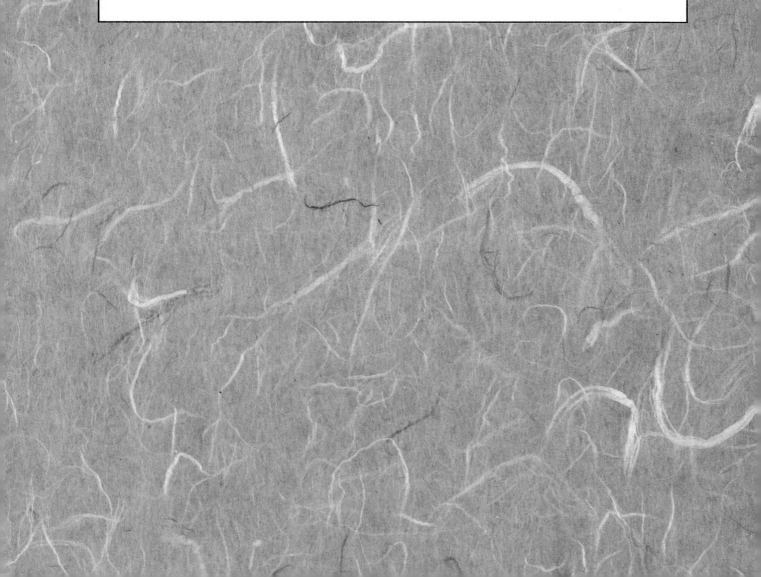

CHAPTER 5

NEUROPSYCHOLOGY

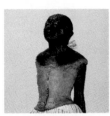 As the name suggests, **neuropsychology** combines two fields—neurology (the study of the nervous system, especially the brain), and psychology. Neuropsychology thus reflects the idea that behavior, thoughts, and emotions can be explained in terms of the nerves and chemicals that make up the human brain.

The origins of this idea may be found in the age-old debate over the mind–body question. Recall that Descartes believed that the mind and the body are distinct entities; the mind is free and voluntary, the body involuntary and subject to the laws of physics and chemistry. Recall also that the materialist philosophers claimed that there is only one reality—the physical reality of the brain (Churchland, 1984). Neuropsychology has adopted the materialist position: The causes of behavior are exclusively physical, and thoughts, emotions, and consciousness are by-products of the normal functioning of the brain. Controlling behavior and producing consciousness are things that the brain does much in the way that it controls or produces physical phenomena like heartbeats.

But can behavior and consciousness really be explained simply in terms of the functioning of the brain? Most neuropsychologists would answer yes, but it is certainly not a simple matter. In fact, it is exceedingly difficult—if not impossible—to know in precise detail how the brain controls behavior and creates consciousness. Imagine dropping a feather from the top of a tall building. Could one ever hope to predict *exactly* where the feather will land? Probably not, because the forces acting on the feather are so complicated and unpredictable. And yet no one doubts that the behavior of the feather results entirely from physical processes acting on it. Similarly, the human brain is so incredibly complex that it may be impossible to gather enough information to determine exactly how it produces thoughts and emotions or how it mediates (influences) or controls (determines) behavior. Neuropsychologists would argue, however, that this complexity does not imply that anything other than physical and chemical processes are involved.

Even though an exact and full account of the relationship between brain and behavior cannot yet be provided, significant progress has been made toward this goal in recent years. Neuropsychologists can now state many of the *general* relationships between behavior and the larger areas of the brain. Those relationships are the subject of this chapter.

EARLY HISTORY

The idea that behavior can be explained in terms of the activity of specific areas of the brain is not new. In the early nineteenth century one of the earliest movements in psychology, known as **phrenology,** focused on this possibility. Phrenologists believed that traits as general as intelligence and as specific as the love of gambling were localized in the brain to such a degree that the size of the bump on the skull just over the brain area associated with a particular trait would reveal the extent to which that trait was developed. In other words, the more an individual possessed a certain trait, the more the appropriate area of the brain—and hence the skull—would bulge.

Phrenologists created elaborate maps of the human skull and used them to construct personality profiles. (See Figure 5-1.) They would first make detailed measurements of a person's skull and then, consulting their maps, identify all the personality traits that were revealed by the measurements. Phrenology ceased to be taken seriously when scientific evidence failed to support its claims: Nerve cells are not like muscles, with larger ones bulging against the skull more than smaller ones.

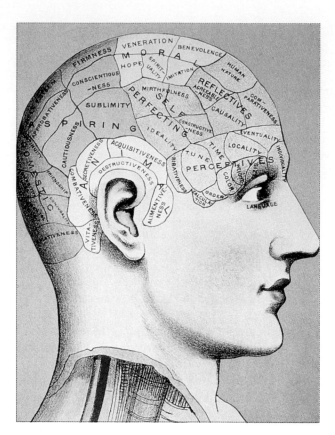

FIGURE 5-1 A phrenologist's map of the areas of the brain and the various characteristics with which they were believed to be associated.

When the reputation of the phrenologists faded, so did the whole idea of localization of functions in the brain.

Interest in the localization of functions was rekindled in the mid- to late nineteenth century with Paul Broca's observation in 1861 of the effects of damage to the left frontal lobe of the brain. Broca examined brains taken from the cadavers of individuals who had been brain-damaged in life and had lost the ability to speak, a condition termed **aphasia.** The autopsies revealed a consistent pattern of damage to a region on the left side of the brain. Broca believed that the correspondence between the location of the damaged area and the loss of speech was more than a coincidence; it suggested that speech production was, in effect, controlled by that part of the brain. In 1874 Karl Wernicke also evaluated the brains of brain-damaged individuals. He was able to identify an area involved not in the production but rather in the comprehension of speech. Although able to speak normally, his patients had been unable to comprehend both spoken and written language, and often had difficulty naming objects (a condition called **anomia**).

The work of these two pioneers represented a breakthrough in the study of the relationships between brain and behavior. Although it would be many years before neuropsychology was recognized as an independent science, the results of their studies focused renewed attention on the notion that the control of certain behaviors could be localized in particular areas of the brain.

INTERIM SUMMARY

An early movement within psychology, known as phrenology, attempted to localize both general and specific traits in the brain; phrenologists believed that if a particular trait was possessed in abundance, a corresponding area of the skull would bulge. Phrenology ceased to be taken seriously when scientific analysis failed to support its claims, but in the midnineteenth century interest in localization of functions was rekindled when Broca linked the condition of aphasia (inability to speak) with a particular region in the victims' brains. Soon thereafter Wernicke was able to identify an area of the brain that plays a role in the comprehension of speech.

NEUROANATOMY

Before we discuss the areas of the brain that have been shown to affect certain behaviors, it is necessary to present some of the basic characteristics of the brain and nervous system. We begin with the individual nerve cell.

NERVE CELLS

There are many kinds of nerve cells, or **neurons,** in the human body; they vary in size, shape, and function.

Structure

A typical nerve cell contains a number of **dendrites,** which, as shown in Figure 5-2, form a branching network of filaments. The dendrites range in length from a few

FIGURE 5 2   A typical nerve cell.

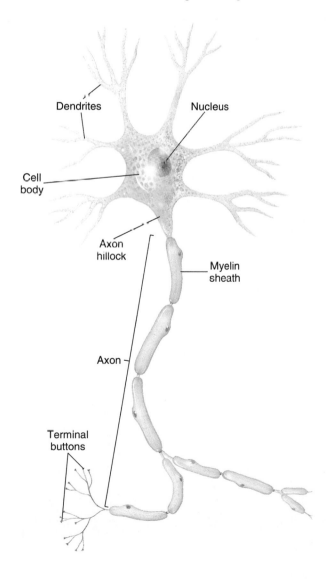

microns (one millionth of a meter) to a millimeter, and their function is to receive information from other neurons.

The dendrites converge onto the **cell body.** At one edge of the cell body is the **axon hillock,** the point of transition between the cell body and the axon. The **axon,** a single fiber extending away from the cell body, can vary from a few microns to over a meter in length. It is covered with a protective **myelin sheath,** which acts much like the insulation on an electrical wire. The function of the axon is to transmit information to other nerve cells.

Electrical Characteristics of Neurons

When salt (sodium chloride) is dissolved in a fluid, the atoms split apart, creating electrically charged molecules called **ions.** The sodium ions (Na+) have a positive charge whereas the chlorine ions (Cl−) have a negative charge. Normally these ions intermingle in the liquid, and because the positively and negatively charged ions bind together, no voltage potential (electrical charge) is produced. In a nerve cell, however, the situation is very different. A mechanism called a **sodium–potassium pump** continuously transfers positively charged sodium ions to the outside of the cell. (See Figure 5-3.) For every three Na+ ions that are so transported outward, only about two potassium (K+) ions enter. Moreover, the cell membrane is not completely permeable to sodium; that is, the Na+ ions do not flow back into the interior of the cell very readily. The result is that the positively charged ions accumulate on the outside of the cell wall, creating an imbalance in the distribution of positive and negative ions across the cell membrane. In effect, the inside and outside of the cell membrane are electrically charged like the two poles of a battery. The electrical potential across the cell membrane of a neuron in a resting state, called the **resting potential,** is about −70 millivolts.

If no other force acts on the neuron, it maintains its resting potential. A disruption of the electrical state of the neuron by some outside force, however, creates a nerve impulse. This occurs when biochemicals emanating from adjacent neurons cause the dendrites to become more permeable to the passage of sodium. It is as if the chemicals open a gate and allow sodium to rush into the cell. When this happens, the proportion of positively charged ions on the inside of the cell increases relative to the proportion on the outside, and the voltage potential at that point on the membrane changes from −70 to about +50 millivolts. This sudden change is called the **action potential.** (See Figure 5-4.)

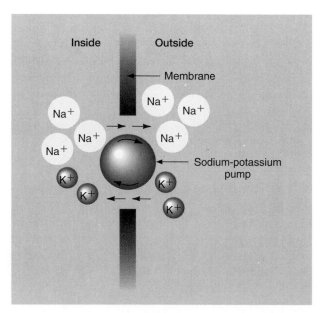

FIGURE 5-3 Schematic diagram of the sodium-potassium pump. This mechanism transfers positively charged sodium ions (Na+) out of the cell. The overall effect, combined with the fact that the cell membrane is relatively more permeable to potassium ions (K+) than to sodium ions, is to maintain the electrical potential of the neuron in its resting state (the resting potential) at about −70 millivolts.

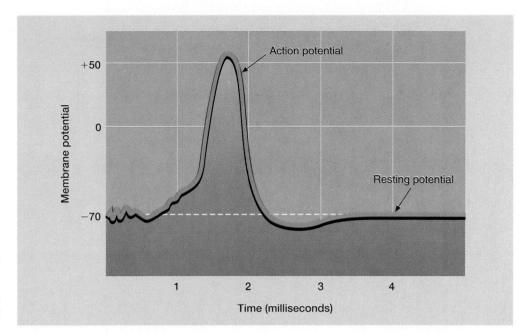

FIGURE 5-4 The action potential. This diagram shows the changes in the electrical characteristics of the cell membrane as it goes from resting potential to action potential and back to resting potential.

The action potential has two important consequences; these are illustrated in Figure 5-5 (see page 120). First, the electrical surge destabilizes the adjacent portion of the axon, causing it, too, to produce an action potential and to stimulate yet another portion of the membrane. In this way the action potential at any given point on the membrane is transmitted down the entire length of the neuron in a chainlike manner, each section triggering an electrical surge in the next portion of the axon.

Second, the sudden rush of positively charged sodium ions into the cell causes positively charged potassium ions to move outward (because like charges repel each other and the cell membrane is permeable to potassium). Meanwhile, the pump continues its task of transporting the Na+ ions to the outside of the membrane. These events reestablish the resting potential and prepare the nerve for further stimulation.

It is important to note that the action potential is an all-or-nothing reaction. Once the stimulation from other neurons is sufficiently intense to cause the cell to reach a threshold value of about −65 to −60 millivolts, the channels are opened to the passage of sodium and the action potential is triggered. And, as noted above, the action potential is self-sustaining: depolarization of one part of the axon causes the adjacent part also to be depolarized.

Chemical Properties of Neurons

The starting point for the action potential (the destabilizing force that triggers a nerve impulse) is a chemical reaction. As shown in Figure 5-6 (see page 121), nerves do not actually connect to each other; they are separated by a small gap called the **synapse.** And at the end of the axon are specialized **terminal buttons** containing, among other things, **synaptic vesicles.** Inside these small sacs are chemicals, called **neurotransmitters,** that diffuse across the synapse and activate the adjacent nerve cell. When an action potential reaches the axon terminal (the **presynaptic membrane),** the vesicles liberate the neurotransmitter substance, which diffuses across the **synaptic cleft** and stimulates the receptor sites on the **postsynaptic membrane**—that is, it stimulates another neuron. (Usually the site of stimulation is the dendrites of the postsynaptic neuron, but other kinds of synaptic arrangements are possible, including a synapse onto an axon).

Although a given neuron contains only one kind of neurotransmitter, the neurotransmitter itself can act on the postsynaptic receptor site in either of two ways. It can excite the membrane, triggering an action potential, or it can inhibit the mem-

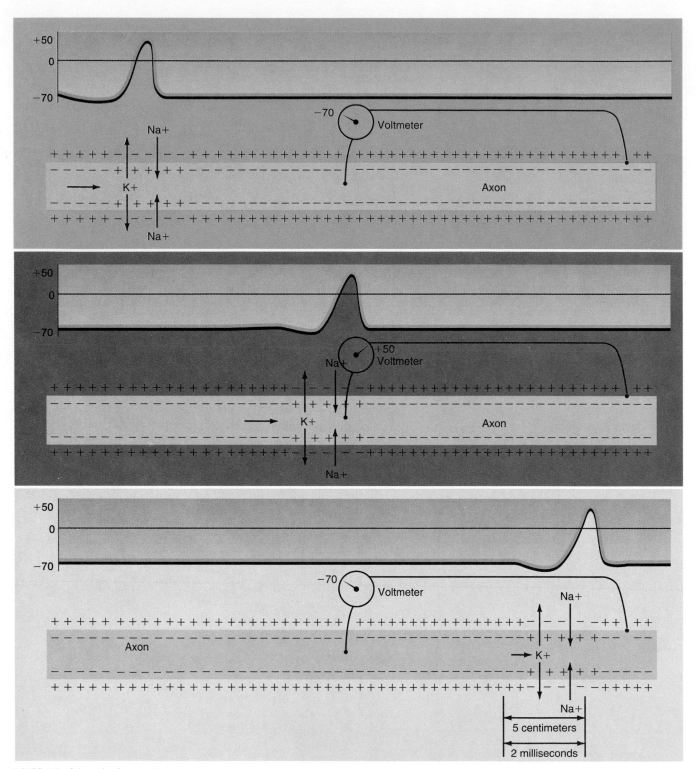

FIGURE 5-5 Schematic diagram showing how the action potential travels along the axon. The dial shows the voltage that a voltmeter would detect at a particular point on the axon as the action potential passed by it.

brane, thus suppressing the action potential. Some neurotransmitters have both an excitatory and inhibitory effect on the postsynaptic membrane depending on the area of the brain in which the neurons are located.

An excitatory reaction occurs when the neurotransmitter causes the postsynaptic membrane to become more permeable to sodium and potassium ions. The Na+ ions rush into the interior of the cell, thus destabilizing the neuron and generating an action potential. The exact opposite happens at inhibitory synapses. The neurotransmitters cause the postsynaptic membrane to become more permeable to chlorine

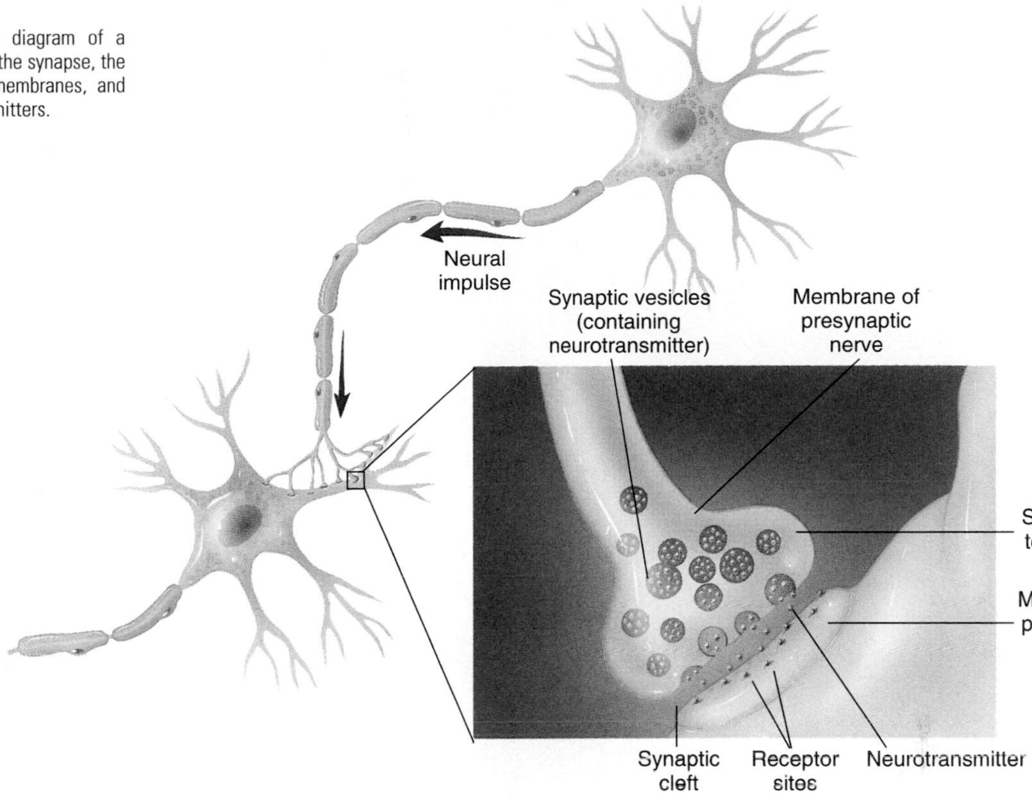

FIGURE 5-6 Schematic diagram of a nerve terminal, showing the synapse, the pre- and postsynaptic membranes, and the action of neurotransmitters.

ions, which enter the cell and cause the differential charge across the membrane to become even greater. Under these circumstances, the action potential is suppressed.

The neurotransmitters operate only briefly. Some are broken down by various enzymes, whereas others are reabsorbed by the presynaptic membrane. Once this happens, of course, the system is ready to fire again.

One of the most common neurotransmitters is **acetylcholine (ACh).** This substance is found in the synapses of nerves that control muscle tissue, as well as in peripheral and brain neurons. Its primary action is to excite skeletal muscles, although it may have the exact opposite action on some muscles, for example the heart. Another important group of chemicals, the **catecholamines,** include the neurotransmitters **dopamine** and **norepinephrine.** These substances may have either an excitatory or inhibitory effect depending on the nature of the postsynaptic neuron. Dopamine is especially important for motor behavior. Nerve fiber tracts containing dopamine, for example, are involved with Parkinson's disease, a condition affecting primarily elderly people that is characterized by tremors, muscle spasms, and difficulty of walking. This serious disease can now be treated rather effectively by the administration of L-Dopa, the biological precursor to dopamine. Dopamine and norepinephrine also seem to be involved in schizophrenia, a severe mental disorder (see Chapter 24). Because this condition has been attributed to an excess of dopamine, its treatment often includes the use of drugs that interfere with the action of that and related neurotransmitters. Finally, **serotonin** is an important neurotransmitter that affects, among other things, body temperature and sleep (see Chapter 7).

Function of Neurons

As noted, there are many kinds of nerves in the human body. **Sensory** (or **afferent,** meaning "to the brain") **neurons** carry information from the various sense organs to the brain. Other nerves, called **motor** (or **efferent,** meaning "away from the brain") **neurons** originate in the brain and extend to the muscle and organs of the body. Generally, nerves travel to and from the brain through the spinal cord. The sensory nerves travel from the sense organs to the spinal cord, connecting with nerves that

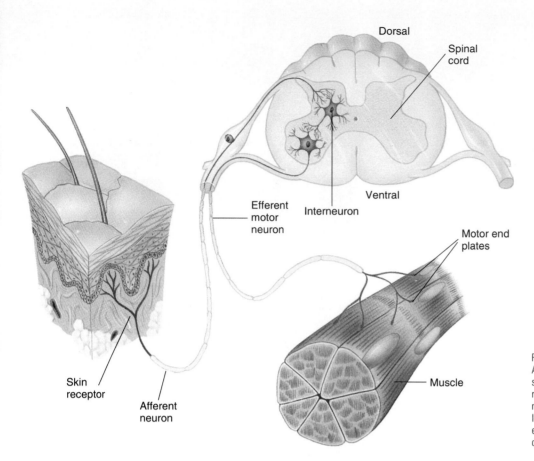

Dorsal

Spinal cord

Ventral

Efferent motor neuron

Interneuron

Motor end plates

Skin receptor

Afferent neuron

Muscle

FIGURE 5-7 Three kinds of neurons. Afferent neurons carry signals from sense organs to the brain. Efferent neurons carry signals from the brain to the muscles and organs of the body. Interneurons connect afferent and efferent neurons directly in the spinal cord, creating a reflex arc.

run along the dorsal (back) side of the cord. (See Figure 5-7.) Efferent nerves, on the other hand, run along the ventral (inner) side of the spinal cord, exiting at various levels and then connecting with muscle tissue. The spinal cord itself really has two functions. First, it provides a suitable conduit for nerves traveling to and from the brain. Second, it contains nerves that are capable of producing simple reflexes, independent of the brain. As suggested in Figure 5-7, sensory neurons may connect with one or more interneurons in the dorsal segment of the spine. The interneuron, in turn, connects directly to an efferent neuron in the ventral portion, which then exits to the motor end plate of a muscle. Thus, some sensory events, such as a pinprick on the skin, may cause a reflexive contraction of the muscle by means of this simple **reflex arc.** The brain itself is not involved.

The nervous system is divided into two major subdivisions: the **peripheral** and **central nervous systems.** The peripheral nervous system includes the sensory and motor neurons in the peripheral areas of the body. The central nervous system, on the other hand, includes the spinal cord and the brain. Traditionally, the peripheral system and spinal cord are grouped together for discussion because both are external to the brain; they are covered in greater detail in Chapter 6. The brain itself, however, is the part of the nervous system on which neuropsychologists have primarily focused. Thus in the following sections we cover the details of the brain.

MAJOR DIVISIONS OF THE BRAIN

Neuroscientists divide the brain into five major sections: myelencephalon, metencephalon, mesencephalon, diencephalon, and telencephalon (Kolb & Whishaw, 1985). Figure 5-8 presents an external view of these areas; Figure 5-9 presents a cross-sectional view, revealing some of the brain's many internal structures.

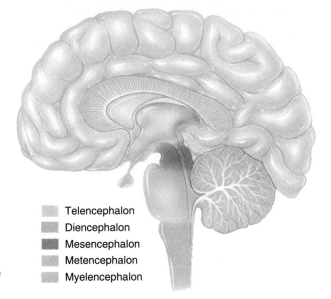

Telencephalon
Diencephalon
Mesencephalon
Metencephalon
Myelencephalon

FIGURE 5-8 The five major divisions of the brain.

Myelencephalon

The first major division of the brain, the **myelencephalon,** is actually an extension of the spinal cord. It contains the **medulla oblongata,** which controls such functions as respiration, cardiovascular functioning, and muscle tone.

Metencephalon

The next level of the brain, the **metencephalon,** contains the **cerebellum.** This structure is concerned primarily with the coordination of movement, equilibrium, and various reflexes. Damage to the cerebellum results in postural impairment and loss

FIGURE 5-9 A cross-sectional view of the brain showing the location of important structures.

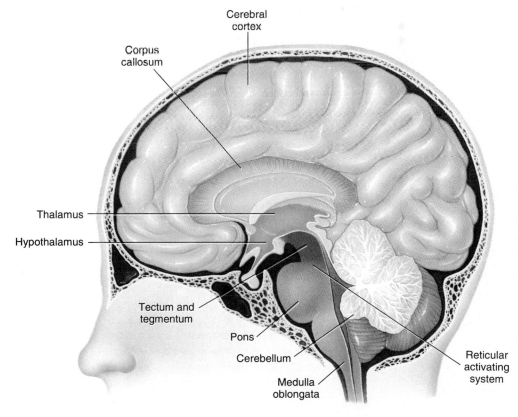

Cerebral cortex

Corpus callosum

Thalamus

Hypothalamus

Tectum and tegmentum

Pons

Cerebellum

Medulla oblongata

Reticular activating system

of skilled motor activity, making even seemingly simple movements such as walking jerky, exaggerated, and uncoordinated. The metencephalon also contains two other structures, the pons and the reticular activating system. The **pons** forms a bridge between the metencephalon and the mesencephalon and helps control sleep and waking. The **reticular activating system (RAS),** which extends forward into the diencephalon, has been shown to affect physiological arousal. For example, activation of the RAS elevates cardiovascular reactions such as heart rate and blood pressure and causes an increase in brain-wave activity (see Chapter 7).

Mesencephalon

The **mesencephalon** has two major subdivisions: the **tectum,** consisting of the **superior** (upper) and **inferior** (lower) **colliculi,** and the **tegmentum.** In mammals the superior colliculi are important because they receive about 20% of the nerves in the optic tract and mediate (coordinate) eye movement in response to visual stimuli. The inferior colliculi mediate movement in response to auditory stimuli. Virtually all the fibers carrying auditory information pass through the inferior colliculi on their way to the higher auditory areas of the brain.

Diencephalon

The **diencephalon** is small but extremely important because it contains nuclei (bundles of nerves) that help to control many cardiovascular and hormonal functions. It also serves as a relay station for fibers traveling from the lower to the higher centers in the telencephalon. Among the most critical structures in the diencephalon is the **thalamus.** The thalamus is the brain's primary relay station: Nearly all the nerves coming from the sense organs go through the thalamus before terminating in the highest levels of the brain, the cerebral cortex. (Olfactory information is the only sensory information that is not transmitted through the thalamus). For example, neurons in the visual tract have synaptic connections in the *lateral geniculate nucleus* of the thalamus and auditory nerves have synaptic connections in the **medial geniculate nucleus.**

Another structure in the diencephalon is the **hypothalamus,** a cluster of nerve cells lying below the thalamus. Although the hypothalamus accounts for only about 0.3% of the brain's weight, it is exceedingly important because it mediates nearly all aspects of behavior, including feeding, drinking, and sexual behavior, as well as physiological functions such as temperature regulation, secretion of hormones, and regulation of vital organs.

Telencephalon

The **telencephalon,** or forebrain, is the highest division of the brain. It contains a number of major areas, including the **limbic system.** (See Figure 5-10.) Originally believed to serve only the sense of smell, the limbic system (also called the limbic lobe) is now known to play an important role in many behaviors and psychological states, including emotion and memory.

By far the most important area of the forebrain is the **cerebral cortex,** or **neocortex,** the large, wrinkled surface that lies on the top of the brain. (See Figure 5-11.) Although the neocortex is only about 1.5 to 3.0 millimeters thick, if one were to iron out the wrinkles one would see that it has a very large surface area—about 2,500 square centimeters, or more than four times the surface area of an 8 1/2×11-inch piece of notebook paper. The folds or creases in the brain evolved so that it could fit into the skull cavity in much the same way that a crumpled piece of paper fits into a small space. The neocortex comprises about 80% of the volume of the brain in humans but is proportionally smaller in lower species.

The neocortex actually consists of two symmetrical halves, or **hemispheres,** joined by a mass of nerve material called the **corpus callosum.** (See Figure 5-9.) As shown in Figure 5-11, the hemispheres are made up of four major subdivisions—the

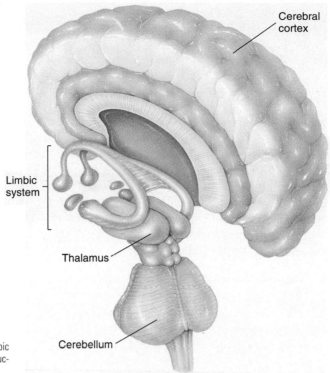

FIGURE 5-10 The location of the limbic system in relation to other brain structures.

occipital, parietal, temporal, and frontal lobes—each of which seems to serve a special function in terms of sensory and motor performance (reception of sensory information or production of muscle movement). The two halves of the brain look about the same, but whether they perform identical functions has long been a subject of debate among neuropsychologists. Today it is known that the two hemispheres have different functions, as we discuss in the next section.

FIGURE 5-11 A lateral (side) view of the human brain showing the four lobes of the cerebral cortex and other structures.

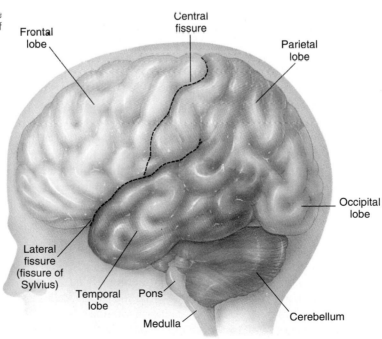

Each nerve cell, or neuron, consists of dendrites, a cell body, and a single fiber called an axon extending away from the cell body. At the end of the axon are specialized terminal buttons containing chemicals (neurotransmitters). When stimulated by an action potential, they diffuse across the space between nerve cells, called the synapse, and stimulate another neuron. Sensory (or afferent) neurons carry information from sense organs to the brain; motor (or efferent) neurons carry signals from the brain to the muscles and organs of the body. Neuroscientists divide the brain into five major sections: myelencephalon, metencephalon, mesencephalon, diencephalon, and telencephalon (or forebrain). The nervous system is controlled by numerous structures within the brain, of which the most important are the thalamus, the hypothalamus, and the neocortex. The cerebral or neocortex consists of two symmetrical halves, called hemispheres, that have different functions. The two hemispheres are connected by the corpus callosum.

LOCALIZATION OF CORTICAL FUNCTIONING

The phrase "localization of function" refers to the idea that particular sensory and motor functions are controlled by specific areas of the brain. Although each area of the cortex does seem to have specialized functions, at least to some degree, the situation is not simple. Nerves that control muscles originate in all of the lobes of the brain, not just selected areas. Similarly, sensory nerves originating in the sense organs extend to more than one area of the brain (Kolb & Whishaw, 1985). This means that there is no one-to-one correspondence between brain area and the function that is predominantly served by that area.

THE OCCIPITAL LOBE

The **occipital lobe,** located at the very back of the brain, is concerned with vision. As shown in Figure 5-12, it contains three interacting systems (Beaumont, 1983; Walsh, 1978). The primary visual cortex, also known as Area 17, receives visual information from the lateral geniculate nucleus of the thalamus; it mediates the perception of simple forms, patterns, and colors. The two surrounding visual systems, Areas 18 and 19, are involved in the conversion of perceptual forms into meaningful images. We know this because if these areas are damaged, a condition called **visual agnosia** (agnosia means "loss of knowing") results: The patient can recognize an object but cannot discriminate that object from others that differ from it only in shape, size, or orientation (Benton, Hannay, & Varney, 1975). For example, the patient may be unable to divide a straight line into two equal parts, or may see the edges of an object as distorted. Some patients can recognize that a face is a face but are unable to identify whose face it is, even if that person is a close friend (Gassel, 1969).

Other types of agnosia may be caused by damage to the occipital lobes. Patients suffering from **color agnosia** can identify individual colors but cannot classify them into groups. Patients with **spatial agnosia** have no depth perception; the world seems to them to exist entirely in two dimensions. Patients with **associative visual agnosia** can draw an object but cannot name the object or state its use. In these cases what appears to be lost is an appreciation of the *meaning* of the object; in other words, the loss is one of perception rather than of sensation (Mack & Boller, 1977).

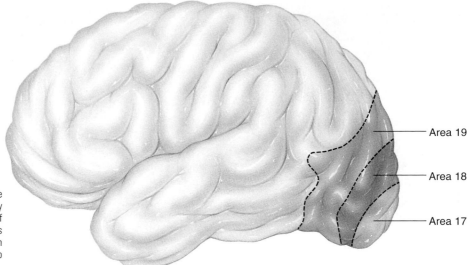

FIGURE 5-12 The three areas of the occipital cortex. Area 17, the primary visual cortex, mediates the perception of simple forms, patterns, and colors. Areas 18 and 19 are involved in the conversion of those simple perceptual elements into meaningful images.

Area 19

Area 18

Area 17

THE PARIETAL LOBE

The **parietal lobe** is located at the top of the brain, in front of the occipital cortex. Its major function is to mediate tactile perception (touch), but it has many other functions as well. Tactile perception is governed primarily by the anterior or forward portion of the parietal lobes. Areas of the body that are especially sensitive to touch, such as the fingers, lips, and face, are connected by means of sensory neurons to larger segments of the cortex; relatively insensitive areas, such as the back, are connected to smaller segments. Figure 5-13 presents a cross section of the parietal cortex, showing the relationship between various parts of the body and the parts of the cortex to which they transmit tactile information. Note the relatively large area of the cortex associated with the lips (a small area of the body) but the small surface of the brain associated with the trunk (which has a large surface area on the body). Clearly, the relative amount of brain tissue to which these areas of the body project does not correspond to the relative size of the body areas themselves.

Damage to the parietal cortex, caused either by a stroke (rupturing of blood vessels in the brain) or by a wound, may produce agnosias of touch; these are termed **asomatognosias.** Patients with this condition may be unaware of their limbs, have

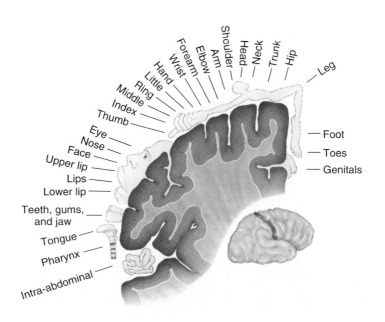

FIGURE 5-13 The area of the parietal cortex that receives sensory information from various parts of the body. The figure superimposed on the diagram of the brain indicates which area in the brain corresponds to which part of the body. Note that some parts of the body are disproportionately represented in the cortex relative to other areas—the hand compared to the trunk, for example.

FIGURE 5-14 Sample stimuli used to test for errors in spatial judgment. Patients with damage to the area of the parietal cortex associated with spatial judgment typically cannot identify which of the comparison stimuli matches the sample stimulus. (Adapted from Butters, Barton, & Brody, 1970.)

trouble getting dressed, and even complain about the presence of strange arms or legs, refusing to believe that they are their own. In another form of this condition, patients cannot identify parts of their own bodies either by moving them or by pointing to them (Beaumont, 1983).

The posterior (back) area of the parietal cortex is associated with spatial judgment. Patients with damage to this area often cannot specify the spatial relations between objects. In one study, illustrated in Figure 5-14, patients were shown a geometric pattern (the sample stimulus) and then were given a number of additional stimuli, only one of which had the same spatial orientation as the sample. When asked to identify the original pattern, they typically were unable to do so (Butters, Barton, & Brody, 1970).

THE TEMPORAL LOBES

The **temporal lobes** lie in front of the occipital cortex and extend around the side of the brain much like the folded wings of a bird. The area is divided into four sections: Heschl's gyrus and the superior, middle, and inferior temporal gyri (gyrus means "convolution"). The primary function of the temporal lobes is auditory perception and the control of speech, but this area of the brain is also involved in memory, attention, and emotion.

The area of the temporal lobes that is most directly involved in auditory perception is near the region where the temporal lobe is connected to the parietal lobe. Mild electrical stimulation of this area can cause a patient to experience tones or even meaningful perceptions such as songs. Predictably, damage to this area causes problems of auditory perception; for example, patients may not be able to discriminate between simple speech sounds such as "ba" and "pa" (Oscar-Berman, Zurif, & Blumstein, 1975).

Damage to this region of the brain may also produce **auditory agnosia,** in which patients cannot identify certain common sounds, such as the sound of footsteps or running water (Critchley & Henson, 1977). In one experiment, subjects suffering from auditory agnosia were shown four pictures of familiar objects; they then heard a sound that would have been produced by one of the objects depicted in the pictures (Vignolo, 1969). The subjects were asked to match the sound with the appropriate picture. (See Figure 5-15.) One of the pictures was a correct match; that is, it accurately portrayed the source of the sound. For instance, if the sound was that of a bird singing, one of the pictures showed a bird singing. Although the other three pictures did not match the sound, the nature of the mismatch differed in each case. One kind of error was semantic, involving a similar agent that produces a dissimilar sound—a

FIGURE 5-15 Examples of the kinds of stimuli used to test auditory agnosia. In these examples the top picture, of a bird singing, correctly matches the sound presented. The second picture down shows a similar agent (a rooster is a kind of bird) that produces a dissimilar sound; the third picture down shows a dissimilar agent (a man) producing a similar sound (a whistle); and the bottom picture shows a dissimilar agent (tugboat) that produces a dissimilar sound (the blowing of a horn). (Adapted from Vignolo, 1969.)

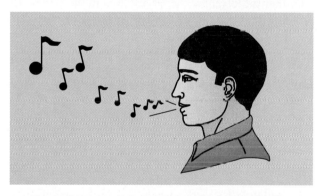

rooster crowing, for instance. A second kind of error was acoustic, involving a dissimilar agent that produces a similar sound—for example, a man whistling. In the third kind of error, both the agent and the sound it produces were unrelated to the original stimulus—a picture of a tugboat sounding its horn, for example. The subjects committed primarily semantic errors; for example, they tended to match the picture of the rooster crowing with the sound of a bird singing. These results indicate that patients with temporal lobe damage can discriminate sounds correctly but cannot associate the sound with its meaning—that is, the objects to which they correspond.

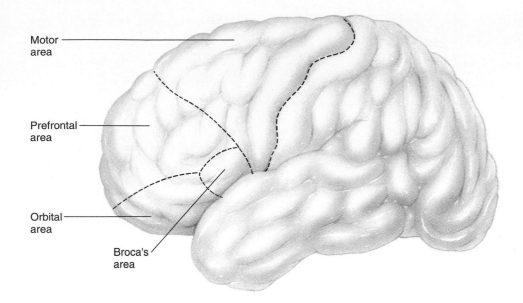

FIGURE 5-16   Areas of the frontal lobes of the cerebral cortex.

Motor area

Prefrontal area

Orbital area

Broca's area

THE FRONTAL LOBES

The **frontal lobes** are the largest area in the cortex. (See Figure 5-16.) Located in the front of the brain, they have four major divisions: the motor area, the prefrontal area, the orbital area, and Broca's area. These areas seem to control many of the behaviors that we consider uniquely human, such as abstract thinking and planning ahead, as well as personality traits. This is an oversimplification, however, because it is unlikely that anything as complex as thinking or intelligence could be confined to a single area of the brain. Nevertheless, the frontal lobes do seem to be involved in mediating these functions, at least in a general way.

The importance of the frontal lobes can be seen in the results of research on the ability to plan ahead. Patients who have suffered damage to the frontal lobes have difficulty constructing geometric designs using building blocks (Lewis, Landis, & King, 1956; Petrie, 1952). Presumably, this is because the task requires that the person visualize beforehand how the final design will appear. Similarly, patients with frontal lobe damage often are unable to follow a simple paper-and-pencil maze because successful performance requires that they plan ahead to avoid dead-end alleys.

Damage to the orbital area can also affect social behavior and personality, although the effects are quite varied. In one case, a middle-aged salesman suffered a fracture of the left frontal skull as a result of an automobile accident. Before the accident he had been a warm, animated, outgoing person, active in church and community affairs. After the accident, however, he was withdrawn and silent; he could speak intelligently but never initiated a conversation. The damage to his brain seemed to have caused a significant change in his personality.

In another case, a quiet, intelligent West Point graduate suffered a bullet wound in the left frontal area while serving in Vietnam. Although he had previously been polite and somewhat reserved, he became brash and disrespectful, making rude and facetious remarks to strangers and acquaintances alike. In sum, frontal brain damage can have a variety of effects on personality and behavior (Blumer & Benson, 1975).

The skull of Phineas Gage. Gage, a railroad laborer, was tamping down a dynamite charge with an iron rod when the blasting powder was accidently ignited. The explosion shot the rod through the frontal portion of his brain. Gage miraculously recovered but showed marked changes in personality and reasoning ability, thus giving some hint as to the function of that portion of the human brain.

130

Each lobe of the cortex seems to have specialized functions. The occipital lobe is concerned primarily with vision, the parietal cortex with tactile perception, the temporal lobes with auditory perception, and the frontal lobes with personality and complex behaviors. No function, however, is confined to a single area of the brain, and most areas are involved in more than one function. Damage to particular areas causes various kinds of agnosia, or loss of ability to assign meaning to stimuli; thus, damage to the occipital lobe causes visual agnosia, whereas damage to the parietal cortex causes asomatognosias (agnosias of touch), and damage to the temporal lobe causes auditory agnosia. Damage to the frontal lobes can affect such behaviors as planning ahead and may cause radical changes in personality.

LOCALIZATION OF MEMORY

It should not be surprising to discover, as our discussion so far has shown, that there are direct connections between the sense organs and the brain. After all, one of the primary functions of the brain is to receive and integrate sensory information. Less obvious, however, is the way the brain creates and stores memories. Unlike sensory inputs, memories are not part of the brain's biological "machinery"; they are acquired through experience and therefore must somehow be created by the neural structures in the brain.

But memories must be encoded and stored in the brain in some way (Goddard, 1980). Some scientists have suggested that the nature of the contact between two nerve cells may change as a result of repeated activation. Perhaps the size of the area or the number of points of contact increases. Or maybe the change is chemical in nature: For example, perhaps there are alterations in the biochemicals that aid in the transmission of nerve impulses (Davis & Squire, 1984). Whatever the exact means by which neurons encode memory, neuropsychologists have long assumed that memories are indeed encoded and stored in the brain; for many years they have been searching for the precise locations where these processes occur.

EARLY RESEARCH

Some of the earliest and most interesting research on memory was done by Penfield (Penfield & Jasper, 1954; Penfield & Perot, 1963).

Penfield's Work

In the course of his career as a neurosurgeon, Penfield operated on more than 1,000 severely epileptic patients. The goal of the surgery was to remove selected areas of the brain that caused the patients' seizures. But in order to identify those areas Penfield had to stimulate the brain electrically and evaluate the patient's responses. This meant that the patient had to be fully awake during the operation. (Because the brain itself has no pain receptors, this process can be carried out with local anesthesia on the surface of the head.)

Penfield found that the stimulation of brain tissue sometimes induced a strong reaction that resembled a memory. Some patients reported hearing voices and music;

others experienced visual images such as people or scenes; still others had both auditory and visual experiences. Many of these experiences were quite specific. For example, one patient reported, "That music, from the stage hit 'Guys and Dolls' . . . I was listening to it" (Penfield & Perot, 1963, p. 653). Another said, "Now I hear people laughing—my friends in South Africa . . . yes they are my two cousins, Bessie and Anne Wheliaw" (Penfield & Perot, 1963, p. 654).

Penfield believed that he had triggered specific memories by stimulating particular areas of the brain. This interpretation has been disputed, however, on the ground that the experiences were more like dreams than actual memories (Loftus & Loftus, 1980). Indeed, some of the reported experiences could not have been real memories because they included descriptions of locations that were unfamiliar to the patient (Halgren, Walter, Cherlow, & Crandall, 1978).

Lashley's Research

Karl Lashley (1950) also conducted research on the localization of memory. He taught animals to run through a complicated maze and then surgically removed various areas of their brains to see whether the animal's memory of the maze was selectively eliminated. The animals showed deficits in performance following the surgery (the greater the amount of tissue damaged, the poorer the performance), but the precise location of the damage seemed to make little difference.

RECENT RESEARCH

The early research just described produced some tantalizing findings, but it failed to demonstrate that memories are localized in specific areas of the brain. Recent research, including studies of brain-damaged individuals and experiments on animals, has made progress in this direction. In this section we review some of the more important results of that research (Squire, 1987).

The Case of N.A.

N.A. was a 22-year-old man who suffered an unfortunate accident: A small fencing foil was plunged through his nasal cavity, penetrating his brain and damaging part of the **medial thalamic region** in the frontal lobe (medial means "toward the center"). After the accident N.A. exhibited various paralyses and neurological disorders, but he recovered nearly all functions within a period of several months. The one deficit remaining after that period was an inability to form new memories; memories that had been present before the accident were not affected. As a result, N.A. had trouble performing many of the simple behaviors of everyday life. It was difficult for him to watch television because he would forget the plot during commercial breaks. Conversations with him were tedious because he asked the same questions over and over again. In fact, psychologists had trouble testing him because he forgot their instructions before he could begin answering the test questions (Squire & Moore, 1979; Teuber, Milner, & Vaughan, 1968).

The Case of H.M.

H.M. had very severe epilepsy that required surgery. The surgery created a lesion in the hippocampus. (See Figure 5-17.) Although his condition improved significantly, he suffered a problem similar to that experienced by N.A.: He was unable to form new memories (Scoville & Milner, 1957), although memories formed prior to the operation appeared to be unaffected. For example, H.M. could direct a person to the neighborhood where he had lived before the operation, but he could not find his way to the house to which he had moved after the operation. During rehabilitation, he was given the job of mounting cigarette lighters on cardboard display frames. He performed the job adequately each day, and yet after six months could not describe his workplace or the nature of his job (Corkin, 1984; Milner, Corkin, & Teuber, 1968; see also Barr, Goldberg, Wasserstein, & Novelly, 1990).

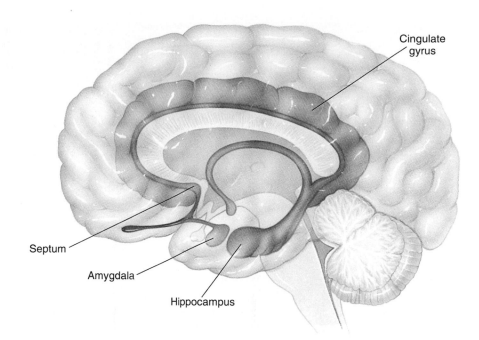

Cingulate
gyrus

Septum

Amygdala

Hippocampus

FIGURE 5-17 The hippocampus and other structures in the limbic system. Research suggests that the hippocampus and the medial thalamic region play an important role in human memory.

Korsakoff's Syndrome

Other evidence for the localization of memory is provided by patients with **Korsakoff's syndrome,** a condition that results from chronic alcoholism (Becker, Furman, Panisset, & Smith, 1990; Kinsbourne & Wood, 1975; Victor, Adams, & Collins, 1971). Like N.A. and H.M., these patients have little ability to use new information, form new memories, or recall recent experiences. The areas of the brain that are affected by Korsakoff's syndrome can vary (Markowitsch, 1982), but in most cases autopsies reveal damage to the medial thalamic region (similar to that suffered by N.A.). In about 36% of the cases, however, damage to the hippocampus (similar to that suffered by H.M.) is found.

Studies of Animals

The research described so far suggests that two areas of the brain—the hippocampus and the medial thalamic region—play a role in human memory. Neuropsychologists, however, obviously cannot create lesions in human brains for the purpose of studying memory processes, so it is not surprising that many have chosen to study those processes in other animals in whom lesions of a specific size and location can be made under highly controlled conditions.

The results of one such study confirm the importance of the medial thalamic region for the formation of short-term memories (Zola-Morgan & Squire, 1985). In this study, the researchers used two groups of monkeys as subjects. The members of one group were normal, but the members of the other had had lesions created in the medial thalamic region of their brains. In the first part of the study, the monkeys were presented with a sample stimulus (a triangle, for example), and then, after a delay interval of eight seconds, two comparison stimuli (a triangle and a circle, for example), one of which was the same as the sample, and one of which was not. The subjects' task was to select the comparison stimulus—the circle—that was different from the sample stimulus. Clearly, this task required that they remember the sample stimulus during the delay interval. Whenever they performed this task correctly, they received a small food reward.

The normal subjects took an average of 140 trials to learn to perform the task at a 90% proficiency level (that is, make the correct response nine times out of ten). The subjects with brain damage, in contrast, took an average of 315 trials to reach the same proficiency level.

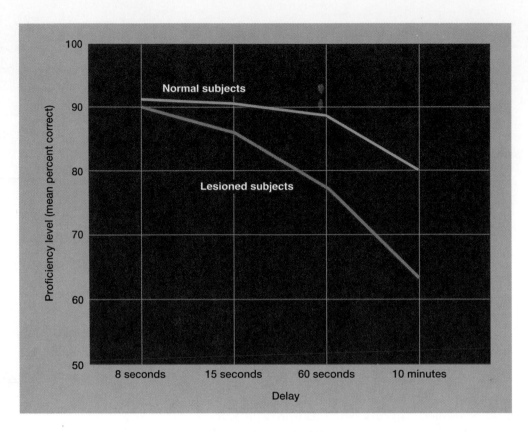

FIGURE 5-18 Mean proficiency level (percent correct) as a function of the delay interval between the sample stimulus and the comparison stimuli for normal (circles) and brain damaged (triangles) monkeys. (Adapted from Zola-Morgan & Squire, 1985.)

In the second part of the study, the researchers continued to test the subjects but varied the delay interval—the time between the presentation of the sample stimulus and the comparison stimuli. The longer the delay interval, the longer the subjects had to remember the sample stimulus to perform the task correctly. As Figure 5-18 shows, as the delay interval increased, the proficiency of both groups decreased, but the proficiency of the brain-damaged group decreased at a greater rate than that of the normal group.

Animal studies have also shown that areas in the temporal lobe are involved in memory. An experiment using a task like the one just described found that damage to either the hippocampus or the amygdala (a structure lying near the hippocampus) also causes performance deficits (Zola-Morgan & Squire, 1985).

In sum, the evidence from brain-damaged human patients and from animal experiments indicates that many areas of the brain are characterized by some degree of specialization in sensory and motor functions, memory, or fundamental patterns of social behavior. This finding should not come as a surprise; the alternative would be to suppose that there is no localization of function in the brain and that each area of the brain is involved in every process. From an evolutionary point of view such extensive redundancy in function would make little sense. Instead, humans have evolved a highly complex brain in which many areas are specialized at least to some degree. As the experimental techniques available to neuropsychologists become even more refined and sophisticated, it is likely that they will discover further evidence of specialization within the brain.

INTERIM SUMMARY

Neuropsychologists have long attempted to determine how and where memories are stored in the brain. Some early research was conducted by Penfield. In the course of operating on severely epileptic patients, he discovered that stimulating particular areas of the brain induced reactions that resembled memories. More recently, evidence from individuals who have suffered damage to the medial thalamic region or the hippocampus has shown that these areas are involved in the formation of short-term memories. These findings are supported by evidence from studies using animals. This research indicates that many areas of the brain are characterized by at least some degree of specialization.

HEMISPHERIC LATERALITY

One of the most important and interesting features of human neural organization is the relationship between sensory and motor control and the two hemispheres of the neocortex. **Hemispheric laterality** refers to the fact that certain functions may be associated with, or controlled by, one half of the brain; it suggests that there may be a significant amount of asymmetry in the way that the brain works (see Previc, 1991).

Figure 5-19 presents a view of the brain from above, showing the two hemispheres. Each hemisphere receives sensory signals from the opposite side of the body and controls the muscles in that side. This occurs largely because the sensory and motor fibers from each side of the body cross over to the opposite side of the brain before reaching their final destinations. The specific way in which this happens differs for different senses. For example, auditory nerves from each ear go to both the **contralateral** (opposite side) and **ipsilateral** (same side of the body) **hemispheres,** but contralateral nerves dominate; that is, the information carried by the nerves going to the contralateral hemisphere takes precedence over the information carried by the nerves going to the ipsilateral hemisphere. In contrast, all tactile information is transmitted to the contralateral hemisphere.

In the visual system, the connections between the eyes and the brain are somewhat more complicated. As shown in Figure 5-20, information on the right side of the visual field stimulates the left side of each retina and vice versa. The nerve tracts that travel from the eye to the brain differ according to the point on the retina where they originate. Nerves from the temporal or outer portion of the retina (that is, farther from the nose) travel to the ipsilateral hemisphere. Nerves from the nasal or inner portion of the retina travel to the contralateral hemisphere. The point at which the fibers cross over is the **optic chiasm.**

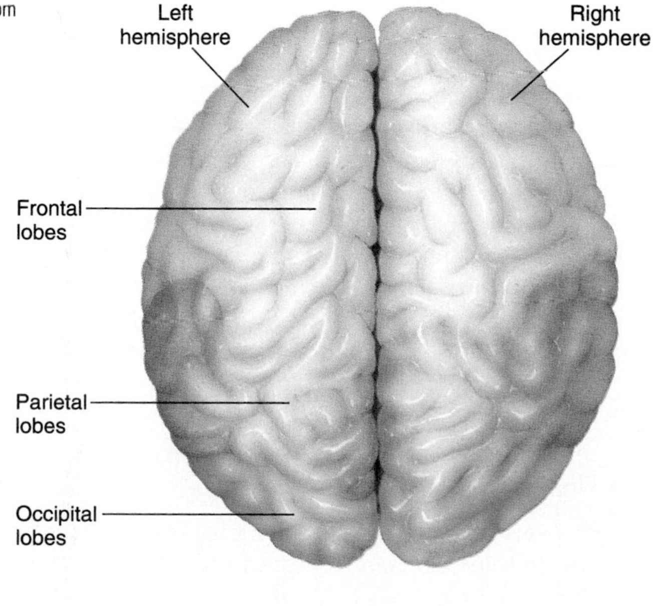

FIGURE 5-19 A view of the brain from above showing the two hemispheres.

Left hemisphere

Right hemisphere

Frontal lobes

Parietal lobes

Occipital lobes

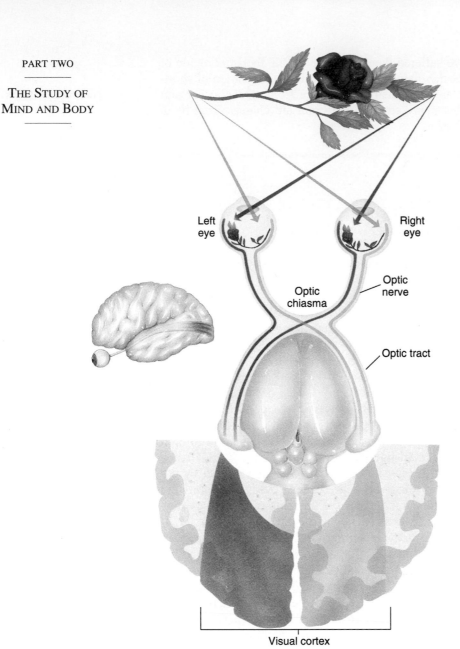

FIGURE 5-20 A schematic view of the connection between the eyes and the visual cortex (occipital lobe) of the brain, showing how visual information in the right visual field is transmitted to the left hemisphere and visual information from the left visual field is transmitted to the right hemisphere.

Because of the way the optic nerves are arranged, the left hemisphere of the brain receives direct information only from the right side of the retina, whereas the right hemisphere receives direct information only from the left side. Recall, however, that the two hemispheres communicate with each other through a mass of connecting fibers called the corpus callosum. As a result, the entire visual field is represented in both hemispheres—directly in the contralateral hemisphere and indirectly, through the corpus callosum, in the ipsilateral hemisphere. (The corpus callosum likewise communicates auditory and tactile information between hemispheres.)

Because the hemispheres appear symmetrical, one might assume that any given area in one hemisphere is equivalent to its mirror image in the other hemisphere. Yet this is not the case (see Annett & Manning, 1990). Evidence of significant differences between the hemispheres has been obtained from an interesting and unique approach to the study of the relationships between the brain and behavior: split-brain experiments.

SPLIT-BRAIN EXPERIMENTS

Severe cases of epilepsy are often characterized by profound and life-threatening seizures. In some patients, a surgical procedure can help alleviate this condition. The procedure involves dividing the brain into two separate and independent hemispheres by severing the major paths of communication between them, notably the corpus callosum. The treatment is based on the premise that a seizure that begins as a localized electrical "storm" in one side of the brain can trigger a more massive seizure if it crosses over to the other side.

One might imagine that anyone who has undergone such an operation would suffer a significant loss of functions, but, surprisingly, this is not the case. The everyday behavior of split-brain patients is remarkably normal, although deficits in performance can be detected by means of special tests (Franco & Sperry, 1977).

As a result of the operation, the neural pathways in the corpus callosum that connect the two hemispheres are severed, but the fibers leading from the retina to the ipsilateral hemisphere are preserved. Therefore, information from the left or right side of the visual field goes only to the opposite hemisphere. (Refer again to Figure 5-20 to understand why this is so.)

One consequence of this treatment is that it offers an opportunity to stimulate each half of the brain independently of the other, providing a unique opportunity for studying brain functioning. For example, one can present visual information to a split-brain subject exclusively from the left (or right) side of the visual field in order to test the abilities of the right (or left) hemisphere, provided the subject is prevented from making eye movements. Neuropsychologists have learned a great deal about the differential functioning of the two hemispheres from experiments of this sort. They have found that the left hemisphere serves primarily to mediate analytic skills, language, and speech production, whereas the right hemisphere is concerned with visual/spatial relations.

A typical experiment, as shown in Figure 5-21, works as follows: A subject focuses (fixates) on a point in the center of a screen. A picture of a coffee cup is flashed to the right of the fixation point and thus is transmitted to the left side of the brain. A normal person would be able to identify the object verbally and by touch with either hand by reaching under the screen and grasping an actual coffee cup from among a collection of other objects. A split-brain patient can identify it by touch only with the right hand. This is because the left hemisphere controls both language production and the muscles in the right hand but not the muscles of the left hand. When the image is flashed to the left of the fixation point—so that the image is transmitted to the right hemisphere—a split-brain subject can grasp the cup with the left hand but cannot name it or point to it with the right hand. This is because the right hemisphere controls the muscles in the left hand but does not control speech production (Gazzaniga, 1970; Gazzaniga & LeDoux, 1978).

Right hand
grasps cup   Left hand
grasps cup

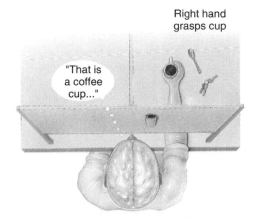 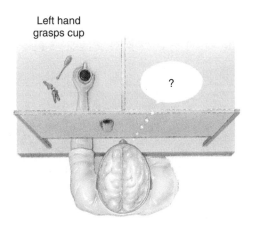

FIGURE 5-21 The format and results of a typical split-brain experiment. In the left panel (a) an image of a coffee cup is projected on the right side of the screen and is transmitted to the left hemisphere of the subject's brain. The subject is able to identify the image verbally as a coffee cup and can use the right hand to identify it by touch from among a collection of other objects. The subject would be unable to identify it with the left hand because the image has not registered in the right hemisphere of the brain, which controls the left hand. In the right panel (b) the image is projected on the left side of the screen and is transmitted to the right hemisphere of the subject's brain. The subject is unable to identify it verbally, but can use the left hand to identify it by touch.

Important and fascinating as this research is, there are some problems associated with it (Whitaker & Ojemann, 1977). First, the number of split-brain patients who have been tested is quite small, so any conclusions drawn from these experiments must be treated with caution. Second, all these patients were epileptic and therefore had abnormal brains to begin with, making it difficult to generalize the findings to the normal population. Finally, the behavior of these patients may have been affected by factors other than their brain surgery, such as the type or dosage of anticonvulsant drugs they were taking, as well as their age and past experience.

The split-brain studies indicate that the most salient difference between the hemispheres has to do with language. The left hemisphere seems to have specialized in language, especially the production of speech, whereas the right hemisphere appears to be stronger in visual/spatial processing. But hemispheric specialization is not an all-or-nothing affair. Each hemisphere is able to handle a variety of tasks, including those related to language, although perhaps not at the same level of efficiency.

OTHER LATERALITY EXPERIMENTS

The split-brain experiments played a significant role in the development of neuropsychology, but it would certainly be more convenient, if not more valid, to study lateralization of function in normal subjects. It is possible to do this using divided visual field experiments (Beaumont, 1983).

Divided Visual Field Experiments

Divided visual field experiments are much like split-brain studies in that stimuli are presented to subjects to the right or left of the fixation point. The special anatomy of the visual system allows researchers to study lateralization of functions. A key point is that the right hemisphere receives information from the left side of the visual field first, through the contralateral connections, before sharing it with the left hemisphere through the corpus callosum; conversely, the left hemisphere receives information from the right side of the visual field before sharing it with the right hemisphere. This is important because the hemisphere that gets the information first has a selective advantage over the other. Perhaps there is a slight loss when information must travel from one hemisphere to the other rather than directly from the eye to one hemisphere. Whatever the reason, there are slight but significant differences in the way the two hemispheres process information, which are revealed as discrepancies in the speed or accuracy of performance.

The results of divided visual field experiments are similar to those obtained from the split-brain studies (Geffen, Bradshaw, & Wallace, 1971). For example, when a face is flashed to the left of the fixation point for only a very short time, it is recognized more quickly than when it is flashed to the right side of the fixation point. This is because the right hemisphere processes visual/spatial information more easily than the left hemisphere does. Conversely, when words or letters are flashed to the right of the fixation point (and therefore transmitted to the left hemisphere first), they are recognized more quickly than when they are flashed to the left of the fixation point, confirming the left hemisphere's dominant role in the control of language (Davidoff, 1982; Klatsky & Atkinson, 1971).

In one experiment of this sort, letter combinations were presented in either the right or the left visual field (Ledlow, Swanson, & Kinsbourne, 1978). In some cases the subject was asked whether the letters matched physically; for instance, "AA" would be a physical match whereas "Aa" would not. In other cases the subject was asked whether the letters matched in terms of their meaning; for example, "Aa" would be a match in terms of meaning but "AB" would not. The results showed that physical matches were reported more accurately and quickly when they were flashed in the left visual field (right hemisphere), whereas matches based on meaning were identified more accurately and quickly when they were flashed in the right visual field (left hemisphere). Again, this indicates that the right hemisphere is better able to make visual/spatial judgments (matches based on physical appearance) whereas the left hemisphere is better able to perform analytic and language-related tasks (matches based on meaning).

Dichotic Listening Experiments

Given the results of split-brain and divided visual field experiments, simple logic would suggest that lateralization might exist in other senses besides vision. This is indeed the case, both for auditory stimuli (Kimura, 1961) and for tactile stimuli (Nachson & Carman, 1975).

As noted earlier, the auditory system is not completely lateralized. That is, auditory nerves transmit information to both the contralateral and the ipsilateral hemispheres. But if both hemispheres receive the auditory signals, how can they respond differently? The answer is that the hemispheres respond differently to auditory information because the contralateral pathway is dominant over the ipsilateral pathway; that is, when both ears are stimulated simultaneously, the information in the ipsilateral pathway is suppressed relative to the information on the contralateral side (Efron, Bogen, & Yund, 1977; Springer & Deutsch, 1985; Springer, Sidtis, Wilson, & Gazzaniga, 1978). Evidence for this comes from **dichotic listening experiments.**

In a typical dichotic ("two-part") listening experiment, pairs of stimuli are presented to the two ears and the subject is asked to identify the stimuli. The stimulus or message that is heard more often or more accurately indicates which hemisphere was dominant. Of course, the messages must be carefully synchronized and balanced for intensity to avoid giving one ear an advantage over the other.

Many studies have found that the left hemisphere has an advantage not only for digits and words (Kimura, 1967) but for all speechlike sounds, including nonsense words (Kimura & Folb, 1968). This should not be surprising in view of the results of the divided visual field experiments. The right hemisphere, in contrast, has an advantage for melodies (Gordon, 1980; Zatorre, 1979) and complex nonverbal stimuli such as traffic, dogs barking, coughing, and the like (Curry, 1967). These results also parallel those of the divided visual field experiments, because melodies, unlike words, have a temporal structure or sequence that does not have to be analyzed for meaning.

INTERIM SUMMARY

Each hemisphere of the brain receives information from the opposite side of the body and controls the muscles on that side. The connections between the eyes and the brain are more complicated, with nerves from the temporal portion of the retina traveling to the ipsilateral hemisphere (the one on the same side) and nerves from the nasal portion traveling to the contralateral hemisphere (the one on the opposite side). Experiments with patients who have undergone an operation in which the two hemispheres of the brain are surgically separated have shown that the hemispheres specialize in different functions, although each hemisphere is able to handle a variety of tasks. The left hemisphere seems to have specialized in language, the right hemisphere in visual/spatial processing. This conclusion is supported by evidence from divided visual field experiments and dichotic listening experiments.

SUMMARY

1. As its name suggests, neuropsychology is a combination of two fields: neurology and psychology. It reflects a materialist assumption that behavior, thoughts, and emotions can be explained in terms of the nerves and chemicals that make up the human brain. Neuropsychologists today can state many of the general relationships between behavior and the larger areas of the brain.

2. *Phrenology,* a now discredited movement in psychology, reflected the first attempt to chart a relationship between particular psychological traits and specific areas of the brain. Phrenologists believed that the size of the bump on the skull just over the brain area presumably associated with a particular trait would reveal the extent to which that trait was developed.

3. In the late nineteenth century, several discoveries of a correspondence between brain damage and behavioral deficits (such as Broca's work on aphasia) helped to legitimize the concept of localization of function.

4. Nerve cells (*neurons*), contain a cell body, axon, and dendrites. Communication between neurons is chemical in nature. When a *neurotransmitter* diffuses across the *synaptic cleft* between nerves, the *postsynaptic membrane* is depolarized, causing an *action potential* to be triggered, which is then propagated down the length of the axon to adjacent neurons.

5. The major divisions of the brain are the *myelencephalon, metencephalon, mesencephalon, diencephalon,* and *telencephalon.* The mesencephalon and diencephalon contain areas that are particularly important for sensory functioning. For example, the *thalamus* in the diencephalon serves as a relay station for most of the sensory nerve tracts. The telencephalon contains, among other structures, the *neocortex,* which provides the areas to which many sensory and motor nerve tracts project.

6. The brain is divided into two *hemispheres.* Most sensory/motor functions are controlled by the contralateral (opposite side) rather than the ipsilateral (same side) hemisphere.

7. The four major lobes of the neocortex are the *occipital, parietal, temporal,* and *frontal* lobes. Although each area is generally associated with the control of a specific function—the occipital lobes with vision, the parietal lobes with touch, the temporal lobes with audition, and the frontal lobes with abstract thinking—there is no simple one-to-one relationship between brain area and function.

8. One source of evidence for the functions associated with the lobes of the cortex is that lesions in each lobe produce certain characteristic *agnosias.* Damage to the occipital lobe produces *visual agnosias;* damage to the parietal lobe produces agnosias of touch *(asomatognosias);* damage to the temporal lobe produces *auditory agnosia,* and damage to the frontal lobes affects personality and the capacity for abstract thinking and planning.

9. Scientists have for many years tried to find the location of memory in the brain. Recent work has shown that the *medial thalamic* area and the *hippocampus* are especially important in this respect.

10. The two hemispheres of the brain do not seem to serve the same functions. Experiments on *split-brain* patients, that is, those in whom the *corpus callosum* has been severed, have shown for example that the left hemisphere is associated more than the right with language, whereas the right hemisphere is associated more with visual/spatial relations.

11. Experiments on normal subjects with intact brains have confirmed this same general picture, although, again, one must be cautious not to accept too simple a characterization of hemispheric functioning.

FOCUS QUESTIONS

1. What is neuropsychology and in what way does it address the mind–body issue?

2. Generally describe the five major areas of the brain and the principal lobes of the cerebral cortex.

3. What evidence do we have to suggest that various sensory functions are localized in the brain?

4. Review the evidence that suggests that memory can be localized in the brain.

5. Describe the differences in the ways in which the two hemispheres of the brain appear to operate.

6. What evidence, stemming from the study of sensory systems other than vision, supports the results of split-brain experiments?

CHAPTER 6

EMOTION

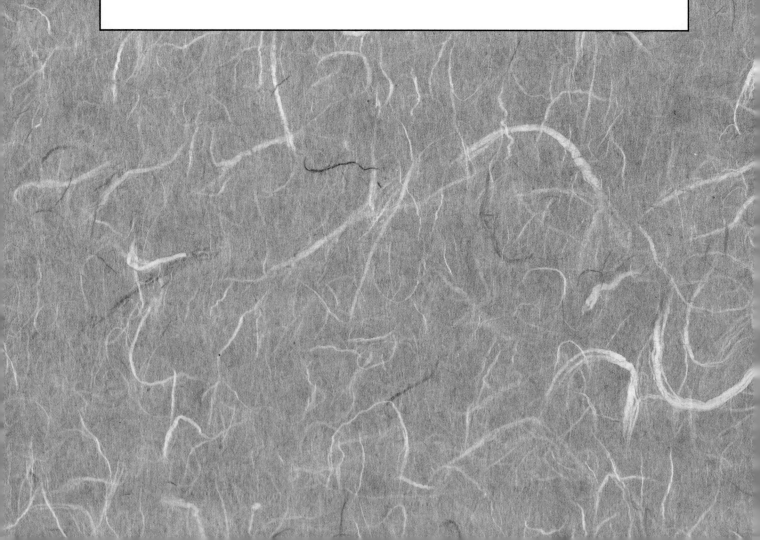

Emotions, in all their endless variety and nuance, are as central to humankind as reason and intellect. Emotions confront us at every turn of our lives; nearly all of our activities are colored in some way by emotions. For this reason, the study of emotion has always been an important area of psychological research (see Carver & Scheier, 1990).

Although we all know intuitively what we mean by emotion, the term is extremely difficult to define precisely. Some theorists (for example, Bindra, 1969) consider emotion to be a form of motivation; others (for example, Candland, 1977) prefer to give examples rather than attempt a definition. The difficulty of defining emotion stems primarily from the fact that psychologists cannot agree on the features that mark a particular event as an instance of emotion. Is an emotion characterized by a specific behavioral reaction or by a particular physiological response? Do emotions involve *both* behavioral and physiological responses? Many so-called emotional events involve one of these but not the other, making it difficult to formulate a definition (Fehr & Russell, 1984). Various forms of physical exercise, for example, involve physiological reactions that are quite similar to those associated with fear or rage, yet it would be inappropriate to say that the exercise actually induced those emotions.

We suggest that a central feature of most, if not all, emotions is the inner psychological state experienced by the individual, that is, the *feelings* generated by an emotional situation. Such a definition has a direct bearing on the mind–body problem: It implies that external physical stimuli give rise to internal psychological experiences, which generate behavioral reactions that enable us to study those experiences. We make inferences about the unobservable experience on the basis of the observable relationship between the stimuli and the reactions.

Consider these examples. An external stimulus, say a red patch, triggers an internal psychological experience of "red"; similarly, a tone may give rise to the experience of "loud." The nature of these experiences can be investigated through study of the subject's reactions. In principle, the study of emotion is similar: Various external (or sometimes internal) stimuli give rise to inner states such as "fear," "rage," "envy," or "joy." We can study these inner states by examining the relationship between the stimulus and the response. In short, the problem of studying joy or rage is, in principle, no different from the problem of investigating red or loud. In each case we specify the conditions that give rise to the experience and the behaviors that result (including physiological reactions) and then make inferences about the intervening psychological state.

There are some significant risks in defining emotion in terms of an inner psychological state (Plutchik, 1980). For example, one can never know what another person's emotional experience is like—how that person "really feels." Indeed, the behaviorist revolution arose out of opposition to such a "mentalistic" approach. Although the behaviorist position has merit, it is nonetheless true that the problem of inferring the properties of emotion from knowledge about environmental inputs and behavioral outputs is very similar to the problem of inferring the properties of other psychological experiences.

What are the behaviors that psychologists use to study emotion? They vary markedly. Some are physiological; for example, heart rate, blood pressure, and sweating often reveal underlying aversive emotions, such as fear or anger. Others are locomotor—subjects tend to move away from stimuli that elicit aversive emotions, whereas they seek out and approach stimuli that trigger a sense of comfort or pleasure. Psychologists also assess emotion by recording verbal statements (such as "I feel frightened") or administering paper-and-pencil tests of mood.

The emotions themselves vary widely and are difficult to classify. Most theories agree that emotions differ in quality. Hate, for example, is qualitatively different from ecstasy. Theories also agree that emotions may vary in intensity. Fear and terror, for example, may be qualitatively similar (both are negative emotions) but different in degree (terror may be an extreme form of fear). Theorists differ, however, on how to classify emotions (see Ortony & Turner, 1990). One noted theory claims that all emotions can be classified according to eight basic or primary categories, much in the way various hues can be accounted for by three primary colors (see Chapter 3). The eight basic emotions are: joy, acceptance, fear, surprise, sadness, disgust, anger, and anticipation (Plutchik, 1980). As shown in Figure 6-1, these emotions may be combined to form other more complex feelings. For example, love is a mixture of joy and acceptance; contempt is a combination of disgust and anger.

Joy, sadness, fear, and anger are four of the eight basic, or primary, categories of emotion according to one theory of emotional classification.

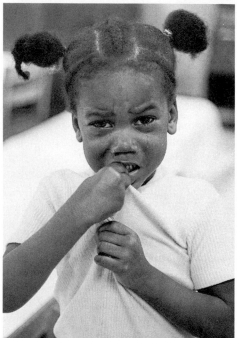

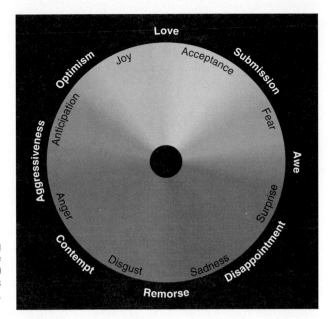

FIGURE 6-1 A scheme for classifying emotions. According to this model, there are eight primary emotions (inside circle) that combine to form complex emotions (on periphery). (Adapted from Plutchik, 1980).

EMOTIONAL EXPRESSION

Because psychologists must use measurable behavior to study emotional states, it is necessary to identify the behaviors—that is, the expressions of emotion—that reflect emotional states. Several were noted above, including physiological reactions, loco-motor behaviors, and responses on mood questionnaires. There are also expressive behaviors or gestures that reflect the inner psychological states that we call emotions (Ekman & Oster, 1979; Leventhal & Tomarken, 1986).

THE EVOLUTION OF EMOTIONAL EXPRESSION

Early studies of emotional expression were based on the idea that such expression may have adaptive value from an evolutionary standpoint. Charles Darwin (1965/1872) made this point in a book titled *The Expression of the Emotions in Man and Animals,* in which he noted that many species of animals, including humans, have similar emotional reactions or expressions. For instance, the bristling of a cat's fur at the sight of a dog is very similar to reactions found in other species, including humans. When we are terrified, our hair "stands on end."

The bristling fur and threatening posture of a frightened cat convey its willingness to fight back against a would-be attacker.

Darwin believed that such reactions convey information that is important for survival. Imagine how useful it would be for an animal to communicate that it is ready to attack. A hissing cat, with its back arched and hair erect, presents a far more ferocious image to its enemy than a cat not showing those reactions. The enemy is, in effect, warned that the cat is ready to fight. To the extent that these reactions scare off enemies, the cat may be able to avoid being hurt. The other animal benefits too, because it can either flee, and thereby avoid being hurt, or prepare to fight. (Presumably an animal that can prepare for a fight is at an advantage relative to one who must fight unprepared.) Either way, its chances of survival are improved. The same kind of argument can be made for almost any form of emotional expression. Greeting gestures—for example, smiles or friendly hand signals—may reduce interpersonal conflicts. Mating signals may help to advertise sexual receptivity. Appeasement displays may signal submission and thus end an aggressive encounter.

FACIAL EXPRESSIONS

Darwin believed that emotional expressions are innate, but many anthropologists have argued that human emotional expressions, like many other aspects of behavior, are learned from culture (Kemper, 1984). Modern research has tended to favor Darwin's position, but there is evidence that learning and culture play an important role as well.

Cross-Cultural Similarities in Emotional Expression

One of the principal means of discovering whether facial expressions of emotion are innate is to examine the reactions of people in different cultures (Ekman, 1984). We can conclude that facial expressions that appear in all cultures are probably innate, whereas any that are unique to a particular culture or group of cultures are probably learned.

There are really two aspects to this issue. The first is whether people from all cultures agree that a given facial expression corresponds to a particular emotion—that a broad smile, for instance, corresponds to, say, unrestrained joy, whereas a smirk signifies contempt. The second is whether people from different cultures express their feelings in the same way. Do people universally smirk when they feel contempt, for example, or do some make various other kinds of expressions? These two aspects are, of course, closely related. In fact, recognizing emotional expressions in others implies a shared use of those expressions. For instance, the fact that one recognizes contempt in another person by observing that person's smirk implies that the observer already knows in some sense that such an expression corresponds to the feeling. Otherwise, the observer could not identify the emotion.

In one study, 30 photographs were chosen by the experimenters to portray facial expressions corresponding to six basic emotions—anger, disgust, happiness, sadness, fear, and surprise. These photos were shown to various observers from the United States, Japan, Argentina, Brazil, and preliterate societies in Borneo and New Guinea (Ekman, Sorenson, & Friesen, 1969). The observers were asked to indicate which emotion was depicted by each of the photos. The observers showed a high level of agreement about which facial expressions corresponded to each emotion. The preliterate subjects, for instance, concurred with the other subjects on the "happy" expressions about 92% of the time, although they agreed less on the other expressions: 56% in the case of anger, 38% in the case of surprise, and only about 31% in the case of disgust. The researchers concluded that even in cultures that are vastly different from our own the same facial expressions are used to express emotions.

In a follow-up experiment, the researchers used only subjects from very isolated communities who were known to have had no contact with Western culture (Ekman & Friesen, 1971). Subjects were asked to select from among three pictures the one whose facial expression corresponded to the feeling expressed by a statement such as "His child died, he felt sad." This procedure enables the observer to match expressions with emotions without using terms or labels provided by the researcher. Again there was a remarkable level of agreement; subjects from preliterate societies generally identified the same pictures as did subjects from Western societies.

Another approach is to film subjects in natural situations as they experience various emotions and then rate the degree of similarity in their expressions. In one such experiment, subjects in different preliterate cultures were filmed in various situations, including greeting, flirting, praying, begging, and interacting with infants (Eibl-Eibesfeldt, 1975). A high degree of consistency of expression was found in the different cultures. (See Figure 6-2.)

Emotional Expression in Children

Yet another way to determine whether or not facial expressions of emotion are innate is to study the facial expressions of very young children. The rationale for these studies is that the younger the children, the more likely it is that their expressions are innate rather than learned. In one experiment, researchers filmed the reactions of children between the ages of 4 and 6 to slides showing familiar people, unfamiliar people, unpleasant images, such as another child crying, and unusual images, such as

FIGURE 6-2 Studies have shown a high degree of consistency in emotional expression across cultures, as these examples of smiling people suggest.

a blurry time-exposed photograph of city traffic (Buck, 1975). Adult judges who did not know which slide the children were viewing rated their facial expressions and attempted to guess which slide had caused them to react in that way. Not only was there a high level of agreement among the judges on the emotion being expressed, but the judges accurately guessed which slide was being viewed.

These results do not prove that emotional expression is innate, because significant cultural learning can occur in the first few years of life. But in other research that used much younger children, including infants a few weeks old (Trevarthen, 1984) the results were comparable to those just described.

The Effect of Culture on Emotional Expression

No one, of course, would deny that culture plays a role in emotional expression (Matsumoto & Ekman, 1989). Cultural rules, it appears, can affect when and how we express our emotions. Japanese men, for example, appear to be encouraged by their culture to smile in the presence of authorities. In an interesting experiment, Japanese and American subjects watched a film about surgery that was intended to induce stress. As they watched, their facial expressions were recorded by a hidden camera (Ekman, 1972). Subjects from both cultures made the same facial movements at about the same point in the film, thus supporting the idea that facial expressions are universal. But when an authority figure (a scientist) came into the room, the Japanese subjects masked their negative feelings. They tended to smile more and showed greater control over their negative facial expressions than the American subjects.

Effects similar to those displayed by the Japanese men, however, occur in almost every culture. For instance, American college students who were waiting to be subjects in a shock experiment were less expressive when they knew they were being observed by the experimenter (an authority figure) than when they were unaware that they were being observed (Kleck et al., 1976).

PHYSIOLOGICAL AROUSAL AND FACIAL EXPRESSION

In addition to facial expressions, responses to emotional experience include various patterns of physiological arousal—changes in heart rate, for example. We discuss the biological aspects of physiological arousal and emotion later in the chapter. Here we will look at a question that has interested many researchers: To what extent are facial expressions and physiological response patterns correlated? Do people who have very expressive facial reactions, for example, also have high levels of physiological arousal? In most of the studies addressing this question, subjects are asked to look at various pictures and to "send" an emotional facial expression over closed-circuit television to a judge who tries to guess what the subject is looking at. At the same time, the subject's heart rate and other physiological reactions are measured. The major finding of this research is contrary to what one would expect: Expressive people who "send" more exaggerated facial expressions typically have *less* intense physiological reactions than people who are not very expressive (Buck, Savin, Miller, & Caul, 1972; Lanzetta & Kleck, 1970; see also Bush, Barr, McHugo, & Lanzetta, 1989; Zajonc, Murphy, & Inglehart, 1989). This inverse relationship between facial expression and physiological arousal suggests that there may be two distinct modes of emotional expression. The so-called externalizing mode is characteristic of people with very expressive faces but low levels of physiological arousal. The internalizing mode is the opposite—minimal facial expression but a high level of physiological arousal.

SEX DIFFERENCES IN EMOTIONAL EXPRESSION

There is evidence that emotional expression differs in males and females. In one experiment, male and female "senders" were shown emotionally loaded slides and were asked to match their emotional reaction to one of the six cultural universals—anger, happiness, fear, sadness, surprise, disgust—or to a neutral expression (Wagner, MacDonald, & Manstead, 1986). The senders' expressions were secretly video-taped, and the edited videotapes were then shown to male and female "receivers." In this experimental setting the receivers' accuracy was less than expected, with better than chance performance only on anger, disgust, and happiness. There was, however, a clear sex difference in sending, with female senders being much better at conveying emotion through their facial expressions. According to some theorists, such differences may occur because young girls have traditionally been encouraged to reveal their emotions, whereas young boys have been discouraged from doing so (Malatesta, 1985).

INTERIM SUMMARY

Darwin believed that expressions of emotion may have adaptive value because they convey information that is important for survival. Although he believed that emotional expressions are innate, many anthropologists have argued that such expressions, like other behaviors, may also be learned from one's culture. Cross-cultural studies have revealed a high degree of consistency in the facial expressions of emotion found among members of different cultures. Studies of emotional expression in children also provide evidence that emotional expressions are universal and may be innate. Researchers have found an inverse relationship between facial expression and physiological arousal, suggesting that there may be two distinct modes of emotional expression: the externalizing mode and the internalizing mode. There are also some sex differences in emotional expression.

BIOLOGICAL FACTORS

The relationship between emotional experiences, which are psychological states, and various physical or biological states has been extensively studied. A portion of this research will be reviewed here.

THE AUTONOMIC NERVOUS SYSTEM

Recall from Chapter 5 that the nervous system is traditionally divided into two parts: the peripheral nervous system and the central nervous system (the spinal cord and brain). (For convenience, the peripheral system and spinal cord are usually described together because both are separate from the brain.) The most important part of the peripheral nervous system for our discussion of emotion is the **autonomic nervous system (ANS).** This system is a specialized set of nerves whose principal job is to regulate the body's vital functions. It begins in the brain, travels along the spine, and exits at various points to connect with the internal organs and glands, including the heart, intestines, spleen, salivary glands, lungs, and pancreas. (See Figure 6-3.)

The function of the ANS can best be understood from an evolutionary perspective. If an organism had to "think" about keeping its heart going, or digesting its food, or maintaining its blood pressure, when distracted it might forget to do so and thus die. From an evolutionary point of view, therefore, vital functions should take care of themselves, that is, be autonomous. The ANS evolved to play this role.

The system is actually composed of two distinct parts: the **parasympathetic nervous system (PNS),** shown on the right side of Figure 6-3, and the **sympathetic nervous system (SNS),** shown on the left side of the figure. The nerves of the PNS leave the spinal column at the cervical (uppermost) and sacral (lowermost) levels of the spinal cord and go directly to organs such as the heart, spleen, and intestines. The

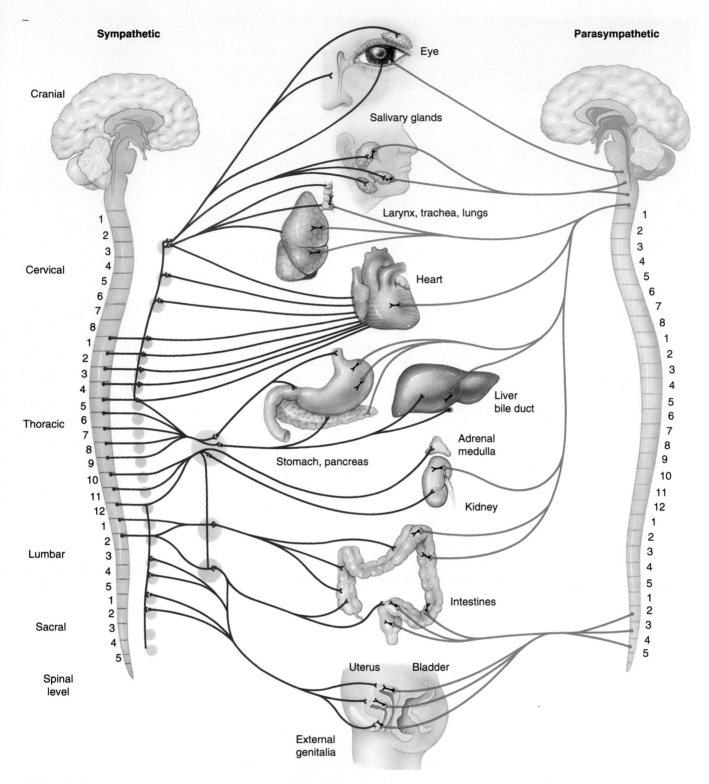

Sympathetic

Parasympathetic

Cranial

Cervical

1
2
3
4
5
6
7
8

Thoracic

1
2
3
4
5
6
7
8
9
10
11
12

Lumbar

1
2
3
4
5

Sacral

1
2
3
4
5

Spinal level

Eye

Salivary glands

Larynx, trachea, lungs

Heart

Liver bile duct

Adrenal medulla

Stomach, pancreas

Kidney

Intestines

Uterus   Bladder

External genitalia

1
2
3
4
5
6
7
8

1
2
3
4
5
6
7
8
9
10
11
12

1
2
3
4
5

1
2
3
4
5

FIGURE 6-3 The autonomic nervous system.

principal function of this system is conservation of energy or recovery following the expenditure of energy. Thus, when the PNS is active there is a decrease in heart rate and blood pressure and an increase in digestion, salivation, and the storage of energy in the form of glycogen.

The nerves of the SNS exit the spinal column at the thoracic and lumbar levels, combine to form concentrated groups of nerve cells called **ganglia,** and then send connecting neurons to vital organs. Because of the interconnection of these nerves in the ganglia, the SNS is a highly integrated system. This means that when one organ is activated, others are also. For example, when the heart is activated, so are the adrenal glands.

The function of the SNS is opposite to that of the PNS: It regulates the use or expenditure of energy. When the organism encounters environmental stressors, a predator for example, the SNS prepares the organism to "fight or flee" (Cannon, 1929). This is done by increasing heart rate, blood pressure, and respiration; converting stored glycogen into usable energy; restricting digestion; and so forth. These responses are designed to cope with the stressor. When the stressor is no longer present, the PNS takes over and the body is restored to its prior condition—digestion increases, heart rate slows, respiration decreases, and, in general, energy is conserved. Responses to stressors are described in detail in Chapter 23.

THE JAMES–LANGE THEORY

The arousal of the ANS is clearly related to the experience of emotion, but what exactly is that relationship? According to the **James–Lange theory of emotion,** formulated independently by William James and the Danish physiologist Carl Lange, the ANS itself is primarily, although not exclusively, responsible for creating emotional feeling (James, 1884; Lange & James, 1967/1885). This theory states, in other words, that the perception of autonomic arousal *is* the feeling of emotion. This is the reverse of what we might expect—namely, that the feeling of emotion *produces* autonomic arousal.

According to the James–Lange theory, whenever the cortex of the brain receives a stimulus through normal sensory processes and then recognizes its emotional significance, the brain automatically produces a reaction involving autonomic arousal and skeletal muscle activity. (See Figure 6-4.) When this ANS arousal and the associated changes in the musculature feed back to the cortex, they are perceived as emotional feeling. In other words, although the emotional *behavior* is triggered automatically, the emotional *experience*, or feeling, occurs because the organism perceives the ANS and musculature reactions. The ANS reactions occur *before* the feeling.

Early in this century Walter Cannon raised several critical points regarding the James–Lange theory (Cannon, 1927, 1931; see Goldstein, 1968). He noted that according to the theory, damage to the ANS should eliminate all emotional feeling,

The sympathetic nervous system prepares an animal for fight or flight.

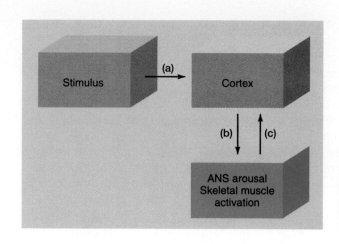

FIGURE 6-4 The James–Lange theory of emotion. An emotionally arousing stimulus directly activates the cortex through normal sensory channels (*a*); the cortex activates the ANS (*b*); feedback from the ANS to the cortex constitutes the emotional feeling (*c*).

yet it does not do so. Similarly, artificial stimulation of the ANS (for example, by a drug) should produce an emotional experience, but again, it does not do so.

Although these criticisms were convincing, more recent information, coupled with a reconsideration of old data, suggests that a version of the James–Lange theory may still be useful (Fehr & Stern, 1970). For example, the argument that damage to the ANS has no effect on emotion is not entirely correct. People who suffer damage to the ANS do still experience emotion, but there is often a partial loss of the extent to which they do so (Hohmann, 1966). The claim that artificial stimulation of the ANS does not produce emotion also is not entirely correct. In fact, as we see in a later section, it may create emotion under certain circumstances.

It appears, therefore, that the James–Lange theory was incorrect in assuming that emotional feeling *follows* the ANS reaction—that is, that emotional feeling results exclusively from the perception of ANS and musculature arousal. Nonetheless, feedback from the ANS to the brain may indeed be important in the experience of emotion, although in a more complicated way than James and Lange proposed (Leventhal & Tomarken, 1986).

CANNON'S THALAMIC THEORY

What the James–Lange theory seems to have ignored is the fact that emotional feeling may precede the ANS reaction, and that various other areas of the brain may be involved in *creating* emotion, not simply in perceiving ANS feedback.

Cannon (1927, 1931) was among the first psychologists to suggest that the brain, in particular the thalamus, plays a significant role in producing emotion. According to Cannon's **thalamic theory of emotion,** illustrated in Figure 6-5, the cortex continually inhibits the thalamus, the major sensory and motor relay station in the brain. When emotion-provoking stimuli reach the cortex from the thalamus through normal sensory pathways, the thalamus is released from this inhibition. While it is in this disinhibited state, the thalamus does two things: It produces emotional *expression* by activating the ANS and skeletal muscles, and it activates emotional *feeling* in the cortex. In this sense, then, the thalamus is the center for both emotional behavior and emotional experience. Rather than preceding the emotional feeling, the ANS reactions are triggered at the same time as the emotional experience.

Cannon offered several kinds of evidence in support of his theory. For example, he noted that animals in which the cortex has been damaged show a form of rage, presumably because the cortex no longer inhibits the thalamus. This rage disappears if the thalamus itself is damaged. Similarly, patients in whom the cortex has been anesthetized often exhibit reactions such as weeping or uncontrolled laughter, again presumably because the cortex is unable to inhibit the thalamus.

Cannon's theory never gained wide acceptance, perhaps because other areas of the brain have been shown to play an even greater role than that of the thalamus in the creation of emotion. Chief among these are various structures in the limbic system.

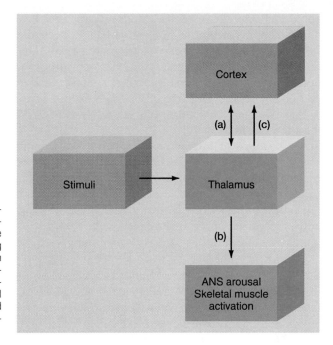

FIGURE 6-5 The Cannon thalamic theory of emotion. The thalamus routes sensory information to the cortex and the cortex sends inhibiting or disinhibiting signals back to the thalamus (*a*). When an emotionally arousing stimulus is perceived, the cortex disinhibits the thalamus, which then triggers emotional expression by activating the ANS and skeletal muscles (*b*) and emotional feeling in the cortex (*c*).

The Role of the Limbic System

As shown in Figure 6-6, the **limbic system** is a loosely defined group of structures in the forebrain that includes the hippocampus, amygdala, septum, mammillary bodies, hypothalamus, and fornix (see also Chapter 5 for a discussion of the limbic system). The original speculation linking these structures to emotion was based on a small amount of clinical data (Papez, 1937), but more recent evidence has confirmed that these areas are indeed important (Panksepp, 1986b; Rolls, 1986).

Many experiments have been conducted on animals in which researchers stimulate various portions of the limbic system to determine whether doing so produces an

FIGURE 6-6 The limbic system in relation to other brain structures. Structures in this system—including the hippocampus, the amygdala, the septum, the mammillary bodies, the hypothalamus, and the fornix—have been shown to be involved in the regulation of emotion.

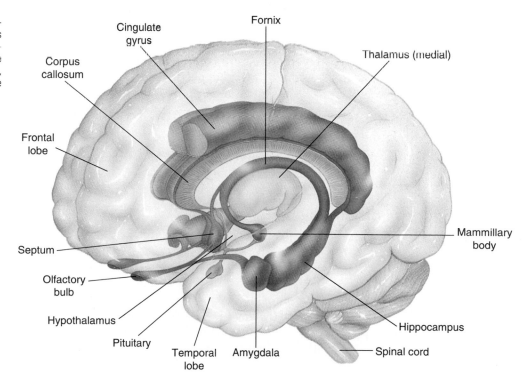

emotional reaction, or create lesions on structures in the system to determine whether doing so eliminates or significantly changes normal emotional behavior. The danger in accepting evidence from such research is that emotional feelings in humans are rarely simple, and the underlying neurological structures are not grouped in clearly defined emotional centers. Nevertheless, these studies have provided valuable information concerning the areas of the brain that are involved in emotion.

For example, the **septum** has been shown to be associated with the inhibition of the rage reaction (Fried, 1972). In one series of studies, researchers created lesions in the septums of cats and assessed them for emotional behavior (Brady & Nauta, 1953; 1955). The subjects' pre- and postoperative behaviors were rated on a 5-point scale; the behaviors studied included resistance to capture in the home cage, resistance to handling, muscular tension, vocalizations, urination and defecation, and rage reaction (hissing) when probed with forceps. Compared to control subjects that did not undergo the operation, subjects with damage to the septum showed immediate increases in most of these indexes of emotional expression.

If damage to the septum leads to rage, the septum must inhibit some other area of the brain that *produces* rage. Studies suggest that this area is the **amygdala** (Aggleton & Mishkin, 1986). Stimulating the amygdala usually causes subjects to exhibit rage (Ursin & Kaada, 1960). Conversely, subjects with a damaged amygdala are emotionally unresponsive and extremely docile (Aggleton & Passingham, 1981; Doty, Negrao, & Yamaga, 1973). This condition of docility is referred to as the **Klüver–Bucy syndrome,** after the investigators who first observed it in cats (Klüver & Bucy, 1937). According to some theorists, the emotional unresponsiveness occurs because damage to the amygdala interrupts the integration of sensory information from the cortex and the activation of other emotional centers in the hypothalamus. In effect, for these animals emotionally arousing stimuli "seem to have lost their naturally frightening or repugnant qualities" (Aggleton & Mishkin, 1986, pp. 292–293).

The Klüver–Bucy syndrome also occurs in humans (Bauer, 1982). In one investigation, researchers examined 25 patients in whom the amygdala had been selectively damaged as a means of treating severe epilepsy (Heimburger, Whitlock, & Kalsbeck, 1966). In 23 of the patients aggression and rage, which had previously been common, were absent after the amygdala was damaged.

The biological basis of pleasurable emotions has also been studied. Many experiments have shown, for example, that small electrical impulses to certain areas of the brain produce what appears to be pleasure (see *Neuroscience and Biobehavioral Reviews,* 1989). In some such studies, animals are allowed to press a lever in order to give themselves a small burst of electrical stimulation (Olds & Milner, 1954). (See Figure 6-7.) It is reasonable to infer that animals press the lever because they find the ensuing stimulation pleasurable. For one thing, they actively seek out and approach the stimulation in much the same way that a hungry animal seeks food. The animal may even forgo food and water to earn more brain stimulation (Routtenberg & Lindy, 1965). Some of the areas involved are in the limbic system; they include the hypothalamus, the amygdala, the hippocampus, and the septum. The predominant **pleasure center,** however, is the **medial forebrain bundle,** which runs near the hypothalamus (Olds, 1962; Olds & Olds, 1963). (See Figure 6-8.)

Comparable studies in humans have shown that stimulation of various portions of the limbic system is accompanied by feelings of extreme pleasure (Heath, 1986). These studies were carried out for the purpose of treating serious neurological disorders like epilepsy. If the investigators were to locate the afflicted areas of the brain, the patients had to be fully awake so that they could report what they felt. (Remember that the brain itself has no pain receptors.) During the treatment the patients reported intense pleasure when certain areas were stimulated—particularly the rear portion of the septum; they also were eager to administer the stimulation to themselves (Bishop, Elder, & Heath, 1963).

In sum, the brain functions in such a complex manner that one risks oversimplifying by identifying specific emotion centers. Nevertheless, certain areas of the limbic system, perhaps in combination with other structures in the brain, appear to provide

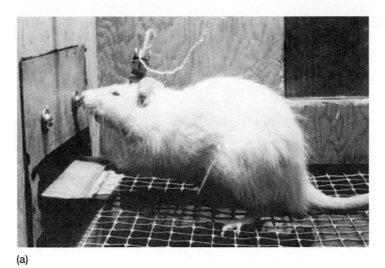

(a)

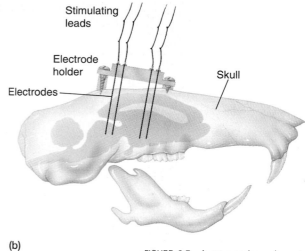

(b)

a neural foundation for emotional expression. Those areas are the amygdala, the septum, and the hypothalamus, as well as the medial forebrain bundle and the hippocampus. The fact that many of these structures are also important for other survival-related behaviors, such as feeding and sexual behavior, suggests that emotions are directly linked to our primitive, life-sustaining neural networks.

CHEMICAL MECHANISMS IN EMOTION

Because neurons transmit impulses by chemical means, it is not surprising that various neurotransmitters affect the experience of emotion (McGeer & McGeer, 1980; Panksepp, 1986b; Thompson, 1988). For example, injecting **carbachol,** a drug that excites neurons in which acetylcholine is the neurotransmitter, into the amygdala of a cat produces a vicious rage reaction (Grossman, 1964). Injecting carbachol into the septum, in contrast, impairs fear reactions such as freezing and fleeing. The converse has also been demonstrated: Injecting **atropine,** an agent that blocks the action of acetylcholine, into the septum produces fear reactions (Kelsey & Grossman, 1969).

FIGURE 6-8 Location of the medial forebrain bundle.

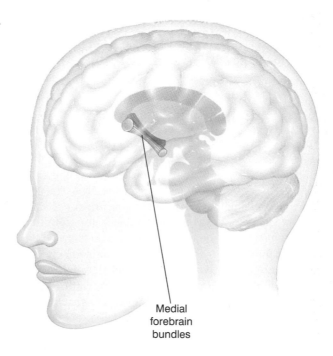

Medial forebrain bundles

Other experiments have provided evidence of a reward–pleasure system in the brain based on the neurotransmitters norepinephrine and dopamine (Panksepp, 1986a). For example, when norepinephrine is injected directly into the brain, self-stimulation increases (Wise & Stein, 1969). When norepinephrine levels are depleted, blocked, or destroyed, rates of self-stimulation decrease (Olds, Killam, & Bach-y-Rita, 1956).

INTERIM SUMMARY

Emotions have long been associated with the autonomic nervous system, a specialized set of nerves whose principal job is to regulate the body's vital functions. It is composed of two parts: the parasympathetic nervous system, which is involved in the conservation of energy, and the sympathetic nervous system, which is involved in the utilization or expenditure of energy. The James–Lange theory of emotion claims that perception of ANS activity constitutes emotional feeling. Although it was convincingly criticized by Cannon, the theory may be correct in some respects. More recent research has shown that structures in the brain are also involved in producing emotion. Cannon's thalamic theory of emotion holds that the thalamus produces emotional expression by activating the ANS and creates emotional feeling by activating the cortex. Other areas of the brain, however, have been shown to play an even greater role in the creation of emotion. Predominant among these are structures in the limbic system, particularly the septum, amygdala, and the medial forebrain bundle. Various neurotransmitters have also been found to affect the experience of emotion.

ENVIRONMENTAL FACTORS

The James–Lange theory predicted that artificial stimulation of the ANS would produce emotion. For example, an injection of epinephrine (adrenaline), the hormone that stimulates the sympathetic nervous system, should produce an emotion resembling fear because its effects on the ANS are like those associated with fear. In fact, however, emotion does not occur under these circumstances. Rather than feeling real emotion, subjects state that they feel "as if" they were afraid. In other words, subjects who have been given epinephrine report that they feel something akin to fear, rather than fear itself.

COGNITIVE INPUTS TO EMOTIONAL EXPERIENCE

Subjects may report feeling "as if" they were afraid because they are tested in an unnatural environment, the laboratory. Perhaps the experience of a true emotion, such as fear, depends not only on the physiological arousal produced by epinephrine but also on the situation in which the arousal occurs. This was the rationale for a famous experiment by Schachter and Singer (1962).

Subjects were brought into the laboratory and told that they were going to participate in a study of the effect of a vitamin supplement on vision. In reality, they were given a mild dose of epinephrine. The subjects were then divided into subgroups. Some were correctly informed about the physiological consequences of the drug: a slight racing of the heart, a blush or warmth in the face, and so forth. Others were misinformed about the physiological consequences of the drug; they were told that they might experience headaches, numbness in the feet, or itching. Subjects in a third subgroup were given no information about the effects of the drug. In addition to these groups, there were several groups of subjects who were given a placebo (a

placebo is a substance that has no physiological effects but is administered to subjects who believe it will have an effect).

After the administration of the drug, each subject was asked to sit in a waiting room so that the drug could take effect. In the room was another person who the subject believed was also there to participate in the experiment. In reality, the second person was an accomplice of the experimenter—that is, an assistant in the experiment whose job was to play the role of a subject. In one situation, the accomplice acted in a euphoric and slapstick manner, claiming to "feel great," throwing paper airplanes around the room, and shooting baskets with wads of paper. In another situation, the accomplice acted angry and complained bitterly about having to complete a questionnaire, which itself was highly insulting. After waiting for 20 minutes with either the euphoric accomplice or the angry accomplice, the real subjects were asked to fill out a questionnaire that measured their mood or emotion.

Two findings of this research are particularly noteworthy. First, subjects who were either misinformed or ignorant about the effects of the epinephrine reported that they felt emotion, but placebo-injected subjects and subjects who were correctly informed about the consequences of the drug reported that they did not experience emotion. Second, the kind of emotion reported—that is, the direction of the mood shift—did not depend on the physiological reaction to the drug (which was the same for all the subjects in the epinephrine groups); instead, it depended on the behavior of the accomplice. Subjects who spent time with the euphoric accomplice experienced an elevation in mood, whereas those who waited with the angry accomplice tended to become angry. In sum, the subjects who were given a mild dose of epinephrine *and* were not informed, or were misinformed, about the effects of the drug experienced a shift in emotion. The *kind* of emotion felt, however, depended on the behavior of the accomplice.

Cognitive Labeling Theory

According to Schachter's **cognitive labeling theory** of emotion, the experience of emotion requires both physiological arousal and an appropriate cognitive label for that arousal (Schachter, 1964). When we are physiologically aroused but have a satisfactory explanation for that arousal (as did the subjects in the experiment who were correctly informed about the effects of the drug), we do not attribute the arousal to an emotion. This is the case, for example, when we exercise. We feel our heart racing and experience shortness of breath, yet we attribute these physiological reactions to the exercise, not to emotion. When we do not have a satisfactory explanation for physiological arousal, however, we search the environment for a logical explanation and label the arousal accordingly. For example, the misinformed or uninformed subjects in the experiment observed a euphoric or angry accomplice and, not having a good explanation for their own arousal, attributed their feelings to an emotion similar to that displayed by the accomplice. It is as if they said, "I don't understand why I feel this way; I notice that this other person is euphoric (or angry); therefore, I must also be feeling euphoric (or angry)."

Assessment of the Theory

A great deal of research has been conducted in an attempt to assess the adequacy of the cognitive labeling theory (Leventhal & Tomarken, 1986; Reisenzein, 1983). Many specific predictions derived from the theory have not been upheld, but the general concept embodied in the theory has won approval. Let us briefly review the evidence for and against the theory.

The cognitive labeling theory predicts that a person will experience less emotion if autonomic arousal is attributed to a nonemotional source, as appeared to be true of the subjects in the original experiment who were correctly informed about the effects of epinephrine. This prediction has been supported by later experiments, although the effect may not occur in certain clinical situations (that is, for some people undergoing psychotherapy) in which the subject already has a strong and immutable

According to cognitive labeling theory, we are unlikely to attribute the racing heart and shortness of breath that accompany exercise like jogging to an emotion because the exercise itself provides a satisfactory explanation for the physiological reactions.

explanation for the source of arousal which in and of itself is the focus of attention in the therapy process (Leventhal & Tomarken, 1986).

The theory also predicts that a mistaken belief that arousal is emotional in nature when in fact it is caused by a drug or exercise will intensify actual emotional feelings. Although the exact causes for such an effect are not entirely known, this prediction is also supported by research findings (Reisenzein, 1983). For example, if a person experiences arousal because of physical exertion and then is placed in a situation that triggers anger, the residue of the physical arousal will intensify the anger (Zillmann, Katcher, & Milavsky, 1972). Similarly, experiencing sexual arousal or arousal caused by a strong unpleasant experience affects the subsequent experience of pleasure (Cantor & Zillmann, 1973). In an experiment demonstrating this effect, subjects were shown one of four 4-minute films, each of which was intended to arouse either positive or negative emotions. Furthermore, the arousal could be moderately intense (a low level of excitation) or quite strong (high excitation). For example, the positive-emotion films showed a couple enjoying a candle-lit dinner (low excitation) and a couple engaged in passionate lovemaking (high excitation). The negative-emotion films portrayed a surgeon performing an operation but without showing the patient (low excitation) and a killer brutally assaulting another person (high excitation). After viewing the movie, subjects heard some unfamiliar pop-rock music that had previously been judged as generally pleasant to listen to. Each subject was asked to rate the music for the overall enjoyment it produced on a 20-point scale (-10 was "worst ever heard" and $+10$ was "best ever heard"). As Figure 6-9 shows, the emotion aroused by the film affected judgments of the music. Subjects who saw either of the two low-excitation films had slightly less-than-neutral feelings about the pleasantness of the music. Subjects who had seen the high-excitation films, on the other hand, liked the music much more; their average ratings were well above the neutral point. In short, the emotion induced by the films had intensified their liking of the music. More important, the same result was found for both the so-called negative and positive films.

Not all experiments using mistaken attribution have supported the cognitive labeling theory, however. In one study, male subjects were told that they would receive a painful shock while participating in an experiment (Allen, Kenrick, Linder, & McCall, 1989). Some of the subjects encountered an attractive female accomplice

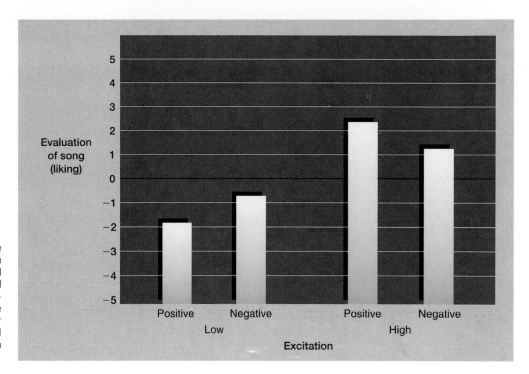

FIGURE 6-9 The effect of arousal on the experience of pleasure. This graph shows the mean evaluation of a recorded song by each of four groups that had viewed an arousing film just before hearing the song. The films differed in the type of emotion they aroused (positive or negative) and the intensity of arousal (low or high excitation). (Adapted from Cantor & Zillman, 1973.)

before being told about the shock; others met the accomplice after being told about the shock. Subjects in a control group—who had not been told they would receive a shock—also met the accomplice. Later, all the subjects were asked to rate their feelings of attraction toward the woman. The cognitive labeling theory would predict that the threat of shock would cause arousal, which would be mistakenly attributed to the attraction felt when meeting the woman. In other words, subjects would report greater attraction if they were *already* aroused by the threat of shock. If the shock threat occurred *after* the meeting with the woman, however, the theory would predict that attraction would not be affected; that is, the arousal caused by the shock threat could not be mistakenly attributed to feelings of attraction because the arousal would occur *after* the encounter with the woman. Contrary to the predictions of the theory, subjects who were told that they would receive a shock gave higher ratings of the woman's attractiveness than subjects in the control group *regardless* of whether the threat of shock occurred before or after the encounter with the accomplice.

Other experiments have found that a person does not necessarily have to experience autonomic arousal in order to feel emotion. In one study, male subjects were told that their heart rate was being measured by an old-fashioned cardiac machine that amplified heartbeats through a loudspeaker, and that the experimenter had to count the beats and then convert the number of beats into a heart-rate score (Valins, 1966). The purpose of this misinformation was to convince the subjects that they were listening to their own heartbeats over the loudspeaker system. In reality, the sounds coming from the loudspeaker were not heartbeats but a false "heart rate" controlled by the experimenter. The subjects were connected to the machine and shown slides of attractive nude women; the experimenter changed the false heart rate—it either increased or decreased noticeably—when certain slides were shown. After all the slides had been viewed, the subjects were asked to rate the women for attractiveness.

The results showed that the subjects preferred the slides that had been accompanied by a change in the "heart rate," regardless of the direction of the change. Moreover, the subjects' real heart rate (which had been recorded without their knowledge) was unrelated to their ratings of the slides. In short, the experiment demonstrated that when the subjects merely believed that their heart rate was changing they experienced emotion; actual changes in the autonomic nervous system were not necessary.

It would be tempting to conclude from such studies that the perception of arousal is all that is necessary for the experience of emotion. This would mean that ANS arousal is neither the principal source of emotion (as James and Lange suggested) nor a necessary one (as Schachter claimed). There are, however, a number of problems with this research. For example, if a person is tested in an experiment like the one just described but is instructed merely to "pay attention" to the sounds coming from the loudspeaker (and is not told that they are heartbeats), the same changes in emotion are observed (Parkinson & Manstead, 1981). Whether or not research ultimately confirms that cognitive inputs alone are necessary and sufficient to produce emotion, it is clear that they play an important role (Hirschman & Clark, 1983; Valins, 1970).

LEARNED EMOTIONS

Why does a person react with a particular emotion to a particular stimulus? For example, in the Schachter and Singer experiment, subjects who watched an accomplice of the experimenter behave in a slapstick manner and throw paper airplanes around reported feeling an elevation of mood. But there is nothing about flying paper airplanes that should necessarily trigger such an emotion. So why did the subjects react as they did?

One answer is that many emotional responses are *learned* responses. In other words, certain stimuli may trigger particular emotions—happiness, sadness, or anger, for example—because we have learned to associate those stimuli with emotional situations.

The concept of learning is discussed in detail in Chapter 12. To explain how emotional reactions can be learned, however, we need to discuss briefly a fundamental form of learning called *classical conditioning*, a process by which an otherwise innocuous stimulus can come to elicit a specific emotional reaction.

Consider a simple situation involving a laboratory rat. Imagine that the animal is placed in one compartment of a box consisting of two interconnecting compartments. A buzzer sounds, and a few seconds later the rat receives an electric shock through the metal bars that make up the floor of the box. The first time the two stimuli are delivered, the rat has no reaction to the buzzer but squeals and jumps when it feels the shock, eventually running to the other compartment where the shock is not being delivered. We can certainly infer from these behaviors that the shock is unpleasant. It is, in other words, an aversive stimulus—one the animal seeks to escape. We can also infer that it produces some type of negative emotion like fear. After repeated presentations of the two stimuli, the rat will react to the buzzer alone in the same way it reacted to the shock, running to the other side of the box as soon as the buzzer sounds. We can infer that the rat has learned to fear the buzzer because it tries to escape from the buzzer just as it had previously tried to escape from the shock. In other words, the buzzer has become an aversive stimulus because it was associated with the shock; the rat has *learned* an emotional reaction, namely *fear*.

Fear is a particularly dramatic example of a learned emotion, but as Figure 6-10 shows, other emotions can be conditioned in a similar manner. The upper-left box represents cases like the one just discussed, in which an innocuous stimulus becomes aversive, producing the emotion of *fear*, when it is paired with an aversive stimulus such as electric shock. The box on the upper right represents cases in which an innocuous stimulus is consistently associated with a pleasant one, producing the emotion of *anticipation* (Mowrer, 1960). As the box on the lower left suggests, a stimulus that always follows an aversive outcome (and therefore signals its absence) will eventually elicit the emotion of *relief*. And finally, as the box in the lower right suggests, *disappointment* is acquired whenever a stimulus consistently follows a pleasant outcome and thus signals the absence of that outcome.

There is every reason to believe that humans also learn emotions through classical conditioning. For example, we respond with positive feelings to images of some buildings (such as our home) but with negative feelings to images of others (such as

	Type of Outcome	
	Aversive (e.g., shock)	Pleasant (e.g., food)
Innocuous stimulus followed by presence of outcome	Fear	Anticipation
Innocuous stimulus followed by absence of outcome	Relief	Disappointment

FIGURE 6-10 Learned emotions. An otherwise innocuous stimulus that is consistently associated with a particular emotionally arousing outcome will itself come to elicit an emotional response. As this matrix shows, the type of learned emotion depends both on the type of outcome and on the relationship between the innocuous stimulus and the outcome.

prisons). While waiting to be picked up by a friend, we feel relief when we see a familiar car approaching but experience disappointment when the car turns out not to be the one we were expecting. In any culture there are countless stimuli that have emotional meaning simply because they have been *associated* with pleasant or unpleasant outcomes in the past.

We must be careful, however, not to assert that all emotions are learned through classical conditioning. In real life, situations are often more complex than those on which this simple model of learning is based. Moreover, there are undoubtedly many stimuli that elicit emotional reactions innately, without first having to be associated with pleasant or aversive outcomes (see Chapter 8 for further discussion). Nevertheless, research on basic learning processes confirms that emotions very often are triggered by stimuli that have taken on meaning through classical conditioning.

INTERIM SUMMARY

Researchers have attempted to determine whether the experience of emotion depends on cognitive inputs as well as physiological arousal. An experiment by Schachter and Singer showed that subjects' experience of emotion was influenced by the behavior of others when the subjects could not explain their feelings in terms of a physiological condition, such as the presence of a drug. According to Schachter's cognitive labeling theory, the experience of emotion requires both physiological arousal and an appropriate cognitive label. Although some specific predictions based on this theory have not been upheld by subsequent research, there is considerable evidence that cognitive inputs play a significant role in emotional experience. Other research has focused on the role of learning in emotion. In simple situations, the process of classical conditioning can result in the acquisition of the emotions of fear, anticipation, relief, and disappointment. In any given culture there are many stimuli that have emotional meaning because they have been associated with pleasant or unpleasant outcomes in the past.

THE DYNAMICS OF EMOTION

So far we have concentrated on single emotions, such as anger, fear, or euphoria. Life outside the laboratory is usually more complicated, however. Emotions are not static; they change over time, and they blend into one another, creating a complex mixture of feelings. Only recently have psychologists attempted to develop theories of emotion that take these dynamic qualities into consideration. In this section we discuss one theory of emotional dynamics: the **opponent-process theory of emotion.**

THE OPPONENT PROCESS THEORY

Following an emotional experience, a person or animal does not return to an emotionally neutral point when the emotion-provoking stimulus is removed, but rather overshoots the initial mood level and feels an emotion that may be described as the opposite of the one initially triggered. This is termed the *rebound effect.*

Consider an example. When a dog is given a mild shock, its heart rate accelerates markedly (Church, LoLordo, Overmier, Solomon, & Turner, 1966). We infer from this reaction that the animal experiences pain and fear. When the shock is terminated, however, the heart rate does not return to its initial level but declines past that level. In other words, the animal's heart rate shows a rebound effect. From this reaction, we infer that the dog feels something akin to relief or even elation during the rebound period.

An explanation of this phenomenon is provided by the opponent-process theory of emotion (Solomon, 1980; Solomon & Corbit, 1974). According to this theory, every emotion-provoking stimulus simultaneously triggers two kinds of reactions. The first, termed the *primary state,* is an unlearned, automatic reaction to the emotion-provoking stimulus. The primary state may be either aversive or pleasant. For example, if the stimulus is a shock, the primary state is fear or aversion. On the other hand, if the stimulus is pleasurable, the primary state is euphoria or pleasure. The primary state reaches its maximum intensity very quickly and declines almost immediately when the stimulus ceases.

A second process is also triggered by the emotion-producing stimulus. It is termed the *opponent process.* This process induces an emotional state—the opponent state—that is the opposite of the primary state. If the automatic or primary reaction to a stimulus is fear and aversion, the opponent state would be pleasure or euphoria. Conversely, if the primary state is pleasure, the opponent process would generate a feeling of fear or aversion. Unlike the primary process, the opponent process has a rather

Bungee cord jumpers experience fear and terror at first and an exhilarating rush of euphoria later.

slow onset and declines slowly. Initially, when the emotion-provoking stimulus is relatively new to the subject, the opponent state is less intense than the primary state. After repeated encounters with the emotion-provoking stimulus, however, the opponent process increases in strength.

According to the opponent-process theory, the emotion that is actually *experienced* by the subject is the algebraic summation of the primary and opponent states. The opponent process "cancels out" the primary process, at least to some degree. This is illustrated in Figure 6-11. Note that in part *a* of the figure the primary state is pleasure or joy, whereas in part *b* it is fear or aversion. The shaded area is the felt emotion, that is, the summation of the primary and opponent processes. When the stimulus is first presented, the primary state predominates because it reaches its maximum strength more quickly. As time passes and the opponent state approaches its maximum strength, the intensity of the felt emotion subsides because the net effect (primary plus opponent process) is gradually reduced.

If the stimulus is suddenly removed, the primary state returns to its zero point rather quickly but the opponent state subsides slowly. Therefore, if the primary state is absent while the opponent state is still active, the felt emotion (the algebraic summation of the two states) is predominantly the opponent state. This is shown as a rebound in Figure 6-11.

FIGURE 6-11 Emotion as an opponent process. In part (*a*) the primary emotion is pleasure and the rebound emotion is aversion. In part (*b*) the primary emotion is aversion and the rebound emotion is pleasure. (Adapted from Solomon & Corbit, 1974.)

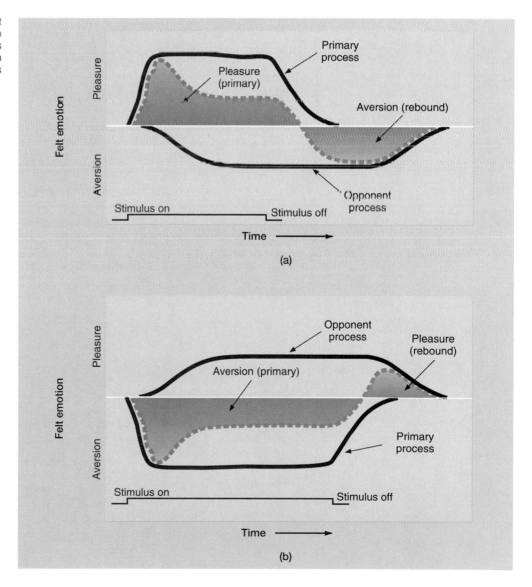

163

EXAMPLES OF OPPONENT PROCESSES

The opponent-process theory has been applied to a number of interesting situations, including the experiences of parachutists, drug addicts, and blood donors (Epstein, 1967; Koob, Stinus, LeMoal, & Bloom, 1989; Solomon, 1977; Piliavin, Callero, & Evans, 1982). Consider the plight of novice parachutists (Epstein, 1967). The intensity of their fear increases as the moment of the first jump draws closer. This is a result of the primary process. Once the jump has been completed, however, the primary process is suddenly reduced to zero, and because the opponent process continues for a while afterward, the parachutists experience a rebound effect. On the first few jumps, the rebound is not very intense; photographs of facial expressions and data from mood questionnaires suggest that the parachutist is more stunned than elated. After repeated jumps, however, the amount of fear experienced before a jump is quite low (because the opponent state is more intense), but the mood experienced after the jump is one of extreme euphoria.

Now consider another example, in which the initial reaction is one of pleasure (Solomon, 1977). A person using heroin for the first time experiences a "rush" of euphoria; this is the primary state. When the effects of the drug wear off, however, the user experiences the rebound. The emotion can be one of fear and despair and is usually accompanied by physiological reactions such as nausea, sweating, and anxiety.

INTERIM SUMMARY

Recently, psychologists have attempted to develop theories of emotion that take into account the fact that emotions change over time and may blend into one another. The opponent process theory of emotion holds that every emotion-provoking stimulus simultaneously triggers two kinds of reactions: a primary state (the reflexive reaction to the stimulus) and an opponent state (the opposite of the primary state). The resulting emotion is the algebraic summation of the primary and opponent states. Because the primary process is initially stronger and reaches its maximum strength more quickly, it predominates at the moment that the stimulus is first presented. But because the opponent process subsides more slowly than the primary process, it predominates after the stimulus is removed. The balance between the primary and opponent states changes with repeated presentations of the stimulus.

SUMMARY

1. A central feature of most emotions is the inner psychological state of the individual that are associated with the emotion—the feelings generated by the emotional situation. The study of emotions requires making inferences about these unobservable internal states based on observable behavior.

2. Emotional expression is the visible product of an inner emotional feeling. It is believed to have adaptive survival value because of the information it conveys to other animals.

3. Cross-cultural research and research on children suggest that facial expressions accompanying various emotions are innate and universal but cultural rules affect when and how we allow ourselves to express our emotions.

4. Research on the relationship between facial expressions and physiological arousal indicates that people who respond to emotional stimuli with strong facial expressions typically have less intense physiological reactions than people who are not as expressive.

5. Evidence suggests that there are differences between men and women in emotional expressiveness, but these differences may have a cultural basis.

6. The *autonomic nervous system,* or *ANS,* is composed of two major parts, the *sympathetic* and *parasympathetic nervous systems* (*SNS* and *PNS*). The role of the ANS in general is to regulate the vital functions of the body. The principal function of the PNS is the conservation of energy or recovery following an expenditure of energy. The principal function of the SNS is to regulate the expenditure of energy.

7. According to the *James–Lange theory of emotion,* the perception of autonomic arousal is the feeling of emotion; we feel emotion only after we behave emotionally. Emotional behavior is triggered automatically, but emotional experience, or feeling, occurs because the organism perceives the ANS reaction.

8. In contrast to the focus on the role of the ANS in the James–Lange theory, *Cannon's thalamic theory* and more recent theories of emotion focus on the role of various brain structures in emotion. In particular, areas in or near the *limbic system,* such as the *amygdala, septum, hippocampus,* and *hypothalamus* have been shown to control, among other emotions, rage, docility, aversion, and pleasure. Neurochemicals, such as *atropine* and *norepinephrine,* also affect emotions primarily by activating relevant areas of the brain.

9. According to Schachter and Singer's *cognitive labeling theory,* emotional feeling depends on the way we interpret physiological arousal and the environmental situation in which we experience it. When we lack a good explanation for feeling physiologically aroused, we will attribute the state to an emotion that seems appropriate to the context.

10. Emotions can be learned through *classical conditioning.* Specifically, when innocuous signals are associated with strong emotion-provoking stimuli, then the signals too come to elicit an emotion. The kind of emotion that gets learned (*anticipation, fear, disappointment,* and *relief*) depends on the relationship between the innocuous signal and its outcome.

11. When an emotion-producing stimulus stops, one often feels a *rebound effect,* that is, an emotion opposite in quality to the original feeling. According to the *opponent-process theory* of emotion, the rebound is attributable to the existence of an opponent process that persists after the primary emotional process has diminished. The emotional experience actually felt at any given point in time is a summation of these two processes.

FOCUS QUESTIONS

1. In what sense can emotional expressions be both universal and also dependent on culture?

2. Describe the way in which the parasympathetic and sympathetic nervous systems interact during an emotional situation.

3. Compare and contrast the James–Lange theory and Cannon's thalamic theory of emotion.

4. Discuss the evidence suggesting that various structures in the limbic lobe are critical for emotion.

5. Outline the cognitive labeling theory of emotion and the evidence that supports it.

6. Describe the opponent-process mechanisms that contribute to emotional dynamics and explain how such a theory accounts for an emotional rebound experience.

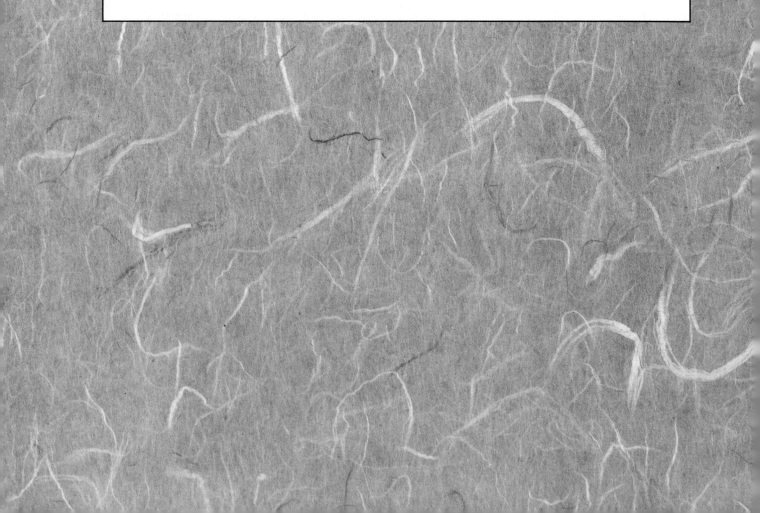

CHAPTER 7

STATES OF CONSCIOUSNESS

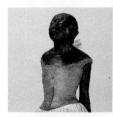 In some ways, the problem of consciousness is the central problem of psychology because it is at the heart of the mind–body controversy. As you will recall, Descartes, in addressing that controversy, asserted that mind and body are separate entities and that mind lacks form and substance. Perhaps the best evidence supporting the existence of mind is the vivid awareness we all have of our own inner, mental experience and our awareness of stimuli coming from the external world. This awareness—both of our inner selves and of the world around us—is what we usually think of as **consciousness.**

If consciousness is defined as self-awareness, however, how can we study it? Our most direct access to self-awareness is through introspection, but as noted in Chapter 2 psychologists since Watson have argued that the study of essentially private inner states is highly problematic. The solution has been to study the way various states of consciousness manifest themselves in overt behavior.

One behavioral indicator of consciousness is *level of arousal,* which refers to the degree to which a person is aware of the world. Arousal is part of what is meant by the term consciousness. For example, we say that a person who is "out cold" as a result of a head injury, or who is asleep, has "lost consciousness." Conversely, we say that a person who is alert and vigilant is "conscious of" the world. Arousal varies along a continuum ranging from coma through deep sleep, light sleep, relaxed wakefulness, and alertness to extreme agitation. We can study consciousness in terms of this continuum. But when we do so, we typically study unusually low or high levels of arousal because they represent altered states of consciousness that are markedly different from the normal waking state. Sleep, for example, is interesting because it involves an unusually low level of arousal.

Overt behavior can also indicate the *quality* of consciousness as, for example, when a person's behavior is disturbed by perceptual distortions, dreams, or hallucinations. Altered states of consciousness, in which a person's awareness of both inner experience and the external world is dramatically different from what is experienced normally, may also occur when the person is influenced by various drugs or has been hypnotized. Here again, these states are interesting to psychologists precisely because they are qualitatively different from the normal waking state.

The following sections discuss states of consciousness as they are revealed in behavior. In some instances, such as sleep, we focus on an altered level of arousal. In others, such as hypnotic or drug-induced states, we concentrate on a qualitatively different kind of experience. In all cases, however, we relate states of consciousness to brain states; that is, we try to describe both the level of awareness (an aspect of mind) and the underlying physiology (a characteristic of the body) involved. (Certain topics related to normal waking states of consciousness are covered in other chapters, for example, attention and vigilance in Chapter 13, and the so-called unconscious mind in Chapter 21.)

SLEEP

What single behavior do you perform for about one-third of your life? The answer, of course, is **sleep.** On the average, a 70-year-old person has spent nearly 27 years asleep and between 6 and 7 of those years dreaming. With sleep occupying so much of our time, it is not surprising that psychologists have devoted a great deal of study to this subject (Mayes, 1983; Mendelson, 1987).

Even after decades of research, the function of sleep remains a mystery. From an

A giant sloth may sleep for up to 20 hours per day.

evolutionary point of view, it is hard to see how such a behavior survived (Meddis, 1983; Tobler, 1984). After all, an organism cannot procreate while sleeping; it cannot feed or engage in other behaviors related to survival; and unless it finds a secure place in which to sleep, it is vulnerable to predators while in such a state of inattention. As one scientist put it, "How could natural selection with its irrevocable logic have 'permitted' the animal kingdom to pay the price of sleep for no good reason? In fact, the behavior of sleep is so apparently maladaptive that one can only wonder why some other condition did not evolve to satisfy whatever need it is that sleep satisfies" (Rechtschaffen, 1971, p. 88).

Despite the apparent disadvantages of sleeping, most animals (at least mammals and birds) spend some time asleep, although the amount of time spent sleeping can vary greatly. Horses and deer spend about 2 hours per day asleep; sheep, goats, and cows about 3 hours; humans and rabbits an average of about 7 hours; chimpanzees, baboons, and foxes about 9 hours; gorillas and raccoons about 12 hours; mice, rats, and wolves 13 hours; giant armadillos 18 hours; and, topping the list, the giant sloth sleeps as much as 20 hours a day (Allison & Cicchetti, 1976).

FUNCTIONS OF SLEEP

Because many species obviously spend much of their time asleep, it therefore appears that sleeping may indeed serve a vital function (Drucker-Colin, Shkurovich, & Sterman, 1979; Horne, 1983; Webb, 1983). One of the earliest ideas was that sleep helps restore an animal's physiological functions (Adam, 1980). Whatever is used up or damaged during wakefulness is replaced or restored during sleep. Indeed, we often say that we feel refreshed after sleeping.

In support of this theory, some investigators have shown that the release of human growth hormone is increased during sleep and that there is a higher rate of protein synthesis, allowing for tissue repair (Drucker-Colin, 1979). In fact, as many as 18 substances in the body may be restored during sleep. In addition, the particular form of brain activity that takes place during sleep may facilitate protein synthesis, increase blood flow and temperature, or even allow for the consolidation of memory traces and information.

According to another theory, sleep may be an instinct, an unlearned behavioral tendency that has survived throughout evolutionary history because it performs functions related to energy conservation and safety (Meddis, 1977; Webb, 1975). This behavioral theory suggests that sleep has survival value because it allows animals to conserve energy and, if they sleep in a relatively safe place, to be free from predators. In other words, the brain periodically causes a state of drowsiness that triggers sleep because in the long run such behavior helps the animal survive.

DEFINITION OF SLEEP

How do we know when an animal is asleep? The precise definition of sleep has two parts: behavioral and electrophysiological. Behaviorally, a sleeping animal assumes typical body postures, shows physical quietness and lack of movement, and displays a reduced sensitivity to external stimuli. Many animals can be said to sleep in the behavioral sense.

The second part of the definition of sleep consists of electrophysiological data and pertains especially to humans. These data are obtained from an **electroencephalogram (EEG),** a recording from the surface of the skull of the electrical signals that originate in the brain tissue below. Because the electrical activity recorded in this way rises and falls, the recordings are called brain waves. Like all waves, they can be characterized in terms of two features: amplitude (measured from the peak of the wave to the trough) and wavelength or frequency (number of peaks or spikes per second). Sleep, then, may be defined in terms of its characteristic EEG patterns. Let us consider this point in greater detail.

STAGES OF SLEEP

During wakefulness, the brain waves are characterized by their low amplitude and high frequency—about 8–14 hertz, or cycles per second. (See Figure 7-1.) EEG waves of this kind are called **alpha waves.** In addition, electrophysiological measurements of the muscles during sleep (called **electromyograms,** or **EMGs**) indicate a high level of muscle tone.

During sleep itself, however, five different EEG patterns, or stages, can be identified. These are illustrated in Figure 7-1. Stage 1 is characterized by low-amplitude, mixed-frequency EEG patterns. The frequencies include both **beta waves** (15–35 hertz) and **theta waves** (4–7 hertz). There is also a reduction in muscle tone and the eyes typically move slowly back and forth under the eyelids.

FIGURE 7-1 Characteristic EEG patterns of the waking state, drowsiness, and the five stages of sleep.

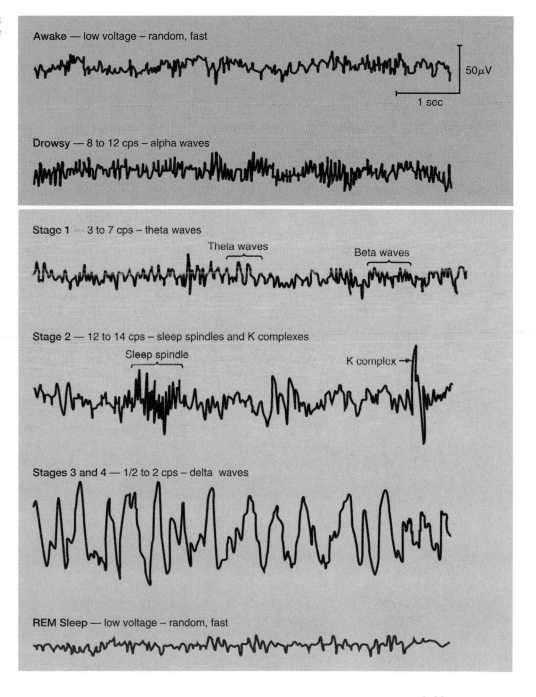

Photographs and accompanying EEG records of a subject in a sleep study.

In stage 2 a somewhat different pattern is observed. There are theta waves (low amplitude, low to high frequency) as there are in stage 1, but in addition there are other patterns known as spindles and K-complexes. **Spindles** are bursts of high-frequency (12–14 hertz) EEG patterns that last for about 0.5 second. A **K-complex,** on the other hand, is a very-high-amplitude, sharp, negative-going wave followed immediately by a sharp, positive-going wave.

Stages 3 and 4 are the deepest levels of sleep and are characterized by a high-amplitude, low-frequency wave form. These slow **delta waves** range from about 0.5 to 3 hertz. During stage 3, delta waves occur about 20–50% of the time. A similar pattern is observed in stage 4, except that delta waves occur more than 50% of the time.

REM Sleep

The most interesting and perhaps most important stage of sleep is the fifth, or **rapid eye movement (REM),** stage (Aserinsky & Kleitman, 1953). In this stage a person is quiet, has very low muscle tone, and is unresponsive to external stimuli. The EEG pattern, however, is the same as that shown during wakefulness—namely, low amplitude and high frequency (15–20 hertz). Thus, in terms of the two-part definition of sleep, REM sleep is paradoxical: While in it a person is behaviorally asleep yet, according to the EEG pattern, awake (Berger, 1961).

REM sleep takes its name from characteristic bursts of rapid eye movement during which the eyeball moves rapidly back and forth underneath the eyelid. REM sleep also involves a decrease in muscle tone, variations in heart rate, penile erection in males, and release of gastric acid. Perhaps the most interesting aspect of REM sleep is that it is associated with dreaming. In fact, about three-fourths of experimental subjects who are awakened during REM sleep report that they were awakened from a dream; others report feeling as if they have just been dreaming, although they cannot remember the details of the dream. In contrast, during non-REM sleep only about 9% of subjects who are awakened report that they were dreaming.

170

CHARACTERISTICS OF SLEEP

The five stages of sleep (stages 1–4 plus REM sleep) constitute a **sleep cycle.** This cycle extends over a period of about 90 minutes and is reenacted from four to six times each night. With each successive cycle, however, the proportion of stage 3 and 4 sleep is reduced and the proportion of REM sleep increases (Feinberg, 1974). This pattern is illustrated in Figure 7-2.

Age Effects

The amount of sleep one needs is related to one's age. As shown in Figure 7-3, newborns sleep about 16 hours a day, adults average about 8 hours a day, and elderly people sleep only a few hours a day (Feinberg & Carlson, 1968; Webb, 1982). In addition, the percentage of a single sleep cycle occupied by REM sleep is highest for infants and decreases with age.

Circadian Rhythm

Another factor that influences sleep is the daily cycle, or **circadian rhythm.** Humans and many other animals have an internal neurological clock that regulates certain functions so that they occur about once a day. (This is reflected in the term *circadian,* which is derived from Latin words meaning "about a day.") The sleep–waking cycle is an example of a circadian rhythm (Aschoff, 1965). Our internal clock is "set" by the rhythm of our normal daily routine. This causes us to be drowsy at about the same time each day and also regulates the length of time we sleep. Changes in routine allow us to see how profoundly we are affected by the circadian rhythm. For example, although the time it takes to fall asleep is related to the duration of wakefulness preceding the sleep, the time of day is actually more critical. Most people find it easier to fall asleep at midnight than at 4.00 in the afternoon even when the duration of wakefulness prior to the sleep is the same (Webb & Agnew, 1975). And people who experience jet lag or who switch from one work shift to another can attest to the disruptive effects of a change in routine.

SLEEP DEPRIVATION

For most animals, sleep is essential. In one study, rats that were deprived of sleep for 33 or more days died (Rechtschaffen, Gilliland, Bergmann, & Winter, 1983). In humans, **total sleep deprivation** for more than 100 hours can result in a number of changes, including episodes of serious thought disturbance, hallucinations, and irri-

FIGURE 7-2 Time spent in the various sleep stages. The dashed vertical lines indicate the boundaries of each cycle; the red bars show periods of REM. (Adapted from Feinberg, 1974.)

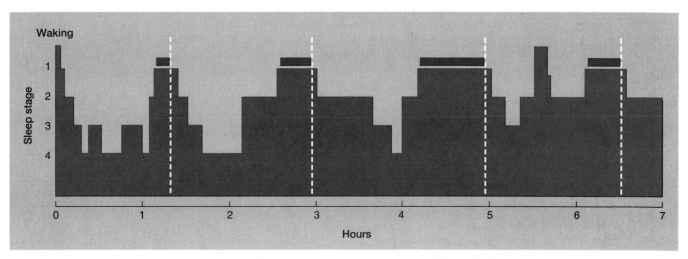

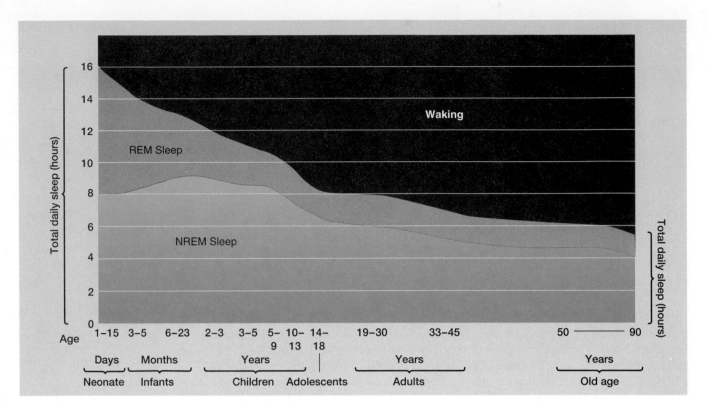

FIGURE 7-3 How sleep patterns change with age. (Adapted from Feinberg & Carlson, 1968.)

tability (Kales et al., 1970). Indeed, sleep deprivation has been used repeatedly as a means of torture, for example with prisoners of war. These effects are not permanent, however; they disappear when the subject is allowed to sleep.

Shorter periods of total sleep deprivation produce other, less severe changes. Experimental subjects who are deprived of sleep for a few days may experience irritability, feelings of persecution, distortions in perception and orientation, and difficulty concentrating on tasks (Morris & Singer, 1961). Again, if the subject is allowed to sleep, these effects disappear.

Selective Sleep Deprivation

Many experiments have selectively deprived subjects of a particular stage of sleep, typically REM sleep (Ellman, Spielman, Luck, Steiner, & Halperin, 1978). Subjects who experience selective sleep deprivation tend afterward to rebound; that is, they enter REM sleep more frequently and for longer periods than normal (Dement, 1960). This effect has also been observed in relation to stage-4 sleep (Agnew, Webb, & Williams, 1964).

Originally it was believed that **REM deprivation** is harmful, perhaps permanently (Dement, 1964). This view has not been supported by the findings of recent research using normal (Sampson, 1966), schizophrenic (Vogel & Traub, 1968), or depressed subjects (van den Hoofdakker & Beersma, 1984). In fact, REM deprivation has been shown to have beneficial effects for depressed people (see also Smith & Wong, 1991).

BIOLOGICAL FOUNDATIONS OF SLEEP

Many studies have focused on the biological foundations of sleep—both the neurological systems involved and the biochemistry of those systems (Jouvet, 1967; Siegel, 1983; Wauquier, Gaillard, Monti, & Radulovacki, 1985). Here we will review the major systems involved in sleep.

It has long been known that the brain stem, particularly the **reticular activating system,** contains structures that are important for arousal and sleep (Moruzzi & Magoun, 1949). A schematic view of the relevant areas is shown in Figure 7-4.

172

Stimulation of these structures arouses sleeping animals; damage to these areas causes them to enter a coma.

Two areas located near the reticular activating system seem to play a central role in sleep. The **raphe system,** often called the sleep center, controls non-REM sleep. When it is stimulated, non-REM sleep is induced; if it is damaged, the subject suffers insomnia (Jouvet, 1974). It appears that the secretion by this area of serotonin, a neurotransmitter, is extremely important: When serotonin secretion is increased, the duration of slow wave, or non-REM, sleep increases, whereas when serotonin secretion is inhibited by special chemicals, insomnia results (Rechtschaffen, Lovell, & Freedman, 1973).

The other important center in the brain stem is the **locus ceruleus,** the arousal center. Neurons in this area control REM sleep and inhibit muscle tone; the neurotransmitter involved is norepinephrine. When the locus ceruleus is stimulated, greater cortical excitation (low-amplitude–high-frequency alpha waves) results. When it is damaged, or when the level of norepinephrine is decreased, the amount of REM sleep decreases (the slower waves typical of stages 3 and 4 predominate) and the subject sleeps excessively (Hobson, 1988).

SLEEP DISORDERS

Judging from the widespread use of sleeping pills, many people have trouble getting a good night's sleep (Mendelson, Gillin, & Wyatt, 1977). Without adequate sleep, people often perform their tasks poorly or simply feel bad. In extreme situations, as noted earlier, they may suffer a variety of symptoms, including irritability and even hallucinations.

Insomnia

When people say they have **insomnia,** they are reporting a subjective judgment or belief that they are not getting enough sleep. In reality, though, there are vast discrepancies between the amount of time people believe they sleep and the amount of time they actually do sleep. Poor sleepers often exaggerate the time it takes them to fall asleep and underestimate the length of time they are asleep (Rechtschaffen & Monroe, 1969). We should add, however, that compared to normal sleepers, insomniacs' sleep patterns are characterized by less REM and more stage-2 sleep, more

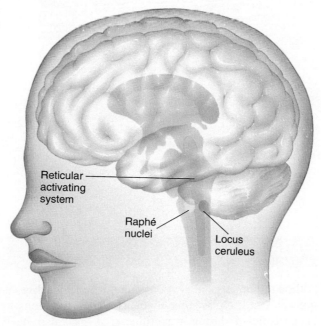

FIGURE 7 4 The reticular activating system of the brain and the two major areas that affect sleep.

Reticular activating system

Raphé nuclei

Locus ceruleus

body movements during sleep, and a greater number of shifts from one stage of sleep to another. Their belief that they have not slept well could therefore be based on these features of their sleep patterns.

Insomnia has many causes. Sometimes insomniacs are anxious, depressed, or even sexually aroused. Other people experience insomnia when there is excessive noise in their surroundings, when they are sleeping in an uncomfortable bed, or when they have undergone a significant change in their normal activity-and-rest cycle (for example, traveling to a different time zone). Insomnia can also be caused by over-sleeping or by a variety of drugs, including stimulants such as caffeine and sedatives such as alcohol.

One of the most disturbing causes of insomnia is **sleep apnea,** a failure to breathe for about 10 seconds or longer during sleep. This condition is thought to reflect a disorder in the neurological mechanisms that control the diaphragm (Mendelson, Gillin, & Wyatt, 1977). Because sleep apnea occurs only at night, it seriously interferes with sleep, causing the sufferer to feel tired and to sleep during the day.

Narcolepsy

A disorder that is the opposite of insomnia is **narcolepsy,** which is characterized by "sleep attacks" that last about 15 minutes and may occur at any time during the waking hours. In addition to experiencing sleep attacks, a person suffering from narcolepsy may exhibit one or more of the following symptoms: a sudden loss of all muscle tone, called cataplexy, which causes a person to nod, buckle at the knees, or collapse entirely; brief paralysis of the muscles, called sleep paralysis, which occurs upon awakening and is often accompanied by feelings of anxiety; or hallucinations, either just before the onset of sleep or just after awakening. Figure 7-5 shows the proportions of a sample of 241 narcoleptic individuals who suffered from one or more of these symptoms (Mendelson, Gillan, & Wyatt, 1977).

The cause of narcolepsy is unknown, although some psychologists have linked it to a disorder in the mechanisms controlling REM sleep. One study of 49 narcoleptic patients found that 90% entered REM sleep during their sleep attacks (Wilson, Raynal, Guillerminault, Zarcone, & Dement, 1973).

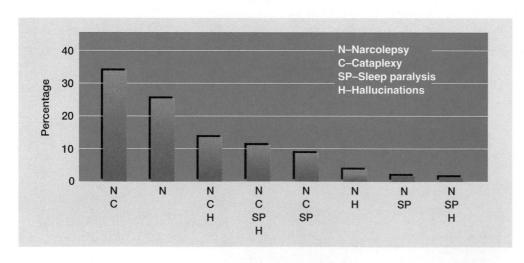

FIGURE 7-5 Percentage of 241 patients with narcolepsy who displayed one or more associated disorders. As the figure shows, only about 25% suffered from narcolepsy alone. (Adapted from Mendelson, Gillan, & Wyatt, 1977.)

INTERIM SUMMARY

Although humans spend about one-third of their lives asleep, the function of sleep is not known. There is some evidence that it functions to restore substances that have been depleted during wakefulness; it has also been theorized that sleep is an unlearned behavioral tendency that allows animals to conserve energy and retreat from predators. Sleep can be defined both behaviorally and electrophysiologically. The behavioral characteristics of sleep include physical quietness and reduced sensitivity to stimuli. The electrophysiological characteristics of sleep are measured by means of an electroencephalogram. Five stages of sleep have been identified on the basis of EEG patterns, of which the most important is REM sleep, during which subjects show bursts of rapid eye movements and other physical changes. The five stages of sleep constitute a sleep cycle that extends for a period of about 90 minutes. The sleep–waking cycle is an example of a circadian rhythm; disturbances of this cycle through either total or selective sleep deprivation can have a variety of effects ranging from irritability to psychoticlike symptoms. The structures that control arousal and sleep are located in the brain stem and include the reticular activating system, the raphe system, and the locus ceruleus. The primary sleep disorders are insomnia (a subjective belief that one is not getting enough sleep) and narcolepsy, a condition characterized by "sleep attacks" or sudden bouts of sleep that last about 15 minutes and may occur at any time.

DREAMING

Dreaming is one of our most exotic and elusive behaviors. It has charmed and puzzled poets, soothsayers, and scientists for many centuries. It is fair to say that kingdoms have been won and lost because of prophecies thought to be contained in the dreams of warriors. Throughout the history of literature, dreams have been a magical device, a dramatic technique for revealing character.

Humans dream much of the time (Foulkes, 1985; Hobson, 1988; Hunt, 1989; Robins, 1988); as noted earlier, dreaming is closely associated with REM sleep. Figure 7-6 shows that between 22 and 28% of sleep is REM sleep; the actual duration of REM episodes increases from about 5 minutes to as much as 45 minutes of the 90-minute cycle. In 80% of instances in which subjects are awakened during a REM episode, the subject reports having just been dreaming (Dement, 1965), although dreaming can occur during non-REM sleep as well (Foulkes & Vogel, 1965). Narrations of dreams usually include reasonably accurate descriptions of real situations. Many dreams (38%) have familiar settings, but 59% have exotic settings. Most dreams include talking and involve the dreamer in the action along with other people. Sensations other than vision and audition are rarely reported. It has been argued that 61% of dreams are in color, but recall of the color fades rapidly after awakening. Dreams involving negative emotions such as depression or anger are twice as common as those involving pleasant emotions such as friendliness. Violence and aggression are reported only about 4% of the time, and bizarre images, though more easily remembered, are not very common. In fact, most dreams are rather mundane.

FIGURE 7-6 Dream episodes (shaded areas) as a function of hours asleep. Numbers refer to the length of the dream episode in minutes. (Adapted from Jones, 1970.)

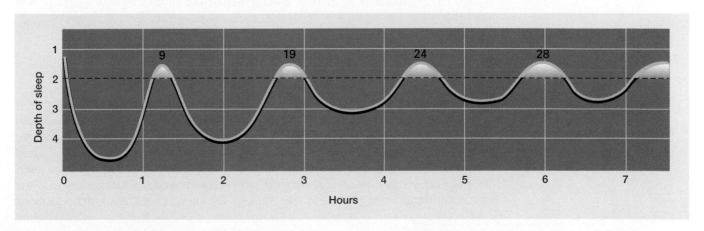

Dreams are usually characterized by a sense of immediacy and reality; that is, normally we are not aware that we are dreaming. But this is not always the case. Recent research has shown that people may engage in so-called **lucid dreaming** (Gackenbach & LaBerge, 1988; LaBerge, 1985), in which the dreamer is aware that he or she is dreaming. Referring to one of his own dreams, one researcher commented, "Fantastic as it may sound, I was in full possession of my waking faculties while dreaming and soundly asleep: I could think as clearly as ever, freely remember details of my waking life, and act deliberately upon conscious reflection. Yet none of this diminished the vividness of my dream. Paradox or no, I was awake in my dream!" (LaBerge, 1985, p. 1).

Not all people engage in lucid dreaming, and for those who do such experiences are not very frequent. It appears, however, that people can be trained to engage in lucid dreaming (Malamud, 1988; Price & Cohen, 1988). And although the content of lucid dreams is similar to that of normal dreams, lucid dreams are characterized by greater auditory activity and conscious reflection about the dream itself (Gackenbach, 1988).

RECALL OF DREAMS

Dreams are difficult to study because they are difficult to recall (Cohen, 1974; Goodenough, 1978). Some investigators believe that there may be important differences between the dreams reported in the laboratory and those recorded in diaries at home (Cartwright & Kaszniak, 1978). The laboratory setting is certainly a significant factor, because the subject must sleep in a strange environment and be awakened periodically. As evidence that the laboratory setting may influence the content of dreams, one study found that 30% of 219 reported dreams made some reference to the laboratory (Domhoff & Kamiya, 1964). Other estimates run as high as 68% (Whitman, Pierce, Maas, & Baldridge, 1962).

It is clear that people differ in the degree to which they recall dreams. In particular, the ability to recall dreams is correlated to a person's overall capacity for visual memory. In one experiment, subjects were given pictures showing different items and asked to recall as many of the items as possible (Cory, Ormiston, Simmel, & Dainoff, 1975). Subjects who could recall the items more accurately tended to be better able to recall dreams.

Despite these differences, most people believe that dreams are difficult to recall. But if (as statistical samples seem to indicate) we spend so much time dreaming, why is our ability to recall dreams so poor?

One possible explanation is the interference we experience upon awakening. Events that occur upon awakening may prevent us from storing our dreams in memory. There is some fairly convincing evidence that this is indeed what happens. For example, if subjects are asked upon awakening to call the weather service and write down the temperature for the previous day, and then to fill out their dream diary, their ability to recall dreams is reduced from about 63% to about 33% (Cohen & Wolfe, 1973). Similarly, if there is a delay before the subject reports a dream, it is more likely that the dream will be forgotten (Goodenough, 1978).

THE CONTENT OF DREAMS

If dreams have any meaning relative to the external environment, it would seem that one could influence their content by changing the external environment. A number of studies have taken this approach (Arkin & Antrobus, 1978). In one experiment, subjects were shown an explicit depiction of childbirth in which surgeons performed emergency measures to deliver the infant, such as using forceps to pull the child from the uterus. The subjects then slept, and upon awakening they reported their dreams. One subject dreamed about girls who were dressed (like surgeons) in white gowns and long white gloves. In later dreams the subject was flying in an airplane

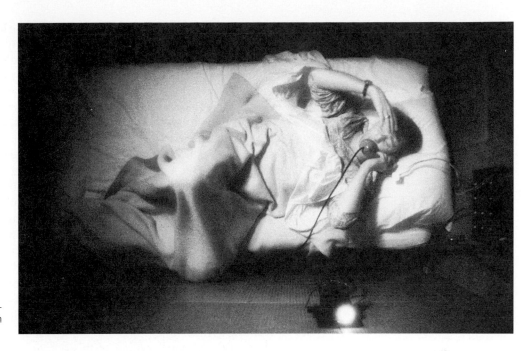

A subject involved in a dream experiment recounts his dream immediately on awakening.

with wires protruding from the door; people were pulling at the wires in much the same way that the surgeon pulled at the baby (Witkin & Lewis, 1965).

Other experiments, however, have had less clear-cut results. In one study, subjects were shown either a violent film or a travelogue before sleeping. The effect of the films on dream content was insignificant, although the violent film was associated with longer REM periods (Foulkes & Rechtschaffen, 1964).

Effects of External Stimuli During REM Sleep

A number of experiments have attempted to manipulate dream content by stimulating the subject during REM sleep. In one such experiment, subjects were deprived of water for 24 hours and given a salty meal before they slept (Bokert, 1968). Immediately prior to their being awakened from REM sleep, the tape-recorded message "A cool delicious drink of water" was played in their presence. The subjects reported an average of 2.11 thirst images per dream, compared to 0.53 per dream for control subjects who were not thirsty and had not heard the message. Subjects who were thirsty but had not heard the message had an intermediate score. It appears, therefore, that stimuli occurring during REM sleep can interact with conditions experienced prior to sleeping. This finding suggests that the content of dreams may be affected, at least in part, by waking experience.

FUNCTIONS OF DREAMING

Clearly, dreaming is an altered state of consciousness, one that is quite different from waking thought. Yet dreams serve no obvious function and we have very little idea why they occur. A number of attempts have been made to identify the function of dreaming; they include Freud's theory and the cognitive model.

Freud's Theory of Dreaming

By far the most influential, yet controversial, theory of dreaming was proposed by Sigmund Freud (1952/1900). For Freud, dreams are an attempt at wish fulfillment, at immediate gratification. In waking, inner wishes, arising from a person's innate sexual or aggressive desires, cannot often be gratified because of social restrictions on behavior. Dreams, however, may represent a compromise between these desires and society's restrictions on their expression. When one is sleeping, one's conscious control over one's thoughts is relaxed and sexual or aggressive images, whose expression would normally be precluded, are released in a dream.

How is this accomplished? Freud believed that these forbidden images were represented symbolically; that is, the elements of a dream are symbols of something else. More specifically, the **manifest content** of the dream, the material reported upon awakening, is symbolic of the dream's **latent content,** the underlying psychological conflict being worked out in the dream.

Freud first applied this theory to one of his own dreams. On the night of July 23, 1895, he dreamed about a young woman named Irma, a close friend whom he had treated for hysteria. The treatment had been discontinued by mutual agreement when a disagreement arose between Freud and the patient. A colleague and friend of Freud named Otto had recently seen Irma and reported that she seemed "better, but not well" (Freud, 1952/1900, p. 182). Freud had taken this as a criticism of his treatment.

In Freud's dream, Irma attended a reception given by the Freuds and complained about pains in her throat, stomach, and abdomen, saying she was "choked by them." A doctor in Freud's dream confirmed the existence of the infection in Irma's throat, agreeing with her that the infection had originated when Otto gave her an injection with an unclean syringe.

According to Freud, the meaning of this dream had to do with wish fulfillment. Freud wished not to be responsible for Irma's pain. He felt guilty because of the implied rebuke in Otto's description of her condition, and he therefore dreamed that Irma's problems had been caused by an infection and not by anything Freud had or had not done. His dream was an attempt to shift the responsibility to Otto and, at the same time, to obtain a sort of revenge for Otto's implied criticism.

Freud's theory of dream interpretation has been strongly criticized. For example, manifest content is not always symbolic. Although *some* dreams seem to include symbolism rather than, say, uncensored sexual images, not all dreams do; blatantly sexual images are frequently contained in a dream. Similarly, dreams do not always involve wish fulfillment, at least not in any obvious way. Freud has even been criticized for not applying his own theory in interpreting the dream about Irma (Jones, 1970; Rycroft, 1979). Although Freud interpreted this dream as involving wish fulfillment, he made no mention of any latent sexual content (in spite of the suggestive image of the syringe), nor did he claim any symbolic significance for the characters in the dream, whom he interpreted as themselves, not as substitutes for someone else.

The Cognitive Model

If the function of dreams is not to express repressed wishes, as Freud believed, then what is their function? Many psychologists have adopted a **cognitive model** according to which "dreams are thoughts" and "dreaming is thinking" (Foulkes, 1978, p. 3; Foulkes, 1982; see also Antrobus, 1991). This model is based on the premise that "the peculiarities of dreaming can be explained in terms of some kind of reorganization of many of those same mental processes and systems that we employ in waking perception and thought" (Foulkes, 1985, p. 13). In other words, the human mind is an information-processing and knowledge-storing system. It produces thoughts, memories, and mental images during waking hours, and it produces dreams during sleep. The processes by which it does so are the same in all cases. And just as we cannot always trace a waking image to its origin, we cannot always trace a dream image to an actual event.

This approach emphasizes the fact that dreams are very much like waking images. For example, think of your best friend. Notice that the image you conjure up is a generalized image, not a picture of your friend in a particular context, performing a particular task. You can, of course, force yourself to focus on the context, but the context is not a natural or necessary part of your image of your friend. Dreams are similar to such images: They are generalized images, detached from context.

In the cognitive model, the mind has a number of organizing principles that become manifest during our waking hours as thoughts, memories, and images; the same organizing principles are manifest during our sleeping hours as dreams. This does not, of course, mean that dreams cannot also be symbolic. Waking consciousness certainly involves symbolism, so if dreaming is an altered form of this type of consciousness, dreams may also be symbolic, at least to some extent (Foulkes, 1978).

INTERIM SUMMARY

Dreaming is closely associated with REM sleep. Usually a dream is one's sole realty; that is, one is not aware that one is dreaming. Sometimes, however, people engage in lucid dreaming, in which they are asleep but are aware that they are dreaming. People differ in the extent to which they recall dreams; those with better visual memory capacity are better able to recall their dreams. Events that occur upon awakening may interfere with the storage of a dream in memory. The content of dreams is influenced by stimuli that occur during REM sleep as well as by conditions that are present prior to sleeping. The function of dreams is not known; attempts to explain dreaming include Freud's theory, according to which the manifest content of a dream is symbolic of its latent content (the underlying psychological conflict), and the cognitive model, according to which dreams are equivalent to waking thoughts, memories, and images.

HYPNOSIS

When most people think of hypnosis they imagine a person in a deep trance, staring off blankly into space with eyes glazed, obedient to the wishes of the hypnotist, showing no willpower or reason whatsoever, perhaps even engaging in bizarre behaviors. The hypnotized person is thought to be in a drastically altered state of consciousness—a sleeplike state in which the normal or conscious self is suppressed. This popular belief is largely inaccurate, however, as this section makes clear. We begin by discussing the history of the complicated but interesting phenomenon called hypnosis (Naish, 1986; Wagstaff, 1981).

MESMER AND ANIMAL MAGNETISM

No one knows precisely when **hypnosis** was discovered, but it is usually associated with the faith healer and physician Franz Mesmer (1734–1815), whose influence was at its height in Paris during the 1770s and 1780s. Mesmer combined two elements to create his theory of animal magnetism. The first was the idea of religious exorcism, in which an evil presence or spirit was thought to be expelled from a "possessed" human body. The second was the belief that magnetism was an invisible force with healing powers. This belief was bolstered by the fact that other invisible forces had apparently magical properties. Helium, for example, was invisible yet, when placed in a balloon, could lift a person from the ground.

Mesmer was one of many people who claimed to have the power to cure illnesses such as paralysis through the use of magnets. But after demonstrating that magnets in and of themselves were not necessary to produce this effect, Mesmer developed the *baquet.* This device, illustrated in Figure 7-7, was a circular oaken cask about 15 inches high and large enough in diameter to allow about 30 people to sit around its

FIGURE 7-7 An artist's depiction of Mesmer's baquet.

periphery. In the bottom of the cask were placed powdered glass and iron filings. In the lid were holes into which metal rods could be inserted in such a way that they could be used to stir the contents of the cask. Some of the people sitting around the baquet grasped a rod with one hand and held onto another person with the other; the result was a "daisy chain" of people, some of whom were holding the "magnetized" rods. In this fashion, the magnetism was thought to spread from the baquet to each person seated around it. Within minutes the participants would become hysterical; many would have convulsions or fall into a trance (hence the word *mesmerized*).

All of Paris succumbed to the lure of this seemingly miraculous treatment. People flocked to Mesmer by the thousands; among them were many with great wealth and power. Stories of wonderful cures were common. Mesmer established a number of "sociétés de l'harmonie" devoted to the development and propagation of animal magnetism. The king, however, worried that these groups were spreading radical politics that could undermine his power. He therefore established two Commissions of Inquiry to validate the claims made by Mesmer and others. The commissions— one of which was chaired by Benjamin Franklin—subjected Mesmer's claims to empirical tests. For example, they studied people who were blindfolded and did not know whether they were connected to the source of magnetism or not; they found that the behavior of those who were not connected was no different from that of people who knew they were connected. They also studied people who were "magnetized" without knowing it; in these cases the hysterical effects were absent. In sum, the commissions found that the effects of animal magnetism were induced by the imagination of the patients. There was no scientific evidence for Mesmer's claims, including the claim that his procedures could cure illnesses.

In the next 50 years the study of animal magnetism, or hypnosis, faded. Mesmer died in obscurity, penniless. In the midnineteenth century, however, interest in the subject revived. Scientists began to think that the trancelike, or hypnotic, state exhibited by Mesmer's patients had resulted from an excited imagination rather than from animal magnetism. Some noted scientists took an interest in this phenomenon, lending it a certain respectability.

Today the study of hypnosis is viewed as scientifically valid. Moreover, it appears that hypnosis may have therapeutic value after all (Udolf, 1987; Wadden & Anderton, 1982). Claims in this area are not entirely proven, but there seems to be some benefit in using hypnosis in the treatment of various problems, including anxiety, headaches, asthma, gastrointestinal distress, and skin diseases like eczema and warts. In addition, there is some evidence that hypnosis can aid in the treatment of psychosexual and personality problems and can serve as a deterrent to pain during dental and obstetrical procedures. On the other hand, the value of hypnosis in the treatment of problems such as obesity, smoking, and alcoholism has not been supported by scientific evidence. If any improvement is observed in a condition like obesity, it is probably due to factors other than hypnotism, such as the diet counseling that accompanies the hypnosis sessions.

THEORIES OF HYPNOSIS

State Theory

An early theory about hypnosis held that it is a specific altered state, a deviation from normal consciousness (Chertok, 1981; Hilgard, 1965). In this view, hypnotized subjects lose their initiative and their ability to plan. Their attention is devoted to the hypnotist and they undergo radical changes in perception accompanied by a heightened ability to fantasize, greater tolerance for distortion of reality, and increased suggestibility.

An important piece of evidence for this **state theory of hypnosis** is that, when questioned later, subjects *believe* that they were hypnotized; that is, they claim to have experienced a different state. In addition, hypnotism seems to eliminate pain (Hilgard & Hilgard, 1984), to enable people to perform impressive feats of strength or skill, and to cause people to act wholly out of character, as if their behavior were totally removed from voluntary control. There is, however, little evidence to support these additional claims (Wagstaff, 1981; see Lynn, Rhue, & Weeks, 1990).

A subject being hypnotized.

The state theory is supported by the so-called hidden observer experiments (Hilgard, 1986). In these experiments subjects are first given a sensitivity test in which they rate the intensity of various painful stimuli. Hypnosis is then induced, and the subjects are told that a "hidden" part of their body has not been hypnotized. This part of the body presumably remains aware of reality. While still hypnotized, the subjects are given another test to determine whether the hypnotic state has changed their perception of pain. Stimuli to the hypnotized part of the body elicit reports of little or no pain. When the subject is questioned about the nonhypnotized (hidden) part, however, a normal level of pain is reported.

Nonstate Theories

A number of **nonstate theories of hypnosis** have been proposed too. These theories take various forms, but all suggest that hypnosis is not a unique state of consciousness and that it is not necessary to hypothesize the existence of special processes in order to explain what happens during hypnosis (Barber, 1969, 1979; Sarbin & Coe, 1972).

Nonstate theories claim that people are naturally prone to experience fantasies and therefore, if given special instructions, will act out those fantasies. The behaviors *appear* to be uniquely related to an altered hypnotic state, but in fact are "normal" behaviors performed because the subjects are reacting strongly to suggestions (Wilson & Barber, 1983). The instructions given to a subject emphasize relaxation, drowsiness, and the ease of responding to the suggestions made by the hypnotist. They work by influencing the subject's attitude and expectations. If the subject *believes* that he or she will be hypnotized and that the situation is conducive to hypnosis, hypnotic behavior will be observed. For example, subjects may respond to the hypnotist by showing muscular rigidity, analgesia (absence of pain), hallucinations, age-regression (childish behaviors), amnesia, posthypnotic suggestions, temporary blindness or color blindness, and so forth. The point is that everyone, to some degree, can increase, say, his or her tolerance to pain; we do not have to resort to an altered state of consciousness to explain that fact.

In sum, modern views of hypnosis no longer attribute exotic or magical properties to this phenomenon. People may unconsciously feel compelled to obey the suggestions of a hypnotist and, at the same time, believe strongly that what they feel is part of a hypnotic trance. The behavior of a hypnotized subject, however, is not so much a function of being in a trance or a special state of consciousness as it is a product of the interaction between the subject's beliefs and desire to comply (Wagstaff, 1981).

INTERIM SUMMARY

The origins of hypnosis are associated with Mesmer's experiments on "animal magnetism." Mesmer claimed to be able to use this force to cure illnesses; among other effects, his treatments caused people to fall into trances. An investigation of Mesmer's work concluded that the effects were induced by the imagination of the patient, and his theory was discredited. In the midnineteenth century interest in hypnosis was revived, and today it is sometimes used in the treatment of problems such as anxiety and psychosexual problems and as a deterrent to pain during dental and obstetrical procedures. There are two basic theories of hypnosis: state theory, which views hypnosis as a special altered state of consciousness, and nonstate theory, which claims that hypnosis results from the interaction between the subject's beliefs and desire to comply with the hypnotist's instructions.

DRUGS AND CONSCIOUSNESS

Drugs obviously affect consciousness, but the effects differ from one drug to another. In this section we review how various drugs affect the brain and how those physiological changes are reflected in consciousness (Julien, 1988; Thompson, 1984).

PRINCIPLES OF DRUG ACTION

Drugs affect the brain by enhancing or interfering with the effects of neurotransmitters. Some drugs adhere to receptor sites on the postsynaptic membrane, making it impossible for the neurotransmitter to do so. Others mimic the action of the transmitter itself, thereby enhancing those functions controlled by the transmitter. Still others alter the manufacture or metabolism of the transmitter substance and thus affect the degree to which the transmitter is available.

The main categories of drugs are hallucinogens (or psychedelics), stimulants, opiates, and depressants (sedatives). Table 7-1 summarizes these categories of drugs and gives several examples. These classes of drugs are alike in that each alters consciousness in a powerful way and, to some degree or under some circumstances, may lead to an addiction. A drug addiction is a physiological dependence on the continued use of the drug. Addicted people do not simply want to continue using a drug, they *need* to continue using it (for example, see File, 1990). Usually, they develop a tolerance to the drug as well; that is, they become progressively insensitive to the effects of the drug and so must use larger amounts in order to satisfy their craving for it and overcome withdrawal symptoms (see Poulos & Cappell, 1991). We should note, however, that not all of the drugs in the following discussion are addictive in this sense. And although the use of drugs is relatively widespread in our culture—at least judging from media reports—the percentage of high school students that has used illicit drugs has been declining in recent years (see Figure 7-8).

PSYCHEDELICS

Psychedelic drugs are substances that have powerful effects on sensory awareness, coordination, and mood (Grinspoon & Bakalar, 1979). In general, they produce an expanded sense of consciousness, strong shifts in mood, and distortions of perception. There are a great many such drugs; we discuss a few of them here.

TABLE 7-1   Four Types of Psychoactive Drugs and Common Examples of Each Type

Type	Examples
Hallucinogens	LSD
	Mescaline
	Marijuana
Stimulants	Amphetamines
	Cocaine
	Caffeine
Opiates (narcotics)	Heroin
	Morphine
Depressants	Barbiturates
	Alcohol
	Nicotine
	Tranquilizers

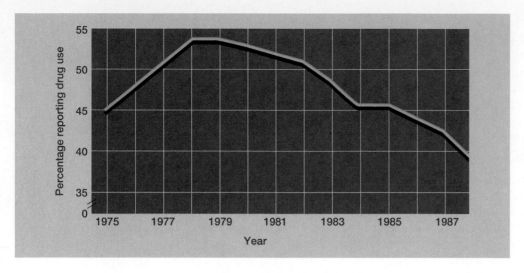

FIGURE 7-8 The percentage of high school seniors, graduating between the years 1975 and 1988, who reported ever having used illicit drugs (that is, drugs not ordered by a doctor). Drugs included hallucinogens, cocaine, heroin, opiates, stimulants, sedatives, tranquilizers, or marijuana. (Adapted from Johnston, O'Malley, & Bachman, 1989).

Acetylcholine Drugs

Many psychedelics produce their effect by disrupting the level or functioning of the neurotransmitter **acetylcholine** in the brain. Some (such as physostigmine) do so by inhibiting a second substance, the enzyme acetylcholinesterase, which is responsible for breaking down acetylcholine. Thus, by inhibiting acetylcholinesterase the drug actually augments the action of acetylcholine. Reactions to drugs of this type may include dreaming, anxiety, delirium, paralysis, and insomnia.

Other psychedelic drugs, such as atropine and scopolamine, tend to block acetylcholine receptors, preventing acetylcholine from having its normal effect. Because a reduction in acetylcholine activity affects the arousal centers in the brain, the psychological effects of these drugs may include sleep, a decline in arousal, drowsiness, fatigue, and a clouded mind.

Norepinephrine Drugs

A number of psychedelics produce their effect by disrupting or changing the level of **norepinephrine,** another neurotransmitter. The most common example of this type of drug is mescaline, a substance derived from the peyote cactus, which grows in the

Below: Artist's rendering of a Native American peyote ceremony. *Below right:* A peyote cactus.

American Southwest. Mescaline has long been used by Native Americans in religious rites (Furst, 1976). Its chemical structure resembles that of norepinephrine. In low doses, it increases heart rate, blood pressure and flow, glucose metabolism, pupil dilation, and adrenaline secretion, and inhibits intestinal contractions. In somewhat higher doses, it may produce clear and vivid hallucinations.

Serotonin Drugs

Another type of psychedelic drug affects the neurotransmitter *serotonin.* The best-known drug in this category is lysergic acid diethylamide-25 (LSD). This drug was first manufactured in the late 1930s but became notorious during the 1960s. Serotonin affects body temperature, sleep, and sensory perception and is important in various brain systems, including the raphe nuclei discussed earlier in connection with sleep. Because it is structurally similar to serotonin, LSD enhances many of these functions. The onset of these effects is rapid (30 to 60 minutes), and the psychological effects last for 10 or 12 hours. In general, the physiological effects (for example, on heart function) are minor. Humans have a strong **drug tolerance** for LSD, meaning that each time the drug is used, a higher dose is required to produce the same effect.

The psychological effects of LSD are profound and dramatic but are hard to predict (Barr, Langs, Holt, Goldberger, & Klein, 1972). Alterations in mood, changes in sensory responsiveness, and hallucinations almost always occur. These effects are collectively known as a "trip." Although many trips are highly euphoric, others can have severe adverse effects, including intense irrational fears, panic, terror, depression (sometimes leading to suicide), and seizures (Schwarz, 1968).

In one experiment on the effects of LSD, subjects were asked to indicate how accurately a set of 156 statements described their feelings while under the influence of the drug (Ditman et al., 1972). The statements described several categories of experience, including pleasantness, self-understanding, religious experience, and sensory alterations. The results showed that LSD has especially strong effects on three of these dimensions. First, it causes vivid distortions of sensory reality, particularly body states and visual stimuli: "I felt as if I were floating in space"; "I saw music." Second, LSD seems to stimulate religious experiences: "I felt in contact with wonderful, unknown forces." Third, hallucinations were common: "My face took different forms in the mirror."

Marijuana

Marijuana, the crushed leaf and flower of the hemp plant (*Cannabis sativa*) has been used for many centuries as a mind-altering substance. Although today the use of marijuana is most prevalent among Americans between the ages of 18 and 25, it is not uncommon for older and younger people to use it as well. For example, in 1980 the U.S. government reported that 60% of high school seniors had used marijuana. Except for alcohol and cigarettes, marijuana is the most commonly tried drug (Jones & Lovinger, 1985).

The active ingredient in marijuana is delta-9-tetrahydrocannabinol (THC). This substance has such varied effects that it is difficult even to classify it pharmacologically or behaviorally. Its action in the brain is largely unknown, although research using monkeys has shown that, when injected, it tends to accumulate in the neocortical, thalamic, and hippocampal areas of the brain. (See Figure 7-9.) At low doses, THC has a sedative effect; like alcohol and antianxiety drugs, it tends to produce relaxation and a decrease in anxiety. At higher doses, THC acts more like a psychedelic; it may produce euphoria, hallucinations, heightened sensation, and, at very high doses, feelings of persecution, confusion, and depersonalization.

Marijuana has been viewed in a very negative light in our culture because its use has been implicated in several highly publicized train accidents, and because many people associate being "stoned" with antisocial behavior. There is little justification,

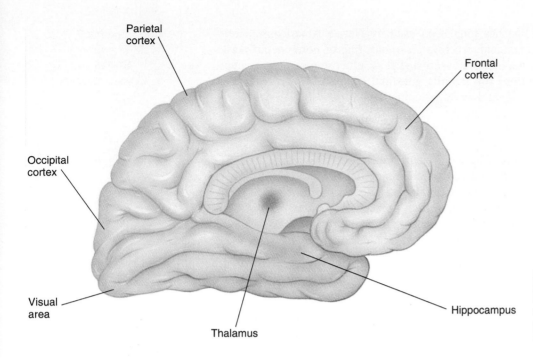

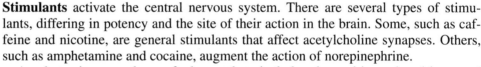

FIGURE 7-9 Areas of the monkey brain (shaded pink to purple) where THC has been shown to accumulate 15 minutes after it has been injected into the bloodstream. (Adapted from McIsaac, Frichie, Idanpaan-Heikkila, Ho, & Englert, 1971.)

however, for placing it in the same category as the psychedelics and narcotics (discussed shortly). Although it tends to decrease motor activity, elevate pain thresholds, and depress reflexes, there is little evidence that THC produces physiological or anatomical abnormalities.

STIMULANTS

Leaves from the coca plant.

Stimulants activate the central nervous system. There are several types of stimulants, differing in potency and the site of their action in the brain. Some, such as caffeine and nicotine, are general stimulants that affect acetylcholine synapses. Others, such as amphetamine and cocaine, augment the action of norepinephrine.

Amphetamine, a class of drugs that includes benzedrine, dexedrine, and methedrine, is structurally very similar to norepinephrine. It increases blood pressure and blood sugar, heart rate, and respiration and blood flow to the muscles; it also dilates the pupils and produces fast, erratic EEG patterns. Psychologically, the drug suppresses appetite and causes an elevation in mood that induces euphoria and alertness and reduces fatigue. At higher doses it has a more dramatic effect: It produces a "speed spree" and can cause disorganized behaviors and excessive activity, irritability, and strong irrational fears. After these effects wear off, the user may experience lethargy and depression.

Cocaine is similar to amphetamine, but it augments the action of norepinephrine by preventing it from being reabsorbed at the presynaptic membrane. Cocaine produces effects similar to those of amphetamine, including increased heart rate and blood pressure and constriction of blood vessels in the nose if it is "snorted." Its psychological effects include euphoria, a sense of well-being, increased mental awareness, reduced fatigue, and increased (though not very coordinated) motor activity (Nuckols, 1989; Yeh & Haertzen, 1991). The negative effects of cocaine have been highly publicized in recent years. They include reactions such as acute anxiety, irritability, sweating, and paranoia. When cocaine is concentrated in the form of smokable "crack," its negative effects can be intensified; there is evidence that the chances of developing an acute panic, or even irrational fears of persecution, are greatly magnified. Cocaine induces a strong desire for more of the drug, accompanied by various withdrawal symptoms, including depression.

186

The widespread use of cocaine in modern societies is common knowledge. Less well known is the fact that the drug was legal until about 1920. Freud used cocaine to relieve depression and ward off fatigue; he called it a "magical drug." At the turn of the century cocaine was an ingredient in products such as Coca-Cola and toothache drops. More recently the use of cocaine has reached epidemic proportions, although the number of frequent users may be declining (Julien, 1988).

OPIATES

A **narcotic** is any drug that induces sleep (that is, a sedative) and relieves pain (that is, an analgesic). The **opiates** are narcotics that have been used for many centuries; opium was used in Egypt as much as 3,000 years ago. In our society the opiates are a mixed blessing: They have valuable medical uses, such as the relief of pain, diarrhea, and coughing, but they are strongly addicting. They induce drug tolerance and dependence; desire for the drug can lead to serious antisocial behavior.

The primary narcotic, one of 20 substances found in the residue of the opium poppy, is morphine. In the United States morphine was as readily available as aspirin until 1914—by which time about one in every 400 Americans was addicted to it.

Morphine reduces pain by altering the perception of pain, not by blocking the sensory information reaching the brain. It also depresses respiratory centers in the brain stem and at high doses may cause a person to enter a coma. Morphine also depresses the cough center in the brain stem (codeine, the cough medicine additive, is also

As this advertisement indicates, opium and its derivative morphine were readily available in the United States in the nineteenth century.

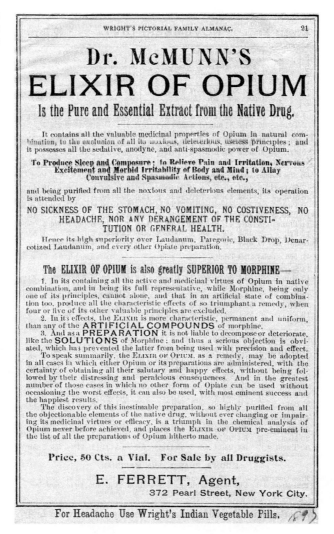

found in opium residue), produces fast, erratic EEG patterns, and suppresses REM sleep.

The psychological effects of morphine include drowsiness, mental clouding, euphoria, and dreamlike contentment. What makes morphine dangerous is that it is so strongly addictive and produces a cross-tolerance for other opiates (such as heroin). Withdrawal symptoms may include extreme irritability, depression, chills and fever, vomiting, panting, cramps, and unbearable aches.

Research has shown that the brain has a number of naturally occurring opiates, including enkephalins and endorphins (Hughes, 1975). Although these substances are distributed throughout the brain, relatively high concentrations are found in the pituitary gland at the base of the brain, in the hypothalamus, and in other structures in the limbic system.

Endorphins and enkephalins act in a similar manner to morphine and thus are built-in analgesics. Indeed, their analgesic effects are so pronounced that people who suffer serious injuries—for example, in automobile accidents—often report feeling no pain whatsoever because the injury stimulates the production of endorphins. Scientists believe that this analgesia is produced when the endorphin or enkephalin inhibits the release of various neurotransmitters (Snyder, 1977). In addition to acting as analgesics, the natural opiates are involved in temperature regulation (Holoday, Wei, Loh, & Li, 1978) and appear to affect moods and reactions to rewards (Belluzzi & Stein, 1977).

ALCOHOL

Clearly, alcohol, a depressant, is used pervasively in American society; just as obviously, it has strong effects on consciousness (Goldstein, 1983; Tarter & Van Thiel, 1985). The physiological effects of alcohol are like those of other sedatives: It tends to depress respiration, dilate blood vessels, and lower body temperature. Psychologically, alcohol produces a mild euphoria (especially at low doses), which is often mistaken for a stimulant effect. It also produces loss of discrimination and memory, decreased concentration, mood fluctuations, and a significant decline in motor performance.

Alcohol enters the gastrointestinal tract and is quickly absorbed into the bloodstream and distributed to the brain cells. The solubility of alcohol in both fat and water helps promote its absorption and distribution. Absorption can be delayed by several factors, including the presence of food in the stomach.

Relatives of the victims of drunk drivers look at photographs on a "victim board" put up by MADD (Mothers Against Drunk Driving) (left). A public service advertisement publicizing the dangers of drunk driving (right).

Alcohol is metabolized by the liver at a rate of about 0.25 to 0.33 ounces per hour. This means that in one hour the equivalent of 1/2 to 2/3 of 1 ounce of 100-proof whiskey, or 6 to 8 ounces of beer, will be eliminated from the digestive system. The rate of metabolism is constant; therefore, alcohol will build up in the bloodstream if it is consumed at a rate of more than 1/3 ounce per hour, but as shown in Table 7-2, the relationship between consumption and levels of blood alcohol depends on both sex and body size.

Because alcohol is a sedative and thus decreases various physiological functions, including reaction time and motor coordination, its use has a number of alarming indirect effects (Bushman & Cooper, 1990; Edkardt, Harford, & Kaelber, 1981; Niven, 1984). For example, nearly 50% of all crimes and automobile accidents are related to alcohol use. Table 7-3 shows the relationship between blood alcohol level and alteration in behavior. Clearly, if a 150-pound male were to drink just four cans

TABLE 7-2   The Effect on Blood Alcohol Level for Males and Females of Various Body Sizes After Consuming Various Quantities of Alcohol Within One Hour

Ounces of alcohol consumed in 1 hour	Amount of beverage	Blood alcohol levels (mg/100 ml)					
		Female (100 lbs)	Male (100 lbs)	Female (150 lbs)	Male (150 lbs)	Female (200 lbs)	Male (200 lbs)
1/2	1 oz 100-proof spirits 1 can beer	0.045	0.037	0.03	0.025	0.022	0.019
1	2 oz 100-proof spirits 2 cans beer	0.09	0.075	0.06	0.05	0.045	0.037
2	4 oz 100-proof spirits 4 cans beer	0.18	0.15	0.12	0.10	0.09	0.07
3	6 oz 100-proof spirits 6 cans beer	0.27	0.22	0.18	0.15	0.13	0.11
4	8 oz 100-proof spirits 8 cans beer	0.36	0.30	0.24	0.20	0.18	0.15
5	10 oz 100-proof spirits 10 cans beer	0.45	0.37	0.30	0.25	0.22	0.18

SOURCE: Adapted from Ray, 1972.

TABLE 7-3   The Effect of Blood Alcohol Level on Behavior

Blood alcohol level (%)	Behavior
0.05	Lowered alertness; usually good feeling
0.10	Slowed reaction times; less caution
0.15	Large, consistent increases in reaction time
0.20	Marked depression in sensory and motor capability; decidedly intoxicated
0.25	Severe motor disturbance, staggering; sensory perceptions greatly impaired
0.30	Semistupor
0.40	Death in about 50% of cases

SOURCE: Adapted from Ray, 1972.

of beer within an hour, a significant decline in reaction time would be observed. Drinking four times that amount would cause his blood to contain between 0.35 and 0.40% alcohol. Half of the people who become that intoxicated die from the experience.

INTERIM SUMMARY

Drugs affect the brain by enhancing or interfering with the effects of neurotransmitters. Psychedelic drugs disrupt the level or functioning of acetylcholine, norepinephrine, or serotonin and have powerful effects on sensory awareness, coordination, and mood. Stimulants activate the central nervous system; they include caffeine, nicotine, amphetamine, and cocaine. A narcotic is any drug that induces sleep and relieves pain; the opiates are narcotic drugs that have valuable medical uses but are strongly addicting. The most commonly used drug is marijuana, the crushed leaf and flower of the hemp plant. It has varied effects that may be either sedative or psychedelic in nature. Finally, alcohol is a pervasive drug that has sedative effects and may have serious direct and indirect consequences when used in excess.

SUMMARY

1. *Consciousness* involves both an awareness of our inner selves and of our environment. And important behavioral indicator of consciouness is level of arousal. Overt behavior can also indicate quality of consciousness, as in the case of perceptual distortions, dreams, or hallucinations.

2. *Sleep* is an important and pervasive behavior, although its actual function is not entirely clear. One theory is that sleep restores substances used up during waking hours. Another theory holds that sleep performs adaptive functions related to energy conservation and safety.

3. Sleep has both behavioral and electrophysiological characteristics. *Electroencephalographic (EEG)* evidence indicates that there are five major stages of sleep. Predominantly low-amplitude–high-frequency waves characterize EEG-patterns in stages 1 and 2; predominantly high-amplitude–low-frequency waves are characteristic of stages 3 and 4.

4. *REM (rapid eye movement)* sleep is the fifth stage of sleep, and it is characterized by EEG patterns similar to those occurring during the waking state.

5. The *sleep cycle* takes place about four to six times per night, each cycle lasting about 90 minutes. Both the amount of sleep and the duration of REM time decrease with age.

6. Both *total sleep deprivation* and *REM deprivation* produce negative effects, such as hallucinations, but the effects disappear after sleep.

7. The *reticular activating system* in the brain stem contains structures that are important for sleep, including the *raphe system* and the *locus ceruleus.* Activation of the former induces non-REM sleep in otherwise awake subjects; stimulation of the latter results in heightened cortical arousal.

8. Most *dreams* occur during REM sleep. Although dreams usually seem real and immediate, so dreamers are unaware they are dreaming, some people experience *lucid dreaming,* in which they are aware that they are dreaming. Dreams are often difficult to recall, probably because interference from events that occur on awakening prevents us from storing dreams in memory. The content of dreams can be influenced by presleep factors or by stimulation during REM.

9. Freud believed that dreams are unconscious wishes, and that their *manifest content* is symbolic of their *latent content,* which in turn reflects the psychological conflicts of the dreamer. According to another, better-documented, theory, the *cognitive model,* dreams are simply thoughts that occur during sleep.

10. The history of *hypnosis* is usually traced to the trancelike states experienced by the subjects of Franz Mesmer's experiments with what he called animal magnetism. Although Mesmer's claims for the therapeutic effects of animal magnetism were discredited, interest in the trancelike hypnotic state revived in the midnineteenth century. Today it appears that hypnosis may have therapeutic value for some psychological problems, although such claims are not entirely proven.

11. According to the state theory of hypnosis, a hypnotized person is actually in an altered state of consciousness. Nonstate theories, in contrast, hold that hypnosis is not a unique state but rather that a hypnotized person is simply in a heightened state of suggestbility.

12. There are many kinds of drugs that affect consciousness. They work primarily by interacting with neurotransmitters in the brain. *Psychedelic drugs,* for example, may affect *acetylcholine, norepinephrine,* or *serotonin.* Their physiological and psychological effects may be very dramatic. Stimulant drugs, such as *amphetamines* and *cocaine,* activate the central nervous system, usually by affecting the action of norepinephrine. *Narcotics,* such as *morphine,* on the other hand, tend to depress the nervous system. *Marijuana* and *alcohol* are widely used in our society. Although their effects may, at times, be less dramatic than other drugs, their overall impact on states of consciousness is often very profound.

FOCUS QUESTIONS

1. How is consciousness defined and how is it measured?

2. Why is it claimed that, from an evolutionary point of view, sleep is maladaptive?

3. Compare and contrast the possible functions served by sleep.

4. Describe the five stages of sleep, giving special attention to the characteristics of REM sleep.

5. Compare and contrast the Freudian and cognitive theories of dreams.

6. Compare and contrast the state and nonstate theories of hypnosis.

7. What are the major classes of psychedelic drugs and what are their primary effects, both physiological and psychological?

PART THREE

FREE WILL VERSUS BEHAVIORAL DETERMINISM

I n our everyday lives, we behave as if we had free will. We make decisions, hold one another accountable for mistakes, and apologize for our failings, all of which suggests that we believe we can control our actions. But are we as free as we believe, or is our behavior determined, especially by our biological makeup? This question lies at the heart of one of the enduring issues in psychology, the issue of **free will versus determinism,** which is the theme of the next four chapters. Chapter 8 examines the biological determinants of instinct and behavior in the context of evolutionary theory and genetics. This biological perspective continues in Chapter 9, which describes the physiological processes that underlie the behavior by which we satisfy our requirements for food and water. Chapter 10 turns to the combination of biological and social factors that influence sexual and aggressive behavior. Perhaps more than any others, these behaviors dramatize the debate between free will and determinism: Are we destined to be aggressive and warlike, and to engage in biologically determined patterns of sexual behavior, or do we have a choice in the matter? Finally, Chapter 11 examines human motives, such as achievement strivings and need for affiliation with others, for which choice, not biology, seems of paramount importance.

CHAPTER 8

ETHOLOGY AND BEHAVIOR GENETICS

Imagine the world as nothing but a seething broth of chemicals, a stormy primordial soup bubbling with ammonia, methane, and hydrogen gases. Primitive life took form in this environment nearly 3.5 billion years ago. We can only speculate about what the first life forms looked like because it was not until much later—a mere 500 million years ago—that creatures began leaving behind the fossil remains that would provide a tangible record of their existence.

The expanse of time during which the processes of biological evolution unfolded is hard to grasp, but we can begin to appreciate it if we imagine the entire fossil record, from the formation of the first fossil until the present time, as being compressed into a single year. (See Figure 8-1.) We can use this single imaginary year as a kind of yardstick for measuring the relative time in which biological forms have evolved. Thus, if we say that early fossil life appeared in the oceans on midnight of January 1, then land plants did not come into existence until early November, and primitive animals did not begin roaming over the land until about mid-November. Reptiles did not appear until the end of November, and mammals, often regarded as among the most complex forms of animal life, did not appear until mid-December. As for human beings, they did not make their entrance until late in the day on December 31. In short, although humans have been evolving for between 2 and 3 million years, compared to the entire span of biological evolution that is but an eye blink in time.

FIGURE 8-1 The span of biological evolution compressed into a single year. As this figure shows, in relation to the history of evolution, the emergence of human beings is extremely recent.

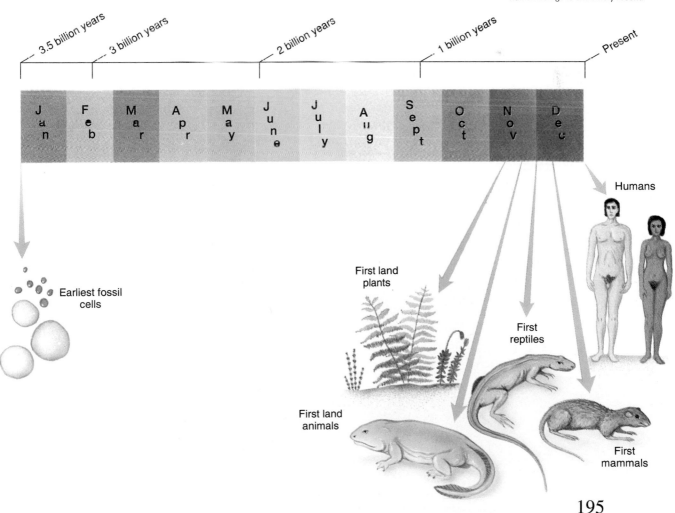

Like all other biological life forms, humans are products of evolution and continue to be subject to evolutionary pressures. Therefore, an evolutionary perspective is valuable in understanding why human beings behave as they do. This perspective is related to several of the themes described at the beginning of the book, but it is particularly relevant to the issue of determinism versus free will. It bears, in particular, on the following question related to that issue: Is human behavior wholly determined by biological forces, or do some human actions occur for reasons that have little to do with biological processes? The fact that humans are as much the result of evolution as are all other biological forms would seem to argue for biological determinism. In this chapter, however, we see that although biological determinism is indeed an important factor in behavior, choice is important too.

EVOLUTION AND BEHAVIOR

As we saw in Chapter 1, Charles Darwin showed how the varied and complex life forms that now inhabit the earth all evolved from simpler forms through **natural selection.** The existence of a natural selection process is based on three facts. First, not all individuals survive to reproduce; many more individuals are born than reach sexual maturity. Second, individuals are not all alike; genetic variations as a result of mutations are commonplace. Sometimes these variations produce structural differences that are obviously important for survival. For example, mutations may improve eyesight in some individuals, or cause them to be stronger or faster. Third, the environment poses a number of challenges that threaten the individual's ability to survive. All creatures must face those challenges because the forces in their environment cannot be altered. Failure to meet the demands of the environment can result in injury or death.

From these three facts—that not all individuals survive to reproduce, that genetic variations due to mutation are commonplace, and that the environment poses threats to individual survival—the theory of natural selection draws the following conclusion: Individuals that possess mutations that give them a slight advantage in coping with environmental challenges are more likely to survive and successfully reproduce than those born without those mutations. As a result, the genes carrying those mutations have a high probability of being passed on to subsequent generations. Eventually, averaged over the countless centuries of biological evolution, the advantageous

Baby turtles run into the sea after hatching. According to the theory of natural selection, those turtles endowed with inherited advantages that help them cope better with the environment compared to their siblings are more likely to survive to reproduce and pass on their traits.

mutations become part of the species' gene pool, the collection of genetically determined traits that characterizes the species as a whole.

In considering the relationships between evolution and behavior, it is important to keep in mind that the process of natural selection does *not* involve a conscious struggle between the individual and the environment. Animals do not stop to ask whether a particular behavior will increase or decrease their chances of survival; they simply respond to the demands of the environment, and the ultimate consequence is either successful reproduction or not. It should also be remembered that survival is a probabilistic notion; it applies to entire species or to groups of animals within a species, not to individual animals. Therefore, what is meant by statements like "Individuals that cope with the environment more effectively than others are more likely to survive" is not that a specific individual will necessarily survive but, rather, that the entire species is more likely to survive over the long term, if indeed the individuals that make up the species *as a group* possess adaptive traits.

An often-cited example of natural selection is the change in coloration of the peppered moth that occurred during the past century. In the early nineteenth century the vast majority of peppered moths in England were quite light in color; only a small percentage were dark. One reason the dark-colored moths were not numerous was that they contrasted with the light green lichen that grew on trees in their environment, making them easy prey for birds. But with the advent of the industrial revolution, with factories belching smoke from coal-fired furnaces, the trees became smudged with soot. Under these conditions the dark-colored moths were at an advantage because they could not be easily seen by hungry birds. (See Figure 8-2.) As a result, the formerly rare gene for darker coloration superseded the formerly common gene for lighter coloration, and the black variety of the moth came to predominate. In rural areas, however, where soot had not blackened the trees, the lighter-colored moths remained predominant.

BEHAVIOR AND NATURAL SELECTION

It is easy to see how the theory of natural selection applies to structural characteristics such as strong muscles, protective coloration, and sharp teeth. But what about behavior? How could behavior—transient actions as opposed to physical structures—be influenced by evolutionary pressures? The two-part answer has to do with the evolution of the brain.

First, an organism's potential for behavior is to a large extent governed by, or dependent on, its brain. We are not concerned here with precisely *how* the brain gov-

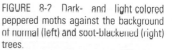

FIGURE 8-2 Dark- and light-colored peppered moths against the background of normal (left) and soot-blackened (right) trees.

erns behavior; that is a problem for physiology and neuropsychology. We merely note the fact that behavior ultimately depends on the functioning of the brain.

Second, the structure of the brain has evolved just as surely as sharp teeth or protective coloration. So if behavior largely depends on the brain and the brain has evolved like other parts of the body, then behavior itself can be said to have evolved.

Similarly, because the structure of the brain is inherited, behavior must, to some extent, be inherited; a major task of psychology is to determine how and to what extent. Accomplishing this task requires exploring the relationship between inherited traits—traits over which an individual has no control—and behavior. Two concepts, genotype and phenotype, are involved in this relationship. **Genotype** refers to an individual's genetic makeup, the sum total of all the genes that the individual has inherited. (We discuss genes and the process by which they are inherited later in the chapter.) **Phenotype** refers to an individual's observable characteristics, including the individual's structure, physiology, and behavior.

THE ROLE OF THE ENVIRONMENT

Although brain structures and thus behavior have evolved, this is not to imply that humans (or other creatures) are born to behave in a fixed way. On the contrary, the environment also has an important effect on behavior. In fact, the causes of behavior make sense only if they are understood as an outcome of the *interaction* between biological and environmental forces.

One way in which the environment contributes to behavior is through culture, in the form of habits that are learned by the individual from others. Culture refers to the manners and customs of a society, the collective behavior of a people, the totality of a society's actions, including, among many things, its social, economic, religious, political, educational, and recreational habits. Culturally derived habits are passed along from one generation to the next, which makes cultural transmission an important alternative to genetic transmission (Dawkins, 1976). As a result, any discussion of evolution must acknowledge the role that the cultural environment plays in maintaining, or changing, behavior over generations.

Normally we think of culture as an exclusively human phenomenon, but in reality many species have cultural traits that they pass from one generation to the next. Wolves, for example, pass hunting techniques along to their young. Similarly, some birds use cactus spines to pry insects out of crevices, and they teach this behavior to younger members of the flock. But perhaps the best example of cultural learning in nonhuman species is the behavior of the Japanese snow monkey (Kawai, 1965). Years ago a troop of these monkeys was isolated on an island off the coast of Japan as part of a wildlife conservation effort. Various food items, including wheat and sweet potatoes, were regularly delivered to the monkeys. Before long a female monkey discovered an efficient way to prepare this food. She separated the wheat grains from the sand and dirt by throwing handfuls of the mixture into the water, waiting for the sand to sink to the bottom, and scooping up the wheat grains that remained afloat. She also washed the sweet potatoes in the seawater, a behavior that snow monkeys normally do not exhibit. (See Figure 8-3.) These behaviors were passed on to other members of the troop—first to the female's offspring, then to other high-ranking adults, and finally to the entire troop.

On the basis of examples like these, some biologists have argued that genes may establish rough potentials for behavior but that experience, or culture, gives shape to behavior patterns. This is especially true of human beings, whose cultural traditions, which are passed on through language, are unusually rich and varied. The noted geneticist Theodore Dobzhansky (1967/1955) stated this view as follows:

FIGURE 8-3 A Japanese snow monkey washing sweet potatoes in the sea. This behavior, learned initially by one female monkey, was passed on to her offspring and then to other adult monkeys in a process of cultural transmission.

> We inherit our genes only from parents and other direct ancestors. We transmit them only to children and direct descendants . . . By contrast, culture can be transmitted to any number of contemporaneous individuals or to future generations, regardless of biological descent or relationships. The founders of great religions, scientists, inventors, poets, philosophers . . . have influenced the cultural heredity of mankind for many generations and perhaps forever. Cultural evolution is vastly more rapid and efficient than biological evolution. (p. 339)

Three facts underlie the theory of natural selection: (1) Not all animals survive to reproduce; (2) genetic variation is commonplace; (3) the environment poses challenges that threaten the individual's ability to survive. From these facts, the theory concludes that individuals possessing mutations that give them a slight advantage are more likely to survive and successfully reproduce than those that lack such advantages. As a result, these advantageous mutations will, over time, characterize the entire species. Evolutionary pressures influence behavior as well as physical structures: They affect the structure and functioning of the brain, which in turn governs or controls behavior. Environmental forces also influence behavior; in fact, behavior must be viewed as an outcome of the interaction between biological and environmental forces. Other animals besides humans are able to learn behaviors and teach them to others.

BEHAVIOR GENETICS

Is it possible to discover the extent to which behavior is determined by biological forces? To answer this question, psychologists and other scientists conduct studies in which they attempt to hold environmental forces constant while observing variations in biological characteristics such as genetic makeup. This area of research— the study of the relationship between genes and behavior—is called **behavior genetics.** In no other field within psychology does the issue of biological determinism come into sharper focus (DeFries & Plomin, 1978; Wahlsten, 1972).

The modern science of genetics began with a paper published by Gregor Mendel in 1865. Mendel had conducted experiments on the nature of plant diversity. (See Figure 8-4.) He noticed that when he crossbred pea plants that yielded white flowers with plants that produced purple flowers, very interesting results occurred in suc-

Gregor Mendel, a pioneer in the field of genetics.

FIGURE 8-4 Mendel's experiments on the effects of breeding on flower color in pea plants. Mendel found that when he cross-bred true-breeding purple-flowered plants (when bred with each other such plants produce only purple-flowered offspring) with true-breeding white-flowered plants (which produce only white-flowered offspring), the offspring were all purple-flowered. When these offspring were self-fertilized—bred with each other—three-fourths of the resulting offspring were purple-flowered, and one-fourth white flowered.

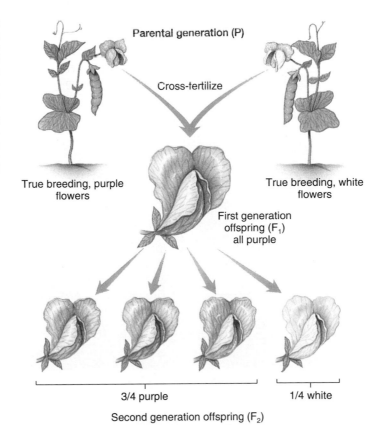

Parental generation (P)

Cross-fertilize

True breeding, purple flowers

True breeding, white flowers

First generation offspring (F₁) all purple

3/4 purple   1/4 white

Second generation offspring (F₂)

cessive generations. In the first generation, called F1 (for "filial 1"), all the plants bore purple flowers. In the second generation (F2), however, both purple and white flowers appeared. The reappearance of the two colors in a specific ratio (three purple to one white) is what gave Mendel insight into the genetic control of physical traits. Although the significance of Mendel's discovery was not fully recognized until years later, genetics has become one of the most important areas of scientific research. In this section we review some of the basic concepts in the field of behavior genetics, beginning with a look at the processes of genetic selection that explain the results of Mendel's experiment (see McClearn & DeFries, 1973).

GENETIC SELECTION

Genes, the fundamental units of heredity, are tiny beadlike structures composed of a protein called deoxyribonucleic acid (DNA). These structures are strung together in long strands of genetic material called **chromosomes.** Each species has a fixed number of chromosome pairs located in the nucleus of each cell of the body. Humans have 23 pairs of chromosomes.

Because most chromosomes occur in pairs, genes are also paired. Each member of a gene pair is called an **allele.** Alleles are of two types: dominant (D) and recessive (d). In an individual's phenotype—that is, the visible and outward expression of the genotype—D alleles dominate d alleles. In other words, **dominant traits** governed by D alleles take precedence over **recessive traits** governed by d alleles. In Mendel's pea plants, one gene governs flower color. The dominant allele (D) is associated with purple flowers; the recessive allele (d) is associated with white flowers. A plant with two D alleles will have purple flowers, as will a plant with one D and one d allele. Only a plant with two d alleles will have white flowers.

Chains of DNA (that is, chromosomes) are made up of millions of subunits called **nucleotides** that are linked together in a specific order. When a normal cell divides (by means of a process called *mitosis*), the DNA chains first unravel and duplicate, or replicate, themselves, and other nucleotides from a free-floating pool are attached to them to form new chains. Once the chromosomes have replicated themselves, the cell begins to divide; one chromosome strand from each pair goes to each of the two resulting cells. Thus, each new cell is an exact replica of the parent cell.

Unfertilized sex cells (**gametes**—the ovum in the female and sperm in the male) are different from other cells in that they contain only one strand of DNA. They are

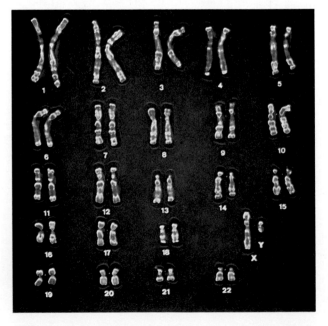

A photomicrograph of human chromosomes.

therefore referred to as **haploid.** When gametes (sperm and egg) unite, they combine to create a fertilized ovum, or **diploid zygote,** which once again has 23 chromosome pairs. As a result of this process, half of the genes in the zygote come from the father and half from the mother.

Figure 8-5 shows how genetic characteristics, in this case the color of pea plant flowers as in Mendel's experiments, are segregated during normal reproduction. In the figure, both original parents are **monozygotic** for the gene governing flower color—that is, both alleles for the gene in each parent are the same. One parent is monozygotic for the dominant allele and has purple flowers (a purple-flowered phenotype); the other is monozygotic for the recessive allele and has white flowers (a white-flowered phenotype). Because all the offspring (the F1 generation) from these parents take one allele from each parent, they all are heterozygous, with one dominant and one recessive allele. As a result, they all have a purple-flowered phenotype.

In the second (F2) generation, which results from the crossing of the heterozygotic F1 individuals, the original characteristics are again segregated. As shown in Figure 8-5, one-fourth of the F2 individuals will be homozygotic dominant (containing only D alleles), one-half will be heterozygotic (combining D and d alleles), and one-fourth will be homozygotic recessive (containing only d alleles). This means that three-fourths of the F2 individuals (the D-D and D-d individuals) will show the dominant trait (purple flowers) and one-fourth (the d-d individuals) will show the recessive trait (white flowers). This 3:1 ratio in the F2 generation was precisely what Mendel observed in his pea plants—three purple-flowered plants for every white-flowered plant.

EXAMPLES OF INHERITED BEHAVIORS

Would it be possible selectively to breed behavioral as well as physical traits? Even though behavior, unlike traits like coloration and size, is not tangible, the answer is

FIGURE 8-5 How the recessive and dominant alleles for the gene that controls flower color in pea plants are segregated to produce the results Mendel observed in his experiments (see Figure 8-4).

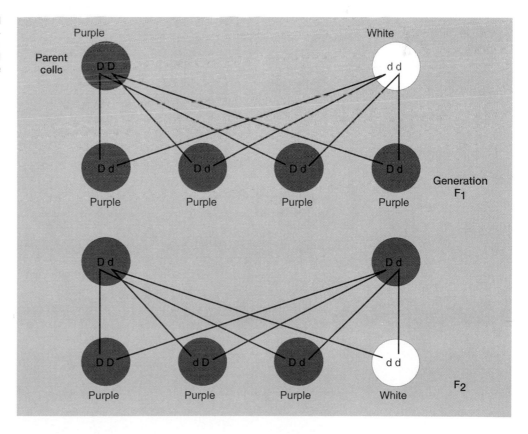

yes. Many experiments using animals have shown that a wide range of behavioral characteristics—including memory, sexual responsiveness, reactivity to novel stimuli, alcohol tolerance, aggressiveness, and susceptibility to noise-induced seizures—are at least partly under genetic control (Wimer & Wimer, 1985). Such experiments are analogous in nearly every respect to the breeding programs that produce prize roses or giant vegetables. In both cases the desired trait—whether it is the color or size of a rose or the behavior of an animal—is encouraged by breeding only individuals that manifest that trait.

Animal Examples

Selective breeding of behaviors is illustrated by a series of experiments using domesticated house mice (Bovet, Bovet-Nitti, & Oliverio, 1969). The mice were first placed in a box with two compartments. When a light came on, the mice had 10 seconds in which to jump into the other compartment through a hole in a partition in order to avoid getting a mild shock. If they failed to jump within the specified time, the shock was presented and they had to jump through the hole to turn it off. As shown in Figure 8-6, on average, the original subjects (generation 0) avoided the shock in only about 15% of 500 trials. The members of this generation that were most successful in avoiding the shock (those that performed better than average) were selected for mating. Their offspring were tested, and again the best learners were mated. By the third generation, the mice were jumping through the partition before the shock was presented on about 85% of the trials. Successive generations also showed greater consistency in performance (that is, greater similarity in scores, not only an improvement in the average score). This is powerful evidence for the notion that a particular behavior can be selectively bred.

Had the behavior of the mice changed in some general way, or only in relation to the particular task used in the experiment? The answer is not entirely clear. In the study just described, the researchers argued that the mice's overall learning ability had improved over the generations: When they were tested on a *different* task, such as traversing a maze to obtain a food reward, the mice that had become efficient shock avoiders learned faster and with fewer errors than those that had not learned the avoidance behavior as well. Other investigators, however, have suggested that selective breeding does not change the ability of the animals to solve problems in general, but instead influences performance indirectly by altering the subjects' emotional reactivity to shock (Brush et al., 1985; Brush et al., 1988). We must therefore be cautious in drawing conclusions from these experiments. Selectively bred animals may show a special talent for learning and memory that generalizes from one task to another, but the effects of genetic selection on behavior may also be indirect.

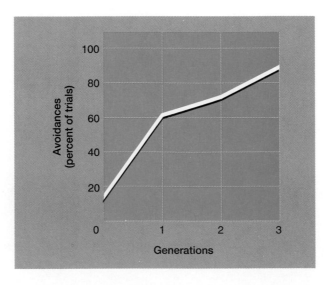

FIGURE 8-6   Mean percent of avoidance behavior for successive generations of mice selected for good avoidance behavior. (Adapted from Bovet, Bovet-Nitti, & Oliverio, 1969.)

Human Examples

Behavior genetics is largely dependent on research in lower species, such as fruit flies or mice, because they are inexpensive and easy to use and because successive generations reach sexual maturity in a relatively short time. It would be impractical as well as unethical to perform similar experiments on humans. Instead, humans must be studied in some fashion other than by using the selective reproduction approach discussed above. The problem, however, is that the contributions of genetics cannot be easily disentangled from those of experience (DeFries & Plomin, 1978). For example, the similarities in behavior between identical (monozygotic) twins (twins that result from the division of a single fertilized egg) could be attributable either to the fact that they are genetically identical or to the fact that they are usually raised in the same household.

There are several ways of circumventing this problem. One is to study adopted individuals (Plomin, DeFries, & Fulker, 1988). As suggested in Figure 8-7, a test of genetically unrelated people who live in the same household can reveal the effects of environmental factors in the absence of genetic determinants (upper-left panel). Conversely, a test of genetically identical twins who were adopted into different families and therefore were raised apart can, at least in theory, indicate the contribution of genetic factors in the absence of environmental determinants (lower-right panel). We say "at least in theory" because, in practice, environmental determinism cannot always be entirely ruled out. For example, identical twins may have been raised apart, but in very similar environments.

A second technique is to examine the characteristics of members of extended families in which the overall genetic relationships are well documented. If a behavioral trait is genetically determined, there should be a statistical correlation between the appearance of the trait and the degree of genetic relatedness between family members. That is, the greater the degree of relatedness, the greater the chance that the trait will appear. For example, if a particular behavior is genetically determined, identical twins should show greater similarity in respect to that behavior than fraternal **(dizygotic)** twins (twins resulting from the fertilization of two separate eggs) because identical twins have a greater genetic relatedness than fraternal twins.

Research on behavior genetics in humans has a long history, and although serious reservations have been expressed about the interpretation of some findings (Henderson, 1982), this research points to the same conclusion as the experiments using animals: A sizable proportion of human behavior is genetically determined, at least to some degree. Among the traits for which there is evidence of a genetic basis are intelligence (Plomin, Pedersen, McClearn, Nesselroade, & Bergeman, 1988), voca-

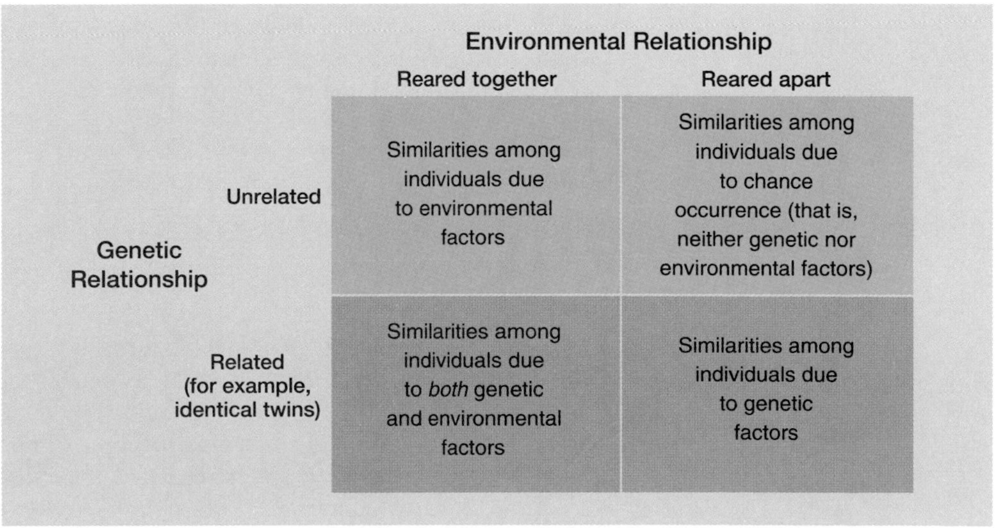

FIGURE 8-7 A scheme for isolating the contribution of genetic and environmental factors to behavior.

	Environmental Relationship	
Genetic Relationship	Reared together	Reared apart
Unrelated	Similarities among individuals due to environmental factors	Similarities among individuals due to chance occurrence (that is, neither genetic nor environmental factors)
Related (for example, identical twins)	Similarities among individuals due to *both* genetic and environmental factors	Similarities among individuals due to genetic factors

tional interests (Plomin, 1989), reading disabilities (DeFries, Fulker, & LaBuda, 1987), and mental retardation (Nichols, 1984; see also Faraone, Kremen, & Tsuang, 1990).

Many behaviors, such as those associated with certain forms of psychopathology, are complex clusters of responses that are difficult to measure, let alone explain (Mendlewicz & Shopsin, 1979). But even these behaviors may have a substantial genetic component (Plomin, 1989). In one survey, for example, 30% of the 164 pairs of identical twins studied manifested similar degrees of psychological disturbance; on average, if one individual was disturbed, the other tended to be too. Only 6.5% of the 268 pairs of fraternal twins studied showed such a correspondence (Kendler & Robinette, 1983).

Other behavior patterns or conditions also seem to be based to some degree on genetic relatedness. For instance, some researchers have investigated the degree to which people inherit certain personality traits, particularly neuroticism (extreme emotionality) and extraversion (extreme sociability) (Loehlin & Nichols, 1976). A study of identical twins who had been raised in different environments found that genetic factors contributed significantly to these personality traits, whereas general environmental factors were less important (Pedersen, Plomin, McClearn, & Friberg, 1988). One researcher commented that "pairs of [genetically] unrelated children reared together in the same house show no more resemblance in personality than pairs of children chosen at random" (Henderson, 1982, p. 420).

In sum, the importance of genetic factors in human behavior has become increasingly clear in recent years. In a recent review of research in this field, one scientist stated that "genetic influence is so ubiquitous and pervasive in behavior that a shift in [our thinking] is warranted: Ask not what is heritable, ask what is not heritable" (Plomin, 1989, p. 108).

INTERIM SUMMARY

Behavior genetics is the study of the relationship between genes and behavior. This field of study began with Mendel's experiments on the nature of plant diversity, which provided insight into the genetic control of physical traits. The appearance of particular traits is determined by the presence or absence of a dominant allele: The combination of a dominant allele with a dominant or recessive allele will produce the dominant trait, whereas the combination of two recessive alleles will produce the recessive trait. Experiments using animals have shown that genes may also govern behavioral characteristics, although it is not always clear whether the influence is direct or indirect. Studies of genetic influences on human behavior are hampered by the fact that humans cannot be subjected to a selective reproduction treatment, but studies of adopted individuals and identical twins, as well as studies of extended families with well-documented patterns of genetic relationships, indicate that genetic factors play an important role in human behavior.

INSTINCT

Behavior genetics suggests that biological determinism takes the form of direct genetic control. We can, however, take a broader view of the issue; that is, we can focus on biologically determined behavior without specifying how it is controlled. This is what we do here in examining the topic of instinct.

Instinct may be defined as "an inherited, specific, stereotyped pattern of behavior . . . [with] its own energy . . . [that] is *released,* rather than guided, by particular environmental stimuli" (Cofer & Appley, 1964, p. 60). This definition clearly indi-

Spinning a web is a complicated but
instinctual behavior pattern.

cates that an instinct has three fundamental characteristics: (1) It is innate and not a
result of experience; (2) it is specific, stereotypical, and wholly inflexible; and (3) it
is triggered in its entirety by particular stimuli, rather than being shaped or guided.
The spinning of a spider's web would be an example.

During the second half of the nineteenth century, instinct was a popular explanation of behavior, especially the seemingly intelligent behavior of nonhuman animals
(Bolles, 1975). Early in this century, however, the use of instincts to explain behavior came under attack. The critics argued that instinct had become an empty concept
(Lashley, 1938). They pointed out that instinctive behavior was often confused with
learned behavior and that to say that a behavior is caused by a certain instinct does
not really explain the behavior, but merely labels it. For example, observing a behavior such as a fearful reaction to snakes and claiming that the behavior is *caused* by an
instinctive fear of snakes does not explain the behavior at all; it simply renames the
behavior without providing any insight into why it occurs.

FIXED-ACTION PATTERNS

As a result of these criticisms, the use of instinct to explain behavior declined in the
United States. In Europe, however, zoologists continued to study animal behavior
from the point of view of instinct. The result of their efforts was twofold. First, these
scientists were able to refine the concept of instinct itself to the point where it once
again became valid and useful for the study of behavior. They were able to do this
because of a second, more general, development—the founding of **ethology.** Modern
ethology is the study of animal behavior largely from an evolutionary perspective.
Its primary purpose is to discover the adaptive (or functional) value of behavior, that
is, the way in which behavior helps an animal cope with environmental pressures
and demands. But ethology is also, to some degree at least, concerned with the
mechanisms that control or cause behavior—for example, the genetic, physiological,
and environmental bases for behavior. Thus, ethology is a broad discipline whose

overall goal is to study animal behavior using both the laboratory approach (which is typical of psychology and physiology), as well as a naturalistic or field-study approach (which is derived from the traditions of European zoology).

One of the most valuable concepts developed by ethologists is the **fixed-action pattern (FAP).** FAPs are a form of instinctual behavior with several characteristics (Lea, 1984). First, they are essentially the same every time they are performed, although some variation can occur. In this regard, they can be compared to a musical score: The "notes" (the specific component behaviors that make up the FAP) are fixed, but the "tempo" (the rate at which the component behaviors are executed) may vary somewhat (Eibl-Eibesfeldt, 1989). Second, they are found in all members of a given species; they are a characteristic of the species, not simply of the individual. This helps rule out learning as a cause of the behavior, because if a single individual were to learn a certain behavior, it would not necessarily be seen in other members of the species.

Third, FAPs are independent of experience; they occur without any previous learning, although experience does play a role in their expression. The fact that they are present at birth has been demonstrated in isolation experiments, in which animals are isolated at birth from any conditions that might affect, or teach, an FAP. When they are tested at a later date, they are able to display the FAP in response to the appropriate stimulus.

Fourth, FAPs have a single function. They are related to achieving a particular goal and occur only in the context of that goal. And finally, FAPs are triggered by a specific **releasing stimulus** (also called a **sign stimulus).** Although a releasing stimulus may have other functions, its major effect on the animal is to stimulate the fixed-action pattern (Lea, 1984).

An example of an FAP is the begging behavior of herring gull chicks. As shown in Figure 8-8, when the mother returns to the nest with food in her crop, the chick pecks at her bill, causing her to regurgitate the food. She then picks the food off the ground and holds it in the tip of her bill so that the chick can take it. A herring gull's bill is yellow, with a small conspicuous red dot about 1/3 of the way from the tip. Researchers have used fake bills like those shown in Figure 8-9 to determine whether the dot functions as a releasing stimulus for the begging FAP.

Although early research suggested that the chick's pecking reaction was determined by the configuration of the mother's head, bill, and red dot (Tinbergen & Perdeck, 1950), more recent studies indicate that the movement of the dot, not its location, is the determining factor (Hailman, 1967; 1969). When the red dot was moved in an arc and its position on the bill was varied as well, pecking was determined by the rate of movement, not by the position of the dot. In addition, the pattern of bill movement (without a red dot) was shown to be a secondary releaser of the pecking behavior: Up-and-down movements of the bill triggered a greater reaction in the chicks than did side-to-side movements.

FIGURE 8-8 A herring gull chick begging for food by pecking its mother's beak.

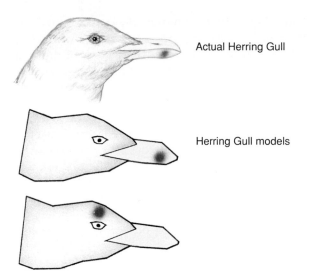

Actual Herring Gull

Herring Gull models

Supernormal stimulus

FIGURE 8-9 Fake herring gull bills like those used to identify the releaser for the herring gull chick's FAP of pecking its mother's beak for food. Research has identified the movement of the red dot as the main factor in releasing the behavior. The supernormal stimulus shown at the bottom of the figure elicited a stronger pecking reaction than any of the other models.

RELEASERS

The sign stimulus, or releaser of an FAP, is often a single but salient part of a more complex stimulus. In the case of the gull chicks' begging reaction, for example, the movement of the red dot is the releaser, even though it is embedded in a complex stimulus that involves the size, shape, coloration, and patterning of the adult gull (or model of a gull) to which the dot belongs.

Supernormal Releasers

Once the critical feature of a releaser has been identified, variations of that feature may produce some interesting effects. For example, large sign stimuli may trigger exaggerated reactions. Such a stimulus is termed a **supernormal stimulus.** In the case of the herring gulls, an artificial supernormal stimulus that is thinner than the mother gull's bill and colored yellow with three small red bars at the tip evokes more begging reactions from newborn chicks than does a realistic copy of the natural head and bill. (See Figure 8-9.)

A more dramatic example of a supernormal stimulus involves the type of egg that female herring gulls prefer to incubate. The larger the egg, the more it stimulates incubation. When a female gull is presented with a large dummy egg, the result is the bizarre and comical situation depicted in Figure 8-10. The gull chooses to sit on the giant egg while ignoring her own egg. Normally, of course, animals do not encounter such supernormal stimuli in their natural environment. Nevertheless, these experiments reveal how strong and inflexible instinctual reactions can be.

COMPLEX INSTINCTUAL PATTERNS

Although some instinctual behavior involves discrete actions, some can also involve complex patterns with a number of component behaviors. An example of such a pattern is the dance of the honeybees.

When a forager bee discovers a new source of food, it flies back to the hive and communicates the precise location of the food source and its quality to other members of the hive by means of various "dances" (von Frisch, 1967; see Dyer & Gould,

FIGURE 8-10 A herring gull attempting to incubate a large dummy egg instead of its own.

207

1983; Gould, 1976; Winston, 1987). The round dance is a relatively simple dance that communicates the fact that a source of food is a short distance from the hive, perhaps 100 meters or less. The pattern of this dance is illustrated in Figure 8-11. The forager turns in a small circle, reversing directions every one or two turns. During this time it exchanges food with other hive members. The other bees then leave the hive and fly in increasingly large circles, searching for the food source on the basis of the odors learned about during the exchange of food with the forager. We know that odors are used because if the forager is allowed to discover a heavily scented sugar solution, the other bees will find the source rather easily. If the experimenter changes the odor of the solution before the other bees arrive, however, the bees will have greater difficulty locating the food.

The waggle dance is somewhat more complicated. A forager performs the waggle dance when the food source is about 100 meters or more from the hive. The dance communicates the direction of the new source, its distance from the hive, and the quality of the food. The pattern of the dance, illustrated in Figure 8-12, is actually a figure eight. It consists of a straight run during which the bee shakes or waggles its abdomen (about 15 times per second), followed by a circle, first in one direction and then in the other. Again the forager stops to exchange food with onlookers (Michelsen, Kirchner, & Lindauer, 1986), thereby giving them an olfactory cue that can help them locate the food source when they are near it.

The distance of the food source from the hive is communicated by the length and duration of the straight run and the number of waggles per second (in other words, the vigor of the dance). As shown in Figure 8-13, the slower the dance and the more time the dancer spends performing the straight run, the greater the distance between the hive and the food.

The exact meaning of a single waggle varies in different races of bees. For Egyptian bees, one waggle is equivalent to about 5 meters; for Italian bees, however, a single waggle is equivalent to about 25 meters, and for German bees one waggle equals 75 meters. By performing more waggles the dancer can communicate distance rather accurately, but the details of the dance are not the same for all races of bees.

The direction of the food source is conveyed in a different manner. If a forager is forced to dance on a horizontal surface, the straight run of the dance is pointed in the same direction as the food source. The other bees simply fly in the direction indicated by the dance. Usually, however, the waggle dance is performed on a vertical surface inside the hive, and the vertical direction of the straight run must be "trans-

FIGURE 8-11 (Below, left) Dance of the honeybees: The round dance. This dance indicates that a food source is a short distance away. (Adapted from von Frisch, 1967.)

FIGURE 8-12 (Below, right) Dance of the honeybees: The waggle dance. This dance communicates the direction of a food source, its distance, and the quality of the food. (Adapted from von Frisch, 1967.)

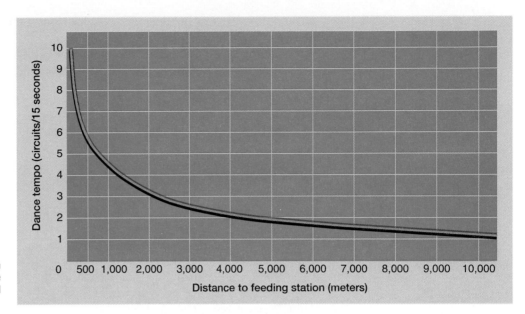

FIGURE 8-13 The relationship between the tempo of the waggle dance and the distance to the food source. (Adapted from von Frisch, 1967.)

lated" into a horizontal direction. The bees accomplish this by equating the upward direction on the vertical surface with the direction of the sun. Thus, if the straight run points directly upward, the food source is located in the direction of the sun; if the straight run is performed downward, the food source is located in the opposite direction from the sun. If the food source is, say, 60 degrees to the left of the sun, the dance will be angled 60 degrees to the left on the vertical surface.

What happens when the sun's position in the sky changes? Bees have a natural "clock" that enables them to correct for such a change. If there is an interval of time between the discovery of the food source and the waggle dance, or between the dance and the arrival of the bees at the food source, the bees automatically correct for the change in the sun's position.

INSTINCTS IN HUMANS

Do humans also perform instinctual behavior patterns like those of other animals? Judging from the fact that humans evolved from ancestral species who surely must have done so, the answer would seem to be yes. In short, the continuity throughout evolution between humans and other species makes it possible, if not plausible, for humans to have instincts too.

Although many claims have been made about the presence of instincts in humans, few of those claims are fully supported by available evidence. As noted earlier, it is not possible to raise humans in isolation and then test them to see if they can perform behaviors that are thought to be innate. But the dilemma is that if researchers use less rigorous methods they cannot rule out learning and experience as sources of the behavior in question. There are, however, other ways of obtaining evidence about instinctual behavior in humans. One way is to observe the similarities between behavior patterns exhibited by humans and those shown by other organisms (Eibl-Eibesfeldt, 1989).

An example of such similarities is the parental instinct. Many different species exhibit parental behaviors. Birds, for example, work ceaselessly to feed the gaping mouths of hungry chicks. Many other species nurture their young for several weeks after birth, often at significant risk to themselves. Because humans are generally similar to other animals in this regard, many scientists claim that humans also possess a parental instinct (Eibl-Eibesfeldt, 1975; Tinbergen, 1951; Wilson, 1978). They argue that over the course of their evolution human beings have cared for their young because they were biologically programmed to do so, not because they were taught

209

to do so. In other words, parenting behavior is innate, not learned (although learning obviously could play a role).

Some support for this theory is provided by the fact that humans respond to certain sign stimuli in a way that is remarkably similar to the responses of many animals. Specifically, we react to so-called baby features in much the same way as do other species. The young of many animal species, including humans, have highly characteristic features. They include a relatively foreshortened face with a large forehead and eyes and protruding cheeks. These features appear to function as releasing stimuli that trigger care-giving behavior.

The possibility that baby features are sign stimuli was first suggested by the noted ethologist Konrad Lorenz (1943). Subsequent research has tended to support this idea (Fullard & Rieling, 1976). In one study, about 200 college students were asked to rate drawings of babies' faces for attractiveness (Sternglanz, Gray, & Murakami, 1977). The subjects were shown dozens of different drawings in which eye height, width, iris size, and vertical position were systematically varied. A representative sample of these drawings is presented in Figure 8-14. The results indicated that certain features were judged to be more attractive than others. The combination of features that was judged to be most attractive is shown in Figure 8-15; this particular combination also most resembles the large eyes, pudgy cheeks, and small nose of the typical baby.

This preference is not limited to laboratory tests. As suggested in Figure 8-16, baby features or the lack thereof account for our adoration of some creatures and our distaste, or even disgust, for others.

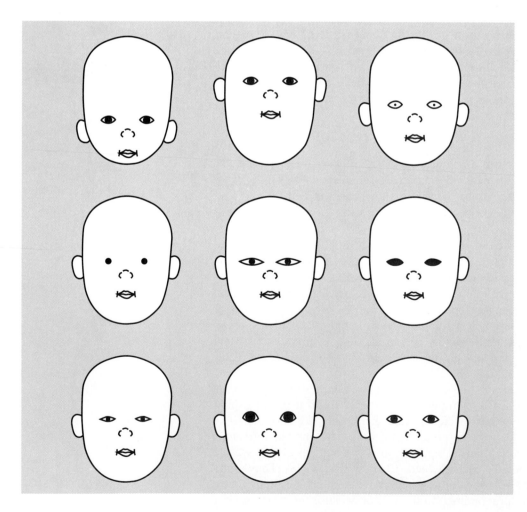

FIGURE 8-14   Examples of the kinds of drawings shown to subjects of a study designed to determine the features that adults find most attractive in the faces of babies. (Adapted from Sternglanz, Gray, & Murakami, 1977.)

FIGURE 8-15 A composite drawing of the features found to be most attractive to adults in the faces of babies. (Adapted from Sternglanz, Gray, & Murakami, 1977.)

FIGURE 8-16 Childlike features in the young of some animals elicit our affection whereas the features of other animals elicit rejection and disgust.

What does the experiment just described demonstrate about the human parental instinct? Although it illustrates that humans are sensitive to certain facial features, it does not unequivocally demonstrate that those features directly elicit a care-giving instinct. There is, however, other evidence suggesting that baby features release care-giving behaviors. For example, care-giving reactions are elicited when subjects are asked to hold a baby or even a kitten (Spindler, 1961). When holding a kitten, subjects tend to express affection and euphoria, pat the animal, and say its name in a high-pitched voice.

There is, unfortunately, evidence for the converse reaction as well: Infants who lack the releasing features may be neglected. Several studies have shown that infants who are most likely to be physically abused are also likely to lack attractive baby features (Martin, 1976). Many of these infants are underweight (Klein & Stern, 1971) or have congenital defects (Hunter, Kilstrom, Kraybill, & Loda, 1978). Of course, the incidence of abuse is strongly related to the characteristics of the abuser, but when one considers cases in which the abusers' characteristics are the same, the features of the child appear to be a significant factor.

INSTINCTS AND THE ENVIRONMENT

So far we have emphasized the biological determinants of behavior, including the possibility that humans, like many other species, have instinctual behavior patterns. Any theory of behavior, however, that failed to recognize the role of the environment would be sadly deficient. Humans clearly are not merely prewired creatures, robots acting out a genetically coded behavior sequence. Behavior patterns are modified by experience. This does not mean that human behavior is simply both innate and learned. Rather, it means that experience actually shapes our biological nature and that genetically coded potentials modify our experience.

An example should help clarify this important point. Most people would assume that bird songs are wholly instinctual and that birds need no experience to be able to sing the song that is typical of their species. This is not the case, however; many species of birds learn their song (Petrinovich, 1985; Slater, 1983). For example, white-crowned sparrows learn their song when they are between 10 and 50 days old. If they are prevented from hearing adult birds singing during this period, they will eventually sing, but their song will be a poor version of the adult song. It appears, therefore, that the birds are biologically "prepared" to sing but that they must have the experience of hearing the song if they are to reproduce it correctly. Biological factors and learning interact; neither factor is sufficient in itself.

The research on herring gulls described earlier also illustrates the interaction of genetic factors and experience. The gull's genes prepare it to respond to the releasing stimulus (movement of the red dot and the bill), but it initially does so clumsily. After three to five days' experience, however, the chick becomes more proficient in its pecking behavior. Thus, experience does not account for the initial appearance of pecking but does improve the accuracy of the behavior.

INTERIM SUMMARY

A basic concept in the study of instinct is the fixed-action pattern (FAP). An FAP has the following characteristics: It is the same each time it is performed, is found in all the members of a given species, occurs independently of experience, has a single function, and is triggered by a specific releasing (or sign) stimulus. Some instincts are discrete actions; others are complex patterns of behavior, like the "dances" used by bees to communicate the location and nature of food sources. Humans also exhibit behaviors that may be instinctual. An example is parental behavior, which resembles the care-giving behavior of other species and is released by specific features of the infant's face; in fact, the absence of those features may be associated with neglect or abuse of the infant. Although experience does not account for the initial appearance of an FAP, it increases the accuracy of the behavior in question.

EVOLUTION OF SOCIAL BEHAVIOR

In the previous sections of this chapter we explored the effects of evolution and natural selection on the behavior of species, including humans, especially the so-called survival behaviors such as feeding and predator defense. Here we turn to a broader issue: What is the effect of evolution on social behavior, including human social behavior? Can social behaviors and norms—things as diverse as, say, dress codes, Easter parades, and children's games—be in some way the products of our genetic makeup? According to the discipline of **sociobiology,** the answer is yes. Sociobiologists maintain that there are fundamental similarities in social behavior, even among the most diverse societies on earth, that reflect the same evolutionary principles that shape other physical and behavioral traits. Many such claims are quite controversial, of course. Critics argue, for example, that the complex behaviors sociobiologists attribute to heredity are much better explained as the result of cultural processes.

Nevertheless, sociobiology has provided a strong case for the heredity of at least some human social behavior. One example is altruism—helping others. It is to this behavior that we now turn.

THE PROBLEM OF ALTRUISM

From an evolutionary perspective individuals should act in a wholly self-interested manner. That is, if survival of the species over time requires success on the part of the individual, and if success entails competition, then any mutation that gives the organism a competitive edge should become part of the gene pool, whereas any mutation that reduces competitive behavior should not. Remember that competition need not be direct or obvious, nor must the individual be consciously aware of it. Competition can be indirect, subtle, and unconscious, as when different species compete for food resources.

If an organism is best served by acting in its own interest, however, there should be little reward for acting altruistically. Yet altruism does exist. Many species, including humans, behave altruistically in countless situations. How can we account for this apparent conflict?

In an evolutionary context, **altruism** may be defined as behavior performed for the benefit of other individuals at the expense of the altruistic individual. That is, a behavior is altruistic if it "reduces the personal reproductive success of the performer while increasing the reproductive success of others" (Barash, 1977, p. 77). "Reproductive success of others" means that the individual that benefits from the altruistic behavior is more likely to survive and have offspring, whereas the altruistic individual is less likely to survive. In practical terms, an altruistic individual may simply sacrifice certain resources, such as food, so that a second individual will have more than it would otherwise; this increases the second individual's chances of survival. Again, it is important to remember that when we refer to altruistic acts we are not implying the presence of any kind of underlying motive, conscious or unconscious.

One of the most common forms of altruistic behavior is parenting. From an evolutionary point of view, parenting involves the sacrifice of resources by the parent for the sake of its offspring. When an individual cares for its offspring, it is giving up part of its own survival potential by sharing resources with the young—finding extra food, chasing away predators, and so forth. Of course, not all animals show parenting behavior. Most fish, for instance, spawn huge numbers of offspring and give them virtually no care. But many species, including humans, display parenting behavior; their offspring are helpless at birth and would die without parental care.

The altruistic nature of parental behavior is also illustrated by the behavior of ground-nesting birds like the killdeer when they see a predator such as a fox. If a mother catches sight of the predator, she scurries from the nest, flapping one wing on the ground as if she were badly wounded. (See Figure 8-17.) This behavior fools the

FIGURE 8-17 A mother killdeer feigns injury to distract a predator from her nest.

predator into following the mother. As the predator pursues the seemingly wounded mother, it is led away from the nest and the young. When the mother has led the predator far enough from the nest, she simply flies away and returns to her chicks, leaving the predator unaware of the location of the nest. This kind of behavior is altruistic because it jeopardizes the life of the mother while increasing the chicks' chances of survival.

SELFISH GENES

How can we explain altruistic acts such as those just described when an evolutionary perspective suggests that individuals should act in a self-interested manner? One answer is that the gene that provides the behavior potential for altruistic acts will be retained in subsequent generations, and thus altruism will evolve within a species, when altruistic acts lead to the survival of genes that are shared with other individuals in that species (Dawkins, 1976). Let us consider this argument in more detail.

Every individual is related to its parents. In most animals that reproduce sexually, an offspring shares half of its genes with each parent. More distant relatives (such as cousins) also share genes with a particular individual, but the more distant the relationship, the lower the degree of genetic relatedness. When an individual acts altruistically toward its relative, it increases the survival chances of the genes they share. Behavior that appears altruistic for a given individual, therefore, is actually selfish behavior from the standpoint of the shared genes. A particular individual may die as a result of altruistic behavior, but the genes it shares with the surviving relative will survive and be passed on to the next generation.

KIN SELECTION

Although the processes just described operate on an unconscious level, the evolution of altruism depends on the presence of one or more of the following conditions. First, the individual must be able to recognize its kin (Wilson, 1975); otherwise an altruistic individual might commit a sacrificial act for an individual that did not share its genes. Altruism as a behavior potential could not evolve under such conditions: If an altruistic individual died, its gene for altruism would cease to exist, whereas the unrelated individual who had been helped would survive and pass on different genes to its offspring. Many animals that exhibit altruism have a keen ability to recognize their kin, although the means by which they do so varies. Some species, including humans, recognize kin by facial features, but in other species kin recognition depends on other signals, such as smell.

Second, altruism can spread through the gene pool if related individuals live near one another. Under such conditions there is a reasonably high probability that an individual that behaves altruistically will be helping a relative.

RECIPROCAL ALTRUISM

Although the processes just discussed make sense in the centuries-long context of evolution, they seem less applicable in contemporary human society. The size of extended families has decreased over the course of human history, and people are less likely to live near their kin now than in the past. In this context, altruistic acts may well benefit unrelated individuals as opposed to related individuals. Consequently, sociobiology must be able to account for altruism among unrelated individuals.

One form of altruistic behavior performed by unrelated individuals is called **reciprocal altruism** (Trivers, 1971). It occurs because the two individuals have an implicit agreement that an act of altruism by one of them will be repaid by the other at a later date. Reciprocal altruism is most likely to evolve in long-lived social ani-

Olive baboons have been shown to demonstrate reciprocal altruism.

mals with relatively high intelligence and the capacity to recognize the other individual. These characteristics, of course, are found in human beings.

Olive baboons provide an example of reciprocal altruism (Packer, 1977). A male baboon normally guards a female with whom it intends to mate by keeping other males at a distance. In order to have an opportunity to mate with the female, however, an excluded male may enlist the help of a third male, who distracts the guardian male. While the guardian and the third male are fighting, the instigator quickly mates with the female. On another occasion the roles will be reversed—the instigator provides the distraction, giving the third male a chance to mate. Thus, the male who shows altruism by distracting the guardian baboon will receive similar assistance in the future; the altruism is reciprocal.

INTERIM SUMMARY

According to the discipline of sociobiology, complex social behaviors are just as much the result of natural selection and evolution as any other physical traits or behaviors. Explanations for the evolution of altruism, a behavior performed for the benefit of other individuals at the expense of the altruistic individual, provides insight into this issue. From an evolutionary perspective, individuals should act in a self-interested manner. Altruism, however, increases the probability that the other individual will survive to reproduce. When such acts favor the survival of genes that are shared with the altruistic individual, the probability that the gene for altruism will survive is enhanced. The evolution of altruism also depends on the ability of an individual to recognize its kin (so that it performs altruistic acts for individuals that share its genes). Altruism can also evolve if related individuals live near one another. Reciprocal altruism occurs between unrelated individuals that have an implicit agreement that altruistic acts by one of them will be repaid by the other at a future date. Critics of sociobiology argue that the complex behaviors sociobiologists attribute to heredity are much better explained as the result of cultural processes.

SUMMARY

1. Because human beings are products of biological evolution, a biological and evolutionary perspective can provide valuable insight into human behavior. In particular, it can help identify the extent to which human actions are determined by biological forces.

2. According to the theory of *natural selection,* individuals in a species that possess mutations that give them a slight advantage in coping with environmental challenges are more likely to survive and reproduce than those born without those mutations. As a result, the genes carrying those mutations have a high probability of being passed on to subsequent generations and becoming part of the species' gene pool.

3. Because an organism's behavior is to a large extent governed by its brain, and because the structure of the brain is inherited, behavior must, to some extent, be inherited. A major task of psychology is to determine how and to what extent. This requires determining the extent to which an individual's *phenotype* is the result of its *genotype* or of environmental forces. Culture provides an important environmental source for human behavior. The cultural transmission of behavior is not limited to humans.

4. *Behavior genetics* is the study of the genetic determination of behavior. *Genes,* the fundamental units of heredity, consist of paired *alleles,* one of which is contributed by each parent. The expression of a genetically controlled trait depends on the particular combination of recessive and dominant alleles the individual receives.

5. Many behaviors of both humans and other animals have been shown to be, in part, genetically determined. Environmental forces, however, also play a critical role.

6. Many scientists have used the concept of *instinct* to explain behavior. Although it fell into disfavor in the United States early in the twentieth century, the concept of the instinct, as refined into the concept of the *fixed-action pattern (FAP),* has been revived thanks to the development of the discipline of *ethol-ogy.* Fixed-action patterns are thought to be inborn, generally fixed and stereotyped, and triggered by specific stimuli called *releasing,* or *sign, stimuli. Supernormal stimuli* have been shown to elicit an exaggerated response.

7. The dance of the honeybees—which enables forager bees to communicate the precise location of a food source to other members of the hive—provides a good example of a complex instinctual behavioral pattern.

8. Although many claims for the existence of instincts in humans have been made, few are fully supported by available evidence. Studies of parenting behavior, however, suggest that the typical features of human infants act as sign stimuli that release instinctive care-giving behavior.

9. Nature and nurture jointly determine behavior. Various birds, for example, are by nature "prepared" to sing, but will not learn their species-typical song unless exposed to it.

10. According to sociobiology, fundamental similarities in the social behavior of all societies reflect the same evolutionary principles that shape other physical and behavioral traits. Critics of sociobiology maintain that these complex behaviors are better explained as the result of cultural processes. The explanation of cooperative behavior (*altruism*), poses a special challenge for evolutionary theory, because altruistic behavior appears to increase the chance for reproductive success of another individual at the expense of the altruistic individual. And yet many species, certainly human beings, show considerable selflessness in their behavior. The explanation favored by many scientists is that altruistic acts, when benefiting a relative with whom the altruist shares genes, increase the survival chances of the shared genes, including those that encode altruism. What is selfless or altruistic on an individual level, therefore, may be selfish on a genetic level.

11. If genes that determine altruism are to survive in the gene pool, however, individuals must be able to recognize kin or

behave altruistically toward those who live nearby. Otherwise, benefit may be given to someone with whom the individual does not share genes. Alternatively, unrelated individuals may mutually profit from *reciprocal altruism* when selfless acts by one are repaid in the future by the other.

FOCUS QUESTIONS

1. Describe how behavior potentials can be said to have evolved in human beings.

2. Identify and discuss examples that illustrate the interaction of genetic and environmental forces.

3. What are fixed-action patterns (FAP) and how do they contrast with learned behaviors?

4. Describe how bees communicate information about food sources.

5. Identify and discuss examples of human instinctual behavior patterns.

6. From an evolutionary perspective, why does altruism appear to be a paradoxical behavior, and how can we explain altruism in terms of natural selection?

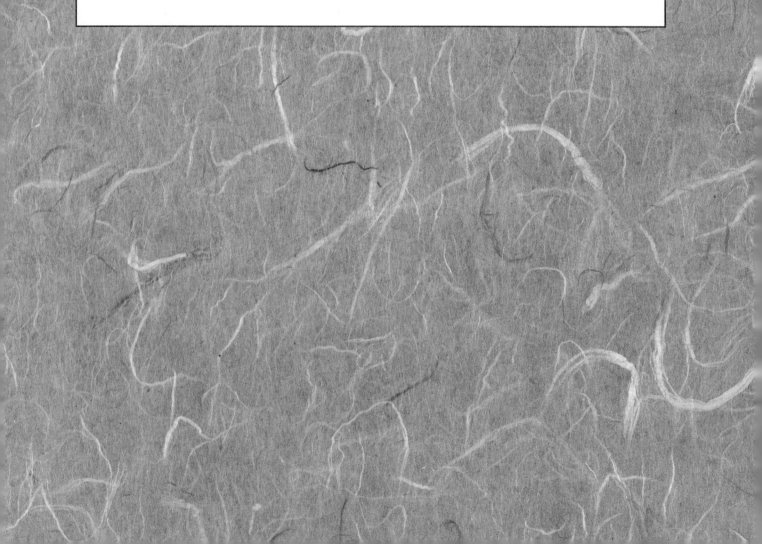

CHAPTER 9

BASIC NEEDS

As we noted in Chapter 1, one of the enduring questions in psychology concerns the origins of human actions. Do we act out of free will or are our actions determined in some way—for example, by our biological makeup? In the last chapter we considered this question from an evolutionary perspective, asking ourselves to what extent human behavior in general is inherited. In this and the rest of the chapters in Part III we consider specific types of behavior and the kinds of forces that give rise to them.

In discussing these forces, psychologists make frequent use of two closely related terms—need and motive. Although defined in various ways, the term **need** is typically associated with a lack of well-being or an "unsatisfying situation" (Murray, 1938, p. 133). A deficiency in some vital substance such as food or water, for example, creates a biological need for that substance. The term **motive,** on the other hand, refers to a psychological state or disposition that energizes behavior. Needs are the objects of motives; motives are the mechanisms by which needs are fulfilled. In this sense, then, hunger is a motive that leads us to satisfy our need for food.

In this chapter we examine the behaviors that satisfy our basic, biological needs for water and food. In Chapters 10 and 11 we look at behaviors that are progressively less tied to biological needs and progressively more tied to forces in our social environment.

To date, research on basic needs has tended to favor a materialist and determinist viewpoint, for the simple reason that various biological states appear to compel us to perform certain actions. Hunger and thirst, for example, seem to affect the behaviors of eating and drinking in a direct and fundamental way. Physiological psychologists have studied how biological states, including the anatomy and physiology of the brain, operate with respect to behavior.

Before we discuss the biological aspects of behavior, however, a word of caution is in order. The materialist viewpoint is an important perspective in psychology, but other views are valuable also. For example, when we say that a person is hungry we are actually *inferring* the presence of hunger from the person's behavior: We note that a particular biological imbalance (lack of food) exists and that a certain behavior (eating) takes place. But the behavior of eating, though seemingly controlled by the biological state of hunger, may be influenced by other factors as well.

Imagine going to an elaborate dinner party. The guests are dressed in formal attire; the table is set with great care and imagination; and the chef has prepared an elegant and sumptuous feast, including exotic hors d'oeuvres and desserts. A prominent response of the guests to these stimuli is to eat; an objective observer might therefore infer that they were biologically hungry. But the guests' behavior is almost certainly affected less by a physiological hunger state than by the social forces that typically

Eating behavior at a state banquet is determined more by social conventions than biological hunger.

operate in such situations—for example, the social stipulation that one should eat slowly and politely, or that one should sample exotic foods even though the thought of them is unappetizing. In other words, a biological framework alone cannot tell us when, why, where, and how people eat.

Similar situations can be found throughout psychology: Behaviors are influenced by so many forces that explanations using only a single perspective are nearly always inadequate. The challenge therefore is not to try to show that a particular perspective is correct by itself, but rather to specify how the perspective provides insight into particular aspects of a situation. To explain hunger, for instance, a physiological or biological perspective may be quite appropriate; eating may indeed be explained in biological terms, *all other things being equal.* If, however, one wishes to explain larger behavioral patterns that are influenced by other psychological states, a simple biological perspective may be inadequate. In the case of the dinner party, the need to be socially compliant also influences the guests' actions.

In the following sections we concentrate on two basic needs—thirst and hunger— and focus on both the physiological and environmental factors that affect these needs. At the end of the chapter we enlarge our focus and consider three common eating disorders: obesity, anorexia, and bulimia.

HOMEOSTASIS

Homeostasis refers to the processes that maintain a state of biological equilibrium in the body. This term was coined over 50 years ago by the noted biologist Walter Cannon to indicate the tendency for the body to maintain an optimal and stable internal environment with an astonishing degree of precision. In Cannon's words:

> When we consider the extreme instability of our bodily structure, its readiness for disturbance by the slightest application of external forces, . . . its persistence through many decades seems most miraculous. The wonder increases when we realize that the system is open, engaging in free exchange with the outer world, and that the structure itself is not permanent but is being continuously broken down by the wear and tear of action, and is continuously built up again by processes of repair. (Cannon, 1967/1932, p. 20)

What causes the disturbances to which Cannon referred? The answer is just about everything. The human body is constantly being affected by the external world. These forces demand a reaction if stability and health are to be protected. To take just one example, as we move about in our environment the temperature is constantly changing, yet our body temperature is maintained at a steady, precise level. We do not become feverish on hot days, nor do we suffer hypothermia (below-normal temperature) when the weather turns cold. Instead, our bodies generate heat when the environment is cold and release heat when it is warm. Such accurate control of body temperature is an example of homeostatic regulation.

NEGATIVE FEEDBACK SYSTEMS

The notion of homeostatic regulation can be represented by a simple feedback system involving a detector and a control mechanism plus associated feedback loops (Ashby, 1956). A thermostat controlling the temperature of a house is an example of such a system (see Figure 9-1). The detector (the thermometer on the wall) has a set-point, a threshold value representing the temperature we wish to maintain. We may, for example, establish the set-point at 68°F, a level we consider comfortable. If the temperature in the house rises above that level, the detector will sense the elevation in temperature and the control mechanism will turn off the furnace, allowing heat to dissipate into the environment (or, in a more sophisticated system, activating an air conditioner). If the temperature falls below the desired level, the control mechanism

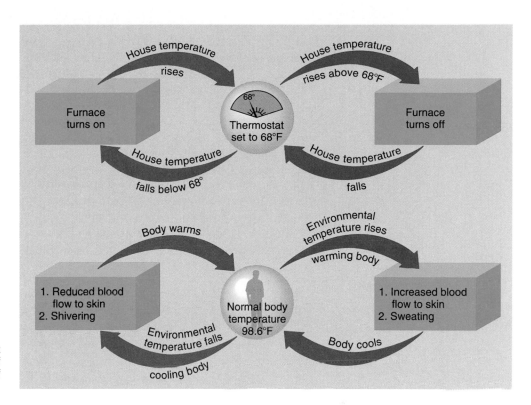

FIGURE 9-1 Two negative feedback systems—the thermostatic control of house temperature and the regulation of body temperature.

is activated, the furnace is turned on, and additional heat is generated. We say that the mechanism provides negative feedback because the greater the discrepancy between the set-point and the current temperature, the more the system will work to eliminate the discrepancy; that is, the consequence of the feedback is to negate the discrepancy. It is important to note that the system is *self*-regulating: Changes in temperature in either direction produce feedback and activate the control mechanism, causing the temperature to hover at or near the set-point.

Body temperature is held constant in an analogous way (see Figure 9-1). When temperature rises, blood flows more readily to the skin surface (allowing the heat to dissipate into the environment) and a person sweats (causing evaporation and thus cooling); both reactions result in a lower body temperature. The reverse occurs when

Evaporation of sweat cools the body; shivering generates heat.

environmental temperature falls: Blood flow to the skin is reduced (thus preventing heat dissipation) and a person shivers (causing stored energy to be converted into heat); the result is an increase in body temperature.

Although some organisms do not have homeostatic mechanisms to control all functions, the feedback system just described is common and has survived throughout the evolutionary process because it provides freedom and flexibility. Imagine what might happen if you could not maintain a steady body temperature. Your mobility would be severely restricted because any change in your environment that resulted in a significant deviation from the optimum temperature would threaten your chances of survival.

The negative feedback system may be viewed as a model of the way many behaviors are biologically determined. Thus psychologists have attempted to identify the particular stimuli that cause the mechanism to be activated, the particular psychological states that accompany those stimuli and influence the resulting adjustments, and the precise mechanisms involved in such a self-regulating system.

INTERIM SUMMARY

The term *homeostasis* refers to the body's ability to maintain an optimal and stable internal environment. It does so by means of negative feedback systems, much the way a thermostat regulates the temperature of a house.

THIRST

The activity of drinking is largely under homeostatic control. The human body is able to maintain its fluids within about 0.5% of the optimum level. Water is obtained from food as well as by drinking, and is lost through evaporation, respiration, and excretion. When the supply of water in the body is diminished, the body attempts both to conserve remaining fluids and to replace, through drinking, that which was lost. Conversely, when the supply of water is excessive, the body excretes water and drinking ceases.

Some homeostatic adjustments in the balance of fluids in the body take place without our being aware of any change; others are obvious to us. For example, we are unaware of the rate at which the body produces urine, but we may experience the sensation of thirst quite strongly (Epstein, Kissileff, & Stellar, 1973; Fitzsimons, 1979; Rolls & Rolls, 1982).

BODY FLUIDS

About two-thirds of the water in the human body is contained within the walls of the cells and is termed the **intracellular fluid.** The **extracellular fluid** makes up the remaining third and lies outside the cells. The third of extracellular fluid contains, approximately 80% (26% of the total) **interstitial fluid,** the warm salty bath that cushions and supports the cells. The remaining 20% (or 7% of the total) is found in the blood plasma and cerebrospinal fluid. All body fluids contain sodium chloride (salt), which, as we saw in Chapter 5, plays a crucial role in neural transmission. In humans, the amount of salt in the fluids is maintained at about 0.9%.

The regulation of these fluids is a complicated task because it entails adjustments not only in the absolute level of fluid but also in the concentrations of sodium chloride and other chemicals within the fluid. If the concentrations of chemicals in the body's fluids are not maintained at the proper levels, the cells cannot perform their normal functions.

When water and various salts are lost through evaporation, they must be replaced.

When the concentrations of sodium chloride in the intra- and extracellular fluids are in balance, the two fluids are said to be **isotonic.** If one of the fluids contains excessive salt, it is termed **hypertonic;** if it contains a lower-than-normal concentration of salt, it is termed **hypotonic.** The body will attempt to correct an imbalance through a process called **osmosis,** in which fluid from the hypotonic side of the membrane (for example, a cell membrane or a blood vessel wall) diffuses through the membrane to balance the concentrations of salt in the fluids on the two sides of the membrane.

CONDITIONS THAT DETERMINE THIRST

Thirst (and therefore drinking) is produced by two conditions, which are called osmotic and hypovolemic thirst. **Osmotic thirst** is caused by an increase in the concentration of salt in the extracellular fluid as a result of the ingestion of salt or the loss of water through respiration and perspiration. Under these conditions water diffuses from the inside of the cells to the interstitial fluid, thus restoring the balance. As a result of the outward flow of water, the cells have less fluid in them than before and actually shrink. This shrinkage, called **cellular dehydration,** is a stimulus for thirst.

The second cause of thirst is a loss of extracellular fluid, a condition known as **hypovolemia.** This occurs primarily through hemorrhaging, vomiting, diarrhea, and evaporation (the last two also change the concentration of salt). The resulting decline in blood pressure and the corresponding increase in the circulation of hormones that regulate the excretion of water appear to trigger thirst.

FLUID REGULATION

The body reacts to osmotic and hypovolemic changes in two ways. First, the remaining supply of water is conserved; second, the supply is replenished through drinking.

Water Conservation

The primary method of conserving water is through the regulation of excretion by the kidneys. For example, when cellular dehydration occurs, the supraoptic area of the hypothalamus activates the posterior pituitary gland, which in turn releases anti-

223

diuretic hormone (ADH). The ADH travels to the kidneys, where it makes the renal tubes more permeable to water. As a result, water is passed back into the body from inside the renal tubes rather than being excreted through the bladder. The net effect is conservation of water.

A complementary process is triggered by hypovolemia. When water is lost through excessive bleeding, for example, blood pressure declines because the blood vessels are not as stretched out as they would be if they contained a larger volume of blood. The change in blood pressure is sensed by **baroreceptors** in the heart and kidneys, which thereupon causes the kidneys to secrete a hormone, renin. This hormone enters the bloodstream and promotes the synthesis of another hormone, angiotensin. Angiotensin circulates in the blood and causes the **adrenal cortex,** an organ located above the kidney, to produce yet another substance, **aldosterone.** The aldosterone travels to the kidneys and causes them to reabsorb sodium. The net effect of this chain of events is a higher concentration of salt in the extracellular fluid and hence greater water retention.

Drinking

As mentioned earlier, thirst stimulates drinking as well as conservation of fluids. When fluid is lost and blood pressure falls, renin is secreted from the kidneys and stimulates the manufacture of angiotensin. (See Figure 9-2.) A derivative of angiotensin, angiotensin II, is detected in an area of the brain called the **subfornical**

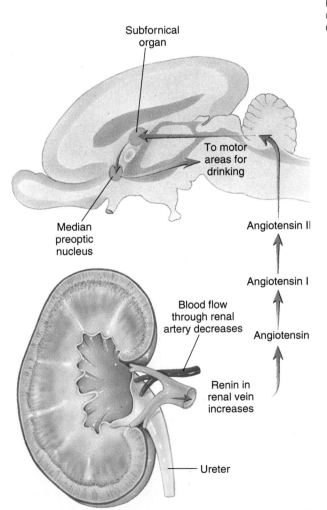

FIGURE 9-2 How fluid loss stimulates drinking in a rat. (Adapted from Galluscio, 1990.)

organ. Neurons connect this site to a second area, the **median preoptic nucleus.** Activation of this area causes an increase in drinking (Fitzsimons & Simons, 1969; Richardson & Mogenson, 1981). Research using rats, for example, has shown that intravenous injection of angiotensin or injection of angiotensin directly into the subfornical organ causes drinking (Fitzsimons & Simons, 1969; Simpson, Epstein, & Canardo, 1978). Conversely, blocking the action of angiotensin causes thirsty rats to cease drinking (Malvin, Mouw, & Vander, 1977).

A similar process results in drinking in response to an increase in the concentration of salt. Certain areas of the hypothalamus and the lateral preoptic area appear to detect the change in salt concentration and induce drinking. Evidence for this comes from several sources. First, if an animal is given an intravenous injection of salty water, it begins drinking within a short time; if the injected water is no saltier than the animal's body fluids, however, drinking does not occur (Fitzsimons, 1972; Holmes & Gregerson, 1947). (Observe what happens to your sense of thirst a few hours after eating a pizza with an anchovy topping.) Second, electrical activity in the hypothalamic areas of an animal's brain increases when a salty solution is injected into the arteries and decreases when pure water is injected (Arnauld, Dufy, & Vincent, 1975). These findings suggest that the brain contains specialized "salt receptors," or **osmoreceptors,** that detect the change in salt concentration and induce the organism to correct the imbalance through drinking.

Both osmotic and hypovolemic thirst are important, but osmotic thirst seems to be the dominant kind. This was shown in an experiment using dogs as subjects (Ramsay, Rolls, & Wood, 1977). (See Figure 9-3.) First the animals were deprived of water; as a result, their blood became hypertonic (saltier). The experimenters then

FIGURE 9-3 Schematic diagram illustrating the technique used to study the effects of osmotic thirst (caused by high concentrations of salt) and hypovolemic thirst (caused by loss of extracellular fluids) in dogs. The researchers changed the concentration of salt in the animals' blood by injecting pure water in the carotid artery. (Adapted from Gallusciu, 1990.)

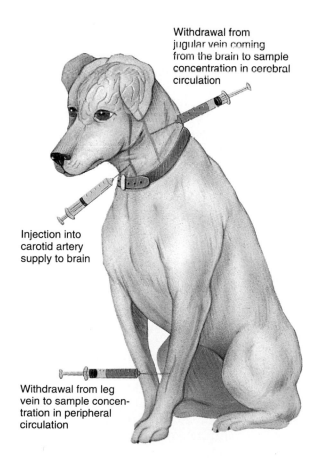

Withdrawal from jugular vein coming from the brain to sample concentration in cerebral circulation

Injection into carotid artery supply to brain

Withdrawal from leg vein to sample concentration in peripheral circulation

injected enough pure water into the dogs' carotid artery to make the concentration of salt in the blood the same as it had been prior to the deprivation period. In other words, they restored the concentration of salt to its initial balanced level without appreciably changing the overall volume of water in the body. While the water was being injected, the dogs were allowed to drink freely. The results indicated that drinking was suppressed by about 75%; that is, relative to control subjects (whose blood salinity was not changed by the injection), the experimental animals exhibited a decline in drinking.

In a second experiment, after the animals had been deprived of water a hypertonic saline solution was injected into the jugular vein, restoring the volume of blood to its predeprivation level without changing the concentration of salt in the body fluids. Under these conditions drinking declined by about 25%; that is, relative to control animals (whose blood volume was not changed), the experimental animals showed a modest decline in drinking. In sum, excessive salt seems to be more important in controlling thirst than a lower-than-normal volume of water, because restoration of the original salt concentration affected drinking more than did restoration of the original fluid volume.

CESSATION OF DRINKING

An interesting characteristic of drinking is that cessation occurs long before the salt balance in the body fluids has been fully restored. It can take as long as 40 minutes after drinking for water to be absorbed into the system (Ramsay, Rolls, & Wood, 1977). The cessation of drinking, and perhaps the feeling of satiety, therefore cannot be attributable to the reestablishment of a balanced salt concentration. The body must have one mechanism for initiating fluid conservation and drinking and a different mechanism for causing drinking to cease.

Stomach Distension

One mechanism for the termination of drinking is located in the stomach and intestines. When the stomach walls are distended by water, an animal drinks less (Rolls, Wood, & Rolls, 1980). Moreover, the transfer of water from the stomach to the small intestine can be an important stimulus for satiety. For example, when the passage between the stomach and intestines is blocked, thus preventing the transfer of water, copious drinking occurs (Hall & Blass, 1977).

Oral Factors

Another key determinant of satiety is the oral sensations accompanying normal drinking. This was demonstrated in a study using rats (Miller, Sampliner, & Woodrow, 1957). The rats were first given 14 milliliters of water. Some of the animals were allowed to drink normally. In others the water was injected directly into the stomach through a surgical tube. Later, all the rats were allowed to drink their fill. As shown in Figure 9-4, the rats that had previously been allowed to drink normally consumed much less water during the later test than the rats that had been injected with water. Satiety levels clearly differed even though both groups of subjects had initially received the same amount of fluid.

It is difficult to determine whether the intestinal or oral stimulus is more important in producing satiety, because the two factors seem to operate together. If, for example, an animal is allowed to drink normally but the water is removed from the esophagus through a surgical tube, satiety occurs only after a large amount of water has been consumed, and is quite temporary (Towbin, 1949). The oral factor *by itself* therefore does not produce satiety. Intestinal factors play a role as well.

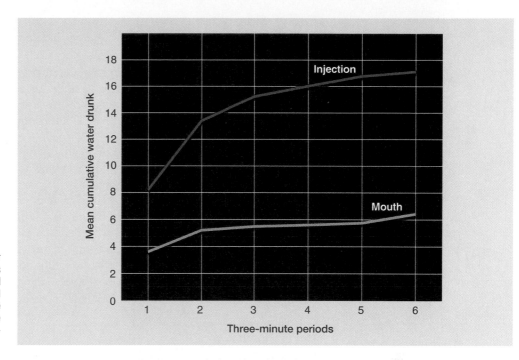

FIGURE 9-4 Mean volume of water drunk as a function of time for animals who had previously been given a fixed amount of water. In one group, the initial water was consumed by mouth; in the other it was injected directly into the stomach. (Adapted from Miller, Sampliner, & Woodrow, 1957.)

INTERIM SUMMARY

Thirst is a psychological state that arises from either of two basic physiological conditions: a higher-than-normal concentration of salt in the extracellular fluids (osmotic thirst) or a loss of extracellular fluid resulting in a decrease in blood pressure (hypovolemia). The body responds to these conditions by conserving its remaining water supply and by drinking. The primary method for conserving water is through the regulation of excretion by the kidneys. Osmotic thirst appears to be the dominant stimulus for drinking. Satiety, or the cessation of drinking, is governed by the interaction of stomach distension and oral factors.

HUNGER

Scientists have been studying the physiological basis of hunger for many years and have accumulated a great deal of information about the biological factors involved. But hunger is a complex state; dozens of processes contribute to the regulation of food intake and energy use. In this section we explore some of these processes.

ENERGY RESERVES

In carrying out their functions, the body's cells use energy; that energy must be replaced. The maintenance of an appropriate energy supply through homeostatic regulation therefore is an important factor in an organism's health. Like fluid reserves, energy reserves are regulated by two means: conservation and replenishment.

227

Energy Storage

It is highly adaptive for an organism to be able to store energy for future use. For one thing, an organism cannot depend on being able to eat at any given time. It may take an appreciable amount of time to find and capture food, and the animal may have to deal with a predator before it can turn its attention to foraging for its next meal. To guard against the possibility of running out of energy, many animals store energy in the form of fat. The fat supply acts as a buffer, enabling the animal to avoid the harmful effects of a food shortage. When food is unavailable, the fat is converted into energy and the appropriate energy level is maintained, at least as long as the fat supply lasts. If the fat stores are depleted, food must be consumed not only to furnish energy but also to replenish the fat supply.

A key element in this process is **insulin,** a hormone secreted by the pancreas. Insulin helps the cells utilize glucose (sugar) and convert it into **glycogen** (the stored form of glucose). If there is no insulin in the circulatory system or if the insulin level is low, as in diabetics, the blood becomes hyperglycemic (that is, it contains an excess of sugar) because the glucose is not being utilized by the cells or being converted into glycogen. Under these conditions, the person's cells may literally die from being starved of glucose.

Energy Utilization

When food is ingested, glucose is absorbed into the bloodstream and either transferred to the cells to serve as energy or converted into glycogen and stored. During a period when food is unavailable, the stored energy must be converted back into usable energy. In this case glycogen in the liver and **glycerol** in the fat tissue is transformed back into glucose. The process is controlled by a hormone, **glucagon,** that is secreted by the pancreas whenever blood sugar falls to a critical level.

CONDITIONS THAT DETERMINE HUNGER AND FEEDING

The storage of glucose as glycogen and fat to be utilized when food is unavailable provides a margin of safety. Normally, however, the organism obtains energy by eating. Psychologists have devoted considerable research to discovering the mechanisms that control this behavior.

One strategy for coping with extended periods during which food is unavailable is to develop layers of fat. Many animals slowly burn their fat during hibernation. Another strategy, shown here, is to hoard food for later consumption.

In people with diabetes, the pancreas does not supply enough insulin and the hormone must be artificially replaced through injection, as these children at a special summer camp are learning to do.

The Role of Glucose

The physiological event that appears to trigger hunger, and hence eating, is a decrease in the availability of glucose. According to the **glucostatic theory,** the brain contains receptors that monitor the amount of glucose in the blood (the blood sugar level). When the blood sugar level falls, the animal experiences hunger and will eat (Mayer, 1955; Oomura, 1976). The stimulus for hunger, however, is the amount of glucose available to the cells as energy, not the absolute amount in the blood (Mayer, 1953). Because insulin makes the cell membranes more permeable to glucose, hunger results when the level of glucose is low and the level of insulin is normal *or* when the glucose level is normal but insulin is lacking.

The location of the **glucoreceptors** has been a subject of intense research. Although the brain certainly plays an important role, the liver seems to be more critical (Friedman & Stricker, 1976). For example, an infusion of glucose will cause the neurons in the liver to fire (Niijima, 1969). Perhaps more convincing is the fact that when the cells are deprived of glucose (by means of an injection of 2-deoxy-D-glucose, which prevents cells from utilizing glucose), laboratory animals immediately begin to eat (Novin, VanderWeele, & Rezek, 1973). It appears, however, that the brain and liver interact, because when the vagus nerve (which carries sensory information from the internal organs to the brain) is severed, the effect of 2-deoxy-D-glucose is eliminated.

Brain Mechanisms

For many years several brain areas were thought to be the primary controllers of hunger. Today, however, some scientists believe that they play a secondary role and that the processes occurring in the liver that were just described are the dominant mechanism in the control of hunger (Friedman & Stricker, 1976).

Until fairly recently psychologists believed that the **lateral hypothalamus** was exclusively responsible for regulating hunger and eating. (See Figure 9-5.) The evidence seemed clear: Electrical or chemical stimulation of this area causes animals to begin eating almost instantly (Miller, 1960; Wyrwicka, Dobrzecka, & Tarnecki, 1960). On the other hand, damage to the lateral hypothalamus causes an animal to

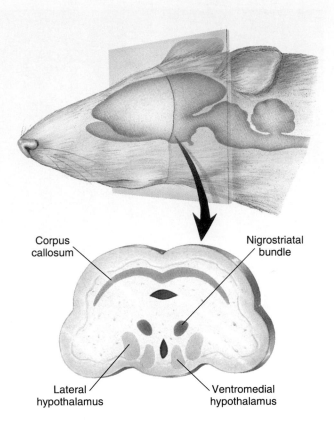

FIGURE 9-5 The location of the lateral hypothalamus and the ventromedial hypothalamus in a rat's brain.

stop eating (a condition termed **aphagia**), which leads to death, usually within days (Teitelbaum & Stellar, 1954). These two facts suggested that the lateral hypothalamus is the brain's "hunger center." When intact and active, it causes the animal to eat; when damaged, eating is inhibited.

We now know that this theory is incorrect. The lateral hypothalamus is not the important area it was thought to be. Instead, a bundle of nerve fibers called the **nigrostriatal bundle,** which runs near the lateral hypothalamus, plays a more significant role (Ungerstedt, 1971). Moreover, damage to the lateral hypothalamus changes the animal's ability to detect and react to sensory changes of all sorts (Marshall, Turner, & Teitelbaum, 1971). By inference, then, animals whose lateral hypothalamus is damaged fail to eat not because they do not feel hunger but because they are insensitive to the stimuli that normally elicit eating, such as the taste and odor of food.

CESSATION OF EATING

As in the case of drinking, satiety for food is governed by mechanisms other than those controlling feeding and hunger.

Peripheral Factors

The stomach distension created by the food itself is an important factor (Smith & Duffy, 1957). If a balloon is surgically implanted in an animal's stomach and then inflated, the receptors in the stomach that detect the stretching of the stomach tissue are stimulated and eating stops. But stomach distension is not the primary mechanism governing satiety, because the satiety created in this way is only temporary and the amount of distension required for the balloon to induce satiety is much greater than the amount of distension created by an ordinary meal.

Another factor governing satiety is the nutritive value of the stomach contents. (See also Geary, 1990.) Rats will eat to compensate for calories that have been removed from their stomachs by a suction device. The more calorie-rich the food that is removed, the more eating occurs. If the process is reversed and the stomach is loaded with nutrients, the rats will cease eating (Deutsch & Gonzalez, 1980).

Oral factors are also involved in the cessation of eating. As with drinking, animals will stop eating when food is allowed to pass through the mouth but is prevented from entering the stomach (Berkun, Kessen, & Miller, 1952). The satiety created in this way is temporary, however, and disappears if the animal has experienced the treatment many times.

Satiety is anticipatory in nature; that is, one must anticipate the appropriate amount of food and stop eating *before* the meal has been fully absorbed. A number of experiments have shown that this is a learned reaction. In an interesting study using human subjects, two groups of subjects received a 100-milliliter drink of "soup" (Booth, Lee, & McAleavey, 1976; see also Booth, 1972, 1977). The caloric content of the soup differed for the two groups. Subjects in one group received a soup that was 65% starch, whereas subjects in the other group received a soup that was only 5% starch. Solutions that are high in starch also have a high caloric content, but starch cannot be detected by its taste. Thus, neither group of subjects could detect the caloric content of the soup by taste alone.

Immediately following the drink of soup, the subjects were given a standard portion of a flavored yogurt in order to provide a distinctive flavor that would become associated with the caloric content of the soup. The subjects were then offered small sandwiches, cookies, and candies and were allowed to eat as much as they wished. Presumably those who were still hungry would eat more food than those whose hunger had been relieved by the previous soup course. This procedure was repeated for four days. (Bear in mind that it takes an appreciable amount of time for calories to be absorbed into the system. Therefore, the amount of food eaten immediately after the soup does not reflect biological satiation so much as it reflects anticipation of being satiated later.)

Subjects in the two groups ate about the same amount of food during the first session: 835 kilocalories (kcal) for the high-starch group and 832 kcal for the low-starch group. In other words, even though they had consumed different amounts of calories, the groups did not show much difference in hunger, because the calories had not had time to be absorbed. By the last session, however, the subjects who unknowingly had become used to consuming a high-calorie soup ate fewer sandwiches and cookies (760 kcal) than those who had become used to consuming the low-calorie solution (946 kcal).

These results are explained as follows: The distinctively flavored yogurt, which had been eaten directly after the soup and thus had become associated with it, served as a signal for the eventual biological consequences of the soup. For the high-calorie group, those consequences included a relatively large increase in calories; the yogurt signal therefore triggered a sense of satiety that suppressed additional eating. People in the low-calorie group ate more sandwiches and cookies after tasting the yogurt because the yogurt signal was not associated with satiety. The biological consequences that they had experienced after drinking the soup and tasting the yogurt involved a relatively small increase in calories.

Brain Factors

Various areas of the brain play a role in satiety. Historically, the **ventromedial hypothalamus** (VMH) (see Figure 9-5) was regarded as central to satiety. For example, when this area is damaged, animals eat incessantly for many days, often gaining two or three times their normal weight and becoming extremely obese (Brobeck, 1946). (See Figure 9-6.) Conversely, stimulation of the VMH causes a decline in eating (Wyrwicka & Dobrzecka, 1960). For these reasons, the VMH was believed to be

FIGURE 9-6 An obese rat with damage to the ventromedial hypothalamus.

the "satiety center," the area of the brain that turns off hunger and causes eating to cease. When this area was missing because of surgical damage, the feeling of satiety was never triggered and the animal continued to eat. When this area was activated by electrical stimulation, however, eating was suppressed.

Further experiments have shown that this theory is incorrect (Friedman & Stricker, 1976; Grossman, 1979). When the VMH is damaged, insulin secretion increases and glucagon secretion is reduced. Because of the increase in insulin secretion, more food is stored as fat; the effect of the lowered glucagon level is that less food is utilized or converted into glucose. Thus, so much food is being converted into fat, and so little fat is being converted into usable energy, that the animal must eat voraciously just to get enough energy for its normal activity.

THE ROLE OF INCENTIVE

Research on hunger and eating indicates that physiological needs cause people to conserve energy and to consume food. We think of people as being driven to find food to satisfy these needs. But physiological factors are only part of the picture; learned reactions are important too. In particular, many food preferences are learned. Animals learn to avoid foods that have made them sick in the past and to prefer foods that contain calories and other needed substances.

In one experiment, rats were given different flavored solutions to drink (Bolles, Hayward, & Crandall, 1981). One solution contained a large number of calories; another contained relatively few calories. The rats developed a preference for the flavor added to the high-calorie food relative to the flavor added to the low-calorie food. Because calories themselves are tasteless, the animals relied on flavor to indicate which food contained the most calories; that is, the nutritional consequences of the food were associated with its flavor. This is an example of a learned food preference based on the caloric content of the food. We learn to distinguish among foods according to flavor and eventually prefer them if they have beneficial effects.

Learned preferences of this sort reflect an important concept: **incentive.** An incentive is a learned source of motivation, a goal object that lures us into action. Consider the following comparison. A starving person is driven to eat a meal in order to

Hunger may goad us to eat, but particularly tasty foods may entice us to eat whether we are hungry or not.

satisfy a biological need; that person can be said to have a hunger drive. Another person, who has just finished eating Thanksgiving dinner and presumably is fully satiated, nevertheless will eat dessert. In each case the behavior—eating—is the same, but in the first case the behavior is "pushed" by a biological drive whereas in the second case it is "pulled" by a food object. In other words, one may be goaded into eating by biological hunger (a temporary physiological state) as well as lured into eating by certain tasty foods (goal objects). Eating thus may occur as a result of a learned habit as well as the presence of the biological state of hunger.

INTERIM SUMMARY

Regulation of the body's energy supply is accomplished by two means: conservation of existing supplies and replenishment through eating. Many animals conserve energy by storing glucose in the form of glycogen or fat, which can be converted into usable energy when food is unavailable. The conservation and replenishment of energy resources is accomplished primarily through the regulation of blood glucose levels. A drop in the level of glucose available to the cells triggers hunger, which stimulates the animal to eat and thereby replenish its energy supplies. Receptors in the brain and the liver interact to produce the sensation of hunger. Satiety is governed by different mechanisms, including stomach distension, the nutritive value of the stomach contents, and oral factors. The most important factor is the anticipation of an increase in calories that is triggered by the flavors previously associated with high-calorie foods. Various areas of the brain, including the ventromedial hypothalamus, play a role in satiety; incentives or goal objects, such as tasty foods, also motivate eating.

OBESITY

By some estimations, obesity has reached near-epidemic levels in the United States. Some surveys claim that between 25 and 45% of middle-aged Americans are at least 20% above their recommended maximum weight (Grinker, 1982). There is little doubt that obesity and other eating disorders constitute a major problem for some people.

Fat protects the organism against famine; from an evolutionary point of view, therefore, it is adaptive. Why, then, is obesity a problem, and what causes it? Although these questions have not been answered fully, much is known about the body's storage of fat and about the conditions leading to obesity. Both physiological and environmental factors contribute to obesity.

PHYSIOLOGICAL FACTORS

The overall quantity of fat is a function of the size and number of fat cells in the body (Hirsh & Knittle, 1970). For any given individual, this number is a result of two factors: genetic makeup and early nutritional experience. Once the fat cells are established, the number of such cells in the body is fixed and stable. Dieting can decrease the size of the fat cells but not the number of fat cells in the body. Not only will resumption of eating enlarge the fat cells once again, but because the metabolism rate changes as well (food is converted into fat at a faster rate so that the body can protect itself from future losses as a result of dieting), their ultimate size will be even greater (Rodin, 1981). In this way the cells are "primed" to become fatter.

Genetic Factors

Considerable evidence suggests a strong genetic component in obesity. Various non-human species have been bred for obesity (Bray & York, 1971). Are some humans genetically predisposed to become fat? The answer is yes, to a considerable degree (Stunkard, Harris, Pedersen, & McClearn, 1990; see also Costanzo & Schiffman, 1989). Among children who have two obese parents, 80% are likely to be obese; among children with only one obese parent, 40% are likely to be obese; among children whose parents are both of normal weight, only 7% are likely to be obese (Mayer, 1965).

These figures obviously do not exclude the effects of environmental factors, but when such factors are eliminated from the analysis, the effect of genetics remains significant. For example, there is a greater correspondence between the weight of parents and that of their natural-born children than there is between the weight of parents and that of adopted children (Grinker, Price, & Greenwood, 1976). One study found a high positive relationship between the weight of children and that of their biological parents—the fatter the parents, the fatter the child, as shown in the left portion of Figure 9-7. Such a relationship was not evident in the case of adoptive parents, as can be seen in the right portion of the figure. The weight of adoptive parents of obese children was no different from that of adoptive parents of thin children. These results led the researchers to conclude that "genetic influences have an important role in determining human fatness in adults, whereas the family environment alone has no apparent effect" (Stunkard, Sorensen, Hanis, Teasdale, Chakraborty, Schull, & Schulsinger, 1986, p. 314).

Fat Stores

Body weight is also determined by processes that regulate fat stores. It has long been thought that fat tissue is the basis for long-term energy regulation. This **lipostatic theory** (Keesey & Powley, 1986) argues that as fat accumulates, appetite decreases, but that as fat stores are depleted and energy is used, appetite increases. This theory resembles the glucostatic theory discussed earlier, except that it is applied to long-term rather than short-term energy regulation. In both cases the system operates much like a thermostat: As fat supplies diminish, appetite is "turned on" and fat stores are built up, at which point appetite declines and fat stores are used to provide energy.

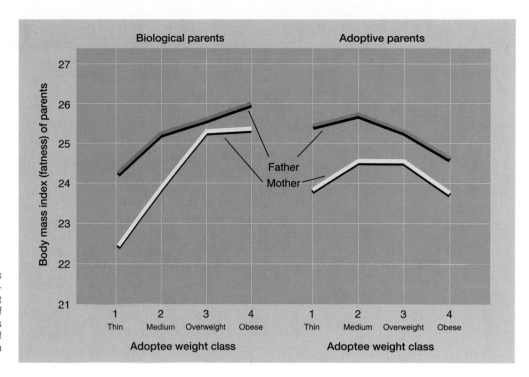

FIGURE 9-7 Mean body mass (an index of fatness) for both biological and adoptive parents in relation to the weight class of adopted offspring. The weight of adopted children more closely matches that of their biological parents than of their adoptive parents. (Adapted from Stunkard et al., 1986.)

There is considerable evidence to support the lipostatic theory. For example, the metabolic rate declines when a person diets. This is a protective mechanism designed to retain fat stores during times of famine (Rodin, 1981). It also means that people burn calories at a slower rate when they are on a diet than when they are not. But the most impressive evidence for the lipostatic theory is that overweight people tend not to overeat (Spitzer & Rodin, 1981). Once their fat stores reach a certain level, they maintain their weight without overeating.

ENVIRONMENTAL FACTORS

Environmental factors also play an important role in obesity. Most animals regulate their body weight quite precisely without ever becoming obese. Under unusual circumstances, however, weight regulation does not occur. Rats, for example, will gain weight and become obese when they are given a tasty high-fat diet. This suggests that sweet, high-calorie diets contribute to obesity (Logue, 1986). Indeed, the taste of a goal object is a powerful attractive force and can lead to obesity (Ramirez, 1990). This occurs because there is normally a strong positive relationship between the perceived pleasantness of a taste and its sweetness. If, however, subjects are satiated with a sweet-tasting solution and then asked to rate its pleasantness, the relationship is negative—the sweeter the taste, the less pleasant it is judged to be (Cabanac, 1971). In other words, people may normally perceive the taste of candy as pleasant but will not consider it pleasant if they have just eaten a large amount of it. This research suggests that taste is an important dimension of a goal object but that such incentives may be less powerful (or even aversive) when the person is satiated.

Stressors

Environmental stressors also contribute to obesity. For example, a mild stressor such as having its tail pinched causes a rat to overeat (Antelman & Rowland, 1981). Analogous effects are seen in humans. College students, for example, tend to eat more during final-examination periods (Pines & Gal, 1977), and obese people tend to eat more when they are anxious (McKenna, 1972).

235

Cognitive Factors

Still another factor contributing to obesity is cognition. In one study, obese and normal subjects were given a liquid as a substitute for one of their usual meals for eight days (Wooley, Wooley, & Dunham, 1972). Half of the meals contained a high number of calories (1.07 calories per cubic centimeter) whereas the other half contained a low number of calories (0.57 calories per cubic centimeter). The flavor of both the high-calorie and the low-calorie liquids was the same. After drinking the liquid, the subjects were asked to rate their hunger and to say whether they had consumed a high- or low-calorie liquid. Presumably they would feel more satisfied after drinking a high-calorie solution than after drinking a low-calorie solution, provided that they were sensitive to their internal satiety cues.

This study produced two major findings. First, the number of calories actually consumed did not affect the subjects' later experience of hunger. Second, subjects showed no ability to identify the caloric content of their liquid meal. They said that they felt fuller and more satiated after drinking what they *believed* to be the high-calorie diet, but this was true whether or not the liquid was actually high in calories. Merely believing that they had received the high-calorie diet caused them to feel less hungry later on. Belief about caloric intake, stemming from information derived externally, thus seems to be one of the factors controlling satiety.

In another study, both obese and normal subjects reported to the laboratory at 9:00 A.M. without having eaten breakfast (Stunkard, 1959; see also Stunkard, 1961). Each subject then swallowed a surgical balloon that, when inflated, provided an electrical recording indicating when the stomach was contracting. Every 15 minutes over the next 4 hours, the subjects were asked if they felt hungry. The results were surprising. First, there were no differences in actual stomach contractions between the obese and normal subjects. Second, normal subjects often said that they felt hungry, and they usually reported these feelings during actual stomach contractions (71% of their contractions were accompanied by reports of hunger). The obese subjects, in contrast, rarely reported feeling hungry, and when they did, they were as likely to do so during a period of no contractions as during a contraction period (only 47% of their contractions were accompanied by reports of hunger). Thus the study indicated that obese subjects do not recognize the internal physiological cues (contractions) associated with hunger.

These and other findings suggested that overweight people are highly susceptible to external cues and highly insensitive to internal hunger signals (Schachter, 1971). Under such conditions overeating is very likely because the world is filled with alluring food-related cues. When an obese person passes a pastry shop, the mere sight of the food in the window (an external cue) is enough to stimulate the desire to eat even though the person is not biologically hungry at the time (an internal cue). If obese people obeyed their internal hunger stimuli, as normal subjects are believed to do, they would wait until they felt hungry before eating.

This theory has been tested in a number of experiments. In one study, a group of obese subjects and a group of normal-weight subjects were first given a large meal consisting of roast beef sandwiches (Schachter, Goldman, & Gordon, 1968). Two other groups were given no food. Then all the subjects were allowed to eat as many crackers as they wished. To conceal the real purpose of the experiment, the subjects were told that their task was to judge the "taste quality" of the crackers. In reality, the purpose was to determine how many crackers they would eat. The results are shown in Figure 9-8. Consistent with the theory, normal-weight subjects ate fewer crackers when their stomachs were already full. This result implies that these individuals were sensitive to their internal hunger cues. Obese subjects, on the other hand, ate as many crackers when they were already full as they did when their stomachs were empty. For them, internal cues seemed to be unimportant.

Although this theory is appealing, it appears to be seriously in error. Recent research has suggested that the response of obese subjects to external cues is not as powerful an explanation as was formerly thought (Rodin, 1981). For example, nor-

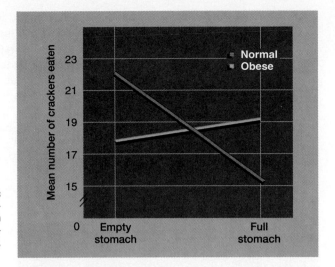

FIGURE 9-8 Mean number of crackers eaten by obese and normal weight subjects after either being preloaded with food (full stomach) or not (empty stomach). (Adapted from Schachter, Goldman, & Gordon, 1968.)

mal subjects appear to be influenced by external cues as much as obese people are. And although some normal-weight subjects who happen to be externally oriented gain more weight than normal subjects who are not externally oriented (Rodin & Slochower, 1976), this finding really says little about the causes of obesity. In sum, responsiveness to external cues can lead to overeating and weight gain, but not all externally oriented people become fat and the amount of weight gain is not determined by the degree of external orientation. As we have seen, obesity also depends on such factors as genetic makeup, number of fat cells, and metabolic rate.

INTERIM SUMMARY

There is evidence that genetic factors play an important role in obesity. It is believed that humans maintain a certain level of fat tissue and that obese people have a higher set-point than normal-weight people. But environmental factors are important, too. Obese people may be far less sensitive to the internal body cues, such as stomach contractions, that normally help regulate eating; they may also be more responsive to external cues such as stress and cognitive factors. These characteristics are not a function of body weight, however, so they say little about the causes of obesity. Responsiveness to external cues may contribute to obesity along with genetic makeup and other physiological characteristics.

OTHER EATING DISORDERS

ANOREXIA NERVOSA

Anorexia nervosa is a debilitating illness that affects up to 16 people per million and is fatal in about 20% of all cases (Bemis, 1978; Garfinkel & Garner, 1982; Gilbert, 1986). Most of the victims are women; the disorder is very rare in men. The symptoms usually become apparent during adolescence and have no known physiological cause.

The primary characteristic of anorexia is a dramatic loss of weight, amounting to as much as 25% of the patient's body weight. (See Figure 9-9.) The patient becomes gaunt and ill. A second key characteristic is a maladaptive attitude toward eating: The patient denies the need to eat and claims not to feel hungry. Daily intake can drop to as low as 200–300 calories, although binge eating sometimes occurs (Leon, 1983). In addition, anorexics usually have a highly distorted body image (Garner, Garfinkel, Stancer, & Moldofsky, 1976). For example, they may express intense fear that they will become fat and may drastically overestimate their body size, believing themselves to be much fatter than they really are (Garfinkel, Moldofsky, Garner, Stancer, & Coscina, 1978). Finally, they may express a strong feeling of helplessness about many aspects of their lives.

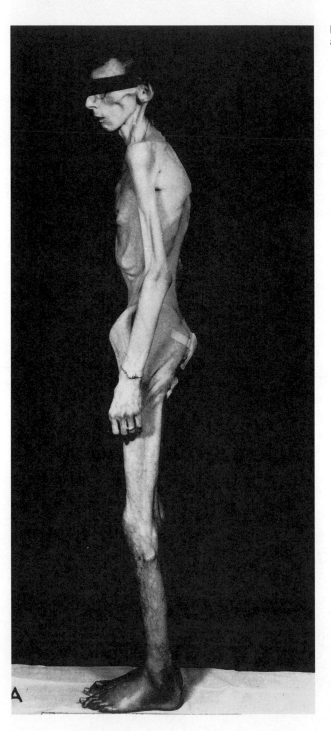

FIGURE 9-9 A woman suffering from anorexia nervosa.

The psychological causes of anorexia are not fully known, but some recurring themes have been identified. Some experts believe that anorexics are seeking attention; others suggest that they are denying their sexuality. It is also believed that anorexia may result from having overdemanding parents. In general, anorexics appear to suffer from severe emotional problems (Logue, 1986), but it is not clear whether the eating disorder is the cause or the result of the emotional stress.

Treatments for anorexia vary widely (Garner & Garfinkel, 1985). They are of two general types: those designed to produce an immediate weight gain and those whose goal is longer-term weight maintenance. In the former category is intravenous feeding (Garfinkel & Garner, 1982). The major problem with such an approach is that, even when successful, the person may believe that all eating leads to weight gain and so may resist maintaining a healthy weight level after being discharged from the treatment facility. In the latter category are psychotherapies, group therapies, and behavior modification. Various drugs have been tried, but their effects are limited; they help the patient gain weight initially but do not contribute to long-term weight maintenance.

One interesting approach uses a structured program related to the preparation and eating of food (Sparnon & Hornyak, 1989). Once weight has stabilized, hospitalized patients are allowed to join other patients in a "cooking group." Each patient plans and prepares a meal once a week for all the group members. The purpose is to give patients practice eating in such situations and to get them to take full responsibility for the meal so that when it is time to leave the hospital they will continue to feel that the preparation and consuming of a meal is a positive and worthwhile event. Close supervision is provided in the early phase of the program. For example, dieticians meet with the patient to help with meal planning and cooks give advice on preparation. Once a patient has performed successfully, however, complete control and independence is granted; the patient now must assume full responsibility for planning and preparing the meal. To be discharged from the hospital, a patient must demonstrate an appreciable weight gain and show evidence that the appropriate behavior will persist. For example, the person must fully consume the meals within 30 minutes and demonstrate a tolerance for new foods.

BULIMIA

Bulimia, a disorder related to anorexia nervosa, is characterized by episodic binging on food followed by fasting and purging by means of strong laxatives or self-induced vomiting. During the binge phase, the person may eat as many as 55,000 calories in a single sitting (Johnson, Stuckey, Lewis, & Schwartz, 1982). Yet, unlike anorexics, bulimics are usually of normal weight.

According to one study, the incidence of bulimia among college students is much higher than that of anorexia—13% compared to 3.8% (Halmi, Falk, & Schwartz, 1981). In this study, 87% of students reporting symptoms of bulimia were female.

The causes of bulimia are unknown; as in the case of anorexia, there is no clear physiological cause. People with bulimia tend to be depressed and express guilt over their binges, together with a feeling of loss of control (Dunn & Ondercin, 1981; see also Heatherton & Baumeister, 1991). One survey found that the factors precipitating an eating binge were difficulty in handling emotions (40%), restrictive dieting (34%), interpersonal conflicts (7%), and loss or separation (6%) (see Johnson, Stuckey, Lewis, & Schwartz, 1982).

Like anorexia, bulimia is difficult to treat. Several approaches have been used to eliminate the binge-purge-starve cycle and to change fundamental attitudes toward eating (Hsu, 1990). One promising treatment is called the "Exposure plus Response Prevention" technique (Hoage, 1989). Here, patients are instructed to binge on various foods during the therapy session until they actually feel the need to vomit. The sessions are conducted individually or in groups; the latter may be even more therapeutic because bulimics often have trouble eating in front of other people. This is done, of course, under the close supervision of the therapist. When the urge to vomit is felt, the person is then instructed to suppress the reaction for up to two and one-half hours (about the time it takes for the food to be absorbed). During this time, the therapist tries to calm the person's fears about eating "forbidden" foods, and gives reassurance that the person *can* control these urges in such a situation. In many cases, the person does eventually learn self-control.

INTERIM SUMMARY

Anorexia and bulimia are eating-related disorders that do not have clear physiological causes. Anorexia is characterized by excessive weight loss and refusal to eat; bulimia involves binge eating and purging. These disorders almost always involve psychological problems such as depression.

SUMMARY

1. Drinking and eating, the behaviors associated with the satisfaction of our basic needs for water and food, are largely the result of biological processes. Many other factors, however, including social pressures, play a role; a biological framework alone cannot tell us when, why, where, and how people eat.

2. *Homeostasis* refers to the processes that maintain a state of biological equilibrium in the body. These processes—for example, the maintenance of a constant body temperature—can be described in terms of simple negative feedback systems. The negative feedback model applies to many biologically controlled behaviors, including those associated with basic needs.

3. Two conditions appear to trigger thirst. *Osmotic thirst* results from an increase in the concentration of salt in the *extracellular fluid,* which causes *cellular dehydration. Hypovolemic thirst* results from *hypovolemia,* a loss of extracellular fluid.

4. The body responds to these osmotic and hypovolemic changes in two ways: by conserving water and by stimulating drinking. Conservation results when a sequence of substances (*renin, angiotensin,* and *aldosterone*) cause the kidneys to reabsorb sodium back into the fluid system, inhibiting water excretion. The increase in angiotensin is detected by *osmoreceptors* in the brain, stimulating drinking. Osmotic thirst appears to

have a greater effect on drinking than does hypovolemic thirst.

5. Drinking ceases before the osmotic balance has been restored, suggesting that one mechanism accounts for fluid conservation and drinking and another for causing drinking to cease. Stomach distension and oral factors are important in this second mechanism.

6. Food is converted into stored energy (*glycogen*), by the pancreatic hormone *insulin.* It is then converted back into usable energy, when needed, by *glucagon.*

7. According to the *glucostatic theory* of hunger, *glucoreceptors* in the liver and brain trigger hunger when glucose levels fall too low. Psychologists once thought that the *lateral hypothalamus* in the brain was exclusively responsible for regulating hunger and eating, but this has been shown not to be the case.

8. As with drinking, separate mechanisms trigger eating and the cessation of eating. One factor contributing to satiety is the stomach distension created by food. Another critical factor is the caloric content of the food consumed. Research suggests that animals learn to associate the stimuli associated with specific foods—flavor, for example—with their caloric content, regulating their consumption accordingly. The *ventromedial hypothalamus* in the brain was once thought to regulate satiety. Later research showed this not to be the case.

9. Learned sources of motivation, or *incentives,* can affect eating behavior independently of physiological motivations. A person might eat an incentive object like a favorite dessert even after eating a filling meal.

10. Both physiological and environmental factors contribute to obesity. Research suggests that genetic makeup has a strong influence on body weight. Body weight is also determined by the physiological processes that regulate fat stores. Environmental factors, such as the taste of particular foods or stress, can influence eating and hence obesity. According to a cognitive theory of obesity, overweight people are highly susceptible to external cues for eating, like the sight of food, and highly insensitive to internal signals of hunger. Recent research, however, suggests that this theory is incorrect.

11. *Anorexia nervosa* and *bulimia* are two eating-related disorders that afflict primarily women. There is no known physiological cause for either of these conditions, but both are almost invariably associated with emotional disorders.

FOCUS QUESTIONS

1. Discuss the way in which the thermostatic control of a heating system can be used as a model for behavioral processes such as eating and drinking.

2. Describe the two primary conditions that determine thirst and the two primary ways by which the body regulates fluid levels.

3. Describe the factors contributing to the cessation of drinking.

4. Describe the mechanisms that control hunger and satiety.

5. In what sense are people motivated to eat by factors other than biological hunger?

6. Discuss the biological and psychological factors that contribute to obesity and other eating-related disorders.

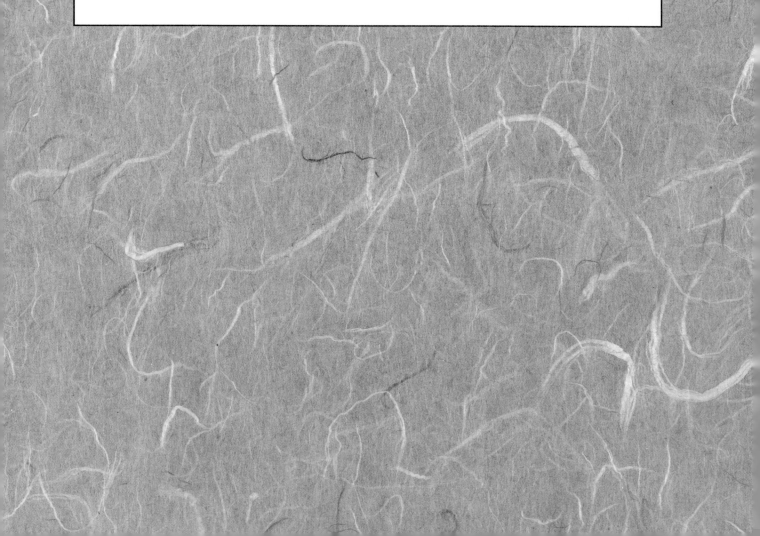

CHAPTER 10

BIOSOCIAL MOTIVES

CHAPTER 10

BIOSOCIAL
MOTIVES

 When discussing the biological foundations of behavior, psychologists often focus on four topics: hunger, thirst, aggression, and sexual behavior. The first two topics, covered in Chapter 9, are usually combined because both involve consumption and both are very closely linked to underlying biological states. Sexual and aggressive behaviors, on the other hand, are often linked for somewhat different reasons: Both share an underlying biological factor—they are dependent on or related to the levels of sex hormones in the body—but both are dramatically influenced by environmental and social factors.

Sexual and aggressive behaviors—to varying degrees the result of an interplay among biological, environmental, and social factors—dramatize perhaps more than any others the issue of free will versus determinism and the debate over the nature of humankind. Does our biological makeup, for example, make warfare an inevitable characteristic of our species? Does it compel us to express our sexuality in fixed ways? Or do we have a choice in these matters?

A simple—and extreme—position on this question is that humans are driven by their biological nature to behave as they do; sexual behavior and aggression are biologically determined. One justification for this position is suggested by the theory of natural selection. Organisms "struggle" for survival and individuals that succeed in this struggle are more likely to survive long enough to reproduce and raise offspring. In other words, organisms may be programmed to be aggressive and to engage in certain sexual behaviors because these behaviors have been adaptive.

Others have argued that human aggression and sexual behavior are not biologically determined; they are learned. According to this position, the forces that predispose us to behave aggressively or to engage in sexual behavior do not reside in our genes but stem rather from our cultures. Some societies are warlike, for example, whereas others are not. Likewise there is an extraordinary variety in sexual expression among societies. This variability suggests that many behavioral options are available to us. Because we can recognize these options, we may have some measure of control over our behavior, some measure of free will.

In the discussion that follows we will try to show how biology and choice interact to shape both sexual and aggressive behaviors.

SEXUAL BEHAVIOR

The study of sexual behavior encompasses a wide variety of concepts. The term **sex,** for example, refers to the physical characteristics of an individual—those aspects pertaining to human reproduction. Thus, biologically speaking, a person with testes is a male and a person with ovaries is a female. The term **gender,** in contrast, refers to the psychological characteristics that a person or society attaches to females or males (Eagly, 1987).

Gender actually has two aspects: identity and role. **Gender identity** is a person's private sense of being male or female; it is the internal experience of "femaleness" or "maleness," the gender with which a person identifies. **Gender role,** in contrast, is the set of expectations society has for women and men. Most gender-related behavior patterns are determined by social or cultural forces—for example, whether a person is dominant or submissive in the presence of a person of the other sex. Indeed, society imposes stereotypical behavior patterns on children from birth. In our society, for example, boys are reinforced for playing with blocks, whereas girls

243

Children often play with toys that reinforce traditional gender roles.

are reinforced for playing with dolls (Grusec & Lytton, 1988). The sexes are perceived as having distinct qualities—females as emotional and gentle, males as dominant and independent (Best, Williams, Cloud, Davis, Robertson, Edwards, Giles, & Fowles, 1977). Although attitudes have changed in recent years, the two sexes are also expected to behave differently as adults. Traditionally, a woman's role has been confined to home and family, but a man's role has always been in the workplace. Men and women will even change their behavior in order to conform to the stereotype gender role (Deaux & Major, 1987). Sex differences in social behavior will be discussed more fully in Chapter 20.

A third important concept related to the study of sexual behavior is **sexual orientation,** which refers to a person's tendency to be sexually attracted either to members of the other sex (heterosexuality) or the same sex (homosexuality).

In the rest of this section we will first highlight the biological factors involved in sexual behavior and then turn to environmental factors. We will end the section with a description of the human sexual response.

BIOLOGICAL DETERMINANTS

Scientists have identified numerous structures in the brain that affect sexual behavior (Whalen, 1977). For example, stimulation of several areas in the hypothalamus causes a male rat to mount and copulate with a female; lesions of these areas eliminate all sexual activity. Perhaps the most important biological determinants of sexual behavior, however, are the sex hormones.

Male sex hormones are called **androgens;** testosterone is the most common of these. There are two classes of female sex hormones: **estrogens** (for example, estrodial) and **progestins** (for example, progesterone). Both males and females have all three kinds of hormones, but in different proportions. Testosterone is predominant in males, but males also have as much as 30% of the estrogen level normally found in females. Estrogen and progesterone are predominant in females, but females may also have up to 20% of the androgen level usually found in males.

Sex hormones are secreted by the adrenal gland and by the sex glands, or **gonads.** The gonads—the **testes** in the male and **ovaries** in the female—are the most important source of these hormones. The levels of sex hormones in the body are controlled by the **gonadotropic hormones,** which are secreted from the pituitary gland. (The action of these hormones, the follicle-stimulating hormone (FSH) and the luteinizing hormone (LH) are discussed later in the chapter in relation to Figure 10-4.)

Sex hormones have two basic functions. They play a critical role in organizing the development of the sex organs and the brain prior to birth and in the development of secondary sexual characteristics at puberty. They are also important in activating sexual behavior later in life.

Hormonal Control of Sexual Development

Among the most interesting areas of research on hormones and sexual behavior is the study of the effects of hormones on prenatal development. To understand this research completely, it is necessary to have some basic knowledge about human reproduction at the cellular level.

As noted in Chapter 8, each human body cell contains 23 pairs of chromosomes. One of these pairs determines sex. The chromosomes in this pair have either an X or Y form. Cells in the female body have a pair of X chromosomes, whereas those in the male body have an X chromosome and a Y chromosome. Sex cells (eggs and sperm) are formed by a process (meiosis) that leaves them with only half of each chromosome pair, including the sex chromosome pair. Thus eggs all have an X chromosome (because both members of the sex chromosome pair in females are X) whereas 50% of sperm have an X chromosome and 50% a Y (because the sex chromosome in males is an XY pair). (See Figure 10-1.) When an egg and a sperm are united following sexual intercourse, the sex of the resulting fetus is determined by whether the sperm contains an X or a Y chromosome. (The egg, of course, contains an X chromosome.) If the sperm–egg union produces an XX combination, the fetus develops into a female; if it produces an XY combination, the fetus develops into a male. Note, however, that the chromosomes do not determine the development of the fetus directly; instead, they establish the sex of the fetus by determining its hormonal status.

FIGURE 10-1 How sex chromosomes determine sex. Sex cells (ova and sperm) are formed through a process called meiosis that leaves them with only half of each of the 23 chromosome pairs, including the sex chromosome pair. Because the sex chromosome pair in females is XX, all ova have an X sex chromosome. Males, however have an XY pair, so half of all sperm have an X sex chromosome and half a Y. When a sperm with an X chromosome unites with an ovum it produces an XX pair, resulting in a female; when a sperm with a Y chromosome unites with an ovum, it produces an XY pair, resulting in a male.

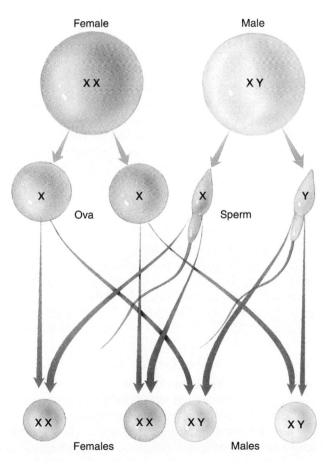

Let us look more closely at how this process works. Initially, the gonads in future males and females are exactly the same. Various proteins in the fetus, however, begin the process of sexual differentiation by controlling the hormonal concentrations the gonads produce. The specific hormonal concentrations determine whether the gonads later develop into ovaries, with the accompanying female sexual organs of vagina and uterus, or testes, with the accompanying male sexual organs of penis and scrotum. In particular, if androgens are present in sufficient quantity, the gonads become male and the fetus develops male sexual organs; if not, they become female and the fetus develops female sexual organs. Evidence for this comes from studies on animals in which the developing gonads are surgically removed from the fetus before sexual differentiation occurs. The effect of this procedure is to stop the production of hormones, including androgens, which in turn stops the process of sexual differentiation. All the fetuses subjected to this procedure develop female sexual organs whether or not they are genetically male (as determined by their chromosomes), suggesting that the natural course of development, in humans as well as other animals, is for the fetus to develop as a female, regardless of genetic factors. It is only the presence of androgens during early prenatal development that masculinizes the fetus.

The **secondary sex characteristics** that appear at puberty are also determined by the sex hormones. In females, those characteristics include breast development, changes in body fat, and maturation of the genitalia. In males, the presence of testosterone stimulates growth of body hair, the lowering of the voice, and development of the muscles and genitalia. Although these secondary sex traits can be changed by injections of the hormones of the other sex, sex itself cannot be altered in this way. If, for example, an adult male were treated with estrogen, he would grow breasts but would not become a female. Similarly, if a woman were given large doses of testosterone in adulthood, she would grow facial hair and her voice would become lower, but her sex would not change.

Hormonal Control of Sexual Orientation

In a debate that is far from resolved, some researchers argue that sexual orientation is the result of biological factors; others claim that it is wholly dependent on cultural factors. One possible biological factor involves the role of hormones. Some studies suggest that heterosexual and homosexual men differ in the way they respond to hormonal changes in their bodies. In one such study, women, heterosexual men, and homosexual men were given an injection of Premarin, a form of estrogen that is known to enhance the concentration of LH in women but not in men (Gladue, Green, & Hellman, 1984). The injection had two results. First, testosterone levels in the blood dropped significantly in the homosexual men relative to the other two groups of subjects. Second, levels of LH, measured as a percentage change from the preinjection level, increased in homosexual men but remained relatively constant in women and in heterosexual men.

These results raise the possibility that sexual orientation has a hormonal basis, at least in men. This claim is, however, highly controversial. In fact, some researchers have found contradictory evidence (Masters & Johnson, 1979), and many psychologists argue that social learning and cultural differences are more important factors (Ehrhardt & Meyer-Bahlburg, 1981; Saghir & Robins, 1973).

Hormonal Control of Gender Identity and Sexual Behavior

Much research has been done on the relationship between exposure to androgens early in development and later gender identity and sexual behavior. If female laboratory rats, for example, are given excessive amounts of testosterone during embryological development or just after birth, when the brain is still developing, they fail to develop normal female sexual behavior patterns in adulthood. Specifically, they do not exhibit female-typical behaviors such as **lordosis** (presenting a suitable copulatory posture to the male), but do exhibit male-typical behaviors such as mounting and copulatory motions.

Subjecting male rats to an analogous treatment—castrating them just after birth so that they stop producing androgens—also affects adult sexual behavior. As an adult the castrated animal shows no sexual interest whatsoever unless he has been injected with replacement doses of testosterone. Moreover, castrated rats injected with female hormones will exhibit female sexual behavior in response to another male rat.

In humans also, hormonal states in the early stages of development affect both the perception of gender (gender identity) and the later expression of behavior consistent with gender role, although the interaction of these hormonal states with environmental factors makes for results that are more ambiguous than those seen in rats. Researchers cannot, of course, experiment directly on humans. They can, however, observe the effects of metabolic disorders that cause the adrenal gland to secrete too much or too little androgen prior to birth. Genetic females who experience excessive androgen levels during fetal development may become **hermaphrodites,** with external genitals that are similar in appearance to those of males but also with ovaries (Money, 1977). Genetic males who lack sufficient androgen during prenatal development may also become hermaphrodites, in their case with abdominal testes and a vaginal-type opening but no ovaries or uterus.

The consequences of such hormonal imbalances are not always predictable. As with laboratory animals, genetically female hermaphrodites may show a propensity for behaviors that are conventionally considered to be typical of boys, for example a preference for rough-and-tumble play, tomboyish behavior, and little interest in play objects conventionally associated with girls, such as dolls (Ehrhardt & Meyer Bahlburg, 1981). Their gender identity is not necessarily confused, however; they may still think of themselves as being distinctly female. Indeed, the attitudes of friends and the actual appearance of their genitals, as well as their overall appearance, may be more important than the genetic, hormonal, and physiological factors themselves in determining the gender with which these individuals ultimately identify. Some have argued, therefore, that gender identity is governed almost exclusively by how the person is treated, not simply by the presence or absence of hormones, and that it is learned by the time of puberty and is more or less fixed thereafter (Ehrhardt & Meyer-Bahlburg, 1981). Others question this position, however, arguing that experience, though important, does not create a fixed identity. According to this position, the original hormonal state may prevail and cause a person to possess a particular gender identity even though he or she was raised as a member of the other sex (Imperato-McGinley, Guerrero, Gautier, & Peterson, 1974; Rubin, Reinisch, & Haskett, 1981). Clearly this is an important but difficult question to study, with many unresolved problems.

Effects of Hormones on Arousal

In male animals testosterone and sexual arousal are highly related. For example, if a male rat is castrated, sexual behavior declines; if the animal is given injections of testosterone, sexual behavior returns to normal levels. Although human males may wish to believe that they are not as dependent on hormones as laboratory rats, the relationship between sexual arousal and testosterone is virtually the same.

The link between hormones and sexual arousal is somewhat different for females. (See Takahashi, 1990; Wallen, 1990.) In species such as rats, sexual receptivity is highly dependent on the level of estrogen; female rats will engage in sexual behavior only at the time of ovulation, when estrogen levels are high (Powers, 1970). In human females, sexual receptivity is generally not related to the level of estrogen and is relatively constant throughout the menstrual cycle. Furthermore, interest in sexual activity does not decline even if the ovaries are removed. Heterosexual arousal in women is actually more sensitive to the level of androgens in the body than it is to estrogen levels (Abplanalp, Rose, Donnelly, & Livingston-Vaughn,

PART THREE

────────

FREE WILL VERSUS
BEHAVIORAL
DETERMINISM

────────

1979). For example, women who have been given testosterone for the treatment of cancer often report an increased interest in sexual activity.

Effects of Experience on Hormones

It is interesting to note that the relationship between hormones and behavior operates in both directions: Experience affects hormone levels just as surely as hormone levels affect behavior. For instance, if an adult male monkey is placed with a receptive female, the male's testosterone levels increase dramatically (Rose, Gordon, & Bernstein, 1972). In humans, when a male views an arousing film the pituitary hormones that regulate the levels of certain sexual hormones increase (LaFerla, Anderson, & Schalch, 1978). Several investigators have shown that when women live together—for example, in a college dormitory—their menstrual cycles become synchronized (Graham & McGrew, 1980). In each of these cases, it is not the biology that controls the behavior, but rather the reverse: The environment influences the hormonal levels. In sum, sexual behavior is in many ways highly determined by biological factors, especially levels of sex hormones. Sexual development, orientation, and behavior are all affected. Environmental influences, however, are also important; in many cases experience actually changes biological variables.

ENVIRONMENTAL DETERMINANTS OF SEXUAL BEHAVIOR

Social and environmental factors obviously contribute to human sexual behavior. Perhaps the clearest evidence for this is the observation that people differ greatly in terms of the stimuli that arouse them, even though they are seemingly in the same biological state; for any given arousal stimulus, some people will be affected, others not. Any theory of sexual behavior therefore must make reference to the many social and environmental conditions that influence that behavior. In this section we briefly consider some of those conditions.

Sexual Signals

Arousal may depend on the presence of sex signals. These are very common in many species of animals. Rats and cats, for example, emit odors, called **pheromones,** that serve to attract mates or advertise sexual receptivity. In other species, hormone-dependent changes may serve the same purpose. An example is the swelling and discoloration of the skin near the genitalia of some nonhuman primates.

In humans, sex signals more often are learned. Among those signals are the dimensions of physical attractiveness, which are culture specific. For example, in our culture slimness is considered "sexy," but one does not have to go back very far in history to discover that this was not always the case (Dion, 1981). Other common examples of human sex signals include jewelry, makeup, or body gestures such as "macho posturing." (See Figure 10-2.)

Testing perfumes. Odors serve as sexual signals in humans as well as in other animals.

Erotic Images

One source of sexual arousal is erotic images. The effects of erotic films, pornography, and other sexual imagery on sexual arousal are more or less the same for both men and women. A famous report of the 1950s on the sexual behavior in American adults, called the Kinsey Report, claimed that men are more easily aroused than women, but it appears to have been wrong. Although it is true that women are, at times, more inhibited than men about reporting their feelings of arousal (which may account for Kinsey's results), more recent evidence suggests that women experience essentially the same degree of arousal as men. In one study, 62 unmarried male and female college students were shown an erotic film, after which they completed a

questionnaire about their level of sexual arousal (Fisher & Byrne, 1978). All the subjects saw the same film, but some of them had been told that the film was about a married couple coming home from a dance whereas others had been told that the film depicted a prostitute and her client coming home from a bar. The results indicated that male and female subjects were equally aroused by the film and that the different scenarios had no effect on arousal. Thus, the study did not support the long-held belief that women are less sexually aroused by erotic images than men, or that they are aroused by them only when they involve a romantic setting.

FIGURE 10-2 Humans send sex signals through jewelry, makeup, clothing, and body gestures. These signals are strongly influenced by cultural factors and vary from place to place and time to time. Compare the sexual suggestiveness in the fashionable clothing and posture of the seventeenth- and eighteenth-century European aristocrats above with that of the late twentieth-century American models below.

In another study, groups of men and women listened to audiotapes depicting erotic or romantic stories and then were asked to engage in sexual fantasies (Heiman, 1977). During this time monitors recorded their genital blood pulse, indicating their level of physiological arousal. Erotic themes caused an increase in physiological arousal when the subjects later fantasized (romantic themes by themselves did not), but again there was no difference between men and women.

HUMAN SEXUAL RESPONSE

The human sexual response cycle consists of four phases, leading from arousal to orgasm (Masters & Johnson, 1966). Figure 10-3 presents a diagram of these cycles for males and females.

During the first phase, the **excitement phase,** an erotic stimulus triggers arousal. In many species, stimulation often involves dramatic sexual displays. For example, many male birds have elaborate courtship rituals that are intended to entice the female to mate. The strut of a peacock with its tail in full array is a stimulus of this kind. Such displays can be seen in humans, too; tight or revealing clothes and provocative postures or gestures are erotic stimuli designed to produce sexual excitement. Advertisers constantly make use of such stimuli to attract attention.

The bodily reactions to erotic stimuli are extensive. In males, they include penile erection and elevation of the scrotal sac. In females they include vaginal lubrication and expansion of the inner vaginal wall.

The second phase of the human sexual response cycle is the **plateau phase.** In this phase, which can be brief or extended, sexual tension levels off, receptivity to extraneous stimuli decreases somewhat, and the diameter of blood vessels is reduced. In males, this is accompanied by an increase in penile swelling; in females, an increase in breast size and an elevation in heart rate, respiration, and blood pressure.

In the **orgasm phase,** the male experiences contractions of the penis and other muscles and organs that cause ejaculation. The female experiences contractions of the uterine and other muscles. In addition, in both men and women the rate of breathing increases and the heart rate may rise to as much as 180 beats per minute, more than twice the normal rate.

The orgasm phase is followed by the **resolution phase.** In males, penile erection is lost and sexual tension is reduced. Females, however, can maintain a high level of tension following orgasm and, if stimulation continues, can experience additional orgasms before the resolution phase and a gradual loss of sexual tension.

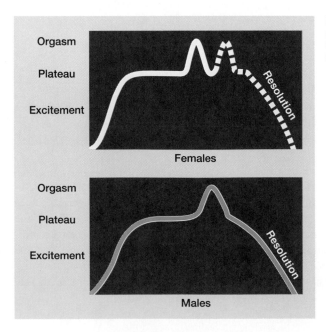

FIGURE 10-3 A schematic representation of the human sexual response cycle in men and women. (Adapted from Masters & Johnson, 1966.)

In many species, peacocks and frigate birds, for example, courtship and mating involve elaborate displays.

INTERIM SUMMARY

Although there are structures in the brain that affect sexual behavior, the most important biological determinants of sexual behavior are the sex hormones—androgens in males and estrogens and progestins in females. Sex hormones organize the development of the sex organs and brain prior to birth. The natural course of development is for a human to become female regardless of genetic factors; the presence of androgen during early prenatal development masculinizes the fetus. Sex hormones determine the secondary sex characteristics at puberty and may play a role in sexual orientation. Gender identity and sexual behavior are also influenced by the sex hormones. In the case of arousal, the relationship between hormone levels and behavior is bidirectional—experience affects hormone levels just as hormone levels affect behavior. Social and environmental factors contribute significantly to human sexual behavior. Arousal may be highly dependent on the presence of sex signals, and erotic images produce sexual arousal in both men and women. The human sexual response cycle consists of four phases: excitement, plateau, orgasm, and resolution.

AGGRESSION

Aggression may be defined as any behavior whose goal is to harm or injure another living being (see Baron, 1977, p. 7). This definition has at least two important implications. First, it stipulates that the goal of the behavior is harm or injury. Thus, inadvertently hitting one's opponent in a racquetball game while swinging at the ball is not aggression, even though it may result in injury. Second, for a behavior to qualify as aggression, it must harm another person. Behaviors directed against inanimate objects, in and of themselves, are not considered to be true acts of aggression.

TYPES OF AGGRESSION

In attempting to specify the kinds of behavior that qualify as aggression, some psychologists distinguish between *inter*species aggression—that is, aggression directed toward a different species, as in predatory behavior—and *intra*species aggression,

251

which is directed toward one's own species, as in territorial defense (Lorenz, 1966). Human intraspecies aggression has been classified into two categories: **instrumental** and **hostile aggression.** Aggression is instrumental when it is designed to achieve a goal beyond the aggressive act itself. Examples are aggression in pursuit of a material gain, such as theft of a wallet, or the use of aggression to gain praise or recognition, such as engaging in heroic acts in wartime. Hostile aggression, in contrast, is intended simply to injure the target; no additional object or motive is involved. Schoolyard bullies often display hostile aggression.

BIOLOGICAL DETERMINANTS OF AGGRESSION

There is considerable evidence linking aggression to specific biological conditions. Factors that may contribute to aggressive behavior include genetic factors, specific brain structures, and hormones.

Genetic Factors

To some extent, aggression has a genetic basis. Animals such as rats, mice, and fowl can be selectively bred for aggressiveness (Fuller & Thompson, 1978; Maxson, 1981). In Thailand, the sport of fish fighting has been popular for centuries. Winning fish were bred; losers were discarded. The result is the modern Siamese fighting fish, which is so aggressive that the male must be isolated from other members of its own species.

It is more difficult to verify that human aggression is *directly* influenced by genetic factors. Because we cannot measure aggression as easily as we measure structural characteristics like eye color, we cannot unequivocally label a person as "aggressive" or "nonaggressive." More important, we cannot perform the same kind of selective breeding experiment with human subjects as we can with other animals such as mice or fish. Nevertheless, there is no reason to believe that humans are different from other animals in this regard (Baron, 1977). As we suggested in Chapter 8, the tendency to behave aggressively may be inherited in the same way that predispositions toward mental disorders are inherited. Studies have shown, for example, that identical twins are far more similar in aggressiveness than fraternal twins (Christiansen, 1978; see also DiLalla & Gottesman, 1991).

Fighting cocks have been bred for aggressiveness, suggesting that some forms of aggression are instinctual.

Brain Structures

The role of specific brain structures in controlling aggression is well documented (Moyer, 1976). Although nearly all the research in this area has used laboratory animals such as rats, it is reasonable to expect that analogous effects may be found in humans.

Most of the areas of the brain that are involved in aggression are the same as those involved in other motivational or emotional reactions, such as thirst and hunger. In one experiment, drugs were injected directly into the lateral hypothalamus of rats through extremely thin stainless steel tubing (Smith, King, & Hoebel, 1970; see also Avis, 1974). For some subjects, the drug was *carbachol*, which stimulates neural activity by mimicking the neurotransmitter acetylcholine. Other subjects received *atropine,* which blocks the action of acetylcholine and thus reduces neural activity. All the subjects had previously been tested for their tendency to attack and kill other rats; some were known to be "killers" and others to be "nonkillers." The injection of carbachol induced the nonkillers to begin killing. Conversely, when injected with atropine, killer rats became docile. When the two drugs were injected into other areas of the brain, changes in aggression did not occur. This study thus showed that an anatomical area (the lateral hypothalamus) and a neural transmitter (acetylcholine) are specific in terms of their effects on aggression.

The relationship between brain anatomy and aggression is not always so simple. Stimulation of structures other than the lateral hypothalamus, including the medial and anterior portions of the hypothalamus (Edwards & Flynn, 1972; Flynn, 1967) and the amygdala (Aggleton & Mishkin, 1986) also produces aggressive reactions. It is therefore unlikely that any specific area of the brain serves as the "aggression center." Nevertheless, this research suggests that some neurological foundation for aggressive behavior exists in the brain. This conclusion is not surprising; virtually all behaviors must somehow depend on or be controlled by structures in the brain. The problem lies in specifying not only which areas are involved for any given behavior but also how environmental stimuli affect those areas.

Hormones and Aggression

The sex hormones also play a role in aggression. In many animals other than humans, for example laboratory rats, males tend to be more aggressive than females (Floody, 1983). There is overwhelming evidence that this tendency is related to the presence of **testosterone,** the male sex hormone produced by the testes; the more testosterone is present, the greater the animal's aggressive tendencies (Leshner, 1978).

Among humans as well, males are more aggresive than females (Hyde, 1984), although the relationship between testosterone and aggression is much less clear (Monti, Brown, & Corriveau, 1977). For any given individual, day-to-day levels of sex hormones are not strongly correlated with feelings of hostility (Doering et al., 1975). Differences in aggressiveness between men, however, have been shown to be related to testosterone levels. For example, if a male is castrated, testosterone levels decline and aggressiveness is correspondingly reduced (Herrmann & Beach, 1976). Similarly, adolescents with high levels of testosterone are significantly more likely to react aggressively to provocation (Olweus, Mattsson, Schalling, & Loow, 1980) than adolescents with lower levels of testosterone. Overall, then, research findings strongly suggest that testosterone (and other male hormones) play a significant role in aggressive behavior in human males (Moyer, 1976).

In adult women, aggressive behavior is correlated with the menstrual cycle and thus with changing hormone levels. Figure 10-4 shows the relationship between hormone levels and the menstrual cycle. Both the follicle-stimulating hormone (FSH) and the luteinizing hormone (LH) are secreted by the anterior lobe of the pituitary

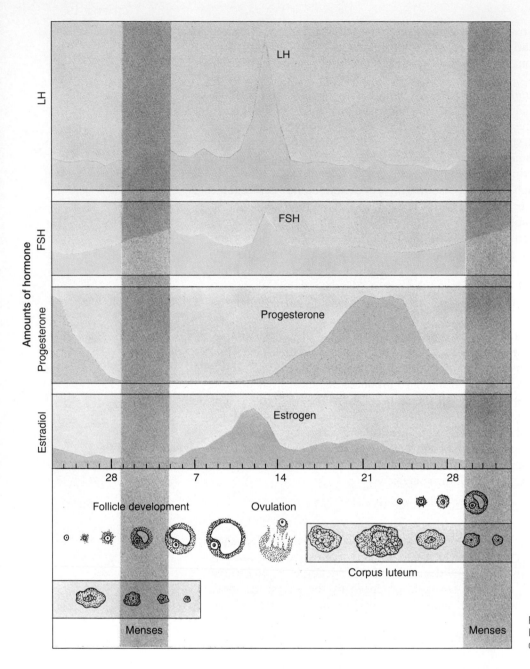

FIGURE 10-4 Changes in sex hormone levels in the human female over the course of the menstrual cycle.

gland, located in the base of the brain. They cause, respectively, growth of the ovarian follicle (a cavity of cells surrounding the unfertilized egg) and ovulation (the eventual rupturing of the follicle and release of the egg). The ovarian follicle (called the *corpus luteum* after ovulation) also produces hormones—namely, estradiol and progesterone. These hormones prepare the uterus to support a fertilized egg. If the egg is not fertilized, progesterone levels decline, menstrual discharge occurs, and the cycle begins again. Surveys have shown that 62% of violent crimes committed by women prisoners were committed during the premenstrual period, that is, when levels of progesterone are relatively high. Only 2% were committed at the beginning of the cycle, immediately after the end of menstruation (Dalton, 1980; Haskett, Steiner, Osmun, & Carroll, 1980). Such correlational studies, of course, do not indicate that the hormonal state necessarily causes aggression, nor do they deny the importance of other factors, such as environmental forces.

Interaction of Hormonal and Environmental Factors

If male rats that have never come into contact with newborn rat pups are given testosterone, they will kill pups if given the opportunity (Rosenberg & Sherman, 1975). If, in contrast, they are castrated before ever coming into contact with newborn pups, they will not kill them. These results are consistent with other findings on the effects of hormones on aggression.

If, however, the rats are exposed to pups *before* experiencing a change in testosterone levels, the effects are radically different. Some male rats kill pups when first exposed to them, others do not. When those that do kill pups are castrated, they continue to kill; castration has virtually no effect. Similarly, when those that do not kill pups are injected with testosterone, they do not begin killing; again, the hormone has no effect on the behavior. In other words, whether or not a change in testosterone levels (through either castration or injection) has an effect on pup-killing behavior depends entirely on whether the animal has been exposed to pups previously and the kind of behavior demonstrated at that time. The experience of engaging in a particular response influenced the later action of the hormone. The study therefore illustrates the important fact that experience and biological factors interact to produce behavior.

SITUATIONAL DETERMINANTS OF AGGRESSION

Aggression is influenced by many situational factors (Mueller, 1983). Stressors of various kinds, such as noise, heat, and crowding, have been shown to influence aggressive behavior (Baron, 1977; Gove, Hughes, & Galle, 1979; Jan, 1980). Focusing on one important situational determinant, frustration, some researchers developed what is called the frustration–aggression hypothesis.

The Frustration–Aggression Hypothesis

As originally formulated, the **frustration–aggression hypothesis** claimed that frustration always produces aggression and that all aggression results from frustration (Dollard, Doob, Miller, Mowrer, & Sears, 1939; Miller, 1941). Although this extreme view is no longer considered correct, the evidence that frustration may cause aggression is impressive.

In one study of the relationship between frustration and aggression, pairs of children competed to earn a reward (Hoving, Wallace, & LaForme, 1979). Each child was instructed to take marbles and put them into a narrow tube until they were all used up. The children were also told they could press either of two buttons while they were filling their tube with marbles. Pressing one of the buttons, they were told, would release the opponent's marbles, causing them to spill back onto the table. For the opponent, this event would be a source of frustration; for the instigator, it would be an act of instrumental aggression intended to retard the opponent's progress. Pressing the other button, the children were told, would produce a loud noise in the opponent's ear. To the opponent, this event would represent a threat or attack; for the instigator, it would be an act of hostile aggression because it would have no instrumental effect on the opponent's progress. Thus, each child competed with the other to complete the task first; while doing so, each could behave aggressively toward the other in one of two ways. In reality, to ensure that the children received equal exposure to these treatments, the releasing of the marbles and the production of the loud noise were not actually controlled by the children but rather by the experimenter.

The results are shown in Figure 10-5. The variable that caused the most hostile aggression (that is, pushing of the noise button) was a hostile attack by the opponent (the blue bar on the left side of the figure). Being frustrated (that is, having one's marbles released by one's opponent) also provoked hostile aggression, but not as much (the blue bar on the right). Instrumental aggression, on the other hand, was

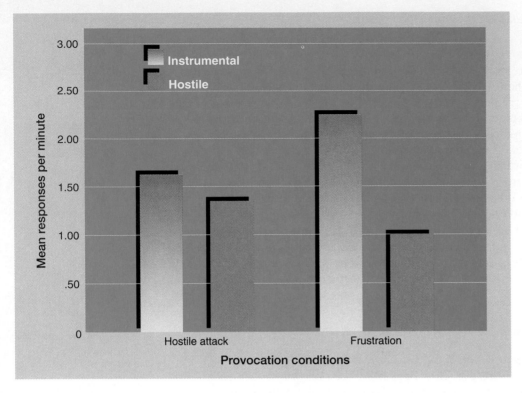

FIGURE 10-5 Mean aggression responses per minute as a function of provocation conditions for children engaged in a competitive game. The children could choose between two types of aggressive, either hostile (delivering a loud noise) or instrumental (releasing opponent's marbles). Likewise, the provocative condition was either a hostile attack (the loud noise) or frustration (having marbles released). (Adapted from Hoving, Wallace, & LaForme, 1979.)

provoked more by frustration (marble release) than by hostile attacks (compare the two pink-yellow bars in Figure 10-5). In other words, the experiment showed that the kind of aggression (instrumental or hostile) committed by a child depended very much on the type of provocation to which the child was responding. A hostile attack provoked more hostile aggression than an instrumental attack, whereas an instrumental attack provoked relatively more instrumental aggression. According to this study, then, frustration may indeed affect aggression, but it does not trigger all forms of aggression to an equal degree (Baron, 1977).

INTERIM SUMMARY

Many studies have shown that aggressive behavior is strongly affected by biological variables, including genetic makeup, brain structures and chemistry, and hormones. It is not determined exclusively by these factors, however; the environment is also important. Indeed, an individual's experience can actually determine what effect biological variables will have on aggressive behavior. Situational factors also play a role in aggression. According to the extreme form of the frustration–aggression hypothesis, all aggression results from frustration. Research on the relationship between frustration and aggression suggests that frustration may indeed affect aggression, but does not elicit all forms of aggression to an equal degree.

SOCIAL LEARNING THEORY AND AGGRESSION

So far we have considered two major factors that are claimed to trigger aggression *directly:* biological factors and frustration. Neither of these factors, however, provides a complete explanation of aggressive behavior because neither accounts for aggressive behavior that arises *indirectly* from experience. Aggressive behavior, in other words, may be learned. This view of aggression is advanced in particular by proponents of **social learning theory,** according to which we learn aggression from other people. The theory identifies several processes by which this occurs (Bandura, 1983). For example, aggressive behaviors may be learned because people are rewarded for using them (**instrumental learning**), or because people observe and imitate others who act aggressively (**modeling**). In this section we review some of the findings of this important area of research.

INSTRUMENTAL LEARNING

As noted earlier, instrumental aggression is a behavior that is designed to produce a positive outcome—a reward—for the aggressor. Such an outcome has the effect of teaching the person the aggressive response, because a response that is followed by a reward is acquired or strengthened. This process has been demonstrated using animal subjects (Scott, 1973). For example, rats were given electric shocks that were terminated whenever the subject engaged in aggressive behavior toward another animal. Aggression thus earned a reward—the termination of the shock. The results indicated that all the rats, even those with no previous history of fighting, learned to attack under these conditions.

Similar effects are believed to occur in humans (Bandura, 1973; Zillmann, 1978). The rewards, of course, are different. In some cases, material incentives such as candy or money may increase the likelihood of aggression. In others, the rewards are social approval or escape from threats and aversive stimuli. In one study, college students were placed in a so-called teacher–learner situation in which they had to administer a shock to a "student" if that person performed a simple task incorrectly; in reality, of course, the "student" was a confederate of the experimenter and did not actually receive any shocks (Geen & Pigg, 1970). Two groups of subjects were used. One was given praise ("That's good" or "You're doing fine") whenever the shock intensity was increased; the other was not given the praise. As shown in Figure 10-6, when the subjects were praised for increasing shock intensity, the mean strength of the shocks that they thought they were giving increased; aggression thus was influenced by the reward of praise. Control subjects who were not praised showed no

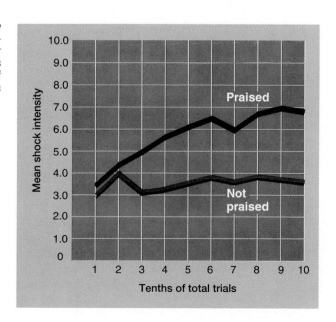

FIGURE 10-6 Mean shock intensity delivered to the "learner" by experimental subjects who were praised for increasing intensity and control subjects who were not, as a function of tenths of the training trials. (Adapted from Geen & Pigg, 1970.)

increase in shock intensity over trials. It is important to realize that a person who rewards aggression with social approval may do so unknowingly; similarly, a person who is acting aggressively may be responding to such a reward without being aware of it.

MODELING AND IMITATION

A second means of learning aggression is through modeling and imitation (Bandura, 1973; 1977). The theory is simple: Humans observe and imitate each other's behavior. This is probably the most common way in which we learn behaviors.

In a classic study of the role of imitation in aggression, a group of children were permitted to observe an adult playing with various toys, including a "Bobo doll," an inflated vinyl toy about 3 feet tall that rights itself after being hit or thrown (Bandura, Ross, & Ross, 1963). The children watched the adult hit the doll with a fist or mallet, throw and kick it around the room, and say things like "Sock him in the nose." A second group of children saw a filmed version of the adult performing the same behaviors. A third group saw the filmed version, but in this case the adult was dressed as a cat. Finally, a control group of children did not observe an adult model of any kind.

In the second stage of the experiment, all the children were led into the playroom and allowed to interact with the toys, including the Bobo doll. (The researchers had actually deliberately frustrated the children immediately before this second stage by allowing them to play only briefly with a favorite toy, on the presumption that aggression required frustration. Subsequent research has shown, however, that the results of the experiment do not depend on prior frustration [Kuhn, Madsen, & Becker, 1967].) During the playtime observers scored the children for aggressive behavior toward the doll, giving them a point for each 5-second period in which they committed an aggressive act, whether or not the act imitated the actions of the model. As shown in Figure 10-7, the mean aggression score was dramatically higher for subjects who had watched the real-life model than for the control subjects. The mean aggression score was somewhat lower for subjects who had watched the movie

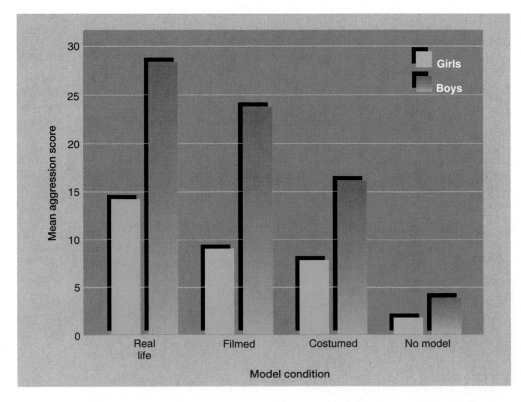

FIGURE 10-7 Mean aggression scores for children who had watched an adult behaving aggressively toward the Bobo doll (real life), a filmed version of the same behavior (filmed), a filmed version in which the adult was dressed as a cat (costumed), and for a control group (no model). (Adapted from Bandura, Ross, & Ross, 1963.)

version and even lower for those who had observed the costumed model. These findings point to a clear and powerful conclusion: Children engaged in exaggerated, *specific* aggressive actions as a result of watching others perform those behaviors. Not only are children more prone to be aggressive after an observation period of this sort, but the tendency can last for up to 6 months (Hicks, 1965).

The fact that the children actually imitated the model is clearly demonstrated in photographs of their behavior. As shown in Figure 10-8, the children's behavior was virtually identical to that of the model.

VIOLENCE AND TELEVISION

The research discussed earlier strongly suggests that humans learn aggressive behavior by observing aggression in models. It is likely, therefore, that violence on television and in other mass media is related to the high level of violence in American society. The premise is that people observe violent behaviors on television and imitate those behaviors in their own lives.

There are literally thousands of studies on the effects of television violence on human behavior. We cannot review this literature in detail, but we can highlight the major arguments and the current status of knowledge in this area (Freedman, 1984, 1986; Friedrich-Cofer & Huston, 1986; Geen, 1983; Wood, Wong, & Chachere, 1991).

Three basic kinds of studies have been done to examine the relationship between television violence and aggression. The first kind involves calculating the degree to which watching violence on television is associated, or correlated, with aggressive behavior. The evidence from these studies reveals a strong positive correlation between exposure to television violence and aggressiveness. People who watch a lot of violent television programs also tend to be aggressive. The most compelling studies of this sort have shown that such a relationship can persist for a long time (Eron, Huesmann, Lefkowitz, & Walder, 1972). For instance, preference for television violence in 8- and 9-year-old subjects was positively correlated with aggressiveness 10 years later.

FIGURE 10-8 Photographs showing the kind of aggressive responses the children made toward the Bobo doll after seeing a movie of an adult behaving aggressively toward it. (Adapted from Bandura, Ross, & Ross, 1963.)

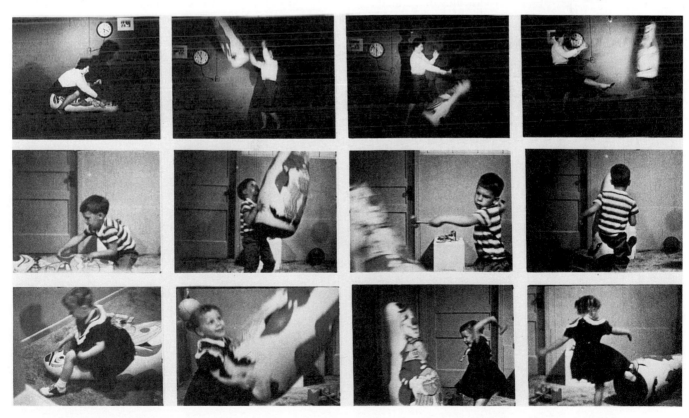

The problem with this approach is that it fails to demonstrate a causal relationship. The fact that people who prefer violent television programs also tend to be aggressive does not necessarily mean that watching violent shows *causes* aggression. It is possible that such people are predisposed both to be aggressive *and* to prefer violent shows. It is also possible that aggressive people prefer to watch violence on television. The correlational studies, though disturbing and suggestive, do not provide definitive proof that watching television violence actually causes aggression.

The second kind of study is the laboratory experiment. The study of children's behavior with the Bobo doll is an example of this approach. According to some theorists, such experiments also fail to demonstrate a causal relationship between viewing of violence and aggressive behavior *in the real world* (Freedman, 1984). Hitting a Bobo doll, they claim, is not true aggression. To show definitively that watching violence causes *real* aggression, one must conduct a third kind of study: a controlled experiment in the real world.

A number of field studies have attempted to do just that. In one such study, nursery school children were shown aggressive cartoons, neutral films, or prosocial programs emphasizing cooperation (such as "Mr. Rogers' Neighborhood") over a 4-week period (Friedrich & Stein, 1973). The measure of aggression used was aggressive behavior directed against peers during free play. The experimenters were careful to record aggressive behavior prior to as well as during and after the viewing of the films. They found that aggressive films stimulated aggressive behavior in children who were already prone to behave aggressively. Already aggressive subjects who were not exposed to violent films showed a decline in aggressive behavior. These findings have the same implications as the correlation and laboratory studies: Aggressive behavior, whether measured by attacks on a Bobo doll or by aggression against peers, seems to be stimulated by the viewing of violent models on television. Some psychologists believe that the causal relationship is bidirectional; that is, watching television violence induces aggression, and being aggressive causes a person to prefer violent television shows (Fenigstein, 1979; Friedrich-Cofer & Huston, 1986).

Although the issue is not fully resolved (Freedman, 1984), the evidence overall indicates that watching television violence does indeed enhance aggression. According to one expert, "Experimental and correlational data strongly support the hypothesis that observation of violence is the *cause* in the relationship and aggression the effect" (Geen, 1983, p. 121; see also Friedrich-Cofer & Huston, 1986).

Imitation—of role models in film and television, for example—may play a role in the development of aggressive behaviors.

Television and Insensitivity to Violence

Research also indicates that televised violence may have an additional, indirect effect on human behavior: It may cause a person to become insensitive to real violence. In one study, 8- to-10-year-old subjects were first shown one of two films (Thomas, Horton, Lippincott, & Drabman, 1977). Some of the subjects saw an edited episode of "S.W.A.T." that involved a shooting, several physical fights, and other violent incidents. The others saw a film of a championship volleyball game. The experimenter then told each subject that there was a group of nursery school children in another room whose teacher had to run an errand, and that the experimenter had been asked to watch the children via a closed-circuit television hookup. At the same moment, however, the experimenter had arranged to be called out of the room by an accomplice to answer a phone call, and so the subject was asked to monitor the children as a favor to the experimenter and to report on their behavior when the experimenter returned. What each subject actually saw was a prerecorded film of an unruly group of children engaged in fighting, damaging property, and other violent behavior.

The fictitious story about monitoring the children was created to convince the subjects that they were witnessing real violence. Throughout the entire experiment (that is, during the movie as well as the monitoring task), the subjects' galvanic skin response (GSR) was being recorded. This physiological reaction is widely used as a measure of emotional reactivity—the greater the GSR, the greater the emotion. The results showed that viewing violence on television caused subjects to be relatively insensitive to real violence. The mean GSR during the monitoring task for subjects who previously saw the film of the volleyball game was much higher than for subjects who had seen the violent television film.

PORNOGRAPHY AND AGGRESSION

Another factor that appears related to aggression is **pornography,** the explicit depiction of sexual acts, such as genital manipulation and penetration, for the purpose of arousing a person sexually. Some but not all pornography involves depictions of aggression and violence, and some violent pornography may depict a compliant victim. These variables complicate the task of evaluating the impact of pornography on aggressive behavior (Donnerstein, 1983).

Nonaggressive pornographic material appears to have two opposing effects on aggression in males. First, the material may enhance aggression against other males, especially if the subject is already angered (Zillmann, 1971). In fact, the effect of pornography on later aggression can be greater than the effect of a nonpornographic but violent film. Second, nonaggressive pornography can actually reduce aggressive behavior (Frodi, 1977). In such cases the pornography appears to divert the person from the anger state (Donnerstein, Donnerstein, & Evans, 1975; Zillmann, Bryant, Comisky, & Medoff, 1981).

The effect of nonaggressive pornography on aggression against women has also been studied (Donnerstein & Barrett, 1978). Generally, the evidence is negative; even highly erotic scenes, which can elicit aggression against males, do not elicit aggression against females. There is evidence that the males are aroused (for example, their blood pressure readings increase), but aggression itself is inhibited.

The effects of aggressive-erotic material are quite different. The combination of depicted violence, which reduces inhibitions on aggressive behavior, and erotic material, which increases arousal, can increase aggression against women. In one experiment, male subjects were met by either a male or a female experimenter who posed as another subject (Donnerstein, 1980). They were told that the purpose of the study was to determine the effect sexual arousal has on performance of a teacher–learner task described earlier in this chapter. Both the subject and his alleged partner were first asked to write a short essay on the topic "marijuana use should be legalized." Then the experimenter in disguise was designated as the "learner" and the real subject the "teacher." The experimenter "learner" then left the room, presumably to practice the learning task. Before engaging in the teacher–learner task, however, the subject was told that he had been judged by his alleged partner, on the basis of his essay, to be lacking in creativity and overall intelligence. This insulting judgment had the effect of angering the subject. The next stage of the experiment was to show the subject one of three types of films—erotic only, both erotic and aggressive, or neither erotic nor aggressive. Finally, the subject and the "learner" were put into the teacher–learner situation and the subject told to deliver shocks of varying intensity to the "learner" when he or she made a mistake (in reality, of course, no shocks were given). The results are shown in Figure 10-9.

The mean shock intensity (the measure of aggression) that a subject chose to administer differed according to the kind of film viewed and the sex of the experimenter. The mean intensity of shocks delivered to male experimenters was higher for those subjects who had viewed either the erotic or the aggressive-erotic film than for those who had viewed the neutral film. The mean intensity of shock delivered to female experimenters, however, was high *only* for those who had viewed the aggressive-erotic film; most significantly, it was higher than that delivered to males. Experiments like this one have caused one investigator to suggest that "there is a direct causal relationship between exposure to aggressive erotica and violence against women" (Donnerstein, 1983, p. 151).

THE CYCLE OF VIOLENCE

There is in our culture a widespread belief that violence breeds violence. In covering an incident of child abuse, for example, the media often end their commentary with the sober observation that the perpetrator knew only violence as a child. On theoretical grounds, there is good reason to believe in the existence of such a **cycle of violence.** Social learning theory contends that violent behaviors can arise in part from modeling and imitation. According to this view, victims of violence become violent themselves because the model to which they were exposed was one of violence and abuse.

The evidence for the cycle of violence includes case histories of child abusers, records of social-service agencies, and self-reports. In a survey that gathered information through interviews, the authors remarked that "without exception in our study group of abusing parents, there is a history of having been raised in the same style which they have re-created in the pattern of rearing their own children" (Steele &

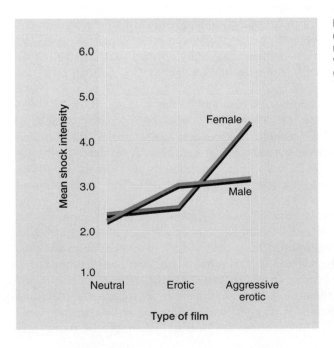

FIGURE 10-9 Mean shock intensity delivered to male or female experimenters as a function of the kind of film viewed (neutral, erotic, or aggressive-erotic). (Adapted from Donnerstein, 1980.)

Pollock, 1968, p. 111). In another survey of 1,146 American parents who had children between the ages of 3 and 17 living at home, the rate of abuse by fathers who had themselves been abused as children was double the rate of abuse by fathers who had grown up in nonviolent homes (Straus, Gelles, & Steinmetz, 1980).

Like the connection between violence and pornography or between aggression and violent television programming, the link between the experience of violence and later violent behavior is not fully understood. In fact, some recent studies have argued that the cycle of violence hypothesis remains unproved (Widom, 1989). Much of the doubt stems from methodological problems. For example, many studies rely on the self-reports of parents concerning their own experiences. Many of these parents may report having been abused in childhood so as to place their own abusive behavior in a more favorable light, or they may simply exaggerate or misremember their childhood experiences. Other problems with research on the cycle of violence include reliance on secondhand reports, unclear definitions of abuse, and failure to include suitable comparison groups. One scientist has summarized the issue as follows: "Being abused as a child may increase one's risk for becoming an abusive parent, a delinquent, or an adult violent criminal. However, on the basis of the findings from the existing literature, it cannot be said that the pathway is straight or certain. It is likely that our conceptualization of the relationship between child abuse and violence has been overly simplistic" (Widom, 1989, p. 24).

CONTROL OF AGGRESSION

Given the high level of violence in our society, it would seem that controlling aggression is a hopeless task. Is there any possibility that humans can live without aggression, or are we condemned to live with the problem forever? If we can indeed learn to live without aggression, the notion that behavior involves a measure of choice is strengthened considerably.

Some investigators have suggested that aggression can be controlled through education, primarily by changing attitudes (Eron & Huesmann, 1984; Linz, Donnerstein, Bross, & Chapin, 1986). In an often-cited study, 170 young boys and girls who were known to watch violent television programs were divided into experimental and control groups (Huesmann, Eron, Klein, Brice, & Fischer, 1983). Over the course of two years, the experimental subjects were given instruction designed to change their attitudes toward aggressive behavior. In particular, they were taught that television does not depict realistic people or situations and that violence is not an effective way to deal with conflict. The control subjects received no such instruction. At the end of the two-year period, peers rated the subjects for aggressiveness. Children in the experimental group were found to be significantly less aggressive than children in the control group, and the typical correlation between watching violence on television and behaving aggressively was no longer present.

In sum, it is not possible to conclude either that "all humans are biologically aggressive" or that "people can choose to behave aggressively." From one perspective, there indeed seems to be a biological basis for aggression and thus some evidence for biological determinism. From other perspectives, however, aggression seems to be highly dependent on learning. Some choice appears to be present, especially in the case of instrumental aggression and the control of aggression.

INTERIM SUMMARY

According to social learning theory, aggressive behaviors may be acquired because people are rewarded for such behavior (instrumental learning) or because people observe and imitate others who act aggressively (modeling). Modeling is probably the most pervasive way in which people learn aggressive behaviors. Some observers believe that the modeling of violence on television leads to aggressive behavior. Psychologists generally are convinced that watching television violence may cause aggression, although some argue that the relationship has not been proved. Research also indicates that excessive exposure to television violence may cause a person to become insensitive to real violence. Studies of the relationship between pornography and aggression have shown that exposure to aggressive-erotic material causes males to become more aggressive toward females. Research on the cycle of violence, in which people who experience abuse in childhood become violent as adults, is less clear-cut and suffers from methodological problems. Research on the possibility of controlling aggressive behavior suggests that such behavior can be controlled through education aimed at changing attitudes toward violence.

SUMMARY

1. Psychologists often link sexual and aggressive behaviors because both are related to the levels of sex hormones in the body and both are dramatically influenced by environmental and social factors.

2. *Sex* refers to the physical characteristics of an individual that pertain to human reproduction. *Gender* refers to the psychological characteristics of a person's sexuality. *Gender identity* is a person's private sense of being male or female. *Gender role* is the set of expectations society has for men and women. Most gender-related behaviors are determined by social or cultural forces. *Sexual orientation* refers to a person's tendency to be sexually attracted to members of the same or other sex.

3. Sexual behavior is affected by a number of biological factors, including male hormones (*androgens*) and female hormones (*estrogens*). Hormones help to determine the sexual development of the fetus, as well as the *secondary sexual characteristics* that appear at puberty.

4. Sex is determined by the sex chromosomes, which regulate the production of androgens during fetal development. In the presence of androgens, the fetus develops as a male; in the absence of androgens, the fetus develops as a female.

5. Abnormal hormonal concentrations during fetal development can cause the fetus to develop as a *hermaphrodite,* a genetic female with male sex organs or a genetic male with female sex organs.

6. The levels of hormones in the body and erotic stimuli in the environment interact to affect sexual arousal and behavior.

7. The *human sexual response cycle* typically involves four distinct phases: *excitement, plateau, orgasm,* and *resolution.*

8. *Aggression* is any behavior whose goal is to harm or injure another living being. *Instrumental aggression* is designed to achieve a goal beyond the aggressive act itself. *Hostile aggression* is intended simply to injure another.

9. The fact that other animals can be bred for aggressiveness suggests that human aggression too has a genetic component. Aggression is also associated with various structures in the brain, particularly the *lateral hypothalamus,* and with neurotransmitters such as *acetylcholine.*

10. *Testosterone,* the male sex hormone, is strongly related to levels of aggression in males, at least in many nonhuman species. Research suggests that testosterone also plays a significant role in aggressive behavior in human males, although the evidence is not as clear as it is for nonhuman species. The effects of hormones on aggression, however, are strongly affected by environmental factors.

11. *Frustration* has long been thought to be a determinant of aggressive behavior, but recent work shows that frustration is likely to elicit instrumental aggression, whereas hostile aggression is more likely to result in a reciprocal hostile aggression.

more suggestive than others. The subject is asked to make up a brief story that answers the following questions: What is happening in the picture? What led up to the situation? What is being thought? What will happen? The subject is given a few minutes to write the story, and then the answer is scored for imagery. The scoring depends on the motive in which the tester is interested. For example, when scoring for achievement motivation, the experimenter decides whether the story contains achievement-oriented imagery, such as a person's inventing something, achieving a goal, or performing some feat. Each image or achievement-related idea expressed in the story is scored according to a predetermined system that awards points based upon the strength and clarity of the image. In sum, Murray believed that each person has certain needs to varying degrees and that when needs are not expressed directly they may be measured indirectly via tests like the TAT.

MASLOW'S HIERARCHY OF NEEDS

Another important theory of needs was proposed by Abraham Maslow (Maslow, 1943; Maslow, 1970/1954). Maslow's most influential idea is that humans strive to actualize, or realize, their individual potential; they are motivated to grow, to enhance the self, and to fulfill their potentials as human beings.

Maslow hypothesized that there are five levels or categories of need, with each level occupying a particular position in a hierarchy. (See Figure 11-3.) The first level is the most primitive and corresponds to the physiological needs—for food, water, nutrients, and so forth. According to Maslow, virtually all living organisms have these needs.

The next highest category consists of the so-called safety needs—for security, order, and freedom from chaos and anxiety. These needs are fulfilled when a person attains a condition of safety, comfort, and calm.

At the third level of the hierarchy is the need for belongingness or love. Maslow believed that people are motivated to reduce the feeling of being unloved by seeking contact, love, and collegiality.

The fourth level includes the needs for esteem, confidence, a sense of mastery, self-regard, independence, and dignity.

The highest level of motivation in Maslow's scheme is the need for **self-actualization,** which is the need to realize one's greatest potential. People who cannot satisfy their need for self-actualization feel alienated and believe that their lives are

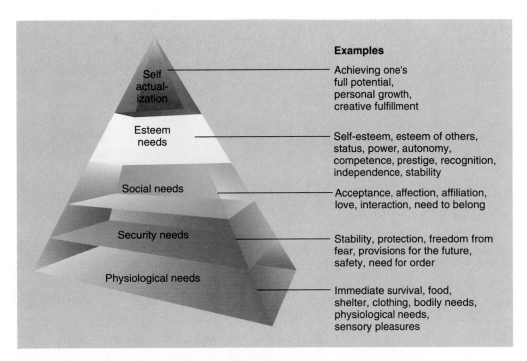

FIGURE 11-3 Maslow's hierarchy of needs.

meaningless. To be self-actualized is to eliminate these feelings, to have a healthy curiosity, to be creative and insightful, and to work at something that brings pleasure.

Maslow argued that we seek to satisfy our higher needs only after we have satisfied our lower ones. In fact, satisfying needs at one level stimulates the desire to satisfy the needs at the next highest level. Lower needs therefore are more powerful than higher needs. As Maslow points out, "Undoubtedly these physiological needs are the most prepotent of all needs. ... A person who is lacking food, safety, love, and esteem would most probably hunger for food more strongly than for anything else" (1970/1954, pp. 36–37). By the same token, individuals who seek esteem and recognition do so only after they have satisfied their need for belongingness.

Although Maslow's theory is appealing from an intuitive standpoint, it has been challenged on at least two grounds (Hall & Nougaim, 1968; Wahba & Birdwell, 1973). First, Maslow offers little empirical evidence either for the existence of his needs or for their arrangement in a hierarchy. Most of his ideas were derived from interviews with rather exceptional people and analyses of famous historical figures such as Thomas Jefferson and Eleanor Roosevelt. It is therefore difficult to know whether the need for self-actualization is as strong in most people as it appears to be in certain highly educated and talented people. A second problem is related to Maslow's notion that higher needs are aroused only after lower needs have been satisfied. A strict interpretation of this notion would suggest, for example, that people who are desperately hungry have little need for self-esteem or love. There is no evidence to support such a contention (Lawler & Suttle, 1972).

Despite these criticisms, Maslow's theory has had an important influence on psychological thought primarily because humans at least *seem* to strive for many of the needs Maslow cites. This optimistic view of human nature has sparked an interest in the development of human potential.

INTERIM SUMMARY

According to Murray, a need is a force in the brain that organizes perception, thought, emotion, and action. Viscerogenic needs are directly related to survival; psychogenic needs are not based on physiological processes. Needs may be overtly expressed in behavior or covertly revealed in fantasies and dreams. Murray developed the Thematic Apperception Test as a means of identifying and measuring covert needs. Maslow believed that humans strive to actualize their individual potential. He hypothesized that there are five categories of needs arranged in a hierarchy, and that people will seek to satisfy lower-level needs before higher-level needs. His ideas have not been fully corroborated, but they have influenced modern psychology's view of human nature.

ACHIEVEMENT MOTIVATION

Achievement has long been thought to be among the most important human motives. The **achievement motive** is aroused whenever a person knows that his or her performance will be evaluated in terms of some standard of excellence and that the consequences will be either favorable (success) or unfavorable (failure) (Atkinson, 1964). As Figure 11-1 shows, Murray called the need to achieve "*n* Achievement"; psychologists often use the shortened term "*n* Ach."

As noted earlier, Murray used the TAT to assess motives; he did not, however, adequately demonstrate that the TAT imagery was dependent on the arousal or activation of a particular motive. To accept the TAT as a useful tool for measuring human needs and motives, researchers had to be convinced that a clear relationship exists between the conditions that arouse a particular need and a high TAT score for that need.

To understand this point, consider the following analogy. Suppose you were to deprive an animal of food, thus establishing a need, and then observe whether the animal performed a certain behavior (like eating) whose purpose was to eliminate the need. If the animal did eat when deprived of food, one could claim with confidence that hunger had been aroused. If, however, one were to deprive an animal of food (create a need for food) and then observe an inappropriate behavior (like sexual behavior) whose purpose was unrelated to the elimination of the need, then one could not claim that hunger had been aroused. By analogy, the same argument applies to the achievement motive and the TAT: People exposed to a situation that arouses or intensifies the motive for achievement should perform achievement-related behaviors, which should include scoring high on TAT imagery for achievement. In short, the use of the TAT as a measure of the need for achievement would seem to depend on whether appropriate achievement-related imagery was elicited in situations that clearly should arouse the achievement motive.

An early investigation attempted to do precisely this—create environmental conditions that presumably would arouse the achievement motive and then observe the use of achievement imagery on the TAT (McClelland, Atkinson, Clark, & Lowell, 1953). Subjects were first given a simple paper-and-pencil test. Then they were divided into six groups, each of which was given different instructions. Those in the achievement group were told that the paper-and-pencil test had been a measure of their IQ and overall ability; these instructions were designed to arouse the achievement motive. Those in the success group and the failure group received the same instructions, except that those in the success group were also told that they had done very well on the previous test and those in the failure group were told that they had done poorly. Subjects in a fourth group, the success/failure group, were given the same instructions but were also told that they had done well on the first half of the test but poorly on the second half. Finally, there were two control groups. Subjects in the relaxed group were told that the paper-and-pencil test was not important at all and did not measure anything relevant. The neutral control subjects, on the other hand, were given virtually no information.

After receiving their instructions, the subjects were shown various TAT pictures and asked to write stories, which were scored for achievement imagery (*n* Ach). The results are shown in Figure 11-4 on page 272. The groups with the lowest scores were the relaxed and neutral groups; the four other groups all scored higher. Overall, then, the instructions appear to have aroused the achievement motive (that is, they elicited achievement-oriented imagery on the TAT) although certain portions of the instructions (such as telling subjects that they had failed) clearly were more powerful in this regard than other portions.

In addition to being elicited by achievement instructions, achievement imagery is also correlated to various behaviors that are indications of an achievement need (Kuhl & Blankenship, 1979). According to one study, men with high *n* Ach scores also prefer to take responsibility; resist social pressure and are motivated by tasks rather than by money; are active in community and college affairs and like to control situations; and tend to be more concerned about the future than men with low scores (McClelland, 1961). Need for achievement may also be manifest in a person's occupational choice. For example, men with high *n* Ach scores tend to be managers, professionals, and proprietors rather than semiskilled or unskilled workers (Veroff, Atkinson, Feld, & Gurin, 1960). A similar result has been found for women. One

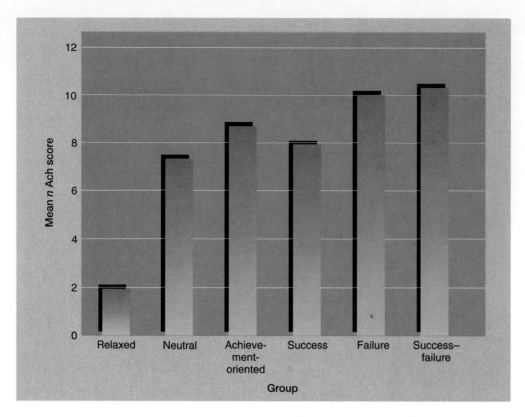

FIGURE 11-4 Mean *n* Ach imagery score on the TAT as a function of the instructions subjects were given in a study of the relationship between TAT imagery and achievement-arousing situations. (Adapted from McClelland, Atkinson, Clark, & Lowell, 1953.)

study, for example, had female college seniors write stories in response to stimuli such as "Carol is looking into her microscope." These stories were then scored for *n* Ach. High *n* Ach women tended later to choose careers that were consistent with their own achievement orientation. Furthermore, these women, like the men studied previously, were concerned with status and mobility and got satisfaction from achieving standards of excellence (Jenkins, 1987).

In sum, human beings have a motive or need to achieve; this motive is aroused when they are placed in an achievement situation; and the strength of *n* Ach as measured by the TAT is correlated with a number of other indexes of achievement. Note, however, that need for achievement as measured by the TAT and self-reported levels of achievement motivation are not highly correlated. That is, what people say about their need for achievement and what the TAT reveals about their motivation are not usually the same (McClelland, Koestner, & Weinberger, 1989).

ATKINSON'S THEORY

One of the most elaborate and successful theories of achievement motivation was proposed by John Atkinson (Atkinson, 1964; Atkinson & Birch, 1978).

Motive to Seek Success

The first tenet of this theory is that the tendency to approach (that is, to perform) an achievement task is a function of the motive for success, the subjective probability of success on the task, and the incentive value of reaching the goal. In formal terms:

$$T_S = M_S \times P_S \times I_S$$

where T_S is the tendency to seek success, M_S is the enduring motive for achievement, P_S is the subjective expectation of success, and I_S is the incentive. Note that M_S is really the same as *n* Ach, so it is measured in terms of imagery on the TAT.

Atkinson's theory makes an important assumption: that incentive is comparable to pride. Pride in the achievement of success increases as the perceived likelihood of

Mountain climbers showing exhilaration on reaching their goal. According to Atkinson, the more difficult a goal is perceived to be, the greater the pride one feels on achieving it.

success decreases. In other words, the inverse relationship between probability of success and incentive (or pride) can be written as $I_S = (1 - P_S)$. If the probability of success is very high, pride will be very low; after all, how can a person take pride in achieving success when the task is so easy? On the other hand, if the probability of success is very low, pride will be relatively high; people do seem to take pride in accomplishing a task that is difficult (see also Skinner, 1971).

The formula for approaching success can now be written as follows:

$$T_S = M_S \times P_S \times (1 - P_S)$$

Note two things. First, the only difference between this equation and the earlier one is that incentive, I_S, has been rewritten as $(1 - P_S)$ to reflect the inverse relationship between probability of success and pride in achievement of that success. Second, because M_S is thought to be an enduring characteristic of the individual, the only factor that varies from one situation to the next is the probability of success. Overall, then, what this equation says is that a person's tendency to seek success on a task is a function of the person's need for achievement, the likelihood of succeeding at the task, and the pride derived from succeeding at that task.

Because of the mathematical properties of this equation, the tendency to approach a task is at its maximum whenever P_S equals 0.5. This is illustrated in Figure 11-5 for various values of P_S. Tasks that are very difficult (low P_S) are not attempted because although the incentive value is high, the probability of attaining the goal is unrealistically low. Similarly, goals that are exceedingly easy to reach (high P_S) are not attempted because very little pride is attached to them. Either way, the tendency to strive toward sucess (T_S) is low. But a person will work hard at a task when the probability of success (P_S) is neither extremely high nor extremely low.

$T_s = M_s \times P_s \times (1 - P_s)$

Assume that $M_s = 0.5$.

The relationship between P_s and T_s will be as follows:

when $P_s =$	$T_s =$
0.1	0.045
0.3	0.105
0.5	0.125
0.7	0.105
0.9	0.045

FIGURE 11-5 The relationship between the strength of the tendency to seek success (T_s) and the probability of success (P_s) in Atkinson's theory of achievement motivation.

Motive to Avoid Failure

The second major tenet of Atkinson's theory has to do with the motive to avoid failure. Whenever a person is in an achievement-oriented situation, the motive to avoid failure is aroused. This motive has traditionally been measured by the Test Anxiety Questionnaire (TAQ) (Mandler & Sarason, 1952). People who score high on the TAQ are said to have a high **fear of failure** (see Birney, Burdick, & Teevan, 1969).

Fear of failure reflects a person's overall tendency to avoid a task for fear of failing at that task. Like the tendency to seek success, the tendency to avoid failure is a function of the motive to avoid failure (measured by the TAQ), the probability of failing, and the shame attached to failing. In formal terms:

$$T_F = M_{AF} \times P_F \times I_F$$

where T_F is the tendency to avoid failure, M_{AF} is the fear of failure as measured on the TAQ, P_F is the probability of failing, and I_F is shame.

In this equation, shame is analogous to pride in the equation presented earlier. It is negatively related to the probability of failure—the greater the probability of failing, the less the shame—and therefore may be rewritten as $I_F = (1 - P_F)$. One would not feel shame at failing at a task if the task was exceedingly difficult—that is, if the probability of success was very low. Conversely, one would feel shame at failing only if the task was relatively easy—that is, if the probability of failing was low.

One can rewrite Atkinson's fear-of-failure equation as follows:

$$T_F = M_{AF} \times P_F \times (1 - P_F)$$

Note that shame (I_F) is rewritten as $(1 - P_F)$ to reflect the inverse relationship between shame and the probability of failure. Just as the tendency to approach sucess is greatest when the probability of success is 0.5, the tendency to avoid failure because of the fear of failure is greatest for intermediate values of P_F.

Achievement Motivation

The third and final tenet of Atkinson's theory is that an individual's tendency actually to engage in achievement-oriented behavior (T_A) is a combination of the person's tendency to approach (T_S) minus his or her tendency to avoid (T_F):

$$T_A = T_S - T_F$$

If we substitute previous terms for those in this equation, we have the following equation:

$$T_A = [M_S - M_{AF}][P_S \times (1 - P_S)]$$

This equation implies that all people are motivated both to seek success and to avoid failure. Every achievement-oriented situation arouses both motives. Whether or not a person actually engages in achievement-related activities depends on two factors: the **resultant achievement motivation** ($M_S - M_{AF}$) and the difficulty of the task [$P_S \times (1 - P_S)$].

Evidence for Atkinson's Model

Atkinson's model is supported by considerable research evidence. In one noted study, subjects were tested for strength of M_S and M_{AF} and then allowed to play a game in which they had to throw a ring onto a peg from a distance of their own choosing (Atkinson & Litwin, 1960). The researchers predicted that success-oriented subjects, whose motivation to achieve is greater than their fear of failure, would choose to throw from an intermediate distance where the difficulty of the task would be neither too low nor too high. Subjects with high fear of failure, in contrast, were expected to avoid intermediate distances and instead to prefer either a very short (easy) or very long (impossibly hard) distance. The results are shown in Figure 11-6. The first prediction was clearly confirmed. Success-oriented subjects showed a distinct preference for intermediate distances—they chose to toss the rings from a point 8 to 11 feet from the peg. The second prediction was also confirmed to some extent. Although subjects with high fear of failure showed a small preference for intermediate distances, they demonstrated a greater relative preference for extreme distances such as 2 to 4 feet or 13 to 15 feet than did the success-oriented subjects.

Other experiments have tested Atkinson's theory in real-life situations such as career choices. In one such study, subjects were divided into success-oriented and

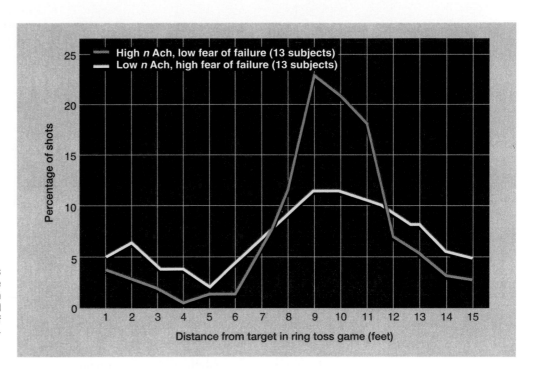

FIGURE 11-6 Percentage of ring-toss shots taken as a function of the distance to the target for subjects with high *n* Ach and low fear of failure (purple line) and subjects with low *n* Ach and high fear of failure (yellow line). Adapted from Atkinson & Litwin, 1960.

fear-of-failure groups and were asked to indicate their occupational goals (Mahone, 1960). A group of psychologists rated each answer according to how realistic it was—that is, whether the career goal could be achieved easily or only with great difficulty. For instance, becoming an astronaut was judged to be a relatively unrealistic or improbable goal, whereas becoming a salesperson was not. As shown in Figure 11-7, the percentage of subjects choosing realistic occupational goals was high in the success-oriented group but rather low in the fear-of-failure group (see also Janman, 1987).

Problems with Atkinson's Model

Despite the evidence supporting Atkinson's model, a number of problems remain. One is that TAT scores are not as reliable as the theory assumes them to be. That is, a

FIGURE 11-7 The relationship between students' vocational choices and their level of achievement motivation and fear of failure. (Adapted from Mahone, 1960.)

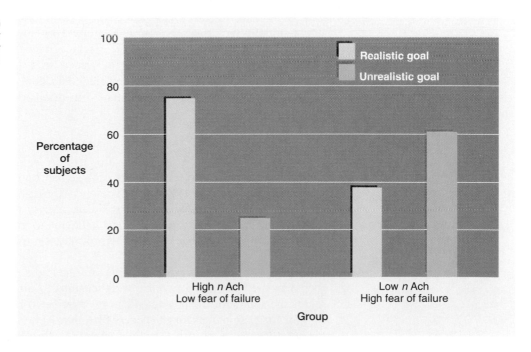

275

Atkinson's success motive (M_S, or the tendency to perform a task) may actually represent many kinds of achievement motives. Motives for extraordinary athletic performance, for example, may include comptitiveness and a concern with excellence, among others.

person's M_S score, which is supposed to measure an enduring trait, is not very consistent from one occasion to the next (Entwisle, 1972). A second problem is that M_S may not represent a single motive but instead may stand for as many as six different kinds of achievement motives (Jackson, Ahmed, & Heapy, 1976). For example, a high-M_S person could be motivated to achieve status with peers or with experts, to be competitive, to be concerned about excellence, and so forth. All of these motivational tendencies could be viewed as distinctly different motives, in which case the use of the TAT as a measure of a single achievement motive would be erroneous.

A third problem is related to Atkinson's claim that pride is equal to $(1 - P_S)$. Some theorists believe that, because of differences in sex role socialization, women may have goals that differ greatly from those of men. And because the term I_S is strongly linked to pride in achieving individual goals that are more typical for men than for women, Atkinson's theory may not apply to women (Parsons & Goff, 1980).

Finally, factors other than the ones used in Atkinson's theory (incentive, probability of success, and motivation to succeed or avoid failure) may affect achievement tendencies. For example, a person's long-range goals (like going to medical school) may affect achievement behavior (like studying) even though the person does not have a high M_S score (Raynor, 1969; 1970).

Despite these problems, Atkinson's model of achievement motivation goes considerably beyond theories that focus only on TAT imagery. Although it assumes that there are motives for success- and failure-avoidance (measured by the TAT and TAQ), it also includes other aspects of achievement-oriented situations, such as the probability of success and the value of success (that is, incentive). Atkinson's model therefore provides a richer and more detailed account of the factors that contribute to achievement behavior than are contained in discussions of the achievement motive alone.

ATTRIBUTION THEORY

A different approach to the study of achievement motivation is based on *attribution theory* (Weiner, 1974, 1985; see Chapter 19). Attribution theory in general claims that people are motivated to understand or explain their behavior. They do this in part by attributing the causes of their behavior to various conditions or agents. In terms of achievement behaviors, a person may, for example, attribute success to talent, or failure to bad luck.

Research findings suggest that the causal factors to which people attribute their behavior can vary along two major dimensions (Weiner, 1985). One dimension concerns the source of the presumed cause—whether it is internal or external. A person might, for example, attribute success or failure at a task to an internal cause like his or her own ability or effort, or to an external cause like luck or the difficulty of the task. This dimension is especially relevant for achievement-related outcomes

(Weiner, Frieze, Kukla, Reed, Rest, & Rosenbaum, 1972). For example, researchers have found that individuals who are high in achievement motivation as measured on the TAT attribute their successes to internal causes ("I succeeded because of my talent") and their failures to external causes ("I failed because the task was too difficult"). In contrast, people who are low in achievement motivation attribute their successes to external causes ("I succeeded because I was lucky"), and their failures to internal causes ("I failed because I don't have the ability").

A second dimension concerns the stability of the cause—the relative permanence of the factors that are thought to affect a given outcome. For example, internal ability and external task difficulty are stable causes; one expects them to remain consistent over time ("I always fail at these tasks" or "Tasks are always too hard for me"). Internal effort and external luck, on the other hand, are variable causes; they are likely to change from one occasion to the next ("I didn't try very hard this time" or "I was unlucky this time").

Evidence for the Attribution Model

A number of interesting experiments have provided evidence that supports the attributional theory of achievement motivation. In one study, subjects were given four trials on a so-called digit-symbol substitution task, in which they were required to cross out each digit on a list and write a special symbol in its place (Weiner & Sierad, 1975). Too little time was allotted for this task, so no subject would be able to succeed at it. The measure of achievement behavior was the number of substitutions per unit of time on four successive trials (relative to the speed of substitution on a pretest).

The subjects in the study were first scored for achievement motivation on the TAT and then divided into four groups. Two of the groups consisted of subjects who had scored high for achievement motivation (high *n* Ach) and two consisted of subjects who had scored low for achievement motivation (low *n* Ach). The members of one of the high *n* Ach groups and one of the low *n* Ach groups were given a harmless sugar pill but told that it was a drug that would slow their performance. The members of the other two groups were not given a pill. The four groups were thus high *n* Ach/drug, low *n* Ach/drug, high *n* Ach/no drug, and low *n* Ach/no drug. (See Figure 11-8.)

FIGURE 11-8 Mean improvement in the number of digit substitutions per trial (relative to a pretest) for high and low *n* Ach subjects who received either the drug or the no drug treatment. (Adapted from Weiner & Sierad, 1975.)

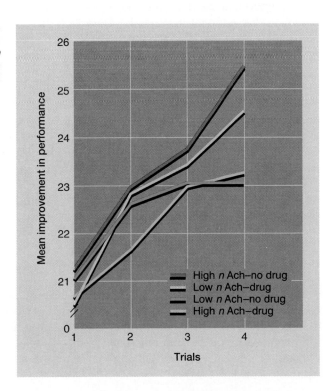

The experimenters made the following predictions. The subjects in the high *n* Ach/drug group, who would normally attribute poor performance to their own lack of effort and thus try harder on successive trials, should in this case attribute their poor performance to the effects of the drug and not try significantly harder on successive trials. The subjects in the high *n* Ach/no drug group, in contrast, unable to attribute poor performance to the effects of a drug, should attribute it to their lack of effort and try harder on successive trials. In other words, wishing to overcome failure, and having no apparent excuse for failure other than their own lack of effort, these subjects should show increased effort and enhanced performance. The subjects in the low *n* Ach/drug group, who would normally attribute poor performance to their lack of ability, should now attribute it to the effects of the drug and not feel the shame they normally associate with failure. They should thus have relatively high levels of performance. Finally, subjects in the low *n* Ach/no drug group should attribute their poor performance to their lack of ability, feel discouraged, and continue to perform poorly.

As Figure 11-8 shows, the results supported these predictions. The high *n* Ach/no drug subjects performed the best, the low *n* Ach/drug group performed at an intermediate level, and the high *n* Ach/drug and low *n* Ach/no drug groups performed the worst.

This study is important because it suggests that the achievement motive does not have a fixed effect on an individual's behavior. The high *n* Ach subjects did not all perform at the same level simply because they were achievement oriented. Instead, their performance depended to a large extent on what they believed to be the cause of their failure.

GENDER AND ACHIEVEMENT MOTIVATION

Investigators have pointed out a problem with this area of research, namely that the traditional findings on achievement motivation, using the TAT, are not reliably found with women subjects. For example, telling women that a test is a measure of IQ does not always result in the production of achievement-related imagery on the TAT as it usually does with men (Veroff, Wilcox, & Atkinson, 1953). A number of explanations have been offered for this discrepancy in results. For example, researchers have argued that the TAT pictures used to assess *n* Ach usually feature male protagonists and therefore do not arouse the achievement motive in women. Researchers have also claimed that the TAT does not work for women because the scoring system is based on conventional male goals (Stein & Bailey, 1973). And they have said that the achievement motive in women, but not in men, is combined with a second motive, namely affiliation (discussed in a later section). Success for women, according to this view, is thus linked more to success in social situations than to conventional achievement goals (Ahlgren & Johnson, 1979).

Although the research in this area is extensive and complex, the generalization that women do not display *n* Ach is surely inaccurate: Need achievement can be aroused in women under a wide array of conditions, including the TAT (Stewart & Chester, 1982). The difficulty in demonstrating arousal of *n* Ach in women has been largely attributable to a methodological discrepancy: The studies that have failed to elicit achievement imagery in women using the TAT have typically compared imagery scores across different groups (for example, those aroused versus those given neutral instructions). In contrast, studies that have shown *n* Ach in women used a pretest/posttest design (Stewart & Chester, 1982).

DEVELOPMENT OF ACHIEVEMENT MOTIVATION

Many psychologists believe that a person's level of achievement motivation is the cause of his or her achievement-related behaviors. In attempting to support this assertion, they have devised various kinds of programs to teach individuals to be high achievers (McClelland & Winter, 1969). In one such program, which was carried out in several cities in India, short seminars were held to teach attitudes and activities that would be conducive to greater achievement in business. Before the seminars, 18% of the participants valued behaviors that typically lead to success in business (such as working long hours, making capital investments, and initiating new programs). After the seminars, however, about 51% of the participants had changed their attitudes and now valued such behaviors. Twenty-two percent of the participants started new businesses within two years, compared to 8% of those in a control group who did not undergo training.

Other studies have not obtained the same result, however (Beit-Hallahmi, 1980; Cover & Johnson, 1976; Frey, 1984). One experiment studied 51 pairs of brothers, each of whom operated a farm in the Punjab region of India (Singh, 1978). In each case one of the brothers was successful and the other was not. Despite the clear differences in economic success, the researcher found no differences in need for achievement. We must be cautious, therefore, in drawing conclusions about the relationship between achievement motivation as measured on the TAT and achievement behavior. On the one hand, motives may have a profound effect on achievement-related behavior even though our tests of this causal relationship are inadequate. On the other hand, an achievement motive in and of itself may not be the cause of achievement-related behavior. As one group of researchers has put it:

> It is hard to doubt that there is some correlation between some kinds of economic behavior and *n* Ach. But considerable doubt remains as to whether *n* Ach is the crucial variable in economic growth or merely a correlate of some other social or psychological process [and as to] the direction of causality between the economic and psychological phenomena concerned. (Lea, Tarpy, & Webley, 1987, p. 441)

INTERIM SUMMARY

The achievement motive is aroused whenever the person knows that performance will be evaluated in terms of some standard of excellence. Some investigators have studied the motivation to achieve by creating environmental conditions that presumably would arouse the achievement motive and observing the consequences in the form of TAT imagery. Achievement-oriented instructions appear to produce higher levels of achievement imagery on the TAT. According to Atkinson's theory of achievement, the tendency to approach a task is a function of the motive for success, the subjective probability of success on the task, and the incentive value of succeeding at that task. Incentive, or pride, is inversely related to the probability of success. Atkinson's theory also states that achievement motivation is influenced by the tendency to avoid failure, which is a function of the motive to avoid failure (measured by the Test Anxiety Questionnaire), the probability of failing, and the shame associated with failure. Shame is inversely related to the probability of failure. The theory claims that an individual's tendency actually to engage in achievement-oriented behavior is a combination of the tendency to approach an achievement-related task minus the tendency to avoid failure. There are some problems with Atkinson's theory stemming from the lack of reliability of TAT scores, the possibility that need for achievement is not a single motive, and the influence of factors other than the ones used in Atkinson's theory. A different approach to the study of achievement motivation is based on attribution theory, or the way people explain the causes of their behavior. People may believe that their behavior is caused internally or may attribute it to external causes. Some have pointed out that the TAT does not always elicit achievement imagery in women subjects, but these results appear to be attributable to differences in methodology. Psychologists have attempted to teach individuals to be high achievers, but with only limited success.

POWER

After achievement, the human motive that has been studied most is power (McClelland, 1975; Winter, 1973; Winter & Stewart, 1978). Power obviously is a salient and pervasive element of human relationships. Both historians and poets have explored the quest for power by nations and their armies, cultural or racial groups, institutions, and individuals. We see evidence for this quest in the development of technology, the control of resources, and the formulation of economic policy, as well as in literature and history, religion and sports, government and business, and social organizations.

THE POWER MOTIVE

The **power motive** (*n* Power), is the stable tendency to seek influence over others, either directly or indirectly. Most psychologists distinguish between the power motive, which is the desire to affect another person's behavior, and influence, which is the resulting change in the other person's behavior.

Like *n* Ach, *n* Power is often measured by the imagery in TAT stories. Typically, the stories involve characters who are concerned with controlling another person, who express strong emotions, or who have an excessive concern for their reputation or position in life.

The power motive is aroused when a person is placed in certain relevant situations. Psychologists have studied several of these situations. In some cases, the subjects were candidates for student government offices who were awaiting the results of the voting (Veroff, 1957; Winter & Stewart, 1977). In others, the subjects were asked to play the role of an experimenter in a psychological study or were shown a film of President John F. Kennedy's inaugural speech. In still other studies the subjects witnessed a demonstration of hypnosis. In all cases the subjects used power imagery in responding to TAT pictures.

The power motive actually consists of two separate components: the **hope for power** and the **fear of power.** Although the imagery evoked by the TAT reflects hope for power and position, the stories also contain negative images suggesting a dislike and mistrust of control. For subjects who fear power, power over others is legitimate only because it may be used to correct an injustice or to help someone who is in a weaker position (Winter, 1973).

POWER BEHAVIOR

The concomitants of the power motive can be seen in interpersonal behaviors and in expressions of power.

Relevant situations—military parades, for example—can arouse the power motive.

FIGURE 11-9 Mean performance evaluation by "managers" (in either a high or low *n* Power group) of subordinates who acted in a neutral or ingratiating manner. (Adapted from Fodor & Farrow, 1979.)

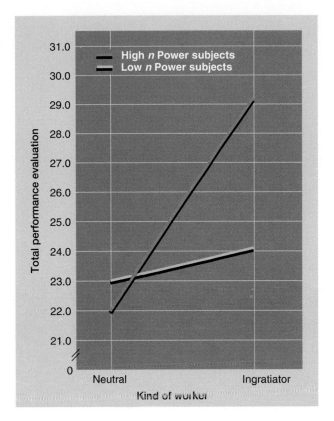

Interpersonal Behaviors

The power motive has a pronounced effect on interpersonal behavior, especially the way power-oriented people interact in group settings. Power-oriented individuals (that is, people with high *n* Power scores) tend to build alliances, especially with others who are not well known but are likely to be loyal (Winter, 1973). They also tend to be subtly manipulative in groups. In one study, for example, groups of students who were unacquainted with one another were given various problems to solve. Those with high *n* Power scores were later judged by the other students in the group to have "most clearly defined the problem," "most encouraged others to participate," and "most influenced others." In other words, these students were able to determine the course of the discussion and influence the participants. At the same time, however, they were judged "not to have the best solution," "not to be the hardest working," and "not to be best-liked" (Winter & Stewart, 1978, pp. 403–404).

An interesting study that simulated an industrial situation used male subjects who were students in a graduate business program (Fodor & Farrow, 1979). The results of this study are shown in Figure 11-9. Subjects were first tested to determine whether they scored low or high in *n* Power. Then they were told that the researchers were conducting a study of managerial style and that their task was to supervise the work of several other men who were building toy models using only pictures of the toy as a guide. The subjects were also instructed to elicit a high rate of production through a variety of techniques, including encouragement, reprisals, promises of higher pay, and advice about construction methods. They were to communicate with the workers, who were supposedly located in another room, through a microphone. In reality there were no workers; the subjects heard only tape recordings of "workers" who acted in either of two ways—in a neutral fashion or in an especially ingratiating manner. For example, the ingratiating workers responded with statements such as "You know, I really like your approach. I can see you're gonna be a good supervisor." In contrast, the neutral responses tended to be, for example, "Well so much for this job. What's next?" Finally, the subjects were asked to evaluate the workers using various managerial categories, such as overall ability, worth to company, prospects for promotion, and likelihood of being hired.

281

People with a personal need for power tend to engage in displays of their prestige, often by wearing a variety of power symbols.

The results showed that the high and low *n* Power subjects reacted to the neutral workers in similar ways. The workers who acted in an ingratiating manner, however, were rated more highly by the high *n* Power subjects than by the low *n* Power subjects. Apparently people with a high need for power attempt to secure and consolidate power by exaggerating the accomplishments of those who act in a subservient and flattering manner toward them.

Expressions of Power

People who are high in *n* Power often have a "high visibility profile" and tend to engage in displays of their prestige. For instance, many high *n* Power college students gain visibility by writing letters to the college newspaper and by displaying prestigious items such as expensive television sets and credit cards (Winter, 1973).

Researchers have identified an important relationship between power and behavior in the form of alcohol consumption (McClelland, Davis, Kalin, & Wanner, 1972; Winter, 1973). Amount of alcohol consumption and *n* Power imagery are positively correlated both in male college students and in male executives: the more imagery, the greater the consumption. In addition, power imagery is affected by alcohol consumption. In a laboratory test, subjects were administered the TAT after they had consumed varying amounts of alcohol. As shown in Figure 11-10, the amount of power imagery increased as a function of the amount of alcohol consumed. Obviously, the alcohol did not create a need for power; it merely reduced the inhibitions on the expression of power imagery. In other words, people may feel more powerful when they have consumed alcohol because inhibitions to the expression of power are reduced. An exception to this finding involves the relationship between alcohol consumption and *n* Power in women: The *n* Power imagery of female subjects remains the same or even declines following consumption of alcohol (Durand, 1975; Wilsnack, 1974).

POWER AND GENDER

A number of experiments have investigated possible differences in *n* Power between males and females. They have found that the same stimuli that tend to arouse the power motive in men also tend to arouse it in women (Steele, 1977; Stewart & Winter, 1976; Winter, 1988). For example, witnessing a demonstration of hypnosis or

282

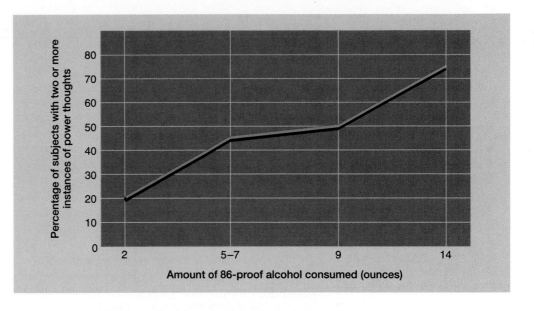

FIGURE 11-10 Percentage of male subjects with two or more instances of power thoughts as a function of amount of alcohol consumed. (Adapted from Winter, 1973.)

hearing excerpts from inspirational speeches tends to arouse *n* Power in women as well as in men. Moreover, the power motive predicts certain behaviors on the part of women, such as having a prestigious position and seeking office (Winter & Stewart, 1978). Thus, female executives tend to have higher *n* Power scores than nonexecutive women who are similar in other important ways, including age, education, and length of employment (Morrison & Sebald, 1974).

POWER AND LEADERSHIP

Scientists have studied *n* Power in relation to political leadership. In particular, they have explored the power motive in twentieth-century U.S. presidents—who are, of course, interesting because of the powerful position they occupy (Winter & Stewart, 1977). None of these presidents has been given the TAT test, but the imagery they used in their inaugural addresses has been scored for *n* Power as well as for *n* Ach and the need for affiliation (discussed in the next section). As shown in Table 11-1, the power imagery used by presidents varies enormously, from a low of 1.97 images per 1,000 words (Taft) to a high of 8.33 (Kennedy).

TABLE 11-1 Power, Achievement, and Affiliation Scores for the Inaugural Speeches of U.S. Presidents.

President	*n* Power	*n* Achievement	*n* Affiliation
T. Roosevelt (1905)	8.25	6.19	2.06
Taft (1909)	1.97	0.90	0.72
Wilson (1913)	5.39	3.00	1.20
Harding (1921)	3.67	2.26	2.82
Coolidge (1925)	3.10	1.67	1.43
Hoover (1929)	3.03	4.04	2.02
F. D. Roosevelt (1933)	6.32	5.26	1.05
Truman (1949)	7.32	4.07	3.66
Eisenhower (1953)	4.07	2.85	4.47
Kennedy (1961)	8.33	6.82	5.30
Johnson (1965)	6.85	7.53	2.05
Nixon (1969)	5.16	8.45	5.16
Ford (1974)	4.72	2.36	10.61
Carter (1977)	5.71	8.16	4.08
Means	5.28	4.54	3.33

SOURCE: Adapted from Winter & Stewart, 1977.

283

In terms of the relationship between power imagery and behavior, the picture is somewhat mixed (Winter & Stewart, 1977). In one study, 50 historians rated the presidents for strength of action, accomplishments, and overall prestige. The *n* Power motive as measured by power imagery in inaugural speeches was positively correlated with each of these categories. Ratings of presidential accomplishments by other historians, however, have not always been correlated with the power imagery. It thus appears that *n* Power is correlated with presidential image—that is, to a president's prestige, perceived strength of action, and enjoyment of the office—but not necessarily with the actual accomplishments of presidents.

INTERIM SUMMARY

The power motive is the tendency to seek influence over others either directly or indirectly. It consists of two separate components: the hope for power and the fear of power. Research on the power motive has revealed a high correlation between power imagery on the TAT and various behavioral expressions of power. People who are high in *n* Power are more likely than those who are low in *n* Power to build alliances, often with those who act ingratiatingly toward them. They are also likely to engage in displays of their prestige. Researchers have found no differences between men and women in need for power.

AFFILIATION

A third motive that has been extensively studied is the **motive for affiliation** (*n* Affil), the tendency to seek the company of others, to find pleasure in being with other people, or to avoid loneliness (Mehrabian & Ksionzky, 1970, 1974; Schachter, 1959). Affiliation is often measured in the same way that achievement and power are measured: in terms of imagery on the TAT. TAT stories may reflect two forms of affiliation (Shipley & Veroff, 1952). Stories with positive imagery emphasize the idea that affiliation is a good thing; they show other people as a source of gratification. Negative imagery, on the other hand, reveals aversive feelings about affiliation with others. A story might, for example, express an aversion for a relationship that had been unpleasant or might reveal painful feelings about the dissolution of a relationship. Although showing concern for others, such imagery expresses that concern in a distinctly negative light. The positive dimension of affiliation is referred to as **hope for affiliation;** the negative dimension is termed **fear of rejection.**

FACTORS INFLUENCING AFFILIATION

Like the achievement and power motives, the affiliation motive is aroused under certain environmental conditions. Perhaps the most important of those conditions is anxiety. In one early study, the subjects were two groups of college women who were not acquainted with one another (reported by Schachter, 1959). A serious-looking experimenter dressed in a white laboratory coat told them that they were to participate in an experiment designed to test the effects of electrical shock on performance (no such experiment was actually planned). Subjects in one group were told that the shock would be quite painful; these were the high-anxiety subjects. Those in the low-anxiety group were told that the shocks would be very mild—they would resemble a tickle and would not be at all painful. All of the subjects were then told that the researchers needed some additional information to conduct the experiment. They were asked to indicate on a 5-point scale the extent to which they liked the idea

Affiliation—the tendency to seek the company of others—is a powerful human motive.

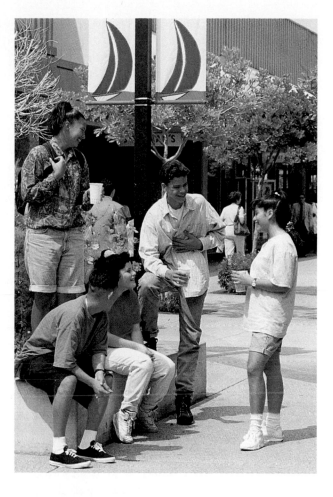

of being a subject in the experiment. (The scale ranged from "I dislike the idea very much" to "I enjoy the idea very much.")

The subjects were then told that there would be a brief delay before the experiment could begin. They were asked to indicate whether they would prefer to wait alone or with others, or whether it did not matter. Their answers were used as the measure of need for affiliation.

Not surprisingly, the results showed that the high-anxiety subjects felt more anxious than the low-anxiety subjects; the experimental manipulation seemed to have succeeded in creating anxiety. In fact, 18.8% of the high-anxiety subjects refused to remain in the experiment, whereas all of the low-anxiety subjects were willing to continue.

Anxiety also affected the subjects' desire to be with others during the waiting period. Of the 32 high-anxiety subjects 20 chose to wait together, compared to only 10 of the 30 low-anxiety subjects. These differences clearly show that anxiety can arouse the affiliation motive, causing the individual to seek the company of others.

Uncertainty and Communication

This basic finding does not explain *why* anxiety arouses the need for affiliation. Several plausible explanations have been suggested (Mehrabian & Ksionzky, 1974). One is that subjects may wish to obtain comfort from other people. Another is that in times of uncertainty people wish to communicate with others in order to clarify the situation and their own feelings. This second explanation was developed by Leon Festinger (1954) in his *social comparison theory* described more fully in Chapter 19. Briefly, this theory argues that people have a drive to evaluate their opinions and abilities, and that when objective means of conducting such an evaluation are unavailable (as in the experiment just described) they will turn to others, especially others who are similar to themselves in some way.

There is considerable evidence that such an evaluation process does indeed occur. In one study, groups of subjects were told that they would receive a painful electric shock (again, no shock was ever administered) and that their physiological reactions to the shock would be measured by means of electrodes on their forearms (Gerard & Rabbie, 1961). Different groups of subjects were given different instructions as to the information they would have about their own reactions and those of others in the experiment. In the low-uncertainty condition, all the subjects were told they would be informed about the reactions of other subjects as well as their own; specifically, they were told that one of four "response meters" located in each subject's testing cubicle registered the subject's own reaction and that the other three meters showed the reactions of other members of the group. In the moderate-uncertainty condition, subjects were told only that they would be informed about their own reaction to getting shocked. In the high-uncertainty condition, subjects were given no information at all—they were not told about the "response meters."

After these instructions had been given, subjects were asked whether they wished to wait alone or together during a 10-minute delay period and to indicate the strength of their desire on a 100-point scale. Nearly all the subjects chose to wait together, but the strength of the choice differed as a function of the instructions they had received. For the low-uncertainty subjects, the mean score on the 100-point scale was 55.1; for the moderate- and high-uncertainty groups, the mean scores were 70.5 and 66.8, respectively. It thus appears that people may seek others in order to obtain information under conditions of uncertainty.

INTERIM SUMMARY

The motive for affiliation is the tendency to seek the company of others, to find pleasure in being with other people, or to avoid loneliness. It has both positive (hope for affiliation) and negative (fear of rejection) dimensions. The need for affiliation is aroused under certain environmental conditions, especially anxiety. Various explanations of this relationship have been offered, including Festinger's theory that people have a drive to evaluate their opinions and abilities, and that under conditions of uncertainty they will turn to others who are similar to themselves in some way.

SUMMARY

1. The study of social motives encompasses the concept of free will to a greater degree than does the study of other motivated behaviors, including behaviors governed by basic needs and biosocial motives.

2. According to Murray's need theory, there are two types of needs: viscerogenic and psychogenic. *Viscerogenic needs* are related to the survival of the organism; *psychogenic needs* are not. Testing techniques like the *Thematic Apperception Test (TAT)* make it possible to infer and measure psychogenic needs from observable behavior.

3. Maslow extended need theory by claiming that a hierarchy of needs exists, ranging from primitive physiological needs to the need for *self-actualization,* which is the need to realize one's greatest potential. According to Maslow, higher needs are aroused only after lower needs have been fulfilled.

4. The *achievement motive* has been studied for many years, often by means of the TAT. For example, various achievement-arousing stimuli have been shown to elicit achievement imagery on the TAT. A detailed theory of achievement motivation was proposed by Atkinson.

He argued that the tendency to work toward success is based on two separate motives—the tendency to approach success (T_S) and the tendency to avoid failure (T_{AF}). Both of these tendencies are at a maximum when the probability of success is 0.5.

5. The *attribution theory* of need achievement was formulated by Weiner, who argued that a person's achievement behavior is related to attributional style. For example, high *n* Ach people tend to explain success in terms of internal causes and failures in terms of external causes. Low *n* Ach people show the opposite kinds of attributions. Recent evidence has tended to support this theory by showing, for example, that achievement performance is affected to a large degree by what people judge to be the cause of their success or failure.

6. The *power motive* consists of two separate motives: the *hope for power* motive (the tendency to seek influence over others) and the *fear of power* motive (a concern for power couched in a negative light, a tendency to dislike and mistrust control). Studies show that people with high *n* Power scores on the TAT tend to form alliances, to be subtly manipulative in groups, and to favor subservient subordinates. There is little difference in *n* Power between men and women, except that men tend to show increased use of power imagery on the TAT when they consume alcohol whereas women do not.

7. The *motive for affiliation* refers to the tendency to seek the company of others. It is strongly influenced by anxiety, possibly because anxious subjects wish to communicate with other people in order to gain comfort or reduce uncertainty.

FOCUS QUESTIONS

1. Compare and contrast the approaches of Murray and Maslow with respect to need theory.

2. Describe the evidence supporting the notion that *n* Ach as measured on the TAT is related to achievement behavior.

3. What are the major tenets of Atkinson's achievement theory and what evidence supports it?

4. Describe the efforts to teach achievement motivation.

5. Describe the way in which *n* Power is related to behavioral expressions of power.

6. Discuss the various kinds of affiliation motives and describe the factors that affect *n* Affil.

PART FOUR

THE ORIGINS OF KNOWLEDGE

 cat pressing a pedal to escape from a puzzle box and a mathematician solving a complex problem are both using knowledge. How is knowledge acquired? How is it organized and structured? And how best can it be manipulated to serve the organism's purposes? These questions involve **the origin of the contents of the mind,** the subject of the next four chapters. Chapter 12 examines basic processes of learning, focusing on the evolutionary value of knowledge. Chapter 13 considers the way information is collected, processed, and represented in memory. Chapter 14 takes a broader perspective, examining cognitive structures and the ways in which units of information might be organized into systems of knowledge. Finally, Chapter 15, on thinking and problem solving, illustrates how acquired knowledge can be put to practical use.

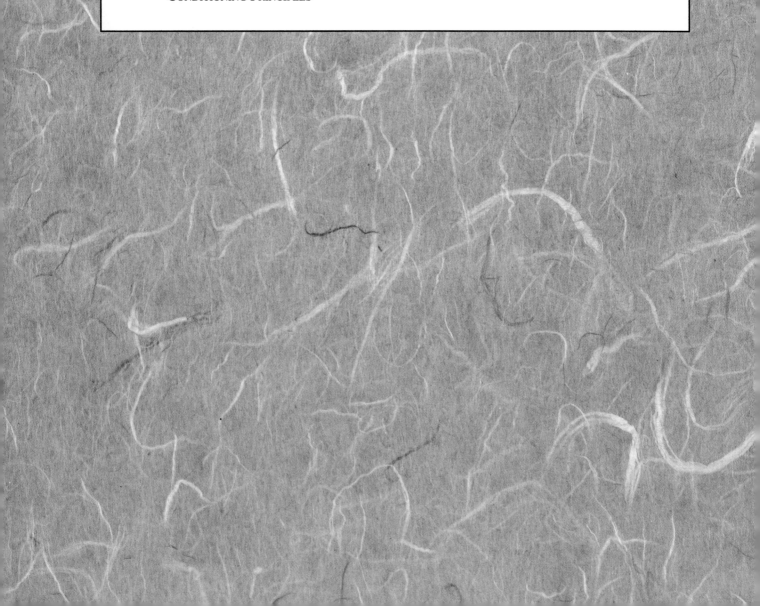

CHAPTER 12

LEARNING

ASSOCIATIONISM
    STIMULUS CONTINGENCY

PAVLOVIAN (CLASSICAL) CONDITIONING
    BASIC TERMS
    ACQUISITION AND EXTINCTION
    TEMPORAL RELATIONSHIPS IN CLASSICAL
        CONDITIONING
    PAVLOVIAN THEORY
    VARIABLES THAT AFFECT CONDITIONING
    PAVLOVIAN PHENOMENA
    APPLICATIONS OF CLASSICAL
        CONDITIONING PRINCIPLES

INSTRUMENTAL (OPERANT)
CONDITIONING
    BASIC TERMS
    REINFORCERS AND PUNISHERS
    INSTRUMENTAL CONDITIONING
        PROCEDURES
    INSTRUMENTAL LEARNING THEORY
    VARIABLES THAT AFFECT INSTRUMENTAL
        CONDITIONING
    INSTRUMENTAL PHENOMENA
    APPLICATIONS OF INSTRUMENTAL
        CONDITIONING PRINCIPLES

Throughout the history of psychology the question of the origins of knowledge has been one of the central themes of the discipline. That question is central to this chapter as well, for here we focus on learning—the basic processes by which organisms acquire knowledge.

Let us begin by considering what we mean by knowledge. Dictionaries typically define knowledge as an organized body of information. For example, we have knowledge about historical facts, the contents of a kitchen drawer, abstract propositions like 2 + 2 = 4, and the menace posed by semi-automatic rifles. But we can also consider knowledge from an evolutionary perspective; that is, we can explore what it might mean for a species that must survive in a challenging and uncertain world. In this context, knowledge is equivalent to meaning or significance. For example, an antelope has knowledge about a source of water—it knows the meaning or significance of features of the landscape that allow it to locate the water. Similarly, a bird has knowledge about the presence of a cat because it has seen it in the same surroundings on many previous occasions.

Knowledge of this sort obviously aids survival. If the antelope can find water by going to the landmarks that are meaningful or significant in this regard, its survival chances are enhanced. If the bird is aware of the cat's presence, it can avoid an encounter with this predator. Individuals that lack knowledge about the meaning of landmarks or danger signals are at a disadvantage (Hollis, 1982).

ASSOCIATIONISM

The British empiricists claimed that knowledge is acquired empirically—that is, from experience—rather than being present at birth. They also tried to show *how* knowledge is acquired through experience. They claimed that two events can become connected through learning, thereby creating an **association**. When two sensations occur together in time or space (that is, are contiguous), the mental reactions to those sensations become associated. Then, whenever the first sensation occurs, it triggers its own reaction (the mental perception of that sensory stimulus) *and* the associated reaction, which is usually triggered only by the second sensation.

Think of a dog that wags its tail in anticipation of being fed every time its owner opens up a kitchen cabinet while gesturing in a particular way. (See Figure 12-1.)

FIGURE 12-1 An example of the formation of an association according to the British empiricists' theory of associationism.

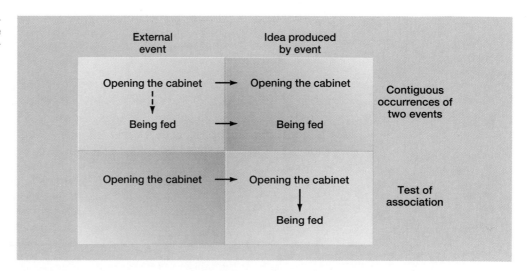

Each of those events ("opening the cabinet" and "being fed") produces a corresponding mental reaction. Because "opening the cabinet" has frequently preceded "being fed," however, the mental reactions to which those events normally give rise have become linked. Thus, when the first stimulus, "opening the cabinet," occurs by itself, it triggers its own mental reaction *as well as* the associated mental reaction to "being fed." This conclusion is supported by the fact that the animal behaves in ways that are appropriate to "being fed"—it wags its tail, approaches the food dish, and salivates.

STIMULUS CONTINGENCY

Why does such an association of ideas develop? The empiricists believed that it was enough simply for two stimuli to occur close together in time or space. But can temporal contiguity alone produce an association? Apparently not. As we will see, modern research suggests that to become associated, two stimuli must not only be contiguous, they must also have a contingent relationship (Rescorla, 1967).

A **contingent relationship** between two stimuli is one in which the second of the two depends on the first; the second occurs in the presence of the first, never in its absence. In other words, the second event or stimulus is consistently preceded by the presence—never by the absence—of the first stimulus. The first stimulus thus acts as a signal for a particular outcome, namely, the second stimulus; the first stimulus can be said to be *informative* in that it predicts the second stimulus.

A contingent relationship between two events need not always be perfect, however; the first stimulus may be an imperfect predictor of the second. To return to our first example, "opening the cabinet" *usually* leads to "being fed," and "not opening the cabinet" *usually* means "not being fed," but many times the dog might see its owner "opening the cabinet" without then "being fed." Moreover, the owner might feed the dog without first "opening the cabinet." Because this is so, the predictive relationship between the signal ("opening the cabinet") and the outcome ("being fed") is not perfect. In fact, if the contingent relationship between the two events were weakened sufficiently, there would come a point at which the stimulus "opening the cabinet" would give the dog no knowledge about what is about to occur. The signal, "opening the cabinet," and the outcome, "being fed," would have become so random relative to each other that the dog could no longer predict whether or not it would be fed when it saw the owner opening the cabinet.

In this chapter we discuss two kinds of knowledge or learning. First, organisms may have knowledge about the stimuli in their environment; they may learn about the meaning of stimuli just as the dog learned about the meaning of the stimulus "opening the cabinet." This kind of learning is called Pavlovian (or classical) conditioning. Second, organisms may have knowledge about their own behavior; they may learn that their own behaviors affect the environment in particular ways that are beneficial to them. This form of learning is called instrumental (or operant) conditioning (see Lieberman, 1990; Mazur, 1990; Schwartz, 1989).

INTERIM SUMMARY

The British empiricists believed that learning occurs when two stimuli are contiguous, and the corresponding mental reactions become linked together or associated. Modern research has shown that for two stimuli to become associated they must not only be contiguous but one must also be contingent on the other. The strength of an association depends on the extent to which one stimulus is a good predictor of the other.

PAVLOVIAN (CLASSICAL) CONDITIONING

We begin our discussion of **Pavlovian,** or **classical, conditioning** by considering the details of Pavlov's famous experiment. Ivan Pavlov (1849–1936) was a Russian physiologist who used the salivation reflex to study digestive processes in dogs (Pavlov, 1927). In the course of doing so, he discovered that his dogs would salivate *before* the experiment had actually begun, that is, when he first entered the room. This curious reaction, which Pavlov called a "psychic secretion" (because the salivation occurred without presentation of any physical stimulus), became the central focus of his study.

Prior to starting an experiment, Pavlov would make a small incision in a dog's cheek so that the saliva could be directed into a flask. (See Figure 12-2.) Then, dur-

FIGURE 12-2 Diagram of the apparatus used by Pavlov to study conditioned salivation.

Ivan Pavlov observing an experiment being conducted in his laboratory.

ing the experiment itself, the dog would be placed in a restraining harness and presented with two stimuli in succession. The first stimulus was usually the clicking sound of a metronome (lights were used in some experiments), whereas the second stimulus, presented, say, 10 seconds later, would be a small amount of food powder delivered directly into the dog's mouth. The first stimulus was relatively innocuous; that is, it would not, on its own, cause the dog to salivate. The second stimulus, however, would always cause the dog to salivate. After repeated pairings of these two stimuli, Pavlov noticed that the metronome *by itself* began to elicit some salivation. That is, the dog began to salivate during the 10 seconds prior to the delivery of food. At first the amount of salivation was rather small, but with repeated presentations of the two stimuli the amount increased considerably.

From many such experiments, Pavlov inferred that the dogs had developed an association between whatever he used as the first stimulus—the light or the metronome—and the delivery of the food powder. If such an association had not developed, then clearly the dogs would have continued to react to the metronome with relative indifference—that is, without salivating.

Since Pavlov's time, studies of conditioning have continued to use animals such as rats and pigeons because their behavior can be conveniently investigated under controlled, laboratory conditions that allow researchers to isolate specific variables and draw valid conclusions about them. Nevertheless, as we shall see, most of the phenomena discussed in this chapter apply to human beings as well. Suppose, for example, that someone were to show you a fresh-cut slice of lemon. The mere sight of the lemon (perhaps even just reading the word *lemon* on this page) would probably cause you to salivate. But surely the sight of a lemon itself cannot cause salivation; the reaction must occur because you learned to associate lemon slices and the taste of lemons (which automatically causes you to salivate) in the past.

BASIC TERMS

A typical Pavlovian experiment has four major components. The **unconditioned stimulus (US)** is the biologically potent stimulus that reliably produces a reflexive reaction. In animal research, food (as in Pavlov's experiments) and electric shock are often used as the US because they are easily administered and controlled, but many

Conditioned stimuli that are not themselves biologically powerful may elicit a Pavlovian reaction because of their past association with an unconditioned stimulus. The mere image of a lemon, for example, may cause you to salivate because of its association with the taste of lemon, which invariably produces salivation.

other stimuli are used as well: mild poisons that cause nausea, bitter-tasting substances, weak puffs of air to the eye, loud noises. All of these stimuli have a strong and predictable effect on the subject, producing a reliable reflexive reaction.

The **unconditioned response (UR)** is the reaction elicited by a US. It is an *unlearned, involuntary* reaction. Any single US, of course, may produce more than one UR. For example, food powder might cause an animal to exhibit an accelerated heart rate as well as to salivate; a shock might produce changes in galvanic skin response (GSR) and withdrawal from the source of the shock. The experimenter's choice of a UR for measurement is often based on convenience as much as on other factors.

The third important component of a Pavlovian experiment is the **conditioned stimulus (CS).** The CS (the metronome or light in Pavlov's experiment) initially provokes little reaction, certainly not a UR. The animal may perk up its ears in response to an auditory CS or turn its head and look at a visual CS, but these responses typically are weak and tend to subside rather quickly. Tones and lights are commonly used as CSs because they are easily administered and measured, but other stimuli, including odors, tastes, and touch stimulation, are often used as well.

The final major component of a Pavlovian experiment is the **conditioned response (CR).** The CR is the reaction elicited by the CS when it is presented alone (after it has been paired with the US); it is the learned reaction, the new behavioral tendency acquired during the conditioning process. The CR is the behavioral evidence that an association has been formed. In Pavlov's experiment, the CR was the number of drops of saliva elicited by the sound of the metronome.

ACQUISITION AND EXTINCTION

The development of the conditioned salivation response, shown on the left in Figure 12-3, reflects the process termed **acquisition.** After the CR has been acquired, if the CS is repeatedly presented without the US, the CR will usually disappear. This process is called **extinction** (see Figure 12-3).

Extinction can be illustrated using our previous example of the dog who reacted by wagging its tail to its master opening the cabinet. If the owner began storing the dog's food in another location, then "being fed" would no longer consistently follow "opening the cabinet." Eventually, the dog would cease to react to the original CS ("opening the cabinet"). That is, the conditioned reaction would eventually extinguish.

FIGURE 12-3 Number of drops of saliva given to the metronome CS during acquisition (left) and extinction (right) in Pavlov's experiment. (Adapted from Pavlov, 1927.)

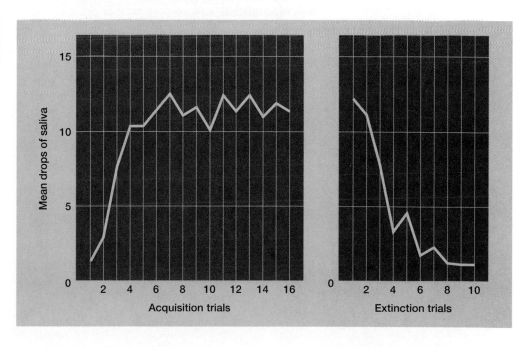

TEMPORAL RELATIONSHIPS IN CLASSICAL CONDITIONING

The temporal relationship between the CS and the US is a critical variable in Pavlovian conditioning. (Indeed, as we noted earlier, the British empiricists identified this factor as critical to the formation of an association.) In general, a CS can occur before, at the same time as, or after the US.

Procedures in which the CS always occurs before the US are called **forward conditioning.** Two common variants of forward conditioning are delayed conditioning and trace conditioning (see Figure 12-4). In delayed conditioning, the CS begins before the US but continues at least until the onset of the US, and may overlap with the US. In trace conditioning, the CS begins and ends before the onset of the US, so that there is a gap of time between the two. Forward conditioning produces stronger CRs than other arrangements, but it is not clear whether or not the delayed and trace variants differ in effectiveness. Some experimenters have found them to be equally effective (Wilson, 1969). Others, however, have found that the delayed arrangement produces superior conditioning (Schneiderman, 1966), although this may be true only when the interval between the onset of the CS and the onset of the US is short (Manning, Schneiderman, & Lordahl, 1969).

In **simultaneous conditioning,** the CS and US are given at precisely the same time (Figure 12-4). This procedure produces an association, but it is much weaker than the associations generated by the forward procedures (Hearst, 1989). In **backward conditioning** (Figure 12-4), the onset of the CS occurs *after* the onset of the US. As with simultaneous conditioning, backward conditioning may produce conditioned reactions, but they are weaker than those produced by forward conditioning (Rescorla, 1969; Spetch, Wilkie, & Pinel, 1981).

PAVLOVIAN THEORY

A major challenge for psychologists studying Pavlovian conditioning is to understand precisely how an association is formed. We noted earlier that stimulus contingency is critical to the formation of an association. We will start this section by considering the evidence underlying this conclusion and then turn to other aspects of Pavlovian theory.

Contiguity and Contingency

The original theory of Pavlovian conditioning was based on the British empiricists' **law of contiguity.** According to this principle, the development of an association

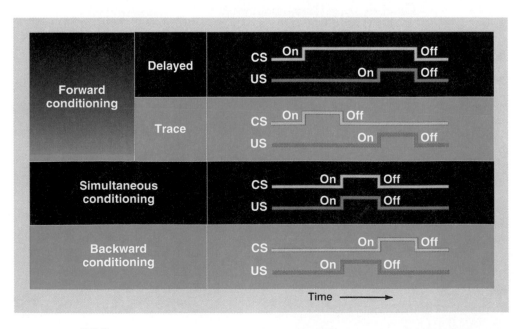

FIGURE 12-4 The temporal arrangement between the CS and US for various conditioning procedures.

depends entirely on the temporal contiguity of the stimuli: Stimuli that are presented close together in time are associated more strongly than stimuli that are presented farther apart in time.

The principle of contiguity seems logical. After all, how could a stimulus function as a signal for an outcome if the outcome were markedly delayed? The principle of contiguity is also supported by research showing that as the interval between stimuli increases, the conditioning becomes weaker. As we discussed earlier, however, temporal contiguity is necessary but not sufficient for an association to occur. If two stimuli are contiguous but do not also have a contingent relationship, no association will form between them (Rescorla, 1967).

A contingent relationship between a CS and a US exists when the two stimuli occur together and do not occur alone. When this is the case, a predictive, or informative, relationship between the stimuli exists. The first stimulus predicts the occurrence of the second; its absence predicts the absence of the second. But recall that a contingent relationship is not always perfect. A particular CS may usually precede a given US, but the US might sometimes occur by itself without the CS first having occurred. For example, the sound of a metronome might be followed by food powder, but the food might also occur by itself on some occasions, that is, without being preceded by the metronome. If contingency is a critical variable for conditioning, then the stronger the contingent (predictive) relationship between a CS and a US, the stronger the resulting CR.

In a study to test this prediction, researchers gave two groups of rats the same number of contiguous presentations of a light (CS) followed by a shock (US) (Rescorla, 1968; see also Goddard & Jenkins, 1987). One of the groups, the extra-US subjects, received additional presentations of the US (shock) alone; the other group, the control subjects, did not. These procedures are diagramed in Figure 12-5. Note that the number of contiguous CS–US pairings was the same for both groups but that the strength of the contingency was not. For the control subjects, the CS more consistently predicted the US than it did for the extra US subjects. If contiguity alone produced an association, there should be no difference between the groups. According to the contingency theory, however, the two groups should differ because the extra USs would weaken the predictive relationship between the CS and the US.

The results confirmed the contingency theory: Conditioning was strong when the subjects did not receive extra presentations of the US. Conditioning was virtually nonexistent when there were as many unpredicted USs as there were predicted USs. In this case the CS and US presentations were thoroughly random with respect to each other, so there was no predictive relationship between the two stimuli.

A predictive (contingent) relationship between a CS and a US is thus essential for learning to take place. This means that conditioning involves the acquisition of knowledge: Based on the CS occurrence, the subject, in a sense, knows about the impending US presentation. When the CS and US are presented randomly, however, the CS cannot come to predict the US and so the subject has no knowledge about the US presentation based on the CS. To illustrate, imagine the preposterous idea that wearing a blue sweater meant that the wearer is ill-tempered. Such an association

FIGURE 12-5 Schematic diagram showing the temporal relations between CS and US for two different contingent relationships. Note that the "extra US" subjects have as many *un*predicted USs as they have predicted USs, but that all the USs are predicted by the CS for the control subjects.

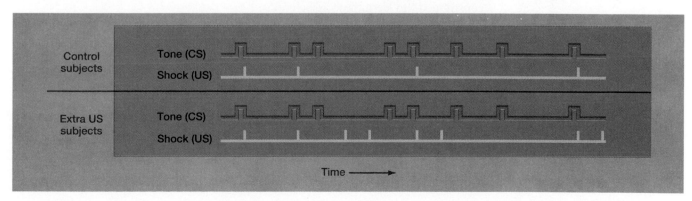

could be true only if blue sweaters were always worn by ill-tempered people, and nonblue sweaters were never worn by ill-tempered people. If such a proposition were true, we could say that we had knowledge of a person's temperament based on sweater color, just as a rat has knowledge of an impending shock upon hearing a tone. But the idea is preposterous precisely because sweater color and temperament are *randomly* paired in the population. That is, no predictive relationship exists between sweater color and temperament and thus no person has knowledge about the temperament of another individual based upon that person's sweater color.

Biological Constraints in Pavlovian Conditioning

For many years, researchers believed that virtually any CS could become associated with any US provided that there was a contingent relationship between them. Research in the last 25 years, however, has suggested that the ease of conditioning may depend in part on the kind of CS–US combinations that are used.

In a classic study, thirsty rats were given a CS (sugar-flavored water along with a tone and flashing light) followed by a US (Garcia & Koelling, 1966). For some subjects the US was a shock; for others it was being injected with a solution that caused mild nausea. According to the law of contiguity, the "bright, noisy, tasty" CS should become associated with either the shock or the poison because the CS is contiguous in both cases. This prediction was tested by giving the components of the CS and observing whether the animals avoided drinking. Specifically, half of the original CS-shock animals and half of the CS-poison subjects were tested for their aversion to the tone/light component; that component was presented whenever they drank from a plain water tube and their aversion to consuming the water was measured. The other half of the CS-shock and CS-poison subjects were tested for their aversion to the flavor component; the sugar-flavored water (without the tone and flashing light) was presented and aversion to consuming it was measured.

The results revealed a selective conditioning effect: Subjects trained with the shock US showed strong aversion to drinking plain water accompanied by the tone/light, but relatively little aversion to the flavored water. In contrast, animals that had been trained with the poison US showed a strong aversion for the flavored water, but little aversion for the plain water plus tone/light. In other words, the tone/light and shock, and the flavor and poison, became strongly associated, but the tone/light and poison, and flavor and shock did not.

Some theorists argued that the two CSs (flavor and tone/light) were not associated with each US (poison and shock) to the same extent because speed of conditioning depends on whether a CS and US "belong" together (Rozin & Kalat, 1971; Seligman, 1970). In a rat's natural environment, for example, flavors and poisonous substances are both components of food; both are "internal" stimuli and therefore belong to the same biological system. Tones/lights and shock, in contrast, impinge on external sense organs. In short, flavors and poison naturally "belong" together and therefore are associated easily; tones/lights and shocks "belong" to a category of externally applied stimuli and thus are easily associated. The alternative combinations, however, do not belong together and thus are not easily associated; subjects are "constrained" to learn these associations.

Belongingness makes sense from an evolutionary perspective. Throughout evolution, individuals who could easily associate the flavor of a food with its subsequent effect (like illness) would be more likely to avoid eating that food a second time, and, therefore, more likely to pass their genes onto future generations. Individuals who could not readily associate flavors with resulting illness, however, would be more likely to eat the poisonous substance a second time and thus more likely to die before successfully raising offspring. Thus, a biologically specialized ability to associate flavors and poison, but not flavors and shock, gradually evolved.

This evolutionary argument has been supported by a number of findings. First, as we discussed previously, conditioning is usually impossible when the US is delayed even for a few seconds; contiguity is essential. In taste aversion learning, however, the CS–US association can develop even when the US (the poison) is delayed for several hours (Andrews & Braveman, 1975). According to an evolutionary perspective, animals who could bridge the long interval between the flavor and poison (an interval that might well be several hours because poison is often slow to act) and still learn the aversion would be at an advantage: If they survived the poison, they would be less likely to consume the food a second time. Animals that could not tolerate such a long delay would not develop the flavor-poison association and thus might not recognize the dangerous food from its flavor when it is once again available.

Researchers now generally believe that taste aversion learning may be a biologically specialized form of learning, but it does not differ markedly from other more conventional forms of Pavlovian conditioning. Animals do not appear to be seriously constrained in their ability to associate CSs and USs (Domjan, 1980, 1983; Logue, 1979). Rats, for example, can learn to associate the appearance of a CS with poison without much difficulty (Revusky & Parker, 1976). Similarly, that taste aversions can be acquired when the US presentation is delayed several hours does not mean that the flavor–poison association is *qualitatively* different from other kinds of Pavlovian associations (such as those involving lights and shocks). Associations differ only in the degree to which US delays are possible (Krane & Wagner, 1975).

In summary, the uniqueness of taste aversion learning has been cited as providing evidence that animals are biologically constrained in their learning ability, that different principles of learning are needed to explain certain forms of learning, and therefore that the laws of conditioning do not apply generally across species and stimuli. Recent analyses, suggest that such an argument is not correct. One researcher noted, "The use of examples from taste-aversion learning to argue against the generality of the laws of learning is no longer very convincing" (Domjan, 1980, p. 327).

VARIABLES THAT AFFECT CONDITIONING

CS–US Interval

If contiguity is not sufficient to cause conditioning, it is, as we noted previously, necessary. No matter how strong the contingent relationship between a CS and a US, if they do not occur close together in time, conditioning will fail to occur.

The general relationship between the CS–US interval and strength of conditioning is a negative one: The longer the interval, the weaker the conditioning. This makes sense. Imagine receiving a CS, such as someone shouting "Watch out!," and then experiencing a painful outcome like a pinprick on a finger. It would not take very many paired presentations of these stimuli to cause you to wince and withdraw your hand at the sound of the warning alone. But would such a reaction develop if the pinprick were delayed for, say, 10 minutes?

The exact relationship between the CS–US interval and the strength of the CR depends to a large extent on the type of response being conditioned. Consider the conditioned eyeblink reaction in rabbits (see Figure 12-6.), which develops when an

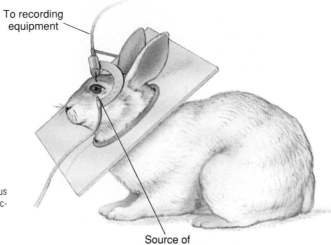

To recording equipment

FIGURE 12-6 Diagram of an apparatus used to study conditioned eyeblink reactions in rabbits.

Source of air puff(US)

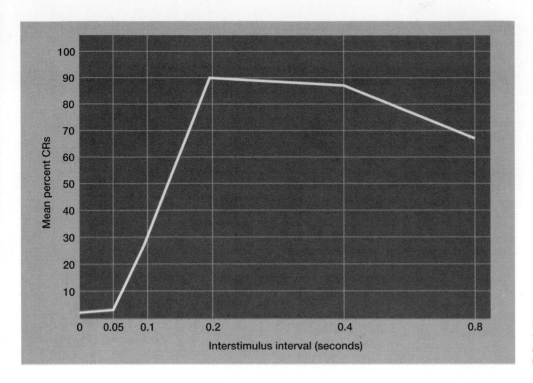

FIGURE 12-7 Mean percent CRs as a function of the CS–US interval for the conditioned eyeblink reaction in rabbits. (Adapted from Gormezano, 1972.)

unpleasant but harmless puff of air, which causes a blink, is delivered to the eye just after a CS such as a tone. As shown in Figure 12-7, the conditioning is strongest when the CS–US interval is between about 0.2 and 0.4 second (Gormezano, 1972), although longer intervals are effective if the time between trials is also lengthened (Levinthal, Tartell, Margolin & Fishman, 1985).

There are other kinds of conditioned reactions, however, for which this degree of contiguity is not required. Consider the case where the CS is, say, a tone and the US is a mild shock. The CR that develops is a physiological reaction, for example a galvanic skin response (GSR) or a change in heart rate. As shown in Figure 12-8, conditioning of an autonomic response such as heart rate in rats is strongest when the CS–US interval is about 6 seconds or longer (Fitzgerald & Martin, 1971).

Finally, consider the case of taste aversion learning discussed previously. Here, rats receive a flavor solution (CS) followed by a weak poison US. The CR is avoidance of the flavored solution later on. As shown in Figure 12-9, the strength of conditioning declines only if the US follows the CS by several hours (Andrews &

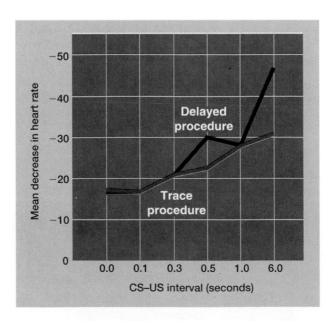

FIGURE 12-8 Mean decrease in heart rate in rats as a function of CS–US interval for both trace and delayed procedures. (Adapted from Fitzgerald & Martin, 1971.)

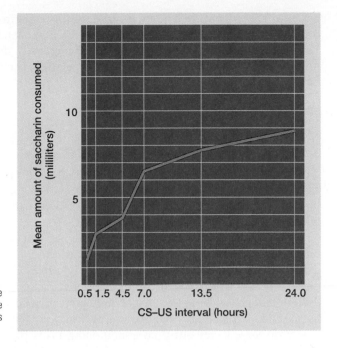

FIGURE 12-9 Mean consumption of the flavor CS (saccharin) as a function of the CS–US interval. (Adapted from Andrews & Braveman, 1975.)

Braveman, 1975). In conclusion, the CS–US interval is important in all cases—strength of conditioning declines as the interval increases, regardless of what kind of CR is being conditioned—but the absolute interval at which learning no longer occurs varies with the kind of response being conditioned.

Stimulus Intensity

The intensity of the stimuli—such as the brightness of a light or the loudness of a tone in the case of a CS and the amount of food or the strength of a shock in the case of a US—also affects conditioning. Conditioning is stronger with more intense stimuli (Andrews & Braveman, 1975; Sheafor & Gormezano, 1972). This is particularly true for USs but is also true for CSs (Kehoe, 1983). Figure 12-10 shows the results of

FIGURE 12-10 Mean change in heart rate as a function of US (shock) intensity for both trace and delayed procedures. (Adapted from Fitzgerald & Teylor, 1970.)

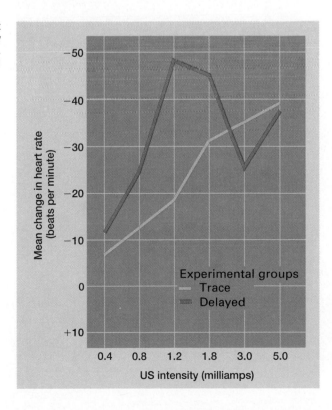

a typical experiment. Using rats as subjects, this experiment gave a tone CS followed by a shock US of varying intensities; the CR was a change in heart rate (Fitzgerald & Teyler, 1970). As the intensity of the shock increased, the magnitude of the response to the CS increased correspondingly; such an effect occurred when either a trace or a delayed conditioning procedure was used.

PAVLOVIAN PHENOMENA

Second-Order Conditioning

An important phenomenon in classical conditioning research is **second-order conditioning.** This occurs when the acquired strength of a CS is transferred to a new CS; the new CS gains strength not because it is paired with a US but because it is paired with another already strong CS (Rescorla, 1980).

Figure 12-11 shows an experimental arrangement for studying second-order conditioning. In phase 1 of the study, normal Pavlovian conditioning is carried out in the experimental subjects. The original CS, a light (CS_L), is followed by a shock US. In phase 2 a new CS, a tone (CS_T), is presented just prior to CS_L. Note that no US is used in this phase. Note also that control subjects receive the two CSs in phase 2, but because the CSs are presented randomly, in accordance with the principle of contingency discussed previously no conditioning takes place; no predictive relationship between the tone and light is present. The strength of CS_T is tested in the experimental subjects in phase 3. The test reveals that CS_T elicits the conditioned reaction in the experimental subjects. What this means is that the CS_T had derived strength from CS_L during phase 2 (Rescorla & Gillan, 1980). No such reaction occurs in the control subjects. In short, the new CS derives meaning or strength from being associated with an already powerful CS; the creation of a Pavlovian conditioned reaction does not depend on the presence of a biological US such as a shock.

This finding has important implications, especially for humans, for whom biologically significant USs are rare. Consider the example of a child becoming fearful at the sight of a kitchen stove because of having previously been burned. Second-order

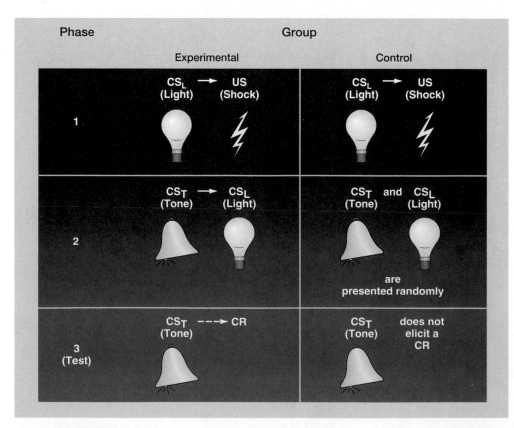

FIGURE 12-11   Procedure used to study second-order conditioning.

conditioning might cause the child to show fear of stimuli associated with the stove such as the hallway leading to the kitchen even though the hallway was not directly associated with the pain of touching the burner.

Sensory Preconditioning

Sensory preconditioning is similar to second-order conditioning except that the first and second phases of the study are reversed (Thompson, 1972). The structure of a sensory preconditioning experiment is shown in Figure 12-12. In phase 1, two innocuous stimuli—CS_T, a tone, and CS_L, a light—are presented sequentially to the experimental subjects. The control group receives random presentations of the two stimuli. There are, of course, no unconditioned responses during this phase because only CSs are used. In phase 2, CS_L is presented with a US to both groups of subjects. In this phase CRs occur: the animal begins to salivate, exhibit an accelerated heart rate, and so on, depending on the kind of US used. Finally, in phase 3 the strength of CS_T is tested. Although CS_T was never paired with *any* powerful stimulus, it nevertheless elicits a conditioned reaction in the experimental subjects (Thompson, 1972). The control subjects show no such reaction.

As suggested in Figure 12-12, the tone produces a conditioned reaction because it elicits the memory of the light, which in turn elicits the CR. In other words, the memory of the light is triggered by the tone because of the association between them that developed in phase 1. The conditioned reaction, on the other hand, is elicited because of the association between CS_L and the US in phase 2.

The importance of this finding cannot be exaggerated. *Any* two stimuli, whether or not one of them is biologically potent, can become associated simply by occurring together. Because of Pavlov's original work using the salivary reflex, Pavlovian conditioning is often thought of as involving merely reflexes, and yet the phenomenon of sensory preconditioning shows that a strong biological US is not needed for an

FIGURE 12-12 Procedure used to study sensory preconditioning.

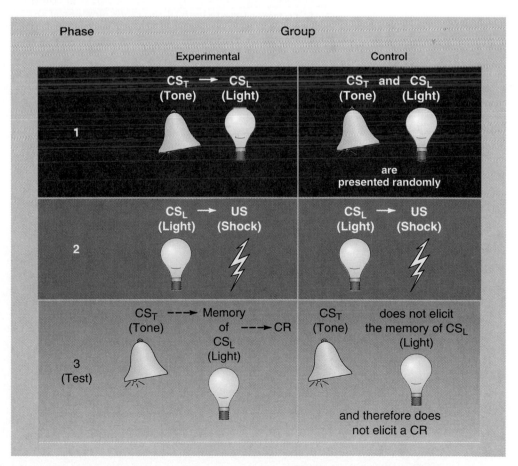

association to develop. Although we cannot directly observe the development of an association between two CSs during phase 1, the lack of an overt reaction does not mean that the two stimuli are not becoming associated.

For an example of sensory preconditioning in humans, imagine that you observe a new neighbor taking a large German shepherd for a walk. The neighbor and the dog are, in essence, two CSs that are being associated at that moment. Now imagine that you are later bitten by the dog. No doubt you will acquire a strong fear reaction to the sight of the dog. But you are also likely to fear the neighbor, because seeing the neighbor will activate a memory of the dog, which in turn will cause a fear reaction.

Blocking

Another important phenomenon related to Pavlovian conditioning is blocking. **Blocking** is the prevention of conditioning to a particular CS by another, already powerful CS. Figure 12-13 shows how a typical experiment is conducted.

In phase 1, subjects in the experimental group receive a CS, a light (CS_L), followed by a US, a shock; subjects in the control group receive no treatment. In phase 2 both groups receive a *compound* CS consisting of the simultaneous presentation of a light and a tone ($CS_L + CS_T$), followed by the US. In phase 3 the strength of CS_T is tested; that is, the tone is given by itself and the strength of the CR is measured.

According to the principle of contiguity, the stimulus that was added in phase 2—namely, CS_T—should become conditioned because it was followed by the US on a number of occasions. Indeed, the control subjects, which do not receive any treatment in phase 1, show an appreciable conditioned reaction to CS_T in phase 3. But CS_T does *not* gain much strength in the experimental subjects. The stimulus that was conditioned in phase 1, CS_L, appears to block or prevent CS_T from gaining strength in phase 2 (Kamin, 1969).

The blocking phenomenon is very important in modern learning theory because it shows that conditioning to one element of a compound stimulus (CS_T in this case) is affected by the strength of the other element of the compound (CS_L) rather than simply by its own relationship to the US. How can we explain this curious finding? As

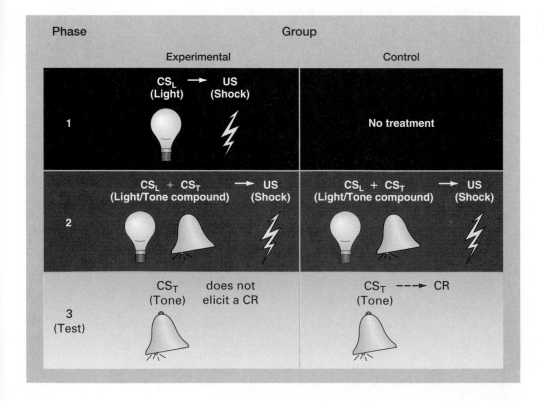

FIGURE 12-13   Procedure used to study blocking.

with simple conditioning, the answer lies in the informational or predictive value of CS_T (Pearce & Hall, 1980). Theorists argue that CS_T is redundant in phase 2 because the US is already predicted by CS_L; CS_T provides no new information about the presentation of the US. And because, as research on the principle of contingency indicates, the predictive value of a CS is so critical to conditioning, CS_T fails to become conditioned. In other words, if a CS lacks predictive validity, conditioning fails to occur even though the CS may be followed by a US on some occasions. The phenomenon of blocking thus confirms the principle of contingency discussed earlier: Conditioning occurs only when there is a predictive relationship between two stimuli.

Generalization and Discrimination

Generalization is another important concept in Pavlovian conditioning (Honig & Urcuioli, 1981). **Generalization** occurs when a subject responds to a CS even though it was not previously used in conditioning. The strength of the reaction to such a novel CS is a function of the similarity between it and the original CS: The greater the similarity, the stronger the CR. This graded relationship between CR strength and CS similarity is termed the **generalization gradient.**

In a typical generalization experiment using rabbits, the subject might be presented with a 1,200-hertz tone CS followed by a mild shock US to the eyelid (the shock is so mild that it merely causes the rabbit to blink). Reactions to other, similar stimuli (such as tones of different frequencies) would then be tested. The results of such an experiment are shown in Figure 12-14 (Moore, 1972). Note the graded relationship between CR strength and CS similarity—the greater the similarity between the generalized CS and the original CS (that is, the closer the pitch of the generalized CS to the pitch of the original), the greater the strength of the CR.

Generalization is not limited to physical stimuli that vary in pitch or intensity; it can occur along other dimensions as well. In one experiment human subjects were given a list of words, some of which were followed by a mild shock (Lacey, Smith, & Green, 1955). Not only did the subjects' heart rate accelerate in response to the various word CSs, but other, semantically related words also elicited the conditioned

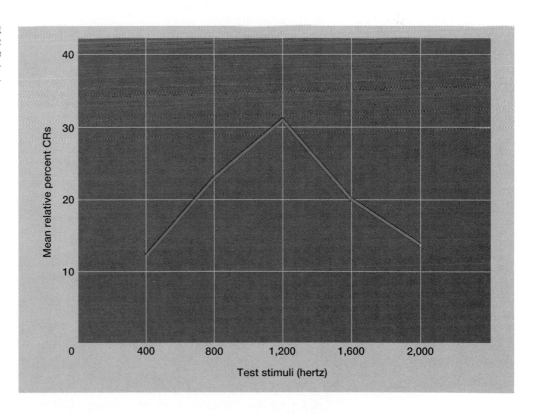

FIGURE 12-14 Mean relative percent eyeblink CRs given to the CS (1,200 hertz tone) and four generalized stimuli. These results show the generalization of conditioned eyeblink reactions in rabbits. (Adapted from Moore, 1972.)

reaction. For example, if a subject had been shocked after the word *cow,* he or she showed a conditioned heart rate response to related words such as *chicken* or *tractor* but not to unrelated words like *skyscraper.*

Discrimination is the opposite of generalization; it occurs when an organism responds differentially to two stimuli on the basis of perceived differences between them. The basic discrimination procedure involves the presentation of two CSs, one of which is followed by the US. The development of the discrimination reaction is measured in terms of the differential response to the two CSs: The CS that is followed by a US triggers the conditioned reaction whereas the other CS does not. For example, imagine that a subject was occasionally presented with a 1,000-hertz tone followed by shock, but on other occasions with a 1,200-hertz tone not followed by shock. Discrimination would be demonstrated if the animal responded *differentially* to the two CSs: conditioned eye blinks to the 1,000-hertz tone but not to the 1,200-hertz CS. Note that if conditioning had involved only a single CS, the 1,000-hertz tone, followed by the US, then the subject would likely have generalized to the other CS had a test of generalization been conducted.

APPLICATIONS OF CLASSICAL CONDITIONING PRINCIPLES

Two outcomes of the conditioning process are especially important for understanding complex human behavior: the conditioning of physiological reactions and the conditioning of emotional responses.

Psychosomatic Illness

As noted earlier, physiological reactions such as heart rate are easily conditioned using Pavlovian procedures. This fact has far-reaching implications for the understanding of **psychosomatic illness,** illness with no physiological cause. Imagine, for example, that a person complains of a "racing heart" but that the condition has no evident biological cause. The symptoms are likely to be labeled as "psychological," or psychosomatic. Although such a diagnosis may be correct, it is important to note that the symptoms are not fake or insignificant. The label *psychosomatic* simply means that the symptoms are based on a psychological process (probably conditioning), not on the direct action of a biological agent.

Conditioned physiological reactions can be extremely subtle (Lubinski & Thompson, 1987). Consider the following experiment using rats (Hutton, Woods, & Makous, 1970; see also Eikelboom & Stewart, 1982). The rats were given five conditioning trials. A blood sample was taken before each trial. Then the rats were placed in a holding cage permeated with the odor of menthol and were injected with insulin. The odor was the CS and the insulin was the US. The investigators confirmed that the insulin triggered a UR (reduced blood-sugar level) by taking a blood sample 20 minutes later and noting that a decline in blood-sugar level had indeed occurred. A group of control subjects received a similar treatment except that their insulin injection did not consistently follow the CS. Instead, they received random presentations of the odor CS and insulin US. (Recall that according to the contingency principle no learning should take place under these circumstances.)

After the five trials, all the animals were tested for their reaction to the CS alone; that is, they were given the odor CS but were not injected with insulin. (Instead, they received an injection of a biologically inactive saline solution.) Any change in blood-sugar level during the subsequent 20 minutes therefore could not be caused by the presence of insulin but must be the result of a conditioned physiological reaction.

The results of the test are shown in Figure 12-15. The control subjects showed virtually no change in blood-sugar level. The experimental subjects, on the other hand, showed a large decline in blood-sugar level. These results demonstrate that an internal reaction such as a change in blood-sugar level can be conditioned to external cues. The implication is that physiological reactions in human beings—reactions that are often referred to as psychosomatic—may be conditioned in a similar way. To return to our earlier example of a young child who had been burned by a kitchen

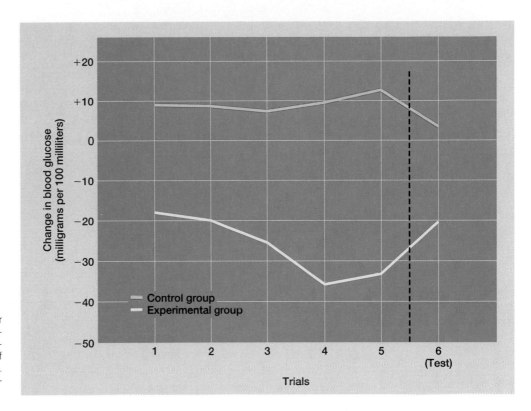

FIGURE 12-15 Change in blood-sugar level following the CS on acquisition trials and on a test in both the experimental and control groups of rats in a study of a conditioned physiological reaction. (Adapted from Hutton, Woods, & Makous, 1970.)

stove, the child's physiological reactions thereafter—racing heart, muscle tension, increased adrenaline in the blood, and so forth—would be triggered by a conditioned stimulus, the sight of the stove, not by a biological agent, the pain of being burned.

Phobias

Another reaction that is frequently learned through Pavlovian conditioning is emotion, such as fear or pleasure. For this reason, scientists believe that Pavlovian conditioning may be a cause of phobias, or maladaptive, irrational fears (Eysenck, 1976). According to this view, a **phobia** is a conditioned fearful response for which the original unconditioned fear-producing stimulus is no longer a threat (thus it can be termed maladaptive).

A famous study of the role of conditioning in phobias used an 11-month-old infant named Albert (Watson & Raynor, 1920). (See Figure 12-16) The child was allowed to hold a pet albino rat (the CS) and then subjected to a loud noise (the US). The loud noise, because it was frightening, established a conditioned fear reaction (crying and withdrawal). Moreover, Albert reacted with fear to the rat as well. This reaction was irrational because the pet rat was tame and had never harmed Albert, and the

FIGURE 12-16 J. B. Watson (behind mask) testing little Albert for conditioned fear reactions.

307

loud noise was never repeated. Not only did Albert develop a fear reaction to the rat, but the reaction generalized to other furry white objects such as a rabbit, cotton wool, and a Santa Claus mask.

The purpose of the experiment with Albert was to show that fears may result from simple classical conditioning rather than from unconscious psychological conflicts. For ethical reasons, such experiments are no longer performed. And although the causes of phobias appear to be more complex than this experiment suggests (Costello, 1970; McNally, 1987), classical conditioning continues to serve as a useful model for the learning of emotions.

INTERIM SUMMARY

Classical conditioning occurs when an organism develops an association between two stimuli that were not previously associated. The unconditioned stimulus (US) is a biologically potent stimulus that produces a reflexive reaction. The reaction is unlearned and involuntary; it is an unconditioned response (UR). The conditioned stimulus (CS) is a stimulus that does not normally provoke the reflex but when paired with the US produces a learned reaction or conditioned response (CR). The development of the CR is known as acquisition; presentation of the CS without the US eventually results in extinction. According to the law of contiguity, the development of an association between a CS and a US depends on the temporal proximity of the stimuli; however, empirical research has shown that there must also be a contingent (predictive) relationship between the stimuli. The intensity of the two stimuli also affects conditioning. Second-order conditioning occurs when the acquired power of a CS is transferred to a new CS. In a related phenomenon, sensory preconditioning, two innocuous stimuli are first associated through repeated pairings. Then one is conditioned through pairing with a US. Finally, the other is shown to elicit a CR. Blocking occurs when conditioning to a CS is prevented by the presence of another, already powerful CS. Generalization occurs when a subject responds to a CS because it is similar to a stimulus that was previously used in conditioning; the opposite process is known as discrimination. The principles of classical conditioning may help explain such phenomena as psychosomatic illness and phobias.

INSTRUMENTAL (OPERANT) CONDITIONING

In addition to learning the meanings of stimuli, an organism learns about the consequences of its own behavior. This second major kind of learning is called **instrumental conditioning** because the organism's behavior is instrumental in bringing about changes in its environment. Many psychologists, following the lead of B. F. Skinner (see Chapter 2), refer to this form of learning as **operant conditioning** because behaviors operate on the environment to produce various outcomes (Skinner, 1953).

BASIC TERMS

Let us begin by describing the simple experiment that E. L. Thorndike (1898) performed on cats to illustrate this kind of learning (see Chapter 2). A cat was placed in a box in which pushing a lever caused the door to open. Initially the cat made apparently random movements—scratching at the cage, walking around, and the like; eventually it hit the lever (presumably by accident), causing the door to spring open and allowing it to eat food placed nearby. The time it took the cat to hit the lever was

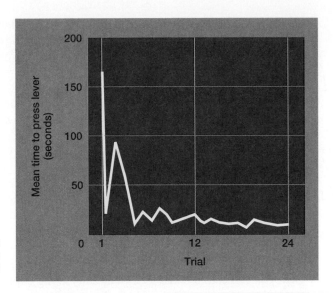

FIGURE 12-17 Mean time for cats to escape from Thorndike's puzzle box as a function of trials. (Adapted from Thorndike, 1898.)

rather long on the first trial. (See Figure 12-17.) In addition, the number of "errors" (that is, random, ineffectual movements) was rather high. When it was repeatedly placed in the apparatus, however, the cat took progressively less time to make the correct response and executed fewer irrelevant or erroneous responses. In other words, it learned to execute a particular motor reaction quickly and efficiently.

Studies of instrumental conditioning today still take the same basic form as Thorndike's experiment. As shown in Figure 12-18, the subjects are often laboratory rats that are trained in a so-called Skinner box to press a lever to obtain a small piece of food. Similar experiments have used pigeons, monkeys, humans, and trained dolphins as subjects. (See Figure 12-19.)

The terms used to describe the components of an instrumental-conditioning experiment are virtually the same as those used in Pavlovian conditioning: *unconditioned stimulus* (US), *unconditioned response* (UR), *conditioned stimulus* (CS), *conditioned response* (CR). The US is usually a biologically powerful stimulus that is contingent (or dependent) on the animal's behavior. Food and water are commonly used as USs, but other stimuli are also used—heat (for a cold animal), sweet-tasting substances, and access to sexual partners are examples. When the US is pleasant, it is called a **reinforcer;** when it is aversive (such as a mild shock or loud noise), it is called a **punisher.**

FIGURE 12-18 The noted psychologist B. F. Skinner watching a laboratory rat earn food in a Skinner box

FIGURE 12-19 Example of instrumental conditioning using a dolphin as a subject.

Instrumental-conditioning situations do not always involve an explicit conditioned stimulus; Thorndike's experiment used no tone or light. Conditioned stimuli can, however, be introduced in these studies. One could, for example, make food available to the cat in Thorndike's box only when a light is on. Animals readily learn such contingencies. The cat, for instance, would learn to hit the lever when the light is on but not when it is off. Conditioned stimuli in instrumental-conditioning experiments are called **discriminative stimuli** because they allow the animal to discriminate when to make the appropriate response.

Discriminative stimuli may be of two kinds. A positive discriminative stimulus signals the availability of a reward; responding in its presence produces the US. A negative discriminative stimulus, on the other hand, signals the *un*availability of the desired outcome; responding in its presence does not produce the US.

In classical conditioning, the CR is usually the same as the UR (for example, salivation in both cases). This is not true of instrumental conditioning. Here, the CR is often a voluntary motor response such as hitting a lever or running down a maze, although many other kinds of behaviors may be used, including changes in heart rate or GSR or even verbal behaviors. In an interesting experiment on the conditioning of verbal behavior, students were brought into the experimenter's office and asked to speak whatever words came to mind (Greenspoon, 1955; see also Williams, 1964). These were their only instructions. Whenever (and only when) a student spoke a plural noun, the experimenter said "mm-hmm." Evidently this "mm-hmm" acted as a reinforcer, because the frequency with which subjects uttered plural nouns increased over the course of the session.

These results demonstrate two interesting and important points. First, virtually any kind of behavior, including verbal utterances, can be a CR; thus, much of human behavior may be affected by instrumental learning. Second, in instrumental conditioning, reinforcers do not have to be powerful biological USs; any outcome that causes a systematic change in the probability of a particular behavior—even a subtle outcome like a person saying "mm-hmm"—can function as a US. The implications for human behavior are clear. Although few of our behaviors are directly reinforced by biological USs, they may be dramatically affected by other kinds of reinforcers, such as encouragement and attention.

Reinforcement is often social. A parent's encouragement and attention, for example, are powerful reinforcers for a child.

REINFORCERS AND PUNISHERS

Instrumental conditioning is common in humans partly because reinforcers and punishers are so pervasive. Think about how many of your everyday behaviors are followed by pleasant consequences. Greeting friends, going to dinner, and playing games are just a few examples of the many kinds of human actions that usually result in reinforcement. Consider also how your behavior is affected by punishers. You may cross the street to avoid talking with a person you dislike; you may refrain from using obscene language in certain situations because you have been punished for doing so in the past; you may avoid certain restaurants because you received slow service or poorly prepared food there.

Most reinforcers or punishers, at least in laboratory experiments, are strong biological USs. But psychologists usually define reinforcers and punishers in more technical terms (Skinner, 1953). According to Skinner, a reinforcer is any stimulus or activity that, when it is contingent on a particular response, causes an increase in the probability of that response. Similarly, a punisher is any stimulus that, when it is contingent on a particular response, causes a decline in the probability of that response. These definitions highlight the fact that any event can be a reinforcer or a punisher, provided that it has these effects on behavior. Not only biologically powerful stimuli such as food or shock but even an innocuous light flash can, under appropriate conditions, serve as a reinforcer (Eisenberger, 1972).

INSTRUMENTAL CONDITIONING PROCEDURES

The four basic kinds of instrumental conditioning procedures are illustrated in Figure 12-20. **Reward conditioning** occurs whenever an instrumental behavior is followed by a pleasant outcome such as food. An example is the conditioning that occurred in Thorndike's original experiment using cats. As noted earlier, the kinds of reactions that can be conditioned in this way vary enormously, ranging from simple motor behaviors to visceral reactions to verbal or social behaviors. Reinforcers also vary greatly, including not only biological stimuli but also such social stimuli as praise.

Punishment occurs when an instrumental behavior produces, or is followed by, an aversive or unpleasant consequence that is termed a *punisher* (Dunham, 1971). A punisher has the effect of suppressing the probability of a contingent behavior; the subject typically reacts by withdrawing. Psychologists often use mild shocks or loud noises as punishers, but nonbiological stimuli, such as criticism or threats, are also effective.

Omission training occurs whenever an instrumental behavior leads to the *nonoccurrence* of a pleasant US. Usually, some other response (or no response) results in the presentation of the reward. The consequence of omission training is a decline in the probability of the behavior that produces the omission of the reward. Parents are using omission training techniques when they promise children a future reward—

FIGURE 12-20 Diagram illustrating the four basic kinds of instrumental conditioning procedures.

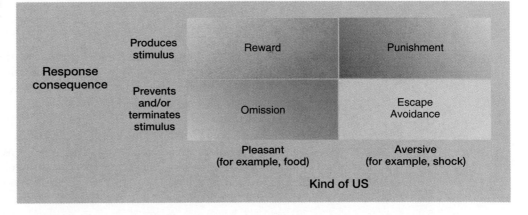

say, a snack or an opportunity to watch television—only if the children do not argue. Arguing causes the omission or cancellation of the reinforcer.

Escape and avoidance learning occur when an instrumental response leads to the termination or nonoccurrence of an aversive US (Bolles, 1972; Higgins & Morris, 1984). Specifically, **escape** occurs whenever the response terminates an aversive US. **Avoidance** learning, in contrast, is somewhat more complicated. Because the subject is allowed to make a response *prior* to the US, the response has the effect of avoiding the aversive US altogether. Often a discriminative signal is given to make this task easier. In a typical avoidance learning study, for example, a 10-second tone might be used to signal an imminent shock. Hitting a lever during the tone, however, would not only terminate the tone but also cancel the shock.

Escape and avoidance reactions are common in humans. Turning down the volume when music is excessively loud is an escape reaction. Going out with an umbrella when rain is predicted or not eating certain foods because they are unpleasantly spicy or bitter are avoidance reactions.

Acquisition and extinction are concepts that apply to instrumental conditioning as well as to Pavlovian conditioning. During acquisition, the instrumental CR is learned because of the contingent relationship between the response and the outcome (either an appetitive or aversive US). During extinction, the CR is not followed by that outcome and so the response declines in strength.

INSTRUMENTAL LEARNING THEORY

How does reinforcement work? Recall that in Pavlovian conditioning a CS becomes powerful whenever there is a *contingent* relationship between the CS and a US; that is, when the US usually occurs in the presence of the CS and not in its absence. The same principle applies to instrumental conditioning. A response is learned when it is followed by a rewarding outcome but not when the reward occurs in the absence of the response. In other words, the consistency of the relationship between the response and the reinforcer—the **reinforcement contingency**—is critical to instrumental learning, just as the consistency of the CS–US relationship is critical to Pavlovian conditioning.

In a study demonstrating the importance of a contingent relationship between a response and a reinforcer, experimental animals (rats) were divided into several groups (Hammond, 1980). All subjects had a 0.1 probability of receiving a food pellet if they pressed the lever in any 1-second interval. This meant that if an animal pressed the lever steadily, it would receive a food reward once every 10 seconds on average. The groups differed, however, in the probability with which they would also receive food independently of pressing the lever—that is, in the probability that they would receive an unearned reward not contingent on lever pressing. In one group, the subjects had a 0.0 probability of receiving unearned reward, so food was entirely contingent on lever pressing. In another group, the probability of the unearned reward was the same as the probability of the reward for bar pressing—0.1, or once in every 10 seconds on average. The members of this group, therefore, were as likely to get food for doing nothing as they were to get it for pressing the lever. In other groups, the probability of the unearned reward was somewhere between 0.0 and 0.1.

The results showed that lever pressing increased as the contingency between lever pressing and the reward increased. The animals that received food only if they pressed the lever became the most dedicated pressers. The animals that were as likely to get food for not pressing the lever as they were for pressing the lever did not learn to press it. Learning in the other groups was intermediate. Instrumental learning thus parallels Pavlovian conditioning. In each case learning requires a contingent relationship between an important event (such as a reward) and a prior event. For Pavlovian conditioning, the prior event is a stimulus; for instrumental conditioning, it is a response.

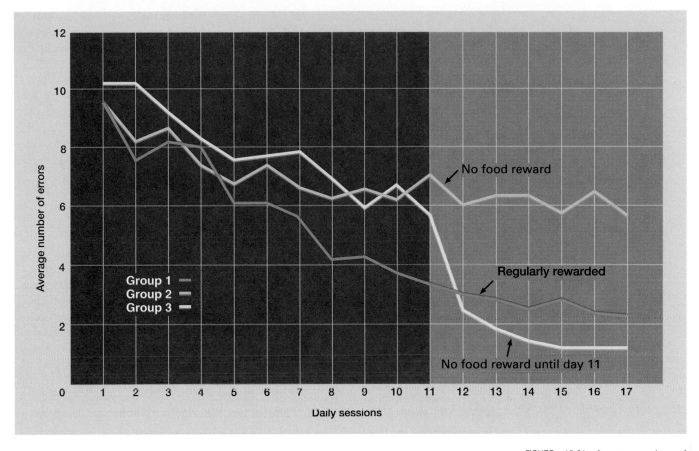

Group 1 —
Group 2 —
Group 3 —

No food reward

Regularly rewarded

No food reward until day 11

FIGURE 12-21 Average number of errors (wrong turns) in the maze as a function of daily sessions for the three groups in an experiment on latent learning. (Adapted from Tolman & Honzik, 1930.)

Is Reward Necessary?

We have seen that a contingency between a reward and a prior behavior produces instrumental learning. But could an organism learn an instrumental response even when no reward is involved?

Some researchers have attempted to answer this question by focusing on **latent learning**. In a classic study intended to demonstrate latent learning, rats were allowed to run through a maze with fourteen choice points (Tolman & Honzik, 1930). Animals in one group always received a reward when they arrived at the goal box. Animals in a second group never received a reward; they were taken out of the maze after a fixed period of time and later fed in their home cage. Figure 12-21 shows the number of errors made by the two groups of subjects. Subjects in group 1 clearly showed a decline in mean number of errors as a function of number of training trials. This is not surprising, because they were rewarded for running through the maze. Subjects in group 2 showed only a slight decline in number of errors with training; even after 17 trials they were still making numerous errors. One could conclude from these findings that learning requires a reward. After all, the no-reward group seemed to be learning very little.

The behavior of a third group of subjects, however, challenged this conclusion. These subjects did not receive a reward on the first 10 trials, but starting on the eleventh trial they were given a reward when they reached the goal box. The change resulted in a dramatic and sudden decline in the mean number of errors, as shown in Figure 12-21. The suddenness of the decline in errors is important, because it suggests that reinforcement was not necessary for the learning to take place. If the animals had not learned anything during the first 10 trials, they should have shown a *gradual* reduction in mean number of errors beginning with trial 11. The only way to explain their dramatic improvement is to suggest that they had indeed learned how to find the goal box during the first 10 trials but had not performed in a way that showed they had. Once they began to receive a reward, their average errors decreased

313

immediately to a level comparable to that of the continually rewarded group. Although there have been some criticisms of this experiment, the results support the conclusion that the effect of reinforcement is more to strengthen the performance of a behavior than the learning of the behavior itself.

Latent learning is common in humans. Imagine, for example, that you had learned the location of your school infirmary by reading a map or walking past it on the way to another building. An observer might not realize that you knew the location of the infirmary, because you never deliberately went there. But now imagine that you suddenly become ill. You could go straight to the infirmary without making any wrong turns; your success in easily finding the infirmary on the first try would thus reveal that you had learned its location previously.

VARIABLES THAT AFFECT INSTRUMENTAL CONDITIONING

Reinforcer Magnitude

Many of the same variables that affect Pavlovian conditioning also affect instrumental learning. For example, larger or more intense USs typically produce better learning. Figure 12-22 presents the results of a study demonstrating this phenomenon. Five groups of rats were trained to run through a straight alleyway to receive food in a goal box (Roberts, 1969). The magnitude of the reward—that is, the number of food pellets—varied among the groups. Three response measures were used: speed of leaving the starting box, running speed in the alleyway, and speed of entering the goal box. All three measures showed a strong positive relationship between performance and US magnitude (the number of food pellets). The same effect, in reverse, is found in punishment situations: The stronger the aversive US, the greater the suppression of the punished behavior (Camp, Raymond, & Church, 1967).

Delay of Reward

A second major variable that affects instrumental learning is delay of reinforcement—the greater the delay, the weaker the learning (Tarpy & Sawabini, 1974). This is true because delay of reinforcement decreases the contiguity between the response and the outcome. Psychologists disagree, however, about how long a delay can be before learning is precluded altogether. Some suggest that the reward can be delayed by only a few seconds, whereas others argue that learning can still occur when the reinforcement is delayed by several minutes or even hours. Delay of punishment also affects instrumental learning: Suppression of behavior by a punisher is reduced when the punisher is delayed (Camp, Raymond, & Church, 1967). Delay of reinforcement certainly affects human learning in a similar way. When a young child accomplishes a new task—identifying the color of a new toy, say—parents usually respond with

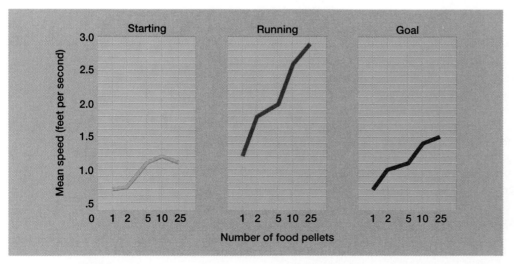

FIGURE 12-22 Mean starting, running, and goal-entry speed as a function of the number of reward pellets in the goal. These results show the relationship between the magnitude of a reinforcer and the resulting learning in rats. (Adapted from Roberts, 1969.)

immediate praise, effectively strengthening the child's learning. If the praise were delayed, however, it would have little impact.

Species-Specific Response Patterns

A factor that affects speed of learning is the extent to which the desired response is compatible with the animal's natural, species-specific behavior patterns. The more compatible the response, the easier the conditioning; the less compatible the response, the longer it takes to learn (Bolles, 1970; Domjan, 1983). For example, in a series of experiments using golden hamsters (Shettleworth, 1975), the researchers found that behaviors that were naturally related to food procurement, such as rearing on the hind legs and digging in the sand, increased in frequency when food rewards were contingent on those behaviors, whereas behaviors unrelated to food procurement, such as scratching or scent marking, did not. Thus, whether a given response was strongly affected by reinforcement depended in part on whether it was compatible with the species-specific behavior patterns commonly used in such a situation.

INSTRUMENTAL PHENOMENA

Schedules of Reinforcement

Although Thorndike initiated the study of instrumental conditioning, B. F. Skinner is credited with promoting its study. One of Skinner's most enduring contributions was his experimental analysis of **schedules of reinforcement** (Skinner, 1938). Skinner pointed out that although an animal may receive a reinforcement after every response, in most situations responses are not reinforced on a continuous basis but rather only occasionally, creating an intermittent schedule of reinforcement.

There are four basic kinds of intermittent reinforcement schedules: fixed ratio, variable ratio, fixed interval, and variable interval. Each of these schedules stipulates a precise relationship between responding and reward delivery and each produces a characteristic pattern of behavior. In a **fixed ratio (FR) schedule** a subject receives a reward for executing a fixed number of responses. For example, in an FR-5 schedule every fifth response would earn a reward. As shown in Figure 12-23, FR schedules

FIGURE 12-23 Typical response patterns for the four basic schedules of reinforcement. Note that responses are cumulative as time passes, so the steeper the slope of the line, the higher the rate of response. The downward slashes indicate when reinforcement was delivered.

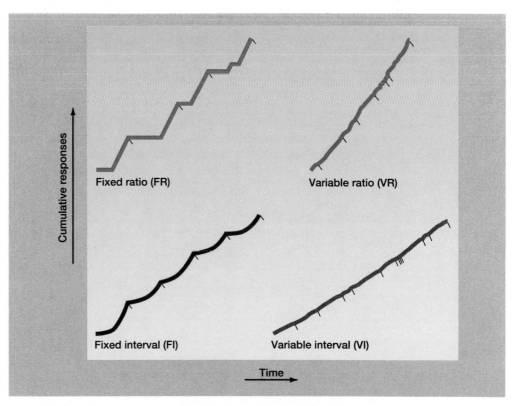

typically cause the animal to respond at a high rate, although it often pauses after each reinforcement (Felton & Lyon, 1966). If the FR value is too high, the rate of responding decreases. Workers who are paid on a piecework basis (that is, for producing or selling a fixed number of items) are being reinforced according to an FR schedule.

Variable ratio (VR) schedules are similar to FR schedules in that reinforcement depends on the number of times the subject performs a behavior. In this case, however, the schedule varies around an average. In a VR-10 schedule, for example, the animal would get a reward, *on average,* after every 10 responses. The actual reward pattern, however, might require the animal to respond correctly 5 times for the first food reward, 12 for the next, 9 for the next, 14 for the next, and so forth; the average number of correct responses required in order to obtain a reward is 10. A VR schedule produces the highest and steadiest rate of responding of all the basic schedules. (See Figure 12-23.) For this reason, slot machines in gambling casinos are programmed to pay on a VR schedule.

There are two types of interval schedules. In a **fixed interval (FI) schedule** reinforcement is delivered after a response, but only if a fixed amount of time has elapsed. The rate of responding on an FI schedule is low overall compared to the rate of responding on a ratio schedule, but the rate accelerates within each time period. (See Figure 12-23.) That is, the animal typically responds either not at all or very slowly immediately after receiving a reward, but it responds increasingly quickly as the time for the next reward approaches (Schneider, 1969). This is because the subject learns to discriminate the temporal interval—it learns approximately when the fixed period of time will elapse and so it begins to respond faster near the end of the period to ensure that the reward will be delivered at the earliest possible moment. If the animal is given signals that help it time the interval even better, the acceleration in response rate is enhanced (Kendall, 1972).

It is difficult to identify pure FI schedules in human environments because few human behaviors are rewarded this way. One example, however, would be a person who is checking on the progress of a cake in the oven. When the cake is first put into the oven, the frequency of the checking response is very low. But as time passes, the frequency of checking increases dramatically.

Variable interval (VI) schedules are similar to FI schedules except that the length of time that must elapse before a single response earns a reward varies around an average from one reward to the next. For example, with a VI 1-minute schedule, a response would produce a reward on average every minute, but the actual pattern might be 30 seconds, then 72 seconds, 48 seconds, 90 seconds, and so forth. As shown in Figure 12-23, the rate of responding on a VI is typically low but steady, and increases as a function of the rate of reinforcement (Catania & Reynolds, 1968). An example from everyday life is trying to reach a telephone number when the line is busy. The response "dialing the number" is performed periodically and is reinforced only when the connection is finally made. But the time it takes to make the connection varies from one occasion to the next.

Human behavior is as profoundly affected by reinforcers and by specific schedules of reinforcement as any other species. Slot machines, for example, are programmed to pay off on variable ratio schedules, which produce the highest, steadiest rate of responding of all the basic schedules.

These four basic schedules can be combined in various ways. For example, imagine a schedule that provides a reward only if a fixed time period has elapsed (FI) *and* the subject has responded five times (FR). Such a schedule is called a *compound schedule.* The behavior patterns of subjects on compound schedules usually reflect a combination of the patterns found on the simpler schedules.

Both simple and complex reinforcement schedules are critical to instrumental learning theory because they probably reflect the way reinforcement occurs in the real world. Humans are like other animals in that their behavior is profoundly influenced by rewards. But neither humans nor other animals receive reinforcement every time they make an appropriate response; rewards are obtained only occasionally. Thus, many human behaviors are affected or maintained by intermittent rewards according to some kind of complex reinforcement schedule. To understand how reinforcement influences behaviors in the real world, it is helpful to know how they function in simple controlled situations (see Reese, 1978).

Consider the following experiment on study time in which the researchers used students in their own psychology course as subjects (Mawhinney, Bostow, Laws, Blumenfeld, & Hopkins, 1971). The researchers placed the reading materials for the course on reserve in the library, stipulating that the materials could not be taken from the library reading room. This meant that they could easily keep track of the number of hours each student spent reading the materials. Early in the semester tests were given on a daily basis, but later they were given every three weeks. The researchers assumed the behavior "reading" is reinforced by the reward "passing the exam."

Figure 12-24 shows the average time spent reading prior to each class session for the first 20 sessions of the semester. When tests were given daily, the rate of responding was fairly constant. This behavior pattern is essentially the same as that of laboratory rats responding on a fairly lenient FR schedule of food reinforcement. When the test interval was changed to once every three weeks, the students' behavior pattern changed markedly. It now resembled what is typically found in laboratory experiments using an FI schedule—a slow rate of response early in the interval (here shown as low amounts of reading time) and a much faster rate near the time when reinforcement will become available (a high amount of reading time). Although this testing schedule is not exactly like the laboratory FI schedule in that reading early in the semester helps a student pass tests later on, there is nevertheless a striking similarity between the schedules and the resulting behavior patterns.

Conditioned Reinforcement

An important concept in instrumental learning theory is **conditioned reinforcement.** A conditioned reinforcer is an originally neutral stimulus that, through consistent

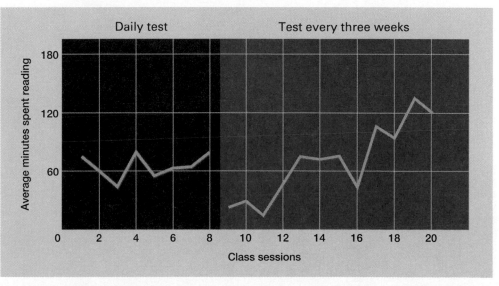

FIGURE 12-24 Mean number of minutes spent reading prior to the class session as a function of sessions when exams were given daily and three weeks apart. These results are from a study of the effects of reinforcement schedules on the studying behavior of students in a psychology class. (Adapted from Mawhinney et al., 1971.)

317

Money is a powerful secondary reinforcer in most modern human societies. It has no intrinsic value itself but is associated with the many reinforcing outcomes it can produce.

pairing with a primary reinforcer such as food, acquires the ability to reinforce behavior. This phenomenon has been demonstrated in a number of ways. In one study, for example, pigeons were first presented with plastic disks that were illuminated from behind with colored lights (Astley & Perkins, 1985). If the subjects pecked at a red disk, food was delivered 90% of the time. If they pecked at a green disk, food was delivered only 10% of the time. During the second phase of the study, subjects could choose between two disks that were both illuminated with white light. If they pecked at the disk on the left, it turned red; if they pecked at the one on the right, it turned green. The results showed that the subjects learned to choose the disk on the left. Red was a stronger conditioned reinforcer than green because it had previously been more frequently associated with the primary reward.

Conditioned reinforcement plays a significant role in everyday human behaviors. Very few of our behaviors are reinforced directly with biologically powerful primary rewards. More often, we earn conditioned reinforcers that have no inherent value but have acquired value by being associated with primary reinforcers. Money is a prime example: It has no inherent value, yet it serves as a reinforcer because it is associated with so many other reinforcing outcomes.

APPLICATIONS OF INSTRUMENTAL CONDITIONING PRINCIPLES

The principles of instrumental learning, especially the concept of reinforcement contingency, can be applied to complex human behaviors. Perhaps the most important and pervasive use of instrumental conditioning is its application to therapeutic and clinical purposes in **behavior modification** (Masters, Burish, Hollon, & Rimm, 1987). Behavior modification techniques are typically aimed at reinforcing adaptive behaviors and extinguishing maladaptive behaviors. Clinical psychologists have used these techniques in a variety of areas, including social skills training, treatment of conditions such as drug dependency and obesity, elimination of maladaptive behaviors such as aggression in school and prison settings, and treatment of chronic mental illness.

The results of the use of behavior modification on a female patient who had been hospitalized in a psychiatric institution for 16 years provide a good example of its effectiveness (Ayllon & Haughton, 1964). The patient's behavior was highly maladaptive, especially her tendency to say psychotic statements such as "I am the queen." The treatment consisted of reinforcing normal statements, such as "What time is it?" or "I'd like some soap" and extinguishing the psychotic utterances. The reinforcement was to give the patient a cigarette and engage in conversation with her

This staged re-creation of a nineteenth-century school room illustrates the use of learning principles—in this case punishment— to modify behavior.

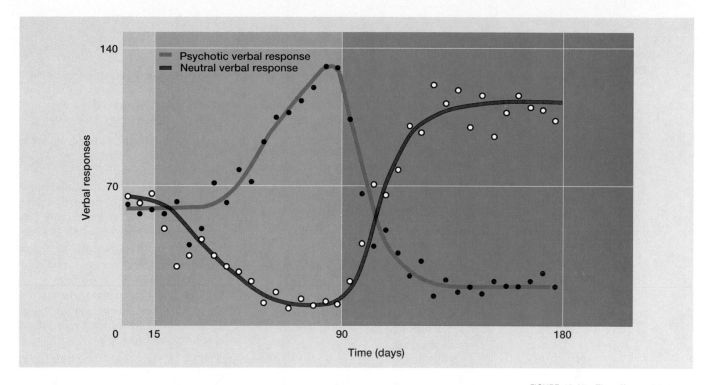

FIGURE 12-25 The effects of behavior modification on the verbal behavior of a mental hospital patient. The graph shows the number of verbal responses, either psychotic or normal, during 15 days baseline, 75 days in which psychotic utterances were reinforced and normal statements were extinguished, and 90 days of treatment in which the contingencies were reversed. (Adapted from Ayllon & Haughton, 1964.)

for three minutes; extinction was accomplished by withholding a cigarette and terminating all social interaction for a fixed period. As shown in Figure 12-25, during a 15-day baseline period, psychotic and normal utterances occurred about equally often. During the next 75 days (days 15–90), the opposite of the treatment procedure was followed: psychotic utterances were reinforced and normal utterances extinguished. The number of psychotic statements rose dramatically and the number of normal statements declined accordingly. During the last 90 days, the treatment procedure was put into effect. The rate of psychotic utterances then declined to a low level and the rate of normal statements increased.

INTERIM SUMMARY

Instrumental conditioning occurs when an organism learns about the consequences of its own behavior on the basis of the consistency of the relationship between its behavior and an important outcome. The US in an instrumental conditioning experiment may be a reinforcer (a pleasant US) or a punisher (an aversive US). The CR is usually a voluntary motor response. Reward conditioning occurs when the CR is followed by a reinforcer; punishment occurs when the CR produces an aversive consequence. Omission training occurs when the CR leads to the nonoccurrence of a pleasant US, and escape and avoidance learning occurs when the CR terminates an aversive US. Studies of latent learning have shown that learning can occur in the absence of direct reinforcement. Among the variables that affect instrumental conditioning are the intensity of the US and delay of reinforcement. Learning is also affected by the compatibility of the learned response with the organism's species-specific behavior patterns. Various schedules of reinforcement (fixed ratio, variable ratio, fixed interval, variable interval) produce characteristic patterns of behavior. In some situations an originally neutral stimulus that is paired with a primary reinforcer acquires the ability to reinforce behavior; this is termed conditioned reinforcement. The most important practical use of instrumental conditioning principles is in behavior modification.

SUMMARY

1. The British empiricists argued that associations between ideas form the basis for acquired knowledge. The reason that ideas become associated, or linked, according to these philosophers, is that the stimuli that give rise to the ideas occur contiguously in time or space. The principle of contiguity has remained central to theories of learning ever since. Current theory, however, stresses the importance of the predictive (contingent) relationship between stimuli for learning.

2. *Pavlovian (classical) conditioning* occurs when an organism develops an association between two stimuli that were not previously associated, such that it recognizes that one stimulus is predictive of the other.

3. In Pavlovian conditioning procedures, a *conditioned stimulus (CS)* is followed by an *unconditioned stimulus (US).* Originally, only the US produces a reaction, called the *unconditioned response (UR).* But after many paired presentations of the two stimuli, the CS also acquires the power to elicit a response—the *conditioned response (CR).*

4. The process of forming the association between the CS and the US is called *acquisition.* The process of breaking the association by presenting the CS without the US is called *extinction.*

5. Classical conditioning is most effective when the CS precedes the US in a *forward conditioning* arrangement.

6. Research indicates that classical conditioning requires a contingent relationship between the CS and the US. Conditioned stimuli come to elicit a CR when there is a strong predictive relationship between the CS and the US, not simply when contiguous CS–US presentations occur.

7. Early research on acquired taste aversions, in which a flavor CS was followed by a mild poison US, suggested that CSs and USs would not necessarily become associated to an equal degree. More recent interpretations, however, tend to discount the notion that conventional principles of learning fail to apply in these cases.

8. Strength of conditioning depends on a number of variables, including the time between the CS and US presentation, and the intensity of the CS and US.

9. *Second-order conditioning* occurs when a new CS is followed by an already powerful CS, rather than by a biologically powerful US. A related phenomenon, *sensory preconditioning,* occurs when two CSs are initially presented together, and then one of them is followed by a US. Results show that the other CS—the one not originally followed by the US—also elicits a CR. Both of these phenomena, therefore, suggest that conditioning can take place even though a biologically powerful US does not follow the CS.

10. *Blocking* occurs when a CS fails to become conditioned after being combined with an already powerful CS. *Generalization* occurs when a subject responds to a CS that is novel yet similar to one that had previously been conditioned. *Discrimination* occurs when a subject reacts differentially to two CSs, presumably because of perceived differences between them.

11. Pavlovian conditioning is relevant to many important areas of human behavior, including *psychosomatic illness* and *phobias.*

12. *Instrumental (operant) conditioning* is the process by which organisms come to learn about the consequences of their own behavior.

13. *Reward conditioning* occurs when a behavior is followed by a pleasant outcome (a *reinforcer*). *Punishment* occurs when a behavior is followed by an aversive or unpleasant consequence (a *punisher*). *Omission training* occurs when a behavior leads to the nonoccurrence of a pleasant US. *Escape* occurs when a behavior terminates an aversive US. *Avoidance learning* occurs when a behavior allows an organism to avoid an aversive US altogether.

14. The essential principle of instrumental conditioning is the *reinforcement contingency.* According to this principle, learning takes place when the reinforcer (or

punisher) occurs soon after the response, and never in the absence of the response. Experiments on *latent learning,* however, suggest that the effect of reinforcement is more to strengthen the performance of a behavior than the learning of the behavior itself.

15. Instrumental learning is affected by many of the same variables that are important in Pavlovian conditioning, such as the magnitude of the US and the delay of reinforcement. In addition, the degree to which a response is compatible with the animal's natural behavior patterns affects speed of learning.

16. *Schedules of reinforcement* greatly affect the pattern with which an animal per-

forms a learned behavior. The four basic kinds of intermittent reinforcement schedules are *fixed ratio (FR), variable ratio (VR), fixed interval (FI),* and *variable interval (VI).*

17. As with classical conditioning, the principles of instrumental conditioning have been applied to human behavior. The concept of a response–reinforcer contingency in particular has been shown to be useful in various educational and clinical settings. *Behavior modification* involves the use of basic instrumental learning principles in the treatment of a wide range of clinical disorders.

FOCUS QUESTIONS

1. Discuss the role of stimulus contingency in learning.

2. Describe Pavlov's experiments and discuss the several factors that affect strength of conditioning.

3. Discuss the Pavlovian phenomena that indicate that a biological unconditioned stimulus is not needed for the development of associations.

4. Compare and contrast instrumental and Pavlovian learning.

5. Discuss the evidence regarding the need for reward in instrumental learning.

6. Discuss the instrumental learning phenomena that are particularly relevant for human behaviors an]d the way in which reinforcement contingencies are used in clinical settings.

INFORMATION PROCESSING AND MEMORY

 How does the mind work? How do we form memories? Questions like these have been debated for centuries. Recall that many philosophers, beginning with Aristotle and extending to the British empiricists, claimed that knowledge is derived from experience rather than being present at birth. Recall also, as we saw in Chapter 12, that an association between two events, such as a conditioned stimulus and an unconditioned stimulus, can be thought of as a unit of knowledge. Surely, however, knowledge is more than a collection of associations. And the fact that knowledge is derived from experience tells us little about the processes involved.

Cognitive psychologists examine in detail the processes that are central to the creation of knowledge: detecting and perceiving information in the environment, evaluating the meaning of that information, encoding the information, storing it as memories, and recalling it.

At the most general level, cognitive psychologists claim that the acquisition of knowledge involves two aspects. First is the input from the environment, or the presentation of sensory information to the subject. Second is a processing system that detects, recognizes, transforms, and rehearses information and forms and stores memories. But if we are to verify that knowledge has been created, there must also be a third aspect—output, or overt expression of the knowledge.

The details of these aspects are, of course, enormously complex, and there are many unanswered questions in this area of psychological research. Some of those questions will be addressed in later sections of the chapter. First, however, we provide a brief introduction to the methods typically used to study cognitive processes.

MEASURES OF MEMORY AND INFORMATION PROCESSING

To a large extent, our ability to make inferences about the way the mind processes and stores information depends on the way we measure the output of the mind. Two general kinds of tests are commonly used: measures of memory or retention and measures of information processing itself.

RETENTION MEASURES

The most straightforward measure of memory is **recall.** In recall tests, subjects are asked to repeat information to which they were exposed previously. Sometimes they are given cues to help them recall, but on other occasions they are not directed in any way. An example of recall is a fill-in-the-blank question on a test.

Another measure of retention is **recognition.** In recognition tests, subjects are given a list of items, some of which were included in information presented previously; they are asked to identify those items. Multiple-choice questions are an example of this approach to measuring retention.

Recognition and recall tests are not equally sensitive measures of memory. Often a subject cannot recall an item of information yet can recognize it when given a choice between it and other items. This is why people usually claim that they easily forget names but not faces; names must be recalled, whereas faces can be identified through recognition.

REACTION TIME

Recall and recognition tests measure the output stage of the memory process—the behavioral expression of a memory. Cognitive psychologists, however, also study the processing of information itself more directly. One way they do this is to measure *reaction time*—the speed and accuracy of performance—for different tasks. Typical reaction time studies compare the way subjects perform on similar tasks that differ in their degree of complexity. Suppose, for example, you are asked to lift your finger from a button as rapidly as possible whenever either of two lights is turned on. To perform this task, you must first receive the visual input, then decide that the input is a light, and finally command your finger to be lifted from the button. (Such information processing, of course, does not necessarily involve conscious decision making.) Now imagine that you are asked to lift your finger as quickly as possible, but only when a red light goes on. In this case two of the stages—the sensory input and the motor output—are more or less the same as before, but the decision process is different. Not only must you recognize that a light is on, but you must also decide whether it is the correct light. Clearly, the number of mental operations (that is, the complexity of the information processing) is greater in the second case than in the first. As a result, the time it takes to respond with the same degree of accuracy should also be greater. Stated differently, if you perform the second task at the same level of accuracy as the first, you should also do so more slowly. Likewise, if you perform the second at the same speed as the first, you should do so with less accuracy. By carefully designing tests like this, researchers can isolate particular mental processes and gain insight into how they work (Meyer, Irwin, Osman, & Kounios, 1988).

STRUCTURE VERSUS PROCESS

So far we have outlined some issues and methods of cognitive psychology. The rest of this chapter fills in details. First, though, it is important to distinguish two concepts: cognitive structures and cognitive processes.

Structures are places or things in the cognitive system, such as memory locations. Structures may even have specific locations in the brain. They are repositories into which information is placed and in which it is manipulated. Processes, on the other hand, are modes of action, the specific ways in which the cognitive system works; examples include attention and rehearsal.

One important question confronting cognitive psychologists is whether or not the information processing and memory system can best be described as a collection of structures or as a series of processes. A good way to understand this issue is to rephrase it in terms of modern computer systems. Suppose you wanted to simulate some aspects of the brain's cognitive functioning on a computer. One strategy would be to restrict various areas of the computer's memory to certain functions (create a collection of structures). No matter what the computer had to do at any given point in time, these areas would remain dedicated to their function. Alternatively, one could use all of the computer's memory to perform whatever function is needed at a particular time (devise a series of processes). If one wished to have the computer perform a task different from the task it was currently doing, one would simply change the software program.

Both the structure model and the process model have been used successfully in cognitive psychology. In the following sections of this chapter we discuss human memory and information processing in terms of both, focusing on what happens to a stimulus when it is first presented to the cognitive system and then on what occurs in the system as the information continues to be processed.

INTERIM SUMMARY

Measures of retention include recall, in which subjects are asked to repeat information to which they were exposed previously, and recognition, in which they are asked to choose from a list of items those to which they were exposed previously. A technique for measuring information processing itself more directly is to measure reaction time—the speed and accuracy with which subjects perform a test. Cognitive structures are repositories into which information is placed and in which it is manipulated. Cognitive processes may be structural, or they simply may be the specific ways in which the cognitive system works.

SENSORY MEMORY

The first event in the processing of information is the detection of information in the environment. Here we consider this stage in terms of visual information.

ICONIC MEMORY

When a visual stimulus activates the sensory system, it enters a cognitive structure called the **iconic memory store** where the visual information is held for a very brief time. To understand why psychologists believe that such a memory store exists, consider the results of experiments such as the following. A matrix of letters consisting of three rows and three columns is flashed on a screen for about 0.05 second. (See Figure 13-1.) The stimulus is presented so briefly that it is impossible to scan the matrix. Instead, the subject sees the display in its entirety in a single flash. The subject is then asked to recall as many of the letters as possible. (This is known as the whole-report technique because the person is asked to recall all of the items.) Most people can recall only four or five items, or an average of one or two items per row. This result suggests that four or five items is all that a person can see in a single glance.

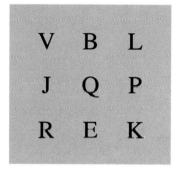

FIGURE 13-1   Example of a matrix of letters used to study iconic memory.

Now suppose the same experiment is performed but the subject is asked to report only some of the items in the matrix (Sperling, 1960). In studies of this type, the subject is typically given one of three tones immediately after the matrix is flashed on the screen. A high-pitched tone means that the subject should recall only the items in the top row; a middle-pitched tone means that the subject should recall only the items in the second row; and a low-pitched tone means that the subject should recall only the items in the bottom row. Bear in mind that the subject does not know *before* seeing the matrix which row he or she will be asked to recall.

Most subjects in such partial-report tests are able to recall nearly all the information from a given row, not just one or two items per row. Because these subjects were not given more time to see the matrix than subjects in the whole-report tests and were not told in advance which row to attend to (the eye sees the same amount in both tests), their performance suggests that the same number of items was available to them in *all* the rows. In other words, multiplying the number of items these subjects reported for a single row by the number of rows in the matrix should give an indication of the total number of items that were available to them. Figure 13-2 (see page 326) shows the results of doing just that compared with the results of the same operation on the performance of whole-report subjects.

How can we explain these curious results? One possibility is that the subject actually detects the entire matrix but forgets many of the items in the process of trying to recall them. In other words, as subjects recite the first items they recall, the others are fading from memory. In whole-report experiments they evidently have time to recall four or five items before the remainder fade. Because a single row contains only three items, however, subjects have time to recall the entire contents of a particular row, as the results of the partial-report studies indicate. In any case, the results of both kinds of studies strongly suggest that a transitory iconic memory exists.

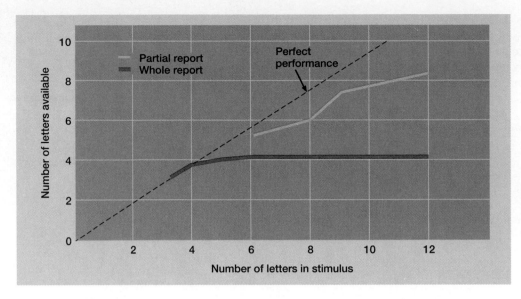

FIGURE 13-2 The number of letters in a matrix available in memory after a brief presentation, for matrices of various sizes, as inferred from the performance of partial-report subjects and whole-report subjects. The dotted line indicates what perfect performance would be. (Adapted from Sperling, 1960.)

Duration of Iconic Memory

If these results do indeed reflect the operation of an iconic memory store, how long does information remain there? This question was addressed in a study in which a matrix of letters was flashed, followed by a second stimulus—a small bar positioned above the location that had been occupied by one of the letters (Averbach & Coriell, 1961). (See Figure 13-3.) The subject was asked to recall the letter that had occupied that location. Subjects recalled the letter correctly about 80% of the time when the bar was presented immediately after the matrix. As the time between the two stimuli increased, however, accuracy of recall declined. In fact, when the presentation of the bar was delayed for about 0.25 second after the presentation of the matrix, the accuracy for any given letter was no better than what is found using the whole-report method. According to these findings, then, iconic memory lasts no longer than 0.25 second (Efron, 1970).

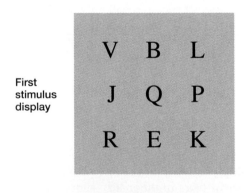

FIGURE 13-3 Sample stimuli used to study the duration of iconic memory. The "bar" in the lower part of the figure is intended to be just over the space previously occupied by the "J."

326

Backward Masking

Iconic memory has been compared to a mental "snapshot"; each new quarter-second snapshot replaces the previous one (see Muise, LeBlanc, Lavoie, & Arsenault, 1991). Evidence for such a notion comes from several experiments. In one, subjects were shown a matrix of letters and then were shown a circle (Averbach & Coriell, 1961). The time between the two stimuli was so short that the circle appeared to be superimposed on the matrix and thus to encircle a letter. (See Figure 13-4.) The subjects were asked to indicate which letter appeared to be encircled. When the circle was flashed immediately after the matrix, they had no trouble performing this task. But when the presentation of the circle was delayed for about 0.25 second, the iconic memory for the letters had faded to such an extent that the circle failed to improve the accuracy of their recall. These two results are in complete agreement with those just described.

An unusual result occurred, however, when the presentation of the circle was delayed for an intermediate amount of time, about 0.1 second. In this case the subjects' recall was even less accurate, indicating that the circle had actually interfered with recall of the matrix. Apparently the circle had masked the iconic memory for the letters—the first "snapshot," the letters, had been displaced by the second, the circle. The implication of this finding is that visual information enters iconic memory as a first step in processing; the iconic memory lasts about 0.25 second unless another image is detected within about 0.1 second, in which case the first image is replaced by the second.

ECHOIC MEMORY

Although much less research has been done in this area, it appears that a comparable system, called **echoic memory,** exists for the processing of auditory information. Experimental results confirm that echoic memory stores auditory information for a very brief time. In one experiment, subjects listened to letters spoken simultaneously through four separate loudspeakers (Moray, Bates, & Barnett, 1965). On some occasions the subjects were asked to recall all of the letters; on other occasions they were asked to recall only the letters they had heard from specific speakers indicated by one of four lights presented shortly after the auditory stimuli. The results were similar to those obtained with visual stimuli; that is, the partial-report method produced greater accuracy. There are, however, some differences between iconic and echoic memory. Studies have shown that echoic memory lasts much longer than iconic memory—up to about 2 seconds—although scientists disagree as to the precise duration.

FIGURE 13-4   Sequence of events in an experiment on backward masking. First the letter matrix is displayed. Then, following a delay interval, the mask (the circle) is presented. What a subject sees depends on the delay interval. If the interval is about 0.1 second, the circle masks the letter. (Adapted from Averbach & Coriell, 1961.)

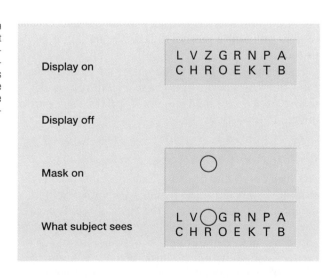

INTERIM SUMMARY

When a visual stimulus activates the sensory system, it enters the iconic memory store, where it is held for a very brief time—about 0.25 second. If another visual stimulus is presented during that time, it will replace the previous memory. A similar store, called echoic memory, exists for auditory information. Echoic memory appears to last up to 2 seconds, considerably longer than iconic memory.

PATTERN RECOGNITION

The next step in information processing is recognition. Recognition of stimulus patterns is obviously an important cognitive function; without it, the world would be a swirling mass of confusing, meaningless stimuli. In discussing theory and data in this area of research, we will emphasize research on the recognition of letters and words. (We discussed pattern recognition in Chapter 4.) Many psychologists believe that the processes involved in letter and word recognition are similar to the general processes involved in the recognition of all incoming information.

BOTTOM-UP PROCESSING

According to one important model, recognition is the end result of **bottom-up processing.** In this model, processing begins with the raw sensory data—the critical elements of the stimulus—then moves to a higher level at which meaning and context are established. In other words, we *construct* the meaning of a stimulus from its simpler sensory features. Let us examine several ways this could take place.

Template Theory

Recognition may involve comparing incoming information with items already stored in memory. Such a process could be carried out in a rather straightforward manner: The incoming image could be compared to a **template** contained in memory. A template is a standardized form of an image; it matches the image the way a cookie cutter matches a particular shape of cookie. (A cookie cutter is, in fact, a template for a particular shape of cookie.) If the image and the template match, the image is recognized.

The problem with the template theory is that it would require the presence of countless templates in memory to enable us to recognize all the things in our environment that have meaning. Consider the letter B. According to the template theory, to recognize any particular example of B as a B, we need to have a template to match that example. We recognize all the objects in Figure 13-5 as B's, however, even though some of them may be entirely novel to us; according to the template theory, if we saw an example of a B that we had never seen before, we would be unable to identify it.

Feature Analysis

Another possibility is that we unconsciously analyze the basic, critical features of a stimulus, compare those features with a list contained in memory, and determine the meaning of the stimulus on the basis of the fit between the features and the list. This concept of **feature analysis** is similar to the concept of a template match, but there are some important differences between them. According to feature analysis, we recognize a stimulus on the basis of only a limited number of *essential* features. For example, the essential features of an A are two intersecting diagonal lines and a hori-

When memory systems break down—as happens, for example, with Alzheimer's disease—the effect can be profoundly debilitating.

FIGURE 13-5 Some of the many forms of the letter "B."

zontal bar. Recognizing that these essential features are part of a stimulus is quite different from recognizing that the entire stimulus pattern matches a representation of it contained in memory.

Experimental evidence suggests that humans do analyze features of stimuli (Rumelhart & Siple, 1974; Treisman & Gormican, 1988). In one experiment, subjects were shown letters and numbers and asked if they had seen the items previously (Kinney, Marsetta, & Showman, 1966). After they had been shown a great many stimuli, the subjects naturally were somewhat uncertain as to whether they had seen any given item before, and they tended to make errors. But the kinds of errors they made were very revealing. For example, they confused items that were *visually* similar. If they were shown a B, for instance, they might claim that they had seen it before when in fact they had seen an 8. Such confusion must have resulted from the fact that the items share certain essential features. In the case of B and 8, both have two rounded sections, one on top of the other. Subjects rarely confused items whose basic features differ, such as A and S. In summary, humans do use a bottom-up processing strategy, although, as we shall discuss below, it is not the only kind of processing that contributes to pattern recognition.

TOP-DOWN PROCESSING

Considerable evidence suggests that recognition is often accomplished by a second kind of processing called **top-down processing.** Top-down processing is selective; it shapes our interpretation of stimuli in light of expectations we derive from prior knowledge and the context (Rumelhart, 1977). Take, for example, this incomplete sentence: "The farmer drove the _____." The context provided by the available words and our prior knowledge of farmers sets limits on the words we *expect* to see in place of the blank. A typical study of top-down processing might use just such a sentence, but the sentence would contain a distorted, hard-to-read word in place of the blank. (See Figure 13-6.) After seeing the sentence displayed briefly on the screen, the subjects would be asked to identify the word. On some occasions the word might be, say, "tractor"; on others it might be "airplane." In line with what top-down processing would lead us to predict, subjects take less time to identify the word "tractor" (presumably because they expect to see it) than they do to identify the word "airplane" even though both would have been displayed for the same length of time.

The Word Superiority Effect

One of the clearest demonstrations of top-down processing can be seen in the **word superiority effect.** In studies of this phenomenon, subjects were given strings of letters that were flashed too quickly to be actually read. The subjects' task was to identify which letter had occurred in a certain position by choosing between two alternative letters as quickly as possible (Johnston, 1978; Reicher, 1969). For example, the subject might have been given either WORD or ORWD and asked to indicate whether the letter in the rightmost position was a D or a K.

The results showed that subjects more quickly identified the D when presented with the letter string WORD than with the string ORWD. The feature analysis model

FIGURE 13-6 Sample stimuli used to test for the effect of top-down processing.

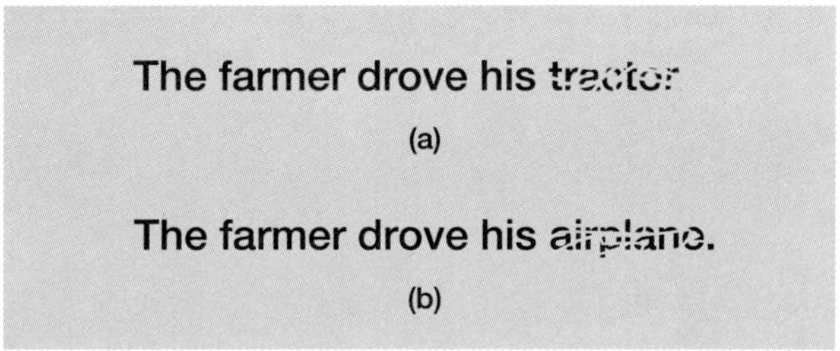

The farmer drove his tractor

(a)

The farmer drove his airplane.

(b)

discussed earlier fails to explain such a result. If subjects had merely analyzed the features of the letter in the rightmost position, there should have been no difference in reaction time. The fact that there was a difference in reaction time supports the existence of top-down processing.

Global Processing

Additional evidence for top-down processing can be seen in the fact that people often recognize holistic (overall) features of a stimulus *before* they recognize its specific features. This is called **global processing.** In one study, stimuli like those shown in Figure 13-7 were flashed briefly in front of subjects (Navon, 1977; see also Broadbent, 1977). On some occasions, the subjects were asked to indicate as fast as they could whether the larger or more global target was an S or an H. On other occasions, they were instructed to say which "small" letter was used to construct the larger letter. The results showed that the global target was recognized much more quickly. Moreover, the reaction times for the global recognition task did not depend on which small letters were used to construct the pattern. For instance, the global H was recognized just as quickly when it was made up of small S's as when it was made up of small H's. In sum, the data suggest that humans may process a stimulus as a whole first (top-down) rather than beginning with the elements or features of the stimulus (bottom-up). This idea is consistent with the Gestalt theories of perception discussed in Chapter 4.

INTERACTION OF TOP-DOWN AND BOTTOM-UP PROCESSING

A number of theorists have suggested that recognition involves both bottom-up and top-down processing (Lindsay & Norman, 1972; Rumelhart, 1977). We analyze the features of a stimulus (bottom-up), but *in addition* our expectations influence the process of recognition (top-down). Stated differently, there are various processes that contribute to recognition. Some involve analyzing specific features of the stimulus; others involve the subject's expectations or the context in which the stimulus occurs.

Our ability to recognize elements within line drawings as representing facial features provides a good example of the interaction between top-down and bottom-up processes (Palmer, 1975). We require a great deal of detail to recognize an eye as an eye if it is drawn out of context. (See Figure 13-8*a*.) Because there is no context to guide the recognition process, the analysis must occur in a bottom-up fashion. In Figure 13-8*b*, however, the eye is represented by a straight line that, by itself, would never be recognized as an eye. Yet in the context of the holistic pattern of facial features, the line is readily identified as an eye. In this instance, then, recognition must occur through a top-down process, because the context provides the only basis for calling the line an eye.

In sum, there is evidence that we process information in two distinct ways. First, we tend to construct the meaning of a stimulus by analyzing its features. Second, we tend to determine the meaning of a stimulus in terms of our expectations, aided by the context in which the stimulus occurs. Both kinds of processing, bottom-up and top-down, occur together.

FIGURE 13-7 Sample stimuli used to study global processing. Note that the smaller letters in the left pattern are consistent with the larger H pattern, whereas the smaller letters on the right are not. (Adapted from Navon, 1977.)

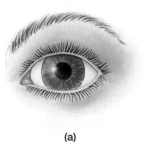

(a)

(b)

FIGURE 13-8 Sample stimuli used to study the interaction of top-down and bottom-up information processing. Without context, we need a lot of information to identify an eye as an eye (*a*); with context, we have no trouble recognizing even a simple horizontal line as an eye (*b*). (Adapted from Palmer, 1975.)

Pattern recognition appears to involve two interacting cognitive processes: bottom-up processing and top-down processing. In bottom-up processing, we first determine the elements of a stimulus and then interpret the meaning of those elements. Two mechanisms have been proposed to explain this process: template theory and feature analysis. According to template theory, we match incoming information with templates contained in memory. According to feature analysis, we recognize a stimulus on the basis of only a limited number of essential features. In top-down processing our interpretation of stimuli is influenced by prior knowledge and context. A result of this process is that we tend to recognize things in a familiar context more readily than the same things in an unfamiliar context.

ATTENTION

Attention is one of the factors that influences the detection and recognition of stimuli. Attention can be extremely selective, allowing us to ignore most of the stimuli in our environment and process only selected items of information (Johnston & Dark, 1986).

SELECTIVE ATTENTION

Perhaps the most famous example of **selective attention** is the so-called cocktail party phenomenon (Cherry, 1953). Imagine that you are talking to a small group of people in a noisy, crowded room. One normally has to "tune out" the party noise just to maintain a conversation under these conditions. But imagine that someone in a different group mentions your name. Even though you have been trying to ignore the noise in the room, you hear your name being spoken. This shows that you are not totally oblivious to the noise; you are able to hear highly significant information, such as your name, despite your effort to ignore it.

Many researchers have studied the cocktail party phenomenon using a technique called **dichotic listening.** In a typical dichotic listening experiment, subjects are fitted with earphones and given two different messages, one in the left ear and the other in the right ear. They are instructed, however, to pay attention to only one of the messages. To confirm that the subjects are indeed attending to a single message, the experimenters ask them to **shadow** the message, that is, to speak the words in the message as they hear them. Later the subjects are asked to recall the other (**unshadowed**) message. Shadowing forces the subjects to devote their full attention to a single message and inhibits them from switching their attention back and forth between messages.

These experiments usually find that the unshadowed message receives very little processing (Treisman & Geffen, 1967; Treisman & Riley, 1969). Subjects can say very little about it. They may be able to say whether the speaker of the message is male or female or whether the message involves spoken words or a tone, but they can report none of the details of the message. In fact, subjects cannot even identify the language in which the unshadowed message is spoken. Only when a highly significant piece of information requiring little attentional resources, such as one's name, occurs in the unshadowed channel does a person recognize the message.

A comparable effect occurs for visual information (Coltheart, 1980). In one study, subjects were shown two videotapes at the same time, one superimposed on the other (Neisser & Becklen, 1975). One of the tapes showed three people throwing a basketball back and forth; the other tape showed two people playing a handslapping game.

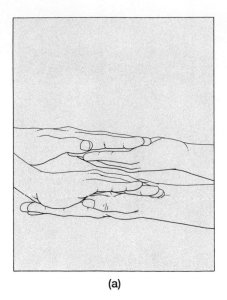
(a)

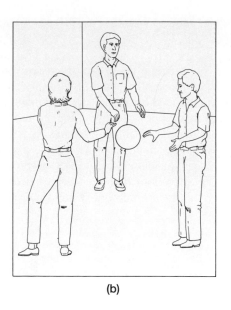
(b)

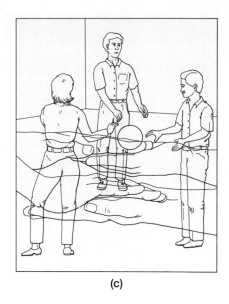
(c)

FIGURE 13-9 Schematic drawings of the two videotaped sequences (*a* and *b*) and the resulting superimposed image (*c*) used in a study of selective attention and visual information. Subjects attended to one of the sequences and later were asked about events that occurred in the other sequence. (Adapted from Neisser & Becklen, 1975.)

(See Figure 13-9.) The subjects were instructed to pay attention to only one of the videos and ignore the other. To verify that they were attending selectively, subjects were asked to press the button on an electronic counter every time a critical event occurred. For example, subjects who attended to the basketball game were told to note each time the ball was thrown from one person to another, whereas those attending to the handslapping game were instructed to note each time the bottom pair of hands tried to slap the top pair. The results were similar to those obtained in dichotic listening experiments. Subjects could selectively attend to only one visual message at a time and had trouble keeping track of the other message. For example, when they attended to the basketball game, subjects rarely saw special events in the handslapping game, as when the two pairs of hands momentarily engaged in a handshake.

MODELS OF SELECTIVE ATTENTION

As the studies just discussed make clear, we attend to our environment selectively. But when in the processing sequence does the selection of information occur? Does it happen early in the sequence, when the information is entering the system, or does it occur later, after the information has been recognized and organized?

The Early Selection Model

One of the first theories about selective attention proposed that the information-processing system includes a filter (Broadbent, 1958). According to this theory, information must pass through this filter at the very earliest stages in the information pro-

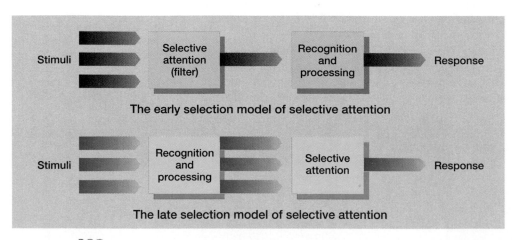

FIGURE 13-10 Two models of selective attention. According to the early selection model, information is selected prior to the point at which it is recognized and processed. According to the late selection model, information is selected after it has been recognized and processed.

cessing sequence, when it is first received. (See Figure 13-10.) The filter admits only one message at a time. Once a message has passed through the filter, it is processed.

This **early selection model** predicts that no message other than the selected one gets through the filter. Therefore, subjects should have no knowledge whatsoever of messages to which they have not attended. This prediction, however, is not supported by experimental evidence (Treisman, 1964). Many studies have found that subjects have *some* knowledge of unshadowed messages. For example, as demonstrated by the cocktail party phenomenon, an unshadowed message may be understood, at least partially, if it contains significant information such as the subject's name (Moray, 1959). Clearly, such a result could not occur if the subject was attending exclusively to a single message.

The Late Selection Model

According to the **late selection model,** *all* the information enters the information processing system and selective attention occurs after the information has been recognized and evaluated (Posner & Snyder, 1975; Shiffrin & Schneider, 1977). According to this model, we do not entirely shut out any messages; we process all of them and then attend selectively on the basis of their meaning. (See Figure 13-10*b*.)

In a dichotic listening experiment testing this model, subjects were given an unpleasant shock whenever they heard particular words in the shadowed message (von Wright, Anderson, & Stenman, 1975). The words were, in a sense, signals for the aversive shocks, and as a result produced a conditioned galvanic skin reaction. Later in the experiment one of the words, a rhyming word, and a synonym were presented in the shadowed and the unshadowed messages. Even though no shocks were given in this stage of the experiment and subjects could not recall the target words when they were included in the unshadowed message, nevertheless they exhibited a galvanic skin reaction to those words whether in the shadowed or unshadowed message. This means that the subjects must have attended to the unshadowed message and processed the words for meaning. In sum, there is strong support for the idea that at least some processing of the unshadowed message may occur, although experimental results in this area are somewhat inconsistent (Dawson & Schell, 1982; Wandlaw & Kroll, 1976).

SHARED ATTENTION

Under certain conditions, attention can be shared among more than one incoming message (Kahneman, 1973). In one study of this phenomenon, subjects were given two tasks (Posner & Boies, 1971). The first task was to indicate as quickly as possible whether two letters matched. Each letter was flashed for 0.05 second, and there was a 1-second interval between letters. The second task was to tap a telegraph key as quickly as possible at the sound of a tone. The tone was given either during the letter presentations or during the gap between letters. Subjects had to attend closely to the second letter in order to match it with the first letter. Giving less than full attention to the letter in order to attend to the tone should therefore cause a reduction in accuracy on the letter-matching task. The intent of the experiment was to discover the extent to which subjects could perform both tasks simultaneously.

The subjects' reaction time on the letter-matching task was fast when the tone was sounded during the gap between letters. That is, performance on the letter-matching task was good if the tone was given at a time when the attention demands of that task were minimal. Their reaction time was slow, however, when the tone was sounded simultaneously with the presentation of the second letter. At that point the attention demands of the letter-matching task were at a maximum, making it difficult to share attention, and performance on that task suffered.

It appears, then, that shared attention can occur but that it depends to a large extent on the difficulty of the tasks involved. When the demands of one task are low, attention can be shared with another task, but when the demands of the first task are high, most or all of the subject's attention is devoted to that task, leaving little for the second task (Moore & Massaro, 1973). An everyday example of this phenomenon is

Research has shown that humans have extreme difficulty paying attention to more than one thing at a time, although attention can shift back and forth between two messages.

engaging in conversation while driving a car. Driving in heavy traffic requires virtually all of one's attention, making it hard to converse. Driving on the open highway, in contrast, requires less attention, making conversation possible.

AUTOMATIC VERSUS ATTENTIONAL PROCESSING

All the evidence discussed so far suggests that attentional resources are limited. In some cases, however, people apparently *can* learn to attend to more than one task at a time. In one study, subjects became relatively proficient at reading a passage while taking dictation of a different passage (Hirst, Spelke, Reaves, Caharack, & Neisser, 1980). It took a great deal of practice for them to achieve even a modest level of proficiency, but the finding nonetheless suggests that the human capacity to process information is greater than the theories discussed so far would suggest.

There is, however, another possible explanation for this finding. Perhaps with practice humans learn to process larger, more holistic patterns of information. Consider the actions involved in slowing down and shifting gears while driving a car: put one foot on the brake; put the other foot on the clutch; manipulate the gear shift; release the clutch while moving the braking foot to the accelerator. A novice driver approaches this task as if all of these actions were separate behaviors, each requiring full attention. Experienced drivers, in contrast, do not attend to each action as a separate behavior but treat them as a single action pattern. Similarly, consider how an experienced typist is able to type words and sentences without having to attend to, or even think about, each letter. The manipulation of the keys is virtually automatic. These examples suggest that improvements in attentional capacity may result not from learning to attend to separate tasks simultaneously but from learning to integrate numerous tasks into a single action pattern.

When we respond in this way, processing becomes automatic. Again consider the act of shifting gears. Experienced drivers might attend to traffic automatically noting when they must slow down and downshift. These examples point to a fundamental distinction between two types of information processing, **automatic processing** and **attentional processing** (Logan, 1988; Schneider & Shiffrin, 1977; Shiffrin & Schneider, 1977).

The Stroop Test

The Stroop test provides a good example of the interaction between these two types of processing (Stroop, 1935; see MacLeod, 1991). In this test, subjects are asked to

With great practice, certain action patterns can become sufficiently automatic such that they do not require attentional processing, making it possible to perform two or more complex tasks at the same time.

indicate the color of the ink used to print various stimuli, including words, like those in Figure 13-11. When the stimuli are everyday words, as in Figure 13-11*a*, the task is easy; it takes little time to name the ink color correctly. When the words are color names that conflict with the color of the ink, as in Figure 13-11*b*, however, the task becomes quite difficult; subjects typically take much longer to perform the task and often make mistakes. The reason for the drop in performance is that the meaning of the words is processed automatically and unconsciously, interfering with the color identification task. In other words, the difference in performance (reaction time) between the two kinds of tasks occurs because of the conflict between attentional processing of the ink color and automatic processing of the color name (Lowe & Mitterer, 1982).

HOUSE	RED
CAR	**GREEN**
PLANT	**BLUE**
(a)	(b)

FIGURE 13-11 Sample stimuli from the Stroop test. Subjects are asked to identify the ink color or the color name.

INTERIM SUMMARY

We ignore most of the stimuli in our environment and process only selected items. This is true of visual as well as auditory information. According to the early selection model of selective attention, information must pass through a filter in order to be processed; only one message can enter the system at a time. According to the late selection model, in contrast, all messages in the environment enter the system; selection occurs later and is based on the meaning of the message. There is evidence that attention can be shared between more than one incoming message, and people can be trained to attend to more than one task at a time. Our ability to master complex skills that seem to require attention to many tasks at once shows that with practice we can learn to integrate many related tasks into action patterns that we perform automatically. Thus, there appear to be two kinds of information processing—attentional and automatic.

SHORT-TERM AND LONG-TERM MEMORY

Detecting and recognizing information are the first steps in information processing. The next step is storage. There are two models that describe how information is stored and processed during this time. The multistore model focuses on cognitive structures; it argues that processing occurs in two separate memory systems—short-term and long-term memory. The levels-of-processing model, on the other hand, focuses on processing; it claims that information is actually processed in different ways within a single memory system.

THE MULTISTORE MODEL

According to the **multistore model,** information can reside in three major storage sites or memory systems: sensory memory, short-term memory, and long-term memory (Atkinson & Shiffrin, 1968). Sensory memory is the iconic or echoic memory described earlier in the chapter. In this section we discuss the other two memory systems.

Short-Term Memory

The evidence for a separate **short-term memory** site is abundant and compelling. Among the earliest and most significant evidence came from studies of the **memory span** (Miller, 1956). In these studies researchers would read subjects a list of about 12 digits and then ask them to recall as many as possible. They found that subjects can recall only between 5 and 9 items, with an average of 7. In words, the memory span is rather limited; only about 7 ± 2 items can be retained in short-term memory at any given time.

The memory span is actually limited in terms of the number of *chunks* of information that can be retained. A chunk is a unit of information. It may consist of a single item or comprise several items. When chunking occurs—that is, when two or more items are combined to form a chunk—the total amount of information that can be held in short-term memory increases. For instance, consider the following string of 14 digits: 7 1 3 9 8 4 4 5 6 1 7 2 6 3. If each digit were treated as an individual unit, a person could retain only about seven of them in short-term memory at a time. Grouping these same digits into two-digit numbers, however, reduces them to seven chunks (71 39 84 45 61 72 63), which a person can retain in short-term memory.

Another major characteristic of short-term memory is its duration. Recall that iconic memory is believed to last for less than a quarter of a second. In contrast, items in short-term memory are thought to last for between 15 and 20 seconds unless they are actively rehearsed. In a noted study of this phenomenon, subjects were given a nonsense syllable like XQM and were asked to recall it after a delay of between 3 and 18 seconds (Peterson & Peterson, 1959). This task seems trivial, especially if one is allowed to rehearse the stimulus during the delay interval. But the researchers prevented rehearsal by giving the subjects a three-digit number immediately after the syllable and asking them to count backward from that number by threes as quickly as possible. As suggested earlier in our discussion of attention, a person normally cannot attend consciously to such a task while attempting to perform another task. Because the subjects had to speak each number, they needed to pay attention to the subtraction task and therefore could not rehearse the nonsense syllable. Thus the experimenters were able to determine how long the syllable could remain in short-term memory.

The results of the study, shown in Figure 13-12, indicate that retention was not perfect even after a 3-second interval; after a 15-second interval, the level of recall was extremely low. In other words, when information cannot be actively rehearsed, it is almost entirely forgotten within 12 to 18 seconds.

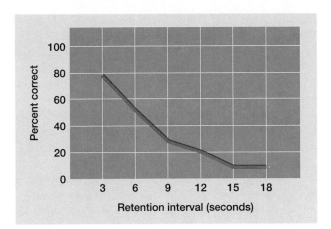

FIGURE 13-12 Mean percent items (three-letter syllables) recalled as a function of the retention interval. The graph shows the duration of short-term memory. (Adapted from Peterson & Peterson, 1959.)

In addition to span and duration, a third characteristic of short-term memory concerns the kind of processing that takes place there. The question here is what specific features of the information are processed. Possibilities would include its meaning, its visual appearance, or its sound (Wickelgren, 1973). There is evidence that the processing that occurs in short-term memory is based largely on sound. Consider the following experiment (Conrad, 1964). Subjects were shown a list of letters and asked to recall as many letters as possible without regard to order. The kinds of errors they made in recalling the letters revealed the way they were encoding the information. The most significant finding was that subjects confused letters on the basis of their sound. For example, they claimed that the list contained an E when in fact the letter had been a V. Rarely did they confuse letters on the basis of their visual appearance (for example, E and F). The results of this experiment therefore suggest that information is treated or processed in short-term memory according to its sound, although people differ somewhat in this regard. Thus, when you try to remember a phone number that you have just looked up (that is, retain the information in short-term memory), you do not "see" the numbers in your head; instead, you "hear" the sound of them being spoken as you process them acoustically.

Long-Term Memory

According to the multistore model, information in short-term memory is transferred (as a result of rehearsal) into **long-term memory** (see Figure 13-13). One major distinction between these two memory systems concerns the amount of information each can hold. Unlike short-term memory, long-term memory can hold a large number of items. In fact, there is no evidence for any kind of limit on the amount of information that can be retained in long-term memory.

Other evidence suggesting that a distinct long-term memory system exists comes from research on brain damage and memory functioning. As we saw in Chapter 5, there have been numerous cases in which patients suffering from various forms of

FIGURE 13-13 The relationship among the three kinds of memory in the multistore model of memory. The process of attention transfers information from sensory memory to short-term memory; the process of rehearsal transfers information from short-term memory to long-term memory.

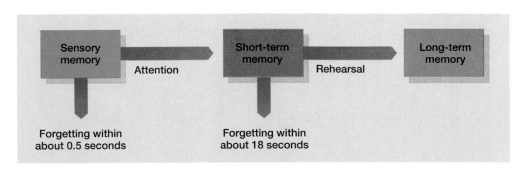

brain damage have been unable to transfer information from short-term, conscious memory to a more permanent long-term memory. In many such cases, to complete any task the patient must focus on it directly and steadily; otherwise within minutes he or she forgets having even discussed it.

Long-term memory also, of course, has a longer duration than short-term memory. Although short-term memories are believed to last only about 12 to 18 seconds, long-term memories can last a lifetime. People often have memories that date back many years and that they are not aware of until the memories are triggered by some relevant event (Bahrick, Bahrick, & Wittlinger, 1975).

Finally, according to the multistore model, information is encoded into long-term memory very differently from its encoding into short-term memory. Long-term memories are believed to be encoded semantically, that is, on the basis of their meaning. In one study of this phenomenon, subjects listened to recorded passages like the one in Figure 13-14 (Sachs, 1967; see also McKoon, 1977). Each passage contained a target sentence. After delay intervals of varying lengths, a sample sentence was presented and subjects were asked to indicate whether the sample had been included in the passage. The sample sentence differed from the target sentence in either structure or meaning, as shown in examples A and B in Figure 13-14.

The results showed that when the sample was presented very soon after the target sentence, subjects noticed both structural and semantic differences. With greater delays between the target and sample sentences, however, subjects tended mistakenly to identify the sample sentence as the target sentence when the meaning of the two sentences was essentially the same. In contrast, subjects rarely confused a sample sentence with the target sentence when the two sentences differed in meaning. The researchers concluded that information in the paragraph had been encoded into long-term memory according to the meaning of the message. Thus, example A in Figure 13-14 might be mistakenly identified as a target sentence because it has the same meaning as that sentence, whereas example B, which has an entirely different meaning, was rarely identified as the target sentence even though some of the same words appeared in the original passage.

FIGURE 13-14 An example of a passage of prose with a target sentence and two sample sentences. One of the sample sentences (example A) differs in structure from the target; the other (example B) differs in meaning. (Adapted from Sachs, 1967.)

Source passage with target sentence

The reality-illusion distinction clearly does not work for plays—the illusion is the reality. If the play is, let us say, a comedy of Shakespeare, there are things inside it that look like real things, such as law courts, and other things, such as fairies and love potions and magic rings, that look impossible. What is important is where all this is going. At the end of the play, a new society is created: four or five couples get married, and things that looked threatening at first, like Shylock, get left behind. We look back over the play and see that what we thought was just fantasy was actually a force strong enough to impose itself on things that looked well established at first and transform them into a quite different shape and direction. The comedy is a miniature example of that drive toward deliverance that has fostered all the great myths of emancipation in the world and is still capable of fostering those of the future.

EXAMPLE A (same meaning): At the end of the play a new order was established.

EXAMPLE B (different meaning): At the end of the play, couples get left behind.

Problems with the Multistore Model

The multistore model has been challenged on several grounds. Critics have claimed that the concept of a "chunk" of information is so poorly defined that the whole notion of the limited capacity of short-term memory is suspect. What does limited capacity really mean if chunking eliminates constraints on storage capacity? Clearly, there is some kind of limitation on short-term memory, but perhaps it is not on storage capacity so much as on the capacity to process information (Craik & Lockhart, 1972).

A second problem has to do with the effects of rehearsal on memory. According to the model, repetition of an item in short-term memory will cause it to be transferred to long-term memory (Rundus, 1971). This notion was challenged in a series of experiments in which subjects were asked to remember four digits for up to about 30 seconds (Craik & Tulving, 1975). During the retention interval the subjects were asked to repeat a word. They were told that this task was designed to prevent them from rehearsing the digits; what they did not know was that they would later be asked to recall the words. The results were surprising in terms of the multistore model: Amount of repetition did not affect accuracy of recall. Words repeated many times were remembered no better than words rehearsed briefly.

This conclusion should be qualified. When the same word was used on more than one trial, recall improved (Rundus, 1977). Similarly, although repetition did not affect performance on a recall test, it did improve performance on a recognition test (Glenberg, Smith, & Green, 1977). Thus, the recognition test detected a relationship between rehearsal and memory, whereas the recall test did not.

A third problem with the multistore model is that studies have shown that humans can encode information visually and semantically as well as acoustically. Short-term memory processing therefore is not exclusively acoustic in nature.

Evidence for visual encoding comes from research on mental rotation of visual images (Cooper & Shepard, 1973; Shepard, 1978; Shepard & Metzler, 1971). Subjects were given two letters and were told to press one button if the pattern of the letters was the same, or another button if the second pattern was the mirror image of the first. The two letters could also differ in degree of rotation. Thus, a letter—say, R—could be in a normal or mirror-image orientation and could also be rotated in either direction up to 180 degrees. (See Figure 13-15.) The results (shown in Figure 13-16 on page 340) indicated that reaction time was a function of the degree of rotation—the greater the rotation, the longer it took for the subject to respond. It appears that subjects rotated the image of the stimulus in their minds when deciding which button to press; thus, their encoding must have been visual in nature.

Other studies have also demonstrated that subjects visually process information in short-term memory (Kosslyn, Ball, & Reiser, 1978). In one, subjects examined a map containing several landmarks. (See Figure 13-17 on page 340.) The maps were taken away and the subjects were asked to visualize one of the landmarks and, using it as a starting point, "scan" the map in their minds as fast as they could until they "reached" a second landmark, at which time they were to press a button. In order to

FIGURE 13-15 Forward (normal) and backward (mirror image) examples of the letter R rotated through six different orientations. (Adapted from Cooper & Shepard, 1973.)

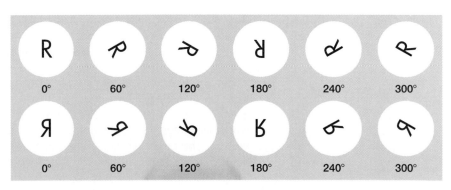

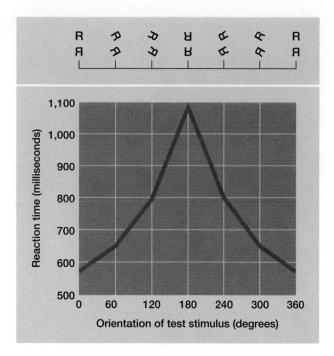

FIGURE 13-16 Mean reaction time as a function of the orientation of the test stimulus. The scales indicate what the stimulus itself would look like relative to a normal "R." The results show that the more the letter is rotated the longer the subjects take to react. (Adapted from Cooper & Shepard, 1973.)

FIGURE 13-17 Map used to study the processing of visual information. Subjects were asked to visualize moving from one position on the map to another. (Adapted from Kosslyn, Ball, & Reiser, 1978.)

verify that a subject really was mentally scanning the image and not just pressing the button as soon as the name of the second landmark was mentioned, so-called catch trials were included. On these trials the name of a landmark that was *not* on the map was given. Clearly, subjects could not "reach" such a landmark in their scan; to confirm that they realized as much, they were told to press a different button. The results showed that reaction times were directly proportional to the actual distance between the two landmarks on the map the subjects had studied. (See Figure 13-18.) Again, the implication is that processing in short-term memory can be visual as well as acoustic.

Finally, research has shown that information can also be encoded semantically in short-term memory. This conclusion was reached in a study in which subjects were given a number of trials, each of which contained 10 words followed by a target word (Baddeley, 1972; Baddeley & Levy, 1971). The subjects' task was to determine whether the target word matched one of the words on the list. The results showed that subjects often confused the target word with a word whose meaning was similar. They were much less likely to say that the target word matched a word on the list when the target word was unrelated to any of the words on the list. It appears, thus, that the information was being encoded semantically.

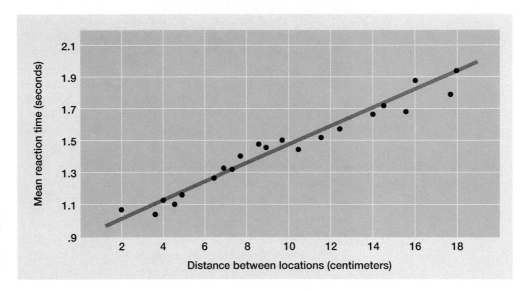

FIGURE 13-18 Mean reaction time required to move, mentally, from one position on the map shown in Figure 13-17 to another as a function of the distance between positions. (Adapted from Kosslyn, Ball, & Reiser, 1978.)

THE LEVELS-OF-PROCESSING MODEL

According to the **levels-of-processing model** of memory, information is not processed by different memory systems but instead is processed at different levels within a single system (Craik & Lockhart, 1972). Specifically, information is first processed according to its sensory qualities. This is the shallowest level of processing. It is then recognized, labeled, and processed according to its sound; this is a somewhat deeper level of processing. Finally, meaning is established through semantic processing. This represents the deepest level of processing. In short, it is the depth of processing, not the transfer from one memory site to another, that affects the duration of memory: the deeper the processing, the longer-lasting the memory.

Types of Processing

Psychologists who study memory from the standpoint of levels of processing distinguish between **maintenance rehearsal** and **elaborative rehearsal** (Craik & Watkins, 1973). Maintenance rehearsal occurs at a single level of processing; it keeps an item of information active in memory but does not affect the permanence of memory for that item. In one study of maintenance rehearsal subjects were given a list of 21 words and were asked to indicate which word was the last one on the list to begin with a particular letter—say, R (Craik & Watkins, 1973). To accomplish this task, the subjects had to recognize that a word began with R and rehearse it either until another word beginning with R occurred (at which point they would begin rehearsing the new word) or until the end of the list was reached (at which point they would report that word). The experimenters could manipulate the amount of rehearsal that took place by varying the number and spacing of words beginning with R. After working through several such lists, subjects were asked to recall as many target words as possible (in our example, the R words). The results showed retention was not a function of amount of rehearsal. Words rehearsed longer were not recalled better at the end of the session than words rehearsed for a short time. The researchers concluded that maintenance rehearsal does not affect retention.

Elaborative rehearsal is rehearsal that occurs at progressively deeper levels of processing. A major tenet of the levels-of-processing model is that the duration of a memory is directly related to the amount of elaborative rehearsal devoted to it. In a study of the effects of this phenomenon, subjects were shown a word for 0.2 second and then were asked to answer one of three questions about it (Craik & Tulving, 1975):

1. "Is the word printed in capital letters?"
2. "Does the word rhyme with ———?"
3. "Does the word fit in the sentence 'The girl placed the ——— on the table'?"

341

Answering the first question required subjects to process or to think about the word only on a visual level; answering the second required them to process it according to its sound, a deeper level; and answering the third required them to process the word according to its meaning, the deepest level.

Subjects were then tested for their ability to remember the words. The results, shown in Figure 13-19, indicate that the deeper the level of processing, the more likely a word was to be remembered (Craik & Tulving, 1975; Fisher & Craik, 1977). Words for which subjects had answered the first question were the least likely to be remembered; words for which they had answered the third question were the most likely to be remembered.

Problems with the Levels-of-Processing Model

Despite the evidence just discussed, there are some problems with the levels-of-processing model. For one thing, the concept of depth of processing is extremely difficult to define. There is no objective way to specify depth other than by the permanence of a memory, and this leads to a circular definition: Items processed at a deeper level are retained better, and items that are retained better are processed at a deeper level (Baddeley, 1978).

A second problem has to do with the prediction that deeper processing will lead to better retention. In a study that questioned this notion, the experimenters read different kinds of sentences to the subjects (Morris, Bransford, & Franks, 1977). Sentences differed in terms of the kind of processing that was required. An example of a sentence that involved semantic processing was "The ———— had a silver engine." An example of a sentence that required phonetic processing (that is, processing according to sound) was "———— rhymes with legal." After a 2-second delay, a target word was given that might or might not be appropriate for the blank (for example, *train* for the first sentence and *eagle* for the second). The subjects were first asked to say whether the target word was appropriate for the blank. Later, they were given a recognition test consisting of the target words or words that rhymed with the target words, and were asked to say whether they had occurred in the sentences. When the words on the recognition test had been used as the original target words, items that had involved semantic processing were more likely to be recognized than words that had been phonetically processed (84% versus 63%). For example, "train" was better remembered than "eagle." This finding agrees with the levels-of-processing model, which predicts that semantically rehearsed information is the most likely to be retained. When the words on the recognition test rhymed with the original items, however, subjects were more likely to recognize rhyming items (49%) than semantic items (33%). For example, the word "regal" was more likely to be recognized as an original target word than the word "brain." This suggests that earlier results showing that semantic memories are more permanent may have been in error,

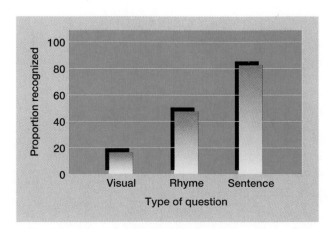

FIGURE 13-19 Proportion of words recognized as a function of the kind of question asked on the recognition text. (Adapted from Craik & Tulving, 1975.) Ivan Pavlov observing an experiment in his laboratory.

and that processing at an acoustic level may, under some conditions, produce more permanent memories than processing on a semantic level.

A third problem with the levels-of-processing model is that it argues that maintenance rehearsal does not improve memory, yet numerous experiments have shown that it does (Geiselman & Bjork, 1980; Maki & Schuler, 1980). For example, in the study discussed earlier, where subjects repeated a word for up to 30 seconds after hearing digits, maintenance rehearsal (mere repetition) did not affect memory for the word when measured by a recall test, but it did affect memory when measured by a recognition test (Glenberg, Smith, & Green, 1977).

Finally, the levels-of-processing model claims that information is processed in a fixed sequence, beginning at a shallow level and progressing to deeper levels. But as noted in our earlier discussion of top-down processing, the overall meaning of an item may be appreciated *before* the item is actually recognized; for instance, the D in WORD is recognized much faster than the D in ORWD. Thus, the first stage in the information-processing sequence is not necessarily the sensory stage.

THE REVISED LEVELS-OF-PROCESSING MODEL

The levels-of-processing model has been revised to account for these criticisms (Craik & Tulving, 1975). The revised version abandons the notion of a fixed sequence of stages. It also argues that memory depends on the degree of elaboration that takes place, not on the depth at which it occurs. Elaboration can occur in one of two ways: within-item elaboration or between-item elaboration.

Within-Item Elaboration

Within-item elaboration involves analyzing or processing information in terms of its own features or characteristics. For example, an item such as the word *tree* could be processed (rehearsed) in terms of the visual appearance of the letters, its sound (rhymes with *flee*), or its meaning (a form of plant life). The more characteristics that are rehearsed for a particular item, the better the memory of that item. Thus, if a word is processed in terms of its visual characteristics *and* its sound *and* its meaning, it will be remembered better than it would be if only one or two of those characteristics were processed.

Between-Item Elaboration

Between-item elaboration involves processing features of an item relative to other memories. The revised levels-of-processing model claims that retention increases when information is processed in relation to information that is already stored in long-term memory. This claim was tested in a study in which subjects were given a list of 60 words and then asked to recall them in any order they wished (Bousfield, 1953). Each word was a member of one of four categories: animals, first names, occupations, and vegetables. The subjects did not recall the words in the order in which they had appeared. Instead, they recalled them in clusters, according to the categories to which they belonged. This finding supports the idea that elaborative processing aids retention, because it suggests that when the subjects heard the words they rehearsed or processed them in terms of the categories.

In sum, psychologists disagree about the nature of memory. Some believe that there are separate memory structures for sensory, short-term, and long-term memories. There is evidence to support this notion in that the duration and characteristics of memories in these three systems differ markedly. Most psychologists, however, now believe that information is processed in different ways or at various levels, and that differences between short- and long-term memories are attributable to the fact that they have been processed in different ways.

According to the multistore model of memory, there are three memory systems: sensory, short-term, and long-term. Short-term memory is of limited span (7 ± 2 items) and of brief duration (3 to 18 seconds), and is encoded largely according to sound. In contrast, long-term memory can hold an unlimited amount of information that can last a lifetime. Items in long-term memory are believed to be encoded semantically. Problems with the multistore model include the lack of a clear definition of the limits on short-term memory, inconsistent evidence for the effectiveness of rehearsal, and the possibility that short-term memories can be encoded visually and semantically as well as acoustically. The levels-of-processing model holds that information is processed at different levels (visual, acoustic, semantic) rather than in different memory systems. This model draws a distinction between maintenance rehearsal (repetition), which occurs at a single level, and elaborative rehearsal, which occurs at progressively deeper levels. There are several problems with this model as well: Depth of processing is difficult to define; deeper processing does not always lead to better retention, whereas maintenance rehearsal can improve the permanence of a memory; and there is evidence that information can be processed in other sequences besides those hypothesized by the model. As a result of these criticisms, the model has been revised so that retention depends on the degree of elaboration that takes place, not on the level at which information is processed. Retention increases when an item is processed in terms of numerous characteristics (within-item elaboration) and in relation to information that is already stored in long-term memory (between-item elaboration).

SUMMARY

1. Cognitive psychologists examine the processes that are central to the creation of knowledge: detecting and perceiving information, evaluating the meaning of that information, encoding it, storing it as memories, and recalling it.

2. Measures of memory and cognitive information processing include retention measures and *reaction time.* Retention measures include *recall* tests, in which subjects are asked to repeat information to which they have been exposed, and *recognition* tests, in which subjects identify items to which they have been exposed. Reaction time studies test the speed and accuracy with which subjects complete tasks of varying complexity, providing insight into the cognitive processes involved in the tasks.

3. The *iconic memory store* is a sensory memory structure in which visual information is held for a very brief time. Its duration is about 0.25 seconds. As new information enters iconic memory, it masks previous information. *Echoic memory* is the comparable sensory memory system for auditory information.

4. Pattern recognition, such as letter or word recognition, is achieved through two general kinds of processes: bottom-up processing and top-down processing. In *bottom-up processing,* the meaning of a stimulus is constructed from its simpler sensory features. According to *template* theory, this process involves comparing incoming information with templates already stored in memory. According to *feature analysis,* we recognize a stimulus on the basis of only a few essential features. In *top-down processing,* our interpretation of stimuli is influenced by prior knowledge and context. Support for the existence of top-down processing comes from research on the *word superiority effect* and *global processing*

5. *Selective attention* refers to the ability to ignore most of the stimuli in the environ-

ment and process only selected items. One way to study selective attention is with the *dichotic listening* technique, in which a subject hears a different message in each ear. Normally, subjects can attend to and process only one of the messages at a time, although some research has shown that the nonattended message may be processed to some degree at least. Psychologists have proposed two models for selective attention: the *early selection model* and the *late selection model.* According to the early selection model, information passes through a selection filter at the earliest stages in processing, and only the selected information is processed. According to the late selection model, selective attention occurs later in the process, after all incoming information has been recognized and evaluated.

6. With sufficient practice, subjects are able to share their attentional resources between two tasks. The reason for this may be that with practice we are able to process larger, more holistic patterns of information that we can perform automatically without devoting attention to them. This suggests that there are two kinds of information processing: *automatic processing* and *attentional processing.*

7. According to the *multistore model* of memory, there are three major storage sites for information—sensory memory (iconic and echoic memory), *short-term memory,* and *long-term memory.* Short-term memory is characterized by its limited capacity (about seven units of information) and its relatively short duration (about 12 to 18 seconds). Information in

short-term memory appears to be encoded acoustically. Long-term memory, on the other hand, is characterized by an apparently limitless capacity for information and a long duration (long-term memories can last a lifetime). Information in long-term memory appears to be encoded semantically. Information is transferred from short-term to long-term memory through rehearsal.

8. Various problems with the multistore model have been noted: Some studies have challenged the relationship between rehearsal and long-term memory; others suggest that short-term memories may be coded visually and semantically as well as acoustically.

9. According to the *levels-of-processing model,* an alternative to the multistore model, information is processed at different levels within a single memory system. Sensory processing is the shallowest level, processing by sound is somewhat deeper, and semantic processing is the deepest. *Maintenance rehearsal* keeps information active in memory, but it does not affect the permanence of the memory. *Elaborative rehearsal* occurs at progressively deeper levels of processing. The deeper the level of processing, the more enduring the information.

10. According to a revised levels-of-processing model, developed in response to weaknesses in the original model, information is processed in terms of its own features or characteristics (*within-item elaboration*), or in terms of other memories (*between-item elaboration*).

FOCUS QUESTIONS

1. Define sensory memory and describe the evidence that suggests that information is held in a sensory store for a very brief period.

2. Compare and contrast bottom-up and top-down processing.

3. Discuss the evidence for the argument that information is processed in both a bottom-up and a top-down fashion.

4. Discuss the evidence for and against the notion that attention is selective.

5. Discuss the major differences between short-term and long-term memory.

6. Compare and contrast the multistore and levels-of-processing models of memory.

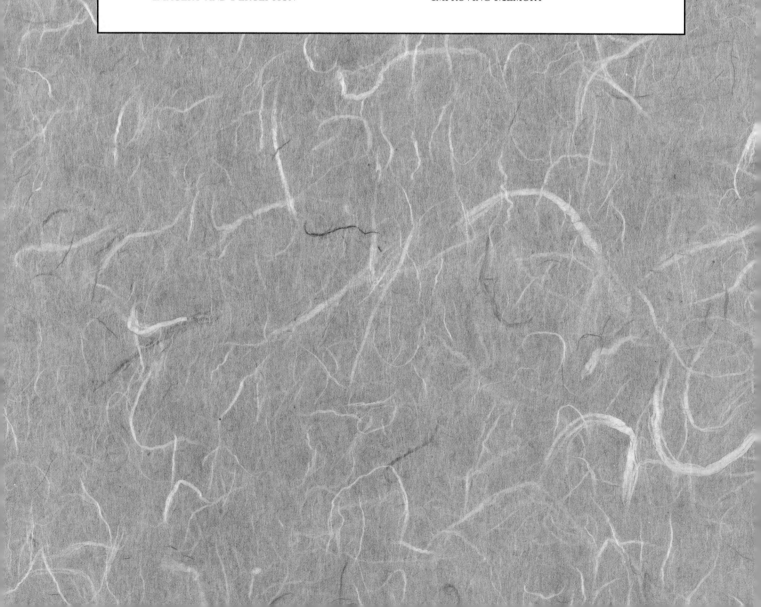

CHAPTER 14

COGNITIVE STRUCTURE AND ORGANIZATION

Theories of the origins of knowledge generally fall into one of two opposing camps: nativism and empiricism. Nativists argue that knowledge is inborn; empiricists argue that it is acquired through experience. Psychologists can hardly claim to have settled this age-old conflict. As we saw in the last two chapters, however, they have identified many of the processes, such as association, attention, recognition, and memory encoding, that affect our acquisition and retention of knowledge. In this chapter, we elaborate on what psychological research has to tell us about these processes, especially the way knowledge is stored and used.

Regardless of its origins, knowledge must consist of more than a collection of discrete memories; it must be *organized* in some way. That is, memories must be related to each other in a coherent fashion. Otherwise we would be unable to gain access to them when we need them.

This point will become clearer if we consider an analogy. Imagine how chaotic a library would be if there were no system for cataloging books. Thousands of books might be stored in the library, but we would have little chance of finding a particular volume except by accident. The amount of *accessible* knowledge represented by the collection of books in the library would be minimal. We can think of discrete memories as analogous to books in a library. Like library books, memories must be organized in some way to be accessible. If there were no system for organizing our memories, for relating one to another, it would be difficult to use them effectively.

There are, however, many possible ways of organizing knowledge. Again consider the library analogy. The Dewey Decimal System is one approach to organizing the books in a library. It classifies knowledge according to 10 categories—general knowledge, philosophy, history, and so forth. The more recent Library of Congress System also organizes books according to categories of knowledge, but the number of categories and the category names are different—"A" for general knowledge, "B" for religion and philosophy, "C" for biography, and so forth. Thus, library books could be organized in many ways; the librarian must adopt a system that reflects, in a sensible and efficient way, the topics contained in a given collection of books.

Determining how human knowledge or memory is structured, however, is a more daunting task than understanding how books are organized in a library. Unlike a library, the human knowledge system is not composed of tangible units of knowledge. Rather, knowledge units—memories, concepts, ideas—are abstract and not easily examined. Nevertheless, in two major areas of cognitive psychology—knowledge representation and categorization—researchers have had some success in creating models of the human knowledge system. In the case of knowledge representation, the models tend to be based on the workings of a modern computer. This is because the components of a digital computer—memory storage, software, interfaces, processing units—provide a rich and compelling metaphor for the human information-processing system called the brain.

ABSTRACT KNOWLEDGE REPRESENTATION

To a large extent, knowledge consists of enduring memories, such as "I had toast for breakfast last Friday" or "England has a Queen." But what are the characteristics of memory? In other words, how is knowledge represented in memory? Psychologists often distinguish between two kinds of long-term memory: episodic and semantic. **Episodic memory** is stored information that is highly linked to the time and place in which it was generated (Tulving, 1983; 1985). **Semantic memory,** in contrast, is abstract general knowledge, including knowledge of words and their referents, the meanings of objects, rules for manipulating words and symbols, and rules for deriving solutions to problems (such as mathematical problems). Most of us know, for example, that fried chicken and rice are foods people sometimes eat for dinner or that England has a queen; these are examples of semantic memory. But consider the question "What did you eat for dinner 10 days ago?" To answer that question, a person must have a memory of the details for that particular meal. Perhaps the meal was memorable because a certain guest was present who had not arrived until that day; perhaps the chicken was flavored with an unusual barbecue sauce that had been discovered by the cook only during the preceding holidays. Regardless of the details, your ability to retrieve the memory is entirely dependent on the context; the knowledge cannot be retrieved in the absence of that context. This is an example of an episodic memory.

EPISODIC MEMORY

Autobiographical Memory

Episodic memory is often called autobiographical memory because it is specifically linked to the context in which the remembered event occurred and cannot be retrieved unless that context is recalled first. In a study illustrating this phenomenon, a researcher recorded more than 2,400 personal events over a six-year period (Wagenaar, 1986). As he entered each item into the diary, he described it in terms of what it was, who was involved, where it had taken place, and when it had occurred. He also noted whether the event was commonplace or unusual and whether it elicited pleasure or some other emotion. Later a colleague helped him test his memory of the events by prompting him with bits of information. For example, the researcher was told what the event had been and then was asked who was involved or where it had taken place. In other instances the researcher was told who was involved and when the event had taken place and was asked what had happened and where. The results showed that the autobiographical context of these episodic memories was especially critical. When given prompts that included who was involved in an event or where it occurred, for example, the researcher was very often able to recall it. When prompted only with information about when an event occurred, he rarely succeeded in recalling it. This study thus confirms that some memories are recalled only because they are closely linked to the context (that is, who and where) in which they were formed; when the context can be recalled, so can the specific event. Simply knowing when an event occurred provides little help in recalling it.

Flashbulb Memories

Episodic memories that are unusually vivid are described as flashbulb memories. According to one definition, "flashbulb memories are memories for the circumstances in which one first learned of a very surprising and consequential (or emotionally arousing) event" (Winograd & Killinger, 1983, p. 414). A contemporary example likely to produce a flashbulb memory is basketball star Magic Johnson's announcement in 1991 that he had tested positive for the human immunodeficiency virus (HIV). In one study of flashbulb memories, subjects were asked what they were doing when they learned of President John F. Kennedy's assassination in 1963. All the subjects were young children (ages 1–7) at the time of the murder (Brown & Kulin, 1977). The results showed that the older the subjects were at the time of the event, the more contextual details they recalled. The study also showed, however, that flashbulb memories are not restricted to surprising events. Many subjects, for example, also demonstrated a vivid flashbulb memory of President Richard M. Nixon's resignation, even though that event did not come as a surprise.

The Challenger explosion is, for many, an event that produced a flashbulb memory.

Is Episodic Memory Unique?

Episodic memories are invariably mixed with semantic memories; that is, context-dependent memories are intertwined with general knowledge. For example, a person may have an episodic memory for President Nixon's resignation—he or she may vividly recall the exact circumstances when learning about the event—but at the same time possess general knowledge about the event (knowledge, for instance, derived from talking with other people after the episode had passed). Because both kinds of memories may occur simultaneously, it is often difficult to distinguish between them.

Given this mixing, is episodic memory really something distinct from semantic memory? In other words, if episodic memories are coded in terms of the context in which they formed and semantic memories are not, does episodic memory therefore operate according to different processes or principles?

Some researchers would answer yes (Tulving, 1983; 1985; 1986). They note, for example, that episodic memories can be selectively impaired by experimental manipulations or by brain damage without affecting general knowledge (Schachter, Harbluk, & McLachlan, 1984). In one study, subjects memorized a list of 15 common words, such as *girl* and *table,* while under hypnosis (Kihlstrom, 1980). After they had completed the learning task but before they were aroused from the trance, they were told that they would not be able to remember the words upon waking unless they were given a specific signal. (This kind of forgetting is called posthypnotic amnesia.) After being awakened, the subjects were given a memory test. First they were asked to recall the words they had learned while under hypnosis. The subjects showed very poor recall, indicating that the hypnotic suggestion to forget the words had been effective. Then they were given words that were closely associated with those on the previously memorized list; for example, *boy* rather than *girl, chair* rather than *table,* and so forth. Here, the subjects demonstrated good recognition memory, suggesting that their overall memory for the meaning of the memorized words had not been affected. Finally, the subjects were given the signal to remember the list, and they were able to do so. This study indicates that episodic memories are separate from general knowledge: During the period of posthypnotic amnesia, the subjects could not recall what they had learned *in that particular context* (episodic memory), but they could remember general information about the items (semantic memory).

Despite evidence of this kind, most cognitive psychologists no longer believe that episodic memory is distinct from general knowledge (McKoon, Ratcliff, & Dell, 1986; Shoben, Wescourt, & Smith, 1978). They argue that both context-dependent information and general information are involved in all memory tasks. In a study supporting this point of view, subjects were asked to repeat out loud a sentence that had been spoken over a distracting hissing noise (Hannigan, Shelton, Franks, & Bransford, 1980). Before performing this task, however, they were given various kinds of information. Some subjects heard the sentence being spoken; others were simply informed of its general meaning; and still others received no information at all. Although subjects who had heard the sentence previously performed better than subjects with no information, those who had been given a general framework for interpreting the meaning of the sentence performed even better. Encountering a particular sentence in a particular context (episodic memory) plus having a general framework for interpreting the meaning of the sentence (general knowledge or semantic memory) improved performance the most. It appears, therefore, that episodic and semantic memories occur together; an event may be remembered because it is both general knowledge and context-linked.

SEMANTIC MEMORY

Psychologists have proposed three models for the structure of semantic memory—that is, for the way we organize and retrieve abstract knowledge (Tien Ming Chang, 1986). These are the hierarchical network model, the feature comparison model, and the spreading activation model.

The Hierarchical Network Model

According to the **hierarchical network model,** knowledge involves three kinds of elements: units, properties, and pointers (Collins & Quillian, 1969). A unit is the name of a concept that refers to a particular set of items, such as *bird* or *canary*. Properties are characteristics of the concept that are not supplied by the name of the concept, such as *yellow, sings,* and *has feathers.* Pointers either connect a concept to a set of properties (for example, *a canary is yellow*) or link together two concepts (for example, *a canary is a bird*). Figure 14-1 illustrates a small portion of such a knowledge network.

A central assumption of this model is that concepts are interconnected hierarchically, so that more general or inclusive concepts, such as *bird,* are located higher in the network than less inclusive concepts like *canary.*

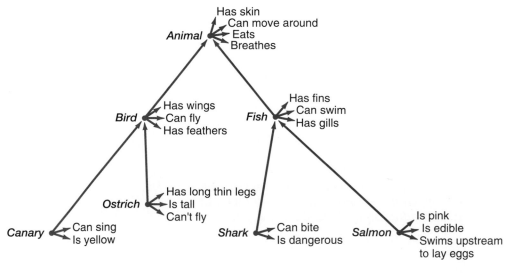

FIGURE 14-1 How the hierarchical network model depicts a small sample of knowledge. (Adapted from Collins & Quillian, 1969.)

A second important assumption is that the properties of a concept are stored in memory at the highest possible level of the hierarchy. For example, the attribute *has skin* is stored at the level of *animal* rather than *bird,* because that property applies both to birds and to other animals. This rule reflects the belief that semantic knowledge is organized in an efficient fashion; if *has skin* were stored at the level of *bird,* it would also have to be stored at the level of *fish.*

How is knowledge used? According to this model, a person unconsciously searches the network systematically, using the pointers to move from one unit to another. Through this process the person is able to determine attributes of various concepts as well as the relationships among concepts. But such processing takes time; indeed, a search that requires the person to traverse a greater number of pathways through the network should take longer than one that involves fewer pathways. Thus, reaction time—the time required for a person to determine the attributes of a concept or the relationships between concepts—should reveal the complexity of the search.

The following experiment shows how reaction time has been used to support the claims of this model. A subject is asked to verify two sentences: "A canary is a bird" and "A canary is an animal." According to the model, it should take a shorter time to verify the first sentence than to verify the second. The reason is that one must traverse only from the level of *canary* to the next-higher level, *bird,* to verify the first sentence, whereas one must traverse two levels—from *canary* to *bird* to *animal*—to verify the second. The findings confirm this prediction: The reaction time required to make a decision about the first sentence is shorter than the time required to make a decision about the second (Collins & Quillian, 1969). This result suggests that knowledge may indeed be organized hierarchically.

There are, however, a number of problems with the hierarchical network model (Rips, Shoben, & Smith, 1973; Smith, Shoben, & Rips, 1974). For example, as illustrated in Figure 14-2, the model predicts that it should take longer to verify "A bear is an animal" than to verify "A bear is a mammal," because *bear* is closer to *mammal* in the network than it is to *animal.* Results of reaction-time studies do not support this prediction.

A second and related problem is that some reaction times that should be the same according to the model are actually different. For example, subjects verify "A robin is a bird" more quickly than "An ostrich is a bird" even though there is no difference between these sentences in terms of the number of levels that must be traversed (McCloskey & Glucksberg, 1979).

The Feature Comparison Model

The **feature comparison model** takes an entirely different approach (Smith, 1978; Smith, Shoben, & Rips, 1974). Whereas the hierarchical network model claims that knowledge structures are stored in memory, the feature comparison model claims that knowledge is computed or *derived* as needed on the basis of certain rules or conditions. What is stored in memory is a list of features.

The model claims that concepts may possess two kinds of features. On the one hand are defining features, the properties that are essential to the definition of the concept. The defining features of *bird,* for instance, might include *feathers, living,* and *two-legged.* On the other hand are characteristic features, which are not essential. The characteristic features of *bird* might include *sings, is chased by cats, sits in trees,* and so forth.

According to the model, we verify propositions not by searching along pathways that tie knowledge units together but by comparing lists of features. For instance, to verify the statement "A robin is a bird," a person might compare the features for *bird* with those for *robin.* Sufficient overlap between the lists leads to the conclusion that the statement is true. Insufficient overlap—as would be the case for a statement like "A robin is a mammal"—leads to the conclusion that the statement is false. An intermediate amount of overlap requires an additional stage of processing in which

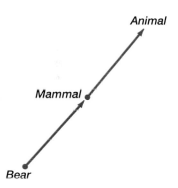

FIGURE 14-2 According to the hierarchical network model, it should take longer to identify a bear as an animal (two steps) than as a mammal (one step). Results of reaction time studies, however, contradict this prediction.

only the defining features of the two concepts are compared. Thus, the feature comparison model can involve two stages: First, a comparison of all features, and second (if necessary), an analysis of the defining features.

The feature comparison model is consistent with many of the results of reaction-time studies that seemed to contradict the hierarchical network model. For example, the feature comparison model predicts that we *should* take longer to identify ostriches as birds than to identify robins as birds because the characteristic features of robins overlap more extensively with the characteristic features of birds. Both robins and ostriches have feathers and two legs, but, like robins and unlike ostriches, most birds fly and are small. Identifying an ostrich as a bird thus requires us to use the second stage of feature comparison and compare only the defining features of the two concepts.

In an important study that supported this model, subjects were first asked to rate various words in terms of semantic relatedness, that is, by how closely related various examples were to an overall category (Rips, Shoben, & Smith, 1973). For instance, they were asked to indicate how close *robin* or *eagle* is to *bird*. A special statistical procedure was used to locate the terms relative to each other. As shown in Figure 14-3, items that were judged, on average, to be similar were placed close together, whereas items that were not judged to be closely related were located much farther from one another. In other words, in Figure 14-3 physical distance is analogous to semantic relatedness as judged by the subjects.

In the second part of the study, these distances were used to predict reaction time. That is, the researchers presented various sentences of the form "An *x* is a *y*" and measured how quickly they were confirmed or disconfirmed by the subjects. The results showed that semantic relatedness (or distance) was highly related to reaction times. The more closely related two words were, the faster the sentence was confirmed.

An interesting aspect of the feature comparison model is that it is consistent with the way people refer to objects. When we speak "strictly" about something, we use its defining features. When we speak "loosely" about it, we use its characteristic features. Thus, strictly speaking, "A porpoise is a mammal" because it suckles its young, but, loosely speaking, "A porpoise is a fish" because it lives in the water and has finlike appendages. The fact that we make these two kinds of statements, speaking strictly sometimes and loosely at other times, suggests that we are indeed comparing lists of features according to the context in which a concept is used.

The feature comparison model is not without problems, however. For one thing, the distinction between defining features and characteristic features is not very clear. It is often difficult even to specify the defining features of a concept. Indeed, some concepts seem to have no defining features—no single characteristic that unequivocally defines it. Can you think of a defining feature, for example, of the concept *furniture?* Is a rug furniture? A framed picture? A wastebasket?

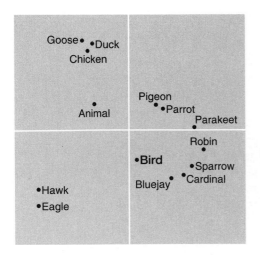
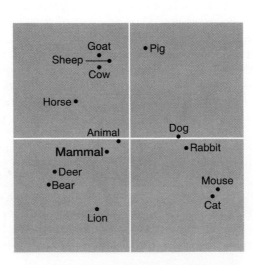

FIGURE 14-3 Schematic diagram of various concepts and their semantic relatedness (represented in terms of physical distance) as depicted by the feature comparison model. (Adapted from Rips, Shoben, & Smith, 1973.)

Another problem is that, as with the hierarchical network model, some research findings are inconsistent with the feature comparison model. Studies have found, for example, that it takes longer to determine that the statement "All collies are birds" is false than to determine that the statement "All collies are terriers" is false (Lorch, 1978). According to the feature comparison model, however, the results should be the other way around—it should take less time to decide that collies are not birds than to decide that collies are not terriers because collies and birds share fewer features than do collies and terriers.

The Spreading Activation Model

In order to overcome the problems encountered in both the hierarchical network and the feature comparison models, some researchers have proposed a different kind of network model called the **spreading activation model** (Collins & Loftus, 1975). According to this model, the relationships between concepts are not hierarchically structured but depend on semantic relatedness. The more two concepts are related semantically, the stronger the connection between them. Furthermore, the strength of the relationship between concepts varies with use. The model thus avoids the need to distinguish between defining and characteristic features.

Figure 14-4 illustrates how a small portion of knowledge may be organized according to the spreading activation model. As in the hierarchical network model, words and concepts are the units of knowledge and they are arranged in a network. And as suggested by the feature comparison model, words may be located near each other as a result of their semantic relatedness. Thus, the concepts *apple* and *banana* are close together because they are semantically related, not because they are part of a logical hierarchy.

Semantic relatedness is determined empirically. For instance, subjects may be asked to rate the degree to which, say, *yellow* and *banana* are related as compared to, say, *yellow* and *daffodil*. The more two concepts are judged to be related in meaning,

FIGURE 14-4 How the spreading activation model depicts a small sample of knowledge. (Adapted from Collins & Loftus, 1975.)

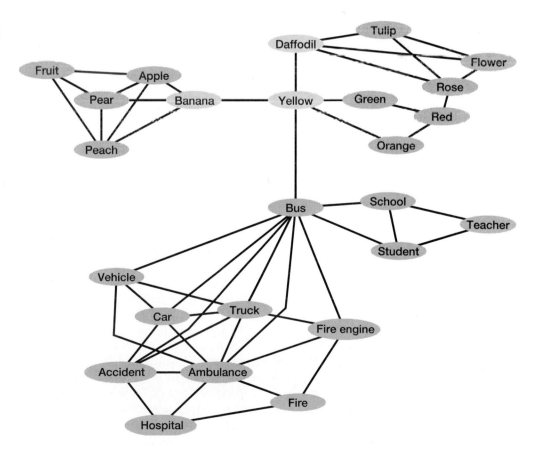

the shorter the distance between them. And the shorter the distance, the more easily the activation of one will trigger the other during a memory search.

A second assumption of this model is that the strength of the link between two concepts varies with use. For example, *robin* is frequently associated with *bird,* whereas *ostrich* is not. Therefore, the link between *robin* and *bird* is stronger than the link between *ostrich* and *bird,* explaining why the reaction time for verifying "A robin is a bird" is shorter than the time for verifying "An ostrich is a bird."

Many findings that are adequately explained by the hierarchical network and feature comparison models are also accounted for by this model. All three models predict, for example, that "A canary is a bird" should be verified more quickly than "A canary is an animal." There are, however, other results that the spreading activation model can explain but the other two models cannot. One of these is the **semantic priming effect,** in which the meaning of words we have just encountered affects our ability to interpret words presented later on (Meyer & Schvaneveldt, 1976; Neely, 1977). In studies of this effect, subjects are asked to indicate as quickly as possible whether a set of letters forms a word or not. The speed and accuracy with which subjects perform this task depends in part on what word is given just prior to the target word. For example, if a subject is given the word *bread* followed shortly afterward by the target word *butter,* the reaction time needed to identify *butter* as a word is much shorter than if the previous word had been, say, *nurse.* It appears that the activation of the unit *bread* spreads to other associated units in the cluster such as *butter,* thus making it more likely that this second unit will become activated when the subject receives the appropriate cue. Activating the unit *nurse,* however, does not spread through the cluster of units containing *butter* because the two concepts are farther apart in the model; that is, they are less semantically related. The spreading activation model explains this result because it claims that activation can spread from one concept to another by virtue of semantic relatedness rather than simply moving from one unit to the next along a given search pathway.

Schemata

Rather than being stored as individual units or concepts within a network, knowledge may be stored in a much larger structure called a **schema.** (The plural form is **schemata.**) Whereas a concept can be viewed as a single unit of information, a schema may be described as an interconnected set of propositions or elements; a schema is a more holistic segment of knowledge.

A schema operates to create expectancies. When information enters the system, a schema may be activated. The person then interprets the incoming information in terms of the schema, perhaps filling in missing information. Later the person reconstructs the meaning of the information partly by using the schema (Thorndyke, 1984).

The experiment in which the idea of schemata was first developed was rather simple (Bartlett, 1932). A subject was asked to read a passage from a native American folk tale entitled "The War of the Ghosts." (See Figure 14-5.) The subject was then instructed to reproduce the story as accurately as possible in writing. This account of the story was passed to a second person, who read it and, in turn, wrote yet another version from memory. This version was given to a third person, who read it and wrote an account of it, and so on through 10 or more subjects. The written accounts were then analyzed to determine what elements of the original story had been retained. (This experiment resembles the game of "telephone," in which a message passed along by a chain of people changes with each retelling.)

The results showed that not only did the story change with each retelling but it changed in a systematic way. Often the details of the original story were eliminated. For example, as shown in Figure 14-5, by the tenth subject the war cries and the noise of the paddles were no longer mentioned, and virtually nothing was written about the battle itself. Sometimes information was exaggerated. For instance, "arrows are in the canoe" became "we have plenty [of arrows] in the canoe." Simi-

Original Version

The War of the Ghosts

One night two young men from Egulac went down to the river to hunt seals, and while they were there it became foggy and calm. Then they heard war-cries, and they thought: "Maybe this is a war-party." They escaped to the shore, and hid behind a log. Now canoes came up, and they heard the noise of paddles, and they saw one canoe coming up to them. There were five men in the canoe, and they said:

"What do you think? We wish to take you along. We are going up the river to make war on the people."

One of the young men said, "I have no arrows."

"Arrows are in the canoe," they said.

"I will not go along. I might be killed. My relatives do not know where I have gone. But you," he said, turning to the other, "may go with them."

So one of the young men went, but the other returned home.

And the warriors went on up the river to a town on the other side of Kalama. The people came down to the water, and they began to fight, and many were killed. But presently the young man heard one of the warriors say: "Quick, let us go home: that Indian has been hit." Now he thought: "Oh, they are ghosts." He did not feel sick, but they said he had been shot.

So the canoes went back to Egulac, and the young man went ashore to his house, and made a fire. And he told everybody and said: "Behold I accompanied the ghosts, and we went to fight. Many of our fellows were killed, and many of those who attacked us were killed. They said I was hit, and I did not feel sick."

He told it all, and then he became quiet. When the sun rose he fell down. Something black came out of his mouth. His face became contorted. The people jumped up and cried.

He was dead.

Version Reproduced by the Tenth Subject

The War of the Ghosts

Two Indians were out fishing for seals in the Bay of Manpapan, when along came five other Indians in a war-canoe. They were going fighting.

"Come with us," said the five to the two, "and fight."

"I cannot come," was the answer of the one, "for I have an old mother at home who is dependent upon me." The other said he could not come, because he had no arms. "That is no difficulty," the others replied, "for we have plenty in the canoe with us"; so he got into the canoe and went with them.

In a fight soon afterwards this Indian received a mortal wound. Finding that his hour was coming, he cried out that he was about to die. "Nonsense," said one of the others, "you will not die." But he did.

FIGURE 14-5   The original version of the "War of the Ghosts" story and the version that was produced by the tenth subject. (Adapted from Bartlett, 1932.)

larly, "they said he had been shot" became "this Indian received a mortal wound." Most significant, however, was that memory for the passage became more compact and more consistent with the readers' expectations. Specifically, details were changed so that the story would fit more easily with the subjects' own experiences. For example, by the tenth subject the story reflected what is often believed in our society, namely that older individuals are dependent on younger family members ("an old mother at home . . . is dependent on me") rather than what was said in the original story ("my relatives do not know where I have gone"). According to the researcher, the story was not recalled accurately because in reconstructing the version they read subjects made the story fit with their existing schemata.

In other experiments that have provided evidence for the existence of schemata, subjects are presented with a passage and are later asked whether certain words or sentences were included in the passage. Subjects invariably recognize a sentence as new when its essential meaning is different from that of the information presented earlier. They often do not recognize a new sentence, however, if the meaning of that sentence is the same as presented earlier. This supports the idea that we assimilate new information into an existing schema and then judge the information in terms of whether it fits the schema or not. Sentences that have a different meaning from information presented earlier do not fit with the schema, so they are easily recognized as new; sentences that have the same meaning are consistent with the schema and are therefore judged to have been part of the information presented earlier (Bransford & Franks, 1971; Sachs, 1967).

Other approaches have also been used to study schemata. In one interesting experiment, two passages were read to college students who were majoring in physical education and music (Anderson, Reynolds, Schallert, & Goetz, 1977; see also Dooling & Christiaansen, 1977). As shown in Figure 14-6, the passages were ambiguous. Previous research had shown that passage 1 is usually interpreted as a description of a night of card playing. It also could be interpreted, however, as a description of a rehearsal of a musical ensemble. Similarly, previous research indicated that passage 2 is usually interpreted as a description of a prison break. Alternatively, however, it

FIGURE 14-6 Two passages of prose, and the subsequent questions asked about them, used in a study of schemata. Subjects' answers depended on their schemata as indicated by their majors. Music majors tended to interpret the first passage as representing a music rehearsal and physical education majors tended to interpret the second passage as describing a wrestling match. (Adapted from Anderson, Reynolds, Schallert, & Goetz, 1977.)

Passage 1

Every Saturday night, four good friends get together. When Jerry, Mike, and Pat arrived, Karen was sitting in her living room writing some notes. She quickly gathered the cards and stood up to greet her friends at the door. They followed her into the living room but as usual they couldn't agree on exactly what to play. Jerry eventually took a stand and set things up. Finally, they began to play. Karen's recorder filled the room with soft and pleasant music. Early in the evening, Mike noticed Pat's hand and the many diamonds. As the night progressed the tempo of play increased. Finally, a lull in the activities occurred. Taking advantage of this, Jerry pondered the arrangement in front of him. Mike interrupted Jerry's reverie and said, "Let's hear the score." They listened carefully and commented on their performance. When the comments were all heard, exhausted but happy, Karen's friends went home.

Passage 2

Rocky slowly got up from the mat, planning his escape. He hesitated a moment and thought. Things were not going well. What bothered him most was being held, especially since the charge against him had been weak. He considered his present situation. The lock that held him was strong but he thought he could break it. He knew, however, that his timing would have to be perfect. Rocky was aware that it was because of his early roughness that he had been penalized so severely—much too severely from his point of view. The situation was becoming frustrating: the pressure had been grinding on him for too long. He was being ridden unmercifully. Rocky was getting angry now. He felt he was ready to make his move. He knew that his success or failure would depend on what he did in the next few seconds.

Sample Questions

Card/Music Passage
What did the four people comment on?
A. The odds of having so many high cards.
B. The sound of their music.
C. The high cost of musical instruments.
D. How well they were playing cards.

Prison/Wrestling Passage
How had Rocky been punished for his aggressiveness?
A. He had been demoted to the "B" team.
B. His opponent had been given points.
C. He lost his privileges for the weekend.
D. He had been arrested and imprisoned.

could be interpreted as a description of a wrestling match. After the passages had been read, the subjects' memory was tested with 10 multiple-choice questions. Two of the answers for each question were correct, one for each possible interpretation. Memory was assessed in terms of the percentage of answers that were correct according to the alternative interpretation (music rehearsal in the first case and wrestling match in the second). For example, a correct answer to the first question shown in Figure 14-6 would be "b" (the people commented on the sound of their music, not on how well they were playing cards); a correct answer to the second question shown in Figure 14-6 would also be "b" (Rocky had been punished by having points awarded to his opponents, not by being imprisoned).

The results showed that the music majors performed better than the physical education majors on the first passage (71% versus 29% correct) because they interpreted the passage in terms of an existing schema, namely, a musical event. In other words, their memory for the information in the passage was better because they could easily assimilate the information into their existing music schemata. For the second passage, the physical education majors performed better than the music majors (64% versus 28% correct), indicating that they interpreted the information in terms of their schemata of a sporting event. Overall, then, the experiment shows that individuals may have different schemata, which influence comprehension and memory by providing knowledge structures into which new information is assimilated.

INTERIM SUMMARY

Episodic memory is stored information that is highly linked to the context in which it was formed. It is sometimes referred to as autobiographical memory. Unusually vivid episodic memories are often called flashbulb memories. Most cognitive psychologists no longer believe that episodic memory is distinct from semantic memory. Various theories have been proposed to describe how semantic memory is structured. According to the hierarchical network model, concepts are interconnected hierarchically; more general concepts are located higher in the network than less inclusive concepts. To verify a proposition, a person systematically searches the pathway from one concept to another. According to the feature comparison model, concepts possess both defining (essential) and characteristic (nonessential) features; verifying a proposition involves comparing lists of features stored in memory. Research findings are not fully consistent with either of these models. A third model, the spreading activation model, overcomes some of the problems of the other two. According to this model, the relationships among concepts are not fixed but depend on semantic relatedness; more closely related concepts are likely to activate each other, whereas more distantly related concepts are not. This model can be used to explain the semantic priming effect, in which the ability to identify a target word is improved if a person is "primed" with a semantically related word. All of these models apply to individual units of knowledge. Larger segments of knowledge called schemata may also exist in memory. Schemata provide knowledge structures into which new information is assimilated.

CONCRETE KNOWLEDGE REPRESENTATION

Up to this point we have considered knowledge in terms of events, words, and concepts. We can think of such knowledge as being abstract in that the encoded form of the knowledge, the units or concept names, bear no resemblance to the objects in the real world to which they refer. There is nothing special about the letters *ROBIN,* for example; they merely form an arbitrary or abstract set of letters that, as a whole, refers to a particular object in the real world that we recognize as a robin. There is, however, a different way in which knowledge can be encoded—as imagery.

IMAGERY

Imagery is perceptually encoded knowledge. It does not represent information as arbitrary, abstract events, words, or statements. Instead, it represents knowledge in a continuous form, much as a visual or auditory image appears in perception. There is an essential correspondence between the encoded knowledge and the object to which that knowledge refers. For example, an encoded image of a building corresponds spatially to the building itself; the memory is not simply an abstract name.

There is considerable support for the notion that knowledge can be stored perceptually. For example, long-term memory for pictures is vastly superior to memory for words (Shepard, 1967). When subjects are asked to memorize a series of pictures and then are tested on their ability to distinguish those pictures from others that are similar, their memory for the original pictures is extremely accurate. The pictures themselves, not simply verbal statements about them, must have been stored in memory. Had words or concepts been the basis for identifying the pictures, then subjects would not have been able to differentiate the test pictures from the new images that were very similar because each would have involved an identical description.

Mental Rotation

The research on image rotation discussed in Chapter 13 lends additional support for the existence of imagery in memory. Recall that in one experiment subjects were asked whether the orientation of two letters was the same or whether one letter was the mirror image of the other (Shepard, 1978). The more the second letter was rotated away from the position of the first, the longer it took subjects to make a match. This implies that to perform the task subjects actually visualized the stimulus and then rotated it in their minds.

Image Space

The existence of imagery is also supported by research on the so-called image space (Kosslyn, 1980). For example, in one study subjects were asked to imagine two animals standing side by side—a rabbit next to an elephant, or a rabbit next to a fly (Kosslyn, 1975). (See Figure 14-7.) Once the subjects had done so, they were asked various questions, such as "Does the rabbit have ears?" If the knowledge "rabbit has ears" was stored in the form of a proposition (that is, as a statement about rabbits), the speed in deriving an answer would not be affected by whether they had visualized the rabbit with an elephant or with a fly; the knowledge should be retrieved equally quickly in either case. If, however, the subjects were actually scanning a mental image to verify that "rabbit has ears," it should take longer to find the ears on a very small image (as would be the case for a rabbit next to an elephant) than on a large and easily visible one (as would be the case for a rabbit next to a fly). The subjects' reaction times suggest that they were indeed scanning an image; they took on average about 211 milliseconds longer to answer the question "Does the rabbit have ears?" when the rabbit had been visualized next to an elephant than when it had been visualized next to a fly.

IMAGERY AND PERCEPTION

Many researchers believe that a recalled or constructed mental image is similar to the perception of a real object. The evidence for such a belief is that subjects answer questions about their imagery as quickly as they answer questions about perceptions.

FIGURE 14-7 The effect on the size of a rabbit of imagining it next to an elephant as opposed to imagining it next to a fly. (Adapted from Kosslyn, 1975.)

In one study, for example, subjects either were shown the outlines of 15 U.S. states or were simply given the names of those states (Shepard & Chipman, 1970). Then all the subjects were asked to rate pairs of states in terms of similarity in shape. Subjects who merely imagined the shapes performed as efficiently as those who actually saw the outlines of the states.

A related finding is that perceptual illusions are experienced in imagery in much the same way as they are experienced visually (Finke, 1980). In one study, subjects were asked to examine the geometric patterns shown in Figure 14-8*a* and *b* (Wallace, 1984). Then they were shown two parallel lines (Figure 14-8*c*) and asked to visualize the geometric patterns (*a* and *b*) superimposed on top of them. Actual images combining these elements, as shown in Figures 14-8*d* and *e,* create the illusion that the parallel lines are bending. While *imagining* this configuration (patterns superimposed on top of the parallel lines), the subjects were asked whether they saw the illusion and, if so, to say by how many millimeters the parallel lines were bent inward or outward. Not only did the subjects report seeing the illusion in their minds, the amount they estimated that the lines were bent was nearly the same as that estimated by subjects looking at the actual images. Note, however, that these results were obtained only with subjects who had claimed they could easily create an image of the patterns in their minds.

FIGURE 14-8 Two perceptual illusions (*d* and *e*) created by a pattern of diagonal lines (*a* and *b*) superimposed over two horizontal parallel lines (*c*). After examining (*a*) and (*b*), subjects were asked to visualize them superimposed on (*c*). (Adapted from Finke, 1980.)

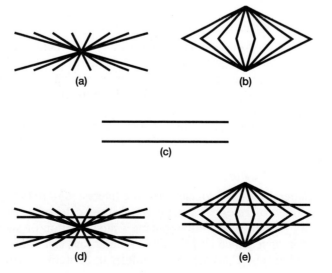

Information stored as imagery is often contrasted with general abstract knowledge. Studies on mental rotation and image space suggest that we tend to scan a picture in our minds in order to use this form of knowledge, which is stored as an image rather than as an event, word, or concept. Some research has suggested that mental images are similar to perceptions of real objects.

CATEGORIZATION

So far we have discussed how knowledge may be represented in the mind, either semantically or spatially, and how it may be structured or organized. This section focuses on the units of knowledge themselves, that is, on the categories of knowledge that are believed to be linked together in a larger knowledge structure.

Think about how we tend to label the things around us. Without exception, we place objects in categories; we create groups of objects that somehow belong together, that define a conceptual class or a collection of similar things. Human knowledge thus involves the arrangement of objects into categories or conceptual classes on the basis of their perceptual or functional properties. **Categorization,** therefore, includes both generalizing from one instance to another and discriminating among different categories (see Anderson, 1991).

Categories are part of the organization of knowledge; they enhance our ability to deal effectively with the myriad stimuli in our environment. It is easy to understand why humans developed the ability to categorize objects. From an evolutionary perspective, imagine the problems that would arise if we did not do so. If each separate sensory experience resulted in a unique mental representation, we would be too overwhelmed to react effectively. If all the objects in our environment were grouped into too few categories, we would not be able to make the distinctions that allow us to cope. For example, if we grouped predators and friends together and therefore viewed them as essentially similar, we would soon perish from our ignorance; that is, by not differentiating between friends and enemies, we would be unable to ensure our survival.

TYPES OF CATEGORIES

Enumeration or Rule Categories

Some categories are designated simply by counting; that is, the members of the category belong together by virtue of being on a particular list. An example of such a category is the category of single-digit numbers (0 through 9).

Categories may also be defined in terms of arbitrary rules, such as the category of "all metallic things weighing over 5 pounds." Presumably one could unambiguously identify members of this category: A half-dollar coin and a wooden desk would not qualify as members, but a 25-pound metal wheelbarrow would.

Natural Categories

Generally, psychologists are more interested in **natural categories** than in categories defined by rules or by counting. Natural categories are used in everyday life to classify stimuli in the environment. Categorization of such stimuli is based largely on their appearance or perceptual similarities, but it may also be based on functional similarities. Consider, for example, three items: a pencil, a quill pen, and an elec-

FIGURE 14-9 Examples of images used to study categorization as a function of both perceptual appearance and functional characteristics. (Adapted from Labov, 1973.)

tronic typewriter. The first two look similar and therefore may be placed in the same category on the basis of their appearance. The third object, although it is decidedly different in appearance, belongs to the same functional category—writing instrument—as the other two.

Categories can combine perceptual and functional characteristics. This was demonstrated in an experiment in which subjects were asked to name pictures (Labov, 1973). Although all the pictured objects were containers with handles, the size of the container's mouth varied. Some looked clearly like conventional coffee cups, whereas others, with wide mouths, looked more like bowls (see Figure 14-9). Before being shown a picture, the subjects were asked to imagine a container being used for a particular purpose—for example, filled with coffee or with mashed potatoes. These instructions were designed to encourage the subjects to think of the pictures they were then shown in terms of a particular function. A container with coffee is likely to function as a cup; a container with mashed potatoes is likely to function as a bowl. The results showed that as the image more closely resembled a bowl because of the increasing width of the mouth, the tendency to call it a cup decreased. In addition, however, a picture was more likely to be called a bowl when the subjects were told that its function was to hold mashed potatoes. Thus, both the appearance and the function of the object determined the category to which it was assigned.

THE STRUCTURE OF CATEGORIES

One would think that categories are defined unambiguously. After all, how else could one determine whether an object is a member of a particular category? Research has shown, however, that categories or conceptual classes often have imprecise definitions. The boundaries of a conceptual class—that is, the conditions that define whether an item is included within a category—may be fuzzy and inexact.

Fuzzy Concepts

When humans say that a stimulus belongs in a certain category or conceptual class, they compare it to items that are already part of the category and determine its

An ambiguous object. Does it belong to the category "car" or the category "boat"?

361

"goodness-of-fit," that is, its degree of similarity to those items. But, as noted earlier, there may be no definitive criteria for judging the goodness-of-fit (Rosch, 1973). In one study, for example, subjects were given a number of stimuli and asked to rate them on a scale of 1 to 7 according to how well they represented one of two categories: fruit and furniture (Rosch, 1975). A rating of 1 meant that the object was "highly typical" of the category, whereas a rating of 7 meant that it was "least typical." Numbers in between provided intermediate ratings of typicality. As Table 14-1 shows, not all the objects were rated equally, that is, not all of the items were considered good examples of either category—furniture or fruit. For example, subjects agreed that a chair and a sofa are "highly typical" examples of furniture (average rating of 1.04), but they did not consider a stove or a sewing machine to be good examples of that category (mean rating of about 5.4). Other items were given an intermediate rating. Similarly, subjects rated an orange and an apple as good examples of fruit, but they did not view a tomato or an avocado as good examples. Given results like these, how can we ever know whether any given item is in fact a member of a particular category?

TABLE 14-1 Examples of Fruit and Furniture, Showing Mean Typicality Score. (Subjects were asked to rate how typical each example was of the category.)

Member	Mean typicality score	Member	Mean typicality score
		Furniture	
Chair	1.04	Chaise longue	2.26
Sofa	1.04	Lamp	2.94
Couch	1.10	Stool	3.13
Easy chair	1.33	Piano	3.64
Dresser	1.37	Cushion	3.70
Coffee table	1.38	Cupboard	4.27
Rocker	1.42	Stereo	4.32
Chest of drawers	1.48	Mirror	4.39
Desk	1.54	Television	4.41
Bed	1.58	Bar	4.46
Davenport	1.61	Wastebasket	5.34
End table	1.61	Radio	5.37
Bookcase	2.15	Sewing machine	5.39
Lounge	2.17	Stove	5.40
		Fruit	
Orange	1.07	Lemon	2.16
Apple	1.08	Watermelon	2.39
Banana	1.15	Cantaloupe	2.44
Peach	1.17	Lime	2.45
Apricot	1.36	Papaya	2.58
Tangerine	1.36	Fig	2.86
Plum	1.37	Mango	2.88
Grapes	1.38	Pomegranate	3.05
Strawberry	1.61	Date	3.35
Grapefruit	1.77	Raisin	3.42
Cherry	1.86	Persimmon	3.63
Pineapple	1.19	Coconut	4.50
Blackberry	2.05	Avocado	5.37
Raspberry	2.15	Tomato	5.58

Note: 1 means highly typical. 7 means least typical.
SOURCE: Adapted from Rosch, 1975.

FIGURE 14-10 Diagram of cards used to study prototypes. The bottom examples show variations of the prototype. (Adapted from Franks & Bransford, 1971.)

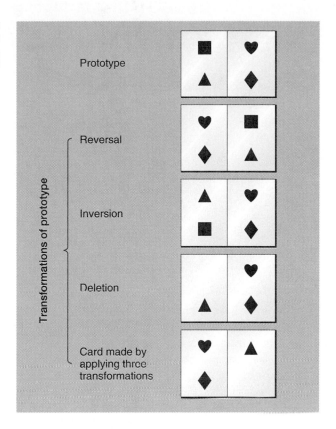

Prototypes

One possible answer is to say that we define categories not by their boundaries but by their most characteristic (or average) members, or **prototypes.** According to this point of view, we base our decision on whether or not an item belongs in a category or conceptual class on the degree to which it resembles the prototype for that category. Items that resemble the prototype are unambiguous members of the category; those that do not resemble the prototype may or may not be members of the category.

Many experiments have supported this idea. In one study, subjects were shown examples of a category—cards on which diamonds, triangles, squares, and hearts were printed (Franks & Bransford, 1971). These are shown in Figure 14-10. On the prototype card these symbols were arranged in a particular position and orientation. Subjects were never shown the prototype itself but they did study cards that resembled the prototype. On some of the cards, the symbols were changed in only one way (for example, reversed or inverted or deleted); on others, they were changed in two or more ways.

After they had studied the cards, the subjects were shown new test cards and were asked to say whether they were members of the category and to rate (on a scale of 1 to 5) how confident they were of their judgment. The new cards included transformations of the prototype, as well as the prototype itself. As shown on page 364 in Figure 14-11, subjects were most confident about the prototype even though they had never seen it before. In fact, as the test cards became progressively different from the prototype, the subjects became less confident that they were members of the category. Because the subjects had originally studied cards that were *like* the prototype, they had inferred what the prototype must be like. In other words, the subjects were confident in identifying the prototype as a category member because in their minds the category itself was represented by the prototype (Fried & Holyoak, 1984). Analogous results have been obtained using musical melodies (Welker, 1982).

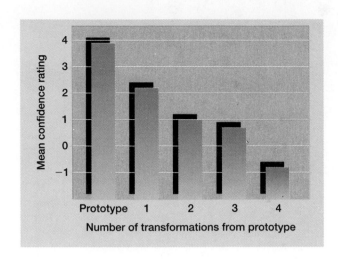

FIGURE 14-11 Mean confidence rating as a function of whether the card was a prototype or one of various transformations. (Adapted from Franks & Bransford, 1971.)

Family Resemblance

Psychologists have attempted to quantify the concept of a prototype in terms of **family resemblance** (Rosch, 1975; 1978). Just as a child may resemble a parent or other relative in certain ways but not in others, a member of a category may belong to the category by virtue of sharing some of the features of that category but not all. This was demonstrated in an experiment in which subjects were given six items (all common nouns), one for each of six categories, and asked to list all the attributes they could think of for each item in 90 seconds (Rosch & Mervis, 1975). The categories were furniture, vehicles, fruit, weapons, vegetables, and clothing. One subject might be asked to list the attributes of "chair," "bicycle," "apple," "bomb," "spinach," and "coat." Another might be asked to list the attributes of "piano," "train," "pear," "knife," "carrots," and "pajamas." In all, 20 items for each category were used, although any one subject was given only one item for each category.

A second group of subjects was given the same items but their task was to rate each item on a scale of 1 to 7 according to how good an example they judged it to be of the category to which it belonged. A rating of 1 meant the subject judged the item

Some of the members of this assortment are more likely to be considered prototypical fruit—for example, apples—than others—for example, persimmons.

to be a good example of the category; a rating of 7 meant the subject judged the item to fit poorly in the category; ratings between 1 and 7 were intermediate fits. The researchers were interested in the extent to which the attributes for any given item in a category overlapped (how many of the attributes listed for "bicycle," for example, were also listed for "train" and the other vehicle category items). They also wanted to know whether the amount of overlap between items had any relationship to ratings for those items given by the second group. They found that the examples of a category did not all have the same attributes but that many shared at least some attributes, and that those judged more typical of the category by the second group shared more attributes than those judged less typical. For example, the five furniture items judged by the second group to be most typical of the concept furniture were claimed by the first group to share 13 attributes; the five least typical items shared only 2. Similarly, the five clothing items that were judged to be most typical of the clothing category (according to the second group of subjects) shared 21 attributes (according to the first group of subjects). To be a "good" member of a category, therefore, an object needed to share more of the attributes of the category with other members.

Basic-Level Categories

Categories differ in terms of how inclusive they are. For example, "motorized vehicles" is a highly inclusive, superordinate category that contains many examples (for example, automobiles, diesel tugboats, tractor mowers). "Pink Cadillacs," on the other hand, is a highly restrictive, subordinate category that contains very few examples. "Automobiles" is a category at an intermediate level of inclusiveness. We are evidently capable of forming, understanding, and using categories at all three levels. Is there, however, a level of category that is somehow more natural to us—a level at which we store most of our knowledge and that we tend to use when naming things?

Some researchers believe that humans tend to group information into **basic-level categories.** As used here, the term *basic* means "average" rather than "irreducible" (Murphy & Smith, 1982). A basic level category is an intermediate level of classification; it is neither too specific nor overly large and inclusive. In fact, the basic level is the most inclusive level at which there is still significant differentiation among members of the category. For example, people tend to refer to an object with four legs and a flat horizontal surface as a table, not as a piece of furniture, because the word *table* provides a clear description of the basic features, whereas the word *furniture* does not; *furniture* is too inclusive. Classification of knowledge on a basic level therefore provides just the right amount of differentiation among objects. This makes sense. If we tended to categorize on a more specific level, we would have to deal with too much differentiation. For example, always having to say "card table" or "end table" or "drafting table" is needlessly detailed. On the other hand, if we tended to categorize on a more superordinate level we would be unable to distinguish effectively among objects. For instance, referring both to a table and chair as "furniture" would fail to differentiate between them.

Research findings support the idea that people form basic-level categories (Rosch, 1978). In one study, subjects wrote down attributes of examples at each level of a category (Rosch, Mervis, Gray, Johnson, & Boyes-Braem, 1976). For example, they listed attributes of "furniture" (superordinate category), "table" (basic-level category), and "kitchen table" (subordinate category). Two results were of particular interest. First, very few attributes were given for the most inclusive (superordinate) category. (After all, how would one describe something as vague and inclusive as "furniture"?) Many more attributes were listed for the basic and subordinate categories, suggesting that information is stored on a basic or subordinate level. Second, the attributes listed for the basic level category did not differ significantly from those listed for the subordinate category. This finding suggests that sufficient differentiation is achieved by classifying objects at a basic level.

Categories may be thought of as the units of knowledge. Sometimes membership in a category is defined by counting or arbitrary rules; natural categories, however, are defined largely on the basis of appearance or function. Often the boundaries of a category are fuzzy and uncertain. In such cases, we tend to place items in categories based on how closely the items resemble a prototype or ideal. Items categorized in this way are said to bear a family resemblance to the prototype. Research findings suggest that people tend to categorize information into basic-level categories, that is, the most inclusive level at which there is still significant differentiation among members of the category.

MEMORY RETRIEVAL

In Chapter 13 we considered many of the factors, such as attention and rehearsal, that affect the formation of memory. In this chapter, our focus has been on the overall structure of knowledge, for example, the extent to which knowledge may be organized in various networks. Our final topic deals with memory retrieval and problems associated with it. Why do we forget? How can we better remember information?

FORGETTING

Decay and Interference Theories

The earliest theories of forgetting suggested that memories faded or decayed gradually during storage. According to this **memory decay theory,** a memory was analogous to a footprint in sand: Just as wind and rain eventually wash away a footprint, so too does the passage of time gradually erase a memory. Although forgetting is indeed related to the length of the retention interval in many situations (the longer the interval, the more forgetting), simple decay of memory appears not to be a very important factor (Baddeley & Hitch, 1977).

Many psychologists favored instead the **interference theory of memory.** According to this theory, forgetting occurs because information that is unrelated to the desired information interferes with its encoding, storage, and retrieval. Thus, what seems to be missing information is really a deficiency in retrieval brought about by a competition between memories. For example, imagine learning a list of nonsense syllables (like XQM, PWK, etc.) and later being asked to recall them. Normally this task would be relatively easy, depending, of course, on how many syllables there were, the length of the retention interval, and so forth. Now imagine learning a second list of syllables after learning the first and then being asked to recall the first. Your performance would almost certainly be impaired by interference from the second list, especially if the two lists contained syllables that were very similar. The implication of the interference theory is that we forget information in our everyday lives because of interference from unrelated memories.

Forgetting in the Real World

One of the problems with the interference theory, however, is that it is more difficult to show interference effects in the real world than it is in the laboratory. We may observe impaired recall of highly artificial laboratory stimuli, such as lists of nonsense syllables, as a result of interference, but we get quite different results when we use real-life stimuli such as written prose. In fact, as discussed in this chapter as well as in Chapter 13, though people may forget details of a passage of prose they usually do not forget its overall meaning.

One of the studies showing lasting memory for meaning was discussed in Chapter 13 (Sachs, 1967; see Figure 13-12). Subjects read a passage of prose and later were asked to say whether a particular sentence had been contained in the passage. When the test sentence had the same meaning as one in the original passage (when it differed only in form), subjects claimed it had been included in the passage. When the test sentence differed in meaning, however, subjects recognized it as being a different sentence altogether. Findings like this imply that our memory of everyday information is based more on its meaning than on specific details. It is thus not subject to the kind of interference effects seen with artificial laboratory stimuli, like nonsense syllables, that have no meaning.

Can interference affect our memory for meaning in the real world? The answer appears to be yes, but the effect is more to distort the memory than to block or eliminate it. In one study that demonstrated this distorting effect, subjects were read a story about a couple, Bob and Margie, who were engaged to be married (Spiro, 1977). In the story, Bob claims that he is strongly opposed to having children, whereas Margie argues that having children is very desirable. About 8 minutes after presenting this story, the experimenter casually told some of the subjects that Bob and Margie were now happily married but told other subjects that the engagement had been broken off. The information in the first statement—that Bob and Margie are happily married—is clearly inconsistent with the tone of the story, whereas the information in the second—that Bob and Margie broke off their engagement—is not. When asked to recall the story either 2 days, 3 weeks, or 6 weeks later, subjects who had been told that Bob and Margie were happily married tended to remember the original dispute about having children as being relatively mild. Some would claim, for example, that "she was only a little upset." Others fabricated details such as "the two people underwent counseling to settle the dispute" or "they agreed on a compromise." In contrast, subjects who had been told that Bob and Margie had broken off their engagement remembered the dispute as being quite severe. Clearly, the statements of the experimenter had in some sense interfered with the subjects' memory of the story. The effect of the interference, however, was not so much to create a loss of recalled detail, but rather to distort the remembered meaning. Subjects apparently *reconstructed* the original story to make it fit with their expectations. This finding is entirely consistent with the research on the effect of schemata on memory, as discussed earlier in the chapter.

Evidence that we reconstruct memories to make them fit existing memory schemata has also been found in research on eyewitness testimony (Loftus, 1979; Yarmey, 1979). In one study, subjects saw a series of slides showing an automobile accident (Loftus & Palmer, 1974) and were then asked questions about it. One group was asked, "How fast were the cars going when they hit each other?" Another group was asked, "How fast were the cars going when they smashed into each other?" This simple difference in wording was associated with a substantial difference in response: The average response of the "hit" group was 34.0 miles per hour, whereas the average response of the "smashed into" group was 40.8 miles per hour. The two groups of subjects also differed in their memories of what they had seen a week later. Specifically, 14% of the "hit" group compared to 32% of the "smashed into" group remembered seeing broken glass in the pictures of the accident. In reality, no broken glass was visible in any of the slides. Subjects thus reconstructed the episode to fit with their existing schemata, and the schemata they used were influenced by the wording of the questions they were asked after viewing the slides. Evidently the schema associated with cars "hitting" each other involves less serious destruction than the one associated with cars "smashing into" each other. The so-called memory for broken glass was thus stronger in the "smashed into" group than the "hit" group.

When does this reconstruction or distortion occur: when the information is first

Eyewitness testimony—as in this case of a traffic accident—is often unreliable because our ability to reconstruct memories is subject to many sources of distortion.

encoded as a memory? when the subject is retrieving the memory? It is difficult to say for sure, but evidence suggests that it may occur at the time of retrieval. In one study subjects read a biographical account of a woman called Carol Harris (Dooling & Christiaansen, 1977). A week later they were asked whether or not they recognized various sentences as having been included in the original passage, such as "She was deaf, dumb, and blind." Some of the subjects were told at this time that the story had really been about Helen Keller, the woman who surmounted all three of those disabilities to become an inspirational educator and writer. These subjects tended to say that the sentence was part of the original story (when in fact it was not) more so than subjects who were not given this information. Apparently, the information provided at the time of retrieval activated a memory schema involving Helen Keller and thus caused a distorted memory for the passage.

IMPROVING MEMORY

As we discussed in Chapter 13, information becomes a more permanent part of memory when it is rehearsed effectively. And according to the levels-of-processing theory, memories that are rehearsed on a semantic (deep) level are more persistent than those rehearsed on a phonetic (shallow) level. Similarly, according to the revised levels-of-processing model, between-item rehearsal is more effective than within-item rehearsal in producing permanent memories. The reason these strategies are so effective is that they allow material to be incorporated into existing knowledge networks or schemata. Certain strategies or devices, however, called **mnemonics,** can improve one's memory for details as well as for meaning. These provide ready-made organizational structures into which new information can be assimilated.

Mnemonics

One of the strategies for improving memory of a list of words is to use them in a story. Assume, for example, that you wished to remember the following list: *airplane, horse, bicycle, toothbrush,* and *lumber.* You might construct a simple story

368

that included each word, such as: "The *airplane* taxied down the runway, just missing the *horse* and the *bicycle,* whose rider was using a *toothbrush* while dragging a piece of *lumber.*" Research has confirmed that using words in meaningful sentences *and* using the sentences to create a coherent story promotes recall. The story must be coherent so that ideas follow in sequence; otherwise the story line itself is forgotten (Belleza, Richards, & Geiselman, 1976). Moreover, the more vivid the story, the more likely one will remember it (and thus the words in it). Thus a sentence like "The *airplane* flew by the head of a *horse* while it rode a *bicycle* and used a *toothbrush* made of *lumber*" might be even more effective at promoting recall than the first sentence.

A second mnemonic is the keyword system. This technique is especially useful for learning vocabulary words for a foreign language (Atkinson, 1975; Presley, Levin, Hall, Miller, & Berry, 1980). The basic idea is to create an image using an English word that rhymes with the to-be-remembered foreign word. Whenever one wishes to recall the foreign word, one simply recalls the image, which then brings to mind the English word that rhymes with the foreign word, and then the foreign word itself. Suppose, for example, you were trying to memorize the French word for "apple," which is *pomme. Pomme* rhymes (approximately) with *palm,* so you might imagine a picture like one of those in Figure 14-12, showing an apple with a human hand (palm up) on top or a large palm with a miniature apple tree growing out of it. When you needed to remember the French word for apple, you could first retrieve the picture and go from there to *palm* and finally to *pomme.*

FIGURE 14-12 Using the keyword system mnemonic. Examples of possible images that relate the idea of an apple to the English word *palm,* which rhymes (approximately) with *pomme,* the French word for apple.

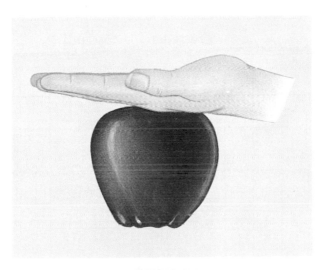

With a third mnemonic, called the peg-word system, information is remembered primarily because it is visualized as part of a well-known (memorized) counting system (Roediger, 1980). To use the system, one must first memorize the following rhyming poem or scheme.

One is a bun
Two is a shoe
Three is a tree
Four is a door
Five is a hive
Six are sticks
Seven is heaven
Eight is a gate
Nine is a line
Ten is a hen

Children's alphabet books rely on the power of imagery for encoding memories concretely.

To use the system one then simply forms an association or image between each successive to-be-remembered item and a successive peg word. For example, assume you wished to remember a list of things you had to do before going to the beach for the day: buy suntan lotion, pack bathing suit, make lunch, lock door, and so forth. You could tie each of these items to a successive peg word. For example, for the first item, buying suntan lotion, you could imagine a cartoon bun with arms, legs, and head dousing itself with suntan lotion. For the second item, the bathing suit, you could think of a large shoe trying to sqeeze into a skimpy bathing suit or modeling a bathing suit in a beauty contest. You would then associate the third item with the

Scholars from the Middle Ages through and beyond the Renaissance in Europe were intensely interested in mnemonics. This woodcut diagram of a mnemonic system dates to the sixteenth century.

370

FIGURE 14-13 Possible images for remembering the word *honor* (*a*) and the word *pail* (*b*). Note that the image for *honor* is a much less concrete representation of its referent than the image for *pail*.

(a)

(b)

third peg word, perhaps picturing a tree with sandwiches and soft drink bottles dangling from its branches or a tree stuffing lunch into its cartoon mouth with its branches. Whatever images you create, recall would involve simply going through the rhyming poem sequentially, thinking of the image or association, and then recalling the exact item. This system works well because the existing network of knowledge, the rhyming poem, is strongly fixed in memory; new information can easily be associated with it.

One of the things that ties all of these mnemonics together is their use of imagery. Imagery allows us to code our memories concretely and to relate things to each other. The more concrete an item is, the easier it is to visualize it. Although it is possible to think of an image for an abstract concept such as *honor*—one could imagine, for example, a person proudly wearing a medal or ribbon (Figure 14-13*a*)—it is obviously easier to do so for a term like *pail,* which has a concrete referent (Figure 14-13*b*). Remembering the word *pail* from the image of a pail is far more likely than remembering the word *honor* from an image of a person wearing a medal. The more concrete you can make an image, therefore, the better the recall.

Images also allow us to tie bits of information together, an interaction that aids retention. For example, assume that you wished to remember that it was Queen Elizabeth I of England who gave orders that eventually led to the defeat of the Spanish armada. You might imagine dozens of toy ships being manipulated on marionette strings by the queen, or a large medieval warship with Queen Elizabeth shouting through a megaphone from the bow. It is the interaction of the two images, even more than the unusual or exceptionally vivid nature of the image, that makes this scene so memorable (Einstein, MacDaniel, & Lackey, 1989).

INTERIM SUMMARY

Research fails to support the idea that a memory simply fades or decays over time, but does suggest that, at least in laboratory situations using nonsense syllables, interference from unrelated information can affect the encoding, storage, or retrieval of desired information. It is more difficult, however, to show interference effects in the real world than in the laboratory. Research suggests that the effect of interference in real-world settings is to distort the meaning of memories rather than the persistence of the memory. Subjects reconstruct incidents based on existing schemata, which can be affected by information received after the incident. This finding has important implications for the reliability of eyewitness testimony. Memory can be improved by the use of mnemonics, devices that help organize information. Many mnemonic strategies involve vivid and concrete images. Relating items within a single image is an especially helpful memory aid.

SUMMARY

1. A central problem for cognitive psychology is to identify how human knowledge is organized and how we gain access to it.

2. Psychologists have traditionally distinguished *episodic memory* (also often called *autobiographical memory*) from *semantic memory*, although recent research has questioned whether they are actually different. *Flashbulb memories* are unusually vivid episodic memories, usually tied to arousing events.

3. Psychologists have proposed three models for the structure of semantic memory. According to the *hierarchical network model*, concepts are organized hierarchically and are linked to other concepts and to properties or characteristics by pointers. Reaction time experiments are consistent with some predictions of this model but not with others.

4. According to the *feature comparison model*, concepts are stored in memory as lists of features, and we verify a proposition by comparing the lists of features that pertain to the concepts in it. In this process we first compare both defining and characteristic features and then, if necessary, compare only defining features. This model is consistent with some of the reaction-time studies that conflict with the hierarchical network model, but inconsistent with others.

5. According to the *spreading activation model*, the relationships between concepts are not hierarchically structured but depend on semantic relatedness. This model is consistent with many of the reaction-time findings that seem to contradict the other models.

6. *Schemata* are interconnected sets of propositions or elements. They are more holistic segments of knowledge than concepts. Their effect is to create expectancies that guide a person's interpretation of incoming information and the later reconstruction of the information. Research, for example, has shown that people change their memories in order to make them fit more easily with their own experiences.

7. *Imagery* is perceptually coded knowledge. It differs from abstract knowledge, which has an arbitrary relationship to the objects to which it refers. Knowledge stored as imagery, in contrast, corresponds to the perception of the objects to which it refers. The existence of this sort of knowledge is supported by research on mental rotation and the image space.

8. *Categorization* is the process of grouping together objects that somehow belong together, that define a conceptual class or a collection of similar things. Although categories can be defined unequivocally by enumeration or arbitrary rules, psychologists are generally more interested in the *natural categories* we use in everyday life to classify stimuli in the environment. Natural categories combine both perceptual and functional characteristics.

9. Natural categories are usually fuzzy, with no clear boundaries, making it difficult to determine unambiguously which examples are members of a particular category and which are not. We may base our judgments of the category to which an example belongs on its resemblance to a *prototype*, an ideal representation of the category. Similarly, a member of a category may belong to the category by virtue of the degree to which it bears a *family resemblance* to other members. In other words, it may share some of the features of the category but not all. Research suggests that humans

form *basic-level categories*—that is, categories that are neither too inclusive nor too exclusive.

10. According to the *memory decay theory,* memories spontaneously fade over time. According to the *interference theory of memory,* forgetting is actually caused by interference from other unrelated information in the memory system. In the real world, people tend to forget details about stored information but not its gist or overall meaning. The effect of interference is thus to distort the meaning of remembered information. This suggests that people tend to reconstruct memories; in the process of doing so, they make the memory conform to existing schemata. This kind of reconstruction process is especially evident in eyewitness testimony.

11. Memory for details may be improved through the use of *mnemonics,* devices that provide ready-made organizational structures into which new information can be assimilated. Effective mnemonic devices include incorporating terms to be memorized into a meaningful story, the keyword system, and the peg-word system. All these systems have in common the use of imagery, which helps us code our memories concretely and to relate things to each other.

FOCUS QUESTIONS

1. Discuss the characteristics of episodic memory and contrast episodic and semantic memory.

2. Identify the models of semantic memory and discuss their basic features.

3. Define schemata and discuss the term in relation to abstract knowledge representation.

4. Discuss the evidence that indicates that knowledge may be represented spatially.

5. Compare and contrast categories defined by enumeration or rules with natural categories.

6. Discuss the evidence that suggests that the boundaries of natural categories are fuzzy.

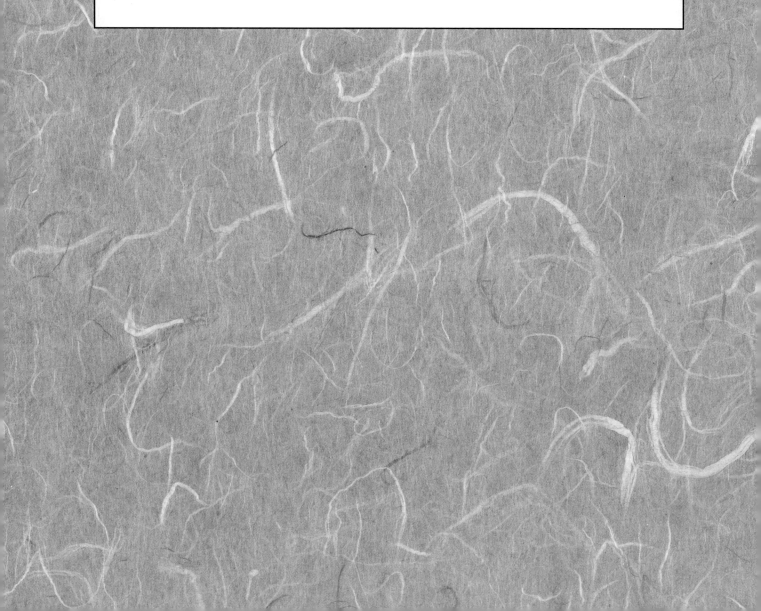

CHAPTER 15

THINKING AND PROBLEM SOLVING

It is often claimed that the ability to think and to reason is what sets humans apart from other animals. It allows us to reconstruct a past that we have never seen, to reflect on our present behavior, and to imagine a future that our descendants will experience but we will not. It enables us to manipulate knowledge, test hypotheses, and make decisions. In contrast to learning, which involves the acquisition of knowledge structures, thinking involves the manipulation of the information contained in those structures (Mayer, 1983).

Some of the earliest recorded discussions of the nature and importance of thinking are found in the writings of the ancient Greek philosophers. Aristotle argued that there are two fundamental forms of thinking. One is contemplation, which entails thinking about what is true—that is, about facts. Contemplation is an assertion of knowledge; it allows the person to state a conclusion. The other basic form of thinking, according to Aristotle, is deliberation, or practical, problem-solving mental activity. When a person deliberates, he or she is making a decision about what to do. Thus, successful deliberation leads to one particular action rather than another.

The two kinds of thinking identified by Aristotle are reflected in the organization of this chapter. First we consider contemplative thinking in the form of reasoning and inference. The second part of the chapter is devoted to problem solving, or deliberative thinking.

The Thinker, Rodin's famous statue.

THINKING

In this section we examine how humans use logical reasoning processes, at least some of the time, to make judgments and arrive at conclusions. We also discuss several kinds of illogical processes that are often used in everyday decision making.

INDUCTIVE REASONING

Inductive reasoning is logical thought in which an examination of particular instances leads to the judgment that a given conclusion is likely to be true. In other words, the inductive reasoning process begins with examples and generates a more global rule. It is important to note that one cannot *know* for sure whether the conclusion based on inductive reasoning is true; however, the instances on which it is based provide good reason to *believe* that it is true.

Consider the following example: It is lunchtime. You are driving through an unfamiliar town and wish to find a particular fast-food restaurant. Although you have no idea of the exact location of the restaurant, you may be able to induce its location based on your experience. For example, in other towns you have seen the same kind of restaurant near convenience stores or in a shopping mall and so you induce that the desired restaurant in this town is likely to be located in similar surroundings. You may, of course, be wrong; the restaurant may, for some unknown reason, be located in a wholly different setting—near farms or undeveloped woodland, for example. But you do not believe this is the case; your inductive reasoning has led you to conclude that the restaurant is likely to be located in the same kinds of surroundings as similar restaurants in other towns. Let us consider the theories that attempt to explain how people make such judgments.

Continuity Theory

According to one of the earliest theories, the **continuity theory,** inductive reasoning involves a gradual and incremental learning process that reflects the principles of association discussed in Chapter 12. The process works this way: Every stimulus has many attributes. A visual stimulus, for example, has attributes of size, shape, and color. We learn to classify stimuli into categories on the basis of these attributes. For example, we say, in effect, that a certain stimulus belongs or does not belong to a certain category because, in the past, we have been told "yes, it does," or "no, it does not." The theory claims that the "yes" responses reinforce the association of the attributes of the stimulus and the category. The attributes that are most consistently reinforced with "yes" come to be associated with the category. Those attributes, in effect, become the defining attributes of the category. To return to our example, you had been reinforced for associating fast-food restaurants and shopping malls (location is an attribute of such restaurants), which enabled you to induce that you would find one in a similar location in the unfamiliar town. In other words, from many encounters with specific examples, you were able to induce a more general rule: Fast-food restaurants are located in shopping malls.

A hypothetical example illustrates this process more fully. Subjects are shown a series of stimuli that have one of two values on three attribute dimensions: size (either small or large), color (either red or green), and shape (either square or round). The researchers tell the subjects that some of these stimuli belong to a category and the others do not. The researchers do not, however, tell them anything about the category itself; that is, they do not say which attributes are positive and which are negative. A subject's task, therefore, is to induce the general rule governing membership in the category—to be able, that is, to say whether or not a given stimulus belongs to the category. The procedure involves showing a subject a stimulus and asking whether or not it belongs to the category. After each guess the researchers tell the subject whether or not the stimulus is indeed a member of the category. According to the theory, the subject sees each stimulus as a collection of attributes. If the subject guesses that a particular stimulus is a member of the category and is then told "yes," then his or her tendency to identify any of the attributes of that particular stimulus with the category is strengthened. Conversely, if the subject is told "no," then his or her tendency to identify any of those attributes with the category is weakened. Ultimately, it is the net effect that counts. That is, after sufficient training, the subject's response to any given attribute depends on whether the positive responses outweigh the negative. For example, if the subject experienced a certain attribute 10 times and was told "yes" on 7 of those occasions and "no" on the other 3, the subject, according to the continuity theory, should associate that attribute with the category.

Figure 15-1 shows a series of trials in our hypothetical study. On trial 1, the researchers identify the stimulus—a large red square—as a member of the category, so "large," "red," and "square" all receive a small increment of strength indicated by the "+" score. The attributes that are not present—"small," "green," and "circle"—receive a "−" score. On trial 2, the stimulus is not a member of the category, so the attributes that are present—"large," "green," and "circle"—receive a "−" score whereas those that are not present—"small," "red," and "square"—receive a "+" score. The cumulative result over all the trials is a gradual, differential buildup of strength for each attribute; that is, the "+" and "−" scores combine to create a net strength score.

After experiencing several trials (for example, six, as in Figure 15-1), the subject is presented with a test stimulus and asked to say whether or not it is a member of the category. The example in Figure 15-1 shows two possible test stimuli—"large green square" and "small red circle." According to the continuity theory, subjects should unconsciously tally the cumulative net strength of each attribute present in

FIGURE 15-1 The procedure in a hypothetical study of induction illustrating the assumptions of the continuity theory. When a stimulus is confirmed as a member of the category ("yes"), its attributes receive an increase in strength (+); when it is said not to be a member of the category ("no"), its attributes decrease in strength (−). After the six test trials a subject would be expected to identify the large green square as a member of the category (because the net strength of its attributes is +4) and to say that a small red circle is not a member (because the net strength of its attributes is −4).

Training Trial	Stimulus		Answer	Direction of incremental changes in attribute strength					
				Size		Color		Shape	
				Small	Large	Red	Green	Square	Circle
1		Large red square	Yes	−	+	+	−	+	−
2		Large green circle	No	+	−	+	−	+	−
3		Small green circle	No	−	+	+	−	+	−
4		Small green square	Yes	+	−	−	+	+	−
5		Large red circle	Yes	−	+	+	−	−	+
6		Small red circle	No	−	+	−	+	+	−
				−2	+2	+2	−2	+4	−4	Cumulative strength

Test Trials		Large green square	Net strength = +4, therefore answer "yes"
		Small red circle	Net strength = −4, therefore answer "no"

the test stimulus and make a decision on that basis. In our example, "large" has a cumulative strength of $+2$ (4 "$+$" scores and 2 "$-$" scores); "green" has a cumulative strength of -2; and "square" has a cumulative strength of $+4$. A "large green square" therefore has a total net score of $+4$ $[(+2) + (-2) + (+4)]$. A "small red circle" has a total net score of -4 ("small" $= -2$, "red" $= +2$, "circle" $= -4$). As a result, a subject presented with a large green square as a test stimulus should infer that it is a member of the category; a subject presented with a small red circle should infer that it is not.

The continuity theory was originally formulated to explain how animals, such as laboratory rats, learn to discriminate among stimuli (Spence, 1936). To discriminate was to induce the rule that defined the stimulus category. At the time the theory was formulated, there was every reason to believe that it would apply to humans as well. Is such a belief justified? Do we, for instance, induce the location of a fast-food restaurant because of such a gradual, continuous buildup of attribute strength?

Noncontinuity Theory

According to the **noncontinuity theory,** the answer is no: The inductive reasoning process is discontinuous; it involves the formation of various hypotheses, which are then confirmed or disconfirmed. In other words, rather than coming to a judgment that a particular stimulus is a member of a category because of the cumulative positive weighting of its attributes, a person forms a hypothesis about the attributes and then tests that hypothesis to confirm or disconfirm it.

Consider once again the hypothetical study and the series of trials illustrated in Figure 15-1. According to the noncontinuity theory, after the first trial the subject might hypothesize that either "red," "large," or "square," or some combination of these attributes, defines the rule for inclusion in the category. Suppose the subject hypothesizes that "large" is the defining attribute. This hypothesis would be disconfirmed on the second trial. Discovering that the hypothesis had been disconfirmed, the subject would presumably now form a new one. But suppose that the subject originally formed a different hypothesis—that "red" is the defining attribute. This hypothesis would appear to be valid until trial 4, at which point it, too, would be disconfirmed. Eventually, of course, a subject will choose the correct hypothesis, which will never be disconfirmed.

In sum, the noncontinuity theory argues that judgments are induced not through a gradual, incremental buildup of strength for a particular cluster of attributes but through the formation and testing of various hypotheses about attributes. When a hypothesis is disconfirmed, the person forms a new one until the correct one is eventually chosen.

Continuity Versus Noncontinuity

Research over the past few decades has tended to support the noncontinuity theory. A number of studies, for example, have tested the predictions of the two theories using so-called shift procedures (Bower & Trabasso, 1963; Kendler & Kendler, 1962; Trabasso & Bower, 1964). Here is how a typical study would be conducted: Assume that the stimuli vary along two attribute dimensions: size of circle (large or small) and color (black or white). There would thus be four possible stimuli—large black circle, small black circle, large white circle, and small white circle. Assume further that the stimuli are presented in pairs and that the subjects are told "yes" during the original learning phase whenever they choose, say, the larger stimulus regardless of color. Most subjects have little trouble learning to do this. At this point, the researchers, of course, have no idea whether the subjects learned to solve the problem because they experienced a gradual strengthening in their tendency to choose "large" (continuity theory) or because they eventually adopted the hypothesis "large is correct" (noncontinuity theory). The researchers, however, can determine which is the case by changing the rules in one of two ways. (See Figure 15-2.)

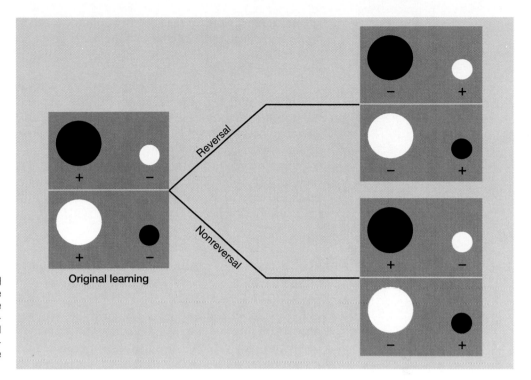

FIGURE 15-2 Examples of stimuli used in shift procedures. In this case, the rule for the original learning phase is "large is correct regardless of color." In a reversal shift, the rule would become "small is correct regardless of color." In a nonreversal shift, the rule would become "black is correct regardless of size."

Original learning

Reversal

Nonreversal

First, they can use a reversal test in which the reinforced attribute becomes the opposite choice in the same dimension. In our example, the subjects would now be reinforced for choosing the small stimulus regardless of color. Second, they can use a nonreversal test (also called an extradimensional shift) in which the reinforced attribute shifts to the previously unimportant dimension. In our example, the subjects would now be reinforced for choosing, say, the black member of the pair regardless of size.

According to the continuity theory, the reversal test should be more difficult than the nonreversal test because it requires a subject gradually to eliminate the positive strength for "large" *before* building up strength for "small." In the nonreversal test, however, the tendency to learn that "black is correct" is no weaker than the tendency to learn that "white is correct." Because neither color has a relative advantage at the beginning of the test, a subject should be able to build up strength for either black or white rather easily.

According to the noncontinuity theory, in contrast, the reversal test should be easier than the nonreversal test because it does not require the subject to attend to a new attribute dimension. If, for example, the subject had hypothesized that "size is the important dimension, and large is the correct attribute," the reversal task would allow the subject to continue to use this hypothesis, merely changing the final choice from large to small. The nonreversal test, on the other hand, would require the subject to form an entirely new hypothesis, namely, that "color, not size, is important." The results of the studies show that the reversal test is indeed easier, thereby supporting the noncontinuity theory.

According to the noncontinuity theory, a subject selects a hypothesis and proceeds to test it. If it is not *dis*confirmed, it is retained; if it proves to be false, a new hypothesis is formed. Thus, the general strategy is "win, stay with hypothesis; lose, shift to a new hypothesis." A number of studies have shown that humans and other animals follow this strategy (Levine, 1975). For example, in one study human subjects were shown a series of stimuli that had one of two attributes on four attribute dimensions: color (black or white), position (left or right), size (large or small), and pattern ("X" or "T") (Levine, 1966). The subjects were told that they could form a hypothesis regarding which one of these eight attributes was correct (combinations of attributes were not considered). Subjects were then given five trials on which they could choose between pairs of stimuli, but they were told whether their choice was correct only on the fifth trial.

The results showed that subjects consistently used the same hypothesis on all five trials. This is not surprising. After all, they were not given any information to the contrary after each of the first four trials, so they had no reason to believe that their initial hypothesis was faulty. If their hypothesis was confirmed on trial 5, they retained it on subsequent trials; if it was disconfirmed on trial 5, they formed a new hypothesis to be tested on subsequent trials. The experiment therefore demonstrated that subjects followed a "win, stay; lose, shift" strategy on such inductive reasoning tasks.

DEDUCTIVE REASONING

The second major kind of logical thought is **deductive reasoning,** which involves reasoning from a general level (or premise) to a specific conclusion (Erickson & Jones, 1978; Evans, 1982).

Let us consider an example similar to the one we discussed previously. Imagine once again that you are in an unfamiliar town and wish to find a particular fast-food restaurant. You could *deduce* its location provided that you know some general facts at the outset. For example, you may know that "the more conveniently a restaurant is located to travelers, the more likely people will eat there." You may also know that "area X is the most densely traveled part of town." From these two general statements (or premises), you could deduce a specific conclusion, that "the sought-after restaurant is likely to be located in area X." In solving this problem, then, you have reasoned from the general to the specific.

Categorical Syllogisms

One formal way to represent deductive reasoning is in a *syllogism.* A syllogism consists of two premises followed by a conclusion, as in this classic example:

All humans are mortal (first premise).
Socrates is human (second premise).
Therefore, Socrates is mortal (conclusion).

Researchers use syllogisms to investigate the deductive reasoning process and thus to develop theories of thinking (see Erickson, 1978; Johnson-Laird, 1983).

In a syllogism truth and validity are two separate issues. The propositions in a syllogism (the statements in the premises and conclusion) are either true or false. "Emily Dickinson was a poet" is a true proposition; "William Shakespeare was a German" is not. The truth of a proposition depends on information external to the syllogism. The conclusion of a syllogism is valid, however, only if it follows logically from the premises, whether or not it is in fact true.

Let us discuss how we can assess the validity of a conclusion based on the logic of the reasoning processes. Two objects can be related in any of four basic ways. A good way to understand these relationships is to visualize them using Euler circles. As shown in Figure 15-3, Euler circles represent a set or collection of objects—say, A's and B's. The extent to which the circles overlap illustrates whether objects contained in A are also contained in B. Parts *a* and *b* of the figure illustrate cases in which all the members of A are included in the collection of B's. Part *c* illustrates the case in which no A's are included in the collection of B's; that is, all the members of A are wholly distinct from the collection of B's. Parts *a, b, d,* and *e* illustrate a third kind of relationship, in which some A's are included in the collection of B's. Note that "some" here means "up to and possibly including all," rather than merely "not all." Thus, if as in parts *a* and *b* all A's are in B, then it is also true that some A's are in B. Parts *d* and *e*, in contrast, illustrate cases in which some but not all A's are included in B. The fourth kind of relationship, in which some A's are not contained

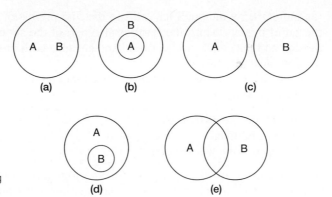

FIGURE 15-3 Euler circles indicating possible relationships between two sets.

in B, is shown in parts *c, d,* and *e.* In the case of part *c,* because none of the members of A are contained in B it follows that some A's are not contained in B.

Euler diagrams are helpful for determining the validity of syllogisms because they can represent visually the relationships implied in the premises and conclusions. If it is possible to construct a Euler diagram that is consistent with the premises of a syllogism but not with its conclusion, then the syllogism is invalid; if not, then the syllogism is valid.

Let us return to the question of validity and truth in deductive reasoning. As just discussed, a conclusion is valid if it logically follows from its premises. Regardless of whether a conclusion is valid or invalid, it can also be characterized as true or false. If the conclusion agrees with facts derived independently of the syllogism in question, it is true whether or not it has been reached through valid reasoning; if it does not agree with the facts, it is false regardless of whether it has been reached through valid reasoning. If the premises are true *and* the reasoning is valid, then the conclusion *must* be true. For example,

All planets revolve around the sun.
Earth is a planet.
Therefore, Earth revolves around the sun.

involves two premises that are true and a valid reasoning process. Independent evidence confirms the truth of the premises and an examination of the logical relationships, with the aid of Euler circles, confirms the validity of the argument. (See Figure 15-4.) The set of planets is a subset of the set of things that revolve around the sun

FIGURE 15-4 Euler circles showing a syllogism for which the conclusion is valid and true.

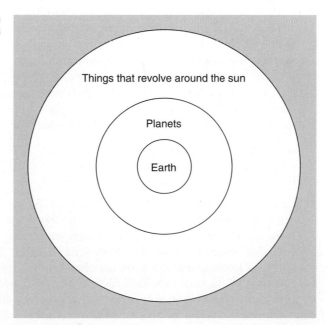

(as indicated by the qualifier "all" in the first premise), and the Earth is a subset of the set of planets. Thus, the Earth is also part of the set of things that revolve around the sun and the conclusion is valid. And because both premises are also true, the conclusion must also be true.

A conclusion can be valid, however, without being true. Consider, for example, the following syllogism:

> All humans have 16 arms.
> John is a human.
> Therefore, John has 16 arms.

The conclusion of this syllogism follows logically from its premises: If indeed all humans had 16 arms and John were human, then John would have 16 arms.

A conclusion can also be true but invalid, as in this example:

> All psychologists are human.
> Some humans are women.
> Therefore, some psychologists are women.

Here, both premises are true, yet the conclusion is not valid because it does not follow logically from the premises. As Figure 15-5 shows, we can conclude from the premises only that the set of humans contains both psychologists and women. We cannot conclude anything about the relationship of those two subsets to each other. We cannot conclude, in other words, that they intersect. As the figure shows, they could be entirely distinct.

FIGURE 15-5 Euler circles illustrating how a syllogism can be invalid even if the conclusion is true.

Psychological Errors in Evaluating Syllogisms

When presented with a syllogism like the one we just discussed, people often claim the conclusion is valid simply because it corresponds to what they believe is true in the real world. Errors of this type have been attributed to a process called the **belief-bias effect** (Revlin, Leirer, Yopp, & Yopp, 1980).

In a study of this effect, subjects were given the following syllogism (Evans, Barston, & Pollard, 1983):

> No highly trained dogs are vicious.
> Some police dogs are vicious.
> Therefore, some highly trained dogs are not police dogs.

The conclusion of this syllogism is not valid. Although the premises clearly indicate that the sets containing police dogs and vicious dogs overlap, they imply nothing about the relationship between the sets containing police dogs and highly trained dogs. They do not preclude, for example, the possibility that all highly trained dogs are police dogs, as in Figure 15-6; they thus provide no grounds for asserting the conclusion. Nonetheless, 92% of the subjects claimed that the conclusion is valid. The reason is that the conclusion conformed to their prior beliefs about dogs—some highly trained dogs, for example seeing-eye dogs, are indeed not police dogs.

Research has shown, in contrast, that people do not accept an invalid conclusion when it is also unbelievable. For example, consider the following syllogism:

> No highly trained dogs are vicious.
> Some police dogs are vicious.
> Thus, no highly trained dogs are police dogs.

FIGURE 15-6 Euler circles showing an invalid conclusion of a syllogism that subjects usually judge to be valid because it conforms to their belief about dogs. (Adapted from Evans, Barston, & Pollard, 1983.)

This conclusion is also invalid. To say that some police dogs are vicious is not to say that all are vicious. The premises thus leave open the possibility that some police dogs are not vicious and that some of these are highly trained, as shown in Figure 15-7. In this instance, however, people tend to agree that the conclusion is invalid because they know that police dogs are often highly trained. Apparently, then, people have a tendency to stop searching for a valid conclusion if the first conclusion they reach is highly believable; only when they encounter an unbelievable conclusion do they continue searching for an alternative (Oakhill & Johnson-Laird, 1985).

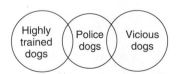

FIGURE 15-7 Euler circles showing an invalid conclusion of a syllogism that subjects tend to agree is invalid because it violates what they believe about dogs. (Adapted from Evans, Barston, & Pollard, 1983.)

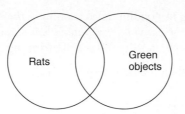

FIGURE 15-8 Euler circles showing the conclusion of a syllogism to be invalid. People are inclined to accept the conclusion simply because it is negative and follows negative premises.

Errors in deductive reasoning can occur for other reasons as well. For example, terms contained in the premises may establish a mental set (expectations) that may, in turn, lead to incorrect reasoning (Begg & Denny, 1969). This is called the **atmosphere effect**—the premises create an atmosphere that favors certain conclusions, regardless of whether the logic is valid or the statements are true. This effect sometimes occurs when people accept a negative conclusion as valid simply because one or both of the premises is negative. For example:

No rats are pets.
No pets are green.
Therefore, no rats are green.

According to the premises, rats and pets are distinct sets of objects ("No rats are pets"); similarly, pets and green objects are distinct sets ("No pets are green"). But the premises say nothing whatsoever about the relationship between rats and green objects. Indeed, as Figure 15-8 shows, these two sets could overlap without contradicting the premises.

A similar kind of error occurs when subjects accept a conclusion that contains "some" because the premises also contain "some." For example:

Some books are novels.
Some books are exciting.
Therefore, some novels are exciting.

According to the premises, novels are contained in books ("Some books are novels"), and exciting books are contained in books ("Some books are exciting"). But as Figure 15-9 shows, the premises do not require that exciting books and novels must overlap, so the conclusion is invalid.

Conditional Reasoning

Conditional reasoning involves premises that consist of two propositions, one of which (called the consequent) depends on a prior condition or statement specified in the other (called the antecedent). In other words, conditional reasoning involves premises that have an "If . . . then" form (Rips, 1981). Here is an example of a syllogism with a conditional first premise and a valid conclusion:

If the car turns left (antecedent), then the coffee spills (consequent).
The car turns left.
Thus, the coffee spills.

In this case the second premise ("The car turns left") *affirms the antecedent* in the first premise. That is, the "If . . ." part of the conditional (first) premise is declared to occur in the second premise. It is thus valid to conclude that the consequent ("the coffee spills") also occurs.

A syllogism in which the second premise *denies the consequent* can also lead to a valid conclusion, as in this example:

If the car turns left, then the coffee spills.
The coffee does not spill.
Thus, the car did not turn left.

Although the coffee could spill for many reasons, if it does not spill and if turning left always causes it to spill, then clearly the car cannot have turned left.

FIGURE 15-9 Euler circles showing the conclusion of a syllogism to be invalid. People are inclined to accept the conclusion because both it and the premises begin with "some."

Two common errors in conditional reasoning—*the fallacy of affirming the consequent* and *the fallacy of denying the antecedent*—lead to invalid conclusions. The following syllogism illustrates the fallacy of affirming the consequent:

If the car turns left, then the coffee spills.
The coffee spills.
Thus, the car turned left.

And this example illustrates the fallacy of denying the antecedent:

If the car turns left, then the coffee spills.
The car does not turn left.
Thus, the coffee does not spill.

Neither of these conclusions is valid. In both cases, the reasoning process involved (affirming the consequent in the first instance and denying the antecedent in the second) ignores the possibility that the coffee might spill for some reason other than a left turn—a right turn, for example.

Research has shown that people have difficulty solving problems in conditional reasoning. In one study subjects were given four cards in an arrangement like that in Figure 15-10. They were told that each card had a letter on one side and a number on the other, and were asked to confirm the validity of a rule by turning over as many cards as necessary (Johnson-Laird & Wason, 1977). The rule was "If a card has a vowel on one side, then it has an even number on the other side." This rule represents, in effect, a conditional first premise; each of the cards in the figure represents a possible second premise. The correct solution to the problem is to turn over the cards with E and 7. Turning over the E-card tests the rule by affirming the antecedent (E is a vowel, so if the rule is correct, the other side of the card must be an even number). Turning over the 7-card tests the rule by denying the consequent (7 is not even, so if the rule is correct the other side of the card must be not a vowel). Turning over the K or 4, however, does not test the rule. Turning over the K is an instance of denying the antecedent; the rule says nothing about what is on the other side of consonants—it could be either an even or odd number. Similarly, turning over the 4-card is an example of affirming the consequent; it provides no information about the validity of the rule because the rule does not claim anything about even numbers—they *could* be on the opposite side of consonants as well as vowels.

Results showed that 96% failed to turn over the correct cards: 46% turned over the E- and 4-cards; 33% turned over only the E-card; and 17% made some other form of error. Only 4% correctly turned over both the E- and 7-cards.

Additional research suggests that even having had a college course in logic does little to improve performance on this kind of task (Cheng, Holyoak, Nisbett, & Oliver, 1986). Other researchers, however, have contested the implications of these studies, claiming that subjects make errors in conditional reasoning because the problems are too abstract (Clement & Falmagne, 1986) or because they tend to match the items they evaluate with those mentioned in the problem (Evans, 1983). For example, the rule in the study just discussed mentioned vowels and even numbers, so the subjects tended to focus on the cards with vowels and even numbers (the E- and 4-cards) rather than the cards that would lead to a valid test of the statement (the E- and 7-cards).

It has also been shown that the familiarity of the task is important (Cheng & Holyoak, 1985). In one study that used a more familiar (less abstract) problem, sub-

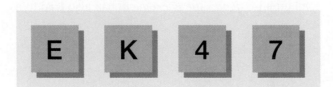

FIGURE 15-10 Sample cards for studying conditional reasoning. Subjects are asked to turn over only the cards that verify the statement "If a card has a vowel on one side, then it has an even number on the other side." (Adapted from Johnson-Laird & Wason, 1977.)

FIGURE 15-11 Sample cards for studying conditional reasoning. Subjects are
asked to turn over the cards that verify
the statement "If a person is drinking
beer, then the person must be over 19
years of age." (Adapted from Cheng &
Holyoak, 1985.)

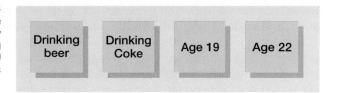

jects were told to verify the statement "If a person is drinking beer, then the person must be over 19 years of age." (The study was conducted in Florida, where 19 was the drinking age at the time.) Subjects were shown four cards (see Figure 15-11) and asked to turn over the cards that would verify the statement. Seventy-four percent selected the correct cards ("drinking beer" and "age 19"). The researchers concluded that the subjects were capable of conditional reasoning, but that the degree to which the concepts involved in a problem are familiar is a critical factor in their performance.

Linear Syllogisms

A different kind of deductive reasoning is used to solve problems involving linear ordering—for example, if A is greater than B (A>B) and B>C, it follows that A>C. The mental processes used in solving such problems have been studied extensively. Some researchers have concluded that subjects construct mental arrays rather than memorize each relationship separately. In one study subjects were given six different comparisons like the following:

The baker is taller than the teacher.
The teacher is taller than the barber.
The barber is taller than the butcher.
The butcher is taller than the farmer.
The farmer is taller than the grocer.
The grocer is taller than the tailor.

Later they were given a series of statements containing two of the terms and were asked to verify each statement; the reaction time required to perform this task was measured (Woocher, Glass, & Holyoak, 1978). The results showed that subjects verified remote pairs (for example, "The baker is taller than the grocer") more quickly than adjacent pairs (for example, "The barber is taller than the butcher"). The average time to verify a relationship was about 1.48 seconds when the terms had been adjacent but only about 0.93 second when the terms had been several steps apart. This suggests that the subjects visualized a line or linear ordering on which the terms were arranged. The items situated at the remote ends of the line are more distinct from each other and hence one is more quickly recognized as being larger (or smaller) than the other, than those located toward the center of the line.

Subjects do not always respond more quickly to remote pairs than to adjacent pairs, however. In one study, some subjects were given adjacent and remote orderings in an abstract format, such as B>C, A>D, and so forth. Other subjects were given the information in a more familiar form, such as "Bill is taller than Dave," "Dave is taller than Frank," and so forth (Mayer, 1979). Subjects in the first group performed as if they had memorized each relationship separately; subjects in the second group performed as if they had formed a linear ordering of items. It is apparently more difficult to order abstract items on a line than it is to arrange concrete items such as proper nouns.

HEURISTICS

Although humans are able to employ both inductive and deductive reasoning, there is no guarantee that they will always do so in arriving at conclusions or judgments.

Indeed, there is considerable evidence that in their everyday lives people make judgments and reach conclusions in a very different way: by using **heuristics.**

Heuristics are shorthand strategies, or rules of thumb, for making decisions. When using a heuristic, a person makes judgments that are consistent with past beliefs or attitudes, initial impressions, vivid memories, hunches, and the like. In other words, the person does not objectively evaluate the available evidence and then proceed to a conclusion; instead, he or she leaps to a conclusion that conforms to a preconceived notion. This is not a logical process but an intuitive one. Needless to say, decisions based on heuristics can be wrong. Humans often make significant errors of judgment when reasoning is absent from their thinking.

Of the several kinds of heuristics, we discuss two: the representativeness heuristic and the availability heuristic (Kahneman, Slovic, & Tversky, 1982; Nisbett & Ross, 1980).

Representativeness

The **representativeness heuristic** is a strategy in which one concludes that items are members of a category simply because they fit a preconceived model (or stereotype) of that category. For example, when we claim that a person is "conservative" simply because he or she is wearing a dark business suit, we are basing our judgment on a stereotype, not on evidence that we have gathered concerning the person's political beliefs.

The representativeness heuristic was demonstrated in a study in which subjects were asked to read five short biographies of people who, they were told, had been chosen randomly from a group of 100 lawyers and engineers (Kahneman & Tversky, 1973). Half of the subjects were told that 70% of the people on the list were lawyers; the other half were told that 70% of the people were engineers. Some of the biographical sketches fit the stereotype of an engineer quite closely, whereas others were closer to the stereotype of a lawyer. A sample is shown in Figure 15-12. The subjects' first task was to indicate how likely it was that a given biography depicted an engineer. Subjects had little difficulty performing this task. They apparently based their decisions on how closely the description fit their preconceived stereotype of an engineer.

All of the subjects were then asked a second question: Given no information whatsoever about an individual chosen at random from the sample, what is the probability that such an individual is one of the 30 engineers? In answering this question, subjects took into consideration what they had been told was the relative frequency of engineers and lawyers on the list. That is, subjects who had been told that the group of 100 people included 70 engineers claimed that the probability of an individual's being an engineer was 0.7, whereas those who had been told that the group contained 30 engineers said that the probability was 0.3. In sum, the subjects used relative frequency of occurrence to judge a person's probable occupation, indicating that they were capable of making an unbiased guess. When they had information in

Jack is a 45-year-old man. He is married and has four children. He is generally conservative, careful, and ambitious. He shows no interest in political and social issues and spends most of his free time on his many hobbies which include home carpentry, sailing, and mathematical puzzles. The probability that Jack is one of the 30 engineers in the sample of 100 is

_____.

FIGURE 15-12 Sample biography used to study the representative heuristic. Note that half of the subjects were told that 30 of the people in the sample of 100 were engineers, whereas the other half of the subjects were told that 70 of the people were engineers. (Adapted from Kahneman & Tversky, 1973.)

the form of the so-called biographies, however, they based their judgments on whether the information fit the occupational stereotypes.

Perhaps the most interesting finding of this study concerned responses to a neutral biographical sketch: "Dick is a 30-year-old man. He is married with no children. A man of high ability and high motivation, he promises to be quite successful in his field. He is well liked by his colleagues." Again, the subjects' task was to state the likelihood that Dick is an engineer. Because the description provided no information whatsoever about Dick's occupation, the subjects ought to have considered the relative frequency of lawyers and engineers on the list of 100 people from which the biography presumably had been drawn. After all, they had nothing else on which to base their judgment. In particular, those who believed that 70% of the people on the list were engineers should have said that the probability that Dick is an engineer is 0.7, whereas those who believed that 30% of the people on the list were engineers should have said that the probability is 0.3. Both groups of subjects, however, said that the probability that Dick is an engineer was 0.5. That is, when given a completely worthless description of Dick, subjects failed to make their judgments on an objective basis (with respect to the relative proportions of lawyers and engineers on the list) but instead decided that the biographical sketch was, in effect, halfway between a description of a typical lawyer and a description of a typical engineer.

Availability

We use the **availability heuristic** whenever we base a decision or judgment on easily remembered instances rather than on actual data. In other words, rather than relying on evidence concerning the frequency of an event, we tend to judge that an event is frequent if others like it easily come to mind.

A good example of the availability heuristic is the finding that people overestimate the frequency of deaths-by-murder relative to deaths-by-stroke (Lichtenstein, Slovic, Fischhoff, Layman, & Combs, 1978). Statistics show that deaths as a result of stroke are far more prevalent than murders, yet when asked subjects argue that the two happen with equal frequency. The reason is that murders are more notorious; they are more memorable than deaths resulting from stroke. Similarly, investigators believe that hindsight (after-the-fact explanations) seems so compelling because of the availability heuristic (Fischhoff, 1975; Hawkins & Hastie, 1990). The outcome, for which hindsight provides an explanation, seems inevitable because it reminds us of similar outcomes in the past. What we tend to forget are the similar instances in the past that had a different outcome.

Utility of Heuristics

The fact that people make judgmental errors by using heuristics is an interesting and perhaps even disquieting message about the human thinking process. There may even be some cause for concern in situations where errors of judgment may be made by people who exercise a responsibility for the well-being of others (Chapman & Chapman, 1967, 1969; Oskamp, 1965). Yet in everyday decision-making situations heuristics work reasonably well over the long run. Ordinary judgments are usually accurate enough to allow a person to behave appropriately. As two researchers in this field have noted:

> Our everyday or "intuitive" strategies serve us well in many judgmental contexts. The availability heuristic [for example] does help us form accurate estimates of frequency or likelihood in many domains ... Similarly, the representativeness heuristic, for all the judgmental folly it can inspire, is a prompt and faithful servant in a great many domains. (Nisbett & Ross, 1980, p. 254)

On balance, then, despite occasional errors, heuristics actually serve our everyday needs reasonably well.

Induction is reasoning from particular instances to a general principle. According to the continuity theory, inductive reasoning results from a continuous learning process that involves calculating the cumulative strength of each attribute of a stimulus in deciding whether it is an instance of a category. According to the noncontinuity theory, the inductive reasoning process involves the formation and testing of various hypotheses about categories. Research evidence tends to support the noncontinuity theory. Deduction is reasoning from a set of general premises to a specific conclusion. We conclude that a certain instance must be true or false on the basis of a prior examination of the more general rule. In everyday life, we often arrive at conclusions based on heuristics rather than inductive or deductive reasoning. Heuristics are shorthand rules for making decisions and arriving at judgments. A judgment may be based on how well the conclusion fits a preconceived model (the representativeness heuristic) or how easily a similar instance comes to mind (the availability heuristic).

PROBLEM SOLVING

In the preceding section we discussed various reasoning processes, or the kinds of thinking that Aristotle labeled "contemplation." In this section we are concerned with Aristotle's other category, deliberation—that is, with how cognitive processes in general and reasoning in particular are used in solving problems.

Humans are continually faced with situations that require action. Some are rather well-defined problems, such as how to open a can of sardines. Others are much less clearly defined problems, such as how to write a good term paper. Whether it is clearly defined or not, however, solving any problem seems to involve the same three basic phases (Newell & Simon, 1972):

1. Defining (representing) the problem in order to identify a starting point and a goal.
2. Choosing an appropriate strategy for solving the problem from among those that are available.
3. Executing the strategy and deciding whether the goal has been reached.

Consider this simple problem: You feel chilly while reading a book. Your first step in solving the problem would be to define it. Here, the problem is that you are cold or that the room is not warm enough. Second, you must stipulate the various strategies that are available for addressing the problem. These might include closing the window, turning up the heat, putting on a sweater, doing some exercise to keep warm, and so forth. One chooses a strategy because it seems most appropriate to the problem. In this example, turning up the heat might take away your chill, but it creates a second problem—it increases the amount of money you would owe to the heating-oil company. Putting on a sweater, in contrast, does not involve such a cost and thus may be the most appropriate action. Finally, of course, the problem is solved by actually executing the action and then by evaluating whether the outcome is satisfactory. If, say, putting on the sweater does not eliminate your chill, then you would presumably have to start over and better define the problem.

REPRESENTATIONAL PROCESSES

Defining or representing the problem may in real life be quite difficult, but here are several ways that, in theory at least, one can accomplish this task.

Problems may be represented in the form of a mathematical equation or set. For instance, the problem "Three oranges cost the same as two apples; an apple is worth 15 cents; how much does an orange cost?" may be represented in the form of a simple algebraic equation:

$$\text{three oranges} = \text{two apples}$$
$$\text{one apple} = \$.15$$
$$\text{therefore: three oranges} = 2 \times \$.15 = \$.30$$
$$\text{one orange} = \$.30/3 = \$.10$$

Problems may also be represented in the form of a visual image. For example, imagine the following:

> A monk began to climb a mountain at sunrise. He reached the temple at the top as the sun was setting and meditated all night. At sunrise of the next day, he came down the mountain, following the same path, but moving at a faster rate, of course. When he reached the bottom he proclaimed: "There is one spot along this path that I passed at exactly the same time of day on my way up the mountain as on my way down." (Mayer, 1983, pp. 75–76)

The problem is to say whether there is a spot along the path that the monk will have occupied at precisely the same time of the day on both trips, despite the fact that he ascended and descended the mountain at different speeds.

When confronted with this scenario, subjects often cannot solve the problem; they do not believe that the monk could have reached a particular point on the path at the same time on both days. Yet one can solve the problem if one creates a visual image of the situation (Kaufmann, 1985; Koestler, 1964). Imagine that there are actually two monks, one starting at the bottom of the mountain and the other at the top. Clearly there is a time during the day when they will pass each other, regardless of how fast each monk walks; at that point, of course, they will be at the same place at the same time. Once the situation is visualized in this manner—that is, once the problem has been recast in a different light using the image of two monks rather than only one—then the solution to the problem becomes obvious.

Representing a problem as a mathematical equation or visual image works only occasionally; most everyday problems cannot be represented so conveniently and clearly (Sinnott, 1989). For example, we often misunderstand (Green, McCloskey, & Caramazza, 1985) or oversimplify (Mayer, 1985) information when we attempt to represent it symbolically. Moreover, problems may be ill-defined, meaning that the starting point and/or the representation of the goals are vague (Chi & Glaser, 1985). One study investigated **ill-defined problems** by asking subjects to imagine they had been named "Minister of Agriculture" for what was then the U.S.S.R. (Voss, Greene, Post, & Penner, 1983). Their task was to recommend a means for increasing crop production. Subjects were either political scientists who specialized in Soviet affairs, students who were taking a college course on Soviet domestic policy, or chemistry professors. The problem as presented was ill-defined because it specified nothing about the many complex forces—economic, political, social, and natural, including highly unpredictable forces such as the weather—that influence crop production.

The strategies devised by the subjects varied considerably. The most detailed and comprehensive recommendations, not surprisingly, were offered by the so-called experts: 24% of these subjects attempted to represent and clarify the problem in terms of the conditions existing then in the U.S.S.R. (for example, its bureaucratic decision-making policies, the amount of arable land, and so forth). Only 1% of the other subjects followed such a strategy. In other respects, however, the approaches made by the experts and other subjects were similar. For example, most of the subjects tended to view the overall solution as involving a series of subgoals. The experts, however, were better able to specify what those subgoals were, suggesting that the more knowledge a person has, the easier it is to formulate appropriate subgoals.

The boundary between ill-defined and clearly defined problems is not exact (Simon, 1973). Nevertheless, many of the problems we face in our everyday lives are ill-defined—for example, writing a term paper. Unfortunately, people are often unable to articulate subgoals and thus they treat clearly defined problems, such as the proof of geometry theorems, as if they were ill-defined (Greeno, 1976).

CONDITIONS AFFECTING PROBLEM REPRESENTATION

The representational process is critical to problem solving because it frames the issue in a problem in terms that permit a person to choose a solution. A number of factors can facilitate or inhibit the representation of a problem. Among them are problem organization, mental set, functional fixedness, and insight.

Problem Organization

As we pointed out in Chapter 4, the Gestalt psychologists maintained that our ability to perceive and distinguish coherent objects from the multitude of sensations that constantly bombard us reflects a number of organizing principles. These principles structure the way we perceive the world. Similar principles govern the way we organize the elements of a problem and consequently the way we go about solving it.

Consider the problem shown in Figure 15-13. The goal is to arrange six matchsticks, shown in part *a*, in such a way as to form four equilateral triangles. Most people confronted with this problem assume that the solution must be two-dimensional—that all the triangles must lie on a single plane. As a result, they try to solve it by forming a square with an "X" in the middle, as in part *b*. The four resulting triangles, however, are not equilateral. The correct solution, shown in part *c*, is a three-dimensional structure. Solving the problem requires us to reorganize our thinking about the elements of the problem from two dimensions to three.

Mental Sets

A number of processes or conditions can inhibit the restructuring of a problem. For example, past experience can cause us to approach a problem with a **mental set** that affects the way we try to solve it.

A classic set of studies on the Luchins water jar problem demonstrated how a mental set for the solution of a particular type of problem could form and then constrain future attempts to solve similar problems (Luchins, 1942; Luchins & Luchins,

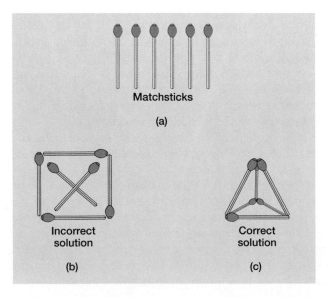

FIGURE 15-13 The matchstick problem is used to study the perceptual organization of a problem.

Trial problems	Number of pints in Jar A	Number of pints in Jar B	Number of pints in Jar C	Final amount
1	21	127	3	100
2	14	163	25	99
3	18	43	10	5
4	9	42	6	21
5	20	59	4	31
Test problem	23	49	3	20

The efficient solution to the trial problems is B − A − C − C
The efficient solution to the test problem is A − C

FIGURE 15-14 Luchins water jar problem. (Adapted from Luchins, 1942.)

1950). In one example, subjects were asked to imagine three containers—a large jar and two smaller jars—and an unlimited supply of water. They were then told that for a series of problems they were to determine how they could fill and empty the jars so that they would be left with a precise amount of water. For each specific problem in the series, the experimenters would specify the volume of water each jar could hold and the amount of water to be left in the end. The subjects were then given the five trial problems and the test problem shown in Figure 15-14. A separate group of subjects was given only the test problem.

Note that the most efficient solution to all five trial problems involves first filling jar B, then emptying water from jar B once into jar A and discarding it, and then twice into jar C and discarding it. In trial 1, this yields 127 pints − 21 pints − 6 pints, or 100 pints, the desired final amount. This pattern can be represented symbolically as follows:

$$B − A − C − C = \text{final amount}$$

The test problem can be solved the same way, but it also has a more efficient solution:

$$A − B$$

Filling jar A (23 pints) and emptying 3 pints into C leaves the desired amount of 20 pints.

Only 26% of the subjects who solved the trial problems before the test problem selected the efficient solution to the test problem. The rest followed the pattern established by the trial problem. In contrast, nearly all the subjects who were asked to solve only the test problem chose the efficient solution. Clearly, the experience of working on the trial problems created a mental set that structured the way the subjects solved the test problem. The subjects were, in a sense, prepared to view the test problem the same way they viewed the trial problems.

A mental set does not necessarily disrupt problem solving; it can be helpful, provided that the set is consistent with the solution. This is illustrated by a study in which subjects were given several poles, some string, and a few clamps and were asked to hang the string from the ceiling without defacing the ceiling in any way (Maier, 1945). The solution is to clamp pairs of poles together so that the fifth pole, around which the string is tied, may be braced against the ceiling. After subjects had solved this problem, they were asked to make a hat-rack using the same objects.

Here the solution is to clamp two poles together so that the entire span can be wedged between the floor and the ceiling, and to use the clamp as the hat-rack. Both solutions are illustrated in Figure 15-15. Only 24% of subjects who had not worked on the first problem were able to solve the hat-rack problem, but 72% of the subjects who had completed the first part of the study were able to solve the second problem. In this case their mental set facilitated problem solution.

Functional Fixedness

Sometimes a mental set can block our ability to solve problems by limiting the way we look at objects and the ways in which they can be used. Psychologists refer to this effect as **functional fixedness.** A well-known study used the candle problem shown in Figure 15-16 to demonstrate this effect (Duncker, 1945). Subjects in the study were given a cardboard box, matches, thumbtacks, and a candle. These objects were lying on a table next to a wall. The subjects' goal was to mount the candle on the wall in such a way that it would burn normally and not drip wax on the table. For some subjects, all the items were initially contained in the box; for others, the items, including the box, were laid out separately (Duncker, 1945). The solution, shown in part *b* of the figure, is to melt some wax onto the box to secure the candle to the top of the box and to use the tacks to attach the box to the wall. Clearly, the box can have more than one function—it can serve as a container and as a platform. The subjects who received the items inside the box had trouble solving the problem because they perceived the box only as a container and did not realize that it could also serve as a platform. The subjects who received the items separately were not affected by this functional fixedness and thus solved the problem relatively quickly.

Functional fixedness can be reduced under some conditions. In one experiment, for example, students sat at a table in front of a small projection screen (Glucksberg

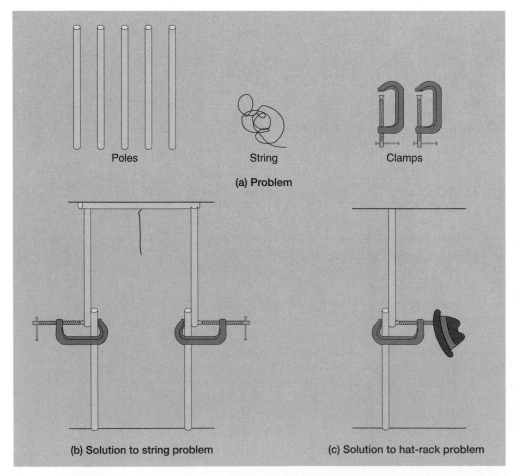

(a) Problem

Poles   String   Clamps

(b) Solution to string problem

(c) Solution to hat-rack problem

FIGURE 15-15 Maier's string problem. Subjects were given several poles, some string, and two clamps and asked to hang the string from the ceiling without defacing the ceiling in any way. The correct solution to this problem is shown in (*b*). A second problem was presented in which the subjects were asked to construct a hat rack with the same materials. The solution is shown in (*c*). (Adapted from Maier, 1945.)

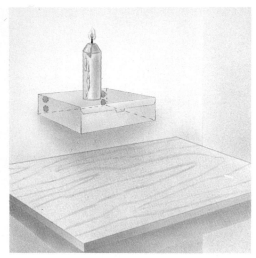

FIGURE 15-16 Duncker's candle problem. The subject was asked to attach the candles to the wall so that wax would not drip on the table below. (Adapted from Duncker, 1945.)

(a)

(b)

& Weisberg, 1966). They were told that a candle and several household items were hidden under a cover and that their task was to affix the candle to a bulletin board, using any of the items they chose. They were then shown a picture of the items. For one group of subjects, none of the items was labeled. For a second group, all the items, including the box, were labeled. For a third group, the box had "tacks" written on it and was the only item with a label. After viewing the picture for 10 seconds, each subject tried to affix the candle to the bulletin board.

The results showed that the subjects for whom all the items were labeled solved the problem in an average of 36 seconds. The other two groups were significantly slower. Members of the "no label" group took, on the average, 8 minutes and 49 seconds, and members of the "tacks" group took an average of 5 minutes and 41 seconds to solve the problem. The researchers concluded that the labels had reduced functional fixedness primarily by reminding the subjects that each item has a named function. In other words, objects often are not noticed, hence their possible functions are not considered. If, however, attention is drawn to them by means of labels, then the subject engages in a more effective analysis of the various functions that are possible (Glucksberg & Danks, 1968).

Insight

Many people have heard the popular, if apocryphal, story about Archimedes (287–212 B.C.), the Greek scientist who jumped from his bathtub and ran naked through the streets shouting "Eureka" ("I have found it"). What Archimedes had "found" was a method of determining whether the king's crown was made of gold. The fact that the water in his bathtub rose in proportion to his body mass gave him the solution—by comparing the amount of water displaced by the crown with the amount of water displaced by a mass of pure gold equal in weight to the crown, one could determine whether the crown was indeed made of gold.

What Archimedes experienced was *insight*, the sudden reorganization or restructuring of a problem so that a solution immediately becomes clear. In a less dramatic way the subjects of many of the studies we have just described—overcoming functional fixedness, say, to see the solution to the candle problem—also experienced insight.

One of the most famous demonstrations of insight used chimpanzees as subjects (Köhler, 1956). A goal object (banana, for example) was placed outside the cage beyond the reach of the chimpanzee. The only way the animal could retrieve the reward was to use some kind of tool. In one case, the chimp could join two short sticks together to make a single pole that was long enough to reach the banana; on other occasions, wooden crates could be piled up to make a platform on which the

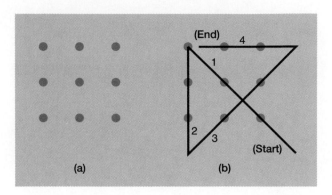

FIGURE 15-18 Nine-dot problem (a) and its solution (b). The problem is to join all the dots with only four straight lines without lifting the pencil from the paper.

chimp could stand and reach a suspended banana. (See Figure 15-17.) According to Köhler, the chimpanzees did not gradually learn to perform these behaviors. Rather, they performed them suddenly, without instruction, as if experiencing insight. Presumably, they had reorganized or represented the problem to themselves in an effective way.

Insight has also been studied in humans but a somewhat different conclusion has been reached. In one study, subjects were given the nine-dot problem shown in Figure 15-18a. They were told to connect all nine dots with just four straight lines without lifting the pencil from the page (Weisberg & Alba, 1981). All subjects were first given 10 practice trials. Those who were unable to solve the problem were then given an additional 10 trials, but some were first given hints about the solution. The members of one group were told to "go outside the square"; the members of another were given the same advice but were also shown line 1 in Figure 15-18b. Subjects in a third group were given the same advice as the others but were also shown lines 1 and 2 in Figure 15-18b. Finally, a group of control subjects was given no information at all.

The results are shown in Figure 15-19. The percentage of subjects who learned to solve the problem varied considerably depending on the group. None of the control subjects solved the problem; rather, they continued to draw lines within the implied square. In contrast, the percent of those finding the solution increased as a function

FIGURE 15-17 Köhler's chimpanzee piling crates to retrieve a reward. The behavior is said to illustrate insight. (Adapted from Köhler, 1956.)

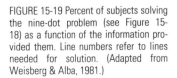

FIGURE 15-19 Percent of subjects solving the nine-dot problem (see Figure 15-18) as a function of the information provided them. Line numbers refer to lines needed for solution. (Adapted from Weisberg & Alba, 1981.)

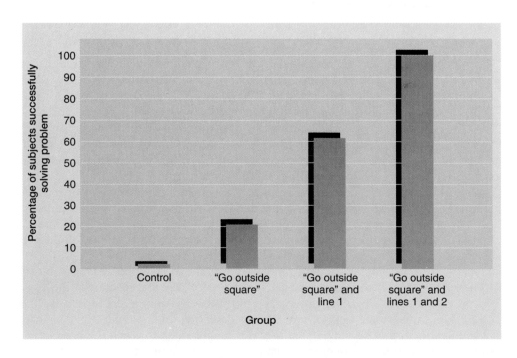

of the amount of information given to them. In fact, 100% of the subjects in the group that had been told "go outside the square" and shown lines 1 and 2 solved the problem. To some degree, the experiment demonstrates the action of insight: The information allowed subjects to restructure the problem and thus devise a solution. On the other hand, however, the study shows that insight really is a matter of degree. Subjects do not immediately leap to the correct solution. They may reorganize or restructure the problem (for example, they may know that one should "go outside the square") and yet still not find a solution. In sum, reorganization of the elements of a problem may eliminate functional fixedness and cause a person quickly to devise a solution, but such insight is likely to occur only when the problem is relatively easy.

SOLUTION STRATEGIES

Representation, as noted earlier, is the first major step in problem solving. The second step is finding a suitable solution (Newell & Simon, 1972). The most straightforward approach to this step would be to choose randomly among a set of alternatives. That is, one might aimlessly sort through possible solutions until one found a solution that worked. Needless to say, problems are rarely solved in this way. Not only does this method provide no justification for choosing one strategy over another, it is also much too cumbersome because most problems have a great number of possible solutions. Clearly, one must search through the available solutions in a more systematic way.

Search Strategies

As shown in Figure 15-20, the decisions one must make in selecting a solution can be abstractly represented as a treelike structure, often referred to as a decision tree. At every decision point, two or more alternatives are available. The choice of any given alternative leads to more alternatives. When one follows such a path, one is not simply testing solutions at random; instead, one is systematically searching along a specific solution path.

The problem with this approach, of course, is that an exceedingly large number of paths could be followed. Even a simple decision tree with only 10 decision points, each involving only two choices, provides 1,024 possible paths. Decision trees with

FIGURE 15-20 Schematic diagram (sideways) of a decision tree. A person has a choice of two possible paths at each juncture. A solution path is shown in bold.

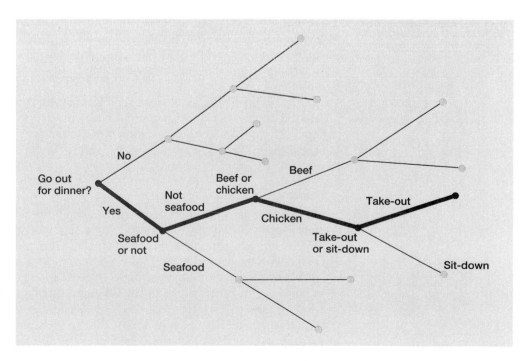

more than two alternatives at each decision point are even more complex. Therefore, one needs a strategy or plan for deciding which path to follow.

One strategy might be to conduct a vertical search (Raphael, 1976)—that is, to follow a given path as far as possible to determine whether it will eventually lead to a solution. Such a strategy is useful, especially if the number of choices on the decision tree is relatively limited. But this strategy obviously precludes the testing of other alternatives because it involves taking only a single path to the point where one is sure that the solution has been reached (or cannot be attained).

Another possible strategy is to conduct a horizontal search. In this case one proceeds along the decision tree in a much more cautious manner. One makes a single decision, observes the alternatives at the next decision point, and then returns to the previous decision point and tests the alternatives that were not originally followed. In other words, instead of going vertically through the decision tree, one attempts to move horizontally across the tree, evaluating all the options at a given level before proceeding to the next level. The primary advantage of the horizontal search is that it avoids commitment to a single solution path. On the other hand, it is a costly approach because it delays arrival at a final solution—one may use up a good deal of time exploring the early choices, many of which would be eliminated if the vertical search strategy were employed.

Consider how these two alternatives might operate for a real problem such as deciding about a career after college. Many factors could have an effect on the final decision—location, salary, opportunity for advancement, working conditions, and so forth. Each factor can be thought of as a choice point on the decision tree. A vertical search would involve following a single path. For example, perhaps the first decision would be to choose a high- rather than a low-salaried job. Taking that branch of the decision tree does not seem to pose a problem until one realizes that many low-salaried jobs might be preferable in other respects (for example, better location or fringe benefits). With a vertical strategy, one would not have the opportunity to explore these other possibilities. With a horizontal strategy, however, one could retrace paths rejected earlier. In our example, one could go back and choose low-salaried jobs and explore whether the final solution—selecting the overall most satisfying job—could be better achieved along such a path.

A compromise strategy to both approaches is known as the progressive deepening strategy (Raphael, 1976). In this approach, one sets limits on the depth of the search (vertical strategy) and explores all the options up to that depth rather thoroughly (horizontal strategy). If no solution is found, new limits are established and the search proceeds in the same way. This strategy combines the advantages of the vertical and horizontal search strategies in that a given solution path is explored thoroughly and the search is spread across the decision tree. Moreover, this approach is guaranteed to find a final solution because it enables one to sample all the available solutions.

The problem with all of these search strategies is that they may be very time-consuming. Other strategies attempt to reduce the "cost" of the search by specifying an optimal way of proceeding along a decision tree. The most important of these approaches is means–end analysis (Newell & Simon, 1972).

Means–End Analysis

A **means–end analysis** is a strategy in which the problem solver achieves the ultimate solution (the end) by first solving a series of subgoals (the means to the end). There are two basic stages in this approach. First, the current state of affairs is compared with the desired or goal state. Second, various measures are taken to reduce the difference between those two states (Greeno, 1978). An example of a means–end analysis is the process used to solve a simple algebraic equation like $bx + a = x + c$. (See Figure 15-21.) The goal (end) of the process is to solve for x, which means defining x in terms of a, b, and c. Achieving the goal requires proceeding by a series of steps (subgoals), each of which reduces the difference between the initial equation

Initial state	$bx + a = x + c$
Step 1	Subtract x from both sides
Result	$bx - x + a = c$
Step 2	Subtract a from both sides
Result	$bx - x = c - a$
Step 3	Factor out x on the left side
Result	$x(b - 1) = c - a$
Step 4	Divide by $b - 1$
Goal state	$x = \dfrac{c - a}{b - 1}$

FIGURE 15-21 Means-end analysis for solving a simple algebraic equation.

(initial state) and the goal. First, subtract x from each side of the equation (step 1). Then subtract a from each side (step 2). Then factor x out in the left term (step 3). Finally, divide each side by the term $b - 1$ to arrive at the goal state.

Many problems are more involved than this example, however, and solving them may require dividing the subgoals themselves into a series of steps (Egan & Greeno, 1974; Simon, 1979). The Tower of Hanoi problem provides a good example of this process. (See Figure 15-22 on page 398.)

The initial state of this puzzle involves three pegs, A, B, and C, and three different-sized disks, 1, 2, and 3, which are placed over peg A as shown in the figure. The problem is to move all the disks from peg A to peg C, moving only one disk at a time and never placing a disk on top of a smaller disk (that is, disk 2 cannot be placed on top of disk 1, and disk 3 cannot be placed on top of disk 2 or disk 1). One can use means–end analysis to solve this problem, but the problem is complicated enough so that subgoals must be established before the final solution is reached. The first subgoal would be to place the largest disk, disk 3, on peg C. In order to achieve this subgoal, one must first remove the other two disks one at a time, making sure that disk 2 is not placed on disk 1. This subgoal is reached by following steps 1–4 in Figure 15-22. The next subgoal is to place disk 2 on top of disk 3. As shown in steps 5–6, it is easy to attain this subgoal—it requires moving disk 1 to peg A and then moving disk 2 to peg C. The final state may then be reached simply by moving disk 1 to peg C.

The Tower of Hanoi problem becomes incredibly complicated when more disks are added. If, for instance, there were 64 disks rather than just 3, and one disk were moved successfully each second, it would take over a trillion years to obtain the final solution (Raphael, 1976)! Nevertheless, the rule for solving the problem is no different in principle than the one just discussed: The attainment of each subgoal provides an incremental reduction in the overall difference between the initial state and the goal state.

EXPERTISE IN PROBLEM SOLVING

Clearly, memory often plays an important role in problem solving. Even simple problems involve memory. For example, solving an algebraic equation involves memory for language and the rules of algebra. But memory is especially important in solving complex problems. This implies that people with good memories ought to be good problem solvers. They should be able to represent a problem and search for a solution faster and more efficiently than people with poor memories. Research has found that this is indeed the case. Much of this research has focused on games, notably chess. Not only does chess involve remembering the moves of various pieces, but it represents a typical problem-solving task in that it contains numerous decision points.

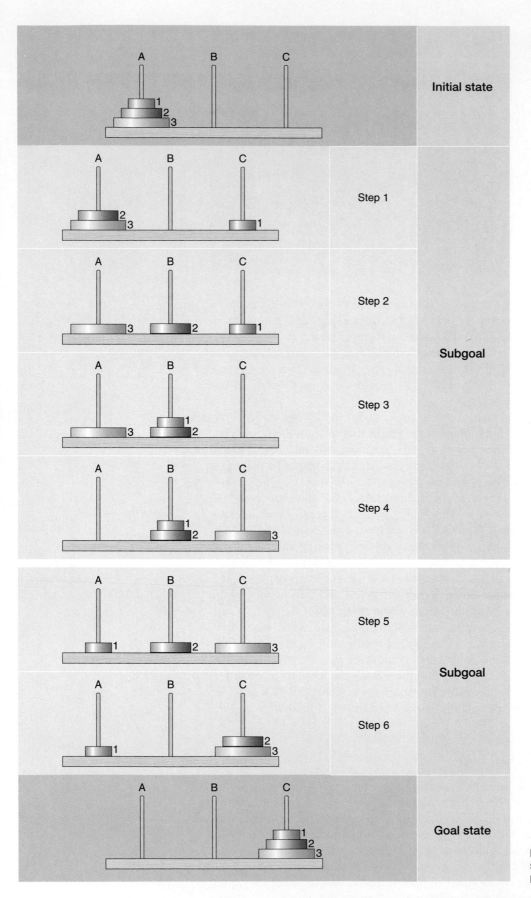

FIGURE 15-22 Means-end analysis, using subgoals, for solving the Tower of Hanoi problem.

World chess champion Gary Kasparov playing several games at once in a demonstration. Chess masters are far better than novices at reconstructing the positions of pieces on a chess board from memory, but only when the pieces are related to one another in a way that would have developed in a real chess game.

To the surprise of many psychologists, early research showed that master (internationally ranked) chess players did not search more solution paths than did novice players. They were no more likely than novice players to look ahead or to plan moves in advance (DeGroot, 1965). But master and novice players differed in other important respects. For example, although masters did not consider more moves than did novices, the moves they considered were better ones and led to greater strategic advantage than the moves considered by novices.

In subsequent research, master players, very good players, and novices were compared on a number of measures (Chase & Simon, 1973). Each player was shown a chessboard for 5 seconds; later the players were asked to reproduce the positions occupied by the various pieces. As shown in Figure 15-23, the master players per-

FIGURE 15-23 Number of chess pieces placed in their correct positions as a function of trials for master, advanced, and beginning players after a brief presentation of a chess board with pieces in real (left) or random (right) chess positions. (Adapted from Chase & Simon, 1973.)

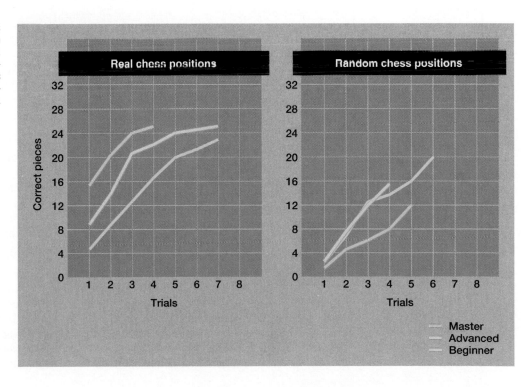

formed far better than the other players when the pieces on the board were in real chess positions. In fact, the better the player, the better that player's memory for the positions.

Interestingly, however, chess masters do not appear to have better memory in general than less advanced players. This was discovered when subjects were shown chess pieces in random positions and asked to reproduce the positions from memory. In this case, of course, the pieces were not related to one another in a way that would have developed in the course of a normal chess game. As shown in the figure, the masters were no better than the novices at remembering the positions occupied by randomly placed pieces; in fact, they were less able to do so. It appears, therefore, that chess masters have an unusual ability to assimilate relevant information into their existing memory structures, but that they do not have better memory overall.

INTERIM SUMMARY

Problem solving involves three stages: representing the problem, choosing an appropriate strategy for solving it, and executing the solution strategy. Several factors affect the way we represent problems to ourselves, including organization of the elements, mental set, and functional fixedness. The search for a solution often involves the exploration of various decision paths. In conducting such a search, one may attempt to sample a variety of alternatives before proceeding toward a solution (horizontal search), or one may follow a single path to discover whether it leads to the correct solution (vertical search). The progressive deepening strategy combines the horizontal and vertical strategies. A related strategy, known as means–end analysis, involves comparing the current state of a problem with the desired end state and then taking measures to reduce the difference between the two states. Research has shown that problem-solving ability is enhanced by the ability to assimilate relevant information into existing memory structures.

SUMMARY

1. Aristotle identified two kinds of thinking: contemplation and deliberation. Contemplation entails thinking about what is true, or inductive and deductive reasoning. Deliberation is practical, problem-solving mental activity.

2. *Inductive reasoning* is logical thought in which one draws a conclusion based on an examination of particular instances. Two theories have been proposed to account for inductive reasoning. According to the *continuity theory,* inductive reasoning involves a gradual and incremental learning process in which the attributes of particular stimuli come to be associated with a particular class through reinforcement. According to the *noncontinuity theory,* on the other hand, inductive reasoning is a discontinuous process; it involves the formation of var-

ious hypotheses that are confirmed or disconfirmed. Research using shift procedures has tended to support the noncontinuity theory.

3. *Deductive reasoning* involves reasoning from general premises to a specific conclusion. The syllogism is one formal way to represent the deductive reasoning process. Research suggests that the *belief-bias effect* and the *atmosphere effect* contribute to errors in the interpretation of syllogisms.

4. Conditional reasoning involves "if . . . then" propositions. Syllogisms in which the second premise either affirms the antecedent or denies the consequent of a conditional first premise lead to valid conclusions. Two common errors in conditional reasoning, the fallacy of affirm-

ing the consequent and the fallacy of denying the antecedent, lead to invalid conclusions. Research suggests that people have difficulty solving problems in conditional reasoning, but that their performance improves when the subject matter of a problem is familiar to them rather than abstract.

5. Research in problems involving linear ordering indicates that subjects tend to verify remote pairs in a sequence more quickly than adjacent pairs, particularly when the items are concrete rather than abstract.

6. Heuristics are shorthand strategies for making decisions and arriving at judgments. The *representative heuristic* is a strategy in which one draws a conclusion based on the fit between an instance and some preconceived model. Prejudices of various kinds result from this process. The *availability heuristic* is a strategy in which one makes a decision based on easily remembered instances, rather than on actual statistical information. Although these heuristics can lead to seriously erroneous judgments, most everyday decision making is reasonably well served by them.

7. Problem solving involves three general processes the representation of the problem, the choice of an appropriate solution strategy, and the execution and evaluation of the strategy.

8. Principles similar to those that govern our perception of objects also govern the way we organize the elements of a problem. Past experience can cause us to approach a problem with a *mental set* that affects the way we solve it. Mental sets can both hinder and facilitate problem solving. *Functional fixedness* occurs when a mental set blocks our ability to solve problems by limiting the way we look at objects and the ways in which they can be used. Research has shown that when the elements of a problem can be seen in a new light, functional fixedness is reduced and problem solving improves.

9. Finding an appropriate solution strategy requires searching among alternative paths in a systematic way, either vertically, horizontally, or in a progressive deepening fashion. *Means–end analysis* involves comparing the current state of a problem to the desired end state and taking intermediate steps (subgoals) gradually to reduce the difference between the two.

10. Research on problem solving has shown that expert problem solvers often have better memories for relevant information, but not better memories in general.

FOCUS QUESTIONS

1. Compare and contrast the two forms of thought first suggested by Aristotle, and relate them to the topics of reasoning and problem solving.

2. Compare and contrast inductive and deductive reasoning and give examples of each.

3. Define and discuss heuristics, and contrast decision making using heuristics with decision making using inductive reasoning.

4. Discuss the three major stages in problem solving.

5. Describe the processes that affect problem representation.

6. Compare and contrast search strategies with means–end analysis.

PART FIVE

THE ROLE OF NATURE AND NURTURE IN DEVELOPMENT

Compared to children, adults possess more extensive cognitive capabilities, greater sophistication in language use, and greater maturity in social relationships. How much of the adult's superior ability is established or limited by genetic endowment—nature; how much is produced as a consequence of experience—nurture? The interplay between nature and nurture can be seen in each of the chapters in this section. Chapter 16 describes the process of cognitive development, in which both heredity and environment play an essential role. Chapter 17 emphasizes the role of nature in the acquisition and use of spoken language, a characteristic that is both unique to humans and universal among them. In contrast, Chapter 18 emphasizes nurture, recognizing the powerful influence that other people have on the social development of the individual.

CHAPTER 16   COGNITIVE DEVELOPMENT

CHAPTER 17   LANGUAGE AND COMMUNICATION

CHAPTER 18   SOCIAL DEVELOPMENT

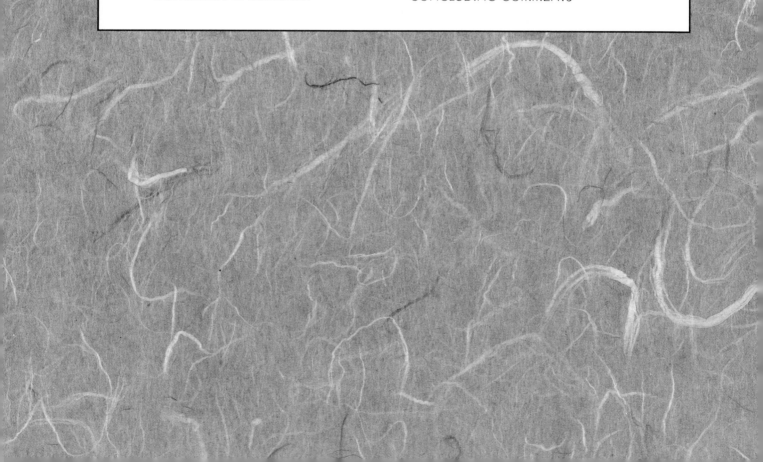

CHAPTER 16

COGNITIVE DEVELOPMENT

Many colleges and universities require students to pass at least one course in advanced mathematics, usually calculus. Why do we not save both the colleges and the students a great deal of trouble by teaching calculus to four-year-olds? One obvious reason is that calculus cannot be taught to a student who has not yet mastered basic arithmetic. But lack of preparation is not really the issue: What makes this suggestion sound silly, rather than merely impractical, is our belief that four-year-olds are simply incapable of learning calculus *at that age.*

How valid is the assumption that a four-year-old cannot learn calculus? More generally, what are the capabilities of a child's mind? How can we study and measure the processes by which those capabilities expand as the child matures? These are fundamental questions in cognitive development, the subfield within psychology that examines processes of change in mental capabilities.

THE CONCEPT OF DEVELOPMENT

Cognitive development is one of the major topic areas within developmental psychology, the branch of psychology devoted to study of change over time in all kinds of psychological capacities and processes.

THE DEVELOPMENTAL APPROACH

An example from the preceding chapter will help clarify the developmental approach. In a study of linear syllogisms, subjects were given a sequence of comparative statements like the following:

> The baker is taller than the teacher.
> The teacher is taller than the barber.
> The barber is taller than the butcher.
> The butcher is taller than . . . etc.

Their reaction times were then measured as they were asked to verify a series of statements comparing both adjacent and remote pairs of terms from the sequence (Woocher, Glass, & Holyoak, 1978).

In our original description of this study we did not mention the age of the subjects, who in fact were college students. It was not important to indicate their age because the focus of the experiment was on the mental representation of a linear problem by subjects who presumably already had sufficient reasoning ability and memory to solve it. Thus the experimental question involved a particular psychological capacity (representation of a linear problem) rather than developmental change in that capacity.

Had the study also tested six-year-old children, the differences between their performance and that of the college students could have shed light on cognitive *development.* Thus, although the research addressed problem solving, a developmental approach to problem solving would have required comparing performance across different age levels. Age comparison need not occur explicitly within the context of a single study for the study to be developmentally oriented, but it must always be at least implicit.

Given developmental psychology's emphasis on the measurement of continuity and change over time, one might wonder why the field is being discussed in terms of the theme of nature–nurture, rather than the theme of stability versus change. To some degree, of course, the placement is arbitrary. But more importantly, the nature–nurture debate has always assumed a central role in the history of developmental psychology. This historical background provides ample justification for describing developmental psychology in the context provided by the nature–nurture debate.

THE NATURE–NURTURE DEBATE AND DEVELOPMENT

Clear intellectual, social, and motivational differences exist between children and adults—age really does make a difference. But what exactly accounts for the difference? One possibility is that adult capabilities are present at birth; the individual simply needs time to discover them all. Another possibility is that no adult capabilities are present at birth; all must be discovered through the individual's experience with the external world. This is the crux of the nature–nurture debate, which has its origins in the writings of the ancients.

Plato, as you will recall from Chapter 1, believed that the mind never contacts the world directly. The information our senses bring us is comparable to what prisoners shackled in a cave can learn about the outside world from shadows cast on the wall of the cave. Only the innate ideas Plato called Forms can be contacted directly, and they can be encountered only through reason, not through experience. Thus, where the origin of knowledge is concerned, Plato's view falls on the nature side of the nature–nurture debate.

In contrast, Aristotle's view, with its emphasis—in both his scientific endeavors and in his philosophy—on the importance of experience, falls on the nurture side. His *Logic* is full of examples drawn from everyday experience, and his physical treatises include descriptions of the heavens and a detailed natural history of animals, demonstrating his belief that experience is a crucial determinant of knowledge. Indeed, Aristotle originated the idea, later popularized by Locke, that the human mind is a *tabula rasa*—a blank slate—at birth. Experience writes on the slate, providing both the contents of mind and the processes by which those contents may change over time.

The nature–nurture debate can also be seen in the contrasting ideas of seventeenth-century philosophers. René Descartes argued for the existence of innate ideas that do not depend on experience—for example, principles of reasoning in arithmetic and the idea of the self. The doctrine of innate ideas was immediately attacked by Thomas Hobbes, a contemporary and acquaintance of Descartes, and later by John Locke. Both Hobbes and Locke believed that all the contents of the mind are obtained from experience.

In the eighteenth century, Immanuel Kant developed what could be considered a compromise between the nature and nurture positions. Kant argued that some of the cognitive content of the mind—the concepts of space, time, and causality, for example—had to be available *a priori*. For example, no person can ever hope to experience all triangles, and yet no one would disagree with the assertion that "all triangles have three sides." The assertion is true in principle, and does not depend on experience. On the other hand, Kant was willing to grant that the items of knowledge about the world that the mind organizes according to its *a priori* concepts (like space, time, and causality) are derived from experience.

ORIGINS OF DEVELOPMENTAL PSYCHOLOGY

The nature–nurture debate was fundamentally changed with the publication of Charles Darwin's *Origin of Species* in 1859. The principle of natural selection reflects an *interaction* between nature and nurture. On the one hand, evolution

ON

THE ORIGIN OF SPECIES

BY MEANS OF NATURAL SELECTION,

OR THE

PRESERVATION OF FAVOURED RACES IN THE STRUGGLE
FOR LIFE.

By CHARLES DARWIN, M.A.,

FELLOW OF THE ROYAL, GEOLOGICAL, LINNÆAN, ETC., SOCIETIES;
AUTHOR OF 'JOURNAL OF RESEARCHES DURING H. M. S. BEAGLE'S VOYAGE
ROUND THE WORLD.'

LONDON:
JOHN MURRAY, ALBEMARLE STREET,
1859.

The right of Translation is reserved.

The title page from Charles Darwin's *On the Origin of Species,* the book that describes his theory of natural selection. The process of natural selection involves an interaction between nature and nurture. Only those individuals best able to cope with the demands of the present will survive to pass their genes on to the future.

depends on genetic transmission from one generation to the next (nature). On the other hand, individuals best able to cope with the demands of the environment (nurture) will be the most likely to transmit their genetic endowment to a new generation. Thus, innate characteristics and environmental pressures together produce change. Although this change is gradual and continuous, it eventually results in the evolution of qualitative differences and the differentiation of species from one another. In short, Darwin's theory provides the connections between nature and nurture, between human and animal, and between child and adult that are the foundation for developmental psychology. "To some extent, all extant . . . views about human development were influenced by, or progressed through, the prism of Darwinian evolutionary thinking" (Dixon & Lerner, 1984, p. 12).

The Organismic Approach

The theory of evolution concentrated on the survival value of various physical characteristics. The first broad developmental approach stimulated by evolutionary theory, called the **organismic model,** extended the principle of adaptation to behavior and to the internal organization of the individual (Dixon & Lerner, 1984; Reese & Overton, 1970). For example, if learning to recognize poisonous snakes is a behavior with obvious survival value, any internal organ (such as a more complex brain) that facilitates learning of this sort also has survival value.

The organismic model emphasizes the adaptive purpose of a process of behavioral development that proceeds through a universal sequence of qualitatively different stages. In each stage, the organism is a relatively active influence on its own environment. Some of the major contributors to developmental psychology whose work follows the organismic tradition include James Mark Baldwin and Jean Piaget (whose comprehensive theory of development we will turn to later in this chapter) (Dixon & Lerner, 1984).

The organismic model's emphasis on the adaptive purpose of behavior made it quite consistent with the more general psychological school of *functionalism,* described in Chapter 2. James Mark Baldwin was a leading figure in functionalism as well as an influential developmentalist. In his genetic theory of development, Baldwin (1895) took Darwin's principle of natural selection—usually seen as acting on whole animals or persons—and applied it to the internal organization of the individual. From this point of view, the simpler the organism, the more limited its potential for adaptation to changes in its environment. The most elementary organisms either alter their physical structure to accommodate changes, or die. More complex organisms can learn to cope with their environment in other ways besides changing their structure. Human beings, for example, can bring the external objects into their minds, consider how their actions might affect these external objects and requirements, and then take intentional actions designed to maximize the adaptive nature of their behavior. A small animal confronted by a wild dog can only run away; a human being can quickly look around for the best escape route, for something to use as a weapon, or for a nearby tree to climb. This ability to consider different options can increase the human's likelihood of surviving.

Because he was influenced not only by Darwin, but also by the empiricism of Locke and Hume, Baldwin did not believe that human infants were born with the ability to consider the consequences of their actions. Rather, he envisioned development as occurring in three phases. In the first phase the child undergoes biological adaptations similar to those of lower animals. These include physical changes, such as changes in the digestive system that enable the child to eat an increasingly wider array of foods, and psychological changes, such as the discovery that the self is separate from others or that movement of an arm or a leg can produce changes in the environment. In the second phase the child becomes capable of learning, especially by imitating the behavior of others. In the third phase the child becomes able to select goals consciously, and to pursue those goals through intentional actions. Thus, through a combination of maturation and experience the relatively helpless infant—entirely dependent on others for its survival—becomes an adult who can live by his or her own wits.

Theories of unconscious motivation as well as theories of conscious motivation reflect the organismic approach (Dixon & Lerner, 1984). The best-known theory involving unconscious processes is Sigmund Freud's theory of *psychosexual stages,* which was first mentioned in Chapter 2 and is covered in detail in Chapter 18. According to this theory, psychological development proceeds through five major stages, each of which involves conflict about sexual gratification derived from a particular bodily organ. For example, in the **oral stage** the young child is presumed to derive sexual gratification from sucking milk from its mother's breast. Another prominent organismic theory of social development (also described in detail in Chapter 18) is Erik Erikson's model of **psychosocial stages.** Erikson concentrates on crises in key interpersonal relationships, rather than on sexual gratification. For example, the **identity crisis** of adolescence involves the teenager's search for a satisfactory role to play in relationships with parents and peers.

The Mechanistic Approach

As important as the organismic model has been to the field of developmental psychology, it is by no means the only approach to development that can be traced to Darwin's influence (Dixon & Lerner, 1984). The **mechanistic model** of development views the human organism as a machine that passively responds to demands imposed on it from the external environment. Where the organismic model combines nature and nurture, the mechanistic model stresses nurture almost exclusively. Major contributors to developmental psychology whose work is in the mechanistic mold include Darwin's half-cousin Sir Francis Galton, whose pioneering measurement of individual differences will be discussed in Chapter 22, and John B. Watson, the founder of behaviorism.

Watson was not really a developmental psychologist, but his well-known assertion that he could make any healthy, well-formed infant into whatever sort of adult he wanted (Watson, 1924) clearly set forth the mechanistic model for development. According to this model, a version of the S–R psychology discussed in Chapter 2, processes within the organism count for virtually nothing. Pressures from the environment reward some actions and punish others, and the developing child's behavior changes gradually and continuously in response to these contingencies. Although the mechanistic model certainly recognizes that the physical and psychological capabilities of a child are different from those of an adult, it postulates none of the dramatic, qualitative reorganizations that characterize the discrete stages so prevalent in organismic theory.

CONCEPTUAL ISSUES IN DEVELOPMENTAL PSYCHOLOGY

In the first few decades of the twentieth century, as the first mechanistic and organismic theories were being proposed, research methods in developmental psychology were primarily descriptive. In other words, rather than attempting to test any of the new theories, researchers focused on describing the characteristic behavior of children at different ages. To do this they had to develop methods for constructing age-based norms for children's behavior. Research by Arnold Gesell (1934, 1954) typifies this approach. Gesell followed the development of children through their early years of life, noting when, on the average, children could first sit unsupported, stand alone, walk, utter two-word sentences, and so forth. Gesell's work took a nature approach, by assuming that children's increasing capabilities would unfold according to a genetically determined sequence with very little influence from the external environment.

Some of the early age-normed tests, such as the Bayley Scales of Infant Development (BSID), are still in use. The first BSID was published in 1933, with a major

Dr. Arnold Gesell was a pioneer in the emerging discipline of developmental psychology. He was among the first to describe accurately the capabilities of infants at various stages.

revision in 1969. The 1969 version (Bayley, 1969) remains a widely respected measure of the mental and motor performance of noninstitutionalized infants (Whatley, 1987). Age-normed tests have been important assessment tools for discovering developmental disabilities and learning disorders, and have been most useful in applied fields such as education and clinical practice.

Since the 1970s, however, the major focus in developmental psychology has been on explanation rather than description (Dixon & Lerner, 1984). Research in the field has accordingly shifted from describing age-related changes to explaining them. This search for explanations frequently involves issues, such as continuity in development and passivity of the child, first raised in the context of the organismic and mechanistic models of development. Is developmental change, for example, really a sequence of discrete stages, with each stage internally coherent but qualitatively different from preceding and succeeding stages, or is development more properly considered continuous and incremental? Do developing children act on the environment, either by temperament or by intention, or do they merely respond to the demands of an environment on which they have no direct influence? These specific questions, and the larger nature–nurture debate from which they are derived, form the background not only for study of cognitive development, but also study of language (Chapter 17) and social development (Chapter 18).

INTERIM SUMMARY

Developmental psychology examines how all forms of psychological capacities and processes change as the individual becomes older. Cognitive development is the study of change in mental capabilities. A fundamental issue for developmental psychology is whether adult capacities are largely inherited (nature) or learned from experience (nurture). The extreme of the nurture position is the idea that the mind is a *tabula rasa,* a blank slate, at birth. Darwin's evolutionary theory argued for the interaction of nature and nurture, and provided the basis for the organismic model of development. This model holds that development proceeds through qualitatively different stages, and that at each stage the organism actively influences its environment. Piaget's theory of cognitive development is the principal modern representative of the organismic model. In contrast, the mechanistic model of development views the human organism as a machine that responds passively to demands imposed by the environment. Behaviorism is the principal mechanistic theory of development. In recent years, the focus of developmental psychology has shifted from a description of age-normed behaviors to an explanation of developmental processes.

HEREDITY, ENVIRONMENT, AND BEHAVIOR

Evolutionary theory suggests that the behavioral capacities of a species may be modified through natural selection. On the other hand, cultural variability suggests that for humans at least, environmental influences play an important role in behavior. Clearly, then, human behavior reflects both nature and nurture. The science of behavior genetics, introduced in Chapter 8, provides developmental psychologists with tools to disentangle these factors and estimate the proportion of an individual's psychological capability that each contributes.

Studies of the inheritance of psychological characteristics have frequently focused on aspects of cognitive development, which provides an excellent natural laboratory for investigating the interplay between nature and nurture. Schooling in industrialized countries subjects children to years of intellectual training that builds on their inherited cognitive capabilities. Unlike personality characteristics, musical talent, physical skill, or other psychological faculties, intellectual ability—often equated with intelligence—is measured with standardized tests. Although intelligence testing is controversial, as we shall see in Chapter 22, its widespread use has made the relative contributions of heredity and environment to intellectual ability a favorite topic of inquiry. We briefly describe it here to provide background for the theories of cognitive development we discuss later in the chapter. After all, theories of cognitive development need to incorporate environmental influences only if nurture plays a role in a person's level of intellectual ability.

MEASUREMENT OF HERITABILITY

The Coefficient of Heritability

As noted in Chapter 8, the *genotype* of an organism is its genetic makeup, the sum total of all the genes it has inherited. The organism's *phenotype,* in contrast, is its observable characteristics. Is the person tall or short? Slim or chunky? Creative, talented, athletic, or none of these? Each phenotypic characteristic is produced by a combination of heredity (genotype) and environment. For example, differences in musculature between individuals will be produced by variations in such things as genetic background, childhood nutrition, exercise history, and specialized activities such as weight training. The **heritability** of a trait is the proportion of phenotypic variation that can be accounted for exclusively by genetic factors, as summarized in the following formula:

$$\text{heritability} = \frac{\text{genotypic variation}}{\text{phenotypic variation}}$$

When a trait is 100% inherited, this fraction (the heritability of the trait) is 1.0. More than 1,500 diseases, for example, have been linked to single genes (McKusick, 1983). One of these, Huntington's disease, is a nervous disorder that involves spasmodic movements and, in its later stages, deterioration of thought. Because the phenotypic cognitive changes accompanying the disease are produced entirely by a single faulty gene, the heritability of those changes is 100%.

None of the complex patterns typical of human behavior, however, has yet been tied to a single gene; given that a structure as simple as the eye of a fruit fly has been shown to be affected by over 100 genes, there is no reason to expect that one ever

The children of the last Russian czar, Nicholas II. Because of their frequent intermarriage, royal families often developed genetically transmitted disorders. The Russian royal family had a high incidence of hemophilia.

will be (Plomin, 1986). It is much more likely that variations in human physical and behavioral characteristics are produced by the joint action of many different genes. Therefore, **quantitative genetics,** the statistical theory that underlies modern behavior genetics, directs us to search for *family resemblances* in inheritance, rather than for specific single genes common to parent and child.

Research Techniques

Because of the way genes are transmitted, parents and their offspring have 50% of their genetic makeup in common. Siblings who have the same parents share 50% of genetic variation, whereas half-siblings, with only one parent in common, share only 25% of genetic variability (Plomin, 1986). Identical (monozygotic) twins, in contrast, have 100% identical genotypes. Whether they are identical twins, siblings, or half-siblings, however, the children in a family obviously share more than genetic inheritance—they also share an environment.

If a trait is heavily influenced by genetic factors, then on the average identical twins should be more similar to one another with respect to that trait than are full siblings, who, in turn, should be more similar to one another than are half-siblings. This general principle of family resemblance is the basis for two research techniques—adoption designs and twin designs—used to separate genetic and nongenetic contributors to variation in psychological characteristics and behavior.

Adoption designs compare genetically related individuals in different environments to genetically *un*related individuals raised in a common environment. For example, suppose two genetic siblings are placed in separate adoptive families that already contain biological offspring of the parents. On a trait strongly influenced by hereditary factors, the two adopted siblings should be similar to one another, and different from the other children in their respective adoptive families. In contrast, on a trait strongly influenced by environment, the two adopted siblings should resemble the other children in their adoptive homes, rather than each other. If a number of siblings are tested on a particular trait, the correlation among their scores is the estimate of their resemblance. As shown in Table 16-1, a significant correlation indicates genetic influence on the measured trait.

Twin studies take advantage of the different genetic characteristics of identical and fraternal twins. Identical twins, because they develop from a single fertilized egg, have identical genotypes. By comparison, fraternal twins, who develop from separate eggs, are no more alike genetically than are siblings born years apart. They do, however, share a common family environment—whatever the parents' ages, parenting experience, and socioeconomic status might be, these factors are the same for fraternal twins (but obviously different for siblings born at different times). Consequently, fraternal twins—same-age siblings—pass through various developmental stages together, enter school together, move together if the family relocates, and experience together any major external events like wars or economic upheavals. Though fraternal twins who do not look alike (and who may of course be of different sexes) might never be confused for one another, their family experiences are still more comparable than those of siblings separated by months or years. Twin studies thus examine differences in the extent to which identical twins, as compared to fra-

TABLE 16-1   The Two Major Research Methods for Determining the Heritability of Psychological Characteristics

Research Design	Indicators of Genetic Influence on Traits and Behaviors
Adoption designs	Significant correlations between scores for siblings reared apart
Twin studies	Greater correlations between scores for identical twins than between scores for fraternal twins

TABLE 16-2 Methods for Deriving Heritability Estimates from Adoption Designs and Twin Studies

	Example Value of Correlation	Multiplier	Heritability Estimate
Adoption designs			
Correlation between siblings reared apart	0.30	2 × Correlation	2 (0.30) = 0.60
Twin studies			
Correlation for identical	0.80		
Correlation for fraternal	0.40		
Difference	0.40	2 × Difference	2 (0.40) = 0.80

ternal twins, share particular traits. To investigate the possibility of genetic influence, the scores of identical twins on a trait are compared to the scores of fraternal twins on the same trait. As shown in Table 16-1, a higher correlation for identical twins than for fraternal twins indicates genetic influence.

Correlations of performance in both adoption designs and twin studies can be used to estimate heritability. Consider the adoption design first. Suppose that scores on a particular trait for siblings placed in adoptive homes produce a correlation of +0.30. Recall that siblings have a genetic background that, on the average, is 50% the same, so even if a trait were 100% heritable, siblings raised apart should show no more than a correlation of +0.50. Thus, doubling the obtained correlation gives the index of heritability. As Table 16-2 shows, this comes to 0.60 in our example (Plomin, 1986).

In twin studies, in contrast, the correlation for fraternal twins provides an estimate of the contribution of environment to a trait, and the *difference* between this correlation and the correlation for identical twins indicates genetic influence. For statistical reasons, this difference only estimates half of the genetic contribution (Falconer, 1981), so it must also be doubled to find the heritability of the trait. Thus, as shown at the bottom of Table 16-2, if the observed correlation for identical twins is +0.80, and the observed correlation for fraternal twins is +0.40, doubling the difference between these two values produces a heritability estimate of +0.80.

HERITABILITY OF COGNITIVE CAPACITIES

One of the first studies of the inheritance of intellectual performance was a combined twin–adoption study (Newman, Freeman, & Holzinger, 1937). There were 119 pairs of twins in the study—50 pairs of identical twins reared together, 50 pairs of

Genetics sets limits on environmental influence. Despite the fact that each of these twins has had a lifetime of different environmental experiences, the two can still be mistaken for one another.

TABLE 16-3   Correlations Between Twins on Measures of Ability, Interests, and Personality. The data in this table summarize the results of 211 studies.

	Intellectual Ability	Interests	Personality
Identical	.74	.48	.48
Fraternal	.54	.30	.29

Adapted from Nichols, 1978.

fraternal twins reared together, and 19 pairs of identical twins reared apart. Each twin completed several psychological tests, including a standardized intelligence test. The results showed that the scores of identical twins reared together were the most similar; those of identical twins reared apart were the next most similar; and those of fraternal twins reared together were least similar (although even their scores were significantly related). The implication of these findings is that intellectual capacity is inherited.

Subsequent twin studies using DNA-based methods to distinguish identical twins from fraternal twins have confirmed these results, although they have rarely incorporated groups of identical twins reared apart. In an extensive review of 211 studies comparing identical and fraternal twins, involving from 1,100 to 4,500 pairs of identical and fraternal twins, Nichols (1978) calculated the average correlations across all of the studies. The results are summarized in Table 16-3.

Note that Nichols's review covered interests and personality as well as intellectual ability, and that the results indicate that twins are more similar in intellectual ability than they are in interests or personality. On all three measures, however, the *difference* between the correlations for identical twins and fraternal twins is roughly the same. This means that the index of heritability for all three is also roughly the same (0.40 for intellectual ability, 0.36 for interests, and 0.38 for personality). Can it really be the case that these highly diverse characteristics have a virtually identical genetic component? Probably not. For statistical reasons, without much larger samples of twins (as many as 2,000 pairs of each kind) we cannot be confident that the true correlations on each of these measures do not vary substantially in either direction from those the study obtained (Plomin, 1986). Thus, the proper overall conclusion is that genetic factors are involved in all three areas, but that most existing research is unable to determine whether any of the three is more heritable than the others.

Although the coefficient of heritability is a useful summary device, two cautions are in order. First, it says nothing about the inheritance of a given trait in a single individual. Knowing that some psychological disorders run in families, for example, does not allow us to conclude that a particular individual's disorder is genetically based. Second, the fact that a trait has a high heritability coefficient does not eliminate environmental influence. For example, one study involving some 1,975 pairs of male identical twins and 2,097 pairs of male fraternal twins found a heritability for body weight of 0.78 (as cited in Plomin, 1986). But someone who interpreted this heritability value as a license to eat everything in sight would find that there was still sufficient environmental influence to make substantial differences in final body weight.

Where intelligence is concerned, both adoption designs (Plomin & DeFries, 1985) and twin studies (Wilson, 1983) find a heritability value of approximately 0.40. Although this number indicates that nature clearly does play a role in cognitive development, it also indicates that there is plenty of variability still remaining to be affected by nurture.

The modern version of the nature–nurture question centers on the notion of heritability, the proportion of variation in behavior that is the result of genetic variation. One way to identify the genetic basis of a trait is to conduct research with identical (monozygotic) and fraternal (dizygotic) twins. Such research indicates that abilities, interests, and personality traits are more highly correlated among identical twins than among fraternal twins. Although the data suggest that heredity plays a major role in these characteristics, they also suggest a substantial role for environmental influences.

PIAGET'S THEORY OF COGNITIVE DEVELOPMENT

Interplay between nature and nurture is the hallmark of the comprehensive and influential theory of cognitive development proposed by the Swiss psychologist Jean Piaget (1896–1980). Originally trained as a biologist, Piaget published his first scientific work, on a rare species of sparrow, at the age of 10 and published several advanced articles on mollusks before he entered college. He received his Ph.D. from the University of Neuchatel at the age of 22; "the intellectual conflict between his biological and philosophical interests turned him to psychology" (Hilgard, 1987, p. 567). Piaget spent a year at two psychological laboratories in Zurich, one of which was the clinical laboratory of Eugen Bleuler, the leading psychiatrist in Switzerland. Piaget left Zurich for the Sorbonne in Paris, where he worked in the laboratory school of Alfred Binet, a pioneer in intelligence testing. Although Piaget was supposed to be working on standardization of childhood reasoning tests, he was more curious to discover the reasons for each child's failures. In Piaget's early interests are the seeds of his approach: theoretical emphasis on biological development and methodological emphasis on detailed analysis of single cases.

Although Piaget's work was read when first translated into English in the 1920s and 1930s, this period was the heyday of behaviorism, and his highly cognitive theory was out of fashion. In the 1950s and 1960s, when behaviorism was on the

The renowned Swiss psychologist Jean Piaget, shown against a backdrop of creative works by children whose behavior Piaget explained with such remarkable insight.

decline and psychologists were once again interested in the origin of cognitive structures, Piaget's theory was rediscovered.

Perhaps because it served as such an effective alternative to strict behaviorism, Piaget's theory has been the dominant explanation of cognitive development. In contrast to the behaviorists, Piaget argues that children are active participants in their own development; development, including cognitive development, occurs in a series of stages as a result of the interaction between maturation and experience. Recent research and theory still support the principle that children are active participants in their cognitive worlds, and that both innate factors and learning influence the course of development. Some scientists, however, supported by methodological advances in developmental research, have begun to challenge the Piagetian idea that cognitive growth occurs in discrete, separable, qualitatively different stages, each of which involves a different sort of reasoning process (Daehler & Bukatko, 1985; Scholnick, 1983). Nonetheless, even recent critics take Piaget's theory as their foil. In the discussion of the process of cognitive development that follows, we concentrate on his ideas, indicating places where recent research challenges them.

THE BIOLOGY OF COGNITION

Organization

Piaget believed that the development of cognition must build on the organism's biological characteristics. A fundamental characteristic of any biological entity is *organization,* the grouping and integration of disparate elements to form more complex systems. Cells are grouped together to form tissues; tissues form organs (such as the heart); organs are linked to others in a system (such as the circulatory system); and systems are linked with others to form the whole biological organism. Each level in the organization, from the cell to the system, has a defined structure, and each has a specialized function. No level can exist independently of the others, but each can profitably be examined individually.

In Piaget's theory, the principle of organization is represented in both structure and process. The basic cognitive structure is the *schema,* a representation of external reality in terms of a perception, idea, memory, or category. Schemata are joined together in ever more complex networks to create systems of thought, just as cells, tissues, and organs are linked together to form biological systems. As the individual matures, the number and sophistication of the schemata increase.

The basic cognitive process is the **transformation,** the mental or physical activity that enables the child to know the external world. In Piaget's words, in order to know objects a child must "act upon them, and therefore transform them: he must displace, connect, combine, take apart, and reassemble them" (1983, p. 104). At first, transformations are physical; for example, a newborn learns about its world by sucking on whatever comes within reach, and a crawling baby handles whatever it can grasp. Later, transformations combine physical and mental activities or are exclusively mental. For example, a 10-year-old may try to take a television set apart to see how it works. Regardless of the nature of the transformation, the child is active, interacting with the environment to increase his or her level of cognitive organization.

Adaptation

Another characteristic of all biological organisms is the ability to adapt to the environment. The process of adaptation has two complementary components—assimilation and accommodation. **Assimilation** is the incorporation of external elements into structures within the organism. An example from the biological realm is the physical and chemical transformation of food into elements that can be absorbed by the body. In the cognitive realm, external information is incorporated into existing cognitive structures. Piaget noted that "no behavior, even if it is new to the individual, constitutes an absolute beginning. It is always grafted onto previous schemes and therefore amounts to assimilating new elements to already constructed structures" (1983, p.

106). By the time a child attempts to dribble a basketball, the child has long since picked objects up, dropped them, watched them bounce, thrown them, and pushed objects down with a hand.

In any biological system, assimilation cannot exist without its counterpart, **accommodation,** the modification of the organism to adjust to the demands of its environment. From the standpoint of a species, adaptation leads to evolutionary change. From the standpoint of individual cognitive development, accommodation is the alteration of cognitive structures—that is, schemata. Such alterations increase both knowledge and the ability to cope with future environmental demands. For example, a toddler who treats every small round object as if it were a ball will get into trouble with a glass paperweight. Through repeated interactions with objects in its environment, the child will alter its schema for "ball"; it will come to recognize that although paperweights are not balls, soccer balls and footballs are.

The Process of Cognitive Development

Repeated instances of assimilation and accommodation progressively alter the individual's cognitive organization. At the level of the schema, such change is continuous. At the level of systems of behavior, Piaget's theory proposes four distinct stages: the sensorimotor period, the preoperational period, the period of concrete operations, and the period of formal operations. The major intellectual tasks accomplished in each of these stages are shown in Table 16-4.

Although the stage-based view of cognitive development has recently come under sustained attack, we discuss each of the stages in Piaget's theory in turn. Where appropriate, we present the important theoretical and methodological alternatives to Piaget's theory.

TABLE 16-4   Piaget's Periods of Cognitive Development

Period	Approximate Age Range	Characteristics or Major Achievements
Sensorimotor	1–2	Representations of absent objects. Means and relationships.
Preoperational	2–7	Development of the symbolic function. Problem of egocentricity.
Concrete Operations	7–11	Learning of conservations. Reversibility, decentration
Formal Operations	11 on	Flexibility and abstraction. Mental hypothesis testing.

THE SENSORIMOTOR PERIOD

The **sensorimotor period** extends from birth to about age 2. At birth, the child is little more than a reflex machine, responding to stimuli with automatic reflexes like sucking. By the second birthday, the child has undergone the "truly momentous cognitive transformation" leading to a symbolic-representational cognitive system (Flavell, 1985, p. 12).

It is easy to see why so much research attention has been devoted to the sensorimotor period. Imagine what it would be like if objects and people ceased to exist when you were not looking directly at them. You would be afraid to close your eyes, for fear your loved ones would never return. Such thoughts never trouble normal adults because they assume the objects they may be looking at do not disappear when they turn their attention elsewhere. This concept of **object permanence**—that objects, animals, and people continue to exist even when they are out of sight—is so fundamental to human thought that one is tempted to conclude it must be innate and

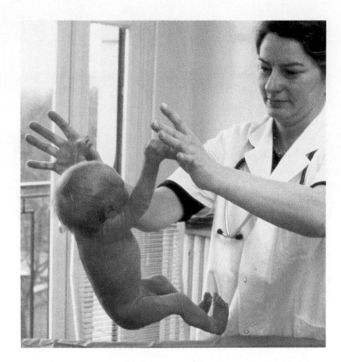

The grasping reflex is so strong that even very young infants can support their own weight.

present from birth. But Piaget's careful observations of his own children, subsequently replicated by other researchers, confirmed that the concept of object permanence develops during the sensorimotor period (Flavell, 1985). (See Figure 16-1.)

This crucial period for cognitive development is subdivided into six phases:

1. *Reflex responding.* According to Piaget, for the first month of life the infant's behavior is limited to innate reflexes; no truly cognitive activity occurs. Recent research employing procedures that were not available to Piaget has shown that visual acuity, pattern recognition, and the specificity of nerve pathways within the visual cortex increase during this phase (Banks & Salapatek, 1983). Whether these enhancements of sensory capability may be considered changes in cognition is open to question, but it is clear that something more than mere reflex action is occurring during this phase.

FIGURE 16-1 Before a child develops object permanence, he or she will act as though an object hidden behind a screen is gone altogether.

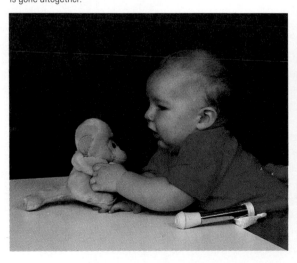

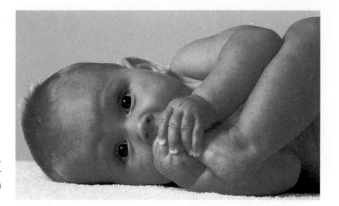

An example of a primary circular reaction. Infants commonly place their hands—or, as in this case, their feet—in their mouths.

2. *Primary circular reactions.* The second phase extends roughly from the first to the fourth month and is characterized by primary circular reactions. These repetitive actions are called "primary" because they involve the infant's own body rather than the external environment. For example, an infant that has inadvertently sucked on its fingers may do so over and over again. Because assimilation and accommodation require repeated interactions with the environment, the circular reaction is viewed as a basic element of cognitive activity.

3. *Secondary circular reactions.* From the fourth to the eighth month the infant's repetitive actions begin to involve external objects and are known as secondary circular reactions. Many of Piaget's insights regarding cognitive development were achieved through very close observation of his own children. As an example of such an action, Piaget recounts how his five-month-old daughter Lucienne kicked a doll that was hanging above her bassinet; delighted in the doll's movement, she kicked it again to make it move.

4. *Coordination of secondary schemata.* Between 8 and 12 months of age, a schema developed in one setting will be used to solve a problem in another, a process referred to as coordination of secondary schemata. To build on the example just

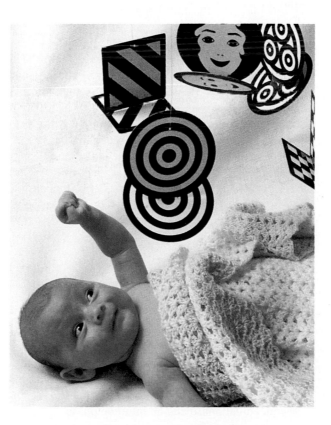

Secondary circular reactions involve external objects. Here an infant who has made a mobile move once is attempting to repeat the action.

419

FIGURE 16-2 An illustration of the development of a schema for solving a particular problem during the tertiary circular reaction phase. The infant realizes that she can bring the stick into the playpen by turning it parallel to the bars.

given, the kicking that moved the doll might be applied to an object placed between the baby and the doll. Note that this reaction must be based on the belief that the doll is still there even though the other object obscures it, indicating an awareness of object permanence. Not only does this stage mark the first transfer of a schema from one situation to another, it also marks the beginning of true imitation of a model. A child to whom an adult waves "bye-bye" will try to match the adult's arm movements, rather than merely waving in a random pattern.

5. *Tertiary circular reactions.* The fifth phase (12 to 18 months) is characterized by tertiary circular reactions. The child performs intentional "experiments" to discover the properties of objects. Unfortunately for parents, a favorite experimental technique is to drop objects to watch them fall, listen for the sound they make, and see whether they bounce on impact. The intentionality that accompanies this experimentation is illustrated by Piaget's description of his daughter Jacqueline's attempts to bring into her playpen a stick that could pass through the bars only if it was held upright (Piaget, 1952). After first holding the stick horizontally and failing to bring it into the playpen, the child quickly learned to change the orientation of the stick before it contacted the bars. As shown in Figure 16-2, such experimentation produces a useful schema that can be repeated whenever desired.

6. *Invention through mental combination.* In the final phase of the sensorimotor period (18 to 24 months), the arena for experimentation shifts from the physical to the mental. To use Piaget's term, experimentation is "interiorized"; the child can now anticipate various possible outcomes of an action. This is known as invention through mental combination. A child who drops a large ball over the side of a playpen can know, without actually manipulating the ball, that it must come back in over the top, rather than through the side openings. An important aspect of invention through mental combination is that it allows the child to imitate the behavior of a model even if the model is absent. On one occasion, for example, a visiting child threw a tantrum upon being placed in Jacqueline's playpen. Although Jacqueline herself had never had a tantrum, on the next day she imitated the tantrum when she was placed in the playpen.

THE PREOPERATIONAL PERIOD

By the end of the sensorimotor period, children have developed the ability to represent to themselves objects and behaviors that are not in sight. Although this capacity is absolutely fundamental for thinking and reasoning, Piaget argues that further cognitive growth is necessary before the child's thought can achieve the level of abstraction that characterizes the adult. This interim phase is known as the **preoperational period.** It extends roughly from age 2 to age 7 and incorporates two separate phases, a preconceptual phase and an intuitive phase.

Mastery of language is the major accomplishment of the preoperational period of development. Language is a complex symbolic system and mastering it requires understanding the distinction between an object or concept and the symbol used to represent it.

The Symbolic Function

In the preconceptual phase (roughly age 2 to age 4), the child builds on the mental representations of particular external objects to construct systems of representation, the major one of which is language. The critical difference between a single representation and a system of representations is that the latter must include not only individual objects but also the relations among them. Generating these systems of representation requires what Piaget calls the **symbolic function,** the cognitive process by which internal symbols (or "signifiers") are differentiated from the external objects and people (the "significates") they represent. For example, the ability to imagine and talk about a cat pushing a ball requires a symbol for the cat, a symbol for the ball, and a mental picture of what the cat is doing to the ball.

In the intuitive phase (age 4 to age 7), having learned language and built schemata that incorporate relations among objects, the child begins to categorize and quantify things. The child learns, for example, the cat is an "animal," whereas the ball is not.

The capacity to form logical classes, however, is not the same as the capacity to draw inferences on the basis of logical relations between classes. Evidence for this assertion comes from the way children respond to a kind of problem initially used by Piaget: When asked "If you have four horses and two dogs, which do you have more of, horses or animals?" most children under 7 will answer that there are more horses (Daehler & Bukatko, 1985). This is a standard "class inclusion" problem, the solution to which requires understanding of the difference between the two subordinate classes (horses, dogs) and the superordinate category to which both belong (animals). According to Piaget, the preoperational child has difficulty recognizing correct relations between concepts or categories, despite knowledge of the categories.

Other limitations in symbolic function that Piaget considered characteristic of the preoperational period are animism, centration, and irreversibility.

Animism

Piaget argued that children in the preoperational period endow inanimate objects with sensations and intentions like those of humans, a tendency called **animism.** A child might say, for example, that a tree is "sad" when it loses its leaves in the fall, or that a flower "hurts" when it is picked. The forest in a fairy tale is frightening not only because of its scary animal inhabitants but also because the trees might hurt people, as suggested in Figure 16-3.

421

FIGURE 16-3 According to Piaget, one characteristic of children in the preoperational period is *animism*, the tendency to endow inanimate objects with human sensations and intentions. The fables and fairy tales that appeal to children in this period, like this scene from *The Wizard of Oz*, often have animistic characters.

Centration

Although the preoperational child has made substantial intellectual progress over the sensorimotor period, his or her thinking is still characterized by **centration,** an exclusive concentration on one aspect or dimension of a problem to the exclusion of other relevant dimensions. One indication of centration is an inability to take the perspective of another person. Piaget developed the "three mountain problem" to study centration (Piaget & Inhelder, 1956). The child sits at one of four chairs around a table, as shown in Figure 16-4. On the table are two small "mountains" and one

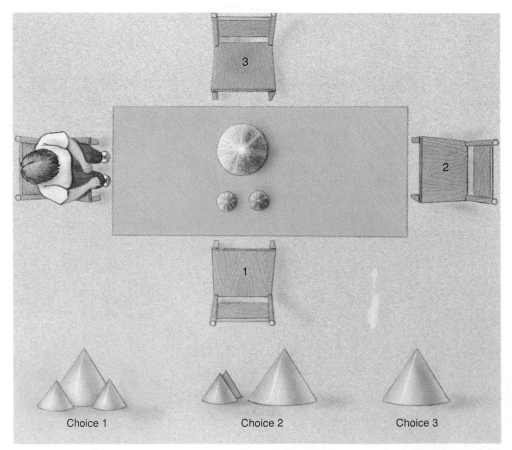

FIGURE 16-4 The three mountain problem. In a typical study using the three mountain problem, a child seated in one chair is asked to say which picture would match the view from each of the three other chairs.

Choice 1   Choice 2   Choice 3

large one; they are cones made of paper and wood. A doll is placed successively in each of the other chairs (numbered 1, 2, and 3 in the figure) and the child is asked to indicate what the doll sees. The child may make a drawing, arrange cardboard cutouts, or select the proper view from the choices provided (see the bottom of the figure). Conceptually, the problem requires that the child transform his or her own view of the three mountains into the doll's view.

In Piaget's own work, and in other early studies, preoperational children were unable to select the correct view on a better than chance basis (Piaget & Inhelder, 1956). More recent research, however, has found that children as young as 3 years of age know that a person looking at a scene from a position other than their own will see something different, provided that the children have some prior experience with the objects in the scene (Gelman & Baillargeon, 1983). One such study used the three-mountain-problem display along with two other displays (Borke, 1975). One of the additional displays showed a small lake with a toy sailboat, a house, and figurines of a house and a cow; the other showed different groupings of miniature people and animals. The children in the study were asked to rotate duplicates of the displays to indicate what the doll would be seeing. On the two displays with familiar objects, the children's performance was much better than on the three-mountain-problem display.

Irreversibility

According to Piaget, the preoperational child is unable to see processes, or cognitive relationships, as reversible. This irreversibility is illustrated by problems involving **conservations** of number, volume, and weight. For example, suppose the child is shown the two beakers in Figure 16-5. The short, wide beaker contains a colored liquid. As the child watches, the experimenter picks up the short beaker and pours all the water into the narrow, tall beaker. Next the experimenter asks the child whether there is now less, more, or the same amount of colored water as before. Typically, the child answers that there is now more colored water.

Piaget's explanation of this surprising result is that the child is concentrating on the height of the beaker and is not able to imagine what would happen if the water were poured back into the short, wide beaker. The child has failed to understand that the volume of water remains the same because his or her thinking is not reversible. Although recent evidence has cast doubt on the all-or-nothing quality of the learning of conservation, it is generally agreed that the preoperational child's cognitive capabilities in this area are qualitatively different from those of an older child.

THE PERIOD OF CONCRETE OPERATIONS

Gradual Discovery of Conservations

The **period of concrete operations** extends from about age 7 to about age 11. During this stage animism virtually disappears, any remaining centration becomes negligible, and the child begins to understand that many operations are reversible. This understanding, however, is not general, but appears to be content-specific, as an example will illustrate.

Imagine two clay balls that are identical in material, shape, and size. If a child older than age 3 or 4 is asked whether one ball is bigger than the other, he or she will say that they are the same. Now suppose that as the child watches, one of the balls is

FIGURE 16-5 Conservation of volume. A preoperational child who watches liquid being poured from the short, wide beaker into the narrow, tall one will say that there is now "more water."

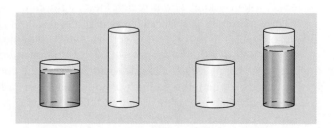

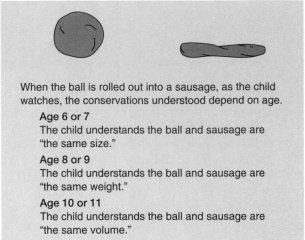

When the ball is rolled out into a sausage, as the child watches, the conservations understood depend on age.

Age 6 or 7
The child understands the ball and sausage are "the same size."

Age 8 or 9
The child understands the ball and sausage are "the same weight."

Age 10 or 11
The child understands the ball and sausage are "the same volume."

FIGURE 16-6 Age variations in the ability to understand conservation within the period of concrete operations. If a ball of clay is rolled into a sausage as the child watches, what the child believes can be conserved—mass, weight, volume—depends on the child's age.

rolled out into the shape of a sausage, as shown in Figure 16-6. A preoperational child will say that the sausage-shaped lump is bigger. A 6- or 7-year-old child will say that the lumps are the same size but will claim that the sausage-shaped lump weighs more. Not until about age 9 will the child say that the two lumps are equal in weight. And not until about age 11 will the child say that the two lumps are equal in volume, even though he or she has been shown that they displace an equal amount of water.

Successful learning of reversibility depends on the child's ability to **decenter,** to think in ever more abstract (and less egocentric) terms. As noted above, Piaget argues that the explanation for a preoperational child's total inability to understand conservation is that the child attends to only one (possibly irrelevant) aspect of the problem. During the several years of the concrete operational period, the child's attention broadens to include multiple dimensions.

A New Look at Decentration

The critical developmental question is "How early does decentration occur?" The traditional Piagetian view is that the preoperational child is incapable of attending to more than one dimension, and that only toward the end of the concrete operational period (roughly at age 7 and up) does the child develop a more balanced view of the problem. Thus, when water is poured from a short (but wide) beaker into a tall (but narrow) beaker, the child attends only to height and claims that there is now more water.

Results from one study, however, suggest that the preoperational child's failure to conserve may have had something to with the liquids, blocks, or pieces of clay used in conservation studies (Anderson & Cuneo, 1978). The investigators who conducted these studies wondered what would happen if children were asked to judge materials, like cookies, about which they might care a great deal, and were asked to provide numerically precise answers in a manner appropriate to their age level. The 5-year-old children in this study were shown rectangular cookies that varied systematically in both width and length. After viewing each cookie, the child was asked to indicate how happy or sad a child would be to eat the cookie just seen.

The scale on which this rating was to be made was a long rod with a happy face at one end and a sad face at the other end. Children had previously been taught how to

424

use the scale, and during testing they were simply to point to a place on the rod to show how happy or sad one would be after eating a particular cookie. This dependent variable differs in two important respects from the dependent variable in a traditional conservation study. First, allowing the child to point to a rod minimizes the linguistic sophistication needed to answer. Second, whereas the traditional conservation study provides only three discrete responses ("more," "less," and "same"), distance along the rod is a continuous variable to which real numbers can be attached. This greater precision permits the use of more powerful statistical techniques to examine the data.

If children were unable to consider more than one dimension, their ratings of happiness/sadness would have reflected changes either in the length of the cookies or in their width, but not both. Results of the study, however, showed that the happiness ratings were a function of length and width, clearly indicating that children were attending to both dimensions. Subsequent research by Cuneo (1980) extended these same findings down to children of ages 3 and 4, a preoperational age previously presumed to be incapable of attending to more than one dimension.

Findings like these indicate that preoperational children are capable of much more abstract cognitive activity than Piaget believed possible. But demonstrating such capabilities in a laboratory in response to precise questions from an experimenter is not the same as using abstract thought in the complex and imprecise environment of the home. It is possible that the cognitive abilities exhibited only in the laboratory during the preoperational period become routine aspects of the child's everyday life during the period of concrete operations.

THE PERIOD OF FORMAL OPERATIONS

At some time between the ages of 11 and 15, children become capable of formal operations, or logical thought. Whereas a child in the concrete operations period attempts to solve problems by direct experience with the materials involved in the problem, an adolescent in the formal operations period first thinks about possible solutions, and only later turns to an empirical test of the hypotheses the thinking process has generated.

The difference between these two approaches can be illustrated by an interesting experiment on the truth value of statements (Osherson & Markman, 1975). In this study the experimenter stood behind a table containing a pile of poker chips of various colors, and asked the subjects to indicate whether a statement the experimenter would make about the chips was true. In one experimental condition, the experimenter pulled a chip out of the pile, concealing its color, and then made two statements about the chip. In another condition, the experimenter pulled a chip out of the pile, but revealed its color and held it up before the subject while making the two statements. The two crucial statements were "Either the chip in my hand is green or it is not green" and "The chip in my hand is green and it is not green."

Notice that the first statement is always true, regardless of the color of the chip held in the experimenter's hand, whereas the second statement is always false, also regardless of the color of the chip held in the experimenter's hand. The point is that knowing this requires the kind of logical thought present during the period of formal operations but missing during the period of concrete operations. Adolescent and adult subjects correctly focus on the statements, assessing their truth value in the abstract. Children in the age range of concrete operations, however, concentrate on the visual cues. These children will judge both statements to be true if the experimenter is holding a green chip, false if the experimenter is holding a red chip, and will say they "can't tell" if the chip is concealed.

Another example of the difference between concrete operations and formal operations is provided by one of Piaget's experimental procedures. Suppose there are four beakers of colorless liquid. One of the liquids is a catalyst; when mixed with another liquid, it produces color. One of the other three liquids, however, is a bleach that can-

Four colorless liquids. One is catalyst and one is bleach. When the catalyst combines with one of the inactive liquids, it produces color. When the catalyst combines with the bleach, however, it produces no color.

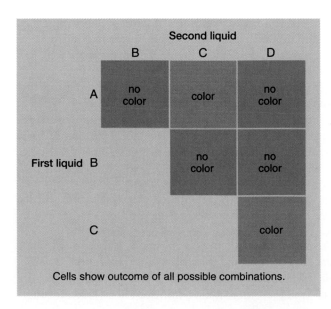

A   B   C   D   C + D

If C + D produces color, how many more combinations must be tested to identify the catalyst and the bleach?

FIGURE 16-7 A problem in formal operations. The colored liquid and bleach problem is a typical example of the kinds of tests psychologists use to study the difference between the cognitive abilities associated with the concrete operations period and those associated with the formal operations period.

cels out the action of the catalyst. The four colorless liquids and one combination are shown in Figure 16-7. The question is which liquid is the catalyst and which is the bleach.

A child in the later years of the period of concrete operations can solve this problem, but only by mixing together all the possible pairs of liquids. This systematic empirical approach guarantees that the problem will be solved, but solved inefficiently. If every pour cost $5, the concrete-operational child would need to spend $30 to find the answer. The outcome is shown in Figure 16-8.

The adolescent or adult capable of formal operations can solve the problem in a much more efficient way. This approach consists of testing combinations of liquids systematically to reduce the number of possible solutions to the problem. Following this procedure, it is possible to arrive at the solution without mixing all possible combinations of liquids. Thus, knowing that the C + D combination produces the colored liquid, we can conclude the following:

Either C is the catalyst or D is the catalyst (because no color occurs without the catalyst), and
Neither C nor D is the bleach (because presence of the bleach eliminates any color), so by elimination,
Either A or B must be the bleach.

The next step would be to mix either C or D with one of the other two liquids. Any test of C or D with A or B that produces color gives the solution to the problem. For example, if C + A produces color, then C must be the catalyst (because it also pro-

Second liquid

	B	C	D
A	no color	color	no color
First liquid B		no color	no color
C			color

Cells show outcome of all possible combinations.

FIGURE 16-8 Concrete operational strategy for the colorless liquids problem. To solve the colorless liquid problem, a child in the concrete operations period would test every single combination to see which produces a colored solution. This particular matrix indicates that C is the catalyst and B is the bleach.

duced color when combined with D), and B must be the bleach (because if A were the bleach, the C + A mixture would have been colorless).

Only if combining C or D with A or B produces a colorless liquid must additional steps be taken. Thus if we test C + B and get a colorless liquid, three possibilities remain:

C is not the catalyst (so D is) and B is the bleach, or
C is not the catalyst (so D is) and A is the bleach, or
C is the catalyst and B is the bleach.

Determining which of these possibilities is correct requires at most two more tests. If we tested D + A and got a colored liquid, we would have the solution. If we got a colorless liquid, however, two possibilities remain:

D is the catalyst and A is the bleach, or
C is the catalyst and B is the bleach.

Combining C with A or D with B would then give the solution. In any event, using formal operations, it is possible to solve the problem with a maximum of an additional three tests instead of six. At a charge of $5 per pour, this difference may not seem significant. Imagine, however, that you are an executive looking for a solution to a problem with millions of dollars at stake on each alternative you try and the superiority of reasoning over trial-and-error becomes obvious.

HEREDITY AND ENVIRONMENT RECONSIDERED

Not all children (or even all adults) reach the stage of formal operations (Neimark, 1981). Attainment of formal-operational thought is related to overall intelligence; some very bright children become capable of such thought relatively early, whereas some less capable individuals never attain this level of cognitive development. But education also plays a role: Training in physics, chemistry, or logic enhances the ability to engage in formal-operational thought (Hetherington & Parke, 1986).

These individual differences illustrate a point that is inherent both in Piaget's theory and in the recent challenges to his theory: Cognitive development depends on a combination of heredity and environment. This point has been made repeatedly in this chapter as well as elsewhere in the book. Here it is important to note that the biological processes of assimilation and accommodation have their counterparts in the cognitive realm. The individual's cognitive structures are at once innate and influenced by experience, and proficiency at various cognitive tasks can be limited by genetic endowment or enhanced by training. The challenge is to show exactly what each of these factors contributes to the increasing cognitive sophistication of the developing child.

INTERIM SUMMARY

Piaget's theory of cognitive development views cognitive structures as analogous to biological units. Schemata, or representations of external reality, are joined together in ever more complex networks to create systems of thought. This is accomplished through the process of adaptation, which consists of assimilation (the incorporation of external elements into structures within the organism) and accommodation (modification of the organism to adjust to environmental demands). The process of cognitive development occurs in four qualitatively distinct stages. During the first stage, the sensorimotor period (birth to age 2), the child develops a concept of object permanence, the knowledge that an object still exists even though it is out of sight. Also during this stage the child's abilities develop through a series of phases in which innate reflexes give way to repetitive actions and eventually to intentional "experiments" to discover the properties of objects. The second stage, the preoperational period (ages 2 to 7), is characterized by the development of the symbolic function, the cognitive process that underlies formation of systems of representation, the most important of which is language. Preoperational thought is limited by animism (endowing inanimate objects with human sensations and intentions), centration (failure to consider more than a single dimension), and irreversibility (inability to see processes as reversible). These limitations disappear during the third stage, the period of concrete operations (ages 7 to 11), during which the child becomes able to decenter, or to consider more than one aspect of a problem at the same time. At some time between the ages of 11 and 15, children become capable of formal operations, or logical thought. In contrast to the concrete-operational child, who solves a problem by empirically testing all the possible solutions, the adolescent can solve a problem by developing and testing hypotheses. Piaget's theory has been challenged by recent research showing that infants and children are often capable of performing various cognitive tasks at earlier ages than the theory would suggest; nevertheless, it remains the most comprehensive and influential theory of cognitive development.

THE INFORMATION-PROCESSING APPROACH TO COGNITIVE DEVELOPMENT

The recent challenge to some of Piaget's conclusions has come from research in information processing that extends the methods and perspective of cognitive psychology into childhood and infancy. This approach presents an alternative to Piaget on several key issues. The picture emerging from this research is of an infant who knows more, and whose cognitive processes are less qualitatively different from those of the adult, than Piaget believed.

THE CONTROVERSY OVER REPRESENTATION

The ability to form a **representation** of an absent object, person, or event is a crucial aspect of cognitive development. As we have just seen, Piaget maintains that this ability develops over the course of the sensorimotor period. Although there is general agreement that the infant changes from a sensory being to a symbolic one during the first two years, questions have been raised about the nature of the representations formed in this period. Piaget argued that mental pictures of external objects are organized into logicomathematical categories with distinct boundaries, but recent research suggests two important qualifications to this conclusion.

The first qualification, regarding the nature of the categories involved in an infant's symbolic thought, can be illustrated by an example. Suppose a family has two pets, and a toddler who sees one of them knows that the other is absent (the toddler has developed object permanence). This knowledge requires some kind of cognitive structure in which each pet is individually identified (such as by name), but in which the two animals are grouped together (as pets). In Piaget's theory, the toddler would have a mental label for each pet, and those two labels would both be included in the mental category of "pets."

An alternative view, however, suggests that the child's own natural categories might be "fuzzy," differing significantly from logical categories like "pets" (Rosch, 1983). As we saw in Chapter 14, the natural cognitive categories of adults are not always logical (for example, whales may loosely be considered "fish," not "mammals"). Even if the infant's cognition is qualitatively different from that of the adult, there is no reason to believe that children's cognitive categories are somehow more logically organized than those of adults. Perhaps instead of a logical category, the child has a cognitive grouping best described as "important things in my immediate environment." Not only the two pets but also several favorite toys might be included in this grouping; anything missing from it would be noticed.

The second qualification has to do with the presumed existence and use of specific category labels. Not all of what is represented in a child's mind is an object that can be placed into a category. The temper tantrum Piaget's daughter Jacqueline imitated was a sequence of events, or, in terms of modern cognitive psychology, a **script** (Schank & Abelson, 1977). A script is a form of procedural knowledge that bears little relation to logical cognitive categories. Moreover, there is reason to believe that children's representations of events are different from their representations of objects (Nelson, 1983). In short, recent research suggests that the process of representation among infants extends beyond the use of cognitive categories to other capabilities more similar to those seen in adults.

ARITHMETIC AMONG PREOPERATIONAL CHILDREN

Despite Piaget's emphasis on logicomathematical categories, his theory assumes that preoperational children are incapable of the complex mental activity needed for such tasks as arithmetic. Piaget uses addition as an example. Addition can be performed either physically or mentally, and is reversible through subtraction. When performed physically, it requires only the conservation of number—a child must be able to recognize, for example, that adding two marbles to a group of six creates a larger group. When performed mentally, it requires a "set theoretical structure" (Piaget, 1983, p. 105), because it involves algebraic grouping (one set of x elements, when added to another set of y objects, produces a total equal to $x + y$). Precisely because he believed children under the age of 7 were unable to perform such logical operations, Piaget posited that the preoperational period extended from age 2 to age 7.

But are young children really incapable of making judgments based on number? Recent research suggests that the answer depends on what is actually meant by "using a counting system." According to one analysis, counting actually involves five principles (Gelman & Gallistel, 1978; see also Gallistel & Gelman, 1990):

1. The principle of one-to-one correspondence—each element in an array must be given a unique "tag."

2. The stable-order principle—the tags must be arranged in an unchanging order.

3. The cardinal principle—the final tag in an array is the "cardinal value" of the array; it answers the question, "How many items are there?"

4. The abstraction principle—the first three principles can be applied to any collection of items, whether the items are like or unlike, real or imagined.

5. The order-irrelevance principle—the items in an array can be tagged in any order, provided that the other principles are followed.

Suppose that a child is asked to count the elements of an array containing two items and responds by saying "3, 7" rather than "1, 2." If the child counts a three-item array by saying "3, 7, 9" instead of "1, 2, 3" and responds to the "How many" question with "9," then according to the principles just listed the child is counting. The difference between this sort of counting and the counting done by adults is that the child is not using the "correct" tags. But if counting is defined as following the principles rather than as using the appropriate tags, children as young as age three and four can not only count one array of items, but can also generalize the principles to count a different array containing more individual elements (Gelman & Baillargeon, 1983). These results are further indication that the cognitive capacities of the preoperational child are substantially more extensive and sophisticated than Piaget believed.

MODELS OF THE NOVICE INFORMATION PROCESSOR

Limits on Processing Capacity

Modern cognitive psychology, as described in several earlier chapters, attempts to understand how the human organism processes information. This approach has now been extended to cognitive development (Flavell, 1985; Klahr & Wallace, 1976; Miller, 1983). One of the central features of the information-processing approach is its "almost compulsive analysis of the experimental or real-life task facing the child or adult" (Miller, 1983, p. 261). How much information is presented to the child by a situation? How much of this information must be stored by the child in order to solve the problem? What general rules might be invoked, once the requirements of the situation have been analyzed? What specific steps must be taken to translate the solution into effective action? How can such action be monitored to ensure that it is progressing toward the desired objective?

Where Piagetian theory posits differences in kind in the capabilities of children in the four stages, the information-processing view concentrates on differences in degree. In an important sense, adults are experts at information processing, whereas children are novices. As novices, children lack the extensive store of additional knowledge that adults possess and many of the strategies that adults use to simplify the processing task; and their information-processing systems can more easily be overloaded. Consider trying to remember this string of numbers: 149217761963. An adult can dramatically simplify this task by chunking the string into three segments tied to events in U.S. history—1492, 1776, and 1963 (the year of President John F. Kennedy's assassination)—but these convenient referents are not available to young children.

The kind of reasoning required to solve the colorless liquid problem discussed earlier provides another example. An adult has learned to play what Flavell (1985) calls the "game" of logical thought, and so has general knowledge of the strategy that should be followed to solve the problem. By contrast, the child, as novice information processor, is much less likely to know that the rules for solving one kind of problem can often be generalized to a substantially different problem.

Rules and Predictions

The cognitive approach is characterized by meticulous analysis of the details involved in accomplishing tasks; appropriately, it accords a central place to the analogy between human information processing and computer information processing. If the information requirements and decision rules of a task can be specified with sufficient precision, then computer models of the task can be used to predict how human subjects will actually perform. Siegler (1978) applied this technique to a traditional Piagetian reasoning problem based on the principle of a balance scale (seesaw). A model of the apparatus appears in Figure 16-9.

As shown in the figure, the balance scale has four equally spaced pegs on each side of the fulcrum. Weights (all equal) can be hung from these pegs. The researcher tells a child how many weights will be placed on each of the pegs, and then asks the child to predict which side of the balance will go down. Two pieces of information are critical for solving this problem: the number of weights used on each side and

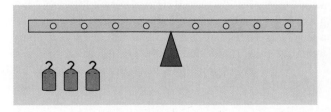

FIGURE 16-9 The weighted balance problem. Various combinations of weights are hung from the pegs on each arm of the balance and children are asked to say which arm will go down.

their distance from the fulcrum. Siegler outlined four decision rules a child might use to solve the problem:

1. Consider only the number of weights (and predict that the side with more weights will go down).
2. Consider only the number of weights unless they are equal, then also take into account the distance.
3. Consider both the number of weights and the distance, but "muddle through" if one side has more weights but the other side's weights are farther away from the center.
4. Measure exact weight and distance by multiplying the number of weights hanging on a peg times the ordinal number of the peg (ordinal numbers can be used because pegs are equally spaced). Use this computation to predict which side will go down.

These four rules progress in sophistication, and only the last, of course, produces consistently accurate predictions. Each, however, is a formal rule (they could all be translated into computer programs) that, if followed consistently, would result in a specific pattern of correct predictions and errors for any given series of problems. It should thus be possible to determine whether or not a child is following one of these rules by comparing the child's performance on a particular series of problems with the results predicted by that rule. Siegler tested children of age 5, 9, 13, and 17 and confirmed his expectation that older children would use more sophisticated rules than the younger ones.

For our purposes it is important to note that the results also showed that all the children, even the youngest, used some formal decision model for making their predictions; the performance of the younger children differed in degree, not kind, from that of the older children. Contrary to what Piaget would lead us to expect, the results did not support the conclusion that children in the preoperational period (age 5) would guess randomly, or that children in the concrete operations stage (age 9) would rely on physical manipulation of the materials.

INTERIM SUMMARY

The information-processing approach presents alternative views on several key issues of Piaget's theory of cognitive development. Children may learn to represent absent objects to themselves not, as Piaget argued, in the form of logicomathematical categories but in the "fuzzy" categories that are, in any case, characteristic of adult thought. The process of representation in infants may also extend beyond the use of cognitive categories to other capabilities similar to those of adults. Also contrary to Piaget's belief, children between 2 and 7 may be capable of arithmetic reasoning even though they do not use the same tags for numbers as adults. The information-processing approach suggests that the cognitive differences between children and adults is one of degree, not of kind. From this point of view, adults are expert information processors whereas children are novices.

CONCLUDING COMMENT

Piaget combined the processes of biological maturation and increasing experience with the world into a comprehensive model that views cognitive development as a progression through four discrete and qualitatively different stages. Improved methodologies and new approaches have led developmental psychologists to the view that children's cognitive capabilities are even more impressive than Piaget believed, and that these capabilities are present much earlier than he thought. Despite recent findings that contradict elements of his theory, the issues in cognitive development that Piaget first framed are likely to influence study in the field for many years to come.

SUMMARY

1. Cognitive development is a subfield of developmental psychology, the branch of psychology devoted to the study of change over time in psychological capacities and processes. Cognitive development examines processes of change in mental capabilities. A central issue for this subfield has always been the degree to which adult skills and capacities are learned as opposed to being innate.

2. The nature–nurture debate began with the ancient Greeks. Plato argued that true knowledge could be obtained only by reasoned consideration of the innate ideas he called Forms, whereas Aristotle took the position that the child's mind was a blank slate, or *tabula rasa,* waiting to be filled by experience.

3. One of the important implications of Darwin's theory of evolution is that mental capacities as well as physical characteristics have survival value. The *organismic model* of development reflects this implication of Darwinian theory. It emphasizes the adaptive purposes of behavioral development and proposes that development proceeds through a universal sequence of qualitatively different stages. Several major developmental theories, such as Piaget's theory of cognitive development and Freud's theory of psychosexual development, follow this model.

4. In contrast to the organismic model, the *mechanistic model* of development views the human organism as a machine that passively responds to demands imposed on it from the external environment. This model emphasizes processes of learning; it views developmental change as gradual and not occurring in stages.

5. The *heritability* of any phenotypic characteristic is the extent to which variations in the characteristic are governed by variations in genotype. This can be expressed as the ratio between genotypic variation and phenotypic variation, giving an index of heritability.

6. Because it is unlikely to find behavioral characteristics that are attributable to single genes, psychologists use *quantitative genetics,* the statistical theory that underlies modern behavior genetics, to search for family resemblances that can distinguish genetic from environmental factors affecting behavior. The two most powerful research designs for assessing the heritability of psychological characteristics are the adoption design, which compares genetically related individuals raised in different environments to genetically unrelated individuals who are raised in a common environment, and the twin study, which compares the behavioral similarity of identical twins to that of fraternal twins.

7. Numerous twin studies have indicated that identical twins are more similar to one another on intellectual capacity, personality characteristics, and even interests, than are fraternal twins.

8. Piaget's theory of cognitive development employs the complementary principles of *assimilation* and *accommodation* to describe how the individual transforms the external world in order to know it. According to Piaget's theory, cognitive development can be separated into four discrete stages: the *sensorimotor period,* the *preoperational period,* the *period of concrete operations,* and the *period of formal operations.*

9. The sensorimotor period extends from birth to about age 2. In this period the child changes from a "reflex organism" to an individual capable of symbolic thought. Particularly important is the child's development of *object permanence,* the knowledge that objects, animals, and people continue to exist even when they are out of sight.

10. During the preoperational period, which extends roughly from age 2 to age 7, the child uses the *symbolic function* to build

systems of representation, the most important of which is language. Although the child's cognitive processes become more sophisticated in this stage, Piaget maintained that they are characterized by *animism, centration,* and *irreversibility.*

11. During the period of concrete operations, from approximately age 7 to approximately age 11, animism disappears and thought processes undergo decentration. The child comes to understand that processes are reversible, and also that material is conserved even when it is transformed to another shape.

12. At some time between the ages of 11 and 15, children become capable of the formal operations that characterize logical thought.

13. Advances in methodology have enabled psychologists to discover that children have more cognitive skills, and at an earlier age, than Piaget believed. These results have led proponents of the *information-processing approach* to cognitive development to suggest that the child's capabilities differ in degree but not in kind from those of the adult.

14. Whereas Piaget's theory argued that mental representation in children consists of logicomathematical categories, the information-processing approach suggests that it consists of "fuzzy" categories, or of event descriptions similar to scripts rather than object categories. It also appears that children are capable of arithmetic reasoning at an earlier age than Piaget thought possible, even though they may not be able to use an "adult" version of counting.

FOCUS QUESTIONS

1. Trace both sides of the nature–nurture debate as it applies to the development of psychological capacities.

2. Discuss the relationship between evolutionary theory and the organismic model of development. What is the major difference between the organismic model and the mechanistic model?

3. Define the concept of heritability. Why are principles of quantitative genetics needed to estimate the genetic basis of most psychological characteristics?

4. How are adoption designs and twin studies used to indicate the heritability of various traits? What qualifications are necessary in the interpretation of heritability?

5. Describe the six phases of the sensorimotor period of cognitive development according to Piaget's theory.

6. According to Piaget, what is the fundamental cognitive change that occurs during the preoperational period? In what way has recent research changed our view of the intellectual capabilities of the preoperational child?

7. What is the major difference in cognitive functioning between a child in the period of concrete operations and one in the period of formal operations?

8. Describe the information-processing approach to cognitive development. Does it assume change is quantitative or qualitative? What does it suggest are the primary limitations of the child information-processor?

auditory channel (it is produced vocally and received by the ears); so do bird songs. Human speech is broadcast in all directions, but hearers can use the sound to locate the speaker; the same is true of bird songs. The sounds of speech are transitory (they fade rapidly); so are bird songs. Humans can hear the sounds they produce; so can birds. Humans can reproduce exactly what they hear others speak; birds can reproduce the songs of their own species and some can mimic the songs of other species. Humans can produce specialized sounds, such as shouts, whispers, a normal speaking volume; birds also make specialized sounds, such as a screeching sound produced in the presence of danger that differs from the song sound produced in safer circumstances.

More important than the physical characteristics of speech sounds for defining language is that these sounds are grouped together to refer to objects and abstract ideas. Five features of language involve this ability to convey meaning. The first of these is *semanticity*, the ability of language forms to stand for things in the external world. All natural human languages use symbols of various kinds (like words) to refer to people, places, things, events, and abstract concepts. Some forms of animal communication also show a degree of semanticity. The bee's dance, for example, is semantic in that its pattern signifies the location of a food source (Hockett, 1960). A computer language, on the other hand, is not semantic because its elements do not stand for anything outside the program.

A second meaning-based feature of language is *arbitrariness*. In language, the relationship between symbols and the things they represent is arbitrary—one symbol could do as well as another. Many animal communication systems lack this feature. The pattern of the bee's dance, for example, depends on the location of a food source relative to the position of the hive and the position of the sun. A human beekeeper could tell someone how to get from a hive to a patch of flowers by describing its distance in meters and its compass location, or by describing the roads and paths to take to reach it. Moreover, the beekeeper could do this regardless of his or her own position or the time of day, and could do so in English or Chinese or any other language. The symbols the beekeeper uses and the things they represent are arbitrarily related to each other.

A third meaning-based feature of language is *displacement*, the ability to describe things that are remote in time and space. A child who sees the family cat being chased up a tree by a dog can later describe the situation to a parent, even though neither the dog, the cat, or the tree is physically present at the time. Displacement is

Ancient Egyptian hieroglyphics are nonarbitrary symbols used to refer to objects and abstract ideas.

not unique to language; to a limited extent it is also a feature of the bee's dance (Hockett, 1960).

The final two meaning-based features are perhaps the most important for distinguishing language from animal communication. The first of these is *productivity,* the ability to use words to describe things the listener, and often the speaker, may never have seen. For example, although no one has ever seen little green Martians, we can easily conceive of them and talk about them. The bee's dance is also productive: The bees that are observing the dance may never have been to the exact location being conveyed, but they can, nevertheless, find the area. The difference between us and the bees is that the bee conveying the information (doing the dance) has seen the flowers, whereas human language can also be used to describe things nobody has seen (such as the future). Moreover, whereas the bee's dance is limited, the words in a language can be used to create an infinite number of sentences. The second of these final meaning-based features is *traditional transmission,* which refers to the fact that many elements of language are transmitted from one generation to the next through social interaction. Thus, whereas all members of a species of birds sing the same song (or minor variations of it), humans speak thousands of different languages whose content is largely determined by culture.

Apart from their other distinctive features, all human languages are characterized by **syntax,** a set of rules that governs the way words are combined into clauses, phrases, and sentences, and that distinguishes acceptable from unacceptable constructions. Recent research and theory in linguistics suggests that syntax plays a critical role in distinguishing human language from animal communication. From a few basic speech sounds, combined sequentially, humans are able to construct words. Then, using syntax, they can talk about what has happened in the past, discuss events, objects, and emotions in the present, and speculate about the future.

A Working Definition of Language

Communication between human beings may have its origin in speech sounds, but the distinctive characteristics of those sounds are not what distinguishes a language from other forms of communication. Rather, it is what the sounds mean that is most important. A true language must have the properties of semanticity, arbitrariness, productivity, and traditional transmission, and must follow rules of syntax. In short, a **language** can be thought of as a rule-governed use of arbitrary symbols to convey meaning.

By contrast, Chinese ideographs, which originally represented objects, have evolved into symbols that have conceptual and phonetic meaning. In this regard the ideographs are much like English words.

(a)

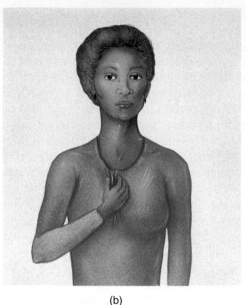

(b)

FIGURE 17-1 The signs for "tree" (*a*) and "Canada" (*b*) in American Sign Language. The sign for "tree" is iconic; the sign for "Canada" is arbitrary.

By this definition, language is not limited to speech. Writing also qualifies, as do sign languages like American Sign Language (ASL) used by the deaf (Gleitman & Wanner, 1986). Although ASL is highly **iconic,** in that many of its symbols mimic the objects they describe, it also contains arbitrary symbols (Klima & Bellugi, 1979). The sign for "tree," for example, could be considered iconic with the upright forearm representing the trunk, the hand and fingers waving gently back and forth representing the branches, and the other hand representing the ground. (See Figure 17-1.) The sign for "Canada," in contrast, which is made by grasping one's shirt, is completely arbitrary. Thus, in spite of its many iconic signs, ASL clearly exhibits semanticity and arbitrariness. ASL is also capable of describing things that are remote in time and space (displacement); it can be used to generate new combinations (productivity); and it must be taught to the next generation (traditional transmission). Finally, ASL, like any other language, is governed by rules of syntax (Klima & Bellugi, 1979). As we see later in the chapter, ASL has played an important role in attempts to determine whether or not nonhuman species can learn and use language.

NATIVISM VERSUS EMPIRICISM IN LANGUAGE

Theories of how we use rules to combine arbitrary symbols into a language capable of conveying meaning—like theories of knowledge in general—usually reflect either a nativist or an empiricist position. According to the nativist position, the capacity for language is an innate and uniquely human characteristic. All children are born with the mental structures that allow them to learn language, even though the particular language they learn depends on the environment in which they are raised. This position can be traced to Descartes, who considered linguistic ability to be one of the two criteria that distinguish humans from other animals (the other is that human actions are guided by reason). Descartes noted that even the most "depraved and stupid" people are capable of arranging "different words together, forming of them a statement by which they make known their thoughts," whereas "no other animal . . . can do the same" (Descartes, 1952/1637, pp. 59–60).

By contrast, the empiricist position (which can be traced to the British philosophers Locke and Hume) holds that learning language, like learning anything else, is the result of experience. Children learn language over a period of time because they are immersed in a linguistic community. In other words, children are not born with a special propensity for language, but must acquire it from parents and others in their

438

environments. Because it holds that language is just another learned behavior, the empiricist position suggests that other animals besides humans can learn language (provided, of course, that they have sufficient cognitive capacity).

In modern **psycholinguistics** (the study of psychological factors involved in language learning and usage) the nativism–empiricism debate has been framed on the empiricist side principally by the work of the linguist Leonard Bloomfield and the behavioral psychologist B. F. Skinner and on the nativist side principally by the work of the linguist Noam Chomsky (Gleitman & Wanner, 1986).

Bloomfield, writing in the 1930s, argued that language can be analyzed as consisting of a set of empirically verifiable rules. These rules can be mastered by reasoning from experience. Children can learn them, in other words, by inferring them from the linguistic behavior of adults in their environment. No innate capacity is required. Similar empiricist arguments were more recently advanced by Skinner (1957), who believed that language is learned according to the principles of operant conditioning described in Chapter 12.

According to Chomsky, humans cannot learn language by example alone. He argued that the collection of utterances available to the child (called the corpus of language) is too incomplete, and too internally inconsistent, to permit effective learning by analogy or reinforcement. Moreover, there are structural similarities among languages that cast doubt on the empiricist position. For example, all languages have a natural order for subject, verb, and object; in English this is subject-verb-object (known as SVO). There are six logically possible orders for S, V, and O, but two of these (OVS and OSV) are not used in any language (Greenberg, 1963). Given that there are thousands of languages spoken throughout the world, the fact that only two-thirds of the possible SVO orders are actually used suggests the presence of innate principles of language structure.

Just as the nature–nurture debate has framed the study of cognitive development, the nativism–empiricism debate has framed the study of language acquisition. And as with the nature–nurture debate, in the nativism–empiricism debate the truth probably lies somewhere between the two extreme positions. Consider our working definition of language as a rule-governed combination of arbitrary symbols. Clearly, the connection between a symbol (word) and the thing to which it refers is learned rather than innate—otherwise there would only be one language in the world. Just as clearly, however, there are structural similarities among languages that strongly suggest the existence of innate cognitive capabilities that make language a universal human attribute.

INTERIM SUMMARY

Three facts form the backdrop for the nativism–empiricism controversy over whether language is innate (nativism) or learned (empiricism): human language is universal; children learn a first language effortlessly; but children learn only the language or languages they hear early in their lives. Language shares many features with other forms of animal communication. The features that most clearly distinguish it from other forms of communication include arbitrariness, productivity, traditional transmission, and syntax. Language can be defined as a rule-governed use of arbitrary symbols to convey meaning. This definition includes writing and American Sign Language as well as speech. The nativist position on language can be traced to Descartes; the empiricist position can be traced to Locke and Hume. In modern psycholinguistics the nativism–empiricism debate has been framed on the empiricist side principally by the work of the linguist Leonard Bloomfield and the behavioral psychologist B. F. Skinner and on the nativist side principally by the work of the linguist Noam Chomsky.

THE STRUCTURE OF LANGUAGE

Language forms a hierarchical structure, with the basic sounds of speech at the bottom, and extended meaningful statements at the top. In this section we will examine that structure.

AIR FLOW AND SPEECH SOUNDS

Vowels and Consonants

Human speech—be it the simplest utterance of a child or the most elaborate statements of a skilled orator—consists of the regulation of the flow of air from the lungs. Air that is forced out of the lungs first encounters the vocal cords, which look more like an interior set of lips than like cords. When the vocal cords are fully closed, no air passes through. When the vocal cords are open, but not vibrating, the air passing through creates voiceless sounds. When the vocal cords are open and vibrating, they produce voiced sounds. These sounds are modified as they pass through the oral and nasal cavities, which filter or interrupt the air flow. (The human vocal tract is shown in Figure 17-2.)

If only filtering occurs, the result is a vowel. If the air flow is stopped or diverted, so that it is released as a hiss or a small explosion, the result is a consonant. Vowels are usually distinguished from one another by the way the tongue, the interior surfaces of the oral cavity, and the lips interact to produce them. Thus the sound of a vowel is affected by which part of the tongue is used (front, middle, or back), how

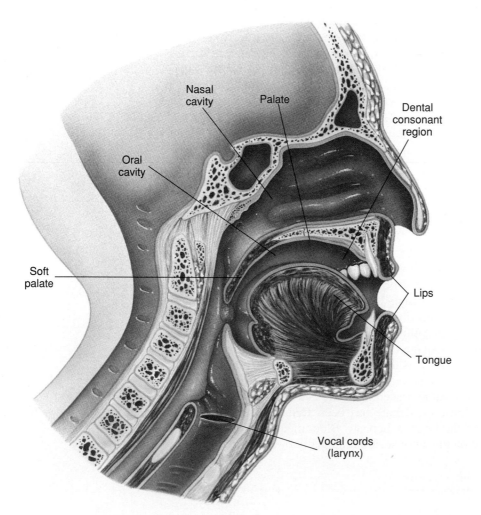

FIGURE 17-2 Elements of the human vocal apparatus.

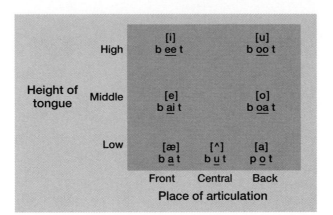

FIGURE 17-3 Anatomical features of some English vowels. Each vowel sound is indicated here by its symbol in the international phonetic alphabet and by a word in which the sound represented by the symbol is underlined.

high the tongue is elevated within the oral cavity, and whether the lips are rounded or unrounded. The result is a three-way classification of vowel sounds. Some of the vowel sounds found in English are shown in Figure 17-3. (Each vowel sound in the figure is indicated by its symbol in the international phonetic alphabet, such as [o], and by a word in which the sound represented by the symbol has been underlined.) In English, the lips are rounded only to pronounce [u] and [o] and other "back" vowels not shown in Figure 17-3 (Clark & Clark, 1977).

Consonants are distinguished from one another by where in the vocal tract the air flow is restricted (for example by the tongue pressing against the teeth or the lips pressing against each other), how complete the restriction is, and whether or not the vocal cords are vibrating during the restriction. Locations at which air flow can be restricted are called **places of articulation,** and as many as 10 of these have been identified (Ladefoged, 1971). Several of the linguistically more common places of articulation are shown in Figure 17-4.

If air flow is completely interrupted, the result is a stop, as with the [p] in "pine." If air flow is constricted to create friction with the articulatory surfaces, the result is

FIGURE 17-4 Some of the places of articulation for the formation of consonants. In a bilabial consonant, the lips press together. In a labiodental consonant, the lower lip presses against the upper teeth. In dental and interdental consonants, the tongue presses against the teeth. In an alveolar consonant, the tongue touches the alveolar ridge, and in a postalveolar consonant, the tongue touches just behind the alveolar ridge.

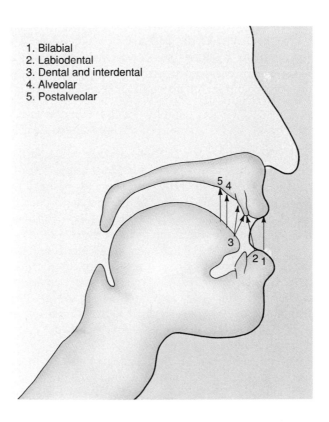

1. Bilabial
2. Labiodental
3. Dental and interdental
4. Alveolar
5. Postalveolar

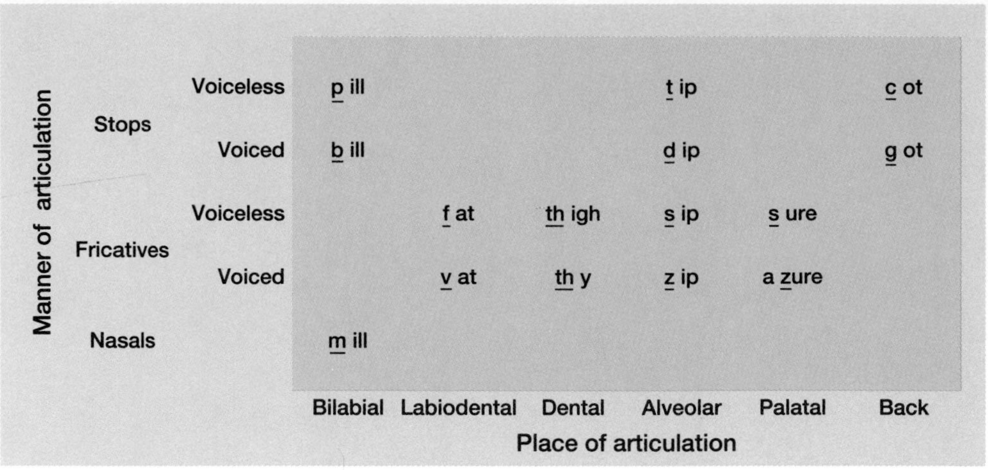

Manner of articulation			Bilabial	Labiodental	Dental	Alveolar	Palatal	Back
Stops	Voiceless		p̲ ill			t̲ ip		c̲ ot
	Voiced		b̲ ill			d̲ ip		g̲ ot
Fricatives	Voiceless			f̲ at	th̲ igh	s̲ ip	s̲ ure	
	Voiced			v̲ at	th̲ y	z̲ ip	a z̲ure	
Nasals			m̲ ill					

Place of articulation

FIGURE 17-5 The place and manner of articulation of some English consonants.

called a fricative, as with the [f] in "father." If air flow is directed out of the nose rather than the mouth, the result is a nasal, as with the [m] in "method." If you find it difficult to believe that a speech sound is really created by shunting air out of the nose, try pinching your nose shut while humming a constant [m]. Stops, fricatives, and nasals occur in all the world's languages; other ways in which air flow can be restricted to produce consonants are much less prevalent.

Voiced consonants are those produced while the vocal cords are vibrating; unvoiced consonants are those produced when the vocal cords are not vibrating. All nasals are voiced, but fricatives and stops can be voiced or unvoiced. For example, the only difference between [f], as in "father," and [v], as in "vine," is that the [v] is voiced. A sample of voiced and voiceless consonants, each with its corresponding phonetic symbol, is shown in Figure 17-5.

Phonemes

Each consonant and vowel discussed to this point has been described by a single phonetic symbol, as if it were always pronounced in exactly the same way. But this is not the case. Natural language is not a sequence of disconnected sounds; it is a flowing pattern, and to some degree the sound associated with a particular consonant or vowel will change depending on its position in this flow. Hold your hand an inch away from your mouth, and quickly read each of the following sentences aloud.

Print your name here.
I think I'll take a trip.

Notice that there was a puff of air when you said the word "print" in the first sentence, but that there was no puff of air at the end of the word "trip" in the second sentence. The "p" in "print" is aspirated, whereas the "p" in "trip" is unaspirated. An exhaustive transcription of the phonetic characteristics of the two sentences would use the symbol [pʰ] for the aspirated consonant, and the symbol [p] for the unaspirated one to reflect the fact that the two *sounds* are different.

As a speaker of English, you know that these phonetically different sounds are merely variations on a theme. In more formal terms, they are **allophones,** phonetically distinct speech elements that are nevertheless members of a single linguistic category. That category is the **phoneme,** the smallest unit of speech that serves to distinguish one utterance from another. Linguists indicate phonemes by enclosing them in slashes. Thus the English phoneme that includes the allophones [p] and [pʰ] is represented by the symbol /p/.

The phoneme is a *linguistic* category that includes acoustically different sounds. Speakers and listeners must share the same phonemic "assumptions," based on their common language, for a phoneme to be correctly perceived. Speakers of English, as we have seen, do not differentiate [p] from [pʰ]. In some of the world's languages,

442

however, an aspirated stop carries a different meaning from the same stop unaspirated. Thus, for example, in Thai, the phonetic combination [t]am means "to pound," whereas the phonetic combination [tʰ]am means "to do" (Ladefoged, 1971). A native speaker of English, accustomed to treating aspirated and unaspirated stops to be equivalent, might have considerable difficulty in learning this distinction and would need to concentrate on the differences when learning to speak Thai.

ELEMENTS OF MEANING

The Morpheme

Whereas the phoneme is the smallest unit of sound that listeners use to discriminate one utterance from another, the **morpheme** is the smallest unit of language that conveys meaning. Morphemes often are entire words, although they can also be only the root, prefix, or suffix of a word. Just as phonemes have allophones, morphemes have **allomorphs**—variants that have the same meaning. Consider the English morpheme that indicates that a noun is plural. As the following examples show, this morpheme can take one of three forms—[s], [z], or [Iz]—depending on the segment preceding it (Lass, 1984):

cat [s], cap [s], and kite [s]
bag [z], dog [z], and bee [z]
dish [Iz], patch [Iz], and buzz [Iz]

The three phonemes involved in these examples are all allomorphs of the morpheme for plural. We can use this example to clarify further the difference between a phoneme and a morpheme. Suppose you heard someone say,

"I saw three cat [Iz]."

You would instantly know that there was something "wrong" with the utterance but that what the person meant was the plural of "cat." You would recognize that the phoneme was the incorrect allomorph, but you would still understand the intended morpheme.

Words

Although people produce and recognize phonemes and use and understand morphemes, they actually speak in words. In English there are two major classes of words—content words, called **contentives,** and function words, called **functors.** Contentives, which name objects, events, and characteristics, are the heart of a sentence. They include nouns, verbs, adjectives, and adverbs; if nouns or verbs are dropped from a sentence, the overall meaning will change. Contentives form what linguists call an open class, which means that their number is virtually limitless. Every science, for example, has its own vocabulary; as discoveries are made, new words are needed to describe them, and these words ultimately find their way into everyday speech.

Functors, in contrast, are a closed class. They include pronouns (I, you, she, him) and relative pronouns (who, which, whose); prepositions (in, on, to); quantifiers (much, many), determiners (a, an, this), and intensifiers (very, a little); conjunctions of various sorts (and, but, although, if, nevertheless, besides); and auxiliary or linking verbs (can, may, be). Although the functors number just a few hundred, they are the most frequently used words; "the," for example, is by far the most common word in English (Clark & Clark, 1977).

Words can be single morphemes, or they can be combinations of morphemes. For example, *truck* is a single-morpheme word. *Truckers,* however, is a combination of three morphemes: {truck} + {er} + {s}. The stem morpheme indicates an object (*truck*), the second indicates "one who" (as in "one who drives a truck"), and the third is the morpheme for plural (more than one). The structure of every language dictates permissible orders for morphemes within words. For example, "erstruck" is easy to recognize as incorrect.

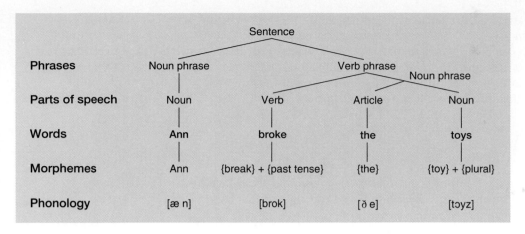

	Sentence			
Phrases	Noun phrase	Verb phrase		Noun phrase
Parts of speech	Noun	Verb	Article	Noun
Words	Ann	broke	the	toys
Morphemes	Ann	{break} + {past tense}	{the}	{toy} + {plural}
Phonology	[æ n]	[brok]	[ð e]	[tɔyz]

FIGURE 17-6 Levels of structure in a sentence.

Sentences

Human language is, of course, more than a series of disconnected words. Consider the sentence in Figure 17-6: "Ann broke the toys." This sentence can be described on any of six levels. At the most basic level, it can be described phonologically, that is, in terms of the sounds of which it is composed when spoken. If the words were unfamiliar, or if you were not already a speaker of English, you could use the phonetic symbols to "sound out" the sentence. (This is why dictionaries include pronunciation guides.)

At the next level, the sentence can be described in terms of the set of morphemes (units of meaning) that make it up. In our example, two of the words actually contain two morphemes, not one. These are the verb "broke," which is composed of the morphemes {break} + {past tense}, and the noun "toys," which is composed of {toy} + {plural}. At the third level are the words of the sentence. These can be described at the fourth level in terms of the parts of speech they represent—noun, verb, and so forth. The parts of speech, in turn, are organized, at the fifth level, into *phrases*. The first noun phrase (NP) consists of the "agent" of the sentence together with its modifiers (in this case there are no modifiers). The verb phrase (VP) consists of the verb and its modifiers (in this case the verb has no modifiers) and another noun phrase. In linguistic terms the verb is the "action," and its object is the "patient" (the entity on which the action is performed). Finally, at the sixth level, the phrases combine to form a sentence consisting of the form agent-action-patient.

PHONOLOGY, SEMANTICS, SYNTAX, AND GRAMMAR

Spoken language begins with sounds; both the speaker and the listener use their knowledge of the *phonology* of a language to distinguish one word from another. These words individually, and as combined in sentences, convey the *semantic* content of an utterance—its meaning. Rules governing the way words combine into phrases and phrases combine into sentences constitute the syntax of a language. Finally, the entire system by which phonology, semantic content, and syntax turn speech sounds into meanings constitutes the **grammar** of a language.

A grammar can be thought of as the total knowledge a native speaker has of his or her language (Aitchison, 1983). Defined this way, a grammar is vastly more inclusive than "the dull prescriptive rules most people are taught about what is, and what is not 'good grammar'" (Clark & Clark, 1977, p. 5). It would include, for example, rules like "In a noun phrase the article always precedes the noun." In fact, the number of rules required to cover both normal and exceptional speech in any language is so large that linguists have not yet written a complete grammar for any language.

How is it possible for people to use grammar so successfully, and for children to learn the rules of language so effortlessly, when linguists cannot fully specify the rules? Four very different answers to this question have been proposed (Aitchison,

1983). According to one, people memorize sentences and then produce appropriate sentences from this memorized store as situations demand. This explanation, although it may account for the way an adult approaches learning a new language before traveling abroad, seems inadequate to explain how anyone becomes a native speaker. It assumes that all sentences one hears will be grammatical, and cannot account for the ability of native speakers to recognize sentences they have never heard before as grammatical or ungrammatical. Neither can it account for the fact that human language is *generative:* People do not search their memories for a previously experienced sentence that might be appropriate in a new context; they simply produce whatever linguistic constructions are demanded by the situation.

If people do not simply memorize sentences, they must use rules of some kind to produce them. According to the second explanation of language production, these rules take the form of a **finite state grammar.** With such a grammar, the number of possible sentences is infinite, but the number of ways to complete a sentence once it has begun is limited, and the limitations increase as more of the sentence is produced. For example, in a sentence like

Would you please pass the _____?

the blank is much more likely to be filled with "salt" than with "carburetor parts" unless one is working in an auto repair shop. Moreover, the sentence as a whole becomes confusing if the blank is filled with "tree stumps." In other words, the range of acceptable words for this last "slot" in the sentence has been restricted by the preceding material. Indeed, the restrictions may begin with the first word: Sentences that begin with "Would" are almost invariably questions. A finite state grammar, then, is organized from left (the beginning of the sentence) to right, and assumes that there are various transition probabilities from one word to the next.

There are, however, major problems with finite state grammars (Best, 1989). First, any competent speaker can insert some other syntactic structure into the middle of an existing sentence. For example,

Would you please *stop talking long enough to* pass the _____?

is more strident than its counterpart above, but it is no less grammatically correct. But how can a subsequent word be dictated by the preceding word, as the finite state grammar requires, if a completely different construction can be inserted between two words? A second problem with a finite state grammar is illustrated by one of Chomsky's famous demonstration sentences:

Colorless green ideas sleep furiously.

It is very difficult to imagine that the word "colorless" ought to be followed by a color name, that an idea can sleep, or that sleep can be done "furiously." Yet, speakers of English immediately recognize this as a grammatically correct, if nonsensical, sentence.

According to the third explanation, language has the hierarchical form of a **phrase structure grammar** (as illustrated in Figure 17-6), rather than the linear form of a finite state grammar. What a native speaker masters is a set of rules about how phrases are organized and combined. Figure 17-7 gives a phrase structure analysis of a shortened version of Chomsky's sentence.

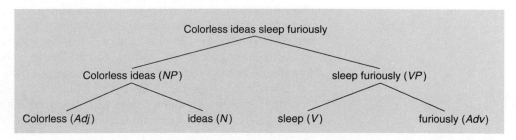

FIGURE 17-7 A phrase structure diagram of a simplified version of a grammatically correct nonsense sentence. Chomsky showed that sentences of this type cannot be explained by finite state grammars.

The phrase structure theory has two major implications. First, native speakers will recognize an utterance as grammatical as long as the phrases and constituents of phrases that compose it follow certain rules. Second, they will recognize sentences with the same phrase structure as similar and those with different phrase structures as dissimilar.

The phrase structure theory has several difficulties (Best, 1989). The most important for our purposes can be illustrated by the following set of three sentences:

> The dog bit the delivery person.
> The dog bit the child.
> The delivery person was bitten by the dog.

The first two sentences have identical phrase structures, but their meanings are entirely different. On the other hand, the first and third sentences have comparable meaning, even though their phrase structures are quite different. Phrase structure theory fails to account for the relationship between the first and third sentences.

In his influential book *Syntactic Structures* (1957), Chomsky described the limitations of finite state and phrase structure grammars and outlined a fourth approach based on the concept of **transformational grammar.** This concept involves a distinction between the underlying meaning of a sentence (its **deep structure**) and the particular organization of the elements or phrases that make up the sentence (its **surface structure**). Looked at this way, the first and third sentences have the same deep structure but different surface structures. According to Chomsky, *transformational rules* govern the way a deep structure sentence is converted into a particular surface structure form. The deep structure sentence itself, however, is also governed by syntactic rules. Thus, syntactic rules dictate semantic content (the deep structure) of a sentence and the phonological content of an utterance (because they specify how the deep structure should be transformed into one spoken sentence or another). The successful use of language requires that a speaker understand its deep structure and the rules for transforming one surface representation into another while preserving the underlying meaning. This understanding, according to the proponents of transformational grammars, is innate.

Meaning and Context

The distinction between surface structure and deep structure helps illuminate some of the reasons for linguistic confusion. Recall the two examples at the beginning of the chapter. The ambiguous sentence in the first example—"The people around you can't read"—could mean either that noise will prevent readers from concentrating or that the library is a resting place for the illiterate. The sentence thus has two possible deep structures, and the child's joke capitalizes on this ambiguity. We infer which of the two meanings is correct from the larger context in which the sentence is embedded.

The second example—"Schedule D is also used to report gains from involuntary conversions of capital assets that are held in connection with a trade or business or a transaction entered into for profit"—is ambiguous in its deep structure as well as on the surface. Not only does it contain a number of expressions that are unfamiliar to the average taxpayer, such as "involuntary conversion" and "capital asset," but it also contains two confusing noun phrases. How can a person gain from an involuntary conversion (whatever that is)? Did someone force the person to act in his or her best interest, as if the person would not have done so voluntarily? And is "a transaction entered into for profit" subordinate to "trade or business" or is it an independent phrase preceded by an implied repetition of "from"? In other words, is Schedule D to be used for reporting both involuntary gains and voluntary ones or for reporting only an involuntary gain that might be obtained in one of three ways? Unfortunately, the tax instructions contain no larger context that could be used to answer these questions.

INTERIM SUMMARY

Speech begins with air flow from the lungs. This flow is modified or interrupted as it passes through the oral and nasal cavities, creating vowels and consonants. The smallest unit of sound that serves to distinguish one utterance from another is the phoneme. A phoneme can have more than one phonetic variant, or allophone. Morphemes are the smallest units of language that convey meaning. Variants of a morpheme that have the same meaning are called allomorphs. English has two major categories of words: contentives, which name objects, events, and characteristics, and functors, the quantifiers, intensifiers, conjunctions, and other function words that bind the contentives together into sentences. The grammar of a language is the set of rules regarding phonology (speech sounds), semantic content (meaning of words), and syntax (structure for combining words into sentences) that represents a speaker's total knowledge of his or her language. Four models have been proposed to account for our ability to learn and use a grammar: memorization, finite state grammars, phrase structure grammars, and transformational grammars. In a transformational grammar, the underlying meaning of a sentence is its deep structure and the particular form it takes is its surface structure. Syntactic rules govern both deep structure and the transformation of deep structure into surface structure.

THEORIES OF LANGUAGE ACQUISITION

When it comes to producing language, human babies are no more competent than puppies or infant monkeys. But as humans develop, they become capable of complex, expressive, and eloquent speech. Are human beings uniquely "preprogrammed" for language, or do they learn it through processes that could be generalized to other animals as well? This is the fundamental issue in the study of language acquisition. Research on the topic has taken three major avenues: investigation of the way humans acquire language, investigation of the linguistic capabilities of nonhuman primates, and investigation of the creation of new languages. In this section we consider each of these lines of research in turn, but first we look briefly at the characteristics of childhood speech.

WHAT CHILDREN SAY

Although the process is subject to a great deal of variation, children normally acquire the elements of language in a specific sequence, as shown in Table 17-1.

TABLE 17-1   Major Milestones in the Acquisition of Language

Approximate Beginning Age	Language Production Stage
Birth	Crying
6 weeks	Cooing
6 months	Babbling
8 months	Differences in intonation patterns
1 year	1-word utterances
18 months	2-word utterances
2 years	Word inflections (plurals, possessives)
2 1/4 years	Questions, negatives
3 years	Complete sentences
5 years	Rare or complex constructions
10 years	Mature speech

SOURCE: Adapted from Aitchison, 1983.

If ever you doubt that language begins in the lungs, spend a few days around a crying baby. Try to think of the noise as exercise for the vocal cords. Crying is not usually regarded as linguistic activity, although most parents can distinguish cries of pain from cries of hunger or frustration. Like crying, cooing involves sounds—mostly vowel-like utterances—that are universal among babies, regardless of the linguistic community into which they have been born (Aitchison, 1983). During the babbling period, infants' utterances begin to sound more like sequences of adult phonemes. Babbling consists of repetitive consonant-vowel strings such as *mama, didididi,* or *papapa.* Parents assume (erroneously) that these babbles are nouns of address, with the result that *mama, dada,* and *papa* are treated as words for mother and father throughout the world (Aitchison, 1983).

Although babbling babies are unable to mimic sequences of adult phonemes, they can hear the differences in sound that distinguish them. Research has shown that adults use what is known as *voice onset time*—the time after release of a stop before voicing begins—to distinguish /p/ from /b/ (Lisker & Abramson, 1970). If voicing begins before the release of air, or up to 10 milliseconds after release, adults almost unanimously perceive the sound to be /b/. If, however, voicing begins after about 20 milliseconds following release, adults regard the sound as a /p/. This is an example of the **categorical perception** of speech sounds: The /b/ does not somehow gradually lose its "b-ness" and gradually acquire "p-ness," but stays a "b" until it switches to a "p."

An ingenious study with babies aged 1 to 4 months showed that they, too, are capable of the categorical perception of sounds (Eimas, Siqueland, Jusczyk, and Vigorito, 1971). The babies were allowed to suck on a special pacifier that permitted the researchers to measure the rate of sucking. Infants respond to changes in their surroundings by changing the rate at which they suck, so the investigators played either the /p/ or the /b/ over and over again until the infant's sucking pattern stabilized. Then the sound was switched. The researchers assumed that if the infants changed their sucking pattern, they had noticed the change. Using variations in voice onset time, Eimas and his associates found not only that the babies were capable of categorical perception of /b/ and /p/, but also that their perception shifted at about the same point in voice onset time (20 milliseconds) as it does for adults.

At about the age of 8 months, children begin to imitate not only speech sounds but also variations in the intonation patterns of adult speech (such as the rise in tone at the end of a question). At about the first birthday, children begin to produce one-word utterances, some 65% of which refer to objects in their environment (Nelson, 1973). These include words about people (Dada, Mama), animals (dog, duck, horse, kitty), toys (ball, block, book, doll), food (juice, milk, cookie, bread, drink), body parts (eye, nose, mouth, ear), and vehicles (car, truck, boat, train). Researchers have been studying the child's "first 50 words" since 1915 (Nice, 1915) and have found that the components of this initial vocabulary are quite similar from one child to another within a given linguistic community; it has also remained remarkably stable through the years (Clark, 1983).

By 18 months to 2 years of age, children begin to produce two-word utterances. From this point, linguistic capability mushrooms, with questions and negatives added at about age $2\frac{1}{4}$, and complete sentences at about age 3. Vocabulary increases from some 300 words at age 2 to nearly 1,000 by age 3. Rare and complex constructions are present by age 5, and by age 10 the child's speech is very much like that of the adult.

Overextension

Detailed study of language acquisition requires almost constant contact with a child, so it is not surprising that much of the research on children's speech takes the form of diaries in which developmental psychologists record the linguistic behavior of their own children. Such studies indicate that as much as one-third of the speech of 12- to 30-month-old children consists of **overextensions,** the use of words in a way that extends their meaning beyond the objects adults normally associate with them to objects that are similar in ways that adults would consider irrelevant (Clark, 1983). Thus a child may use "ball" to refer not only to balls but also to oranges, balloons, the moon, and doorknobs.

Children's use of overextended words arises from their desire to communicate despite limitations in vocabulary. Parents are active participants in this communication process, inferring the likely meaning of the child's word from the physical context and then elaborating on the child's utterance (Maratsos, 1983). One form of elaboration is expansion, in which the parent imitates and adds to the child's utterance, as in this example: Child (pointing): "Ball." Parent: "Yes, that's a ball."

Telegraphic Speech

The two-word utterances that children begin to produce toward the end of their second year are known as telegraphic speech. Research in which children are asked to imitate a spoken sentence shows that the incomplete imitations usually omit everything but nouns and verbs (Brown & Fraser, 1964). Thus, "I see a cow" becomes "See cow."

During this period children speak telegraphically not only when imitating adult sentences but also when uttering their own thoughts. Telegraphic utterances are limited primarily to contentives, omitting functors. How is it possible for researchers to tell what is missing when examining a child's spontaneous conversation (instead of the child's imitation of a model sentence)? The answer is that language contains a variety of obligatory elements. As psycholinguists note, whenever a particular kind of noun, for instance "ball," is modified by a cardinal number greater than 1, the noun requires a plural (Brown, 1973). So the utterance "three ball," which omits the required plural, is in error. Similarly, when the same kind of noun is preceded by a transitive verb, the utterance requires an article. So the utterance "throw ball," which omits the required article "the," is also in error.

Two features of telegraphic speech bear on the nativism–empiricism debate. First, the characteristic omissions of telegraphic speech are unlikely to reflect the child's experience, because they are not typically found in the speech of the surrounding adults. Second, the characteristics of telegraphic speech appear to be universal, occurring among children with such diverse native languages as Swedish, Hebrew, Mandarin Chinese, and Samoan (Brown, 1973). Thus the existence of telegraphic speech provides evidence in favor of the nativist position.

EMPIRICIST THEORIES OF LANGUAGE ACQUISITION

Now that we have discussed the "what" of language acquisition, we can return to the "how." From the standpoint of the empiricists, there are two major explanations for the acquisition of language forms—imitation and conditioning.

Imitation

Given the obvious fact that children learn the language they normally hear spoken in their presence, it has been suggested that imitation plays a central role in language acquisition. By this account, children listen to the sounds they hear, and when their vocal organs become capable of doing so, they reproduce those sounds. This explanation, however, fails to account for many of the characteristics of childhood speech. If children are imitating adults, for example, why do they progress from one-word utterances to telegraphic speech and then to complete sentences instead of imitating complete sentences from the beginning?

An even stronger argument against imitation is based on the fact that children make errors because of **overregularization,** the application of a grammatical rule for regular words to irregular words. The rule for constructing the past tense of regular verbs in English is "Add -ed." Children typically overregularize by applying this

This is a wug.

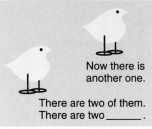

Now there is another one.

There are two of them.
There are two _____.

FIGURE 17-8 Pictures of the sort used to elicit plurals in a study by Berko (1958).

rule to irregular as well as regular verbs, saying "goed," for example, instead of "went."

Overregularization is a problem, of course, only when the underlying form is irregular. In most circumstances the use of morphological rules allows the child to produce the proper form for a word never before encountered. In one study, for example, children were shown a picture of an invented, birdlike creature like that in Figure 17-8 and told "This is a wug" (Berko, 1958). They were then shown a picture with two of the creatures and told "Now there is another one." Finally they were told "There are two of them" and were asked to complete the sentence "There are two _____." The regular rule for creating the plural of a noun like "wug" is to add "s," and most of the children answered "wugs." Even when the root word requires an unusual plural, children's performance is remarkably good. When the researcher used similar pictorial methods to ask children for a plural of "heaf," nearly 80% of preschoolers produced a correct form. Demonstrations like this have shown that imitation cannot account for language development.

Conditioning

The second empiricist explanation for the acquisition of language is based on behaviorist learning theory and the principles of conditioning discussed in Chapter 12. According to the behaviorist argument, language, like any other behavior, is acquired gradually through learning. Before they can talk themselves, infants hear their parents and older siblings talk. In a process akin to conditioning, they come to recognize verbal sounds (words) and to make connections between them and the objects to which they refer. At the same time, the infant makes babbling noises, which the parents selectively reinforce, and those reinforced babbles become primitive words ("dada" becomes "Daddy"). As the child grows older, individual words become word strings, which increase in complexity and gradually evolve into the spoken language of adulthood.

Support for this view of language acquisition can be found in some research on the content of children's speech. For example, the infant's production of sounds follows a consistent pattern similar to the one shown in Table 17-1. Crying begins at birth, cooing after about one month, babbling roughly halfway through the first year, and patterned speech around the first birthday (Aitchison, 1983; Kaplan & Kaplan, 1971). Moreover, when patterned speech first appears, it typically occurs one word at a time; as noted earlier, over 65% of those words refer to objects (Nelson, 1973).

Proponents of the empiricist position interpret these findings as indicating that language develops through the refinement or elaboration of early sounds and references to concrete objects. Taking this perspective to its extreme, Skinner (1957) claimed that verbal behavior results entirely from operant conditioning. He argued that the infant's early sounds are shaped into words, and those words are shaped into coherent utterances, through reinforcement.

Although it seems likely that learning processes like conditioning could account for the way children acquire vocabulary, this approach has a number of fundamental problems when it comes to other aspects of language. First, observational research has shown that mothers are more likely to reinforce children for true but ungrammatical statements than for grammatically correct falsehoods (Brown, 1973). Yet adult speech is more likely to be grammatical than truthful. Second, children in different cultures learn the structural elements of language in the same order. Children who have learned a particular construction, such as the formation of a plural form, in relation to one set of objects will employ the same construction in novel situations. Learning theory cannot account for this fact, or for the ease with which children understand sentences that have the same deep structure but different surface structures. Third, the linguistic environment of most children is fragmented; their speech is reinforced in inconsistent ways and they receive little feedback about its grammatical correctness (Chomsky, 1965). Under these conditions it is not likely that reinforcement could account for the tremendous consistency in the way children acquire grammatical rules. Finally, as noted earlier, the conditioning approach cannot account for the fact that language is productive, that children and adults alike can generate new utterances for which they have never been reinforced.

A CRITICAL PERIOD?

Some psychologists who oppose the learning theory approach claim that there is a *critical period* for language acquisition (Lenneberg, 1967). A critical period is a limited span of time, usually in infancy, during which a particular species-specific behavior develops (see Chapter 8). During such a period baby ducks will follow whoever or whatever leads them around; infant birds that are prevented from hearing the song of their species during a critical period will not learn the song correctly. In the case of human speech, it is claimed that the critical period extends until puberty, when the lateralization of brain hemispheres is complete and the brain loses its "plasticity" (Lenneberg, 1967).

Evidence for the existence of a critical period for language learning comes from two kinds of clinical cases, those involving people suffering physical damage to areas of the brain that affect speech, and those involving children raised in isolation.

As we saw in Chapter 5, damage to the left hemisphere of the brain can produce aphasia, the inability to comprehend or produce language. In some cases, the underlying neurological problem can be successfully treated. Whether or not recovery from the neurological problem is accompanied by full recovery of the ability to use language, however, depends on age. In a pattern that supports the existence of a critical period, young children who recover can learn language as well as their peers do, but adults typically cannot regain the use of language (Reynolds & Flagg, 1977).

The cases of children raised in isolation—either in wilderness areas, where they have lived with animals, or at home, where they have been denied contact with other people—present a more complicated picture. A well-documented case of a child deprived of contact with others is that of Genie, a girl who was isolated from the time she was 20 months old until she was discovered 3 months before her 14th birthday (Curtiss, Fromkin, Krashen, Rigler, & Rigler, 1974). For 12 years her only human contact was with her blind mother, who fed her mainly cereal and baby food. Genie "was physically punished by her father if she made any sounds. Most of the time she was kept harnessed into an infant's potty chair; otherwise she was confined in a home-made sleeping bag in an infant's crib covered with wire mesh" (Curtiss et al., 1974, p. 529). When she was discovered in 1970, she was mute, incontinent, and badly undernourished.

Because Genie had experienced no linguistic communication until after the presumed critical period for language learning, her case was considered a test of the existence of such a period. The results were mixed. During the two years following her rescue, she gained the ability to utter strings of verb phrases (such as "Want go shopping") and to use possessives, the conjunction *and,* and comparative adjectives. But although her vocabulary grew quickly, her ability to use the structural features of language developed slowly. By two years after she was rescued, many of the structural features characteristic of the language of 2-year-olds—such as question words and some transformation rules—were absent from her speech. In contrast to Genie, at least two isolated children who were found at younger ages developed language capabilities more like those of adults (Reynolds & Flagg, 1977). Taken together, these cases suggest that at least some elements of language are regulated by a critical period.

ANIMAL COMMUNICATION

Humans easily acquire a spoken language, whereas other species obviously do not. Many theorists believe that this fact alone proves that language is unique to humans, and is unlike any other form of animal communication. From this nativist point of view, although many differences between humans and other animals may be only

Helen Keller, who triumphed over blindness and deafness, is shown here using a Braille typewriter to write a biography of Anne Sullivan Macy, who first taught her language. Helen Keller's accomplishment is one indication of the depth of the human capacity for language.

quantitative, the human capacity for language represents a qualitative difference. This claim has been put to the test in research designed to teach human language to other animals, particularly chimpanzees and gorillas. Success in this enterprise would support the empiricist view that language learning is only quantitatively different, not qualitatively different, from other kinds of learning.

Research Using Sign Language

Although animals are clearly capable of communicating, sometimes using transmitted sounds, their vocal apparatus is less well suited to producing spoken language than that of humans (Aitchison, 1983). Specifically, human teeth are upright, evenly spaced, and touch each other. These characteristics are not needed for eating, but are essential for articulation of a number of language sounds, especially the fricatives. In addition, the human mouth is relatively small, can be opened and shut rapidly, and has lips in which the muscles are much more highly developed than in the lips of other species. Finally, the human tongue is thick, muscular, and highly mobile, and thus is capable of restricting the air flow in a variety of ways.

Because of the unique features of the human vocal apparatus, attempts to teach spoken language to animals such as chimpanzees were doomed to failure. If speech were an essential defining characteristic of language, then by definition other animals would be incapable of it. As we saw earlier in the chapter, however, linguists consider American Sign Language to be a true language in and of itself. Primates like chimpanzees and gorillas may be physically incapable of speech, but they are capable of manipulating visual symbols in various forms. Recent attempts to teach them language have focused on these capabilities.

In the 1960s a series of dedicated investigators began trying to teach sign language to chimpanzees. The most successful of these efforts was with a female chimpanzee named Washoe (Gardner, Gardner, & Van Canfort, 1989). The attempt to teach sign language to a chimpanzee begins in the chimp's infancy because it is necessary to establish the equivalent of a parent-child relationship with the chimp. (An adult chimpanzee is not as easily domesticated or trained.) In her early years Washoe enjoyed a stimulating and language-rich environment: "We amplified and expanded on the chimpanzee's fragmentary utterances, added known-answer questions,

FIGURE 17-9 Washoe being shown a lollipop by a researcher whose hand gestures represent the question "Whose that?"

attempted to comply with requests and praised correct, well-formed utterances" (Gardner, Gardner, & Van Canfort, 1989, p.15). Washoe had her own house trailer, considerable freedom from restraint, and constant human company when she was awake. The Gardners were her principal companions, playing games with her and using only ASL. (See Figure 17-9.)

During the first year Washoe began learning language one word at a time, just as a human child might. Compared to the early words of humans, Washoe's initial language contained fewer "naming" words and more "action" words; this is not surprising in view of the chimp's greater mobility. By the end of the year, although she had not been taught how to make sentences, Washoe began producing combinations of signs such as "more fruit," "open blanket," and "out open please hurry." At the age of 4 Washoe could produce 160 signs, but her understanding of sign language was more extensive (Hetherington & Parke, 1986). Her most impressive feat was the creativity she demonstrated in language (Aitchison, 1983). Chimpanzees enjoy being tickled, and one of her spontaneous two-sign productions was "gimme tickle"; a three-sign sequence was "roger washoe tickle." Another three-sign sequence was "open food drink," Washoe's name for her refrigerator, although the humans had referred to this appliance as "cold box" (Gardner, Gardner, & Van Canfort, 1989). Although Washoe's use of signs showed semanticity and displacement, it did not demonstrate dependence on any structure that could be likened to syntax.

Research Using Manipulation of Shapes

The Gardners' work with Washoe and other chimps represents only one of the possible ways of teaching animals to communicate with humans. Another technique, manipulation of shapes, has also produced some important results. There are two major variants of this method, one developed in California by Premack and his associates (Oden, Thompson, & Premack, 1988; Premack, 1971, 1985) and the other at the Emory University primate research center by Savage-Rumbaugh and her associates (Savage-Rumbaugh, Rumbaugh, & McDonald, 1985; Savage-Rumbaugh, 1987; Savage-Rumbaugh, Pate, Lawson, Smith, & Rosenbaum, 1983). Both methods rely on the fact that shapes, like words, can be arbitrary symbols for semantic content, can be used to describe objects not present in the immediate environment (displacement), and in principle can be strung together in sequences according to rules that are analogous to syntax.

453

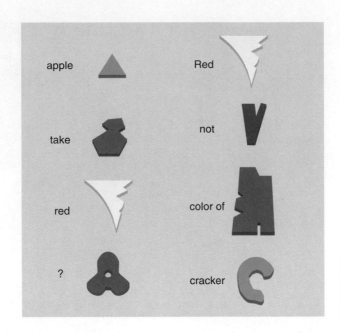

FIGURE 17-10 Some of the plastic shapes and the words they represented in Premack's research on the capacity of animals for language. (Adapted from Premack, 1976.)

Premack's group developed a large set of plastic shapes, each of which represented a word; examples are shown in Figure 17-10. Each shape had a metal back so that it would stick to a magnetic board, enabling the chimpanzee to build a sentence by placing several shapes in a column. For example, the right column in Figure 17-10 represents the sentence "Red not color of cracker."

Unlike Washoe, the Premack group's first chimpanzee, Sarah, lived in standard laboratory conditions. Virtually all of her contact with humans occurred when she was being trained to recognize and use the shapes. Much of this training used standard operant-conditioning procedures, in which the chimp was reinforced for successful use of the plastic shapes. The teacher would show Sarah an object and give her a food reward if she chose the shape that matched the object. After $2^{1}/_{2}$ years Sarah was able to produce sentences, identify concepts such as color and shape, use negation, conjunction, and interrogatives, and even express the conditional (*if . . . then*). On the other hand, in six years of training, Sarah never learned to initiate a conversation, and, in testing, her responses were correct only 70% to 80% of the time (Aitchison, 1983).

The second variant of this approach, developed by the Emory team, used the large computer keyboard shown in Figure 17-11. Ninety-two of the keys on the board con-

FIGURE 17-11 The language keyboard used in the Rumbaughs' research on the capacity of animals for language.

tained **lexigrams,** symbols representing an object such as food or a tool. Other keys were either nonfunctioning or had photographs of teachers. Grammatical rules can be illustrated by sequences of key presses. Although the keyboard has the disadvantage of being limited to a single location (unlike the hands of the chimp using sign language), it has two important advantages: It is connected to a computer that records every key press, and it can be used when humans are not present, thereby avoiding the criticism that the experimenter is cueing the chimp.

Using this keyboard, the Emory group has studied several chimpanzees and a few pygmy chimpanzees. The results have been consistent with those of other studies using shapes. After training, the chimps can not only associate the lexigrams with the objects they represent but also combine them in the equivalent of sentences. Indeed, some of the pygmy chimps have acquired this ability through observation and imitation, without specific training (Savage-Rumbaugh, Rumbaugh, & McDonald, 1985).

Nim Chimpsky

The idea that language acquisition in chimpanzees is analogous to human language acquisition was challenged by research conducted by Terrace and his associates at Columbia University (Terrace, 1979; Terrace, Petitto, Sanders, & Bever, 1979). The research was originally designed to teach ASL to a chimpanzee named, with what turned out to be more than a touch of irony, Nim Chimpsky (after the linguist Noam Chomsky). Teaching Nim ASL was not the goal of the research but a means to study aspects of the chimpanzee's problem solving capability. Because of intermittent funding, Nim did not have the constant attention that Washoe enjoyed; more important, Nim had a series of language teachers. In both these respects, Nim's linguistic environment more closely matched that of a human infant than did the language-intensive environment of Washoe.

While they were teaching Nim ASL, the Columbia group made detailed transcripts of his linguistic activity available, unedited, to psycholinguists specializing in children's language acquisition. These transcripts were scored for the number of morphemes included in each utterance (mean length of utterance) according to criteria used in studies of children. The result, according to one critic, was that "the market crashed, and you couldn't sell stock in a linguistic chimp for a nickel a share" (Brown, 1986, p. 440).

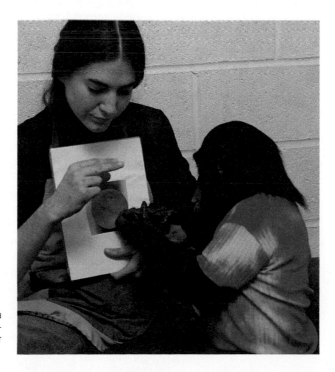

A researcher shows Nim Chimpsky a picture of an orange, and signs the question "What?" Nim signs the answer "Orange."

Examination of the unedited transcripts showed that Nim's "language" was deficient in two respects. First, it contained fewer morphemes than the speech of young children. Research by Brown (1973) has shown that mean length of children's utterances increases steadily. Children who are just beginning to speak produce utterances that, on the average, contain 1.5 morphemes. Two years later their utterances average 3.75 morphemes in length. In contrast, the average length of Nim's utterances ranged from 1.0 to 1.6 morphemes. Nim's longest utterance consisted of 16 signs that meant "Give orange me give eat orange me eat orange give me eat orange give me you" (Brown, 1986, p. 441). The telegraphic utterance "Give orange" would omit nothing of real importance communicated by this construction.

Second, Nim's communication was much less informative than that of a child. A typical six-sign sequence for the chimp would be "You me sweet drink give me," whereas a typical six-word sentence uttered by a preschool child might be "Johnny's mother poured me some Kool-Aid" (Brown, 1986, p. 442). There is an obvious difference in the amount of information conveyed by these two constructions.

In view of the findings of the Columbia group, there is reason to doubt that the language of chimpanzees is comparable to that of human children in structure and productivity. On the other hand, chimps' language does show semanticity and displacement. Perhaps the best summary of the evidence is that "even though intelligent animals seem capable of coping with some of the rudimentary characteristics of human language, they do not seem predisposed to cope with them. . . . The apparent ease with which humans acquire language, compared with apes, supports the suggestion that they are innately programmed to do so" (Aitchison, 1983, p. 58).

THE CREATION OF NEW LANGUAGES

New evidence for the nativist claim that humans are innately programmed to acquire language comes from research on the origins of **creole languages** (Bickerton, 1984). A creole language is one that is based on two or more other languages, but serves as the native language for its speakers. A child's linguistic environment normally consists of adult speakers of a single language, and in that environment language acquisition proceeds as described earlier. But this is not always the case. Consider what happens when speakers of numerous mutually unintelligible languages are thrown together, as occurred in plantation colonies in South America and elsewhere. In 1695, for example, one plantation in Cayenne had a labor force of 65 slaves who spoke 12 different languages (Curtin, 1969, cited in Bickerton, 1984). To communicate with one another in these settings, adult speakers developed pidgin languages—simplified speech with few if any grammatical rules. For example, because pidgins are "contact languages" spoken in face-to-face settings, they tend to have only a single locative preposition (Clark & Clark, 1977). (Locative prepositions in English are *at, in, by, from, on,* and *to.*)

Pidgins were barely sufficient for communication among adults, all of whom had their own native languages but could not use them to communicate with speakers of other languages. Children in these settings might be exposed to their parents' native language at home, but the demands of everyday living—including interaction with other adults and children—made pidgin their primary linguistic environment. But a pidgin cannot serve as a true native language, and children who learn one as a first language rapidly turn it into a creole with many of the syntactic complexities found in native languages (Clark & Clark, 1977).

Recently, an explanation for the shift from pidgin to creole has been suggested that explicitly makes the nativist case. This explanation is termed the **language bioprogram hypothesis,** and it contains three major claims (Bickerton, 1984). First, the innovative aspects of a creole grammar are invented by the first generation of children whose linguistic environment consists of pidgin. Second, different creoles show a degree of grammatical similarity—despite wide variation in the parent languages from which they are formed—that is too great to be attributed to chance. And third, this similarity is the result of innate linguistic capabilities; it "derives from the structure of a species-specific program for language, genetically coded and expressed, in ways still largely mysterious, in the structures and modes of operation of the human brain" (Bickerton, 1984, p. 173).

Although a number of plantation colonies had pidgin languages, Hawaii is the only one in which it is still possible to interview original speakers of the pidgin. Using material obtained from such interviews, the researchers compared the language of pidgin-speaking immigrants and creole-speaking, first-generation native-born residents. Detailed linguistic analysis revealed a more stable word order (subject-verb-object), more verbs, and more fully elaborated syntax in the creole as contrasted with the pidgin.

The researchers then compared the structures of different creole languages, finding important similarities among Saramaccan (from Suriname in South America), Haitian, Jamaican, Guyanese (from Guyana in South America), Mauritian (from the island of Mauritius in the Indian Ocean), and Hawaiian. These findings support the first two claims of the bioprogram hypothesis: that creoles are invented by children and that they are more similar to one another than would be expected by chance.

Do these linguistic similarities reflect the workings of an innate "program" for language or could they be the result of social or cultural factors common to plantation colonies? The researchers attempted to answer this question by analyzing the social composition of the colonies involved. Early in the development of a plantation colony the European colonial population far outnumbered the slaves brought in to build the colony. Because they were outnumbered, the first slaves had an opportunity to learn at least some of the dominant (colonial) language. But within a short time the colonial population was outnumbered by the slaves, and increasing numbers of new arrivals were taught not by native speakers of the dominant language but by the first generation of slaves. Over a short period of time, the native speakers of the colonial language constituted as few as 3% of the inhabitants of the colony (Bickerton, 1984). The lower this percentage, the less influence the colonial (dominant) language would have on the development of any subsequent creole.

What does this mean for the language bioprogram hypothesis? As the percentage of native speakers of the dominant language decreases, the influence of that language on the development of any subsequent creole should also decrease. In the same way, as the number of different linguistic backgrounds of the immigrants increases, the influence of any one language on the development of the creole should decrease. Faced with an utterly confusing linguistic environment, children create a new language of their own. According to the language bioprogram hypothesis, the more confusing the environment, the more the result should reflect the influence of an innate language bioprogram. Thus the more diverse the linguistic environments that give rise to them, the greater should be the similarity between two creoles. To test this prediction of the hypothesis, the researchers analyzed social and demographic factors such as the degree of contact a colony had with countries where the colonial language was still spoken, how quickly the colonial language lost its dominance because of a rapid influx of slaves, and the proportion of the population consisting of pidgin-speakers. Their results confirmed the prediction: The less the influence of the dominant language, the greater the grammatical similarity among creoles.

Although these and other findings support the language bioprogram hypothesis (see a review by Cziko, 1989), it remains controversial. The research just described has been criticized for confusing a product (a creole language) with a cognitive process (an innate capacity for language with certain specified elements) (Bates, 1984). By analogy, the fact that all people eat with their hands (with or without utensils) does not require us to "invoke an innate hand-feeding principle to account for this universal tendency" (Bates, 1984, p. 189). Moreover, the particular evolutionary processes that might have produced a language bioprogram have not been identified. Despite these criticisms, the language bioprogram hypothesis raises the exciting possibility that psycholinguists may soon discover how much of the human capacity for language is innate and how much is learned.

INTERIM SUMMARY

Children normally acquire the elements of language in a specific sequence that begins with crying and proceeds through cooing, babbling, one-word utterances, telegraphic speech, complete sentences, and, by age 10, mature speech. Empiricist theories of language acquisition attribute it to imitation and conditioning. Although these processes may account for the acquisition of vocabulary, they fail to explain the acquisition of many of the structural features of language. Evidence from case studies suggests that there may be a critical period for language acquisition that begins at birth and ends at puberty. Research on the ability of nonhuman primates to acquire language suggests that although they appear to be capable of semanticity and displacement, there is reason to doubt that their use of language is comparable to that of human children in structure and productivity. According to the language bioprogram hypothesis, the formation of creole languages reflects the operation of an innate, genetically coded program for language.

SUMMARY

1. The features of *language* that distinguish it from other forms of animal communication include semanticity, arbitrariness, productivity, traditional transmission, and syntax. Language can be thought of as a rule-governed use of arbitrary symbols to convey meaning. This working definition includes the written word and systems such as American Sign Language (ASL) as well as the spoken word.

2. According to the nativist position on language, which can be traced to Descartes, the capacity for language is an innate and uniquely human characteristic. According to the empiricist position, which can be traced to Locke and Hume, language, like anything else, is acquired through experience; children are not born with a special propensity for it. The nativism–empiricism debate continues to frame research and theory on language acquisition.

3. Speech begins with the expulsion of air from the lungs. This flow is modified or interrupted as it passes through the oral and nasal cavities, creating vowels and consonants. *Phonemes* are the smallest units of language that serve to distinguish one utterance from another. *Morphemes* are the smallest units of language that convey meaning. Words can be single morphemes or combinations of morphemes. Following rules of syntax, words can be combined into phrases and sentences.

4. A *grammar* is the entire system by which phonology, semantic content, and syntax relate speech sounds into meanings. Functionally, a grammar is a person's total knowledge of his or her language.

5. Four models have been advanced to describe how people might learn and use sentences to convey meaning: memorization, *finite state grammars, phrase structure grammars,* and *transformational grammars.* In a transformational grammar, the underlying meaning of a sentence is its deep structure and the particular form it takes is its surface structure.

6. Children's language develops in a universal sequence, beginning with crying, cooing, and babbling. These nonlinguistic patterns are followed, in order, by one-word utterances, *telegraphic speech,* questions and negatives, and, by age 3, the utterance of complete sentences.

7. Some 65% of children's first words refer to objects in their environments, and there is remarkable stability of this initial vocabulary. Many of the child's first words are *overextensions,* labels that fail to denote distinctions that adults would make among the objects to which the labels are applied.

8. Two major empiricist explanations for language acquisition are imitation and conditioning. Although these explanations may account for the acquisition of

some aspects of language, including vocabulary, they fail to explain the acquisition of many of the structural features of language.

9. The study of language acquisition among nonhuman animals has focused primarily on chimpanzees and has used either ASL or some form of *lexigram* to represent objects. Although chimps clearly possess conceptual ability, their

"linguistic" performances—even after considerable detailed training—are at best no better than the performances of very young human beings.

10. According to the *language bioprogram hypothesis,* the formation of creole languages reflects the operation of an innate, genetically coded program for language.

FOCUS QUESTIONS

1. What features of language distinguish it from the communication system of other animals?

2. Describe the primary organs involved in human speech.

3. How are vowel sounds and consonant sounds produced in the human vocal apparatus?

4. Describe the elements of meaning, from the morpheme to the sentence.

5. What is a "grammar"? Describe the four grammar-based explanations for the production of meaningful and grammatical sentences. Which account is most plausible?

6. What is the difference between the surface structure of an utterance and its deep structure?

7. Trace the major steps in the development of speech among children.

8. Which of the following is currently the most plausible account of language acquisition: imitation, conditioning, or an approach that relies more heavily on innate factors? Why?

9. Attack or defend the proposition "Animals use language."

10. Describe the language bioprogram hypothesis, and evaluate the evidence in favor of it.

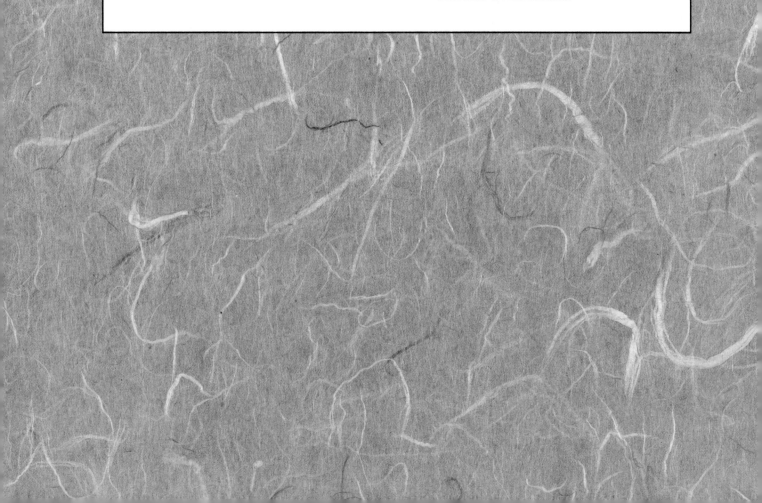

CHAPTER 18

SOCIAL DEVELOPMENT

As originally used within developmental psychology, the term *social development* referred specifically to the changes in social behavior that occur during childhood and adolescence. Examples of topics encompassed by the term in this sense include peer relations among children and adolescents, the internalization of moral standards, and the development of a sense of identity in adolescents. Today, recognizing that change in social behavior is a life-long process that does not end at adolescence, developmental psychologists take a *life-span* approach to social development. Despite this broadened focus of the field in general, however, research in social development tends to concentrate on specific age-defined periods—the traditionally investigated periods of infancy, childhood, and adolescence as well as the more recently investigated periods of adulthood and old age. This chapter presents prominent theories that have been applied to each of these major life stages.

Like the child that is often its subject, the field of social development is itself undergoing continuous change. As in the case of cognitive development and language acquisition, a critical question in the field is the degree to which social development is determined or limited by innate genetic factors as opposed to experience. Early research on social development emphasized biological factors. During the 1920s, for example, developmental psychologists concentrated on the behavior of infants and asserted that experience would have no effect until biological maturation had reached a certain level (Gesell, 1928). Soon the pendulum swung to the other extreme of Watson's strict behaviorism, with its exclusive focus on the role of experience in human development. Recent work in the field attempts to account for both the biological and social factors influencing social development.

An important difference between language acquisition and social development suggests that of the two processes, social development may be more subject to environmental factors. The universal character of language acquisition (the process is essentially the same for all children no matter what their native language) strongly suggests that it has a biological basis—nature. Furthermore, the vast majority of the 250 million inhabitants of the United States speak variations of a single language, and the same is true in many other countries. In contrast, the personality characteristics that are the result of social development are more diverse than languages, and the process of social development, although tied to the biological processes of physical maturation, is far more variable than the process of language acquisition. This variability strongly suggests the influence of experience—nurture.

THE ROLE OF EXPERIENCE

People are born, mature into adulthood, and eventually die. The human infant, initially unable to support its own head, becomes a toddler capable of walking upright; the toddler becomes a child and then an adolescent; the sexual organs mature and the adolescent becomes a young adult; as aging occurs, the adult loses muscle mass and bone elasticity. These obvious changes, and others like them, are the universal physical foundation on which experience constructs individual differences in personality and social behavior. All established theories of social development recognize the importance of such changes. Where they differ is in the degree to which they link the processes of biological change to the process of psychological growth.

Physical changes set limits on development, but learning and environmental influences shape the individual. Indeed, some differences among individuals that appeared at first to be innate have been shown to be produced by environmental factors. For example, a review of the elementary school experience of boys and girls shows that girls receive consistently higher grades, are criticized less by teachers, and are more highly regarded for their skills, motivation, and conduct than are boys (Dweck & Goetz, 1978). Yet despite this positive treatment girls are much less likely to persist at a task following failure. Girls, moreover, are more likely than boys to attribute their failures to lack of ability, even on tasks where their ability exceeds that of boys.

These paradoxical findings might at first seem to indicate an innate difference between boys and girls, but careful studies have identified environmental factors that can account for them. In one such study, psychologists observed the ways in which fourth- and fifth-grade boys and girls were treated in the classroom (Dweck & Goetz, 1978). Every instance of evaluative feedback by teachers was coded to indicate whether it was positive or negative, whether it was for conduct or for schoolwork, and, if it was for schoolwork, whether it was for nonintellectual aspects such as neatness or for intellectual aspects such as correctness. The results showed that boys received more criticism than girls did, but that most of the difference was in the area of conduct. On the average, boys and girls received the same amounts of praise and criticism for the quality of their work. But when the nature of the feedback was considered, it became clear that boys and girls were treated differently, as shown in Figure 18-1. For the boys, almost half of the criticisms dealt with matters of form, such as messiness or failure to follow instructions. For the girls, only 12% of the criticisms were of this kind.

What might students conclude from these patterns? A boy, who is as likely to be criticized for his behavior as for his work, might conclude that his teachers are "always nagging" him, but would not feel that the criticisms were directed exclusively at his intellectual ability. As a result, should the boy fail at a particular intellectual task, he would have no reason to assume that the failure reflected a lack of underlying ability. He could easily conclude that if he tried again, or if he were able to perform for someone who was not "always on his case," he would succeed. On the other hand, a girl, who is likely to be criticized only for her work, could conclude that the teachers think her intellectual abilities are second-rate. Unlike the boy, she would attribute her failure at a task to her underlying lack of ability, become discouraged, and give up.

A subsequent study corroborated this interpretation (Dweck, Goetz, & Strauss, 1980). Fifth-grade children were given four trials of a task in which they were to

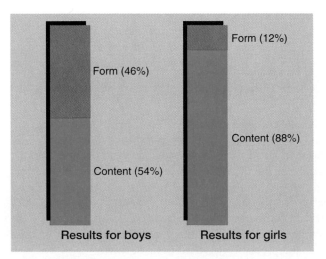

FIGURE 18-1 Results of a study comparing the way teachers criticized boys and girls. Although the total amount of criticism was about the same, boys and girls were equally likely to be criticized for form and content, whereas girls were far more likely than boys to be criticized for content only. (Adapted from Dweck & Goetz, 1978.)

Form (46%)

Content (54%)

Form (12%)

Content (88%)

Results for boys   Results for girls

draw a Chinese pictogram representing a number. Before they began, they were asked to estimate how well they would perform on the task. All of the children were told that both correctness and neatness would be scored. On each trial the children were given insufficient time to complete the task and were told that their performance was unsatisfactory. After four trials they were asked to estimate how well they would do on a fifth trial. Before making this estimate, the children were told how the fifth trial was going to be conducted. Specifically, half of the boys and half of the girls were told that the person judging their performance (the "evaluator") would be the same as on the first four trials, whereas the other half of the boys and girls were told that the evaluator would be a different person. Within the same-evaluator and different-evaluator groups, half of the children were told that the task on the fifth trial would be the same as it had always been, whereas the other half of the children were told that the task would be different.

The question of interest to us is whether children's performance expectations (their estimates of how well they will do) change when the task on the fifth trial is to remain the same but the evaluator is to differ. There had been wide variations in the children's performance estimates for the first trial, before any of the experimental conditions were introduced. To remove the effects of these initial differences, children's performance estimates for the fifth trial were expressed as a percentage of their original estimate. Thus, a child whose fifth-trial performance estimate was exactly the same as his or her first-trial estimate would have a score of 100%; a child whose fifth-trial estimate was only two-thirds of the initial estimate would have a score of 67%. The actual percentage estimates are shown in Figure 18-2 for the experimental conditions in which the task was to remain the same.

Not surprisingly, neither the boys nor the girls expected to do very well when they thought the same person was to evaluate their performance. When they thought they would have a different evaluator, boys had considerably higher expectations, whereas girls' expectations remained low. This result is consistent with the argument that boys attribute failure partly to the person evaluating them, rather than solely to their lack of ability to perform the task, whereas girls attribute failure to their lack of ability, regardless of who is evaluating their performance.

Clearly, the factors that govern social development are complex. In this case a sharp difference in the behavior of boys and girls—boys are more likely to persist after failure—that might at first glance seem attributable to innate factors was found, on close examination, to be caused by environmental factors. Specifically, the effect seems to arise because of the different ways that teachers treat boys and girls. It is useful to keep this complexity in mind as we now turn to consider prominent theories of social development.

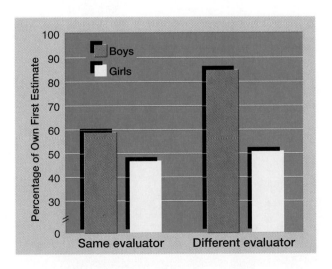

FIGURE 18-2 Performance expectations of boys and girls following a series of failures. Expectations are expressed as a percentage of the performance estimates the children made *before* any failure experiences. Children expected that the task would remain the same. (Adapted from Dweck, Goetz, & Strauss, 1980.)

Physical changes set limits on individual development, but within those limits the individual is shaped by environmental influences. Some differences among individuals are caused by environmental factors even though they may appear to be based on innate capabilities. An example is the greater tendency of boys than girls to persist at a task following failure. This tendency has been shown to result from differences in the criticism boys and girls receive in school, rather than from an innate difference between the sexes.

INFANCY: ORIGINS OF SOCIAL DEVELOPMENT

Social development obviously begins in infancy. During this stage of life—before the emergence of language—the relationship between a human infant and its parent is in many ways comparable to the parent-offspring relationship in other species. Therefore, we begin this section with a look at some of the factors that affect the social development of infant animals in other species.

IMPRINTING

As we noted in Chapter 8, an important contribution of *ethology,* the study of animal behavior in natural settings, is the identification of the role of *fixed-action patterns* in animal behavior. Fixed-action patterns are predictable, species-specific, stereotypical behaviors triggered by a *releasing stimulus.* When herring gull chicks, for example,

Dr. Konrad Lorenz, whose ethological studies of imprinting in natural settings showed the critical role played by fixed-action patterns in the social development of young animals. Lorenz is especially well known for his studies of geese and gulls.

peck at their mother's bill to receive food she has brought home for them, they are engaging in a fixed-action pattern released by the movement of the red dot on her bill. **Imprinting** is a fixed-action pattern that prompts the young of certain species of birds to follow a parent. This following behavior effectively attaches the chicks to the parent and helps create a protective environment for them.

Imprinting is most noticeable in birds whose chicks are well developed at birth and that leave the nest soon after the chicks hatch. Early in the lives of the chicks there appears to be a *critical period* for imprinting, after which it is unlikely to occur. Imprinting is established in ducks when the mother duck, after briefly caring for her chicks at the nest, vocalizes repeatedly. She then slowly walks away from them and they soon follow. The releasing stimulus for this very strong fixed-action pattern is not the mother duck herself but her movement. Chicks will, in fact, follow virtually any moving object soon after birth, as shown in Figure 18-3.

Cloth and Wire Mothers

According to an early view of social behavior, the infant's relationship to a care giver is nothing more than an outgrowth of the basic need to satisfy hunger. Specifically, in terms of the learning theory described in Chapter 12, by satisfying the newborn's hunger through feeding, the mother herself becomes a secondary reinforcer (Dollard & Miller, 1950). Because this explanation was one of the few to accord with both learning theory and Freudian psychoanalytic theory, "no one seriously questioned [it] for several decades" (Lamb, Thompson, Gardner, & Charnov, 1985, p. 11). A now-famous series of studies, however, showed this explanation to be wrong (Harlow & Zimmerman, 1959).

In the studies, infant rhesus monkeys were separated from their mothers and reared in an experimental chamber containing a "wire mother" and a "cloth mother." As shown in Figure 18-4, each of these mother surrogates had the general shape of an adult monkey. The wire mother contained a nipple through which the infant monkey could obtain food, but the cloth mother did not. Presented with this choice, the infant monkeys spent most of their time clinging to the cloth mother, climbing over to nurse from the wire mother only when they were hungry. The contact, not the food, was the main source of comfort.

Cloth surrogate mothers obviously lack facial, vocal, and gestural language, cannot protect their infants, and cannot respond to the infant's behavior. Nevertheless, when surrogate-raised infants were given extensive opportunities to interact with

FIGURE 18-3 Although ducklings normally imprint on their mother, they may also imprint on whatever moving object is present during the critical period.

FIGURE 18-4 A baby rhesus monkey with a "cloth mother" and a "wire mother" in Harlow's primate laboratory. The wire mother had a nipple through which the monkey could obtain food; the cloth mother did not. Nevertheless, the research showed that infant monkeys preferred the contact with the cloth mother, reaching over to nurse from the wire mother only when they were hungry.

465

peers, they still showed "remarkably effective social and sexual development" (Harlow & Harlow, 1969, p. 28). Infants raised by their real mothers were more advanced in "rough and tumble" play, but the differences lessened over time. Compared to infants raised in isolation, both the surrogate-with-peers infants and the mother-raised infants showed more complete adult patterns of social and sexual behavior. Specifically, adults that had been raised in isolation exhibited inadequate social play, avoided physical contact, did not engage in normal heterosexual activity, and behaved aggressively toward other adults. These findings lend support to the idea that a bond with some other member of the species is important to subsequent social development.

ATTACHMENT THEORY

There are obvious pitfalls in generalizing directly from the imprinting of young birds or the development of young monkeys to the socialization of human beings. Human infants, after all, are helpless at birth; unlike ducklings, they cannot follow their mothers, and unlike rhesus monkeys, they cannot cling to them. Nonetheless, from an evolutionary point of view, maintaining proximity to the parent has obvious advantages for the newborn of any species, including humans. Given that human infants cannot stay close to their parents, perhaps we have evolved behaviors that cause parents to stay close to their infants. Thus, smiling, cooing, and crying may have the evolutionary function of bringing parents to infants, despite the fact that the first two normally signal pleasure whereas the third signals distress.

This evolutionary interpretation of infant behavior provides the foundation for **attachment theory,** a widely accepted theory of the effect of infant-parent interaction on social development (Bowlby, 1969, 1973, 1980, 1988). According to this theory, both the infant's proximity-seeking behaviors and the parent's responses to those behaviors are important in the struggle for survival. Human infants are incapable of feeding themselves or keeping themselves safe, so infants with strong attachment bonds to an adult care giver (usually the mother) have better odds of surviving to a reproductive age. Moreover, although attachment behavior is most obvious among the very young,

> it can be observed throughout the life cycle, especially in emergencies. . . . The biological function attributed to it is that of protection. To remain within easy access of a familiar individual known to be ready and willing to come to our aid in an emergency is clearly a good insurance policy—whatever our age (Bowlby, 1988, p. 27).

One feature of attachment theory is the principle of *monotropy,* the idea that the infant is predisposed to form an attachment to one caring and responsive person. In most cases this will be the mother, but it could also be the father or a grandparent or other care giver. For example, one study of 2-year-old children found 70% of them displaying more attachment behavior to the mother and 30% displaying more attachment behavior to the father (Lytton, 1980).

Regardless of whether the primary attachment figure is the mother or the father, children show a strong attachment bond to the other parent as well (Grusec & Lytton, 1988); during childhood and adolescence the individual will form still other attachments. The prevalence and importance of such secondary attachment bonds has led some authors to argue that the principle of monotropy is incorrect (Lamb, Thompson, Gardner, & Charnov, 1985). Whether or not he or she is the only important attachment figure, however, the primary attachment figure can still be seen as what Ainsworth (1967) has called a secure base from which the child can make forays into the physical and social worlds. This relationship between the care-seeking child and a care-giving parent is the infant's first emotional tie to another person.

Although precursors to attachment behavior are present among newborns, the pattern of seeking to reestablish a secure base appears only in the second half of the first year (Bowlby, 1988). By this time the child has acquired the cognitive capacity for representation (discussed in Chapter 16). As a result, the child can tell the difference between a stranger and his or her mother (or other primary care giver) and will fret or cry in her absence. Faith in the secure availability of a primary attachment figure "is built up slowly during the years of immaturity—infancy, childhood, and adolescence" (Bowlby, 1973, p. 235). An adult who as a child interacted regularly with an attachment figure (not necessarily the child's biological parent) will "be much less prone to either intense or chronic fear" (p. 235) than an adult whose childhood attachment figure was less dependable.

THE "STRANGE SITUATION"

An early methodological problem for attachment theory was the absence of a standard procedure for measuring the degree of security provided by an attachment figure. Suppose, for example, that a child cries when its mother leaves the room. Does this indicate that the child believes the mother has vanished forever? Does it indicate that the child is frustrated because it has lost contact with a person who helps satisfy its needs? Or is it an indication that the infant has lost the feeling of safety normally provided by the primary attachment figure?

The research procedure known as the *Strange Situation* was developed to enable investigators to distinguish among these various interpretations (Ainsworth, Blehar, Waters, & Wall, 1978; Ainsworth & Wittig, 1969). This procedure consists of a series of eight interaction episodes involving a baby, its primary care giver, and a person who is a stranger to both. After an introduction (episode 1), the care giver sits quietly in the room, allowing the baby to explore (2). The stranger comes in, converses with the care giver, then approaches the child, and the care giver leaves (3). After this first separation (4), the care giver returns and the stranger departs, leaving the baby with the care giver (5). Then the care giver departs, leaving the baby alone (6) until the stranger returns (7). Finally the care giver returns, greets the baby, and picks it up, and the stranger leaves (8). The entire sequence is completed in a little over 20 minutes.

This set of episodes allows researchers to assess the child's use of the care giver as a base for exploration, its reactions to an unfamiliar person, and its distress at separation and isolation. The reunion episodes show how easily the child can be soothed by a stranger or by the care giver. Attachment theory holds that attachment behavior is most likely to occur when fear and distress are aroused. Thus, the procedure takes place in a setting that is unfamiliar to the care giver and the child. (See Figure 18-5.)

Researchers have developed a threefold classification of attachment based on children's behavior during the entire session, but especially the reunion episodes

According to attachment theory, a child's primary care giver serves as a secure base for forays into the social world.

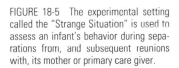

FIGURE 18-5 The experimental setting called the "Strange Situation" is used to assess an infant's behavior during separations from, and subsequent reunions with, its mother or primary care giver.

467

(Ainsworth, Blehar, Waters, & Wall, 1978). *Secure* children explore the environment before separation, but periodically return to reestablish contact if they are distressed. *Avoidant* children stay apart from their care givers, do not cling when picked up, and treat the stranger as positively as they do the care giver. *Resistant* (sometimes called *ambivalent*) children seek proximity and contact, but at the same time resist the approaches of the care giver; these children cry a great deal during separation, and continue crying after reunion.

If attachment to a parent is developmentally important because it is a child's first social bond, one would expect the quality of that attachment to affect later social behavior. And if the way children are classified as a result of their behavior in the Strange Situation reflects the quality of parental attachment, the classifications should correlate with later behavior. Several studies have investigated the degree to which classification in these categories does in fact correspond to later social behavior and most have shown that securely attached children, compared to others, are more flexible, adaptable, and skilled in interactions with peers, and are less emotionally dependent on teachers (for example, Main & Weston, 1981; Sroufe, Fox, & Pancake, 1983; Waters, Wippman, & Sroufe, 1979). One study involved preschool children who had been assessed in the Strange Situation in infancy (Sroufe, 1983, 1988). Later, the children were evaluated by several sorts of independent observers. Preschool teachers provided detailed ratings of the children, other observers coded their fantasy play, clinical psychologists rated them for symptoms of depression, and other children rated them for friendship. In all cases these evaluators were unaware of the children's initial attachment classification. The results revealed that, compared to children in the other two classifications, securely attached children had higher-rated self-esteem, fewer depressive symptoms, greater interpersonal competence, and higher friendship ratings from peers (Sroufe, 1988). Other studies have shown comparable results on self-esteem, and have also found securely attached children to possess greater resilience in social settings (Bretherton, 1985). Thus there is good evidence that secure attachment forms a firm foundation for subsequent social development.

Despite these positive results, it is important not to overstate the case. Because the concept of attachment is often thought of in terms of the nature of the bond between child and care giver, a child's behavior in the Strange Situation is often erroneously equated with security of attachment. The result is that the concept of attachment may be confused with the way in which it has been assessed (Lamb, Thompson, Gardner, & Charnov, 1985). This is a mistake for a number of reasons. First, some studies have failed to replicate the relationship between the security of the attachment bond (secure, avoidant, or resistant) and the sensitivity of the care giver when that sensitivity is measured independently, rather than being inferred from care-giver behavior in the Strange Situation (Campos, Barrett, Lamb, Goldsmith, & Stenberg, 1983). Second, the child's behavior may be influenced as much by his or her own temperament as by the bond with the care giver. That is, some babies may be temperamentally more distressed and agitated than others, whether in the Strange Situation or not (Grusec & Lytton, 1988). Third, there is reason to wonder how well a child's everyday behavior corresponds to behavior in the experimental setting. For example, one study found no consistency in attachment behaviors when reunions in the Strange Situation were compared to reunions with the mother in a day-care setting (Ragozin, 1978). Finally, some investigators have suggested that the three attachment categories used in Strange-Situation studies do not reflect fundamentally distinct psychological types, but rather are an artificial trichotomy that has been forced onto what are really continuous underlying dimensions (Lamb, Thompson, Gardner, & Charnov, 1985).

ATTACHMENT AND ADULT BEHAVIOR

Measurement of attachment behavior is recent enough that there has not yet been time for the long-term prospective studies needed to describe the adult behavior of individuals whose security of attachment was assessed in infancy. But at least one retrospective study suggests that the nature of childhood attachment can influence one particular aspect of adulthood—the experience of romantic love (Hazan & Shaver, 1987). Adults who responded to a newspaper questionnaire were asked to comment on their most important love relationship and also to indicate which of three self-descriptive statements (secure, avoidant, and resistant) best characterized them. For example, the "secure" statement read: "I find it relatively easy to get close to others and am comfortable depending on them and having them depend on me. I don't often worry about being abandoned or about someone getting too close to me" (Hazan & Shaver, 1987, p. 515). Fifty-six percent of the respondents indicated that this statement best characterized them. These self-designated secure subjects described their most important love experience as happy, friendly, and trusting. In contrast, avoidant respondents (25%) expressed fear of intimacy together with emotional highs and lows; resistant respondents (19%) described their love experience as involving obsession, extreme sexual attraction, and jealousy (Hazan & Shaver, 1987).

The fact that this study depended on self-reports of both attachment and love experiences raises a number of problems. For example, there is no guarantee that a person who in fact might have shown securely attached behavior as an infant will be able to verbalize that experience as an adult. Another problem is that people may have been responding to the questionnaire on the basis of their most recent interpersonal experiences, rather than on the basis of the sum total of their relationships with other people. In other words, they may have been responding on the basis of the availability heuristic discussed in Chapter 13: If their most recent love relationship was emotionally wrenching, it may not have been very important to them that others had been much more positive. Finally, because respondents identified their attachment patterns and their love experiences at the same time, it is impossible to assert a causal relationship between attachment and love life.

ATTACHMENT THEORY AND SOCIAL POLICY

Although we know virtually nothing about the consequences for adult behavior of various kinds of attachment patterns in infancy, there has still been an attempt to apply attachment theory and research to social policy questions. Two examples—one having to do with hospital obstetrical practices, and one dealing with nonparental day care of children—illustrate this trend.

Maternal Bonding

For years, hospitals treated births as surgical procedures: Only hospital personnel were permitted in the delivery room, newborn babies were kept in nurseries except when they were taken to the mother for feeding; mothers, themselves, were not allowed to have visitors (including the baby's father) except during rigidly controlled visiting hours, and if these hours happened not to correspond with feeding times, it might not be until it was time to leave the hospital that a father saw the baby. Such hospital practices have now been dramatically changed, partly in response to new theories about attachment.

Specifically, some researchers have argued that the process of attachment begins in the first few hours after birth, provided that there is skin-to-skin contact between mother and child (Klaus & Kennell, 1982). According to this theory, a critical period begins immediately after delivery and extends for a few days. During this time, repeated opportunities for the mother to hold her naked baby will establish an affectionate bond between them. The theory has received some empirical support, and hospitals have taken it very seriously, establishing detailed maternity procedures designed to enhance bonding.

There is, however, little evidence for a critical period in humans during which skin-to-skin contact enhances later emotional interaction between mother and baby (Campos, Barrett, Lamb, Goldsmith, & Stenberg, 1983). Moreover, critics have identified a number of methodological deficiencies in the original research, such as failures to control for preexisting family characteristics or for the possibility that mothers guessed the research hypotheses and were trying to be especially affectionate toward their newborns (Anisfeld & Lipper, 1983; Svejda, Campos, & Emde, 1980). Unfortunately, as for the current state of the evidence, "In truth, we do not know when bonding takes place—and the process is probably never completed—nor is there general agreement on the kind of maternal behavior that clearly indicates the presence of attachment" (Grusec & Lytton, 1988, p. 147).

Nonparental Day Care

For many two-parent families, and for all single-parent households, parental employment outside the home is an economic necessity. As a result, the need for quality day care of infants has reached crisis proportions: In major metropolitan areas parents begin their search for day care almost upon learning that they are to have a child. As if merely finding satisfactory day care were not enough of a problem, the attachment literature has led some observers to wonder whether reliance on nonparental day care is producing a generation of insecurely attached children at risk of developing psychological problems as adults (Belsky, 1988; Belsky & Rovine, 1988). To the extent that there is a "typical" family unit, the mother is the primary attachment figure, and the child's attachment behavior begins in earnest in the second half of the first year. Thus, if both parents work outside the home, they will most likely be placing their infant in day care before the attachment process has run its natural course. This raises the possibility that the "primary care giver" to whom the child becomes attached may be a day-care provider, rather than one parent or the other. Moreover, the opportunities for secure attachment would seem to be reduced still further by the increasingly frequent staff turnover in day-care centers.

The issue is dramatically illustrated in one study that assessed nearly 150 infants in the Strange Situation when they were 12 or 13 months old (Belsky & Rovine, 1988). Infants who were in the day-care setting for more than 20 hours per week were more likely to be classified as insecurely attached than were infants whose day-care experience amounted to fewer than 20 hours per week. This pattern was especially notable for boys, with sons whose mothers worked full-time being the most insecurely attached, not only to their mothers, but also to their fathers (Belsky & Rovine, 1988). Results of this study are consistent with other findings from research on the effects of day care. As one review notes, day-care children, especially children who entered day care as infants, "interact more with peers rather than adults, are

Although children in day-care and nursery school settings interact more with peers than with adults, there are occasions, such as "story time," during which all the children concentrate on the adult care giver.

Conflict over toys is one of the precipitating causes of aggressive behavior among preschool-age children.

inclined to be more assertive and aggressive both verbally and physically, and are more given to running about; they are also less conforming to adult standards and less cooperative" (Grusec & Lytton, 1985, p. 452).

Not surprisingly, the question of what psychological consequences follow early participation in day care remains the subject of intense scrutiny, as evidenced by special issues of major psychological journals devoted to the topic (*American Psychologist*, 1989; *Early Childhood Research Quarterly*, 1988). Critics of the attachment-based research have correctly pointed out that, as noted above, behavior in the Strange Situation should not be equated with security of attachment (Lamb & Sternberg, 1990), and that the entire separation-reunion sequence that characterizes the Strange Situation may well produce less stress in a day-care-sophisticated child for whom such separations are routine (Clarke-Stewart, 1989). Moreover, the observed behavioral differences between day-care children and home-care children may be attributable not to the day-care experience itself, but rather to a variety of economic, social, educational, and psychological characteristics of the parents who choose to place their infant children in day care (Clarke-Stewart, 1989). The one point on which all commentators agree is that much more detailed study of the day-care experience is warranted.

INTERIM SUMMARY

Social development begins with the establishment of a bond between the infant and an adult care giver. In many animals this bond involves the fixed-action pattern known as imprinting, in which the young follow the parent shortly after birth. Although early developmental theories suggested that social bonds between mother and infant resulted from secondary reinforcement, research on monkeys provided with cloth mothers showed that attachment needs could be separated from requirements for food. According to a major theory of child development—attachment theory—the attachment of an infant to a primary care giver is no less important for human beings than for other animals. The nature of the relationship between children and their care givers can be observed in the Strange Situation procedure. Using this procedure, researchers have identified three categories of attachment: secure, avoidant, and resistant. Little is known about the consequences for adult behavior of various kinds of attachment patterns in infancy. Principles of attachment theory have been used to justify changes in hospital birthing practices, and to raise questions about the psychological consequences of nonparental day care.

PSYCHOSOCIAL DEVELOPMENT FROM CHILDHOOD THROUGH ADOLESCENCE

Despite its recent applications to adult behavior, attachment theory and research have historically concentrated on infancy and early childhood. We now turn to theories that devote more of their attention to the developmental issues that arise during childhood and adolescence. These theories—Freud's theory of psychosexual stages, Erikson's theory of psychosocial development, and Kohlberg's theory of the development of moral reasoning—concentrate on the acquisition of moral standards. Many developmental psychologists would agree with Kagan's claim that "The capacity to evaluate the actions of self and others as good or bad is one of the psychological qualities that most distinguishes *Homo sapiens* from the higher apes" (Kagan, 1984, p. 112). For developmental theory, the critical issue is how children come to possess such moral standards, and how they refer to the standards when asked to evaluate their own behavior and the actions of others.

FREUD'S THEORY OF PSYCHOSEXUAL STAGES

Of the explanations offered for the internalization of moral standards, Sigmund Freud's theory of psychosexual stages, part of his comprehensive theory of personality (see Chapter 21), is by far the most revolutionary (Freud, 1952/1932). As we mentioned in Chapter 2, Freud's theory of personality is a form of *biological determinism*. Freud maintained that all psychic energy is derived from metabolic processes—that mind is impossible without the body—and that just as there are physical limits on metabolic processes, there are also limits on psychic energy, or **libido.** Freud also maintained that in an important sense the child is the parent of the adult: Unless the psychological conflicts that accompany development are satisfactorily resolved, they will remain as psychological problems.

According to Freud's theory, the organs involved in digestion and procreation that are critical to the survival of the organism and the species are also **erogenous zones**—instinctual sources of sexual pleasure. The developing child passes through a series of psychosexual stages, each of which is linked to the pleasurable sensations associated with a specific erogenous zone (Freud, 1952/1932). Conflicts associated with the control of those sensations play a major role in the formation of the adult personality. Specifically, to reach psychological maturity the individual must successfully resolve the conflicts associated with each stage. People who experience either excessive frustration or excessive gratification of the sexual feelings associated with one of the early stages will become psychologically *fixated* at that stage.

The Oral Stage

Freud believed that an infant's nervous system develops outward from the brain, so the first source of gratification is the mouth (Maddi, 1989). He argued that the mouth not only satisfies the infant's need for sustenance, but is also an erogenous zone—a source of sensual pleasure. One indication of this is that infants put virtually anything they can pick up, not just food, into their mouths. According to Freudian theory, the fundamental psychological concerns of the *oral stage* are receiving and taking. Early in the stage, the infant is capable only of receiving; when it begins teething, the somewhat more aggressive taking becomes possible.

In this stage, either too much or too little attention to the infant's instinctual desire for oral gratification can lead to oral fixation. The oral character type can therefore be described as including several so-called bipolar dimensions, with one pole representing overindulgence and the other pole representing deprivation (Maddi, 1989). Some of these dimensions are optimism–pessimism, gullibility–suspiciousness, and admiration–envy. Thus, a Freudian would consider an adult who was highly pessimistic, suspicious, and envious of others to be fixated at the oral stage, and to have been deprived during that stage.

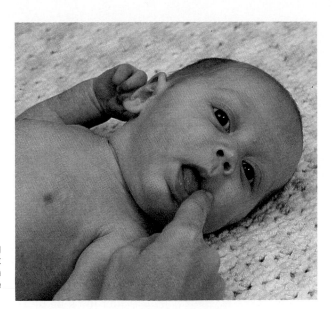

A graphic illustration of the "rooting reflex" in a newborn. The infant responds to a touch on the cheek, even as far back as the ear, with a reflexive search for a breast.

Whatever the merits of Freud's theory as a whole, considerable evidence suggests that an infant's earliest contacts with the world are associated with the mouth. Typically a baby's first social contact occurs during nursing shortly after birth. Newborns respond to any touch on their cheeks, even as far back as their ears, with a reflexive search for the breast called the rooting reflex. Having made contact with the nipple, the infant begins a pattern of sucking in bursts and pauses. The bursts consist of from 5 to 24 sucks, followed by a pause for recovery (Brazelton, 1990).

Research indicates that this burst–pause pattern is associated only with breast milk. In the research, infants were fed different liquids through a nipple. Infants can recognize a change in sweetness of a liquid after as few as two sucks (Lipsitt, 1977), and their sucking pattern changes depending on the liquid (Johnson & Salisbury, 1975). Salt water produces choking, a formula made from cow's milk produces continuous sucking, but only breast milk produces the burst–pause sequence.

These differences suggest that babies expect social interaction during breast feeding, and observations of mothers show how the interaction develops (Kaye, 1977). During the bursts of sucking, mothers are usually inactive, but during the pauses they look down at their babies, talk softly to them, stroke them, and jiggle them. These signals actually prolong the pauses between bursts. "In other words, it seems as if human infants are programmed with a special kind of sucking pattern which they come to associate with breast milk" (Brazelton, 1990, p. 61).

The Anal Stage

Once food has been digested, it accumulates in the rectal vault until pressure on the anal sphincter muscles causes a reflex discharge. This discharge relieves tension and is thus pleasurable. Not until the second year of life do children begin to develop rudimentary muscular control over their defecation; at the same time parents begin to attempt to control the process. Thus, the source of gratification for the child in the second psychosexual stage, the **anal stage,** is the release of feces, and the source of conflict in this stage is the parents' attempts to control it through toilet training. (It is worth noting that in Freud's time a child's expulsion of feces was more than the minor inconvenience it presents in these days of plastic pants and disposable diapers.) In Freud's theory, if toilet training is too strict, the child will either hold feces back and become constipated, or choose inopportune times to release. The psychological dimensions involved in the anal stage are *giving* and *withholding.* If toilet training is either too restrictive or too lenient, the result can be an adult who is either an *anal retentive* (obstinate, stingy, orderly, and meticulous) or *anal expulsive* (acquiescent, overgenerous, messy, and dirty).

473

The Phallic Stage

When Freud proposed his theory at the turn of the century, during the Victorian era, many critics were distressed at the notion of an infant's obtaining anything like sexual gratification either from sucking on its mother's breast or from defecating. But Freud's description of the young child's next stage was even more controversial.

He maintained that in the years between the second and fifth birthdays the child enters the **phallic stage.** During this stage the genitals become the focus of libido. It is not clear in Freudian theory why the "outward development" of the nervous system should result in the phallic stage's following the anal stage, because the two bodily regions are so close together (Maddi, 1989). The period involved, however, is certainly one in which boys and girls begin to explore their own bodies, discover that male and female bodies are different, and begin to consider that interaction between people is sexual in nature (Maddi, 1989).

According to Freud, the phallic stage differs in boys and girls. The young boy, who has discovered the pleasure of manipulating his genitals, develops a sexual desire for his mother. His attraction to his mother is accompanied both by resentment of his father and fear that his father will retaliate against him. Freud labeled this set of feelings the *Oedipus complex,* after the king of Thebes in Greek mythology who inadvertently killed his father and married his mother. The boy's fear of his father produces what Freud called "castration anxiety," and this anxiety, in turn, causes him to push his lust for her out of consciousness—in other words, to repress his desire for her. **Repression** lays the foundation for the development of conscience: The boy identifies with (becomes like) his father, or at least like his conception of what his father represents. Identification with the father, and with the father's moral standards, protects the boy from fears of castration and at the same time enables him to gain vicarious satisfaction from the father's relationship with the mother.

The young girl experiences a not-quite-equivalent set of feelings that is sometimes called the *Electra complex,* after the heroine of Greek tragedy who induced her brother to kill their mother. The girl discovers that boys her age possess protruding sexual organs, whereas she does not. She comes to believe that her mother is responsible for her "castration," and this belief weakens her love for the mother. Finally, according to the theory, the girl develops "penis envy," which only intensifies her desire for the father, specifically to have a child by him, thereby symbolically acquiring a penis. Both her father and mother resist this idea, and she then identifies with her mother in order to gain vicarious satisfaction from the mother's relationship with the father.

For both boys and girls, the psychologically healthy outcome of the phallic stage is the internalization of the attitudes, values, and moral prescriptions of the parent of the same sex, together with the development of a sense of themselves as worthwhile sexual beings. As before, fixation in the phallic stage can arise either from overindulgence or severe frustration of the child's sexual fantasies. The phallic character type thus may include personality dimensions such as pride–humility, flirtatiousness–avoidance of heterosexuality, and chastity–promiscuity.

The Genital Stage

Between the ages of 5 and 11, both boys and girls enter a latency period. At puberty, they enter the **genital stage.** During this stage the adolescent begins to obtain pleasure from others rather than from narcissistic self-manipulation. Not only sexual activity but also friendship, group activities, and vocational planning reflect this outward orientation. Now able to engage in reproductive behavior, the young man or woman no longer needs any of the pregenital substitutes. There is no "genital character type," because in Freudian theory the genital stage is the final step in psychosexual development. Having reached this stage without becoming fixated at one of the pregenital stages, the man or woman is now ready for the heterosexual responsibilities of adulthood.

Freud's stages of psychosexual development are listed in Table 18-1.

TABLE 18-1   Freud's Stages of Psychosexual Development

Stage	Approximate Age	Presumed Psychological Content or Activity
Oral	Infancy	Eating as pleasure, biting as aggression
Anal	Age 1–2	Overly strict toilet training presumed to lead either to retentive or expulsive character
Phallic	Age 2–5	Oedipus and Electra complexes; resolution of these through identification with same-sex parent
Latency	Age 5–11	No identified erogenous zone
Genital	Puberty	Beginning of time for obtaining pleasure from others, both through sexual activity and through friendship

Evaluation of Freud's Theory

Terms from Freud's theory permeate popular culture. A whole generation of adults in Western societies was raised by parents who were concerned about the harshness of toilet training, and "anal-retentive" has become a virtual synonym for "stingy." Even without formal instruction in psychology, people have some idea of what the Oedipus complex entails, and the notion of infantile sexuality has tempered our impressions of the innocence of childhood.

Despite this popular attention, Freud's theory has been severely criticized in the professional literature (Robinson, 1979). Researchers have found little empirical evidence to support the notion of discrete psychosexual stages. Another problem, which may superficially seem not to be a problem at all, is that the theory is difficult to prove false. The logic of scientific investigation, however, dictates that theories can never be proved to be "true," because the possibility can never be eliminated that an as yet undiscovered, disconfirming example exists. The best a theory can do is achieve the credibility that accompanies frequent testing that fails to prove it wrong. But for this credibility to accrue to the theory, it must be falsifiable: It must be possible in principle to specify outcomes that would prove it wrong. In this regard, Freudian theory leaves much to be desired.

Suppose, for example, that a young adult male identifies with his father. The theory can claim that his Oedipus complex has been resolved. If the boy does not identify with his father, the theory can claim that his Oedipus complex has not been resolved. It is impossible to construct conditions that would demonstrate that the boy *never had an Oedipus complex at all.* After considering evidence from clinical cases, experimental studies, and comparisons of childhood sexual behavior in different societies, one investigator described the Oedipus complex as "an unverified hypothesis" (Fernald, 1984). Current interest in attachment theory is in part attributable to the fact that the principles of attachment theory, in contrast to those of Freudian psychosexual development, can be falsified, and thus tested.

ERIKSON'S STAGES OF PSYCHOSOCIAL DEVELOPMENT

Although the details of Freud's theory have been discredited, two of its generalizations have been accepted. First, maturity is not reached without some conflict, and second, the way in which conflict is resolved in childhood will affect the behavior of the adult. These two general principles are also part of Erik Erikson's theory of psycho*social* development (Erikson, 1950).

In contrast to Freud's theory, which asserts that the most critical events in development occur before the age of 5, Erikson's theory outlines what he terms the eight "ages of man," a set of developmental stages that extend from the first year of life

Erik Erikson's theory of development concentrates on the resolution of a series of psychosocial crises. His theory is best known for its description of identity formation in adolescence.

through old age. The first five of these stages, ending with adolescence, are summarized in Table 18-2; the remaining three are discussed in the section on adult development. All of the stages emphasize the interaction between biological maturation and social influences, and like the stages in Freudian theory, each also is characterized by a central conflict or crisis. Because of Erikson's psychoanalytic background, it is not surprising that the age range of his stages corresponds approximately to that of Freud's.

TABLE 18-2   The First Five of Erikson's Stages of Social Development

Approximate Age	Developmental Task for the Stage	Psychosocial Crisis
0–1.5 years	Attachment to the mother based on consistency of attention to needs.	Basic trust versus basic mistrust.
1.5–3 years	Gaining control of self (movement) and impulses (e.g., toilet training).	Autonomy versus shame and doubt.
3–6 years	Becoming self-directive and using energy in productive ways, not in activities that produce guilt.	Initiative versus guilt.
6–puberty	Developing persistence, especially in school activities, but also in physical and social skills.	Industry versus inferiority.
Adolescence	Making transition from dependency of childhood to independent identity and possible career choice.	Identity versus role diffusion.

SOURCE: Adapted from Erikson, 1963.

Tasks of Childhood

In the first year, the infant's primary developmental task is to form a secure attachment to the care giver. If maternal care is consistent, affectionate, and reliable, the infant will develop basic trust; if care is not affectionate or consistent, the infant may develop a basic mistrust of others that will persist through life.

During the second year, and extending into the third, the toddler develops muscular control and is able to move about. This enables the child to make choices regarding where to go and whether or not to engage in forbidden behaviors. The popular label "terrible twos" reflects the conflict between the child's desires and controls imposed by parents. According to Erikson, a child who is able to gain some control over his or her own actions will become autonomous; one who is not allowed to make guided choices may develop doubt; and one who is unable to control his or her impulses will experience shame.

During the preschool years self-control is expanded into self-direction. The child develops real initiative, using his or her boundless energy to achieve new successes. Occasionally, however, this energy is channeled into activities that produce harm. Thus, the central crisis at this age can be described as "initiative versus guilt." A child may be able to hit another child hard enough to hurt but may not realize this beforehand. Because physical capabilities exceed the capacity for moral reasoning, parents and care givers are likely to say, "Imagine how it would feel if somebody did that to you." During the early school years, initiative becomes focused, producing persistence at a single task, be it schoolwork, the nurturance of a friendship, or practicing of physical skills.

Adolescence and Identity Formation

Erikson's theory is best known for its view of adolescence as a period of identity formation. Adolescence is a transitional stage during which the dependent child becomes an independent adult. The adolescent who previously has known only one social role—that of child—is now confronted with a large number of important

476

Adolescents spend a great deal of time trying on possible roles for themselves. The result is often a desire to "fit in." Note for example that all the clothes in this picture are minor variations on the same theme.

choices reflecting new social opportunities. Should I stay in school or drop out? If I continue my education, should I seek job training or higher education, and which school would be best? What about sex and its consequences? What would happen if I became a teenage parent? What kinds of friends are best for me? Am I a good friend who can be trusted?

According to Erikson's theory, adolescents spend a great deal of time trying on various possible roles before making a selection. This process of self-evaluation is so important that, at least in Western cultures, it may lead to **adolescent egocentrism** (Elkind, 1984). Unlike the egocentrism of Piaget's theory of cognitive development, adolescent egocentrism is not an inability to take another's viewpoint. Rather, it reflects the adolescent's assumption that everyone else is focused on just one person, "me." This creates heightened sensitivity to the opinions of others and a desire to fit in at almost any cost. After all, if you think that everyone is looking at you, you do not want to be "different."

Most of the research inspired by Erikson's theory has focused on adolescence and the concept of identity formation. This emphasis reflects the importance of the concept to the theory as a whole. As one observer has noted, identity formation is "the most important single concept, and the only truly structural one, in Erikson's theory of psychosocial development" (Marcia, 1988, p. 211). It accounts for the transition from a childhood identity framed by parents to the beginning of an adult identity framed by one's own choices of occupational role and moral values.

Studies of identity formation employ what is known as the identity status interview (Marcia, 1980). The intent of this interview is to determine whether or not an adolescent has evaluated the life alternatives he or she has available, and whether or not he or she feels a personal commitment to an alternative. Together, these processes of evaluation and commitment produce four outcomes reflecting four possible resolutions to the problem of identity formation as shown in Figure 18-6 (Marcia, 1980; see also Adams, Abraham, & Markstrom, 1987).

FIGURE 18-6 The role of commitment and evaluation in the resolution of the identity crisis of adolescence. To achieve an independent identity, an adolescent needs to have examined the available life alternatives, and to have committed himself or herself to one of these possible paths. (Adapted from Marcia, 1980.)

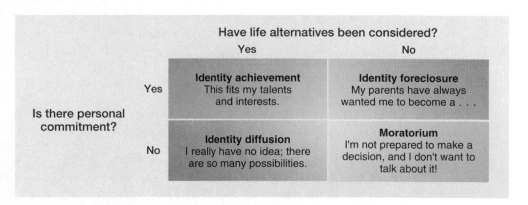

477

Adolescents who have both considered alternative life courses and selected a path in which they have a substantial personal investment fall into the **identity achievement** category—they are considered to have achieved an independent identity. Rather than blindly accepting what parents and peers have suggested for them, these adolescents have examined the occupational and social choices available to them, have narrowed this field to a few, and have devoted their energies to making their personal beliefs and plans a reality. After thorough evaluation, they have committed themselves to a particular course. For example, when asked by a high school teacher, "What do you plan to do after graduation," a young adult in the identity achievement category might respond by saying: "I'm going on to college, because I plan to be a veterinarian. I'm good in science, I've always loved animals, and I want to do something to help them." Young adults who fit this category are characterized by flexible strength. They have their own internal standards but are open to new ideas; they have a sense of humor, are thoughtful, and function well under stress.

Adolescents who have internalized the standards imposed by others—parents or other authorities in society—without examining any alternatives fall into the **identity foreclosure** category. Asked about postgraduation plans, such an adolescent might reply, "My parents have always wanted me to be a doctor, so I'm going to take a general premedical program in college." Although identity foreclosure adolescents are happy and self-assured, they become dogmatic when their beliefs are challenged.

Adolescents who have not made a commitment to any particular role fall into the **identity diffusion** category. They have looked briefly at some of the alternatives, have considered many of these to be attractive, but have not yet settled on one or a few, and have not made any personal commitment to a single path. Asked about postgraduation plans, such an adolescent might answer by saying: "I'm not really sure. There are so many things I might like to do that it is hard to choose among them. So I really don't know now." An adolescent whose identity is so diffuse that he or she has no clear sense of self or purpose will drift, and can be superficial, unhappy, and unable to form strong bonds with others.

Finally, some adolescents fall into the **moratorium** category. They are struggling with the need to make some important life choices, but have not yet examined any alternatives seriously and have made no personal commitment to any particular path. These individuals tend to be competitive and anxious, wanting intimacy but unable to achieve it.

Evaluation of Erikson's Theory

Erikson's concept of adolescent identity formation has permeated the popular culture to almost the same degree as have some of Freud's concepts. Erikson's view of the process of identity formation, however, has received extensive support from decades of research. There is now little doubt that the formation of an identity is crucial to bridging the gap between the attachment and dependency of childhood and the independence of adulthood (see, for example, Lapsley & Power, 1988). Moreover, Erikson's theory, first proposed over 40 years ago, outlined a series of life crises that continued well beyond adolescence into late adulthood. In so doing, it foreshadowed the life-span approach now so prevalent in developmental psychology.

MORAL DEVELOPMENT

As noted earlier, one of the major tasks facing a young person is the development of a personal sense of morality. In Freudian theory, the internalization of a conscience that results from the successful resolution of the Oedipus or Electra complex lays the foundation for a moral sense. This internalization is presumed to occur without conscious thought. In Erikson's theory, a sense of morality emerges gradually with the successful resolution of the psychosocial crisis of each developmental stage.

In an alternative to both these views modeled on Piaget's theory of cognitive development, Kohlberg (1981) proposed that moral reasoning develops in tandem with cognitive abilities generally. Kohlberg's theory emphasizes the connection between morality and conscious reasoning processes. It suggests that as children's cognitive capacity increases, so does their ability to make increasingly complex moral judgments.

Stages of Moral Reasoning

According to Kohlberg, there are six stages of moral development, as indicated in Table 18-3. These are grouped into three categories: **preconventional** (stages 1 and 2, which cover the preschool and early school years), **conventional** (stages 3 and 4, which cover the middle school years), and **postconventional** (stages 5 and 6, which cover adolescence and adulthood). Although the order of these stages is invariable, not every person will reach the final stage.

Early in the preconventional period the child's interaction with moral authorities is governed by a simple principle: Right and wrong are determined by reward and punishment. Correct behavior is behavior that enables the child to avoid punishment by a person with power. The child is egocentric in the Piagetian sense and is unable to recognize the perspectives and needs of other people. This changes in the latter part of the preconventional period (stage 2), as the child begins to recognize that people have different needs, which sometimes create conflicts. Rather than considering every moral dilemma to be a new case, the stage 2 child begins to follow rules based on concepts of fairness and equal exchange.

During the conventional period, moral behavior is behavior that avoids guilt, rather than punishment. Stage 3 morality is based on approval obtained by conforming to the expectations of people such as parents and teachers, but principles of fair exchange remain important. Living up to the expectations of others and abiding by a variant of the Golden Rule (do not do to others what you would not want them to do to you), the stage 3 child lets mutual agreements take precedence over individual

TABLE 18-3 Stages of Moral Development According to Kohlberg's Theory	
Stage	What Is Considered Morally Right
Preconventional Morality (Preschool to early school years)	
Stage 1: Punishment and obedience orientation.	Physical consequences of action determine its goodness or badness regardless of the human meaning. Avoidance of punishment and unquestioned deference to power are valued in their own right.
Stage 2: Instrumental relativist orientation.	Right action is that which satisfies one's own needs. Elements of fairness present, but interpreted in pragmatic way.
Conventional Morality (Middle school years)	
Stage 3: Interpersonal concordance orientation.	Good behavior is that which pleases or helps others and is approved by them. Behavior frequently judged by intention, approval earned by being "nice."
Stage 4: Society maintaining orientation.	Orientation toward authority, fixed rules, and maintenance of the social order. Right behavior consists of doing one's duty, respecting authority, maintaining social order for its own sake.
Postconventional Morality (Adolescence to adulthood)	
Stage 5: Social contract orientation.	Right action defined by general individual rights and standards that have been critically examined and agreed upon by the society. Awareness of relativism of personal values; emphasis on procedural rules for reaching consensus. Possibility of changing law through rational discussion of social utility.
Stage 6: Universal ethical principle orientation.	Right defined by decision of conscience in accord with self-chosen ethical principles appealing to logical comprehensiveness, universality, and consistency. Universal principles of justice, not concrete moral rules. Respect for dignity of human beings as individuals.

SOURCE: Adapted from Kohlberg, 1981.

The Reverend Martin Luther King (pointing) and his wife, Coretta Scott King, at a history-making, civil-rights demonstration: the 1963 March on Washington. Many regard King's principled views on nonviolence and human dignity as excellent examples of the moral reasoning that characterizes Kohlberg's stage 6.

interests. In stage 4, adherence to fixed social rules that derive either from laws or religious teachings takes precedence over informal agreements among individuals. Because of this emphasis on laws for their own sake, stage 4 has been called the "law and order" stage. Only in exceptional circumstances will children in this stage consider behaving in ways that contradict rules and laws, even though by some other principle it might be morally "right" do to so.

In the postconventional stages the individual begins to base his or her behavior on internalized principles, rather than on specific externally imposed rules. In stage 5 the person begins to distinguish the rules and laws of a particular society from universal principles, such as liberty and equality, that ought to apply in every society. Here the emphasis is on rational argument, and the individual comes to recognize, for example, that what is "legal" may not always be what is "moral." Finally, in stage 6, allegiance to universal principles is carried into action (stages 5 and 6 are rarely distinguished from one another in research). The fundamental principle of postconventional reasoning is that when an existing law appears to contravene a universal moral principle, the law may be disobeyed. The civil disobedience that characterized the initial days of the civil rights movement in the United States provides numerous examples of postconventional behavior. When lunch counters were segregated by law, many people expressed their moral outrage at segregation by breaking the law and being arrested for trespassing.

Measurement of Moral Development

An individual's level of moral development can sometimes be inferred from his or her behavior. Studies of moral development, however, more typically examine the way the individual responds to moral dilemmas like the one shown in Figure 18-7. The scoring of a response is based on the reasoning by which a person arrives at an answer, rather than on the answer itself (Colby, et al., 1978). For example, a preconventional child responding to the story in the figure is likely to say that stealing is wrong because "someone could see you and call the police," a reference to the possibility of punishment. A conventional child might explain that "stealing is against the law; people have to follow the laws, even when it might not be convenient to do so, because the laws are there to protect everyone." Finally, a postconventional person might condone the theft, saying that "Heinz's wife's right to life is being compared to the druggist's right to protect his investment. In this case, I think the right to

FIGURE 18-7 One of the dilemmas used in Kohlberg's research on moral reasoning and moral development. (From Kohlberg, 1981, p. 12.)

An Example of a Moral Dilemma

In Europe, a woman was near death from a very bad disease, a special kind of cancer. There was one drug that the doctors thought might save her. It was a form of radium that a druggist in the same town had recently discovered. The drug was expensive to make, but the druggist was charging ten times what the drug cost him to make. He paid $200 for the radium, and charged $2,000 for a small dose of the drug. The woman's husband, Heinz, went to everyone he knew to borrow the money, but he could get together only about $1,000, which was half of what it cost. He told the druggist that his wife was dying and asked him to sell it cheaper or let him pay later. But the druggist said, "No, I discovered the drug and I'm going to make money from it." Heinz got desperate and broke into the man's store to steal the drug for his wife.

life predominates, especially because I think that the druggist is charging way too much."

The processes of moral reasoning reflected in responses to moral dilemmas are presumed to be universal, so should apply to all cultures (Kohlberg, 1981). To test this presumption, the moral dilemmas have been used to gauge moral development in children of various ages in more than two dozen countries in Europe, Asia, and Africa, as well as in the United States and Canada (Snarey, 1985). In most cases, the dilemmas have been adapted to the local culture by translating the material into the native language, changing the names and settings appropriately, and altering the content (for example, in nonindustrialized countries the essential "drug" becomes essential "food"). Over 45 separate studies have now been conducted; taken as a whole, these studies have found reasoning at stages 1–4 in almost all of the samples. Moreover, regardless of cultural background, there is a general increase in the level of moral reasoning as the respondent's age increases; the few longitudinal studies that have been conducted have found virtually no regression from one stage to a previous one (Snarey, 1985). Across all of these studies, there was one important cultural differences: Stage 5 moral reasoning was found in nearly all urban societies but not in any tribal or village cultures. Although this might suggest that urban cultures are somehow more morally advanced than tribal cultures, a better explanation is that there is bias in the scoring system (Snarey, 1985). Specifically, whereas the coding categories used with stages 1–4 are empirically based, the descriptions of reasoning in stages 5 and 6 are based primarily on ideas drawn from Western philosophy, restricting the cultures to which the analysis can apply.

Moral Reasoning About Sex

Although as just noted studies have found no regression from one stage to an earlier one, there appears to be one exception to this general pattern. In one study, the moral dilemmas were translated into ones with sexual themes. One example described the situation of a high school girl who was alone in the house because her parents were away for the weekend. Her boyfriend came over to the house unexpectedly. The two of them spent the evening together in the house, and after a short time began necking and petting (Gilligan, Kohlberg, Lerner, & Belensky, 1971). Subjects were asked whether this behavior is right or wrong, whether there are circumstances that would make it right, and whether it would be right or wrong for the couple to engage in sexual intercourse. The results showed that when teenagers were asked to evaluate such dilemmas their level of moral development was lower than it was when measured by dilemmas lacking sexual content; that is, when they were evaluating sexually charged situations, their level of moral reasoning regressed to a more primitive stage. It is worth noting that this research was conducted in the late 1960s, before there was widespread concern about sexually transmitted diseases, especially AIDS.

Evaluation of the Theory

Despite the cross-cultural evidence for the existence of stages of moral reasoning, Kohlberg's theory has had its share of criticism. Three specific problems have been noted in a number of reviews (for example, Grusec & Lytton, 1988). First, by presenting moral dilemmas that are outside the everyday experience of children, Kohlberg may have underestimated the moral capabilities of youngsters. In other words, what Kohlberg considers an age-related change in moral reasoning may actually be little more than an age-related change in familiarity with the kinds of problems being described. Second, the moral dilemmas used to assess level of moral reasoning carry what some regard as political overtones. For example, as noted earlier, stages 5 and 6 are defined in terms of Western philosophical ideas. In addition, in almost all studies the moral dilemmas have been phrased with male protagonists, and too frequently have been tested on exclusively male subjects. This concentration on males has led one critic to argue that the theory is biased against women (Gilligan, 1977), although a review of over 75 published studies has found no consistent sex differences in level of moral reasoning (Walker, 1984). A third general problem is that the traditional means of measuring moral development requires detailed coding of the subject's open-ended discussion of each moral dilemma, raising the possibility that the coders are imposing their own views of moral development on the free responses. This problem is particularly important, because Kohlberg has changed the stage definitions many times since he first began using the system (Rest, 1986). Indeed, to solve this problem one researcher has developed an objective test of moral reasoning that has now been used in more than 500 studies (Rest, 1986). It is important to note, however, that this objective test has provided strong evidence that there are indeed six stages of moral reasoning.

SOCIAL BEHAVIOR OF ADOLESCENTS

Adolescence is often considered a time of turmoil, and statistics are readily available to support this view. For example, in the United States there are over half a million teenage pregnancies each year (U.S. Department of Health and Human Services, 1991). Moreover, individuals under the age of 21 account for 30% of all arrests (FBI Uniform Crime Reports, 1991), and large numbers of teenagers die each year as a result of accidents or suicide. Statistics like these indicate that adolescence can be a troubled and difficult stage of life. Some important recent research, however, suggests that the true picture may not be this bleak.

Part of the reason that we have such a negative impression of adolescence is that the study of this age group has been "problem driven." Teenage pregnancy and juvenile delinquency are social problems unique to adolescence, and a disproportionate number of adolescents commit suicide. In an effort to understand these problems, researchers have concentrated primarily on adolescents who become known to law enforcement and social welfare agencies. Because the majority of teenagers, who are leading more normal lives, rarely come to the attention of researchers, their everyday behavior has been virtually ignored.

One study of students from a predominantly middle-class high school has begun to fill this gap (Csikszentmihalyi & Larson, 1984). Because few teenagers will permit adult interviewers to follow them around all day, the researchers recruited 75 students to wear electronic pagers for a week. These students agreed to stop what they were doing and fill in a reporting form whenever they were paged. The form asked for information about the subject's surroundings, activities, thoughts, and feelings. During the course of the week, the researchers buzzed each participant about 40 times. On weekdays the buzzings occurred between 7:30 A.M. and 10:30 P.M.; on weekends they occurred between 7:30 A.M. and 1:30 A.M.

The results of any self-report study may be influenced by the subjects' desire to present themselves in a positive light. On the other hand, as the range of responses

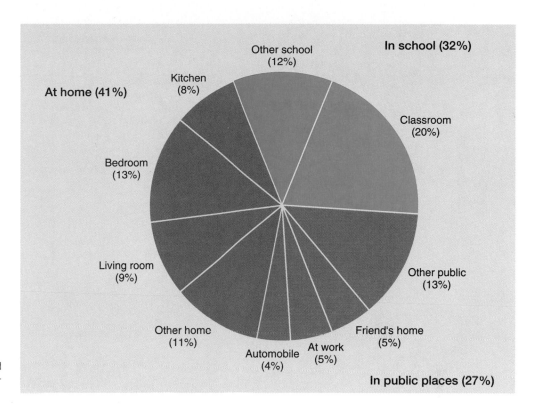

FIGURE 18-8 Where adolescents spend their time. (Adapted from Csikszentmihalyi & Larson, 1984.)

received in this study included socially disapproved actions and feelings as well as more constructive emotions and behaviors, the respondents appear to have been reasonably honest.

As shown in Figure 18-8, the results of the study suggest that adolescents spend their time in three very different social worlds. One of these, in which they spend more than one-third of their waking time, is the home. No longer really children, they are nevertheless dependent on their parents, and these contradictory roles can contribute to misunderstanding and rebellion. Thus, it is not surprising that the largest segment of the adolescent's time at home is spent in his or her own room, away from other members of the family.

The second social world of the adolescent, at least in the United States, is the school. In many respects the school is the adolescent's workplace. One may negotiate patterns of interaction with one's family, but at school one must follow uniform rules or pay a penalty.

More than a quarter of the adolescent's time is spent in settings other than home and school. In what may be a uniquely American phenomenon, a significant fraction of this time—nearly 4% of the teenager's total waking activity—is spent in an automobile.

What are teenagers doing during their waking hours? Again the responses, shown in Figure 18-9, suggest three major kinds of activity. Given the amount of time spent in school, a significant portion of the teenager's time is devoted to productive activity. It is worth noting, however, that although nearly 20% of the adolescent's time is spent in the classroom, only 12% is spent doing classwork. Thus, students claim to be doing schoolwork for just over half of the time they are physically in the classroom.

Teenagers spend about one-third of their time in what the researchers call "maintenance" activities—errands, eating, personal care, and grooming—with almost one-third of this time, or 8.8% of total time, devoted to napping and eating. Without the responsibilities of career and family, the adolescent can devote more than 40% of his or her waking time to leisure activities, primarily socializing with peers.

483

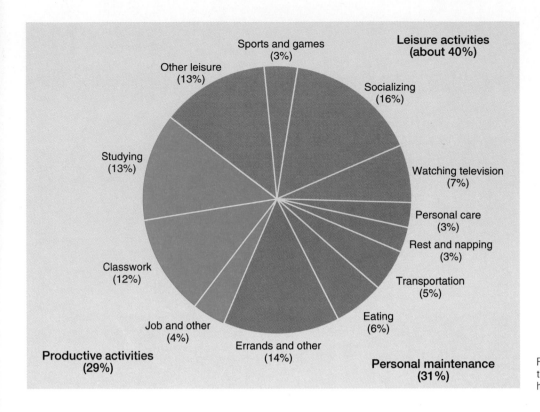

FIGURE 18-9 How adolescents spend their time. (Adapted from Csikszentmihalyi & Larson, 1984.)

There is no better indicator of the psychological changes that occur during adolescence—especially the search for identity—than the data showing with whom adolescents spend their time. As shown in Figure 18-10, more than one-quarter of the teenager's time is spent alone. This matches the popular view of teenagers as withdrawn or not communicating with other members of their families. But it contradicts the equally common notion that teenagers are highly dependent on interactions with peers. And despite the typical parent's complaint that all teenagers do at home is eat and sleep, nearly 20% of the adolescent's time is spent in the company of other family members, including siblings as well as parents. Finally, almost 30% of the teenager's time is spent with friends.

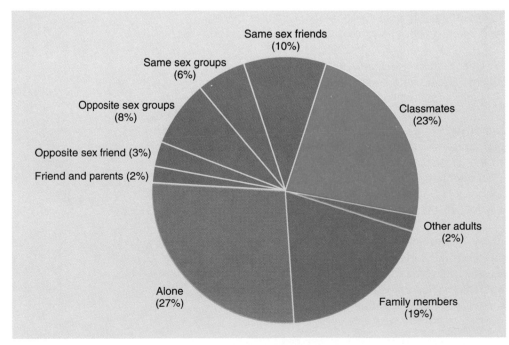

FIGURE 18-10 With whom adolescents spend their time. (Adapted from Csikszentmihalyi & Larson, 1984.)

484

Freud's theory of psychosexual stages holds that particular erogenous zones are the focus of pleasure during different stages of development in early childhood. Each stage is characterized by conflicts between the child's desire for pleasurable sensations and the parent's desire to control the child's behavior; these conflicts may have a lasting impact on personality. In contrast to Freud's theory, which focuses on the biological development of the individual, Erikson's theory emphasizes interpersonal challenges. In each stage the individual must resolve a specific challenge or crisis. The theory is most frequently applied to adolescence, in which the central challenge is the formation of an identity. An adolescent who has carefully considered available life alternatives and has made a conscious choice from among them is said to have achieved identity. A major task facing a young person is the development of a sense of morality. According to Kohlberg, moral development occurs in a series of stages that reflect the development of cognitive capacity. Recent research on the everyday behavior of high school students who have not come to the attention of the authorities has documented where they spend their time, what they do, and with whom they do it. Findings from this research are consistent with Erikson's contention that one of the adolescent's primary psychological tasks is to develop an independent identity.

ADULT DEVELOPMENT

As noted at the beginning of the chapter, when developmental psychology began as a separate subfield early in the twentieth century, it focused almost exclusively on the behavior of infants and children. In a sense, developmental psychology was interested in "first times." How does an infant learn to walk for the first time? What is involved in a child's first production of language? What social and psychological changes accompany the sexual maturation that first occurs in adolescence? Implicit in this view is the assumption that an infant is different from a toddler, who is different from a child, who is different from an adolescent, who is different from an adult; but one adult is the same as another. In part, this tendency to treat all adults as equivalent reflected demographic realities: At the turn of the twentieth century, a baby born in the United States could expect to live only to age 48 (Belsky, 1990). A child born in the mid-1980s, however, can expect to live to age 74, an increase in life expectancy of an entire generation in only eight decades (Belsky, 1990). As life expectancy has increased, developmental psychologists have come to recognize that adulthood also has its share of "firsts," and have begun to focus attention on it.

ERIKSON'S THEORY

We noted before that Erikson was the first developmental theorist to address adulthood. He divided adulthood into three stages: young adulthood, middle age, and old age, as indicated in Table 18-4. Young adults, in contrast to adolescents, are confident of their identities, and are capable of showing commitment to another person. Whereas the adolescent's interest in others is motivated by the search for identity, the young adult shows real concern for the interests and welfare of another; that concern is reciprocated, producing intimacy. A young adult who avoids commitment— whether to friends, causes, or a sexual partner—loses the responsibility that devotion requires, and is likely to become isolated. Although Erikson focused on interpersonal relationships, the need for commitment that makes intimate relationships possible is also a prerequisite for another task of the young adult—embarking on a career.

TABLE 18-4   Erikson's Three Adult Stages of Social Development

Approximate Age	Developmental Task for the Stage	Psychosocial Crisis
Young adulthood	Fusing one's own identity with that of another person through mutuality and commitment.	Intimacy versus isolation.
Middle age	Fulfilling family and personal goals, demonstrating concern for future generations.	Generativity versus stagnation.
Old age	Reviewing one's life and deciding that it contains order and meaning.	Ego integrity versus despair.

SOURCE: Adapted from Erikson, 1963.

Individuals in middle age are faced with the task of evaluating their accomplishments to determine whether or not they have accomplished both personal and socially imposed goals. It is this challenge that has been popularized as the "midlife crisis." If one feels that one's accomplishments measure up to expectations, the crisis is resolved in favor of what Erikson terms *generativity,* the belief that further growth is still possible. If, however, one feels that one does not measure up, the result will be stagnation. Of all the developmental crises described in Erikson's theory, the crisis between generativity and stagnation is most heavily influenced by social factors. Social expectations, rather than internal ideals, provide the standards against which individuals judge their success.

Upon reaching old age, the individual must confront his or her mortality. No longer is it possible to think that an alternate path might be more successful; one must be able to find order and meaning in the path already taken. According to Erikson, the individual who experiences ego integrity accepts the limitations of life, and obtains satisfaction from having been part of a larger history that includes previous generations. Achieving ego integrity leads to *wisdom;* failure to reach this state of acceptance leads to despair.

The young interviewer is taking an oral history from the older woman. According to Erikson's theory, the developmental task for old age is to review one's life and to decide that it has meaning, especially in regard to past and future generations.

THE SELF IN TRANSITION

More than other developmental theories, Erikson's emphasizes the transitions from one stage of life to another. When a developmental crisis is resolved, the person achieves an equilibrium that lasts until the next challenge presents itself. Taking their cue from Erikson's general position, researchers have only recently begun to explore the transitions that occur during the adult years. The first major study of this kind was conducted among men representing four occupations—business executives, hourly workers in industry, novelists, and university biologists—in the northeastern United States. There were 40 subjects, all of whom were between the ages of 35 and 45 at the beginning of the study. Extensive interviews with these men suggested that there are three broad classes of life transitions in adulthood, each of which is further subdivided into specific phases.

The first class of transitions includes those involved in the individual's need to become established, in social relationships and in an occupation. In the "early adult transition," beginning in the late teens, the man enters the adult world and faces four developmental tasks. The first two—getting married and starting a family, and choosing an occupation—are self-explanatory. The third task, "forming a Dream," is to establish general expectations about what one will become or would like to become. The fourth task is to choose a mentor, a more experienced person who can provide both professional and personal guidance. Over the next several years the young adult becomes more established in his occupation. At the "age 30 transition" he works out the flaws in his original life structure. During the next phase, "settling down," he no longer considers a large number of options but instead engages in concerted effort in a few areas. During this phase the principal motivation among the men studied was professional advancement.

The second class of transitions can be thought of as involving a review of what has gone before. The "midlife transition" typically occurs between the ages of 40 and 45. The researchers found what could be described as a midlife crisis in nearly 80% of the subjects. These men were reexamining their prior values, expectations, and career choices. This reevaluation tended to be more pronounced for those who had pursued their prior goals most singlemindedly. For some, the crisis culminated in a dramatic event such as a divorce or job change; for most, however, it involved little more than a self-examination imposed by the limitations that the structure of business in the United States imposes on career goals. Because most businesses are organized as pyramids, with fewer opportunities at higher levels, not everyone who hopes to can make it to the top. If continued advancement is part of one's "Dream," failure to attain it would necessarily lead to a rethinking of goals. The choices made as a result of this reexamination are solidified in the "age 50 transition."

The third class of transitions reflects the shift from an occupation to retirement and later life. The "late adult transition" concludes middle adulthood and forms the basis for late adulthood, which usually begins around the time of retirement. At the time of the study, few of the subjects had reached retirement age, so data for this final stage were sparse.

This study had two significant limitations. First, most of the subjects were professionals, so the results cannot safely be generalized to the far more numerous part of the population in manufacturing and service jobs. Second, as already noted, the study included no women. This limitation is currently being remedied in a comparable study of life transitions among adult women that is underway (Levinson, 1986). In addition, other research on women's adult development has found that they progress through a series of stages during early adulthood that is virtually the same as the progression that Levinson found for men (Roberts & Newton, 1987).

Developmental psychology's interest in aging is so recent that the first textbook on the psychology of aging was only published in 1984 (Belsky, 1984). As the population of the United States, and of most developed countries, becomes increasingly older on the average, there will no doubt be more attention paid to the many changes that occur during adulthood and old age.

INTERIM SUMMARY

Lifespan developmental psychology explores social and psychological development in adults and the elderly as well as infants, children, and adolescents. According to Erikson, the challenge for a young adult is to show commitment to another, leading to intimacy rather than isolation. The middle-aged individual must judge his or her achievements against the expectations of others; if those accomplishments are viewed as productive, the crisis is resolved in favor of generativity rather than stagnation. Upon reaching old age, the individual must confront mortality and find order and meaning in his or her life. Successful resolution of this crisis produces ego integrity rather than despair. Researchers have also explored the nature of the transitions that occur in adult life. They have identified three broad types of transitions: the early adult transition, the midlife transition, and the late adult transition.

SUMMARY

1. As originally used, the term *social development* referred to the changes in social behavior that occur during childhood and adolescence. Today, developmental psychologists take a life-span approach to the subject. Physical changes associated with maturation set limits on social development, but learning and environmental influences shape the individual. The interaction of biological and environmental factors is complex, and some differences in social behavior that might appear to be innate may be attributable to environment.

2. *Imprinting* is a fixed-action pattern that prompts the young of certain species to follow a parent. The behavior effectively attaches the young to the parent, creating a protective environment for them. Research with infant rhesus monkeys suggests that physical contact with the mother plays an important role in social development.

3. According to *attachment theory,* the behaviors of human infants—like smiling, cooing, and crying—that prompt parents to take care of them have an evolutionary basis similar to those that attach the young of other species to their parents. The theory suggests that secure attachment provides a firm foundation for later social development.

4. The quality of a child's attachment to its primary care giver can be measured by a procedure called the *Strange Situation.* This procedure has been used to distinguish children who are securely attached to their care giver from children whose relationships to their care givers are either avoidant or ambivalent. Research suggests that behavior in the Strange Situation does correlate with behavior later in childhood.

5. According to Freud's theory of psychosexual stages, the developing child passes through a series of stages—oral, anal, phallic, and, following a latency period, genital—each of which is linked to the pleasurable sensations associated with a specific *erogenous zone.* Conflicts associated with the control of those sensations play a major role in the formation of adult personality. Despite its substantial influence on popular culture, Freud's theory has received very little scientific support.

6. Erikson's theory of psychosocial development identifies eight stages through which individuals pass from infancy to old age. In each stage a central conflict must be resolved. Perhaps the best-known of these conflicts is the *identity crisis,* which can characterize the period of adolescence.

7. According to Kohlberg, moral reasoning develops in tandem with cognitive abilities. He identified six stages of moral development grouped into three more general categories. In the preconventional stages, reward and punishment are the basis for morality. In the conventional stages, the focus shifts to the following of rules. In the postconventional stages, these explicit societal rules are

replaced by more abstract ethical principles.

8. Adolescence is often considered to be a time of turmoil because of the social problems associated with it, like teenage pregnancy and suicide. There is, however, remarkably little information on the everyday behavior of "normal" teenagers. Recent research has begun to change this imbalance. A study of the behavior of high school students documents the importance to them of school, friends, and time alone. These findings are consistent with Erikson's contention that the primary task of adolescence is the development of an independent identity.

9. Reflecting the recent emphasis on development through the life span, developmental psychologists have undertaken long-term studies of adult development. This research has begun to identify the important transitional phases from young adulthood through old age.

FOCUS QUESTIONS

1. Describe the process of attachment in both animals and humans, citing relevant research.

2. Describe the Strange Situation. What are the three classes of attachment outcome that result from the Strange Situation, and what is the implication of each for social development?

3. Describe Freud's stages of psychosexual development. Has research confirmed the importance of these stages for the psychological functioning of the adult

4. Describe Erikson's stages of psychosocial development from birth through adolescence.

5. Discuss the process of adolescent identity formation.

6. How is it possible to measure a person's level of moral reasoning? What relationship does moral reasoning have to overall cognitive development?

7. According to the research on high school students, what are the major socializing influences on adolescents?

8. According to Erikson's theory, what are the major life crises facing adults?

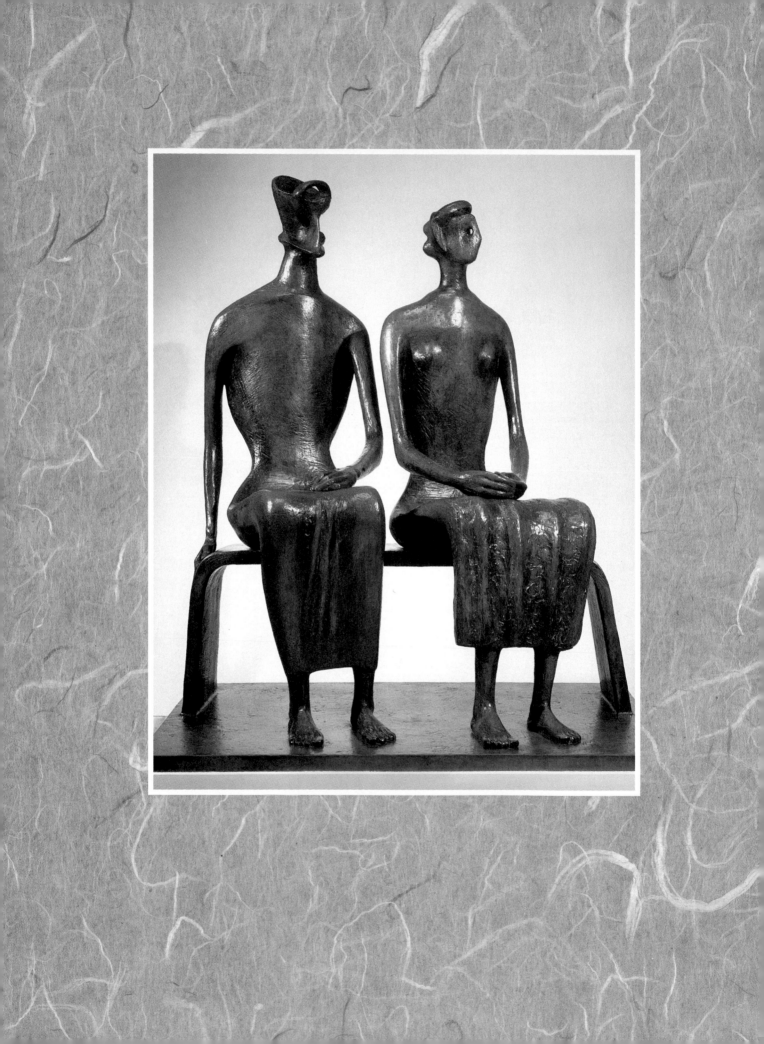

PART SIX

INDIVIDUAL AND GROUP PROCESSES

nly rarely do people live in isolation; individual behavior is affected by the actual or implied presence of others. The two chapters in Part VI consider how the **individual functions within the larger group.** Chapter 19 takes the perspective of the individual, showing how the larger social context affects representations of the environment, attitudes toward objects and people, and the development of a sense of self. Chapter 20 turns to interpersonal processes, describing social exchange among individuals, the influence that people have over one another, and aspects of the way people participate in groups.

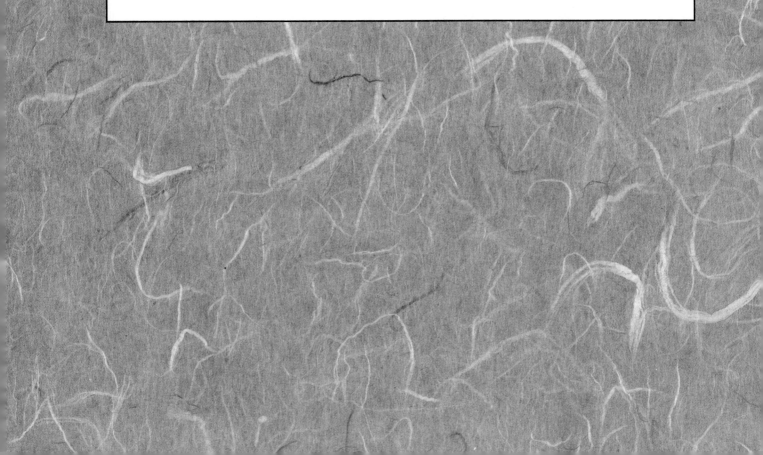

CHAPTER 19

SOCIAL COGNITION, ATTITUDES, AND THE SELF

Rarely do human beings live a solitary existence, isolated from others. In fact, such a state of nature, as imagined by Rousseau, Hobbes, and other philosophers of the seventeenth and eighteenth centuries, probably never existed—humans have probably been social animals since they first evolved. Today people live in increasingly complex societies in which rules for social conduct limit the individual's freedom of action. The concept of a state of nature may nonetheless be useful for addressing broad philosophical and ethical issues about the nature of humankind. Would individuals free from social rules be in harmony with nature, animals, and the few other humans encountered as Rousseau believed? Or would life without society be, in Hobbes's words, "solitary, poor, nasty, brutish, and short" (1651/1952, p. 85)? For psychology, the key issue is not what the individual would be like without society, but rather what the individual is like within society. The relationship between individual and group is the subject matter for social psychology, the subfield that examines the personal and situational influences on individual behavior. This chapter concentrates on the individual, examining how the individual thinks about others, forms attitudes toward others, and constructs a self-concept based in part on information provided by others. Chapter 20 moves beyond the individual, examining the relationships between and among people.

To a great extent the reciprocal influence of individual and group depends on **social cognition**—the cognitive processes involved in gathering, organizing, and interpreting information about social beings. These processes are in many ways so automatic that we become aware of them only when confronted by an unfamiliar situation. Suppose, for example, that it is your first day at work on a job you obtained through an interview at school during your senior year. You may have visited your employer-to-be during the interview process, but this is still your first encounter with most of your new co-workers. Most of the morning has been spent in brief introductions and exchanges of small talk, and now one of your colleagues, a person who has been with the company for five years, invites you out for lunch. You are delighted not to have to grab a sandwich somewhere by yourself on your first day at work, but suddenly a torrent of questions intrudes. You have been told the company's official policy on lunch time, but how long should you really take? On your first day, should you go at all? Is your co-worker merely being friendly, or is there some ulterior motive? Are you being sized up for something? Will others be pleased or offended if you accept the invitation? How can you tell what this person is like, deep down? Assuming you go, what topics are appropriate for you to discuss? How much of your own opinions, about the company or about unrelated issues, should you divulge? What will your co-worker think of you? All of these questions involve social cognition, which is fundamentally different from the perceptual and cognitive processes discussed earlier in Chapters 4, 13, 14, and 15.

GATHERING SOCIAL INFORMATION

Ask people to describe what makes a good friend, and you are likely to get some common themes among the answers: someone I can talk to, someone who shares my values, someone who cares what happens to me. But how do we separate the sympathetic and trustworthy listeners from those who cannot keep a confidence, or distinguish a person who truly accepts us as we are from people who only like the public face we put on? The answers begin with the gathering of social information.

PEOPLE ARE DIFFERENT FROM THINGS

The difference between social cognition and the cognitive processes discussed earlier begins with the stimulus for social perception. Compared to things, people are more complex, with many important characteristics hidden from view. People have wants, needs, ideas, friends, relatives, a past and a future, all of which may be affecting their actions in ways not obvious to you. The range of possible causes behind the movement of an object or the behavior of an animal is restricted; the range of possible causes of human behavior is vast. Consequently, the search for the causes of action is an important part of social cognition. A second important difference between things and people is that people manage their public images, either because doing so will serve their purposes or because the social situation calls for particular kinds of behavior. For example, in contemporary American society there are social rules that discourage the expression of negative emotions in public; indeed, so many people tell others to "have a nice day" that the phrase has become a cliché.

The extent to which smiling in public reflects these rules, rather than actual happiness, was demonstrated in an ingenious series of observational studies in which researchers examined the facial expressions of bowlers, hockey fans at a home game, and pedestrians walking along a city street (Kraut & Johnston, 1979). If facial expressions reflect actual feelings, there should be more smiles among bowlers after a strike or a spare than after a miss; hockey fans should smile more when the home team fares well than when it does not; and there should be more smiles among pedestrians on sunny days than on dreary ones. Although the researchers found that this is indeed the case, the social involvement of the person being observed was a much better predictor of smiling than the situation. In other words, individuals who were observed in the presence of bowling partners, other spectators, or walking with companions smiled more than individuals who were bowling, attending a hockey game, or walking along the street alone. Thus, the social rules governing displays of emotion in public settings were at least as important as internal feeling states in determining the facial expressions observed.

Most—but not all—people follow the social rules for public displays of emotion. Human beings are capable of intentional action; they can choose whether to behave according to the rules or not. In contrast, objects have no choice in the matter; their "behavior" is governed by physical laws. Animals obviously can regulate their movements in response to features of the environment, but there is no evidence that they respond to each other's intentions. As perceivers who recognize that people act intentionally, we look behind any particular action to find dispositional properties—enduring features of the person that will affect behavior in many settings. These dispositional properties can include such things as personality characteristics, personal styles, or long-term goals—anything that helps us understand what the person has already done, or predict what the individual will do in the future.

EXPECTATIONS CAN PRODUCE REALITY

When we infer dispositional properties from another person's behavior, we develop expectations about what the person is likely to do. But because this individual, called the stimulus person, or target person, is busily perceiving us at the same time, we can produce responses from the stimulus person that are consistent with our expectations (Snyder, 1984). For example, in one study, each of 48 male students held a "get-acquainted" telephone conversation with one of 48 female students. Before the conversation began, each male was given a folder containing real biographical information provided by the target female and a Polaroid photograph that was said to be her picture. In reality the photograph was of someone else—one of eight different photographs, four of females previously rated by other undergraduate males as very attractive, four of females rated as unattractive. (The women in the photographs knew that their pictures would be used in a social-perception study.)

The conversation was unstructured, lasted for 10 minutes, and was tape-recorded so that the male's portion of the conversation could later be separated from the female's portion. These separate portions were then rated by undergraduate judges who were unaware of the nature of the study or the purported attractiveness of the female conversationalists. Not surprisingly, males who believed they were talking to attractive females were rated (among other things) as more confident, animated, comfortable, socially adept, outgoing, and sexually warm than were males who believed they were talking to unattractive females. What is more interesting is the effect that the males' expectations regarding attractiveness produced on the females. On 17 of 21 variables, judges who heard only the females' portion of the conversation rated as more attractive the females who were talking to males who thought that they were attractive: "What had initially been reality in the minds of the men had now become reality in the behavior of the women with whom they had interacted" (Snyder, Tanke, & Berscheid, 1977, p. 661).

CUES TO INTERNAL STATES

Although in some instances stimulus persons can mask their true feelings, and perceivers can produce what they expect, the fact remains that most of our perceptions of others are relatively accurate representations of reality. One reason for this is the diversity of cues from which emotional states may be inferred. The kinds of cues that have received the most attention are facial expressions and other nonverbal cues such as body position and ways of speaking.

Facial Expressions

As noted in Chapter 6, the idea that many emotions are accompanied by facial expressions that are *universal*—that is, constant across cultures—originated in Darwin's (1872) comparisons of emotional expressions in animals and humans. But more than a century went by before scientists were able to put this idea to a critical test. Popular wisdom holds that "a smile is a smile in any language." And, as studies described in Chapter 6 indicate, in this instance the popular wisdom is correct. Facial expressions for six emotions—anger, disgust, fear, happiness, sadness, and surprise—are recognized across cultural boundaries (Ekman & Friesen, 1975; Ekman, Sorenson, & Friesen, 1969; Izard, 1971).

Early research on the recognition of emotion through facial expressions was concerned with the accuracy of the perception, not with distinguishing one expression from another. Subjects were typically shown photographs of actors producing various expressions and were asked to identify the emotion. As initially designed, these studies made no provision for distinguishing the degree of error involved in a misidentification (Woodworth, 1938). Thus, a subject who identified a presumably happy expression as one of contentment would be counted as just as wrong as a subject who identified it as an expression of anger. Not surprisingly, under these conditions subjects did not appear to be very good at labeling emotional expressions.

To solve this problem, Woodworth argued that emotional expressions can be arranged in a continuum of categories. The continuum begins at one end with happiness, love, and mirth (a), proceeds through surprise (b), fear and suffering (c), anger and determination (d), and disgust (e), and ends with contempt (f). Note that this research preceded and made possible the studies that demonstrated which expressions were universally perceived across cultures; the categories it uses are not exactly those that are accepted today. Specifically, psychologists now separate fear and suffering into two expressions—fear and sadness—and no longer consider contempt to be a universally recognized facial expression.

Woodworth's contribution to the study of facial expressions was to show that errors in perception of one step (such as mistaking surprise for fear) were different in magnitude from errors of more than one step (such as mistaking happiness for disgust). Building on this work, another researcher argued that the pattern of emotional

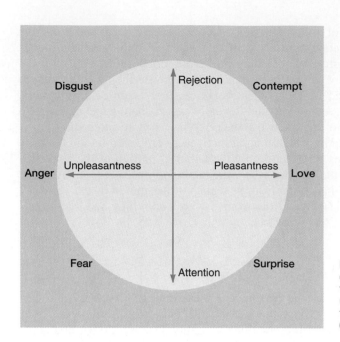

FIGURE 19-1 The circular model of emotional expressiveness. According to this model, emotions differ on two underlying dimensions, attention/rejection and pleasantness/unpleasantness. (Adapted from Schlosberg, 1952.)

expressions is really best regarded as a circle, created by joining Woodworth's category (a) of happiness, love, and mirth to his category (f) of contempt (Schlosberg, 1952). This circular classification scheme, shown in Figure 19-1, has had a substantial influence on later research in the perception of facial expressions of emotion.

The circular model's success in accounting for data from studies of posed states of emotion attests to the perceiver's ability to make the necessary distinctions. But what, exactly, is being distinguished? Are perceivers merely reacting to a posed state described by a particular linguistic label? Or are they discerning an outward expression of a real emotional experience that is independent of the particular language used to construct the categories? The latter would have to be true for there to be universally recognized emotional expressions.

It is relatively simple to show that people can successfully recognize unposed emotional expressions. To obtain images of unposed facial expressions, for example, people viewing emotionally arousing videotapes can themselves be videotaped by cameras concealed in the video monitors. Still photographs of their expressions can then be produced. The result would be images of ordinary people (not trained actors) experiencing (not posing in) specific emotional states. Research employing just such techniques with American and Japanese subjects showed cross-cultural consistency in the identification of unposed emotional expressions, regardless of whether the people evaluating the expressions were looking at images of people from their own or the other culture (Ekman, 1972).

It is more complicated to demonstrate that the identification of emotional expressions is independent of the words in a language that label emotional states. For example, is fear next to anger in the circular classification in Figure 19-1 because the two emotions are indeed related, or because the labels—the words "fear" and "anger"—are related? This question was addressed in a study that compared the judgments of adults (presumably capable of making subtle linguistic distinctions among emotional states) to the judgments of preschoolers (presumably without comparable linguistic skills) (Russell & Bullock, 1985).

The research employed a statistical analysis tool known as **multidimensional scaling (MDS),** which requires only that subjects be able to judge the *similarity* of stimuli to be scaled, regardless of whether they can attach linguistic labels to them. Every stimulus in a set is paired with every other. For each pairing, a subject rates how similar the members of the pair are to one another. The similarity judgments of all the subjects are then analyzed by a computer program that produces a picture rep-

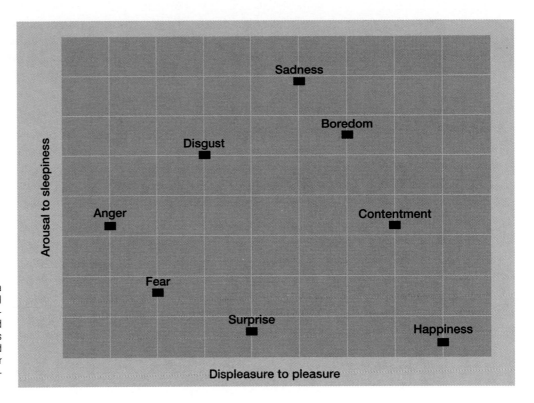

FIGURE 19-2 Plot of results from a multidimensional scaling of 20 facial expressions. The major categories follow the circular pattern first suggested by Schlosberg (1952). Note that subjects were shown only unlabeled pictures and asked to pair them according to their degree of similarity. (Adapted from Russell & Bullock, 1985.)

resenting the position of every stimulus relative to every other stimulus in the set. In this case, subjects were shown pairs of pictures of 20 different emotional expressions and asked, "How much alike are the two people feeling?" This is a question that both adults and children understand, and it completely avoids any linguistic labels for the expressions. Figure 19-2 presents a two-dimensional plot of the similarities among the expressions. Rather than include all 20 expressions used as stimulus materials, Figure 19-2 shows only the eight expressions most like the six universally recognized facial emotions. The points in the figure are ones derived from the study without linguistic labels; the words representing each emotional expression have been added for clarity. The arrangement of expressions in the plot is comparable to the circular classification shown in Figure 19-1. Moreover, there were no important differences between the judgments of adults and preschoolers, suggesting that the "universal" emotions are independent of the labels used to describe them.

Nonverbal Leakage and Detection of Deception

Although facial expressions are important sources of social information, they are not the only cues available for the perceiver. Other cues, such as body position and gestures, also contribute to the perceiver's impression. No matter how much your face might reflect sadness when you learn of a good friend's misfortune, you convey your sympathy more effectively if you accompany your facial expression with a comforting arm around the friend's shoulders.

Why do gestures and body position carry such power? Part of the answer lies in the fact that people normally exert relatively little control over their body position (Ekman & Friesen, 1969). We are social beings and social rules often govern the emotions we are expected to display. Sometimes, however, the expected emotion is not the emotion we are actually feeling. We may nonetheless attempt to control our expressions of emotion to conform to the social rules—to "put on a happy face" and, in effect, lie about what we are feeling. Of the three channels we use to communicate emotion—speech, facial expression, and body position—speech, at least insofar as the words we utter are concerned, is the easiest to control. Speech, however, involves many elements besides words. These include dialect, rate of speaking, pitch, and loudness. We are more likely to control some of these elements, like loudness, than others, like rate and pitch (Apple, Streeter, & Krauss, 1979). Next to speech, the most easily controlled channel of communication is facial expression. By comparison, the ability to control the position of body and limbs is a distant third. Thus, putting on a happy face will rarely be accompanied by straightening one's shoulders and keeping one's feet still.

In nonverbal communication, the opposite of control is **nonverbal leakage,** the nonverbal cues that conflict with a spoken message. A person who "talks a good game," and may even control his or her facial expression during delivery of a false message, may not attend to the position of body and limbs. As a result, these nonverbal cues can indicate when the person is lying. Indeed, an entire industry has been built on the assumption that it is the body, rather than speech, that tells the truth. This industry uses various physiological measures in efforts to detect deception. Prominent among these are the Psychological Stress Evaluator (PSE) and the more familiar polygraph, or "lie detector." The developers of the PSE claim that it detects deception by measuring stress-related tremors in the voice. An authoritative review concluded, however, that there is insufficient evidence to support this claim (Zuckerman, DePaulo, & Rosenthal, 1981).

Because of its widespread use, the current status of the polygraph is much more controversial. One fundamental point must be made as clearly as possible: The polygraph does not detect lies. Rather, it records respiration rate, changes in blood pressure, and galvanic skin response, each of which changes in response to physiological arousal. Because there is substantial evidence that intentional deception produces arousal (Zuckerman, DePaulo, & Rosenthal, 1981), the polygraph is believed to detect lies. It should be noted, however, that factors other than lying—such as fear of the interrogation, anxiety about losing one's job, guilt over a transgression that is not the subject of the polygraph test—can also produce arousal. When this occurs, the subject may appear to be lying when in fact this is not the case.

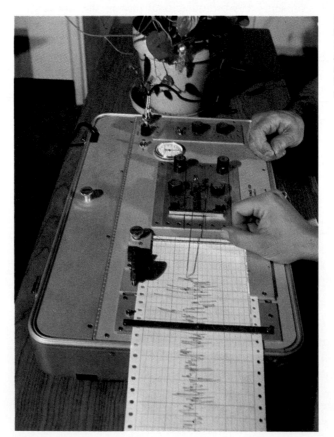

Early polygraphs, such as the one shown here, recorded only one or two physiological measures related to psychological arousal. More recent models measure respiration rate, heart rate, changes in blood pressure, and galvanic skin response.

Social cognition begins with the gathering of social information. Although it involves many of the same processes as the perception of inanimate objects, it differs in two major ways. First, because people are capable of intentional action, they can manage the impressions they create. Second, because impression-formation involves contact between stimulus person and perceiver, the perceiver's own expectations can influence the stimulus person's actions. Despite these differences, social perception is usually quite accurate. One reason for this is the diversity of cues from which emotional states may be inferred. These include facial expressions, six of which—anger, disgust, fear, happiness, sadness, and surprise—are recognized across cultural boundaries. Other nonverbal cues include body position and gestures; these are thought to be more revealing than facial expressions and verbal communication. Two physiological measures, the Psychological Stress Evaluator and the polygraph, attempt to use nonverbal cues to detect intentional deception.

ORGANIZATION OF INFORMATION

A stimulus person's verbal statements and nonverbal behavior, and the social context in which this behavior occurs, provide the raw material for social cognition. But imagine trying to keep track of every statement made, every facial expression presented, and every nonverbal behavior performed by every person with whom you have any contact, even during a single day. Obviously, to be useful, the vast array of available information must be simplified and organized; this is where the "cognition" part of social cognition comes into play.

PERSON MEMORY

Social knowledge, like other knowledge, is organized in mental structures such as those described in Chapter 14. Storage begins with memory, but just as social perception is different from object perception, *person memory* is different from memory for things. Specifically, because people are such complex stimuli, the memory filing cabinet for a person contains three main drawers—one for aspects of the person's appearance, one for the person's behavior, and one for the person's traits (Fiske & Taylor, 1991).

With regard to appearance, people's memory for faces of members of their own race is, under laboratory conditions, truly amazing, with nearly perfect accuracy over long periods of time. The qualification "under laboratory conditions" is necessary because a substantial amount of research on eyewitness testimony shows that under normal conditons the accuracy of facial identification varies considerably depending on the circumstances of the initial observation and subsequent attempts at recall (Shapiro & Penrod, 1986).

Whereas memory for faces is likely to be stored in concrete, individual units, memory for behavior is likely to be stored with an attached *temporal* code. That is, social behaviors occur in a time-bound sequence, and there is evidence that this sequence is preserved in memories of actions: "You did that, and then I did this, and then you did . . ." The stored sequences are frequently grouped into larger time units, such as phases of one's life (high school, college, and so on), but within those larger units the sequences do not appear to be stored in an invariant serial order (Fiske & Taylor, 1991).

Finally, memory for traits appears to be coded *semantically,* usually in a mental network that relates one trait to another. Traits are inferences from behavior, and collections of traits are used to place individuals into cognitive categories (such as friend, enemy, conscientious worker). This placement is usually done on the basis of actual behavior, but is sometimes done on the basis of stereotypes, in the absence of any actual behavior.

KNOWLEDGE STRUCTURES

In Chapter 14 we described a number of cognitive structures into which information is organized. These include *categories, schemata,* and *prototypes,* each of which has its place in the organization of social information. Early research and theory in social cognition focused exclusively on cognitive categorization—the placing of individuals into mental "boxes" on the basis of whether or not they possess the defining characteristics of a member of a particular class. From this point of view, for example, only one characteristic—having had a child—defines the social category of "parent."

The categorization approach, however, fails to account fully for the meaning of the word "parent." Being a parent involves more than having had children; it also involves a set of interrelated personal responsibilities and societal expectations. In short, it is more like a schema than a category. Recognizing complexities like these, and taking a cue from their colleagues in cognitive psychology, social psychologists began to look at the organization of social knowledge in terms of schemata. Thus a schema for "parent" would include, among other things, responsibilities to children, relationships to schools and other organizations that involve children, and possible conflicts between work and home responsibilities.

To some social psychologists, the overlapping expectations, some of which are more important than others, suggests that social knowledge might best be described in terms of prototypes (Cantor & Mischel, 1979). A prototype is an ideal—a collection of all the features that would define an instance. So the prototypical "parent" would have all of the features that anyone might associate with the concept. But a prototype is a *fuzzy* cognitive structure, so a particular instance will be seen as representing the prototype if it shares a *family resemblance* to the prototype. The prototypical parent might thus be one member of a male/female couple who together live with and care for their biological offspring. People whose characteristics bear a sufficient family resemblance to the prototype—for example, single parents or adoptive parents—would be classified as parents, whereas others—celibate hermits, for example—would not.

JUDGMENTAL HEURISTICS

As is the case for the cognition of nonsocial objects, the formation of knowledge structures is not always conscious and deliberative. Consequently, the accuracy of social cognition can be reduced by judgmental heuristics (Kahneman, Slovic, & Tversky, 1982). These heuristics were discussed in Chapter 15, but two of them—the availability heuristic and the representativeness heuristic—merit further discussion here. The availability heuristic involves the use of an easily remembered instance to judge the frequency of an event. A political advertisement that personalizes an issue such as crime, tax cheating, or welfare takes advantage of the availability heuristic to lead perceivers to overestimate the prevalence of each of these problems. The representativeness heuristic also involves probability judgments, such as judgments about whether an individual belongs to a specific category, but in this case the judgment is made on the basis of the extent to which the person's attributes "fit" what is expected of category members rather than on statistical base rates.

The interpretation of social information can also be influenced by the **priming effect,** a bias that results from other cognitive activities performed previously. For example, if you are asked to make three-word sentences from sets of words related to hostility, such as *leg break arm his,* and later are asked to evaluate a person whose actions could be interpreted as showing hostility, you are more likely to say that the person is hostile than if you had not been "primed" by creating the hostile sentences. Such priming effects have been shown to last up to 24 hours (Higgins, Bargh, & Lombardi, 1985).

SOCIAL STEREOTYPING

When a stimulus person is a member of a readily identifiable social category, such as a racial, occupational, or gender-based group, some of the processes of social cognition can lead to the formation of a **stereotype,** an inflexible image of the members of a particular group that is held without regard to whether it is true. Stereotyping can be thought of as the reverse of the availability heuristic. Whereas the availability heuristic involves a faulty generalization from one easily remembered individual to all members of the social group, stereotyping involves a faulty generalization from characteristics believed to be common to all members of a group or category to an individual. Both kinds of error simplify the cognitive task at the expense of accuracy in social perception.

Measuring Stereotypes

Because stereotypes about various social groups have been related to discriminatory behavior against members of those groups, psychologists have for years been interested in measuring, and changing, stereotypes. Early research on stereotyping used what has come to be known as the "checklist" method (Katz & Braly, 1933). Male subjects were asked to evaluate a variety of national and cultural groups, including Americans, Chinese, English, Germans, Irish, Italians, Japanese, Jews, Negroes, and Turks (the ethnic labels here are those of the original study), using a list of 84 descriptive adjectives. Each subject was asked to list those adjectives he considered most "characteristic" of each national or ethnic group. The specific dependent variable was the proportion of subjects who assigned each trait to a particular group.

This method has several drawbacks. For one thing, people who know that they are taking part in psychological research are reluctant to attribute negative characteristics to any national or ethnic group (Karlins, Coffman, & Walters, 1969). For another, the checklist procedure reveals the percentage of a *group* of subjects who endorse any given stereotype (Brigham, 1971). Yet stereotyping is defined as a faulty generalization on the part of an *individual* perceiver. Thus, the checklist procedure will show how many subjects believe that members of a particular group possess a particular trait, but it cannot show whether an individual subject believes that members of the group possess a particular *collection* of traits.

A more useful method is the estimation of subjective probabilities (McCauley & Stitt, 1978). Subjects are asked questions such as "What percent of all the world's people are snobbish?" Their answers reveal their subjective appraisal of the likelihood that any person they encounter will be snobbish. Subjects are then asked "What percent of [a particular target group] are snobbish?" Their answers reveal their subjective appraisal of the likelihood that a member of the target group will be snobbish. If the perceiver considers members of the target group no more likely to be snobbish than anyone else, the two percentage estimates should be the same, and dividing the second by the first should yield a quotient of 1.00. This quotient is called the **diagnostic ratio** because to the degree that it exceeds 1.00 it is diagnostic of the perceiver's view of the target group. In principle, a similar ratio could be calculated for any conceivable trait.

Illusory Correlation

Sometimes the motivation for stereotyping may be clear, at least to an outside observer, as, for example, when an etablished group derogates the members of a new immigrant group that appears to pose an economic threat. Even when such motivations are absent, however, the cognitive act of classifying people can itself produce stereotypes. For example, in one study college undergraduates were asked to read sets of sentences describing individuals belonging to two groups, which were identified only as Group A and Group B (Hamilton, Dugan, & Trolier, 1985). Of 26 sentences describing members of Group A, 18 mentioned desirable traits and 8 noted undesirable traits. Of 13 sentences describing members of Group B, 9 contained desirable descriptions and 4 contained undesirable ones. Thus, the desirable/undesirable ratio was 9:4 for both target groups. Nevertheless, the subjects' opinions of Group B were more negative than their opinions of Group A. How could this happen?

The researchers concluded that the subjects formed an **illusory correlation** (Chapman, 1967) between negative statements and membership in Group B. The correlation was illusory because it was perceived by the subjects but was not present in the data on which the judgment was based. In this case the illusory correlation was based on the distinctiveness of the negative information. There were fewer statements about Group B, so the negative ones stand out more and lead to the erroneous conclusion that members of Group B had undesirable characteristics. And as the researchers pointed out, the subjects had no underlying motivation to conclude that members of Group B were undesirable. A cognitive bias of this sort can affect comparisons of any majority group to any minority group. Members of minority groups are encountered less frequently than members of majority groups; undesirable traits are encountered less often than desirable ones. When the two occur together, they are associated in an illusory correlation.

INTERIM SUMMARY

Once social information has been perceived, it must be simplified and organized. Although much social cognition leads to valid conclusions, there are a number of sources of error. These include priming and judgmental heuristics, such as the representativeness heuristic and the availability heuristic. Incorrect conclusions may also be attributable to stereotyping, in which a faulty generalization is made to an individual from characteristics thought to be common to the members of a group. Some stereotypes may be attributable to illusory correlations between negative information and a particular minority group.

INTERPRETATION OF BEHAVIOR

No matter how much information about another person's behavior you might gather and organize, you must complete the final step in the process of social cognition—interpretation—before you act on the information. If you are approached by a large dog that you have never seen before, and the dog, vigorously wagging its tail, comes close to you and nuzzles your hand, you will have no doubt that the dog is friendly. On the other hand, if a stranger walks up to you and offers to do you a favor, you will wonder what the person really wants. Should the person's behavior be attributed to a desire to take advantage of you, or should it be attributed to the person's underlying friendliness? Because people are not things, you must look behind their observable behavior to determine its causes; this search for the causes of behavior is the subject of attribution theory.

ATTRIBUTION PROCESSES

Like judgmental heuristics, **attribution processes** function to simplify the social world. Rather than keeping a running tally of all the actions another person performs, it is more efficient to record the person's underlying *personal dispositions—*

his or her relatively enduring personality characteristics, behavioral styles, or reasons for acting. Not only are there far fewer dispositions than there are behaviors, but knowledge of those dispositions enables you to predict the person's actions in other circumstances besides the present ones. If you have worked on several projects with a person who consistently takes more than a fair share of the credit, for example, you will come to think of the person as self-aggrandizing. It would then not surprise you to find the person exhibiting other behaviors—seeking publicity, always having something to say in a conversation, or being overzealous about classwork—that reflect this underlying personal disposition. In other words, personal dispositions find expression in a wide variety of behaviors performed in different settings.

How do you discover the dispositions behind a person's behavior? This is the central question addressed by several attribution theories. The first of these, which provided a basic model for most subsequent developments in attribution theory, was outlined in 1958 by Fritz Heider. Trained in the Gestalt tradition (discussed in Chapter 4), Heider was interested in the way people without any scientific background used everyday language to describe people's actions. He called this "naive psychology" to distinguish it from explanations made in scientific terms.

According to Heider, people perceive the social world as divided into forces within the actor (*personal force*) and forces and obstacles in the actor's environment (*environmental force*). Personal force includes a person's intention, effort, and ability. The more personal force underlies an action, the more the result is attributed to the actor. Environmental force typically determines the difficulty of a task. The difference between task difficulty and a person's ability determines whether the person "can" perform the task. This model of attribution is summarized in Figure 19-3. Let's consider an example. If you have the ability to do college-level work in a subject, then you "can" succeed in that subject. Whether you will succeed then depends on how hard you try: you must intend to succeed, and must study hard enough to understand and remember the material.

Heider's model describes the way an outside observer—a perceiver—would interpret the forces underlying another person's choices, but it does not tell us how a perceiver explains why the person chooses a particular action over another in a given situation. The way a perceiver might do this has been described by **correspondent inference** theory (Jones & Davis, 1965; Jones & McGillis, 1976). This theory assumes that every action results from a choice between two alternatives, even if one alternative is to do nothing at all. Each action, the one performed as well as the one

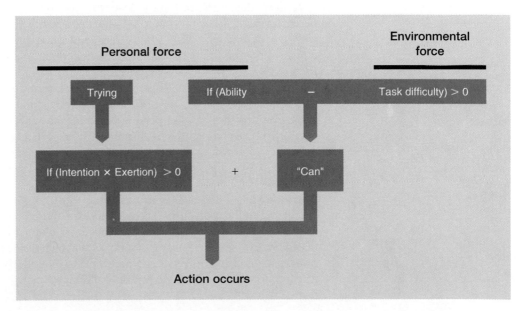

FIGURE 19-3 The relation between personal force and environmental force in Heider's attribution theory.

After the crash of an Air Florida plane in Washington, DC, in January of 1982, one of the bystanders dove into the icy water to help rescue passengers and crew. Consistent with correspondent inference theory, we describe this unusual and dangerous behavior, and the person who performed it, by the same term: heroic.

not performed, will produce a variety of effects. Some of these effects would have been brought about by either action; those are common to the two choices. For example, your selection of a college major will not normally change the minimum number of credits you need to graduate. Other effects are unique to each course of action, and these noncommon effects are the primary focus of the theory. Although your choice of major will not change the graduation requirements, it will begin to open up some career opportunities while closing off others. For a perceiver trying to evaluate another's behavior, the fewer noncommon effects produced by an action, the clearer the reasons behind the choice.

Actions that produce highly desirable noncommon effects, however, provide the perceiver with little information about the actor. This is because under similar circumstances *anyone* would choose an action that produced a highly desirable outcome. In contrast, actions that produce noncommon effects that are low in desirability for a person in the actor's position are informative. Such out-of-role actions are presumed to reveal the actor's underlying personal dispositions. For example, a person who behaves kindly toward a friend who has met with a misfortune may or may not be perceived as a kind person, but a person who behaves kindly toward a bitter enemy who has met with a misfortune will be seen as truly compassionate.

CAUSAL JUDGMENTS

Correspondent inference theory assumes that the perceiver has already determined that the stimulus person is the real cause of the effects being explained, but that is not always the case. For example, the legal claim of self-defense recognizes that occasionally the true causes of one's own behavior reside in the prior actions of other people. Thus, inferences about a person's underlying dispositions must follow a search for the causes of the person's actions.

Two Different Processes

That search proceeds in different ways, depending on the number of observations one is able to make. In normal everyday interactions, you see your friends performing a wide variety of actions in a multitude of settings. If you are asked to explain one of those actions, you can use all of these observations as a guide. In contrast, if you were a member of a jury deciding the fate of a criminal defendant, you would learn about only one of the defendant's actions—the alleged crime—and would discover almost nothing about his or her other behavior.

With repeated observations of a person's behavior, you attribute causality for any given act according to a principle of *covariation:* You note what presumed causes are present when the act occurs and what causes are absent when the act does not occur (Kelley, 1967). Consider an example: Suppose you have a roommate who claims to be "crazy about" a certain person whom you have not yet met. Three possible causes of your roommate's reaction might come to mind: (1) your roommate is easily smitten; (2) the other person is tremendously attractive and would appear so to anyone; and (3) the two of them have suddenly become very interested in each other. How can you determine which of these possibilities or combination of possibilities is the cause of your roommate's reaction?

Perhaps the first question you might ask yourself is, "Does my roommate say this kind of thing about everyone?" If the answer is no, then, according to the principle of covariation, the person in question is *distinctive.* Next you might want to know whether the attraction is a passing one: "Will my roommate feel this way next week, or next month?" If the answer is yes, your roommate's reaction to the person is *consistent.* Finally, you might ask, "Do other people who have seen the person agree that the person is attractive?" If they do, there is *consensus* among the perceivers. When the target (in this case, the special person) is distinctive, consistency of perception (by your roommate) is high, and there is consensus about how attractive the person is, then that person (rather than some feature of your roommate, or a developing relationship between the two people) will be seen as the cause of your roommate's reaction. Unfortunately, of course, the very consensus indicates that if your roommate chooses to pursue the special person, there will be plenty of competition.

Covariation explains how we determine causes when repeated observations are possible, but how can we identify causes when the event or action occurs only once? In this case, obviously, it is not possible to observe similar actions under a variety of circumstances. But people do attribute causality, and even criminal responsibility, for actions that occur only once, despite the relative lack of information. A widely accepted explanation of this phenomenon is that perceivers rely on *causal schemata* to fill in missing data (Kelley, 1972; 1973). A causal schema is like other comparable knowledge structures, except that it consists of information about how things happen instead of, for example, what collections of traits people might possess.

Discounting and Augmentation

Very few social events are a result of only one cause. Put more technically, most social behavior has *multiple sufficient causes.* That is, most instances of social behavior could have been produced in any of several different ways, as suggested by the adage, "There are three sides to every story: your side, my side, and the truth." A single act of kindness, for example, could be a genuine expression of friendship or an ingratiating tactic designed to cause the other person to reciprocate.

The same theorist who suggested that we rely on causal schemata to help fill in missing data we need to explain a social action also identifies two principles that help us weight and choose from among the causes (Kelley, 1972; 1973). According to the *discounting principle,* the more potential causes an action has, the less important any one cause of the action is likely to be. According the *augmentation principle,* in contrast, we attribute more weight to causes that appear to affect an action despite obstacles that may be standing in the way of the action.

You have a good friend who

    Chooses a major in chemistry.
    Decides to become engaged to be married.
    Takes a summer job with a law firm.

You, yourself

    Choose to major in economics.
    Decide to date one person exclusively.
    Take a summer job with an architectural firm.

FIGURE 19-4 Questions designed to elicit the attributional error of correspondence bias.

Errors in Attribution

Like other aspects of social cognition, the attribution process produces its share of errors. To see how these might occur, read the statements at the top of Figure 19-4, imagining that each of them describes something a good friend of yours has done. Now decide, for each action, whether it tells us:

1. Something about your friend,
2. Something about the situation involved, or
3. It depends.

Now read the three statements at the bottom of the figure, imagining that they describe something you yourself have done, and again decide, for each action, whether it tells us something about you, something about the situation, or "it depends."

If your answers are like those of most people, you will use the "it depends" category more for yourself than for your imagined friend (Kelley & Michela, 1980). This difference reflects what has been termed the *fundamental attribution error* (Ross, 1977) or **correspondence bias** (Gilbert & Jones, 1986; Jones, 1990)—the tendency to attribute other people's actions to their personal dispositions while ignoring the situational influences on their behavior.

One explanation for this error is that it reflects perceptual problems like those involved in the differentiation of figure and ground (see Chapter 4). When you are the actor, the situational requirements are the figure and your personality is the ground. But when another person is the actor, from your perspective his or her personality traits are the figure and any situational constraints present are the ground.

Other errors in attribution reflect what is called *self-serving bias*. These often occur when a perceiver is evaluating his or her own actions. For example, people are more willing to take credit for success than they are to take responsibility for failure (Weary & Arkin, 1981).

INTERIM SUMMARY

Because people are not things, we must look behind people's actions to discover their true causes. This aspect of social cognition—the interpretation of behavior—is the subject of various attribution theories. In their everyday explanations of behavior, people divide the social world into personal force—forces within the actor—and environmental force—obstacles in the actor's environment. An action is seen as the outcome of the interaction of these forces. Every action produces a set of unique effects, and these can be examined to infer the person's reasons for acting. Our attempts to infer the causes of other people's actions depend partly on the number of observations we can make. With repeated observations of a person's behavior, we attribute causality according to the principle of covariation. When faced with the need to explain behavior observed in isolation, people rely on causal schemata to fill in missing data. Strategies for evaluating the multiple causes involved in most social behavior include the discounting principle and the augmentation principle. Sources of error in attribution include the correspondence bias and self-serving biases.

ATTITUDES

Picture this scene. A person stands at the front of a small room, writing with a large felt-tip pen on a flip-chart placed at the head of a table. Seated around the table are six other people, all of whom are munching popcorn that they have just seen described in a commercial. One wall of the room appears to be a mirror, but it is really a one-way vision screen. Behind the screen, technicians are audiotaping the popcorn munchers' conversation about the product and recording data from physiological measuring devices. After the six subjects have eaten the popcorn, they will answer a lengthy series of standardized questions about their income, education, occupation, leisure activities, consumer preferences, and political choices.

What is going on here? This is a "focus group" conducted by a market research firm to determine how to market a new brand of popcorn. With television advertising costing enormous sums, few corporations can afford to waste advertising dollars on a segment of the viewing audience that is not interested in their product. Taking physiological measurements and asking background questions helps determine whether the message being presented is changing the attitudes of the listeners; those changes are reflected in the measures. The focus group is an example of the kinds of activities undertaken by advertisers in the belief that the way to a person's wallet is through his or her attitudes.

ATTITUDE FUNCTIONS AND COMPONENTS

The social context provided by groups and other individuals is even more crucial in attitude formation than it is in social cognition. This is so for two reasons. First, attitudes are even farther removed from direct sensory experience than are social perceptions. Not only do attitudes involve multiple inferences regarding the dispositions of others, they also involve value judgments about those dispositions. These value judgments are strongly influenced by the values of other people who are important to the perceiver.

Holding particular attitudes can serve a "value expressive" function. This tuna company's expression of its support for particular fishing methods may serve its overall marketing goals.

Second, holding particular attitudes can serve strategic purposes in social interaction. Indeed, attitudes may perform a "value expressive" function, serving as public statements of one's position on issues of importance (Katz & Stotland, 1959). In addition, they may perform an "instrumental" function by indicating agreement with important people (Katz & Stotland, 1959). Thus, whereas in social perception the principal source of error is the fact that the stimulus person may be hiding his or her true feelings, in the realm of attitudes one's own motives are a more important source of bias.

A social **attitude** has three basic components: a *cognitive* component representing the person's beliefs about a target, an *affective* component representing the person's evaluative or emotional reaction to the target, and a *behavioral* component representing the person's likely actions toward the target (Allport, 1935). These components can best be understood as answers to three questions:

What characteristics does the object possess (cognitive component)?
How much do I like those characteristics, or the object as a whole (affective component)?
What will I do about it (behavioral component)?

The cognitive component of an attitude consists of all of the person's beliefs about the target object or person. In the example of the focus group, the participants' beliefs about the popcorn would include their estimates of its nutritional value and ease of preparation. The affective component is the sum total of the person's feelings toward the attitude object. People's values, past experience, and emotions will lead them to evaluate an attitude object in positive or negative terms, to rate it on a good–bad scale. In the focus group, the market researchers ask how the popcorn smells and tastes, measure the participants' physiological state as they eat it, and ask questions about their life-style and values in order to gauge their positive or negative feelings about the product. Finally, the behavioral component is the person's "predisposition to respond" on the basis of his or her beliefs and evaluative judgments. Attitude theory assumes that a positive evaluation of an attitude object will, when circumstances permit, be translated into actions that are favorable toward the object. The people who spend several billion dollars a year on advertising surely assume that by altering beliefs and evaluations, advertising can lead people to buy products.

Attitudes consist of cognitive, affective, and behavorial components. Here demonstrators on both sides of an important social issue are turning their beliefs, and emotions, into action.

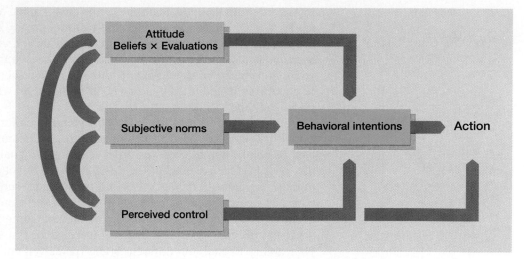

FIGURE 19-5 The attitudinal model of planned action. According to this model, the underlying attitude, the subjective norms, and the person's perceived control interact to create behavioral intentions that lead to action. (Adapted from Ajzen & Madden, 1986.)

Turning Attitude into Action

The qualification just noted, that *when circumstances permit* a positive evaluation results in positive action, is an important one. No matter how positive the attitude, favorable action can result only if certain other conditions are met. For example, factors outside the individual—such as a store's being out of popcorn—may prevent a positive attitude from being translated into action. Two theories—the theory of reasoned action (Fishbein & Ajzen, 1975) and its sequel, the theory of **planned action** (Ajzen & Madden, 1986)—present a model of the chain that links beliefs and evaluations to behavior (see Figure 19-5). The model begins with an attitude and then specifies the way external pressures on the individual interact with the attitude either to produce or preclude a *behavioral intention,* a specific plan to take action consistent with the attitude.

As indicated in the upper-left portion of Figure 19-5, an attitude is constructed from two components: beliefs and evaluations. Beliefs are estimated probabilities that the attitude object has certain characteristics. Each belief (such as "this popcorn will be easy to prepare") is multiplied by an evaluation, the value the person places on that particular characteristic (such as "ease of preparation is very important to me"). The general attitude is the sum of all the belief × evaluation products. Thus, the specific cognitive components (beliefs) and their associated affective reactions (evaluations) combine in a multiplicative fashion to generate an attitude.

One external factor interacting with attitudes is subjective **norms**—expectations held about an attitude object by people important to the attitude holder. No matter how positively you regard popcorn, you will not buy it if you are on the way to visit your grandparents, who do not permit any snacks that might be the slightest bit messy. There is a separate subjective norm for each person whose opinion matters to the attitude holder. Each norm is multiplied by the attitude holder's motivation to comply with the expectations of that person. The overall subjective norm is the sum of these norm × motivation products.

To general attitudes and subjective norms the model adds the degree of control people perceived themselves to have in relation to an attitude object (Ajzen & Madden, 1986). Perceived control is defined as including both actual constraints present in the environment and the person's view of those constraints. You may not attempt to reach a particular goal either because you (correctly) know you will be unable to overcome the obstacles in the way or because you (incorrectly) see those obstacles as insurmountable. In the example, you may normally expect to have control over your choice among brands of popcorn. If everyone else has stocked up just before an expected snowstorm, and there is only one brand remaining when you reach the shelves, your actual control is greatly diminished.

According to the model, attitude, subjective norms, and perceived control interact to create a behavioral intention. These can vary greatly in specificity. For example, if you are attracted to a person of the other sex—that is, you have a generally favorable attitude toward that person—you might intend to date the person (behavior specific), you might intend to go to a movie with the person (behavior and situation specific), or you might intend to go to a movie on Friday night with the person (behavior, situation, and time specific).

Obviously, the more specific the behavioral intention, the more predictive it is of actual behavior, provided that the person has sufficient control over events. That a lack of control might keep you from reaching the goal, however strong your intention might be, is indicated in Figure 19-5 by the direct arrow from control to action. Finally, the curved arrows connecting the attitude, subjective norms, and perceived control to each other indicate that these separate elements affect one another. For example, if the company convinces your current dating partner that its popcorn is the best, that person's expectations for your behavior (the subjective norm) will reduce your ability to choose a different brand (perceived control), while at the same time making your overall attitude toward the product more positive (the attitude).

COGNITIVE DISSONANCE THEORY

Implicit in the way attitude, norms, and perceived control combine to affect behavioral intentions, and ultimately action, is the idea of motivation. We want to possess objects that will enhance our self-esteem, and we desire to be kind to people who help us. Personal goals we consider attainable are more desirable than goals we think can never be achieved. All of this impetus toward action leads to decisive behavior when there is only one attitude object in mind. But what happens when there are competing goals or when there are conflicts between internal attitude and overt behavior? Such questions are at the heart of the **cognitive consistency models** of attitude formation and change.

According to these models, people seek to maintain harmony among their attitudes, or between their attitudes and their actions. This cognitive "keeping of the peace" serves the same function as the cognitive simplification discussed in the sections on social cognition: It increases one's effectiveness in dealing with the social world by minimizing internal distractions.

Leon Festinger's (1957) theory of **cognitive dissonance** holds that there are three fundamental relationships possible among what the theory calls "cognitive elements." Most often these elements are beliefs, but they can also be statements of plans for the future or memories of the past. Elements that have nothing to do with one another (such as "today is Tuesday" and "it is raining") are irrelevant to each other. Elements that agree with, or support, one another (such as "it is raining" and "I'm going to stay inside") are *consonant* with one another. Finally, if one element implies the opposite of another ("I dislike being out in the rain" and "I am walking two miles in the rain without an umbrella"), the two are *dissonant*. When two elements are dissonant, there is pressure to change one or the other.

FORCED COMPLIANCE

The findings of one experiment account for the early impact of dissonance theory (Festinger & Carlsmith, 1959). Imagine that you are a subject in this experiment. On a table in front of you is a simple box about the size of a briefcase. Several rows of holes have been cut into the top of the box, and in each of those holes is a large peg. Your task is to turn each peg a quarter-turn to the right, beginning with the peg in the upper-left corner of the box. When you have turned the last peg, you are to start all over again. You dutifully begin the task and continue, becoming increasingly bored, until the experimenter stops you after about 20 minutes.

The experimenter explains that the purpose of the experiment is to study the effects of prior motivation on performance of a motor task; because you were in the control group, you received no instructions. (In fact, none of the subjects are given instructions.) The experimenter notes that subjects in the experimental group are to be told that the task is interesting and fun. He then says that the next subject is supposed to receive these motivating instructions but that the "other student" who was supposed to deliver the instructions has not shown up. The experimenter wonders whether you would be willing to tell the waiting subject that the task was interesting. For your trouble, and for being willing to do the job again if the need arises, the experimenter offers to pay you. The amount of the payment is either $1 or $20. (The experiment was conducted in the late 1950s; these payments would be worth about $3.50 and $70 today.)

You agree to help, regardless of how much the experimenter offers you, never suspecting that the same request has been made of every participant and that the "waiting subject" is really an accomplice of the experimenter. This experimental technique, known as *forced compliance,* causes you to engage in a *counterattitudinal behavior,* an action that disagrees with your attitude, while leaving you with the illusion that you have freely chosen to help. You found the task boring, but now find yourself telling someone else that it was really interesting. What happens to your attitude?

Cognitive dissonance theory states that when a payment or reward provides *insufficient justification* to perform an action that is dissonant with an attitude, the result is an unpleasant state of tension called cognitive dissonance. The experimenters assumed that the $1 payment would be insufficient justification for lying to the waiting subject. Your lie was public and so cannot be ignored or taken back. According to the theory the only way to resolve cognitive dissonance in such a situation is to change one's attitude. In contrast, with sufficient justification, as the experimenters assumed would be the case for the $20 payment, there is no tension and no need for an attitude change. The experimenters thus predicted that subjects offered the $1 reward would be more likely to change their attitude toward the boring task than those offered the $20 reward. The results confirmed the prediction: Evaluations of the task were much more positive for subjects in the $1 condition than for those in the $20 condition.

Alternatives to Cognitive Dissonance

The results of this study were immediately controversial, because the outcome appeared to contradict one of the most fundamental principles in psychology: People will like that for which they are rewarded. This general principle of reinforcement, discussed in detail in Chapter 12, is inherent in a wide variety of psychological theories. Yet here were people expressing a more positive attitude when paid $1 than when paid $20!

In the specific domain of attitudes, the reinforcement position is called *incentive theory.* This theory holds that attitude change increases as the strength of reinforcement increases. In other words, this theory would have predicted that attitudes toward the boring task would have been more positive in the $20 condition than in the $1 condition. Confronted with results that so clearly contradicted their own view, the incentive theorists were quick to point out various shortcomings in the procedures. For example, one critic pointed out that subjects in psychological experiments are careful to behave in what they think is a "typical" fashion, so that they will not reveal any of their psychological frailties (Rosenberg, 1965). This **evaluation apprehension** would have led subjects in the $20 condition to want to appear *not* to have been "bought," so they would maintain their original (negative) attitude toward the task.

A second alternative explanation accepted the validity of the experiment's results, but merely argued that no real motivation was involved (Bem, 1972). This *self-perception theory* is based on the principles of attribution described earlier. According to self-perception theory, subjects in the experiment observed themselves much as they would have observed other people, and used the same processes to draw inferences from their own behavior. Specifically, the subjects could attribute to themselves two causes for saying the task was interesting: the intrinsic interest value of the task and the size of the payment. In the $1 condition, only one of the causes could apply—the intrinsic interest value of the task—because the $1 payment would not be enough to serve as a cause. In the $20 condition, however, both could apply, and the size of the payment would make it the more important of the two. Thus, the subjects in the study might not have felt any unpleasant arousal that needed to be reduced, but might only have been looking objectively at their behavior.

Modifications of Dissonance Theory

The controversy among proponents of dissonance, incentive, and self-perception theories continued for several years, resulting in important contributions to research methodology along the way, and in time leading to a major revision of dissonance theory. In the modified theory, four elements combine in a sequential process that ultimately leads to cognitive dissonance and attitude change (Cooper & Fazio, 1984). (See Figure 19-6.) The first element is *consequences.* Counterattitudinal behavior must produce aversive consequences, such as the possibility of being reminded later that one has publicly taken two conflicting positions on an issue of importance. The second element is *personal responsibility.* If a person believes that he or she had no choice about performing an action, or could not have foreseen the consequences, no dissonance will result. The addition of this element is a response to criticisms of cognitive dissonance theory from incentive theory. The modified theory thus suggests that the size of a payment is irrelevant for people who have been forced into action or who do not consider themselves responsible for the action.

Accepting personal responsibility for the aversive consequences will produce a generalized physiological *arousal.* If the arousal is incorrectly labeled as pleasant or as unrelated to the counterattitudinal behavior, no dissonance will result. For example, in the experiment described earlier, if you explained your discomfort by saying "I am always nervous when I am in an experiment," no dissonance would result. This modification is dissonance theory's response to criticisms from self-perception theory. It suggests that for cognitive dissonance to occur a person must not only feel aroused by the situation but must attribute the arousal to having taken personal responsibility for producing aversive consequences.

The final step, once all the other conditions have been met, is *dissonance motivation,* which results either in denial of personal responsibility or real attitude change. According to this modified theory, then, subjects in the $1 condition of the original experiment, unable to deny personal responsibility for an action that they believed

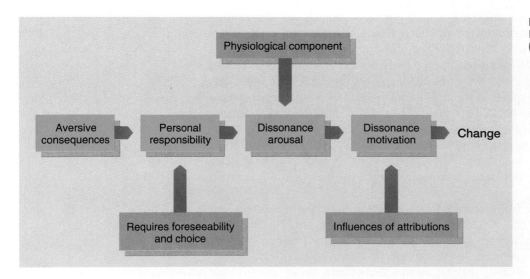

FIGURE 19-6 Elements in the reformulated theory of cognitive dissonance. (Adapted from Cooper & Fazio, 1984.)

they had freely chosen, experienced dissonance motivation and changed their attitude about the boring task. Where the original theory argued that any behavior inconsistent with one's attitudes would lead to attitude change, the modified theory argues that this process is limited by a variety of conditions suggested by incentive theory and self-perception theory.

BALANCE THEORY

Although cognitive dissonance theory adds to our understanding of the relationship between motivation and attitude change, its scope is limited. Only an individual's own actions influence his or her level of dissonance; the actions of other people are largely irrelevant. Dissonance theory is thus an *intra*personal theory of consistency; it cannot be used to describe the relationships between people. In contrast, **balance theory** is an *inter*personal model of consistency.

Fritz Heider originated balance theory in the same book (1958) in which he introduced attribution theory. According to balance theory, there are two ways in which beliefs, or people, might be related to one another. The first way is through liking (or disliking). Our social worlds include places, things, and other people, some of which we approve of, some of which we do not. As this suggests, the *liking relation* between a person and a target is balance theory's version of the affective component of an attitude. The second way is through connection (or lack of connection) to the liked (or disliked) objects. For example, during the workday people are in close proximity to their co-workers; this physical proximity is the basis for the relation known as *unit formation*. Physical proximity, however, is not the only basis for connections among people. We form a unit with members of our families, and with our friends, despite the fact that we may not be in their immediate vicinity. Finally, we are connected to our possessions, and to our public behavior.

In its simplest terms, balance theory specifies two values for each relation: liking or disliking; unit formation or denial of unit formation. Other things being equal, one positive value should lead to another (unit formation leads to liking, and vice versa), and one negative value should lead to another (disliking should produce avoidance). When the signs of the two relations match (both positive or both negative), the system is in balance, and there is no motivation to change. When the signs do not match, however, the imbalance is a force for change.

Unlike dissonance theory, balance theory can accommodate more than two elements at a time. Imagine that you have just made a public speech in favor of preserving green spaces in the city. You and your speech form a unit, and you also like its content. Now suppose that an old friend of yours heard your speech. In balance theory, this triad of you, your speech, and your friend can be represented as shown in Figure 19-7.

FIGURE 19-7 The p-o-x triadic formulation of balance theory. The person, other, and object (x) are joined to one another by a unit-formation relation, and by liking relations. If the signs multiplied together produce a positive, the triad is in balance.

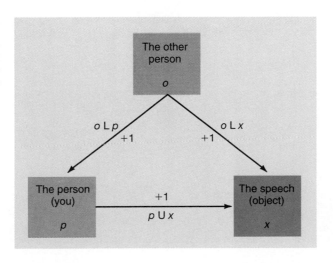

The person from whose perspective the diagram is drawn (in this case you) is designated as p, for person. From your perspective, your friend is the other (designated as o), and your speech is an object (designated as x). Because of your past association, your friend likes you (the arrow in the diagram that is designated by o L p). The connection (association) between you and your speech is designated by p U x. Your friend, who shares your views, also likes the speech (o L x). As the figure shows then, each of these relations is positive, and as a consequence the triad is balanced.

If each positive relation is thought of as the number $+1$, then multiplying the three relations together also produces $+1$ ($+1 \times +1 \times +1 = +1$), reflecting a balanced system. This multiplicative rule applies even if some of the relations in the system are negative. For example, think of the adage, "My enemy's enemy is my friend." In this triad my dislike of my enemy gives a value of -1, my enemy's dislike for the third person also gives a value -1, but my liking for third person gives a value of $+1$. Multiplying these values produces $+1$, a balanced triad.

Conversely, any triad that multiplies out to -1 is unbalanced. Thus, to return to our previous example, if your friend for some reason had not liked the speech you presented (-1) the triad represented by you, your friend, and the speech would be unbalanced.

By including a third element, balance theory illustrates how attitudes can change without the aversive consequences that are demanded by dissonance theory. For example, one technique of attitude change that is commonly used by advertisers is known as *prestige suggestion*. This technique, involves a celebrity endorsing a product. The advertiser relies on the positive attitude of potential buyers toward the celebrity, and the celebrity's positive attitude toward the product, to create a positive attitude toward the product in the buyers. As balance theory suggests, this triad involves no aversive relationships; attitude change results from the motive to reduce imbalance.

The attitude change technique of prestige suggestion relies on a transfer of our positive feelings toward a celebrity to a product that person endorses.

514

INTERIM SUMMARY

Attitudes consist of a cognitive component (such as beliefs), an affective component (desires and evaluations), and a behavioral component (predispositions toward behavior). These are combined in a model of planned action that suggests how a person's beliefs and evaluations, coupled with subjective norms and perceived control over events, produce behavioral intentions toward the attitude object. According to cognitive dissonance theory, when behavior runs counter to a person's attitudes, the resulting cognitive dissonance may lead to attitude change. The claims of dissonance theory have been challenged by the incentive and self-perception theories, and dissonance theory has been modified to account for the claims of these two theories. In the revised theory, counterattitudinal behavior produces aversive consequences, for which the actor assumes personal responsibility; this produces a generalized arousal that, if correctly labeled, results in dissonance motivation and, ultimately, attitude change. Like dissonance theory, balance theory claims that cognitive inconsistency is a motivation for attitude change. Balance theory, however, can account for relationships between people, whereas cognitive dissonance theory cannot.

INFLUENCES ON SOCIAL INFORMATION

As we have seen, people gather social information, organize it, and use beliefs derived from this information in the development of attitudes. But because people live among other human beings, merely having a storehouse of social information is not enough. People want to know how their views compare with those of others and they want to change the minds of people who disagree. We now consider these processes of informal social communication and persuasion.

SOCIAL COMPARISON THEORY

One prominent theory of informal social communication claims that people have a drive to evaluate their opinions and abilities; it assumes that people will be better able to achieve their goals if they know their strengths, their limitations, and their position relative to others (Festinger, 1954). For example, a person who overestimates his or her abilities will suffer one failure after another until the truth becomes obvious. The pain that accompanies this realization might have been avoided if the person had somehow estimated his or her ability more accurately in the first place.

But how is such information to be obtained? One obvious possibility would be to use objective standards that do not depend on the opinion of anyone else. For example, if you want to know how fast you can run, you can find out using a measured distance and a stopwatch. No other people are necessary. When objective standards are not available or sufficient, social comparison theory argues that we rely on information obtained from others—that is, on **social comparison.** For example, once you have learned to play a game—say, tennis—you can determine how well you play only through competition with others. How often do you win? When you lose, is it to people who routinely win against others or to people who typically lose? Information like this can be used to build a network of relative standings against which you can measure your own level of performance.

Some comparisons will provide more information than others. This is especially true for opinions, but also applies in the case of abilities. Do you learn much about your relative placement in the network of amateur tennis players when you lose pitifully in an exhibition match with a touring professional? Of course not. Does it help you to locate your political attitudes to learn that your views are more liberal than

In social comparison we learn most about our abilities from others who are similar to us. Thus, the young tennis players will learn more about their ability by playing each other than by playing against their coach. Social comparison also involves a unidirectional drive upward; the high jumper is always striving to clear just one notch higher.

those of a right-wing extremist, but more conservative than the views of a left-wing radical? Again, probably not. What this means is that you gain the most information from social comparison with other people who are similar to you on attributes related to the comparison (Goethals & Darley, 1977).

In the case of an ability, the comparison choice is also affected by what the theory calls the "unidirectional drive upward": the natural tendency to try to improve one's abilities. Consequently, in many ability-related tasks, one's preferred source for comparative information about one's performance will be the performance of a person slightly better at the task (Wheeler, Koestner, & Driver, 1982). If, however, the trait being examined is a negative one (for example, "insincerity"), then the desire to improve—or at least to see oneself in a positive light—will be reflected in *downward comparison* to a person who is slightly less sincere (Wills, 1981).

Like attitude formation, social comparison involves a cognitive component (the opinions being determined or evaluated), an affective component (reactions of pride or shame to the outcome of a comparison), and a behavioral component (task performance). It also involves some of the motivational processes described by the cognitive dissonance and balance theories. For example, our tendency to select targets for comparison that allow us to see ourselves in a positive light resembles our tendency to change our attitudes to resolve cognitive dissonance.

PERSUASIVE COMMUNICATION

Where social comparison involves an individual's need to obtain reliable information about his or her own position in a social context, persuasive communication involves the efforts of one or more people to change the beliefs or attitudes of others.

The elements of persuasive communication are shown in Figure 19-8. The *source* of a persuasive message is an individual or group whose purpose is to cause a change in the attitudes or beliefs of others. To return to our earlier example, the popcorn manufacturer trying to market its product would be such a source. Through its advertising agency, this source would construct a *message*—based in part on what

FIGURE 19-8 The components of persuasive communication.

had been learned through focus groups like the one described—that would be sent through a variety of *channels,* including radio, television, and print advertising, to *receivers.* Although the person-as-a-whole is usually considered the receiver, the ultimate *target* of the message is within the person. This target can be the person's specific beliefs about the product, a change in evaluation of the product, or an increase in the probability that the person will purchase that brand of popcorn.

Given the number of persuasive messages that we encounter every day, what makes some effective and others not? This question has been at the heart of research on persuasion for decades. The first systematic attempt by social psychologists to answer it was made by the Yale Communication and Attitude Change Program, which began in the 1950s (Hovland, Janis, & Kelley, 1953; Sherif & Hovland, 1961).

Some findings from this program have subsequently been challenged, but one that is still accepted is that the **credibility of a communicator** affects the likelihood that he or she will succeed in changing the attitudes of others. Credibility involves both expertise and trustworthiness: A knowledgeable expert will be a more effective persuader than a nonexpert, as will a person who is perceived to have little to gain personally from succeeding in the persuasive effort.

More recent research has produced the **elaboration likelihood model** of persuasion (Petty & Cacioppo, 1986). This model draws a distinction between *central* and *peripheral* routes to persuasion. Persuasive messages that take a central route require receivers to think about and evaluate them. Persuasive messages that take a peripheral route rely on less important aspects of a communication—the celebrity status of the communicator, for example.

The fundamental principle of the elaboration likelihood model is that the greater the cognitive effort a message requires of the receiver, the greater the chances are that it will have an effect. Messages that involve central processing (thought about the topic, rehearsal of the message, intriguing aspects of the communication) will produce more change than those that engage the receiver only peripherally. This principle clearly reflects findings from the study of memory that suggest that the greater the cognitive depth at which a message is processed, the greater the likelihood that it will be retained (see Chapter 13).

INTERIM SUMMARY

There are two basic sources of beliefs: informal social communication and formal persuasive messages. Some beliefs can be validated through direct physical tests, but others must be evaluated through social comparison with other people. Social comparison is most informative when it is to someone similar on the attributes related to the comparison. Persuasive communication involves the efforts of one or more people to change the beliefs or attitudes of others. The elements of a persuasive communication are the source, the message, various channels, a receiver, and a target. The persuasiveness of a communication is strongly influenced by the credibility of the communicator—that is, the expertise and trustworthiness of the source. According to the elaboration likelihood model of persuasion, the more cognitive work a message requires of its recipient, the more effective it will be.

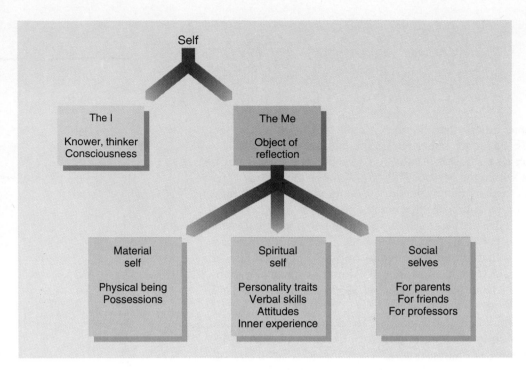

FIGURE 19-9 The structure of the self. (Adapted from James, 1892.)

THE SOCIAL SELF

The abilities and opinions that are evaluated through social comparison make up much of the individual's social **self.** The self, to a large extent, may be viewed as a set of answers to the question "Who am I?"

COMPONENTS OF THE SELF

In his classic psychology text, William James (1892) distinguished between the self as an object of reflection (the *Me*) and the self as a conscious agent (the *I*) (see Chapter 2). This distinction remains valid today. Figure 19-9 illustrates the structure of the self, with some of the subdivisions identified by James.

The Me is the sum total of all that a person can call his or her own. It is further subdivided into the *material self,* the *spiritual self,* and various *social selves.* The material self is a single entity consisting of one's physical being and possessions. The spiritual self is also a single entity, incorporating psychological faculties such as personality traits, verbal skills, social perceptions, and attitudes. In contrast, there are numerous social selves, which vary for each category of people who recognize you as an individual. Thus, you might have one self that you reveal to your parents, one that you present to your close friends, one that you take with you to your job, and one that you offer to your professors.

Rather than being a collection of elements, the I is the ongoing process of consciousness: the thinker, the knower, the pure ego. It can reflect on the contents of the Me, but it is separate from them. It can direct the individual's purposive behavior, but it is separate from that behavior.

THE INTERACTING SELF

In reflecting upon the contents of the Me, the I places a value on what it sees; this fundamental estimate of personal worthiness is known as **self-esteem.** James (1892) defined self-esteem as the ratio of successes to pretensions. In this definition, a person's pretensions are internal standards over which he or she has some control, both in terms of the aspects of the self considered important and in terms of the level of performance anticipated in each chosen area. The latter is known as the person's **level of aspiration,** the self-imposed expectation (such as a hoped-for grade on an examination) that will determine whether a given performance will be evaluated positively or negatively.

Our expectations of ourselves are not limited to levels of aspiration for particular tasks. We also set personal goals for how to behave in a friendship; for wit, charm, and social skills; for integrity, trustworthiness, and other personal characteristics. Taken together, these goals constitute our *ideal self,* the collection of traits that we consider desirable. Very few individuals are all that they would like to be, so for most of us our *real self* falls short of the ideal. The extent of the discrepancy between the ideal self and the real self is sometimes taken as a measure of the individual's self-esteem (Bills, Vance, & McLean, 1951). This discrepancy, like the gap between successes and pretensions, is further evidence that self-esteem is a relative judgment of self-worth. Consequently, it is possible to find people who, though possessing virtually identical talents and characteristics, have quite different levels of self-esteem.

The view of self-esteem as relative suggests that it can vary over time, depending on the circumstances of the individual's life. Some of the resulting variations are influenced more or less deliberately by the individual's own behavior or by the behavior of others. Among the behaviors of individuals that affect self-esteem are self-presentation, self-monitoring, and self-handicapping.

Self-Presentation

As noted in the section on social perception, one of the major differences between the perception of a person and that of an inanimate object is that a stimulus person is capable of intentional action. Specifically, people engage in **self-presentation,** the creation and maintenance of a public self (Goffman, 1959).

Self-presentation is an individual behavior, but it requires the presence of a social group. A public self involves at least two people, an actor and an audience. Each participant brings to the interaction a *line,* a view of the situation and the people involved. A central element of the line is the individual's *face*—the claim of positive social value for oneself. In a normal interaction, the roles of actor and audience alternate, with each person playing both roles over time. Consequently, if the interchange is to continue there must be an implicit commitment by each person to keep the other from "losing face." This tacit social contract helps both parties maintain their self-esteem.

Self-Monitoring

People do not depend exclusively on the actions of others for the enhancement and protection of their self-esteem. They also attend to the social requirements for the interaction and tailor their behavior to those requirements. Normally this *self-monitoring* works quite well, but occasionally it fails miserably. No doubt you can think of a person who does not "get the idea" that a conversation is over (despite the glazed look in your eyes and your frequent glances around the room) until you say outright that you have to leave. Such a person might score very low on a self-monitoring scale that measures, among other things, the use of social comparison to identify the actions that are appropriate under particular circumstances, and that also measures the ability to modify actions in response to the demands of the situation (Snyder, 1979).

As much as we might wish for a higher level of self-monitoring in some insensitive individuals, there is a certain shallowness about the behavior of people whose level of self-monitoring is too high. Such people tend to concentrate on appearances, ignoring the less readily apparent positive qualities of temperament and character. One study found this to be the case among dating partners, especially in the formative stages of a relationship (Snyder, Berscheid, & Glick, 1985). Male undergraduates with different scores on a self-monitoring scale were asked to choose an actual date on the basis of folders that included pictures and personality descriptions. There were only two choices. One of the young women was physically plain but had several desirable personality characteristics (for example, sociable, emotionally stable, willing to listen to others), whereas the other was physically attractive but had several undesirable personal traits (for example, reserved, moody, self-centered). Low self-monitoring men were more likely to base their choice on personality, whereas high self-monitoring men were more likely to base their choice on appearance.

Self-Handicapping

Successful management of the impression one creates requires more than an awareness of the demands of the situation. It also requires the ability and willingness to change one's own behavior to conform to those demands. The degree to which attention to the requirements of the situation, coupled with reflection on one's own capabilities, can affect behavior is suggested by research on what is known as *self-handicapping* (Jones & Berglas, 1978). This strategy for impression management involves placing obstacles in one's own way when confronted with a task to perform.

Consider the high school senior who goes to a party the night before taking the Scholastic Aptitude Test and gets only three hours of sleep. People who behave like this, in effect, handicap themselves. How can this be a strategy for maintaining a positive impression? Recall the discounting and augmentation principles from attribution theory, and you will see the advantages. Should the person do well on the SAT, he or she can claim even greater ability ("Look how well I did on three hours of sleep!"). Should the person do poorly, the failure can be attributed to lack of sleep, not to lack of ability or effort. Of course the fundamental risk in self-handicapping is the failure itself: If one fails to gain admission to any college, looking good in the eyes of some of one's peers may not be worth the eventual cost.

When looking good in failure is more important than actually succeeding in fact, the self-handicapper may turn to drugs or alcohol. For example, in two studies male and female undergraduates took part in research ostensibly dealing with the effects of drugs on intellectual performance (Berglas & Jones, 1978). Subjects first completed a set of 20 analogies and progressions like those included in standard intelligence tests. They were then asked to choose between an allegedly performance-depressing drug and an allegedly performance-enhancing drug before completing a second set of analogies and progressions.

Half of the subjects (the noncontingent group) were told that they had answered 16 of the 20 questions correctly, but in fact only 4 of the questions they had been given were solvable. They thus were led to wonder what might have caused their success. The remaining subjects (the contingent group) were given problems that they could solve, and most of them achieved an actual score of 12 to 14. The researchers expected that subjects who were uncertain about the cause of their first performance would self-handicap by choosing the drug that was supposed to depress performance so as to minimize the possibility that the second test would reveal that they had low ability.

The results of this experiment showed that male and female subjects responded differently, as illustrated in Figure 19-10. Males in the noncontingent group chose the performance-depressing drug 70% of the time, whereas males in the contingent group chose that drug only 13% of the time. Among females, the direction of the difference was the same but the gap was smaller (40% for the noncontingent group and 26% for the contingent group). Thus, male subjects accounted for most of the self-handicapping that was observed. Subsequent research using only male subjects has

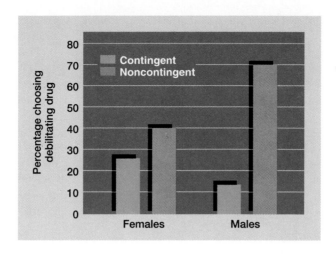

FIGURE 19-10 Sex differences in self-handicapping behavior. The graph summarizes the results of a study of self-handicapping among male and female undergraduates. The subjects were told they were participating in a study of the effects of drugs on intellectual performance, but in fact no drugs were ever adminstered. The researchers were interested in the percentage of subjects who would *choose* a drug they thought would handicap their performance on a test (indicted as "percent choosing debilitating drug" on the graph). The subjects in the noncontingent group were given an initial test of 20 questions, 16 of which were impossible to solve. They were told, however, that they had answered 16 correctly. The subjects in the contigent group were given 20 solvable questions, and most of them got 12 to 14 of them correct. All subjects were then asked to choose between an allegedly performance-enhancing drug and an allegedly performance-depressing drug before taking a second test. (Adapted from Berglas and Jones, 1978.)

shown comparable self-handicapping (again following noncontingent success) using alcohol rather than a drug (Tucker, Vucinich, & Sobell, 1981). It is important to note, however, that this research found no self-handicapping when subjects could choose between alcohol and performance-enhancing study materials.

Many of the processes described in this section paint a picture of a self that is at risk in social interaction. We wish to set goals for ourselves that are reasonable, but that will be attainable. We approach each other with a face we hope to maintain; we enter into a mutual compact to avoid loss of face. We attend carefully to the requirements of the situation, and try to change our behavior when the situation demands change. Faced with the possibility of failure, we arrange our excuses in advance. In all of these ways, we attempt to enhance and protect self-esteem.

INTERIM SUMMARY

The self can be divided into the "I" and the "Me," following the distinction originally made by William James. The I is the ongoing process of consciousness, whereas the Me is the object of reflection. The Me is further subdivided into the material self, the spiritual self, and various social selves. Much social behavior is affected by the tension between accurate self-perception and distortion in order to protect self-esteem. Many people's real selves fall short of their ideal selves, just as their level of performance may fall short of their level of aspiration. Self-esteem thus should be understood as a relative judgment of self-worth. Self-esteem may be enhanced by various individual behaviors, including self-presentation (the creation and maintenance of a public self), self-monitoring (using social comparison to identify appropriate actions and modifying one's behavior accordingly), and self-handicapping (behaving in such a way that failure can be attributed to a handicap whereas success can be attributed to augmented ability).

SUMMARY

1. *Social cognition* refers to the cognitive processes involved in gathering, organizing, and interpreting information about social beings.

2. As objects of perception, people are quite different from things. People have wants, needs, ideas, a past, and a future, all of which may affect their behavior in

ways that are not immediately obvious. Moreover, people are capable of managing their public images, occasionally hiding their true feelings because of social rules for emotional displays.

3. Six facial expressions—anger, disgust, fear, happiness, sadness, and surprise—are recognized across cultures. Such expressions, and the stimulus person's other *kinesic cues,* can be used by the perceiver to infer the person's underlying emotional state. When the verbal and nonverbal messages conflict, *nonverbal leakage* can be a clue to deception.

4. Just as social perception differs from object perception, *person memory* differs from memory for things. Specifically, a person's appearance, behavior, and traits seem to be stored in different kinds of codes. Social information is organized in cognitive *categories, schemata,* and *prototypes.* The latter are "fuzzy" structures into which people are placed on the basis of the family resemblance of their characteristics to the characteristics that define the prototype.

5. Judgments about others can be adversely affected by a variety of inferential errors, including the cognitive heuristics of availability or representativeness, *priming effects,* and *social stereotyping.* Although stereotypes frequently have a motivational basis, purely cognitive effects such as the *illusory correlation* may also produce stereotypes.

6. In the attempt to infer the causes of actions, perceivers rely on principles of covariation, or on cognitive schemata that guide their search. Judgments of causality may also be affected by motivational processes, such as a perceiver's *self-serving biases.*

7. Social attitudes are usually considered to consist of cognitive, affective, and behavioral components. The *theory of planned action* combines these elements to suggests how beliefs and evaluations, together with norms imposed by other people, combine into the behavioral intentions that lead to action.

8. Once an attitude structure is organized, there is a motivation to keep its elements consistent. An important attitude theory suggests that people will go to great lengths to avoid the *cognitive dissonance* that arises from an inconsistency between private attitude and overt action.

9. A significant amount of information about oneself is obtained through *social comparison processes,* in which one uses standards provided by others as a frame of reference.

10. The effectiveness of persuasive communication is dramatically affected by the *credibility* of the communicator.

11. The *self* consists of both an object of reflection (the Me) and the ongoing process of consciousness (the I). One's *self-esteem* is the result of a comparison of one's ideal self to one's real self.

12. People differ in self-monitoring, the degree to which they are sensitive and responsive to the demands of the social situation. They also differ in willingness to use self-handicapping as a tool to protect self-esteem in the face of possible failure.

FOCUS QUESTIONS

1. Describe the elements of the process of social perception. In what ways does social perception differ from the perception of inanimate objects?

2. What are the six universally recognized emotional expressions? Are these independent of language?

3. In what way is social information stored, and how does this process differ from the way information about objects is stored?

4. What is a social stereotype, and can stereotypes be measured?

5. Describe the attribution processes used in perceptions of causality. Discuss the augmentation and discounting principles, and mention possible errors in attribution.

6. How are the cognitive, affective, and behavioral components of an attitude represented in the model of planned action?

7. Distinguish the revised formulation of cognitive dissonance theory from the original version. Show how alternative explanations have been incorporated in the revised model.

8. Describe the elements of social comparison theory.

9. What are the components of the social self? How are the pressures to maintain self-esteem reflected in self-monitoring and self-handicapping?

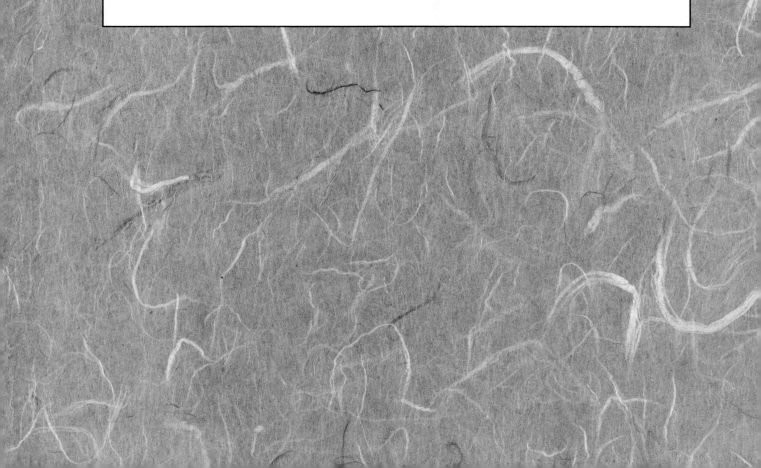

CHAPTER 20

INTERPERSONAL BEHAVIOR

As we saw in the preceding chapter, the individual's contact with the social environment begins with the cognitive processes used to gather, store, and interpret social information. Social context affects both the development and maintenance of attitudes and the creation of the social self. Where interpersonal behavior is concerned, social context is more than an influence; it is essential. Without the social context provided by others, there can be no interpersonal behavior. This chapter begins where the preceding one ended—with the self. But now, instead of concentrating on the internal constituents of the self, we consider its relation to other people. Then we examine the formation of social relationships, the standards people use to determine whether they are being treated fairly, the ways they compete with and attempt to influence one another, and how they behave in groups.

SEX DIFFERENCES IN SOCIAL BEHAVIOR

People speak thousands of different languages, originate from hundreds of ethnic backgrounds, come in an infinite variety of shapes, sizes, and have a variety of interests. But on one dimension—sex—this entire world of diversity can be separated into two classes. Before turning to some of the behavioral differences between females and males, issues of terminology need to be mentioned. Some writers have argued that the term "sex differences" should be used to describe biological differences between males and females and the term "gender differences" used to denote any behavioral differences that are environmentally caused (Deaux, 1985; Macaulay, 1985). Other writers, however, have noted that the issue of biological versus environmental causality regarding female–male differences is still so highly controversial that **sex differences** should be used to refer to any well-established difference between males and females, regardless of how that difference might have come about (Eagly, 1987; Grusec & Lytton, 1988). We shall follow this convention, and shall use the term *gender* to refer to "the meanings that societies and individuals ascribe to female and male categories" (Eagly, 1987, p. 6).

METHODS OF COMPARISON

Until the mid-1970s most reviews of research on sex differences used what has become known as a "box-score" method (Eagly, 1987). This method proceeds in three steps. First, the reviewer selects the domain of inquiry (such as sex differences in nurturance) and identifies all relevant studies. Second, the reviewer may choose to discard or ignore studies with obvious methodological failings. Third, the reviewer examines the remaining research for occurrences of sex differences on the topic in question, and compares the number finding a sex difference to the number in which no such difference occurs. A simple majority rule then dictates the reviewer's conclusion as to whether the behavior in question involves a sex difference. A variant of this approach was used in a major review of sex differences on all forms of psychological characteristics (Maccoby & Jacklin, 1974).

About the time this major review was published, however, the statistical technique known as **meta-analysis** was developed. In contrast to the earlier box-score method, meta-analysis permits a *quantitative* generalization from the findings of earlier research studies. In the area of sex differences, the meta-analytic technique begins by including all studies in which a female–male difference was tested. It then uses a statistical technique to standardize the difference between the female mean score and the male mean score in each study. This standardization permits direct quantitative comparisons among studies that may vary greatly in methods or content. In her authoritative review of the literature on sex differences, Eagly (1987) notes that because of its inherently quantitative nature, meta-analysis avoids both the paternalistic views of women once offered in psychology and the "popular 1970s verdict that sex differences are typically small or nonexistent" (p. 39).

BIOLOGICAL DIFFERENCES

Sex differences begin with the fertilization of the egg by the sperm. As noted in Chapter 8, an embryo with two X chromosomes will become a female, and an embryo with one X and one Y chromosome will become a male, provided that the secretion of androgens occurs in the normal fashion. Among humans, as with other mammals, the major biological difference between females and males is the obvious fact that only the females can give birth to, and provide breast milk for, the young. In an evolutionary sense, human behaviors that maximize contact between mother and infant should increase the species' chances for survival. Moreover, as noted in Chapter 18, the typical newborn's first social experience is sucking at its mother's breast: during the pauses between bursts of sucking the mother strokes and talks to the baby. For humans and other primates, secure attachment to a parent provides much of the foundation for later social development.

In industrialized societies it is easy to lose sight of how recently cultural expectations for females and males have been added to evolutionary pressures. But in most preindustrial societies, the division of labor necessary to maintain a family group reflects sex differences in physical capabilities and in caring for the young. One extensive study of 224 preindustrial societies identified a number of subsistence activities and determined the extent to which each activity was performed by men or women (D'Andrade, 1966). A partial listing of these activities appears in Table 20-1. Men are involved in aggressive activities away from the home; women are involved in nonaggressive activities that can be done near the home; both sexes participate in agriculture.

The cross-society consistency with which some activities are performed almost exclusively by women or by men suggests that biological differences, or evolution-

---

TABLE 20-1   Division of Labor on Subsistence Activities in 224 Preindustrial Societies. Some activities are performed almost exclusively by males, some almost exclusively by females, and others are shared almost evenly by the two sexes.

	Number of societies in which activity is performed by:				
Activity	Men always	Men usually	Either sex	Women usually	Women always
Hunting	166	13	0	0	0
Trapping	128	13	4	1	2
Fishing	98	34	19	3	4
Clearing land	73	22	17	5	13
Preparing soil	31	23	33	20	37
Gathering fruits	12	3	15	13	63
Cooking	5	1	9	28	158
Carrying water	7	0	5	7	119
Grinding grain	2	4	5	13	114

SOURCE: D'Andrade (1966).

ary purposes, may be involved. But if this may be true for preindustrial societies, in modern industrialized societies the division of labor is more likely to reflect cultural patterns. Indeed, when virtually all subsistence needs can be satisfied by a trip to the supermarket, breast-feeding may be the only subsistence activity limited to one sex. In short, sex differences in behavior that may be biologically based in a preindustrial society are likely to be culturally based in an industrial society, if they are found there at all.

PSYCHOLOGICAL DIFFERENCES BETWEEN THE SEXES

Although the activities performed by males and females have become more alike in modern societies, the division of labor endures in stereotyped views of gender roles (Williams & Best, 1982). Specifically, males are often considered to be *agentic*— assertive and controlling—whereas females are thought to be *communal*—concerned with the welfare of others (Bakan, 1966; Eagly, 1987). Research on gender stereotypes shows expectations consistent with this agency/communion distinction. Women are expected to be caring and nurturant, sympathetic, understanding, warm, and expressive; men are expected to be aggressive, dominant, independent, self-sufficient, and adventurous (Bem, 1974; Broverman, Vogel, Broverman, Clarkson, & Rosenkrantz, 1972; Spence & Helmreich, 1978). It is worth keeping these stereotyped views of gender roles in mind as we review research on actual sex differences.

Sex in the Self Concept

Although biological sex is the most fundamental of human distinctions, the degree to which this distinction is part of an individual's working self-concept is affected by the social context. In a program of research on people's spontaneous self-descriptions, this working self-concept, or *phenomenal self,* is operationalized as a subject's response to the request, "Tell me about yourself" (McGuire & McGuire, 1988). Participants in this research respond for several minutes by describing themselves in whatever terms come to mind; the resulting material is analyzed, and common themes are extracted.

One of the studies involved 560 elementary and secondary school students (70 boys and 70 girls from each of four grade levels—first, third, seventh, and eleventh) (McGuire, McGuire, & Winton, 1979). Overall, approximately 10% of the students mentioned their sex, although the proportion was much smaller at the first-grade level (3%) than at the eleventh-grade level (19%). The research was not, however, primarily interested in age-related differences. Instead, it was investigating the effects of *distinctiveness*—the degree to which one's personal characteristics are unlike those of other people in one's immediate surroundings.

The researchers predicted that students who were sexually distinctive, that is, whose sex was in the minority in their family setting, would spontaneously mention their sex more frequently than would those whose sex was in the majority. The data testing this prediction are shown in Figure 20-1 on page 528 and indicate that, for both females and males, reports of one's own sex were more frequent when it was in the minority in the household. These findings show how much the immediate social context can influence reports about the self. Distinctiveness influences not only reports of one's sex, but also one's ethnicity and such physical characteristics as height, hair color, and handedness. Hispanic and black students mentioned their ethnicity more frequently than did white students; taller- or shorter-than-average students more frequently commented on their height; blonds and redheads more frequently mentioned their hair color than did the modal brunettes; left-handed students mentioned their handedness more frequently than did right-handed students (McGuire & McGuire, 1988).

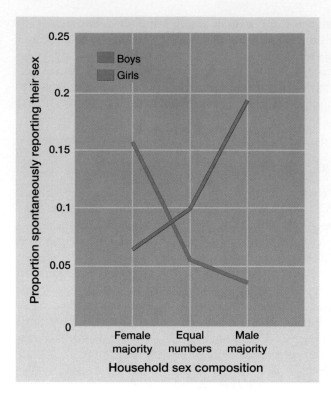

FIGURE 20-1 Effects on the spontaneous self-concept of living in a family where one's own sex is in the minority or majority. Numbers are the proportion of times that boys and girls mentioned their sex when asked to describe themselves. Boys in female-majority households and girls in male-majority households were the most likely to mention their sex spontaneously. (Source: Adapted from McGuire & McGuire, 1988.)

Activity and Aggression

Sex differences in social behavior begin in early childhood. One early pattern that continues into adulthood encompasses physical activity, risk-taking, and aggressiveness. Among nonhuman primates, young males engage in more rough-and-tumble play than do young females (Harlow, 1962). The same is true for humans, beginning in preschool: Boys are more physically active than girls, use more space for their play outdoors, and climb more on structures (Grusec & Lytton, 1988). Boys also show less ability to control their impulses than girls, are less able to delay gratification, and are more prone to take risks (Block, 1983). Finally, two meta-analyses of sex differences in aggression found that males were consistently more aggressive than females. One of these reviews concentrated on studies involving children and found a difference as large as any other known male–female behavioral difference (Hyde, 1984). The other concentrated on experimental studies involving adults and found a smaller, but still important, difference (Eagly, 1987). The entire male pattern of activity, impulsivity, and aggressiveness can be summarized in the words of one popular humorist: "When we look at actual children, no matter how they are raised, we notice immediately that little girls are in fact smaller versions of real human beings, whereas little boys are Pod People from the Planet Destructo" (Barry, 1990, p. 64).

Communication Patterns

There are two well-documented sex differences in cognitive abilities, one of which is relevant to the social expectation that females will be more communal than males. These differences are in mathematical and verbal ability. Both qualitative reviews and meta-analyses of the psychological literature show that boys are superior in mathematical and spatial abilities, whereas girls are superior in verbal abilities (Grusec & Lytton, 1988; Hyde, 1981; Maccoby & Jacklin, 1974).

In addition to being verbally superior to males, meta-analysis indicates that females are *non*verbally superior (Hall, 1984). That is, as noted in Chapter 19, women are better than men at decoding facial expressions. Women are also superior in recognizing faces and interpreting body cues. Moreover, women are more expressive communicators than men are: They laugh more, gaze at other people more (and are gazed at more), and produce more expressive gestures and head movements. Finally, in conversation, women make fewer speech errors than men, and use fewer pause-fillers (such as "um").

Another meta-analysis, this one of behavior in small group discussions, reveals other male–female differences consistent with agency versus communion (Carli, 1982, cited in Eagly, 1987). When communication activity in small groups is separated into two categories—task-focused versus relationship-maintaining—men on the average make more task-related contributions, whereas women on the average make more relationship-maintaining contributions. Thus, in these settings, men tend more to engage in what one sociolinguist has called "report-talk"—exchange of factual information to maintain or emphasize status differences—whereas women tend to engage in "rapport-talk"—exchange of personal and emotional information in order to establish or maintain connections (Tannen, 1990). Although both kinds of talk are valuable to the small group, the sex differences in communication patterns can also leave men and women talking *past* each other, leading to fundamental misunderstandings.

EXPLANATIONS FOR SEX DIFFERENCES

Three kinds of explanations can be offered for sex differences in social behavior. First, there are known biological differences between females and males. For example, autopsies on children as young as 4 years old showed that the brain's left hemisphere (the language center) was more mature in girls than in boys, whereas the right hemisphere (specializing in spatial relations) was more mature in boys than in girls (Levy, 1980). Moreover, it is generally accepted that androgens, the organizing hormones that turn the XY embryo into a male, also increase levels of aggression (see Chapter 10). Thus there may be a biological basis for sex differences in behaviors such as language use and aggression.

A second kind of explanation emphasizes the fact that females and males can have quite different experiences as children. According to this view, the differential process begins before birth, when parents and friends of the family-to-be select everything from the color of the baby clothes (pink or blue) to the toys for the newborn. There is some evidence in favor of differential socialization. For example, two studies showed that adults who were told that an infant was a girl offered the infant dolls to play with, whereas adults told that the same infant was a boy offered the infant hammers and mechanical toys (Frisch, 1977; Smith & Lloyd, 1978).

Considering aggressiveness, one of the two major behaviors that differ by sex, the evidence for differential socialization is decidedly mixed (Grusec & Lytton, 1987). For example, parents are not very tolerant of aggression by their children, no matter whether they are boys or girls. On the other hand, girls receive more warmth and affection, including touching, from their parents than boys do, particularly during the school years. And as the children reach adolescence, girls are permitted less freedom of movement outside the home, probably in response to parental fears of danger to their daughters. Although it is theoretically possible that differences in warmth and freedom of movement contribute to some of the observed difference in aggression, socialization does not appear to be a promising explanation of this difference.

The third kind of explanation for sex differences derives from the social roles prescribed for females and males (Eagly, 1987). According to this explanation, even in a modern society the agentic/communal distinction stems from the different roles men and women play in the economy and in the family. Despite recent increases in women's employment outside the home, the ratio of paid employees to homemakers is still much greater for males than for females. And paid employees are expected to be assertive, aggressive, and task-focused, whereas homemakers are expected to be

Studies of preschool children show that boys take more risks than girls.

529

One explanation for sex differences in social behavior centers on the social roles prescribed for females and males in the economy and the family.

nurturant, accommodative, and person-focused. Furthermore, society accords higher status to paid employment than to homemaking. According to the social role analysis, the result of these societal expectations can be seen in the behavioral differences between men and women: Higher status (more powerful) participants in paid employment are aggressive people who must take decisive action; lower status (less powerful) homemakers are conciliatory people who must use language effectively to persuade, because they are not in a position to command. Meta-analyses of sex differences in aggression, helping behavior, and nonverbal behavior have supported predictions derived from this social role view perspective (Eagly, 1987).

At the beginning of this section we noted that the question of what *causes* behavioral sex differences is still unanswered. This is true not because of an absence of explanations but because few possible explanations can be ruled out. Indeed, it appears that biology, socialization by parents and peers, and societally constructed sex roles all combine to maintain sex differences in social behavior.

INTERIM SUMMARY

In addition to their obvious physical differences, females and males show differences in social behavior. These differences have been identified both through qualitative reviews of research and through the now-preferred quantitative technique of meta-analysis. In cognitive abilities, females are superior in verbal skills, whereas males are superior in mathematical skills. In social behavior, males are more aggressive, whereas females are more conciliatory and effective in interpersonal communication. The agentic male behavior pattern and the communal female behavior pattern have been explained by biological differences, differential socialization experiences, and disparate social roles.

ATTRACTION AND FRIENDSHIP

There are some 5 billion people in the world; most of us know only a few hundred, and count as good friends only a very few. In this section we examine the social processes by which some of the many become the select few.

MAKING ACQUAINTANCES

Without knowing that they are doing it, some professors are helping to arrange dating relationships and marriages—simply by assigning seats. How can this be true, when we believe so strongly that we choose our friends and dating partners? The answer is *propinquity:* physical proximity. Your romantic partners come from among your friends, your friends come from among your acquaintances, your acquaintances come from among the people you see on a regular basis. Which brings us to assigned seats in a classroom. Research shows that if seats are assigned alphabetically, during the term students come to know best those whose names begin with the same letter (Segal, 1974). This propinquity effect extends to student housing units, and far beyond students to residents in housing projects for the elderly (Festinger, Schachter, & Back, 1950; Nahemow & Lawton, 1975).

INTERPERSONAL EXCHANGE

People who come into contact with each other in class, in their dormitories or housing units, or in the work setting will soon begin to talk to one another, sharing experiences, interests, and feelings. Each participant in such an interaction comes with certain attitudes, a sense of self, expectations for the interaction, and goals to be achieved. **Exchange theory** describes how interactions might proceed. This theory begins with one important simplifying assumption: Each person seeks to maximize his or her own benefits from participating in the interaction (Kelley & Thibaut, 1978).

Transformation of Selfish Motives

How does this rather selfish motivation produce a mutually satisfactory interaction? Consider what happens when two people begin talking as they meet for the first time. Does either begin a conversation by announcing a dogmatic position on a con-

Without knowing that they are doing so, professors can be helping to arrange dating relationships and marriages. See the text to find out how.

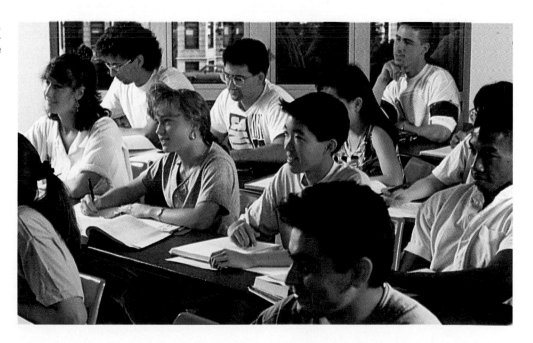

troversial social issue—poverty, AIDS, affirmative action, abortion, or the death penalty for murder—even if one holds such a position? Of course not. What happens is more like:

> "It certainly is hot today."
> "Yeah, but in the winter we'll wish for a day like this."
> "Actually, I like winter a lot. I enjoy skiing."
> "Really? So do I. Where do you usually go?"

Even the most innocuous opening line provides what exchange theory refers to as the opportunity to *sample* some of the interaction possibilities, to determine whether there is anything of mutual interest. If a particular line of conversation is a dead end, the one who opened it switches to something else; if another topic piques curiosity, that topic will be explored in greater detail. This is known as the *win-stay–lose-change rule.* If the sampling of interaction possibilities identifies an activity that both parties consider positive, then the interaction is likely to continue. What began as indifference to one another then shifts to what is known as *mutual behavior control:* Both people realize that their own favorite choices can be achieved in concert with the other.

Exchange theory argues that each interactant evaluates his or her outcomes against two different standards. The first is the **comparison level (CL)**—the average goodness of outcomes from past relationships. The second is the **comparison level for alternatives (CL_{alt})**—the goodness of outcomes to be found in the best other relationship currently available. The theory argues that one's ties to a relationship will depend on the level of one's outcomes relative to the CL and the CL_{alt}, as shown in Figure 20-2. Specifically, the best relationships, to which a person is *attracted,* are those in which one's outcomes exceed both standards. Thus, the ideal relationship is one in which your own outcomes are better than they have been in the past, and better than they could be in a present interaction with anyone else. In contrast, a person is *dependent* on a relationship in which outcomes exceed only the CL_{alt} because there are no other reasonable possibilities; this will be true even if those outcomes are not up to the expectations represented in the CL. This, according to the theory, is the explanation of why one might remain in a relationship with which one is dissatisfied.

It is important to note that the CL and CL_{alt} are unique to each person and may change. This point was confirmed in recent research by Johnson and Rusbult (1989). In one study undergraduate students were asked to describe their commitment to a current dating relationship and to comment on the attractiveness of other potential partners. The results of this study are shown in Figure 20-3. During the seven

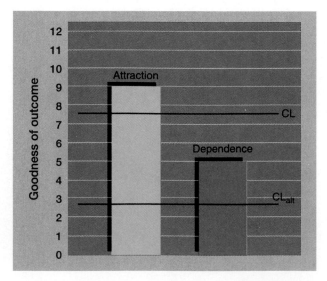

FIGURE 20-2 Definition of attraction to a relationship, and dependence on a relationship. People are attracted to relationships that provide outcomes that exceed both their expectations from the past (the comparison level, CL) and the outcomes currently available elsewhere (the comparison level for alternatives, CL_{alt}).

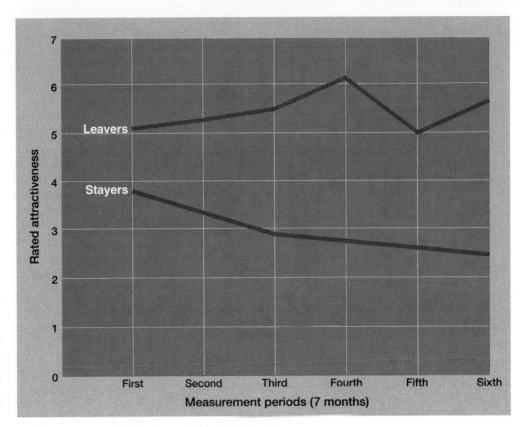

FIGURE 20-3 Changes over time in the rated attractiveness of alternative relationship partners. Those who stay in their initial relationship see alternative partners as less and less attractive. (Source: Adapted from Johnson & Rusbult, 1989.)

months covered by the research, subjects who eventually left their current partners expressed increasing attraction toward other partners, whereas subjects who stayed with their current partners devalued the attractiveness of alternative partners. These results illustrate changes in the CL_{alt}.

Measuring the Strength of a Relationship

A critical element of exchange theory is the principle of **correspondence of outcomes,** the degree to which one's selfish pursuit of one's own goals also rewards the other person. People who enjoy the same sports, share common interests, or have similar attitudes have a high correspondence of outcomes: They can do together what each might otherwise do alone. On the other hand, if one person's greatest rewards are achieved at the expense of the other, then the two people have a low correspondence of outcomes. This is the case in competition, to which we shall return later in this chapter. Exchange theory holds that the more one participant's outcomes correspond to those of the other person, the stronger the relationship will be.

The recently developed Relationship Closeness Inventory (RCI) was designed to assess the strength of relationships (Berscheid, Snyder, & Omoto, 1989). This inventory measures three aspects of relationships: frequency of contact, diversity of joint activities, and strength of mutual influence. For frequency of contact, respondents indicate the amount of time they spend alone with the partner in the morning, afternoon, and evening. For diversity of joint activities, the inventory lists 38 activities ranging from the mundane (doing the laundry) to the unusual (wilderness activities) and respondents indicate those in which the partners are alone together. For strength of mutual influence, the inventory inquires about the influence of each partner on the activities and plans of the other. The value of this approach is suggested by a study of the continuation of romantic relationships (Berscheid, Snyder, & Omoto, 1989), in which RCI scores were a better predictor of dissolution of the relationship than either the longevity of the relationship or the partners' subjective ratings of their closeness.

533

FACTORS INFLUENCING ATTRACTION

The simple way to describe the factors influencing interpersonal attraction, from the choice of acquaintances to the choice of friends and romantic partners, is, in the words of a once popular song, "accentuate the positive." As one recent study demonstrated, this emphasis on the positive begins with the mood of the people involved, at least for males (Cunningham, 1988). The male subjects in this study were divided into four groups. In two of the groups mood was induced by telling subjects they had performed either exceedingly well or exceedingly poorly on a test of social insight; in the other two groups mood was induced by having subjects view elating or depressing films that had no effect on self-esteem. After the mood manipulation, all subjects—individually—were asked to wait in an adjoining lounge while equipment was set up for a second part of the experiment.

Shortly after the subject arrived in this lounge, a second experimenter showed up, accompanied by a female student. As these two people entered the lounge the experimenter was telling the student that she was about 20 minutes early for his study but that she could wait in the lounge until the scheduled time. In fact, both of these people were part of the set-up: The idea was to provide the opportunity for the male subject to begin a conversation with the female student. To keep the conversations as standard as possible, all of the females who played the role of waiting student had been trained to participate in conversation without dominating it. If the conversation lagged for more than a minute, the female used a set series of seven topics (such as asking the subject his academic major, whether he held a part-time job, what his home town was, what his pastimes were) to keep the interchange going.

The subject's part of the conversation was coded into categories representing very little personal disclosure (such as only factual comments), moderate personal disclosure (such as expressions of personal opinions), and high personal disclosure (such as expressions of liking for the female). Analysis of the results showed that regardless of the source of the mood (test feedback or film) there were more high disclosure or moderate disclosure statements when the subject had received the positive mood induction.

One's own mood is only one way in which interactions are influenced by the positive. Despite warnings not to "judge a book by its cover," people have a strong preference for interaction partners they judge to be more attractive (Hatfield & Sprecher, 1988). Both males and females believe in a stereotype known as "what is beautiful is good," expecting physically attractive people to be more interesting, poised, successful, well-adjusted, sexual, dominant, and exciting than people who are less physically attractive (see, for example, Moore, Graziano, & Millar, 1987).

This consistent emphasis on the positive, like the effects of propinquity, can be described in terms of exchange theory. According to the theory, continuation of interaction requires the exchange of rewards. Such exchange is impossible without contact (hence, the importance of propinquity) and is facilitated by one's own mood (happy people might be more receptive to many activities) and the attractiveness of others (who presumably have more rewards to offer).

INTERIM SUMMARY

Although we think of ourselves as choosing acquaintances and friends, we overlook the fact that those choices are made from among the people in our immediate social environments. Thus, propinquity is an important, although largely invisible, constraint. Processes of attraction have been explained by exchange theory, which begins with the assumption that people seek to maximize their outcomes. This admittedly selfish motive is transformed, through such things as the win-stay–lose-change rule, into mutual behavior control. For a relationship to be maintained, one person's outcomes must have some correspondence with those of the other person, and outcomes for both must be above the comparison level for alternatives. The strength of a relationship has been assessed by the Relationship Closeness Inventory. In keeping with exchange theory, interaction is facilitated if the participants are happy and physically attractive.

FAIRNESS IN SOCIAL EXCHANGE

Initial encounters may be based on mutual attraction and friendships may involve the mutual exchange of rewards. But in many of our relationships, and with social groups such as employers, the central issue may be *fairness*. We are concerned not only with the outcome—the reward received—but also with the manner in which that outcome was determined.

DISTRIBUTIVE AND RECTIFICATORY JUSTICE

Aristotle was the first social thinker to write at length about fairness in social relationships. In the *Nichomachean Ethics* he distinguished between two kinds of fairness, or justice. The first is "manifested in distributions of honor or money" (Aristotle, 1952, p. 378) and therefore is called *distributive justice.* The nature of this kind of fairness can be seen in the workplace: Employees make positive contributions to their employer's business and are rewarded for their efforts. If they feel that the rewards are commensurate with their contributions, distributive justice will prevail.

The second kind of justice "plays a rectifying part in transactions between man and man" and therefore is called *rectificatory justice* (Aristotle, 1952, p. 378). The criminal justice system provides the best example of this kind of fairness. When one person steals from another, a third party (society) steps in to bring the situation back into balance. Sometimes this can be accomplished through restitution alone, but more often society insists that the offender pay an additional penalty in the form of a fine or jail term. With a crime of violence, restitution is obviously a less appropriate part of the solution, so the system concentrates on punishment. The crucial difference between distributive and rectificatory justice lies in whether one of the parties has *lost* something before the attempt to achieve justice. In contemporary social psychology, both the distribution of rewards and the rectification of wrongdoing can be described in terms of **equity theory,** to which we now turn.

The saying "a day's work for a day's pay" is one expression of the principle of distributive justice.

EQUITY THEORY

Like exchange theory, equity theory assumes that people seek to maximize their outcomes in their interactions with other individuals, groups, or organizations. That is, they try to minimize the personal costs of their actions and to maximize the rewards gained. On the other hand, equity theory recognizes that "if everyone were unrestrained in his attempts to get what he wanted, everyone would suffer. . . . Only by working out a compromise can the group avoid continual warfare and maximize collective reward" (Walster, Berscheid, & Walster, 1976, p. 2). The theory further assumes that to ensure such a compromise, groups will "generally reward members who treat others equitably and generally punish . . . members who treat others inequitably" (Walster, Berscheid, & Walster, 1976, p. 2).

What exactly does it mean for a person to be treated equitably? In the original formula, an equitable situation was described as one in which each person's outcomes are proportional to his or her inputs (Adams, 1965).

$$\text{Equity results if } \frac{Outcomes_A}{Inputs_A} = \frac{Outcomes_B}{Inputs_B}$$

For example, suppose that you have studied hard for an examination and have done very well. You would feel that equity had prevailed if, when comparing test scores with a person who had put in very little effort, you discovered that the person had received a low grade. This description assumes that both parties have made positive inputs (lots of study or minimal study) for which they are rewarded (by a high grade or a low grade). It thus represents what Aristotle identified as distributive justice.

Over time the equity formula has been broadened to include cases in which at least one of the participants does something bad—that is, contributes *negative* inputs. The need for this change can be illustrated by putting numbers on a version of the study/test score example. Suppose that your conscientious studying is a positive input of 2, but that instead of receiving the B you expected you were shocked to see a D on your returned examination. Given your expectation this is a negative outcome, say a -10. To make matters worse, you discover that instead of studying at all, your colleague went to an all-night party before the exam. This person's inputs are, therefore, negative, say -4. Now, what outcome would the other person need to receive for the situation to be equitable by the original formula? Your -10 divided by $2 = -5$, and to produce an identical -5 your friend's input of -4 would have to be divided into a positive outcome of $+20$. In other words, by the original formula the situation would be equitable only if your friend's score for slacking off were substantially *better* than your score for studying hard. This is arithmetically correct but is psychological nonsense.

To bring the numbers back into correspondence with the psychological reality, the new version of the formula makes three specific changes. First, the numerator (outcomes) for each person is replaced by *profits* (outcomes minus inputs). Second, the original sign of each person's inputs is removed by making the inputs into an absolute value. And third, the influence of the original sign of the inputs is preserved with an exponent that takes the numerical value of either $+1$ or -1. The numerical value of this exponent is determined by multiplying the *sign* of each person's original inputs times the *sign* of the same person's profits (outcomes − inputs). If the exponent, k, is positive, the profits are divided by the absolute value of the inputs, as in the original formula. On the other hand, if the exponent is negative, then its effect is to move the inputs to the numerator, where they are multiplied by the profits. The formula thus becomes

$$\text{Equity results if } \frac{(Outcomes_A - Inputs_A)}{(|Inputs_A|)^{k_A}} = \frac{(Outcomes_B - Inputs_B)}{(|Inputs_B|)^{k_B}}$$

Putting in the numbers from the example,

$$(2)(-10 - 2) \neq (4)[20 - (-4)]$$
$$\text{or } -24 \neq 96.$$

Now the formula more accurately represents your view that you have been punished for studying whereas your friend has been greatly rewarded for goofing off, a clearly inequitable result. In short, the revised formula can now describe relationships in which one of the parties has a negative input.

The Individual's Viewpoint

Regardless of the relationship, equity theory assumes that fairness, or lack of it, is a matter of individual perception. The participants need not agree on whether a particular outcome is fair. For example, two employees who receive the same amount of praise from a supervisor might interpret that praise differently. One might consider it adequate under the circumstances, but the other might not. There may also be differences of opinion about inputs, with one employee believing that merely showing up on time is sufficient for reward, and another believing that a high quality of work is also needed.

To be included in the definition of equity, an input must be *relevant* to the issue at hand and all parties must *recognize* its relevance. Disagreements often center on the relevance of an input. For example, the controversy over affirmative action involves, among other things, a disagreement about whether or not ethnic origin or sex are relevant inputs for a hiring decision. For a company with a preponderance of white male employees, implementing an affirmative action plan requires hiring female and minority candidates. Even when inputs are recognized as relevant, they can conflict with one another. For example, if an economic setback forces the company to lay off workers, the principle of affirmative action will require distributing the layoffs across all levels of the employee hierarchy. But another important input principle is seniority, which would require laying off first the most recently hired workers. Where two or more input principles conflict, what is "fair" will depend on each viewer's perspective on both principles.

Reactions to Inequity

People who feel inequitably treated may, according to the theory, respond in one of five general ways.

1. They may change their own inputs or outcomes, in effect taking justice into their own hands. Thus, employees who feel poorly paid may pilfer from their employer (increase outcomes) or take long lunches or unwarranted sick leaves (lower inputs).

2. They may change the inputs or outcomes of a person they believe to be receiving preferential treatment. Thus, one employee might harass another to make that

If workers believe that their efforts for a company are not being fairly rewarded, their reactions to this perceived inequity can include direct action against the company.

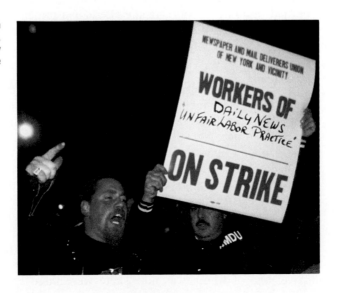

person's life miserable (decrease outcomes) or put obstacles in the person's way (requiring an increase in inputs).

3. They may distort the value of their own inputs or outcomes so that they no longer perceive the situation as inequitable. For example, an employee who believes he or she deserves more credit than an equally paid co-worker might convince himself or herself that the boss "likes me better."

4. They may distort the value of the other person's inputs or outcomes. For example, an employee who learns that a co-worker makes more money for the same job might convince himself or herself that the difference arose because the other person was willing to work on weekends.

5. They may avoid comparing themselves to others, or may leave the situation entirely.

EQUITY, PRODUCTIVITY, AND HARMONY

Apart from choosing the "right" people for comparison, what can make a situation appear fair? Researchers have identified three major factors that must be considered in answering this question: the principles underlying the distribution of rewards, the gender of the person dispensing the rewards, and the goals that person is trying to achieve.

Distribution Principles

Equity theory assumes that perceived fairness is achieved if rewards are *proportional* to effort. This principle is the basis for any meritocracy: Work harder, get paid more; work less, earn less. But other principles can also be used. Even in the United States, where the educational and economic systems generally follow the proportionality rule, there are some social benefits that are not based on this principle.

An alternative rule is the principle of *equality*. At least in theory every American citizen is equal before the law. In other words, regardless of social position, education, or power, all citizens should have a single vote regarding the laws that govern them, all should have the protection of the law, and all should be treated equally should they violate the law. Thus, in some circumstances fairness demands equality, not the proportionality inherent in equity theory.

Another alternative is the principle of *need*. Compassion dictates that people who need food or medicine should be able to obtain it whether or not they, as individuals, are able to pay for it. Programs that provide aid to families with dependent children or financial aid for college students are based on demonstrated need, as opposed to the proportionality that underlies equity theory. In sum, what people regard as fair in a particular situation may depend on whether the principle of proportionality (as specified in equity theory), or the alternative principles of equality and need seem most appropriate in the circumstances.

Sex Differences

When the situation itself does not dictate which distribution principle will be applied, individual inclinations will affect the way rewards are dispensed. Some studies show an important sex difference in those inclinations (Major & Deaux, 1981). When asked to allocate rewards among participants in a task, women tend toward equality (ignoring differences in productivity) whereas men tend toward proportionality based on productivity.

One explanation for this difference, consistent with the agentic–communal distinction noted earlier, is that women seek to maintain harmonious relations within groups, whereas men are more concerned about task performance.

A recent study shows, however, that the picture is somewhat more complicated. Female and male subjects were asked to assume the role of a supervisor who was deciding how to divide a reward between two workers, one of whom was very productive, one of whom was not. There were three experimental conditions. In the

Compassion dicates that people in need should receive help. This principle of need underlies our willingness to contribute to charities.

first, the supervisors were asked to allocate rewards in a way they considered "fair," with no definition of this term provided. The researchers expected that in this condition the highly productive worker would receive a greater reward than the less productive worker. This differential in favor of the more productive worker constituted the baseline against which results in the other two conditions were evaluated. In the second condition, the supervisors were asked to distribute rewards in a way that would "maintain harmonious relationships" between the two workers. The researcher expected that in this condition the reward differential would be minimized; that is, that the difference between what the highly productive worker and the less productive worker were paid would be smaller. In the third condition the supervisors were asked to distribute rewards in a way that would "emphasize productivity." The researchers expected that in this condition the reward differential would be exaggerated; that is, that to enhance productivity, the difference between payment to the highly productive worker and to the less productive worker would be larger.

The results of the study are shown in Figure 20-4. In the "fair" condition, both male and female supervisors allocated roughly $4.25 more to the highly productive worker than to the less productive worker (shown as a horizontal line at the $4.25 level). In the "maintain harmonious relationships" condition, male and female supervisors made reward allocations that reduced the productivity differential, with females reducing this differential more than males did. In the "emphasize productivity" condition, both males and females increased the productivity differential, with males tending to do so to a greater degree than females. The general conclusion is that males emphasize productivity more than females do, but that both sexes also respond appropriately to the demands of the situation (Stake, 1985, Study 1).

A second study suggested that males are more likely to attribute variations in performance to differences in motivation, whereas females are more likely to attribute them to factors other than motivation, such as training or experience (Stake, 1985, Study 2). Thus, a person's appraisal of what is fair is influenced by numerous factors, including the characteristics of the situation, the gender of the person allocating the rewards, the specific task objectives, and individual judgments about the causes of variations in performance. The complexity of the appraisal of fairness should be kept in mind as we turn to a consideration of cooperation, competition, and social influence.

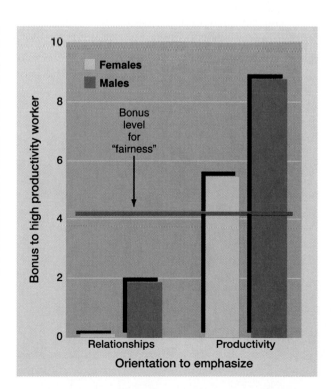

FIGURE 20-4 Reward allocations made by female and male supervisors of two hypothetical workers under three different experimental conditions. One worker was highly productive, the other was less productive. In the "fair" condition, the subjects were asked to allocate a reward for performance between the two workers strictly on the basis of fairness. The results of this condition, in which men and women both allocated about $4.25 more to the productive worker, serve as a baseline for evaluating the results of the other conditions. In the relationships condition, the subjects were asked to allocate the reward in a way that would maintain harmonious relationships, and in the productivity condition, they were asked to allocate the reward in a way that would emphasize productivity. (Source: Adapted from Stake, 1985.)

INTERIM SUMMARY

Aristotle distinguished between two kinds of fairness (justice): distributive justice and rectificatory justice. In contemporary social psychology, both forms of justice are addressed in equity theory. The original equity formula stated that an equitable situation is one in which each person's outcomes are proportional to his or her inputs. The formula has since been broadened to include negative inputs. For an input to be included in the definition of equity, it must be relevant to the issue at hand and all parties must recognize its relevance. Disagreements about what inputs are relevant can be seen at the core of a number of social disputes. A person may react to the perception of inequity by trying to change his or her own outcomes or inputs or the other person's outcomes or inputs, by distorting outcomes or inputs, or by avoiding comparisons with others. Other factors that can influence the perception of equity are the principles underlying the distribution of rewards (proportionality, equality, or need), the gender of the person dispensing the rewards, and the goals that person is trying to achieve.

COMPETITION

We noted in Chapter 1 that a central issue for psychology is whether the life of an individual is improved or made worse by social contact. Are we better off as individuals because of our social bonds, or does society stifle individual freedom? Rousseau (1952/1762) argued that in a state of nature, without social groups or social organizations, humans would (and once did) live in equality and without conflict. In his view, society replaced this inherent equality with a social hierarchy that, in turn, created conflict and war. Hobbes (1952/1651) had also believed that humans are inherently equal in their physical and mental gifts, but he considered them equal in their desire for mates and possessions. Because these resources are limited, conflict and war are inevitable unless individuals sacrifice some of their independence for the protection offered by the state.

The state of nature envisioned by Rousseau and Hobbes may never have existed. Archaeological evidence suggests that humans have been social animals since they first evolved, although the size and complexity of social groups has increased dra-

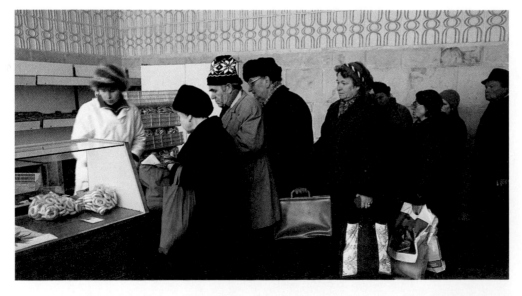

Are individuals better off, or worse off, because of their participation in organized society? This question can become especially acute when a society's resources are limited.

Individuals who sacrifice too much of their independence for the protection offered by the state can sometimes find the state's power used against them.

matically. Still, there is no question that individuals are often in conflict with each other and with the larger society. For psychologists, the study of conflict begins with competition between two individuals.

A DEFINITION OF COMPETITION

Recall that in exchange theory a high correspondence of outcomes occurs if one person's pursuit of his or her best outcomes also increases the outcomes of the other participant in the interaction. Thus, in exchange theory terms, *competition* is a *low* correspondence of outcomes. Specifically, if one person's most positive outcomes are achieved in joint activities that provide little or no reward for the other, then the two people are in competition. In the extreme, this creates a **zero-sum game,** an interaction in which all the gains of one person are obtained at the expense of the other. In a poker game, for example, the monetary gains of the winners exactly match the monetary losses of the losers.

Situations with a clear winner and a clear loser are not the only instances of competition, however. Many situations—plea bargaining between prosecutors and defense attorneys, labor negotiations, ratification of international treaties—also involve a low correspondence of outcomes. In contrast to a poker game, in which the sum of winnings and losses is zero, these examples can be characterized as **nonzero-sum games.**

Treaty negotiations are a nonzero sum game. Each side gives up something and gets something else in return. As history makes clear, however the results are not always fair.

541

One key ingredient in any nonzero-sum game is negotiation. Prosecutors settle for a sure conviction on a lesser charge rather than risk possible acquittal of the accused. Defense attorneys trade possible conviction on serious charges for a reduced penalty. Usually, labor negotiators do not obtain as lucrative a contract as they would like, and management pays more than it wants to. Nations must relinquish claims to complete sovereignty and freedom of action if they are to take advantage of protections afforded by international treaties.

THE PRISONER'S DILEMMA

To simplify the experimental task, psychologists have often separated the process of negotiation in a nonzero-sum game from the structural properties of the game itself. One widely used nonzero-sum game without a negotiation component is known as the Prisoner's Dilemma (Luce & Raiffa, 1957). It is based on the situation that arises when two coconspirators are taken into custody for a minor infraction but are suspected of having committed a much more serious crime. The prosecutor separates them and makes each the following offer: "Confess, and turn state's evidence against your partner for the more serious crime. I'll let you off and throw the book at your friend. By the way, I'm going to make the same offer to your friend." What is the offender to do? Obviously, if both offenders confess to the serious crime the prosecutor will easily convict both of them, but will recommend less than the maximum sentence. If neither confesses, both will be tried for the minor infraction. If, however, one confesses and the other does not, the one who confesses will be spared and the other will receive the law's full sanctions.

A sample set of outcomes (known as a *payoff matrix*) for such a game is shown in Figure 20-5. There are two numbers in each cell, one above the diagonal line in the cell, one below the diagonal. All payoffs are negative, as they represent months in prison. The outcomes above the diagonal in each cell go to prisoner 1 and those below it go to prisoner 2. Because the coconspirators cannot communicate with each other, the key issue in this dilemma is trust; each prisoner can resist confessing ("stonewall") only by trusting the other to stand firm as well. Not surprisingly, research has shown that competition (betrayal) increases with increases in the rewards to be gained for confessing (Enzle, Hansen, & Lowe, 1975).

In an experimental setting, subjects typically play games such as the Prisoner's Dilemma for repeated trials and usually are playing for positive points that can be converted into money at the end of the game. The structure of such a positive game is shown in Figure 20-6, with the respective payoffs indicated by the letters R, S, T,

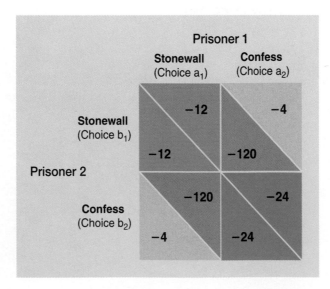

FIGURE 20-5 Example outcomes in a Prisoner's Dilemma game. Numbers shown are negative because they represent months of lost freedom, or time in jail.

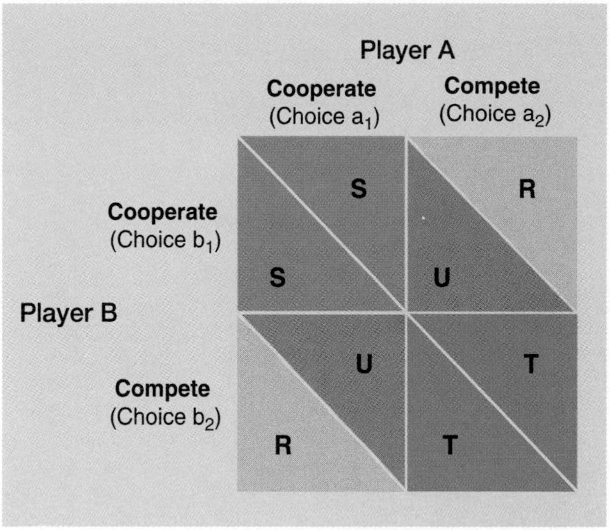

FIGURE 20-6 Definition of a Prisoner's Dilemma game. Any payoff matrix in which the labeled cells satisfy the inequality $R > S > T > U$ is a Prisoner's Dilemma game, whether the outcomes are all negative, all positive, or mixed.

and U. A Prisoner's Dilemma is any game in which the highest payoff (R) goes to a person who competes when the other person cooperates, the next highest payoff (S) is achieved by joint cooperation, the next highest payoff (T) is obtained by joint competition, and the lowest payoff (U) goes to the person who cooperates when the other person competes. Thus any game that satisfies the inequality

$$R > S > T > U$$

is a Prisoner's Dilemma game, regardless of the actual numbers used.

Over several trials, players of the Prisoner's Dilemma game gradually develop strategies for minimizing their own losses. One common strategy is *alternation*, in which players take turns defecting on one another. With this strategy, on any given trial one player makes the maximum amount of money and the other makes the least. The situation is reversed on the next trial, and if

$$(R + U) > 2S$$

then alternation will produce the *maximum joint profit*. If alternation does not develop, another likely strategy to emerge is the *contingent* strategy. In this case, person A's response on trial N produces what person B does on trial N + 1. The contingent strategy is usually regarded as a way for one subject to communicate with the other. The communication is, admittedly, accomplished by threat, but it is rudimentary communication nonetheless. When subjects playing the Prisoner's Dilemma game are provided with an explicit opportunity to threaten their opponent (by imposing a "fine" or sending a warning that a fine of a particular size is imminent), a cycle of retaliation develops (Youngs, 1986). Not only the number of warnings, and the size of the warnings, but also the size of the actual fines is reciprocated. Thus, threat produces defiance rather than compliance, leading to a spiral of escalating conflict.

THE TRAGEDY OF THE COMMONS

Although the Prisoner's Dilemma is limited to two players, the same general principles apply to situations involving many individuals. One of these is known as the "tragedy of the commons" (Hardin, 1968). Many New England towns were built on a plan in which houses surrounded an open commons on which residents could graze their cattle. The amount of pasture land was usually sufficient, provided that no family kept more cattle than were needed for its own use. Overuse of the commons would destroy the grazing land for everyone. From the perspective of any given family, this situation is a **social dilemma**—immediate self-interest is in conflict with long-term collective interest.

The commons dilemma applied to a modern environmental problem: Each person who commutes to work by car pursues his or her own individual convenience, but the result may be air that nobody can breathe.

Maximizing one's own short-term outcomes would mean increasing one's own use of the commons. This greed would be rewarded as long as other families did not increase their use of the land. On the other hand, if other families increased their cattle holdings and yours did not, your family would suffer both in the short term (by having fewer cattle) and in the long term (because the commons would disappear despite your sacrifice). One study modeled the commons dilemma by having four-person groups manage a computerized "forest" in which trees could be planted or harvested (Sato, 1987). Trees grew in size and value across 10 stages, so the best group outcome was to wait to harvest until after the trees completely matured. For individuals, however, waiting carried the risk of personal losses, because others in the group might harvest trees first. Within each group, the costs of planting and maintaining seedlings were either shared equally or were allocated exclusively to the one individual who harvested the most trees. Results of the study showed that overall group profits were highest when the harvesting costs were individualized. This outcome suggests that the way out of the commons dilemma is to make those who profit from use of a resource responsible for the costs of maintaining it.

The social dilemma represented by the use of the commons applies to any situation in which a renewable resource can be depleted through overuse. Thus, the dilemma serves as a model for numerous environmental issues. Many of those issues involve the automobile. Interstate highways are fast, efficient means of transportation—unless everyone uses them at the same time. Should people be permitted to drive their cars without restriction during city ozone alerts? As fears of a global greenhouse effect increase, because of the burning of fossil fuels, should limits be placed on the amount of fuel used by passenger cars in the United States? Although public policy moves slowly in these areas, the institution of carpool lanes, greater interest in emission control, and changes in fuel efficiency requirements suggest that industrialized societies are becoming more aware of the need to protect long-term collective interest (Zarega, 1981).

INTERIM SUMMARY

Psychological study of conflict begins with a definition of competition as a low correspondence of outcomes. In the extreme case, competition is a zero-sum game, in which one person's winnings exactly match the other person's losses; in less extreme instances the situation is a nonzero-sum game. Competition is frequently studied using the Prisoner's Dilemma game, in which the combination of choices that produces the best outcome for one person simultaneously produces the worst outcome for the other person. Partly in an effort to communicate with one another, players of this game often adopt a contingent strategy. When explicit communication is permitted that uses threats of punishment, a cycle of retaliation develops that reduces the outcomes for everyone. Similar effects can be seen in the tragedy of the commons, a social dilemma in which the best short-term individual outcome is detrimental to the long-term success of the group. In such a social dilemma, the best group outcomes are achieved when the individuals who profit from using the resources are made fully responsible for the costs of those resources.

SOCIAL INFLUENCE AND SOCIAL POWER

When two people are attracted to one another, their mutual interest in maintaining the relationship gradually begins to affect each person's choices. In other words, the relationship to some extent controls their behavior. We now consider aspects of more direct social control: social power and social influence. At first glance, these two terms appear equivalent. Most people would equate a person's social power with the influence that person is able to exercise, on the assumption that the more influence produced, the more powerful the person. As we shall see, however, social power and social influence are different. Using the terms interchangeably overlooks the fact that both the person who would exercise power (often called the "change agent") and the person subject to that power (the "target person") exist in a social context that encompasses other people.

FIELD THEORY

The importance of the social context, the *field,* was indicated in a theory of social behavior proposed by Kurt Lewin (1890–1947). Lewin, who came to the United States as a refugee from Berlin during World War II, founded the Research Center for Group Dynamics (originally at the Massachusetts Institute of Technology; now at the University of Michigan). Respected not only for his writings but also for his ideas and his insistence that scientific theories of behavior should have practical implications, Lewin is generally regarded as one of the founders of social psychology.

Lewin's **field theory** (1951) holds that social behavior is jointly produced by personal factors and environmental forces. "Personal factors" refers to the personal desires and objectives present at the time of an action; "environmental forces" refers to the part of the environment, including other people, perceived by the person. These combine to create the **life space.** Figure 20-7 illustrates the life space of a student who is deciding between spending the weekend studying for a quiz or going

FIGURE 20-7 Forces in the life space of a student trying to decide whether to study or go skiing for the weekend. (Source: Adapted from Lewin, 1951.)

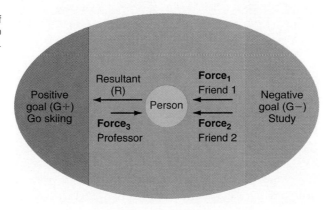

skiing with friends. The life space contains two goal regions, indicated by G+ (a positive goal) and G− (a negative goal, to be avoided). In this example G+ represents going skiing and G− represents studying. The diagram also shows three forces, representing the pressures put on the person by two friends who want the person to join them on a weekend ski trip, and one professor, who announced on Friday that there would be a special quiz on Monday. Each force is conceptualized as a mathematical vector, having a specified length and direction. The length indicates the strength, and the resultant (R) is the algebraic combination of all the forces.

This resultant brings us to the critical difference between power and influence. **Social power** is a person's capacity to affect the behavior of others. **Social influence** is a result; it is the actual change in a target person's behavior. Power and influence will be equal only when the change agent (the person exercising power) is the sole force acting on the target person—not a frequent situation.

In the example illustrated in Figure 20-7, if F_3 were the power exerted by one change agent (the professor), it would fail to produce influence because of the greater forces (F_1 and F_2) applied by the two friends. The resultant (R) would cause the student to choose the ski trip, showing the effect of the friends. Because of the other forces that are typically present in a social context, a particular change agent's power is not diminished by a target person's failure to respond. In our example, the professor's power may become evident at the time of the quiz, when the person may come to regret having gone skiing.

SOURCES OF SOCIAL POWER

A change agent's power is likely to be most effective when the nature of the power matches the situation in which the power is exercised. Five general bases of social power have been identified—reward, coercive, legitimate, referent, and expert (French & Raven, 1959).

1. *Reward power* derives from the change agent's ability to provide positive reinforcements. For example, best friends share interests and activities, are enjoyable companions for each other, and provide mutual support.

2. *Coercive power* derives from the agent's ability to punish the target person. The school bully who controls the behavior of anyone who gets in the way is an example of coercive power.

Referent power derives from the target person's desire to emulate an admired role model. Movie stars can attract people to a social cause not because they have specialized knowledge, but because they are admired.

3. *Legitimate power* derives from the target person's having been socialized to accept influence from change agents in positions of authority. This is the basis for police officers' power.

4. *Referent power* derives from the target person's desire to emulate an admired role model. Movie stars and rock bands can attract thousands of people to social causes, not because they have special knowledge about the causes but because they are admired celebrities.

5. *Expert power* derives from a change agent's specialized skills or knowledge that the target person needs. An example is a mathematics tutor who tells students how to solve the kinds of problems that are likely to appear on the next exam.

Although the bases of power are listed separately, they are rarely found alone. For example, consider what is involved in a carpool lane. The lane was established through the legitimate authority of the local government on the recommendation of experts who believed it would reduce the percentage of single-occupant vehicles on the road, a percentage now estimated at 75% (Zarega, 1981). Lone drivers stay out of the lane because they recognize its value to society (legitimate power), like to think of themselves as law-abiding citizens (referent power), and want to avoid the $100 fine for improper use of the lane (coercive power).

MACHIAVELLIANISM: POWER AS INTERPERSONAL STYLE

Regardless of the source of their power, some change agents seem to be more effective than others. These people may be high in **Machiavellianism,** an interpersonal style that embodies a cool, calculating manipulativeness. In his advice to a prince of the Medici about how to rule effectively, Niccolo Machiavelli (1952/1513) noted that at times it would be necessary to resort to force. In those instances, he said the prince should adopt certain qualities of the fox and the lion, because "the lion cannot defend himself against snares and the fox cannot defend himself against wolves. Therefore, it is necessary to be a fox to discover the snares and a lion to terrify the wolves" (p. 25).

Social psychologists have devoted considerable study to whether people who agree with Machiavelli's views have a distinctive style of interacting with others. In one study, researchers extracted a large pool of statements about social influence from Machiavelli's original book, *The Prince,* added statements of their own, and created a questionnaire designed to measure a person's Machiavellian interpersonal style. The questionnaire has two subscales, one reflecting the respondent's views of human nature and the other the person's interpersonal tactics (Christie & Geis, 1970). Two items from the questionnaire are shown in Figure 20-8.

Engraving of Niccolo Machiavelli, whose views on social influence form the basis for a measure of individual differences in manipulativeness.

FIGURE 20-8 The Machiavellianism scale contains two subscales, one of which deals with the respondent's views of human nature, the other with the person's position on various interpersonal tactics. (Reprinted from Christie & Geis, 1970.)

Sample items from the Machiavellianism scale
Interpersonal tactics
Positive wording: The best way to handle people is to tell them what they want to hear.
Reversed wording: Honesty is the best policy in all cases.
Views of human nature
Positive wording: It is hard to get ahead without cutting corners here and there.
Reversed wording: Most people are basically good and kind.

Research using this questionnaire shows that people who are high in Machiavellianism ("high Machs") are cool, cerebral individuals who view interactions as opportunities to manipulate others. They initiate and control the structure of the interaction, concentrate on the rules of the game rather than on the people involved, and resist social pressure. From the standpoint of high-Mach individuals, the most favorable situation involves face-to-face interaction in which there is latitude for improvisation; under these conditions they can create irrelevant emotions in the other participants. When all others are responding emotionally, the high Mach has the greatest opportunity to manipulate them. Thus, interpersonal style can enhance social influence.

OBEDIENCE TO AUTHORITY

In many social settings the change agents are people in positions of authority. In the military, those who fail to follow a superior officer's orders may be court-martialed; workers who are insubordinate to their supervisors may be fired; police officers may arrest and imprison those who violate the laws. These examples all involve a combination of legitimate and coercive power, so it is not surprising that the targets of such power tend to comply. One of the most widely cited studies in social psychology suggests, however, that in certain circumstances people may be overly obedient to those who have apparent authority, even though they may have no coercive power whatsoever.

This research was conducted by Stanley Milgram, who realized that the systematic murder of civilians by the Nazis during World War II "could only be carried out on a massive scale if a very large number of persons had obeyed orders" (Milgram, 1963, p. 371). Milgram wanted to determine whether anyone (not just people of German extraction, and not just during wartime) would follow orders that caused suffering to others. He devised an experiment in which adult men recruited for a learning experiment through newspaper advertisements were asked to administer a series of increasingly intense shocks to another middle-aged man, ostensibly as punishment for errors in performing a simple learning task.

Through a ruse the subject was chosen to be the "teacher" and the other person (an accomplice of the experimenter) was chosen to be the "learner." At the beginning of the session the learner mentioned that he had suffered some heart problems; the experimenter replied that although the shocks might be quite painful there would be no permanent damage. Next, the subject/teacher himself experienced a 45-volt shock, to prove to him that it was indeed real, then he watched the learner sit in a chair and have his arm strapped to a shock plate. Next, he went to an adjoining room containing the shock generator. Although the 45-volt shock experienced by the subject at the beginning of the session was real, no shocks were ever actually administered to the learner. The experimental setting is shown in Figure 20-9.

Everything was done to make the subject believe that he was about to cause potentially serious shocks to another person. Each of the switches on the authentic-looking shock generator represented a 15-volt increment over the one to its left. The shock scale ran from a low of 15 volts to a high of 450 volts, with the last groups of switches labeled "Extreme Intensity Shock," "Danger: Severe Shock," and "XXX." The subject was directed to administer increasing levels of shock each time the learner made an error, despite his cries of pain. The learner was then taught a list of paired words (nice-day, blue-girl, and so on); next, the teacher read the first word of each pair and waited for the learner to say the second word. The learner began with several correct responses, but then began to make mistakes. At every mistake the experimenter directed the teacher to administer the (increasing) shock. As the shock level increased, the learner showed increasing signs of pain and distress. At the 300-volt level the learner fell silent.

The study was designed to determine the point at which the subject would refuse to continue the experiment. Before conducting the study Milgram had asked a num-

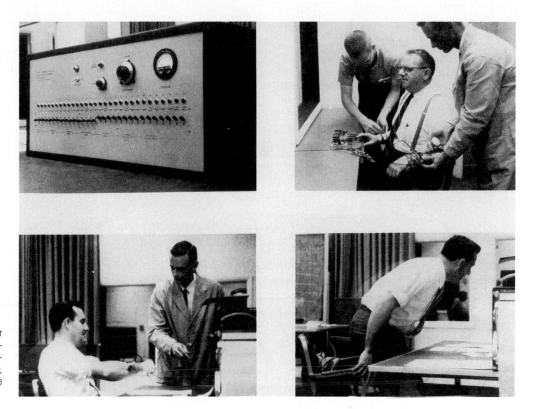

FIGURE 20-9 Experimental setting for Milgram's study of behavioral obedience. (Source: Copyright 1965 by Stanley Milgram. From the film *Obedience*, distributed by the Pennsylvania State University, PCR.)

ber of professional colleagues and senior psychology majors for estimates of the proportion of subjects who would continue through the 450-volt level. The most pessimistic estimate was 3%—but in reality 65% of the subjects administered shocks through the 450-volt level, and no subject refused until after the learner fell silent at the 300-volt level.

This is a profoundly disturbing experiment. Critics objected to aspects of the procedure, such as the deception itself and the debriefing procedure used to explain the study to subjects (Baumrind, 1964). For example, the debriefing necessarily explained that the idea of the study was to see when individuals would stop administering shock, which can be seen as suggesting to subjects that they were people who could easily injure others. The estimates that Milgram obtained in advance would have led one to conclude that few, if any, subjects would have to deal with such knowledge—yet when Milgram did a follow-up interview with participants to determine whether there had been residual psychological effects, there did not seem to be any.

Subjects who asked who would be responsible for what happened to the learner were told that the experimenter would accept the responsibility—exactly what any authority figure might say. Keep in mind that the subject was free to leave at any time. But no subjects turned around to say, "This is an experiment, and I am leaving." What is important is the climate for obedience created in the experiment. Subjects were too caught up in the power of the situation to step back, examine their own behavior against their moral standards, and decide to stop. Very much the same failure of independent judgment was part of the My Lai massacre of Vietnamese civilians by U.S. forces during the Vietnam War (Kelman & Hamilton, 1990). Although only one junior officer, Lieutenant William Calley, was convicted following the massacre, there is good reason to believe that the climate created by his military and civilian superiors contributed to the massacre. Despite the continuing controversy over Milgram's research methods, his study raises fundamental questions about blind obedience to authority.

Lieutenant William Calley, the only officer convicted for the My Lai massacre of civilians during the Vietnam War.

CONFORMITY TO GROUP NORMS

Specific demands by people in positions of authority are strong influences on social behavior, but they are by no means the only ones. Our actions are also affected by the formal and informal norms of the social groups to which we belong. As noted in Chapter 19, people evaluate their opinions and abilities by comparing them with those of people like themselves. Whether the social group is a small collection of friends or an organized club with stated goals and scheduled meetings, the result of this social comparison among group members will be a **social reality** for the group—that is, a group consensus regarding which attitudes are acceptable and which group objectives are important.

Informational and Normative Influence

Any group that is used as a basis for comparison is serving as a **reference group.** If the group provides a model of desirable behavior it is a positive reference group; conversely, if it provides a model of undesirable behavior, it is a negative reference group. If the group is one that the person belongs to or wishes to join, it is a membership group as well as a reference group.

To the extent that opinions and actions are molded by comparisons with a reference or membership group, that group is exerting **informational social influence.** This influence need not be direct, as it is in the case of obedience to authority. Most of the time it is the individual, not the group, who initiates the social comparison. Nevertheless, because the individual's behavior after the comparison is different from what it would have been otherwise, the group has influenced the individual. If, on the other hand, the group actually dictates behavior in a particular setting and imposes sanctions for failure to comply, it is exerting **normative social influence.** For example, convergences in opinions among members of fraternal organizations may be the result of informational social influence, whereas required attendance at meetings, if enforced by fines, would be normative social influence.

Pressure to Conform

People frequently compare their opinions with those of other people. Ordinarily this comparison serves a useful purpose, preventing people from responding inappropriately to situations that they do not understand fully. But sometimes the desire to fit in, like the desire to follow legitimate directions from an authority figure, can lead to serious mistakes. This was first indicated in a classic study of perceptual judgment conducted by Solomon Asch (1951).

The subjects in Asch's experiment were told that they were taking part in a study involving visual discrimination. Each subject arrived at the laboratory to find eight other subjects (actually accomplices of the experimenter) already seated in a semicircle in front of a blackboard. After describing the visual-discrimination task that the subjects were to perform, the experimenter placed on the chalk rail two large cards, one containing a standard line and the other containing three comparison lines, as shown in Figure 20-10. Each subject was to say which of the comparison lines was the same length as the standard line. The real subject, having taken the only empty seat, was the seventh person to express a judgment.

There were several trials. On most trials all nine people agreed on what, perceptually, was a trivially simple discrimination. On several "critical" trials, however, the six accomplices who spoke before the real subject all gave an obviously wrong answer. The subject thus was confronted with a dilemma: Conform to the erroneous group judgment or give a correct answer that disagreed with the majority opinion.

The results showed that subjects who maintained their opinions in the face of a unanimous majority tended either to be quite sure of their answers or to be nervous and withdrawn. Subjects who conformed to the group opinion on more than half of

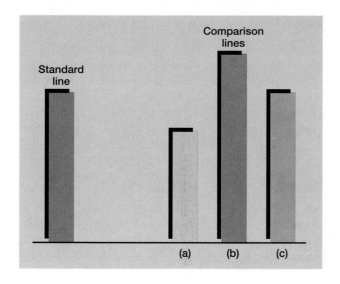

FIGURE 20-10 Stimulus materials like those used in a study of conformity (left) and the experimental setting (right). The student in the center is the only real subject; the others are accomplices. On selected trials the accomplices claim that either line (*a*) or line (*b*) is the length of the standard line.

the critical trials, on the other hand, seemed torn between the perceptual facts as they saw them and the majority opinion. Subsequent conformity studies have shown that increasing the number of forces on the individual—for example, by making the group more desirable, having responses spoken out loud rather than written down, and increasing the similarity of group members in terms of sex or ability—will increase the likelihood of conformity (Allen, 1975). By far the most important factor is the *unanimity* of the majority. When there is even one person who agrees with the real subject, the proportion of subjects who conform to the erroneous group opinion decreases from approximately one-third to just over 5% (Moscovici, 1985).

INTERIM SUMMARY

Social power is the capacity to affect the behavior of others; social influence is measured by the actual change that occurs in the behavior of the target person. The social context can be thought of as a field of forces acting in concert to influence the individual's actions. There are five kinds of social power—reward, coercive, legitimate, referent, and expert. Regardless of their actual social power, people who score high in the manipulative interpersonal style known as Machiavellianism seem able to exercise control over others, especially in face-to-face interactions with plenty of latitude for improvisation. The influence of the group on the individual can be seen in obedience to authority and conformity to group opinion.

GROUP PROCESSES

So far we have described interpersonal processes from the standpoint of the individual: Equity is a matter of individual perception; exchange theory explains the relationship between two people who each seek good outcomes; the bases of social power enable some individuals to influence others. Even the study of conformity focuses on the effect of social pressure on the individual. There are, however, numerous social situations in which several individuals influence one another. Two that have been extensively studied by social psychologists are the relationship between the members of a group and its leader, and the decision-making processes of groups.

LEADERSHIP

Who is a better group leader—a charismatic person with no organizational skills or a competent organizer who lacks the ability to inspire others? Psychologists have long been interested in the qualities of effective leaders. A review of early research found that leaders tend to be taller, more attractive, more intelligent, better adjusted, and more dominant than other people (Gibb, 1969). Yet the most striking thing about these presumed leadership characteristics is how rarely the people possessing them are successful leaders in more than one setting. This point has been emphasized in more recent reviews: Despite occasional historical examples to the contrary, the evidence does not support the "great man" theory—the idea that a particular combination of traits will produce a renowned leader (Hollander, 1985).

On the contrary, much of the research evidence shows that a leader's success is contingent both on his or her personal qualities and on the nature of the group interaction (Fiedler, 1964; 1978). The **contingency model** of leadership effectiveness focuses on one dimension of the leader's personal style—the degree to which he or she is permissive or controlling. A leader whose effectiveness is being evaluated is asked to use a series of bipolar adjectives, such as productive–unproductive, to describe his or her *least preferred co-worker* (LPC). In identifying an LPC, the leader is asked to consider all of his or her past work relationships and to recall the one person with whom it was most difficult to get along. A leader who rates even this person positively (a "high-LPC" leader) is said to be permissive and considerate and to be concerned primarily with human relations. A leader who rates the LPC negatively (a "low-LPC" leader) is said to be managing and controlling and to be task oriented; that is, "all business."

Dimensions of the Situation

The effectiveness of these leader orientations depends on three dimensions of the situation: *leader–member relations, task structure,* and *position power.* The first dimension is self-explanatory. Is there a good feeling between the group members and the leader, or are they continually at each other's throats? The second dimension has to do with the degree of ambiguity in what the group is trying to accomplish. At one extreme would be a team of assembly-line workers assigned a task that contains a known number of discrete elements, each of which must be performed in a prescribed sequence within a set time. At the other extreme would be a committee—whose task, say, is to discuss whether to change a college curriculum—that might have no time limit, no set agenda, and no prescribed way to go about the task. The third dimension refers to the legitimate power vested in the leader's position. Some organizations (such as the military) endow leaders with considerable power, whereas other organizations (such as a student government) endow leaders with little more than a forum for persuading others to adopt their ideas.

To keep the explanatory task manageable, the contingency model of leadership considers each of the three factors to be a dichotomy: Relations between the leader and the members are either good or poor; the situation is either structured or unstructured; the leader's position power is either strong or weak. Combining the three factors produces an overall dimension termed *favorability of the situation.* The relationship between the leader and the group is the most important influence on favorability, the structure of the situation is the next most important, and the leader's authority is the least important. The most favorable situation is one in which leader–member relations are good, the task is highly structured, and the leader's position power is strong. Merely changing the leader–member relations from good to poor makes the situation substantially less favorable. If an unstructured task and low position power are added to the poor affective relations, the leader's situation becomes highly unfavorable.

A task-oriented leader will be most effective in the most favorable situations, those in which relations between leader and members are good, the task is struc-

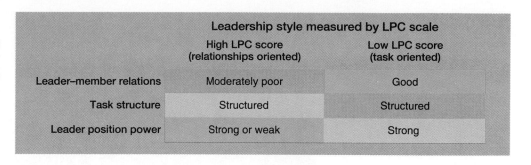

FIGURE 20-11 The contingency model of leadership effectiveness argues that both the leader's characteristics (measured by the LPC score) and the characteristics of the situation (in terms of leader–member relations, the structure of the task, and the leader's position power) affect the quality of leadership. This figure summarizes the conditions under which the two kinds of leaders are likely to be most effective.

	Leadership style measured by LPC scale	
	High LPC score (relationships oriented)	Low LPC score (task oriented)
Leader–member relations	Moderately poor	Good
Task structure	Structured	Structured
Leader position power	Strong or weak	Strong

tured, and the leader's position is powerful. In such a case, the daily activities of the group normally proceed smoothly; when a decision *is* required, an autocrat will make it most efficiently. (See Figure 20-11.) This task-oriented leader is also thought to be most effective when the situation is unfavorable. For example, when leader–member relations are poor, the task is unstructured, and the inherent power of the leader's position is low, a leader who concentrates on getting the job done will be more effective than one who attempts to make everyone feel better.

In contrast, a relationships-oriented leader will shine when the situation is neither very favorable nor highly unfavorable. Such a situation occurs when group relations are poor but the task is structured and the leader has clear authority. An example is a job in which workers are paid on a piece-work basis to accomplish a very specific task and the group's supervisor is the only one who can legitimately check on a worker's output. In these circumstances, unless the leader exercises his or her authority with sensitivity and good humor, the work group will never achieve its objectives.

Some difficulties remain with aspects of the contingency model. Researchers disagree, for example, about the exact meaning of the LPC scale (Hollander, 1985). Nevertheless, a review of more than 100 studies found general support for the contingency model predictions (Strube & Garcia, 1981). Popular as the idea of a "great leader" is, in reality a leader's effectiveness is jointly determined by the leader's actions, the task, and the group members.

GROUP DECISIONS

Suppose that instead of having decisions made by the leader and announced to the group, the decision-making authority rests wholly or in part in the group? How will the interaction among members affect the outcome? The answer to this question centers on the commitment to the group by its members.

Whether a social organization is formed to protect its members, as in Hobbes's view of the function of government, or to allow them to attain collective goals, participation in the group requires that individuals forgo some of their freedom. People will be willing to do so to the extent that participation satisfies their emotional needs for belonging and friendship while also helping them attain their personal goals. In terms of field theory, some forces will act to keep the person in the group while others will act to propel the person out of the group. The sum of the forces binding group members together is the **cohesiveness** of the group. A group with low cohesiveness is likely to have diffuse objectives and to find it difficult to make a decision that will be accepted by the entire group. (Members dissatisfied with the decision will simply leave.)

A highly cohesive decision-making group is much more effective at creating a shared social reality for its members, but high cohesiveness is not always an advantage. When such a group has an important decision to make, it may lose touch with reality. The maintenance of cohesiveness can require absolute unanimity of opinion, so the group cannot move directly toward its goal if there is any dissension. Recog-

A tragedy of charismatic leadership. In 1978 Jim Jones, the self-proclaimed leader of the People's Temple, led hundreds of his followers to commit mass suicide.

nizing this, members who value their position may seek concurrence rather than a thorough examination of all alternative courses of action.

This situation can lead to **groupthink,** the mode of thinking that arises when "members' strivings for unanimity override their motivation to realistically appraise alternative courses of action" (Janis, 1982, p. 9). Although some decisions are not adversely affected by the pressure for concurrence, others may turn into policy disas-

The Watergate cover-up scandal, which led to the resignation of then-President Richard Nixon and the criminal conviction of many of his close advisers, can be seen as an example of the flawed decision making so characteristic of groupthink.

ters (McCauley, 1989). A number of decisions by government officials appear to have been influenced by groupthink. An example is the cover-up of the break-in at the Watergate headquarters of the Democratic National Committee in 1972, which created the scandal that led to the resignation of President Richard M. Nixon and criminal convictions for several of his advisers. Analysis of this incident suggests that the small decision-making group surrounding the president maintained its unanimity until one of its members, John Dean, faced criminal prosecution (Janis, 1982). Another example is the NASA decision in 1986 to launch the ill-fated space shuttle *Challenger,* resulting in America's worst space-related disaster (Moorhead, Ference, & Neck, 1991).

An episode that could be considered the prototype of groupthink is the decision-making process that led to the abortive invasion of Cuba that was initiated in 1961 by President John F. Kennedy and his close advisers (McCauley, 1989). The plan was to land an invasion group of 1,400 Cuban exiles at the Bay of Pigs. It was expected that the invasion would precipitate a popular uprising that would overthrow Cuba's dictator, Fidel Castro. But instead the popular opposition to Castro was overestimated, and the landing troops, poorly equipped and supported, were quickly overcome by Cuban troops loyal to Castro. About 1,200 of the invaders were later ransomed by the United States for $53-million-worth of food and medicine.

Why did a group of intelligent and sophisticated decision makers fail to anticipate an outcome that in hindsight seems so predictable? There had been rumors that popular opposition to Castro was soft, and standard military tactics argue against sending an invasion force without full naval and air support. Analysis of the transcripts of the meeting at which the decision was made, together with the public statements made by participants, revealed a flawed decision process. The group was highly cohesive and insulated from outside opinion, and members who had reservations about the plan were unwilling to risk their status by raising objections. In any such group the reluctance to speak out leads to an *illusion of unanimity* regarding the decision, and this translates into an *illusion of invulnerability* regarding the course of action. Each participant believes that if none of the other capable people in the group can discover a flaw, the plan must be perfect.

The way to reduce the likelihood of groupthink is to counter the illusion of unanimity. The leader should refrain from expressing his or her opinion before the discussion, outside experts should be brought in to challenge the group's position, and one member of the group should be appointed to take the role of devil's advocate. All these actions reassert the power of the individual relative to the group.

Finally, it is worth noting again that the effort to obtain concurrence does not always create problems for the group (Longley & Pruitt, 1980). Indeed, for a wide variety of group decisions, seeking agreement on minor matters enables the group to consider the major issues at length.

INTERIM SUMMARY

Psychologists have long been interested in the qualities of effective leaders. Early research suggested that leaders tend to be more attractive, more intelligent, and better adjusted than other people, but such leaders do not seem to be equally effective in all contexts. More recent research shows that a leader's success is contingent on the nature of the group interaction as well as on his or her personal qualities. The contingency model of leadership effectiveness concentrates on one dimension of the leader's personal style—concern with human relations versus concern for the task at hand—and three dimensions of the situation—leader–member relations, task structure, and position power, which combine to determine the favorability of the situation. In this model, a task-oriented leader will be effective in the most and least favorable situations, whereas a relationships-oriented leader will be effective in the neither very favorable nor very unfavorable situations. The sum of the forces binding members to one another is known as the cohesiveness of the group. A highly cohesive group is susceptible to groupthink, in which the desire for unanimity overrides that for considering alternative courses of action. Groupthink can be prevented by measures designed to counter the illusion of unanimity.

SUMMARY

1. *Sex differences* refer to any well-established behavioral difference between females and males, regardless of whether the presumed causes of the differences are biological or cultural. *Gender* refers to the set of meanings that individuals ascribe to the female and male categories.

2. *Meta-analysis* is a powerful quantitative method for examining the findings of a large number of research studies. Use of this technique has identified several important sex differences. Females are superior in verbal abilities; males are superior in mathematical and spatial abilities. Females are more effective in interpersonal communication; males are higher in activity and aggression. This pattern of differences has been interpreted as reflecting a distinction between agency, generally more characteristic of males, and communion, generally more characteristic of females.

3. *Propinquity,* the physical proximity between people, has a profound effect on the development of interpersonal attraction and friendship. Other factors that enhance attraction are positive mood and physical attractiveness.

4. The effects of propinquity, mood, and attractiveness can be accounted for by *exchange theory,* which claims that people seek to maximize their outcomes from interaction with others. Through interaction and a developing commitment to the relationship, this selfish motive results in mutual behavior control.

5. Exchange theory identifies two internal standards, the *comparison level (CL)* and the *comparison level for alternatives CL$_{alt}$)*, against which people judge their outcomes from an interaction. Studies using a Relationship Closeness Inventory (RCI) suggest that the quality and range of joint outcomes achieved are better predictors of the maintenance of romantic relationships than are such things as prior longevity of the relationship or subjective estimates of closeness.

6. People's continued participation in informal social groups depends in large part on the belief that rewards derived from participation are *equitable.* An interchange is equitable if the ratio of one participant's profits to inputs is equal to that of the other participant.

7. People who feel inequitably treated can remedy the situation by directly altering their own or the other person's outcomes or inputs, by cognitively distorting the nature of the reward distribution, or by leaving the field.

8. Exchange theory can distinguish cooperation, characterized by high correspondence of outcomes, from *competition,* in which one person's best outcomes are obtained at the expense of the other.

9. Competition can take the form of a *zero-sum game,* in which one person's winnings match the other person's losses, or *nonzero-sum game,* in which winnings do not necessarily match losses. The *Prisoner's Dilemma game* is a specific form of nonzero-sum game designed to examine interpersonal trust. It serves as a model for a variety of social negotiations.

10. *Social dilemmas* are a form of nonzero-sum game in which the long-term interest of a group of people is compromised if each individual relentlessly pursues his or her own short-term objectives.

11. *Social power* is an individual change agent's capacity to affect a target person, other things being equal. *Social influence,* reflecting that other things are rarely equal, is the actual change in the target person.

12. There are five bases of social power—reward, coercive, legitimate, referent, and expert.

13. A person high in *Machiavellianism* can often produce compliance, even without any formal power, particularly in face-to-face situations with latitude for improvisation that permit the high-Mach individual to inject irrelevant affect.

14. The degree to which people will follow orders from authority figures has been shown in a powerful series of laboratory experiments by Stanley Milgram. Although this research has raised ethical questions, its results—showing how willing people are to accede to authority—serve as a strong warning against blind obedience, even to legitimate authority.

15. Pressure to conform to a group's judgment can originate from either *informational social influence* or *normative social influence.* Unanimity of the majority is the most important factor in producing conformity.

16. Notwithstanding a few historical examples to the contrary, effective leadership is not generally a property of the person. Rather, it depends on the relationship between the interpersonal style of the leader and the demands of the situation as described by the *contingency model* of leadership.

17. Any highly *cohesive* group runs the risk that its decisions will be adversely affected by *groupthink,* a tacit failure to consider the ramifications of a policy about to be adopted.

FOCUS QUESTIONS

1. What are the major sex differences in social behavior? How do the recognized sex differences compare with differences in the division of labor in preindustrial societies?

2. Describe the principles of exchange theory. How do people evaluate the outcomes received from an interaction?

3. What is the essential principle represented in equity theory? What are the possible responses to inequity?

4. Describe the Prisoner's Dilemma game. What is the underlying psychological problem for participants in such an interaction?

5. Illustrate the forces and goals present in the life space. How can this model be used to distinguish social power from social influence?

6. What are the five bases of social power?

7. Attack or defend this statement: People can be made to hurt others only under the most unusual circumstances.

8. Describe research on conformity to group opinion. What factors make such conformity more likely?

9. Describe the contingency model of leadership effectiveness.

10. What factors make groupthink more likely? How can this decision-making bias be avoided?

PART SEVEN

STABILITY AND CHANGE
IN BEHAVIOR

L ife is a balance between **stability and change.** A person whose identity remains unquestionably the same can nevertheless change behavior from one setting to the next. This last part of the book considers issues involved in the stability and integrity of the individual over time and from one situation to another. Chapter 21 discusses theories of personality, the core of enduring characteristics that defines us as individuals. Chapter 22 confronts the methodological challenges involved in the definition and measurement of individual differences in personality and intelligence. Chapter 23, on stress and coping, examines the consequences of an individual's attempts to adapt to a variety of external pressures. Chapter 24, on psychopathology, describes the dramatic change in everyday behavior that results, in a general sense, from failures to adapt. Chapter 25, on the treatment of disorders, considers ways that some kinds of structured change can restore the individual's stability.

CHAPTER 21

PERSONALITY STRUCTURE AND FUNCTION

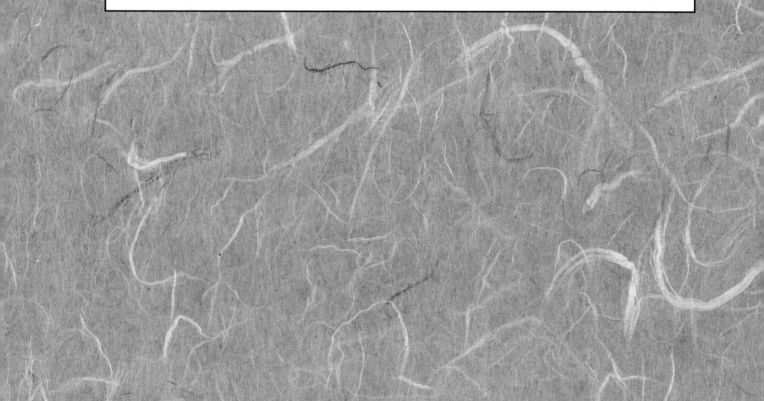

How can people have so much in common with one another and yet each be unique? How can people change behavior from one setting to another and still remain essentially the same? These questions reflect a fundamental theme of psychology: stability versus change.

We live in a world of constantly shifting social, emotional, and physical demands to which we have to adapt appropriately—we behave differently in an office, for example, than in a classroom or on an informal outing with friends. Throughout our lives we experience emotional changes, changes in things we know or believe, and changes in our physical capabilities. Even the way we answer the question "Who am I?" changes with our moods, the other people around us, and the things we happen to be thinking or talking about (Markus & Kunda, 1986). Nonetheless, each of us can reasonably say, "I am still basically the same person I was before." In this chapter we consider the structure and function of personality, the enduring human feature that makes each of us a distinctive entity.

PERSONALITY AND SITUATION

The word *personality* is derived from the ancient Greek *persona,* which originally referred to a mask worn to perform a role in a play but later came to mean the role itself. The idea of a mask, coupled with the actor's talent, is an apt metaphor for the modern concept of personality, which includes both the enduring characteristics of the individual and the way those characteristics are expressed. Personality has been defined as the "stable set of tendencies and characteristics that determine those commonalities and differences in people's psychological behavior (thoughts, feelings, and actions) that have continuity in time and that may not be easily understood as the sole result of the social and biological pressures of the moment" (Maddi, 1989, p. 8). Three aspects of this definition deserve expansion. First, stability over time is critical: The characteristics that constitute personality are presumed to be stable, and the behaviors that result from these characteristics show continuity. Second, personality is confined to humans: Detailed study of how thoughts and feelings find their way into actions requires a rich and expressive language. Third, personality is what remains when social and biological pressures are removed: Personality accounts for differences between the actions of various people who face identical social and biological pressures, and it accounts for the consistency in one individual's actions despite changes in social and biological pressures.

CROSS-SITUATIONAL CONSISTENCY

The assumption that an individual's personality structure will guide almost all of his or her behavior is at the heart of the idea of **cross-situational consistency.** The personality characteristics that are assumed to endure within the individual are referred to as *person variables,* and researchers who study them are known as *personologists* (Maddi, 1989). As we will see, the assumption of cross-situational consistency in person variables has been a feature of numerous major personality theories, beginning with Freud's theory in the early 1900s and extending to the humanistic theories of the 1960s.

Such an assumption is necessary from a scientific standpoint and also makes sense in practical terms. From a scientific standpoint, psychology involves a search for regularities in behavior. The scientific study of personality therefore presumes that there are causes of action that can be identified and that among those causes are internal factors associated with what we loosely call "personality." On the practical side, much of our behavior toward other people is based on the belief that what those people did yesterday is a reasonable predictor of what they will do tomorrow. Given that an individual's past history is fixed, and that physiological characteristics remain relatively constant, it is no surprise that there is a high level of cross-situational consistency in behavior.

SITUATIONISM

There must, however, be more to behavior than cross-situational consistency alone. Nobody's actions are exactly the same from one setting to the next. Even a person's scores on measures of personality will change if social conditions change. Research has shown that the results of personality tests are only moderately correlated from one setting to another (Bem & Allen, 1974). To reduce this variability, personologists try to control for biological and social pressures when they look for ways in which people are similar to, or different from, one another (Maddi, 1989). The logic of this approach, however, raises a troubling question. If there is so much variation in the way any individual acts from one situation to another, how can the underlying "personality" still be considered an important influence on action?

According to one school of thought, **situationism,** the answer to this question is that the causes of regularities in behavior are to be found in the situations themselves, not in the person's internal personality characteristics (Mischel, 1968). If this position sounds familiar to you, it should. In its extreme form, situationism in personality theory is another version of the stimulus–response (S–R) approach to behavior that was prevalent in the early decades of the twentieth century. Specifically, situationism's claim that regularities in a person's behavior are built up from repeated experiences of similar situations is comparable to S–R theory's claim that knowledge is built up from associations.

PERSON-BY-SITUATION INTERACTION

There are strong arguments against situationism, not the least of which is that if situationism were true, then in situations where there are very strong social pressures on behavior everyone would behave in an identical fashion. For example, anyone who chooses to have sexual relations would use protection, and nobody who had imbibed several drinks too many would drive home. After all, few social messages are stronger or more prevalent than "practice safe sex" and "don't drink and drive." But as health statistics demonstrate, these admonitions produce far less than total compliance. Obviously some people heed the message, others do not.

If neither cross-situational consistency nor situationism provides a complete explanation for behavior, then the truth must lie somewhere in between these extremes (Bowers, 1973). The question then becomes, "What proportion of the variability in people's actions can be attributed to the person, what proportion to the situation, and what proportion to the combination of person and situation?" Researchers have examined this question and have discovered that the **person-by-situation interaction** explains much of an individual's behavior. (See Figure 21-1.)

Variations in the Situation

If the demands of a situation are strong, virtually all people will behave in the way dictated by the situation, regardless of their personality structure. For example, when a state police officer, with siren on and lights flashing, pulls up behind a car and motions the driver to stop, only a fool, a drunk, or someone who has just committed a major crime will step on the gas. In the language of the person-by-situation debate, the demands of this situation are so powerful that there will be substantial uniformity of behavior among individuals (for example, see Funder & Colvin, 1991).

FIGURE 21-1 The mutual influence of personality and situation on the predictability of human behavior. Consistency in action from one situation to the next is likely when the person variables are strong and the situational demands are weak; uniformity in the actions of different individuals is likely when the situational demands are strong and the person variables are weak.

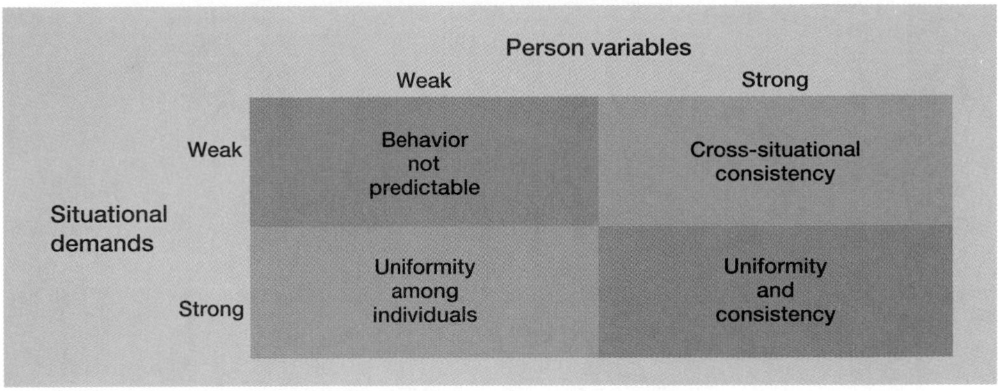

When the situational demands are weak, however, person variables also affect behavior, with the extent of the effect depending on the variables' strength. If the person variables also are weak, they will have little effect on behavior. The exchange, "What kind of salad dressing do you want?" "I don't care; what is there?" is an example of a case in which both situation and person variables are weak. On the other hand, when the person variables are strong, behavior can be expected to show considerable consistency across a variety of situations. A committed religious fundamentalist, for example, will follow an unwavering moral imperative in a wide range of settings, regardless of the strength of the situational demands.

Explaining the Interaction

Many of the traditional personality theories to be discussed later in this chapter (such as any of the psychodynamic theories) would predict that personality characteristics could account for behavior in a wide variety of settings. Reviews of the literature, however, indicate that this is not necessarily so (Mischel & Peake, 1982). The general failure of personality characteristics to predict behavior has been explained in three ways.

The first explanation is methodological (Epstein, 1979; 1980). According to this view, personal characteristics really are good predictors of behavior, although most research techniques make this difficult to demonstrate. Specifically, with only a few exceptions (Block, 1971; Hartshorne & May, 1928) most studies of the relationship between personality and behavior take only one measure of a personality characteristic and then assess behavior in only one setting. For example, a study might measure a person's "optimism" and then attempt to determine whether this characteristic was related to the person's expected success on a single experimental task. But the relationship between personality and behavior should be discovered much more reliably when the personality characteristic is measured in several ways and multiple behaviors are examined (Epstein, 1979; 1984). For example, if there were several measures of optimism, and if the one experimental task were supplemented by other behavioral measures—such as whether the people involved bet on the lottery, believe that they will keep their jobs in bad times, and expect that their children will get into the college of their choice—then the correlations between the multiple measures of the trait and those of the behavior should improve significantly.

A second explanation emphasizes that people differ in the degree to which a particular personality characteristic is *consistently* relevant for their behavior (Bem & Allen, 1974). For example, people differ widely in their desire to be dominant in social settings. A person whose dominance varies dramatically from one situation to the next would fall into the upper-left box of Figure 21-1, whereas one whose dominance is extremely consistent would fall in the upper-right box. But if many people are measured on dominance, predictions based on the average measures will be inac-

563

| Personality dispositions | DOMINANT submissive |
| Situational template | DOMINANT |

FIGURE 21-2 Illustration of the idea that personal dispositions, such as submissiveness or dominance, will correlate with behavior only when those dispositions fit the "template" provided by the situation.

curate because they draw on both people who are weak in dominance as well as those who are strong in it.

The third explanation focuses on the match between the individual's personality characteristics and the demands of the situation (Bem & Funder, 1978). This approach is termed *template-matching*. It assumes that a high correlation between personality characteristics and behavior will be achieved only if the individual's personality matches the behavioral "template" inherent in the situation, as shown in Figure 21-2. For example, a person's dominance should be more closely related to performance in a setting that requires individual achievement than in one that demands equal and cooperative contributions from members of a team.

The controversy over the relative influences of person and situation points up the complexity of the task facing psychologists who theorize about, and conduct research on, the way that personality influences behavior. Strong situational demands may change behavior without changing personality, and personality characteristics that influence behavior are likely to be identified only if the demands of the situations are weak. The theories of personality presented in this chapter therefore should be regarded as descriptions of the ways in which personality affects behavior in settings in which the situational demands are not overwhelming. We begin with two concepts—type and trait—central to personality theory, and then turn to detailed discussion of specific personality theories.

INTERIM SUMMARY

To meet the social demands of a situation, a person's behavior will change from one setting to another. Despite these changes, a central core of the person remains constant. This stable set of tendencies and characteristics constitutes the individual's personality. When biological and social pressures are removed, individual differences will remain; these person variables are the focus of personality theory and research.

TYPES, TRAITS, AND PERSONALITY DYNAMICS

As early as the fourth century B.C., the Greek philosopher Theophrastus outlined some 30 personality types, and described regularities in each type's behavior that were presumed to be consistent regardless of the setting (Aiken, 1989). The Greek physician Hippocrates suggested that there were four "humours," or basic sub-

Illustration of the four humoral personality types: phlegmatic, choleric, sanguinic, and melancholic.

stances in the body—blood, yellow bile, black bile, and phlegm. Building on this idea, the Roman physician Galen identified four personality types, each involving an overabundance of one of the humours. A person with too much blood was sanguine (active and confident), whereas a person with excess phlegm was phlegmatic (slow-moving and emotionally flat). A person with too much yellow bile was choleric (quick to anger and violence), whereas a person with an excess of black bile was melancholic (sad and depressed). It is interesting that although modern personality theory no longer subscribes to such a simple view, the adjectives—sanguine, phlegmatic, choleric, and melancholic—are still found in popular personality descriptions.

Personality Types

The modern derivative of Galen's idea is the view that all individuals can be classified into a few personality types. These types are often based on the presumption that specific physical features are accompanied by particular personality characteristics—that very thin people, for example, have a personality structure that is different from that of very heavy people. Each type is defined as a prototype (see Chapter 14), an ideal member who has all the psychological features that illustrate the type. Individuals are assessed and categorized according to the prototype they most closely

Galen, the second-century Roman who served as physician and surgeon to gladiators and Marcus Aurelius, as imagined by a later artist, and the title page of a sixteenth-century edition of one of Galen's hundreds of treatises.

resemble. Because a person's physical features remain relatively constant, personality characteristics are also presumed to be quite stable.

One well-known type theory classified people into three **somatotypes**—mesomorphs, ectomorphs, and endomorphs—based on physique (Sheldon & Stevens, 1942). Mesomorphs are well-proportioned and -muscled, ectomorphs are thin, and endomorphs are fat. Individuals were classified into one type or another on the basis of their physical features, then researchers assessed their personality characteristics (Sheldon & Stevens, 1942). As promising as this idea sounds, years of research have failed to establish any straightforward relationship between physical features and personality structure. Consequently, although type theories were popular from the beginning to the middle of the twentieth century, they are now regarded as simplistic (Aiken, 1989).

Traits: The Language of Personality Description

Where the somatotype theory concentrated on a few physical characteristics that many people share, trait theories of personality emphasize the conscious strivings that make each individual unique. The major trait theory was proposed by Gordon Allport (1897–1967), who believed that although people were unique individuals, their personalities could nevertheless be described by common organizational principles. At first it might seem contradictory to claim that people who are unique can be described by a relatively few common dimensions. But this is exactly what is done in genetics—a few fundamental genetic elements are the basis for all of human variation. The use of a few dimensions to characterize individuals is also what is done with fingerprint identification (Hilgard, 1987). "All persons have lines in their skin composed of such 'traits' as arches, loops, and whorls which appear when an ink impression is taken. These are patterned uniquely, however, so that an individual can be identified by fingerprints as one among countless others" (Hilgard, 1987, p. 499). Allport's theory will be discussed in greater detail later in the chapter.

Because of its attempt to characterize the unique aspects of each person, a trait theory depends more heavily on descriptive language than does any other personality theory. Indeed, the classic study that laid the foundation for the trait approach began by culling from an unabridged dictionary over 18,000 words that could be used to describe a person (Allport & Odbert, 1936). These words were separated into **traits** (stable and enduring structures that guide the person's adaptation to the environment), *states* (temporary moods or activities), and *character evaluations.*

If the type theories suffered from having too few central types, trait theories suffered from having too many dimensions on which an individual's personality might be described. As a result, the objective of much personality trait research has been to reduce the number of personality descriptors from several thousand to something more manageable. This objective has usually been achieved through the application of **factor analysis,** a statistical technique for identifying the common dimensions among a large number of variables.

In one such factor analytic study, researchers began with the list of traits found in the dictionary and another set of terms gleaned from the psychological literature (Cattell, 1946; 1957). The resulting list was then reduced, by combining synonyms, to 171 items. A sample of 100 people was then recruited from all walks of life. Friends and associates of these people, who knew them well, were asked to rate them using the 171 descriptive terms. Elimination of terms that appeared redundant produced a shorter list of trait words, which was then used by friends of another group of over 200 target persons. Factor analyses of the latter ratings formed the basis for the construction of a personality test designed to measure what Cattell called the "primary source traits" of personality. This test is Cattell's *16 Personality Factors Questionnaire* (Cattell, Saunders, & Stice, 1950). The primary source traits identified in the *16pf* are really *classes* of items rather than individual items. Thus, for example, one class is called "cultured mind versus boorishness." The category names, however, are not as important as the content of the items comprising each of the 16 categories.

Gordon Allport , author of the major trait theory of personality. In his theory, Allport attempted to develop a way to describe the unique characteristics of every individual.

The factor-analytic method has been used by numerous other researchers either to construct standardized personality tests or to reduce the number of trait words that must be used to describe an individual. Perhaps the most prominent factor-analytically derived alternative to the *16pf* is Eysenck's personality inventory, which groups 32 separate factors into two higher-order dimensions—*introversion–extraversion* and *neuroticism* (Eysenck & Eysenck, 1975).

The most prominent classification system that is not a personality test is Norman's, used with his reduction of Allport and Odbert's list of 18,000 terms to 75 (Norman, 1967). These 75 were then grouped into three major categories—traits, states, and activities. This classification, like the rationale for constructing factor-analytic personality tests, turns on the distinction between stability and change: Traits are enduring; states and activities are temporary.

Although the trait–state distinction has been part of trait theory from the very beginning, it has always been imposed on the data by theorists. This fact has led some researchers to suggest that the distinction reflects the requirements of theory rather than the way we actually use the language to describe attributes of other people (Allen & Potkay, 1981).

To test this idea, one group of investigators (Chaplin, John, & Goldberg, 1988) presented subjects with a list of 75 personality-descriptive terms, 25 of which were from Norman's (1967) research and the remaining 50 of which were drawn from other sources. In several studies, the researchers asked subjects to indicate whether they believed each descriptive word represented a personality trait, a human state or condition, or a human activity. Overall, the results showed that subjects easily distinguished among the three. Examples from each category are shown in Table 21-1. The results of this research have two implications for our discussion. First, they reinforce the idea that a complex language is necessary for adequate description of personality. Second, they show that, where personality is concerned, natural language supports the distinction between stability and change.

Personality Dynamics

Where trait theories concentrate on each individual's conscious strivings, other personality theories emphasize the interplay among unconscious processes. For these *psychodynamic* theories, stability in personality is the result of constant internal turmoil. The human being's animal heritage gives rise to sexual and aggressive drives that must be tempered by moral principles internalized from the culture. Unconscious sexual and aggressive instincts are part of the biological creature, so they are present from birth. Principles of moral behavior, however, are learned through processes of socialization. The result is that psychodynamic theories devote a great deal of attention to developmental stages through which the individual is presumed to pass. Each stage is characterized by a specific conflict between biological desires and the demands of the external situation. Satisfactory resolution of the conflict allows psychological development to proceed to the subsequent stage. Unsatisfactory resolution of a conflict produces *fixation* at the present stage, thus stunting the individual's psychological growth in ways that will later be reflected in adult behavior patterns.

TABLE 21-1   Sample Trait Words, Human States, and Activities

Person Descriptions	Human States	Activities
Gentle	Infatuated	Carousing
Domineering	Miserable	Bickering
Gracious	Resigned	Welcoming
Cunning	Displeased	Hovering

SOURCE: Adapted from Chaplin, John, & Goldberg (1988).

In Freudian theory, unconscious processes give rise to *anxiety,* and much of the organization of the personality is designed to minimize that anxiety. Not all personality theories, however, assume that unconscious processes are the primary motivation for behavior. For example, despite their intellectual debt to the psychodynamic approach, the theories of Alfred Adler and Harry Stack Sullivan emphasize interpersonal sources of anxiety. The learning theories of personality, also discussed later in this chapter, take this externalization of motivation one step further. For them, behavioral conflicts are the product of competing environmental demands; an internal psychological state of "anxiety" may be a useful explanatory concept, but it is not seen as an essential ingredient in behavior. Finally, for trait theory and the humanistic theories, also discussed later, the fundamental motivation for the formation of personality is *positive,* not negative. That is, instead of describing internal anxieties, or even external sources of behavioral conflict, these theories assume that an individual's personality reflects the characteristic ways that the person strives for positive goals and objectives.

COMPONENTS OF PERSONALITY THEORIES

The Greek actor's mask, the persona, was directly observable by the audience, but in modern research the characteristics of an individual's personality must be inferred from behavior that, as we have seen, may be constrained by the situation. Each personality theory described in this chapter has a slightly different view of what this inferred personality system is really like. But whether it concentrates on inner conflict, conscious striving, personality traits, or learned behaviors, each theory includes at least three common elements. Each describes the structure of the personality, relates personality to motivation, and implies what sort of behavior should be regarded as abnormal (Hall & Lindzey, 1957; Mischel, 1981).

Structure

Every personality theory makes claims about the internal structure, or organization, of the person. Some theories provide detailed descriptions of "mental topography"—the interior landscape of competing aspects of the personality. Because of their interest in the internal struggle between conscious and unconscious, psychodynamic theories—especially Freud's—devote the most attention to this interior landscape. Other accounts of personality provide less detailed descriptions but still embody structural principles.

Motivation

Because the concept of personality is a way of explaining the internal forces impelling human behavior, personality theories are theories of motivation. Some of them assume that the individual is consciously aware of the needs, drives, and motives underlying behavior; others incorporate unconscious motivations. Some theories include physiological components; others rely on cognitive sources of motivation. For psychodynamic theories, the ultimate source of motivation is internal; for theories that emphasize conscious goals, the ultimate source is external. But for all, the concept of motivation is crucial.

Abnormal Behavior

In their reliance on structure and their emphasis on motivation, personality theories are comparable to many of the theories considered in earlier chapters. In one important respect, however, they are quite different. By describing the functioning of a normal person, models of personality imply what behavior is *abnormal* and how normal functioning might be restored to a person suffering from a disorder. Many personality theorists have been practicing psychotherapists whose views on normal personality were derived from insights obtained in their work with disturbed people. Moreover, models of personality are frequently tested in clinical practice rather than in laboratory research. Thus, many of the features of classical personality theories are based on the analysis of individual cases rather than on evidence obtained from empirical studies using large numbers of subjects. This connection between theory and application should be kept in mind as we discuss some of the best-known theories of personality.

INTERIM SUMMARY

The earliest descriptions of personality types were provided by the ancient Greeks, who believed that an individual's personality reflected the balance among four bodily "humours." The modern derivative of this idea is the somatotype theory of personality, which holds that particular patterns of personality are associated with distinctive physical features. Research has failed to find a consistent relationship between physique and personality, so type theories are now regarded as simplistic. A prominent alternative view is provided by trait theories of personality, which concentrate on the conscious strivings of the individual as reflected in characteristic traits. Because of the huge number of descriptive terms that can be applied to a person, research on personality traits has depended on the statistical method of factor analysis to identify common dimensions on which personalities can be compared. In contrast to trait and type theories, the psychodynamic theories emphasize unconscious processes and the conflict between the human being's animal heritage and the internalized requirements of culture. Regardless of the position they take on the importance of conscious processes, all personality theories describe the internal structure of the person and the motivational processes that influence behavior. In addition, by describing the functioning of a normal person they imply what behavior is abnormal and how normal functioning should be restored.

FREUDIAN THEORY

Sigmund Freud's collected papers fill some 24 volumes (Strachey, 1953–1974). His influence on modern thought is often considered on a par with that of Charles Darwin. Darwin's theory of natural selection challenged many of humankind's claims to uniqueness, leaving the capacity for reflective thought and rational action as one of the few distinctions between humans and "lower" animals. Freud's theory removed this last claim to intrinsic nobility by suggesting that human behavior is influenced by numerous socially undesirable unconscious forces. But whereas Darwin's theory has withstood one scientific test after another, Freud's ideas have gained only modest empirical support. They have, nonetheless, had a profound influence on psychological theory and practice.

MENTAL TOPOGRAPHY

The Unconscious

What do dreams, slips of the tongue, and the development of morality have in common? According to Freudian theory, all involve the **unconscious,** a region of the mind containing instincts, wishes, and impulses, many of which are socially unacceptable.

Freud compared the mind to an iceberg. The conscious mind, he suggested, is like the small tip of the iceberg visible above the surface of the sea; the unconscious mind is like the vast remainder that lies hidden beneath the surface. This unconscious mind is the repository of biologically based instincts, wishes, and motives.

Two of the fundamental categories of instincts are **Eros** and **Thanatos.** Eros is the collection of life instincts that assure the satisfaction of basic needs for food, water, and sex. Thanatos is the death instinct that underlies all aggressive and destructive behavior. All instincts operate on a tension-reduction principle to maintain psychic equilibrium. Thus, hunger is a state of tension that stimulates a search for food and is reduced by eating; sexual desire is a state of tension that produces behavior designed to achieve sexual gratification; anxiety and anger lead to behavior designed to reduce these forms of tension. Freud conceived of the death instinct in this context—death, after all, is the ultimate state of equilibrium.

The Preconscious and the Conscious

Freud believed that everyday living is a constant struggle among the instincts for control of a limited supply of psychic energy, or *libido.* Both the life and the death instincts give rise to tension, and this tension is reduced by attaching psychic energy to objects that will reduce the tension. This attachment of energy is termed **cathexis.** Thus, a hungry person will form a cathexis for food; a frustrated person will form a cathexis for retaliation against the frustrating agent. Because there is only a limited amount of libido available, the more that is attached, the less there is left to be used for other purposes. An example would be a person so consumed by anger at a co-worker that he or she has virtually no time or energy for anything else.

The struggle for control of psychic energy cannot be contained within the unconscious; some interaction with the environment is necessary. For example, unconscious cathexes of food will not satisfy hunger; only seeking, finding, and eating food will do so. In short, although the unconscious is the source of motivation, it cannot survive on its own. The personality must also have a *conscious* aspect, one that can deal with the external world.

Freudian theory argues that there is a third, **preconscious** aspect of the mind that consists of thoughts, feelings, and emotions that are capable of being called into consciousness. In fact, Freud viewed mental life as being arrayed along a continuum extending from the very deep unconscious to immediate consciousness. Thus, the three categories—conscious, preconscious, and unconscious—should be regarded as arbitrary labels for three nonoverlapping ranges of mental activity.

THE STRUCTURE OF THE PERSONALITY

The limited nature of psychic energy and the need for the individual to interact with the external world together create a personality structure with three components: the **id,** the **ego,** and the **superego.** (See Figure 21-3.)

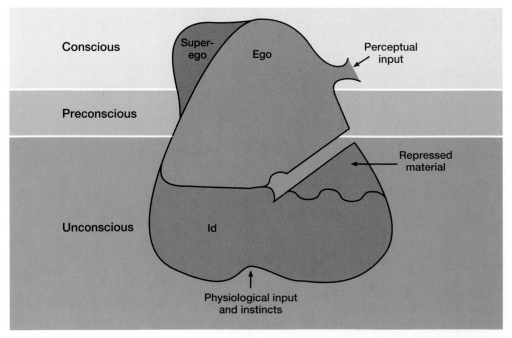

FIGURE 21-3 Elements of mental topography according to Freud's personality theory. There are three major structural elements—the id, the ego, and the superego—as shown by the curved lines. The id is entirely unconscious and contains some material that the ego has repressed (banished from consciousness). The ego is mostly conscious and preconscious (capable of being called into consciousness) but has some direct contact with the unconscious. The superego is a combination of conscious and preconscious.

The Id

At birth, according to Freud, the human personality consists only of the id, the unorganized, uninhibited, and irrational seat of the instincts. As shown in Figure 21-3, the id is entirely unconscious, receiving energy from the biological functioning of the organism. It is the source of all motivation and operates according to the *pleasure principle,* the homeostatic principle that demands immediate reduction of any form of tension. According to Freudian theory, a newborn infant is virtually nothing but id: The infant's immature psychological structure has no contact with external reality. A hungry infant can do little but cry until it is fed.

The Ego

Because the id lacks contact with reality, it cannot reduce tension without external help. To solve this problem, a rudimentary ego, the rational and largely conscious component of the personality, emerges from the id. As shown in Figure 21-3, the ego extends a short distance into the unconscious, reflecting its relationship with the id.

The ego is partly preconscious but mostly conscious. It operates according to the *reality principle,* according to which efforts to reduce tension must conform to the demands of the external environment. In contrast to the pleasure principle, the reality principle demands delay of gratification of impulses until an appropriate object can be found in the environment. The ego finds such objects by using the perceptual input (the senses) available only to it. Freud compared the id and the ego, respectively, to a horse and its rider. The ego must hold in check the superior strength of the horse, although sometimes "a rider, if he is not to be parted from his horse, is obliged to guide it where it wants to go" (Freud, 1952, p. 702). In many instances, however, the ego attempts to prevent or delay the gratification of the id, or to substitute another object for the desired one, usually to protect the psychological or physical well-being of the individual. For example, the ego prevents a hungry person from stealing food in front of a police officer.

Freud pointed out that the ego uses psychic energy it borrows from the id to meet the id's demands. This borrowing is of immense psychological importance because the ego is free to use for its own purposes whatever libido remains after each impulse of the id has been satisfied. And by finding ever more efficient ways to satisfy the id's impulses and manage its own energy, the ego builds what has been described as "a virtual monopoly over the store of psychic energy" (Hall & Lindzey, 1957, p. 42). Making yourself a sandwich is a much more efficient way of satisfying an id wish for food than is crying for 20 minutes until someone notices that you are hungry. All the id "knows" in each case, however, is that the tension from hunger has been reduced.

The Superego

The child's parents are an especially important element of its environment. In attempting to satisfy the desires of the id, the child's ego must negotiate among the rewards and punishments provided by the parents. The rewards are *introjected,* or internalized, as part of the child's *ego ideal.* The punishments become internalized as part of the child's *conscience.* Following resolution of the Oedipal conflict, described in Chapter 18, societal prescriptions for correct behavior become crystallized in the *superego,* which by this time includes both ego ideal and conscience. As shown in Figure 21-3, the superego also includes both conscious and preconscious elements. This internalized moral judge attempts to block id impulses. Moreover, it continually strives for perfection and attempts to substitute moralistic goals (such as never telling lies) for realistic ones (such as telling a white lie to protect someone's feelings).

INTRAPSYCHIC CONFLICT

Given the vastly different goals of the three components of personality, it is not surprising that Freud's theory emphasizes intrapsychic conflict. Suppose that the id has an aggressive impulse. The superego will try to block the expression of that impulse while the ego attempts to find a way of displacing it onto a safe, acceptable target. For example, a person angered by frustration on the job may discharge the tension by shouting at a child upon arriving home. Notice that "acceptable" here may mean "safe" only in the sense that there will be no retaliation.

Repression

When the id's impulses cannot be safely gratified, they must be opposed by the ego. If the ego controls enough psychic energy it can generate anticathexes, or defenses against the id's object choices. When an impulse is too unacceptable or frightening to be dealt with, a resourceful ego can literally force it out of the conscious—and even the preconscious—by locking it into the id with sufficient energy to prevent its recurrence. This *repression* is, however, very costly in terms of libido. A preferable alternative is to permit disguised expressions of the unacceptable impulse. Examples include slips of the tongue, which let out the true feeling but can be dismissed as a mistake, and the images contained in dreams. So the complete answer to the question of what slips of the tongue, dream images, and the development of morality have in common is that all three are part of the personality's attempt to cope with id impulses that would otherwise be unacceptable. If repression is successful, the result is the chasm shown in Figure 21-3, which effectively blocks the repressed wish from bubbling up into the rest of the personality.

Other Defense Mechanisms

Repression is not, however, always completely effective. When it fails, the person feels neurotic anxiety, that is, the fear that instincts will get out of control. Such anxiety can itself be countered with repression, or the person can engage in other **defense mechanisms,** such as those shown in Table 21-2. Although Freud originally described defense mechanisms, including repression, as responses to internal neurotic anxiety, they are now seen as part of the ego's normal response to external threats, provided that they are not used to excess (A. Freud, 1946).

According to Freudian theory, defense mechanisms can be placed into an order, based on the amount of cognitive effort that each requires. For example, denial is simpler than projection, which in turn is simpler than identification. Denial consists of the withdrawal of attention from a threat, a solution requiring no real cognitive work. Projection requires the presence of internal standards (an existing cognitive structure) against which certain thoughts can be judged unacceptable (through a cog-

TABLE 21-2	Psychological Defense Mechanisms
Mechanism	Characteristics
Repression	Blocks threatening ideas, impulses, or feelings from conscious awareness.
Denial	Reinforcing one's strength or importance by denying failings and weaknesses.
Projection	Attributing to other people one's own "bad" characteristics.
Displacement	Impulses or anger unconsciously felt toward one person are directed at another (usually less powerful) person.
Reaction-formation	Transformation of dangerous impulses or feelings into conscious, but socially acceptable opposites, such as turning anger into "affection."
Identification	Overcoming one's own failings by emulating the personal characteristics and moral principles of others.
Sublimation	Channeling of unacceptable unconscious desires into socially approved activities, such as venting interpersonal hostility through sports.

SOURCE: Adapted from Willerman & Cohen (1990).

nitive process of comparison). Identification requires the differentiation of self from others (a still more complex cognitive process) and the ability to construct mental representations of others (Cramer & Gaul, 1988). Finally, the theory assumes that, when confronted by a threat, people have a tendency to regress to simpler forms of defenses.

If it is true that external threats cause people to regress to simpler defenses, then failure should lead to overuse of the simpler defenses. This idea was tested in a study that compared the use of denial, projection, and identification by elementary school children playing a timed marble-rolling game (Cramer & Gaul, 1988). Half of the children were told that they had beaten the average time, whereas half were told that they had not. (Before the end of the experiment all the children were given an opportunity to perform successfully, and care was taken to ensure that no child left the study upset.) Upon learning of their performance, children were given the chance to explain it, and their responses were scored for the presence of each of the three defense mechanisms. The results of the study, shown in Figure 21-4, were consistent with the idea of regression to simpler forms. Children who were told they had failed used more denial and projection but less identification than those who were told they did well. These findings suggest that the children regressed to more primitive defenses in response to the external threat.

Psychosexual Stages

Although Freud's *psychosexual stages* were discussed in detail in Chapter 18, it is worth noting here that each stage represents a fundamental psychic conflict. In the *oral stage* the conflict is between the id's wish for immediate reduction of tension from hunger and the parent's need to extend the time between feedings, ultimately weaning the infant from the breast or bottle. In the *anal stage* the conflict is between the id's wish for immediate expulsion of feces and the social prohibitions against soiling oneself. In the *phallic stage* the conflict is between the id's sexual wish for the parent of the opposite sex and the social and cultural taboos against incest. Even in the *genital stage* the id's desire for immediate reduction of sexual tension comes into conflict with social rules for courtship and consent to sexual activity. Finally, as noted in Chapter 18, fixation at any of the early stages is presumed to lead to problems in the adult personality.

EVALUATION OF THE THEORY

Freud's writings have provided a comprehensive view of human nature and society, a prescription for clinical practice, and a spur for hundreds of empirical studies. Support for the theory, however, has been disappointingly sparse (Smith & Vetter, 1982).

Freud's main contribution to the study of personality is the conception of the

FIGURE 21-4 Use of defense mechanisms in explanations for success and failure. Theoretically, denial is simpler than projection, which is simpler than identification. Thus, if failure causes regression to simpler forms of defense, there should be greater use of denial and projection than of identification among subjects who are having to explain why they failed—which is what the study results confirmed. (Source: Adapted from Cramer & Gaul, 1988.)

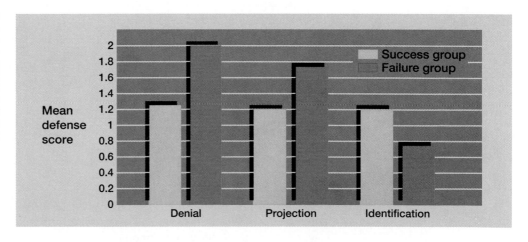

human personality as driven by unconscious forces. The processes embodied in the id, ego, and superego are dynamic and ongoing, and although the ego usually maintains control, lapses—both trivial and serious—occur with some regularity. The assumption that every individual has a dark side struggling to break free of ego control helps us understand examples of humankind's seeming inhumanity—murder, terrorism, torture. And despite lack of convincing experimental support for some key elements of the theory, Freud's view of people as inherently sexual creatures, even in childhood, has become a key feature of psychoanalytic theory. Finally, many aspects of the theory are reflected in popular culture and have served as the point of departure, or as the foil, for other personality theories. The post-Freudian idea of personality is profoundly different from the *persona* as it was conceived of before Freud's writings.

INTERIM SUMMARY

Freud's theory of personality emphasizes the unconscious, the portion of the mind that contains biologically based instincts, wishes, and motives. Among the most basic instincts are life instincts such as hunger and sex (Eros) and the death instinct (Thanatos). All human behavior has its ultimate source in the unconscious, but mental activity includes preconscious and conscious processes as well. According to Freud, the structure of the personality has three components: the id (the seat of the instincts, which operates according to the pleasure principle), the ego (the rational aspect of personality, which operates according to the reality principle), and the superego (the internalized judge of morality). Intrapsychic conflict among these three structural components may lead to repression, in which id impulses are locked out of consciousness, or to the use of other defense mechanisms such as denial, projection, and identification. The influence of Freud's theory on popular culture greatly exceeds the limited empirical support it has received.

OTHER PSYCHODYNAMIC THEORIES

THE ANALYTIC PSYCHOLOGY OF CARL JUNG

The Swiss psychologist Carl G. Jung (1875–1961) was an early admirer of Freud's psychoanalytic theory. In 1910 he became the first president of the International Psychoanalytic Association. But although Freud regarded Jung as his likely successor as leader of the psychoanalytic movement, the two developed irreconcilable differences, and in 1914 Jung resigned from the presidency of the association (Hall & Lindzey, 1957).

The main reason for the rift between Jung and Freud was their disagreement over the importance of sexuality in the functioning of the personality (Hall & Lindzey, 1957). The childhood sexuality embodied in Freud's stages of development, especially the Oedipal conflict arising from desire for the opposite-sex parent, is largely absent from Jung's **analytic psychology.** Moreover, where Freud's theory claims that the adult personality is shaped entirely by the individual's biological and psychological history, Jung's theory claims that the individual's goals for the future contribute significantly to personality development.

The Collective Unconscious

Like Freud, Jung believed in the importance of unconscious processes. Jung's theory includes a *personal unconscious,* a region of the mind that contains experiences that were suppressed, forgotten, ignored, or too weak to enter consciousness in the first

Carl G. Jung, the Swiss psychologist, was the first president of the International Psychoanalytic Association. Jung's psychodynamic theory emphasizes the importance of archetypes in personality dynamics.

place. This is roughly equivalent to what Freud identified as the preconscious. Jung argued, however, that the most powerful element of the personality system is the *collective unconscious,* a psychological vestige of evolution that is the same for all people. The collective unconscious contains remnants of our distant animal ancestry as well as the history of humankind as a separate species. Just as people are born with the capability to perceive three-dimensional space, they are born with predispositions for thinking and feeling that reflect the collective experience of the human species through thousands of years. For example, Jung would argue that people instinctively fear snakes, even on a first encounter, because of the danger they posed in humankind's ancestral past.

According to Jung's theory, the collective unconscious contains a large number of specific structural elements. These elements are known as *archetypes*—universal ideas that provide a way of interpreting aspects of conscious experience. Archetypes arise from generations of human experience: Countless humans have watched the sun rise in the morning, warm the land during the day, and set in the evening; this produces an archetype of the sun-god, a powerful and benevolent deity that should be worshiped. Other archetypes also reflect constants in human experience—birth, death, the hero, the child. Forty of the most prominent archetypes have been collected in the Archetypal Symbol Inventory, used to test the effects of archetypes on memory and recall (Rosen, Smith, Huston, & Gonzales, 1991).

Five archetypes have become so highly developed that they are regarded by the theory as separate systems within the personality. The first of these is the *persona,* the archetype derived from the fact that human beings are social creatures. (Although this use of the word *persona* is specific to Jung's personality theory, it incorporates the original use of the word to refer to a mask.) The second and third are the *anima* and *animus,* archetypes that embody the similarities and differences between females and males. The fourth archetype is the *shadow,* the repository of the animal instincts acquired in the course of evolution. The aggressive and socially disapproved contents of this archetype correspond roughly to the contents of the id in Freudian theory. Finally, there is the *self,* the center of the personality. The self holds the rest of the personality together, providing unity, stability, and the balance between conscious and unconscious. This striving for wholeness can be seen in humankind's search for religious experiences or perfect artistic forms such as the *mandala* symbol, the "magic circle" shown in Figure 21-5, which is prevalent in art, architecture, and even city planning (Jung, 1964).

FIGURE 21-5 Three illustrations of the *mandala* symbol that represents unity and wholeness in Jung's personality theory. The Tibetan sand painting, the Colosseum, and the sixteenth-century map of Paris all show this important circular arrangement. The fact that circular symbols are so aesthetically satisfying to humans is taken as evidence for the psychological unity that they represent.

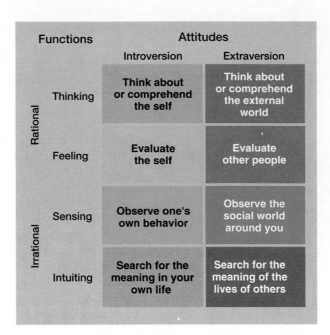

Functions		Attitudes	
		Introversion	Extraversion
Rational	Thinking	**Think about or comprehend the self**	**Think about or comprehend the external world**
Rational	Feeling	**Evaluate the self**	**Evaluate other people**
Irrational	Sensing	**Observe one's own behavior**	**Observe the social world around you**
Irrational	Intuiting	**Search for the meaning in your own life**	**Search for the meaning of the lives of others**

FIGURE 21-6 The attitudes and functions as outlined in Jung's personality theory. There are two attitudes (introversion–extraversion) and two sets of opposing functions. The rational functions are thinking and feeling; the irrational (meaning only "not deliberative") are sensing and intuiting. The theory argues that people will have a single dominant function, and that the opposite member of that function pair will be the person's inferior function, with the other two functions falling somewhere in between.

Attitudes and Functions

According to Jung's theory, the functioning personality typically involves a balance between opposing forces. This is especially true in the case of attitudes and functions. (See Figure 21-6.) A person may take either of two major attitudes toward life—*introversion* or *extraversion*. An introverted individual is oriented toward the inner, subjective world built around the ego, whereas an extraverted individual is oriented toward the external world, especially other people.

Cross-cutting these two fundamental attitudes are the functions of thinking, feeling, sensing, and intuiting. These functions are actually two sets of opposing pairs: Thinking and feeling are opposing rational functions, whereas sensing and intuiting are opposing irrational functions. (For Jung, the term *irrational* simply means "not deliberative" and does not carry the negative connotations attached to it in Freud's theory.) Thus, thinking is the rational function through which we attempt intellectually to understand ourselves and the world around us, and feeling is the rational function that allows us emotionally to evaluate our experiences. Through thinking we answer the question, "What is it?" Through feeling we answer the question, "Do I like it?" Sensing is the irrational process of perceiving, through which information is obtained for conscious awareness, and intuiting is the irrational function—often influenced by unconscious processes—that enables us to apprehend, or discover the meaning behind sensory information. According to Jung, the attitudes are more important than the functions in determining the nature of the adult personality. Thus, any person is first characterized either as introverted or as extraverted. Only after this does one turn to the functions. One of the four functions will then be *dominant* in the person's behavior; the opposite member of that pair will be the least developed, or *inferior* function. The two members of the other pair of functions will be moderately developed. So, for example, an extraverted person in whom the dominant function happened to be thinking would be least well developed in feeling, with sensing and intuiting both being moderately well developed.

Evaluation of the Theory

By far the most controversial aspect of Jung's theory is the claim that behavior is driven by forces found in a collective unconscious inherited from preceding generations. Critics have argued that it is implausible to believe that knowledge and personality characteristics can be transmitted genetically. Moreover, archetypes are immune to scientific scrutiny, and in any case the patterns of action ascribed to archetypes can be explained without reference to any inherited characteristics (Smith & Vetter, 1982). The last of these three criticisms remains viable, but the first two have become less persuasive with advances in the science of genetics. It is clear that elements of intelligence are transmitted genetically and that predispositions for some emotional disorders are inherited. It would be a mistake, therefore, to rule out the possibility of genetic transmission of the psychological predispositions described by Jung's theory.

The most widely accepted element of Jung's theory is the distinction between introversion and extraversion. This distinction provided the theoretical basis for Eysenck's factor-analytic view of personality, mentioned earlier. The distinction has also been the basis for a wide variety of research studies with both normal individuals and clinical populations (Eysenck & Eysenck, 1975). This research has shown that introversion–extraversion is indeed a key dimension of human personality.

INTERPERSONAL DYNAMIC THEORIES

The motivating forces in Freud's personality theory are almost entirely unconscious and biological in origin. In Jung's theory, some motivation arises from the conscious strivings of the self, although unconscious processes still play a major role. But there are other theories of personality structure that build on Freud's psychodynamic view while giving substantially greater weight to interpersonal sources of motivation. We shall describe two such theories—Adler's and Sullivan's—here.

Adler's Theory

Several human organs—the kidneys, lungs, and eyes, for example—occur in pairs. When one member of the pair is defective, the other increases its functioning to compensate. Alfred Adler, a contemporary of Freud, brought this notion of defect and compensation into the psychological realm. He noted that human infants are biologically and psychologically frail. Unconsciously recognizing their inadequacies, they develop feelings of inferiority, and those feelings have become the basis for later personality development (Ansbacher & Ansbacher, 1956).

Feelings of inferiority can have many sources, including small physical size, comparisons to older siblings, or lack of social skills relative to adults. Whatever the source, people feel a need to compensate by *striving for superiority* over their past. This striving differs from the motivating forces in Freudian theory in two respects. First, the sources of inferiority are social rather than biological, hence, Adler viewed defense mechanisms as reactions to external threats rather than to internally generated anxiety. Second, the effort to compensate is conscious rather than unconscious. This purposive effort is central to Adler's view of the self.

Whereas the person described by Freud is a creature of his or her past, the person described by Adler is his or her own creation. Adler believed that a person's abilities (provided by heredity) and impressions (provided by experience) are "the bricks which he uses in his own 'creative' way in building up his attitude toward life" (1935, p. 5). This attitude toward life, not heredity or sensory experience, defines the person's place in the world and relationships with other people. One person may strive for superiority through athletic accomplishment, another through intellect, a third through political power.

Although many of Adler's ideas are not strongly supported by empirical evidence, his view of the self as the organizing force in the personality is reflected in much current research (such as Carver & Scheier, 1981).

Sullivan's Theory

Although Harry Stack Sullivan's work was directed primarily at clinical practice, it does have implications for the structure of personality. Sullivan maintained that personality cannot be separated from interpersonal behavior, defining personality as

According to Alfred Adler's personality theory, in our effort to compensate for unconscious feelings of inferiority developed in childhood, we use our abilities and impressions to "create" our attitudes toward life.

577

Harry Stack Sullivan, whose personality theory concentrated on the interpersonal setting for the development of both normal and abnormal behavior.

"the relatively enduring pattern of recurrent interpersonal situations which characterize a human life" (Sullivan, 1953, p. 111). In terms of the person-by-situation interaction described earlier, this definition places Sullivan's theory at the extreme situationism end of the continuum. Sullivan acknowledged biological influences on the person, but asserted that social interaction is what makes people distinctively human.

In Sullivan's theory, the smallest unit of behavior that can be studied is a *dynamism*—a recurring "energy transformation," or pattern of interpersonal behavior. For example, a person who routinely behaves in an underhanded manner toward others would be showing a dynamism of deceit. Dynamisms are presumed to satisfy the individual's needs. The primary dynamism, the *self-system,* arises out of the anxiety created by the individual's interactions with others. Although the self-system develops to shield the person from anxiety, its relative independence can become a disadvantage—if, for example, it disregards feedback and criticism that, if adopted, would actually improve the person's functioning. By serving its protective function too well, the self-system can easily become so isolated from the rest of the personality that the individual is unable to see his or her behavior objectively.

From the standpoint of internal personality dynamics, Sullivan's theory emphasizes conscious processes. Specifically, the theory identifies three cognitive modes for understanding experience. *Prototaxic* experiences are momentary sensations. This is "raw" experience, involving no reflective thought, and is comparable to the "stream of consciousness" described by William James. *Parataxic* thinking involves a primitive form of conscious reflection on experiences, but leads to the erroneous conclusion that events that occur close together in time are causally related. Such thinking is illustrated by superstitious beliefs. *Syntaxic* thinking is the most sophisticated cognitive mode, using "consensually validated symbols," such as words and numbers with standard meanings, to describe and organize experiences. Thus, in contrast to Freud's theory, which emphasizes the unconscious forces that shape personality, Sullivan's theory endows conscious cognitive processes with the capability of shaping personality.

The most important contribution of Sullivan's theory is its insistence that personality structure is interpersonal. For example, Sullivan's claim that successful treatment of emotional disturbances requires a therapeutic social environment, not just individual therapy, led to the creation of "therapeutic communities" within hospitals. These, in turn, provided a model for programs such as the Synanon drug treatment program and Alcoholics Anonymous (Smith & Vetter, 1982).

Sullivan's insistence on the importance of interpersonal interaction for personality development and the treatment of emotional disturbance provides the theoretical rationale for "therapeutic communities" that treat various forms of substance abuse in a controlled and supportive social environment.

In Jung's analytic psychology, the individual's goals contribute to personality development. The most controversial aspect of Jung's theory is the concept of a collective unconscious containing archetypes, or universal forms of thought, inherited from past generations. The most important archetypes are the persona, anima, animus, shadow, and self. The self serves to organize the personality and includes the attitudes of introversion or extraversion and the functions of thinking, feeling, sensing, and intuiting. Other theories of personality structure, such as those of Adler and Sullivan, emphasize the importance of interpersonal sources of motivation. Adler believed that children develop feelings of inferiority and that the need to compensate causes them to strive for superiority. The sources of the feeling of inferiority are social rather than biological, and the effort at compensation is purposive and conscious. Sullivan argued that the individual's personality cannot be separated from his or her behavior in interpersonal settings, and that the self-system arises out of the anxiety created by interactions with others. Successful treatment of emotional disturbance therefore requires a therapeutic environment, not just individual therapy.

LEARNING THEORIES

With the exception of Sullivan's theory, psychodynamic approaches view personality as the result of processes—conscious or unconscious—that originate within the individual. Other psychologists have drawn on research in learning theory (see Chapter 12) to develop theories that focus on the role of external factors—the environment—in shaping personality. We shall describe two such theories in this section.

STIMULUS–RESPONSE LEARNING THEORY

The first learning theory of personality was formulated by John Dollard and Neal Miller, both of whom had received training in psychoanalysis. Impressed with the ideas underlying psychoanalysis but dissatisfied with its complexity and vagueness, Dollard and Miller attempted to translate some of Freud's principles into the language of learning theory. They asserted that there are four major factors underlying the learning of personality characteristics: drive, cue, response, and reinforcement (Dollard & Miller, 1950). Notice that the terms, summarized in Table 21-3, are described in words that apply equally well to humans or to animals.

A *drive* is any stimulus that is strong enough to evoke behavior. Some drives, such as hunger and thirst, are internal, and thus correspond to what recent learning theory

TABLE 21-3 Elements of the S–R Personality Theory

Element	Description
Drive	Any stimulus sufficiently strong to impel the individual into activity. Primary drives are usually physiological in nature, secondary drives are learned.
Cue	Features of the stimulus environment that direct the energy inherent in a drive, thus determining the nature of the response.
Response	The actual behavior of the organism. Responses initially follow an innate hierarchy, but the hierarchy changes through learning.
Reward	Stimulus events that act to strengthen the connection between a given response and the cue that gave rise to that response.

would describe as a *need.* Others, however, are external, such as loud noises, physical threats, or a potential sexual partner. Not all stimuli are drives, however. Some are merely *cues* indicating the appropriate response to a drive stimulus (in the language we used in Chapter 12, cues would be *discriminative stimuli*). Cues may be as simple as a light that signals the availability of a reward, or as complex as the social setting that signals what sort of conversation is (or is not) appropriate at a formal dinner party. When a cue occurs in the presence of a relevant drive, the result will be a *response.* In most settings some responses will be more likely than others, and the order of preference for responses is known as the individual's *initial response hierarchy.* If the response reduces the drive, the individual will receive *reinforcement.* Drive reduction is an essential feature of reinforcement in this model, and in this respect it is similar to the idea of tension reduction found in many psychodynamic theories.

The Role of Conflict

From the psychodynamic viewpoint, personality is characterized by conflict, such as the conflict between the id and the ego or superego. Dollard and Miller also consider conflict to be very important, but they propose a model, influenced by Lewin (1935), that depends less on inference and is more easily tested. The model begins by recognizing that wishes, goals, or features of the environment can be either positive or negative; that is, some stimuli (goals) are approached whereas others are avoided. Next, it assumes that the closer one is to the object, the greater the tendency either to approach it (if it is positive) or avoid it (if it is negative). This assumption is reflected in the *goal gradients* shown in Figure 21-7, with the slope of the avoidance gradient rising more quickly than the slope of the approach gradient. Finally, the overall strength of both the goals and the gradients depends on the strength of the underlying drive, itself induced by a different stimulus.

   The result of these assumptions is a model that includes three kinds of conflict. If a person is faced with a choice between two equally attractive, but mutually exclusive, alternatives, there is an *approach–approach conflict.* This is not a real conflict, however, because a positive outcome will be achieved regardless of which alternative is chosen. If the person is faced with a choice between two equally unattractive alternatives, the result will be an *avoidance–avoidance conflict,* which will lead to vacillation. As the person approaches one of the unattractive choices, the tendency to avoid it will become stronger, causing the person to backtrack and approach the other negative choice, which will also stimulate an avoidance reaction. Imagine a novice skier whose more experienced friends urge trying an advanced run. In the lodge, away from the slopes, the person most wants to avoid being called a

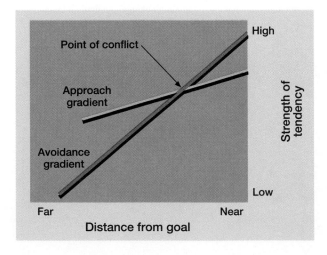

FIGURE 21-7 An approach–avoidance conflict as characterized by Dollard & Miller's stimulus–response theory of personality organization. The different slopes of the approach and avoidance gradients reflect the fact that the positive qualities of a goal are most noticeable from a far psychological distance, whereas the negative qualities of the same goal are most noticeable from a close psychological distance.

coward, so agrees to try; as the person nears the chair lift, however, the prospect of actually beginning the long ride to the top becomes more threatening than the thought of "wimping out."

The third sort of conflict involves goals that have both positive and negative features. This is an *approach–avoidance conflict,* shown graphically in Figure 21-7. For example, should a politician answer a question with the unvarnished truth, thereby gaining the esteem of his or her constituents (approach) but alienating a special-interest group that has contributed to past campaigns (avoidance)? As the figure shows, at a great distance from the goal, the approach gradient exceeds the avoidance gradient. Closer to the goal, the avoidance gradient is the more powerful. Thus, when considering this question from a distance, the politician, responding to the height of the approach gradient, might assert that he or she would respond candidly, but upon nearing the podium, responding to the steeply rising avoidance gradient, might decide not to.

Features of the stimulus–response theory have been extensively tested in both humans and animals (Miller, 1959). For example, researchers have investigated the approach–avoidance conflict in animals by placing small harnesses on laboratory rats and measuring the strength of their pull on the harness. Animals placed near an aversive goal pull harder to get away from it than when they are placed far from it. Conversely, animals placed near an attractive goal pull harder to reach it than when they are placed far from it. Comparisons of the strength of the pulls indicates that avoidance gradients are more steeply sloped than approach gradients. When applied to humans, the learning theory model places *outside* the individual many of the behavioral conflicts that other personality models would attribute to internal psychodynamics. Thus, where Freudian theory, for example, considers the source of human motivation to be unconscious processes, the learning theory model considers it to be the result of external stimuli. Like Sullivan's theory, Dollard and Miller's theory is on the situationism end of the person–situation continuum.

SOCIAL LEARNING THEORY

Despite the success of Dollard and Miller's model, some critics argue that it cannot do justice to the complex learning involved in the development of the human personality. One such critic is Albert Bandura, whose **social learning theory** emphasizes the role of observational learning in explaining behavior.

Modeling

A central feature of the social learning approach is the claim that people can learn indirectly, by observing the behavior of others, as well as through direct reinforcement of their own actions. In Bandura's theory (1977) this observational learning process is called **modeling** and consists of four related components. First, for modeling to occur, the observer must be attending to the relevant stimulus. This is not as simple as it sounds, because any stimulus situation includes interference. In the language of Chapter 12, every stimulus situation includes irrelevant information as well as the relevant cues on which the model's behavior is contingent. Second, because the observer typically does not perform the modeled behavior immediately, that behavior must be retained in memory. Third, the observer must be able to reproduce the modeled behavior successfully. As the skills and proficiency required increase, this becomes increasingly difficult to do. For instance, an avid fan may watch professional golfers hit dozens of straight, long shots off the tee but still be unable to reproduce their behavior. Finally, even though the observer may have acquired the skill to repeat the model's actions, an actual performance of the modeled behavior will not occur unless the reinforcement conditions are favorable. Again, in the terms of Chapter 12, the performance will not occur unless discriminative stimuli in the environment signal that reinforcement will follow performance of the behavior.

Engraving of offenders being punished by public humilation in the stocks. Observers watching this spectacle might learn, through vicarious reinforcement, to behave so as to avoid a comparable fate.

Reinforcement

In Dollard and Miller's personality theory, reinforcement is regarded as a direct influence on the behavior that precedes it. As we saw in Chapter 12, however, reinforcement can play an informational as well as a motivational role. That is, reinforcement identifies contingencies between responses and subsequent rewards. Social learning theory emphasizes the informational role of reinforcement.

The theory describes three kinds of reinforcement. The first, *external reinforcement,* is the overt consequence, positive or negative, that follows the performance of a behavior; it is the equivalent of what is traditionally meant by reinforcement. The second kind is the *vicarious reinforcement* an observer receives by watching the reward or punishment received by the model. Businesses that give merit awards to employees are providing direct rewards to the recipients and vicarious rewards to other employees; the legal system routinely metes out sentences to offenders that serve as vicarious punishment—and therefore warnings—for would-be offenders. Finally, in a break with other learning approaches, Bandura argues that *self-reinforcement* plays an important role in maintaining behavior. A person who has met a self-defined standard of performance can administer self-reinforcement by taking the rest of the day off, going shopping, or enjoying a feeling of accomplishment.

Triadic Reciprocal Interaction

Bandura's theory emphasizes the role of the *self-system,* which regulates behavior not as an independent agent but as a collection of largely cognitive processes. In other words, the self-system is not a specific psychological entity, as suggested by Jung and Sullivan. Rather than viewing behavior as directed wholly from inside or outside the self, Bandura (1978) argues that behavior results from what he terms *triadic reciprocal interaction,* in which person variables, environmental variables, and the individual's own behavior in a given setting all influence one another. An example of this interaction is provided by the effects of televised violence. The effects of a particular violent television show will depend on the viewer's initial preferences (a person variable), the content of the show (an environmental variable), and the nature of the viewing behavior (the behavioral variable). The viewer's initial preferences and the amount of violence portrayed by the program will matter only if the viewer is actually paying attention. Not only does social learning theory describe such situations, it also suggests that some of the cross-situational consistencies in behavior that psychodynamic approaches would attribute to internal, even biological, processes, are in fact response tendencies built up gradually during prior experience. Thus, social learning theory, like Dollard and Miller's theory, takes a situationist view of personality development and structure.

INTERIM SUMMARY

Dollard and Miller's stimulus–response theory of personality holds that four major factors—drive, cue, response, and reinforcement—underlie the learning of personality characteristics. This simplified view of personality is most effective in accounting for behavior in situations characterized as approach–avoidance conflicts, which involve goals that have both positive and negative features. Largely because its propositions are readily testable, this theory has been supported by research results. It does not, however, provide a detailed explanation of the learning processes involved in the development of the personality. Bandura's social learning theory attempts to do this. In it, not only direct reinforcement but also modeling, vicarious reinforcement, and self-reinforcement contribute significantly to the development of personality. Behavior results from triadic reciprocal interaction, or the mutual influences of person variables, environmental variables, and the individual's behavior in a particular setting.

THEORIES FOCUSING ON THE INDIVIDUAL

The descriptions of personality structure considered so far all seek to describe commonalities among people. For example, Freudian theory assumes that all people have ids, egos, and superegos; moreover, the conflict among these three aspects of personality is roughly comparable from one person to another. Similarly, the learning theory approaches to personality assume that the external stimuli that are reinforcing, or punishing, to one person will be reinforcing, or punishing, to others. Both kinds of theory suggest how individual differences might develop, but each focuses most of its attention on processes presumed to be comparable from one person to another. In short, none takes the individual person as the unit of analysis. In this section we describe two theories that ask, "In what ways are individual personalities *unique?*" instead of, "What processes are common to all?"

ALLPORT'S PERSONALITY THEORY

Emphasis on Individual Traits

Gordon Allport (1897–1967) claimed that there is greater similarity in psychological functioning among all the animals in any nonhuman species than there is between any two human beings (Allport, 1937). What makes each human being unique is his or her set of individual personality traits. In Allport's view, a personality *trait* is a "focalized neuropsychic system" that actually exists in the brain. It is unique to the individual and has "the capacity to initiate and guide consistent forms of adaptive and expressive behavior" (Allport, 1937, p. 295). This is an even bolder claim than Jung's argument for a genetically transmitted collective unconscious. Recall from Chapter 13 that—at least as of this writing—researchers have not yet discovered particular points in the brain that can be associated with something as simple as a specific memory trace. But by almost any conception of personality, a personality trait would have to be much more complex than a single memory. It may be that future neuropsychological research will identify groups of brain cells that participate in what is best regarded as a personality trait. But at this point, Allport's claim has to be regarded as nothing more than an interesting speculation.

Traits themselves can occur at varying levels of intensity. There are *cardinal traits* that are so influential that they are reflected in all of the person's activities. Not everyone has cardinal traits, but those who do may become famous for them; the

Mother Theresa visiting the survivors of the Bhopal disaster in India. Her well-known altruism is an excellent example of a cardinal trait—a trait so influential that it characterizes all of the person's behavior.

altruism of Albert Schweitzer and Mother Theresa is an example of such a trait. Less influential are the *central traits,* the few highly characteristic tendencies that are easily inferred from a person's behavior. People can be described in terms of fewer than a dozen central traits (many of which would find their way into the factor analyses of personality descriptions discussed earlier). Finally, there are *secondary traits* that come into play in only a few settings and are more difficult to infer.

Functional Autonomy

In Allport's view, personality traits provide much of the motivation for human behavior. This idea is quite different in one fundamental way from the notion of motivation contained in psychodynamic theories. It treats motivation as contemporaneous with behavior. That is, there is no Jungian collective unconscious of racial memories, no Freudian idea that adult behavior reflects childhood conflicts. Allport's theory argues that adult motivation reflects the current desires and objectives of the adult, not the biological needs or developmental conflicts of the child. Moreover, any individual behavior may gain *functional autonomy*—it may become an end in itself, continuing as part of the individual's pattern of action long after the initial impetus is gone. A college student taught to write clearly in a series of writing classes may come to value clarity of expression as an end in itself, regardless of the particular topic being described.

The principle of functional autonomy embodies Allport's view that normal adult behavior shows two discontinuities that have been overlooked by other personality theorists (Hall & Lindzey, 1957). The first is the discontinuity between the actions of the adult and the emotions and motivations of childhood. The second is the discontinuity between the everyday behavior of normal individuals and that of people with emotional disorders; in Allport's view, normal and abnormal differ in kind, not in degree. Thus, whereas psychodynamic theories would lead to therapies based on discovering and resolving conflicts presumed to have originated in childhood, Allport's approach would argue that the normal adult personality must be understood for what it is, rather than as a possible model against which abnormal behavior can be understood.

Maslow's Humanistic Theory

Psychologists who take a humanistic approach, such as Henry Murray, Carl Rogers, and Abraham Maslow (1908–1970), argue that the two major forces that have dominated psychological explanations in the past—behaviorism and Freudian theory—provide inadequate accounts of human behavior. According to Maslow, neither force does justice to the purposive quality of human behavior. Although there are some similarities in psychological functioning between humans and other animals, many motives—such as the need for freedom, for dignity, and to realize one's potential—are uniquely human. Humanists in general, and Maslow in particular, maintain that they have developed a new theoretical perspective—a *third force*—that better accounts for human behavior motives than do the mechanistic explanations of behaviorism or the biological determinism of Freudian theory.

This is not to say that Maslow and other humanists ignore biological motivation entirely. Recall from Chapter 9 that Maslow's theory of self-actualization (1954) takes biological needs into account. Moreover, Maslow's hierarchy of needs is based on the principle that higher order (psychological) needs will not be addressed until the more fundamental biological needs have been satisfied. Specifically, recall that deficiency needs are at the lowest level of the hierarchy and include the physiological needs for food and water. Safety needs, belongingness needs, and esteem needs can be satisfied only after the physiological needs are met.

Like Allport, Maslow concentrated on the psychological characteristics of the healthy personality. The idea behind his theory is to identify the personal characteristics and situations that contribute to the everyday behavior of the vast majority of people who lead normal lives. Maslow's theory begins with the assumption that human nature is fundamentally good and that problems in living arise because of unhealthy influences from the environment (Hall & Lindzey, 1957). Note that this assumption directly contradicts Freud's view that the original element of the personality is the id—a repository for socially undesirable wishes for sex or aggression.

During the person's development, environmental obstacles and the requirement to satisfy basic needs impede the person's progress toward self-actualization (of one's inherently good nature). Maslow noted, however, that there are especially vivid and powerful "peak experiences" (extreme ecstasy, rapture, or bliss) that enable people to experience at least momentary self-actualization. Peak experiences result in a temporary loss of defensiveness and anxiety, temporal or spatial disorientation, and momentary loss of contact with reality; these conditions can be seen in the mystic experiences associated with some religions. Not everyone will have a peak experience in such situations. But for many people, peak experiences provide a window onto the possibilities and a positive goal for which the person can strive. In terms we have used before, much of Maslow's theory deals with person variables—safety, belongingness, and esteem needs. The psychological insight achieved during a peak experience, however, is an example of the person-by-situation interaction.

Abraham Maslow, whose humanistic theory of personality concentrates on the satisfaction of needs. Once basic needs have been satisfied, the individual can pursue self-actualization.

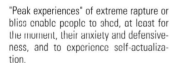

"Peak experiences" of extreme rapture or bliss enable people to shed, at least for the moment, their anxiety and defensiveness, and to experience self-actualization.

INTERIM SUMMARY

Allport's trait theory emphasizes the uniqueness of the individual, although it recognizes that there are broadly recurring patterns of behavior. According to the theory, personality traits are of three general kinds: cardinal, or very influential characteristics; central, or highly characteristic tendencies easily inferred from the person's behavior; and secondary. Because motivation is contemporaneous (not dependent on childhood events), patterns of adult behavior may become functionally autonomous, and will be maintained long after their original impetus has disappeared. Maslow's humanistic theory of personality describes a hierarchy of needs that is common to all people but emphasizes the importance of peak experiences in producing a self-actualized and thoroughly unique individual.

SUMMARY

1. A great deal of human behavior is regarded as the product of *person-by-situation interactions.* The challenge for personality theory is to discover those relatively enduring traits or dispositions that increase the *cross-situational consistency* of action. One recent development in this area is the *template-matching* view, which holds that the correlation between personality variables and behavior will be substantial only when the individual's traits match the requirements of the situation.

2. The ancient Greeks first suggested that different personality types would be found among people with different physical characteristics, and the modern version of this idea is the *somatotype* theory. This theory classified people into three physical types—ectomorphs, endomorphs, and mesomorphs—and claimed that each type had a particular set of personality traits.

3. Trait theories of personality distinguish *traits* (stable and enduring structures that guide a person's adaptation to the environment) from *states* (temporary moods) or *activities.* Trait theories attempt to describe an individual's personality as a unique collection of traits.

4. Because of the large number of words available in the language to describe personality, researchers interested in the trait approach have used the statistical technique of *factor analysis,* along with studies of natural language, to identify the most important and inclusive personality traits. Among these traits, a dimension of *introversion–extraversion* has proved to be important.

5. Every major personality theory makes three important claims. First, the personal characteristics that comprise the personality are organized into a coherent internal structure. Second, personality structure is a source of motivation for the individual's behavior. And third, by specifying the dimensions of a normal personality, theories can distinguish normal from abnormal behavior.

6. Freud's psychodynamic view of personality divides the mental topography into three sections—the *unconscious, preconscious,* and *conscious.* The unconscious is a vast repository of biologically based instincts (such as *Eros* and *Thanatos*), wishes, and motives.

7. The instincts are represented in the *id,* a wholly unconscious part of the personality that operates according to the *pleasure principle.* The *ego,* which is the person's link to the external world, operates according to a *reality principle* and is largely conscious, although it also extends through the preconscious into the unconscious. The *superego* is primarily conscious, and attempts to lead the ego to substitute moral goals for rational ones.

8. According to Freudian theory, intrapsychic conflict among ego, id, and superego can lead to *displacement* of

undesirable wishes onto desirable objectives, or outright *repression* of the disapproved wishes. People may use a variety of *defense mechanisms* to protect themselves from unpleasant realizations.

9. Compared to Freud's theory, Jung's *analytic psychology* emphasized the importance of future goals and minimized the importance of sexual conflict. According to Jung, the personality contains a *collective unconscious* that is the psychological vestige of evolution. It consists of five *archetypes*, representing the public personality, the masculine and feminine, the animal instincts, and the self.

10. Other psychodynamic personality theories have been developed by Adler, who emphasized the person as creator of his or her own destiny, and Sullivan, who stressed that the personality arises out of social interaction.

11. In addition to the psychodynamic theories, there are learning theories of personality, such as Dollard and Miller's translation of psychodynamic principles into the more readily measurable behaviors familiar from learning theory. Their analysis of the *approach–avoidance conflict* has been particularly influential.

12. The social learning approach to personality structure emphasizes the role of reinforcement, and especially the power of *modeling* to shape the adult personality.

13. The major *personality trait* theory, proposed by Allport, assumes that personality traits have a biological basis in the brain, and that they initiate and guide both adaptive and expressive behavior. Some of these behaviors then become ends in themselves, *functionally autonomous* from the initial impetus behind them.

14. The *humanistic* personality theories concentrate on the *needs* of the individual. These theories assume that once basic biological and shelter needs have been satisfied, the healthy person will pursue *self-actualization*, the development of an authentic and nondefensive self.

FOCUS QUESTIONS

1. Attack or defend the following assertion: Human behavior is entirely determined by the situation.

2. Everyday language provides a huge number of words that can be use to describe personality characteristics. Discuss the methods researchers use to reduce this vast amount to a manageable number of personality traits.

3. What are the three components of virtually all personality theories? How does each component reflect the definition of personality?

4. Describe the mental topography as specified in Freud's personality theory.

5. According to Freudian theory, how does the individual cope with anxiety?

6. In Jung's personality theory, what are the archetypes? How do the attitudes and functions combine into behavior?

7. What is the major difference between Adler's theory and Sullivan's theory?

8. Compare and contrast the two major learning theories of personality. In each theory, what is the central mechanism for learning?

9. Describe Allport's principle of functional autonomy. Where might this principle fit into Maslow's hierarchy of needs?

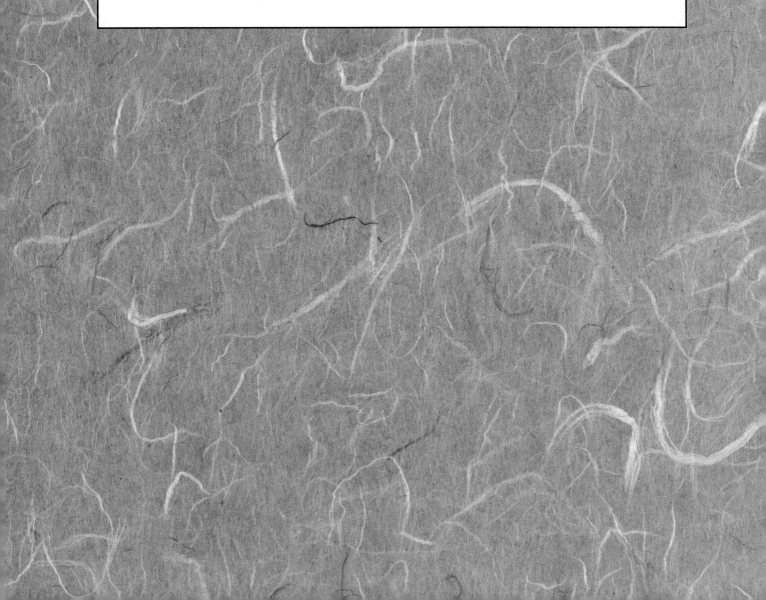

CHAPTER 22

INDIVIDUAL DIFFERENCES

The science of psychology is founded on the assumption that observation and measurement can identify regularities over time in human behavior. For example, consider how the concept of personality was defined in Chapter 21. Personality is the stable set of characteristics that account for both variations in the way different individuals respond to a common situation, and commonalities in the way one person behaves in different situations after biological pressures and situational demands have been ruled out.

In principle, this definition asserts that a person's behavior in any situation will be determined by at least three separate factors—biological pressures, situational demands, and person variables. To see how all of these are involved, let us expand a bit on the example from Chapter 9 of a hungry person at a formal dinner party by examining the person's conversation with others during the party. Assuming that the party begins fashionably late, the biological pressures involved are obvious: the guests have lowered blood sugar levels, their stomachs are contracting, and they are experiencing the psychological state we call hunger. Despite being hungry, they will wait until everyone at the table has been served, and until the host or hostess has lifted a fork, the accepted signal that diners may begin to eat. This shows the influence of the situation.

So far, the guests have all behaved in pretty much the same way. But now, during dinner, they will talk to each other while eating. Some will converse in reserved tones, others will speak as if they were on stage. Some will take a real interest in what their dinner partners have to say, others will make only minimal attempts at polite conversation. Some will talk very little about themselves, others will do nothing but boast. These are the kinds of differences between people that provide a clue to personality. Now suppose we follow one of the loud, disinterested, and boastful diners to the office the next day, where we see the same kind of behavior repeated. We have now supplemented our observation of individual differences in a common situation (the dinner party) with the discovery of commonalities in behavior from that situation to another (the office). As a result, we would claim that we had discovered at least one person's enduring personality characteristics. In other words, we would claim that we had discovered how one person's behavior was *consistently different* from the behavior of others.

Although our claim is intuitively plausible, our informal observations would not meet scientific standards of measurement. This chapter describes how psychologists assess individual differences in both personality and intellectual functioning in ways that do satisfy scientific standards. Although many of the specific procedures are presented in greater detail in the appendix on research methods and statistics at the end of this book, some introduction is needed here as a foundation for the discussion of personality assessment and intelligence testing.

REGULARITY AND VARIATION

From the origin of psychology as a separate discipline until the present day, measurement issues have been at the center of theoretical controversies. For example, recall from Chapter 2 the turn-of-the-century debate between structuralism (which attempted to identify the irreducible elements of consciousness) and functionalism (which attempted to discover what evolutionary purposes might be served by various psychological capacities). Structuralists insisted that subjects could not provide useful data until they had been trained, whereas functionalists were more interested in the fact that subjects' response times changed (through learning) during training. This example makes three critical points.

First, the disagreement could not have arisen at all without meticulous measurement of the subjects' performance. To say that a subject's responses show the effects of training requires an accurate measure of performance both before and after training. There must be a way to measure regularities in behavior with precision.

Second, there must be some statistical procedure—accepted by both sides in a disagreement—for determining when a real change has occurred. In short, when posttraining performance is compared to pretraining performance there must be some accepted method for determining how much of a difference is enough to assert that a real change has taken place. Any time a psychological measurement is taken more than once, there will be some variation between the two values obtained.

Such variation with repeated observations is not unique to psychology. The next time you drive on an interstate highway made of concrete, notice the transverse joints every hundred feet or so. These are expansion joints, places where two concrete slabs are separated by a rubberized material. Expansion joints are needed because the concrete slab shrinks a bit during the cold winter and expands a bit during the hot summer. The point is that if the question "How long is this concrete slab?" were to be answered with precision, the answer would vary from one time to another, depending on whether the measurement were taken in winter or summer. This variation occurs even though the length of the concrete slab can be measured directly, using universally accepted units of length. Although observable behaviors can also be measured directly, many important psychological states must be inferred from these behavioral measurements. Moreover, there can be fundamental disagreements among psychologists about what techniques, and what units, are appropriate for measuring psychological states. Consequently, the question "How much variation is enough?" may have more than one answer.

Third, the example illustrates that what one researcher considers a nuisance, another may consider the variable of primary interest. For the structuralists, all that mattered was a subject's posttraining performance; the change in response during training was merely a nuisance to be ignored or discarded. But for the functionalists, this change was what really mattered. Again, this difference in interest is not unique to psychology. Construction crews building the highway need only ensure that the individual slabs are approximately the same length between expansion joints. Thus, the crew's focus is on how much commonality there is from one slab to another. But for the engineers designing the material to fit in the expansion joints, the minor variations based on weather and construction methods are of critical importance. The material must be wide enough to fill the gap during the winter, but narrow enough so that it will not pop out of the joint when the road expands during the summer. Thus the engineer's focus is on the possible differences between slab lengths. Keep in mind the idea that one researcher's nuisance variable is another's variable of interest when we turn to assessment of individual differences in personality and intellectual functioning.

NUMERICAL MEASURES OF RESPONSES

Understanding how psychologists measure regularity and variation requires familiarity with four elementary concepts—operational definitions, distributions of scores, central tendency, and dispersion.

Operational Definitions

Let us return to the dinner party conversation for a moment. Suppose that a personality researcher wished to determine, for example, which people were "boastful." This task is not like determining the length of concrete slabs on the interstate: There is no universally acceptable scale (such as metric units of length) by which boastfulness can be measured. Moreover, although boastful behavior can be observed directly, the enduring personality trait, boastfulness, can only be inferred from this overt behavior. Thus, the personality researcher must first justify the method for measuring boastfulness in behavior, then justify the inferential link by which that observable behavior is taken as evidence that an underlying personality disposition of boastfulness exists.

Psychologists solve the first of these problems with what is known as an *operational definition,* a definition of a theoretical concept in terms of the procedures used to measure it. No one measurement procedure is likely to do justice to the full meaning of a theoretical concept, so researchers typically vary the operational definition from one study to the next. What an operational definition does provide, however, is explicit instructions to other researchers concerning how the concept was measured. Thus, any researcher who chooses to do so can *replicate* the earlier research using exactly the same operational definition. In our example, let us suppose that the personality researcher chose to operationalize boastfulness as "number of self-referent statements made in 10 minutes of conversation." To collect this measure, one would simply listen to each diner's conversation for 10 minutes and count the number of times the person refers to himself or herself.

Distributions of Scores

Now suppose that during the lengthy dinner the personality researcher and a colleague listen for 10 minutes to the conversations of 20 diners. Each researcher counts the number of self-referent statements made during the observation period. Over the 20 diners, the researchers in this hypothetical study heard the following set of self-referent statements: 8, 6, 4, 4, 3, 2, 1, 2, 4, 5, 5, 5, 4, 0, 6, 7, 2, 4, 3, 5. This set of data can be understood more easily if the results are presented as shown in Figure 22-1. As the figure shows, one person made 8 self-referent statements, one person made 7, five people made 4, and one person made none at all. The figure thus shows a **distribution** of scores—how many cases (people) there were who made each number (from 0 to 8) of self-referent statements. Scores on any variable—number of errors in a learning task, number of seconds taken to solve a problem, decibel levels at which a tone can be detected, numbers of people considered close friends, strength of attitudes in favor of the death penalty—could be arrayed on the X axis instead of the number of self-referent statements made in a 10-minute observation period. In all of these examples the Y axis would remain the number of individuals whose scores fell at each point identified on the X axis.

Central Tendency

It is immediately apparent from the distribution that more people made 4 self-referent statements than made any other number, although 5 was a close second. Moreover, as Figure 22-1 shows, more people have scores near the middle of the distribution than at either end. In other words, the distribution has a **central tendency,** a central value around which the scores tend to cluster. The central tendency of a dis-

FIGURE 22-1 Hypothetical distribution of scores based on observations of boastful behavior at a formal dinner party. Most scores cluster around the central tendency of the distribution.

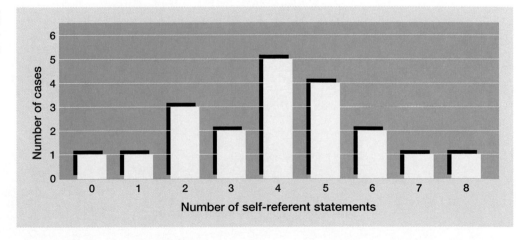

tribution can be shown graphically, as in Figure 22-1, or it can be summarized arithmetically by the **mean,** the **median,** or the **mode.** The mean of a distribution is the arithmetic average of the scores, computed by adding all the scores together and then dividing this total by the number of scores used. In the distribution shown, the mean is 4. The median is the numerical value above and below which half of the distribution lies, and the mode is the most frequently occurring score. The mode of a distribution can be determined simply by counting.

Dispersion

As useful as the central tendency is for characterizing a distribution of scores, it must be supplemented by an indication of the variability in the distribution. For example, consider the distribution of self-referent statements shown in Figure 22-2. This distribution, like the previous one, shows the scores of 20 individuals. Moreover, like the previous distribution, this one has a mean of 4. Yet the two are obviously different. Where the first one was bell-shaped (as are distributions of many psychological characteristics), this one is virtually flat.

What does this difference between the distributions mean, psychologically? In the first distribution, because most of the behavior clusters around the central tendency, the two people with scores of 7 and 8 can be said to have shown behavior that looks boastful by comparison to the others. Similarly, the two people with scores of 0 and 1 can be said to have shown behavior that looks modest by comparison to the others. The second distribution of scores, however, is so flat that it provides no way to distinguish one person's behavior from another.

In statistical terms, the second distribution has a **dispersion** (degree of variability) that is greater than that of the first distribution. How can this be represented as a number, when the mean of each distribution is 4, and each distribution contains scores that range from a low of 0 to a high of 8? The answer is in a measure of dispersion, called the **standard deviation,** that is based on the squared difference between each score in the distribution and the mean score. Computation of the standard deviation is illustrated in the appendix to this book. For now it is sufficient to note that the more peaked distribution will have a standard deviation that is smaller (2.0 for Figure 22-1) than the one for the flatter distribution (2.6 for Figure 22-2). Thus, a thorough description of a distribution of scores requires both the mean and the standard deviation.

How Much of a Mean Difference Is Enough?

We are now ready to discuss how psychologists determine whether two distributions of scores (such as responses before and after training) are different. The mean scores of the two distributions are compared in statistical procedures that also take into

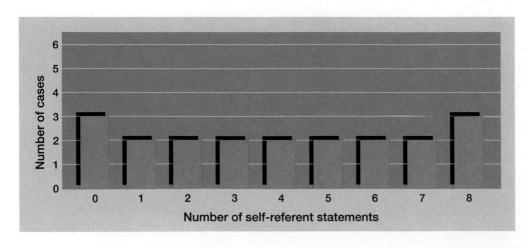

FIGURE 22-2 A hypothetical distribution of boastfulness scores that does not show the bell-shaped form that is typical of many measures of psychological characteristics.

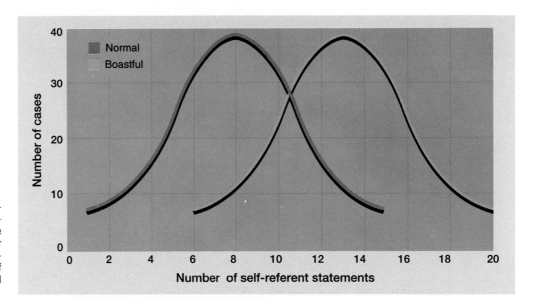

FIGURE 22-3 Two bell-shaped distributions of scores on a measure of boastfulness: One distribution describes the behavior of normal individuals, the other describes the behavior of boastful individuals. Because of the dispersion of each distribution, there is substantial overlap between the two.

account the dispersion of each distribution. The procedures are described in the statistical appendix, but can be illustrated conceptually here.

Suppose that, as a result of observing individual differences in boastfulness at the dinner party, a researcher identifies a group of people who are expected to be in the normal range of boastfulness and a group (perhaps politicians, guests on television talk shows, news commentators) expected to be high. After observing members of each group for 20 minutes, the researcher obtains the two distributions of scores shown in Figure 22-3. The mean score for the normal group is 8 self-referent statements in the 20 minutes; the mean score for the boastful group is 13.

Does this indicate that the members of the boastful group are *really* more boastful than the members of the normal group? The mean scores are clearly not the same, but as Figure 22-3 indicates, there is substantial overlap between the two distributions. A score as low as 6 could still belong to a person in the boastful group; a score as high as 15 could still belong to a person in the normal group. In other words, a substantial proportion of the scores in both distributions fall into a region of *overlap* between the distributions. Contrast this situation with the results shown in Figure 22-4. These two distributions also have mean scores for the normal and boastful

FIGURE 22-4 Two steeply peaked distributions of scores on a measure of boastfulness: One distribution describes the behavior of normal individuals, the other the behavior of boastful individuals. Because of the narrow dispersion of each distribution, there is very little overlap between the two.

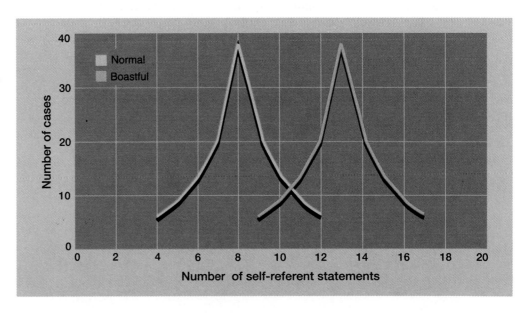

593

groups, respectively, of 8 and 13. But the distributions are so sharply peaked that there is virtually no overlap. The range of scores that could have come from either distribution is now reduced from 9 points in Figure 22-3 (6 to 15) to 3 points (9 to 12) in Figure 22-4. Thus, although the two sets of mean scores are the same, the likelihood of confusing the two distributions is much less in Figure 22-4.

Thus the answer to the question "Are the mean scores really different?" depends on both the mean scores and the dispersions involved. Let us return to the first observation of 20 diners. Suppose that we chose to divide this group of 20 into two groups of 10 by flipping a coin to determine group placement. Because the placement was random, the resulting two distributions of 10 scores each might have the same mean score, or they might not, even though we know that the people were all drawn from the same group of origin, or **population.** In most real-world studies we cannot know for certain whether two or more samples have come from the same population. We can infer the likelihood that they have, however, by examining the mean scores and dispersions of the samples. The less the overlap in scores between two samples the less the likelihood that the two samples are really from the same population. By convention, psychologists generally conclude that two samples are not from the same population (that the difference between the two samples is **statistically significant**) if a mean difference as large as the one obtained between the two samples would occur by chance fewer than 5 times in 100. To return to the two groups shown in Figures 22-3 and 22-4, in either of these cases we would consider the boastful group to be significantly more boastful than the normal group only if the observed mean difference of 5 self-references (8 versus 13) would have occurred fewer than 5 times out of 100, assuming that the samples had been drawn randomly from the same population.

ASSESSMENT OF INDIVIDUAL DIFFERENCES

Thus far the discussion of elementary statistical principles has concentrated on ways to determine whether two groups of scores are significantly different from one another. But many of the same ideas—operational definition, central tendency, dispersion—also enter into the assessment of psychological differences between individuals.

Reliability

As noted earlier, although behaviors are observable, the psychological states presumed to be involved in these behaviors must be inferred. Because the psychological measurements cannot be performed *directly,* there must be standards of performance against which any test can be judged. Two such standards are generally used. The first is **reliability**—the consistency of the measurement procedures used. One way to assess reliability is to measure the behavior twice or more, with some time lapse between measurements. For example, one might observe people's conversation at several formal dinners over a period of a few weeks. A measurement procedure that was perfectly reliable would yield exactly the same results each time, but in practice such reliability is never achieved. Not only might there be minor variations in the procedure itself, but also behavior might vary from one time to the next because of differences in the setting, variations in mood, or even a conscious effort not to produce exactly the same response pattern the second time around.

Behavioral variation over time is illustrated in Figure 22-5. Suppose that we have observed the dinner party conversations of 10 individuals at 5 different dinner parties. Each vertical line in Figure 22-5 represents the scores for one person and indicates both the *range* of scores achieved by that person and the person's mean score. So, for example, if person 1 had made 6 self-referent statements during the first observation period, 7 the second, 5 the third, 4 the fourth, and 8 the fifth, that person's distribution of scores would have had a mean score of 6. The horizontal tick

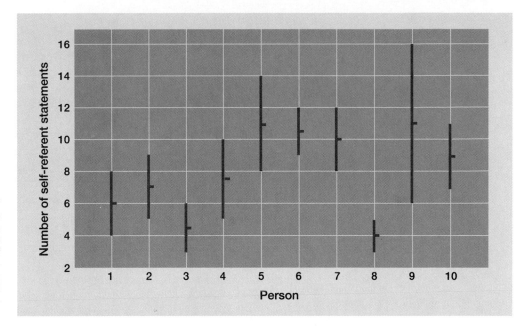

FIGURE 22-5 Repeated measures of individuals over time. Each person's number of self-referent statements was counted on five different occasions. The vertical line represents the range of scores that person achieved; the horizontal tick mark on each line is the mean score for the person. Shorter vertical lines indicate less variability in individual performance over different settings.

mark at 6 for person 1 indicates this mean score. Notice that some individuals, like person 8, have a very narrow range of self-referent statements, whereas people like person 9 have a very wide range.

Conceptually, reliability is the degree to which our observational technique produces the same scores for each individual over the five testing sessions. Thus, an extremely reliable test would produce a set of very short vertical lines; an unreliable test would produce a series of quite long ones. The overall reliability of the test is then expressed as a numerical average across all subjects whose behavior was observed multiple times.

Validity

A second standard against which a psychological measure can be judged is **validity**—the extent to which a psychological test actually measures what it is supposed to measure. We might have developed an exceedingly reliable conversation-scoring technique, one that consistently obtains virtually the same number of self-references from people whose behavior is observed through several dinner parties. But is our operational definition, "number of self-referent statements," really what we mean conceptually by *boastfulness*?

Validity may be established in several ways. One way is to use the testing procedure on what are known as **criterion groups:** groups of people who have already been classified as having the target trait or capacity on the basis of some procedure other than the one being developed. For example, we might get a number of people to nominate several individuals whom they consider boastful, and several others they consider self-effacing. Then we would observe several conversations in which each of these people participates, expecting that those nominated as boastful would make significantly more self-references than would those nominated as self-effacing. Again, if this did not happen, we would be concerned that our operational definition did not match what at least some people consider boastfulness.

Although criterion groups are occasionally constructed by nomination, they are more frequently defined in some formal way. For example, suppose researchers were developing a new test for a particular kind of mental disorder. Scores of hospitalized mental patients diagnosed by other methods as having the disorder could be compared with scores of patients considered not to have it and with scores from normal individuals. If the new test failed to discriminate among these groups, it would most likely not be considered valid.

Discriminative Efficiency of a Test

Psychological testing is frequently used to identify the personal characteristics and psychological capacities of an individual. For example, one might wish to discover what other personality attributes accompany boastfulness. Or in intelligence testing, one might wish to have a measure of the person's overall intellectual capability.

But at other times the end result of the testing is either the placement of an individual into a group or the exclusion of the person from it. For example, schoolchildren are moved from standard classrooms into special education classes, or into classes for the gifted and talented, on the basis of tests of intellectual capacity. Hospitalized patients with mental disorders are placed into one kind of treatment program or another depending on their diagnoses, and these diagnoses are made largely on the basis of psychological testing (broadly conceived to include interviews by the staff). The outcome of a criminal trial can depend on the success of an insanity defense, a judgment about a person's knowledge of right and wrong at the time a crime was committed, with this judgment influenced by the outcome of psychological testing.

All these instances share a common method: Each uses a person's location within a *distribution* of scores to make a *binary* choice about placement. For example, elementary school students will, as a group, show a wide range of abilities and talents. Yet some will be placed in special education classes, whereas others will not. Usually decisions such as this are not made on the basis of a single test, but on the basis of a **test battery**—a collection of psychological assessment procedures. In effect, a test battery consists of multiple operational definitions of a concept (such as "learning disabled"). Theoretically, although each test might have specific limitations, these limitations vary from one test to another. As a result, the entire battery should not suffer from the shortcomings of any one test.

Although a test battery is likely to be superior to any single test, the battery as a whole can still lead to incorrect placements. A recent analysis by Wiggins (1988) shows how this can happen. Suppose we have a test battery designed to distinguish those elementary school students eligible for placement into a gifted/talented program from those who are not. Let us assume that on the basis of educational theory and psychological research we know that there is a group of students who will not profit from the gifted/talented program; we also know that there is a group who will profit.

Suppose that we were able to identify these two groups on some grounds other than the test battery. Then, if we were to give the test battery to those who would not profit from the program, we would obtain a distribution of scores. This would be a distribution of "actual negatives"—the shaded curve shown in Figure 22-6. Now suppose the cutoff score for determining who should be placed in the gifted program were set at the point shown on the figure. All students in the actual negative group testing below this score would be correctly excluded from the program; they would be valid negatives. Those who tested above the cutoff score would be incorrectly placed in the program; they would be false positives. Shifting the cutoff score to the right decreases the number of false positives; shifting it to the left increases it.

Similarly, suppose that we also tested schoolchildren known to be capable of profiting from the gifted/talented program. Their scores would form a distribution, as shown in Figure 22-7, of actual positives. Students with scores to the right of the cutoff score shown on the figure—valid positives—would be correctly placed in the program. Students with scores to the left of the cutoff—false negatives—would be incorrectly excluded from the program. Shifting the cutoff score to the left decreases the number of false negatives; shifting it to the right increases it.

When we combine the two distributions, as shown in Figure 22-8, we find that they overlap. This overlap is the reason that test batteries inevitably result in some error of placement. As the figure indicates, no matter where we place the cutoff score, we get either false negatives, false positives, or both. To phrase this dilemma in terms of signal detection theory, which we discussed in Chapter 3, both the false

FIGURE 22-6 Distribution of scores produced by a test battery designed to place individuals into two categories, one negative for a particular trait, one positive. If the test battery is given to people known to be "actual negatives" on the trait, the normal dispersion of scores will produce at least some "false positives," unless the cutoff score is located beyond the tail of the distribution.

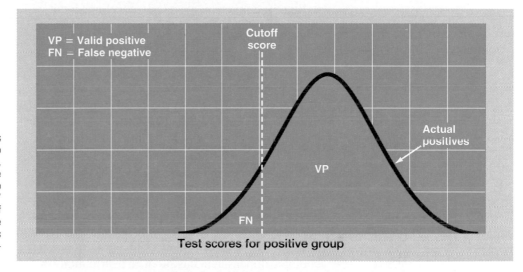

FIGURE 22-7 Distribution of scores produced by a test battery designed to place individuals into two categories, one negative for a particular trait, one positive. If the test battery is given to people known to be "actual positives" on the trait, the normal dispersion of scores will produce at least some "false negatives," unless the cutoff score is located beyond the tail of the distribution.

FIGURE 22-8 Combination of the distributions from Figures 22-6 and 22-7. The greater the degree of overlap between the two distributions, the lower the discriminative efficiency of the test battery. If, for example, there was complete overlap between the two distributions, then assigning individuals to the positive and negative groups on the basis of the test battery would be no more efficient than doing so by flipping a coin.

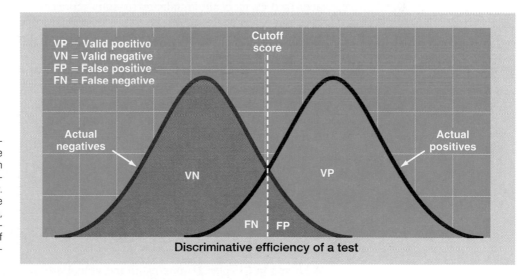

positives and the false negatives are misses—incorrect placements. The less any two distributions overlap, the smaller the area of misses relative to the area of hits (correct placement) and the better able the test battery is to discriminate members of one criterion group from members of another.

597

STATISTICAL STABILITY AND CHANGE

Statistical concepts can be used to refine the definitions of stability and change. First, assume that the test is reliable and valid. Next, imagine that it is possible to assess the individual's behavior more than once. These multiple measures will produce a distribution of scores for that individual. As indicated in Figure 22-5, that distribution will have a central tendency (the mean score). Each of these person-based distributions of behavior will also have dispersion (indicated by the standard deviation). The mean score can be considered the person's stable position within the possible range of the behavior or trait being measured. Just how stable that position is can be indicated by the degree of variability (the greater the dispersion, the less stable the behavior or trait).

If over time (or in different circumstances) the central tendency of the behavior or trait shifts, we can conclude that the individual has changed in some way. For example, consider a person who seeks psychological treatment for depression. Before treatment, that person's distribution of emotional states could be expected to have a central tendency represented by a negative number. If the therapy is successful, it will not totally eliminate negative feelings but it will shift the central tendency of the entire distribution toward the positive end of the emotional scale.

In sum, stability of behavior can be regarded as the central tendency on a reliable and valid test; change in behavior can be measured in terms of differences from this central tendency. These statistical devices allow psychologists to describe the underlying themes of a person's behavior, despite the variations that occur: The central tendency represents the theme and the standard deviation represents the variation.

INTERIM SUMMARY

Individual differences in personality and intellectual capability are two of the major regularities in human behavior that can be assessed with appropriate scientific methods. These methods begin with operational definitions—definitions of concepts in terms of the procedures that will be used to measure the concepts. The resulting psychological measurements produce distributions of scores, each of which can be characterized by its central tendency (usually represented by the arithmetic mean) and its dispersion (typically represented by the standard deviation). Statistical comparisons between groups of scores must take both the central tendency and the dispersion into account: As the mean difference increases or the dispersion of each distribution decreases, the likelihood increases that the two distributions will be significantly different. Measurement procedures must be reliable and valid to provide scientifically acceptable conclusions. The discriminative efficiency of a reliable and valid measurement procedure is its ability to distinguish between valid and false positives and valid and false negatives.

PERSONALITY ASSESSMENT

As noted in Chapter 21, interest in individual differences in personality dates back to the ancients, especially Hippocrates' identification of four bodily humors—blood, yellow bile, black bile, or phlegm—and Galen's suggestion that people could be classified into four personality types on the basis of the predominant humor. Type theories of personality persisted through the first half of the twentieth century, when they were largely supplanted by trait theories, psychodynamic theories, and social learning theories.

Throughout this historical record of theoretical change, one thing has remained constant: Theory has dictated assessment. That is, the particular personality assessment method one selects depends on one's theoretical beliefs about what constitutes the human personality. A personality researcher whose theoretical orientation was psychodynamic would look for assessment methods that permitted exploration of the unconscious forces that impel behavior. In assessment terms, this kind of researcher would use a **projective test.** These tests, such as the Thematic Apperception Test (TAT, discussed in Chapter 11), present subjects with an ambiguous stimulus that must be described or explained. The researcher then searches the subject's description for evidence of unconscious processes or motives. In contrast, a personality researcher who was interested in a trait theory would select a form of **objective personality test.** Rather than present subjects with an ambiguous stimulus, objective tests present them with concrete ways to characterize themselves (using either self-descriptive statements or personality-trait words). What the subject says is what the researcher gets—there is no search for unconscious motives behind the choices of words.

We next consider some of the most common personality assessment techniques, beginning with the most thoroughly documented objective test, the Minnesota Multiphasic Personality Inventory (MMPI).

THE MINNESOTA MULTIPHASIC PERSONALITY INVENTORY (MMPI-2)

The Minnesota Multiphasic Personality Inventory (MMPI) was designed to distinguish psychologically normal individuals from those with serious psychological disorders. The developers of the test began by collecting nearly 1,000 statements about psychological symptoms from clinical reports and textbooks (Hathaway & McKinley, 1943). When ambiguous and similar statements were eliminated, some 500 were left. These statements were then given to institutionalized patients, diagnosed as suffering from various kinds of mental disorders, and several hundred individuals with no history of psychiatric problems, all of whom indicated whether each of the items was true or false for them. Items that successfully distinguished between a particular clinical diagnostic group and the normal individuals were retained for use in a clinical scale; the others were discarded. Thus, if five items were answered one way by people diagnosed as being depressed and another way by normals, those five items would become part of a "depression scale."

The MMPI has undergone extensive revision through the years. The most recent version, called the MMPI-2, consists of 567 true–false items that are used to produce 13 different scales (Butcher, Dahlstrom, Graham, Tellegen, & Kaemmer, 1989), nine of which are clinical scales that identify particular psychological problems, such as depression, paranoia, and schizophrenia. (Examples of scale items like those used are shown in Table 22-1.) In addition to the clinical scales, the MMPI-2 contains a masculinity–femininity scale and three validity scales. (Examples of items like the latter are also shown in the table.) These three scales exemplify any personality test's need to guard against response biases. One of them assesses the person's tendency to claim too much virtue; another tests the tendency to deny normal problems; and the third tests faking or incoherence (by examining the internal consistency of answers to items in the scale).

The MMPI was originally designed as a diagnostic tool, in the hope that a person with a particular psychological problem would have a high score on the corresponding scale. In clinical practice, however, it soon became apparent that such precision was not going to be achieved (Graham, 1990). For example, a person suffering from depression would have a high score on the depression scale, but might have elevated scores on other scales as well. Moreover, because a number of the scales use the same items (74 items on the MMPI-2 are used in more than one scale), many of the

TABLE 22-1 Simulated Items Representing MMPI Scales

Scale	Item Content
Items Exemplifying Clinical Scales	
Depression (57 actual items)	"I sometimes think there's no purpose to my life."
Paranoia (40 actual items)	"People are trying to control my thoughts."
Schizophrenia (78 actual items)	"Sometimes my dreams are more real than my experiences while awake."
Items Exemplifying Validity Scales	
Lie Scale (15 actual items)	"I always clean my plate."
Correction (30 actual items)	"I enjoy having my work criticized."
Frequency (60 actual items)	"I enjoy activities that involve other people." followed later in the test by: "I am uncomfortable in social situations."

clinical scales are not independent of one another. In statistical terms, such scales are **intercorrelated:** responses on one are related to responses on another.

Despite its lack of diagnostic precision, the MMPI's objective scoring made it extremely popular as a research and clinical tool; it has been used in more than 10,000 studies (Graham, 1990), and together these studies provide some of the diagnostic precision missing from the individual scales. So as not to detract from the usefulness of this literature, test revisions have kept item changes to a minimum. Fewer than 15 percent of the original items have been deleted or changed, with changes designed primarily to remove sexist language, clarify meaning, or put words into contemporary idiom. The revised test is the most frequently used criterion-based personality test; it is preferred by about 90% of clinical psychologists (Aiken, 1989).

THE CALIFORNIA PERSONALITY INVENTORY (CPI)

The original MMPI served as a model for a number of other tests, including some designed for use only with normal individuals. One of these is the California Personality Inventory (CPI), which includes 15 scales that measure dimensions of personality and three that detect response biases (Gough, 1957). Brief descriptions of the scales are presented in Table 22-2. The CPI consists of 480 true–false items (of which 178 were taken from the MMPI) written at a fourth-grade level and most suitable for testing high school and college students and young adults.

When one is attempting to characterize a normal personality, one cannot use clinical criterion groups. Instead, *norms* are established by administering tests to large numbers of people. Norms for the CPI were obtained by testing a geographically and socioeconomically diverse sample of some 7,000 females and 6,000 males of varying ages; this process is called *standardization*. Separate norms (both mean scores and standard deviations) were established for females and males on each scale in the inventory. Thus, an individual's scores are compared to the norms derived from the standardization sample.

Results of the CPI will inform the respondent about how typical his or her answers are, not how healthy or abnormal they might be. Making any value judg-

TABLE 22-2   Descriptions of Scales from the CPI

Class I Scales: Poise, Ascendancy, Self-Assurance, Adequacy

Dominance	To identify dominant and influential individuals capable of initiative and leadership.
Capacity for Status	To measure qualities of ambition that can lead to achieved status in the culture.
Sociability	To distinguish outgoing and social people from those who shun involvement.
Social Presence	To identify those whose self-confidence and verve may be slightly manipulative.
Self-Acceptance	To assess sense of personal worth and capacity for independent thinking and action.

Class II Scales: Maturity, Responsibility, Intrapersonal Structuring of Values

Responsibility	To identify temperamentally conscientious and responsible people.
Socialization	To assess social maturity, integrity, and rectitude.
Self-Control	To measure self-regulation and freedom from impulsivity and self-centeredness.
Tolerance	To identify permissive, accepting, and nonjudgmental individuals.

Class III Scales: Achievement Potential and Intellectual Effectiveness

Achievement Conformance	To identify factors that facilitate achievement when conformance is positive.
Achievement Independence	To identify factors that facilitate achievement when autonomy is positive.
Intellectual Efficiency	To indicate degree of intellectual efficiency.

Class IV Scales: Intellectual and Interest Modes

Psychological-Mindedness	To measure interest in, and responsiveness to, inner needs of others.
Flexibility	To indicate degree of adaptability of person's thinking and social behavior.
Femininity	To assess the femininity or masculinity of interests.

SOURCE: Adapted from Aiken (1909) and Megargee (1972).

ments about a particular scale position requires the assumption that most people are psychologically healthy and that deviations from the norm necessarily reflect psychological problems. In many instances this may be a tenuous assumption.

THE PROJECTIVE METHOD

Like objectively scored personality inventories, projective tests face the problem of finding appropriate criterion groups. When a test is used as a clinical diagnostic tool, the criterion group consists of patients previously classified as having a particular disorder. But when a test is used to try to understand the unconscious forces that drive normal personality, there are no criterion groups. In addition to this problem, projective tests must also deal with inconsistencies in scoring by different examiners.

The history of the Rorschach test illustrates the effort to reduce examiner effects in the interpretation of projective tests. The Rorschach is a psychodiagnostic test based on the interpretation of a person's responses to a series of 10 large inkblots similar to the one pictured in Figure 22-9 on page 602 (Rorschach, 1921). Each inkblot is printed on a 5.5 × 9.5 inch card; five inkblots are printed in shades of black and gray, two are printed in black and red, and the remaining three are multicolored. The respondent's perceptions of the inkblots, associations to them, and stories constructed about them reveal critical features of his or her personality.

The interview takes place in two phases. In the free-association phase, the respondent is shown each inkblot and is asked to say whatever comes to mind. This

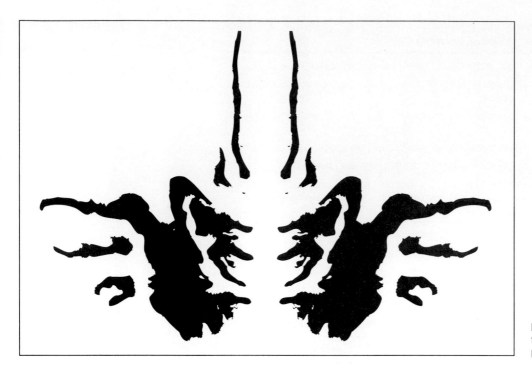

FIGURE 22-9 An inkblot similar to those used in the Rorschach projective personality test.

response is recorded verbatim by the examiner. In the inquiry phase, the examiner asks the respondent to indicate how each free association came about—that is, whether it occurred through references to color, form, or other characteristics of the inkblot.

Hermann Rorschach died unexpectedly in 1922, only a year after publishing his psychodiagnostic method, and in the succeeding years five different scoring systems were developed by students of the method. Each system had its own peculiarities, and each attracted a number of adherents; the result was widespread inconsistency in the administration and interpretation of the test. Critics seized on this chaos as an indication that the personality characteristics identified by the Rorschach test were located not in the respondent but in the eye of the examiner.

In the first phase of a Rorschach interview, the interviewee is shown one of the standard cards and is asked to say whatever comes to mind. The examiner records this response verbatim and then asks the interviewee to describe how each free association came about.

Beginning in the mid-1970s, one researcher reviewed some 700 published studies on the Rorschach, using them as data against which to test aspects of each of the five scoring systems (Exner, 1974, 1978, 1982). He then combined the empirically valid features of each system to create a comprehensive system that is now the standard. Exner's work illustrates the principle that consistency in scoring is critical to the usefulness of a projective test. With an objectively scored test, only its creator needs to know in detail how it should operate; the examiner does not need to know whether an item "really" belongs in one scale or another. In contrast, with a projective test, examiners must be trained in the scoring method until their proficiency begins to match that of the test creator. Only then can they draw appropriate conclusions from the test results. Even under these circumstances, however, only reliability is guaranteed; validity of the results as indicators of particular personality characteristics is not.

STABILITY, CHANGE, AND ETHICS

Issues of reliability and validity are critical for personality testing. Test–retest reliability can be established relatively easily for an objectively scored inventory like the MMPI-2. When the same examiner both administers and interprets a projective test, the test–retest reliability of some of them is also acceptable (Aiken, 1989). In other words, there seems to be stability in tested personality over time.

The validity of personality testing, in contrast, is more controversial. When the test is used as a clinical diagnostic tool, comparisons with known diagnostic groups provide significant validity. On the other hand, when the test is being used to elucidate the personality structure of a presumably normal person, there is no obvious criterion group. The test can be judged only in terms of *convergent validity* (does it give the same answers as similar tests?) and *discriminant validity* (does it give different answers from those provided by tests designed to measure different characteristics?). Any resulting inferences made about the respondent's psychological health depend on the risky assumption that giving a "typical" answer is equivalent to being "healthy."

In view of these limitations, the ethical guidelines of the American Psychological Association require that standardized personality tests be administered only by professionals, who are aware of the test's reliability and validity limits. They treat the personality test as a privileged communication, given with full informed consent, and provide the detailed feedback that respondents deserve.

INTERIM SUMMARY

Personality assessment is driven by the theoretical orientation of the researcher. Those who believe in unconscious processes are likely to use projective tests; those who believe in the primacy of conscious processes are more likely to use some objective form of personality testing. One of the first objective tests of personality was the Minnesota Multiphasic Personality Inventory, most frequently used in clinical settings. Several tests for normal individuals have been derived from the MMPI; foremost among these is the California Psychological Inventory. Important projective personality tests include the Thematic Apperception Test and the Rorschach test. The latter is used primarily for personality testing in connection with diagnosis of psychological disorders. Whether objective or projective, personality tests face serious difficulties in establishing their validity. Despite attempts at providing both convergent validity and discriminant validity, there is no obvious criterion group available against which to compare the results of personality testing.

INTELLIGENCE

The measurement of human intellectual ability began with Sir Francis Galton (1822–1911), who first discussed the influences of heredity and environment on psychological capacities (Hilgard, 1987). Galton's first major work traced the history of a few eminent families and made a strong case for the importance of heredity in the development of talent (Galton, 1952/1869).

To assess human capabilities, Galton tested people's visual acuity, keenness of hearing, hand strength, and reaction time. He was the first scientist to examine the degree of association among such faculties, using scatterplots like those in Figure 22-10 (Hilgard, 1987). In the figure, part *a* shows a positive relationship between the variable plotted on the *X* axis (horizontal) and the one on the *Y* axis (vertical). The two axes, which are not labeled, could represent any sorts of measures. In part *a*, as a point is farther away from the origin (0, 0) on the *X* axis, it tends also to be farther from the origin on the *Y* axis. In part *b*, which shows a scatterplot of a negative relationship between two variables, points closer to the origin on the *X* axis tend to be farther away from the origin on the *Y* axis. Finally, part *c* shows no relationship between the two variables: Regardless of their location on the *X* axis, points in this plot tend to cluster in the 8-to-17 range on the *Y* axis.

Galton's student Karl Pearson developed a statistical method for representing the degree of association between two variables (Hilgard, 1987). This method, described in the appendix, produces what is known as the Pearson product-moment **correlation coefficient.** The correlation coefficient, represented by the symbol *r,* reflects the degree to which knowing an individual's score on the *X* variable permits prediction of the score on the *Y* variable. For example, knowing a person's hand strength would permit you to make a prediction about the upper-arm strength. Your prediction of arm strength would not be perfect, of course, but it would certainly be better than it would be with no knowledge of hand strength. The arithmetic value of the correlation coefficient ranges from +1 (a perfect positive correlation) through zero to −1 (a perfect negative correlation).

TESTS OF INTELLECTUAL CAPACITY

Although Galton measured individual differences in ability, he concentrated mainly on physical and sensory faculties. Modern testing of intellectual capacity is founded on the materials devised by Frenchmen Alfred Binet and Théophile Simon in the early decades of the twentieth century.

Sir Francis Galton, whose work tracing the history of a few eminent families began the psychological study of hereditary influences on intellectual capacity.

Alfred Binet, creator of one of the first standardized intelligence tests, is shown here with a youth whose mental age was being tested.

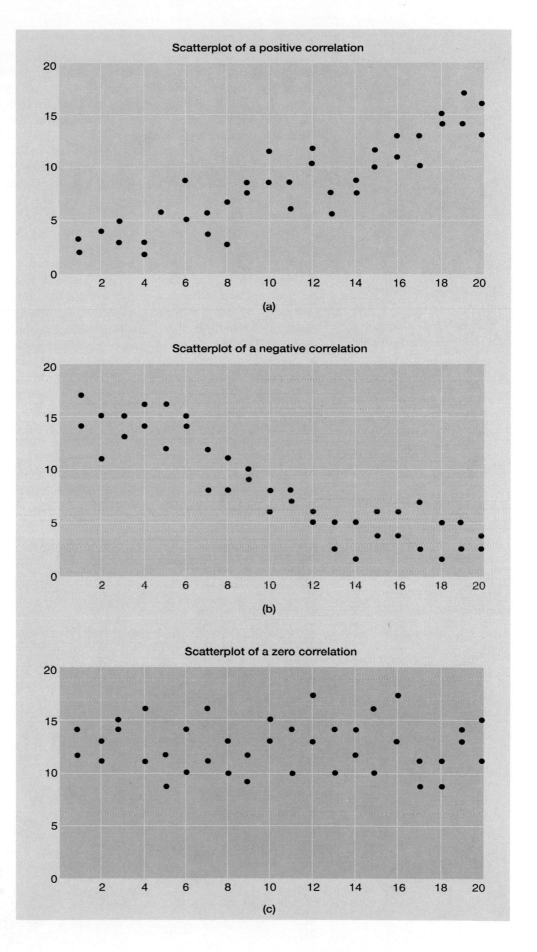

FIGURE 22-10 Scatterplots representing different associations between two variables. In part (a) the association is positive: As a person's score on the X axis increases, the score on the Y axis also increases. In part (b) the association is negative: As a person's score on the X axis increases, the score on the Y axis decreases. In part (c) there is no relationship between scores on the two axes.

Origins of the Test

Every spring, when college admission decisions are mailed to anxious applicants, newspapers carry stories about the SAT and other intelligence tests. There are ongoing controversies over whether the tests measure anything of value, whether they are culturally fair, and whether they play too great a role in college selection procedures. The general tenor of the arguments is that the tests have become a means of restricting access to educational opportunities.

Ironically, Binet's work in mental testing was originally conducted to *expand* educational opportunities. In the early 1900s the minister of public instruction in Paris appointed a commission to determine how to provide education for children who were unable to compete successfully in the public schools. This meant devising a fair way of identifying which children should be sent to special schools. For this purpose, Binet and Simon attempted to construct tests of intellectual ability that were as objective as possible.

For Binet and Simon, intelligence was reflected in the quality of the individual's judgment, that is, "the faculty of adapting oneself to circumstances. To judge well, to comprehend well, to reason well, these are the essential activities of intelligence" (1916, pp. 42–43). From this perspective, tests of intelligence should involve more than mere knowledge. They should give the person being tested an opportunity to monitor his or her progress toward a predefined goal, on the assumption that a child of normal intelligence will persevere at a task until it has been done correctly, whereas one of marginal intelligence will settle for a rough approximation.

The tests used age-appropriate materials. For example, the modern version of the Binet test for a 2-year-old includes a form board with three holes—one triangular, one circular, and one square—into which the child must place pieces of the proper shape; a paper doll to be used in identifying the major parts of the body; and pictures of familiar objects to be named. The test is administered to one child at a time by a person who has been trained in the assessment method. Because it is generally recognized that mental processes become more complex with age, the test elements for

AT A PSYCHOLOGICAL CLINIC

THE FORM BOARD

Early assessment of psychological capacities (top) included primitive devices for testing coordination, hand strength, and color perception. The form board (bottom) was one tool for distinguishing mentally retarded children from those of normal intelligence.

A child takes the Wechsler Intelligence Scale for Children, Revised (WISC-R).

a 14-year-old include arithmetic word problems, reasoning about spatial directions, and the cognitive categorization skills involved in saying how two opposites such as hot and cold might be alike. The problems correctly solved were presumed to indicate the child's *mental age.* This could be compared to the chronological age to determine whether the child was behind or ahead of other same-age children in mental development.

Binet's materials and instructions were soon translated into several languages. An American version was prepared by Lewis Terman at Stanford University and came to be known as the Stanford–Binet (Terman & Merrill, 1937). Although the Stanford–Binet is the most widely used individual test of intelligence, it is by no means the only one (Sternberg & Powell, 1983). The major alternative to it is the Wechsler Intelligence Scale. There are two versions of this test: the Wechsler Intelligence Scale for Children-Revised (WISC-R), published in 1974 (Wechsler, 1974), and the Wechsler Adult Intelligence Scale-Revised (WAIS-R), published in 1981 (Wechsler, 1981).

The Numerical IQ

In any intelligence test for children the initial items should be easy, but subsequent items should become sufficiently complex to produce repeated failure. Like Binet's original tests, Terman's tests emphasized the mental age of the individual being tested, defined as his or her standing relative to the average performance of individuals of the same chronological age. Building on the previous work of Stern (1914) and others, Terman converted this comparison of mental and chronological age into the familiar **intelligence quotient (IQ):**

$$IQ = 100 \times \frac{\text{Mental age}}{\text{Chronological age}}$$

If mental age is greater than chronological age the IQ will be above 100, but if it is less, the IQ will be below 100.

Although the concept of an intelligence quotient is easy to understand, it presents a number of problems. First, there is the question of the stability of the IQ over time. For a 5-year-old child to attain an IQ of 120, the child must have a mental age of 6 [120 = 100(6/5)], one year more than his or her chronological age. To maintain that

IQ at age 10, the child must have a mental age of 12 [120 = 100(12/10)]—in other words, the absolute difference between the child's mental and chronological ages must be double what it was previously. This arithmetic requirement is inconsistent with the idea that a person's capabilities are roughly comparable over time. Consequently, numerical measures of IQ are now expressed in *deviation units* from children of the same age, rather than in terms of a comparison between mental age and chronological age. Specifically, most age groups tested with the Stanford–Binet produce distributions of scores with a mean of 100 and a standard deviation of plus or minus 15 points (Cronbach, 1985).

A second problem with a numerical expression of intelligence is that the number itself, rather than what it represents, becomes the focus of discussion. An individual with a low IQ may feel stigmatized, regardless of whatever other talents he or she has. Public disputes over IQ scores rarely consider the dispersion of the subgroups sampled, the potential for measurement error, or issues of reliability and validity. Consequently, public commentary on IQ tends to be more dogmatic than it would be if the requisite statistical qualifications had been included. To avoid this problem, some experts recommend avoiding the term IQ or any numerical definition of IQ in terms of its deviation from 100 (Cronbach, 1985).

KINDS OF INTELLIGENCE

One example of the problems created by the focus on a single IQ number is that it could lead the unwary to conclude that there is only one kind of intellectual capability—namely, that which is measured by IQ tests. Some of the modern theories we discuss in a moment suggest, however, that "intelligence" is multifaceted, including a variety of intellectual skills that are not measured by the standard IQ test.

Measured Correlations

As an example of a multifaceted intelligence, suppose that a person is given five intellectual tasks to perform. Suppose that these tasks include some of the sensorimotor capabilities that Galton might have measured—visual acuity and manual dexterity—and some of the more cognitive tasks—spatial ability, vocabulary, and the solving mathematical word problems—that characterize more recent measures of intelligence. The result would be five separate scores for each person. Now suppose that 199 other people take the same set of tests. There will now be a total of 1,000 scores. By using statistical procedures, we can estimate the degree to which the 200 scores on one of the tests are related to the 200 scores on each of the other tests. The outcome is the Pearson product-moment *correlation coefficient* mentioned earlier. There will be one correlation coefficient for each pair of tests.

A set of hypothetical correlation coefficients for the five intellectual tasks is presented in Figure 22-11. The figure shows a typical *correlation matrix* in which the

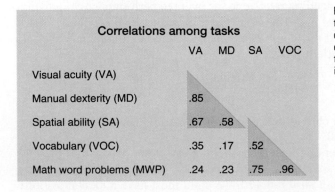

Correlations among tasks

	VA	MD	SA	VOC
Visual acuity (VA)				
Manual dexterity (MD)	.85			
Spatial ability (SA)	.67	.58		
Vocabulary (VOC)	.35	.17	.52	
Math word problems (MWP)	.24	.23	.75	.96

FIGURE 22-11 Hypothetical correlations among various possible measures of intellectual abilities. The triangles enclose clusters that seem to go together. In this example each cluster includes spatial ability.

five tasks are listed on the left side and four of the tasks are also listed at the top. The correlation of any task or test with itself is 1, so these values are typically omitted from the correlation matrix. Similarly, only half of the matrix is shown, because correlations in the other half are the mirror image of those shown. For example, the correlation of +0.17 between vocabulary (row 4) and manual dexterity (column 2) is exactly the same as the correlation—not shown—between manual dexterity (row 2) and vocabulary (column 4).

Factor Analysis

Few real data sets are as easily interpreted as this example, so psychologists use statistical techniques such as *factor analysis* to reveal the fewest number of underlying dimensions that can account for the variability observed in the correlations. If such an analysis were performed on the hypothetical correlations shown in Figure 22-11, three factors would most likely emerge. The first would be a general intelligence factor involved in all of the tests; this is evident because all the correlations are positive. The second factor would be a sensorimotor factor; it is involved in the high intercorrelations shown in the upper triangle. Visual acuity, manual dexterity, and spatial ability are more highly correlated with one another than with vocabulary or the solution of word problems. The third factor would be a vocabulary factor, as shown in the lower triangle. Vocabulary scores are more highly correlated with word problem scores than with anything else, and these two scores are also related to scores in spatial ability. Thus, in this hypothetical example both the sensorimotor factor and the vocabulary factor are involved in spatial ability.

Aspects of Intellectual Performance

Research since Galton's time has found results comparable to those illustrated in this example, suggesting that both some overall intellectual capability and some specific task competencies are involved in intelligence. The analysis of intellectual functioning into terms of separate factors was originated by Spearman (1904), who argued that a general intellectual performance factor, which he termed *g,* will be reflected in the results of any test. More intelligent people will perform better than less intelligent people on almost any intellectual task. In addition, Spearman argued that specific factors are associated with particular intellectual tasks.

Just how many such factors there may be has been a matter of controversy. One factor-analytic study, which led to the creation of the Primary Mental Abilities Test, found evidence of seven abilities: verbal comprehension, number usage, memory, perceptual speed, spatial ability, verbal fluency, and inductive reasoning (Thurstone & Thurstone, 1962).

Another study suggested that the number of separate abilities identified may depend on the age of the person being tested, although there is a core of intellectual capability, such as that represented by *g,* that persists through time. This research, known as the Berkeley Growth Study, followed a selected sample of individuals from birth well into adulthood and included a number of age-appropriate measures of intelligence (Bayley, 1968). In infancy most individual differences are found in sensorimotor alertness (Hofstaetter, 1954), whereas after age 4 most are accounted for by the ability to manipulate symbols. Research typically shows very little correlation between the performance of infants and the performance of the same children after age 4, the earliest age at which a reasonably stable estimate of IQ can be obtained (Sternberg & Powell, 1983). Given that sensorimotor activity is all a preverbal child has to show, and that so much later cognitive activity involves processing verbal and symbolic information, these low correlations are not surprising. What does seem to be common across age is "the seeking, finding, learning, and solving of novel problems . . ." (Sternberg & Powell, 1983, p. 363), a notion quite similar to the "mental energy" that Spearman believed accounted for his *g* factor.

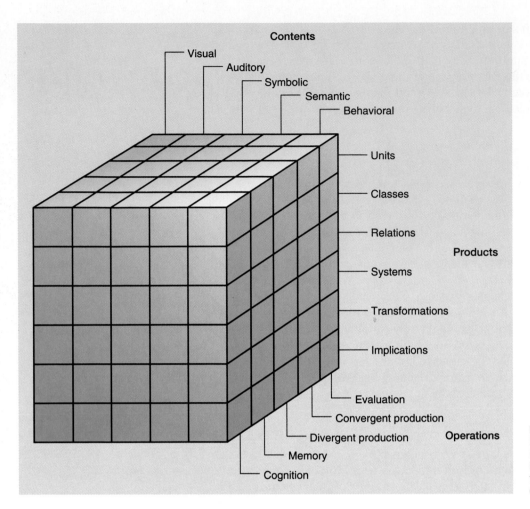

Contents

— Visual
— Auditory
— Symbolic
— Semantic
— Behavioral

— Units
— Classes
— Relations
Products
— Systems
— Transformations
— Implications

— Evaluation
— Convergent production
— Divergent production   Operations
— Memory
— Cognition

FIGURE 22-12 Guilford's Structure of Intellect model of intellectual functioning. The combination of 5 operations, 5 kinds of content, and 6 kinds of cognitive product produces a total of 150 specific abilities.

Finally, the extreme of the multifacet approach to intelligence suggests that there may be as many as 150 factors contributing to intellectual performance (Guilford, 1967; 1985). This "Structure of Intellect" theory defines intelligence as "a systematic collection of abilities or functions for processing information of different kinds in various forms" (Guilford, 1985, p. 230). In an attempt to specify all the functions and abilities, the theory argues that every mental task requires three elements, each of which can be represented on one side of a three-dimensional solid as shown in Figure 22-12. The first dimension, extending from front to back, represents mental operations such as evaluation, memory, and cognition. These are the mental tools used to process information. The second dimension, extending from left to right, represents the specific content of the task, such as numerical symbols, figural images, or the behavior of other people. This dimension provides the raw material for the cognitive processes. Finally, the third dimension, extending from top to bottom, represents the products of mental operations, such as classes, relations, and transformations. Individual blocks in the three-dimensional solid are identified by the initials of the relevant elements with the order of the initials always being operation-content-product. For example, CVR refers to cognition of visual relations and represents the kind of ability needed to solve a multiple-choice visual analogy. In all, there are five operations, five contents, and six products. Because any operation may be performed on any kind of content and may result in any product, there are $5 \times 5 \times 6 = 150$ possible elements of intelligence, each represented by one of the small blocks in Figure 22-12 (Guilford, 1985).

Whether the actual number of factors or elements of intelligence is 3, 7, or even 150, it is clear that intellectual functioning involves more than one sort of ability. To

610

be fair, it should be noted that standard measures of IQ include tests of multiple abilities, a fact that is often overlooked in public discussions of intelligence testing. Nevertheless, there is considerable variation in those factors within any individual, and an individual's scores on any given factor will therefore change over time and cannot be reflected in a single test score. For all of these reasons, the first question for anyone who makes a claim about the intelligence of an individual or group should be, "According to what measure?"

Multiple Intelligences

Despite Galton's early interest in aspects of physical coordination such as manual dexterity, most of the factor-analytic approaches to the study of intellectual capability have focused almost exclusively on cognitive functioning. But an important recent theory argues that there is much more to human potential than cognitive ability (Gardner, 1983). Building on research in neuropsychology as well as on more traditional psychometric methods, the theory first specifies criteria for determining whether a particular capability is a separate intelligence. For example, if brain damage can eliminate one capability while leaving all others intact, then that one is a candidate for a separate intelligence. Alternatively, the fact that some individuals have a particular capability to a truly exceptional degree suggests that that capability might be a distinguishable intelligence.

Applying these and other criteria to human performances, Gardner finds seven different "intelligences," as outlined in Table 22-3. Three of these—linguistic, logical–mathematical, and spatial—have a familiar ring. Indeed, many more traditional intelligence tests incorporate measures of language capability, problems in logic and mathematics, and rotations or reversals of complex figures.

The other four ability sets, however—musical intelligence, bodily–kinesthetic intelligence, and two personal intelligences (knowledge of oneself and knowledge of others)—substantially broaden the scope of what has usually been meant by "intelligence." The theory offers evolutionary, neuropsychological, and behavioral evidence for these distinguishable abilities. A few examples can illustrate the point. Regarding musical intelligence, the complete works of Mozart fill nearly 200 compact disks; many of the best jazz pianists, such as Art Tatum, were self-taught; musical talent is evident early in childhood—as noted by John Lennon, "People like me are aware of their so-called genius at ten, eight, nine . . ." (cited in Gardner, 1983, p. 115). Regarding bodily–kinesthetic intelligence, ballet dancer Mikhail Baryshnikov, track star Florence Joyner, and basketball star Michael Jordan all have an amazing combination of physical capability and bodily control. Watching these people in action, it is easy to believe that their athletic capabilities differ in kind, not merely in degree, from those of most other people.

TABLE 22-3   Seven Intelligences

Kind of Intelligence	Characteristic Functions, Exemplars
Linguistic	Poetry, rhetoric, explanation.
Musical	Composition, performance, sense of pitch and rhythm.
Logical–mathematical	Extensive chains of logical reasoning. Love of abstraction.
Spatial	Visual perceptions of forms, mental manipulation of images.
Bodily–kinesthetic	Fine control over motor behavior. Mimes, dancers, athletes.
Personal–self	Access to one's own feeling life.
Personal–others	Ability to notice moods, motivations, intentions of others.

SOURCE: Adapted from Gardner (1983).

The fact that some individuals possess a particular capability to a truly exceptional degree—Mozart's musical talent, for example, or Florence Joyner's physical prowess—is one justification for the claim that the term "intelligence" should be broadened to include more than the usual cognitive capabilities associated with it.

It remains to be seen whether future research will support the theory of multiple intelligences, but by expanding the domain usually associated with the term *intelligence,* the theory brings into focus the need for the study of human capability to expand its view beyond cognitive processes.

HEREDITY AND ENVIRONMENT

Ever since Galton began measuring individual differences in intellectual performance, psychologists have been interested in whether those differences should be attributed to heredity or to environment. Greatly impressed with Darwin's theory of evolution, Galton ascribed intellectual variation to hereditary factors: "I have no patience with the hypothesis . . . that babies are born pretty much alike" (1952/1869, p. 4). Not surprisingly, his research conducted with eminent families obtained results consistent with this position.

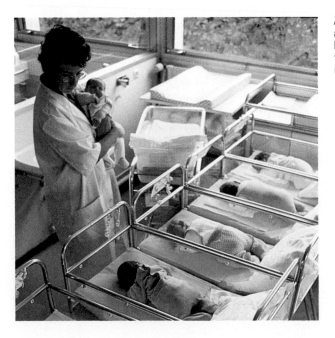

Are babies born pretty much alike? Or are they substantially different in capability before their first experiences with the world? This is the essence of the nature–nurture controversy.

Genetically speaking, identical twins like these are 100% alike, whereas fraternal twins are, on the average, only 50% alike. Comparisons among the two kinds of twins are used to estimate the heritability of various traits.

Although there have been numerous defenders of the hereditarian position in the twentieth century since Galton's work (Sternberg & Powell, 1983), most modern research makes it abundantly clear that intellectual functioning is influenced by environmental variables as well. Recall that years of twin studies and adoption studies have now established that some 30% to 50% of intellectual capability is inherited (Plomin, 1988; Vandenberg & Vogler, 1985). What this means is that at least half of the variability in scores of intellectual functioning is *not* attributable to genetic factors.

As noted earlier, modern behavior genetics permits us to make separate estimates of the contributions that heredity and environment might make to any particular intellectual performance. Genetically speaking, identical twins are 100% alike, whereas fraternal twins are, on the average, only 50% alike. Thus the heritability of a particular trait can be determined by subtracting the fraternal-twin correlation from the identical-twin correlation and doubling the difference. Because identical twins raised in the same family share not only 100% of genetic heritage, but also a common environment, identical-twin correlations are typically larger than the estimate of heritability. Thus, subtracting the estimate of heritability from the identical twin correlation gives a measure of the contribution of the common environment. Finally, any behavioral difference between members of a pair of identical twins living in the same home can be used to estimate what is known as the *specific,* or within-pair, environment. Together, heritability, common environment, and specific environment account for all of the variability in any behavior (Thompson, Detterman, & Plomin, 1991).

One recent study illustrating the partitioning of behavioral variability into these three components compared children's cognitive ability to their school achievement (Thompson, Detterman, & Plomin, 1991). These investigators tested the verbal ability, spatial ability, cognitive speed, and memory of 132 pairs of like-sexed fraternal twins and 146 pairs of identical twins. In addition, the investigators measured the scholastic achievement—in reading, mathematics, and language—of the children. Separate estimates of heritability, common environment, and specific environment were computed for each measure. The results are shown in Figure 22-13 (on page 614), presented as an average over the several ability measures and as an average over the several achievement measures. Three points should be made about these results. First, heritability is approximately three times as important for the cognitive abilities as it is for the achievement measures, on which experience and motivation would be expected to make a greater difference. Second, common environment is the

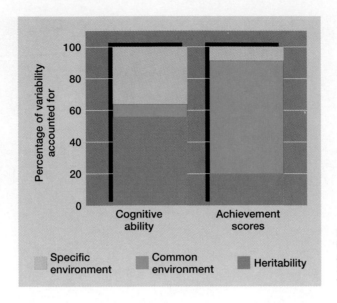

FIGURE 22-13 Relative contributions of heredity and environment to cognitive abilities and scholastic achievement. Source: Adapted from Thompson, Detterman, & Plomin (1991).

single most important influence on the achievement measures. And third, the effects of common environment and specific environment together account for an average of just over 41% of the variability in ability scores, and an average of nearly 80% of the variability in achievement scores. This important contribution of the environment should be kept in mind as we consider one of the most controversial current issues in psychology—group differences in intelligence.

In the United States, years of testing have established that, on the average, the mean IQ for black children is 85, whereas the mean for white children is 100 and the mean for Asian children is 104 (Scarr, 1981). There is, of course, substantial overlap among these distributions of IQ scores, but the difference between mean scores has been a source of intense social, political, and scientific debate (Flynn, 1980; Herrnstein, 1973; Kamin, 1974). The debate results in part from the fact that "Higher test scores [are] associated with higher levels of education, greater occupational success (measured in a variety of ways), and higher social class standing" (Keating, 1984, p. 6). Thus it is not surprising that a furor erupted when one educational researcher, noting that within-group differences reflect heritability, suggested that *between*-group differences might also contain a substantial component based on inheritance (Jensen, 1969). It is worth noting that Jensen began his studies of this subject out of concern that black children were being erroneously classified as retarded because IQ tests were being misused (Flynn, 1980). Almost immediately, however, the issue exploded. Fuel was added to the fire when the genetic hypothesis was used to justify the denial of equal educational opportunity to black children.

The argument is that if genetic factors are implicated in within-group differences and if IQ differences persist when environmental factors are statistically removed, the only explanation left is the genetic one. There is, however, a significant problem with this argument. It commits what has been called the *hereditarian fallacy* (Mackenzie, 1984): "the assumption that unless an IQ difference can be given a detailed and specific environmental explanation, it can most reasonably be concluded to have a genetic one" (p. 1222). This is a fallacy because it assumes that the only environmental variables that might be associated with intelligence differences are those that have typically been measured, such as family structure, level of education, and socioeconomic status. But of course the fact that these are the most obvious choices to measure cannot be taken as proof that they are the only possibilities.

The fact that a substantial amount of the variation in intellectual performance is attributable to environmental influences is one justification for programs, such as Head Start, designed to expand the educational opportunities of very young children.

INTERIM SUMMARY

Although the measurement of psychological capabilities began with Sir Francis Galton, modern intelligence testing can be traced to the work of Alfred Binet. Today the Stanford–Binet and the Wechsler Adult Intelligence Scale-Revised are the most commonly used intelligence tests. The numerical IQ is the quotient of mental age divided by chronological age, multiplied by 100. Theories of intelligence differ in the number of specific abilities or factors included. Studies have found evidence of up to 150 possible elements of intelligence. Theories also disagree about whether intelligence is a unitary concept or a collection of related but distinct capabilities. More than half of the variability in cognitive abilities can be traced to genetic factors, but scholastic achievement is much more heavily influenced by environmental factors. There are well-established group differences in measured intelligence, but at this point no firm conclusions can be drawn about the relative contributions of heredity and environment to such group differences.

SUMMARY

1. We know intuitively that when biological pressures and situational demands are removed people will show consistent individual differences in behavior. Two of the most important of these are differences in personality characteristics and intellectual functioning.

2. Scientific measurement of regularity and variation in behavior requires *operational definition* (definition of concepts in terms of the procedures used to measure the concept). Scores obtained will form distributions that have an identifiable *central tendency* and dispersion.

3. Measures of central tendency include the *median, mode,* and the arithmetic *mean.* The mean is computed by adding all the scores in the distribution together and then dividing this number by the number of scores. An important measure of dispersion is the *standard deviation,* based on the squared difference between each score in the distribution and the mean score.

4. The question "How much of a difference is enough?" is answered by statistical procedures that consider both the mean scores and the dispersions of two (or more) distributions. By convention, psychologists agree that a difference between distributions is *statistically significant* if there is less than a 1 in 20 probability that a difference as large as the one obtained would have come about through chance alone.

5. In the assessment of individual differences, psychologists strive for measures that are both reliable and valid. The *reliability* of a measure is its ability to produce the same results from one time to another; its *validity* is the degree to which the psychological test measures what it is supposed to measure. Validity is often established using *criterion groups,* although for personality tests on normal individuals such criterion groups can be difficult to identify.

6. The *discriminative efficiency* of a psychological *test battery* is its ability to distinguish hits (valid positives and valid negatives) from misses (false positives and false negatives).

7. The Minnesota Multiphasic Personality Inventory (MMPI-2) is an *objective test* of personality that consists of 567 true–false statements, from which nine clinical scales, a masculinity–femininity scale, and three validity scales are derived.

8. Although the MMPI was designed as a clinical diagnostic tool, it has given rise to other scales designed for assessment of normal personality functioning. One of these is the California Personality Inventory (CPI). A person's scores on the various CPI scales are compared to group norms rather than to clinical criterion groups.

9. The Rorschach inkblot test is an important *projective test* of personality functioning used in clinical settings and by personality researchers who stress the importance of unconscious processes.

10. The first test of intellectual functioning was constructed by Alfred Binet and Théophile Simon. Designed to measure comprehension, reasoning, and ability to adapt to new circumstances, this test consisted of age-appropriate materials from which a child's *mental age* could be derived. The Stanford–Binet is the most widely used version in the United States.

11. The *intelligence quotient (IQ)* is obtained by dividing a measured mental age by the child's chronological age and multiplying the result by 100. Because of a number of problems with the IQ as a measure, current intelligence tests usually provide scores expressed as a deviation from the central tendency of a group norm.

12. The relationships among various intellectual abilities can be expressed in *correlation coefficients,* and the statistical procedure of *factor analysis* can be used to determine the number of fundamental dimensions underlying a particular set of scores.

13. Although Spearman considered intellectual capacity to be reflected in a single underlying dimension, *g*, other theories have identified numerous factors that might be involved. The Structure of Intellect model, for example, consists of three dimensions—operations, contents, and products—that together identify 150 separable mental abilities.

14. Recent theories of intelligence suggest that the term should include such things as musical talent, bodily–kinesthetic skill, and knowledge of oneself and others, as well as the more traditional aspects of cognitive functioning.

15. Twin- and adoption-studies have shown that about 50% of the variation in intelligence scores is attributable to genetic factors. Although tests reveal what are referred to as racial differences in IQ, the causes of such differences have not yet been conclusively established.

FOCUS QUESTIONS

1. How do psychologists measure and quantify individual differences?

2. How can one determine whether two distributions of scores are significantly different from each other?

3. What is the difference between the relia-

bility of a psychological assessment tool and its validity? Between convergent validity and discriminant validity?

4. What is a criterion group, and how were criterion groups used in the development of the MMPI?

5. What are the similarities and differences between an objective personality test like the California Personality Inventory and a projective test like the Rorschach?

6. What is the IQ? What are the conceptual and methodological problems associated with this measure of intellectual functioning?

7. How many aspects of intellectual ability are there? Should such things as musical ability and control over one's body be regarded as additional features of intelligence? Why or why not?

8. Is the heritability of intellectual performance the same, regardless of the measure used?

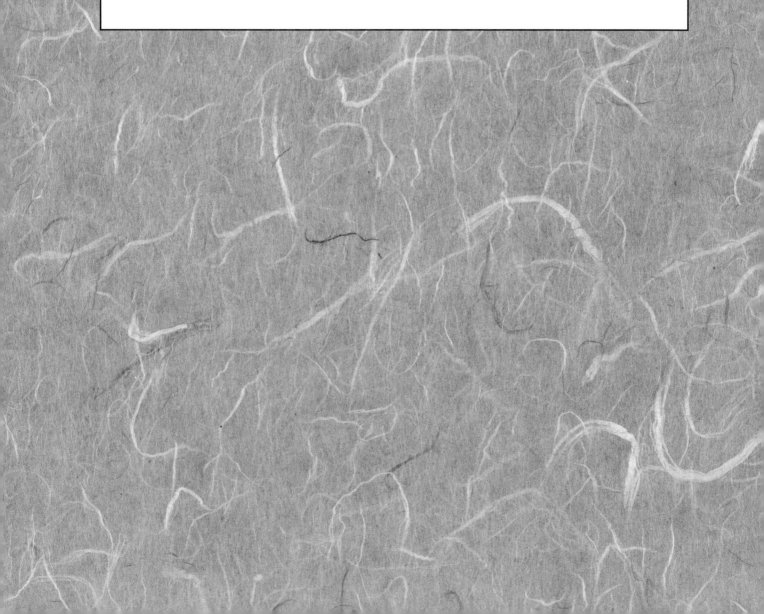

CHAPTER 23

STRESS AND COPING

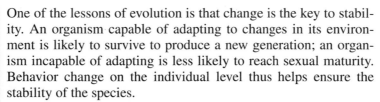

One of the lessons of evolution is that change is the key to stability. An organism capable of adapting to changes in its environment is likely to survive to produce a new generation; an organism incapable of adapting is less likely to reach sexual maturity. Behavior change on the individual level thus helps ensure the stability of the species.

Often an organism's adaptive behavior begins with a physiological response to external demands. This response, which prepares the individual to fight or to flee, evolved as a way of coping with the threats posed by predatory animals. Few modern human beings, however, come into contact with predators. Much more common today are the stressful events of urban life: the pressure of deadlines, the irritation of construction noise, the frustration of being trapped in a huge traffic jam. Nevertheless, the physiological response to these external demands remains much as it was when we were confronting sabre-tooth tigers. The sources of pressure and the methods of coping have changed, but the underlying physiological reactions have not.

Before discussing these physiological responses, we should note that the term *stress* has been defined in two quite different ways: (1) as the body's response to a noxious stimulus, and (2) as the stressful stimulus itself. The first definition is based on the work of Hans Selye (1936, 1976a, 1976b) and is most commonly found in medical and biological research. The second definition derives from engineering, in which stress is an external force exerted on a structure, producing "strain." Although psychological research often views stress as a stimulus (Singer, 1986), we will use the term **stressor** to denote the stimulus and **stress** to denote the response.

PHYSIOLOGICAL RESPONSES TO STRESSORS

There is a voluminous literature describing the body's response to external demands, but it all began with the work of two investigators—Walter Cannon and Hans Selye—each of whom was attempting to study something else (Cannon, 1935; Selye, 1936). Recall from Chapter 6 that William James (1892) believed that emotional states result from visceral sensations triggered by the arousal of the autonomic nervous system. Cannon criticized this view, arguing that changes in visceral organs are

Walter B. Cannon (left) and Hans H. B. Selye, the two pioneers credited with originating research on the body's response to environmental stressors.

not specific to external stimuli, and are, therefore, unable to reproduce a full range of emotional experience. As an alternative, Cannon proposed a *central* theory of emotional experience that placed the source of emotional experience in the brain. One way to make this case is to show that a single stressor can produce changes in a variety of visceral organs. This is just what Cannon did, by recording all the effects produced in cats that were frightened by barking dogs.

What happens when an organism is afraid? For many species, survival depends on one of two responses—fight or flight. An animal must be able either to defend itself or to outrun its adversary. Through Cannon's research, amplified by subsequent work, we know that when an animal is threatened its **adrenal glands** (two small endocrine glands located just above the kidneys) secrete adrenaline *(epinephrine)*, one of the *catecholamines,* neurotransmitters that activate the organism (see Chapter 5). Traveling through the bloodstream, the released epinephrine creates a diverse set of effects that together prepare the organism either to fight or to flee. As shown in Table 23-1, this emergency response includes increases in bodily processes (such as heart rate, muscle tone, respiration) that would strengthen a counterattack and decreases in processes (such as digestion, blood flow to the gut) that would reduce capability or exacerbate injury.

Cannon's purpose in summarizing the components of the emergency response was to show that a single stimulus could produce a wide variety of visceral effects. He thereby cast doubt on the idea that there is a one-to-one correspondence between a visceral change and an emotional experience. But Cannon's findings also revealed the commonality among visceral effects, a commonality that is very important, as will become clear shortly.

THE GENERAL ADAPTATION SYNDROME

At about the time that Cannon was doing his research, Selye was studying the physiological effects of sex hormones by injecting rats with extracts from the ovaries or placentas of other animals. When the rats were killed and dissected, the hormones were found to have had wholly unanticipated effects on three sets of organs: the adrenal glands, the lymphatic structures, and the stomach. Before describing those effects, let us take a brief look at each of the organs involved.

Adrenal Glands

The two adrenal glands, near the kidneys, are composed of an internal portion (the adrenal medulla) and an outer covering (the adrenal cortex). When stimulated, the adrenal gland secretes hormones into the bloodstream. The adrenal cortex secretes steroids, including the male sex hormone *androgen* (in both males and females), and

TABLE 23-1	Elements of the Emergency Response[a]	
	Increases In	Decreases In
	Heart rate	Digestive activity
	Blood pressure	Blood flow to gut
	Respiration rate	Kidney activity
	Dilation of:	
	Coronary arteries	
	Lung blood vessels	
	Blood flow to muscles	

[a]When confronted by a potential threat, the body prepares itself to fight or flee by increasing internal activities designed to enhance physical performance and decreasing those that would make the organism more vulnerable to infection should there be any injury.
SOURCE: Adapted from Selye, 1976a.

cortisone, a hormone often used in treating rheumatoid arthritis and certain skin disorders. The adrenal medulla secretes epinephrine (adrenaline) and *norepinephrine,* another catecholamine.

Lymphatic Structures

The lymph nodes, in the armpits, groin, and neck, produce *lymphocytes,* cells that circulate in the bloodstream and play a part in the body's defenses against infection. Certain organs, such as the thymus and spleen, are also composed primarily of lymphocytes. Together, these tissues and circulating cells constitute the *lymphatic structures.* An animal's immune reactions involve all these structures; damage to them leaves the organism more susceptible to infection.

The Stomach

Digestion is normally aided by hydrochloric acid secreted in the stomach, especially in the duodenum. The stomach lining is normally protected from the effects of the acid by a covering of mucus, but under certain conditions this protective shield fails and the stomach develops *ulcers.*

The Nonspecific Response to Stressors

What do stomach ulcers have in common with abnormal changes in the adrenal glands and lymphatic structures? The answer, discovered by Selye, is that all three occur in response to stressors. When Selye examined rats that had been injected with ovarian hormones, he discovered a consistent pattern: enlargement of the adrenal glands; shrinking of all the lymphatic structures, including fewer lymphocytes circulating in the blood; and bleeding ulcers. These effects are obvious when organs from injected rats are shown next to organs from noninjected rats, as in Figure 23-1 (Selye, 1976a).

Reasoning that the reactions might have been due to the biochemical nature of the hormones used, Selye experimented with other chemical agents and with forced restraint of the animal. Different stressors did produce different physiological results, but regardless of the stressor used, the triadic physiological pattern also occurred—enlarged adrenals, atrophy of lymphatic structures, and stomach ulcers. This pattern represents the body's *nonspecific* response to stressors; it is analogous to the fever that occurs as a result of any bacterial infection.

Three Stages of Response

Through research with noxious agents and stimulation, Selye discovered three distinct stages in the organism's response to stressors. (See Figure 23-2 on page 622.) These stages occur in addition to specific responses to the agent used. In the first stage, *alarm,* the body's defenses are aroused and the organism is prepared to fight or flee. When the stressor is a noxious agent or an injury to the body, most of the "fighting" is done in the bloodstream; when the stressor is an attack, the internal preparations are also accompanied by behavioral responses.

The alarm stage is an emergency response that cannot be maintained. If it is unsuccessful in reducing or eliminating the stressor, the organism's internal organs move into the second stage, *resistance.* In this stage the body's defenses are replenished for a sustained attack against the invading agent. Again, most of this attack is carried on in the bloodstream to eliminate a noxious agent or to kill an infection. Thus the internal changes supplement the organism's behavioral responses to attack.

If the stressor is so persistent that it outlasts both the alarm and resistance stages, the organism may suffer from the third stage, *exhaustion.* This can occur if a noxious agent is continually introduced into the body, or if a behavioral response continually fails to eliminate a stressor. With its resources severely depleted, the body is susceptible to illness or, in extreme cases, death. Exhaustion produces the triadic pattern of

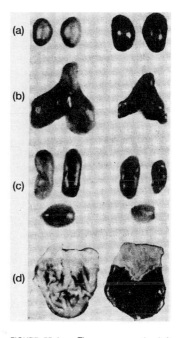

FIGURE 23-1   The organs on the left are those of a normal rat, those on the right are from a rat exposed to a prolonged environmental stressor. In the rat exposed to stress, the adrenal glands *(a)* are enlarged, the thymus *(b)* and lymph nodes *(c)* are smaller than normal, and the stomach lining *(d)* shows numerous ulcers. This pattern of organ damage is a typical result of the exhaustion stage of the General Adaptation Syndrome. (Source: Selye, 1976a.)

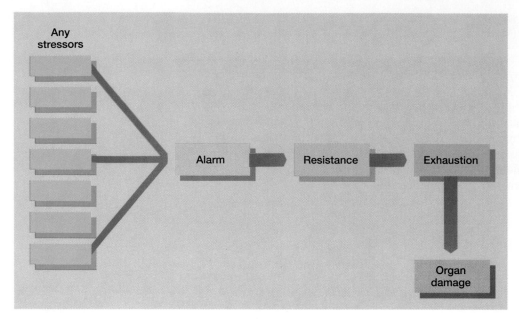

FIGURE 23-2 Elements of the general adaptation syndrome describing the body's response to environmental stressors. During the initial alarm phase the body's emergency mobilization prepares it to fight or flee; if this immediate reaction does not remove the stressor, the internal organs mount a sustained resistance. If there is continued failure to resolve the problem, there will be exhaustion, followed by damage to the adrenal glands, lymphatic structures, and stomach lining. (Source: Adapted from Selye, 1976.)

organ damage described earlier. Temporary changes in adrenal glands and lymphatic structures also accompany the alarm stage, but stomach ulcers take time to develop. Consequently, the full triadic pattern is unlikely to occur before exhaustion.

Together, the stages of alarm, resistance, and exhaustion make up what Selye called the **general adaptation syndrome.** Later research has shown that some stressors produce one kind of adrenal secretion whereas others produce different kinds (see, for example, Mason, 1975). Thus, some aspects of the body's response are specific to the particular noxious agent introduced. A review of all the physiological evidence suggests, however, that the reaction to stressors is a whole-body response that is *nonspecific* in that any stressor can cause it (Baum, Davidson, Singer, & Street, 1987).

WEAR AND TEAR

The extensive organ changes illustrated in Figure 23-1 represent the body's failure over time to cope with the effects of noxious agents or extreme environmental conditions. But long before devastating organ changes occur, the stress response adds to the wear and tear caused by everyday life.

Hormone Changes

The alarm phase of the general adaptation syndrome includes increased secretion of **adrenocorticotropic hormone (ACTH)** from the pituitary gland. This hormone stimulates the adrenal cortex to produce a substance known as cortisol. Elevated levels of cortisol have been found in chronic medical and psychiatric patients and in normal individuals suffering temporary distress from such events as oral examinations or surgery (Baum, Davidson, Singer, & Street, 1987). In women, the abnormal secretion of other hormones, such as follicle stimulating hormone (FSH) or luteinizing hormone (LH), may produce ovulation in response to acute stressors, or abnormal cessation of menstruation in response to chronic stressors (Selye, 1976b).

Organ Changes

Even during the early stages of response to stressors, ACTH and cortisol stimulate increases in the amount of hydrochloric acid secreted in the gastrointestinal tract. Thus, it is not surprising that ulcers are one of the results of chronic stress. But there are other results as well. In laboratory animals chronic stress damages the liver and pancreas and causes changes in the kidneys (Baum, Davidson, Singer, & Street,

1987). Most important for humans, chronic stress responses are implicated in many changes in the cardiovascular system, including damage to the blood vessel walls, increased resting blood pressure, and the likelihood of developing heart disease (Baum, Davidson, Singer, & Street, 1987). Because cardiovascular diseases cause more than half of all deaths in the United States, and because personality variables are implicated in the relationship between stress and heart disease, this topic will be covered in detail in a later section. Here it is enough to note that stressful life events clearly contribute to wear and tear on the body.

INTERIM SUMMARY

A stressor is an external force exerted on the body, which experiences stress as a result. The stress response consists of a predictable pattern of physiological responses known as the general adaptation syndrome. This syndrome affects the adrenal glands, lymphatic structures, and stomach, and occurs in three stages: alarm, resistance, and exhaustion. Long-term stress can cause elevated secretions of adreno-corticotropic hormone (ACTH), increases in hydrochloric acid in the stomach, and increased likelihood of heart disease.

THE STRESS OF DAILY LIVING

Most early research on the physiological stress response used animal subjects exposed to extreme stressors such as injections of powerful biochemical compounds in large doses. If these noxious agents were the only sources of stress, the study of stress would have remained an esoteric medical specialty. What makes the study of stress and coping so important for psychology is that cognitive processes are also involved in the production of stress, as well as in alleviating its effects.

COGNITIVE FACTORS IN STRESS

According to one investigator, stress is "in the mind of the beholder" (Cohen, 1986, p. 66). Consider two characteristics of modern urban life: noise and crowding. Much research has shown that the *perceived* qualities of sound or population density can make them stressful (Cohen, 1986; Suedfeld, 1986). If they are extreme, of course, they will produce stress in any case. But if the objective conditions are moderate,

Cognitive factors affect the way we perceive stressors. The person who finds the crowding and loud noise of a club enjoyable might feel stress if confined in some other environment that was equally crowded and noisy.

cognitive processes will make a difference. Imagine, for example, that you were listening to your car radio, tuned to a station that plays a kind of music you enjoy. Now suppose that without changing the volume, you switched to a station that plays a kind of music you dislike. You would immediately feel the urge to turn down the volume. Or imagine that a large group of people packed into a friend's small apartment for a party was transported to an equally small college office to register for an oversubscribed class. What had been a friendly group of revelers would become a large number of competitors, causing the room to seem crowded.

The Appraisal Process

The importance of cognitive factors in stress is related to the nature of stressors in the modern world. As a biological process that prepares the individual to fight or flee, the stress response obviously serves evolutionary purposes. For modern human beings, however, survival has been redefined:

> Stress nowadays is not so much associated with survival as with a certain idea of survival. . . . Sitting for an exam, applying for a job, the climate of competition in which money and power are the criteria of success—these are some of today's stressors that elicit the old physiological response preparing the human organism for physical activity. [Tache & Selye, 1986, pp. 19–20]

Figure 23-3 illustrates the role of cognitive processes—specifically the appraisal process—in mediating between the stressor and the perceived stress (Lazarus & Folkman, 1984). An example will clarify the relationships shown in the figure. Imagine a person who is late for an important meeting, driving on a narrow road, and caught behind another car that is traveling well below the posted speed limit. Situational factors affecting the perception of this stressor would include the road and traffic conditions. If oncoming traffic is light and the road is straight, our tardy driver should be able to pass the slow car promptly, thus removing it as a stressor. If oncoming traffic is heavy and the road is tortuous, our driver could be stuck for a long time. Personal factors affecting the perception of the stressor could include the driver's disposition and status in the company. If the driver is usually relaxed and holds an important position, then being late might not be much of a problem. But if the driver is usually tense and holds a lesser position, then the effect of the stressor will be exaggerated.

The appraisal process includes several judgments. First, the person decides whether a particular transaction with the environment is relevant to his or her well-being. In this case the transaction includes the environment's restriction of the per-

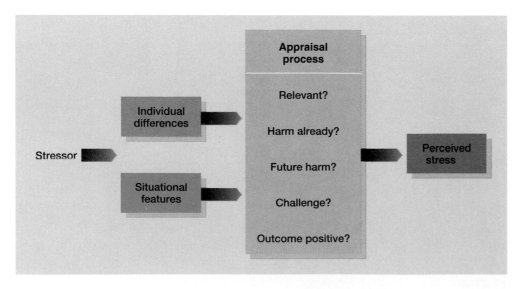

FIGURE 23-3 The cognitive appraisal model of adaptation to stressors. Environmental stressors occur in a situational context that may influence their action on the individual; not all people respond to these stressors in exactly the same fashion. Despite individual differences, people are thought to ask themselves whether the stressor is relevant to them and whether it has produced harm already or will do so in the future. Then they examine their resources to determine whether they will be able to meet the challenge, and estimate the probability of a positive outcome. Ultimately all these cognitive factors act to create perceived stress, which may or may not be the same as the original environmental stressor.

son's travel and what the person will do to eliminate that restriction. It also involves deciding what will be lost by being even more tardy. At this point, appraisal leading to an ultimate reduction of stress might be, "My secretary will cover for me at the beginning of the meeting, and they won't get to the things they need me for right away." Next, the person determines whether the transaction has already produced harm that requires a response, or may produce such harm in the future. This appraisal might be, "So far, I've only been behind this slowpoke for a minute. If I get lucky, I can make up the time." The process also includes consideration of the challenges posed by the situation and the estimated possibility of a positive outcome, such as, "There's a four-lane stretch just ahead, so I can pass there without any real danger." Despite its positive outcome in this case, the demands placed on the body by the appraisal process generate the typical stress response, which can itself be modified by cognitive factors such as thinking of a plausible excuse for tardiness.

Effects on the Body

When a person's body is invaded by bacteria or viruses, the invader is immediately attacked by three kinds of cells. The first of these, *macrophages,* circulate in the bloodstream and engulf the bacteria or virus at the point of invasion. The second kind consists of *T cells*—lymphocytes that originate in the bone marrow. When they pass through the thymus, the T cells become immunocompetent, or capable of a normal immune response. In cooperation with the macrophages, the T cells secrete other biochemicals (**lymphokines,** specifically interleukin-1 and interleukin-2) that cause the T cells to multiply and to activate *B cells.* The B cells also originate in the bone marrow, but they become immunocompetent by passing through the spleen and lymph nodes. Once activated, the B cells secrete antibodies specific to the invading entities, thereby killing them (Campbell & Cohen, 1985; see also Vollhardt, 1991).

Notice that both the T cells and the B cells mature into immunocompetent cells by passing through the thymus, spleen, and lymph nodes—which are among the organs that are damaged by extended exposure to stress. When we remember that the effective stressor is not an external stimulus but the stimulus *as perceived by the individual,* it becomes apparent that people might, through their cognitive responses to stressors, suppress the functioning of the immune system. In short, people might almost "think themselves sick." Although little of the available research evidence has been able to show how cognitive processes might directly produce change to the immune system, there is substantial evidence of a relationship between chronic stress and the onset of disease. Stressful life events have been implicated in the development of heart disease (Rahe, 1987), depression (Weiss & Simson, 1985), and hypertension (Anderson, 1985). We will consider two well-documented sources of potential stress.

MAJOR LIFE EVENTS

Earlier we discussed two stressors—noise and crowding—that are common to most modern urban environments. In industrial societies, the impact of these stressors is compounded by competition, frustration, and a variety of significant life changes that are not encountered in primitive societies. Research suggests that an "overdose" of such changes can increase the likelihood of coronary heart disease (Holmes & Rahe, 1967; Rahe, 1987).

Measuring Life Changes

One problem that immediately arises in the study of psychosocial stressors is definitional. Although there are generally accepted ways of measuring the intensity of many potential stressors, this is not so for psychosocial stressors. In laboratory studies with animals, for example, the form of restraint can be specified, the concentration of an injected chemical can be noted, or the decibel level of a sound can be assessed. But there is no operational definition of "life changes." Moreover, everyday life *is* change; how can one determine when those changes are stressful?

These issues are addressed in a questionnaire called the Recent Life Changes Questionnaire (RLCQ) (Rahe, 1987), an expansion of the Schedule of Recent Experiences questionnaire originally designed by Holmes and Rahe (1967). The RLCQ lists 55 life experiences divided into five major sections: health, work, home and family, personal and social, and financial. Respondents are asked to indicate how recently, if at all, they have undergone each experience listed. The questionnaire is designed to predict the likelihood of coronary heart disease (CHD); because the vast majority of CHD patients are males, some of the questions are worded for men. All but a few questions, however, are equally appropriate for women. Some items from each major section of the RLCQ are shown in Table 23-2 (with their original numbering).

Two aspects of the questionnaire deserve comment. First, what is important is *change,* not whether the change is positive or negative. Vacations, marriages, births of grandchildren, and purchases of new automobiles are desirable, whereas major dental work, serious illnesses of family members, sexual difficulties, and foreclosure on a mortgage are undesirable. The point is that regardless of whether a change is positive or negative, it places a demand on the person that can produce stress.

A second key aspect of the questionnaire is that not all the changes are equally important. The death of one's spouse obviously is more catastrophic than damage to personal property. The scoring of responses to the RLCQ takes into account the relative intensity of life experiences by stating weights for each item in terms of *life change units.* Such units are shown in parentheses for those items in the RLCQ that were scaled in the questionnaire from which the RLCQ was developed (Holmes & Rahe, 1967). In this weighted system, the death of a spouse has, on the average, twice the impact of marriage. The scoring also takes into account the amount of change that typically occurs in most people's lives; this is represented as a baseline of some 150 life-change units per year. This amount of change is considered "background noise" (Rahe, 1987), and only if total life change deviates significantly from this level is there thought to be a major effect on health.

TABLE 23-2   Items from the Recent Life Changes Questionnaire[a]

Within the time periods listed, have you experienced:

A. Health

2.	major dental work?
3.	a major change in eating habits? (15)
5.	a major change in your usual type and/or amount of recreation? (19)

B. Work

7.	a change in your work hours or conditions? (20)
10.	a major business readjustment? (39)
11.	a retirement? (45)

C. Home and Family

17.	a major change in the health or behavior of a family member (illnesses, accidents, drug, or disciplinary problems, etc.)?
18.	marriage? (50)
30.	the birth of a grandchild?
31.	death of a spouse? (100)

D. Personal and Social

36.	a change in your political beliefs?
39.	a vacation? (13)
43.	sexual difficulties? (39)

E. Financial

52.	a loss or damage of personal property?
53.	a moderate purchase (such as an automobile, a stereo, a home computer, etc.)?
55.	foreclosure on a mortgage or loan? (30)

[a]These items indicate the range of environmental changes that can serve as stressors. Numbers in parentheses represent the presumed impact (as scaled in an earlier questionnaire) of the item.

In terms of reducing overall stress, sometimes the best response to an environmental disaster is to "relax and enjoy it."

Life Change and Heart Disease

What exactly is the effect of life changes on health? In particular, will taking a vacation put you at risk of a heart attack? Obviously the answer is no. Life changes need to be considered in the context of the major risk factors in coronary heart disease. A sedentary, overweight male smoker with a high cholesterol level is a prime candidate for a heart attack regardless of how stressor-free his life might be. In contrast, an active, slim female nonsmoker with a low cholesterol level is an unlikely candidate for heart disease even if she has had a high level of recent life changes.

Life changes apparently affect the timing of heart attacks, not the risk of ever having an attack. Risk factors such as smoking, overweight, lack of exercise, and high cholesterol levels remain relatively constant. Why, then, does a person have a heart attack at one time rather than another? One answer is that the demands of increased life changes outstrip the person's ability to cope with those changes.

A number of studies have compared people who have had a heart attack with other people who have not. Researchers began by obtaining retrospective reports from patients who had just had a first attack. These patients were asked to indicate their life changes for each quarter-year preceding the attack. A recent review combined the results of several such studies; the trend revealed by these findings is clear (see Figure 23-4). The level of life changes immediately before a heart attack is, on the average, significantly higher than it was two years earlier (Rahe, 1987).

FIGURE 23-4 Recent life changes during the 3-month (quarter-year) periods before a heart attack. Individuals who had heart attacks also had significant life changes during the period from 9 to 12 months before the attack. (Source: Adapted from Rahe, 1987.)

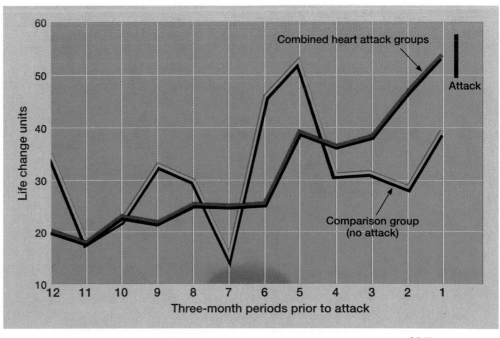

627

Retrospective research designs of this kind have three problems. First, recent experiences may be more vivid than those that occurred years ago, and some from years ago may have been forgotten completely. Second, the patients are 3 years older at the time of their attacks than they were during the first period they are asked to describe so their bodies have had more time to deteriorate. Third, to the degree that the patients themselves believe that life events may be precursors of heart attacks, they may be overestimating the level of recent changes. Recognizing these difficulties, the investigators conducted a number of studies designed to reduce or eliminate the problems. For example, they used interviews with family members to compare events in the lives of patients who had survived an attack with those of patients who had died. Another alternative to retrospective methods were prospective studies that followed patients after their first heart attack and compared changes in the life experiences of patients who had a second attack, or died, with those of patients who did not. Regardless of the method used, the basic pattern was repeated: More serious health problems were preceded by increases in life changes (Rahe, 1987).

PERSONALITY STYLE

Life changes, in and of themselves, are not the sole cause of CHD. They are *potential* stressors, and, like other demands, they are filtered through the individual's cognitive processes and personal characteristics. Some people deal with life changes productively; others find them devastating. Consequently, another mediating influence on the stress response is personality style. One personality style, or set of traits, has been so frequently associated with heart disease that it has virtually become a risk factor itself. This is the so-called *Type A* personality style.

For decades physicians have shared anecdotes about individuals whose hard-driving aggressiveness makes them prime candidates for heart attacks. Two cardiologists first described the specific elements of this coronary-prone behavior pattern (Friedman & Rosenman, 1959). As more recently elaborated, the Type A pattern involves extremes of competitiveness, striving for achievement, aggressiveness and hostility, time urgency (impatience, haste, restlessness, feelings of time pressure), and willingness to oppose others if necessary to achieve one's own goals (Jenkins, 1971). In contrast, the so-called *Type B* pattern is more relaxed, low in competitiveness and hostility, and interested in accommodation rather than opposition.

These characteristics can be assessed by means of a structured interview, but more important than the content of the subject's responses is the manner in which those responses are given. Several voice cues are used to infer the presence of Type A behavior. These include loud, explosive, rapid, and accelerated speech; quick responses; verbal competitiveness; and indications of hostility toward the interviewer. The Type A pattern can also be assessed by a paper-and-pencil measure, the Jenkins Activity Survey (Jenkins, Zyzanski, & Rosenman, 1979), but this measure obviously cannot provide any indication of interpersonal hostility.

Type A Behavior and Heart Disease

A prospective study begun in 1960, the Western Collaborative Group Study, extended over eight and a half years. It included more than 3,500 males recruited from 10 corporations in northern California. All subjects were initially free of any symptoms of CHD. These men had annual medical examinations that included measures of blood pressure, cholesterol, and general health habits. In addition, researchers obtained information about their medical history, level of education, and annual income. The Type A pattern was assessed at the beginning of the study and again after 18 months. Study results showed that Type A behavior was an *independent* risk factor for the development of CHD, roughly comparable in importance to traditional risk factors such as smoking, high blood pressure, or a high cholesterol level (Krantz, Lundberg, & Frankenhaeuser, 1987).

Some investigators have expressed reservations about the WCGS (Dembroski & MacDougall, 1985). Not only have several other studies failed to find a relationship between the overall Type A behavior pattern and heart disease, but a new prospective study of more than 3,100 subjects (the Multiple Risk Factor Intervention Trial, or MRFIT) has not found the overall Type A pattern to be an independent risk factor (Shekelle et al., 1983). These discrepancies have led investigators to reexamine the importance of the elements of the overall Type A pattern. Although this research is still under way, the best present suggestion is that the patient's *hostility* (both toward others and toward himself) accounts for the differences. When scores for hostility are a major influence on whether a person is classified as Type A or Type B, as they are in the structured interview that assesses the manner in which questions are answered, there is a relationship between the overall pattern and heart disease. But when factors other than hostility are the principal means for classifying subjects as Type A or Type B, as in the questionnaire methods, there seems to be little correlation between the Type A pattern and CHD. Whether the global Type A pattern, or only the hostility component of the pattern, is ultimately established as an independent risk factor for CHD, it is still evident that individual differences can affect the course of the stress response.

OTHER POTENTIAL STRESSORS

Recent life experiences and personal style of dealing with them are not the only factors involved in stress responses. As noted earlier, noise and crowding are potential stressors, and there are numerous others in the modern industrialized environment. Hardly a week goes by without the publication of articles about "stress in the workplace," but there has not yet been much controlled experimental research, including careful measurements of physiological markers of the stress response, among white-collar workers. Studies of blue-collar workers show, however, that occupational

Occupational noise can be stressful.

Stress can be produced not only by major life traumas that occur infrequently, but also by the "everyday hassles" that are a normal part of living in an urbanized society.

noise and rotating shifts produce increases in norepinephrine secretion; that job dissatisfaction and plant noise interact to increase blood pressure; and that sawmill employees with dangerous jobs have higher levels of epinephrine secretion than workers with less hazardous jobs in the same mill (Cottington & House, 1987).

One model suggests that two critical factors, acting in concert, increase the risk of job-related heart disease (Karasek, Russell, & Theorell, 1982). The first factor consists of demands inherent in the job, such as time pressure or monotony; the second is the extent of the individual's control over job-related decision making. According to the model, workers with high job demands and little say in how to cope with them should be at greater risk of developing CHD. The results of several studies provide support for this model (Cottington & House, 1987).

Some researchers have drawn attention to the "little things" that make life stressful (Kanner, Coyne, Schaefer, & Lazarus, 1982). Being concerned about events in the news, suffering through traffic congestion, having to wait in line, not getting enough sleep, and being lonely are everyday "hassles" that create stress by the regularity of their recurrence. Because these hassles are viewed as routine and nonserious, one is expected to take them in stride. This is in marked contrast to the way people regard major life changes such as those assessed by the RLCQ. Those major changes are expected to lead to the mobilization of the individual's coping resources. For example, a person whose spouse has died is expected to grieve and is given time off from work (and/or forgiven for decreased job performance). The bereaved individual also receives extensive social support from family, friends, and co-workers, and will not be stigmatized for seeking professional help. These life events are comparatively rare, with the result that ordinary rules about appropriate responses are suspended. On the other hand, the everyday annoyances of life are just that—daily irritants that affect everyone. We expect both ourselves and others to be able to deal with them effectively.

Consequently, routine irritants can be regarded as *microstressors* that place continuing demands on the individual. Researchers have attempted to assess the health effects of these everyday hassles, using a scale for measuring them (DeLongis, Coyne, Dakof, Folkman, & Lazarus, 1982; Kanner, Coyne, Schaefer, & Lazarus, 1981). This scale consists of 117 items dealing with annoyances associated with household duties, health, time pressure, inner concerns (such as being lonely), environmental problems (such as noise), financial responsibility, work, and concerns about future security. Responses to the scale have been correlated with self-reported psychological symptoms (Kanner et al., 1981). There is, however, no evidence as yet that physiological variables mediate the relationship between daily hassles and the psychological stress response.

Research has shown that cognitive factors influence the stress response. The perception of a stimulus as harmful can generate the physiological components of the stress response; in other words, people can "think themselves sick." When major life changes substantially exceed their baseline level, they can affect the timing of coronary heart disease. The personal style known as the Type A behavior pattern, which includes such things as competitiveness, time urgency, and hostility, may also increase the risk of coronary heart disease. Recent research suggests that hostility is the most significant of these characteristics. Microstressors, everyday hassles that place continuing demands on the person, also produce psychological symptoms of stress, but there is no evidence yet that these symptoms are mediated physiologically.

COPING WITH STRESS

Logically, there are three ways in which an individual can react to a stressor: Do nothing; change or eliminate the stressor; or modify the response. We have already discussed the consequences of doing nothing; in this section we will consider the other two options.

REMOVING OR ALTERING THE STRESSOR

An individual who wishes to remove a stressor has a choice: Take unilateral action to protect himself or herself, or participate in collective action to remove stressors on a larger scale. Many policies of government and industry can be viewed as collective actions against stressors. For example, virtually all the activities of the Occupational Safety and Health Administration (OSHA) reduce the frequency and intensity of stressors in the workplace. Limits on noise levels in manufacturing plants, regulations requiring protective clothing for workers exposed to hazardous chemicals, and standards for the safe operation of heavy machinery have eliminated stressors that otherwise might affect the health of industrial employees. Contemporary business practices also contribute to the removal or reduction of stress. Examples include the pension plans, health insurance or health maintenance programs, and educational or training opportunities offered by corporations. At the community level, individuals

Collective policies of government and industry can both contribute to, and reduce, the influence of environmental stressors. Here, regulations requiring protective clothing for those who work directly with hazardous materials reduce the danger for the workers. But the presence of large amounts of such hazardous materials in our society raises the level of danger for everyone.

Even on the level of an individual neighborhood, people can band together to reduce the influence of stressors. However, some fear that sometimes such collective action can result in vigilantism. In this picture, a group called the Guardian Angels seeks to reduce the likelihood of crime in a neighborhood.

form voluntary groups to protect aspects of their environment, or participate in neighborhood watch programs that can be highly successful in reducing crime rates in the covered area.

Not all collective activity reduces stressors. The same government that sponsors OSHA is responsible for an annual stressor—people's filing and payment of income tax. The same corporations that offer stress management seminars for their employees may also transfer managers to other locations, and such transfers are a major stressor. Even well-meaning community organizations can decrease individual privacy.

At the individual level, "reducing stress sometimes entails refusing to be placed under stress and, up to a point, refusing to meet challenges" (Tache & Selye, 1986, p. 22). More and more business managers are electing to change companies rather than relocate. Some people choose to live in the city rather than face a long daily commute; others commute because they consider life in the suburbs less stressful (and some of them join vanpools to eliminate the driving). Anyone who makes a life-style choice instead of a professional or economic choice may be doing so to avoid at least some stressors.

MANAGING THE LEVEL OF STRESS

Collective or individual action against stressors usually takes place through conscious choice. Stress management can likewise involve conscious choice, but it can also entail less effective defenses that occur without conscious consideration.

A Decision-making Model of Coping

According to one model, coping involves a reasoning process—analysis of the stressor and a proper response to it (Janis, 1986). This decision-making model focuses on the way people evaluate and respond to an impending danger for which they are able to prepare in advance. (See Figure 23-5.)

As shown in the figure, the model suggests that coping involves a series of decisions about the danger. One decision path leads to effective coping; the others to

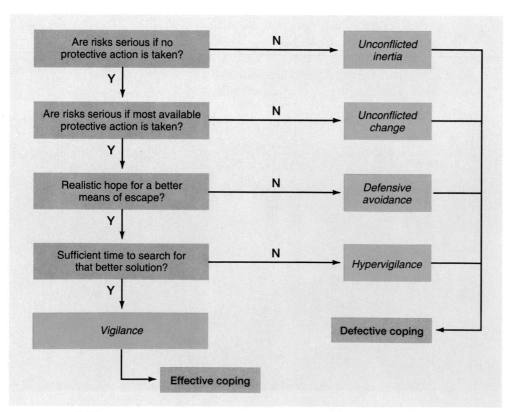

FIGURE 23-5 The decision-making model of effectiveness in responding to environmental stressors. Successful coping with a threat is presumed to occur if the person accurately assesses the risks, believes there is a realistic way to escape from or deal with those risks, has time to find an appropriate solution, and remains vigilant regarding the dangers and how to counter them. If this process is interrupted, ineffective coping is apt to result. (Source: Adapted from Janis & Mann, 1977.)

ineffective coping. The first decision involves assessing the degree of risk posed by the danger. If the risk is deemed insignificant, the individual continues as before, in a state called *unconflicted inertia.* If the risk is deemed serious, the individual must decide whether his or her usual repertoire of responses is sufficient to cope with it. If it is, then the result is *unconflicted change* to another available alternative. Both unconflicted inertia and unconflicted change will be ineffective coping responses should the danger materialize and be more serious than expected.

If the risks are considered serious even if protective action is taken, then the individual assesses the prospects of finding a solution. Failing to identify any better means of escape will lead to *defensive avoidance.* But if there is hope, then the last question is whether there is still time to find a solution. If there is not, then the result is *hypervigilance,* a state of near panic in which the individual may commit to a hastily contrived solution. Defensive avoidance and hypervigilance, like unconflicted inertia and change, lead to ineffective coping if the danger materializes.

According to the model, only in the state called **vigilance** will there be successful coping should the threatened stressor actually occur. Vigilance comes about only if the person has recognized the seriousness of the risks, recognized that immediately available protective actions may not suffice, realized that other avenues of escape exist, and had the time or opportunity to investigate those avenues thoroughly.

Principles of this model have been tested with hospitalized patients awaiting surgery or stressful diagnostic procedures. In one study, patients in an experimental group were given instructions designed to encourage an optimistic view of the decision to have surgery, to identify the positive consequences of the decision, but to be realistic about the setbacks that might be encountered (Langer, Janis, & Wolfer, 1975). Compared to patients who were not given this advance preparation, the patients who were encouraged to be realistically optimistic showed less preoperative stress, as rated by nurses who were unaware of the instructions received by the patients, and less postoperative desire for and use of pain relievers and sedatives.

Stress Inoculation

Anyone who has ever been in a hospital can understand how a thorough discussion of posttreatment outcomes can aid in recovery. This is especially true if the discussion includes realistic yet optimistic recommendations for coping with the stress created by the treatment. Removing the element of uncertainty will not reduce pain, but it will reduce the level of perceived stress. Previous experience of mastery of the anticipated stressors would be even more effective than cognitive preparation. This is the idea behind a procedure known as *stress inoculation* (Meichenbaum & Novaco, 1986), which combines cognitive preparation with graded mastery over mild stress of the sort that will be encountered in larger doses later.

Some occupations are notoriously stress-inducing. Police, for example, routinely experience the anger of a public they are sworn to protect and defend. Stress inoculation techniques have been used successfully to prepare police officers for their everyday activities.

Occupations can be sources of stressors, and some people's jobs are especially stress-inducing—air traffic controllers, hazardous waste emergency response team members, police officers, and firefighters, for example. Stress inoculation has been used successfully in the training of police officers (Meichenbaum & Novaco, 1986), for whom a major stressor is the anger they experience in dealing with the public. Officers are taunted by belligerent youths, frustrated by citizens who refuse to help, and second-guessed by lawyers and judges who have plenty of time to contemplate decisions made by the officers in the heat of a crisis.

The stress-inoculation procedure for police consisted of three phases. In the *cognitive preparation phase* officers were asked to distinguish among provocations and to identify the factors that contribute to anger. Those factors include predisposing events, such as equipment trouble, that may have nothing to do with the eventual provocation; cognitive determinants, such as expectations about danger in a particular neighborhood; and situational cues, such as a suspect's appearance or demeanor. The cognitive preparation phase allows officers to see their anger as the culmination of a long sequence of irritating events. This insight opens the possibility of short-circuiting the script leading to stress by dealing with the minor irritants before they can build into the background for the precipitating event.

In the second phase, *skill acquisition,* officers were taught how to cope with provocations. They were shown how to prepare for confrontations, recognize and reduce the arousal that accompanies the stress response, and deal with the psychological effects of conflict (regardless of how the conflict was resolved). In the third phase, *application,* the officers participated in role playing that allowed them to practice their newly acquired skills. Results of this study suggest that stress inoculation training may improve the officers' effectiveness in dealing with provocations.

THE IMPORTANCE OF CONTROL

Like virtually all approaches to successful coping, the decision-making model of coping and the stress-inoculation technique emphasize the individual's personal control over stressors. People who are exposed to high levels of noise suffer less stress if they believe they can control the noise, regardless of whether they choose to exercise that control (Glass & Singer, 1972). Patients who are told explicitly how they themselves can deal with anticipated setbacks require less pain medication. Police officers who are taught how to respond to provocation are better able to deal with the stressful aspects of their job. In these and numerous other instances, control is a key element.

Individual Differences

People differ in their desire to exert control over stressors—some strive for complete control over environmental threats; others try not to think about potential threats unless they materialize. Over the years, researchers have proposed a number of labels for this dimension, including *repression–sensitization* (Byrne, 1964), *avoidance–vigilance* (Cohen & Lazarus, 1973; Janis, 1958), and *blunting–monitoring* (Miller, 1980). Each dimension is expressed as a pair of opposites, reflecting the fact that it is presumed to extend on a continuum from people whose orientation toward stressors is passive to those whose orientation is active.

One distinction among the dimensions is based on the pervasiveness with which each is presumed to influence behavior. Specifically, repression–sensitization is viewed as a relatively stable personality trait; repressors are people who avoid anxiety-arousing stimuli through selective attention or forgetting, whereas sensitizers are oriented toward such stimuli. This enduring personality trait, like any other such trait, is thought to affect a wide variety of behavior, with response to potential stressors being only one aspect. In contrast, avoidance–vigilance is more of a personal style than an enduring trait; avoidance involves procrastinating, giving up responsibility for the outcome, and failing to make appropriate contingency plans, whereas vigilance involves attention, accepting of responsibility, and planning ways to deal with anticipated stressors. As a personal style, avoidance–vigilance is a way of dealing with stressors that does not affect behavior unless environmental threats are salient. Finally, blunting–monitoring involves attention to the stressor itself, as expressed in preference for distraction from versus orientation toward the threat.

These and other coping styles have been categorized as involving either approach to or avoidance of the threat (Roth & Cohen, 1986). Each considers coping to be a dynamic process, an interchange between the individual's own predilections and the demands of the situation. But commitment to an initial response does not obligate the person to continue that response indefinitely.

At any point, a person may alter a response that seems not to be productive. An important benefit of approaching stressors is that doing so increases the likelihood that one will take appropriate action. The major costs of approach are increases in distress and worry about what *might* happen. In contrast, the central benefit of avoidance is stress reduction. But that may come with a very high price—disruptive emotional responses that get in the way of taking effective action. One cannot be an effective problem-solver when one is emotionally distraught. Consequently, the ideal strategy is a mixture of approach (to those stressor aspects over which the individual has some control) and avoidance (of the more emotion-arousing components of the situation).

Regaining Control

Coping techniques that involve preparing for an impending stressor have little to offer people who are trapped in a stressful environment or who are suddenly victimized. Stressors such as constant exposure to environmental hazards or occupational pressures, for example, can seldom be reduced significantly except by removing oneself from them. When leaving would result in unemployment or homelessness, however, it may not be an option. Similarly, stressors such as sudden health crises, serious accidents, or criminal assault rarely allow for preparation. Even in these situations, however, the individual's ability to regain some sense of control—even if it is only illusory—plays an important role in reducing the stressor's effect.

Engaging in a program of vigorous exercise, for example, can have positive effects on health although it has no effect on environmental stressors (Blumenthal & McCubbin, 1987). A number of studies have compared responses to short-term

Attempting to regain control over one's life and finding a helpful source of social support are two of the best means for coping with the acute stress that follows an incident of victimization.

Norman Cousins, the author whose report of his success in "thinking" his cancer into remission suggests the important role that cognition may play in the functioning of the immune system.

stress among physically fit and sedentary individuals. Those studies have found few differences in initial physiological response to stress, but the physically fit individuals typically *recovered* more quickly (Blumenthal & McCubbin, 1987).

Another technique for managing stress is obtaining social support (Coyne & Downey, 1991). Participating in a company-sponsored stress management program, spending time with friends, or having a supportive companion can provide health benefits. Unfortunately, the investigation of the health benefits of social support has been plagued by conceptual and methodological problems. For one thing, people who seek social support may already be more effective at coping with stressors than people who do not seek help (Wortman & Dunkel-Schetter, 1987). Recently, however, a number of studies involving the random assignment of individuals to social-support or no-social-support conditions, together with the use of physiological outcome measures rather than self-reports, have shown that social support can be beneficial (Wortman & Dunkel-Schetter, 1987).

Finally, to restate: regaining a sense of control can be important even if that control is illusory. Interviews with victims of breast cancer have found that nearly two-thirds believe they can personally prevent the cancer from returning (Taylor, Lichtman, & Wood, 1984). This belief may have been stimulated by a popular book reporting one person's success in "thinking" cancer into remission (Cousins, 1979), but the more researchers learn about the relationship between stress and suppression of the immune system, the more it becomes apparent that a positive attitude may indeed enhance healing. Attempts to regain control have also been found to have positive effects on coping with accidents and criminal victimization (Bulman & Wortman, 1977; Janoff-Bulman, 1979).

These findings have led to a theory that emphasizes *cognitive* adaptation to stress (Taylor, 1983). This theory argues that adjustment involves three themes: a search for the meaning of the experience, an attempt to gain mastery over the particular event and over one's life in general, and an effort to restore one's self-esteem through self-enhancing comparisons to other people in the same situation. Aspects of this theory have yet to be fully tested, but the findings of early research (Taylor, 1983) reinforce the view that regaining a sense of personal control is an essential ingredient of coping.

INTERIM SUMMARY

One way of coping with stress is to remove or alter the stressor. This may be accomplished through collective action (for example, government or industry policies) or individual action. Anyone who makes a life-style choice instead of a professional or economic choice may be doing so to avoid stress. Another way of coping is to manage the level of stress. A decision-making model of coping describes the response to a realistic threat of impending danger as consisting of a reasoning process in which the individual assesses the risks and takes appropriate protective action. According to this model, only when the process results in vigilance (recognition of the threat and investigation of alternative protective actions) will there be successful coping if the threatened stressor actually occurs. Another approach, stress inoculation, combines cognitive preparation with graded mastery over mild stress of the kind that will be encountered later. Stress inoculation occurs in three phases: cognitive preparation, skill acquisition, and application. Virtually all approaches to successful coping emphasize the importance of personal control over stressors, even when the stressor has already occurred. Regaining a sense of control can be important even if that control is illusory.

SUMMARY

1. When an organism is afraid, its survival may depend on the success with which it can fight or flee. To prepare for either alternative, the *adrenal glands* secrete *epinephrine* that begins the emergency response. This response includes increases in heart rate, muscle tone, and respiration, and decreases in digestion and blood flow to the skin. Modern humans rarely confront hungry tigers, but other external stressors in the urban environment can produce many of the same physiological changes.

2. The body's response to external stressors—called the *general adaptation syndrome*—consists of three stages. During the alarm stage the body's defenses are aroused. This arousal cannot last long, so if the defenses are unsuccessful the organism moves into the resistance stage, during which the resources of the adrenals and lymphatic structures are replenished. Finally, if the organism remains unsuccessful, it may reach exhaustion, which is accompanied by damage to the adrenals, lymphatic structures, and stomach.

3. Although the stress response is physiological, it can be mediated by a cognitive appraisal process. Individual differences in personality may either reduce or exacerbate the external threat.

4. In the modern urban environment, noise and crowding are two common stressors.

But variable *life events*—changes in health, work, home and family, finances, or personal/social life—may also produce the stress response.

5. Recent life changes have been implicated in coronary heart disease. Not only major life changes, but also the minor hassles of daily living in the modern urban environment are contributors to the stress response.

6. The way a person approaches the world can also affect medical outcomes. An example is the difference between the so-called *Type A* person and the *Type B* person. Type A involves competitiveness, striving for achievement, time urgency, willingness to use other people, and, most important, aggressiveness and hostility. Type B is more relaxed and less competitive or hostile. The hostility associated with Type A has been linked to heart attacks.

7. Responses to environmental stress can involve collective action to reduce or eliminate the problem, or individual actions, including decisions to enhance coping with a stressor that cannot be eliminated.

8. Whether the particular strategy for coping is the *vigilance* suggested by one model or the *stress inoculation* identified by another, a critical variable is the individual's perceived *control* over life events and other stressors.

FOCUS QUESTIONS

1. Describe the general adaptation syndrome, concentrating on the three organ groups that are harmed by this nonspecific response to stressors.

2. Describe the process for cognitive appraisal of stress. How might such processes be involved in immunosuppression?

3. How should Type A and Type B personalities be measured? How is the Type A behavior pattern related to heart attacks?

4. What are the health implications of both major life changes and minor irritations? Which do you think might be more of a problem?

5. Describe some of the collective actions that can be taken to minimize responses to stressors.

6. What are the elements of the decision-making model of coping with stressors? Show how personal control can be important in the coping process.

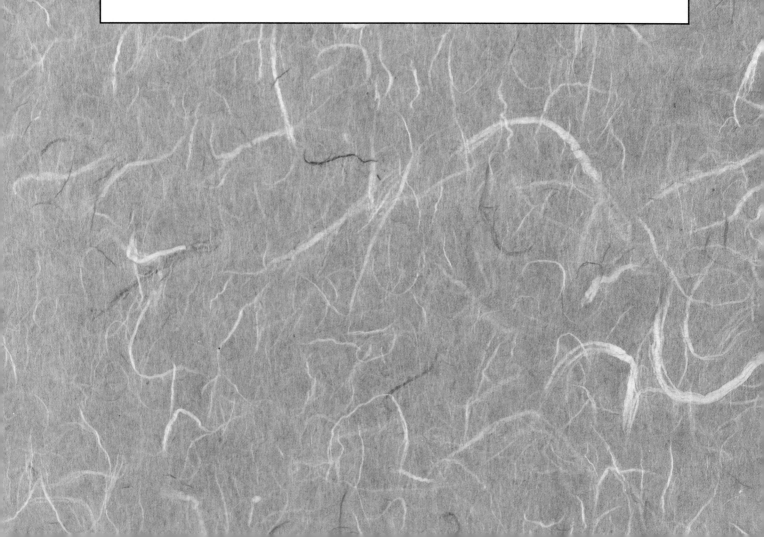

CHAPTER 24

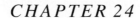

PSYCHOLOGICAL DISORDERS

 Emotionally disturbed individuals seem to have turned the relationship between stability and change inside out—to the unpracticed observer such people appear consistent only in their unpredictability. But as with any human behavior, careful observation reveals regularities. The study of abnormal behavior involves research, theory, and clinical interviews designed to discover the failures of adaptation that underlie emotional disturbance. The enormity of this task was noted by the fifth-century Greek physician Hippocrates, who wrote that "all the most acute, most powerful, and most deadly diseases, and those which are most difficult to be understood by the inexperienced, fall upon the brain" (1952, p. 360). This chapter describes the major forms of psychological disturbance, and the final chapter describes the varieties of psychotherapy used in attempts to help clients develop more adaptive behavior patterns.

CHANGING VIEWS OF PSYCHOPATHOLOGY

People have contradictory feelings toward those with psychological disturbances. On the one hand, they fear bizarre or unusual behavior. On the other, they frequently feel compassion toward those who display it. As a result, the history of psychology is replete with conflicting definitions of sanity and insanity, theories about the causes of psychological disturbance, and experimentation with methods of treatment, many of which are at least as troubling as the behavior they were designed to correct.

EARLY VIEWS OF MENTAL DISORDER

Hippocrates believed that mental disorders arise from imbalances among the four "humours"—blood, black bile, yellow bile, and phlegm (see Chapter 21). Building on this view, Plato stated that "madness" is actually a result of "acid and briny phlegm and other bitter and bilious humours [that] wander about in the body," creating "infinite varieties of ill-temper and melancholy" (1952, p. 474). These ideas are the first expression of what has come to be known as the **medical model** of emotional disturbance. Formally known as the theory of **somatogenesis** (from the Greek *soma*, "body"), the medical model holds that psychological disorder is the outward manifestation of an inner physiological disturbance, and that anyone with the physiological condition will develop the corresponding psychological symptoms, regardless of his or her social circumstances. Obviously, psychologists no longer believe in a humoural theory of disorder, but they still assert that such things as irregularities in brain construction or imbalances in neurotransmitter substances are the cause of observed psychological symptoms. (Note that this is a materialistic view: Just as ordinary mental events depend on brain function, disturbed mental events can be traced to brain dysfunction.)

The medical model is usually contrasted with the **behavioral model** of emotional disorder. Formally termed **psychogenesis,** this model argues that pathogenic psychological or social conditions, not physiological disturbances, are the principal causes of psychopathology.

EMOTIONAL DISTURBANCE AND RATIONAL THOUGHT

Part of the ambivalence that the emotionally disturbed generate in the rest of society may reflect the view that they lack the self-reflective consciousness that is the hallmark of ordinary human behavior. Indeed, the focus of the Greek philosophers on

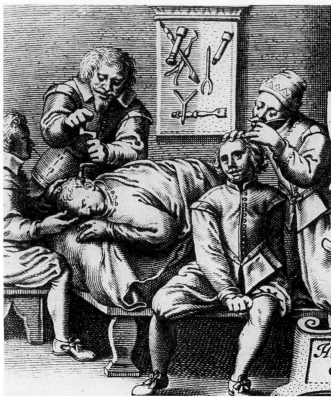

In the middle ages in Europe the mentally disturbed were thought to be possessed by demons that could be exorcised through religious rites. Trephining, the practice of drilling holes in the skulls of living people (right panel), presumably to release demons, dates from paleolithic times.

the physiological causes of mental disorder effectively excluded consciousness from discussion. Because the emotionally disturbed were thought to lack reason, they were considered to be more like animals than humans. In the *Ethics,* Aristotle described "madmen" as characterized by "incontinence," or lack of control over their impulses, which he considered "brutish" (Aristotle, 1952, p. 400).

The notion that the emotionally disturbed have lost the most human of qualities, the ability to reason, has justified extreme treatments of them since at least the Stone Age. Archaeologists have uncovered skulls dating from paleolithic times in which holes have been chipped, presumably to release demons (Rosenhan & Seligman, 1989). This practice, called *trephining,* was performed on living individuals, as indicated by the fact that some skulls show bone growth beginning to close the holes. Centuries later, during the medieval period, emotionally disturbed people were still thought to be possessed by demons. Extreme measures such as flogging and forced ingestion of poisonous potions were used in an effort to discourage demons from remaining in the body.

Over time, voices were raised in opposition to harsh treatment of the mentally disturbed. The British empiricist John Locke considered "madmen" to have "jumbled thoughts," in contrast to retarded individuals, who lacked thought altogether (Locke, 1952/1670). For Locke, if a person had thought of any sort, no matter how jumbled, it raised that person above the level of animals and entitled him or her to at least minimum standards of humane treatment. Furthermore, J. S. Mill, writing about liberty, noted that governments might have ulterior motives for finding a person insane: The courts could then assume control over the person's assets (Mill, 1952/1859). The implication of Mill's argument is that if governments can deprive the insane of liberty, as they can deprive the sane (such as criminals) of liberty, then the insane should be entitled to protections comparable to those accorded the sane. Despite the views of these respected thinkers, English common law continued to compare the insane to animals until the early nineteenth century. This doctrine, known as *furiosis* (Robinson, 1969), held that the insane could not be accountable for any criminal activities they might perform while in an animal-like frenzy. Modern law continues

640

to provide an insanity defense, but not because the emotionally disturbed are thought equivalent to animals.

When disturbed people are viewed as animals, society does not need to give them much in the way of comfort or dignity. After all, the reasoning seems to have gone, if people are "out of their minds," they will neither comprehend nor object to degradation. An example is the Priory of St. Mary of Bethlehem, founded in England in 1243, which over five centuries gradually became a hospital almost exclusively for mentally disturbed patients. These patients were put on display for the amusement of visitors who paid an admission charge, and in time the contraction of the hospital's name—"Bedlam"—came to mean a place of uproar and confusion. At the "insane asylum" in Paris, La Bicêtre, patients were shackled to the walls with chains on their hands and feet and iron collars around their necks (Selling, 1940).

The first mental hospital to unshackle its psychiatric patients was the Italian St. Boniface, in 1774 (Rosenhan & Seligman, 1989). This eighteenth-century liberation of mental patients reached its peak in 1792, when the newly appointed administrator of La Bicêtre, Philippe Pinel, initiated a comprehensive change in treatment. Believing that the patients were human beings, not beasts, he removed their chains, allowed them to live in rooms with windows (instead of dungeons), and eventually was able to discharge some recovered patients. At about the same time, the English Quakers established a humane institution for mental patients, and the first mental hospital in the United States was founded in Williamsburg, Virginia.

The trend toward hospitalization continued in the United States, with increasing numbers of mentally disturbed individuals being confined to state-run mental hospitals. Admission to mental hospitals took one of two forms. First, people who believed they needed help could choose *voluntary commitment,* effectively signing themselves into a hospital for treatment. Such voluntary patients were free to leave on their own initiative, even if the treatment staff was opposed to their doing so. Second, procedures in local and state courts allowed *involuntary commitment* of individuals who were thought either to be unable to care for themselves or to be dangerous to themselves or other people.

In the 1970s, however, public attitudes toward institutionalization began to change (Wrightsman, 1990). Perhaps the general public's skepticism about the power of

Engraving of the conditions that prevailed at the Priory of St. Mary of Bethlehem in England, the hospital whose contracted name—"Bedlam"—came to mean a place of uproar and confusion.

Reactions against the stark conditions present even in modern mental hospitals, coupled with the increasing use of psychotropic medication, led to the policy of deinstitutionalization: release of all but the most severely disturbed patients.

government, fueled in part by the country's experience in the Vietnam War, led to the belief that involuntary commitment had been too easy to do. Additionally, there were significant advances in drug treatments for serious psychological disorders (see Chapter 25). No longer was institutionalization the only alternative. Finally, a series of legal challenges to existing commitment practices both restricted involuntary commitments and guaranteed a *right to treatment* for those who were involuntarily committed (*Rouse* v. *Cameron,* 1966; *Wyatt* v. *Stickney,* 1971). These and other factors created legislative support for a policy known as **deinstitutionalization,** the discharge of all but the most seriously disturbed patients. Some recent commentators, however, have suggested that the pendulum has swung too far in the direction of deinstitutionalization (see Wrightsman, 1990).

MODERN CONCEPTIONS OF EMOTIONAL DISORDER

Deinstitutionalization is likely to remain controversial. One reason this is so is that there is no broad agreement on what behaviors should be defined as *abnormal.* There is consensus about what mental disorder is not: The mentally disturbed are no longer thought to be possessed by demons. There are, however, three competing approaches to defining abnormal behavior. Each categorizes a disturbed individual somewhat differently, and each is open to serious objections.

The three approaches can be illustrated with an example. Suppose that you believe that extraterrestrial aliens are controlling your mind. You further believe that the aliens will grant your every wish if only you will always walk backward. You also believe, however, that if you ever walk forward the aliens will be angry and cause your brain to explode. Let us examine how each approach to abnormality would deal with this example.

The first way of defining abnormal behavior is to use a *statistical* approach: Abnormal behavior is behavior that occurs infrequently. In the discussion of individual differences (Chapter 22) we noted that people's behavior can be described by a distribution of scores that can be characterized by its central tendency (mean score) and dispersion (standard deviation). On a distribution of scores representing beliefs about aliens, the belief that aliens will destroy your mind if you walk forward would be far out in one of the tails of the distribution shown in Figure 24-1. The belief is infrequent in the extreme, and so, statistically speaking, is abnormal.

There are two related problems with the statistical definition. First, desirable behaviors such as winning a gold medal in the Olympics may be as infrequent as undesirable behaviors such as believing one is controlled by aliens. But we would not call winning an Olympic event abnormal. Second, what makes a particular behavior seem disturbed is not its relative frequency but its quality.

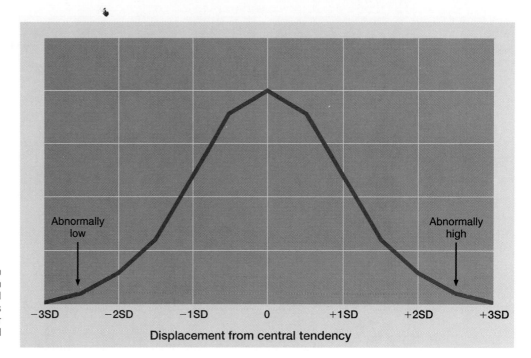

FIGURE 24-1 The statistical definition of abnormality considers the distribution of scores on a particular psychological trait. Individuals whose scores on this trait are either extremely high or extremely low would be considered "abnormal."

Abnormally low ↓

Abnormally high ↓

−3SD   −2SD   −1SD   0   +1SD   +2SD   +3SD

Displacement from central tendency

A second approach to the definition of abnormality takes into account the *personal discomfort* it causes the person who displays it, that is, the extent to which the behavior interferes with the person's everyday activities. By this definition, too, the person controlled by aliens qualifies as abnormal—he or she walks backward everywhere, risks tripping over things and bumping into people, and lives in constant fear of the consequences of walking forward. No doubt this behavior causes personal discomfort. The problem with this definition, however, is that it excludes some behavior we would consider abnormal even though the person who displays it experiences no discomfort. For example, we would consider abnormal a person who derives pleasure from sadistically inflicting pain on other people or animals.

The nature of the objection to the "personal discomfort" standard suggests a third approach: Abnormal behavior may be defined in terms of the *violation of social norms*. Societies have expectations for how their members should behave in most settings. People who violate those norms will be considered deviant and may be ostracized. This definition relies on the fit between expectations and behavior, not on the relative frequency of a behavior. An action that is relatively common in one setting may be considered abnormal in another. In years past, custom dictated that people should back out of a room containing royalty; one did not turn one's back on the king. But even then, to walk backward in all circumstances would violate expectations about how people should behave. Thus, by being contrary to social norms, persistent walking backward is abnormal.

This definition, however, presents a simple if difficult problem: Who decides what behavior is abnormal enough to warrant treatment? Rarely is there either unanimity or consistency regarding acceptable behavior. For example, drinking one's own alcohol is against the norm for behavior of fans at many sporting events, but drinking beer sold by concessionaires is encouraged at others. Does drinking at sporting events violate social norms, or not?

Even when there is broad social consensus regarding the norm, there may be disagreement about the need for treatment. In recent years there has been so much concern about drunk driving that even commercial messages from beer producers have urged moderation. Does this mean that anyone who drives after drinking is mentally ill and in need of treatment? The seriousness of this kind of question becomes especially evident in totalitarian states. In the former Soviet Union, for example, political dissent was often defined as abnormal, and dissidents who were mentally well were diagnosed as having serious psychiatric problems (Bloch, 1991). These dissidents

In the former Soviet Union, political dissent was often defined as abnormal behavior, a reason for involuntary confinement in mental institutions. The political dissent expressed since the collapse of the Soviet Union (right) might have led, in a previous time, to the kind of confinement suffered even by a Red Army General like Pyotr Grigorenko (left) for his participation in human rights campaigns.

were involuntarily committed to mental institutions and given drugs as a means of social control; some were forced to renounce their longstanding political views to show that they had "recovered" (Bloch, 1991).

Proponents of a sociocultural theory called **labeling theory,** which outlines the social consequences of attaching a disapproved label to a person's actions, have objected to defining abnormality in terms of the violation of norms. Applying this theory, one prominent critic of psychotherapy argues that what society labels "mental illness" may merely reflect problems in living, forms of adjustment (or failure to adjust) that society finds unacceptable (Szasz, 1961). Why should a person lose liberty (by being involuntarily committed to a mental institution) because *other* people disapprove of his or her actions? Should everyone who has driven a car after drinking be forced into treatment? Most psychologists believe that there is more to mental disorder than mere social disapproval, but they also recognize the dangers inherent in a definition of abnormality that concentrates too heavily on social judgments about violations of norms.

THE CLASSIFICATION OF MENTAL DISORDERS

Because no single definition of abnormal behavior is entirely satisfactory, many psychologists now believe that the concept should be regarded as fuzzy, best defined in terms of examples or elements (Cantor & Genero, 1986; Rosenhan & Seligman, 1989). According to this view, abnormality should be defined by its family resemblance to a prototype (see Chapter 14). Specifically, it should include *elements* such as personal discomfort, maladaptiveness, violation of moral standards, irrationality, loss of control (Rosenhan & Seligman, 1989). Each instance of emotional disturbance will then bear a family resemblance to other instances, although it need not include all the elements. This approach recognizes that abnormality is continuous with normal behavior rather than completely distinct from it—the more bizarre a person's actions, the more personal suffering they cause, and the more they contradict prevailing social norms, the greater the likelihood that the person will be deemed to need treatment.

The Diagnostic and Statistical Manual

Although recognizing the fuzziness of the definition of abnormality, psychologists and psychiatrists have attempted to specify as objectively as possible the behavior patterns that might signify the presence of emotional disturbance. The first modern classification of mental disorders, by Emil Kraepelin, was published in 1883. Krae-

644

pelin identified two major mental disorders, *dementia praecox* (what is now known as schizophrenia) and **manic-depressive psychosis** (now referred to as bipolar affective disorder).

Since Kraepelin's initial efforts, several international organizations, including the World Health Organization, have attempted to develop a uniform worldwide standard for the classification of psychological disorders. In the United States this effort has led to the development of the system published by the American Psychiatric Association in its *Diagnostic and Statistical Manual* (DSM). First published in 1952, the DSM is continually undergoing revision. The current version is the DSM-III-R, a major revision of the DSM-III (American Psychiatric Association, 1987).

The DSM-III-R takes what is called a *multiaxial* approach to the classification of mental disorder. The individual's behavior is rated on five axes, or dimensions. A brief list of elements from these dimensions is shown in Table 24-1. The first axis (dimension) consists of the clinical **syndromes,** which are collections of symptoms that regularly appear together. The second axis consists of disorders that either occur during childhood (school-related), or are thought to originate from the personality development that occurs in childhood. The third axis consists of physical disorders

---

TABLE 24-1   Elements of the DSM-III-R Classification System

Axis I: Clinical Syndromes

Organic disorders
Psychoactive substance abuse disorders
Schizophrenia
Mood disorders
    Bipolar disorders
    Depressive disorders
Anxiety disorders
Somatoform disorders (e.g., hypochondriasis)
Dissociative disorders (multiple personality)
Sexual disorders
Sleep disorders
Impulse control disorders
Adjustment disorders

V Codes for conditions not attributable to a
    mental disorder (such as academic
    problems or adult antisocial behavior)

Axis II: Developmental Disorders

Mental retardation
Pervasive developmental disorders (autism)
Specific developmental disorders
    Reading, arithmetic, writing, and language
        disorders
Personality disorders
    Cluster A (paranoid, schizoid, and schizo-
        typal personality disorders)
    Cluster B (antisocial, narcissistic)
    Cluster C (avoidant, dependent, obsessive
        compulsive, passive aggressive)

Axis III: Physical disorders and conditions

*Axis IV: Severity of Psychosocial Stressors
(acute events shown, enduring events also
possible)*

1 None
2 Mild (broke up with boyfriend or
    girlfriend)
3 Moderate (marriage, separation, job loss,
    miscarriage)
5 Severe (divorce, birth of first child)
6 Extreme (death of spouse, victim of rape,
    serious physical illness diagnosed)
7 Catastrophic (death of child, suicide of
    spouse, devastating natural disaster)

Axis V: Global Assessment of Functioning Scale

90–81 Absent or minimal symptoms

80–71 If symptoms are present, they are
      transient and expectable consequences
      of external stressors

70–61 Some mild symptoms, but generally
      functioning pretty well, with some
      meaningful interpersonal relationships

60–51 Moderate symptoms or difficulty in
      school or occupation

50–41 Serious symptoms or impairment in
      social, occupational, or school functioning

40–31 Some impairment in reality testing in
      communication, or major impairment in
      school, occupational, or interpersonal
      settings

30–21 Considerable delusions or hallucinations;
      or inability to function in almost all areas

20–11 Some danger of hurting self or others, or
      gross impairment in communication, or lack
      of minimal personal hygiene

10–1 Persistent danger of hurting self or others;
      suicide attempt with expectation of death.

SOURCE: American Psychiatric Association (1987).

and conditions, such as asthma, that may have a psychological component. The fourth axis reflects the fact that environmental stressors can produce serious psychological symptoms. Finally, the fifth axis takes into account how effectively the individual has functioned—socially, occupationally, and psychologically—during the previous year.

The approach to classification embodied in the DSM has substantially increased diagnostic precision compared to the ways in which mental disturbances were categorized in the past. Until the advent of the DSM, diagnosis of disorders was heavily influenced by the theoretical position—Freudian, Jungian, Adlerian, and so forth—of the clinical practitioner doing the assessment. Consequently, there was a tendency for clinicians to diagnose what they could treat. In contrast, the DSM categorization is based on empirically assessed symptom clusters. The basis for assessment has therefore shifted from a set of symptoms that a particular clinician might think go together to a description of all the symptoms that a particular client actually has. Revisions of the DSM have attempted to incorporate findings from the research literature and clinical insights from advisory groups of mental health professionals. These advisory groups have included psychiatrists (physicians who have completed a residency in psychiatry), clinical psychologists (doctoral-level psychologists who have completed an internship in psychological treatment), psychiatric social workers (master's-level social workers with specialized training in psychopathology), and psychiatric nurses. Moreover, the DSM and its revisions have maintained diagnostic categories that are compatible with those in the *International Classification of Diseases,* a publication of the World Health Organization, so that there is some international standardization of psychiatric diagnosis.

Although the DSM-III and its revision, the DSM-III-R, are an advance over earlier attempts at categorization, the DSM approach has not been immune to criticism (see Wideger & Shea, 1991). For example, compared to its predecessors, the DSM-III included in its list of psychiatric disorders a greatly expanded list of childhood problems such as developmental arithmetic disorder, developmental reading disorder, and developmental expressive writing disorder. Critics have noted that these diagnoses are often made without regard to the cognitive capabilities of normal children, and that it is a mistake to label as a psychiatric disorder what is really a learning problem (see, for example, Bemporad & Schwab, 1986).

The DSM-III was also criticized for the way it dealt with homosexuality. This version of the DSM did not claim that homosexuality itself was a psychiatric problem. It only included "ego-dystonic homosexuality"—homosexuality that adversely affected other aspects of psychological health. Critics noted, however, that there was almost no evidence of adjustment differences between homosexuals and heterosexuals. In the absence of such adjustment differences, it appears that the sociopolitical climate of the time influenced the content of the classification system (Rothblum, Solomon, & Albee, 1986). The category of ego-dystonic homosexuality was removed from the DSM-III-R for several reasons, including that "it suggested to some that homosexuality itself was considered a disorder" (American Psychiatric Association, 1987, p. 426).

More generally, the DSM-III came under attack for ignoring both theory and data regarding psychopathology (Corning, 1986; Salzinger, 1986). The use of advisory groups in preparing DSM-III-R may have countered the criticisms regarding data, but no attempt was made to incorporate the prevailing theories about the nature and origins of emotional disturbance. In sum, although the DSM-III-R is an important clinical tool, these criticisms indicate that the process of clinical assessment is still evolving.

CLINICAL ASSESSMENT

A clinical diagnosis of an individual, whether based on the axes involved in the DSM-III-R or not, should be preceded by an assessment of the person's physical and psychological condition. The comprehensiveness of such an assessment will depend on a number of factors, including the nature of the disturbance, the manner in which the person was referred for treatment, and the resources of the clinician. The ideal described here would involve an assessment team that includes, at minimum, a physician and a clinical psychologist; this ideal is not always achieved in the real world.

Medical Condition

Numerous disorders of emotion and behavior—such as the tremors associated with Parkinson's disease, the delirium produced by systemic infections, and the hallucinations and delusions that may accompany substance abuse—involve physical functioning. Consequently, clinical assessment should begin with a physical examination. This examination typically includes a personal history, because traumatic events in a person's past may show up years later in emotional disturbances. (An example is the posttraumatic stress disorder suffered by many Vietnam veterans.) Questions are also asked about the mental health of family members; some emotional disturbances, such as schizophrenia, appear to run in families.

The physical examination will include sensory abilities as well as neurological functioning. Sensory examinations concentrate on vision and audition, to rule out sensory impairment as an explanation for the apparent psychological problems. For example, a child's inability to persevere in school-related tasks could be the result of a significant hearing impairment. Without a hearing test, the child's lack of concentration might be erroneously diagnosed as attention deficit disorder. Neurological examination will include a battery of tests designed to discover the presence of organic brain dysfunction. If the test results are positive, a sophisticated procedure such as a computerized axial tomography (CAT) scan or a positron emission tomography (PET) scan will determine whether the problem is caused by brain tumors or other abnormalities.

Cognitive Functioning

If medical tests give no clear indication of the source of the problem, testing will turn to measures of cognitive functioning, including motor performance, language, and intelligence. Much cognitive assessment, especially among adults, consists of

One reason that a clinical assessment includes an extensive personal history is that traumatic events from past years can produce long-delayed effects on psychological health. Many Vietnam veterans did not begin to suffer from posttraumatic stress disorder until years after their return to the United States.

intelligence testing. Such testing serves two very different clinical purposes: (1) It provides the foundation for a diagnosis (such as mental retardation), and (2) it helps the clinician decide how the rest of the assessment procedure (especially the clinical interview) should be carried out.

Personality Testing

Many personality tests were originally developed for clinical applications. These include the revised Minnesota Multiphasic Personality Inventory (MMPI-2), the Rorschach, and the Thematic Apperception Test (TAT). As noted in Chapter 22, the MMPI-2 is an empirically derived test, meaning that it was designed to distinguish one kind of emotional disorder from another, independent of psychological theory. In contrast, the Rorschach and the TAT are theoretically based. The Rorschach originated in psychodynamic theory, whereas the TAT is closely tied to Murray's system of needs. Consequently, these two tests are likely to be preferred by clinicians with the corresponding theoretical orientations.

The Clinical Interview

Traditionally, the clinical interview has been a central element of the assessment process. In the interview a psychotherapist (who may be, by training, a counselor, clinical psychologist, clinical social worker, or psychiatrist) holds a special kind of conversation with the client. Because people are usually ill at ease when they first encounter a psychotherapist, the clinician initially attempts to establish rapport. Active, sympathetic, and nonjudgmental listening help to create the desired atmosphere. Once rapport has been established, the interview proceeds along lines largely determined by the clinician's theoretical orientation.

The client's statements are only part of the information obtained in the interview. The client's emotional state is almost as important as the content of the responses, as is illustrated by the structured interview used to assess the hard-driving, hostile, time-urgent Type A personality (see Chapter 23). The main purpose of that interview is to observe the hostility with which questions are answered (Dembroski & Mac-Dougall, 1985; Friedman & Rosenman, 1959). In short, the interview is not merely a way to obtain verbal information; it is also an opportunity to observe the client's behavior.

Clinical Versus Statistical Prediction

Making a diagnostic classification of a person's behavior is exceedingly difficult. If obvious neurological causes of disorder are ruled out, the clinician combines information from cognitive and personality assessments with information from in the clinical interview and direct observation of the client's behavior.

Unfortunately, a substantial body of research, beginning with a review by Meehl (1954), shows serious limits on the clinician's intuitive interpretation of all this information. The individual clinician's judgment is called **clinical prediction.** It is typically contrasted with **statistical prediction,** the use of formal statistical procedures to combine the information. All psychological assessment is an attempt to answer the question, "What do I now know about this person that I did not know before the assessment?" The principal difference between clinical prediction and statistical prediction is in the choice of standards against which the person's responses are compared. This difference between the two can be illustrated with an example. Imagine that as part of the assessment, the client or patient has been given the MMPI-2 (along with other tests). In clinical prediction the comparison is to the clinician's prior experience, with no attention paid to the psychometric properties (such as reliability and validity) of the assessment tools. In statistical prediction, the comparison is to established norms for the tests used, and tests with better psychometric properties are given more weight than tests with poorer reliabilities and validities.

Statistical prediction has repeatedly been found superior to clinical prediction. A recent review of more than 100 research studies on differences between the two has again found statistical prediction more effective (Dawes, Faust, & Meehl, 1988). Why might this be? Simply because clinicians are human. Their judgments about clients suffer from the same biases that affect other cognitive tasks. Clinicians have preconceived notions, based partly on their theoretical orientation and partly on *illusory correlations* between distinctive symptom patterns and equally distinctive psychiatric syndromes. There is also a tendency for the clinicians who are least accurate in their assessments to be most confident in their judgments (Arkes, 1985).

INTERIM SUMMARY

The medical model of emotional disturbance (somatogenesis) holds that psychological disorders are the outward manifestation of physiological disturbances. An alternative model, the behavioral model (psychogenesis), argues that psychopathology is caused by pathogenic psychological or social conditions. Historically, mentally disturbed individuals were believed to lack the capacity for rational thought, a view that justified harsh treatment. In the late eighteenth century Philippe Pinel initiated more humane treatment of mental patients. In modern societies the mentally disturbed are no longer thought to be possessed by demons, but this does not mean that there is complete agreement about what behaviors are abnormal. Behaviors may be defined as abnormal because they are statistically infrequent, because they interfere with the individual's everyday activities, or because they violate social norms. According to labeling theory, "mental illness" may consist of forms of adjustment that society considers unacceptable. To avoid problems of definition, psychologists and psychiatrists have developed an extensive system for classifying emotional disturbances on the basis of symptom patterns. The most recent version of this system is the *Diagnostic and Statistical Manual* (DSM-III-R). The DSM-III-R takes a multiaxial approach in which the individual's behavior is rated on five dimensions: clinical syndromes (symptom patterns), personality and childhood disorders, physical disorders, environmental stressors, and the individual's previous social, psychological, and occupational functioning. The DSM is used in conjunction with clinical assessment to arrive at a diagnosis. Clinical assessment procedures include a physical examination, tests of cognitive functioning, personality testing, and a clinical interview. Numerous studies have shown that statistical prediction (the use of formal statistical procedures) is superior to clinical prediction (the individual clinician's judgment).

SCHIZOPHRENIA

Classification and assessment procedures are designed to identify clusters of symptoms, or psychopathological syndromes. Only after a proper diagnosis can a therapist provide effective treatment. Although present classification systems are less than perfect and clinical judgment is sometimes faulty, there is general agreement on the features of major categories of emotional disturbance. We describe these categories in the remainder of the chapter, beginning with the class of disorders that accounts for the vast majority of psychiatric inpatient hospitalizations: schizophrenia.

As noted earlier, Kraepelin termed this pathological condition *dementia praecox,* or "premature mental deterioration," referring to its presumed onset in adolescence. In 1911 Eugen Bleuler, an influential Swiss psychiatrist, argued that a better term would be **schizophrenia,** which combines the Greek words for "to split" and "mind." It should be emphasized that what is "split" is *not* the personality but the connection between thought and action or affect (emotion). The proper term for the disorder popularly known as "split personality" is *multiple personality,* with which, unfortunately, the term schizophrenia is all too often confused.

FUNDAMENTAL SYMPTOMS

Bleuler identified four fundamental symptoms of schizophrenia, and these remain at the core of the diagnosis today. These symptoms, which have been called the "four A's," are shown in the left panel of Table 24-2 (Bootzin & Acocella, 1984). The first of these, *association,* refers to the profound thought disorder that is typical of the syndrome. The normal cognitive rules that connect one image or idea to another (see Chapter 13) seem not to apply. The result is that the patient's spoken and written language mixes coherent expressions with incoherent ones. Schizophrenic individuals frequently commit errors in syllogistic reasoning, such as "Aristotle was mortal; I am mortal; therefore I am Aristotle." This disordered thought is often accompanied by secondary symptoms such as hallucinations and delusions.

In addition to problems of association, schizophrenic individuals suffer from blunted, flat, or inappropriate *affect.* For example, a patient's claim that invaders from space are controlling his or her mind would be made in a matter-of-fact tone with none of the emotion (such as anger, fear) that would normally be expected to

---

TABLE 24-2   Schizophrenia Symptoms: Then and Now

Bleuler's Description (1911)	DSM-III-R Description (1987)
Association Patient shows evidence of thought disorder, usually apparent through use of language.	▪ Bizarre delusions that others in the culture would regard as absurd, such as having one's mind controlled by thought broadcasts. ▪ Prominent hallucinations, such as a voice constantly commenting on one's activities. ▪ Incoherence, marked loosening of associations, markedly illogical thinking. ▪ Digressive, vague, overelaborate, or circumstantial speech. ▪ Unusual perceptual experiences, recurrent illusions. ▪ Odd beliefs or magical thinking, belief in telepathy or clairvoyance.
Affect Patient's emotional responses are blunted or inappropriate for the situation.	▪ Blunted, flat, or inappropriate affect.
Ambivalence Patient is indecisive and unable to carry on normal activities to attain goals.	▪ Marked lack of initiative, interests, or energy. ▪ Marked impairment in role functioning as wage-earner, student, or homemaker.
Autism Patient is socially withdrawn; self-absorbed.	▪ Social isolation or withdrawal. ▪ Marked impairment in personal hygiene and grooming.

SOURCE: Adapted from Bootzin and Acocella (1984) and the American Psychiatric Association (1987).

accompany such a statement. On the other hand, inappropriate affect may be expressed by something such as deep sorrow over a leaf that has died and fallen from a tree.

The other two fundamental symptoms, *autism* and *ambivalence,* are now considered much less important than thought disorder and inappropriate affect, but they remain part of the description of schizophrenia. Autism refers to the schizophrenic person's isolation from others and tendency to exist in a private world that he or she has created. In this world apart from normal social contact, personal grooming and hygiene may be unimportant, and behavior that markedly contradicts everyday social expectations may occur frequently. Ambivalence can be in behavior (indecision and vacillation, as suggested by Table 24-2), or it can be in emotion (intense, but opposite, feelings toward a person or situation).

KINDS OF SCHIZOPHRENIA

Kraepelin originally described three categories of schizophrenia—hebephrenic (now called disorganized), catatonic, and paranoid—and these continue to be recognized today. The *disorganized* type has a symptom pattern that includes most of the elements shown in Table 24-2 (Davison & Neale, 1986). Patients with this form of schizophrenia commonly display bizarre thoughts, often involving deterioration of the body, as well as hallucinations and delusions. Their affective responses are likely to be inappropriate rather than blunted or flat. For example, a disorganized schizophrenic patient may giggle much of the time in response to no evident stimulus, but shout with anger when given a present. He or she may neglect personal grooming and may become incontinent, voiding at whim regardless of the circumstances. This symptom pattern best fits the stereotypical image of a "crazy" person and may be deeply upsetting to people who are unaccustomed to dealing with mental disorder. Consequently, it is important to note that, contrary to popular opinion, disorganized schizophrenic individuals are not usually dangerous to others.

Catatonic schizophrenics, in addition to thought disorder and affective disturbance, exhibit a characteristic pattern of motor disorder (Davison & Neale, 1986). They may hold a pose for hours at a time, until the affected limbs become stiff and swollen. Unless the patient's limbs are moved, there may even be permanent physiological damage. In some patients this catatonic stupor alternates with a state of great agitation and wild movement. Fortunately, the motor pattern associated with catatonia responds well to drug therapy, so the sight of a catatonic patient frozen into place is rare today (Morrison, 1974).

Paranoid schizophrenia is defined in terms of the content of the delusions experienced by those who suffer from the disorder (Davison & Neale, 1986). These individuals may be quite lucid except for extensive delusions of grandeur, accompanied by delusions of persecution. Kraepelin's description of these delusions remains accurate:

> People are watching them, intriguing against them, they are not wanted at home, former friends are talking about them and trying to injure their reputation. These delusions are changeable and soon become *fantastic.* The patients claim that some extreme punishment has been inflicted upon them, they have been shot down into the earth, have been transformed into spirits, and must undergo all sorts of torture. Their intestines have been removed by enemies and are being replaced a little at a time; their own heads have been removed, their throats occluded, and the blood no longer circulates. [1902, p. 257]

Because they are likely to incorporate therapists into their delusions, paranoid schizophrenic patients present a unique challenge. For example, a therapist who suggests a treatment may be seen as one more torturer. Despite the content of their delusions, however, paranoids pose very little threat to the general public.

In addition to Kraepelin's three original categories, modern diagnosis recognizes two additional diagnostic categories of schizophrenia. *Chronic undifferentiated*

651

schizophrenia describes patients who show elements of more than one symptom pattern or no distinguishable group of symptoms. *Residual* schizophrenia is a classification reserved for people whose symptoms have passed from the active phase to a less intense form.

ORIGINS OF SCHIZOPHRENIA

Why do people suffer from disorders like schizophrenia? This question is as old as the recognition that some people are normal whereas others are "mad." Because schizophrenia affects about 1% of the population of the United States and accounts for between 30% and 40% of psychiatric hospital admissions (National Institute of Mental Health, 1990), its causes have been the subject of extensive investigation and debate. Explanations of schizophrenia are of two main classes—biological and social.

Genetic Factors

Foremost among the biological explanations for schizophrenia is the view that some people have a genetic predisposition toward developing the disorder. The possibility of genetic predisposition is usually isolated by comparing (1) families to one another, (2) identical (monozygotic) twins to fraternal (dizygotic) twins, or (3) siblings reared apart to siblings reared together. All three kinds of studies suggest that there is a significant genetic predisposition toward schizophrenia in some individuals.

Comparisons of families with and without schizophrenic members indicate that the more closely one is related to a schizophrenic individual, the more likely one is to develop the disorder (Gottesman & Shields, 1977; 1982). As shown in Figure 24-2, the general risk for schizophrenia is about 1%. When one has a schizophrenic sibling, the risk as indicated by 13 studies involving nearly 10,000 siblings of schizophrenics was 10.1%; when one has a schizophrenic parent, 7 studies of over 1,500 children of schizophrenics showed an incidence of 12.8% (Gottesman & Shields, 1982). Despite the fact that first-degree relatives of schizophrenics are 10 times more likely to develop the disorder than the general population, over 90% of schizophrenics do *not* have a schizophrenic relative (Plomin, 1988).

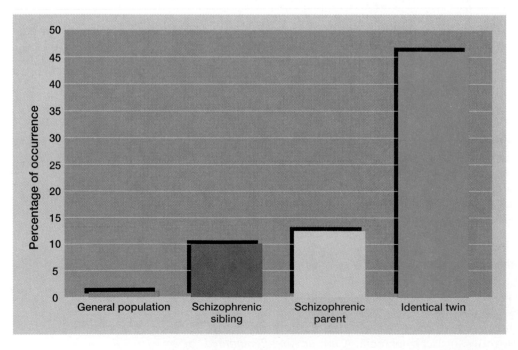

FIGURE 24-2 Family similarities that suggest a genetic influence on the predisposition to develop symptoms of schizophrenia. The risk of schizophrenia in the general population is about 1%, but this risk is increased more than tenfold if one has a schizophrenic sibling or parent. The risk is still higher if one has a schizophrenic identical twin. (Source: Adapted from Gottesman & Shields, 1982.)

Of course, comparisons of prevalence rates among families do not establish that the disorder is inherited. The environment in a family with schizophrenic members is surely different from that in a family without such members. Indeed, recent research has found that certain aspects of the family environment have a significant effect on the likelihood of relapse, suggesting that those variables may also be involved in the initial onset of the disorder (Falloon et al., 1985).

Twin studies provide a better indication of the role of genetic factors in schizophrenia. A well-known study of all twins treated at the Maudsley and Bethlehem hospitals in London between 1948 and 1964 provided data that support the argument for genetic influence (Gottesman & Shields, 1972). Members of a twin pair are said to be **concordant** if they share a personality trait or a diagnosis (of schizophrenia, for example). The London study compared the degree of concordance among fraternal and identical twins in three categories: diagnosed, hospitalized, and abnormal. The diagnosed category included twins who had been hospitalized *and* diagnosed as schizophrenic, the hospitalized category included those who had been hospitalized but not diagnosed as schizophrenic, and the abnormal category included those who were abnormal but had not been hospitalized.

As Figure 24-3 shows, there was greater difference in concordance between identical and fraternal twins among the diagnosed group than among either of the other groups. That is, the similarity between identical twins was much greater than the similarity between fraternal twins only in the diagnosed group. This suggests a strong genetic influence on the most serious disorders.

These results, however, have also been interpreted from an environmentalist perspective. Specifically, it is argued that compared to fraternal twins, identical twins may be more likely to define their own identities in terms of their twin. For example, many fraternal twin pairs are opposite sex, so a major component of each twin's identity—gender role—may be quite different. Identical twins, of course, are always the same sex. Furthermore, parents and friends of the family may be more likely to respond in the same way to members of an identical twin pair (who are more likely to be dressed the same, for example) than to members of a fraternal twin pair. These environmental pressures could make identical twins more likely than fraternal twins to believe that "what happens to my twin will happen to me." Thus, having a schizophrenic identical twin could be more threatening than having a schizophrenic fraternal twin, and this added threat could increase the likelihood of schizophrenia.

On the other hand, researchers have also found a higher incidence of schizophrenia among children who were born to schizophrenic mothers and put up for adoption than among a control group of children placed by the same adoption agencies (Heston, 1966; Kety, 1987). The methods used in these studies have been criticized, how-

FIGURE 24-3 Differences in concordance for schizophrenia among identical and fraternal twins in three diagnostic categories. Concordance rates are relatively similar for abnormal behavior and for hospitalization for mental disorder. They are quite different, however, for twins hospitalized and diagnosed as schizophrenic, suggesting that genetic factors play an important role in the more serious disorders. (Source: Adapted from Gottesman & Shields, 1972.)

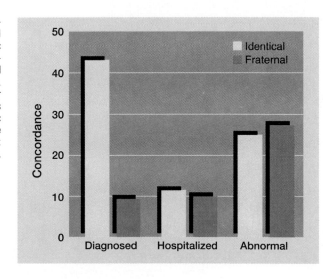

ever. For example, because the adoption agencies knew the children's backgrounds, the placements obviously were not random.

The contribution of genetic as opposed to environmental influences on the development of schizophrenia has yet to be resolved. Because the disorder could be polygenic rather than produced by a single allele pair, the concordance rate among identical twins might never reach 100%. The concordance rate typically obtained is from 40% to 65%, suggesting that environmental factors could play a significant role (Plomin, 1988; Rosenhan & Seligman, 1989).

Biochemical Factors

Results of family, twin, and adoption studies suggest that there is a physiological or biochemical basis for schizophrenia. A number of potent **psychotropic** drugs—substances that act on the central nervous system—have been found to be effective in reducing or controlling the symptoms of schizophrenia. Autopsies of schizophrenic individuals who have died of natural causes, as well as CAT scans of living patients, reveal that the brains of some schizophrenics have enlarged ventricles (open spaces within the brain), suggesting pathology in the limbic system (Weinberger, Wagner, & Wyatt, 1983). These findings have spurred a search for biochemical agents that might be involved in schizophrenia.

That search has led to the discovery that the blood platelets of chronic schizophrenics contain much lower levels of monoamine oxidase (MAO) than do those of normal individuals. Recall from Chapter 5 that MAO is an enzyme involved in neural transmission; it can inactivate the neurotransmitter dopamine. This is significant in light of another important finding: One of the drugs effective in treating schizophrenia, **phenothiazine,** produces side effects resembling the symptoms of

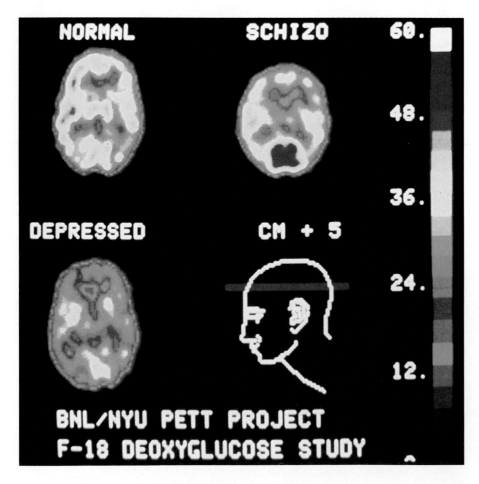

Recent research has begun to identify the physiological correlates of schizophrenia. These computer images, based on PET scans of the brains of patients with different psychological disorders, show quite different patterns of brain activity.

Parkinson's disease, which is caused in part by low levels of dopamine. Researchers have inferred, therefore, that phenothiazine reduces schizophrenic symptoms by lowering dopamine levels.

This line of reasoning and the fact that schizophrenics have low levels of MAO together suggest that the biochemical problem underlying schizophrenia is an excess of dopamine. Researchers have been unable, however, to establish a clear causal relationship between excess dopamine and schizophrenia. The kind of study that would provide conclusive evidence would involve injecting normal individuals with large amounts of dopamine to determine whether it causes them to become schizophrenic. Clearly, such a study is ethically out of the question. Hence, the biochemical factors, like the genetic factors, are as yet only tantalizing clues to the origins of this debilitating emotional disorder.

Social Factors

Like so many other psychological characteristics, schizophrenia appears to be related to environmental factors as well as genetic and biochemical ones. For example, investigators have found that the prevalence of schizophrenia is greater among those of lower socioeconomic classes than among those of higher classes (Hollingshead & Redlich, 1958). This difference could be attributed to *social drift,* the tendency for emotionally disturbed individuals to perform poorly at higher-paying jobs and consequently to drift to lower socioeconomic strata. Or it could be *sociogenic,* that is, largely caused by the living conditions of the poorer groups.

Indirect evidence for a sociogenic explanation comes from studies that show increased stress among people who lose control over situations that affect their lives (see, for example, Taylor, Lichtman, & Wood, 1984). If people in higher economic classes are in fact better able to control factors that otherwise would create stress, then low socioeconomic status may contribute to emotional disturbance. At present the data do not rule out either the social drift or the sociogenic explanation (Davison & Neale, 1986).

Some researchers have suggested that family interaction patterns play a causal role in the development of emotional disorder. Of particular interest is the **double-bind hypothesis**—the belief that in certain families the parents' communications to a child are so confused that the child does not know how to respond (Bateson, Jackson, Haley, & Weakland, 1956). The parent who says "I love you" while holding the child away in a fashion that conveys the opposite message is putting the child in a double bind. The verbal message can be neither accepted nor outwardly questioned, so the only available alternative is to withdraw from social interaction. This hypothesis has obvious relevance for the withdrawal that is characteristic of schizophrenic individuals, but it has received only moderate empirical support (Davison & Neale, 1986).

Studies of families with schizophrenic members have found that there is more conflict between the parents of schizophrenic children than between those of normal children and that the former are also characterized by inadequate communication (Fontana, 1966). Recent studies of the families of schizophrenic individuals have found that those families have higher levels of **expressed emotion (EE)**—hostility and criticism—than families of normal individuals. Moreover, when families with schizophrenic members are rated on expressed emotion, the results show that patients from high-EE families need additional treatment sooner than patients from low-EE families (Vaughn & Leff, 1976).

The problem with such studies is that it is impossible to know whether the conflict and poor communication are the cause of the child's condition or a consequence of that condition. They do, however, suggest a need for further experimentation. For example, training high-EE families to deal with their emotions in more constructive ways could affect the likelihood of relapse among their schizophrenic members (Hogarty et al., 1986).

Schizophrenia is a debilitating mental disorder that accounts for the majority of inpatient psychiatric hospitalizations. It is characterized by failures in association (profound thought disorder, accompanied by hallucinations and delusions), flattening of affect, and withdrawal from interpersonal relationships. There are three subtypes of schizophrenia—disorganized, catatonic, and paranoid—as well as two additional diagnostic categories: chronic undifferentiated and residual. Evidence suggests that there is a genetic predisposition toward schizophrenia, although social factors such as confused communication patterns in the family may also play an important role. Biochemical evidence suggests that abnormally high levels of dopamine may also contribute to the development of schizophrenia.

MOOD AND OTHER DISORDERS

A second major class of psychopathological syndromes consists of disorders characterized by mood disturbances rather than by incoherent thought. Mood disorders are those in which the complex and diverse human emotions are carried to extremes that interfere with normal life. In the past, many of these disorders, especially those involving anxiety, were called *neuroses,* but this term was discarded when the multiaxial classification system introduced in DSM-III-R came into widespread use.

MAJOR DEPRESSION

Prevalence of Depression

The disorder known as **major depression** is by far the most prevalent mood disorder, so prevalent that it has been called "the common cold of mental illness" (Rosenhan & Seligman, 1989, p. 307). Approximately 1 in 20 Americans now suffers from severe depression; epidemiological studies show that from 5% to 12% of men and from 9% to 26% of women will have a clinically significant episode of depression during their lifetimes (American Psychiatric Association, 1987).

Moreover, the lifetime risk of depression has been increasing dramatically. One study interviewed 10,000 adults randomly selected from New Haven, Baltimore, and St. Louis, asking whether respondents had suffered from symptoms of depression (Robins et al., 1984). The idea was to examine the risk of depression for individuals born at different times. A group of people born at approximately the same year is known as an *age cohort,* and the researchers split their subjects into four age cohort categories: people who were 65 years old or more at the time of the study, between 45 and 64, between 25 and 44, and between 18 and 24. Note that lifetime risk is cumulative: The longer you have lived, the greater your risk, provided that the overall prevalence of the disorder remains constant. One can obtain a rough estimate of the *yearly* risk, however, by dividing the lifetime risk for a cohort by the midpoint age of that cohort. So, for example, the yearly risk for the 45-to-64 cohort is the lifetime risk for that cohort divided by 55, the midpoint age of the cohort. This estimate is only approximate, because the divisor (midpoint age) does not take into account the proportion of members of the cohort who fall above or below it (in other words, the midpoint of the category is not the same as the median age of the category). The results of the study are shown in Figure 24-4, expressed in yearly risk units.

These results show that the yearly risk for a person in the 25-to-44 cohort is roughly 10 times that for a person in the over-64 cohort. This dramatic increase in risk for depression from one generation to another, along with comparable findings from other epidemiological studies, has led some psychologists to conclude that "we now live in an Age of Melancholy" (Rosenhan & Seligman, 1989, p. 317).

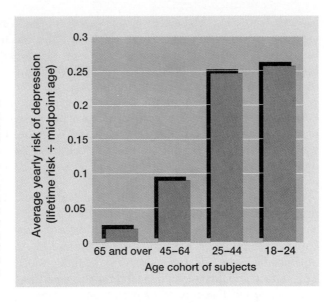

FIGURE 24-4 The average yearly risk of major depression has been increasing in recent years. For this comparison the average yearly risk has been computed by dividing the lifetime risk by the midpoint of each age category. For example, the lifetime risk among people in the 45-to-64 age category is 4.5%—which means that 4.5% of the people in this category will have had at least one episode of major depression during their lifetimes. Because the midpoint of this category is age 55, the average yearly risk can be estimated by dividing the lifetime risk (4.5%) by 55, to produce an average yearly risk value of 0.08%.

Nature and Origin of Depression

Major depression is manifest in emotional, cognitive, motivational, and somatic symptoms (Rosenhan & Seligman, 1989). The predominant emotional tone of a person who has major depression is a pervasive sadness. This is not a touch of "the blues," or the temporary response to a personal setback or loss; it is a generalized feeling of hopelessness. The patient may be miserable to the point of tears for a substantial portion of waking hours. A principal cognitive symptom of depression is pessimism. Depressed individuals believe that they are responsible not merely for their own problems, but for the problems of the world. They think of themselves as worthless and ineffective; they expect to fail in the future as they believe they have failed in the past. Not surprisingly, these cognitive symptoms shade over into motivation: Depressed individuals have great difficulty getting started. In severe cases, a depressed person can take several hours just to get out of bed in the morning. Once up and around, such a person's movements are in slow motion. The somatic symptoms of depression include loss of appetite and loss of sleep. There is increased concern over bodily aches and pains, and in severe cases there can be substantial weight loss.

There are three competing explanations—biological, psychodynamic, and cognitive—for the origin of depression. The biological explanation involves principles also seen in the account of schizophrenia: genetics and neurotransmitters. First, the biological view of depression holds that people inherit a genetic predisposition

The predominant emotional tone of a person suffering from major depression is a pervasive sadness. Depressives think themselves responsible not only for their own problems, but also for the problems of the world.

toward depression. Evidence on this point comes from twin studies and adoption studies, but the results are mixed. Identical twins are not more likely than fraternal twins to be concordant for major depression (Torgerson, 1986). On the other hand, biological relatives of depressed patients are several times more likely to develop depression themselves than are adoptive relatives (Wender et al., 1986).

The second element of the biological explanation holds that the motivational deficits seen in depression reflect abnormally low levels of the neurotransmitter norepinephrine. This hypothesis is based, as was the dopamine hypothesis of schizophrenia, on the action of drugs. Recall from Chapter 23 that norepinephrine is one of the substances that prepares the body to fight or flee—it helps increase the individual's level of activation. Two classes of drugs are effective in treating the symptoms of major depression. One of these groups, the **tricyclic antidepressants,** prevents the *reuptake* of norepinephrine by the nerve cell that released it (see Chapter 5). The other group, the **MAO inhibitors,** prevents the *breakdown* of norepinephrine by the enzyme monoamineoxidase (MAO). In other words, both groups of drugs have the effect of increasing the amount of norepinephrine in the synapses. This effect and the fact that norepinephrine is an activation-increasing substance have suggested that a norepinephrine deficit may be involved in major depression. Because both the tricyclics and the MAO inhibitors have other neurophysiological effects, the norepinephrine deficit hypothesis has not yet been conclusively established (Rosenhan & Seligman, 1989).

The psychodynamic approach to depression, based on Freud's view of personality development, argues that depression is anger turned inward. Recall from Chapter 21 that in the normal course of development the child's sexual desire for the opposite-sex parent is presumed to be replaced by identification with the same-sex parent. The psychodynamic approach to depression argues that if this early relationship, or another intense love, leads to disappointment, the person will "incorporate" the lost person. The anger that would have been directed at that individual will, instead, be turned on the self. The result is that as an adult the person will be desperate for approval and love, and any disappointment will bring back the anger and the sense of worthlessness.

The third explanation of major depression concentrates on cognitive processes. One of the most influential cognitive theories traces depression to a *cognitive triad:* negative thoughts about the self, about one's present experience, and about the future (Beck, 1967). According to this theory, depressives believe that they are defective and worthless, that the normal setbacks of everyday life are major obstacles, and that the future holds no promise for improvement. The theory argues that, in addition to the cognitive triad, the thought processes of depressives are characterized by *errors in logic.* Depressives magnify small problems, minimize positive experiences, take the slightest criticism as an indication of their complete worthlessness, and infer personal failings from events that have nothing to do with their own performance.

LEARNED HELPLESSNESS

Perhaps the best evidence for the influence of psychological factors on the occurrence of depression comes from research on the phenomenon known as **learned helplessness.** Although this phenomenon was originally demonstrated in experiments with laboratory animals, it has since become one of the cognitive explanations for the occurrence of depression. The original discovery of learned helplessness was made in studies designed to show the effects of prior Pavlovian conditioning on instrumental learning (see Chapter 12). Laboratory dogs were suspended in harnesses and given a series of some sixty 5-second electric shocks intense enough to be unpleasant, but not intense enough to cause any physiological damage (Maier, Seligman, & Solomon, 1969). In one condition the dogs could escape from these shocks, but in another condition they could not. Both of these groups were then placed in a shuttle box used for aversive conditioning (see Chapter 12). Half of the box contained a grid floor that could be electrified; the other half was safe. Nor-

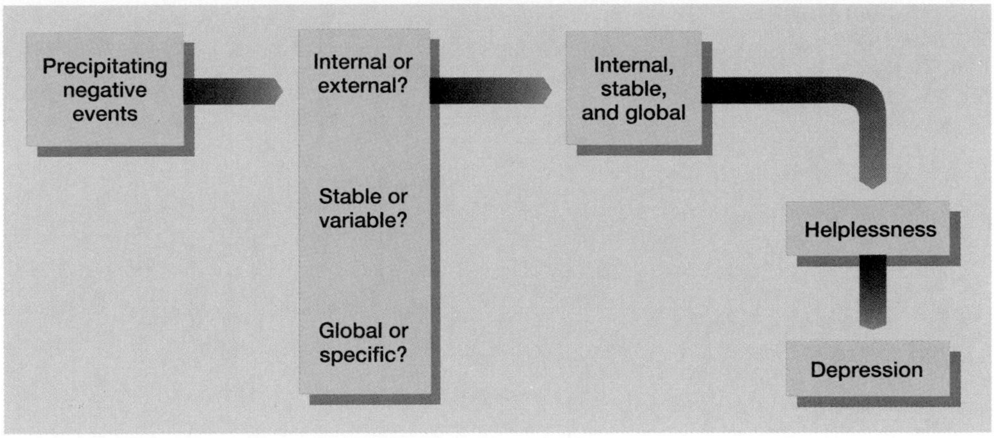

FIGURE 24-5 The reformulated model of learned helplessness suggests that people evaluate the negative events that affect them. If they decide that these negative events are the result of their own stable, internal characteristics, and that these characteristics are likely to produce negative outcomes in a wide variety of domains, they are likely to become helpless. That perceived inability to prevent or correct what is wrong can lead to depression.

mally, when animals are tested in such an apparatus, they quickly learn to jump from the electrified side to the safe side—this is aversive conditioning. Results of the study showed that dogs given prior experience with escapable shock, and dogs given no prior training, both learned to jump to the safe side. In contrast, dogs with prior experience of *in*escapable shock showed no tendency whatsoever to jump to the safe side. Their training had taught them to be helpless (Seligman, 1975). Recall that in discussing stress and coping we noted the importance of control in reducing both physiological and psychological effects of stressors. Learned helplessness, and the resulting depression, may be the organism's response to a perceived loss of control.

The word *perceived* here is important, as the learned helplessness position has been reformulated specifically to explain how humans might perceive the causes of negative events that affect them (Abramson, Seligman, & Teasdale, 1978). The reformulation thus builds in principles of social cognition to construct the model of depression shown in Figure 24-5. According to this model, when a person is confronted by negative life events such as academic or social failure, a search is made to determine whether the perceived causes are internal or external, stable (and therefore persistent) or variable, and global (affecting a broad range of experiences) or specific. If this search suggests that the causes of negative events are internal, stable, and global, the model predicts that the person will become helpless and severely depressed (Abramson, Seligman, & Teasdale, 1978). A substantial amount of research has been done testing the learned helplessness theory of depression. At least one study has failed to find a loss of perceived control among depressed individuals (Alloy & Abramson, 1979), and other reservations have been raised concerning the model (Flannery & Harvey, 1991; Pillow, West, & Reich, 1991), but overall there is good support for the learned helplessness approach (Peterson & Seligman, 1984).

BIPOLAR DISORDER

In earlier classification schemes, "manic-depressive psychosis" was considered to be a single, unified disorder: Some people had the manic phase of the disorder, others did not. Present diagnostic methods, however distinguish between the major depression we have just been discussing and what is now known as **bipolar disorder,** which involves fluctuations between positive and negative emotions. A person suffering from bipolar disorder goes through extreme mood swings—from despair, through relatively normal functioning, to elation, and back again. The endpoints of this sequence—mania and depression—are termed *episodes*. Each episode includes many of the symptoms listed in Table 24-3 on page 660. The disorder may begin with either mania or depression, although mania is more prevalent.

Bipolar disorder is relatively rare, affecting between .4% and 1.2% of the adult population at some point in their lives (American Psychiatric Association, 1987). Bipolar disorder typically begins before the age of 30. Unlike major depression,

TABLE 24-3 Features of Manic and Depressive Episodes

The Manic Episode	The Depressive Episode
Elevated, expansive, or irritable mood	*Depressed mood*
This is the fundamental feature of a manic episode. Marked impairment of occupational functioning or social interaction.	The essential feature of the depressive episode. Loss of interest in almost all activities for at least a two-week period.
Hyperactivity	*Disturbance of appetite*
Increase in goal-directed activity in social, occupational, or sexual realm.	Loss of appetite is most common, although increased appetite is sometimes evident.
Talkativeness	*Sleep disruption*
Loud and rapid speech that is difficult to interrupt, replete with puns, jokes, and irrelevant details.	Insomnia is common, and may be manifest as difficulty in falling asleep, awakening during the night, or waking too early.
Flight of ideas	*Psychomotor disturbance*
Abrupt shifts from one topic to the next, with the shifts sometimes based on understandable ideas, but sometimes merely on plays on words.	May be manifest either as agitation, an inability to sit still; or as retardation, including slowed body movements and excessive fatigue.
Inflated self-esteem	*Feelings of guilt and worthlessness*
Uncritical self-confidence, ranging to grandiosity (including claims to some special relationship with God or a celebrity).	Exaggeration of minor failings, unrealistic negative evaluation of self-worth.
Sleeplessness	*Difficulties in thinking*
Manics typically need little sleep, waken after a few hours, or may go for days without sleep with no apparent loss of energy.	Difficulty concentrating or thinking. Mental processes slowed. Indecisiveness.
Distractability	*Recurrent thoughts of death*
Abrupt changes in attention resulting from attention to various irrelevant external stimuli, such as pictures on a wall.	Thoughts of death, belief that self or others would be better off dead, perhaps suicidal thoughts with no specific plan for carrying them out.
Reckless behavior	
Engaging in buying sprees, reckless driving, or foolish business ventures.	

SOURCE: American Psychiatric Association (1987).

bipolar disorder affects men and women in roughly equal proportions, and is more prevalent in the higher socioeconomic groups than in lower socioeconomic groups. Also unlike major depression, bipolar disorder tends to run in families: Relatives of manic-depressives are five times more likely to develop the disorder than are people who do not have an affected relative (Rice et al., 1987). Finally, the drug **lithium carbonate** is effective in treating the symptoms of bipolar disorder, but has no appreciable effect on major depression. The cause of bipolar disorder is not known, but these differences between it and major depression have led some clinicians to suggest that the two disorders are fundamentally different despite the fact that both involve negative affect (Bootzin & Acocella, 1984).

SUICIDE

Although not all depressed individuals attempt suicide, the majority of people who kill themselves have suffered from depression (Barraclough, Nelson, Bunch, & Sainsbury, 1969). There are an estimated 20,000 to 60,000 suicides each year in the

United States. Because of the intense social stigma attached to suicide, the fact that in many jurisdictions it is a crime, and that insurance companies typically refuse to pay death benefits to the survivors, individuals who commit suicide may make the death look like an accident.

Despite the difficulty of obtaining overall figures for suicides, researchers have been able to identify the demographic characteristics of people who attempt, and commit, suicide (Schneidman, 1976; Schneidman & Farberow, 1970). Women are three times more likely than men to attempt suicide, but men are three times more likely than women to succeed in the attempt. Most likely this difference reflects the choice of methods. Women select means that are less immediately lethal—slitting their wrists, taking overdoses of sleeping pills—whereas men select means that are more immediately effective—shooting themselves, jumping off buildings (Rosenhan & Seligman, 1989).

Although most suicides occur among adults, suicide is the second leading cause of death among people between the ages of 15 and 24 (accidents are the most frequent cause of death in this age group). The problems of everyday life can seem insurmountable to an adolescent who is undergoing profound physiological changes and trying to construct an acceptable identity. One important study compared more than 500 adolescents who had attempted suicide with the same number of nonsuicide attempters of the same age and sex (Garfinkel, Froese, & Hood, 1982). The results showed that among the attempters girls outnumbered boys by three to one and were, on the average, six months older (mean age = 15.3 years). Compared to the controls, attempters had more experience with substance abuse, more psychological difficulties, and more psychiatric disorder in their families.

Because the vast majority of people who commit suicide have made at least one previous attempt, it is important for friends and family members to take attempts seriously and to encourage the attempter to obtain immediate professional help.

INTERIM SUMMARY

Mood disorders are a second major class of emotional disturbances. The primary disorders of this group are major depression and bipolar disorder (alternating episodes of mania and depression). There are three explanations for the origin of major depression. The biological explanation suggests that there may be a genetic predisposition, and that vulnerability to the disorder is increased by a deficiency of norepinephrine. The psychodynamic explanation views depression as the turning inward, onto the self, of anger felt over the loss of an early love. The cognitive approach encompasses a variety of specific explanations, such as a negative view of the self and the future, errors in logic, and the learned helplessness that results from assuming that one's stable characteristics are the cause of all the negative events that happen. A substantial number of individuals who suffer from depression (as well as some who do not) attempt to commit suicide. Women outnumber men among those who attempt suicide, but men account for nearly three times as many completed suicides as do women.

OTHER PSYCHOLOGICAL DISORDERS

Schizophrenia and the mood disorders are the most serious emotional disturbances, but people can also suffer from other psychological disorders. In this section we briefly describe some of these disorders.

ANXIETY DISORDERS

When an organism is confronted with an identifiable threat, it responds with fear. When there is no identifiable threat or when the stimulus would not be threatening to most people, some individuals experience an unwarranted fear called *anxiety.* Anxiety disorders are the most prevalent of all psychological disorders. These include simple phobia, panic disorder, obsessive-compulsive disorder, and posttraumatic stress disorder. Simple phobia is most common form of anxiety disorder, but panic disorder is most common among people who seek treatment (American Psychiatric Association, 1987).

Simple phobia is the persistent fear of a particular feature of the environment. The feared object may be inanimate (such as elevators, heights, enclosed places) or animate (such as snakes, insects, cats, dogs). People typically do not seek treatment for these phobias, partly because they often can simply avoid the feared object. This solution is not possible for a person suffering from **panic disorder,** which is characterized by recurring attacks of intense fear or discomfort that are not related to the situation. For example, it is normal for a person to have symptoms such as shaking, sweating, abdominal distress, palpitations, and fear of losing control immediately before giving a speech to a large group of people; if the same symptoms occur when the situation is not threatening, the individual may be suffering from panic disorder.

Panic disorder is frequently accompanied by **agoraphobia,** which means "fear of open places" but in fact refers to a fear of leaving home. Consequently, people suffering from panic disorder and/or agoraphobia generally seek help.

Phobic reactions often represent an attempt to cope with anxiety by tying it to an object that can be avoided without greatly disturbing one's everyday behavior. Efforts to control anxiety also underlie the less common **obsessive-compulsive disorder,** but in this case the efforts typically have a greater impact on everyday behavior. An obsession is a recurring image or thought that cannot be put out of mind even though it is upsetting. In contrast, a compulsion is an action that the person feels compelled to repeat again and again. Whereas obsessions are often of a violent or sexual nature, with socially disapproved content, compulsions typically exaggerate behaviors that are approved unless they are performed to excess, such as being careful to lock doors and windows. Washing one's hands before meals is an approved way of protecting oneself against infection; washing one's hands 80 times a day reflects an exaggerated concern about infection. Obsessions and compulsions can interfere with a person's productivity on the job and ability to carry on normal interpersonal relationships.

The final major kind of anxiety-related disorder, **posttraumatic stress disorder (PTSD)** differs from those discussed so far in an important way: The precipitating event is real and would be intensely disturbing to anyone. Consequently, the reaction is to an event, not to feelings of anxiety. Although PTSD is frequently associated with wartime experiences, it can also be produced by personal victimization (assault, rape), natural disasters (floods, earthquakes), or catastrophic accidents (plane crashes, building collapses). Not all people who suffer from such experiences or catastrophes will develop symptoms of PTSD, but the number who do can be quite high. It is estimated, for example, that some 20% to 25% of Vietnam War veterans have suffered from PTSD (Walker & Cavenar, 1982). Symptoms—including insomnia, pain from constantly reliving the experience, or guilt from having survived when others died—usually occur shortly after the precipitating event, but in some cases months may pass before any effects are evident.

PERSONALITY DISORDERS

We saw in Chapter 21 that personality traits are relatively enduring ways of perceiving, organizing, and relating to aspects of the environment. We also noted that current personality theory and research generally regard behavior as resulting from person-by-situation interactions. That is, behavior shows some consistency from one situation to another, but that consistency is not perfect. Translating the DSM-III-R

The precipitating factor for posttraumatic stress disorder is a real event, such as a catastrophic accident, that would be disturbing to anyone.

criteria into these terms, a **personality disorder** exists when there is virtually no situational effect on behavior. That is, a personality *trait* becomes a personality *disorder* when the trait is so inflexible it dictates all behavior regardless of the situation.

One of the most thoroughly studied personality disorders, the **antisocial personality disorder,** illustrates this principle. We can all think of people we would describe as impulsive, others who are thoughtless, and still others who are shallow. Combine these traits, in the extreme, into one person, and you have the antisocial personality disorder (which used to be called the "sociopath"). The antisocial personality disorder is characterized by inability to form attachments to others and consistent lack of concern for or violation of the rights of other people.

Estimates place the prevalence of antisocial personality disorder at roughly 2% to 3% of the population, with males outnumbering females by a ratio of 4:1 (Cadoret, 1986; Regier et al., 1984). This disorder typically begins in adolescence with illegally or socially disapproved actions, failure to show responsibility in work or financial obligations, reckless and impulsive behavior, and disregard for truth.

According to the DSM-III-R, people can be diagnosed as having antisocial personality disorder if they are incapable of conducting themselves according to the normal social rules, if there is longstanding evidence of this inability to conform to the rules, and if their antisocial behavior can be seen in at least four classes of behavior. These classes include such things as irresponsible parenting, unlawful activities, and inability to sustain a relationship with a sexual partner (Rosenhan & Seligman, 1989). In other words, emotional shallowness, impulsivity, and a complete lack of remorse about behavior that harms others characterizes virtually all the activities of the antisocial personality disorder. The difference between a person diagnosed with this disorder and a person we would simply consider a criminal is that the criminal is assumed to have *chosen* to act against normal morality, whereas the person with antisocial personality disorder is considered unable to have made such a conscious choice.

If the antisocial personality disorder resembles the "normal" criminal, several other personality disorders bear an obvious relationship to more serious forms of pathology. *Paranoid personality disorder,* for example, is characterized by pervasive mistrust and suspiciousness. The paranoid personality consistently interprets the actions of other people as deliberately threatening or demeaning; believes associates are scheming and disloyal; and is moralistic, argumentative, and quick to counterattack when any threat is perceived. Although individuals with these personality traits can function well in society and rarely seek help, their symptoms show a strong resemblance to those of the paranoid schizophrenic.

Schizotypal personality disorder is characterized by disordered thought, though the condition is not serious enough to warrant a diagnosis of schizophrenia. *Schizoid personality disorder* is characterized by some of the flattened affect found in schizophrenia, without the disordered thought. *Compulsive personality disorder* is manifested in a preoccupation with rules, efficiency, or detail and is accompanied by inability to express warm emotions. All of these personality disorders have a pervasive influence on the individual's behavior but do not involve loss of contact with reality.

Some forms of personality disorder are less similar to psychoses. The *avoidant* person shows hypersensitivity to rejection and consequently withdraws from social interaction. The *dependent* person relies excessively on others and refuses to take responsibility for his or her own life. The *passive-aggressive* person resists requests for adequacy in personal relationships or job performance, but does so indirectly rather than through direct confrontation. The *narcissistic* person is exhibitionistic and preoccupied with his or her self; the *histrionic* person engages in exaggerated emotional expressions, as if he or she were performing for an audience.

INTERIM SUMMARY

Anxiety disorders include panic disorder and agoraphobia as well as simple phobias such as fear of snakes. The fundamental problem in these disorders is intense anxiety that may or may not arise from an identifiable event. A final category consists of personality disorders, which develop when particular personality traits become maladaptive and inflexible ways of responding to the social world. Some of these disorders, such as paranoid personality disorder and schizotypal personality disorder, are related to other forms of pathology.

SUMMARY

1. The *somatogenic,* or *medical model,* of emotional disturbance holds that psychological disorders are the manifestation of physiological dysfunction. In contrast, the *psychogenic,* or *behavioral model,* argues that pathogenic psychological or social conditions, not neurochemical imbalances, are the principal causes of psychopathology.

2. Historically viewed as an absence of rational thought, or as possession by demons, psychopathology is now considered a problem for medical and behavioral science.

3. Three criteria may be used to determine whether a behavior is "abnormal." The *statistical* definition considers any infrequently occurring behavior abnormal; the *personal discomfort* definition considers the degree to which the individual's everyday behavior is disrupted; the *violation of social norms* definition labels as abnormal any behavior that is

wholly inappropriate for the social setting. None of these definitions is entirely satisfactory.

4. The *Diagnostic and Statistical Manual* (DSM) and its revisions, published by the American Psychiatric Association, is the most widely used system of classification of psychopathology and behavior problems.

5. The DSM-III-R rates a person's behavior on five dimensions. The first consists of the clinical *syndromes* (collections of symptoms); the second consists of personality disorders and disorders related to childhood; the third enumerates physical conditions that might have a psychological component; the fourth relates to environmental stressors; and the fifth takes into account the level of the person's adjustment in the preceding year. The DSM-III-R continues to be revised.

6. Clinical assessment ideally begins with tests of vision, audition, motor perfor-

mance, language, and intelligence. These are followed by general personality testing, and then by a specialized clinical interview. When information from all of these sources is to be combined into a coherent picture of the client, substantial research evidence indicates that *statistical prediction* is far superior to *clinical prediction.*

7. The fundamental symptoms of *schizophrenia* are thought disorder (lack of coherence in spoken and written language), flattened or inappropriate affect, ambivalence (inability to pursue a task to completion), and autism (retreat into one's own private world).

8. Studies of identical and fraternal twins suggest that there is a substantial genetic predisposition for schizophrenia.

9. The blood platelets of chronic schizophrenics contain much lower levels of *monoamine oxidase (MAO),* a critical neurotransmitter substance. This suggests that biochemical factors play an important role in the disorder.

10. In addition to biochemical factors, aspects of the communication within a schizophrenic's family may influence the course of the disorder. These include the *double-bind* that can lead to social withdrawal, and the level of *expressed emotion* in the family.

11. A second general class of psychopathology includes disorders of affect such as *bipolar disorder* (which involves swings between elation and depression) and *major depression* (a unipolar disorder involving only negative affect). The latter may be caused in part by the individual's loss of control over events, or *learned helplessness.*

12. The extreme of affect disorder is suicide. Although three times as many females attempt suicide as males, males succeed more often and account for three-quarters of successful attempts. Suicide is the second leading cause of death (after accidents) among people aged 15 to 24.

13. The anxiety disorders include *phobias,* with the most prevalent of these being *panic disorder with agoraphobia* (literally fear of open places, but usually expressed as a fear of leaving the home). Other anxiety disorders are *obsessive-compulsive disorder* and *posttraumatic stress disorder.*

14. An enduring personality trait becomes a *personality disorder* when the trait is so inflexible that it dictates virtually all behavior, with maladaptive consequences.

FOCUS QUESTIONS

1. Describe how the treatment of people with mental disorders has changed since the first "insane asylums" were constructed.

2. What are the three kinds of definitions for abnormal behavior? Which one do you think is best? Why?

3. Describe the multiaxial approach to diagnosis taken by the DSM-III-R. What are the weaknesses of this system?

4. Describe all the information that a clinical practitioner should have before making a conclusive diagnosis. How should this information be combined?

5. Describe the major symptoms of schizophrenia. Distinguish among the various types of the disorder.

6. Compare and contrast the biological and environmental theories regarding the origin of schizophrenia.

7. Describe the essential symptoms of major depression. Compare and contrast the three theories regarding the origin of depression.

8. Describe the symptoms of bipolar disorder. How is this disorder different from major depression?

9. Describe the prominent anxiety disorders. Which of these is the most prevalent?

10. What is the difference between a personality trait and a personality disorder? Describe the antisocial personality disorder.

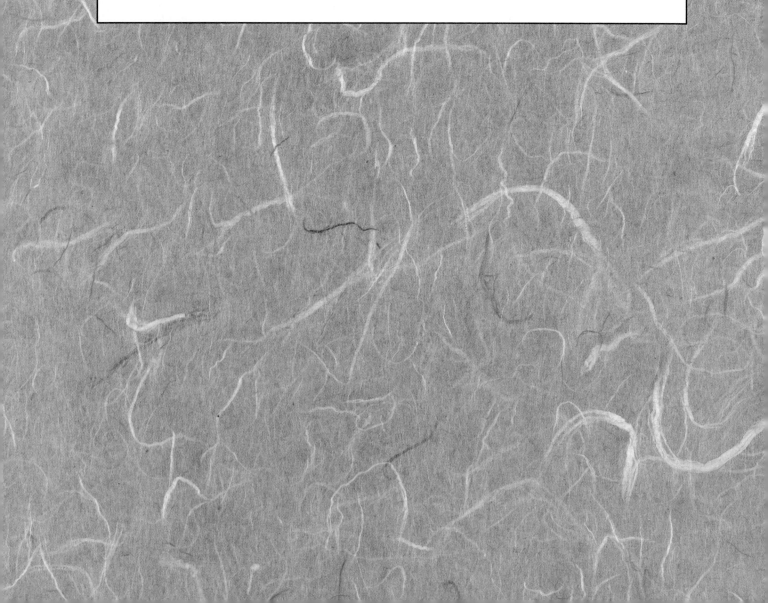

CHAPTER 25

TREATMENT OF DISORDERS

 How many times have you heard a network news anchor describe an accused criminal as "a former mental patient"? This all-too-frequent comment reinforces an unfortunate stereotype—that of the "dangerous crazy person"—in two ways. First, it leads viewers to overestimate the number of crimes committed by former mental patients because the newscasters never give the relevant base rate information (the number of accused criminals who are not former mental patients). Second, it suggests that the former emotional disturbance, rather than some characteristic of the individual's present environment, is the cause of the criminal act.

The "former mental patient" label also brings into sharp focus the theme of stability versus change. No one is ever described as a "former broken arm." We consider a broken arm to be a temporary disorder, caused by some external event such as an accident. Once a broken arm is treated and healed, we consider it whole and expect it to remain normal in the future. Where emotional disturbance is concerned, however, the comments of newscasters and others suggest that *disorder* is the stable state and that treatment produces an unstable "normality" that could disappear at any moment. Is there any justification for this view? Just how permanent are the benefits of psychotherapy, and how can we tell? Questions like these underlie much of the following discussion.

ISSUES IN TREATMENT OF MENTAL DISORDERS

Three fundamental issues have dominated discussions of psychotherapy through the years. The first concerns the tension between the medical and behavioral models of treatment. The second concerns an ongoing struggle over society's ability and authority to impose treatment on individuals who do not seek it. The third concerns a long-standing debate over the effectiveness of both medical and behavioral therapies. In this section we consider each of these issues in turn.

MODELS OF TREATMENT

As noted earlier, there are two dominant models of psychopathology. According to the *medical model*, particular psychological problems are equivalent in every respect to medical conditions. That is, each separate psychological problem has an identifiable physical cause or set of causes that produces a limited set of symptoms. These symptoms dictate the proper treatment, which, if followed, suggests a prognosis for the likely course of the disorder. Although the American Psychiatric Association's *Diagnostic and Statistical Manual* (DSM-III-R) does not specify treatments, its structured approach to diagnosis, described in Chapter 24, is very much in keeping with the medical model.

In contrast to the medical model, the *behavioral model* claims that psychological disturbances reflect problems in living. Events that precipitate these disturbances are traumatic occurrences external to the person, and the resulting emotional disorder is essentially a failure to adapt or cope. This view of disorder corresponds to the person-by-situation approach to personality characteristics and social behavior (see Chapter 21). Traumatic events differ in the threats they pose to individuals, and individuals differ in their resilience—one might be overwhelmed by an external threat that another could tolerate.

Accordingly, treatment should reflect which of the two variables—person or situation—is most likely the cause of the problem. First, an individual who is unable to

A memorial service in front of Luby's Cafeteria in Kileen, Texas, for the victims of the gunman who opened fire when the restaurant was crowded with lunch-time customers. Immediate psychological intervention can help support the survivors and the families of victims of random violence.

cope effectively with the demands of daily living can be taught more effective ways of dealing with problems. Second, people who are overwhelmed by unusual traumatic events—an earthquake, a flood, a random attack by a mass murderer—can be helped to deal with the psychological aftermath of an event that would strain anyone's coping skills. In either case, learning processes, not psychoactive drugs, are the key to long-term psychological well-being.

Both of these models are supported by empirical evidence, although neither provides a complete explanation of psychological disturbance. For example, proponents of the medical model argue that schizophrenia is produced by a neurochemical imbalance and that if this imbalance is corrected, the patient will recover completely. This position has empirical support in the documented effectiveness of antipsychotic medications. On the other hand, it is also true that among individuals with the same degree of neurochemical imbalance some cope more effectively than others; moreover, the probability of relapse is influenced by the nature of the social environment to which a schizophrenic patient returns after treatment, even if drug therapy is continued (Vaughn & Leff, 1976).

Clinicians search for neurochemical imbalances only when they are dealing with a person who comes to them with symptoms. (These initial symptoms are often called the *presenting* symptoms, to distinguish them from other problems that may be discovered later.) The presence of such imbalances in "normal" individuals has not been studied. Thus, the neurochemical abnormalities and the symptoms of emotional disorder are correlated, but such correlation does not establish a causal connection. As noted earlier, psychological stressors have been shown to produce dramatic changes in the neuroendocrine system, suggesting the possibility that the psychological problems actually preceded the neurochemical abnormalities.

We will see in this chapter that some emotional disturbances respond best to psychoactive drugs whereas others respond best to behavioral therapies. So although the debate between proponents of the medical and behavioral models remains lively, there is clearly some value in each approach.

PSYCHOPATHOLOGY AND THE LAW

Disagreements over the role of neurochemical and behavioral causes of psychopathology have occurred largely among psychologists and clinicians. But unlike most other areas of psychology, psychotherapy also must deal with an important force outside the discipline of psychology: the law. The relationship between psychotherapy and the law has often been a subject of intense controversy centering on two related but distinct issues—the insanity defense and involuntary civil commitment.

The Insanity Defense

In industrialized societies the law sets limits on individual conduct. These limits differ in different countries, depending on the nature of the society and the objectives of the state. In all countries, however, a person who violates the limits risks legal sanction. As one commentator has noted, the law is written by rational beings for rational beings (Robinson, 1980). Penalties for violations of the law assume that offenders have the mental capacity to understand the difference between right and wrong, that they have sufficient control over their behavior to avoid doing wrong, and that they will understand why violations are punished.

A society that makes these assumptions should not impose punishment on a person who does not know the difference between right and wrong, who clearly cannot control his or her behavior, or who is unable to understand why the punishment is being imposed. These are the rational capacities that are legally presumed to be lacking in people who suffer from serious psychopathology. For example, it is difficult to argue that a schizophrenic who follows the instructions of "voices" has the same degree of self-control as a normal individual. Consequently, jurisprudence in the English tradition makes an exception to the normal criminal penalties. This exception rests on the **insanity defense**—the claim that the defendant was, by reason of mental disease or defect, unable to distinguish right from wrong or to make his or her behavior conform to that knowledge.

As civilized as this principle sounds, the insanity defense has been subjected to severe criticism in its application (Robinson, 1980). Specifically, it places psychologists and psychiatrists in the position of making claims about the defendant's mental state *at the time of the crime* on the basis of tests and interviews conducted much later. In the easy cases this is not a problem. If the defendant is obviously deranged and has behaved in a bizarre fashion ever since arrest, the opinion of a mental health professional adds little to what the jury can see for itself. In difficult cases, however, the defendant appears outwardly calm and rational, and the prosecution and defense present contradictory expert testimony by mental health professionals. The verdict can then turn on which clinician was the most persuasive, making the mental health testimony most important when it is most in doubt.

In some jurisdictions recognition of the limits of psychological assessment, together with public objections to the frequency of the insanity defense (including a case in which a Florida defendant claimed that his violent attack on an innocent victim was a result of temporary insanity caused by an allergic reaction to Hostess Twinkies), has led to the adoption of a different legal standard. Rather than acquitting a person by reason of mental disease or defect, the new laws enable judges and juries to find a defendant guilty as charged but mentally ill and in need of treatment

The insanity defense is one of the most controversial points of interaction between psychology and the law. Does a defendant know right from wrong? Does he or she have sufficent control over self-behavior to act in accordance with this knowledge? The issue of self-control was a critical part of the insanity defense offered by Jeffrey Dahmer who was tried in 1992 for murdering and dismembering over a dozen victims. Dahmer is shown here flanked by his attorneys. The jury apparently did not believe that Dahmer lacked control over his actions; they found him guilty.

(as opposed to mentally whole and deserving of imprisonment). Typically, these *guilty but mentally ill* laws require that the defendant be given a criminal sentence upon being "cured" of the mental disorder. This kind of verdict retains control over offenders, thereby reducing the public outcry at acquittals by reason of insanity. Whether it will in the long run provide a good balance between the need to regulate conduct and the desire for compassionate treatment of emotionally disturbed people remains to be seen.

Involuntary Civil Commitment

Criminal defenses of insanity are not the only point of interaction—and friction—between psychology and the law. Another such point, outside the bounds of the criminal law, is **involuntary civil commitment.** Mental health professionals receive training that leads them to see government as an ally in the delivery of services. Legal professionals receive training that leads them to be suspicious of the use of government power, even for socially desirable ends. Consequently, the question of whether a severely disturbed person should be compelled to receive treatment can often put mental health workers and attorneys in opposition, although each group will be doing what it considers is in the person's best interest.

As noted in Chapter 24, people suffering from psychological disorders enter state mental hospitals through one of two routes. Either they choose to sign themselves into the facility (voluntary commitment), or, as the result of a court proceeding, they are placed in the hospital against their will (involuntary commitment). In the United States there are two fundamental criteria for involuntary civil commitment: The person must be mentally ill and, in typical legal language, either "a danger to himself or others" or "substantially unable to care for himself." If a court decides, on the petition of a family member, physician, or law enforcement agent, that a person meets either of these criteria, the person will be placed in a state mental hospital for a limited observation period (usually no more than a week). During this time the hospital staff will evaluate the patient to determine whether the court's opinion is valid and, if it is, to propose a time-limited treatment program. This treatment program is reviewed periodically by the court, and the person is released when treatment has been successfully completed.

In theory, involuntary commitment deprives a disturbed person of liberty so that the person can benefit from treatment. In practice, however, the procedure is only as good as the clinical judgment about the person's mental disturbance. The problem can be illustrated by comparing involuntary commitment to the imprisonment of a criminal offender. A criminal offender can be deprived of liberty for something he or she *has done.* An involuntarily committed patient, however, is deprived of liberty because of what he or she *might do* (fail to care for himself or herself; commit violence). Thus, the involuntary commitment is a prediction task similar to the signal detection and sensory judgment tasks discussed in Chapter 5 and the identification of personality traits discussed in Chapter 22 (see Figure 25-1).

A person who has been involuntarily committed either does or does not have a disorder serious enough to warrant treatment without consent. The clinical staff assigned to evaluate the patient will assert to the court that a serious disorder either is or is not present. An assertion that the patient has a serious disorder will result in that patient's continued confinement for treatment, but only if that judgment corresponds to the actual state of the patient (a "hit"), will involuntary confinement be justified.

Unfortunately, there is evidence that clinical judgment can be far from perfect. In one widely cited study, for example, a number of volunteer "pseudopatients" arrived at the admitting offices of several psychiatric hospitals complaining of hearing voices that said "empty," "hollow," and "thud"—one of the key symptoms of schizophrenia (Rosenhan, 1973). (The pseudopatients had been screened by the researchers to make sure they were not in fact suffering from any form of emotional disorder.) The pseudopatients reported no other symptoms and accurately described their own medical histories. All were initially diagnosed as psychotic and admitted

FIGURE 25-1 Clinical diagnosis for involuntary commitment can be regarded as a sensory judgment problem in which there is a "hit" only if the clinician diagnoses the patient as having a disorder the patient actually has. Other possibilities are the "miss" that occurs when the clinician fails to diagnose an existing disorder, a valid negative (no disorder, no diagnosis), and a false alarm (diagnosis, but no actual disorder). In the last instance, however, a patient will be incorrectly committed.

for treatment; the average stay was 19 days. In no instance did a hospital staff member ever discover that the pseudopatients were in reality quite sane, although in some instances other patients became aware of the deception. When they were released, most of the pseudopatients were described as suffering from schizophrenia "in remission."

It should be noted that people without psychological problems rarely arrive at the admitting desk of a psychiatric hospital, so it is not surprising that the hospital staff had what in sensory judgment terms is a bias toward false alarms (believing that the pseudopatients really needed help). The problem, however, is that the initial diagnosis remained unchanged, despite a detailed examination, until the pseudopatient was discharged. It appears that the hospital personnel were guided by expectations rather than by reality. And those expectations must be more powerful in the case of an involuntarily committed individual. Such a person is brought in by the police after a judge has signed a commitment order, usually on the petition of a physician. It is evident, therefore, that at least some people in the community consider the patient to be suffering from a mental disorder.

If an individual is being involuntarily committed because of being substantially unable to care for himself or herself, there are likely to be some outward appearances: The person may be malnourished, filthy, even incontinent. Even then, the clinician's judgment task is difficult. When the reason behind the commitment is the presumption that the individual is dangerous, the clinician's task is much more likely to be in error. Consider the structure of the decision task as shown in Figure 25-1. A mental health professional whose judgment is a "miss"—a patient released as nondangerous kills somebody—will not only suffer the community's outrage, but also may be successfully sued for damages. In contrast, the same professional's "false alarm"—confinement of a nondisturbed individual—may never even be discovered. So the decision is clearly biased toward overprediction of dangerousness.

One highly cited incident illustrates how much in error predictions of dangerousness can be (Ennis, 1970). At one time in the state of New York, criminal offenders who became mentally disturbed during their incarceration were routinely transferred to a maximum-security hospital run by the Department of Corrections. Once their original sentences were served, such disturbed offenders were released, transferred to civil hospitals, or—if they were considered dangerous—kept in the maximum security facility. A Supreme Court case challenging this procedure (*Baxtrom* v. *Herold,* 1966) resulted in the immediate transfer to civil hospitals of 967 patients who had been certified dangerous. Four years later, only 2.7% of these released patients had behaved dangerously and were either imprisoned or back in a hospital for the criminally insane (Steadman & Keveles, 1972). Some experts believe that the prediction of dangerousness has not improved much since the time of the *Baxtrom* case (Steadman, 1983), whereas others argue that improvements in prediction have taken place (Monahan, 1984). Despite these improvements, predictions of long-term

671

People can be involuntarily committed to mental institutions if they are substantially unable to care for themselves. In many urban environments, however, it can be difficult to distinguish people who are *psychologically* unable to care for themselves from people who are *economically* unable to care for themselves.

dangerousness are "so inaccurate that the official policy of the American Psychiatric Association is that psychiatrists are incapable of making them" (Miller, 1991).

Debates over involuntary commitment have led to the development of three principles that have been incorporated into U.S. law. First, the deprivation of liberty should be minimized (*Lessard* v. *Schmidt,* 1972). In the words of the law, people should be treated in the **least restrictive alternative** setting. Only patients who cannot be supervised adequately in community mental health centers should be hospitalized; once hospitalized, only violent patients should be isolated or physically restrained. Second, a person deprived of liberty for the sake of treatment should actually receive treatment (*Rouse* v. *Cameron,* 1966; *Wyatt* v. *Stickney,* 1971; *O'Connor* v. *Donaldson,* 1975). Again using the words of the law, an involuntarily committed person has an affirmative **right to treatment,** described by Judge Frank Johnson in *Wyatt* v. *Stickney:* "To deprive any citizen of his or her liberty upon the altruistic theory that the confinement is for humane therapeutic reasons and then fail to provide adequate treatment violates the very fundamentals of due process." The law now states minimum conditions necessary to justify institutionalization (minimum standards that are below those recommended by the American Psychiatric Association [Rosenhan & Seligman, 1989]). Third, despite restrictions on their movements, people should retain as much freedom of choice as possible. This means that patients have a *right to refuse treatment.* It is not clear how this right can be reconciled with the right to treatment without significantly interfering with hospital treatment programs. Not since the beginning of the asylum reform movement (see Chapter 24), late in the eighteenth century, has the legal system weighed in so heavily on the side of involuntarily committed patients. This relatively recent establishment of a whole series of *patient's rights* will continue to affect the treatment of psychological disorders for the foreseeable future.

EVALUATING PSYCHOTHERAPY

The effectiveness of psychotherapy in relieving the symptoms of mental disorder has always been a matter of concern to patients, clinicians, and government agencies in charge of mental hospitals. As the preceding discussion indicates, however, another institution—the law—now has a vested interest in the effectiveness of psychotherapy. And the law is not alone. In modern industrialized societies such as the United States, relatively few patients (or patients' families) pay the entire cost of their treatment. Instead, the costs of psychotherapy are now largely borne by third-party payers—private insurance companies, federal assistance programs such as Medicare and

One reason it is difficult to evaluate the effectiveness of psychotherapy is that clients choose therapists with whom they expect to have substantial rapport.

Medicaid, legislatively mandated subsidies for state mental hospitals. Not surprisingly, these third-party payers seek to maximize the effectiveness of the treatment dollars they spend. As a result of all of these pressures, there is intense interest in the study of psychotherapy outcomes.

Measuring Outcome

The goal of research on the effectiveness of psychotherapy is to determine whether a particular treatment actually changes the target behavior. Assuming that behavioral change can be measured (an assumption that is open to debate), such research must perform three tasks: It must establish that the behavior actually changed, it must show that the treatment was the cause of the change, and it must demonstrate that nothing else could account for the change. If all three of these conditions are met, the investigators can conclude that the therapy changed the target behavior.

Treatment outcomes are typically measured with data from one of five sources, as indicated in Figure 25-2 (Lambert, 1983). The primary source of data on outcome is

FIGURE 25-2 A review of 216 psychotherapy outcome studies published during a five year period in the *Journal of Consulting and Clinical Psychology* found five data sources used to judge the effectiveness of psychotherapy. These were patient self-reports, the opinions of trained observers, physiological measures (instrumental), the therapists themselves, and significant other people in the patient's life. No studies used more than three of the possible sources.

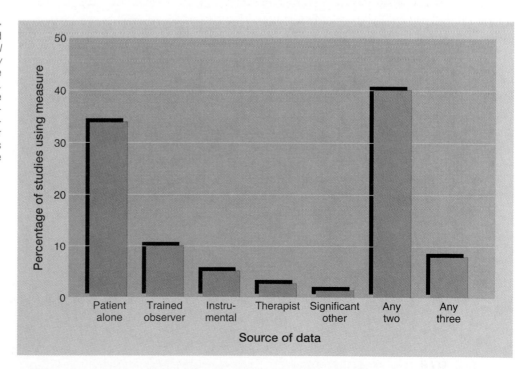

the self-report of the patient, which was the only data source found in nearly 34% of 216 outcome studies that appeared in a major journal during a five-year period (Lambert, 1983). The next most frequently used single source (in roughly 10% of the studies reviewed) is the trained observer who has been instructed in the use of standardized scales to assess symptoms or behavior. About 5% of the studies employed physiological measuring instruments to monitor such things as heart rate, muscle tension, blood pressure, or sweating palms, all of which might be related to arousal or anxiety. Only some 2% of the studies included therapist ratings of the patient's improvement as the sole source of outcome data. Roughly 1% based outcome effectiveness judgments only on ratings by friends, relatives, or co-workers of the patient. Nearly 40% of the studies used two of these five data sources; about 8% of the studies used three of the five data sources; not a single study used more than three separate sources of data. Across the total of 216 studies, self-reports were one of the data sources in nearly 80%.

Given the high proportion of outcome studies involving patient self-reports, it would be valuable to know more precisely what measures were involved. Another review of 150 outcome studies involving self-reports placed these measures into four broad categories, shown in Figure 25-3 (Beutler & Crago, 1983). Most of the studies used more than one self-report measure. Nearly 40% (59 of the 150) included a direct assessment of the patient's belief that he or she had *improved* as a consequence of therapy. Almost as popular were standardized measures of personality, such as the Minnesota Multiphasic Personality Inventory (MMPI), the most recent version of which was discussed in detail in Chapter 22. Indeed, the MMPI was by far the most frequently used personality test, employed in almost half of the studies that used a personality inventory. Twelve measures of general symptomatology were used in 25 of the studies. Single symptoms were assessed in 45 of the studies, with the State-Trait Anxiety Inventory (STAI) (Spielberger, Gorsuch, & Lushene, 1970) used in one-quarter of these. Finally, the 150 studies reported use of an additional 62 self-report measures—only 4 of which appeared more than twice—that are not shown in Figure 25-3. As the authors of the review concluded, "we are impressed with the lack of consistency in the use and selection of specific measures" (Beutler & Crago, 1983, p. 467). Only self-ratings of improvement, the MMPI, and the STAI were used in more than 10 of the 150 studies.

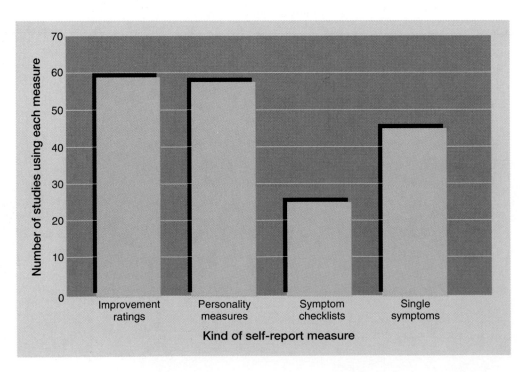

FIGURE 25-3 A detailed examination of the patient self-report measures used in 150 selected studies of psychotherapy outcome. Patient self-ratings of improvement were used in nearly 40% of the studies (59 out of 150), and a comparable number of studies used standardized personality measures such as the Minnesota Multiphasic Personality Inventory (MMPI). Studies also used general symptom checklists and measures of the occurrence of specific symptoms. Aside from the MMPI, the State-Trait Anxiety Inventory (STAI) was the only measure used in more than 10 studies.

Problems in Measurement

Lack of uniformity in measures of psychotherapy outcome is just one problem in determining whether psychotherapy is effective. Three other problems—the meaning of change, the self-selection of subjects, and the placebo effect—also complicate the task.

One of the most prevalent measures of outcome is the patient's self-rating of *improvement*. Does this measure indicate that real change has occurred, and if so, can the amount of change be quantified? Unfortunately, there is reason for concern on both counts. Self-ratings of improvement are, in other terms, customer satisfaction surveys. And for the most part, the customers are happy, with most patients indicating that they are satisfied with their outcome (Rosenhan & Seligman, 1989). Satisfaction measures, however, are affected by the amount of money and time the client may have invested in treatment (nobody wants to think that all that expense was for nothing). Moreover, the improvement the client sees may be in an area (such as "I learned how to talk about my problems with someone") quite different from the one that initially led him or her to seek treatment. Finally, improvement is a relative measure: The worse one's psychological state at the beginning of treatment, the more room for improvement there is (Beutler & Crago, 1983). For all of these reasons, self-ratings may not be valid indicators of real change.

If it were ethically acceptable to conduct psychotherapy outcome studies using standard experimental techniques, some individuals seeking help would be randomly assigned to a treatment group, and others to a no-treatment group. Because simple experiments of this sort are scarcely possible, client self-selection is a serious problem for psychotherapy outcome research. Having freely chosen a therapist (and, by extension, that therapist's theoretical orientation), the clients arrive with expectations about how well the particular form of therapy will work for them. Thus, what is being evaluated is a combination of the client and the therapy, not the therapy alone. Even if the treatment is of great benefit to those who have chosen it, we still do not know whether it would work equally well for people who had not chosen it for themselves.

Finally, there is the possibility that the patient will improve not as a direct result of the therapy but because participating in therapy leads to the expectation that change will take place. The term for this, borrowed from medicine, is the **placebo effect.** One study provides an excellent demonstration of this effect (Lowinger & Dobie, 1969). At the beginning of this two-part study some patients were given actual medication and some were given a placebo. Approximately 35% of the patients improved, regardless of whether they had received the placebo or the actual medication. In the second part of the study, the dosage rates for both the medication and the placebo were doubled, and the improvement rates also doubled—for each of the groups. This change occurred although neither the patients nor the physicians involved knew whether patients were receiving placebos or medication. The placebo effect is not well understood (Rosenhan & Seligman, 1989), and until it is understood, and can be eliminated, it will continue to compromise research on the effectiveness of psychotherapy.

Drawing Conclusions

Because of client self-selection and the placebo effect, it is virtually impossible to draw conclusions about the effectiveness of psychotherapy from a single study. On the other hand, because of the lack of standardization in methods, it used to be difficult to draw conclusions even from a sizable group of studies. This latter problem was fundamentally altered when a new statistical technique, *meta-analysis,* was applied to research on the outcomes of psychotherapy (Smith & Glass, 1977). Because it compares the statistical results, not the procedures, from one study to the next, meta-analysis can overcome the lack of standardization.

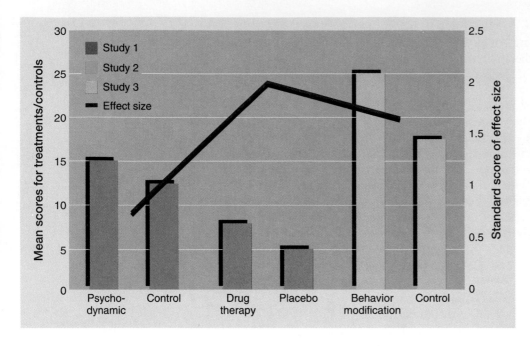

FIGURE 25-4 The statistical technique of meta-analysis can be used to compare effect sizes across studies with widely differing objectives, methods, and subject populations. Effect size is computed by subtracting the mean score of the control group from the mean score of the treatment group and dividing the result by the standard deviation of the control group. The result for these three hypothetical studies is shown as the single line.

Exactly how this works can be illustrated with an example. Imagine that a psychotherapy outcome study has been conducted that compares a psychodynamic treatment program to a placebo control group. Subjects in each group would be tested on some measure of psychological well-being, producing a mean score for psychological adjustment within the treatment group (M_T) and another for adjustment within the control group (M_C). The difference between the two scores is then divided by the standard deviation within the control group (SD_C) to obtain a measure that Smith and Glass (1977) called "effect size" (ES):

$$ES = \frac{M_T - M_C}{SD_C}$$

Now imagine that two other studies have been conducted. One of these compares a drug treatment to a placebo treatment among hospitalized schizophrenics; the other compares behavior modification techniques to a group-discussion control in the treatment of a snake phobia. Hypothetical results of all three studies are shown in Figure 25-4. In this figure the bars, which are scaled by the left Y axis, indicate the mean scores for the two groups in each of the three studies. The single line, which is scaled on the right Y axis, indicates the ES (mean difference divided by standard deviation of the control group). In this hypothetical example, the ES is shown as larger in Studies 2 and 3 than in Study 1.

The point is that use of ES permits us to make this kind of comparison across three studies that differ not only in subject population and particular dependent variable, but also in theoretical orientation. Thus, ES is a measure of the relative improvement resulting from the treatment. If the ES is positive, the treatment has, on the average, increased psychological adjustment. Because the ES is a *standard score* (a score expressed in standard deviation units), an ES of +1.0 would mean that the average person in the treatment group is better adjusted than 84% of the people in the control group, representing a substantial improvement.

The first meta-analysis of 375 studies of psychotherapy outcomes found an average ES of +0.68, which means that "the average client receiving therapy was better off than 75 percent of the untreated controls" (Smith & Glass, 1977, p. 354). The problem with this conclusion, as critics were quick to point out, is that it is only as sound as the studies included in the meta-analysis. Many of the studies analyzed compared one form of psychotherapy to another rather than making direct comparisons either to untreated controls or to placebo controls. To correct this problem, Landman and Dawes (1982) began with 468 outcome studies, randomly selected 65 for detailed scrutiny, and retained for meta-analysis only the 42 that had a true no-treatment (or placebo) control condition. The meta-analysis of these studies found an average *ES* of +0.78, confirming the earlier conclusion that psychotherapy has some effect. A more recent meta-analysis focusing on the comparison between psychotherapy and various kinds of control conditions found that psychotherapy was "approximately twice as effective" as well-designed control conditions (Barker, Funk, & Houston, 1988, p. 579).

In sum, despite the procedural difficulties that can affect individual outcome studies, the results of these three meta-analyses justify the conclusion that psychotherapy is effective. What the findings do not tell us is whether a particular form of therapy is effective; studies were included in the meta-analyses without regard to the particular kind of therapy involved. As we will see in later sections, questions can still be raised about the effectiveness of some forms of psychotherapy.

INTERIM SUMMARY

The medical model of psychopathology holds that psychological disorders are produced by physiological factors and can be diagnosed and treated in the same way as physical disorders. In contrast, the behavioral model holds that psychological disturbance is a reflection of problems in living. Both models have received empirical support, but neither alone provides a complete explanation for psychological disturbance. The legal system is an important force affecting the treatment of emotionally disturbed individuals. The law demonstrates compassion for the mentally disturbed in the provision of an insanity defense against criminal charges, which has recently been modified to require that defendants be given criminal sentences upon being cured of their mental disorder. Involuntary civil commitment is the court proceeding by which a person is placed in a state mental hospital. Ethical issues related to involuntary commitment have led to modification of the law so that people are treated in the least restrictive alternative setting, have a right to treatment, and have the right to refuse treatment. Both the insanity defense and involuntary civil commitment assume that psychotherapy is effective. Although research on the results of therapy cannot match the standards of experimental research, the statistical technique of meta-analysis provides strong evidence that psychotherapy is effective in treating psychological disorders.

SOMATIC THERAPIES

Just as psychological disorders have been explained by two models—the medical and the behavioral—treatments for disorder have also been of two forms—somatic and psychological. In the remainder of this chapter we shall discuss both forms, beginning with the somatic therapies.

Since the 1950s emotional disorders such as schizophrenia have been treated with psychoactive medication. As understanding of the neurochemistry of transmission of nerve impulses increased, the variety of drug therapies increased dramatically, as did the precision with which particular drugs could be applied to specific emotional disturbances. The disorders that are most responsive to drug therapy are schizophrenia and bipolar affective disorder.

TREATMENT OF SCHIZOPHRENIA

Before discussing the treatment of schizophrenia, let us review the basic elements of neurosynaptic transmission (described in detail in Chapter 5). Recall that the body's internal messages are carried across neural synapses by *neurotransmitter substances.* Depending on the neurotransmitter substance involved, the receiving dendrite is either activated or inhibited. Once the transmission has occurred, much of the neurotransmitter substance is deactivated by enzymes that break it down into its component substances; the remainder is reabsorbed into the terminal bulb's vesicles in a process known as *reuptake.* At this point the terminal bulb is primed to fire again.

Transmitter Substances

Because the fleeting electrochemical changes that occur at the synapse are difficult to measure, it has not been possible to make a complete list of neurotransmitter substances and their effects. Some substances that have been identified are acetylcholine, norepinephrine, serotonin, gamma-aminobutyric acid (GABA), and dopamine.

One of these substances, dopamine (DA), is most important for our purposes here. When an action potential causes DA to be released, it diffuses across the synaptic cleft. After the neural impulse, most of the excess DA in the synapse is metabolized by monoamine oxidase (MAO) and catechol methyltransferase (COMT); some of the excess is reabsorbed and then metabolized by MAO.

In 1950 a French surgeon, Henri Laborit, was testing drugs to reduce incidents of dangerously low blood pressure during surgery. Quite by accident he discovered that one of these drugs reduced presurgical anxiety. Laborit collaborated with a chemist, Paul Charpentier, to examine the chemical structure of the drug, and Charpentier later developed **chlorpromazine,** the first drug to be used successfully in treating the symptoms of schizophrenia.

Chlorpromazine and other drugs in the family known as *phenothiazines* act on the brain by preventing the release of DA from the presynaptic membrane and by blocking the DA receptors on the postsynaptic membrane (Galluscio, 1990). As noted in Chapter 24, the effectiveness of these drugs and other families of drugs that block DA led to the development of the **dopamine hypothesis of schizophrenia:** The symptoms of schizophrenia are caused by excessive activity in brain structures in which DA is a primary neurotransmitter.

Psychoactive Drugs

The chance discovery of the antipsychotic effects of phenothiazines led to an explosion of interest in drug therapy for various psychological disorders. Numerous psychoactive drugs were developed and tested in the ensuing years. Two major classes of psychoactive drugs are shown in Table 25-1. The first class, the **minor tranquil-**

TABLE 25-1   Psychotherapeutic Medications for Anxiety and Schizophrenia

Psychological Effect	Generic Name	Trade Name
Minor tranquilizers (antianxiety)	Chlordiazepoxide	Librium
	Diazepam	Valium
	Meprobamate	Miltown, Equanil
Antipsychotics (neuroleptics)	Chlorpromazine	Thorazine
	Fluphenazine	Prolixin
	Haloperidol	Haldol
	Thioridazine	Mellaril
	Trifluoperazine	Stelazine

SOURCE: Adapted from Rosenham & Seligman (1989).

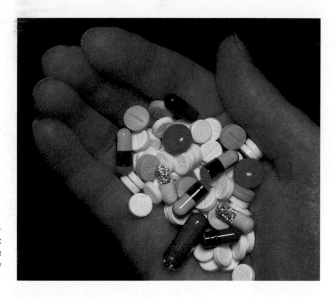

Since the chance discovery of the phenothiazines, there has been a dramatic increase in the number of psychoactive drugs used in the treatment of a variety of psychological disorders.

izers, includes Valium, Librium, Miltown, and other antianxiety drugs that are typically prescribed for the treatment of stress. These drugs are so common that according to some estimates they will have been used at one time or another by half of the adult population of the United States (Bootzin & Acocella, 1984). Usually they are a substitute for psychotherapy.

A second class of drugs consists of the **antipsychotic** drugs that reduce psychotic symptoms. This category includes the original antipsychotic medication, chlorpromazine, as well as other phenothiazines that reduce the hallucinations and disordered thought that are characteristic of schizophrenia. Although the antipsychotic drugs are sometimes called "major tranquilizers," this label inaccurately suggests that their principal effect is to reduce anxiety rather than reduce thought disorder. They are also referred to as *neuroleptic* drugs (from leptikos, the Greek word for "seize") and have an unfortunate side effect: They can produce symptoms that resemble the stiffness and tremors of neurological diseases such as Parkinson's disease. Despite their side effects, these drugs are usually credited with much of the reduction in the hospitalization of schizophrenics that has occurred since they came into widespread use.

Problems in Treatment

Although the vast majority of previously hospitalized schizophrenic patients now take daily maintenance doses of antipsychotic medication, it would be a mistake to conclude that these patients are cured. For one thing, the medication affects only the active symptoms (hallucinations, confusion); it does not change the flat emotional responding, nor does it raise the patient's overall level of social skills. That level is frequently so low that the patient still needs a great deal of psychological assistance and support.

A more serious problem arises from the strength of the medication. In ways that are not yet fully understood, these drugs may produce symptoms such as muscular rigidity and a peculiar twisting posture, inability to stand still, and tremors in the fingers. Moreover, a significant proportion of phenothiazine recipients over the age of 30 suffer from **tardive dyskinesia,** a loss of control over particular muscle groups that develops long after the patient first takes the drug. The symptoms of tardive dyskinesia include involuntary movements of the head, mouth, and tongue. The most troubling aspect of these side effects is that they remain even after the antipsychotic medication is discontinued, although recent studies have shown that they can be mitigated somewhat with other medication. Thus, although the antipsychotic drugs have allowed large numbers of schizophrenics to return to a more nearly normal life outside the hospital, this has been achieved at some cost.

TREATMENT OF AFFECTIVE DISORDERS

Somatic therapy has been found to be effective in the treatment of affective disorders. In considering the therapies used to treat these disorders, recall that bipolar affective disorder (manic-depressive disorder) differs in important ways from major depression. These differences seem to be reflected in the kinds of psychoactive drugs that provide relief from the symptoms of the disorders.

Treatment of Major Depression

As Table 25-2 shows, two families of antidepressants are used in the treatment of major depression. The *tricyclics,* so named because of their three-ring molecular structure, were first used in treating schizophrenia in the hope that they would provide the benefits of the phenothiazines without the damaging side effects. They proved ineffective in alleviating confusion or hallucinations, but they did produce an elevated mood (Davison & Neale, 1986). Consequently, they have come to be used in treating depression. The other major family of antidepressants is the *monoamine oxidase inhibitors (MAOIs).* Like the tricyclics, the MAOIs were originally intended for treatment of a disorder other than depression (in this case, tuberculosis), and were found to be ineffective for this purpose, but produced an elevated mood among the patients who received them.

TABLE 25-2   Psychotherapeutic Medications for Affective Disorders

Psychological Effect	Generic Name	Trade Name
Antidepressants	Tricyclics	
	Amitriptyline	Elavil
	Imipramine	Tofranil
	Monoamine oxidase inhibitors	
	Phenelzine	Nardil
Antibipolar disorder	Lithium carbonate	Lithonate, Lithane

SOURCE: Adapted from Rosenham & Seligman (1989).

Both classes of drug take from two to four weeks to make a difference in the patient's mood, and both produce undesirable side effects. The tricyclics produce dryness in the mouth, constipation, dizziness, palpitations, and blurred vision. (Many of these symptoms are also produced by phenothiazines.) The MAOIs are the most toxic of the psychotherapeutic medications. In combination with other drugs, or even with foods containing large amounts of the amino acid *tyramine* (such as foods preserved through pickling and beverages produced through fermentation), the MAOIs can produce serious illness or even death. For this reason, they are used with great care and only with patients who do not respond to tricyclics.

It was originally thought that both families of antidepressants produce their effects by increasing the amount of monoamines available at critical synapses in the brain. Tricyclics were thought to do this by blocking the reuptake of catecholamines, whereas MAOIs were believed to block the breakdown of catecholamines. Recent research, however, has complicated the picture. It has been shown that some tricyclics have no effect on catecholamines, although they do block *histamine* receptors in the medial forebrain bundle (stimulation of this part of the brain is reinforcing; see Chapter 5), but that MAOIs have no effect on histamine receptors (Galluscio, 1990). This suggests that more than one kind of neurochemical condition may be involved in major depression, but conclusive evidence has yet to be found.

Treatment of Bipolar Disorder

Since the mid-1970s the most prevalent drug therapy for the mania and depression experienced by people with bipolar affective disorder has been the inorganic salt **lithium carbonate.** (See Table 25-2.) This light metallic ion affects both catecholaminergic neurons and amino acid–based neurotransmitters (Galluscio, 1990). Interestingly, lithium carbonate has virtually no effect on the symptoms of unipolar affective disorder, and the tricyclics or MAOIs have virtually no effect on the symptoms of bipolar disorder. As noted in Chapter 24, the fact that lithium is ineffective in treating major depression and the trycyclics are ineffective in treating bipolar disorder suggests that the two affective disorders have different bases in brain chemistry.

Although its neurological effects are not well known, lithium carbonate appears to have the ability to prevent future episodes of mania and depression in patients who are given a maintenance dose, and it does not produce the neurological symptoms that appear as side effects of the phenothiazines. It does, however, require careful monitoring of dosage level because an overdose can be fatal.

OTHER SOMATIC THERAPIES

In addition to drug therapy, two other somatic therapies have been used to treat emotional disorders. They are psychosurgery and electroconvulsive therapy.

Psychosurgery

Psychosurgery is the surgical destruction of brain tissue. The most infamous of these operations is the **prefrontal lobotomy,** a procedure in which a surgical instrument is inserted into the front of the brain (either through a hole drilled in the side of the head or through the transorbital structure separating the eye and the brain). The instrument is then rotated in an arc of some 60 degrees around the point of insertion, destroying up to 120 square centimeters of brain tissue, mostly in the prefrontal lobes of the cortex, and severing the connections between the prefrontal lobes and other areas of the brain. Before the introduction of phenothiazines, this operation was performed in an attempt to reduce violent and aggressive behavior in some patients. Since then the operation has been thoroughly discredited, and it is no longer performed.

Electroconvulsive Therapy

Electroconvulsive therapy (ECT) is used in cases of severe depression. The procedure typically consists of a series of six to ten treatments administered over a period of a few weeks. The patient is first given a sedative and muscle relaxant; electrodes are then placed on each side of the head. A current of 70 to 130 volts is passed between the electrodes for a fraction of a second, inducing a seizure that mimics a grand mal epileptic seizure and briefly interrupts most electrical activity in the brain. ECT causes some confusion in the patient, who also suffers temporarily from **retrograde amnesia** (inability to remember things learned before the ECT) and **anterograde amnesia** (inability to remember events that occurred immediately after the treatment). These effects largely disappear over time.

In popular culture ECT has a tarnished reputation. Indeed, it is among a very few therapeutic techniques that are specifically regulated by state laws. Patients and their families are reluctant to resort to ECT, and even with careful anesthesia and restraint the patient may be bruised by the convulsion. As noted, the treatment causes electri-

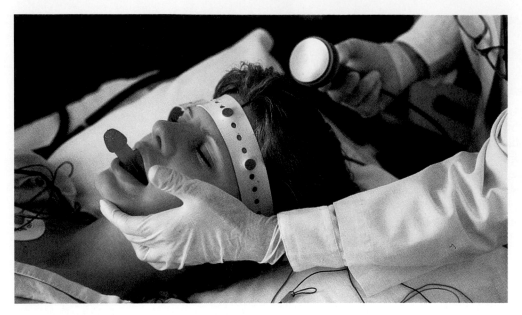

Electroconvulsive therapy (ECT) causes a seizure that temporarily interrupts the brain's electrical activity. Although this therapy has been effective in some cases of extreme depression, it is highly controversial, and usually regulated or prohibited by state laws.

cal activity in the brain to cease momentarily, even when unilateral techniques are used in which current is applied only to the patient's nondominant hemisphere. Yet ECT works both rapidly and effectively in the treatment of profound depression; controlled studies have shown that it is more effective in these cases than treatment with antidepressant medication (Rosenhan & Seligman, 1989). Moreover, drug therapy can take as long as two to three weeks to work, during which time the patient is at risk for suicide. The problem is that very few of the neurochemical effects of ECT are known, and it is possible that researchers may discover additional risks associated with the procedure.

INTERIM SUMMARY

Schizophrenia and affective disorders are most responsive to somatic therapies. Compounds known as phenothiazines interfere with the production and reception of the neurotransmitter dopamine and produce dramatic reductions in the hallucinations and disordered thought that characterize schizophrenia. Unfortunately, these medications can also produce a movement disorder known as tardive dyskinesia. Tricyclics and monoamine oxidase inhibitors reduce the symptoms of major depression, apparently by very different underlying neural mechanisms. Like the antipsychotics, these antidepressants can have damaging side effects. Among the nonchemical somatic treatments are psychosurgery (now virtually unknown) and electroconvulsive therapy. Although the latter is effective in producing immediate reductions in depressive symptoms, its long-term neurological effects are not known.

PSYCHOLOGICAL AND BEHAVIORAL THERAPIES

The range of disorders that can be treated effectively using somatic therapies is limited primarily to schizophrenia and major affective disorders. This leaves a large number of disorders inappropriate for a medical approach. Moreover, even when they are most effective, somatic treatments cannot by themselves produce a total cure. For both of these reasons, a variety of other therapeutic techniques are also used. Three of these—psychoanalysis, humanistic–existential therapies, and behavior

Many psychological disorders are more appropriately treated with psychological and behavioral therapies than with medication.

therapy—will be discussed in this section. These psychological and behavioral therapies, unlike somatic therapies, are related to the theories of personality organization and learning discussed in earlier chapters. These theories contribute the key assumptions on which the therapeutic methods are based, and form part of the background for criticisms of one method by proponents of others.

PSYCHOANALYSIS

Psychoanalysis, the psychotherapeutic technique originally developed by Freud, has served either as the model or as the target for most of the psychological and behavioral treatments of emotional disorder that have evolved since Freud's day. This technique hinges on some of the central concepts of Freud's theory of personality. As we saw in Chapter 21, that theory assumes that most of the crucial events of mental life happen in the unconscious and that the three structural elements of the personality—id, ego, and superego—are in constant tension. The id is the repository of sexual and aggressive instincts, and it seeks instant gratification of those desires. The ego attempts to mediate between the wishes of the id and the constraints of reality, and must also deal with the moralistic prescriptions of the superego. Because it cannot accomplish this task completely, the ego suffers *anxiety.* If the defense mechanisms used to counter this anxiety fail, psychopathology will result. Freud thus believed that psychoanalysis would be an effective treatment for what are now classified as anxiety disorders, not for more serious disorders such as schizophrenia.

The Anxieties of Childhood

Freud believed that the anxiety an individual suffers in adulthood is based on conflicts that arose during childhood that were not adequately resolved. In particular, he believed that such conflicts were often a product of sexual desire for the opposite-sex parent. Freud's analysis of the case of Little Hans, a boy who was so fearful of horses that he refused to leave his home, is the most celebrated example of this view.

Freud's description of the case occupies more than 100 pages in his *Collected Works,* so a very brief description cannot do justice to the analysis. A few details can, however, give the flavor of Freud's approach. In letters written to Freud, Hans's father reported that at age 3 Hans had shown great interest in his penis. When he was 3 1/2, Hans's mother had caught him with his hand on his penis and had threatened to have it cut off if he didn't stop playing with it. When he was 4 1/2, on one occasion when his mother was powdering him around his penis, being careful not to touch it,

Hans had asked her to put her finger on it, saying that this would be "great fun." She had admonished him, saying that it would not be proper for her to touch it. Some six months later, when Hans was out walking with his nursemaid, he had been frightened by a horse-drawn van that turned over. This fear had quickly generalized to all horses, which Hans thought might bite him and which he described as having "black things" around their mouths and "things in front of their eyes."

In keeping with his developing view of infantile sexuality, Freud concluded that Hans had strong sexual feelings toward his mother. When these were rejected, and the rejection was accompanied by the threat of castration, Hans became anxious in his father's presence. But because his father (who had a mustache and wore glasses) could not be avoided, the source of anxiety shifted to a father symbol, namely, the horses with "black things" around their mouths and "things in front of their eyes." The solution to this phobia of horses was to deal with the original source of conflict, identified through careful interpretation of all the details the patient was able to report. Because Freud founded both his personality theory and his clinical approach on lessons learned from individual cases, he generalized from this case to anxiety disorders in general, which he believed could be treated most effectively by thorough interpretation of deep-seated conflicts.

Psychoanalytic Techniques

Interpretation is a crucial element of psychoanalysis because the presumed origin of anxiety is sexual desire for a parent, something most people would not readily admit to. Consequently, when he began his clinical practice Freud used hypnosis to overcome patients' reluctance to discuss their sexual desires and fantasies. Soon, however, he recognized that *free association*, a technique that requires the client to relax and say anything that comes to mind, would accomplish the same purpose. Free association is usually supplemented by analysis of the patient's dreams, in which ego control is reduced and the wishes of the id are more directly expressed.

Throughout the process of psychoanalysis, which typically takes several years, the client talks and the therapist interprets. At a crucial point in the treatment the patient

Psychoanalysis relies extensively on the technique of free association, in which the client—relaxing in a comfortable position on a couch—says anything that comes to mind. Shown here is Sigmund Freud's office in London, where he lived after Hitler's annexation of Austria.

develops a **transference** reaction, beginning to treat the therapist in an emotionally charged fashion that would ordinarily be appropriate only for a person who was significant to the patient in his or her childhood. Psychoanalysts take the transference reaction as a sign that they can begin to discuss the childhood fears that gave rise to the patient's problem. Ultimately, the patient achieves **insight** and is said to be cured.

Evaluation of the Procedure

Freud was trained as a medical doctor, and most psychoanalysis is still practiced by physicians who have completed a psychiatric residency. Contemporary psychoanalysis places more emphasis on the role of the ego than Freud did, although the wishes of the id are still seen as the fundamental cause of anxiety. Given the importance of the psychodynamic perspective in psychology, one would expect to find a large number of research studies that show the power of psychoanalysis in treating many kinds of emotional disorders. Yet one review was able to find only 11 such studies (Prochaska, 1984). Most of them failed to include a placebo control, and "no study has found either psychoanalysis or psychoanalytically oriented psychotherapy to be significantly more effective than either a placebo treatment or some alternative form of therapy" (Prochaska, 1984, p. 55). Critics have also pointed out that even the case of Little Hans provides "unsatisfactory evidence for the psychoanalytic view of phobias," which are better explained in terms of the conditioning principles discussed in Chapter 12 (Rosenhan & Seligman, 1989, p. 206). Although its influence on popular culture has been significant, psychoanalysis as a therapeutic method has a very poor record.

HUMANISTIC–EXISTENTIAL THERAPIES

Like psychoanalysis, the humanistic and existential therapies attempt to alleviate anxiety. But these approaches concentrate on the adult ego rather than on the possible effects of childhood experiences. Most of the humanistic therapies subscribe to the personological view of personality, maintaining that conscious processes of self-actualization predominate over unconscious desires.

Client-centered Therapy

A fundamental tenet of the humanistic approach is that the individual can be understood only in terms of his or her unique perspective on the world. The way the person views the world, not the actual nature of the world, is of central importance. This emphasis on the perspective of the *client* (as opposed to *patient*) is illustrated in the **client-centered therapy** of Carl Rogers (1951; 1961). Client-centered therapy assumes that people undertake purposive actions rather than simply responding either to external environmental forces or to unconscious instincts. In a view reminiscent of Rousseau's description of the "state of nature" in which independent humans tended to their own needs without attempting to impose their will on others, Rogers believed that people are inherently good and that psychopathology is a result of faulty learning. Given a client who is aware of his or her motives, wants to be a self-actualized and effective person, and is capable of purposive behavior, the role of the therapist is to facilitate change, not to direct it. Whereas a psychoanalyst interprets the client's free associations in accordance with the tenets of Freudian theory, a client-centered therapist concentrates on seeing the world from the perspective of the client.

Unlike psychoanalysis, which has a single theory for every client, client-centered therapy has a different "theory" for each client. The fact that there is no specific theoretical structure within which to interpret the client's remarks places a significant burden on the therapist. Rogers argues, therefore, that the successful therapist must have three qualities. First, the therapist must be *genuine,* spontaneous, self-disclos-

Carl Rogers's client-centered therapy assumes that psychological disorders are the result of faulty learning. By providing clients with unconditional positive regard, Rogerian therapists hope to facilitate the client's own attempts to change.

According to the existential approach, a primary human goal should be the achievement of *fusion*—the development of an open, spontaneous, and loving connection to another human being—that serves as protection against the fundamental fear of dying.

ing, and willing to take responsibility for his or her own emotions. Second, the therapist must be able to express *unconditional positive regard* for the client—to accept the person without reservation. Third, the therapist must be capable of *empathy*—able to see the world from the client's perspective and to use that perspective to identify the client's problem.

Existential Therapy

Whereas humanistic therapy sees clients as engaged in a positive search for self-actualization, existential therapy sees clients as searching for meaning in events that are essentially negative. Life consists of choices, and because people are able to contemplate alternative courses of action, those choices are accompanied by responsibility and often by sadness. Thus, from the standpoint of existential therapy some anxiety is a normal aspect of the human condition. Anxiety arises both from things that are beyond the individual's control (such as catastrophic accidents) and from things that are under his or her control (such as the need to take responsibility for his or her actions).

The source of psychopathology, according to the existential approach, is failure to accept responsibility for one's actions (along with the anxiety that accompanies that responsibility). The goal of therapy is to help the client recognize that life consists of choices: "I can't" is all too often a substitute for "I don't want to." Taking responsibility for one's actions is a necessary prelude to achieving **authenticity,** or truth in relationships with others. Authenticity is more than success at interpersonal relations; it is frank, honest, spontaneous, open, and loving interaction with other human beings. The result is a psychological connection, or *fusion,* to others that serves as protection against the fundamental fear, fear of dying. If people can achieve authentic connections with others, then they are reassured that when they die they will at least live in the memories of others.

Evaluation of the Humanistic–Existential Approaches

The effectiveness of humanistic therapy has not yet been conclusively established (Davison & Neale, 1986). Most of the research on the outcomes of therapy has relied on clients' self-reports about their psychological state following therapy, but there are problems with this research technique. Specifically, the attempt to restructure the client's worldview through therapy is based on the assumption that the client does not know exactly what he or she thinks and feels. Hence, one cannot accept uncritically the same client's report regarding the effectiveness of the therapy.

Research on the effectiveness of existential therapy may be more than problematic, it may be theoretically impossible (Davison & Neale, 1986). For one thing, the existential approach is just that, an approach based on a philosophical position. It is not a specific set of therapeutic techniques. Moreover, the very act of gathering data is, in the eyes of many existential therapists, inauthentic. Reducing a person's experiences in the world and attempts to grapple with the meaning of personal choices to a set of data is dehumanizing. Consequently, from the perspective of existential therapy the entire notion of outcome research may be irrelevant.

BEHAVIOR THERAPY

The collection of procedures known as **behavior therapy** includes techniques based on conditioning, social learning, and cognitive restructuring of situations. What these have in common is the assumption that the general knowledge obtained by all experimental branches of psychology should be helpful in improving clinical practice. For the behavioral approaches, outcome data are not merely a form of assessment; they are a justification for choosing one procedure over another. Some of the most widely used approaches—systematic desensitization, the token economy, modeling, and cognitive restructuring—will be discussed here.

Systematic Desensitization

As we saw in Chapter 12, John Watson conditioned a child to fear a rabbit by pairing presentations of the rabbit with a loud noise. Some 40 years later, this conditioning procedure was reversed in treating individuals with phobias (Wolpe, 1958). Reasoning that a phobia is a conditioned fear, and recognizing that conditioning can be extinguished, Wolpe created the technique that is now known as **systematic desensitization.** This technique combines deep relaxation with increasingly powerful representations of the feared stimulus. After undergoing relaxation training, the client begins by imagining a weak and distant version of the feared setting or stimulus. The anxiety evoked by this remote threat is overcome through relaxation procedures. Then the client imagines a more immediate version of the stimulus, which again is overcome through relaxation. This process continues, cycling back to earlier stages if necessary, until the client is able to confront the source of the fear directly. At that point he or she has been systematically desensitized to the threat. An excellent example of the technique is provided by training programs designed to overcome phobic reactions to flying. People who are terrified of flying are first placed in secure and relaxing settings and then asked to think of seeing a plane off in the distance. Over many sessions, this procedure graduates to a trip to an airport, followed by getting on a plane that will only taxi on unused runways, and culminates in a flight to a vacation spot.

The Token Economy

Conditioning principles have also been applied in the treatment of schizophrenia. One important study tested some highly disturbed adults: long-term chronic schizophrenics (Paul & Lentz, 1977). Most of the patients ate with their hands; many were incontinent; and some were mute whereas others screamed for hours at a time.

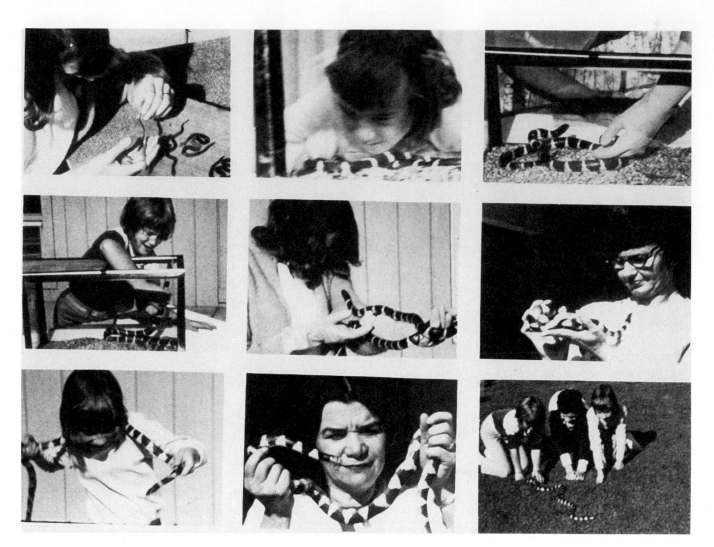

The behavioral therapy of systematic desensitization is especially effective in treating phobic reactions, such as fear of snakes. In this series of pictures people are shown overcoming their initial fears enough to hold a snake in their hands. Previously, just watching the snake would have been threatening to them.

Groups of patients were matched in terms of age, sex, socioeconomic level, symptoms, and length of hospitalization and were randomly assigned to one of three conditions. In the "routine hospital maintenance" condition, patients continued in the standard therapeutic routine of the hospital, receiving large doses of antipsychotic drugs and otherwise being left alone (except for the 5% of their waking time occupied by individual therapy, group therapy, and recreation). In the "milieu therapy" condition, patients were kept busy for 85% of their waking time. The were expected to participate individually and collectively in decisions affecting their ward. They were also expected to behave appropriately and were praised when they did so.

Finally, in the "social learning" condition patients were confronted with a **token economy.** In this system they paid for their meals and luxuries using tokens, which became secondary reinforcers through their connection to primary reinforcers such as food. Tokens could be earned by behaving appropriately at mealtime, taking part in classroom activities, making one's bed, maintaining an acceptable appearance, and even by socializing with others during free time. Each patient also received an individualized behavior treatment to deal with his or her specific symptoms. These patients, too, were kept busy for 85% of their waking time.

The results of the study showed that both milieu therapy and the social learning condition reduced the prevalence of symptoms; some patients improved enough to be discharged from the hospital. Of these patients, those who had been in the social learning group were significantly better able to function outside the hospital. Considering that the average length of hospitalization was some 17 *years,* these results are impressive. Critics have, however, raised questions about the extent to which this regimented approach can be generalized to the "real world," in which reinforcements are not always reliably associated with correct behavior. These are legitimate questions, but they do not detract from the fact that a token economy was effective with patients in whom no other treatment had made any noticeable difference. It is worth noting that tokens can also be used as part of a behavioral treatment of depression (Lewinsohn, 1975).

Modeling

Social learning theory indicates that direct reinforcement is not always necessary in changing behavior. Imitation and *vicarious reinforcement* (reinforcement of a model for appropriate behavior) can also lead to learning. The effects of modeling of appropriate behavior have been tested in a variety of clinical settings, often using films prepared for this purpose. An example is a film of an initially fearful child preparing for and coping with a visit to the dentist (Melamed, Hawes, Heiby, & Glick, 1975). Similar procedures, with the therapist, not a film, serving as a model, have been used successfully to train schizophrenics in more effective social behavior upon release (Bellack, Hersen, & Turner, 1976).

Cognitive Restructuring

We noted in the preceding chapter that one possible source of depression is a faulty attributional pattern; compared to normal people, depressed individuals are more likely to attribute the negative events in their lives to stable, internal factors (such as incompetence) that extend across several behavioral domains (Abramson, Seligman, & Teasdale, 1978). To relieve depression, therefore, the patient must be encouraged to think more positively about himself or herself. This cognitive restructuring typically involves identifying the emotions associated with an upsetting situation, listing the *automatic thoughts* (self-destructive cognitions such as "I can never do anything right") that cause feelings of depression, and then neutralizing these by silently repeating rational responses ("My co-workers always ask me for help on their projects") that counter the automatic negative thoughts (Bedrosian & Beck, 1980).

Comments on the Behavioral Approach

The cognitive restructuring techniques included here under the heading "Behavior Therapy" are often described as "cognitive." We refer to them as behavioral for two reasons: (1) Like the other methods described here, they depend on research to suggest how they might be used and to determine their effectiveness; and (2) as noted earlier, even classical conditioning of behavior involves the organization and use of knowledge, so there is no clear boundary between cognitive and behavioral approaches.

Another point about the behavioral therapies is that they are often criticized by proponents of a psychodynamic approach. These therapies are said to substitute one symptom for another rather than resolving the underlying psychological problem. For example, if a phobic is cured of the fear of snakes, a Freudian psychologist would expect the unresolved anxiety to spill out into a new phobia. Moreover, it is argued that real improvement in psychological health takes place largely in the mind rather than in outward behavior. Whether this improvement takes the form of greater insight into one's problems (as in psychodynamic therapy) or a recognition that one must assume responsibility for one's own behavior (as in existential therapy), the goal of treatment, according to these critics, should be more than mere elimination of symptoms.

Finally, behavioral therapies assume that the treatment of individual patients can be improved by applying of principles learned through psychological research. Research results are used both to design therapy programs and to evaluate the effectiveness of those programs. This assertion of a mutually beneficial relationship between science and clinical practice contrasts sharply with the views of existential therapy, and to a lesser degree with the way that psychoanalysis is often practiced.

INTERIM SUMMARY

Psychoanalysis is based on Freud's personality theory, in which the structural elements of the personality—id, ego, and superego—are in constant tension, producing anxiety and in some cases psychopathology. The solution is to deal with the original source of conflict through interpretation of the patient's dreams and free associations. Client-centered therapy (a humanistic approach) attempts to facilitate, rather than direct, change. The therapist concentrates on seeing the world from the perspective of the client. This requires that the therapist be genuine, able to express unconditional positive regard for the client, and capable of empathy. Whereas humanistic therapy sees clients as engaged in a positive search for self-actualization, existential therapy sees them as searching for meaning in events that are essentially negative. The goal is to assist clients in accepting responsibility for their actions and achieving authenticity in relationships with others. Behavioral therapies apply knowledge gained from psychological research to change maladaptive behaviors. These techniques include systematic desensitization, the token economy, modeling, and cognitive restructuring.

SUMMARY

1. The *medical model* of psychiatric disorder assumes that each disorder has an identifiable physical cause that produces a limited set of symptoms that, in turn, imply what treatment ought to be employed.

2. The *behavioral model* of psychiatric disorder emphasizes the role of traumatic events external to the person, and concentrates on teaching people how better to cope with these externally induced problems.

3. Although the legal insanity defense was designed to protect defendants who by reason of mental disease or defect were unable to distinguish right from wrong, the defense has been criticized in its application. Many jurisdictions have recently adopted a verdict of "guilty but mentally ill" as an alternative to acquittal by reason of insanity.

4. People who pose a danger to themselves or others, or who are substantially unable to care for themselves, may be placed in mental hospitals by a process of involuntary civil commitment. Such patients have a right to treatment, which should take place in the least restrictive setting.

5. It is difficult to evaluate the effectiveness of psychotherapy, because of both ethical and methodological limitations. Despite these difficulties, meta-analyses of outcome studies have concluded that psychotherapy is more effective than placebo control treatment.

6. Four classes of psychoactive drugs are regularly used in therapy. These are the *minor tranquilizers,* the *antipsychotic drugs* (predominantly phenothiazines), the *antidepressants* (including trycyclics and MAOIs), and the antibipolar medications.

7. The psychotherapy of *psychoanalysis,* developed by Freud, has been a predominant model for the psychological treatment of mental disorders, primarily anxiety disorders. The technique typically involves *free association,* and transference of emotion to the therapist, leading ultimately to insight.

8. *Client-centered therapy* is a major humanistic alternative to psychodynamically oriented therapies. The therapist's role in this procedure is to provide unconditional positive regard for the client, and to facilitate the client's discovery—without interpretive intervention from the therapist—of the nature of his or her problem.

9. The behavior therapies include *systematic desensitization,* which combines deep relaxation with increasingly powerful representations of a threatening stimulus; token economies, which eliminate environmental support for aberrant actions; and *cognitive restructuring,* which is designed to modify the person's conception of the self.

FOCUS QUESTIONS

1. What are the similarities and differences between the medical model of psychological disorder and the behavioral model?

2. Describe the process of involuntary civil commitment. Is there reason to be skeptical about initial diagnosis under these conditions? What rights does a mental patient now have?

3. What are the sources of data regarding the effectiveness of psychotherapy? What are the most prevalent forms of patient self-reports of treatment outcome?

4. Describe the process of meta-analysis as it applies to the problem of determining the effectiveness of psychotherapy. Which of the typical problems with psychotherapy outcome research does this technique help overcome? Which remain?

5. What are the antipsychotic drugs? Neurochemically, how are they presumed to deal with the symptoms of schizophrenia? Do they work on all schizophrenia symptoms?

6. What forms of drug therapy work most effectively with the affective disorders of major depression and bipolar disorder? What conclusion do psychologists draw from these results?

7. Describe the psychoanalytic approach to therapy. Is there evidence that it is effective?

8. Describe the humanistic and existential approaches to psychotherapy.

9. Describe the forms of behavioral therapy for psychological disorders. How do these therapies demonstrate their effectiveness?

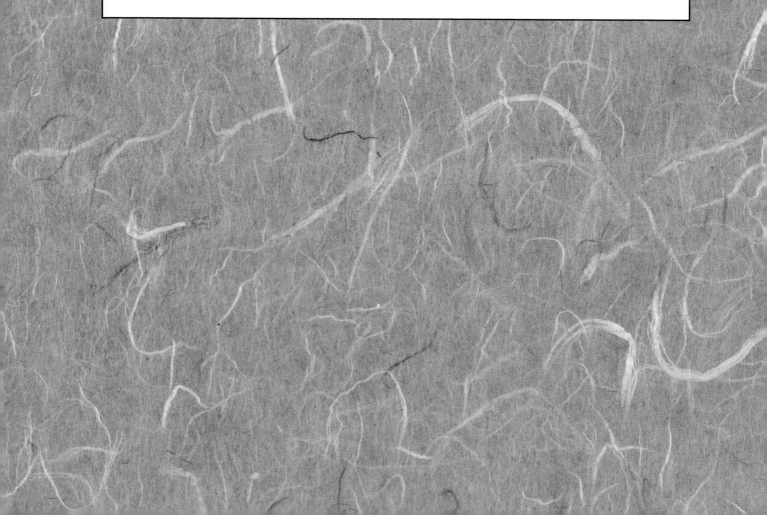

APPENDIX

AN INTRODUCTION TO RESEARCH METHODS AND STATISTICS IN PSYCHOLOGY

sychologists consider themselves scientists and have almost universally adopted a scientific approach to the study of behavior. The scientific approach, a general method of inquiry based on logic, emphasizes control of the circumstances under which information is collected and assessed. It also requires researchers to make the methods and results of their studies public so that others can replicate and verify them.

THE GOALS OF PSYCHOLOGICAL RESEARCH

Scientific research in general has four major goals: description, explanation, prediction, and control. The first goal of psychological research is thus to describe behavior. The second goal is to explain behavior, which means to identify its causes. Successful explanation makes it possible to achieve the third goal—to predict behavior. Psychologists are interested in predicting many things—who will succeed in college, for example, or whether a particular therapeutic approach will help in the treatment of mentally ill patients. The fourth and final goal is control. If we understand certain behaviors and can predict when they will occur, then we are in a position to control the circumstances that cause them. If we can understand and predict depression, for example, we may be able to control it. Likewise, if we understand the process of learning sufficiently well, we can create conditions to improve the ability to learn.

There are five major stages in psychological research: hypothesis formation, research design, data collection, data analysis, and interpretation.

HYPOTHESIS FORMATION

The first step in any research is to identify a problem and express it as a testable proposition, or hypothesis. Problems in psychology are derived from many sources, including experiences in our everyday lives, theories or previous studies, and various practical issues. For example, after noting the results of studies that show that the degree of a rat's hunger affects its ability to solve mazes, a psychologist might become interested in the effect of hunger on humans' ability to learn.

Whatever the source of the problem, studying it requires framing it, or some aspect of it, as a hypothesis. A hypothesis states a theoretical relationship among variables. It generally takes an "If . . . then" form relating an outcome to a prior condition. An example would be, "If a person is hungry (prior condition) . . . then the person should engage in food-oriented behaviors (the outcome)."

RESEARCH DESIGN

The next task in any research project is to specify a research design, which is an overall plan or scheme for conducting the research on the problem and testing the hypothesis.

The first, and perhaps most important, step in research design is to identify the variables under study. In scientific research there are generally two types of variables: independent and dependent.

693

Independent Variables

An independent variable is a condition that is claimed to affect or cause a behavioral outcome. The independent variable can be isolated in several ways. First, a group of subjects in which a condition is present can be compared to a group in which the condition is absent. If, for example, we had identified food deprivation as our independent variable, we could compare subjects who had been deprived of food (the condition is present) to subjects who had not been deprived (the condition is absent).

Second, individuals can be subjected to one of several levels or intensities of a condition and then compared in terms of the graded differences in their behavior. For instance, subjects could be deprived of food for 0, 5, 10, or 15 hours, and then the subjects could be tested for differences in their behavior. A comparison of these groups would reveal how the strength or degree of the treatment (condition), not just its presence, affected the behavior.

Finally, the independent variable might simply be a property or condition that is characteristic of the subjects, such as education, age, or sex. These conditions, although they cannot be manipulated, represent some underlying dimension on which the subjects can be differentiated. When such a condition is the *only* basis for differentiating among subjects, it can be claimed to be the underlying cause of any behavioral differences that are observed.

Dependent Variables

A dependent variable is a behavioral measure; it is affected by the independent variable, and thus measures or reflects the action of the independent variable. A dependent variable must be sensitive, valid, and reliable. To be sensitive it must change noticeably when the independent variable changes. To be valid it must measure what it is intended to measure. Psychologists can never be entirely sure that a dependent variable is valid, but if a variety of measures, all of which are conceptually related to the independent variable, tend to change systematically with the independent variable, then any one of them is very likely valid. To be reliable a dependent variable must act consistently in relation to the independent variable. If subjects respond a certain way on one occasion but an entirely different way on another occasion when the independent variables remain the same, the dependent variable would be unreliable.

Research designs generally fall into one of two broad categories: descriptive and experimental.

DESCRIPTIVE RESEARCH

The goal of descriptive research, as the name suggests, is to describe behavioral phenomena rather than to establish their causes in any direct fashion.

Naturalistic Observation

In naturalistic observation, the researcher observes the behavior of subjects from a distance without interacting with them. Often, subjects in this sort of research are unaware of the experimenter's presence. For example, a psychologist interested in the effect of familiarity (independent variable) on social interaction (dependent variable) might discover that eye contact—a form of social interaction—is more frequent among friends than among strangers simply by observing people from a distance.

Field Studies

In field studies, as opposed to naturalistic observation, subjects are aware that they are being studied. Field study techniques include, among others, the use of surveys and questionnaires. When subjects know they are being studied, their behavior can be affected. For example, being asked to complete a survey can put subjects on guard—they may react in an unusually cooperative manner, or in a way that puts them in the best possible light. Similarly, the characteristics of the person conducting a survey may alter responses. Subjects, for example, might respond differently to a questioner dressed in jeans and a T-shirt than to one dressed in a business suit.

Case Studies

A case study is an in-depth analysis of an individual or group. It can draw on a variety of sources, including interviews, records, and surveys. Case studies are particularly useful for studying rare or interesting events or people.

EXPERIMENTAL RESEARCH

Experimental research differs from descriptive research in that it involves the deliberate manipulation or control of an independent variable to determine its effect on a dependent variable. Descriptive research may indicate relationships between variables, but only experimental research permits reliable inferences about the causes of behavior.

Experimental research can take place in the natural environment as well as in a laboratory. One could, for example, study altruistic behavior in the natural environment by staging an emergency (having someone call for help) and then observing whether subjects complied to the request for assistance. Most experimental research, however, takes place in the laboratory where researchers can best control the experimental conditions.

After-only Designs

Perhaps the simplest experimental research design is the after-only design. Here, subjects are chosen randomly from the population and allocated to experimental and control groups that differ in only one respect: Subjects in the experimental group receive some treatment or manipulation related to the independent variable, and subjects in the control group do not. Although subjects may vary somewhat in their reactions as a result of extraneous uncontrolled factors, any *consistent* variation in the dependent variable must logically be the result of the single difference between the two groups of subjects, namely the independent variable.

Before-after Designs

In before-after designs, experimental and control subjects are first given a pretreatment test (that is, the dependent variable is measured in both groups). Following this pretest, the experimental subjects are given the manipulation or treatment whereas the control subjects are not. Finally, all subjects are tested once again. Usually members of the control group show little change from the first to the second test because they received no treatment. The experimental subjects typically show a change from the first to the second measure as a result of the treatment. Thus, the researcher can compare results *between* the two groups, as well as from one time to the next *within* a single group.

Multiple Factor Designs

The two basic research designs previously discussed involve only a single treatment. It is, however, possible to give *combinations* of treatments to various groups and discover how two or more factors operate, simultaneously, to affect behavior. For example, imagine that researchers want to know how children's age *and* feedback affect their ability to learn a list of vocabulary words. The researchers could select children who were, say, 5 and 6 years old, and then, within each of those age groups, reward half of the children and not reward the other half. In essence, the researchers would identify four separate groups of children: 5 years old/reward, 6 years old/reward, 5 years old/no reward, and 6 years old/no reward. A comparison of the differences in their ability to learn the vocabulary words would reveal not only the effects of age and the effects of reward, but also the combined effects of the two factors.

COLLECTING DATA

The validity of any psychological research depends on the careful, systematic collection of data. Two important requirements of this process are to select a valid sample of subjects and to identify potential sources of error.

SAMPLING

Psychologists want to discover laws that apply to human or animal behavior in general, that is, to *all* individuals. But because it is impossible to study all the individuals of any species, a smaller subset—a **sample**—must be used that is presumably representative of the larger population. Although there is no way to guarantee that a sample is representative, we can maximize the likelihood that it is by selecting its members at random. Random, in this sense, means that each member of the population has an equal opportunity of being selected and that the selection of one member does not influence the chances of another member's being selected.

ERROR SOURCES

Various conditions can produce erroneous data. One source of distortion, called experimenter bias, results from characteristics or expectations of the experimenter. The sex of the experimenter, for example, can affect the results of certain sorts of studies. Imagine that you were asked by an experimenter to reveal something personal about yourself. You might unconsciously react differently to a man than to a woman. Similarly the attitudes or behaviors of the experimenter can affect subjects' behavior. The experimenter, for example, could seem to be acting in a dominant and confrontational manner, or seem warm and friendly, or stern and aloof. Each style could affect the kind of information that the subjects provide.

Subjects can also have biases that influence their reactions. For example, being observed by an experimenter often causes subjects to "try extra hard" or to respond in a way that puts them in a favorable light.

ANALYZING DATA

The fourth step of psychological research is to analyze the data the research generates. Because data are almost always quantitative, this process requires the use of statistics. Although a full discussion of the use of statistics in psychology is beyond the scope of this appendix, we will discuss a few important statistical techniques here.

There are two major areas of statistics: descriptive and inferential.

DESCRIPTIVE STATISTICS

Descriptive statistics, as the name implies, provides a way of describing the observations of psychological research. Among other things, it includes methods for assigning numbers to observations, for summarizing observations with averages, and for calculating how discrepant numbers are from one another.

Frequency Distributions

Once we have chosen a random sample from the population and have made our behavioral measurement, we need to organize the resulting data. If we do not, all we have is a group of meaningless numbers.

One way of organizing data is to distribute the original observations among a limited number of categories, noting the frequency of occurrence in each category. This process results in a **frequency distribution.** Assume, for example, that we have measured the IQ of a random sample of 17 children (see Table A-1). The ungrouped data tell us little. To create a frequency distribution from them, we first must designate several classes or categories of scores. In this example, the categories 71–80, 81–90, 91–100, 101–110, 111–120, and 121–130 would seem appropriate. Next, we count the number of occurrences (the number of children) whose IQ score falls into each category. Finally, we plot these frequency values as a function of the categories, with frequency on the vertical axis and the category name on the horizontal axis (as in Figure A-1). We can now determine at a glance the pattern of IQ scores in this particular sample. We can see, for example, that although the scores extend from the lowest to the highest category, most fall toward the middle of the distribution.

TABLE A-1 A Sample of IQ Scores	
Child	IQ Score
1	96
2	108
3	105
4	108
5	79
6	92
7	93
8	104
9	95
10	97
11	98
12	126
13	98
14	118
15	101
16	99
17	109

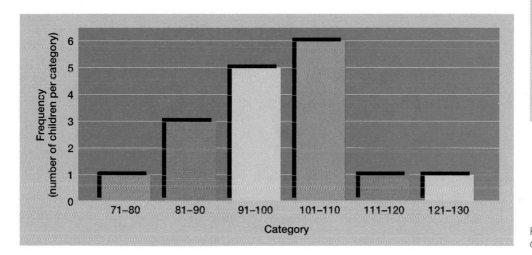

FIGURE A-1 Frequency distribution derived from the data in Table A-1.

Central Tendency

Frequency distributions give an overall picture of a collection of scores, but they do not specify the average IQ score in any precise way. Measures of **central tendency** do this—they summarize the central point, that is the average, of a group of scores in a single value.

The most common measure of central tendency is the **mean,** which is defined as follows:

$$M = \frac{\Sigma X}{n}$$

In this equation, X stands for an individual score, n refers to the total number of X scores, and Σ is the general term for summation; thus, $\Sigma X/n$ means sum all X scores and divide by n. Figure A-2 applies this formula to the data in Table A-1. The sum of all the scores is 1726.0. Dividing that figure by the number of scores, 17, gives a mean of 101.5. Because all the scores in a sample contribute to the mean (that is, all are summed together and thus all affect the size of the mean), it is the most powerful measure of central tendency.

A second measure of central tendency is the **median,** which is the middle score in a distribution. Of the scores, 50% fall above the median and 50% fall below. When the number of scores is odd, the median is the middle value; when the number of scores is even, the median is halfway between the two middle values. Finding the

$$\Sigma X = 1726$$
$$n = 17$$

$$M = \frac{\Sigma X}{n} = \frac{1726}{17} = 101.5$$

FIGURE A-2 Calculating the mean of the data in Table A-1.

697

Rank	Child	IQ score	
1	5	79	
2	6	92	
3	7	93	
4	9	95	
5	1	96	
6	10	97	
7	11	98	
8	13	98	
9	16	99	Median
10	15	101	
11	8	104	
12	3	105	
13	2	108	
14	4	108	
15	17	109	
16	14	118	
17	12	126	

FIGURE A-3   Calculating the median of the data in Table A-1.

median for the data in Table A-1 requires ordering the IQ scores from lowest to highest and identifying the middle score. As Figure A-3 indicates, the result is 99.

After the mean, the median is the next most commonly used measure of central tendency. It is useful for distributions with only a small number of scores or for highly irregular distributions—those, for example, with one or more exceptionally high (or low) values. This is because a few highly discrepant scores will affect the mean (they contribute to the sum of the numbers) but not the median (no matter what the value of the highest and lowest numbers are, the middle few scores remain unchanged).

The fact that the mean and median can differ often has important implications. For example, consider the average salary in a corporation. If the majority of employees earn, say, $20,000, but a few highly paid executives earn as much as, say, $500,000, the median salary would be $20,000 but the mean would be appreciably higher. In other words, the few high executive salaries would not affect the median, but they would affect the mean, causing it to be greater than the median. The executives, if they wanted to suggest that the average salary at the corporation was quite generous, would likely cite the higher of the two measures of central tendency—the mean. The workers, on the other hand, if they wanted to portray themselves as being poorly paid, would use the lower of the two measures—the median. Both measures would be correct, but their messages would be dramatically different.

Variability

The second major characteristic of a distribution of numbers is its variability, that is, the degree to which the numbers differ from each other. Consider the three distributions in Figure A-4. (Note that these distributions are represented as line drawings rather than as bar graphs. A distribution of this kind is created essentially by taking a bar distribution and drawing a line that connects the middle of the top of each bar.) All three distributions in the figure have the same mean value, but they differ in terms of variability. In the tallest distribution scores are tightly clustered around the mean and variability is relatively low. In the bottom distribution scores are widely dispersed around the mean and variability is relatively high. The third distribution shows relatively moderate variability.

The least informative measure of variability is the **range,** which is the highest score minus the lowest. The range gives only a rough index of variability. It indicates the boundaries of a distribution, but gives no information about the values that lie near the center. It does not indicate, for example, whether most of the numbers are widely dispersed between the boundaries or clustered near a central value.

The more commonly used (and more powerful) measures of variability are the **variance** and **standard deviation.** As Figure A-4 indicates, the greater the standard deviation, the greater the variability of a distribution.

The variance is defined as follows:

$$V = \frac{\Sigma(X - M)^2}{n}$$

The standard deviation is defined as the square root of the variance.

The expression $(X - M)$ refers to the difference between an individual score and the mean and gives a measure of the extent to which the score *deviates* from the mean. In any distribution, some of these deviations will be positive (those X values that are greater than the mean), some will be negative (those X values that are less than the mean), and the sum of all of them will be zero. For this reason, calculating an average deviation requires converting all the deviations to positive numbers. This is accomplished by squaring them, as indicated by the expression $(X - M)^2$. The expression $\Sigma(X - M)^2/n$ refers to the sum of all the squared deviations divided by the total number of scores. The square root of the result—the standard deviation—is thus a measure of the average discrepancy of the X scores from the mean, just as the mean itself is a measure of the average value of all the X scores.

698

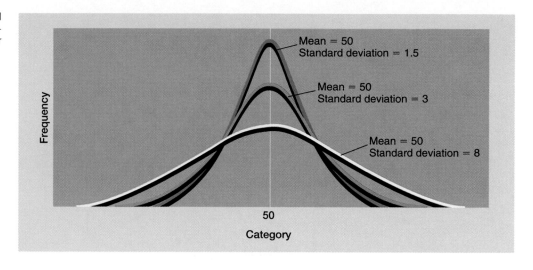

FIGURE A-4 Variability versus central tendency. Each of these three distributions has the same mean but they differ in their degree of variability.

Mean = 50
Standard deviation = 1.5

Mean = 50
Standard deviation = 3

Mean = 50
Standard deviation = 8

Frequency

50

Category

Correlation

Another important technique in descriptive statistics is called **correlation.** The purpose of a correlation is to describe, quantitatively, the relationship between two sets of scores taken from a single set of individuals. One score for each of the subjects is typically called X, the other Y. Consider, for example, the relationship between weight (X) and height (Y). Is it a fact that taller people usually weigh more than shorter people? Is there a systematic relationship between height and weight? Calculating the correlation allows us to answer just such questions.

We can represent a correlation visually with a **scatterplot** (see Figure A-5 on page 700). Such a graph plots each pair of scores as a single point positioned at the intersection of the X value and its Y counterpart. That is, for each pair of scores, one moves along the X axis to the point corresponding to the X value, and then upward along the Y axis to the point corresponding to the Y value. This is the intersection point for that pair. Once all the pairs of scores have been plotted in this fashion, one can determine whether they form a systematic pattern. Three general patterns are possible. First, when high Y scores tend to be associated with high X scores, the correlation is said to be positive. Height and weight are an example of a positive correlation; taller people do indeed tend to weigh more than shorter (see Figure A-5a). Second, when high Y scores tend to be associated with low X scores the correlation is said to be negative. An example of a negative correlation is the relationship between the amount of time spent studying and the number of errors on a subsequent exam (see Figure A-5b). On average, the more the studying, the *fewer* the errors. Finally, there are relationships in which no correlation exists. Here, there is no tendency for the Y values to vary systematically with the X values. An example might be GPA and shoe size (see Figure A-5c). Presumably, people with high GPAs *and* people with low GPAs have small as well as large feet. There is no consistent relationship between the size of the X values and the size of the corresponding Y values.

The degree to which a relationship exists between two sets of scores can be represented quantitatively by a **correlation coefficient.** Coefficients vary between -1 and $+1$. A coefficient value, designated by the term of -1, would indicate a perfect negative correlation; a coefficient of $+1$ would indicate a perfect positive correlation; and a coefficient of zero would indicate no correlation. A correlation coefficient, in other words, gives a measure of *degree* or *strength* of a relationship. This is important because few, if any, correlations in psychology are perfect, or even close to perfect, even for clear-cut examples. For instance, although height and weight are clearly correlated in a positive direction, nevertheless there are some very tall slender people and some very short heavy people who do not fit the general pattern. Similarly, studying *usually* is associated with fewer errors on exams, but not always; some people (for reasons that are not always clear) make few errors with little studying, whereas others commit numerous errors despite lots of study time.

699

(a)

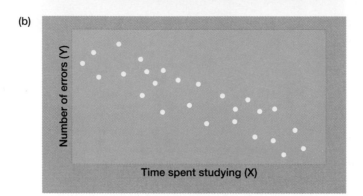

(b)

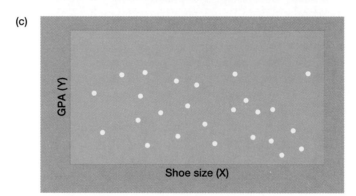

(c)

FIGURE A-5 Scatterplots showing a positive correlation *(a)*, a negative correlation *(b)*, and no correlation *(c)*.

Consider the data shown in Table A-2 on hours of food deprivation (X) and the amount subsequently eaten (Y) for 10 experimental subjects. The numbers alone give no clear sense of the overall relationship between the two variables. A scatterplot derived from the data (Figure A-6) shows that the relationship is positive—the hungrier an animal, the more it tends to eat—but it gives only a subjective indication of the strength of the relationship. A correlation coefficient, however, will give a precise measure of the strength of the relationship.

The most widely used correlation coefficient is the Pearson product-moment coefficient, designated by the letter r and calculated as follows:

$$r = \frac{n\Sigma XY - \Sigma X \Sigma Y}{\sqrt{[n\Sigma X - (\Sigma X)^2][n\Sigma Y - (\Sigma Y)^2]}}$$

The purpose of this imposing-looking formula (we will not subject you to a full explanation of it) is to calculate the degree to which the discrepancy of each X from the mean of the X values is, on average, identical to the discrepancy of its corresponding Y from the mean of the Y values. In other words, r is a measure of "agreement-in-position" of the X and Y pairs relative to their respective means. As Figure A-7 on page 702 shows, performing the appropriate calculations on the data in Table A-2 gives an r of .987, indicating a strong positive correlation between length of food deprivation and amount of food eaten.

TABLE A-2   Relationship Between Food Deprivation and Amount of Food Eaten for 10 Subjects

Subject	Hours of Food Deprivation (X)	Amount of Food Eaten (Y)	Subject	Hours of Food Deprivation (X)	Amount of Food Eaten (Y)
1	6.6	10.1	6	8.4	8.9
2	13.6	18.9	7	11.2	19.4
3	2.5	6.3	8	26.2	41.0
4	14.3	27.9	9	29.1	46.2
5	18.0	30.9	10	23.5	34.6

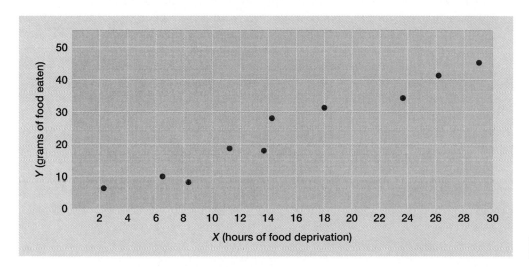

FIGURE A-6 A scatterplot of the data in Table A-2.

Subject	Hours of food deprivation (X)	Amount of food eaten (Y)	X^2	Y^2	XY
1	6.6	10.1	43.6	102.0	66.7
2	13.6	18.9	185.0	357.2	257.0
3	2.5	6.3	6.3	39.7	15.8
4	14.3	27.9	204.5	778.4	399.0
5	18.0	30.9	324.0	954.8	556.2
6	8.4	8.9	70.6	79.2	74.8
7	11.2	19.4	125.4	376.4	217.3
8	26.2	41.0	686.4	1681.0	1074.2
9	29.1	46.2	846.8	2134.4	1344.4
10	23.5	34.6	552.3	1197.2	813.1

$\Sigma X = 153.4$ $\Sigma Y = 244.2$ $\Sigma X^2 = 3044.9$ $\Sigma Y^2 = 7699.3$ $\Sigma XY = 4818.5$

$$r = \frac{n(\Sigma XY) - (\Sigma X)(\Sigma Y)}{\sqrt{[n(\Sigma X^2) - (\Sigma X)^2][n(\Sigma Y^2) - (\Sigma Y)^2]}}$$

$$= \frac{10(4818.5) - (153.4)(244.2)}{\sqrt{[10(3044.9) - 153.4^2][10(7699.3) - 244.2^2]}}$$

$$= \frac{48185 - 37460.3}{\sqrt{[6917.4][17369.3]}}$$

$$= \frac{10724.7}{10961.0}$$

$$= .98$$

FIGURE A-7 Calculating the correlation coefficient r from the data in Table A-2.

A note of caution is needed when interpreting correlation coefficients. Although a coefficient reflects the degree to which sets of numbers are related, it does *not* indicate that one set (e.g., the *Y* values) is caused by the other set (the *X* values). For example, weight does not *cause* a person to be taller. The two are related but both are caused by some third condition. Similarly, study time may be negatively *related* to exam errors, but the coefficient does not conclusively prove that study time *causes* fewer errors. It may be that smarter people study more and tend to have fewer exam errors; intelligence, then, might cause both things to happen.

INFERENTIAL STATISTICS

The second major area of statistics in psychology is called **inferential statistics.** The purpose of inferential statistics is to allow us to infer something about a treatment and its effect on behavior. For example, assume we conducted an experiment to determine the exact relationship between study time and test errors. Depending upon the outcome of our experiment, inferential statistics might allow us to conclude, say, that greater study time is associated with fewer exam errors *in general*. In other words, inferential statistics allows us to infer that what is true of the experimental subjects—a sample of the population—is also true of the whole population.

The mean of a random sample of numbers drawn from a population of numbers is very likely to be similar to the mean of the population itself. For example, assume that you wrote the names of each student at your university on a piece of paper, put all the pieces in a box, and then drew out a sample of 15 names. Assume further that you measured the average height of those 15 individuals. If the sample is truly representative of the population, then the mean height of the sample should be similar to the true mean height of the population. It *could* happen that you draw a very unusual sample, all the members of the university's basketball team, perhaps, whose mean height would be very much greater than the average height of the students in the population. But the chance of such an event occurring would be very low.

Sampling Distribution

An important concept in inferential statistics is that of the **sampling distribution,** a set of numbers calculated from the many samples that *could be* drawn from a population. In our previous example, we noted that one could take a sample of 15 subjects and calculate the mean height, but one could also imagine taking many such samples—two, fifty, several thousand, or even an infinite number. Each sample would contain 15 individual subjects and each would yield a single value (in this example the mean height). The collection of these many mean values, then, would comprise the sampling distribution of the mean.

Any one sample value that you take in reality, that is any one mean value, can be located among the many sample values that would be possible to take. "Locate" in this sense means to determine how unusual the sample value is relative to the other values in the sampling distribution. Unusually large (or small) sample values are rare. One would expect to get these infrequently by chance alone. Stated differently, the *probability* of drawing an unusually large (or small) sample value is quite low. In contrast, sample values close to the mean of the other sample values (close to the mean of the sampling distribution) are quite common. One would often expect to get such values; the probability of obtaining these by chance alone is high.

Normal Distribution

Figure A-8 shows the exact relationship between the probability of drawing a random sample with a given mean and the degree to which that sample mean deviates from the population mean. The distribution in the figure is a **normal distribution** (often called the "bell-shaped" curve). Many psychological characteristics are distributed in this fashion. Note that 68% of the sample means fall within ±1 standard deviation of the population mean. In other words, the probability is .68 that any given sample drawn randomly from a population will fall within ±1 standard deviation from the mean of the population. A sample of 15 university students that included only basketball players would be a very rare sample indeed. The discrepancy between the mean of that sample and the mean of the population would be very large and correspondingly the chance of randomly drawing such a sample would be very small.

By convention, we usually say that a sample is significantly deviant if its mean differs from the population mean by more than 1.96 standard deviation units. (On Figure A-8 this would be at a point very close to +2 or −2 standard deviations.) Significant here does not mean "meaningful" but simply improbable, so much so that the mean falls within the two small tails of the sampling distribution.

If a random sample is representative of the population, why should its mean deviate from the population mean? There are two possible reasons for obtaining a deviant sample mean. First, as just discussed, a sample mean could deviate from the population mean simply by chance. Second, something could be systematically biasing the numbers. Typically, we do not know whether a deviant sample mean is the result of random sampling error or bias. If, however, the sample mean is *very* discrepant, for instance if the probability of getting that sample is less than 5 in 100, then we are inclined to say that something *probably* biased the numbers. In sum, whenever we have a sample that deviates drastically from what we would expect, that is, whenever the probability of getting such a discrepant mean by chance alone is very low, say less than 5 in 100, we argue that something special has likely happened to bias the numbers.

Testing the Difference Between Two Groups

What typically biases a group of numbers is a treatment that is given to the subjects. For example, assume that we have a sample of 10 students and, as a way to measure their level of activity, we calculate the number of times each of them moves 3 feet or more in any direction during a 1-hour period. Initially we have no reason to believe that our sample of 10 subjects is unusual. That is, we suspect that the sample is representative of all students and so we would argue that the mean activity level (the mean number of movements) is likely to be very close to the mean activity level of students in general. The mean of our sample could, of course, be somewhat higher or somewhat lower than the real population mean simply due to random sampling error, but we know that such a discrepancy is not very likely.

Assume now that we have a different sample of students who have been treated with a special drug (for example, caffeine) and that we do not know the full effect of the drug but we suspect that it could be an increase in activity level. Assume further that the mean activity level of this second sample is indeed much larger than that found in the first group. Have we discovered a manipulation (drug ingestion) that meaningfully affects activity? If both the first and second groups are representative of normal people, then both should have a mean that is reasonably close to the popu-

FIGURE A-8   The normal distribution.

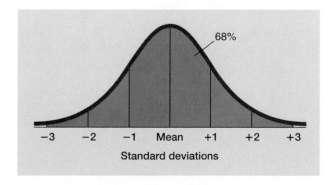

lation mean *and* therefore close to each other. Their means should vary from each other due to random sampling error but only by a small amount. If, however, the mean of the caffeine group is much higher than the mean of the no-drug group, then we can say that the experiment "worked"; the drug significantly affected (biased) the activity scores.

INTERPRETING RESULTS

Once the data have been analyzed, the researcher can consider whether the original hypothesis is true. That is, the researcher can formulate an experimental conclusion—confirm the hypothesis, for example. In doing so, the researcher is able to fulfill the real purpose of doing the research—to provide additional knowledge or a deeper understanding of the original problem.

Inferential statistics involves many tests for evaluating experiments of this kind. The details of these tests are, of course, beyond the scope of this text. Nevertheless, in each case, the experimenters attempt to determine whether the mean of a treated (experimental) group of subjects is markedly higher or lower than the mean of an untreated (control) group. If it is, they conclude that the treatment affected (biased) the numbers; if it is not, they attribute any small differences that do exist to random sampling error. In other words, depending on the outcome of the analysis, the experimenters may be able to conclude that the treatment affected behavior and thus to generalize that such a treatment would affect all subjects in the population.

GLOSSARY

Numbers in brackets following definitions refer to the chapter in which the term is discussed. (APP refers to the Appendix, "An Introduction to Research Methods and Statistics in Psychology.")

absolute threshold: The energy intensity of a stimulus that is sufficient to cause a person to first sense the stimulus. [3]

accommodation: An adjustment in the shape of the lens to compensate for the distance of the object. [4] In Piaget's theory of cognitive development, the modification of the child's cognitive structures in response to the demands of the external environment. [16]

acetylcholine (ACh): A common neurotransmitter substance. [5]

achievement motive (n Ach): A person's need to achieve aroused whenever a person knows that his or her performance will be evaluated in terms of some standard of excellence and that the consequences will be either favorable or unfavorable. [11]

acquisition: The process during which a CR or association is acquired. [12]

action potential: Sudden change in electrical potential when a neuron is stimulated. [5]

adolescent egocentrism: The adolescent's assumption that all attention is focused on the adolescent. Unlike the egocentrism of childhood, this is not an inability to take another's viewpoint, but rather the belief that all others are interested in the self. [18]

adrenal cortex: Part of the adrenal gland, lying above the kidney, which produces aldosterone. [9]

adrenal glands: Two small endocrine glands located just above the kidneys. These glands secrete adrenaline (epinephrine), a neurotransmitter substance that increases activation. [23]

adrenocorticotropic hormone (ACTH): A hormone, secreted from the pituitary gland, that stimulates the production of cortisol by the adrenal cortex (often in response to an external stressor). [23]

aerial perspective: A cue for depth created by the fact that distant objects appear blurry or hazy. [4]

aggression: Any behavior whose goal is to harm or injure another living being. [10]

aggressive-erotic: Erotic material involving the depiction of aggressive acts. [10]

agoraphobia: A psychological disorder that involves intense fear of leaving home (literally, "fear of open places"). [24]

aldosterone: Substance produced in the adrenal cortex that causes the kidneys to reabsorb sodium. [9]

allele: One member of the gene pair. [8]

allomorphs: Phonetically distinct forms that together constitute the linguistic category of a morpheme. For example, the allomorph *es* attached to the word *watch* and the allomorph *s* attached to the word *light* both signify the plural, even though they sound different. [17]

allophones: Phonetically distinct speech elements that are, nevertheless, members of a single linguistic category; the category is the phoneme. [17]

alpha wave: EEG pattern characterized by its low amplitude and high frequency (about 8 to 14 Hz). [7]

altruism: Behavior performed for the benefit of other individuals at the expense of the altruistic individual. [8]

amplitude: The height of a wave measured from peak to trough; intensity. [3]

amygdala: Structure in the limbic system associated with rage. [6]

anal stage: In Freudian theory, the second psychosexual stage. This stage is presumed to involve conflict between the child and parents over toilet training. [18]

analytic psychology: Jung's psychodynamic theory of personality that combines the individual's racial and personal past with his or her conscious goals for the future. [21]

androgen: Male sex hormone. [10]

animism: A kind of primitive thought that characterizes children in the preoperational phase of cognitive development: the tendency to endow inanimate objects with sensations and intentions like those of humans. [16]

anomia: A difficulty in naming objects. [5]

anorexia nervosa: An eating disorder characterized by extreme weight loss, maladaptive attitudes toward eating, distorted body image, and feelings of helplessness. [9]

anterograde amnesia: Inability to remember events and material from the time period immediately following the administration of electroconvulsive therapy (ECT). [25]

antidiuretic hormone: A substance produced in the posterior pituitary gland of the brain that causes the kidneys to be more permeable to water. [9]

antipsychotic: Any of several psychotropic drugs that has the effect of reducing the symptoms of schizophrenia. Includes, for example, the phenothiazines. [25]

antisocial personality disorder: A psychological disturbance characterized by extremes of impulsiveness, thoughtlessness, and shallowness. Once referred to as a "sociopath," a person with this disorder is unable to form attachments to others and shows a consistent lack of concern over violations of the rights of others. [24]

aphagia: The absence of eating caused by damage to the lateral hypothalamus. [9]

aphasia: Loss of language ability. [5]

apparent motion (phi) phenomenon: The perception of motion of a stationary visual stimulus. [4]

asomatognosias: A condition associated with parietal lobe damage in which a person shows defective touch perception. [5]

assimilation: In Piaget's theory of

cognitive development, the child's incorporation of information about the external world into existing cognitive structures. [16]

association: Connection between two events or sensations that occur together in time or space. [12]

associative visual agnosia: A condition associated with occipital lobe damage in which a person shows a loss of the ability to appreciate the meaning of objects. [5]

atmosphere effect: Faulty deductive reasoning based on the fact that the premises create an atmosphere that favors certain conclusions, regardless of whether the logic is valid or the statements are true. [15]

atropine: A drug that blocks the action of acetylcholine and produces fear reactions when injected into the septum. [6]

attachment theory: Bowlby's theory of social development, which holds that an infant's proximity-seeking behaviors and the parent's responses to those behaviors are important in the struggle for survival of the species. [18]

attentional processing: Information processing requiring deliberate reflection. [13]

attitude: An organized predisposition to behave in a favorable or unfavorable manner toward a specified class of social objects; consists of a cognitive component (beliefs about the object), an affective component (feelings or evaluations), and a behavioral component (the likely actions). [19]

attribution processes: Processes of social cognition that are used to infer the causes of events or the motivations behind behavior. [19]

auditory agnosia: A condition associated with temporal lobe damage in which a person shows defective auditory perception. [5]

authenticity: In existential therapy, the state of being capable of frank, honest, spontaneous, and loving relationships with other people. Responsibility, without defensiveness, for one's own choices. [25]

automatic processing: Information processing not involving deliberate reflection. [13]

autonomic nervous system (ANS): A part of the peripheral nervous system involved with regulation of vital functions. [6]

availability heuristic: Kind of heuristic in which a subject bases a decision or judgment on easily remembered instances rather than on actual data. [15]

avoidance: A form of instrumental learning in which execution of the designated response leads to the nonoccurrence of an aversive stimulus. [12]

axon hillock: The point of transition between a cell body and the axon. [5]

axon: A fiber extending away from the cell body that carries the neuronal impulse to adjacent nerves. [5]

backward conditioning: Classical conditioning procedure in which the CS is presented following the US. [12]

balance theory: A cognitive consistency theory of attitude organization and change that posits two relations—liking and unit-formation—between cognitive elements. [19]

baroreceptor: Receptor in the heart or kidney that senses a change in blood pressure. [9]

basic-level category: An average or intermediate level of classification, neither too specific nor overly inclusive. [14]

basilar membrane: Part of the cochlear partition containing hair cells that connect with auditory nerves. [3]

behavior genetics: The area within psychology that is interested in the relationship between genetic makeup and behavior. [8]

behavior modification: The use of behavioral techniques to change maladaptive behavior patterns. [12]

behavior therapy: A collection of procedures, usually involving principles of conditioning in combination with other techniques, for treating phobias and other psychological disorders. [25]

behavioral model: The model of psychological disturbance that holds that psychological disorders reflect pathogenic social or psychological conditions, not physical disturbances. [24, 25]

behaviorism: The school of psychological thought founded by John B. Watson, who believed that psychology could advance as a science only by discarding all references to internal mental states. Modern behaviorism thus concentrates on stimulus-response connections, often ignoring the organism's potential contribution to the behavior. [2]

belief-bias effect: The finding that subjects may agree that a conclusion is valid simply because it conforms to what they believe is true in the real world. [15]

beta wave: EEG pattern characterized by its high frequency (about 15 to 35 Hz). [7]

between-item elaboration: Analyzing or processing features of an item relative to other memories. [13]

Bezhold-Brücke effect: The change in color, for example, violet becomes bluer, when the intensity of a stimulus is changed. [3]

binocular disparity: A difference between two retinal images produced by the fact that each eye has a slightly different view of an object. [4]

bipolar cell: Nerve cell to which rods and cones connect. [3]

bipolar disorder: A serious psychological disorder, previously known as "manic-depressive psychosis," characterized by extreme mood swings from despair through elation. [24]

blocking: The prevention of conditioning to a particular CS by the addition of another already powerful CS. [12]

bottom-up processing: Kind of information processing or recognition in which a subject processes the critical elements of the stimulus and then moves to a higher level of processing at which meaning and context are established. [13]

brightness: Perceived intensity of a visual stimulus. [3]

brightness contrast: Perceived difference in the intensity of a visual stimulus as a result of the stimulus bordering on another stimulus having a different intensity. [3]

bulimia: An eating disorder related to anorexia characterized by eating binges followed by fasting and purges. [9]

carbachol: Cholinergic neurotransmitter that stimulates neural activity by mimicking the neurotransmitter acetylcholine; has been shown to lead to rage when injected into the amygdala. [6]

catecholamine: A class of neurotransmitter substances. [5, 23]

categorical perception: The fact that speech sounds are perceived as discrete phonological categories rather than as sounds that gradually shade into one another. [17]

categorization: Arranging objects into categories or conceptual classes on the basis of their perceptual or functional properties. [14]

cathexis: In Freudian theory, the attachment of psychic energy (libido) to an object that can reduce tension. The object may be a real one or it may only be a convenient mental substitute. [21]

cell body: An integral portion of a neuron containing the nucleus. [5]

cellular dehydration: A condition in which cells contain less fluid as a result of the outward flow of water. [9]

central nervous system: Part of the nervous system containing the brain and spinal cord. [5]

central tendency: In a distribution of scores on a variable, the central value around which the scores tend to cluster. This central tendency can be described by the mean, the median, or the mode of the distribution. [22]

centration: The exclusive concentration on one aspect of a problem, or one dimension of a stimulus, that characterizes the thought processes of the preoperational child. [16]

cerebellum: A structure in the metencephalon that is concerned with coordinated movement. [5]

cerebral (or neo-) cortex: Large surface area of the forebrain containing the various lobes of the brain. [5]

chlorpromazine: One of the phenothiazines, or chemical compounds, that reduce the levels of dopamine in the brain synapses and in so doing reduce some of the thought disorder that characterizes schizophrenia. [25]

choroid coat: Pigmented layer of tissue in the eye. [3]

chromosome: Strand of genetic material contained within cell nuclei. [8]

cilia: Hairlike projections from the olfactory rods that protrude into the mucous membrane. [3]

ciliary muscle: The muscle that helps to focus light by causing the lens to be stretched. [3]

circadian rhythm: Internal neurological "clock" that helps regulate sleep patterns. [7]

client-centered therapy: The humanistic psychological treatment program, originated by Carl Rogers, in which the therapist acts only as a facilitator for change that the client is assumed to desire. [25]

clinical prediction: The clinician's intuitive judgment, often based on prior experience, of the meaning of the results of a battery of psychological tests. Contrasted with statistical prediction. [24]

cochlea: Coiled structure in the inner ear containing the receptor organs for hearing. [3]

cochlear partition: Structure that divides the cochlea lengthwise. [3]

cognitive consistency models: Any of several models of attitude organization and change based on the assumption that people seek to maintain consistency among their attitudes or between their attitudes and their behavior. [19]

cognitive dissonance: The motivation for attitude change that arises when one cognitive element (such as a belief) implies the opposite of another element. [19]

cognitive labeling theory: Theory claiming that the joint occurrence of physiological arousal and the use of a cognitive label is the source of emotion. [6]

cognitive model of dreams: Theory claiming that dreams can be explained in terms of those same mental processes and systems that we employ in waking perception and thought. [7]

cohesiveness: The mutual commitment and attraction of members of a social group; the sum of the forces binding the group together. [20]

color agnosia: A condition associated with occipital lobe damage in which a person cannot easily classify colors. [5]

color mixture by addition: Creation of new hues by combining colored lights. [3]

color mixture by subtraction: Creation of new hues by combining colored pigments. [3]

comparison level: In exchange theory, the salient average value of outcomes achieved in past relationships. [20]

comparison level for alternatives: In exchange theory, the value of the best available alternative to the present relationship. [20]

complementary: Colors occupying the opposite position on the color circle. [3]

concordant: Term used to describe members of a twin pair who share a personality trait or a clinical diagnosis. [24]

conditioned reflexes: Stimulus-response connections that are established through learning. [2]

conditioned reinforcement: An originally neutral stimulus that, through consistent pairing with a primary reinforcer such as food, acquires the ability to reinforce behavior. [12]

conditioned response (CR): The reaction elicited by the conditioned stimulus when presented alone; the new behavioral tendency acquired during the conditioning process. [12]

conditioned stimulus (CS): A relatively innocuous stimulus that later develops the ability to trigger a CR. [12]

cone: Chromatic photoreceptor in the retina. [3]

consciousness: Awareness of our inner selves and the world around us. [7]

conservations: In Piaget's theory of cognitive development, the concrete-operational child's discovery that properties (size, weight, and volume) of objects do not change when the shape of the object changes. [16]

constancy: The perceptual similarity of an object despite variations in the conditions of observation. [4]

contentives: Words (nouns, verbs, adjectives, adverbs) that name the objects, actions, and characteristics that are at the heart of a sentence. [17]

contingency model: A model of leadership effectiveness that holds that the efficacy of various leadership styles (permissive versus controlling) will depend on the match between style and the characteristics of the setting. [20]

contingent relationship: A relationship between stimuli in which the second of the two depends on the first; i.e., the second occurs in the presence of the first, never in its absence. [12]

continuity theory: Theory claiming that inductive reasoning involves a gradual and incremental learning process that reflects the principles of association. [15]

contour: An abrupt change in luminance; an edge between areas of light and dark. [4]

contralateral hemisphere: Hemisphere lying on the opposite side of the body from the sensory and motor functions that it controls. [5]

conventional morality: The second major phase of moral development in which right action is defined by social standards (such as the approval of others or the rules imposed by society). [18]

convergence: The turning of the eyes inward to focus on an object. [4]

cornea: The transparent outer layer of the eye covering the iris and pupil. [3]

corpus callosum: A mass of neurons that connects the two hemispheres of the brain. [5]

correlation coefficient: A measure of association between scores on two or more variables; the degree to which knowing an individual's score on one variable permits prediction of the person's score on the other variable(s). The numerical value for the correlation coefficient ranges from +1 (a perfect positive correlation) through zero (no association between the two sets of scores) to −1 (a perfect negative correlation). [22, APP]

correspondence bias: In social perception, the pervasive tendency to overestimate the personal causes of behavior while underestimating the influence of the environment; sometimes referred to as the "fundamental attribution error." [19]

correspondence of outcomes: The degree to which the outcomes of one person in a relationship are interdependent with the outcomes of the other; high correspondence represents cooperation, low correspondence represents competition. [20]

correspondent inference theory: A theory of social perception in which an underlying personal motivation is inferred from the effects produced by the person's actions. [19]

credibility of a communicator: The believability of a person who attempts persuasive communication; usually a combination of the person's trustworthiness and expertise. [19]

creole languages: Languages that are based on two or more other languages, but nevertheless serve as the native language for speakers of the creole. [17]

criterion groups: In the development of a new psychological measurement technique, a group of individuals who are believed—on the basis of some measurement procedure *other than* the one being developed—to possess a target trait or capacity. [22]

critical fusion frequency (CFF): The frequency of light flashes that produces the flicker-fusion phenomenon. [3]

critical period: A time-limited period during which a particular capability is thought to be acquired. [17]

cross-situational consistency: The idea that an individual's internal personality structure will guide the person's behavior in a wide variety of settings, and that the setting itself will have only minimal influence on action. [21]

cutaneous sensation: Sensation related to the skin. [3]

cybernetics: The study of control (feedback) processes in animals and machines. [2]

cycle of violence: Theory claiming that violence breeds violence; that victims of violence become violent themselves. [10]

dark adaptation: Process of adjustment of eyes to low light intensities causing replenishment of rhodopsin levels. [3]

decenter: In Piaget's theory of cognitive development, the child's ability to think in ever more abstract, and less egocentric, terms. The ability to take another's viewpoint. [16]

decibel (db): Measure of loudness of sound. [3]

deductive reasoning: Logical thought in which a person reasons from a more general level to a more specific level. [15]

deep structure: The underlying meaning of a sentence, regardless of the particular organization of the words that make up the sentence. [17]

defense mechanisms: Any of several means—such as repression, denial, or displacement—of coping with anxiety. [21]

deinstitutionalization: The social policy of discharging from mental hospitals all but the most severely disturbed patients. As originally intended, the policy was designed to place discharged patients on maintenance doses of medication to be supervised on an outpatient basis either by the hospitals or by community-based treatment centers. [24]

delta wave: EEG pattern characterized by its high amplitude and low frequency (.5–3 Hz). [7]

dementia praecox: The original term, coined by Kraepelin, for the psychological disorder now known as schizophrenia. Literally, "premature mental deterioration." [24]

dendrite: Branching filament extending from the cell body of a neuron. [5]

dermis: A main layer of the skin. [3]

determinism: The philosophical, and psychological, view that all events are caused. [1]

diagnostic ratio: In social perception, the ratio of two probability estimates: the probability that a defined group possesses a particular characteristic divided by the probability that people in general possess the characteristic. [19]

dichotic listening experiment: Technique in which a different message is presented to each ear. The subject shadows (repeats) one of them and later attempts to recall aspects of the other (unshadowed) message. [5, 13]

diencephalon: A division of the brain containing the thalamus and hypothalamus. [5]

difference threshold: The difference in intensity levels that is sufficient to cause a person to sense that the two stimuli are indeed different. [3]

diploid zygote: Fertilized ovum. [8]

discrimination: Phenomenon occurring when an organism responds differentially to two stimuli on the basis of perceived differences between them. [12]

discriminative stimulus: A stimulus that sets the occasion for a reinforcer by signaling when the reinforcer is available through responding. [12]

dispersion: The degree of variability in a distribution of scores. Although the dispersion is sometimes represented by the range of scores—the highest score minus the lowest—it is more typically represented by the standard deviation. [22]

distribution: A collection of scores on a variable, usually displayed as an X-Y plot in which the X axis represents the possible categories of scores and the Y axis represents the number of scores in each of the categories. [22, APP]

dominant trait: Phenotype determined by the dominant allele, observable in the F_1 generation. [8]

dopamine: A catecholamine neurotransmitter. [5]

dopamine hypothesis of schizophrenia: The hypothesis that the symptoms of schizophrenia are caused by excess levels of dopamine in synapses in the brain. The hypothesis was suggested by the fact that phenothiazines, which reduce the level of dopamine, reduce the symptoms of schizophrenia. [25]

double-bind hypothesis: An explanation for the withdrawal from social interaction that often characterizes patients with schizophrenia. The inconsistency between a parent's verbal message of love and nonverbal message of disgust is presumed to create such confusion in the child that the only available

option for the child is withdrawal from any interaction. [24]

drug tolerance: A condition in which a drug-dependent person requires progressively more of the substance to have the same effect. [7]

dualism: The philosophical view, attributable to Descartes, that the mind and the body are separate entities. [1]

echoic memory store: Memory system in which auditory information is held for a very brief time. [13]

ego: In many psychodynamic theories, the rational and largely conscious aspect of the personality. [21]

elaboration likelihood model: A model of persuasion that distinguishes the cognitive effort required on the part of the message recipient from aspects of the message itself. Change is presumed to be more likely as more cognitive effort is required. [19]

elaborative rehearsal: Kind of rehearsal that occurs at progressively deeper levels of processing; elaborative rehearsal affects the permanence of memory. [13]

Electra complex: In Freudian theory, a daughter's sexual desire for her father during the phallic stage of psychosexual development that places her in competition with her mother for her father's attentions. [2]

electroconvulsive therapy (ECT): A procedure for the treatment of severe depression that involves passing a current of 70 to 130 volts for a fraction of a second between electrodes placed on each side of the patient's head. This current induces a seizure that briefly interrupts most electrical activity in the patient's brain. ECT has been effective in treating very severe depression, but it is a highly controversial method. [25]

electroencephalogram (EEG): Brain wave pattern. [7]

electromyogram or EMG: Electrophysiological recording of muscle activity. [7]

Emmert's Law: A formal claim that the perceived size of an object is equal to the retinal image size created times the perceived distance of the object. [4]

epidermis: A main layer of the skin. [3]

episodic memory: Kind of stored information that is highly linked to the time and place in which it was formed. [14]

epistemology: The philosophical study of the nature and origins of knowledge. [1]

equity theory: A theory describing the processes by which individuals evaluate the fairness of their outcomes from interaction. People feel equitably treated if the ratio of their outcomes to inputs is equal to the same ratio for other participants. [20]

erogenous zones: In Freudian theory, bodily regions involved in digestion and procreation that are thought to be instinctual sources of sexual pleasure. [18]

Eros: In Freudian personality theory, the collection of life instincts that assure the satisfaction of basic needs for food, water, and sex. [21]

escape: A form of instrumental learning in which execution of the designated response leads to the cessation of an aversive stimulus. [12]

estrogen: Female sex hormone. [10]

ethology: The study of animal behavior from an evolutionary perspective. [8]

evaluation apprehension: An experimental subject's concern about attaining a positive evaluation of his or her behavior from the experimenter, usually reflected in an attempt to behave in a "typical" manner. [19]

exchange theory: A theory of interpersonal behavior that holds that (a) social encounters can best be described as exchanges of rewards and punishments, and (b) in such encounters people seek to maximize their own outcomes. [20]

excitement phase: First phase of the human sexual response cycle involving the reception of stimuli from the environment. [10]

expressed emotion (EE): The level of hostility and criticism present in a schizophrenic's family of origin. High levels of expressed emotion are associated with early relapse among schizophrenics who have returned home after release from mental institutions. [24]

G-5

extinction: The process during which the CR or association is weakened. [12]

extracellular fluid: Water not contained within the body's cells. [9]

factor analysis: A statistical technique for determining the commonalities among a large number of descriptors. The technique analyzes the entries in a correlation matrix to identify the few dimensions that underlie the observed correlations. [21]

family resemblance: Membership in a category by virtue of sharing some but not all of the features of that category. [14]

fear of failure: Motive to avoid failure measured by the Test Anxiety Questionnaire. [11]

fear of power: One component of the power motive characterized by negative feelings about power. [11]

fear of rejection: One component of the affiliation motive characterized by expressions of the negative aspects of relationships. [11]

feature analysis: Process by which a subject determines the meaning of the stimulus on the basis of the fit between the features of the stimulus and an implicit list in memory of possible features. [13]

feature comparison model: Theory claiming that knowledge is computed or derived as needed on the basis of certain rules or conditions and a list of features stored in memory. [14]

field theory: Kurt Lewin's topological theory that views human motivation as the product of various forces (personal, external) acting on the individual. [20]

figure: An integrated unit of perception; a group of contours having shape and coherence. [4]

filter model: Theory claiming that information must pass through a filter at the very earliest stages in the information-processing sequence prior to being processed. [13]

finite state grammar: A theory of language production. The key assumption is that in any sentence the words are organized from left to right, with the number of ways to complete the sentence decreasing dramatically with each transition

point in the sentence. For example, if the first word in a sentence is "How," the sentence will almost invariably be a question. [17]

fixed interval (FI) schedule: A basic reinforcement schedule in which a reward is delivered once the organism performs the desired responses and an interval of time has elapsed. [12]

fixed ratio (FR) schedule: A basic reinforcement schedule in which a reward is delivered once the organism has performed a fixed number of responses. [12]

fixed-action pattern (FAP): A form of instinctual behavior having a relatively stereotyped pattern of execution. [8]

flicker-fusion phenomenon: The perception of a series of light flashes as a single continuous light. [3]

forward conditioning: Classical conditioning procedure in which the CS is presented prior to the US. [12]

fovea: The central part of the retina containing only cone receptors. [3]

free association: A therapeutic technique, originally associated with Freudian psychoanalysis, in which the client is required to say everything that comes to mind, with no censorship. [2]

free nerve ending: Nerve ending thought to mediate the sensation of pain. [3]

frequency: The number of peaks per unit time. [3]

frequency distribution: A distribution in which observations are grouped in a limited number of categories (along the X axis), noting the frequency of occurrence of scores in each category (along the Y axis). [APP]

frequency theory: Theory of hearing claiming that perception of sound frequency depended on the rate of vibration of the basilar membrane. [3]

frontal lobe: The front portion of the neocortex that mediates many higher functions including the ability to plan ahead. [5]

frustration-aggression hypothesis: Theory claiming that frustration always produces aggression and that all aggression results from frustration. [10]

functional fixedness: A process or condition that blocks the ability to solve problems by limiting the way in which subjects look at objects and the ways in which those objects can be used. [15]

functional materialism: One of the several forms of *monism.* Specifically, the philosophical view that the mind is what the mind does: Activities of thinking and decision making, whether performed by a person or by a computer, constitute the mind. [1]

functionalism: An early approach to psychology that concentrated on the adaptive value (function) of mental processes and behavior. [2]

functors: Words (such as pronouns, prepositions, intensifiers) that provide connections among the contentive words in a sentence. [17]

gamete: Sex cell—ovum in the female, sperm in the male. [8]

ganglia: Concentrated groups of nerve cells. [6]

ganglion cell: Nerve cell in the retina connected to the optic tract. [3]

gender: The meanings that societies and individuals ascribe to the female and male categories. [10]

gender identity: A person's private sense of being male or female; the gender with which a person identifies. [10]

gender role: A person's public expression of identity; an individual's pattern of gender-related behavior. [10]

gene: Fundamental unit of inheritance. [8]

general adaptation syndrome: The sequential process of attempting to adapt to the continuing presence of environmental stressors. The syndrome consists of three stages: alarm, resistance, and exhaustion. [23]

generalization: A phenomenon shown when a subject responds to a CS that was not previously used in conditioning but is similar in some respect to the CS originally used. [12]

generalization gradient: Graded relationship between the strength of the CS, as measured by the magnitude or rate of the CR that is elicited, and the similarity of the new CS to the CS originally involved in conditioning. [12]

genital stage: In Freudian theory, the fourth psychosexual stage at which a now-adolescent's sexual interest turns outward to peers. [18]

genotype: An individual's genetic makeup. [8]

Gestalt: A school of psychology claiming that perceptual phenomena could be understood only if viewed as organized wholes. [4]

global processing: Processing of holistic features of a stimulus. [13]

glucagon: Pancreatic hormone controlling the conversion of glucogen and glycerol into glucose. [9]

glucoreceptor: Receptor in the brain and liver that senses levels of blood glucose. [9]

glucostatic theory: Theory claiming that the brain contains receptors that monitor glucose availability in the blood. [9]

glycerol: Component of fat tissue that is transformed into glucose by the hormone glucagon. [9]

glycogen: The stored form of glucose. [9]

gonad: Sex gland. [10]

gonadotropic hormone: Pituitary hormones that control the levels of the sex hormones. [10]

grammar: An entire system by which phonology, semantic content, and syntax turn speech sounds into meanings. [17]

ground: The formless extense seen to lie behind a figure. [4]

groupthink: The preoccupation with unanimity of opinion within a group (usually to facilitate achievement of a desirable but risky group goal) that renders ineffective any critical evaluation of the proposed course of action. [20]

gustation: Sense of taste. [3]

gustatory cell: Cell contained in the taste buds that come into contact with taste substances. [3]

habituation: The gradual reduction in responding created when a stimulus is repeatedly presented. [4]

haploid: Cells (e.g., gametes) having only one chromosomal strand. [8]

hemisphere: A symmetrical half of the cortex. [5]

hemispheric laterality: Concept referring to the finding that the two hemispheres of the cortex are not symmetrical in their functioning. [5]

heritability: The proportion of phenotypic variation in a trait or characteristic that is accounted for exclusively by genetic factors. When a trait is 100 percent inherited, the fraction of phenotypic variation to genotypic variation is 1.0. [16]

hermaphrodite: A female who suffers excessive androgen levels or a male who suffers insufficient androgen levels during fetal development. [10]

hertz (Hz): Measure of wave frequency as cycles per second. [3]

hierarchical network model: Theory claiming that knowledge involves conceptual units linked together in a hierarchical fashion. [14]

hippocampus: An important area in the limbic system that is associated with memory (the patient H. M. experienced damage to this area). [5]

homeostasis: Processes that maintain a state of biological equilibrium in the body. [9]

hope for affiliation: One component of the affiliation motive characterized by a tendency to seek the company of others. [11]

hope for power: One component of the power motive characterized by a tendency to seek influence over others. [11]

hostile aggression: Aggression intended simply to injure another individual. [10]

hue: The perceived color of a visual stimulus. [3]

human sexual response cycle: Characteristic phases of the human sexual response. [10]

hypertonic: Containing an excess or higher-than-normal level of salt ions. [9]

hypnosis: A sleep-like condition, possibly a state, in which a person may experience a change in consciousness such as heightened suggestability. [7]

hypothalamus: An important structure in the diencephalon that helps regulate many vital functions. [5]

hypotonic: Containing a lower-than-normal level of salt ions. [9]

hypovolemia: A reduction in the volume of extracellular fluid due to hemorrhaging, vomiting, diarrhea, or evaporation. [9]

iconic: As applied to a sign language, the fact that many of the language's symbols mimic the objects they describe. [17]

iconic memory store: Memory system in which visual information is held for a very brief time. [13]

id: In Freudian theory, the unorganized, uninhibited, and irrational set of unconscious instincts present at birth. [21]

identity achievement: One of the four categories of adolescent identity development; the result of the combination of consideration of life alternatives and personal commitment to a choice among those alternatives. [18]

identity crisis: In Erikson's theory of psychosocial development, the key crisis for adolescence that marks the transition between a childhood framed by the parents and an independent adulthood. [16]

identity diffusion: One of the four categories of adolescent identity development; the result of consideration of life alternatives without any personal commitment to a particular role. [18]

identity foreclosure: One of the four categories of adolescent identity development; the result of personal acceptance of parental (or other external) standards for one's life and future. [18]

ill-defined problems: Problems for which the starting point and/or the representation of the goals are vague. [15]

illusory correlation: In social perception, a perceived association—such as the traits ascribed to members of a group—that is not actually present in the data. [19]

imagery: Perceptually encoded knowledge. [14]

imprinting: The development of filial attachment among animals, typically as shown by "following" behavior. [18]

incentive: A learned source of motivation; a goal object. [9]

incus: Bone in the middle ear connecting the tympanic membrane and the oval window. [3]

indeterminism: The philosophical and psychological view that some events (particularly internal mental activities) are not governed by physical laws. [1]

induced movement: The perception of motion of a stationary object produced by the real motion of another stimulus in the viewing field. [4]

inductive reasoning: Logical thought in which an examination of particular instances leads to the judgment that a given conclusion is likely to be true. [15]

inferior colliculi: Structures in the tectum that are part of the auditory pathways. [5]

informational social influence: The social power of persuasion that produces private acceptance by providing the target person with the information needed to make a wise decision. [20]

insanity defense: A legal defense against criminal charges; the defense argues that at the time the offense was committed the accused was—by reason of mental disease or defect—unable to distinguish right from wrong or to behave according to knowledge of the difference between the two. [25]

insomnia: A belief that one is getting insufficient sleep. [7]

instinct: An inherited, specific, stereotyped pattern of behavior with its own energy that is released, rather than guided, by particular environmental stimuli. [8]

instrumental aggression: Aggression designed to achieve a goal beyond the aggressive act itself. [10]

instrumental (operant) conditioning: Basic learning process in which an organism learns to perform a response that produces or eliminates some outcome, for example, a reward or punisher. [12]

instrumental learning: A form of learning involving rewards or punishers for contingent behaviors. [10]

insulin: A pancreatic hormone that helps the body's cells utilize glucose and convert glucose into glycogen. [9]

intelligence quotient (IQ): As origi-

nally described by Terman, the ratio of a person's measured "mental age" to the person's chronological age, multiplied by 100. [22]

intercorrelated: Two or more measures of psychological characteristics or capacities are intercorrelated if individuals' responses on one scale are related to their responses on the other scale(s). [22]

interference theory of memory: Theory claiming that forgetting occurs because information that is unrelated to the to-be-remembered memory interferes with the encoding, storage, or retrieval of the memory. [14]

interposition: A cue for distance created when one object partially blocks the view of another. [4]

interstitial fluid: Fluid surrounding, and giving support to, the body's cells. [9]

intracellular fluid: Water contained within the walls of the body's cells. [9]

introspection: The examination of inner perceptual experience by trained subjects in controlled conditions. [2]

involuntary civil commitment: A judicial proceeding by which an individual is placed in a state mental hospital. The proceeding takes place in civil (not criminal) courts, and commitment occurs if the court is convinced that the person is either "a danger to self or others," or "substantially unable to care for himself." [25]

ion: Electrically charged particle. [5]

ipsilateral hemisphere: Hemisphere lying on the same side of the body as the sensory and motor functions that it controls. [5]

isotonic: Having an equal concentration of salt ions, i.e., having the same osmotic pressure or tension. [9]

James-Lange theory of emotion: Theory claiming that perception of feedback from the ANS is the source of emotion. [6]

judgmental heuristic: A shorthand strategy, or rule of thumb, for making decisions. [15]

just noticeable difference (jnd): The difference in intensity levels that is sensed as being "just noticeable";

the change in stimulus intensity needed to reach the difference threshold. [3]

K-complex: EEG pattern involving a very high amplitude and a sharp, negative-going wave followed immediately by a sharp, positive-going wave. [7]

kinetic depth effect: An experience of depth created when stationary two-dimensional objects are rotated. [4]

Klüver-Bucy Syndrome: A condition of docility following damage to the amygdala. [6]

Korsakoff's syndrome: A condition associated with severe alcoholism involving damage to either the medial thalamic region or the hippocampus and resulting in an associated loss of memory function. [5]

Krause end bulb: Nerve ending thought to mediate the sensation of cold. [3]

labeling theory: The socio-cultural theory that claims that psychological disturbance is too often defined in terms of the violation of social norms. According to this theory, behavior that is unexpected or distasteful to society is labeled as "abnormal," and treated as "illness" rather than as a different pattern of adjustment. [24]

language: As used in this text, a rule-governed collection of arbitrary symbols used to convey meaning. Must have the properties of semanticity, arbitrariness, productivity, and traditional transmission, and must follow the rules of syntax. [17]

language bioprogram hypothesis: The nativist view that humans are genetically prepared to acquire language by virtue of the structures and modes of operation of their brains. [17]

late selection theory: Theory claiming that information enters the information-processing system and selective attention occurs only after the information has been recognized and evaluated. [13]

latent content: The latent dream material said to reflect underlying conflicts. [7]

latent learning: Procedure (and phenomenon) in which learning takes place without the use of any obvious reward. [12]

lateral geniculate nucleus (LGN): Nuclei in the thalamus that connect with the optic tract. [3]

lateral hypothalamus: Area of the diencephalon that helps to control certain vital functions including feeding and drinking; originally considered to be the hunger center of the brain. [9]

law of closure: A Gestalt law arguing that incomplete objects are perceived as being complete. [4]

law of contiguity: Claim that the development of an association depends entirely on the temporal contiguity of the stimuli. [12]

law of effect: Thorndike's law of conditioning: Behavior that is rewarded is "stamped in," and behavior that produces discomfort is "stamped out." [2]

law of good continuation: A Gestalt law arguing that contours will be continued along the line of the implied direction of a perceptual pattern. [4]

law of Prägnanz: A Gestalt law arguing that objects will be perceived as simpler, more stable, symmetrical, and meaningful. [4]

law of proximity: A Gestalt law arguing that elements in the perceptual field that are spatially near each other will be perceived as constituting a coherent whole object. [4]

law of similarity: A Gestalt law arguing that elements in the perceptual field that are similar to each other will be perceived as constituting a coherent whole object. [4]

learned helplessness: The conditioned response to aversive but inescapable events. Also a theory of the origin of depression based on an internal and stable explanation for the occurrence of negative events. [24]

least restrictive alternative: A legal principle governing the involuntary civil commitment of a psychologically disturbed individual: A person should be deprived of liberty only to the minimum extent needed to guarantee proper treatment. [25]

lens: Transparent structure behind the pupil that focuses light onto the retina. [3]

level of aspiration: A self-imposed expectation for task performance that will determine whether the self-evaluation following task completion is positive or negative. [19]

levels-of-processing model: Theory claiming that information is not processed by different memory systems but instead is processed at different levels within a single system. [13]

lexigram: A symbol, often used in the attempt to teach language to chimpanzees, that represents an object or tool. [17]

libido: In Freudian theory, psychic energy. [18]

life space: In field theory, the total field of personal factors and environmental forces perceived by the person at any given moment in time. [20]

limbic system (or lobe): An important area of the forebrain (telencephalon) containing the septum and amygdala. [5]

linear perspective: A cue for distance created by the convergence of two apparently parallel lines in the distance. [4]

lipostatic theory: Theory claiming that as fat accumulates, appetite decreases, and that as fat stores are depleted and energy is used, appetite increases. [9]

lithium carbonate: A form of lithium salt with psychotropic properties; useful in reducing the symptoms of bipolar disorder. [25]

locus ceruleus: Structure in the brain that induces cortical excitation when stimulated. [7]

long-term memory: Memory storage system in which an unlimited amount of information may be retained for an indefinite length of time. Evidence suggests that the primary basis according to which the information is stored is its meaning. [13]

lordosis: Behavior typical of female rats presenting a suitable copulatory position. [10]

lucid dream: A dream in which the person is aware that he or she is dreaming. [7]

luminance: Amplitude or intensity of light waves. [3]

lymphocytes: Cells, produced by the lymph glands, that circulate in the bloodstream and play a part in the body's defenses against infection. [23]

lymphokines: Biochemicals, specifically interleukin-1 and interleukin-2, that are secreted by the T-cells (lymphocytes that originate in bone marrow). The lymphokines are involved in the body's response to infection. [23]

Machiavellianism: The interpersonal style characterized by manipulation of other people, especially in face-to-face interactions with great latitude for improvisation. [20]

maintenance rehearsal: Kind of rehearsal that occurs at a single level of processing; maintenance rehearsal keeps an item of information active in memory but does not affect its permanence. [13]

major depression: The psychological disorder characterized by pervasive sadness, pessimism, slowness of movement, and loss of appetite and sleep. More than "the blues," depression is quite debilitating and is one of the most prevalent forms of psychological disorder. [24]

malleus: Bone in the middle ear connecting the tympanic membrane and the oval window. [3]

manic-depressive psychosis: The original term, coined by Kraepelin, for the psychological disorder now known as bipolar affective disorder. [24]

manifest content: The dream material reported upon awakening. [7]

MAO inhibitors: A class of psychotropic drugs useful in treating the symptoms of depression. These drugs act to prevent the breakdown of norepinephrine by monoamine oxidase (MAO), thereby having the effect of increasing the activation level. [24]

materialist identity theory: The philosophical view, attributable to Hobbes, that the mind is nothing more, and nothing less, than the physical brain. This is one of the several forms of monism. [1]

mean: A measure of central tendency. The arithmetic average of a distribution of scores computed by adding all of the scores together and dividing by the total number of scores. [22, APP]

means-end analysis: A strategy in which the problem solver achieves the ultimate solution (the end) by first solving a series of subgoals (the means to the end). [15]

mechanistic model: A model of psychological development that views the human organism as a machine that passively responds to demands imposed upon it from the external environment. [16]

medial forebrain bundle: The primary pleasure center. [6]

medial geniculate nucleus: Nuclei in the thalamus in which auditory neurons synapse. [5]

medial thalamic region: An important area in the frontal lobe that is associated with memory (the patient N. A. experienced damage to this area). [5]

median: A measure of central tendency. The point (which may or may not be an actual score) in a distribution of scores above which and below which half of the scores lie. [22, APP]

median preoptic nucleus: Area of the brain near the hypothalamus, which when stimulated causes drinking. [9]

medical model: The model of emotional disturbance that holds that psychological disorder is the outward manifestation of an internal physiological problem. The model thus assumes that there are physical causes for all psychological disorders, and that correction of these physical problems will eliminate the psychological disturbance. [24]

medulla oblongata: A structure in the myelencephalon that controls respiration, cardiovascular functioning, and muscle tone. [5]

Meissner's corpuscle: Nerve ending thought to mediate the sensation of touch. [3]

memory decay theory: Theory of forgetting that claims that memories fade or decay gradually during storage. [14]

memory span: Number of items of information that a subject can simultaneously retain (i.e., reproduce) at any given time. [13]

mental set: A process or condition stemming from experience that inhibits the restructuring of a problem. [15]

mesencephalon: A division of the brain containing the tectum and tegmentum. [5]

meta-analysis: A statistical technique for comparing results across diverse research studies by standardizing the effect sizes. [20, 25]

metencephalon: A division of the brain containing the cerebellum. [5]

mind-body problem: The philosophical and psychological problem of describing exactly how mental events become translated into actions of the body. [1, 3]

minor tranquilizers: A class of psychotropic drugs that is effective in reducing the symptoms of anxiety. [25]

mnemonic: Strategy or device that can be used to improve memory. [14]

mode: A measure of central tendency. The most frequently occurring score in a distribution. [22]

modeling: Learning through the imitation of others. [10, 22]

monism: The philosophical view that mind and body are one, rather than being separate entities. [1]

monotropy: The idea that a human infant is predisposed to form an especially powerful attachment to just one caring and responsive person. [18]

moon illusion: The illusion that the moon appears larger when on the horizon than when viewed overhead, despite the fact that the retinal image is the same in both cases. [4]

moratorium: One of the four categories of adolescent identity development; the failure to examine life alternatives coupled with the failure to make any personal commitment to one choice. [18]

morpheme: The smallest unit of language that conveys meaning. Morphemes are often entire words, although they can also be prefixes or suffixes (such as the "s" that constitutes the plural). [17]

motion detector: Neuron in the cat's brain that responds only when lines of a certain slant are passed across the visual field. [4]

motion parallax: A difference in retinal image produced by the fact that the retina changes position relative to objects in the visual field. [4]

motive: A state or disposition that energizes and directs behavior. [11]

motive for affiliation (n Affil): Tendency to seek the company of others, to find pleasure in being with other people, or to avoid loneliness. [11]

motor (efferent) neuron: Nerve that carries information from the brain to the various muscles and organs of the body. [5]

Müller-Lyer illusion: The illusion that two horizontal lines of equal length are perceived as being unequal because of the shape and size of the oblique lines at each end. [4]

multidimensional scaling: A statistical technique for discovering the patterns underlying a set of stimuli, based on judgments of the similarity between members of all possible pairs of the stimuli. [19]

multistore model: Theory claiming that information resides in one of three major storage sites or memory systems: sensory memory, short-term memory, and long-term memory. [13]

myelencephalon: A division of the brain containing the medulla oblongata. [5]

myelin sheath: A fatty protective covering around axons. [5]

narcolepsy: A sleep disorder in which a person experiences sleep "attacks" during waking hours. [7]

narcotic: Drug that induces sleep and lessens pain. [7]

natural category: Categories used in everyday life to classify stimuli in the environment. [14]

natural selection: Darwin's claim concerning the primary mechanism of evolution—heritable traits that endow an organism with a relative advantage in the struggle for existence will, on average, tend to be passed on to future generations. [8]

need: A force that organizes perception, thought, emotion, and action; a state of affairs that would improve the well-being of an organism. [11]

Neoplatonism: Any philosophical position that incorporates Plato's distinction between the sensory world, known indirectly from experience, and the world of truth, known only through contemplation and reason. [1]

neuropsychology: The study of behavior in relation to the nervous system, especially the brain. [5]

neurotransmitter: Biochemical substance that diffuses across synaptical clefts to stimulate adjacent nerve endings. [5]

nigrostriatal bundle: A bundle of neurons running near the lateral hypothalamus which, when destroyed, causes eating abnormalities including aphagia. [9]

nonaggressive erotica: Erotic material not involving the depiction of aggressive acts. [10]

noncontinuity theory: Theory claiming that the inductive reasoning process is discontinuous, involving the formation of various hypotheses, which are then confirmed or disconfirmed. [15]

nonstate theories of hypnosis: Theory claiming that hypnosis does not involve a special state of consciousness. [7]

nonverbal leakage: The nonverbal cues, typically emanating from the position of the body and the limbs, that conflict with a spoken message. [19]

nonzero-sum game: A social interaction in which the interests of the parties conflict, but in which the sum of winnings and losses is not zero. [20]

norepinephrine: A catecholamine neurotransmitter. [5]

normal distribution: A symmetrical "bell-shaped" curve produced by a particular mathematical formula. The normal curve represents the likelihood of various chance events; many psychological characteristics are distributed in a way that approximates the normal distribution. [APP]

normative social influence: The social power of reward and punishment that produces behavioral compliance but may not produce any private acceptance of the position advocated. [20]

norms: General social expectations for behavior in particular settings. [19]

nucleotide: Genetic material (DNA) that forms units of a chromosome. [8]

object permanence: The idea that objects, animals, and people continue to exist even when they are out of sight. This fundamental idea does not seem to be present from birth but rather is learned through interaction with the environment. [16]

objective personality test: A personality test that presents individuals with concrete ways to characterize themselves (often in terms of self-descriptive statements or personality-trait words). [22]

obsessive-compulsive disorder: A psychological disturbance characterized by recurring images or thoughts that, although upsetting, cannot be put out of mind (obsessions) or by actions the person feels compelled to repeat over and over (compulsions). [24]

occipital lobe: The rear portion of the neocortex that mediates vision. [5]

Oedipus complex: In Freudian theory, a son's sexual desire for his mother during the phallic stage of psychosexual development that places him in competition with his father for his mother's attentions. [2]

olfaction: Sense of smell. [3]

olfactory epithelium: Portions of the mucous membrane that contain smell receptors. [3]

olfactory rod: Nerve ending of smell receptor. [3]

omission training: A form of instrumental learning in which execution of the designated response leads to the nonoccurrence of an appetitive stimulus. [12]

operant conditioning: A form of learning in which the provision of reinforcement following the performance of a behavior increases the future likelihood that the behavior will be repeated. Also known as instrumental conditioning. [2, 12]

operational definition: Definitions of conceptual variables, especially states internal to the organism, in terms of the experimental procedures used to produce the stimuli and measure the responses. For example, "24 hours of food deprivation" is an operational definition for an internal state called "hunger." [2]

opiate: A type of narcotic, such as morphine, that is derived from the opium plant. [7]

opponent-process theory of emotion: Theory claiming that emotion-provoking stimuli induce both a primary and an opponent (opposite) hedonic state; felt emotion is a summation of these two states. [6]

opponent-process theory: Theory of color vision claiming that various hues are produced through the combined action of three color processes or systems, each system sensitive to a pair of colors. [3]

optic chiasm: Point in the brain where visual nerves cross to the contralateral cortex. [5]

oral stage: In Freudian theory, the stage of psychosexual development, from birth to roughly age 2, during which the infant is presumed to obtain gratification from sucking milk from its mother's breast. [16]

organ of Corti: Structure containing cochlear partition, basilar membrane, and hair cells. [3]

organismic model: The first broad approach to the study of developmental psychology. This model assumed that the internal (cognitive) organization of the individual is affected by the same evolutionary pressures that make certain kinds of physical characteristics particularly advantageous for the species. [16]

orgasmic phase: Third phase of the human sexual response cycle involving muscular contractions. [10]

osmoreceptor: Specialized receptor in the brain for detecting the salt concentration in fluids. [9]

osmosis: A process in which fluid from the hypotonic side of the membrane diffuses through the membrane to balance the concentrations of salt in the fluids on the two sides of the membrane. [9]

osmotic thirst: Thirst that is caused by an increase in the concentration of salt in the extracellular fluid due to the ingestion of salt or to the loss of water through respiration and perspiration. [9]

oval window: Membrane on the wall of the cochlea connected to the stapes whose vibrations are transmitted to the inner ear. [3]

ovary: Female sex gland. [10]

overextension: In the early stages of language acquisition, the child's use of a single word to describe objects superficially similar to the target object. [17]

overregularization: In the early stages of language acquisition, the child's tendency to apply a grammatical rule to irregular forms that is only appropriate for regular forms. [17]

panic disorder: A psychological disorder characterized by recurring attacks of intense fear or discomfort that are not related to the demands of the situation. [24]

papillae: Lobes of tissue on the tongue containing taste buds. [3]

parallax: The difference in appearance of an object that results from the fact that it is perceived from two viewing positions. [4]

parasympathetic nervous system: One portion of the ANS associated with conservation and restoration of energy. [6]

parietal lobe: The top portion of the neocortex that mediates touch. [5]

Pavlovian (classical) conditioning: Basic learning process in which an organism develops an association between two stimuli based on their contingent relationship. [12]

perception: The processes that give coherence and meaning to sensory inputs; study of the phenomenological world. [4]

perilymph fluid: Fluid contained in the cochlear regions. [3]

period of concrete operations: In Piaget's theory of cognitive development, the period from roughly age 7 to age 11 during which the child discovers that processes and operations are reversible, and becomes able to take another's viewpoint. [16]

peripheral nervous system: Part of the nervous system that is external to the brain and spinal cord. [5]

person-by-situation interaction: The modern view of the relationship between personality and behavior: Both an individual's enduring characteristics and the requirements of the situation interact to determine behavior. [21]

personality disorder: A psychological disturbance characterized by extremes of normal personality traits: The trait becomes an inflexible and powerful influence on behavior, regardless of the demands of the situation. [24]

phallic stage: In Freudian theory, the third psychosexual stage. During this stage the genitals become the focus of attention; children are believed to have primitive feelings of sexual attraction toward their parent of the opposite sex. [18]

phenothiazine: A class of psychotropic medications that reduces the thought disorder associated with schizophrenia, perhaps by lowering levels of dopamine in the brain. Phenothiazines can produce side effects that resemble the movement disorders usually considered symptomatic of Parkinson's disease. [24]

phenotype: An individual's observable characteristics. [8]

pheromone: Sexual odors that serve to attract mates or advertise sexual receptivity. [10]

phobias: An intense fear reaction for which the original unconditioned fear-producing stimulus is no longer a realistic threat. [12]

phoneme: The smallest unit of speech that serves to distinguish one utterance from another. The phoneme is a linguistic category, not a particular acoustic pattern, and consists of allophones (phonetically distinct members of the category). [17]

phrase structure grammar: A theory of language production that concentrates on the hierarchical structure of sentences. The theory holds that people learn a set of rules about how phrases are organized and combined; they then use these rules to generate new combinations. [17]

phrenology: The study of the relationship between mental faculties and specific areas of the brain. [5]

placebo: A substance that has no physiological effects. [6]

placebo effect: The possibility that a person's psychological condition will improve upon receiving a treatment (either a medication or a psychological procedure) that is known *not* to produce any real behavioral change. [25]

place-resonance theory: Theory of hearing claiming that perception of sound frequency depended on the length, and thus the position on the basilar membrane, of the resonating hair cells. [3]

places of articulation: Locations in the human vocal apparatus where the air flow from the lungs can be restricted to produce sounds. These include the lips, the teeth, and various locations along the palate. [17]

planned action: A theory of the relationship between attitude and behavior. Favorable predispositions toward an attitude object will be translated into specific behavioral intentions influenced by subjective norms and by perceived control. [19]

plateau phase: Second phase of the human sexual response cycle in which receptivity to extraneous stimuli decreases somewhat. [10]

pleasure center: Area of the brain associated with pleasure when stimulated. [6]

pons: A structure in the metencephalon that bridges the mesencephalon and the metencephalon. [5]

population: In statistical terms, an entire group of individuals. Examples are "all people in the United States," or "all children in kindergarten." [22]

pornography: The explicit depiction of sexual acts, such as genital manipulation and penetration, for the purpose of arousing a person sexually. [10]

postconventional morality: The third major phase of moral development in which right action is determined by reference to critically examined social contracts or universal ethical principles. [18]

postsynaptic membrane: Site containing receptors for receiving stimulation from another neuron. [5]

posttraumatic stress disorder (PTSD): A psychological disorder brought about by the stress of wartime or an intense victimization experience. The disturbance is characterized by insomnia, pain from constantly reliving the experience, or guilt from having survived when others nearby have died. [24]

power motive (n Power): A disposition that is aroused in particular situations and results in the tendency to seek influence over others, either directly or indirectly. [11]

preconscious: In Freudian theory, the region of the mind that consists of thoughts, feelings, and emotions that are capable of being called into consciousness. [21]

preconventional morality: The first major phase of moral development, with right and wrong determined by the consequences (such as reward, punishment, satisfaction of personal needs) of action. [18]

prefrontal lobotomy: A technique of psychosurgery in which a surgical instrument is inserted into the front of the brain (either through a small hole drilled in the side of the head or through the transorbital structure) and rotated through an arc of some 60° around the point of insertion, thus destroying brain tissue in the prefrontal lobes. [25]

preoperational period: In Piaget's theory of cognitive development, the period extending roughly from age 2 to age 7 during which the child develops language and extends a variety of other symbolic activities. [16]

presynaptic membrane: Site at the end of an axon that contains synaptic vesicles. [5]

primary color: The hue associated with the three kinds of cone receptors—red, green, blue. [3]

priming effect: A bias in social perception that results from cognitive activities performed previously: New information is interpreted in terms of the previous activity. [19]

progestin: A class of estrogen. [10]

projective test: A psychological measurement technique in which individuals are presented with ambiguous stimuli and required to assign meaning to them. Projective tests rely on the assumption that what the individual sees in the ambiguous stimulus is a reflection of his or her underlying psychological motivations. [22]

prototype: A single item that serves as an ideal example of a category. [14]

psychedelic drug: Mind-altering drug that affects awareness, coordination, and mood. [7]

psychoanalysis: The psychotherapeutic technique based on Freud's theories of personality and abnormal behavior. [25]

psychogenesis: The "behavioral model" of psychological disturbance in which psychological disorders reflect pathogenic social or psychological conditions, not physical disturbances. [24]

psychogenic need: A need related to the psychological (nonorganic) state of an organism. [11]

psycholinguistics: The study of the psychological factors involved in language learning and usage. [17]

psychophysics: The scientific study of the relationship between physical states (such as sound) and psychological events (such as the experience of loudness). [3]

psychosexual stages: The four stages—oral, anal, phallic, genital—of psychological development according to Freud's personality theory. If the parent's behavior at any stage is either overly permissive or overly restrictive, the child is said to become fixated at that stage, with adverse consequences for later personality development. [2]

psychosocial stages: In Erikson's model of social development, the series of eight "crises" in interpersonal relations that must be resolved to ensure healthy development.[16, 18]

psychosomatic illness: Illness not based on organic factors but on psychological factors, often conditioning. [12]

psychosurgery: Any of several surgical techniques designed to alleviate psychological disorders by severing particular brain connections. [25]

psychotropic drugs: Substances that act on the central nervous system; these can include both medications prescribed to alleviate particular psychological symptoms and illicit drugs (such as LSD) that produce intense psychological effects. [24]

punisher: An event or outcome that decreases the probability of a behavior on which it is contingent. [12]

punishment: A form of instrumental learning in which execution of the designated response leads to the occurrence of an aversive stimulus. [12]

pupil: Opening in the eye through which light passes. [3]

Purkinje effect: The decrease in perceived brightness of the long-wavelength hues (e.g., red), relative to the short-wavelength hues (e.g., green), as a function of a decrease in overall illumination. [3]

quantitative genetics: The statistical theory that underlies modern behavior genetics. [16]

random: As applied to sampling from a population, random means that every member of the population has an equal chance of being included in the sample, and that the selection of one member of the sample will not alter the probability that any other member might be selected. [APP]

range: In a distribution of scores, the numerical value of the highest score minus the lowest score. [APP]

raphe system: Structure in brain that induces non-REM sleep when stimulated. [7]

rapid eye movement (REM): Phenomenon that occurs during deep sleep in which the person is behaviorally asleep but shows a waking (low amplitude, high frequency) EEG pattern and accompanying movements of the eyeballs. [7]

reaction time: The period of time that it takes to make a muscular response (such as pressing a key or lifting a finger) after receiving a sensory input (like a light or a flash). Provided that the muscular response remains the same, variations in reaction time are presumed to reflect complexity of the cognitive processes that precede the muscular movement. [2]

recall: Measure of memory in which subjects are asked to repeat information to which they were exposed previously. [13]

recessive trait: Phenotype determined by the subordinate allele, observable only when both alleles are recessive. [8]

reciprocal altruism: Altruistic acts performed by individuals who are genetically unrelated. [8]

recognition: Measure of memory in which subjects are asked to identify items of information to which they were exposed previously. [13]

reductionism: The assertion that theories about any system (such as behavior) should be expressed in the most elementary units involved. For example, if all behavior involves neural communication within the brain, then a thorough description of that communication should constitute a full explanation of the behavior. [2]

reference group: Any group that is serving as a basis for comparison or self-evaluation; the group may be either a positive or a negative reference. [20]

reflex arc: A simple nerve circuit containing an afferent neuron, an interneuron or connecting nerve, and an efferent nerve. [5]

reinforcement: Provision of reward for behavior. This reward can take either the form of presentation of a pleasant stimulus ("positive reinforcement") or removal of a noxious stimulus ("negative reinforcement"). [2]

reinforcement contingency: Basic principle of instrumental conditioning in which the delivery of the reinforcer or punisher depends on the prior execution of the response. [12]

reinforcer: An event or outcome that increases the probability of a behavior on which it is contingent. [12]

releasing stimulus: An environmental stimulus that triggers a fixed-action pattern. [8]

reliability: A measure of the consistency of a psychological test. [22]

REM deprivation: Procedure in which a subject is awakened upon entering REM sleep. [7]

replication: Repeating an experimental procedure in a different setting (and perhaps with minor changes in method) in an attempt to corroborate findings achieved from an earlier study. Replication is made simpler if there have been operational definitions of the terms. [2]

representation: A mental "picture" of an absent object, person, or event. An internal symbolic substitute for the external object or person. [16]

representativeness heuristic: Kind of heuristic in which a subject concludes that items are members of a category simply because they fit a preconceived model of that category. [15]

repression: The Freudian defense mechanism through which psychic energy is used to force unwanted thoughts out of conscious awareness. [18]

resolution phase: Fourth phase of the human sexual response cycle involving a decline in tension in the male but not necessarily in the female. [10]

resting potential: The electrical potential across the membrane of a neuron while in the unstimulated state. [5]

resultant achievement motivation: Summation of motive to succeed and motive to avoid failure. [11]

reticular activating system (RAS): A structure in the metencephalon that is involved with physiological arousal. [5]

retina: The innermost, light-sensitive surface on the interior of the eye. [3]

retrograde amnesia: Inability to remember material learned prior to the administration of electroconvulsive therapy (ECT). [25]

reward conditioning: A form of instrumental learning in which execution of the designated response leads to the occurrence of an appetitive stimulus such as food. [12]

rhodopsin: Light-sensitive, visual pigments in the rod receptors. [3]

right to treatment: A legal principle governing the psychological treatment of a person involuntarily committed to a mental institution: The deprivation of liberty for the purpose of providing treatment requires that legitimate treatment be provided by the state. [25]

rod: Achromatic photoreceptor in the retina. [3]

Ruffini ending: Nerve ending thought to mediate the sensation of heat. [3]

S-O-R model: The view of psychology, traced to Woodworth, that observable responses (R) reflect not only observable stimuli (S), but also any of several mediating processes within the organism (O). This view contrasts with radical behaviorism. [2]

sample: A subset of a population, a group selected from the members of a population according to some consistent principle. [APP]

sampling distribution: A distribution of values, each of which has been computed from one of the samples of size *n* taken from a population. [APP]

saturation: Purity of hue. [3]

scala tympani: Section of the cochlea created by the cochlear partition. [3]

scala vestibuli: Section of the cochlea created by the cochlear partition. [3]

scatterplot: A visual representation of the correlation between two variables. Each observation in the scatterplot is a single point positioned at the intersection of the X value for one individual and the Y value for the same individual. [22, APP]

schedule of reinforcement: System or rule for presenting reinforcement intermittently. [12]

schema (pl: **schemata**): An interconnected set of propositions or elements; a more holistic segment of knowledge. [14]

schizophrenia: The term, coined by Bleuler, for the set of psychological symptoms characterized primarily by profound thought disorder. Derived from the Greek words for "to split" and "mind," the term describes the lack of connection between thought and emotion or action. [24]

sclerotic coat: Outermost protective layer of the eye. [3]

script: A sequence of behavioral events; a form of procedural knowledge. [16]

second-order conditioning: Phenomenon in which a CS gains strength because of being paired with another already strong CS. [12]

secondary sex characteristic: Manifest sexual characteristic such as the developed genitalia. [10]

selective attention: Finding that subjects ignore most stimuli and process only selected items of information. [13]

self: The totality of answers to the question "Who am I?" usually including inner experience, awareness, observable capabilities, and material possessions. [19]

self-actualization: The highest level of motivation according to Maslow's theory is the need for self-actualization. [11]

self-esteem: Positive feelings of self-worth, usually defined as the ratio of one's successes to one's pretensions. [19]

self-presentation: The social behavior involved in the creation and maintenance of a public self. [19]

semantic memory: Abstract general knowledge, including knowledge of words and their referents, the meanings of objects, rules for manipulating words and symbols, and rules for deriving solutions to problems. [14]

semantic priming effect: Phenomenon showing that the meaning of words just encountered affects one's ability to interpret words presented later on. [14]

semicircular canals: Three semicircular tubes in the inner ear, lying roughly at right angles to each other, that help control balance. [3]

sensation: Experience of feeling or awareness produced by stimulation of a sense receptor; the process of sensing. [3]

sensorimotor period: In Piaget's theory of cognitive development, the period extending from birth to about age 2. During this period, subdivided into six stages, the child changes from responding purely by reflex action to inventing new behaviors through mental combinations of elements. [16]

sensory (afferent) neuron: Nerve that carries information from various locations in the body to the brain. [5]

sensory preconditioning: Phenomenon in which two CS's become associated. [12]

sensory threshold: The point at which a physical stimulus becomes strong enough to trigger a psychological sensation. [1]

septum: Structure in the limbic system that inhibits the amygdala. [6]

serotonin: A neurotransmitter that affects sleep; important in the raphe system. [5]

sex: Physical characteristics of an individual pertaining to human reproduction. [10]

sex differences: Any well-established differences in behavior between males and females, regardless of how that difference might have come about. [20]

shadowed message: Message in a dichotic listening experiment that is repeated as it is received in one of the ears. [13]

shadowing: A cue for depth created by the shadows either cast upon an object or cast by the object onto another surface. [4]

shape constancy: The perception of an object as retaining the same shape despite a change in the viewing angle. [4]

short-term memory: Memory storage system in which about seven items of information may be retained for up to about 15 seconds. Evidence suggests that the primary basis according to which the information is stored is its sound. [13]

sign stimulus: A releasing stimulus. [8]

simple phobia: A psychological disturbance characterized by a persistent fear of a particular feature of the environment. [24]

simultaneous conditioning: Classical conditioning procedure in which the CS is presented at the same time as the US. [12]

situationism: The view that behavior is largely determined by forces in the situation; that in any setting people will respond in much the same manner regardless of their own personality structure. [21]

size constancy: The perception of an object as being the same size despite a change in the size of the retinal image. [4]

sleep: A state of decreased awareness or loss of consciousness involving behavioral inactivity and various brain-wave patterns. [7]

sleep apnea: A sleep disorder in which breathing stops for ten seconds or more. [7]

sleep cycle: Five stages of sleep. [7]

social cognition: The cognitive processes of perception, categorization, memory, and inference that are involved in gathering, organizing, and interpreting information about social beings. [19]

social comparison: Evaluation of one's opinions and abilities by reference to the opinions or abilities of similar other people. [19]

social dilemma: A social exchange in which the immediate short-term interests of any individual are in conflict with the collective long-term interest of the group. [20]

social influence: Attitudinal or behavioral change brought about by the application of social power. Actual change in a target person's behavior. [20]

social learning theory: Theory claiming that aggression and other forms of behavior are learned from other people. [10]

social power: The capacity of a person to affect the behavior of another person or a group in the absence of forces to the contrary. [20]

social reality: The consensus about a situation or an attitude issue reached by social comparison among members of a group. [20]

sociobiology: The study of social behavior from an evolutionary perspective. [8]

sodium-potassium pump: A neuronal mechanism that transports positively charged sodium ions to the outside of the cell wall. [5]

soft determinism: The philosophical and psychological view that human behavior is caused by prior events, some of which might be choices made by the individual. [1]

somatogenesis: The "medical model" of psychological disorder. The model thus assumes that there are physical causes for all psychological disorder and that correction of these physical problems will eliminate the psychological disturbance. [24]

somatotypes: Sheldon's type theory of personality that classified people according to body type—mesomorphs, ectomorphs, and endomorphs—and assumed that each body type was associated with a different collection of personality traits. [21]

spatial acuity: The extent to which two objects can be distinguished in space. [3]

spatial agnosia: A condition associated with occipital lobe damage in which a person has defective depth perception. [5]

specific nerve energies: The early physiological theory, proposed by Muller, that the nature of a psychological situation depends on the kind of nerve that is stimulated, rather than on the characteristics of the external objects causing the stimulation. [1]

spindle: Half-second burst of high-frequency EEG pattern. [7]

spreading activation model: Theory claiming that the relationships between concepts depends on their semantic relatedness. [14]

standard deviation: A measure of the variability in a distribution of scores; the square root of the variance. [22, APP]

stapes: Bone in the middle ear connecting the tympanic membrane and the oval window. [3]

state theory of hypnosis: Theory claiming that during hypnosis, a person is in an altered state of consciousness. [7]

statistical prediction: The use of formal statistical procedures to combine the information from a battery of psychological tests. Statistical prediction, which typically takes into account the psychometric properties (such as reliability and validity) of the tests involved, is often contrasted with clinical prediction. [24]

statistically significant: A way to describe the strength of a statistical test. Any statistical comparison, such as a measure of association or difference, produces a numerical value for what is known as the "test statistic." If the test statistic is large enough that there is only a 1 in 20 probability that it could have been produced by random variation, then by convention it is considered statistically significant. [22]

stereochemical theory: "Lock and key" theory of smell claiming that perceived odorant quality results from a physical match between the odorous molecule and a particular kind of receptor. [3]

stereoscope: A device for presenting each eye with a slightly different two-dimensional view of an object, thus creating a sense of depth. [4]

stereotype: An inflexible image of the members of an identifiable group; a belief that each group member possesses all of the attributes ever associated with the group. [19]

stimulant: Drug such as caffeine, nicotine, amphetamine, or cocaine that activates the central nervous system. [7]

stress: The psychological and physiological reaction to noxious stimuli (stressors) outside the individual. [23]

stressor: Any noxious stimulus in the environment. [23]

structuralism: An early approach to psychology that concentrated on searching for the irreducible building blocks of conscious mental experience. [2]

subcutaneous tissue: A main layer of the skin. [3]

subfornical organ: Area of the brain responsible for detecting angiotensin II. [9]

superego: In Freudian theory, the idealized internal moral judge consisting of the conscience and the ego ideal (the internalized version of parental expectations). [21]

superior colliculi: Structures in the tectum that are part of the visual pathways. [5]

supernormal stimulus: A stimulus containing a critical feature of a releasing stimulus such that an exaggerated reaction occurs. [8]

surface structure: The particular sequence of words and phrases that make up a sentence, as opposed to the underlying meaning of the sentence (which might be expressed in many different ways). [17]

sustentacular cell: Cell in the olfactory epithelium that provides physical support for the smell receptors. [3]

symbolic function: In Piaget's theory of cognitive development, the cognitive process by which internal symbols ("signifiers") are differentiated from the external objects and people ("significates") they represent. [16]

sympathetic nervous system: One portion of the ANS associated with the regulation of energy expenditure. [6]

synapse: Small gap between neurons. [5]

synaptic cleft: Small space between the terminal buttons of the presynaptic neuron and the postsynaptic neuron. [5]

synaptic vesicle: Sac containing a transmitter substance. [5]

syndromes: Collections of psychological symptoms that regularly occur together. [24]

syntax: The orderly system of language that regulates the way words are combined into clauses, phrases, and sentences. [17]

systematic desensitization: A behavioral therapy for anxiety that combines deep relaxation with increasingly vivid and powerful representations of the feared stimulus. [25]

tabula rasa: Literally, "blank slate," referring to the idea that the human mind is empty at birth. On this view the contents of mind and the processes by which those contents might change are provided by experience. [1, 15]

tardive dyskinesia: A loss of control over particular muscle groups (such as muscles of the head, mouth, and tongue) that occurs long after treatment with antipsychotic medication. These drug side effects are often quite difficult to distinguish from the effects of other neurological disorders, such as Parkinson's disease. [25]

taste bud: Taste receptor. [3]

tectum: A structure in the mesencephalon that is made up of the superior and inferior colliculi. [5]

tegmentum: Anterior portion of the mesencephalon. [5]

telencephalon: A division of the brain containing the limbic system. [5]

template: A standardized form of an image. [13]

temporal acuity: The extent to which two objects can be distinguished in time. [3]

temporal lobe: The side portion of the neocortex that mediates audition, speech, memory, and emotion. [5]

terminal button: Structure found at the end of the nerve axon containing transmitter substances. [5]

test battery: A collection of psychological assessment procedures. [22]

testes: Male sex glands. [10]

testosterone: Male sex hormone; most common androgen. [10]

texture gradient: A cue for depth created by the change in density of the elements that constitute a perceived object. [4]

thalamic theory of emotion: Theory claiming that the disinhibiting of the thalamus is the source of emotion. [6]

thalamus: An important relay junction for sensory neurons lying in the diencephalon. [5]

Thanatos: In Freudian personality theory, the death instincts that underlie all aggressive and destructive behavior. [21]

Thematic Apperception Test (TAT): Projective test of various needs including need for achievement. Subjects are shown ambiguous pictures and asked to relate a story. The person's needs are determined from the imagery used to describe the picture. [11]

theta wave: EEG pattern characterized by its low frequency (about 4 to 7 Hz). [7]

token economy: A structured social system, usually in a mental hospital, in which psychologically healthy responses and behaviors are reinforced with tokens that can be exchanged for meals and luxuries. [25]

top-down processing: Kind of information processing in which a subject recognizes stimuli in light of expectations derived from prior knowledge and the context. [13]

total sleep deprivation: Procedure in which subject is deprived of all sleep. [7]

traits: Dispositional characteristics of personality; enduring structures that guide the person's adaptation to the demands of the environment. [21]

transference: In psychoanalytic treatment, the point at which the client begins to react to the therapist in an emotionally charged fashion that would really be appropriate only for a person (i.e., a parent) from the client's childhood. [25]

transformation: The basic cognitive process in Piaget's theory of cognitive development; the mental or physical activity that enables a child to know the external world by taking it apart and reassembling it. [16]

transformational grammar: A theory of language production. The theory holds that sentences have a deep structure (fundamental meaning) that can be modified by transformational rules to produce different sentences that nevertheless retain the original meaning. [17]

trichromatic theory: Theory of color vision claiming that various hues are produced through a combination of three kinds of cone receptors. [3]

tricyclic antidepressants: A class of psychotropic medication, named for the shape of its chemical structure, useful in treating the symptoms of depression. Tricyclics act to prevent the reabsorption of norepinephrine, thereby increasing activation. [24]

tympanic membrane: Membrane separating the outer ear from the middle ear, vibrations of which are transmitted to the middle ear; eardrum. [3]

Type A: A personality style characterized by hostility, aggressiveness, and extremes of time urgency and competitiveness. The hostility component, at least, has been implicated as an independent risk factor for the development of coronary heart disease. [23]

unconditioned response (UR): The reaction elicited by an unconditioned stimulus. [12]

unconditioned stimulus (US): A biologically potent stimulus that reliably produces a reflexive reaction. [12]

unconscious: In Freudian and other psychodynamic theories of personality, the region of the mind that contains instincts, wishes, and impulses, many of which are socially unacceptable. [21]

unshadowed message: Message in a dichotic listening experiment not shadowed by the subject. [13]

validity: The extent to which a psychological test actually measures what it was designed to measure. [22]

variable interval (VI) schedule: A basic reinforcement schedule in which the reward is delivered once the organism performs the desired responses and an interval of time has elapsed, although the exact length of the interval varies from one reward to the next. [12]

variable ratio (VR) schedule: A basic reinforcement schedule in which reward is delivered once the organism has performed a certain number of responses, although the actual number varies from one reward to the next. [12]

variance: A measure of variability in a distribution of scores; the average discrepancy of scores from their mean. [APP]

ventromedial hypothalamus: Area of the diencephalon originally believed to be the satiety center. [9]

vestibule: Middle portion of the inner ear. [3]

vigilance: According to the decision-making model of coping with stress, the psychological state that best prepares the individual for successful coping. Vigilance comes about only if the person recognizes the seriousness of the risks, knows that immediately available responses may not be sufficient, and has had the opportunity to investigate alternative avenues of escape. [23]

viscerogenic need: Need, such as food or water, related to the biological survival of an organism. [11]

visual agnosia: A condition associated with occipital lobe damage in which a person cannot easily discriminate visual stimuli. [5]

visual cliff: An apparatus used to test depth perception. [4]

volley principle: Groups of fibers on the basilar membrane fire in a synchronized fashion as squads rather than in unison. [3]

wavelength: The distance between peaks of a wave. [3]

within-item elaboration: Analyzing or processing information in terms of its own features or characteristics. [13]

word superiority effect: Phenomenon demonstrating top-down processing in which letters are recognized more quickly when they help form sensible words than when they do not. [13]

zero-sum game: A social interaction in which all the gains achieved by one party are obtained at the expense of the other parties involved. [20]

REFERENCES

Numbers in brackets refer to chapters in which entries are cited. (APP refers to the Appendix, "An Introduction to Research Methods and Statistics in Psychology.")

Abplanalp, J. M., Rose, R. D. M., Donnelly, A. F., & Livingston-Vaughn, L. (1979). Psychoendocrinology of the menstrual cycle: II. The relationship between enjoyment of activities, moods, and reproductive hormones. *Psychosomatic Medicine, 41,* 605–615. [10]

Abramson, L. Y., Seligman, M. E. P., & Teasdale, J. D. (1978). Learned helplessness in humans: Critique and reformulation. *Journal of Abnormal Psychology, 87,* 49–74. [24, 25]

Adam, K. (1980). Sleep as a restorative process and a theory to explain why. *Progress in Brain Research, 53,* 289–305. [7]

Adams, G. R., Abraham, K. G., & Markstrom, C. A. (1987). The relations among identity development, self-consciousness, and self-focusing during middle and late adolescence. *Developmental Psychology, 23,* 292–297. [18]

Adams, J. S. (1965). Inequity in social exchange. In L. Berkowitz (Ed.), *Advances in experimental social psychology* (Vol. 2, pp. 267–299). New York: Academic Press. [20]

Adler, A. (1935). The fundamental views of individual psychology. *International Journal of Individual Psychology, 1,* 5–8. [21]

Aggleton, J. P., & Mishkin, M. (1986). The amygdala: Sensory gateway to the emotions. In R. Plutchik & H. Kellerman (Eds.), *Emotion: Theory, research, and experience: Vol. 3. Biological foundations of emotion* (pp. 281–299). Orlando, FL: Academic Press. [6, 10]

Aggleton, J. P., & Passingham, R. E. (1981). Syndrome produced by lesions of the amygdala in monkeys (*Mucaca mulatta*). *Journal of Comparative and Physiological Psychology, 95,* 961–977. [6]

Agnew, H. W., Webb, W. B., & Williams, R. L. (1964). The effects of stage four sleep deprivation. *Electroencephalography and Clinical Neurophysiology, 27,* 68–70. [7]

Ahlgren, A., & Johnson, D. W. (1979). Sex differences in cooperative and competitive attitudes from the 2nd through the 12th grades. *Developmental Psychology, 15,* 45–49. [11]

Aiken, L. R. (1989). *Assessment of personality.* Boston: Allyn & Bacon. [21, 22]

Ainsworth, M. D. S., Blehar, M., Waters, E., & Wall, S. (1978). *Patterns of attachment.* Hillsdale, NJ: Lawrence Erlbaum Associates. [18]

Ainsworth, M. D. S., & Wittig, B. A. (1969). Attachment and exploratory behavior of one-year-olds in a strange situation. In B. M. Foss (Ed.), *Determinants of infant behaviour* (Vol. 4, pp. 111–136). London: Methuen. [18]

Aitchison, J. (1983). *The articulate mammal: An introduction to psycholinguistics* (2nd ed.). New York: Universe Books. [17]

Ajzen, I., & Madden, T. J. (1986). Prediction of goal-directed behavior: Attitudes, intentions, and perceived behavioral control. *Journal of Experimental Social Psychology, 22,* 453–474. [19]

Allen, B. P., & Potkay, C. R. (1981). On the arbitrary distinction between states and traits. *Journal of Personality and Social Psychology, 41,* 916–928. [21]

Allen, J. B., Kenrick, D. T., Linder, D. E., & McCall, M. A. (1989). Arousal and attraction: A response-facilitation alternative to misattribution and negative-reinforcement models. *Journal of Personality and Social Psychology, 57,* 261–270. [6]

Allen, V. L. (1975). Social support for nonconformity. In L. Berkowitz

(Ed.), *Advances in experimental social psychology* (Vol. 8, pp. 2–43). New York: Academic Press. [20]

Allison, T., & Cicchetti, D. V. (1976). Sleep in mammals: Ecological and constitutional correlates. *Science, 194,* 732–734. [7]

Alloy, L. B., & Abramson, L. Y. (1979). Judgment of contingency in depressed and nondepressed students: Sadder but wiser? *Journal of Experimental Psychology: General, 108,* 441–485. [24]

Allport, G. W. (1935). Attitudes. In C. Murchison (Ed.), *Handbook of social psychology* (pp. 798–884). Worcester, MA: Clark University Press. [19]

Allport, G. W. (1937). *Personality: A psychological interpretation.* New York: Holt, Rinehart, & Winston. [21]

Allport, G. W., & Odbert, H. S. (1936). Trait names: A psycholexical study. *Psychological Monographs, 47* (1, Whole No. 211). [21]

American Psychiatric Association. (1987). *Diagnostic and statistical manual of mental disorders* (3rd rev. ed.). Washington, DC: Author. [24, 25]

Amoore, J. E. (1969). A plan to identify most of the primary odors. In C. Pfaffmann (Ed.), *Olfaction and taste III* (pp. 158–171). New York: Rockefeller University Press. [3]

Amoore, J. E. (1970). *Molecular basis of odor.* Springfield, IL: Thomas. [3]

Anderson, D. E. (1985). Behavioral stress and experimental hypertension. In T. M. Field, P. M. McCabe, & N. Schneiderman (Eds.), *Stress and coping* (pp. 117–133). Hillsdale, NJ: Lawrence Erlbaum Associates. [23]

Anderson, J. R. (1991). The adaptive nature of human categorization.

Psychological Review, 98, 409–429. [14]

Anderson, N. H., & Cuneo, D. O. (1978). The height + width rule in children's judgments of quantity. *Journal of Experimental Psychology: General, 107,* 335–378. [16]

Anderson, R. C., Reynolds, R. E., Schallert, D. L., & Goetz, E. T. (1977). Frameworks for comprehending discourse. *American Educational Research Journal, 14,* 367–382. [14]

Andrews, E. A., & Braveman, N. S. (1975). The combined effects of dosage level and interstimulus interval on the formation of one-trial poison-based aversions in rats. *Animal Learning and Behavior, 3,* 287–289. [12]

Angell, J. R., & Moore, A. W. (1896). Reaction time: A study in attention and habit. *Psychological Review, 3,* 245–258. [2]

Anisfeld, E., & Lipper, E. (1983). Early contact, social support, and mother-infant bonding. *Pediatrics, 72,* 79–83. [18]

Annett, M., & Manning, M. (1990). Arithmetic and laterality. *Neuropsychologia, 28,* 61–69. [5]

Ansbacher, H. L., & Ansbacher, R. (Eds.). (1956). *The individual psychology of Alfred Adler.* New York: Basic Books. [21]

Antelman, S. M., & Rowland, N. (1981). Endogenous opiates and stress-induced eating. *Science, 214,* 1149–1150. [9]

Antrobus, J. (1991). Dreaming: Cognitive processes during cortical activation and high afferent thresholds. *Psychological Review, 98,* 96–121. [7]

Apple, W., Streeter, L. A., & Krauss, R. M. (1977). Effects of pitch and speech rate on personal attributions. *Journal of Personality and Social Psychology, 37,* 715–727. [19]

Aristotle. (1952). *Metaphysics* (W. D. Ross, Trans.). In R. M. Hutchens (Ed.), *Great books of the Western world* (Vol. 8, pp. 499–626). Chicago: Encyclopaedia Britannica. [1]

Aristotle. (1952). *Nichomachean ethics* (W. D. Ross, Trans.) In R. M.

Hutchens (Ed.), *Great books of the Western world* (Vol. 9, pp. 335–436). Chicago: Encyclopaedia Britannica. [20, 24]

Aristotle. (1952). *On the soul* (J. A. Smith, Trans.). In R. M. Hutchens (Ed.), *Great books of the Western world* (Vol. 8, pp. 631–668). Chicago: Encyclopaedia Britannica. [1]

Arkes, H. R. (1987). Clinical judgment. In R. J. Corsini (Ed.), *Encyclopedia of psychology* (pp. 198–199). New York: Wiley. [24]

Arkin, A. M., & Antrobus, J. S. (1978). The effects of external stimuli applied prior to and during sleep on sleep experience. In A. M. Arkin, J. S. Antrobus, & S. J. Ellman (Eds.), *The mind in sleep: Psychology and psychophysiology* (pp. 351–391). Hillsdale, NJ: Lawrence Erlbaum Associates. [7]

Arnauld, E., Dufy, B., & Vincent, J. D. (1975). Hypothalamic supra optic neurons: Rates and patterns of action potential firing during water deprivation in the unanesthetized monkey. *Brain Research, 100,* 315–325. [9]

Asch, S. (1951). Effects of group pressure on the modification and distortion of judgments. In H. Guetzkow (Ed.), *Groups, leadership, and men* (pp. 177–190). Pittsburgh: Carnegie Press. [20]

Aschoff, J. (1965). Circadian rhythms in man. *Science, 148,* 1427–1432. [7]

Aserinsky, E., & Kleitman, N. (1953). Regularly occurring periods of eye motility and concomitant phenomena during sleep. *Science, 118,* 273–274. [7]

Ashby, W. R. (1956). *An introduction of cybernetics.* London: Methuen. [9]

Astley S. L., & Perkins, C. C. (1985). Stimulus duration and conditioned reinforcing value measured by a learning-tests procedure. *Animal Learning and Behavior, 13,* 18–24. [12]

Atkinson, J. W. (1964). *An introduction to motivation.* New York: Van Nostrand. [11]

Atkinson, J. W., & Birch, D. (1978). *An introduction to motivation* (2nd ed.). New York: Van Nostrand. [11]

Atkinson, J. W., & Litwin, G. H. (1960). Achievement motive and test anxiety conceived as a motive to approach success and to avoid failure. *Journal of Abnormal and Social Psychology, 60,* 52–63. [11]

Atkinson, R. C. (1975). Mnemotechnics in second-language learning. *American Psychologist, 30,* 821–828. [14]

Atkinson, R. C., & Shiffrin, R. M. (1968). Human memory: A proposed system and its control processes. In K. W. Spence & J. T. Spence (Eds.), *The psychology of learning and motivation* (Vol. 2, pp. 89 195). New York: Academic Press. [13]

Attneave, F. (1954). Some informational aspects of visual perception. *Psychological Review, 61,* 183–193. [4]

Attneave, F. (1955). Symmetry, information, and memory for patterns. *American Journal of Psychology, 68,* 209–222. [4]

Avant, L. L. (1965). Vision in the ganzfeld. *Psychological Bulletin, 64,* 246–258. [4]

Averbach, E., & Coriell, A. S. (1961). Short-term memory in vision. *Bell Systems Technical Journal, 40,* 309–328. [13]

Avis, H. H. (1974). The neuropharmacology of aggression: A critical review. *Psychological Bulletin, 81,* 47–63. [10]

Ayllon, T., & Haughton, E. (1964). Modification of symptomatic verbal behaviour of mental patients. *Behavior Research and Therapy, 2,* 87–97. [12]

Baddeley, A. D. (1972). Retrieval-rules and semantic coding in short-term memory. *Psychological Bulletin, 78,* 379–385. [13]

Baddeley, A. D. (1978). The trouble with levels: A reexamination of Craik and Lockhart's framework for memory research. *Psychological Review, 85,* 139–152. [14]

Baddeley, A. D., & Hitch, G. J. (1977). Recency re-examined. In

S. Dornic (Ed.), *Attention and performance* (Vol. 6, pp. 646–667). Hillsdale, NJ: Lawrence Erlbaum Associates. [14]

Baddeley, A. D., & Levy, B. A. (1971). Semantic coding and memory. *Journal of Experimental Psychology, 89*, 132–136. [13]

Bahrick, H. P., Bahrick, P. O., & Wittlinger, R. P. (1975). Fifty years of memory for names and faces: A cross-sectional approach. *Journal of Experimental Psychology: General, 104*, 54–75. [13]

Bakan, D. (1966). *The duality of human existence: An essay on psychology and religion.* Chicago: Rand McNally. [20]

Baldwin, J. M. (1895). *Mental development in the child and the race: Methods and processes.* New York: Macmillan. [16]

Baldwin, J. M., & Shaw, W. J. (1895). Types of reaction. *Psychological Review, 2*, 259–273. [2]

Bandura, A. (1973). *Aggression: A social learning analysis.* Englewood Cliffs, NJ: Prentice-Hall. [10]

Bandura, A. (1977). *Social learning theory.* Englewood Cliffs, NJ: Prentice-Hall. [10, 21]

Bandura, A. (1978). The self system in reciprocal determinism. *American Psychologist, 33*, 344–358. [21]

Bandura, A. (1983). Psychological mechanisms of aggression. In R. G. Geen & E. I. Donnerstein (Eds.), *Aggression: Theoretical and empirical reviews* (Vol. 1, pp. 1–40). New York: Academic Press. [10]

Bandura, A., Ross, D., & Ross, S. A. (1963). Vicarious reinforcement and imitative learning. *Journal of Abnormal and Social Psychology, 67*, 601–607. [10]

Banks, M. S., & Salapatek, P. (1983). Infant visual perception. In P. H. Mussen (Ed.), *Handbook of child psychology* (4th ed., Vol. 2; pp. 435–571). New York: Wiley. [16]

Barash, D. P. (1977). *Sociobiology and behavior.* New York: Elsevier. [8]

Barber, T. X. (1969). *Hypnosis: A scientific approach.* New York: Van Nostrand-Reinhold. [7]

Barber, T. X. (1979). Suggested ('hypnotic') behaviour: The trance paradigm versus an alternative paradigm. In E. Fromm & R. E. Shor (Eds.), *Hypnosis: Developments in research and new perspectives* (pp. 217–271). New York: Aldine. [7]

Barker, S. L., Funk, S. C., & Houston, B. K. (1988). Psychological treatment versus nonspecific factors: A meta-analysis of conditions that engender comparable expectations for improvement. *Clinical Psychology Review, 8*, 579–594. [25]

Baron, R. A. (1977). *Human aggression.* New York: Plenum. [10]

Barr, H. L., Langs, R. J., Holt, R. R., Goldberger, L., & Klein, G. S. (1972). *LSD: Personality and experience.* New York: Wiley. [7]

Barr, W. B., Goldberg, E., Wasserstein, S., & Novelly, R. A. (1990). Retrograde amnesia following unilateral temporal lobectomy. *Neuropsychologia, 28*, 243–255. [5]

Barraclough, B. M., Nelson, B., Bunch, J., & Sainsbury, P. (1969). The diagnostic classification and psychiatric treatment of 100 suicides. *Proceedings of the Fifth International Conference for Suicide Prevention.* London. [24]

Barry, D. (1990). *Dave Barry turns 40.* New York: Fawcett Columbine. [20]

Bartlett, F. C. (1932). *Remembering: A study in experimental and social psychology.* Cambridge, England: Cambridge University Press. [14]

Bates, E. (1984). Bioprograms and the innateness hypothesis. *Behavioral and Brain Sciences, 7*, 188–190. [17]

Bateson, G., Jackson, D. D., Haley, J., & Weakland, J. H. (1956). Toward a theory of schizophrenia. *Behavioral Science, 1*, 251–264. [24]

Battig, W. F., & Montague, W. E. (1969). Category norms for verbal items in 56 categories: A replication and extension of the Connecticut category norms. *Journal of Experimental Psychology, 80*(3, Pt. 2). [17]

Bauer, R. M. (1982). Visual hypoemotionality as a symptom of visual-limbic disconnection in man. *Archives of Neurology (Chicago), 39*, 702–708. [6]

Baum, A., Davidson, L. M., Singer, J. E., & Street, S. W. (1987). Stress as a psychophysiological process. In A. Baum & J. E. Singer (Eds.), *Handbook of psychology and health: Vol. 5: Stress* (pp. 1–24). Hillsdale, NJ: Lawrence Erlbaum Associates. [23]

Baumrind, D. (1964). Some thoughts on the ethics of research: After reading Milgram's "Behavioral study of obedience." *American Psychologist, 19*, 421–423. [20]

Baxtrom v. Herold, 383 U.S. 107 (1966). [25]

Bayley, N. (1933). *The California First-Year Mental Scale.* Berkeley: University of California Press. [16]

Bayley, N. (1968). Behavioral correlates of mental growth: Birth to thirty-six years. *American Psychologist, 23*, 1–17. [22]

Bayley, N. (1969). *Bayley scales of infant development.* San Antonio, TX: The Psychological Corporation. [16]

Beaumont, J. G. (Ed.). (1983). *Introduction to neuropsychology.* New York: Guilford Press. [5]

Beck, A. T. (1967). *Depression: Clinical, experimental, and theoretical aspects.* New York: Hoeber. [24]

Becker, J. T., Furman, J. M. R., Panisset, M., & Smith, C. (1990). Characteristics of the memory loss of a patient with Wernicke-Korsakoff's syndrome without alcoholism. *Neuropsychologia, 28*, 171–179. [5]

Bedrosian, R. C., & Beck, A. T. (1980). Principles of cognitive therapy. In M. J. Mahoney (Ed.), *Psychotherapy process: Current issues and future directions.* New York: Plenum. [25]

Begg, I., & Denny, P. (1969). Empirical reconciliation of atmosphere and conversion interpretations of syllogistic reasoning errors. *Journal of Experimental Psychology, 81*, 351–354. [15]

Beit-Hallahmi, B. (1980). Achievement motivation and economic growth: A replication. *Personality* and *Social Psychology Bulletin, 6,* 210–215. [11]

Békésy, G. von. (1960). *Experiments in hearing.* New York: McGraw-Hill. [3]

Békésy, G. von. (1964). Sweetness produced electrically on the tongue and its relation to taste theories. *Journal of Applied Physiology, 19,* 1105–1113. [3]

Békésy, G. von. (1966). Taste theories and the chemical stimulation of single papillae. *Journal of Applied Physiology, 21,* 1–9. [3]

Bellack, A. S., Hersen, M., & Turner, S. M. (1976). Generalization effects of social skills training in chronic schizophrenics: An experimental analysis. *Behavior Research and Therapy, 14,* 391–398. [25]

Belleza, F. S., Richards, D. L., & Geiselman, R. E. (1976). Semantic processing and organization in free recall. *Memory & Cognition, 4,* 415–421. [14]

Belluzzi, J. D., & Stein, L. (1977). Enkephalin may mediate euphoria and drive-reduction reward. *Nature (London), 226,* 556–558. [7]

Belsky, J. K. (1984). *The psychology of aging: Theory, research, and interventions.* Pacific Grove, CA: Brooks/Cole. [18]

Belsky, J. K. (1988). The "effects" of infant day care reconsidered. Special issue: Infant day care. *Early Childhood Research Quarterly, 3,* 235–272. [18]

Belsky, J. K. (1990). *The psychology of aging: Theory, research, and interventions* (2nd ed.). Pacific Grove, CA: Brooks/Cole. [18]

Belsky, J. K., & Rovine, M. J. (1988). Nonmaternal care in the first year of life and the security of infant-parent attachment. *Child Development, 59,* 157–167. [18]

Bem, D. J. (1972). Self-perception theory. In L. Berkowitz (Ed.), *Advances in experimental social psychology* (Vol. 6, pp. 2–62). New York: Academic Press. [19]

Bem, D. J., & Allen, A. (1974). On predicting some of the people some of the time: The search for cross-situational consistencies in behavior. *Psychological Review, 81,* 506–520. [21]

Bem, D. J., & Funder, D. C. (1978). Predicting more of the people more of the time: Assessing the personality of situations. *Psychological Review, 85,* 485–501. [21]

Bem, S. L. (1974). The measurement of psychological androgyny. *Journal of Consulting and Clinical Psychology, 42,* 155–162. [20]

Bemis, K. M. (1978). Current approaches to the etiology and treatment of anorexia nervosa. *Psychological Bulletin, 85,* 593–617. [9]

Bemporad, J. R., & Schwab, M. E. (1986). The DSM-III and clinical child psychiatry. In T. Millon & G. L. Klerman (Eds.), *Contemporary directions in psychopathology* (pp. 135–165). New York: Guilford Press. [24]

Benton, A. L., Hannay, H. J., & Varney, N. R. (1975). Visual perception of line direction in patients with unilateral brain disease. *Neurology, 25,* 907–910. [5]

Berger, R. J. (1961). Tonus of extrinsic laryngeal muscles during sleep and dreaming. *Science, 134,* 840. [7]

Berglas, S., & Jones, E. E. (1978). Drug choice as a self-handicapping strategy in response to noncontingent success. *Journal of Personality and Social Psychology, 36,* 405–417. [19]

Berko, J. (1958). The child's learning of English. *Word, 14,* 150–177. [17]

Berkun, M. M., Kessen, M. L., & Miller, N. E. (1952). Hunger reducing effects of food by stomach fistula versus food by mouth measured by a consummatory response. *Journal of Comparative and Physiological Psychology, 45,* 550–554. [9]

Berscheid, E., Snyder, M., & Omoto, A. M. (1989). The Relationship Closeness Inventory: Assessing the closeness of interpersonal relationships. *Journal of Personality and Social Psychology, 57,* 792–807. [20]

Best, D. L., Williams, J. E., Cloud, J. M., Davis, S. W., Robertson, L. S., Edwards, J. R., Giles, E., & Fowles, J. (1977). Development of sex-trait stereotypes among young children in the United States, England, and Ireland. *Child Development, 48,* 1375–1384. [10]

Best, J. B. (1989). *Cognitive psychology* (2nd ed.). St. Paul, MN: West. [17]

Beutler, L. E., & Crago, M. (1983). Self-report measures of psychotherapy outcome. In M. J. Lambert, E. R. Christensen, & S. S. DeJulio (Eds.), *The assessment of psychotherapy outcome* (pp. 453–497). New York: Wiley. [25]

Bickerton, D. (1984). The language bioprogram hypothesis. *Behavioral and Brain Sciences, 7,* 173–221. [17]

Bills, R. E., Vance, E. L., & McLean, O. S. (1951). An index of adjustment and values. *Journal of Consulting Psychology, 15,* 257–261. [19]

Bindra, D. (1969). A unified interpretation of emotion and motivation. *Annals of the New York Academy of Sciences, 159,* 1071–1083. [6]

Binet, A., & Simon, T. (1916). *The development of intelligence in children* (E. S. Kite, Trans.). Baltimore, MD: Williams & Wilkins. [22]

Birney, R. C., Burdick, H., & Teevan, R. C. (1969). *Fear of failure motivation.* New York: Wiley. [11]

Bishop, M. P., Elder, S. T., & Heath, R. G. (1963). Intracranial self-stimulation in man. *Science, 140,* 394–396. [6]

Bloch, B., & Trager, G. L. (1942). *Outline of linguistic analysis.* Baltimore, MD: Linguistic Society of America. [17]

Bloch, S. (1991). The political misuse of psychiatry in the Soviet Union. In S. Bloch & P. Chodoff (Eds.), *Psychiatric ethics* (2nd ed., pp. 493–515). Oxford: Oxford University Press. [24]

Block, J. H. (1971). *Lives through time.* Berkeley, CA: Bancroft Books. [21]

Block, J. H. (1983). Differential premises arising from differential socialization of the sexes: Some conjectures. *Child Development, 57,* 1335–1354.

Bloomfield, L. (1933). *Language*. New York: Henry Holt. [17]

Blumenthal, J. A., & McCubbin, J. A. (1987). Physical exercise as stress management. In A. Baum & J. E. Singer (Eds.), *Handbook of psychology and health: Vol. 5: Stress* (pp. 303–331). Hillsdale, NJ: Lawrence Erlbaum Associates. [23]

Blumer, D., & Benson, D. F. (1975). Personality changes with frontal and temporal lobe lesions. In D. F. Benson & D. Blumer (Eds.), *Psychiatric aspects of neurologic disease* (pp. 151–170). New York: Grune & Stratton. [5]

Bokert, E. (1968). The effects of thirst and a related verbal stimulus on dream reports. *Dissertation Abstracts, 28,* 4753B. [7]

Bolles, R. C. (1970). Species-specific defense reactions and avoidance learning. *Psychological Review, 77,* 32–48. [12]

Bolles, R. C. (1972). The avoidance learning problem. In G. H. Bower (Ed.), *The psychology of learning and motivation* (Vol. 6, pp. 97–145). New York: Academic Press. [12]

Bolles, R. C. (1975). *Theory of motivation* (2nd ed.). New York: Harper & Row. [8]

Bolles, R. C., Hayward, L., & Crandall, C. (1981). Conditioned taste preferences based on caloric density. *Journal of Experimental Psychology: Animal Behavior Processes, 7,* 59–69. [9]

Booth, D. A. (1972). Conditioned satiety in the rat. *Journal of Comparative and Physiological Psychology, 81,* 457–471. [9]

Booth, D. A. (1977). Satiety and appetite are conditioned reactions. *Psychosomatic Medicine, 39,* 76–81. [9]

Booth, D. A., Lee, M., & McAleavey, C. (1976). Acquired sensory control of satiation in man. *British Journal of Psychology, 67,* 137–147. [9]

Bootzin, R. R., & Acocella, J. R. (1984). *Abnormal psychology: Current perspectives* (4th ed.). New York: Random House. [24, 25]

Boring, E. G. (1950). *A history of experimental psychology* (2nd ed.). New York: Appleton. [5]

Borke, H. (1975). Piaget's mountains revisited: Changes in the egocentric landscape. *Developmental Psychology, 11,* 240–243. [16]

Bouman, M. A. (1955). Absolute threshold conditions for visual perception. *Journal of the Acoustical Society of America, 45,* 36–43. [3]

Bousfield, W. A. (1953). The occurrence of clustering in recall of randomly arranged associates. *Journal of General Psychology, 49,* 229–240. [13]

Bovet, D., Bovet-Nitti, F., & Oliverio, A. (1969). Genetic aspects of learning and memory in mice. *Science, 163,* 139–149. [8]

Bower, G. H., & Trabasso, T. R. (1963). Reversals prior to solution in concept identification. *Journal of Experimental Psychology, 66,* 409–418. [15]

Bower, T. G. R. (1964). Discrimination of depth in premotor infants. *Psychonomic Science, 1,* 368. [4]

Bower, T. G. R. (1965). Stimulus variables determining space perception in infants. *Science, 149,* 88–89. [4]

Bowers, K. S. (1973). Situationism in psychology: An analysis and a critique. *Psychological Review, 80,* 307–336. [21]

Bowlby, J. (1969). *Attachment and loss: Vol. 1. Attachment.* New York: Basic Books. [18]

Bowlby, J. (1973). *Attachment and loss: Vol. 2. Separation: Anxiety and anger.* New York: Basic Books. [18]

Bowlby, J. (1980). *Attachment and loss: Vol. 3. Loss.* New York: Basic Books. [18]

Bowlby, J. (1988). *A secure base: Parent-child attachment and healthy human development.* New York: Basic Books. [18]

Brady, J. V., & Nauta, W. J. H. (1953). Subcortical mechanisms in emotional behavior: Affective changes following septal forebrain lesions in the albino rat. *Journal of Comparative and Physiological Psychology, 46,* 339–346. [6]

Brady, J. V., & Nauta, W. J. H. (1955). Subcortical mechanisms in emotional behavior: The duration of affective changes following septal and habenular lesions in the albino rat. *Journal of Comparative and Physiological Psychology, 48,* 412–420. [6]

Bransford, J. D., & Franks, J. J. (1971). The abstraction of linguistic ideas. *Cognitive Psychology, 2,* 331–350. [14]

Bray, G., & York, D. A. (1971). Genetically transmitted obesity in rodents. *Physiological Review, 51,* 598–646. [9]

Brazelton, T. B. (1990). *The earliest relationship.* Reading, MA: Addison-Wesley. [18]

Bretherton, I. (1985). Attachment theory: Retrospect and prospect. *Monographs of the Society for Research in Child Development, 50*(1 & 2), 3–35. [18]

Brigham, J. C. (1971). Ethnic stereotypes. *Psychological Bulletin, 76,* 15–38. [19]

Broadbent, D. E. (1958). *Perception and communication.* London: Pergamon. [13]

Broadbent, D. E. (1977). The hidden preattentive processes. *American Psychologist, 32,* 109–118. [13]

Brobeck, J. R. (1946). Mechanisms of the development of obesity in animals with hypothalamic lesions. *Physiological Review, 26,* 541–549. [9]

Broverman, I. K., Vogel, S. R., Broverman, D. M., Clarkson, F. E., & Rosenkrantz, P. S. (1972). Sex-role stereotypes: A current appraisal. *Journal of Social Issues, 28*(2), 59–78. [20]

Brown, N. R., Rips, L. J., & Shevell, S. K. (1985). The subjective dates of natural events in very-long-term memory. *Cognitive Psychology, 17,* 139–177. [14]

Brown, P. K., & Wald, G. (1964), Visual pigments in single rods and cones of the human retina. *Science, 144,* 45–52. [3]

Brown, R. (1958). *Words and things.* Glencoe, IL: Free Press. [17]

Brown, R. (1973). *A first language.* Cambridge, MA: Harvard University Press. [17]

Brown, R. (1986). *Social psychology: The second edition.* New York: Free Press. [17]

Brown, R., & Fraser, C. (1964). The acquisition of syntax. *Monographs of the Society for Research in Child Development, 29*(1), 43–79. [17]

Brown, R., & Kulin, K. (1977). Flashbulb memories. *Cognition, 5,* 73–99. [14]

Brown, T. S. (1975). Olfaction and taste. In B. Scharf (Ed.), *Experimental sensory psychology* (pp. 187–214). Glenview, IL: Scott Foresman. [3]

Brush, F. R., Baron, S., Froehlich, J. C., Ison, J. R., Pellegrino, L. J., Phillips, D. S., Sakellaris, P. C., & Williams, V. N. (1985). Genetic differences in avoidance learning by *Rattus norvegicus:* Escape/avoidance responding, sensitivity to electric shock, discrimination learning, and open-field behavior. *Journal of Comparative Psychology, 99,* 60–73. [8]

Brush, F. R., Del Paine, S. N., Pellegrino, L. J., Rykaszewski, I. M., Dess, N. K., & Collins, P. Y. (1988). CER suppression, passive-avoidance learning, and stress-induced suppression of drinking in the Syracuse high- and low-avoidance strains of rats (*Rattus norvegicus*). *Journal of Comparative Psychology, 102,* 337–349. [8]

Buck, R. (1975). Nonverbal communication of affect in children. *Journal of Personality and Social Psychology, 31,* 644–653. [6]

Buck, R., Savin, V. J., Miller, R. E., & Caul, W. F. (1972). Nonverbal communication of affect in humans. *Journal of Personality and Social Psychology, 23,* 362–371. [6]

Bulman, R. J., & Wortman, C. B. (1977). Attributions of blame and coping in the "real world": Severe accident victims react to their lot. *Journal of Personality and Social Psychology, 35,* 351–363. [23]

Bundesen, C., Larsen, A., & Farrell, J. E. (1983). Visual apparent movement: Transformations of size and orientation. *Perception, 12,* 549–568. [4]

Bush, L. K., Barr, C. S., McHugo, G. J., & Lanzetta, J. T. (1989). The effects of facial control and facial mimicry on subjective reactions to comedy routines. *Motivation and Emotion, 13,* 31–52. [6]

Bushman, B. J., & Cooper, M. M. (1990). Effects of alcohol on human aggression: An integrative research review. *Psychological Bulletin, 107,* 341–354. [7]

Butcher, J. N., Dahlström, W. G., Graham, J. R., Tellegen, A., & Kaemmer, B. (1989). *Minnesota Multiphasic Personality Inventory (MMPI-2). Manual for administration and scoring.* Minneapolis: University of Minnesota Press. [22]

Butters, N., Barton, M., & Brody, B. A. (1970). Role of the right parietal lobe in the mediation of cross-modal associations and reversible operations in space. *Cortex, 6,* 174–190. [5]

Byrne, D. (1964). Repression-sensitization as a dimension of personality. In B. A. Maher (Ed.), *Progress in experimental personality research* (Vol. 1, pp. 169–220). New York: Academic Press. [23]

Cabanac, M. (1971). Physiological role of pleasure. *Science, 173,* 1103–1107. [9]

Cadoret, R. (1986). Epidemiology of antisocial personality. In W. H. Reid, D. Dorr, J. L. Walker, & J. W. Bonner (Eds.), *Unmasking the psychopath: Antisocial personality and related syndromes* (pp. 28–44). New York: Norton. [24]

Camp, D. S., Raymond, G. A., & Church, R. M. (1967). Temporal relationship between response and punishment. *Journal of Experimental Psychology, 74,* 114–123. [12]

Campbell, D. T., & Stanley, J. C. (1966). *Experimental and quasi-experimental designs for research.* Chicago: Rand McNally. [25]

Campbell, F. W., & Maffei, L. (1974). Contrast and spatial frequency. *Scientific American, 231,* 106–114. [4]

Campbell, P. A., & Cohen, J. J. (1985). Effects of stress on the immune response. In T. M. Field, P. M. McCabe, and N. Schneiderman (Eds.), *Stress and coping* (pp. 135–145). Hillsdale, NJ: Lawrence Erlbaum Associates. [23]

Campos, J. J., Barrett, K. C., Lamb, M. E., Goldsmith, H. H., & Stenberg, C. (1983). Socioemotional development. In P. H. Mussen (Ed.), *Handbook of child psychology* (4th ed., Vol. 2, pp. 783–915). New York: Wiley. [18]

Campos, J. J., Langer, A., & Krowitz, A. (1970). Cardiac responses on the visual cliff in prelocomotor human infants. *Science, 170,* 196–197. [4]

Candland, D. K. (1977). The persistent problems of emotion. In D. K. Candland, J. P. Fell, E. Keen, A. I. Leshner, R. M. Tarpy, & R. Pultchik, *Emotion* (pp. 1–84). Monterey, CA: Brooks/Cole. [6]

Cannon, W. B. (1927). The James-Lange theory of emotions: A critical examination and an alternation. *American Journal of Psychology, 39,* 106–124. [6]

Cannon, W. B. (1929). *Bodily changes in pain, hunger, fear, and rage* (2nd ed.). New York: Appleton. [6]

Cannon, W. B. (1931). Again the James-Lange and the thalamic theories of emotion. *Psychological Review, 38,* 281–295. [6]

Cannon, W. B. (1935). Stress and strains of homeostasis. *American Journal of Medical Science, 189,* 1. [23]

Cannon, W. B. (1966). *The wisdom of the body.* New York: Norton. (Original work published 1933) [9]

Cantor, J. R., & Zillmann, D. (1973). The effect of affective state and emotional arousal on music appreciation. *Journal of General Psychology, 89,* 97–108. [6]

Cantor, N., & Genero, N. (1986). Psychiatric diagnosis and natural categorization: A close analogy. In T. Millon & G. L. Klerman (Eds.), *Contemporary directions in psychopathology* (pp. 233–256). New York: Guilford Press. [24]

Cantor, N., & Mischel, W. (1979). Prototypes in person perception. In L. Berkowitz (Ed.), *Advances in experimental social psychology*

(Vol. 12, pp. 3–52). New York: Academic Press. [19]

Cartwright, R. D., & Kaszniak, A. (1978). The social psychology of dream reporting. In A. M. Arkin, J. S. Antrobus, & S. J. Ellman (Eds.), *The mind in sleep: Psychology and psychophysiology* (pp. 277–294). Hillsdale, NJ: Lawrence Erlbaum Associates. [7]

Carver, C. S., & Scheier, M. F. (1981). *Attention and self-regulation: A control-theory approach to human behavior.* New York: Springer-Verlag. [21]

Carver, C. S., & Scheier, M. F. (1990). Origins and functions of positive and negative affect: A control-process view. *Psychological Review, 97,* 19–35. [6]

Catania, A. C., & Reynolds, G. S. (1968). A quantitative analysis of the responding maintained by interval schedules of reinforcement. *Journal of the Experimental Analysis of Behavior, 11,* 327–383. [12]

Cattell, R. B. (1946). *Description and measurement of personality.* New York: World Book. [21]

Cattell, R. B. (1957). *Personality and motivation structure and measurement.* New York: World Book. [21]

Cattell, R. B., Saunders, D. R., & Stice, G. F. (1950). *The 16 Personality Factor Questionnaire.* Champaign, IL: Institute for Personality and Ability Testing. [21]

Chaplin, W. F., John, O. P., & Goldberg, L. R. (1988). Conceptions of states and traits: Dimensional attributes with ideals as prototypes. *Journal of Personality and Social Psychology, 54,* 541–557. [21]

Chapman, L. J. (1967). Illusory correlation in observational report. *Journal of Verbal Learning and Verbal Behavior, 6,* 151–155. [19]

Chapman, L. J., & Chapman, J. P. (1967). Genesis of popular but erroneous diagnostic observations. *Journal of Abnormal Psychology, 72,* 193–204. [15]

Chapman, L. J., & Chapman, J. P. (1969). Illusory correlation as an obstacle to the use of valid psychodiagnostic signs. *Journal of*

Abnormal Psychology, 74, 271–280. [15]

Chase, W. G., & Simon, H. A. (1973). The mind's eye in chess. In W. G. Chase (Ed.), *Visual information processing* (pp. 215–281). New York: Academic Press. [15]

Cheng, P. W., & Holyoak, K. J. (1985). Pragmatic reasoning schemas. *Cognitive Psychology, 17,* 391–416. [15]

Cheng, P. W., Holyoak, K. J., Nisbett, R. E., & Oliver, L. M. (1986). Pragmatic versus syntactic approaches to training deductive reasoning. *Cognitive Psychology, 18,* 293–328. [15]

Cherry, E. C. (1953). Some experiments on the recognition of speech with one and with two ears. *Journal of the Acoustical Society of America, 25,* 975–979. [13]

Chertok, L. (1981). *Sense and nonsense in psychotherapy: The challenge of hypnosis.* Oxford: Pergamon. [7]

Chi, M. T. H., & Glaser, R. (1985). Problem-solving ability. In R. J. Sternberg (Ed.), *Human abilities: An information-processing approach* (pp. 227–250). New York: Freeman. [15]

Chomsky, N. (1957). *Syntactic structures.* The Hague: Mouton. [17]

Chomsky, N. (1959). Review of *Verbal behavior* by B. F. Skinner. *Language, 35,* 26–58. [17]

Chomsky, N. (1965). *Aspects of a theory of syntax.* Cambridge, MA: MIT Press. [17]

Chomsky, N., & Halle, M. (1968). *The sound pattern of English.* New York: Harper. [17]

Christiansen, K. O. (1978). The genesis of aggressive criminality: Implications of a study of crime in a Danish twin study. In W. W. Hartup & J. deWit (Eds.), *Origins of aggression* (pp. 99–120). The Hague: Mouton. [10]

Christie, R., & Geis, F. L. (Eds.). (1970). *Studies in Machiavellianism.* New York: Academic Press. [20]

Church, R. M., LoLordo, V. M., Overmier, J. B., Solomon, R. L., &

Turner, L. H. (1966). Cardiac responses to shock in curarized dogs. *Journal of Comparative and Physiological Psychology, 62,* 1–7. [6]

Churchland, P. M. (1984). *Matter and consciousness.* Cambridge, MA: MIT Press. [5]

Churchland, P. M. (1988). *Matter and consciousness* (rev. ed.). Cambridge, MA: MIT Press. [1]

Clark, E. V. (1983). Meanings and concepts. In P. H. Mussen (Ed.), *Handbook of child psychology* (4th ed., Vol. 3, pp. 787–840). New York: Wiley. [17]

Clark, H. H., & Clark, E. V. (1977). *Psychology and language: An introduction to psycholinguistics.* New York: Harcourt Brace Jovanovich. [17]

Clarke-Stewart, K. A. (1989). Infant day care: Maligned or malignant? *American Psychologist, 44,* 266–273. [18]

Clement, C. A., & Falmagne, R. J. (1986). Logical reasoning, world knowledge, and mental imagery: Interconnections in cognitive processes. *Memory & Cognition, 14,* 299–307. [15]

Cofer, C. N., & Appley, M. H. (1964). *Motivation: Theory and research.* New York: Wiley. [8]

Cohen, D. B. (1974). Toward a theory of dream recall. *Psychological Bulletin, 81,* 138–154. [7]

Cohen, D. B., & Wolfe, G. (1973). Dream recall and repression: Evidence for an alternative hypothesis. *Journal of Consulting and Clinical Psychology, 41,* 349–355. [7]

Cohen, F., & Lazarus, R. S. (1973). Active coping processes, coping dispositions, and recovery from surgery. *Psychosomatic Medicine, 35,* 375–389. [23]

Cohen, S. (1986). Cognitive processes as determinants of stress. In C. D. Spielberger & I. G. Sarason (Eds.), *Stress and anxiety: Vol. 10. A sourcebook of theory and research* (pp. 65–81). Washington, DC: Hemisphere. [23]

Colby, A., Kohlberg, L., Gibbs, J., Candee, D., Speicher-Dubin, B.,

Hewer, A., & Power, C. (1978). *Measuring moral judgment: Standardized scoring manual.* Cambridge, MA: Harvard University, Moral Education Research Foundation. [18]

Collins, A. M., & Loftus, E. F. (1975). A spreading-activation theory of semantic memory. *Psychological Review, 82,* 407–428. [14]

Collins, A. M., & Quillian, M. R. (1969). Retrieval time from semantic memory. *Journal of Verbal Learning and Verbal Behavior, 8,* 240–247. [14]

Coltheart, M. (1980). Iconic memory and visible persistence. *Perception & Psychophysics, 27,* 183–228. [13]

Conrad, R. (1964). Acoustic confusions in immediate memory. *British Journal of Psychology, 55,* 75–84. [13]

Cook, T. D., & Campbell, D. T. (1979). *Quasi-experimentation: Design and analysis in field settings.* Chicago: Rand McNally. [25]

Cooper, J., & Fazio, R. H. (1984). A new look at dissonance theory. In L. Berkowitz (Ed.), *Advances in experimental social psychology* (Vol. 17, pp. 229–266). Orlando, FL: Academic Press. [19]

Cooper, L. A., & Shepard, R. N. (1973). Chronometric studies of the rotation of mental images. In W. G. Chase (Ed.), *Visual information processing* (pp. 75–176). New York: Academic Press. [13]

Coren, S. (1972). Subjective contours and apparent depth. *Psychological Review, 79,* 359–367. [4]

Coren, S., & Girgus, J. S. (1972). Differentiation and decrement in the Müller-Lyer illusion. *Perception & Psychophysics, 12,* 446–470. [4]

Coren, S., Porac, C., & Ward, L. M. (1984). *Sensation and perception* (2nd ed.). Orlando, FL: Academic Press. [3]

Corkin, S. (1984). Lasting consequences of bilateral medial temporal lobectomy: Clinical course and experimental findings in H.M. *Seminar in Neurology, 4,* 249–259. [5]

Corning, W.C. (1986). Bootstrapping toward a classification system. In T. Millon & G. L. Klerman (Eds.), *Contemporary directions in psychopathology* (pp. 279–303). New York: Guilford Press. [24]

Cornsweet, T. N. (1962). Changes in the appearance of stimuli of very high luminance. *Psychological Review, 69,* 257–273. [3]

Cornsweet, T. N. (1970). *Visual perception.* New York: Academic Press. [3]

Cory, T. L., Ormiston, D. W., Simmel, E., & Dainoff, M. (1975). Predicting the frequency of dream recall. *Journal of Abnormal Psychology, 84,* 261–266. [7]

Costanzo, P. R., & Schiffman, S. S. (1989). Thinness—not obesity—has a genetic component. *Neuroscience and Biobehavioral Reviews, 13,* 55–58. [9]

Costello, L. G. (1970). Dissimilarities between conditioned avoidance responses and phobias. *Psychological Review, 77,* 250–254. [12]

Cottington, E. M., & House, J. S. (1987). Occupational stress and health: A multivariate relationship. In A. Baum & J. E. Singer (Eds.), *Handbook of psychology and health: Vol. 5. Stress* (pp. 41–62). Hillsdale, NJ: Lawrence Erlbaum Associates. [23]

Cousins, N. (1979). *Anatomy of an illness as perceived by the patient: Reflections on healing and regeneration.* New York: Norton. [23]

Cover, J. D., & Johnson, N. R. (1976). Need achievement, phase movement and the business cycle. *Social Forces, 54,* 760–774. [11]

Coyne, J. C., & Downey, G. (1991). Social factors and psychopathology: Stress, social support, and coping processes. *Annual Review of Psychology, 42,* 401–425. [23]

Craik, F. I. M., & Lockhart, R. S. (1972). Levels of processing: A framework for memory research. *Journal of Verbal Learning and Verbal Behavior, 11,* 671–684. [13]

Craik, F. I. M., & Tulving, E. (1975). Depth of processing and the retention of words in episodic memory. *Journal of Experimental Psychology: General, 104,* 268–294. [13]

Craik, F. I. M., & Watkins, M. J. (1973). The role of rehearsal in short-term memory. *Journal of Verbal Learning and Verbal Behavior, 12,* 599–607. [13]

Cramer, P., & Gaul, R. (1988). The effects of success and failure on children's use of defense mechanisms. *Journal of Personality, 56,* 729–742. [21]

Critchley, M., & Henson, R. A. (Eds.). (1977). *Music and the brain: Studies in the neurology of music.* London: Heinemann Medical Books. [5]

Csikszentmihalyi, M., & Larson, R. (1984). *Being adolescent.* New York: Basic Books. [18]

Cuneo, D. O. (1980). A general strategy for quantity judgments: The height and width rule. *Child Development, 51,* 299–301. [16]

Cunningham, M. R. (1988). Does happiness mean friendliness? Induced mood and heterosexual self-disclosure. *Personality and Social Psychology Bulletin, 14,* 283–297. [20]

Curry, F. K. W. (1967). A comparison of left-handed and right-handed subjects on verbal and non-verbal dichotic listening tasks. *Cortex, 3,* 343–352. [5]

Curtiss, S., Fromkin, V., Krashen, S., Rigler, D., & Rigler, M. (1974). The linguistic development of Genie. *Language, 50,* 528–554 [17]

Cziko, G. A. (1989). A review of the state-process and punctual-nonpunctual distinctions in children's acquisitions of verbs. *First-Language, 9*(25, Pt.1), 1–31. [17]

Daehler, M. W., & Bukatko, D. (1985). *Cognitive development.* New York: Knopf. [16]

D'Agostino, P. R., O'Neill, B. J., & Paivio, A. (1977). Memory for pictures and words as a function of levels of processing: Depth or dual coding? *Memory & Cognition, 5,* 252–256. [13]

Dalton, K. (1980). Cyclical criminal acts in premenstrual syndrome. *Lancet, 2,* 1070–1071. [10]

D'Andrade, R. G. (1966). Sex differences and cultural institutions. In E. E. Maccoby (Ed.), *The develop-*

ment of sex differences (pp. 174–204). Stanford, CA: Stanford University Press. [20]

Darwin, C. (1859). *On the origin of species*. London: Murray. [1, 17]

Darwin, C. (1952). *The descent of man*. In R. M. Hutchens (Ed.), *Great books of the Western world* (Vol. 49, pp. 253–659). Chicago: Encyclopaedia Britannica. (Original work published 1871) [17]

Darwin, C. (1965). *The expression of emotions in man and animals*. Chicago: University of Chicago Press. (Original work published 1872) [6, 19]

Davidoff, J. (1982). Studies with nonverbal stimuli. In J. G. Beaumont (Ed.), *Divided visual field studies of cerebral organization* (pp. 29–55). London: Academic Press. [5]

Davies, J. T., & Taylor, F. H. (1965). A theory of quality of odours. *Journal of Theoretical Biology, 8,* 1–7. [3]

Davis, H. P., & Squire, L. P. (1984). Protein synthesis and memory: A review. *Psychological Bulletin, 96,* 518–559. [5]

Davis, J. M., Klerman, G., & Schildkraut, J. (1967). Drugs used in the treatment of depression. In L. Efron, J. O. Cole, D. Levine, & J. R. Wittenborn (Eds.), *Psychopharmacology: A review of progress*. Washington, DC: U.S. Clearinghouse of Mental Health Information. [25]

Davison, G. C., & Neale, J. M. (1986). *Abnormal psychology: An experimental clinical approach* (4th ed.). New York: Wiley. [24, 25]

Dawes, R. M., Faust, D., & Meehl, P. E. (1989). Clinical versus actuarial judgment. *Science, 243* (March), 1668–1674. [24]

Dawkins, R. (1976). *The selfish gene*. Oxford: Oxford University Press. [8]

Dawson, M. E., & Schell, A. M. (1982). Electrodermal responses to attended and nonattended significant stimuli during dichotic listening. *Journal of Experimental Psychology: Human Perception and Performance, 8,* 315–324. [13]

Deaux, K. (1985). Sex and gender. *Annual Review of Psychology, 36,* 49–81. [20]

Deaux, K., & Major, B. (1987). Putting gender into context: An interactive model of gender-related behavior. *Psychological Review, 94,* 369–389. [10]

DeFries, J. C., Fulker, D. W., & LaBuda, M. C. (1987). Evidence for a genetic etiology in reading disability in twins. *Nature (London), 329,* 537–539. [8]

DeFries, J. C., & Plomin, R. (1978). Behavioral genetics. *Annual Review of Psychology, 29,* 473–515. [8]

De Groot, A. D. (1965). *Thought and choice in chess*. The Hague: Mouton. [15]

DeLongis, A., Coyne, J. C., Dakof, G., Folkman, S., & Lazarus, R. S. (1982). Relationship of daily hassles, uplifts, and major life events to health status. *Health Psychology, 1,* 119–136. [23]

Dembroski, T. M., & MacDougall, J. M. (1985). Beyond global Type A: Relationships of paralinguistic attributes, hostility, and anger-in to coronary heart disease. In T. M. Field, P. M. McCabe, and N. Schneiderman (Eds.), *Stress and coping* (pp. 223–242). Hillsdale, NJ: Lawrence Erlbaum Associates. [23, 24]

Dement, W. C. (1960). The effect of dream deprivation. *Science, 131,* 1705–1707. [7]

Dement, W. C. (1964). Experimental dream studies. *Science and Psychoanalysis, 7,* 129–184. [7]

Dement, W. C. (1965). Recent studies on the biological role of REM sleep. *American Journal of Psychiatry, 122,* 404–408. [7]

Descartes, R. (1952). *Discourse on the method of rightly conducting the reason and seeking for truth in the sciences* (E. S. Haldane & G. R. T. Ross, Trans.) In R. M. Hutchens (Ed.), *Great books of the Western world* (Vol. 31, pp. 41–67). Chicago: Encyclopaedia Britannica. (Original work published 1637) [17]

Descartes, R. (1952). *Meditations on first philosophy* (E. S. Haldane & G. R. T. Ross, Trans.). In R. M. Hutchens (Ed.), *Great books of the Western world* (Vol. 31, pp. 69–293). Chicago: Encyclopaedia Britannica. (Original work published 1641) [1]

Deutsch, J. A., & Gonzalez, M. F. (1980). Gastric nutrient content signals satiety. *Behavioral and Neural Biology, 30,* 113–116. [9]

DeValois, R. L., & DeValois, K. K. (1975). Neural coding of color. In E. C. Carterette & M. P. Friedman (Eds.), *Handbook of perception: Vol. 5: Seeing* (pp. 117–162). New York: Academic Press. [3]

DeVries, H., & Stuiver, M. (1961). The absolute sensitivity of the human sense of smell. In W. A. Rosenblith (Ed.), *Communication processes* (pp. 159–167). New York: Wiley. [3]

DiLalla, L. F., & Gottesman, I. I. (1991). Biological and genetic contributors to violence—Widom's untold tale. *Psychological Bulletin, 109,* 125–129. [10]

Dion, K. K. (1981). Physical attractiveness, sex roles and heterosexual attraction. In M. Cook (Ed.), *The bases of human sexual attraction* (pp. 3–22). New York: Academic Press. [10]

Ditman, K. S., Moss, T., Forgy, E. W., Zunin, L. M., Lynch, R. D., & Funk, W. A. (1972). Dimensions of the LSD, methylphenidate, and chlordiazepoxide experiences. In D. W. Matheson & M. A. Davison (Eds.), *The behavioral effects of drugs* (pp. 212–221). New York: Holt, Rinehart, & Winston. [7]

Dixon, R. A., & Lerner, R. M. (1984). A history of systems in developmental psychology. In M. H. Bornstein & M. E. Lamb (Eds.), *Developmental psychology: An advanced textbook* (pp. 1–35). Hillsdale, NJ: Lawrence Erlbaum Associates. [16]

Dobzhansky, T. (1967). *Evolution, genetics, and man*. New York: Wiley. (Original work published 1955) [8]

Doering, C. H., Brodie, K. H., Kraemer, H. C., Moos, R. H., Becker, H. B., & Hamburg, D. A. (1975).

Negative affect and plasma testosterone: A longitudinal human study. *Psychosomatic Medicine, 37,* 484–491. [10]

Dollard, J., Doob, L., Miller, N., Mowrer, O. H., & Sears, R. R. (1939). *Frustration and aggression.* New Haven, CT: Yale University Press. [10]

Dollard, J., & Miller, N. E. (1950). *Personality and psychotherapy: An analysis in terms of learning, thinking, and culture.* New York: McGraw-Hill. [18, 21]

Domhoff, B., & Kamiya, J. (1964). Problems in dream content study with objective indicators: II. Appearance of experimental situation in laboratory dream narratives. *Archives of General Psychiatry, 11,* 525–528. [7]

Domjan, M. (1980). Ingestional aversion learning: Unique and general processes. In J. S. Rosenblatt, R. A. Hinde, C. Beer, & M. C. Busnel (Eds.), *Advances in the study of behavior* (Vol. 11, pp. 275–336). New York: Academic Press. [12]

Domjan, M. (1983). Biological constraints on instrumental and classical conditioning: Implications for a general process theory. In G. Bower (Ed.), *The psychology of learning and motivation* (Vol. 17, pp. 215–277). New York: Academic Press. [12]

Donaldson, I. M. L., & Long, A. C. (1980). Interactions between extraocular proprioceptive and visual signals in the superior colliculus of the cat. *Journal of Physiology (London), 298,* 85–110. [4]

Donnerstein, E. (1980). Aggressive erotica and violence against women. *Journal of Personality and Social Psychology, 39,* 269–277. [10]

Donnerstein, E. (1983). Erotica and human aggression. In R. G. Geen & E. I. Donnerstein (Eds.), *Aggression: Theoretical and empirical reviews* (Vol. 2, pp. 127–154). New York: Academic Press. [10]

Donnerstein, E., & Barrett, G. (1978). The effects of erotic stimuli on male aggression towards females. *Journal of Personality and Social Psychology, 36,* 180–188. [10]

Donnerstein, E., Donnerstein, M., & Evans, R. (1975). Erotic stimuli and aggression: Facilitation or inhibition. *Journal of Personality and Social Psychology, 32,* 237–244. [10]

Dooling, D. J., & Christiaansen, R. E. (1977). Episodic and semantic aspects of memory for prose. *Journal of Experimental Psychology: Human Learning and Memory, 3,* 428–436. [14]

Doty, R. W., Negrao, N., & Yamaga, K. (1973). The unilateral engram. *Acta Neurobiologiae Experimentalis, 33,* 711–728. [6]

Drucker-Colin, R., Shkurovich, M., & Sterman, M. B. (Eds.). (1979). *The functions of sleep.* New York: Academic Press. [7]

Drucker-Colin, R. (1979). Protein molecules and the regulation of REM sleep: Possible implications for function. In R. Drucker-Colin, M. Shkurovich, & M. B. Sterman (Eds.), *The functions of sleep* (pp. 99–111). New York: Academic Press. [7]

Duncker, K. (1945). On problem solving. *Psychological Monographs, 58*(Whole No. 270). [15]

Dunham, P. J. (1971). Punishment: Method and theory. *Psychological Review, 78,* 58–70. [12]

Dunn, P. K., & Ondercin, P. (1981). Personality variables related to compulsive eating in college women. *Journal of Clinical Psychology, 37,* 43–49. [9]

Durand, D. E. (1975). Effects of drinking on the power and affiliation needs of middle-aged females. *Journal of Clinical Psychology, 31,* 549–553. [11]

Dweck, C. S., & Goetz, T. E. (1978). Attributions and learned helplessness. In J. H. Harvey, W. Ickes, & R. F. Kidd (Eds.), *New directions in attribution research* (Vol. 2, pp. 157–179). Hillsdale, NJ: Lawrence Erlbaum Associates. [18]

Dweck, C. S., Goetz, T. E., & Strauss, N. L. (1980). Sex differences in learned helplessness: IV. An experimental and naturalistic study of failure generalization and its mediators. *Journal of Personality and Social Psychology, 38,* 441–452. [18]

Dyer, F. C., & Gould, J. L. (1983). Honey bee navigation. *American Scientist, 71,* 587–597. [8]

Dzendolet, E., & Meiselman, H. L. (1967). Gustatory quality changes as a function of solution concentration. *Perception & Psychophysics, 2,* 29–33. [3]

Eagly, A. H. (1987). *Sex differences in social behavior: A social role interpretation.* Hillsdale, NJ: Lawrence Erlbaum Associates. [20]

Edkardt, M. J., Harford, T. C., & Kaelber, C. T. (1981). Health hazards associated with alcohol consumption. *JAMA, Journal of the American Medical Association, 246,* 648–666. [7]

Edwards, S. B., & Flynn, J. P. (1972). Corticospinal control of striking in centrally elicited attack behavior. *Brain Research, 41,* 51–65. [10]

Efron, R. (1970). The relationship between the duration of a stimulus and the duration of a perception. *Neuropsychologia, 8,* 37–55. [13]

Efron, R., Bogen, J. E., & Yund, E. W. (1977). Perception of dichotic chords by normal and commissurotomized human subjects. *Cortex, 13,* 137–149. [5]

Egan, D. E., & Greeno, J. G. (1974). Theory of rule induction: Knowledge acquired in concept learning, serial pattern learning, and problem solving. In L. W. Gregg (Ed.), *Knowledge and cognition* (pp. 43–103). Hillsdale, NJ: Lawrence Erlbaum Associates. [15]

Ehrhardt, A., & Meyer-Bahlburg, H. F. L. (1981). Effects of prenatal sex hormones on gender-related behavior. *Science, 211,* 1312–1318. [10]

Eibl-Eibesfeldt, I. (1975). *Ethology: The biology of behavior.* New York: Holt, Rinehart, & Winston. [6, 8]

Eibl-Eibesfeldt, I. (1989). *Human ethology.* New York: Aldine de Gruyter. [8]

Eikelboom, R., & Stewart, J. (1982). Conditioning of drug-induced physiological responses. *Psychological Review, 89,* 507–528. [12]

Eimas, P. D. (1985). The perception of speech in early infancy. *Scientific American, 252,* 46–52. [17]

Eimas, P. D., Siqueland, E. R., Jusczyk, P., & Vigorito, J. (1971). Speech perception in infants. *Science, 171,* 303–306. [17]

Einstein, G. O., McDaniel, M. A., & Lackey, S. (1989). Bizarre imagery, interference, and distinctiveness. *Journal of Experimental Psychology: Learning, Memory, and Cognition, 75,* 64–72. [14]

Eisenberger, R. (1972). Explanation of rewards that do not reduce tissue needs. *Psychological Bulletin, 77,* 319–339. [12]

Ekman, P. (1972). Universal and cultural differences in facial expression of emotion. In J. K. Cole (Ed.), *Nebraska Symposium on Motivation, 1971* (pp. 207–283). Lincoln: University of Nebraska Press. [6, 19]

Ekman, P. (1984). Expression and the nature of emotion. In K. R. Scherer & P. Ekman (Eds.), *Approaches to emotion* (pp. 319–343). Hillsdale, NJ: Lawrence Erlbaum Associates. [6]

Ekman, P., & Friesen, W. V. (1969). Nonverbal leakage and clues to deception. *Psychiatry, 32,* 88–106. [19]

Ekman, P., & Friesen, W. V. (1971). Constants across cultures in the face and emotion. *Journal of Personality and Social Psychology, 17,* 124–129. [6]

Ekman, P., & Friesen, W. V. (1975). *Unmasking the face: A guide to recognizing emotions from facial clues.* Englewood Cliffs, NJ: Prentice-Hall. [19]

Ekman, P., & Oster, H. (1979). Facial expressions of emotion. *Annual Review of Psychology, 30,* 527–554. [6]

Ekman, P., Sorenson, E. R., & Friesen, W. V. (1969). Pan-cultural elements in facial displays of emotion. *Science, 164,* 86–88. [6, 19]

Elkind, D. (1984). *All grown up and no place to go.* Reading, MA: Addison-Wesley. [18]

Ellman, S. J., Spielman, A. J., Luck, D., Steiner, S. S., & Halperin, R. (1978). REM deprivation: A review. In A. M. Arkin, J. S. Antrobus, & S. J. Ellman (Eds.), *The mind in sleep: Psychology and psychophysiology* (pp. 419–457). Hillsdale, NJ: Lawrence Erlbaum Associates. [7]

Ennis, B. J. (1970). The rights of mental patients. In N. Dorsen (Ed.), *The rights of Americans: What they are and what they should be* (pp. 484–498). New York: Pantheon. [25]

Entwisle, D. R. (1972). To dispel fantasies about fantasy-based measures of achievement motivation. *Psychological Bulletin, 77,* 377–391. [11]

Enzle, M. E., Hansen, R. D., & Lowe, C. A. (1975). Causal attribution in the mixed-motive game: Effects of facilitory and inhibitory environmental forces. *Journal of Personality and Social Psychology, 31,* 50–54. [20]

Epstein, A. N., Kissileff, H. R., & Stellar, E. (1973). *The neuropsychology of thirst: New findings and advances in concepts.* Washington, DC: Winston. [9]

Epstein, S. (1979). The stability of behavior: I. On predicting most of the people much of the time. *Journal of Personality and Social Psychology, 37,* 1097–1126. [21]

Epstein, S. (1980). The stability of behavior: II. Implications for psychological research. *American Psychologist, 35,* 790–806. [21]

Epstein, S. (1984). A procedural note on the measurement of broad dispositions. *Journal of Personality, 52,* 318–325. [21]

Epstein, S. M. (1967). Toward a unified theory of anxiety. In B. A. Maher (Ed.), *Progress in experimental personality research* (Vol. 4, pp. 2–89). New York: Academic Press. [6]

Erickson, J. R. (1978). Research on syllogistic reasoning. In R. Revlin & R. E. Mayer (Eds.), *Human reasoning* (pp. 39–50). Washington, DC: Winston. [15]

Erickson, J. R., & Jones, M. R. (1978). Thinking. *Annual Review of Psychology, 29,* 61–91. [15]

Erikson, E. (1950). *Childhood and society.* New York: Norton. [18]

Erlebacher, A., & Sekuler, R. (1969). Explanation of the Müller-Lyer illusion: Confusion theory examined. *Journal of Experimental Psychology, 80,* 462–467. [4]

Eron, L. D., & Huesmann, L. R. (1984). The control of aggressive behavior by changes in attitudes, values, and the conditions of learning. In R. J. Blanchard & D. C. Blanchard (Eds.), *Advances in the study of aggression* (Vol. 1, pp. 139–171). Orlando, FL: Academic Press. [10]

Eron, L. D., Huesmann, L. R., Lefkowitz, M. M., & Walder, L. O. (1972). Does television violence cause aggression? *American Psychologist, 27,* 253–263. [10]

Evans, J. St. B. T. (1982). *The psychology of deductive reasoning.* London: Routledge & Kegan Paul. [15]

Evans, J. St. B. T. (1983). Selective processes in reasoning. In J. St. B. T. Evans (Ed.), *Thinking and reasoning: Psychological approaches* (pp. 135–163). London: Routledge & Kegan Paul. [15]

Evans, J. St. B. T., Barston, J. L., & Pollard, P. (1983). On the conflict between logic and belief in syllogistic reasoning. *Memory & Cognition, 11,* 295–306. [15]

Exner, J. E. (1974). *The Rorschach: A comprehensive system* (Vol. 1). New York: Wiley. [22]

Exner, J. E. (1978). *The Rorschach: A comprehensive system: Vol. 2. Current research and advanced interpretation.* New York: Wiley. [22]

Exner, J. E. (1982). *The Rorschach: A comprehensive system: Vol. 3. Assessment of children and adolescents.* New York: Wiley. [22]

Eysenck, H. J. (1976). The learning model of neurosis. *Behavior Research and Therapy, 14,* 251–267. [12]

Eysenck, H. J., & Eysenck, S. B. G. (1975). *Manual of the Eysenck Personality Questionnaire.* San Diego, CA: Educational and Industrial Testing Service. [21, 22]

Falconer, D. S. (1981). *Introduction to quantitative genetics* (2nd ed.). London: Longman. [16]

Falloon, I. R., Boyd, J. L., McGill,

C. W., Williamson, M., Razini, J., Moss, H. B., Gilderman, A. M., & Simpson, G. M. (1985). Family management in prevention of morbidity in schizophrenia. *Archives of General Psychiatry, 42,* 887–896. [24]

Faraone, S. V., Kremen, W. S., & Tsuang, M. T. (1990). Genetic transmission of major affective disorders: Quantitative models and linkage analyses. *Psychological Bulletin, 108,* 109–127. [8]

Federal Bureau of Investigation. (1991). *Uniform crime reports* (August 11). Washington, DC: United States Department of Justice, Government Printing Office. [18]

Fehr, B., & Russell, J. A. (1984). Concept of emotion viewed from a prototype perspective. *Journal of Experimental Psychology: General, 113,* 464–486. [6]

Fehr, F. S., & Stern, J. A. (1970). Peripheral physiological variables and emotion: The James-Lange theory revisited. *Psychological Bulletin, 74,* 411–424. [6]

Feinberg, I. (1974). Changes in sleep cycle patterns with age. *Journal of Psychiatric Research, 10,* 283–306. [7]

Feinberg, I., & Carlson, V. (1968). Sleep variables as a function of age in man. *Archives of General Psychiatry, 18,* 239–250. [7]

Fellows, B. J. (1967). Reversal of the Müller-Lyer illusion with changes in the length of the inter-fin lines. *Quarterly Journal of Experimental Psychology, 19,* 208–214. [4]

Felton, M., & Lyon, D. O. (1966). The post-reinforcement pause. *Journal of the Experimental Analysis of Behavior, 9,* 131–134. [12]

Fenigstein, A. (1979). Does aggression cause a preference for viewing media violence? *Journal of Personality and Social Psychology, 37,* 2307–2317. [10]

Fernald, D. (1984). *The Hans legacy: A story of science.* Hillsdale, NJ: Lawrence Erlbaum Associates. [18]

Festinger, L. (1954). A theory of social comparison processes. *Human Relations, 7,* 117–140. [11, 19]

Festinger, L., & Carlsmith, J. M. (1959). Cognitive consequences of forced compliance. *Journal of Abnormal and Social Psychology, 58,* 203–210. [19]

Festinger, L., Schachter, S., & Back, K. (1950). *Social pressures in informal groups: A study of human factors in housing.* New York: Harper. [20]

Fiedler, F. E. (1964). A contingency model of leadership effectiveness. In L. Berkowitz (Ed.), *Advances in experimental social psychology* (Vol. 1, pp. 149–190). New York: Academic Press. [20]

Fiedler, F. E. (1978). Contingency model and the leadership process. In L. Berkowitz (Ed.), *Advances in experimental social psychology* (Vol. 11, pp. 59–112). New York: Academic Press. [20]

File, S. E. (1990). The history of benzodiazepine dependence: A review of animal studies. *Neuroscience and Biobehavioral Reviews, 14,* 135–146. [7]

Finke, R. A. (1980). Levels of equivalence in imagery and perception. *Psychological Review, 87,* 113–132. [14]

Fischhoff, B. (1975). Hindsight = foresight: The effect of outcome knowledge on judgment under uncertainty. *Journal of Experimental Psychology: Human Perception and Performance, 1,* 288–299. [15]

Fishbein, M., & Ajzen, I. (1975). *Belief, attitude, intention and behavior.* Reading, MA: Addison-Wesley. [19]

Fisher, R. P., & Craik, F. I. M. (1977). The interaction between encoding and retrieval operations in cued recall. *Journal of Experimental Psychology: Human Learning and Memory, 3,* 701–711. [13]

Fisher, W. A., & Byrne, D. (1978). Sex differences in response to erotica? Love versus lust. *Journal of Personality and Social Psychology, 36,* 117–125. [10]

Fiske, S. T., & Taylor, S. E. (1991). *Social cognition* (2nd ed.). New York: McGraw-Hill. [19]

Fitzgerald, R. D., & Martin, G. K. (1971). Heart-rate conditioning in rats as a function of interstimulus interval. *Psychological Reports, 29,* 1103–1110. [12]

Fitzgerald, R. D., & Teyler, T. J. (1970). Trace and delayed heart-rate conditioning in rats as a function of US intensity. *Journal of Comparative and Physiological Psychology, 70,* 242–253. [12]

Fitzsimons, J. T. (1972). Thirst. *Physiological Review, 52,* 468–561. [9]

Fitzsimons, J. T. (1979). *The physiology of thirst and sodium appetite.* Cambridge, England: Cambridge University Press. [9]

Fitzsimons, J. T., & Simons, B. J. (1969). The effect on drinking in the rat of intravenous infusion of angiotensin, given alone or in combination with other stimuli of thirst. *Journal of Physiology (London), 203,* 45–57. [9]

Flannery, R. B., & Harvey, M. R. (1991). Psychological trauma and learned helplessness: Seligman's paradigm reconsidered. *Psychotherapy, 28,* 374–378. [24]

Flavell, J. H. (1985). *Cognitive development.* Englewood Cliffs, NJ: Prentice-Hall. [16]

Floody, O. R. (1983). Hormones and aggression in female mammals. In B. B. Svare (Ed.), *Hormones and aggressive behavior* (pp. 39–89). New York: Plenum. [10]

Flynn, J. P. (1967). The neural basis of aggression in cats. In D. C. Glass (Ed.), *Neurophysiology and emotion* (pp. 40–60). New York: Rockefeller University Press. [10]

Flynn, J. R. (1980). *Race, IQ, and Jensen.* London: Routledge & Kegan Paul. [22]

Fodor, E. M., & Farrow, D. L. (1979). The power motive as an influence in the use of power. *Journal of Personality and Social Psychology, 37,* 2091–2097. [11]

Fontana, A. (1966). Familial etiology of schizophrenia: Is a scientific methodology possible? *Psychological Bulletin, 66,* 214–228. [24]

Foulkes, D. (1978). *A grammar of dreams.* New York: Basic Books. [7]

Foulkes, D. (1982). A cognitive-psychological model of dream production. *Sleep, 5,* 169–187. [7]

Foulkes, D. (1985). *Dreaming: A cognitive-psychological analysis*. Hillsdale, NJ: Lawrence Erlbaum Associates. [7]

Foulkes, D., & Rechtschaffen, A. (1964). Presleep determinants of dream content: The effect of two films. *Perceptual and Motor Skills, 19*, 983–1005. [7]

Foulkes, D., & Vogel, G. (1965). Mental activity at sleep onset. *Journal of Abnormal Psychology, 70*, 231–243. [7]

Fox, R., Aslin, R. N., Shea, S. L., & Dumais, S. T. (1980). Stereopsis in infants. *Science, 207*, 323–324. [4]

Franco, L., & Sperry, R. W. (1977). Hemisphere lateralization for cognitive processing of geometry. *Neuropsychologia, 15*, 107–114. [5]

Franks, J. J., & Bransford, J. D. (1971). Abstraction of visual patterns. *Journal of Experimental Psychology, 90*, 65–74. [14]

Freedman, J. L. (1984). Effect of television violence on aggressiveness. *Psychological Bulletin, 96*, 227–246. [10]

Freedman, J. L. (1986). Television violence and aggression: A rejoinder. *Psychological Bulletin, 100*, 372–378. [10]

French, J. R. P., Jr., & Raven, B. (1959). The bases of social power. In D. Cartwright (Ed.), *Studies in social power* (pp. 150–167). Ann Arbor, MI: Institute for Social Research. [20]

Freud, A. (1946). *The ego and the mechanisms of defence*. New York: International Universities Press. [21]

Freud, S. (1913). *The interpretation of dreams* (A. A. Brill, Trans.) (3rd ed.). New York: Macmillan. (Original work published 1900) [2]

Freud, S. (1952). *The interpretation of dreams*. New York: Basic Books. (Original work published 1900) [7]

Freud, S. (1952). *A general introduction to psychoanalysis* (J. Riviere, Trans.). In R. M. Hutchens (Ed.), *Great books of the Western world* (Vol. 54, pp. 449–638). Chicago: Encyclopaedia Britannica. (Original work published 1917) [1]

Freud, S. (1952). *The ego and the id*. In R. M. Hutchens (Ed.), *Great books of the Western world* (Vol. 54, pp. 697–717). Chicago: Encyclopaedia Britannica. (Original work published 1923) [21]

Freud, S. (1952). *New introductory lectures on psychoanalysis* (W. J. H. Sprott, Trans.). In R. M. Hutchens (Ed.), *Great books of the Western world* (Vol. 54, pp. 807–884). Chicago: Encyclopaedia Britannica. (Original work published 1932) [18]

Freud, S. (1960). *Psychopathology of everyday life*. In J. Strachey (Ed. & Trans.), *The standard edition of the complete psychological works of Sigmund Freud* (Vol. 6). London: Hogarth Press. (Original work published 1901) [2]

Frey, R. S. (1984). Need for achievement, entrepreneurship, and economic growth: A critique of the McClelland thesis. *Social Science Journal, 21*, 125–134. [11]

Fried, L. S., & Holyoak, K. J. (1984). Induction of category distributions: A framework for classification learning. *Journal of Experimental Psychology: Learning, Memory, and Cognition, 10*, 234–257. [14]

Fried, P. A. (1972). Septum and behavior: A review. *Psychological Bulletin, 78*, 292–310. [6]

Friedman, M. I., & Rosenman, R. H. (1959). Association of a specific overt behavior pattern with increases in blood cholesterol, blood clotting time, incidence of arcus senilis and clinical coronary artery disease. *JAMA, Journal of the American Medical Association, 169*, 1286–1296. [23, 24]

Friedman, M. I., & Stricker, E. M. (1976). The physiological psychology of hunger: A physiological perspective. *Psychological Review, 83*, 409–431. [9]

Friedman, R. C., Hurt, S. W., Arnoff, M. S., & Clarkin, J. (1980). Behavior and the menstrual cycle. *Signs, 5*, 719–738. [10]

Friedrich, L. K., & Stein, A. H. (1973). Aggression and prosocial television programs and the natural behavior of preschool children. *Monographs of the Society for Research in Child Development, 38*(4, Serial No. 151). [10]

Friedrich-Cofer, L., & Huston, A. C. (1986). Television violence and aggression: The debate continues. *Psychological Bulletin, 100*, 364–371. [10]

Frisch, H. L. (1977). Sex stereotypes in adult-infant play. *Child Development, 48*, 1671–1675. [20]

Frodi, A. (1977). Sexual arousal, situational restrictiveness, and aggressive behavior. *Journal of Research in Personality, 11*, 48–58. [10]

Fullard, W., & Rieling, A. M. (1976). An investigation of Lorenz' baby babyness. *Child Development, 47*, 1191–1193. [8]

Fuller, J. L., & Thompson, W. R. (1978). *Foundations of behavior genetics*. St. Louis, MO: Mosby. [10]

Funder, D. C., & Colvin, C. R. (1991). Explorations in behavioral consistency: Properties of persons, situations, and behaviors. *Journal of Personality and Social Psychology, 60*, 773–794. [21]

Furst, P. T. (1976). Hallucinogens and culture. San Francisco: Chandler & Sharp. [7]

Gackenbach, J. (1988). Psychological content of lucid versus nonlucid dreams. In J. Gackenbach & S. LaBerge (Eds.), *Conscious mind, sleeping brain: Perspectives on lucid dreaming* (pp. 105–134). New York: Plenum. [7]

Gackenbach, J., & LaBerge S. (1988). *Conscious mind, sleeping brain: Perspectives on lucid dreaming*. New York: Plenum. [7]

Gagge, A. P., & Stevens, J. C. (1968). Thermal sensitivity and comfort. In D. R. Kenshalo (Ed.), *The skin senses* (pp. 345–367). Springfield, IL: Thomas. [3]

Gallistel, C. R., & Gelman, R. (1990). The what and how of counting. *Cognition, 34*, 197–199. [16]

Galluscio, E. H. (1990). *Biological psychology*. New York: Macmillan. [9, 25]

Galton, F. (1952). *Hereditary genius: An inquiry into its laws and conse-*

quences. New York: Horizon. (Original work published 1869) [22]

Ganz, L. (1975). Vision. In B. Scharf (Ed.), *Experimental sensory psychology* (pp. 116–263). Glenview, IL: Scott Foresman. [3]

Garcia, J., & Koelling, R. A. (1966). Relation of cue to consequence in avoidance learning. *Psychonomic Science, 4,* 123–124. [12]

Gardner, H. (1983). *Frames of mind: The theory of multiple intelligences.* New York: Basic Books. [22]

Gardner, R. A., Gardner, B. T., & Van Canfort, T. E. (1989). *Teaching sign language to chimpanzees.* Ithaca: State University of New York Press.

Garfinkel, B. D., Froese, A., & Hood, J. (1982). Suicide attempts in children and adolescents. *American Journal of Psychiatry, 139,* 1257–1261. [24]

Garfinkel, P. E., & Garner, D. M. (1982). *Anorexia nervosa.* New York: Brunner/Mazel. [9]

Garfinkel, P. E., Moldofsky, H., Garner, D. M., Stancer, H. C., & Coscina, D. V. (1978). Body awareness in anorexia nervosa: Disturbances in "body image" and "satiety." *Psychosomatic Medicine, 40,* 487–498. [9]

Garner, D. M., & Garfinkel, P. E. (1985). *Handbook of psychotherapy for anorexia nervosa and bulimia.* New York: Guilford Press. [9]

Garner, D. M., Garfinkel, P. E., Stancer, H. C., & Moldofsky, H. (1976). Body image disturbances in anorexia nervosa. *Psychosomatic Medicine, 38,* 327–336. [9]

Garner, W. R. (1962). *Uncertainty and structure as psychological concepts.* New York: Wiley. [4]

Garner, W. R. (1974). *The processing of information and structure.* Potomac, MD: Lawrence Erlbaum Associates. [4]

Garner, W. R., & Clement, D. E. (1963). Goodness of pattern and pattern uncertainty. *Journal of Verbal Learning and Verbal Behavior, 2,* 446–452. [4]

Gassel, M. M. (1969). Occipital lobe syndromes (excluding hemianopia). In P. J. Vinkin & G. W. Bruyn (Eds.), *Handbook of neurology* (Vol. 2, pp. 640–679). Amsterdam: North-Holland. [5]

Gazzaniga, M. S. (1970). *The bisected brain.* New York: Appleton-Century-Crofts. [5]

Gazzaniga, M. S., & LeDoux, J. E. (1978). *The integrated mind.* New York: Plenum. [5]

Geary, N. (1990). Pancreatic glucagon signals postprandial satiety. *Neuroscience and Biobehavioral Reviews, 14,* 323–338. [9]

Geen, R. G. (1983). Aggression and television violence. In R. G. Geen & E. I. Donnerstein (Eds.), *Aggression: Theoretical and empirical reviews* (Vol. 2, pp. 103–125). New York: Academic Press. [10]

Geen, R. G., & Pigg, R. (1970). Acquisition of an aggressive response and its generalization to verbal behavior. *Journal of Personality and Social Psychology, 15,* 165–170. [10]

Geffen, G., Bradshaw, J. L., & Wallace, G. (1971). Interhemispheric effects on reaction time to verbal and nonverbal visual stimuli. *Journal of Experimental Psychology, 87,* 415–422. [5]

Geiselman, R. E., & Bjork, R. A. (1980). Primary versus secondary rehearsal in imagined voices: Differential effects on recognition. *Cognitive Psychology, 12,* 188–205. [13]

Geldard, F. A. (1972). *The human senses* (2nd ed.). New York: Wiley. [3]

Gelman, R., & Baillargeon, R. (1983). A review of some Piagetian concepts. In P. H. Mussen (Ed.), *Handbook of child psychology* (4th ed., Vol. 3, pp. 167–230). New York: Wiley. [16]

Gelman, R., & Gallistel, C. R. (1978). *The child's understanding of number.* Cambridge, MA: Harvard University Press. [16]

Gerard, H. B., & Rabbie, J. M. (1961). Fear and social comparison. *Journal of Abnormal and Social Psychology, 62,* 586–592. [11]

Gesell, A. L. (1928). *Infancy and human growth.* New York: Macmillan. [18]

Gesell, A. L. (1934). *An atlas of infant behavior.* New Haven, CT: Yale University Press. [16]

Gesell, A. L. (1954). The ontogenesis of infant behavior. In L. Carmichael (Ed.), *Manual of child psychology* (2nd ed., pp. 335–373). New York: Wiley. [16]

Gibb, C. A. (1969). Leadership. In G. Lindzey & E. Aronson (Eds.), *Handbook of social psychology* (2nd ed., Vol. 4, pp. 205–282). Reading, MA: Addison-Wesley. [20]

Gibson, E. J. (1969). *Principles of perceptual learning and development.* New York: Appleton-Century-Crofts. [4]

Gibson, E. J., & Walk, R. D. (1960). The "visual cliff." *Scientific American, 202,* 64–71. [4]

Gibson, J. J. (1950). *Perception of the visual world.* Boston: Houghton-Mifflin. [4]

Gilbert, D. T., & Jones, E. E. (1986). Perceiver-induced constraint: Interpretations of self-generated reality. *Journal of Personality and Social Psychology, 50,* 269–280. [19]

Gilbert, S. (1986). *Pathology of eating: Psychology and treatment.* London: Routledge & Kegan Paul. [9]

Gilligan, C. (1977). In a different voice: Women's conceptions of self and morality. *Harvard Educational Review, 47,* 481–517. [18]

Gilligan, C., Kohlberg, L., Lerner, M., & Belensky, M. (1971). *Moral reasoning about sexual dilemmas* (Technical report of the U.S. Commission on Obscenity and Pornography, VI, pp. 141–174). Washington, DC: U. S. Government Printing Office. [18]

Gladue, B. A., Green, R., & Hellman, R. E. (1984). Neuroendocrine response to estrogen and sexual orientation. *Science, 225,* 1496–1499. [10]

Glass, D. C., & Singer, J. E. (1972). *Urban stress: Experiments on noise and social stressors.* New York: Academic Press. [23]

Gleitman, L. R., & Wanner, E. (1986). Current issues in language learning. In M. H. Bornstein & M. E. Lamb (Eds.), *Developmental psychology: An advanced textbook* (pp. 181–240). Hillsdale, NJ: Lawrence Erlbaum Associates. [17]

Glenberg, A., Smith, S. M., & Green, C. (1977). Type I rehearsal: Maintenance and more. *Journal of Verbal Learning and Verbal Behavior, 16,* 339–352. [13]

Glucksberg, S., & Danks, J. (1968). Effects of discriminative labels and of nonsense labels upon availability of novel function. *Journal of Verbal Learning and Verbal Behavior, 7,* 72–76. [15]

Glucksberg, S., & Weisberg, R. W. (1966). Verbal behavior and problem solving: Some effects of labeling in a functional fixedness problem. *Journal of Experimental Psychology, 71,* 659–664. [15]

Goddard, G. V. (1980). Component properties of the memory machine: Hebb revisited. In P. W. Jusczyk & R. M. Klein (Eds.), *The nature of thought: Essays in honour of D. O. Hebb* (pp. 231–247). Hillsdale, NJ: Lawrence Erlbaum Associates. [5]

Goddard, M. J., & Jenkins, H. M. (1987). Effect of signaling extra unconditioned stimuli on autoshaping. *Animal Learning and Behavior, 15,* 40–46. [12]

Goethals, G. R., & Darley, J. M. (1977). Social comparison theory: An attributional approach. In J. M. Suls & R. L. Miller (Eds.), *Social comparison processes: Theoretical and empirical perspectives* (pp. 259–278). Washington, DC: Hemisphere/Halsted. [19]

Goffman, E. (1959). *The presentation of self in everyday life.* Garden City, NY: Doubleday. [19]

Goldstein, D. B. (1983). *Pharmacology of alcohol.* New York: Oxford University Press. [7]

Goldstein, M. L. (1968). Physiological theories of emotion: A critical historical review from the standpoint of behavior theory. *Psychological Bulletin, 62,* 89–109. [6]

Goodenough, D. R. (1978). Dream recall: History and current status of the field. In A. M. Arkin, J. S. Antrobus, & S. J. Ellman (Eds.), *The mind in sleep: Psychology and psychophysiology* (pp. 113–142). Hillsdale, NJ: Lawrence Erlbaum Associates. [7]

Gordon, H. W. (1980). Degree of ear asymmetries for perception of dichotic chords and for illusory chord localization in musicians of different degrees of competence. *Journal of Experimental Psychology: Human Perception and Performance, 6,* 516–527. [5]

Gordon, I. E. (1989). *Theories of visual perception.* New York: Wiley. [4]

Gormezano, I. (1972). Investigations of defense and reward conditioning in the rabbit. In A. H. Black & W. F. Prokasy (Eds.), *Classical conditioning: II. Current research and theory* (pp. 151–181). New York: Appleton-Century-Crofts. [12]

Gottesman, I. I., & Shields, J. (1972). *Schizophrenia and genetics: A twin study vantage point.* New York: Academic Press. [24]

Gottesman, I. I., & Shields, J. (1977). Twin studies and schizophrenia a decade later. In B. A. Maher (Ed.), *Contributions to the psychopathology of schizophrenia* (pp. 253–266). New York: Academic Press. [24]

Gottesman, I. I., & Shields, J. (1982). *Schizophrenia: The epigenetic puzzle.* Cambridge, England: Cambridge University Press. [24]

Gough, H. C. (1957). *California Psychological Inventory manual.* Palo Alto, CA: Consulting Psychologists Press. [22]

Gould, J. L. (1976). The dance-language controversy. *Quarterly Review of Biology, 51,* 211–244. [8]

Gove, W. R., Hughes, M., & Galle, O. R. (1979). Overcrowding in the home: An empirical investigation of its possible pathological consequences. *American Sociological Review, 44,* 59–80. [10]

Graham, C. A., & McGrew, W. C. (1980). Menstrual synchrony in female undergraduates living on a coeducational campus. *Psychoneuroendocrinology, 5,* 245–252. [10]

Graham, C. H. (Ed.). (1965). *Vision and visual perception.* New York: Wiley. [3]

Graham, J. R. (1990). *MMPI-2: Assessing personality and psychopathology.* New York: Oxford University Press. [22]

Green, B. F., McCloskey, M., & Caramazza, A. (1985). The relation of knowledge to problem solving, with examples of kinematics. In S. F. Chipman, J. W. Segal, & R. Glaser (Eds.), *Thinking and learning skills* (Vol. 2, pp. 127–139). Hillsdale, NJ: Lawrence Erlbaum Associates. [15]

Greenberg, J. H. (Ed.). (1963). *Universals of language.* Cambridge, MA: MIT Press. [17]

Greeno, J. G. (1976). Indefinite goals in well-structured problems. *Psychological Review, 83,* 479–491. [15]

Greeno, J. G. (1978). Natures of problem-solving abilities. In W. K. Estes (Ed.), *Handbook of learning and cognitive processes: Vol. 5. Human information processing* (pp. 239–270). Hillsdale, NJ: Lawrence Erlbaum Associates. [15]

Greeno, J. G., & Bjork, R. A. (1973). Mathematical learning theory and the new "mental forestry." *Annual Review of Psychology, 24,* 81–116. [1]

Greenspoon, J. (1955). The reinforcing effect of two spoken sounds on the frequency of two responses. *American Journal of Psychology, 68,* 409–416. [12]

Grinker, J. A. (1982). Physiological and behavioral basis of human obesity. In D. W. Pfaff (Ed.), *The physiological mechanisms of motivation* (pp. 145–164). New York: Springer-Verlag. [9]

Grinker, J. A., Price, J. M., & Greenwood, M. R. C. (1976). Studies of taste in childhood obesity. In D. Novin, W. Wyrwicka, & G. Bray (Eds.), *Hunger: Basic mechanisms and clinical implications* (pp. 441–457). New York: Raven Press. [9]

Grinspoon, L., & Bakalar, J. B. (1979). *Psychedelic drugs reconsidered.* New York: Basic Books. [7]

R-15

Gross, C. G., Rocha-Miranda, C. E., & Bender, D. B. (1972). Visual properties of neurons in inferotemporal cortex of the macaque. *Journal of Neurophysiology, 35,* 96–111. [4]

Grossman, S. P. (1963). Chemically induced epileptiform seizures in the cat. *Science, 142,* 409–411. [6]

Grossman, S. P. (1964). Effects of chemical stimulation of the septal area on motivation. *Journal of Comparative and Physiological Psychology, 58,* 194–200. [6]

Grossman, S. P. (1979). The biology of motivation. *Annual Review of Psychology, 30,* 209–242. [9]

Gruber, H. E., & Clark, W. (1956). Perception of slanted surfaces. *Perceptual and Motor Skills, 6,* 97–106. [4]

Grusec, J. E., & Lytton, H. (1988). *Social development. History, theory, and research,* New York: Springer-Verlag. [18, 20]

Guilford, J. P. (1967). *The nature of human intelligence.* New York: McGraw-Hill. [22]

Guilford, J. P. (1985). The Structure-of-Intellect model. In B. B. Wolman (Ed.), *Handbook of intelligence: Theories, measurements, and applications* (pp. 225–266). New York: Wiley (Interscience). [22]

Gulick, W. L. (1989). *Hearing: Physiological acoustics, neural coding, and psychoacoustics.* New York: Oxford University Press. [3]

Hailman, J. P. (1967). The ontogeny of an instinct. *Behaviour, Supplements, 15,* 1–159. [8]

Hailman, J. P. (1969). How an instinct is learned. *Scientific American, 221,* 98–106. [8]

Halgren, E., Walter, R. D., Cherlow, A. G., & Crandall, P. H. (1978). Mental phenomena evoked by electrical stimulation of the human hippocampal formation and amygdala. *Brain, 101,* 83–117. [5]

Hall, C. S., & Lindzey, G. (1957). *Theories of personality.* New York: Wiley. [21]

Hall, D. T., & Nougaim, K. E. (1968). An examination of Maslow's need hierarchy in an organizational setting. *Organizational Behavior and Human Performance, 3,* 12–35. [11]

Hall, J. A. (1984). *Nonverbal sex differences: Communication accuracy and expressive style.* Baltimore, MD: Johns Hopkins University Press. [20]

Hall, W. G., & Blass, E. M. (1977). Orogastric determinants of drinking in rats: Interactions between absorptive and peripheral controls. *Journal of Comparative and Physiological Psychology, 91,* 365–373. [9]

Halmi, K. A., Falk, J. R., & Schwartz, E. (1981). Binge-eating and vomiting: A survey of a college population. *Psychological Medicine, 11,* 697–706. [9]

Hamilton, D. L., Dugan, P. M., & Trolier, T. K. (1985). The formation of stereotypic beliefs: Further evidence for distinctiveness-based illusory correlations. *Journal of Personality and Social Psychology, 48,* 5–17. [19]

Hammond, L. J. (1980). The effect of contingency upon the appetitive conditioning of free operant behavior. *Journal of the Experimental Analysis of Behavior, 34,* 297–304. [12]

Handel, S., & Garner, W. R. (1966). The structure of visual pattern associates and pattern goodness. *Perception & Psychophysics, 1,* 33–38. [4]

Hannigan, J. L., Shelton, T. S., Franks, J. J., & Bransford, J. D. (1980). The effects of episodic and semantic memory on the identification of sentences masked by white noise. *Memory & Cognition, 8,* 278–284. [14]

Hardin, G. (1968). The tragedy of the commons. *Science, 162,* 1243–1248. [20]

Harlow, H. F. (1962). The heterosexual affectional system in monkeys. *American Psychologist, 17,* 1–9. [20]

Harlow, H. F., & Harlow, M. K. (1962). Social deprivation in monkeys. *Scientific American, 207,* 136–146. [18]

Harlow, H. F., & Harlow, M. K. (1969). Effects of various mother-infant relationships on rhesus monkey behaviors. In B. M. Foss (Ed.), *Determinants of infant behaviour* (Vol. 4, pp. 15–36). London: Methuen. [18]

Harlow, H. F., & Zimmermann, R. R. (1959). Affectional responses in the infant monkey. *Science, 130,* 421–432. [18]

Hartshorne, H., & May, M. A. (1928). *Studies in the nature of character: Vol. 1. Studies in deceit.* New York: Macmillan. [21]

Haskett, R. F., Steiner, M., Osmun, J. N., & Carroll, B. J. (1980). Severe premenstrual tension: Delineation of the syndrome. *Biological Psychiatry, 15,* 121–139. [10]

Hatfield, E., & Sprecher, S. (1988). *Mirror, mirror . . . The importance of looks in everyday life.* Albany: State University of New York Press. [20]

Hathaway, S. R., & McKinley, J. C. (1943). *The Minnesota Multiphasic Personality Inventory.* Minneapolis: University of Minnesota Press. [22]

Hawkins, S. A., & Hastie, R. (1990). Hindsight: Biased judgments of past events after the outcomes are known. *Psychological Bulletin, 107,* 311–327. [15]

Hazan, C., & Shaver, P. (1987). Romantic love conceptualized as an attachment process. *Journal of Personality and Social Psychology, 52,* 511–524. [18]

Hearst, E. (1989). Backward associations: Differential learning about stimuli that follow the presence versus absence of food in pigeons. *Animal Learning and Behavior, 17,* 280–290. [12]

Heath, R. G. (1986). The neural substrate for emotion. In R. Plutchik & H. Kellerman (Eds.), *Emotion: Theory, research, and experience: Vol. 3. Biological foundations of emotion* (pp. 3–35). Orlando, FL: Academic Press. [6]

Heatherton, T. F., & Baumeister, R. F. (1991). Binge eating as an escape from self-awareness. *Psychological Bulletin, 110,* 86–108. [9]

Hecht, S. (1931). The interrelations of various aspects of color vision. *Journal of the Optical Society of America, 21,* 615–639. [3]

Hecht, S., & Shlaer, S. (1938). An adaptometer for measuring human dark adaptation. *Journal of the Optical Society of America, 28,* 269–275. [3]

Hecht, S., Shlaer, S., & Pirenne, M. H. (1942). Energy, quanta, and vision. *Journal of General Physiology, 25,* 819–840. [3]

Heider, F. (1958). *The psychology of interpersonal relations.* New York: Wiley. [19]

Heiman, J. R. (1977). A psychophysiological exploration of sexual arousal patterns in females and males. *Psychophysiology, 14,* 266–274. [10]

Heimburger, R. F., Whitlock, C. C., & Kalsbeck, J. E. (1966). Stereotaxic amygdalectomy for epilepsy with aggressive behavior. *JAMA, Journal of the American Medical Association, 198,* 741–745. [6]

Heinemann, E. G. (1955). Simultaneous brightness induction as a function of inducing- and test-field luminance. *Journal of Experimental Psychology, 50,* 89–96. [3]

Heller, D. (1968). Absence of size constancy in visually deprived rats. *Journal of Comparative and Physiological Psychology, 65,* 336–339. [4]

Henderson, N. D. (1982). Human behavior genetics. *Annual Review of Psychology, 33,* 403–440. [8]

Hering, E. (1964). *Outlines of a theory of the light sense.* Cambridge, MA: Harvard University Press. (Original work published 1877) [3]

Herrmann, W. M., & Beach, F. C. (1976). Psychotropic effects of androgens: A review of clinical observations and new human experimental findings. *Pharmakopsychiatrie/Neuro-Psychopharmakologie, 9,* 205–219. [10]

Herrnstein, R. J. (1973). *IQ in the meritocracy.* Boston: Atlantic Monthly Press. [22]

Hershberger, W. (1970). Attached shadow orientation perceived as depth by chickens reared in an environment illuminated from below. *Journal of Comparative and Physiological Psychology, 73,* 407–411. [4]

Hershenson, M. (1982). Moon illusion and spiral aftereffect: Illusions due to the loom-zoom system? *Journal of Experimental Psychology: General, 111,* 423–440. [4]

Heston, L. L. (1966). Psychiatric disorders in foster home reared children of schizophrenic mothers. *British Journal of Psychiatry, 112,* 819–825. [24]

Hetherington, E. M., & Parke, R. D. (1986). *Child psychology: A contemporary viewpoint* (3rd ed.). New York: McGraw-Hill. [16, 17]

Hicks, D. J. (1965). Imitation and retention of film mediated aggressive peer and adult models. *Journal of Personality and Social Psychology, 2,* 97–100. [10]

Higgins, E. T., Bargh, J. A., & Lombardi, W. (1985). The nature of priming effects on categorization. *Journal of Experimental Psychology: Learning, Memory, and Cognition, 11,* 59–69. [19]

Higgins, S. T., & Morris, E. K. (1984). Generality of free-operant avoidance conditioning to human behavior. *Psychological Bulletin, 96,* 247–272. [12]

Hilgard, E. R. (1965). *Hypnotic susceptibility.* New York: Harcourt, Brace & World. [7]

Hilgard, E. R. (1986). *Divided consciousness: Multiple controls in human thought and action, expanded edition.* New York: Wiley. [7]

Hilgard, E. R. (1987). *Psychology in America: A historical survey.* San Diego, CA: Harcourt Brace Jovanovich. [2, 16, 21, 22]

Hilgard, E. R., & Hilgard, J. R. (1984). *Hypnosis in the relief of pain.* Oxford: Freeman. [7]

Hippocrates. (1952). *On the sacred disease* (Francis Adams, Trans.). In R. M. Hutchens (Ed.), *Great books of the Western world* (Vol. 10, pp. 154–160). Chicago: Encyclopaedia Britannica. (Original work published ca. 400 B.C.) [24]

Hirschman, R., & Clark, M. (1983). Bogus physiological feedback. In J. T. Cacioppo & R. Petty (Eds.), *Social psychophysiology: A sourcebook* (pp. 177–214). New York: Guilford Press. [6]

Hirsh, J., & Knittle, J. L. (1970). Cellularity of obese and nonobese human adipose tissue. *Federation Proceedings, 29,* 1516–1521. [9]

Hirst, W., Spelke, E. S., Reaves, C. C., Caharack, G., & Neisser, U. (1980). Dividing attention without alternation or automaticity. *Journal of Experimental Psychology: General, 109,* 98–117. [13]

Hoage, C. M. (1989). The use of in-session structured eating in the outpatient treatment of bulimia nervosa. In L. M. Hornyak & E. K. Baker (Eds). *Experiential therapies for eating disorders* (pp. 60–77). New York: Guilford Press. [9]

Hobbes, T. (1952). *Leviathan.* In R. M. Hutchens (Ed.), *Great books of the Western world* (Vol. 23, pp. 45–283). Chicago: Encyclopaedia Britannica. (Original work published 1651) [19, 20]

Hobson, J. A. (1988). *The dreaming brain.* New York: Basic Books. [7]

Hochberg, J. (1971). Perception. II. Space and movement. In J. W. Kling & L. A. Riggs (Eds.), *Woodworth and Schlosberg's experimental psychology* (3rd ed., pp. 475–550). New York: Holt, Rinehart, & Winston. [4]

Hockett, C. F. (1960). The origin of speech. *Scientific American, 203*(3), 88–96. [17]

Hofstaetter, P. R. (1954). The changing composition of intelligence: A study of the *t*-technique. *Journal of Genetic Psychology, 85,* 159–164. [22]

Hogarty, G. E., Anderson, C. M., Reiss, D. J., Kornblith, S. J., Greenwald, D. P., Javna, C. D., & Madonia, M. J. (1976). Family psychoeducation, social skills training, and maintenance chemotherapy in the aftercare treatment of schizophrenia: I. One-year effects of a controlled study on relapse and expressed emotion. *Archives of General Psychiatry, 43,* 633–642. [24]

Hohmann, G. W. (1966). Some effects

of spinal cord lesions on experienced emotional feelings. *Psychophysiology, 3,* 143–156. [6]

Holding, D. H. (1970). A line illusion with irrelevant depth cues. *American Journal of Psychology, 83,* 280–282. [4]

Hollander, E. P. (1985). Leadership and power. In G. Lindzey & E. Aronson (Eds.), *Handbook of social psychology* (3rd ed., Vol. 2, pp. 485–537). New York: Random House. [20]

Hollingshead, A. B., & Redlich, F. C. (1958). *Social class and mental illness: A community study.* New York: Wiley. [24]

Hollis, K. L. (1982). Pavlovian conditioning of signal-centered action patterns and autonomic behavior: A biological analysis of function. In J. S. Rosenblatt, R. A. Hinde, C. Beer, & M.-C. Busnel (Eds.), *Advances in the study of behavior* (Vol. 12, pp. 1–64). New York: Academic Press. [12]

Holmes, J. H., & Gregerson, M. I. (1947). Relation of the salivary flow to the thirst produced in man by intravenous injection of hypertonic salt solution. *American Journal of Physiology, 151,* 252–257. [9]

Holmes, T. H., & Rahe, R. H. (1967). The social readjustment scale. *Journal of Psychosomatic Research, 11,* 213–218. [23]

Holoday, J. W., Wei, E., Loh, H., & Li, C. H. (1978). Endorphins may function in heat adaptation. *Proceedings of the National Academy of Sciences of the U.S.A., 75,* 2923–2927. [7]

Honig, W. K., & Urcuioli, P. J. (1981). The legacy of Guttman and Kalish (1956): 25 years of research on stimulus generalization. *Journal of the Experimental Analysis of Behavior, 36,* 405–445. [12]

Horne, J. A. (1983). Mammalian sleep functions with particular reference to man. In A. Mayes (Ed.), *Sleep mechanisms and functions in humans and animals—an evolutionary perspective* (pp. 262–312). Wokingham, England: Van Nostrand-Reinhold. [7]

Horney, J. (1979). Menstrual cycles and criminal responsibility. *Law and Human Behavior, 2,* 25–36. [10]

Hoving, K. L., Wallace, J. R., & LaForme, G. L. (1979). Aggression during competition: Effects of age, sex, and amount and type of provocation. *Genetic Psychology Monographs, 99,* 251–289. [10]

Hovland, C. I., Janis, I. L., & Kelley, H. H. (1953). *Communication and persuasion.* New Haven, CT: Yale University Press. [19]

Hsu, L. K. G. (1990). *Eating disorders.* New York: Guilford Press. [9]

Hubel, D. H., & Wiesel, T. N. (1962). Receptive fields, binocular interaction and functional architecture in the cat's visual cortex. *Journal of Physiology (London), 160,* 106–154. [4]

Hubel, D. H., & Wiesel, T. N. (1968). Receptive fields and functional architecture of monkey striate cortex. *Journal of Physiology (London), 195,* 215–243. [4]

Huesmann, L. R., Eron, L. D., Klein, R., Brice, P., & Fischer, P. (1983). Mitigating the imitation of aggressive behaviors by changing children's attitudes about media violence. *Journal of Personality and Social Psychology, 44,* 899–910. [10]

Hughes, J. (1975). Isolation of an endogenous compound from the brain with pharmacological properties similar to morphine. *Brain Research, 88,* 295–308. [7]

Hull, C. L. (1943). *Principles of behavior.* New York: Appleton-Century. [2]

Hume, D. (1952). *An enquiry concerning human understanding.* In R. M. Hutchens (Ed.), *Great books of the Western world* (Vol. 35, pp. 451–509). Chicago: Encyclopaedia Britannica. (Original work published 1739) [1]

Hunt, H. T. (1989). *The multiplicity of dreams: Memory, imagination, and consciousness.* New Haven, CT: Yale University Press. [7]

Hunter, R. S., Kilström, N., Kraybill,

E. N., & Loda, F. (1978). Antecedents of child abuse and neglect in premature infants: A prospective study in a newborn intensive care unit. *Pediatrics, 61,* 629–635. [8]

Hurvich, L. M., & Jameson, D. (1957). An opponent-process theory of color vision. *Psychological Review, 64,* 384–404. [3]

Hutton, R. A., Woods, S. C., & Makous, W. L. (1970). Conditioned hypoglycemia: Pseudoconditioning controls. *Journal of Comparative and Physiological Psychology, 71,* 198–201. [12]

Hyde, J. S. (1981). How large are cognitive gender differences? *American Psychologist, 36,* 892–901. [20]

Hyde, J. S. (1984). How large are gender differences in aggression? A developmental meta-analysis. *Developmental Psychology, 20,* 722–736. [20]

Imperato-McGinley, J., Guerrero, L., Gautier, T., & Peterson, R. E. (1974). Steroid 5–reductase deficiency in man: An inherited form of male pseudohermaphroditism. *Science, 186,* 1213–1215. [10]

Internal Revenue Service. (1988). *1987 federal income tax forms and instructions.* Washington, DC: Department of the Treasury. [17]

Ittelson, W. H. (1951). Size as a cue to distance: Static localization. *American Journal of Psychology, 64,* 54–67. [4]

Izard, C. E. (1971). *The face of emotion.* New York: Appleton-Century-Crofts. [19]

Jackson, D. N., Ahmed, S. A., & Heapy, N. A. (1976). Is achievement a unitary construct? *Journal of Research in Personality, 10,* 1–21. [11]

James, W. (1884). What is an emotion? *Mind, 9,* 188–205. [6]

James, W. (1890). *Principles of psychology* (Vols. 1 & 2). New York: Holt. [1, 2]

James, W. (1892). *Psychology, briefer course.* New York: Holt. [1, 2, 19]

Jameson, D., & Hurvich, L. M. (1959). Note on factors influencing the relation between stereoscopic acuity and observation distance. *Journal of the Optical Society of America, 49,* 639. [4]

Jan, L. (1980). Overcrowding and inmate behavior: Some preliminary findings. *Criminal Justice and Behavior, 7,* 293–301. [10]

Janal, M. N., Clark, W. C., & Carroll, J. D. (1991). Multidimensional scaling of painful and innocuous electrocutaneous stimuli: Reliability and individual differences. *Perception & Psychophysics, 50,* 108–116. [3]

Janis, I. L. (1958). *Psychological stress.* New York: Wiley. [23]

Janis, I. L. (1972). *Victims of groupthink: A psychological study of foreign policy decisions and fiascoes.* Boston: Houghton-Mifflin. [20]

Janis, I. L. (1982). *Groupthink* (2nd ed.). Boston: Houghton-Mifflin. [20]

Janis, I. L. (1986). Coping patterns among patients with life-threatening diseases. In C. D. Spielberger & I. G. Sarason (Eds.), *Stress and anxiety: Vol. 10. A sourcebook of theory and research* (pp. 461–476). Washington, DC: Hemisphere. [23]

Janis, I. L., & Mann, L. (1977). *Decision-making: A psychological analysis of conflict, choice and commitment.* New York: Free Press. [23]

Janman, K. (1987). Achievement motivation theory and occupational choice. *European Journal of Social Psychology, 17,* 327–346. [11]

Janoff-Bulman, R. (1979). Characterological versus behavioral self-blame: Inquiries into depression and rape. *Journal of Personality and Social Psychology, 37,* 1798–1809. [23]

Jenkins, C. D. (1971). Psychologic and social precursors of coronary disease. *New England Journal of Medicine, 284,* 244–255, 307–317. [23]

Jenkins, C. D., Zyzanski, S. J., & Rosenman, R. H. (1979). *Jenkins Activity Survey: Manual.* New York: Psychological Corporation. [23]

Jenkins, S. R. (1987). Need for achievement and women's careers over 14 years: Evidence for occupa-

tional structure effects. *Journal of Personality and Social Psychology, 53,* 922–932. [11]

Jensen, A. R. (1969). How much can we boost IQ and scholastic achievement? *Harvard Educational Review, 39,* 1–123. [22]

Johnson, C. L., Stuckey, M. K., Lewis, L. D., & Schwartz, D. M. (1982). Bulimia: A descriptive survey of 316 cases. *International Journal of Eating Disorders, 2,* 3–16. [9]

Johnson, D. J., & Rusbult, C. E. (1989). Resisting temptation: Devaluation of alternative partners as a means of maintaining commitment in close relationships. *Journal of Personality and Social Psychology, 57,* 967–980. [20]

Johnson, P., & Salisbury, D. (1975). Breathing and sucking during feeding of the newborn. In M. Hofer (Ed.), *Parent-infant interaction.* Amsterdam: Elsevier. [18]

Johnson-Laird, P. N. (1983). *Mental models: Towards a cognitive science of language, inference, and consciousness.* Cambridge, MA: Harvard University Press. [15]

Johnson-Laird, P. N., & Wason, P. C. (1977). A theoretical analysis of insight into a reasoning task, and postscript. In P. N. Johnson-Laird & P. C. Wason (Eds.), *Thinking: Readings in cognitive science* (pp. 143–157). Cambridge, England: Cambridge University Press. [15]

Johnston, J. C. (1978). A test of the sophisticated guessing theory of word perception. *Cognitive Psychology, 10,* 123–153. [13]

Johnston, L. D., O'Malley, P. M., & Bachman, J. G. (1989). *Drug use, drinking, and smoking: National survey results from high school, college, and young adult populations, 1975–1988.* Rockville, MD: National Institute on Drug Abuse. [7]

Johnston, W. A., & Dark, V. J. (1986). Selective attention. *Annual Review of Psychology, 37,* 43–75. [13]

Jones, E. E. (1990). *Interpersonal perception.* San Francisco: Freeman. [19]

Jones, E. E., & Berglas, S. (1978).

Control of attributions about the self through self-handicapping strategies: The appeal of alcohol and the role of underachievement. *Personality and Social Psychology Bulletin, 4,* 200–206. [19]

Jones, E. E., & Davis, K. E. (1965). From acts to dispositions: The attribution process in person perception. In L. Berkowitz (Ed.), *Advances in experimental social psychology* (Vol. 2, pp. 219–266). New York: Academic Press. [19]

Jones, E. E., & McGillis, D. (1976). Correspondent inferences and the attribution cube: A comparative reappraisal. In J. H. Harvey, W. J. Ickes, & R. F. Kidd (Eds.), *New directions in attribution research* (Vol. 1, pp. 389–420). Hillsdale, NJ: Lawrence Erlbaum Associates. [19]

Jones, H. C., & Lovinger, P. W. (1985). *The marijuana question.* New York: Dodd, Mead. [7]

Jones, R. M. (1970). *The new psychology of dreaming.* New York: Grune & Stratton. [7]

Jouvet, M. (1967). Neurophysiology of the state of sleep. *Physiological Review, 47,* 117–177. [7]

Jouvet, M. (1969). Biogenic amines and the states of sleep. *Science, 163,* 32–41. [7]

Jouvet, M. (1974). Monoaminergic regulation of the sleep-waking cycle in the cat. In F. O. Schmitt & F. G. Worden (Eds.), *The neurosciences: Third study program* (pp. 499–508). Cambridge, MA: MIT Press. [7]

Julien, R. M. (1988). *A primer of drug action* (5th ed.). New York: Freeman. [7]

Jung, C. G. (Ed.). (1964). *Man and his symbols.* London: Aldus. [21]

Kagan, J. (1984). *The nature of the child.* New York: Basic Books. [18]

Kahneman, D. (1973). *Attention and effort.* Englewood Cliffs, NJ: Prentice-Hall. [13]

Kahneman, D., Slovic, P., & Tversky, A. (Eds.). (1982). *Judgment under uncertainty: Heuristics and biases.* New York: Cambridge University Press. [15, 19]

Kahneman, D., & Tversky, A. (1973).

On the psychology of prediction. *Psychological Review, 80,* 237–251. [15, 19]

Kales, A., Tan, T. L., Kollar, E. J., Naitoh, P., Preston, T. A., & Malmstrom, E. J. (1970). Sleep patterns following 204 hours of sleep deprivation. *Psychosomatic Medicine, 32,* 189–200. [7]

Kamin, L. J. (1974). *The science and politics of IQ.* Hillsdale, NJ: Lawrence Erlbaum Associates. [22]

Kamin, L. J. (1969). Predictability, surprise, attention, and conditioning. In B. A. Campbell & R. M. Church (Eds.), *Punishment and aversive behavior* (pp. 279–296). New York: Appleton-Century-Crofts. [12]

Kanner, A. D., Coyne, J. C., Schaefer, C., & Lazarus, R. S. (1982). Comparisons of two modes of stress measurement: Daily hassles and uplifts versus major life events. *Journal of Behavioral Medicine, 4,* 1–39. [23]

Kant, I. (1952). *Critique of pure reason* (J. M. D. Meikeljohn, Trans.). In R. M. Hutchens (Ed.), *Great books of the Western world* (Vol. 42, pp. 1–250). Chicago: Encyclopaedia Britannica. (Original work published 1781) [1]

Kaplan, E., & Kaplan, G. (1971). The prelinguistic child. In J. Elliot (Ed.), *Human development and cognitive processes* (pp. 359–381). New York: Holt. [17]

Karasek, R. A., Russell, R. S., & Theorell, T. (1982, March). Physiology of stress and regeneration in job-related cardiovascular illness. *Journal of Human Stress,* pp. 29–42. [23]

Karlins, M., Coffman, T. L., & Walters, G. (1969). On the fading of social stereotypes: Studies in three generations of college students. *Journal of Personality and Social Psychology, 13,* 1–16. [19]

Katz, D. (1989). *The world of touch.* Hillsdale, NJ: Lawrence Erlbaum Associates. [3]

Katz, D., & Braly, K. W. (1933). Racial stereotypes of one hundred college students. *Journal of Abnormal and Social Psychology, 28,* 282–290. [19]

Katz, D., & Stotland, E. (1959). A preliminary statement to a theory of attitude structure and change. In S. Koch (Ed.), *Psychology: Study of a science* (Vol. 3, pp. 423–475). New York: McGraw-Hill. [19]

Katzner, K. (1975). *The languages of the world.* New York: Funk & Wagnalls. [17]

Kaufman, L., & Rock, I. (1962). The moon illusion. I. *Science, 136,* 953–961. [4]

Kaufmann, G. (1985). A theory of symbolic representation in problem solving. *Journal of Mental Imagery, 9,* 51–70. [15]

Kawai, M. (1965). Newly acquired pre-cultural behavior of the natural troop of Japanese monkeys on Koshima Islet. *Primates, 6,* 1–30. [8]

Kaye, H. (1977). Infant sucking behaviour and its modification. In L. P. Lipsitt & C. C. Spiker (Eds.), *Advances in child development and behaviour* (Vol. 3, pp. 2–52). London & New York: Academic Press. [18]

Keating, D. P. (1984). The emperor's new clothes: The "New Look" in intelligence research. In R. J. Sternberg (Ed.), *Advances in the psychology of human intelligence* (Vol. 2, pp. 1–45). Hillsdale, NJ: Lawrence Erlbaum Associates. [22]

Keesey, R. E., & Powley, T. L. (1986). The regulation of body weight. *Annual Review of Psychology, 37,* 109–133. [9]

Kehoe, E. J. (1983). CS-US contiguity and CS intensity in conditioning of the rabbit's nictitating membrane response to serial compound stimuli. *Journal of Experimental Psychology: Animal Behavior Processes, 9,* 307–319. [12]

Kelley, H. H. (1967). Attribution theory in social psychology. In D. Levine (Ed.), *Nebraska Symposium on Motivation 1967* (pp. 192–238). Lincoln: University of Nebraska Press. [19]

Kelley, H. H. (1972). Causal schemata and the attribution process. In E. E. Jones, D. E. Kanouse, H. H. Kelley, R. E. Nisbett, S. Valins, & B. Weiner (Eds.), *Attribution: Perceiving the causes of behavior* (pp. 151–174). Morristown, NJ: General Learning Press. [19]

Kelley, H. H. (1973). The processes of causal attribution. *American Psychologist, 28,* 107–128. [19]

Kelley, H. H., & Michela, J. L. (1980). Attribution theory and research. *Annual Review of Psychology, 31,* 457–501. [19]

Kelley, H. H., & Thibaut, J. W. (1978). *Interpersonal relations: A theory of interdependence.* New York: Wiley. [20]

Kelman, H. C., & Hamilton, V. L. (1990). *Crimes of obedience.* New Haven, CT: Yale University Press. [20]

Kelsey, J. E., & Grossman, S. P. (1969). Cholinergic blockage and lesions in the ventromedial septum of the rat. *Physiology and Behavior, 4,* 837–845. [6]

Kemper, T. D. (1984). Power, status, and emotions: A sociological contribution to a psychophysiological domain. In K. R. Scherer & P. Ekman (Eds.), *Approaches to emotion* (pp. 369–383). Hillsdale, NJ: Lawrence Erlbaum Associates. [6]

Kendall, S. B. (1972). Some effects of response-dependent clock stimuli in a fixed-interval schedule. *Journal of the Experimental Analysis of Behavior, 17,* 161–168. [12]

Kendler, H. H., & Kendler, T. S. (1962). Vertical and horizontal processes in problem solving. *Psychological Review, 69,* 1–16. [15]

Kendler, K. S., & Robinette, C. D. (1983). Schizophrenia in the National Academy of Sciences–National Research Council twin registry: A 16-year update. *American Journal of Psychiatry, 140,* 1551–1563. [8]

Kenshalo, D. R., Decker, T., & Hamilton, A. (1967). Spatial summation on the forehead, forearm, and back produced by radiant and conducted heat. *Journal of Comparative and Physiological Psychology, 63,* 510–515. [3]

Kenshalo, D. R., & Nafe, J. P. (1962). A quantitative theory of feeling: 1960. *Psychological Review, 69,* 17–33. [3]

Kety, S. S. (1987). The significance of genetic factors in the etiology of schizophrenia: Results from the national study of adoptees in Denmark. *Journal of Psychiatric Research, 21,* 423–429. [24]

Kihlstrom, J. F. (1980). Posthypnotic amnesia for recently learned material: Interactions with "episodic" and "semantic" memory. *Cognitive Psychology, 12,* 227–251. [14]

Kimura, D. (1961). Some effects of temporal lobe damage on auditory perception. *Canadian Journal of Psychology, 15,* 156–165. [5]

Kimura, D. (1967). Functional asymmetry of the brain in dichotic listening. *Cortex, 3,* 163–178. [5]

Kimura, D., & Folb, S. (1968). Neural processing of backward speech sounds. *Science, 161,* 395–396. [5]

Kinney, G. C., Marsetta, M., & Showman, D. J. (1966). *Studies in display symbol legibility. Part XII. The legibility of alpha-numeric symbols for digitalized television* (ESD-TR-66–117). Bedford, MA: Mitre Corp. [13]

Kinsbourne, M., & Wood, F. (1975). Short-term memory processes and the amnesic syndrome. In D. Deutsch & J. A. Deutsch (Eds.), *Short-term memory* (pp. 258–291). New York: Academic Press. [5]

Klahr, D., & Wallace, J. G. (1976). *Cognitive development: An information processing view.* Hillsdale, NJ: Lawrence Erlbaum Associates. [16]

Klatsky, R., & Atkinson, R. (1971). Specialization of the cerebral hemispheres in scanning for information in short-term memory. *Perception & Psychophysics, 10,* 335–338. [5]

Klaus, M., & Kennell, J. (1982). *Parent-infant bonding.* St. Louis, MO: Mosby. [18]

Kleck, R. E., Vaughan, R. C., Cartwright-Smith, J., Vaughan, K. B., Colby, C. Z., & Lanzetta, J. T. (1976). Effects of being observed on expressive, subjective, and physiological responses to painful stimuli. *Journal of Personality and Social Psychology, 34,* 1211–1218. [6]

Klein, M., & Stern, L. (1971). Low birth weight and the battered child syndrome. *American Journal of Disorders in Children, 122,* 15–18. [8]

Klerman, G. L. (1975). Drug therapy of clinical depressions: Current status and implications for future research on neuropharmacology of the affective disorders. In D. F. Klein & R. Gittelman-Klein (Eds.), *Progress in psychiatric drug treatment.* New York: Brunner/Mazel. [25]

Klima, E. S., & Bellugi, U. (1979). *The signs of language.* Cambridge, MA: Harvard University Press. [17]

Klüver, H., & Bucy, P. C. (1937). "Psychic blindness" and other symptoms following bilateral temporal lobectomy in rhesus monkeys. *American Journal of Physiology, 119,* 352–353. [6]

Koestler, A. (1964). *The act of creation.* London: Hutchinson. [15]

Koffka, K. (1935). *Principles of Gestalt psychology.* New York: Harcourt. [4]

Kohlberg, L. (1969). Stage and sequence: The cognitive-developmental approach to socialization. In D. A. Goslin (Ed.), *Handbook of socialization theory and research* (pp. 347–480). Chicago: Rand McNally. [18]

Kohlberg, L. (1981). *The philosophy of moral development: Moral stages and the idea of justice: Vol. 1. Essays on moral development.* San Francisco: Harper & Row. [18]

Köhler, W. (1947). *Gestalt psychology.* New York: Liveright. [4]

Köhler, W. (1956). *The mentality of apes.* London: Routledge & Kegan Paul. [15]

Kolb, B., & Whishaw, I. Q. (1985). *Fundamentals of human neuropsychology* (2nd ed.). New York: Freeman. [5]

Kolers, P. A., & von Grunau, M. (1976). Shape and color in apparent motion. *Vision Research, 16,* 329–335. [4]

Koob, G. F., Stinus, L., LeMoal, M., & Bloom, F. E. (1989). Opponent process theory of motivation: Neurobiological evidence from studies of opiate dependence. *Neuroscience and Biobehavioral Reviews, 13,* 135–140. [6]

Kosslyn, S. M. (1975). Information representation in visual images. *Cognitive Psychology, 7,* 341–370. [14]

Kosslyn, S. M. (1980). *Image and mind.* Cambridge, MA: Harvard University Press. [14]

Kosslyn, S. M., Ball, T. M., & Reiser, B. J. (1978). Visual images preserve metric spatial information: Evidence from studies of image scanning. *Journal of Experimental Psychology: Human Perception and Performance, 4,* 47–60. [13]

Kraepelin, E. (1883). *Lehrbuch der Psychiatrie* (1st ed.; 8th ed., 1915). *Clinical psychiatry* (A. R. Diefendorf, Trans. from 7th German edition). Delmar, NY: Scholars' Facsimiles and Reprints, 1981. [24]

Krane, R. V., & Wagner, A. R. (1975). Taste aversion learning with a delayed shock US: Implications for the "generality of the laws of learning." *Journal of Comparative and Physiological Psychology, 88,* 882–889. [12]

Krantz, D. S., Lundberg, U., & Frankenhaeuser, M. (1987). Stress and Type A behavior: Interactions between environmental and biological factors. In A. Baum & J. E. Singer (Eds.), *Handbook of psychology and health: Vol. 5. Stress* (pp. 203–228). Orlando, FL: Academic Press. [23]

Kraut, R. E., & Johnston, R. E. (1979). Social and emotional messages of smiling: An ethological approach. *Journal of Personality and Social Psychology, 37,* 1539–1553. [19]

Kuhl, J., & Blankenship, V. (1979). Behavioral change in a constant environment: Shift to more difficult tasks with constant probability of success. *Journal of Personality and Social Psychology, 37,* 551–563. [11]

Kuhn, D. Z., Madsen, C. H., & Becker, W. C. (1967). Effects of exposure to an aggressive model and "frustration" on children's aggressive behavior. *Child Development, 38,* 739–745. [10]

Kuhn, T. S. (1962). *The structure of scientific revolutions.* Chicago: University of Chicago Press. [1]

LaBerge, S. (1985). *Lucid dreaming.* Boston: Houghton-Mifflin. [7]

Labov, W. (1973). The boundaries of words and their meanings. In C. J. N. Bailey & R. W. Shuy (Eds.), *New ways of analyzing variation in English* (pp. 340–373). Washington, DC: Georgetown University Press. [14]

Lacey, J. I., Smith, R. L., & Green, A. (1955). Use of conditioned autonomic responses in the study of anxiety. *Psychosomatic Medicine, 17,* 208–217. [12]

Ladefoged, P. (1971). *Preliminaries to linguistic phonetics.* Chicago: University of Chicago Press. [17]

LaFerla, J. J., Anderson, D. L., & Schalch, D. S. (1978). Psychoendocrine response to sexual arousal in human males. *Psychosomatic Medicine, 40,* 166–172. [10]

Lamb, M. E., & Sternberg, K. J. (1990). Do we really know how day care affects children? *Journal of Applied Developmental Psychology, 11,* 351–379. [18]

Lamb, M. E., Thompson, R. A., Gardner, W., & Charnov, E. L. (1985). *Infant-mother attachment: The origins and developmental significance of individual differences in strange situation behavior.* Hillsdale, NJ: Lawrence Erlbaum Associates. [18]

Lambert, M. J. (1983). Introduction to assessment of psychotherapy outcome: Historical perspective and current issues. In M. J. Lambert, E. R. Christensen, & S. S. DeJulio (Eds.), *The assessment of psychotherapy outcome* (pp. 3–32). New York: Wiley. [25]

Landman, J. T., & Dawes, R. M. (1982). Psychotherapy outcome: Smith and Glass' conclusions stand up under scrutiny. *American Psychologist, 37,* 504–516. [25]

Lange, C. G., & James, W. (1967). *The emotions.* New York: Hafner. (Original work published 1885) [6]

Langer, E. J., Janis, I. L., & Wolfer, J. A. (1975). Reduction of psychological stress in surgical patients. *Journal of Experimental Social Psychology, 11,* 155–165. [23]

Lanzetta, J. T., & Kleck, R. E. (1970). Encoding and decoding of nonverbal affect in humans. *Journal of Personality and Social Psychology, 16,* 12–19. [6]

Lapsley, D. K., & Power, F. C. (Eds.). (1988). *Self, ego, and identity: Integrative approaches.* New York: Springer-Verlag. [18]

Lashley, K. S. (1938). Experimental analysis of instinctive behavior. *Psychological Review, 45,* 445–471. [8]

Lashley, K. S. (1950). In search of the engram. *Symposia of the Society for Experimental Biology, 4,* 454–482. [5]

Lass, R. (1984). *Phonology: An introduction to basic concepts.* New York: Cambridge University Press. [17]

Lawler, E. E., & Suttle, J. L. (1972). A causal correlation test of the need hierarchy concept. *Organizational Behavior and Human Performance, 7,* 265–287. [11]

Lazarus, R. S., & Folkman, S. (1984). *Stress, appraisal, and coping.* New York: Springer. [23]

Lea, S. E. G. (1984). *Instinct, environment and behavior.* London: Methuen. [8]

Lea, S. E. G., Tarpy, R. M., & Webley, P. (1987). *The individual in the economy: A survey of economic psychology.* New York: Cambridge University Press. [11]

Ledlow, A., Swanson, J. M., & Kinsbourne, M. (1978). Reaction times and evoked potentials as indicators of hemispheric differences for laterally presented name and physical matches. *Journal of Experimental Psychology: Human Perception and Performance, 4,* 440–454. [5]

Lenneberg, E. *Biological foundations of language.* New York: Wiley. [17]

Leon, G. R. (1983). Anorexia nervosa: The question of treatment emphasis. In M. Rosenbaum, C. M. Franks, & Y. Jaffe (Eds.), *Perspectives on behavior therapy in the eighties* (Vol. 9, pp. 363–377). New York: Springer. [9]

Lepper, M. R., & Greene, D. (Eds.). (1978). *The hidden costs of reward.* Hillsdale, NJ: Lawrence Erlbaum Associates. [19]

Leshner, A. I. (1978). *An introduction to behavioral endocrinology.* New York: Oxford University Press. [10]

Lessard v. Schmidt, 349 F. Supp. 1078 (E. D. Wisc. 1972), vacated and remanded on other grounds, 94 S. Ct. 713 (1974), *reinstated* 413 F. Supp. 1318 (E. D. Wisc. 1976). [25]

Leventhal, H., & Tomarken, A. J. (1986). Emotion: Today's problems. *Annual Review of Psychology, 37,* 565–610. [6]

Levine, M. (1966). Hypothesis behavior by humans during discrimination learning. *Journal of Experimental Psychology, 71,* 331–338. [15]

Levine, M. (1975). *A cognitive theory of learning.* Hillsdale, NJ: Lawrence Erlbaum Associates. [15]

Levinson, D. J. (1978). *The seasons of a man's life.* New York: Ballantine. [18]

Levinson, D. J. (1986). A conception of adult development. *American Psychologist, 11,* 3–13. [18]

Levinthal, C. F., Tartell, R. H., Margolin, C. M., & Fishman, H. (1985). The CS-US interval (ISI) function in rabbit nictitating membrane response conditioning with very long intertrial intervals. *Animal Learning and Behavior, 13,* 228–232. [12]

Levy, J. (1980). Cerebral asymmetry and the psychology of man. In M. C. Wittrock (Ed.), *The brain and psychology* (pp. 245–321). New York: Academic Press. [20]

Lewin, K. (1935). *A dynamic theory of personality.* New York: McGraw-Hill.

Lewin, K. (1951). Problems of research in social psychology. In D. Cartwright (Ed.), *Field theory in social science: Selected theoretical papers by Kurt Lewin* (pp. 155–169). New York: Harper & Row. [20]

Lewinsohn, P. M. (1975). The behavioral study and treatment of depression. In M. Hersen, R. M. Eisler, & P. M. Miller (Eds.), *Progress in behavior modification*. New York: Academic Press. [25]

Lewis, N. D. D., Landis, C., & King, H. E. (1956). *Studies in topectomy*. New York: Grune & Stratton. [5]

Lichtenstein, S., Slovic, P., Fischhoff, B., Layman, M., & Combs, B. (1978). Judged frequency of lethal events. *Journal of Experimental Psychology: Human Learning and Memory, 4*, 551–578. [15]

Lieberman, D. A. (1990) *Learning: Behavior and cognition*. Belmont, CA: Wadsworth. [12]

Lindsay, P. H., & Norman, D. A. (1972). *Human information processing*. New York: Academic Press. [13]

Linz, D., Donnerstein, E., Bross, M., & Chapin, M. (1986). Mitigating the influence of violence on television and sexual violence in the media. In R. J. Blanchard & D. C. Blanchard (Eds.), *Advances in the study of aggression* (Vol. 2, pp. 165–194). Orlando, FL: Academic Press. [10]

Lipsitt, L. P. (1977). The study of sensory and learning processes of the newborn. *Clinical Perinatology, 4*(1), 163–186. [18]

Lisker, L., & Abramson, A. S. (1970). The voicing dimension: Some experiments in comparative phonetics. *Proceedings of the Sixth International Congress of Phonetic Sciences*. Prague: Academia. [17]

Lloyd, C. W. (1964). Treatment and prevention of certain sexual behavioral problems. In C. W. Lloyd (Ed.), *Human reproduction and sexual behavior* (pp. 498–510). Philadelphia: Lea & Febiger. [10]

Locke, J. (1952). *An essay concerning human understanding*. In R. M. Hutchens (Ed.), *Great books of the Western world* (Vol. 35, pp. 85–395). Chicago: Encyclopaedia Britannica. (Original work published 1690) [1, 24]

Loehlin, J. C., & Nichols, R. C. (1976). *Heredity, environment, and personality: A study of 850 sets of twins*. Austin: University of Texas Press. [8]

Loftus, E. F. (1979). *Eyewitness testimony*. Cambridge, MA: Harvard University Press. [14]

Loftus, E. F., & Loftus, G. R. (1980). On the permanence of stored information in the human brain. *American Psychologist, 35*, 49–72. [5]

Loftus, E. F., & Palmer, J. C. (1974). Reconstruction of automobile destruction: An example of the interaction between language and memory. *Journal of Verbal Learning and Verbal Behavior, 13*, 585–589. [14]

Logan, G. D. (1988). Toward an instance theory of automatization. *Psychological Review, 95*, 492–527. [13]

Logue, A. W. (1979). Taste aversion and the generality of the laws of learning. *Psychological Bulletin, 86*, 276–296. [12]

Logue, A. W. (1986). *The psychology of eating and drinking*. New York: Freeman. [9]

Longley, J., & Pruitt, D. G. (1980). Groupthink: A critique of Janis's theory. In L. Wheeler (Ed.), *Review of personality and social psychology* (Vol. 1, pp. 74–93). Beverly Hills, CA: Sage. [20]

Lorch, R. F. (1978). The role of two types of semantic information in the processing of false sentences. *Journal of Verbal Learning and Verbal Behavior, 17*, 523–538. [14]

Lorenz, K. (1943). Die angeborenen Formen moglicher Erfahrung. *Zeitshrift für Tierpsychologie, 5*, 235–409. [8]

Lorenz, K. (1966). *On aggression*. New York: Harcourt Brace & World. [10]

Lowe, D. G., & Mitterer, J. O. (1982). Selective and divided attention in a Stroop task. *Canadian Journal of Psychology, 36*, 684–700. [13]

Lowinger, P., & Dobie, S. (1969). What makes the placebo work? A study of placebo response rates. *Archives of General Psychiatry, 20*, 84–88. [25]

Lubinski, D., & Thompson, T. (1987). An animal model of the interpersonal communication of interoceptive (private) states. *Journal of the Experimental Analysis of Behavior, 48*, 1–15. [12]

Luce, R. D., & Raiffa, H. (1957). *Games and decisions*. New York: Wiley. [20]

Luchins, A. S. (1942). Mechanization in problem solving. *Psychological Monographs, 54*, (Whole No. 248). [15]

Luchins, A. S., & Luchins, E. H. (1950). New experimental attempts at preventing mechanization in problem solving. *Journal of General Psychology, 42*, 279–297. [15]

Lynn, S. J., Rhue, J. W., & Weeks, J. R. (1990). Hypnotic involuntariness: A social cognitive analysis. *Psychological Review, 97*, 169–184. [7]

Lytton, H. (1980). *Parent-child interaction: The socialization process observed in twin and singleton families*. New York: Plenum. [18]

Macaulay, J. (1985). Adding gender to aggression research: Incremental or revolutionary change? In V. E. O'Leary, R. K. Unger, & B. S. Wallston (Eds.), *Women, gender, and social psychology* (pp. 191–224). Hillsdale, NJ: Lawrence Erlbaum Associates. [20]

Maccoby, E. E., & Jacklin, C. N. (1974). *The psychology of sex differences*. Stanford, CA: Stanford University Press. [20]

Machiavelli, N. (1952). *The prince*. In R. M. Hutchens (Ed.), *Great books of the Western world* (Vol. 23, pp. 1–37). Chicago: Encyclopaedia Britannica. (Original work published 1513) [20]

Mack, J. L., & Boller, F. (1977). Associative visual agnosia and its related deficits: The role of the minor hemisphere in assigning meaning to visual perceptions. *Neuropsychologia, 15*, 345–350. [5]

Mackenzie, B. (1984). Explaining race differences in IQ: The logic, the methodology, and the evidence. *American Psychologist, 39*, 1214–1233. [22]

MacLeod, C. M. (1991). Half a century of research on the Stroop effect: An integrative review. *Psychological Bulletin, 109,* 163–203. [13]

Madden, T. M., & Burt, G. S. (1981). Inappropriate constancy scaling theory and the Muller-Lyer illusion. *Perceptual and Motor Skills, 52,* 211–218. [4]

Maddi, S. R. (1989). *Personality theories: A comparative analysis* (5th ed.). Chicago: Dorsey. [18, 21]

Mahone, C. H. (1960). Fear of failure of unrealistic vocational aspiration. *Journal of Abnormal and Social Psychology, 60,* 253–261. [11]

Maier, N. R. F. (1945). Reasoning in humans: III. The mechanisms of equivalent stimuli of reasoning. *Journal of Experimental Psychology, 35,* 349–360. [15]

Maier, S. F., Seligman, M. E. P., & Solomon, R. L. (1969). Pavlovian fear conditioning and learned helplessness: Effects on escape and avoidance behavior of (a) the CS-US contingency and (b) the independence of the US and voluntary responding. In B. A. Campbell & R. M. Church (Eds.), *Punishment and aversive behavior.* New York: Appleton-Century-Crofts. [24]

Main, M., & Weston, D. (1981). The quality of the toddler's relationship to mother and father: Related to conflict behavior and the readiness to establish new relationships. *Child Development, 52,* 932–940. [18]

Major, B., & Deaux, K. (1981). Individual differences in justice behavior. In J. Greenberg & R. L. Cohen (Eds.), *Equity and justice in social behavior* (pp. 43–76). New York: Academic Press. [20]

Major, B., & Testa, M. (1989). Social comparison processes in judgments of entitlement and satisfaction. *Journal of Experimental Social Psychology, 25,* 101–120. [20]

Maki, R. H., & Schuler, J. (1980). Effects of rehearsal duration and level of processing on memory for words. *Journal of Verbal Learning and Verbal Behavior, 19,* 36–45. [13]

Malamud, J. R. (1988). Learning to become fully lucid: A program for inner growth. In J. Gackenbach & S. LaBerge (Eds.), *Conscious mind, sleeping brain: Perspectives on lucid dreaming* (pp. 309–319). New York: Plenum. [7]

Malatesta, C. Z. (1985). Developmental course of emotion expression in the human infant. In G. Zivin (Ed.), *The development of expressive behavior: biological-environment interactions* (pp. 183–219). Orlando, FL: Academic Press. [6]

Malvin, R. L., Mouw, D., & Vander, A. J. (1977). Angiotensin: Physiological role in water-deprivation-induced thirst of rats. *Science, 197,* 171–173. [9]

Mandler, G., & Sarason, S. (1952). A study of anxiety and learning. *Journal of Abnormal and Social Psychology, 47,* 166–173. [11]

Manning, A. A., Schneiderman, N., & Lordahl, D. S. (1969). Delay vs. trace heart rate classical discrimination conditioning in rabbits as a function of ISI. *Journal of Experimental Psychology, 80,* 225–230. [12]

Maratsos, M. (1983). Some current issues in the study of the acquisition of grammar. In P. H. Mussen (Ed.), *Handbook of child psychology* (4th ed., Vol. 3, pp. 707–786). New York: Wiley. [17]

Marcia, J. E. (1980). Identity in adolescence. In J. Adelson (Ed.), *Handbook of adolescent psychology* (pp. 159–187). New York: Wiley. [18]

Marcia, J. E. (1988). Common processes underlying ego identity, cognitive/moral development, and individuation. In D. K. Lapsley & F. C. Power (Eds.), *Self, ego, and identity: Integrative approaches* (pp. 211–225). New York: Springer-Verlag. [18]

Markowitsch, H. J. (1982). Thalamic mediodorsal nucleus and memory: A critical evaluation of studies in animals and man. *Neuroscience and Biobehavioral Review, 6,* 351–380. [5]

Marks, W. B., Dobelle, W. H., & MacNichol, E. F. (1964). Visual pigments of single primate cones. *Science, 143,* 1181–1183. [3]

Markus, H., & Kunda, Z. (1986). Sta-bility and malleability of the self-concept. *Journal of Personality and Social Psychology, 51,* 858–866. [21]

Marshall, D. A., & Moulton, D. G. (1981). Olfactory sensitivity to α-ionine in humans and dogs. *Chemical Senses, 6,* 53–61. [3]

Marshall, G. O., & Zimbardo, P. G. (1979). Affective consequences of inadequately explained arousal. *Journal of Personality and Social Psychology, 37,* 970–978. [6]

Marshall, J. F., Turner, B. H., & Teitelbaum, P. (1971). Sensory neglect produced by lateral hypothalamic damage. *Science, 174,* 523–525. [9]

Martin, H. P. (1976). Which children get abused: High risk factors in the child. In H. P. Martin (Ed.), *The abused child* (pp. 27–41). Cambridge, MA: Ballinger. [8]

Maslach, C. (1979). Negative emotional biasing of unexplained arousal. *Journal of Personality and Social Psychology, 37,* 953–969. [6]

Maslow, A. H. (1943). A theory of human motivation. *Psychological Review, 50,* 370–396. [11]

Maslow, A. H. (1954). *Motivation and personality.* New York: Harper. [21]

Maslow, A. H. (1970). *Motivation and personality.* New York: Harper & Row. (Original work published 1954) [11]

Mason, J. W. (1975). A historical view of the stress field. *Journal of Human Stress, 1*(2), 22–36. [23]

Masters, J. C., Burish, T. G., Hollon, S. D., & Rimm, D. C. (1987). *Behavior therapy: Techniques and empirical findings* (3rd ed.). San Diego, CA: Harcourt Brace Jovanovich. [12]

Masters, W. H., & Johnson, V. J. (1966). *The human sexual response.* Boston: Little, Brown. [10]

Masters, W. H., & Johnson, V. J. (1979). *Homosexuality in perspective.* Boston: Little, Brown. [10]

Matsumoto, D., & Ekman, P. (1989). American-Japanese cultural differences in intensity ratings of facial expressions of emotion. *Motivation and Emotion, 13,* 143–157. [6]

Maurer, D., & Salapatek, P. (1976). Developmental changes in the scanning of faces by young infants. *Child Development, 47,* 523–527. [4]

Mawhinney, V. T., Bostow, D. E., Laws, D. R., Blumenfeld, G. J., & Hopkins, B. L. (1971). A comparison of students' studying behavior produced by daily, weekly, and three-week testing schedules. *Journal of Applied Behavior Analysis, 4,* 257–264. [12]

Maxson, S. C. (1981). The genetics of aggression in vertebrates. In P. F. Brain & D. Benton (Eds.), *The biology of aggression.* (pp. 69–104). Alphen aan den Rijn: Noordhoff-Sijthoff. [10]

Mayer, J. (1953). Glucostatic mechanism of regulation of food intake. *New England Journal of Medicine, 249,* 13–16. [9]

Mayer, J. (1955). Regulation of energy intake and the body weight: The glucostatic theory and the lipostatic hypothesis. *Annals of the New York Academy of Sciences, 63,* 15–43. [9]

Mayer, J. (1965). Genetic factors in human obesity. *Annals of the New York Academy of Sciences, 131,* 412–421. [9]

Mayer, R. E. (1979). Qualitatively different encoding strategies for linear reasoning premises: Evidence for single association and distance theories. *Journal of Experimental Psychology: Human Learning and Memory, 5,* 1–10. [15]

Mayer, R. E. (1983). *Thinking, problem solving, cognition.* New York: Freeman. [15]

Mayer, R. E. (1985). Implications of cognitive psychology for instruction in mathematical problem solving. In E. A. Silver (Ed.), *Teaching and learning mathematical problem solving* (pp. 123–138). Hillsdale, NJ: Lawrence Erlbaum Associates. [15]

Mayes, A. (1983). *Sleep mechanisms and functions in humans and animals: An evolutionary perspective.* Wokingham, England: Van Nostrand-Reinhold. [7]

Mazur, J. E. (1990). *Learning and*

behavior (2nd ed.). Englewood Cliffs, NJ: Prentice-Hall. [12]

McCauley, C. L. (1989). The nature of social influence in groupthink: Compliance and internalization. *Journal of Personality and Social Psychology, 57,* 250–260. [20]

McCauley, C. L., & Stitt, C. L. (1978). An individual and quantitative measure of stereotypes. *Journal of Personality and Social Psychology, 36,* 929–940. [19]

McClearn, G. E., & DeFries, J. C. (1973). *Introduction to behavioral genetics.* San Francisco: Freeman. [8]

McClelland, D. C. (1961). *The achieving society.* Princeton, NJ: Van Nostrand. [11]

McClelland, D. C. (1975). *Power, the inner experience.* New York: Irvington. [11]

McClelland, D. C., Atkinson, J. W., Clark, R. A., & Lowell, E. L. (1953). *The achievement motive.* New York: Appleton-Century-Crofts. [11]

McClelland, D. C., Davis, W. N., Kalin, R., & Wanner, E. (1972). *The drinking man.* New York: Free Press. [11]

McClelland, D. C., Koestner, R., & Weinberger, J. (1989). How do self-attributed and implicit motives differ? *Psychological Review, 96,* 690–702. [11]

McClelland, D. C., & Steele, R. S. (1972). *Motivation workshops: A student workbook for experiential learning in human motivation.* New York: General Learning Press. [11]

McClelland, D. C., & Winter, D. G. (1969). *Motivating economic achievement.* New York: Free Press. [11]

McCloskey, M., & Glucksberg, S. (1979). Decision processes in verifying category membership statements: Implications for models of semantic memory. *Cognitive Psychology, 11,* 1–37. [14]

McCutcheon, N. B., & Saunders, J. (1972). Human taste papilla stimulation: Stability of quality judgments over time. *Science, 175,* 214–217. [3]

McDougall, W. (1908). *An introduction to social psychology.* London: Methuen. [1]

McGeer, P. L., & McGeer, E. G. (1980). Chemistry of mood and emotion. *Annual Review of Psychology, 31,* 273–307. [6]

McGuire, W. J. (1985). Attitudes and attitude change. In G. Lindzey & E. Aronson (Eds.), *Handbook of social psychology* (3rd ed., Vol. 2, pp. 233–346). New York: Random House. [19]

McGuire, W. J., & McGuire, C. V. (1988). Content and process in the experience of self. In L. Berkowitz (Ed.), *Advances in experimental social psychology* (Vol. 21, pp. 97–144). San Diego, CA: Academic Press. [20]

McGuire, W. J., McGuire, C. V., & Winton, W. (1979). Effects of household sex composition on the salience of one's gender in the spontaneous self-concept. *Journal of Experimental Social Psychology, 15,* 77–90. [20]

McIsaac, W. M. Frichie, G. E., Idanpaan-Heikkila, J. E., Ho, B. G., & Englert, L. F. (1971). Distribution of marihuana in monkey brain and concomitant behavioral effects. *Nature (London), 230,* 593–594. [7]

McKenna, R. J. (1972). Some effects of anxiety level and food cues on the eating behavior of obese and normal subjects: A comparison of the Schachterian and psychosomatic conceptions. *Journal of Personality and Social Psychology, 22,* 311–319. [9]

McKoon, G. (1977). Organization of information in text memory. *Journal of Verbal Learning and Verbal Behavior, 16,* 247–260. [13]

McKoon, G., Ratcliff, R., & Dell, G. S. (1986). A critical evaluation of the semantic-episodic distinction. *Journal of Experimental Psychology: Learning, Memory, and Cognition, 12,* 295–306. [14]

McKusick, V. A. (1983). *Mendelian inheritance in man* (7th ed.). Baltimore, MD: Johns Hopkins University Press. [16]

McNally, R. J. (1987). Preparedness

and phobias: A review. *Psychological Bulletin, 101,* 283–303. [12]

Meddis, R. (1977). *The sleep instinct.* London: Routledge & Kegan Paul. [7]

Meddis, R. (1983). The evolution of sleep. In A. Mayes (Ed.), *Sleep mechanisms and functions in humans and animals—an evolutionary perspective* (pp. 57–106). Wokingham, England: Van Nostrand-Reinhold. [7]

Meehl, P. E. (1954). *Clinical versus statistical prediction: A theoretical analysis and a review of the evidence.* Minneapolis: University of Minnesota Press. [24]

Megargee, E. I. (1972). *The California Psychological Inventory handbook.* San Francisco: Jossey-Bass. [22]

Mehrabian, A., & Ksionzky, S. (1970). Models for affiliative and conformity behavior. *Psychological Bulletin, 74,* 110–126. [11]

Mehrabian, A., & Ksionzky, S. (1974). *A theory of affiliation.* Lexington, MA: Heath. [11]

Meichenbaum, D., & Novaco, R. (1986). Stress inoculation: A preventative approach. In C. D. Spielberger & I. G. Sarason (Eds.), *Stress and anxiety: Vol. 10. A sourcebook of theory and research* (pp. 419–435). Washington, DC: Hemisphere. [23]

Melamed, B. G., Hawes, R. R., Heiby, E., & Glick, J. (1975). Use of filmed modeling to reduce uncooperative behavior of children during dental treatment. *Journal of Dental Research, 54,* 797–801. [25]

Melzack, R., & Wall, P. D. (1962). On the nature of cutaneous sensory mechanisms. *Brain, 85,* 331–356. [3]

Mendelson, W. B. (1987). *Human sleep: Research and clinical care.* New York: Plenum. [7]

Mendelson, W. B., Gillin, J. C., & Wyatt, J. (1977). *Human sleep and its disorders.* New York: Plenum. [7]

Mendlewicz, J., & Shopsin, B. (1979). *Genetic aspects of affective illness.* New York: Spectrum. [8]

Meyer, D. E., Irwin, D. E., Osman, A. M., & Kounios, J. (1988). The dynamics of cognition and action: Mental processes inferred from speed-accuracy decomposition. *Psychological Review, 95,* 183–237. [13]

Meyer, D. E., & Schvaneveldt, R. W. (1976). Meaning, memory structure, and mental processes. *Science, 192,* 27–33. [14]

Michelsen, A., Kirchner, W. H., & Lindauer, M. (1986). Sound and vibrational signals in the dance language of the honeybee, *Apis mellifera. Behavioral Ecology and Sociobiology, 18,* 207–212. [8]

Milgram, S. (1963). Behavioral study of obedience. *Journal of abnormal and Social Psychology, 67,* 371–378. [20]

Mill, J. S. (1952). *On liberty.* In R. M. Hutchens (Ed.), *Great books of the Western world* (Vol. 43, pp. 267–323). Chicago: Encyclopaedia Britannica. (Original work published 1859) [24]

Miller, G. A. (1956). The magical number seven, plus or minus two: Some limits on our capacity for processing information. *Psychological Review, 63,* 81–97. [13]

Miller, G. A., Galanter, E., & Pribram, K. H. (1960). *Plans and the structure of behavior.* New York: Holt. [1, 2]

Miller, N. E. (1941). The frustration-aggression hypothesis. *Psychological Review, 48,* 337–342. [10]

Miller, N. E. (1959). Liberalization of basic S-R concepts: Extensions to conflict behavior, motivation, and social learning. In S. Koch (Ed.), *Psychology: Study of a science* (Vol. 2, pp. 196–292). New York: McGraw-Hill. [21]

Miller, N. E. (1960). Motivational effects of brain stimulation and drugs. *Federation Proceedings, 19,* 846–853. [9]

Miller, N. E., Sampliner, R. I., & Woodrow, P. (1957). Thirst-reducing effects of water by stomach fistula vs. water by mouth measured by both a consummatory and an instrumental response. *Journal of Comparative and Physiological Psychology, 50,* 1–5. [9]

Miller, P. H. (1983). *Theories of developmental psychology.* San Francisco: Freeman. [16]

Miller, R. (1991). The ethics of involuntary commitment to mental health treatment. In S. Bloch & P. Chodoff (Eds.), *Psychiatric ethics* (2nd ed., pp. 265–289). Oxford: Oxford University Press. [25]

Miller, S. (1980). When is a little knowledge a dangerous thing? Coping with stressful events by monitoring vs. blunting. In S. Levine & H. Ursin (Eds.), *Coping and health* (pp.145–179). New York: Plenum. [23]

Milner, B., Corkin, S., & Teuber, H. L. (1968). Further analysis of the hippocampal amnesic syndrome: 14-year follow-up study of H.M. *Neuropsychologia, 6,* 215–234. [5]

Mischel, W. (1968). *Personality and assessment.* New York: Wiley. [21]

Mischel, W. (1981). *Introduction to personality* (3rd ed.). New York: Holt, Rinehart, & Winston. [21]

Mischel, W., & Peake, P. K. (1982). Beyond déjà vu in the search for cross-situational consistency. *Psychological Review, 89,* 730–755. [21]

Mitchell, D. (1981). Sensitive periods in visual development. In R. Aslin, J. Alberts, & M. Petersen (Eds.), *Development of perception* (pp. 1–43). New York: Academic Press. [4]

Monahan, J. (1984). The prediction of violent behavior: Toward a second generation of theory and policy. *American Journal of Psychiatry, 141,* 10–15. [25]

Moncrieff, R. W. (1967). *The chemical senses* (rev. ed.). Cleveland, OH: Chemical Rubber Co. [3]

Money, J. (1977). Human hermaphroditism. In F. A. Beach (Ed.), *Human sexuality in four perspectives* (pp. 62–86). Baltimore, MD: Johns Hopkins University Press. [10]

Monti, P. M., Brown, W. A., & Corriveau, D. P. (1977). Testosterone and components of aggressive and sexual behavior in man. *American*

Journal of Psychiatry, 134, 692–694. [10]

Moore, J. J., & Massaro, D. W. (1973). Attention and processing capacity in auditory recognition. Journal of Experimental Psychology, 99, 49–54. [13]

Moore, J. S., Graziano, W. G., & Millar, M. G. (1987). Physical attractiveness, sex role orientation, and the evaluation of adults and children. Personality and Social Psychology Bulletin, 13, 95–102. [20]

Moore, J. W. (1972). Stimulus control: Studies of auditory generalization in rabbits. In A. H. Black & W. F. Prokasy (Eds.), Classical conditioning II: Current research and theory. (pp. 206–230). New York: Appleton-Century-Crofts. [12]

Moorhead, G., Ference, R., & Neck, C. P. (1991). Group decision fiascoes continue: Space shuttle Challenger and a revised groupthink framework. Human Relations, 44, 539–550. [20]

Moray, N. (1959). Attention in dichotic listening: Affective cues and the influence of instructions. Quarterly Journal of Experimental Psychology, 11, 56–60. [13]

Moray, N., Bates, A., & Barnett, T. (1965). Experiments on the four-eared man. Journal of the Acoustical Society of America, 38, 196–201. [13]

Morgan, C. D., & Murray, H. A. (1935). A method for investigating fantasies. Archives of Neurological Psychiatry, 34, 289–306. [11]

Morris, C. C., Bransford, J. D., & Franks, J. J. (1977). Levels of processing versus transfer appropriate processing. Journal of Verbal Learning and Verbal Behavior, 16, 519–533. [13]

Morris, G., & Singer, M. T. (1961). Sleep deprivation: Transactional and subjective observations. Archives of General Psychiatry, 5, 453–465. [7]

Morrison, J. R. (1974). Changes in subtype diagnosis of schizophrenia: 1920–1966. American Journal of Psychiatry, 131, 674–677. [24]

Morrison, R. F., & Sebald, M. (1974).

Personal characteristics differentiating female executive from female nonexecutive personnel. Journal of Applied Psychology, 59, 656–659. [11]

Moruzzi, G., & Magoun, H. W. (1949). Brain stem reticular formation and activation of the EEG. Electroencephalography and Clinical Neurophysiology, 1, 455–473. [7]

Moscovici, S. (1985). Social influence and conformity. In G. Lindzey & E. Aronson (Eds.), Handbook of social psychology (3rd ed., Vol. 2, pp. 347–412). New York: Random House. [20]

Moskowitz, H. R. (1970). Ratio scales of sugar sweetness. Perception & Psychophysics, 1, 315–320. [3]

Mowrer, O. H. (1960). Learning theory and behavior. New York: Wiley. [6]

Moyer, K. E. (1968). Kinds of aggression and their physiological bases. Communications in Behavioral Biology, 2, 65–87. [10]

Moyer, K. E. (1976). The psychobiology of aggression. New York: Harper & Row. [10]

Mueller, C. W. (1983). Environmental stressors and aggressive behavior. In R. G. Geen & E. I. Donnerstein (Eds.), Aggression: Theoretical and empirical reviews (Vol. 2, pp. 51–76). New York: Academic Press. [10]

Muise, J. G., LeBlanc, R. S., Lavoie, M. E., & Arsenault, A. S. (1991). Two-stage model of visual backward masking: Sensory transmission and accrual of effective information as a function of target intensity and similarity. Perception & Psychophysics, 50, 197–204. [13]

Murphy, G. L., & Smith, E. E. (1982). Basic-level superiority in picture categorization. Journal of Verbal Learning and Verbal Behavior, 21, 1–20. [14]

Murray, H. A. (1938). Explorations in personality: A clinical and experimental study of fifty men of college age. New York: Oxford University Press. [11, 21]

Myers, I. B., & McCaulley, M. H.

(1985). Manual: A guide to the development and use of the Myers-Briggs type indicator. Palo Alto, CA: Consulting Psychologists Press. [21]

Nachson, I., & Carman, A. (1975). Hand preference in sequential and spatial discrimination tasks. Cortex, 11, 123–131. [5]

Nahemow, L., & Lawton, M. P. (1975). Similarity and propinquity in friendship formation. Journal of Personality and Social Psychology, 32, 205–213. [20]

Naish, P. L. N. (1986). What is hypnosis? Current theory and research. Philadelphia: Open University Press. [7]

Navon, D. (1977). Forest before trees: The precedence of global features in visual perception. Cognitive Psychology, 9, 353–383. [13]

Neely, J. H. (1977). Semantic priming and retrieval from lexical memory: Roles of inhibitionless spreading activation and limited-capacity attention. Journal of Experimental Psychology: General, 106, 226–254 [14]

Neimark, E. (1981). Confounding with cognitive style factors: An artifact explanation for the apparent nonuniversal incidence of formal operations. In I. Sigel, D. Brodzinsky, & R. Golinkoff (Eds.), New directions in Piagetian research and theory. Hillsdale, NJ: Lawrence Erlbaum Associates. [16]

Neisser, U., & Becklen, R. (1975). Selective looking: Attending to visually specified events. Cognitive Psychology, 7, 480–494. [13]

Nelson, K. (1973). Structure and strategy in learning to talk. Monographs of the Society for Research in Child Development, 38, (1 & 2). [17]

Nelson, K. (1983). The derivation of concepts and categories from event representations. In E. K. Scholnick (Ed.), New trends in conceptual representation: Challenges to Piaget's theory? (pp. 129–149). Hillsdale, NJ: Lawrence Erlbaum Associates. [16]

Newell, A., & Simon, H. A. (1972). Human problem solving. Englewood Cliffs, NJ: Prentice-Hall. [15]

R-27

Newman, H. H., Freeman, F. N., & Holzinger, K. J. (1937). *Twins: A study of heredity and environment.* Chicago: University of Chicago Press. [16]

Nice, M. M. (1915). The development of a child's vocabulary in relation to environment. *Pedagogical Seminary, 22,* 35–64. [17]

Nichols, P. L. (1984). Familial mental retardation. *Behavior Genetics, 14,* 161–170. [8]

Nichols, R. C. (1978). Heredity and environment: Major findings from twin studies of ability, personality, and interests. *Homo, 29,* 158–173. [16, 22]

Niijima, A. (1969). Afferent impulse discharges from glucoreceptors in the liver of the guinea-pig. *Annals of the New York Academy of Sciences, 157,* 690–700. [9]

Nisbett, R., & Ross, L. (1980). *Human inference: Strategies and shortcomings of social judgment.* Englewood Cliffs, NJ: Prentice-Hall. [15]

Niven, R. G. (1984). Alcoholism—A problem in perspective. *JAMA, Journal of the American Medical Association, 252,* 1912–1914. [7]

Norman, D. A. (1981). *Perspectives in cognitive science.* Hillsdale, NJ: Lawrence Erlbaum Associates. [1]

Norman, W. T. (1967). *2800 personality trait descriptors: Normative operating characteristics for a university population.* Ann Arbor: Department of Psychology, University of Michigan. (As cited in Chaplin, John, & Goldberg, 1988) [21]

Novin, D., VanderWeele, D. A., & Rezek, M. (1973). Hepatic-portal 2-deoxy-D-glucose infusion causes eating: Evidence for peripheral glucoreceptors. *Science, 181,* 858–860. [9]

Nuckols, C. C. (1989). *Cocaine: From dependency to recovery* (2nd ed.). Blue Ridge Summit, PA: Tab Books. [7]

Oakhill, J. V., & Johnson-Laird, P. M. (1985). The effects of belief on the spontaneous production of syllogistic conclusion. *Quarterly Journal of Experimental Psychology, 37A,* 553–569. [15]

O'Connor v. Donaldson, 422 U.S. 563 (1975). [25]

Oden, D. L., Thompson, R. K., & Premack, D. (1988). Spontaneous transfer of matching by infant chimpanzees *(Pan troglodytes). Journal of Experimental Psychology: Animal Behavior Processes, 14,* 140–145. [17]

Olds, J. (1958). Self-stimulation of the brain. *Science, 127,* 315–324. [6]

Olds, J. (1962). Hypothalamic substrates of reward. *Psychological Review, 42,* 554–604. [6]

Olds, J., Killam, K. F., & Bach-y-Rita, P. (1956). Self-stimulation of the brain used as a screening method for tranquilizing drugs. *Science, 124,* 265–266. [6]

Olds, J., & Milner, P. (1954). Positive reinforcement produced by electrical stimulation of the septal area and other regions of the rat brain. *Journal of Comparative and Physiological Psychology, 47,* 419–427. [6]

Olds, J., & Olds, M. E. (1963). Approach-avoidance analysis of rat diencephalon. *Journal of Comparative Neurology, 120,* 259–295. [6]

Olweus, D., Mattsson, A., Schalling, D., & Loow, H. (1980). Testosterone, aggression, physical and personality dimensions in normal adolescent males. *Psychosomatic Medicine, 42,* 253–269. [10]

Oomura, Y. (1976). Significance of glucose, insulin, and free fatty acid on the hypothalamic feeding and satiety neurons. In D. Novin, W. Wyrwicka, & G. A. Bray (Eds.), *Hunger: Basic mechanisms and clinical implications* (pp. 145–157). New York: Raven Press. [9]

Ortony, A., & Turner, T. J. (1990). What's basic about basic emotions? *Psychological Review, 97,* 315–331. [6]

Oscar-Berman, M., Zurif, E. G., & Blumstein, S. (1975). Effects of unilateral brain damage on the processing of speech sounds. *Brain and Language, 2,* 345–353. [5]

Osherson, D. N., & Markman, E. M. (1975). Language and the ability to evaluate contradictions and tautologies. *Cognition, 2,* 213–226. [16]

Oskamp, S. (1965). Overconfidence in case-study judgments. *Journal of Consulting Psychology, 29,* 261–265. [15]

Packer, C. (1977). Reciprocal altruism in *papio anubis. Nature (London), 265,* 441–443. [8]

Palmer, S. E. (1975). Visual perception and world knowledge: Notes on a model of sensory-cognitive interaction. In D. A. Norman, D. E. Rumelhart, & the LNR Research Group (Eds.), *Explorations in cognition* (pp. 279–307). San Francisco: Freeman. [13]

Panksepp, J. (1986a). The neurochemistry of behavior. *Annual Review of Psychology, 37,* 77–107. [6]

Panksepp, J. (1986b). The anatomy of emotions. In R. Plutchik & H. Kellerman (Eds.), *Emotion: Theory, research, and experience: Vol. 3. Biological foundations of emotion* (pp. 91–124). Orlando, FL: Academic Press. [6]

Papez, J. W. (1937). A proposed mechanism of emotion. *AMA Archives of Neurology and Psychiatry, 38,* 725–743. [6]

Parkinson, B., & Manstead, A. S. R. (1981). An examination of the roles played by meaning of feedback and attention to feedback in the "Valins effect." *Journal of Personality and Social Psychology, 40,* 239–245 [6]

Parks, T. E., & Hui, L. (1989). Pictorial depth and the Poggendorff illusion. *Perception & Psychophysics, 46,* 465–468. [4]

Parsons, J. E., & Goff, S. B. (1980). Achievement motivation and values: An alternative perspective. In L. J. Fyans (Ed.), *Achievement motivation: Recent trends in theory and research* (pp. 349–373). New York: Plenum. [11]

Paul, G. L., & Lentz, R. J. (1977). *Psychosocial treatment of chronic mental patients: Milieu versus social learning programs.* Cambridge, MA: Harvard University Press. [25]

Pavlov, I. P. (1927). *Conditioned reflexes* (G. V. Anrep, Trans.). London: Oxford University Press. [6, 12]

Pearce, J. M., & Hall, G. (1980). A model for Pavlovian learning: Variations in the effectiveness of conditioned but not of unconditioned stimuli. *Psychological Review, 87,* 532–552. [12]

Pedersen, N. L., Plomin, R., McClearn, G. E., & Friberg, L. (1988). Neuroticism, extraversion, and related traits in adult twins reared apart and reared together. *Journal of Personality and Social Psychology, 55,* 950–957. [8]

Penfield, W., & Jasper, H. (1954). *Epilepsy and the functional anatomy of the human brain.* Boston: Little, Brown. [5]

Penfield, W., & Perot, P. (1963). The brain's record of auditory and visual experience. *Brain, 86,* 595–696. [5]

Peterson, C., & Seligman, M. E. P. (1984). Causal explanations as a risk factor for depression: Theory and evidence. *Psychological Review, 91,* 347–374. [24]

Peterson, L. R., & Peterson, M. J. (1959). Short-term retention of individual verbal items. *Journal of Experimental Psychology, 58,* 193–198. [13]

Petrie, A. (1952). A comparison of the psychological effects of different types of operations on the frontal lobes. *Journal of Mental Science, 98,* 326–329. [5]

Petrig, B., Julesz, B., Kropfl, W., Baumgartner, G., & Anliker, M. (1981). Development of stereopsis and cortical binocularity in human infants: Electrophysiological evidence. *Science, 213,* 1402–1405. [4]

Petrinovich, L. (1985). Factors influencing song development in the white-crowned sparrow (*Zonotrichia leucophrys*). *Journal of Comparative Psychology, 99,* 15–29. [8]

Petty, R. E., & Cacioppo, J. T. (1986). The elaboration likelihood model of persuasion. In L. Berkowitz (Ed.), *Advances in experimental social psychology* (Vol. 19, pp. 123–205). Orlando, FL: Academic Press. [19]

Pfaffmann, C. (1962). Sensory pro-

cesses and their relation to behavior: Studies on the sense of taste as a model S-R system. In S. Koch (Ed.), *Psychology: A study of a science* (Vol. 4, pp. 380–416). New York: McGraw-Hill. [3]

Piaget, J. (1952). *The origins of intelligence in children* (M. Cook, Trans.). New York: International Universities Press. (Original work published 1936) [16]

Piaget, J. (1983). Piaget's theory. In P. H. Mussen (Ed.), *Handbook of child psychology* (4th ed., Vol. 1, pp. 103–128). New York: Wiley. [16]

Piaget, J., & Inhelder, B. (1956). *The child's conception of space.* London: Routledge & Kegan Paul. [16]

Pike, K. L. (1943). *Phonetics: A critical analysis of phonetic theory and a technic for the practical description of sounds.* Ann Arbor: University of Michigan Press. [17]

Piliavin, J. A., Callero, P. L., & Evans, D. E. (1982). Addiction to altruism? Opponent-process theory and habitual blood donation. *Journal of Personality and Social Psychology, 43,* 1200–1213. [6]

Pillow, D. R., West, S. G., & Reich, J. W. (1991). Attributional style in relation to self-esteem and depression: Mediational and interactive models. *Journal of Research in Personality, 25,* 57–69. [24]

Pines, A., & Gal, R. (1977). The effect of food on test anxiety. *Journal of Applied Social Psychology, 7,* 348–358. [9]

Plato. (1952). *Meno* (B. Jowett, Trans.). In R. M. Hutchens (Ed.), *Great books of the Western world* (Vol. 7, pp. 174–190). Chicago: Encyclopaedia Britannica. [1]

Plato. (1952). *Republic* (B. Jowett, Trans.). In R. M. Hutchens (Ed.), *Great books of the Western world* (Vol. 7, pp. 295–441). Chicago: Encyclopaedia Britannica. [1, 2]

Plato. (1952). *Timaeus.* In R. M. Hutchens (Ed.), *Great books of the Western world* (Vol. 7, pp. 442–477). Chicago: Encyclopaedia Britannica. (Original work published ca. 350 B.C.) [24]

Plomin, R. (1986). *Development,*

genetics, and psychology. Hillsdale, NJ: Lawrence Erlbaum Associates. [16, 24]

Plomin, R. (1988). The nature and nurture of cognitive abilities. In R. J. Sternberg (Ed.), *Advances in the psychology of human intelligence* (Vol. 4, pp. 1–33). Hillsdale, NJ: Lawrence Erlbaum Associates. [22]

Plomin, R. (1989). Environment and genes. *American Psychologist, 44,* 105–111. [8]

Plomin, R., & DeFries, J. C. (1980). Genetics and intelligence: Recent data. *Intelligence, 4,* 15–24. [22]

Plomin, R., & DeFries, J. C. (1985). *Origins of individual differences in infancy: The Colorado Adoption Project.* Orlando, FL: Academic Press. [16]

Plomin, R., DeFries, J. C., & Fulker, D. W. (1988). *Nature and nurture during infancy and early childhood.* New York: Cambridge University Press. [8]

Plomin, R., Pedersen, N. L., McClearn, G. E., Nesselroade, J. R., & Bergeman, C. S. (1988). EAS temperaments during the last half of the life span: Twins reared apart and twins reared together. *Psychology and Aging, 3,* 45–50. [8]

Plutchik, R. (1980). *Emotion: A psychoevolutionary synthesis.* New York: Harper & Row. [6]

Popper, K. R. (1959). *The logic of scientific discovery.* New York: Basic Books. [22]

Posner, M. I., & Boies, S. W. (1971). Components of attention. *Psychological Review, 78,* 391–408. [13]

Posner, M. I., & Snyder, C. R. R. (1975). Attention and cognitive control. In R. L. Solso (Ed.), *Information processing and cognition: The Loyola Symposium.* (pp. 55–85). Hillsdale, NJ: Lawrence Erlbaum Associates. [13]

Poulos, C. X., & Cappell, H. (1991). Homeostatic theory of drug tolerance: A general model of physiological adaptation. *Psychological Review, 98,* 390–408. [7]

Powers, J. B. (1970). Hormonal control of sexual receptivity during the estrous cycle of the rat. *Physiology and Behavior, 5,* 831–835. [10]

Premack, D. (1971). Language in chimpanzee? *Science, 172,* 808–822. [17]

Premack, D. (1976). *Intelligence in ape and man.* Hillsdale, NJ: Lawrence Erlbaum Associates. [17]

Premack, D. (1985). "Gavagai": The future history of the animal language controversy. *Cognition, 19,* 207–296. [17]

Presley, M., Levin, J. R., Hall, J. W., Miller, G. E., & Berry, J. K. (1980). The keyword method and foreign word acquisition. *Journal of Experimental Psychology: Human Learning and Memory, 6,* 163–173. [14]

Previc, F. H. (1991). A general theory concerning the prenatal origins of cerebral lateralization in humans. *Psychological Review, 98,* 299–334. [5]

Price, R. F., & Cohen, D. B. (1988). Lucid dream induction: An empirical evaluation. In J. Gackenbach & S. LaBerge (Eds.), *Conscious mind, sleeping brain: Perspectives on lucid dreaming* (pp. 105–134). New York: Plenum. [7]

Prien, R. E., Kupfer, D. J., Mansky, P. A., Small, J. G., Tuason, V. B., Voss, C. B., & Johnson, W. E. (1984). Drug therapy in the prevention of recurrences in unipolar and bipolar affective disorders. *Archives of General Psychiatry, 41,* 1096–1104. [25]

Prochaska, J. O. (1984). *Systems of psychotherapy* (2nd ed.). Homewood, IL: Dorsey. [25]

Ragozin, A. (1978). A laboratory assessment of attachment behavior in day-care children. In H. Beex (Ed.), *Social issues in developmental psychology* (pp. 218–232). New York: Harper & Row. [18]

Rahe, R. H. (1987). Recent life changes, emotions, and behaviors in coronary heart disease. In A. Baum & J. E. Singer (Eds.), *Handbook of psychology and health: Vol. 5. Stress* (pp. 229–254). Hillsdale, NJ: Lawrence Erlbaum Associates. [23]

Ramirez, I. (1990). Stimulation of energy intake and growth by sac-

charin in rats. *Journal of Nutrition, 120,* 123–133. [9]

Ramsay, D. J., Rolls, B. J., & Wood, R. J. (1977). Thirst following water deprivation in dogs. *American Journal of Physiology, 232,* R93–R100. [9]

Raphael, B. (1976). *The thinking computer.* San Francisco: Freeman. [15]

Ray, O. S. (1972). *Drugs, society, and human behavior.* St. Louis, MO: Mosby. [7]

Raynor, J. O. (1969). Future orientation and motivation of immediate activity: An elaboration of the theory of achievement motivation. *Psychological Review, 76,* 606–610. [11]

Raynor, J. O. (1970). Relationship between achievement-related motives, future orientation, and academic performance. *Journal of Personality and Social Psychology, 15,* 28–33. [11]

Rechtschaffen, A. (1971). The control of sleep. In W. A. Hunt (Ed.), *Human behavior and its control* (pp. 75–92). Cambridge, MA: Schenkman Press. [7]

Rechtschaffen, A., Gilliland, M. A., Bergmann, B. M., & Winter, J. B. (1983). Physiological correlates of prolonged sleep deprivation in rats. *Science, 221,* 180–183. [7]

Rechtschaffen, A., Lovell, R. A., & Freedman, D. (1973). The effect of parachlorophenylalanine on sleep in the rat: Some implications for the serotonin-sleep hypothesis. In J. Barchas & E. Usdin (Eds.), *Serotonin and behavior* (pp. 401–418). New York: Academic Press. [7]

Rechtschaffen, A., & Monroe, L. J. (1969). Laboratory studies of insomnia. In A. Kales (Ed.), *Sleep: Physiology and pathology* (pp. 158–169). Philadelphia: Lippincott. [7]

Reed, C. F. (1984). Terrestrial passage theory of moon illusion. *Journal of Experimental Psychology: General, 113,* 489–500. [4]

Reese, E. P. (1978). *Human operant behavior: Analysis and application* (2nd ed.). Dubuque, IA: Brown. [12]

Reese, H. W., & Overton, W. F.

(1970). Models of development and theories of development. In L. R. Goulet & P. B. Baltes (Eds.), *Lifespan developmental psychology: Research and theory* (pp. 116–144). New York: Academic Press. [16]

Regier, D., Mathews, J., Kramer, M., Robins, L., Blayer, D., Hough, R., Eaton, W., & Locke, B. (1984). The NIMH epidemiological catchment area program: Historical context, major objectives, and study population characteristics. *Archives of General Psychiatry, 41,* 934–941. [24]

Reicher, G. M. (1969). Perceptual recognition as a function of meaningfulness of stimulus material. *Journal of Experimental Psychology, 81,* 275–280. [13]

Reid, T. (1863a). *The works of Thomas Reid* (W. Hamilton, Ed.) (Vol. 1). Edinburgh: Machlachlan & Stewart. [1, 2]

Reid, T. (1863b). *The works of Thomas Reid* (W. Hamilton, Ed.) (Vol. 2) Edinburgh: Machlachlan & Stewart. [1, 2]

Reisenzein, R. (1983). The Schachter theory of emotion: Two decades later. *Psychological Bulletin, 94,* 239–264. [6]

Rescorla, R. A. (1967). Pavlovian conditioning and its proper control procedures. *Psychological Review, 74,* 71–80. [12]

Rescorla, R. A. (1968). Probability of shock in the presence and absence of CS in fear conditioning. *Journal of Comparative and Physiological Psychology, 66,* 1–5. [12]

Rescorla, R. A. (1969). Pavlovian conditioned inhibition. *Psychological Bulletin, 72,* 77–94. [12]

Rescorla, R. A. (1980). *Pavlovian second-order conditioning: Studies in associative learning.* Hillsdale, NJ: Lawrence Erlbaum Associates. [12]

Rescorla, R. A., & Gillan, D. J. (1980). An analysis of the facilitative effect of similarity on second-order conditioning. *Journal of Experimental Psychology: Animal Behavior Processes, 6,* 339–351. [12]

Rest, J. R. (1986). *Moral develop-*

ment: *Advances in theory and research.* New York: Praeger. [18]

Revlin, R., Leirer, V., Yopp, H., & Yopp, R. (1980). The belief-bias effect in formal reasoning: The influence of knowledge on logic. *Memory & Cognition, 8,* 584–592. [15]

Revusky, S., & Parker, L. A. (1976). Aversions to unflavored water and cup drinking produced by delayed sickness. *Journal of Experimental Psychology: Animal Behavior Processes, 2,* 342–353. [12]

Reynolds, A. G., & Flagg, P. W. (1977). *Cognitive psychology.* Cambridge, MA: Winthrop. [17]

Rice, J., Reich, T., Andreasen, N. C., Endicott, J., VanEerdewegh, M., Fishman, R., Hirschfeld, R. M. A., & Klerman, G. L. (1987). The familial transmission of bipolar illness. *Archives of General Psychiatry, 44,* 441–447. [24]

Richardson, D. B., & Mogenson, G. (1981). Water intake elicited by injections of angiotensin II into the preoptic area of rats. *American Journal of Physiology, 240,* R70–R74. [9]

Rips, L. J. (1981). Cognitive processes in propositional reasoning. *Psychological Review, 90,* 38–71. [15]

Rips, L. J., Shoben, E. J., & Smith, E. E. (1973). Semantic distance and the verification of semantic relations. *Journal of Verbal Learning and Verbal Behavior, 12,* 1–20. [14]

Rivest, J., Ono, H., & Saida, S. (1989). The roles of convergence and apparent distance in depth constancy with motion parallax. *Perception & Psychophysics, 46,* 401–408. [4]

Roberts, P., & Newton, P. M. (1987). Levinsonian studies of women's adult development. *Psychology and Aging, 2,* 154–163. [18]

Roberts, W. A. (1969). Resistance to extinction following partial and consistent reinforcement with varying magnitudes of reward. *Journal of Comparative and Physiological Psychology, 67,* 395–400. [12]

Robins, L. N., Helzer, J. E., Weissman, M. M., Orvaschel, H., Gruen-

berg, E., Burke, J. D., & Regier, D. A. (1984). Lifetime prevalence of specific psychiatric disorders in three sites. *Archives of General Psychiatry, 41,* 949–958. [24]

Robins, P. R. (1988). *The psychology of dreams.* Jefferson, NC: McFarland. [7]

Robinson, D. N. (1979). *Systems of modern psychology: A critical sketch.* New York: Columbia University Press. [1, 2, 18]

Robinson, D. N. (1980). *Psychology and law: Can justice survive the social sciences?* New York: Oxford University Press. [24, 25]

Rock, I. (1975). *An introduction to perception.* New York: Macmillan. [4]

Rock, I., & Kaufman, L. (1962). The moon illusion. II. *Science, 136,* 1023–1031. [4]

Rock, I., Tauber, E. S., & Heller, D. (1965). Perception of stroboscopic movement: Evidence for its innate basis. *Science, 147,* 1050–1052. [4]

Rodin, J. (1981). Current status of the internal-external hypothesis for obesity: What went wrong? *American Psychologist, 36,* 361–372. [9]

Rodin, J., & Slochower, J. (1976). Externality in the nonobese: Effects of environmental responsiveness on weight. *Journal of Personality and Social Psychology, 33,* 338–344. [9]

Roediger, H. L. (1980). The effectiveness of four mnemonics in ordering recall. *Journal of Experimental Psychology: Human Learning and Memory, 6,* 558–567. [14]

Rogers, C. R. (1951). *Client-centered therapy.* Boston: Houghton-Mifflin. [25]

Rogers, C. R. (1961). *On becoming a person: A therapist's view of psychotherapy.* Boston: Houghton-Mifflin. [25]

Rolls, B. J., & Rolls, E. T. (1982). *Thirst.* Cambridge, England: Cambridge University Press. [9]

Rolls, B. J., Wood, R. J., & Rolls, E. T. (1980). Thirst: The initiation, maintenance, and termination of drinking. In J. M. Sprague & A. N. Epstein (Eds.), *Progress in psychobiology and physiological psy-*

chology (Vol. 9, pp. 263–321). New York: Academic Press. [9]

Rolls, E. T. (1986). Neural systems involved in emotion in primates. In R. Plutchik & H. Kellerman (Eds.), *Emotion: Theory, research, and experience: Vol. 3. Biological foundations of emotion* (pp. 125–144). Orlando, FL: Academic Press. [6]

Rorschach, H. (1921). *Psychodiagnostik.* Berne: Bircher. [22]

Rosch, E. (1973). On the internal structure of perceptual and semantic categories. In T. E. Moore (Ed.), *Cognitive development and the acquisition of language* (pp. 111–144). New York: Academic Press. [14, 17, 19]

Rosch, E. (1975). Cognitive representations of semantic categories. *Journal of Experimental Psychology: General, 104,* 192–253. [14]

Rosch, E. (1978). Principles of categorization. In E. Rosch & B. Lloyd (Eds.), *Cognition and categorization* (pp. 27–48). Hillsdale, NJ: Lawrence Erlbaum Associates. [14]

Rosch, E. (1983). Prototype classification and logical classification: The two systems. In E. K. Scholnick (Ed.), *New trends in conceptual representation: Challenges to Piaget's theory?* (pp. 73–86). Hillsdale, NJ: Lawrence Erlbaum Associates. [16]

Rosch, E., & Mervis, C. B. (1975). Family resemblances: Studies in the internal structure of categories. *Cognitive Psychology, 7,* 573–605. [14]

Rosch, E., Mervis, C. B., Gray, W., Johnson, D., & Boyes-Braem, P. (1976). Basic objects in natural categories. *Cognitive Psychology, 8,* 382–439. [14]

Rose, J. E., Brugge, J. F., Anderson, D. J., & Hind, J. E. (1967). Phase-locked response to low-frequency tones in single auditory nerve fibers of the squirrel monkey. *Journal of Neurophysiology, 30,* 769–793. [3]

Rose, R. M., Gordon, T. P., & Bernstein, I. S. (1972). Plasma testosterone levels in the male rhesus: Influences of sexual and social stimuli. *Science, 178,* 643–645. [10]

Rosen, D. H., Smith, S. M., Huston, H. L., & Gonzales, G. (1991). Empirical study of associations between symbols and their meanings: Evidence of collective unconscious (archetypal) memory. *Journal of Analytical Psychology, 36,* 211–228. [21]

Rosenberg, K. M., & Sherman, G. F. (1975). Influence of testosterone on pup killing in the rat is modified by prior experience. *Physiology and Behavior, 15,* 669–672. [10]

Rosenberg, M. J. (1965). When dissonance fails: On eliminating evaluation apprehension from attitude measurement. *Journal of Personality and Social Psychology, 1,* 28–42. [19]

Rosenbloom, J. (1986). *696 silly school jokes & riddles.* New York: Sterling. [17]

Rosenhan, D. L. (1973). On being sane in insane places. *Science, 179,* 250–258. [25]

Rosenhan, D. L., & Seligman, M. E. P. (1989). *Abnormal psychology* (2nd ed.). New York: Norton. [24, 25]

Ross, L. D. (1977). The intuitive psychologist and his shortcomings. In L. Berkowitz (Ed.), *Advances in experimental social psychology* (Vol. 10, pp. 173–220). New York: Academic Press. [19]

Roth, S., & Cohen, L. J. (1986). Approach, avoidance, and coping with stress. *American Psychologist, 41,* 813–819. [23]

Rothblum, E. D., Solomon, L. J., & Albee, G. W. (1986). In T. Millon & G. L. Klerman (Eds.), *Contemporary directions in psychopathology* (pp. 167–189). New York: Guilford Press. [24]

Rouse v. Cameron, 373 F. 2d 451 (D. C. Cir. 1966). [24, 25]

Rousseau, J. J. (1952). *The social contract* (G. D. H. Cole, Trans.). In R. M. Hutchens (Ed.), *Great books of the Western world* (Vol. 38, pp. 387–439). Chicago: Encyclopaedia Britannica. (Original work published 1762) [1, 19, 20]

Routtenberg, A., & Lindy, J. (1965). Effects of the availability of reward-ing septal and hypothalamic stimulation on bar pressing for food under conditions of deprivation. *Journal of Comparative and Physiological Psychology, 60,* 158–161. [6]

Rozin, P., & Kalat, J. W. (1971). Specific hungers and poison avoidance as adaptive specializations of learning. *Psychological Review, 78,* 459–486. [12]

Rubin, R. T., Reinisch, J. M., & Haskett, R. F. (1981). Postnatal gonadal steroid effects on human behavior. *Science, 211,* 1318–1324. [10]

Rumelhart, D. (1977). *Introduction to human information processing.* New York: Wiley. [13]

Rumelhart, D. E., & Siple, P. (1974). Process of recognizing tachistoscopically presented words. *Psychological Review, 81,* 99–118. [13]

Rundus, D. (1971). Analysis of rehearsal processes in free recall. *Journal of Experimental Psychology, 89,* 63–77. [13]

Rundus, D. (1977). Maintenance rehearsal and single-level processing. *Journal of Verbal Learning and Verbal Behavior, 16,* 665–681. [13]

Russell, J. A., & Bullock, M. (1985). Multidimensional scaling of emotional facial expressions: Similarity from preschoolers to adults. *Journal of Personality and Social Psychology, 48,* 1290–1298. [19]

Rycroft, C. (1979). *The innocence of dreams.* New York: Pantheon. [7]

Sachs, J. D. S. (1967). Recognition memory for syntactic and semantic aspects of connected discourse. *Perception and Psychophysics, 2,* 437–442. [13, 14]

Saghir, M. E. T., & Robins, E. R. (1973). *Male and female homosexuality: A comprehensive investigaton.* Baltimore, MD: Williams & Wilkins. [10]

Salapatek, P. (1975). Pattern perception in early infancy. In L. Cohen & P. Salapatek (Eds.), *Infant perception: From sensation to cognition: Vol. 1. Basic visual processes* (pp. 133–248). New York: Academic Press. [4]

Salzinger, K. (1986). Diagnosis: Distinguishing among behaviors. In T. Millon & G. L. Klerman (Eds.), *Contemporary directions in psychopathology* (pp. 115–134). New York: Guilford Press. [24]

Sampson, H. (1966). Psychological effects of deprivation of dreaming sleep. *Journal of Nervous and Mental Disease, 143,* 305–317. [7]

Sanders, R. J. (1985). Teaching apes to ape language: Explaining the imitative and nonimitative signing of a chimpanzee *(Pan troglodytes). Journal of Comparative Psychology, 99,* 197–210. [17]

Sarbin, T. R., & Coe, W. C. (1972). *Hypnosis: A social psychological analysis of influence communication.* New York: Holt, Rinehart, & Winston. [7]

Sato, K. (1987). Distribution of the cost of maintaining common resources. *Journal of Experimental Social Psychology, 23,* 19–31. [20]

Savage-Rumbaugh, E. S. (1987). Communication, symbolic communication, and language: Reply to Seidenberg and Pettito. *Journal of Experimental Psychology: General, 116,* 288–292. [17]

Savage-Rumbaugh, E. S., Pate, J. L., Lawson, J., Smith, S. T., & Rosenbaum, S. (1983). Can a chimpanzee make a statement? *Journal of Experimental Psychology: General, 112,* 457–492. [17]

Savage-Rumbaugh, E. S., Rumbaugh, D. M., & McDonald, K. (1985). Language learning of two species of apes. *Neuroscience and Biobehavioral Reviews, 9,* 653–665. [17]

Scarr, S. (Ed.). (1981). *Race, social class, and individual differences in IQ.* Hillsdale, NJ: Lawrence Erlbaum Associates. [22]

Scarr, S., & Kidd, K. K. (1983). Developmental behavior genetics. In P. H. Mussen (Ed.), *Handbook of child psychology* (4th ed., Vol. 2, pp. 345–433). New York: Wiley. [22]

Schachter, D. L., Harbluk, J. L., & McLachlan, D. R. (1984). Retrieval without recollection: An experimental analysis of source amnesia. *Journal of Verbal Learning and Verbal Behavior, 25,* 593–611. [14]

Schachter, S. (1959). *The psychology of affiliation*. Stanford, CA: Stanford University Press. [11]

Schachter, S. (1964). The interaction of cognitive and physiological determinants of emotional state. In L. Berkowitz (Ed.), *Advances in experimental social psychology* (Vol. 1, pp. 49–80). New York: Academic Press. [6]

Schachter, S. (1971). Some extraordinary facts about obese humans and rats. *American Psychologist, 26*, 129–144. [9]

Schachter, S., Goldman, R., & Gordon, A. (1968). Effects of fear, food deprivation, and obesity on eating. *Journal of Personality and Social Psychology, 10*, 91–97. [9]

Schachter, S., & Singer, J. E. (1962). Cognitive, social and physiological determinants of emotional state. *Psychological Review, 69*, 379–399. [6]

Schank, R. C., & Abelson, R. P. (1977). *Scripts, plans, goals, and understanding.* Hillsdale, NJ: Lawrence Erlbaum Associates. [16]

Schiff, W., & Foulke, E. (1983). *Tactual perception: A sourcebook.* New York: Cambridge University Press. [3]

Schlosberg, H. (1952). The description of facial expressions in terms of two dimensions. *Journal of Experimental Psychology, 44*, 229–237. [19]

Schneider, B. A. (1969). A two-state analysis of fixed-interval responding in the pigeon. *Journal of the Experimental Analysis of Behavior, 12*, 677–687. [12]

Schneider, W., & Shiffrin, R. M. (1977). Controlled and automatic human information processing: I. Detection, search and attention. *Psychological Review, 84*, 1–66. [13]

Schneiderman, N. (1966). Interstimulus interval function of the nictitating membrane response of the rabbit under delay versus trace conditioning. *Journal of Comparative and Physiological Psychology, 62*, 397–402. [12]

Schwartz, B. (1989). *Psychology of learning and behavior* (3rd ed.). New York: Norton. [12]

Schwarz, C. J. (1968). The complications of LSD: A review of the literature. *Journal of Nervous and Mental Disease, 146*, 174–186. [7]

Scott, J. P. (1973). Agonistic behavior of mice and rats: A review. *American Zoologist, 6*, 683–701. [10]

Scoville, W. B., & Milner, B. (1957). Loss of recent memory after bilateral hippocampal lesions. *Journal of Neurology, Neurosurgery and Psychiatry, 20*, 11–21. [5]

Segal, M. W. (1974). Alphabet and attraction: An unobtrusive measure of the effect of propinquity in a field setting. *Journal of Personality and Social Psychology, 30*, 654–657. [20]

Sekuler, R. (1975). Visual motion perception. In E. C. Carterette & M. P. Friedman (Eds.), *Handbook of perception* (Vol. 5, pp. 387–433). New York: Academic Press. [4]

Seligman, M. E. P. (1970). On the generality of the laws of learning. *Psychological Review, 77*, 406–418. [12]

Seligman, M. E. P. (1975). *Helplessness: On depression, development, and death.* San Francisco: Freeman. [24]

Selling, L. S. (1940). *Men against madness.* New York: New Home Library. [24]

Selye, H. (1936). A syndrome produced by diverse nocuous agents. *Nature (London), 138*, 32. [23]

Selye, H. (1976a). *The stress of life* (rev. ed.). New York: McGraw-Hill. [23]

Selye, H. (1976b). *Stress in health and disease.* Boston: Butterworth. [23]

Senden, M. von. (1960). *Space and sight: The perception of space and shape in congenitally blind patients before and after operation.* London: Methuen. [4]

Shank, M., & Walker, J. T. (1989). Figure-ground organization in real and subjective contours: A new ambiguous figure, some novel measures of ambiguity, and apparent distance across regions of figure and ground. *Perception & Psychophysics, 46*, 127–138. [4]

Shannon, C. E., & Weaver, W. (1949). *The mathematical theory of communication.* Urbana: University of Illinois Press. [2]

Shapiro, P. N., & Penrod, S. (1986). Meta-analysis of facial identification studies. *Psychological Bulletin, 100*, 139–156. [19]

Sheafor, P. J., & Gormezano, I. (1972). Conditioning the rabbit's (*Oryctolagus cuniculus*) jaw-movement response: US magnitude effects on URs, CRs, and pseudo-CRs. *Journal of Comparative and Physiological Psychology, 81*, 449–456. [12]

Shekelle, R. B., Hulley, S., Neaton, J., Billings, J., Borhani, N., Gerace, T., Jacobs, D., Lasser, N., Mittlemark, M., Stamler, A., & the MRFIT Research Group. (1983, January). The MRFIT behavior pattern study II: Type A behavior pattern and incidence of coronary heart disease. *CVD Epidemiology Newsletter*, p. 34. [23]

Sheldon, W. H. (with the collaboration of S. S. Stevens). (1942). *The varieties of temperament: A psychology of constitutional differences.* New York: Harper & Row. [21]

Shepard, R. N. (1967). Recognition memory for words, sentences and pictures. *Journal of Verbal Learning and Verbal Behavior, 6*, 156–163. [14]

Shepard, R. N. (1978). The mental image. *American Psychologist, 33*, 125–137. [13, 14]

Shepard, R. N., & Chipman, S. (1970). Second-order isomorphism of internal representations: Shapes of states. *Cognitive Psychology, 1*, 1–17. [14]

Shepard, R. N., & Metzler, J. (1971). Mental rotation of three-dimensional objects. *Science, 171*, 701–703. [13]

Sherif, M., & Hovland, C. I. (1961). *Social judgment: Assimilation and contrast effects in communication and attitude change.* New Haven, CT: Yale University Press. [19]

Sherrick, C. E. (1968). Studies of apparent tactual movement. In D. R. Kenshalo (Ed.), *The skin senses* (pp. 331–344). Springfield, IL: Thomas. [3]

R-33

Shettleworth, S. J. (1975). Reinforcement and the organization of behavior in golden hamsters: Hunger, environment, and food reinforcement. *Journal of Experimental Psychology: Animal Behavior Processes, 1,* 56–87. [12]

Shiffrin, R. M., & Schneider, W. (1977). Controlled and automatic human information processing: II. Perceptual learning, automatic attending and a general theory. *Psychological Review, 84,* 127–190. [13]

Shipley, T. E., & Veroff, J. (1952). A projective measure of need for affiliation. *Journal of Experimental Psychology, 43,* 349–356. [11]

Shneidman, E. S. (1976). *Suicidology: Contemporary developments.* New York: Grune & Stratton. [24]

Shneidman, E. S., & Farberow, N. L. (1970). Attempted and completed suicide. In E. S. Shneidman, N. L. Farberow, & R. E. Litman (Eds.), *The psychology of suicide.* New York: Science House. [24]

Shoben, E. J., Wescourt, K. T., & Smith, E. E. (1978). Sentence verification, sentence recognition and the semantic-episodic distinction. *Journal of Experimental Psychology: Human Learning and Memory, 4,* 304–317. [14]

Shopsin, B., Gershon, S., Thompson, H., & Collins, P. (1975). Psychoactive drugs in mania. *Archives of General Psychiatry, 32,* 34–42. [25]

Siegel, J. M. (1983). REM sleep control mechanisms: Evidence from lesion and unit recording studies. In A. Mayes (Ed.), *Sleep mechanisms and functions in humans and animals—An evolutionary perspective* (pp. 217–231). Wokingham, England: Van Nostrand-Reinhold. [7]

Siegler, R. S. (1978). The origins of scientific reasoning. In R. S. Siegler (Ed.), *Children's thinking: What develops?* (pp. 109–149). Hillsdale, NJ: Lawrence Erlbaum Associates. [16]

Simon, H. A. (1973). The structure of ill-structured problems. *Artificial Intelligence, 4,* 181–202. [15]

Simon, H. A. (1979). *Models of thought.* New Haven, CT: Yale University Press. [15]

Simpson, J. B., Epstein, A. N., & Canardo, J. S. (1978). The localization of dipsogenic receptors for angiotensin II in the subfornical organ. *Journal of Comparative and Physiological Psychology, 92,* 581–608. [9]

Singer, J. E. (1986). Traditions of stress research: Integrative comments. In C. D. Spielberger & I. G. Sarason (Eds.), *Stress and anxiety: Vol. 10. A sourcebook of theory and research* (pp. 25–33). Washington, DC: Hemisphere. [23]

Singh, S. (1978). *n* achievement, decision making, orientation, and work values of fast and slow progressing farmers in India. *Journal of Social Psychology, 106,* 153–160. [11]

Sinnott, J. D. (1989). *Everyday problem solving: Theory and applications.* New York: Praeger. [15]

Skinner, B. F. (1938). *The behavior of organisms.* New York: Appleton-Century-Crofts. [12]

Skinner, B. F. (1953). *Science and human behavior.* New York: Macmillan. [12]

Skinner, B. F. (1957). *Verbal behavior.* New York: Appleton-Century-Crofts. [17]

Skinner, B. F. (1963). Behaviorism at fifty. *Science, 140,* 951–958. [11]

Skinner, B. F. (1971). *Beyond freedom and dignity.* New York: Knopf. [1, 11]

Slater, P. J. B. (1983). Bird song learning: Theme and variation. In A. H. Brush & G. A. Clark (Eds.), *Perspectives in ornithology* (pp. 475–499). Cambridge, England: Cambridge University Press. [8]

Smith, B. D., & Vetter, H. J. (1982). *Theoretical approaches to personality.* Englewood Cliffs, NJ: Prentice-Hall. [21]

Smith, C., & Lloyd, B. (1978). Maternal behavior and perceived sex of infant: Revisited. *Child Development, 49,* 1263–1266. [20]

Smith, C., & Wong, P. T. P. (1991). Paradoxical sleep increases predict successful learning in a complex operant task. *Behavioral Neuroscience, 105,* 282–288. [7]

Smith, D. E., King, M. B., & Hoebel, B. C. (1970). Lateral hypothalamic control of killing: Evidence for a cholinoceptive mechanism. *Science, 167,* 900–901. [10]

Smith, E. E. (1978). Theories of semantic memory. In W. K. Estes (Ed.), *Handbook of learning and cognitive processes* (Vol. 5, pp. 1–56). Hillsdale, NJ: Lawrence Erlbaum Associates. [14]

Smith, E. E., Shoben, E. J., & Rips, L. J. (1974). Structure and process in semantic memory: A featural model for semantic decision. *Psychological Review, 81,* 214–241. [14]

Smith, M. L., & Glass, G. V. (1977). Meta-analysis of psychotherapy outcome studies. *American Psychologist, 32,* 752–760. [25]

Smith, M. P., & Duffy, M. (1957). Some physiological factors that regulate eating behavior. *Journal of Comparative and Physiological Psychology, 50,* 601–608. [9]

Snarey, J. R. (1985). Cross-cultural universality of social-moral development: A critical review of Kohlbergian Research. *Psychological Bulletin, 97,* 202–232. [18]

Snyder, M. (1979). Self-monitoring processes. In L. Berkowitz (Ed.), *Advances in experimental social psychology* (Vol. 12, pp. 85–128). New York: Academic Press. [19]

Snyder, M. (1984). When belief creates reality. In L. Berkowitz (Ed.), *Advances in experimental social psychology* (Vol. 18, pp. 247 305). Orlando, FL: Academic Press. [19]

Snyder, M., Berscheid, E., & Glick, P. (1985). Focusing on the exterior and the interior: Two investigations of the initiation of personal relationships. *Journal of Personality and Social Psychology, 48,* 1427–1439. [19]

Snyder, M., Tanke, E. D., & Berscheid, E. (1977). Social perception and interpersonal behavior: On the self-fulfilling nature of social stereotypes. *Journal of Personality and Social Psychology, 35,* 656–666. [19]

Snyder, S. H. (1977). Opiate receptors and internal opiates. *Scientific American, 236,* 44–56. [7]

Sokal, M. M. (Ed.). (1984). *Psychology, briefer course* by William James (Authorized scholarly edition). Cambridge, MA: Harvard University Press. [1]

Solomon, R. L. (1980). The opponent-process theory of motivation. *American Psychologist, 35,* 691–712. [6]

Solomon, R. L. (1977). An opponent-process theory of acquired motivation: IV. The affective dynamics of addiction. In J. D. Maser & M. E. P. Seligman (Eds.), *Psychopathology: Experimental models* (pp. 66–103). San Francisco: Freeman. [6]

Solomon, R. L., & Corbit, J. D. (1974). An opponent-process theory of motivation: I. Temporal dynamics of affect. *Psychological Review, 81,* 119–145. [6]

Sommer, B. (1983). How does menstruation affect cognitive competence and psychophysiological responses? In S. Golub (Ed.), *Lifting the curse of menstruation* (pp. 53–90). New York: Haworth. [10]

Sparnon, J. L., & Hornyak, L. M. (1989). Structured eating experiences in the inpatient treatment of anorexia nervosa. In L. M. Hornyak & E. K. Baker (Eds.), *Experiential therapies for eating disorders* (pp. 207–233). New York: Guilford Press. [9]

Spearman, C. (1904). "General intelligence," objectively defined and measured. *American Journal of Psychology, 15,* 201–293. [22]

Special issue: The neural basis of reward and reinforcement. (1989). *Neuroscience and Biobehavioral Reviews, 13,* 59–186. [6]

Spence, J. T., & Helmreich, R. L. (1978). *Masculinity & femininity: Their psychological dimensions, correlates, and antecedents.* Austin: University of Texas Press. [20]

Spence, K. W. (1936). The nature of discrimination learning in animals. *Psychological Review, 43,* 427–449. [15]

Spence, K. W. (1956). *Behavior theory and conditioning.* New Haven, CT: Yale University Press. [2]

Sperling, G. (1960). The information available in brief visual presentations. *Psychological Monographs, 74,* 1–29. [13]

Spetch, M. L., Wilkie, D. M., & Pinel, J. P. J. (1981). Backward conditioning: A reevaluation of the empirical evidence. *Psychological Bulletin, 89,* 163–175. [12]

Spielberger, C. D., Gorsuch, R. L., & Lushene, R. E. (1970). *The State-Trait Anxiety Inventory (STAI) test manual for form X.* Palo Alto, CA: Consulting Psychologists Press. [25]

Spindler, P. (1961). Studien zur Vererbung von Verhaltensweisen. 3. Verhalten gegenuberjungen Katzen. *Anthropologischer Anzeiger, 25,* 60–80. [8]

Spiro, R. J. (1977). Remembering information from text: The "state of schema" approach. In R. C. Anderson, R. J. Spiro, & W. E. Montague (Eds.), *Schooling and the acquisition of knowledge* (pp. 137–165). Hillsdale, NJ: Lawrence Erlbaum Associates. [14]

Spitzer, L., & Rodin, J. (1981). Human eating behavior: A critical review of studies in normal weight and overweight individuals. *Appetite, 2,* 293–329. [9]

Springer, S. P., & Deutsch, G. (1985). *Left brain, right brain.* New York: Freeman. [5]

Springer, S. P., Sidtis, J., Wilson, D., & Gazzaniga, M. S. (1978). Left ear performance in dichotic listening following commissurotomy. *Neuropsychologia, 16,* 305–312. [5]

Squire, L. R. (1987). *Memory and brain.* New York: Oxford University Press. [5]

Squire, L. R., & Moore, R. Y. (1979). Dorsal thalamic lesion in a noted case of human memory dysfunction. *Annals of Neurology, 6,* 503–506. [5]

Sroufe, L. A. (1983). Infant-caregiver attachment patterns of adaptation in preschool: The roots of maladaptation and competence. In M. Perlmutter (Ed.), *Minnesota Symposium in Child Psychology* (Vol. 16, pp. 41–81). Minneapolis: University of Minnesota Press. [18]

Sroufe, L. A. (1988). The role of infant-caregiver attachment in development. In J. Belsky & T. Nezworski (Eds.), *Clinical implications of attachment* (pp. 18–38). Hillsdale, NJ: Lawrence Erlbaum Associates. [18]

Sroufe, L. A., Fox, N. E., & Pancake, V. R. (1983). Attachment and dependency in developmental perspective. *Child Development, 54,* 1615–1627. [18]

Stace, W. T. (1952). *Religion and the modern mind.* Philadelphia: Lippincott. [1]

Stake, J. E. (1985). Exploring the basis of sex differences in third-party allocations. *Journal of Personality and Social Psychology, 48,* 1621–1629. [20]

Statistical abstract of the United States: 1990. (1990). Washington, DC: U. S. Bureau of the Census. [10]

Steadman, H. J. (1983). Predicting dangerousness among the mentally ill: Art, magic, and science. *International Journal of Law and Psychiatry, 6,* 381–390. [25]

Steadman, H. J., & Keveles, G. (1972). The community adjustment and criminal activity of the Baxtrom patients: 1966–1970. *American Journal of Psychiatry, 129,* 304–310. [25]

Steele, B. J., & Pollock, C. B. (1968). A psychiatric study of parents who abuse infants and small children. In R. E. Helfer & C. H. Kempe (Eds.), *The battered child* (pp. 103–147). Chicago: University of Chicago Press. [10]

Steele, R. S. (1977). Power motivation, activation, and inspirational speeches. *Journal of Personality, 45,* 53–64. [11]

Stein, A. M., & Bailey, M. M. (1973). The socialization of achievement orientation in women. *Psychological Bulletin, 80,* 345–364. [11]

Stern, W. (1914). *The psychological methods of testing intelligence* (G. M. Whipple, Trans.) Education Psychological Monographs, No. 13. Baltimore, MD: Warwick & York. [22]

Sternberg, R. J., & Powell, J. S. (1983). The development of intelligence. In P. H. Mussen (Ed.), *Handbook of child psychology* (4th ed., Vol. 3, pp. 341–419). New York: Wiley. [22]

Sternglanz, S. H., Gray, J. L., & Murakami, M. (1977). Adult preferences for infantile facial features: An ethological approach. *Animal Behaviour, 25,* 108–115. [8]

Stevens, S. S. (1936). A scale for the measurement of a psychophysical magnitude: Loudness. *Psychological Review, 43,* 405–416. [3]

Stevens, S. S. (1957). On the psychophysical law. *Psychological Review, 64,* 153–181. [3]

Stevens, S. S. (1958). Problems and methods of psychophysics. *Psychological Bulletin, 55,* 177–196. [3]

Stevens, S. S. (1966). Matching functions between loudness and ten other continua. *Perception and Psychophysics, 1,* 5 8. [3]

Stevens, S. S. (1969). Sensory scales of taste intensity. *Perception & Psychophysics, 6,* 302–308. [3]

Stevens, S. S. & Guirao, M. (1962). Loudness, reciprocality, and partition scales. *Journal of the Acoustical Society of America, 34,* 1466–1471. [3]

Stewart, A. J., & Chester, N. L. (1982). Sex differences in human social motives: Achievement, affiliation, and power. In A. J. Stewart (Ed.), *Motivation and society* (pp. 172–218). San Francisco: Jossey-Bass. [11]

Stewart, A. J., & Winter, D. G. (1976). Arousal of the power motive in women. *Journal of Consulting and Clinical Psychology, 44,* 495–496. [11]

Stokols, D. (1986). A congruence analysis of human stress. In C. D. Spielberger & I. G. Sarason (Eds.), *Stress and anxiety: Vol. 10. A sourcebook of theory and research* (pp. 35–64). Washington, DC: Hemisphere. [23]

Stone, A. A. (1975). *Mental health and law: A system in transition.* Rockville, MD: National Institute of Mental Health. [25]

Strachey, J. (Ed. & Trans.). (1953–1974). *The standard edition of the complete psychological works of Sigmund Freud* (Vols. 1–24). London: Hogarth Press. [2, 21]

Straus, M., Gelles, R., & Steinmetz, S. K. (1980). *Behind closed doors: Violence in the American family.* Garden City, NY: Anchor. [10]

Stroop, J. R. (1935). Studies of interference in serial verbal reaction. *Journal of Experimental Psychology, 18,* 643–662. [13]

Strube, M. J., & Garcia, J. E. (1981). A meta-analytic investigation of Fiedler's contingency model of leadership effectiveness. *Psychological Bulletin, 90,* 307–321. [20]

Stunkard, A. (1959). Obesity and the denial of hunger. *Psychosomatic Medicine, 21,* 281–289. [9]

Stunkard, A. (1961). Hunger and satiety. *American Journal of Psychiatry, 118,* 212–217. [9]

Stunkard, A., & Koch, C. (1964). The interpretation of gastric motility: I. Apparent bias in the reports of hunger by obese persons. *Archives of General Psychiatry, 11,* 74–82. [3]

Stunkard, A. J., Harris, J. R., Pedersen, N. L., & McClearn, G. R. (1990). The body-mass index of twins who have been reared apart. *New England Journal of Medicine, 322,* 1483–1487. [9]

Stunkard, A. J., Sorensen, T. I. A., Hanis, C., Teasdale, T. W., Chakraborty, R., Schull, W. J., & Schulsinger, F. (1986). An adoption study of human obesity. *New England Journal of Medicine, 314,* 193–198. [9]

Suedfeld, P. (1986). Stressful levels of environmental stimulation. In C. D. Spielberger & I. G. Sarason (Eds.), *Stress and anxiety: Vol. 10. A sourcebook of theory and research* (pp. 83–104). Washington, DC: Hemisphere. [23]

Sullivan, H. S. (1953). *The interpersonal theory of psychiatry.* New York: Norton. [21]

Svejda, M. J., Campos, J. J., & Emde, R. N. (1980). Mother-infant "bonding": Failure to generalize. *Child Development, 51,* 775–779. [18]

Szasz, T. (1961). *The myth of mental illness: Foundations of a theory of personal conduct.* New York: Harper (Hoeber). [24]

Tache, J., & Selye, H. (1986). On stress and coping mechanisms. In C. D. Spielberger & I. G. Sarason (Eds.), *Stress and anxiety: Vol. 10. A sourcebook of theory and research* (pp. 3–24). Washington, DC: Hemisphere. [23]

Takahashi, L. (1990). Hormonal regulation of sociosexual behavior in female mammals. *Neuroscience and Biobehavioral Reviews, 14,* 403–413. [10]

Tannen, D. (1990). *You just don't understand: Women and men in conversation.* New York: Ballantine. [20]

Tanner, J., Whitehouse, R., & Takaishi, M. (1966). Standards from birth to maturity for height, weight-height velocity, and weight velocity: British children, 1965. *Archives of the Diseases of Childhood, 41,* 468. [18]

Tarpy, R. M., & Sawabini, F. L. (1974). Reinforcement delay: A selective review of the last decade. *Psychological Bulletin, 81,* 984–997. [12]

Tarter, R. E., & Van Thiel, D. H. (1985). *Alcohol and the brain: Chronic effects.* New York: Plenum. [7]

Tauber, E. S., & Koffler, S. (1966). Optomotor responses in human infants to apparent motion: Evidence of innateness. *Science, 152,* 382–383. [4]

Taylor, S. E. (1983). Adjustment to threatening events: A theory of cognitive adaptation. *American Psychologist, 38,* 1161–1173. [23]

Taylor, S. E., Lichtman, R. R., & Wood, J. V. (1984). Attributions, beliefs about control, and adjustment to breast cancer. *Journal of Personality and Social Psychology, 46,* 489–502. [23, 24]

Tees, R. C., & Midgley, G. (1978). Extent of recovery of function after early sensory deprivation in the rat. *Journal of Comparative and Physiological Psychology, 92,* 768–777. [4]

R-36

Teitelbaum, P., & Stellar, E. (1954). Recovery from the failure to eat produced by hypothalamic lesions. *Science, 120*, 894–895. [9]

Terman, L. M., & Merrill, M. A. (1937). *Measuring intelligence.* Boston: Houghton-Mifflin. [22]

Terman, L. M., & Merrill, M. A. (1973). *Stanford-Binet intelligence scale: Manual for the third revision, form L-M.* Boston: Houghton-Mifflin. [22]

Terrace, H. S. (1979). *Nim.* New York: Columbia University Press. [17]

Terrace, H. S., Petitto, L. A., Sanders, R. J., & Bever, T. G. (1979). Can an ape create a sentence? *Science, 206*, 891–902. [17]

Teuber, H. L., Milner, B., & Vaughan, H. G. (1968). Persistent anterograde amnesia after stab wound of the basal brain. *Neuropsychologia, 6*, 267–282. [5]

Thomas, M. H., Horton, R. W., Lippincott, E. C., & Drabman, R. S. (1977). Desensitization to portrayals of real-life aggression as a function of exposure to television violence. *Journal of Personality and Social Psychology, 35*, 450–458. [10]

Thompson, J. G. (1988). *The psychobiology of emotions.* New York: Plenum. [6]

Thompson, L. A., Detterman, D. K., & Plomin, R. (1991). Association between cognitive abilities and scholastic achievement: Genetic overlap but environmental differences. *Psychological Science, 2*, 158–165.

Thompson, R. F. (1972). Sensory preconditioning. In R. F. Thompson & J. S. Voss (Eds.), *Topics in learning and performance* (pp. 105–129). New York: Academic Press. [12]

Thompson, R. F. (1984). *The brain: An introduction to neuroscience.* New York: Freeman. [7]

Thorndike, E. L. (1898). Animal intelligence. An experimental study of the associative processes in animals. *Psychological Monographs, 2* (No. 8). [12]

Thornkyke, P. W. (1984). Applica-

tions of schema theory in cognitive research. In J. R. Anderson & S. Kosslyn (Eds.), *Tutorials in learning and memory: Essays in honor of Gordon Bower* (pp. 167–191). San Francisco: Freeman. [14]

Thurstone, L. L., & Thurstone, T. G. (1962). *SRA Primary Mental Abilities.* Chicago: Science Research Associates. [22]

Tien Ming Chang (1986). Semantic memory: Facts and models. *Psychological Bulletin, 99*, 199–220. [14]

Tinbergen, N. (1951). *The study of instinct.* London: Oxford University Press. [8]

Tinbergen, N., & Perdeck, A. C. (1950). On the stimulus situation releasing the begging response in the newly-hatched herring gull chick *(Larus argentatus). Behaviour, 3*, 1–38. [8]

Titchener, E. B. (1898). The postulates of a structural psychology. *Philosophical Review, 7*, 449–465. [2]

Tobler, I. (1984). Evolution of the sleep process: A phylogenetic approach. In A. Borbely & J.-L. Valatx (Eds.), *Sleep mechanisms* (pp. 207–226). Berlin: Springer-Verlag. [7]

Tolman, E. C., & Honzik, C. H. (1930). Introduction and removal of reward, and maze performance in rats. *University of California, Berkeley, Publications of Psychology, 4*, 257–275. [12]

Torgersen, S. (1986). Genetic factors in moderately severe and mild affective disorders. *Archives of General Psychiatry, 43*, 222–226. [24]

Towbin, E. J. (1949). Gastric distension as a factor in the satiation of thirst in esophagastomized dogs. *American Journal of Physiology, 159*, 533–541. [9]

Trabasso, T. R., & Bower, G. H. (1964). Presolution reversal and dimensional shifts in concept identification. *Journal of Experimental Psychology, 67*, 398–399. [15]

Treisman, A. M. (1964). Verbal cues, language and meaning in selective attention. *American Journal of Psychology, 77*, 206–219. [13]

Treisman, A. M., & Geffen, G. (1967). Selective attention: Perception or response? *Quarterly Journal of Experimental Psychology, 19*, 1–17. [13]

Treisman, A. M., & Gormican, S. (1988). Feature analysis in early vision: Evidence from search asymmetries. *Psychological Review, 95*, 15–48. [13]

Treisman, A. M., & Riley, J. G. A. (1969). Is selective attention selective perception or selective response? A further test. *Journal of Experimental Psychology, 79*, 27–34. [13]

Trevarthen, C. (1984). Emotions in infancy: Regulators of contact and relationships with persons. In K. R. Scherer & P. Ekman (Eds.), *Approaches to emotion* (pp. 129–157). Hillsdale, NJ: Lawrence Erlbaum Associates. [6]

Trivers, R. L. (1971). The evolution of reciprocal altruism. *Quarterly Review of Biology, 46*, 35–57. [8]

Tucker, J. A., Vucinich, R. E., & Sobell, M. B. (1981). Alcohol consumption as a self-handicapping strategy. *Journal of Abnormal Psychology, 90*, 220–230. [19]

Tulving, E. (1983). *Elements of episodic memory.* New York: Oxford University Press. [14]

Tulving, E. (1985). How many memory systems are there? *American Psychologist, 40*, 385–398. [14]

Tulving, E. (1986). What kind of a hypothesis is the distinction between episodic and semantic memory. *Journal of Experimental Psychology: Learning, Memory, and Cognition, 12*, 307–311. [14]

Tversky, A., & Kahneman, D. (1974). Judgment under uncertainty: Heuristics and biases. *Science, 185*, 1124–1131. [19]

Udolf, R. (1987). *Handbook of hypnosis for professionals* (2nd ed.). New York: Van Nostrand-Reinhold. [7]

Ungerstedt, U. (1971). Adipsia and aphagia after 6–hydroxydopamine induced degeneration of the nigrostriatal dopamine system. *Acta Physiologica Scandinavica, 82* (Suppl. 367), 95–122. [9]

United States Department of Health and Human Services (1991a). *Monthly vital statistics report* Vol. 40(8). Washington, DC: National Center for Health Statistics, Centers for Disease Control, Public Health Service, U.S. Government Printing Office. [18]

United States Department of Health and Human Services (1991b). *Morbidity and mortality weekly report. CDC Surveillance Summaries* (Vol. 39, No. SS-2). Washington, DC: U.S. Government Printing Office. [18]

Ursin, H., & Kaada, B. R. (1960). Functional localization within the amygdaloid complex in the cat. *Electroencephalography and Clinical Neurophysiology, 12,* 1–20. [6]

Valins, S. (1966). Cognitive effects of false heart-rate feedback. *Journal of Personality and Social Psychology, 4,* 400–408. [6]

Valins, S. (1970). The perception and labeling of bodily changes as determinants of emotional behavior. In P. Black (Ed.), *Physiological correlates of emotion* (pp. 229–243). New York: Academic Press. [6]

Valvo, A. (1971). *Sight restoration after long-term blindness: The problems and behavior patterns of visual rehabilitation.* New York: American Foundation of the Blind. [4]

Valzelli, L. (1981). *Psychobiology of aggression and violence.* New York: Raven Press. [10]

Vandenberg, S. G., & Vogler, G. P. (1985). Genetic determinants of intelligence. In B. B. Wolman (Ed.), *Handbook of intelligence: Theories, measurements, and applications* (pp. 3–57). New York: Wiley (Interscience). [22]

van den Hoofdakker, R. H., & Beersma, D. G. M. (1984). Sleep deprivation, mood, and sleep physiology. In A. Borbely & J.-L. Valatx (Eds.), *Sleep mechanisms* (pp. 297–309). Berlin: Springer-Verlag. [7]

van der Meer, H. C. (1979). Interrelation of the effects of binocular disparity and perspective cues on judgments of depth and height. *Perception & Psychophysics, 26,* 481–488. [4]

Vaughn, C. E., & Leff, J. P. (1976). The influence of family and social factors on the course of psychiatric illness: A comparison of schizophrenic and depressed neurotic patients. *British Journal of Psychiatry, 129,* 125–137. [24, 25]

Veroff, J. (1957). Development and validation of a projective measure of power motivation. *Journal of Abnormal and Social Psychology, 54,* 1–8. [11]

Veroff, J., Atkinson, J. W., Feld, S. C., & Gurin, G. (1960). The use of thematic apperception to assess motivation in a nationwide interview study. *Psychological Monographs: General and Applied, 74,* 1–32. [11]

Veroff, J., Wilcox, S., & Atkinson, J. W. (1953). The achievement motive in high school and college age women. *Journal of Abnormal and Social Psychology, 18,* 108–119. [11]

Verrillo, R. T. (1975). Cutaneous sensation. In B. Scharf (Ed.), *Experimental sensory psychology* (pp. 151–184). Glenview, IL: Scott Foresman. [3]

Victor, M., Adams, R. D., & Collins, G. H. (1971). *The Wernicke-Korsakoff syndrome.* Philadelphia: Davis. [5]

Vignolo, L. A. (1969). Auditory agnosia: A review and report of recent evidence. In A. L. Benton (Eds.), *Contributions to clinical neuropsychology* (pp. 172–208). Chicago: Aldine. [5]

Vogel, G. W., & Traub, A. C. (1968). REM deprivation. I. The effect on schizophrenic patients. *Archives of General Psychiatry, 18,* 287–299. [7]

Vollhardt, L. T. (1991). Psychoneuroimmunology: A literature review. *American Journal of Orthopsychiatry, 61,* 35–47. [23]

von Frisch, K. (1967). *The dance language and orientation of bees.* Cambridge, MA: Harvard University Press. [8]

von Wright, J. M., Anderson, K., & Stenman, U. (1975). Generalization of conditioned GSRs in dichotic listening. In P. M. A. Rabbitt & S. Dornic (Eds.), *Attention and performance* (Vol. 5, pp. 194–204). New York: Academic Press. [13]

Voss, J. F., Greene, T. R., Post, T. A., & Penner, B. C. (1983). Problem solving skill in social sciences. In G. H. Bower (Ed.), *The psychology of learning and motivation: Advances in research and theory* (Vol. 17, pp. 165–213). New York: Academic Press. [15]

Wadden, T. A., & Anderton, C. H. (1982). The clinical use of hypnosis. *Psychological Bulletin, 91,* 215–243. [7]

Wagenaar, W. A. (1986). My memory: A study of autobiographical memory over six years. *Cognitive Psychology, 18,* 225–252. [14]

Wagner, H. L., MacDonald, C. J., & Manstead, A. S. R. (1986). Communication of individual emotions by spontaneous facial expressions. *Journal of Personality and Social Psychology, 50,* 737–743. [6]

Wagstaff, G. F. (1981). *Hypnosis, compliance and belief.* New York: St. Martin's. [7]

Wahba, M. A., & Birdwell, L. G. (1973). Maslow reconsidered: A review of research on the need hierarchy theory. *Proceedings of the 33rd Annual Meeting of the Academy of Management,* pp. 514–520. [11]

Wahlsten, D. (1972). Genetic experiments with animal learning: A critical review. *Behavioral Biology, 7,* 143–182. [8]

Walk, R. D., & Gibson, E. J. (1961). A comparative and analytical study of visual depth perception. *Psychological Monographs, 75*(Whole No. 519). [4]

Walker, J. I., & Cavenar, J. O. (1982). Vietnam veterans: Their problems continue. *Journal of Nervous and Mental Disease, 170,* 174–180. [24]

Walker, L. J. (1984). Sex differences in the development of moral reasoning. *Child Development, 55,* 677–691. [18]

Wallace, B. (1984). Apparent equivalence between perception and imagery in the production of various visual illusions. *Memory & Cognition, 12,* 156–162. [14]

Wallach, H., O'Connell, D. N., & Neisser, U. (1953). The memory effect of visual perception of three-dimensional form. *Journal of Experimental Psychology, 45,* 360–368. [4]

Wallen, K. (1990). Desire and ability: Hormones and the regulation of female sexual behavior. *Neuroscience and Biobehavioral Reviews, 14,* 233–241. [10]

Walsh, K. W. (1978). *Neuropsychology: A clinical approach.* Edinburgh: Churchill-Livingstone. [5]

Walster, E., Berscheid, E., & Walster, G. W. (1976). New directions in equity research. In L. Berkowitz & E. Walster (Eds.), *Advances in experimental social psychology* (Vol. 9, pp. 1–42). New York: Academic Press. [20]

Wandlaw, K. A., & Kroll, N. E. A. (1976). Autonomic responses to shock-associated words in a nonattended message: A failure to replicate. *Journal of Experimental Psychology: Human Perception and Performance, 2,* 357–360. [13]

Waters, E., Wippman, J., & Sroufe, L. A. (1979). Attachment, positive affect, and competence in the peer group: Two studies in construct validation. *Child Development, 50,* 821–829. [18]

Watson, J. B. (1913). Psychology as the behaviorist views it. *Psychological Review, 20,* 158–177. [2]

Watson, J. B. (1914). *Behavior: An introduction to comparative psychology.* New York: Holt. [1, 2]

Watson, J. B. (1919). *Psychology from the standpoint of a behaviorist.* Philadelphia: Lippincott. [2]

Watson, J. B. (1925). *Behaviorism.* New York: Norton. [16]

Watson, J. B., & Raynor, R. (1920). Conditioned emotional reactions. *Journal of Experimental Psychology, 3,* 1–14. [12]

Watson, R. I. (1968). *The great psychologists: From Aristotle to Freud* (2nd ed.). Philadelphia: Lippincott. [1, 2]

Wauquier, A., Gaillard, J. M., Monti, J. M., & Radulovacki, M. (1985). *Sleep: Neurotransmitters and neuromodulators.* New York: Raven Press. [7]

Weary, G., & Arkin, R. M. (1981). Attributional self-presentation. In J. H. Harvey, W. Ickes, & R. F. Kidd (Eds.), *New directions in attribution research* (Vol. 3, pp. 223–246). Hillsdale, NJ: Lawrence Erlbaum Associates. [19]

Webb, W. B. (1975). *Sleep: The gentle tyrant.* Englewood Cliffs, NJ: Prentice-Hall. [7]

Webb, W. B. (1982). Sleep in older persons: Sleep structures of 50–to–60–year-old men and women. *Journal of Gerontology, 37,* 581–586. [7]

Webb, W. B. (1983). Theories in modern sleep research. In A. Mayes (Ed.), *Sleep mechanisms and functions in humans and animals—an evolutionary perspective* (pp. 1–17). Wokingham, England: Van Nostrand-Reinhold. [7]

Webb, W. B., & Agnew, H. W. (1975). Sleep efficiency for sleep-wake cycles of varied length. *Psychophysiology, 12,* 637–641. [7]

Wechsler, D. (1974). *Manual for the Wechsler Intelligence Scale for Children—Revised.* New York: Psychological Corporation. [22]

Wechsler, D. (1981). *Manual for the Wechsler Adult Intelligence Scale—Revised.* New York: Psychological Corporation. [22]

Weinberger, D. R., Wagner, R. L., & Wyatt, R. J. (1983). Neuropathological studies of schizophrenia: A selective review. *Schizophrenia Bulletin, 9,* 193–212. [24]

Weiner, B. (1974). *Achievement motivation and attribution theory.* Morristown, NJ: General Learning Press. [11]

Weiner, B. (1985). An attributional theory of achievement motivation and emotion. *Psychological Review, 92,* 548–573. [11]

Weiner, B., Frieze, I. H., Kukla, A., Reed, L., Rest, S., & Rosenbaum, R. M. (1972). Perceiving the causes of success and failure. In E. E. Jones, D. E. Kanouse, H. H. Kelley, R. E. Nisbett, S. Valins, & B. Weiner (Eds.), *Attribution: Perceiving the causes of behavior* (pp. 95–120). Morristown, NJ: General Learning Press. [11]

Weiner, B., & Sierad, J. (1975). Misattribution for failure and enhancement of achievement strivings. *Journal of Personality and Social Psychology, 31,* 415–421. [11]

Weinstein, S. (1968). Intensive and extensive aspects of tactile sensitivity as a function of body part, sex, and laterality. In D. R. Kenshalo (Ed.), *The skin senses* (pp. 195–222). Springfield, IL: Thomas. [3]

Weisberg, R. W., & Alba, J. W. (1981). An examination of the alleged role of "fixation" in the solution of several "insight" problems. *Journal of Experimental Psychology: General, 110,* 169–192. [15]

Weiss, J. M., & Simson, P. G. (1985). Neurochemical mechanisms underlying stress-induced depression. In T. M. Field, P. M. McCabe, and N. Schneiderman (Eds.), *Stress and coping* (pp. 93–116). Hillsdale, NJ: Lawrence Erlbaum Associates. [23]

Welker, R. L. (1982). Abstraction of themes from melodic variations. *Journal of Experimental Psychology: Human Perception and Performance, 8,* 435–447. [14]

Wender, P. H., Kety, S. S., Rosenthal, D., Schulsinger, F., Ortmann, J., & Lunde, I. (1986). Psychiatric disorders in the biological and adoptive families of adopted individuals with affective disorders. *Archives of General Psychiatry, 43,* 923–929. [24]

Wertheimer, M. (1976). The Gestalt movement. In G. M. Murch (Ed.), *Studies in perception* (pp. 104–123). Indianapolis, IN: Bobbs-Merrill. [4]

Wever, E. G. (1949), *Theory of hearing.* New York: Wiley. [3]

Whalen, R. E. (1977). Brain mechanisms controlling sexual behavior. In F. A. Beach (Ed.), *Human sexuality in four perspectives* (pp. 215–246). Baltimore, MD: Johns Hopkins University Press. [10]

Whatley, J. L. (1987). Bayley scales of infant development. In D. J. Keyser & R. C. Sweetland (Eds.), *Test critiques compendium: Reviews of major tests from the Test Critiques series* (pp. 14–23). Kansas City, MO: Test Corporation of America. [16]

Wheeler, L., Koestner, R., & Driver, R. E. (1982). Related attributes in the choice of comparison others: It's there, but it isn't all there is. *Journal of Experimental Social Psychology, 18*, 489–500. [19]

Whitaker, H. A., & Ojemann, G. A. (1977). Lateralization of higher cortical functions: A critique. *Annals of the New York Academy of Sciences, 299*, 459–473. [5]

Whitman, R., Pierce, C., Maas, J., & Baldridge, B. (1962). The dreams of the experimental subject. *Journal of Nervous and Mental Disorders, 134*, 431–439. [7]

Wickelgren, W. A. (1973). The long and the short of memory. *Psychological Bulletin, 80*, 425–438. [13]

Widiger, T. A., & Shea, T. (1991). Differentiation of Axis I and Axis II disorders. Special issue: Diagnoses, dimensions, and DSM-IV: The science of classification. *Journal of Abnormal Psychology, 100*, 399–406. [24]

Widom, C. S. (1989). Does violence beget violence? A critical examination of the literature. *Psychological Bulletin, 106*, 3–28. [10]

Wiener, N. (1948) *Cybernetics*. New York: Wiley. [2]

Wiggins, J. S. (1988). *Personality and prediction: Principles of personality assessment*. Malabar, FL: Krieger. [22]

Willerman, L., & Cohen, D. B. (1990). *Psychopathology*. New York: McGraw-Hill. [21]

Williams, J. E., & Best, D. L. (1982). *Measuring sex stereotypes: A thirty-nation study*. Beverly Hills, CA: Sage. [20]

Williams, J. H. (1964). Conditioning of verbalization: A review. *Psychological Bulletin, 62*, 383–393. [12]

Willis, C. G. (1984). Myers-Briggs Type Indicator. In D. J. Keyser & R. C. Sweetland (Eds.), *Test critiques* (Vol. 1, pp. 482–490). Kansas City, MO: Test Corporation of America. [21]

Wills, T. A. (1981). Downward comparison principles in social psychology. *Psychological Bulletin, 90*, 245–271. [19]

Wilsnack, S. (1974). The effects of social drinking on women's fantasy. *Journal of Personality, 42*, 43–61. [11]

Wilson, E. O. (1975). *Sociobiology*. Cambridge, MA: Harvard University Press. [8]

Wilson, E. O. (1978). *On human nature*. New York: Bantam Books. [8]

Wilson, R., Raynal, D., Guilleminault, C., Zarcone, V., & Dement, W. (1973). REM sleep latencies in daytime sleep recordings of narcoleptics. *Sleep Research, 2*, 166. [7]

Wilson, R. S. (1969). Cardiac response: Determinants of conditioning. *Journal of Comparative and Physiological Psychology Monograph, 68*(Pt. 2). [12]

Wilson, R. S. (1983). The Louisville twin study: Developmental synchronies in behavior. *Child Development, 54*, 298–316. [16]

Wilson, S. C., & Barber, T. X. (1983). The fantasy prone personality: Implications for understanding imagery, hypnosis, and parapsychological phenomena. In A. A. Sheikh (Ed.), *Imagery: Current theory, research, and application* (pp. 340–387). New York: Wiley. [7]

Wimer, R. E., & Wimer, C. C. (1985). Animal behavior genetics: A search for the biological foundations of behavior. *Annual Review of Psychology, 36*, 171–218. [8]

Winograd, E., & Killinger, W. A. (1983). Relating age at encoding in early childhood to adult recall: Development of flashbulb memories. *Journal of Experimental Psychology, 112*, 413–422. [14]

Winston, M. L. (1987). *The biology of the honey bee*. Cambridge, MA: Harvard University Press. [8]

Winter, D. G. (1973). *The power motive*. New York: Free Press. [11]

Winter, D. G. (1988). The power motive in women and men. *Journal of Personality and Social Psychology, 54*, 510–519. [11]

Winter, D. G., & Stewart, A. J. (1977). Content analysis as a technique for assessing political leaders. In M. G. Hermann (Ed.), *A psychological examination of political leaders* (pp. 27–61). New York: Free Press. [11]

Winter, D. G., & Stewart, A. J. (1978). The power motive. In H. London & J. E. Exner (Eds.), *Dimensions of personality* (pp. 391–447). New York: Wiley. [11]

Wise, C. D., & Stein, L. (1969). Facilitation of brain self-stimulation by central administration of norepinephrine. *Science, 163*, 299–301. [6]

Witkin, H., & Lewis, H. (1965). The relation of experimentally induced presleep experiences to dreams: A report on method and preliminary findings. *Journal of the American Psychoanalytic Association, 13*, 819–849. [7]

Wolpe, J. (1958). *Psychotherapy by reciprocal inhibition*. Stanford, CA: Stanford University Press. [25]

Woocher, F. D., Glass, A. L., & Holyoak, K. J. (1978). Positional discriminability in linear orderings. *Memory & Cognition, 6*, 165–173. [15, 16]

Wood, W., Wong, F. Y., & Chachere, J. G. (1991). Effects of media violence on viewer's aggression in unconstrained social interaction. *Psychological Bulletin, 109*, 371–383. [10]

Woodruff, R. A., Clayton, P. J., & Guze, S. B. (1975). Is everyone depressed? *American Journal of Psychiatry, 132*, 627–628. [24]

Woodworth, R. S. (1921). *Psychology: A study of mental life*. New York: Holt. [2]

Woodworth, R. S. (1938). *Experimental psychology*. New York: Holt. [19]

Wooley, D. W., Wooley, S. C., & Dunham, R. B. (1972). Can calories be perceived and do they affect hunger in obese and nonobese humans? *Journal of Comparative* and *Physiological Psychology, 80,* 250–258. [9]

Wortman, C. B., & Dunkel-Schetter, C. (1987). Conceptual and methodological issues in the study of social support. In A. Baum & J. E. Singer (Eds.), *Handbook of psychology and health: Vol. 5: Stress* (pp. 63–108). Hillsdale, NJ: Lawrence Erlbaum Associates. [23]

Wrightsman, L. S. (1990) *Psychology and the legal system* (2nd ed.). Pacific Grove, CA: Brooks/Cole. [24]

Wyatt v. Stickney, 325 F. Supp. 781 (M. D. Ala., 1971), enforced in 334 F. Supp. 1341 (M. D. Ala., 1971), 344 F. Supp. 373, 379 (M. D. Ala., 1972). [24, 25]

Wyrwicka, W., & Dobrzecka, C. (1960). Relationship between feeding and satiation centers of the hypothalamus. *Science, 132,* 805–806. [9]

Wyrwicka, W., Dobrzecka, C., & Tarnecki, R. (1960). The effect of electrical stimulation of the hypothalamus feeding center in satiated goats on alimentary conditioning reflexes, type II. *Acta Biologiae Experimentalis (Warsaw), 20,* 121–126. [9]

Yarmey, A. D. (1979). *The psychology of eyewitness testimony.* New York: Free Press. [14]

Yeh, S. Y., & Haertzen, C. A. (1991). Cocaine-induced locomotor activity in rats. *Pharmacology, Biochemistry and Behavior, 39,* 723–727. [7]

Yodogawa, E. (1982). Symmetropy, an entropy-like measure of visual symmetry. *Perception & Psychophysics, 32,* 230–240. [4]

Youngs, G. A., Jr. (1986). Patterns of threat and punishment reciprocity in a conflict setting. *Journal of Personality and Social Psychology, 51,* 541–546. [20]

Zajonc, R. B., Murphy, S. T., & Inglehart, M. (1989). Feeling and facial efference: Implications of the vascular theory of emotion. *Psychological Review, 96,* 395–416. [6]

Zarega, A. M. (1981). Transportation energy conservation policy: Implications for social science research. *Journal of Social Issues, 37*(2), 31–50. [20]

Zatorre, R. J. (1979). Recognition of dichotic melodies by musicians and nonmusicians. *Neuropsychologia, 17,* 607–617. [5]

Zillmann, D. (1971). Excitation transfer in communication-mediated aggressive behavior. *Journal of Experimental Social Psychology, 7,* 419–434. [10]

Zillmann, D. (1978). *Hostility and aggression.* Hillsdale, NJ: Lawrence Erlbaum Associates. [10]

Zillmann, D., Bryant, J., Comisky, P. W., & Medoff, N. J. (1981). Excitation and hedonic valence in the effect of erotica on motivated intermale aggressive behavior. *European Journal of Social Psychology, 11,* 233–252. [10]

Zillmann, D., Katcher, A. H., & Milavsky, B. (1972). Excitation transfer from physical exercise to subsequent aggressive behavior. *Journal of Experimental Social Psychology, 8,* 247–259. [6]

Zola-Morgan, S., & Squire, L. R. (1985). Amnesia in monkeys following lesions of the mediodorsal nucleus of the thalamus. *Annals of Neurology, 17,* 558–564. [5]

Zuckerman, M., DePaulo, B. M., & Rosenthal, R. (1981). Verbal and nonverbal communication of deception. In L. Berkowitz (Ed.), *Advances in experimental social psychology* (Vol. 14, pp. 1–59). New York: Academic Press. [19]

CREDITS

LINE ART AND TABLE CREDITS

Chapter 2

Figure 2-3: From *Plans and the Structure of Behavior* (p. 26) by G. A. Miller, E. Galanter, and K. H. Pribam, 1960. Reprint. New York: Adams, Bannister, Cox, 1986. All rights reserved. Reprinted by permission.

Chapter 3

Figure 3-6: From "An Adaptometer for Measuring Human Dark Adaptation" by S. Hecht and S. Schlaer, 1938, *Journal of the Optical Society of America, 28,* pp. 269–275. Reprinted by permission.

Chapter 5

Figure 5-18: From "Amnesia in Monkeys Following Lesions of the Mediodorsal Nucleus of the Thalamus" by S. Zola-Morgan and L. R. Squire, 1985, *Annals of Neurology, 17,* pp. 558–564. Reprinted by permission of *Annals of Neurology.*

Chapter 8

Figures 8-14 and 8-15: From "Adult Preferences for Infantile Facial Features: An Ethological Approach" by Sternglanz, Gray, and Murakami, 1977, *Animal Behavior, 25,* pp. 108–115. Reprinted by permission of Academic Press, Inc.

Chapter 9

Figure 9-7: From "An Adoption Study of Human Obesity" by A. J. Stunkard, T. I. A. Sorenson, C. Hanis, T. W. Teasdale, R. Chakraborty, W. J. Schull, and F. Schulsinger, 1986, *The New England Journal of Medicine, 314,* pp. 193–198. Reprinted by permission of *The New England Journal of Medicine.*

Chapter 10

Figure 10-6: From "Acquisition of an Aggressive Response and Its Generalization to Verbal Behavior" by R. G. Geen and R. Pigg, 1970, *Journal of Personality and Social Psychology, 15,* pp. 167–170. Copyright 1970 by the American Psychological Association. Adapted by permission.

Chapter 11

Figure 11-8: From "Misattribution for Failure and Enhancement of Achievement Strivings" by B. Weiner and J. Sierad, 1975, *Journal of Personality and Social Psychology, 31,* pp. 415–421. Copyright 1975 by the American Psychological Association. Adapted by permission.

Table 11-1: From "The Power Motive" by D. G. Winter and A. J. Stewart, in *Dimensions of Personality* (pp. 391–447) by H.

London and J. E. Exner (Eds.), 1978, New York: John Wiley and Sons. Copyright © 1978 by John Wiley & Sons, Inc. Reprinted by permission of John Wiley & Sons, Inc.

Chapter 12

Figure 12-23: From *Learning and Behavior* (2nd ed.) (p. 126) by J. E. Mazur, 1990, Englewood Cliffs, NJ: Prentice-Hall. Copyright 1990 by Prentice-Hall, Inc.

Figure 12-24: From "A Comparison of Students' Studying-behavior Produced by Daily, Weekly, and Three-week Testing Schedules" by V. T. Mawhinney, D. E. Bostow, D. R. Laws, G. J. Blumenfeld, and B. L. Hopkins, 1971, *Journal of Applied Behavior Analysis, 4,* pp. 257–264. Adapted by permission.

Figure 12-25: From "Modification of Symptomatic and Verbal Behavior of Mental Patients" by T. Ayllon and E. Haughton, 1964, *Behaviour Research and Therapy, 2,* pp. 87–97. Copyright Pergamon Press PLC. Adapted by permission.

Chapter 13

Figure 13-9: From "Selective Looking: Attending Visually Specified Events" by U. Neisser and R. Becklen, 1975, *Cognitive Psychology, 7,* pp. 480–494. Adapted by permission of Academic Press, Inc.

Figures 13-15 and 13-16: From "Chronometric Studies of the Rotation of Mental Images" by L. A. Cooper and R. N. Shepard, in *Visual Information Processing* (pp. 75–176) by W. G. Chase (Ed.), New York: Academic Press. Reprinted by permission of Academic Press, Inc.

Figures 13-17 and 13-18: From "Visual Images Preserve Metric Spatial Information: Evidence from Studies of Image Scanning" by S. M. Kosslyn, T. M. Ball, and B. J. Reiser, 1978, *Journal of Experimental Psychology: Human Perception and Performance, 4,* pp. 47–60. Copyright 1978 by the American Psychological Association. Adapted by permission.

Chapter 14

Figure 14-1: From "Retrieval Time from Semantic Memory" by A. M. Collins and M. R. Quillan, 1969, *Journal of Verbal Learning and Verbal Behavior, 8,* pp. 240–247. Reprinted by permission of Academic Press, Inc.

Figure 14-3: From "Semantic Distance and the Verification of Semantic Relations" by L. J. Rips, E. J. Schoben, and E. E. Smith, 1973, *Journal of Verbal Learning and Verbal Behavior, 12,* pp. 1–20. Reprinted by permission of Academic Press, Inc.

Figure 14-6: From "Frameworks for Comprehending Discourse" by R. C. Anderson, R. E. Reynolds, D. L. Schallert, and E. T. Goetz, 1977, *American Educational Research Journal, 14,* pp. 367–382. Copyright 1977 by the American Educational Research Center. Adapted by permission of the publisher.

Table 14-1: From "Cognitive Representations of Semantic Categories" by E. Rosch, 1975, *Journal of Experimental Psychology: General, 104,* pp. 192–253. Copyright 1975 by the American Psychological Association. Adapted by permission.

Chapter 15

Figure 15-23: From "The mind's eye in chess" by W. G. Chase and H. A. Simon, 1973, in *Visual Information Processing* (pp. 215–281) by W. G. Chase (Ed.), New York: Academic Press. Reprinted by permission of Academic Press.

Chapter 17

Table 17-1: From *The Articulate Mammal: An Introduction to Psycholinguistics* (2nd ed.) (p. 90) by J. Aitchison, 1983, New York: Universe Books. Adapted by permission.

Figure 17-8: From "The Child's Learning of English" by J. Berko, 1958, *Word, 14,* pp. 150–177.

Figure 17-10: From *Intelligence in Ape and Man* (pp. 41, 285) by D. Premack, 1976, Hillsdale, NJ: Lawrence Erlbaum Associates. Used by permission.

Chapter 18

Figure 18-6: From "Identity in Adolescence" by J. E. Marcia, in *Handbook of Adolescent Psychology* (pp. 159–187) by J. Adelson (Ed.), 1980, New York: John Wiley & Sons. Copyright © 1980 by John Wiley & Sons, Inc. Reprinted by permission of John Wiley & Sons, Inc.

Figure 18-7: From *The Philosophy of Moral Development: Moral Stages and the Idea of Justice: Vol. I. Essays on Moral Development* (p. 12) by L. Kohlberg, 1981, San Francisco: Harper and Row. Adapted by permission.

Figures 18-8, 18-9, and 18-10: From *Being Adolescent* by M. Csikszentmihalyi, 1984, New York: Basic Books, a division of HarperCollins Publishers. Copyright © 1984 by Basic Books, Inc. Reprinted by permission.

Chapter 19

Figure 19-5: From "Prediction of Goal-Directed Behavior: Attitudes, Intentions, and Perceived Behavioral Control" by I. Ajzen and T. J. Madden, 1986, *Journal of Experi-*

mental Social Psychology, 22, pp. 453–474. Adapted by permission from Academic Press, Inc.

Figure 19-6: From "A New Look at Dissonance Theory" by J. Cooper and R. H. Fazio, in *Advances in Experimental Psychology, 17,* (pp. 229–266) by L. Berkowitz (Ed.), 1984, New York: Academic Press. Adapted by permission from Academic Press, Inc.

Chapter 20

Figure 20-1: From "Sex Differences and Cultural Institutions" by R. D. Andraw, in *The Development of Sex Differences* (pp. 174–204) by E. E. Macoby (Ed.), 1966, Stanford: Stanford University Press. © 1966 by the Board of Trustees of the Leland Stanford Junior University. Adapted by permission of the publishers, Stanford University Press.

Figure 20-3: From "Resisting Temptation: Devaluation of Alternative Partners as a Means of Maintaining Commitment in Close Relationships" by D. J. Johnson and C. E. Rusbult, 1989, *Journal of Personality and Social Psychology, 57,* pp. 967–980. Copyright 1989 by the American Psychological Association. Adapted by permission.

Figure 20-8: From *Studies in Machiavellianism,* pp. 17–18 by R. Christie and F. L. Geis (Eds.), 1970, New York: Academic Press. Reprinted by permission of Academic Press, Inc.

Chapter 21

Table 21-1: From "Conceptions of States and Traits: Dimensional Attributes with Ideals as Prototypes" by W. F. Chaplin, O. P. John, and R. L. Goldberg, 1988, *Journal of Personality and Social Psychology, 54,* pp. 541–557. Copyright 1988 by The American Psychological Association. Adapted by permission.

Chapter 22

Figure 22-12: From "The Structure-of-Intellect Model" by J. P. Guilford, in *Handbook of Intelligence: Theories, Measurements and Applications* (pp. 226–266) by B. B. Wolman (Ed.), 1985, New York: Wiley-Interscience. Adapted by permission of John Wiley & Sons, Inc.

Chapter 23

Figure 23-3: From *Stress, Appraisal, and Coping* by R. S. Lazarus and S. Folkman, 1984, New York: Springer Publishing Company, Inc., New York 10012. Used by permission.

Table 23-2 and Figure 23-4: From "Recent Life Changes, Emotions and Behaviors in Coronary Heart Disease" by R. H. Rahe, in *Handbook of Psychology and Health, Volume V: Stress,* (pp. 229–254) by A. Baum and J. E. Singer (Eds.), 1987, Hillsdale, NJ: Lawrence Erlbaum Associates. Reprinted by permission.

Figure 23-5: From *Decision Making: A Psychological Analysis of Conflict, Choice, and Commitment* by Irving L. Janis and Leon Mann. Copyright © 1977 by The Free Press, a Division of Macmillan, Inc. Adapted with the permission of the publisher.

Chapter 24

Tables 24-1 and 24-3: From *Diagnostic and Statistical Manual of Mental Disorders* (3rd ed., rev.), (pp. 3–11, 217–218, 222–223) by American Psychiatric Association, 1987. Washington, DC: American Psychiatric Association. Reprinted by permission.

PHOTO CREDITS

Part One: A Historical Overview of Psychology
Constantin Brancusi, "Sleeping Muse," 1910. The Metropolitan Museum of Art, The Alfred Stieglitz Collection, 1949 (49.70.225).

Chapter 1: Foundations for Understanding Behavior
Page 5 © The Bettmann Archive; *page 6 (top)* © The Bettmann Archive; *page 6 (bottom)* © The Bettmann Archive; *page 7* © The Bettmann Archive; *page 9* © Yale Joel/Life Magazine © 1950 Time Inc.; *page 12* © Art Resource; *page 11* © Nicholas Devore/Photographers Aspen; *page 14 (top)* © R. and S. Michaud/Woodfin Camp & Assoc.; *page 14 (bottom)* © The Bettmann Archive; *page 15* © The Bettmann Archive; *page 17* © Culver Pictures, Inc.; page 18 © Historical Pictures Service; *page 19 (bottom left)* © Brown Brothers; *page 20* © Erwin and Peggy Bauer/Bruce Coleman; *page 22* © Culver Pictures, Inc.; *page 23* © FPG International; *page 25 (bottom left)* © Alvin E. Staffan/Photo Researchers, Inc.; *page 25 (bottom center)* © Steven Maslowski/Photo Researchers, Inc.; and *page 25 (bottom right)* © Richard Parker/Photo Researchers, Inc.

Chapter 2: Psychology as a Science
Page 31 (top) © Brown Brothers; *page 31 (bottom)* The Ferdinand Hamburger, Jr. Archives. Collection of the Johns Hopkins University; *page 32* D. Mosakowski/Archives and Special Collections, Goddard Library, Clark University, MA; *page 34* © The Bettmann Archive; *page 36* © The Bettmann Archive; *page 40* © Jim Selby/SPL/Photo Researchers, Inc.; *page 41 (top)* © The Bettmann Archive; *page 41 (bot-*

tom) © C. Field/Bruce Coleman, Inc.; *page 42* © Diego Goldberg/Sygma; *page 43* Courtesy of GMFanuc Robotics Corp.; and *page 45* © The Bettmann Archive.

Part Two: The Study of Mind and Body
Hilaire Germain Edgar Degas (1834–1917). The Metropolitan Museum of Art, bequest of Mrs. H. O. Havemeyer, 1929. The H. O. Havemeyer Collection (#29.100.370).

Chapter 3: Sensation
Page 56 © Diego Goldberg/Sygma; *page 60 (both)* © David Parker/Photo Researchers, Inc.; *page 61 (bottom)* Courtesy of the National Eye Institute; *page 63 (bottom)* Courtesy of the National Eye Institute; *page 64* © The Bettmann Archive; *page 67 (top)* © Life Picture Service, Life Magazine; and *page 90 (bottom)* © 1960, Circle Limit IV (Heaven and Hell), M. C. Escher/Cordon Art—Baarn-Holland.

Chapter 4: Perception
Page 91 (top) Kaiser Porcelain Ltd., UK; *page 95 (top)* © The Bettmann Archive; *page 98 (top left)* © R. Michael Stuckey/Comstock; *page 98 (top right)* © Martin Dohrn/SPL/Photo Researchers, Inc.; *page 98 (center)* © Wernher Krutein/Liaison International; *page 98 (bottom)* © Bullaty Lomeo/The Image Bank; *page 99 (bottom)* © The Image Bank; *page 101 (top)* © Art Resource; *page 101 (bottom)* © William Vandivert; and *page 105 (top)* © J. Scowen/FPG International.

Chapter 5: Neuropsychology
Page 116 (both) © The Bettmann Archive

and *page 130 (bottom)* Warren Anatomical Museum, Harvard Medical School.

Chapter 6: Emotion
Page 144 (top left) © Jill Fineberg/Photo Researchers, Inc., *(top right)* © Alice Kandell/Photo Researchers, Inc., *(bottom left)* © Erika Stone/Photo Researchers, Inc., *(bottom right)* © Ulrike Welch/Photo Researchers, Inc.; *page 145 (bottom)* © Frank Siteman/Stock-Boston; *page 147 (top left)* © Jonathan T. Wright/Photographers Aspen, *(top right)* © Nicholas Devore/Photographers Aspen, *(bottom left)* © Mork Bernheim/Woodfin Camp & Assoc., *(bottom right)* © Momatiuk/Eastcott/ Woodfin Camp & Assoc.; *page 151* © Stouffer Productions/Animals Animals; *page 155 (top left)* Dr. Marianne Olds/California Institute of Technology, Division of Biology; *page 158* © David Madison/Bruce Coleman, Inc.; and *page 162* © Philippe Poulet/Gamma-Liaison.

Chapter 7: States of Consciousness
Page 168 © Jim Tuten/Animals Animals; *page 170* © Ted Spagna/Photo Researchers, Inc.; *page 177* © Ralph Morse/Life Picture Service/Life Magazine © 1966; *page 180* © Historical Pictures Service; *page 181* © David Parker/Photo Researchers, Inc.; *page 184 (bottom right)* © Michel Viard Jacana/Photo Researchers, Inc.; *page 184 (bottom left)* Eospybuck, "Delaware Peyote Ceremony," watercolor. National Museum of the American Indian; *page 186 (bottom)* © C. Carrion/ Sygma; *page 187* Culver Pictures, Inc.; and *page 188* © Robert Hollister Davis/The Bettmann Archive.

C-3

NAME INDEX

SUBJECT INDEX